KT-440-635

Trademark Acknowledgements

Wrox has endeavored to provide trademark information about all the companies and products mentioned in this book by the appropriate use of capitals. However, Wrox cannot guarantee the accuracy of this information.

Credits

Authors
Rahim Adatia
Faiz Arni
Craig A. Berry
Kyle Gabhart
John Griffin
Matjaz B Juric
Jeremiah Lott
Tim McAllister
Aaron Mulder
Nathan Nagarajan
Dan O'Connor
Ted Osborne
Dr. P. G. Sarang
Andre Tost
Dave Young

Contributing Authors
Cedric Beust
Paul Done
Scott McReynolds
Erwin Vermassen

Additional Material
Richard Anderson
Keyur Shah

Technical Architect
Craig A. Berry

Technical Editors
Mathew Moodie
Christian Peak
Steve Rycroft
Robert FE Shaw
Mark Waterhouse

Category Manager
Viv Emery

Author Agents
Emma Batch
Nicola Phillips

Technical Reviewers
Vishwajit Aklecha
Kapil Apshankar
Roberto Baglioni
Carl Burnham
Ramu Choppa
John Davies
Brian Higdon
Rahul Kumar
Paul Langan
Alex Linde
Eric Ma
Jim MacIntosh
Jacob Matthew
Ant Mitchell
Hemant More
Dave Morris
Ron Philips
Mike Slinn
Andrew Watt

Project Administrator
Simon Brand

Index
Andrew Criddle
Bill Johncocks

Production Project Coordinator
Tom Bartlett

Additional Layout
Emma Eato

Illustrations
Paul Grove

Cover
Dawn Chellingworth

Proof Reader
Chris Smith

About the Authors

Rahim Adatia

Rahim is a founder and the CEO of Lokah Limited – although he has been able to maintain his technical skills based on over 15 years of industry experience. Originally, starting from a C/C++ and CORBA background, he made the transition to Java when it first appeared in 1995, and is currently tackling the challenges in developing systems to support the emerging wireless data services markets.

Rahim graduated with a degree in Computer Engineering from The University of Ottawa, in Canada. He can be reached at rahimadatia@yahoo.com.

Rahim contributed Chapters 18 and 21 to this book.

Faiz Arni

Faiz Arni is the President and co-founder of InferData Corporation, a training, consulting, and mentoring company specializing in object-oriented methodologies and enterprise software development. Faiz has more than 15 years of experience in designing and developing high-performance, large scale enterprise class applications. As a courseware developer and instructor, Faiz provides training in J2EE, CORBA, and other enterprise technologies while sharing his practical and real-world experiences with his students. He also serves as a mentor and consultant for InferData's clients.

Faiz has published articles in numerous technical journals and is a frequent speaker at various conferences and industry events. He developed the J2EE seminar content for Sun Microsystems and is a member of faculty at Java University. His research interests include distributed systems, database management systems, financial applications, rule-based expert systems, object-oriented technology, and mobile computing.

Faiz received an M.S. in Computer Engineering from the University of Texas at Austin. For more information about Faiz and his company, go to http:// www.inferdata.com. He can be contacted at farni@inferdata.com.

Thanks to Ning Xiao for invaluable technical discussions and to Barbara Garrett for facilitating opportunities such as this one. Thanks to Melissa Faust for making the content conform to the formatting standards of Wrox. Thanks to my friends and partners, Vladimir Bacvanski and Petter Graff, for taking time off from their busy schedules and helping me with the illustrations. Thanks to my friend Unnikrishnan for all the support and help over the years. I would also like to acknowledge Craig Berry at Wrox for his support and immense patience with me throughout this project. Finally, this would not have been possible without the help and support of my lovely wife, Rani and my year old daughter, Aliya. My deepest gratitude to them for always being there and putting up with my crazy schedule.

To my lovely wife, Rani, and daughter, Aliya.

Faiz contributed Chapter 10 to this book.

Professional EJB

Rahim Adatia
Faiz Arni
Craig A. Berry
Kyle Gabhart
John Griffin
Matjaz B Juric
Jeremiah Lott
Tim McAllister
Aaron Mulder
Nathan Nagarajan
Dan O'Connor
Ted Osborne
Dr. P. G. Sarang
Andre Tost
Dave Young

with
Cedric Beust
Paul Done
Scott McReynolds
Erwin Vermassen

Wrox Press Ltd. ®

Professional EJB

Published by Wrox Press Ltd,
Arden House, 1102 Warwick Road, Acocks Green,
Birmingham, B27 6BH, UK
Printed in the United States
ISBN 1-861005-08-3

Craig A. Berry

Craig Berry is a technical architect for Wrox Press in Birmingham, UK, where he has worked for the past three years. He insists on using his middle initial, which stands for Adrian, as he used to go by that name in college. Craig came to Java and publishing by the rather round about route of zoology and film journalism, so when not masterminding the latest Wrox Java titles, he can usually be found in the bowels of a cinema somewhere. After his latest trip to JavaOne this year, Craig has now decided he wants to move there, so if anyone reading this is willing to offer him a job in the San Fran area, he would be most gratified.

Craig contributed Chapter 19 and 22 as well as additional material to this book.

Cedric Beust

Cedric Beust is a senior software engineer in the EJB team at BEA Systems. He's been involved in implementing the EJB 2.0 version of the WebLogic EJB container and holds a Ph.D. in computer science, from the University of Nice, France. Before that, he was working at Sun Microsystems where he focused mainly on CORBA. Over the years, Cedric has been involved in several committees such as EJB, CORBA, and C++. His interests range from everything that relates to distributed computing and software engineering in general, to hobbies such as golf, squash, tennis, and volleyball.

Cedric contributed Appendix C to this book.

Paul Done

Paul is a Product Specialist for SilverStream Europe, concentrating on emerging Java, J2EE, and Web-based technologies. Before SilverStream, Paul spent 4 years as a Software Engineer for Oracle UK in the product development team that develops the Oracle Designer/2000 modelling and generation tool. He has a background in C and C++ development and has been engineering client and server-side Java applications for the past 3½ years. Outside of Java, Paul can often be found with a beer in his hand watching his beloved Everton Football Club lose badly.

I would like to thank my wife Helen for making me happy, and Mum, Dad, and Bazz for teaching me what is important in life. Thanks to Kris D'Hooghe for making my contribution to this book possible.

Paul contributed Appendix E to this book.

Kyle Gabhart

Kyle Gabhart is the Director of the Java/EJB Group within Objective Solutions Inc. http://www.objectsoln.com, a high-end engineering services company focusing on the medical, semiconductor, and telecommunications domains. His group provides professional J2EE training and consulting services in the Dallas-Fort Worth metroplex. Prior to joining Objective Solutions, Kyle worked as a Senior Software Engineer for Brainbench in Chantilly, VA, the premier provider of online skills certification testing. Before that, Kyle lived in the Dallas-Fort Worth metroplex working as an independent Java trainer and consultant.

In addition to his work experience, Kyle has been involved in a number of professional development activities. He currently serves as the DevX Java Pro http://www.devx.com answering questions online and writing 1-2 articles each month. Early this year, he contributed two chapters *to "Professional Java XML"* published by Wrox Press. Kyle also serves as an Associate Member of the Worldwide Institute of Software Architects (www.wwisa.org). He serves as the Subject Chair for Architectural Patterns and the moderator for a working group on certification within that organization.

Kyle lives in Dallas, TX, with his beautiful wife Elizabeth and adorable little girl, Kati.

I love you both.

Kyle contributed Chapter 8 to this book.

John Griffin

John Griffin is a software consultant specializing in large-scale distributed application architecture and development. In 1997, John founded Aries Software Technologies, Inc., an IT consulting company providing software solutions and testing services to the financial and healthcare industries. John has designed, built, and deployed n-tier applications using CORBA and/or Java for many Fortune 500 companies, spanning platforms from handhelds to mainframes.

I dedicate my chapter to my parents Theresa and John and my brother Daniel, whose support and encouragement put everything within reach.

John contributed Chapter 20 to this book.

Matjaz B Juric

Matjaz B. Juric holds a Ph.D. in computer and information science and is an Assistant Professor at the University of Maribor. His research area covers all aspects of object technology, with special emphasis on distributed object systems (CORBA, EJB, RMI, COM+), component development, performance, analysis, and design. He has been involved in the RMI-IIOP (integral part of Java 2 platform) development for performance analysis and optimization. Matjaz is author of several scientific and professional articles in journals like *Java Report, Information and Software Technology*, ACM journals, etc. He published a chapter in the book *More Java Gems* and has presented at conferences like OOPSLA, ICPADS, PDCS, and SCI. He is also a reviewer, program committee member, and conference co-organizer.

Matjaz contributed Chapter 15 to this book.

Jeremiah Lott

Jeremiah Lott is a software engineer who specializes in data integration. His work over the past few years has included implementing EJB persistence mechanisms. He currently resides in Pittsburgh, Pennsylvania with his wife Beth. Although this is his first foray into writing, he has enjoyed sharing his knowledge of EJBs, and hopes that you enjoy reading about BMP in his chapter.

Jeremiah contributed Chapter 16 to this book.

Tim McAllister

Tim McAllister is an independent consultant and director of Object Answers http://www.ObjectAnswers.com. His expertise is in Java, J2EE, Web services, XML, and UML.

Tim spent much of the eighties in the music industry. He released several albums of his own material and produced records for numerous other artists. Tired of peanut butter sandwiches, Tim left the music industry in 1989 returning to college to find a more stable career.

His interest in computers dated back to the days of the TRS-80 and Commodore-64, so he naturally fell into the software industry, graduating with a degree in Management Information Systems. He learned the ropes while doing client-server development at Nike and Hewlett Packard. Tim's interest in object technologies lead him to adopting UML and Java as his tools of choice.

Tim now lives in the Pacific Northwest, spending most of his time in front of a computer. He somehow finds time to fish the rivers of Oregon, and play guitar in a blues band. His next big project involves building a combat robot with his son. He can be reached at tim@ObjectAnswers.com.

Tim contributed Chapter 13 to this book.

Scott McReynolds

Scott McReynolds is a Technical Evangelist with Sybase and has worked for them for 6 years. He has been working with java for the past 2 ½ years. Scott works with the Sybase engineers on the application server and eBusiness platforms. He also works with customers to help them understand the technology and how best to use it. He has spoken at such events as JavaOne, Linux World, and Sybase's User Conference Techwave.

Scott contributed Appendix F to this book.

Aaron Mulder

Despite graduating with a degree in Aerospace Engineering, Aaron was quickly hooked on Java. His personal projects have included an e-mail client, a web client, an FTP server, a car design applet, convention management software, a news reader that downloads articles from the Internet, reads them out loud, and responds to voice commands, a 3D Studio file loader for Java 3D, a database of books and DVDs that interfaces with a barcode scanner to download reviews and information from the Internet, satellite tracking software, a stereo vision package for robotic eyes, and a natural language processing package for MUD AIs.

For work, Aaron has designed and developed a variety of n-tier CORBA and J2EE applications, as well as contributing to two open-source EJB servers in the areas of configuration, deployment, persistence, J2EE Connectors, proxies, and clustering. He has presented at several industry conferences, including JavaOne. Aaron is currently a Java Architect with Skylight Systems, where he is designing next-generation J2EE accounting software.

Aaron contributed Chapter 17 and Appendix G to the book.

Nathan Nagarajan

Vaidyanathan Nagarajan (a.k.a. Nathan) has been programming in the Java language since he started his career with Enherent Corporation in 1996. He consulted for Netscape in their professional services from Dec '98 to Dec '99. Currently, Nathan is pursuing his M.B.A. at a leading business school.

Thank you Padma for supporting me. My gratitude goes to my parents and mother-in-law, and sincere thanks to Mr. James McGovern for encouraging me to write a book. Thanks also to Ms. Sandie Evans and Mr. D.C.S. for their support at work, and to all my colleagues at Enherent.

Nathan contributed Chapter 12 to this book.

Dan O'Connor

Daniel O'Connor is the President of MVCSoft Inc. http://www.mvcsoft.com and author of the MVCSoft EJB 2.0 Persistence Manager. He is a member of the board of directors for JBoss (www.jboss.org), the governing organization for an open-source application server featuring an EJB container. He is one of the authors of "*Professional Java Server Programming J2EE Edition*" and "Professional Oracle 8i Application Programming," both published by Wrox Press.

I would like to dedicate my efforts in this book to my nieces and nephews: Nicolas, Lauren, Brian, Ryan, Kaylie, and Molly.

Dan contributed Chapters 5 and 6 as well as additional material to this book.

Ted Osborne

Over the past 15 years, Ted Osborne has designed, developed, tested, documented, maintained, and explained a variety of software products and technologies. He currently works for Empirix as a developer on the Bean-test$^{(TM)}$ engineering team. Ted holds a degree in Jazz Composition from Berklee College of Music.#

Ted contributed Chapter 14 to this book.

Poornachandra G. Sarang

A contractor to Sun Microsystems, Dr. Sarang trains Sun's corporate clients on various courses from Sun's official curriculum. He also conducts the "Train The Trainers" program and "Instructor Authorization Tests" on behalf of Sun.

As CEO of ABCOM Information Systems Pvt. Ltd., Dr. Sarang specializes in training and project development on the Java/CORBA platform. With almost 20 years of industry experience, Dr. Sarang has developed a number of products and successfully completed various industry projects. He is a regular speaker in national and international conferences and regularly contributes technical articles to international journals and magazines of repute.

"I would like to thank my mother and my wife Nita without whose patience and support this writing would not have been possible."

Dr. Sarang contributed Chapters 1 to 4, Chapter 7 and Appendix B to this book.

Andre Tost

Andre Tost works as a Solution Architect for IBM's Software Group in Rochester, Minnesota. In his current assignment, he works with some of IBM's strategic software partners. Before that, he had various development and architecture roles in IBM's SanFrancisco and WebSphere Business Components projects. He started Java programming in early 1996 in the SanFrancisco Project and has been developing in this language ever since. Lately, XML and XSL have caught his attention, and he is closely following how things evolve in this space.

He was born and raised in northern Germany and moved with his family to Minnesota in 1998. Being a big football fan (i.e. the *real* football that Americans call soccer), he likes to play and watch the game. Fortunately, Rochester has a quite active soccer scene, with plenty of playing opportunities. Besides spending his time on programming and soccer, he likes to be with his wife and his two boys, who are four years and one year old (and who think being a programmer at IBM must be the biggest fun one can possibly have – oh well...).

Andre contributed Chapter 22 and Appendix D to this book.

Erwin Vermassen

At the moment Erwin is working as a product specialist for SilverStream Software, concentrating mainly on the SilverStream J2EE-compliant application server. He graduated a long time ago as an Electronics Engineer and then became involved in industrial-oriented software projects. Erwin participated in the development of a real-time operating system used in the digital signal processing area by using such notorious programming languages as C/C++ and assembler.

I would like to thank Misha Davidson, Kris D'Hooghe, Paul Done, and the guys over in Billerica for the assistance they gave me while writing my piece for the SilverStream.

Erwin contributed Appendix E to this book.

Dave Young

Dave Young has worked with Java since its inception and was one of the first lecturers on Enterprise JavaBeans. He has spoken on EJB-related topics at many conferences, including JavaOne and the International Conference for Java Development. He is president of Z-Systems, Inc. http://www.zs.com, a New York metro systems integration firm that specializes in mentoring companies in distributed application design, as well as its implementation.

Dave would like to dedicate this book to his beautiful wife, Lynette, without whose support, patience, and understanding would never let him achieve half of the things he sets out to do, and to his lovely daughter, Bailey Veronica, who has given him the reasons for trying. He would also like to thank his friends and family for their encouragement and support.

You can reach Dave at dyoung@zs.com.

Dave contributed Chapters 9 and 11 to this book.

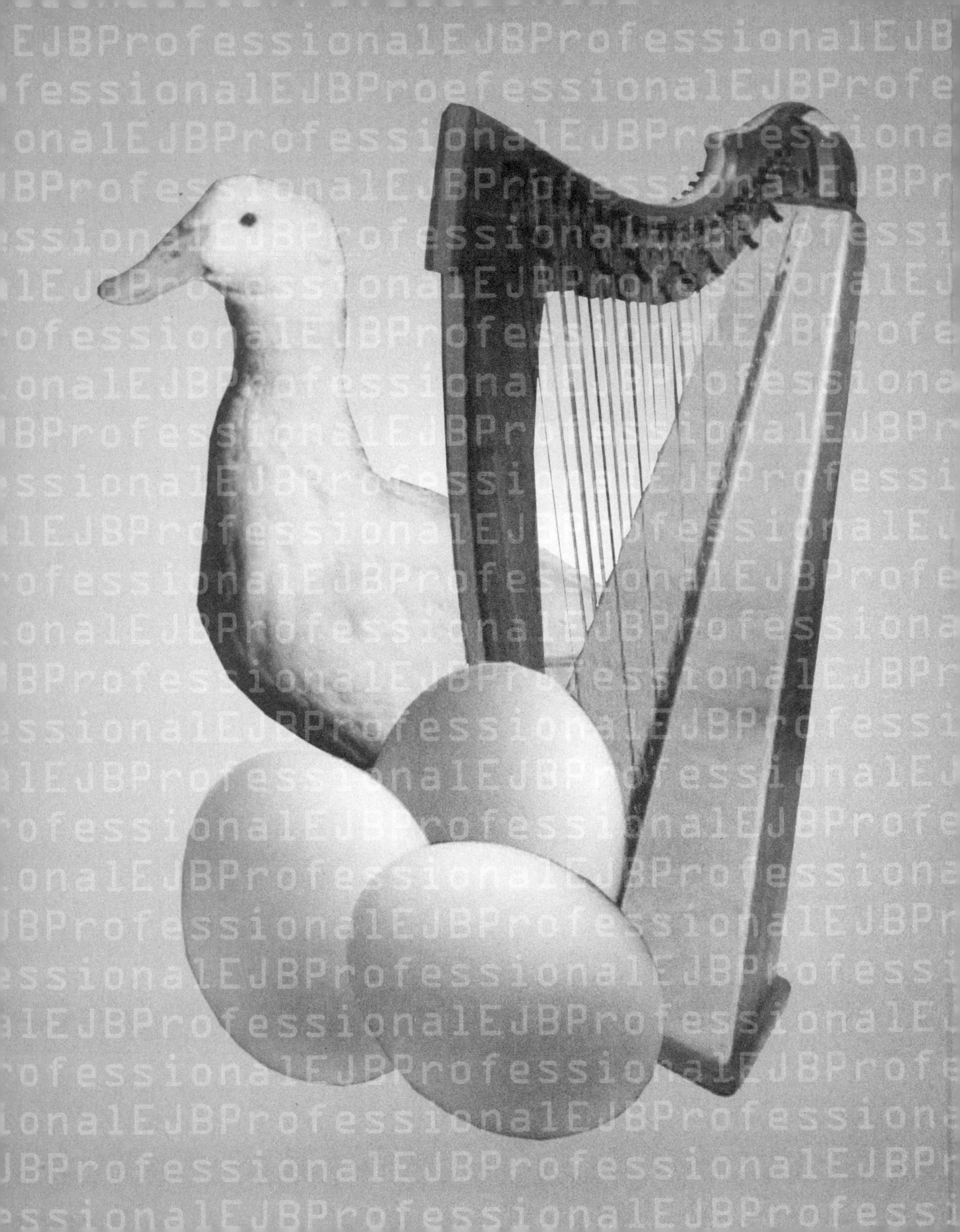

Table of Contents

Table of Contents

Table of Contents

Table of Contents

Table of Contents

Table of Contents

Table of Contents

Table of Contents

Table of Contents

Table of Contents

Table of Contents

Table of Contents

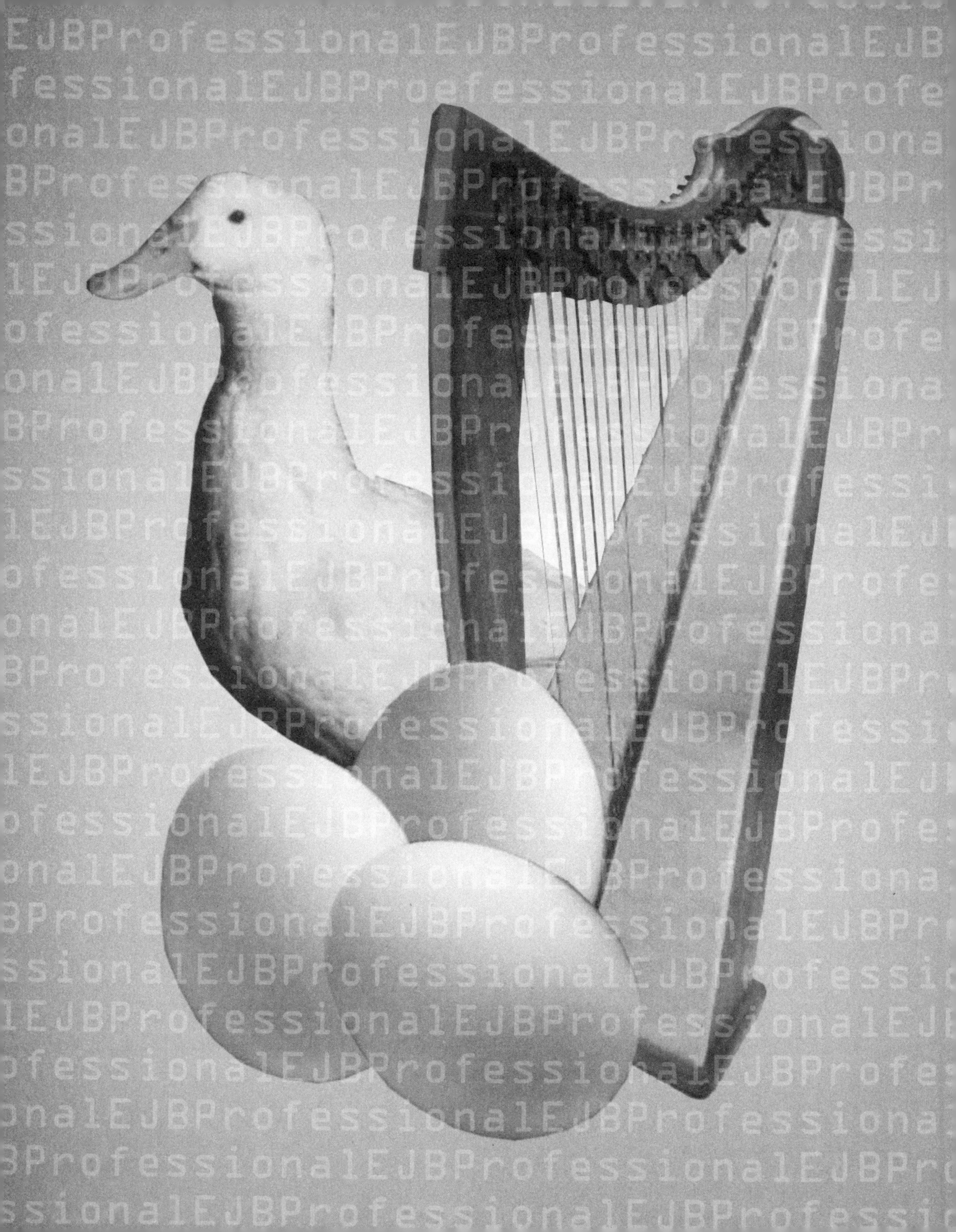

Introduction

Welcome to Professional Enterprise JavaBean Development. This book will demonstrate the basics of developing web-based enterprise applications using Enterprise JavaBeans (EJBs) within the architecture of Java 2 Platform, Enterprise Edition (J2EE). In doing this, we'll be dealing with EJB 2.0 (at Proposed Final Draft 2 at time of press), and EJB 1.1 specifications; where there are differences, we'll highlight them for you.

EJB architecture represents the primary distributed component model for creating business applications. Arguably the most mature and robust model for enterprise development, J2EE and EJBs offer a significant technology for the development of many of today's large, secure, scalable, and transactional applications. Specifically, EJBs enable the separation of business logic implementation from system-level services, thus allowing the developer to concentrate on the business issues at hand. Furthermore, recent improvements in the specification, now in version 2.0, mean that EJBs are an even more attractive proposition.

This book will take you through the fundamentals of learning to develop with the EJB architecture, through to more advanced issues such as design strategies, performance, testing, and integration issues.

Who is this Book For?

The purpose of this book is to teach the EJB architecture and the development of EJBs to a Java programmer. It is assumed that the reader is well conversant with Java Programming and the core APIs, and has some knowledge of server-side Java programming. However, all concepts that relate to programming EJBs will be covered assuming no prior knowledge.

This book not only covers all the basics of developing EJBs to the API, but also gets into more advanced topics about what to do with this knowledge. As we've already said, this book aims to develop to the EJB 2.0 specifications.

What's Covered in this Book

The book has the following basic structure:

❑ **EJB Architecture** – including details of the four elements of an EJB: home and component interfaces, implementation class, and deployment descriptor.

❑ **Developing with EJBs** – Session Beans, Entity Beans (highlighting the significant difference between the EJB 1.1 and 2.0 specifications), and Message-Driven Beans.

❑ **EJB Services** – Resource, Transaction, and Security Management.

❑ **EJB Applications** – Design Strategies and Patterns, Modelling, Testing, and Performance.

❑ **The EJB Container** – how the container handles Deployment, Run-time Services, Resource Management, and Clustering.

❑ **Integration** – with J2EE, COM, CORBA, Wireless, and Web Services.

There are also several appendices, which take the form of a deployment guide to application servers. Here we present useful information and step-by-step details regarding installing and configuring some of the most popular EJB containers that you can use to deploy your Enterprise JavaBeans on. For a comparison, we'll be deploying the same sample EJB using the following software: J2EE Reference Implementation, BEA WebLogic, IBM WebSphere, SilverStream, Sybase EAServer, and JBoss.

What You Need to Use this Book

Most of the code in this book was tested with the Java 2 Platform, Enterprise Edition SDK 1.3 Reference Implementation, which is available for download from http://java.sun.com/j2ee/j2sdkee-beta/index.html. However, for some of the chapters, certainly the appendices, you will need some additional software:

EJB Containers

As well as the Reference Implementation, the appendices deal with the following readily available application servers and EJB containers:

❑ BEA WebLogic Server 6. or 6.1:
http://commerce.beasys.com/downloads/weblogic_server.jsp#wls

❑ IBM WebSphere Application Server 4.0:

http://www-4.ibm.com/software/webservers/appserv/

❑ SilverStream Application Server 3.7.2: http://www.silverstream.com/

❑ Sybase EAServer 3.6: http://www.sybase.com/products/applicationservers/easerver/

❑ JBoss 2.0 Application Server: http://www.jboss.org/

Databases

Several of the chapters also require access to a database. For these chapters we used a mixture of:

❑ Oracle

❑ Cloudscape (an in-process version comes with the J2EE RI): http://www.cloudscape.com/

❑ Microsoft Access 2000

Additional Software

Finally, there are a few additional pieces of software that a couple of chapters also require:

- ❑ Sun's JNDI SDK, which is included with JDK 1.3
- ❑ The JavaIDL ORB, also bundled within the Java SDK
- ❑ ORBacus C++ ORB from Object Oriented Concepts, Inc: http://www.ooc.com/
- ❑ A C++ compiler for your particular platform – for compilation of the ORBacus product as well as our sample client application
- ❑ CapeConnectTwo from Cape Clear: http://www.capeclear.com/products/download/index.shtml
- ❑ IBM Web Services Toolkit 2.2.1: http://www.wrox.com
- ❑ J-Integra: http://www.intrinsyc.com/products/deviceintegration/jintegra.html
- ❑ J2EE Client Access Services (CAS) COM Bridge: http://developer.java.sun.com/developer/earlyAccess/j2eecas/download-com-bridge.html
- ❑ Bean-test from Empirix: http://www.empirix.com/
- ❑ JUnit: http://www.xprogramming.com/software.htm

The code in the book will work on a single machine, provided it is networked (that is, it can see http://localhost/ through the local browser).

The complete source code from the book is available for download from:

http://www.wrox.com/

Online discussions relating to this and other Wrox titles can be found at:

http://p2p.wrox.com/

Conventions

To help you get the most from the text and keep track of what's happening, we've used a number of conventions throughout the book.

For instance:

> **These boxes hold important, not-to-be forgotten information that is directly relevant to the surrounding text.**

The background style is used for asides to the current discussion.

As for styles in the text:

- ❏   When we introduce them, we **highlight** important words.
- ❏   We show keyboard strokes like this: *Ctrl-A*.
- ❏   We show filenames and code within the text like so: doGet().
- ❏   Text on user interfaces and URLs are shown as: Menu.

We present code in three different ways. Definitions of methods and properties are shown as follows:

```
protected void doGet(HttpServletRequest req, HttpServletResponse resp)
                   throws ServletException, IOException
```

Example code is shown:

```
In our code examples, the code foreground style shows new, important,
    pertinent code
while code background shows code that's less important in the present context,
    or has been seen before.
```

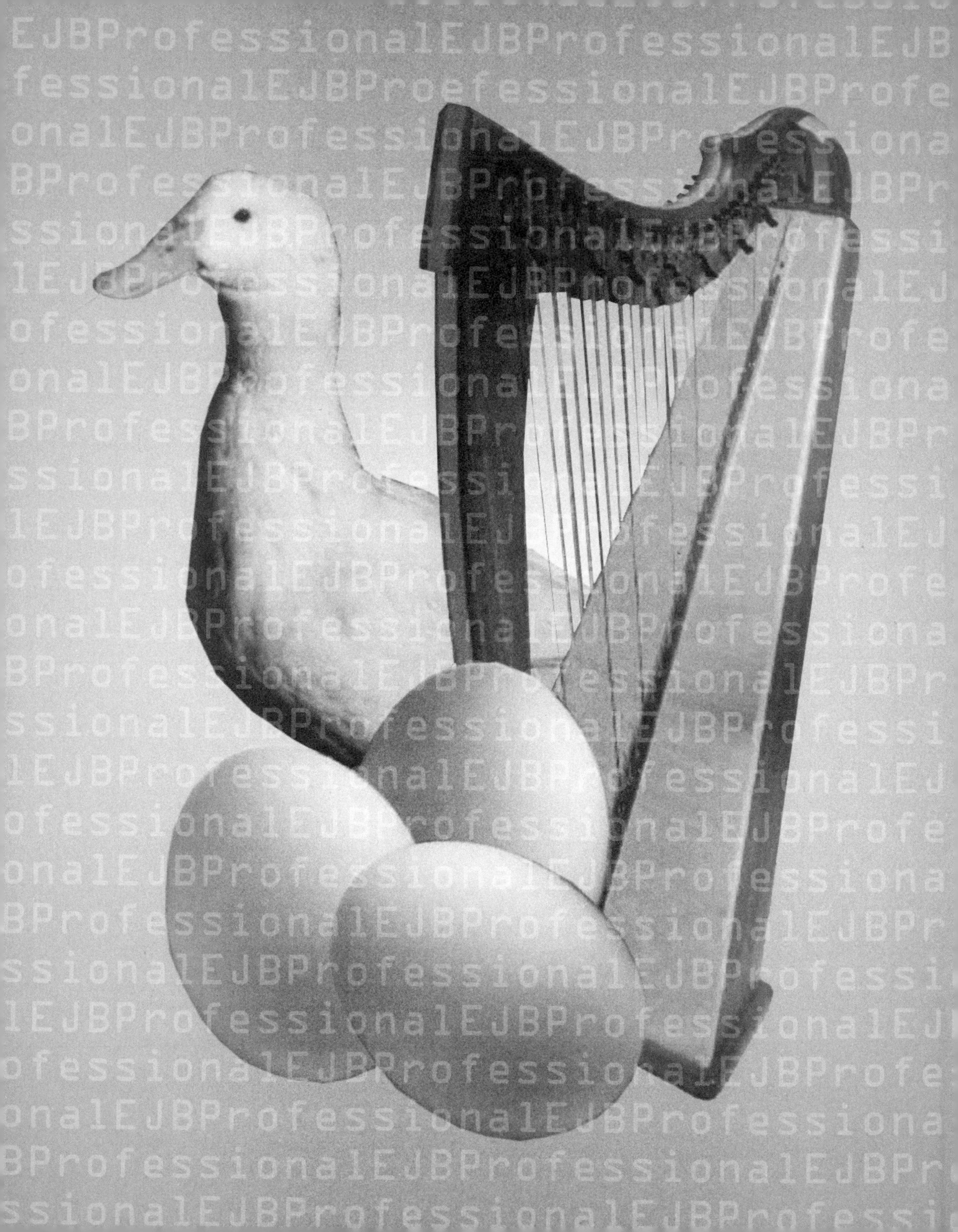

1

The Enterprise JavaBeans Architecture

Since Sun first released the **Enterprise JavaBeans (EJB)** specification in early 1998, EJBs have been growing in popularity and production use. The early drafts of the specification provided many of the basic concepts that make the EJB architecture so attractive to developers, even if many of the implementation details were too vague, and performance was far from ideal. However, recent improvements in the specification – now reaching version 2.0 – mean that EJBs are a more attractive proposition than ever.

EJBs also play a crucial role in the **Java 2 Platform, Enterprise Edition (J2EE)** architecture (now entering version 1.3), as the primary component responsible for the implementation of your application's business logic. As one of the most durable and sophisticated enterprise development models available, J2EE is a significant technology in the development of many of today's large, scalable, and secure applications.

This book will take you through the basics of learning to develop with the EJB architecture, through to more advanced issues such as performance, testing, and design. In this first chapter, we will be taking a high-level view of the EJB architecture: Why it has evolved; the basic advantages of the EJBs; the main pieces in how EJBs actually function; and how today's architecture is helping application developers to develop, deploy, and manage large distributed applications in a realistic time frame.

As a guide, in this chapter we will discuss the following:

❑ The evolution of distributed computing systems

❑ The need for a new architecture for distributed computing

❑ The J2EE architecture

❑ The Enterprise JavaBeans architecture

❑ EJB container services

❑ Application servers

Before we look at EJBs then, we'll briefly spend some time looking at the reasons why architectures such as EJB and J2EE have evolved.

The Evolution of Distributed Computing

Before the introduction of personal computers in the 1980s, computing generally took place on large centralized, non-distributed systems consisting of dumb terminals linked to a mainframe. PCs did not really change the computing model; they simply brought the processing power to the user's desktop. All the different parts of the application, from the data to the user interface, had to be collocated. Retrospectively, we call the applications running in a single processing space **monolithic**, and we can define such systems as being **single tier**.

The disadvantage of such monolithic applications was that any change in any part of the program would require the generation of a new executable. Even a small change in the user interface would require the re-compilation of the entire code – the larger the application and the more copies of it, the more time this would take. Besides, such applications could not be shared between users and remained in a single user domain. The personal computers in the early 80s did not have enough processing power to handle medium to large size jobs – processing the company's payroll for instance – so a mainframe installation was still required to run these kinds of jobs. Then came the introduction of a new computing model – the popular **client-server** systems of the late 80s.

As PCs provided at least some processing power on the user's desktop, it was possible to do off-line data entry using a personal computer and feed such data into a mainframe at a later time. Slowly, PCs were connected to mainframes or mid-range servers. The PCs were either used as dumb terminals to mainframes, or a small application running on the PC would allow data entry and basic validation for direct input to the application running on a mainframe.

The user interface from the monolithic applications was taken out and run on a PC. Often, the application was split in two parts (tiers), one responsible for data entry and business logic processing, while the other portion would take care of persistent data storage. The first part would run on a PC-based client.

In other cases, the client application would consist of only data entry and some validation, while the business processing would still be done on the database tier. In this case, the user interface would provide for data entry and validation; so any changes in the user interface would necessitate changing only the client code run on the PC. The server code that essentially implemented the business rules and persistent storage for the corporate data remained unaffected by changes in the client code. This movement of the application into separate tiers reduced the time spent maintaining the application dramatically.

Indeed, such client-server systems could also be implemented by connecting PCs to a centralized server using a local area network (LAN), avoiding the need for a mainframe. The processing power required by the application could be derived from the more powerful server. Since the application was deployed on a server, it was possible to share the same application among many users, increasing the productivity. This also resulted in a much more efficient use of (expensive) computing resources.

n-tier Architecture

In the two-tier client-server system, any changes in the business logic still necessitated changes to a large portion of the application. Also, because the database and the business logic were both embedded in the application on the server, migrating from one database vendor to another resulted in the modification of the server code too. To ease these difficulties, further code modularization was needed, so a **3-tier** concept was introduced. In this concept, the business logic is separated from the database server, so any changes in the business rules or the database server do not affect the other layers. The client layer still remains the same as for the case of client-server technology. Thus the application is split across three tiers:

❑ Presentation

❑ Business logic

❑ Data

The presentation tier provides the user interface, the business logic tier obviously implements the business logic, and the data tier takes care of the persistence of data used in the business tier. This came to be known as **distributed processing**.

The introduction of 3-tier architecture also resulted in better scalability of the business logic, now located exclusively in the middle tier, the most process-intensive block of the entire application. Initially, this kind of 3-tier architecture was used in intranet scenarios. However, with the growing popularity of the Internet in the early 90s, corporations wanted their applications to be web-enabled so that company personnel (and customers and suppliers) could run the same centralized application from anywhere in the world while traveling on business.

Thus, the **n-tier** architecture of today was developed. n-tier architecture is simply about further modularizing (an therefore distributing) the component architecture. The main additional distribution under the n-tier architecture is the need for a dedicated web processing space to handle most of the presentation logic while the client merely becomes a dumb web browser.

Developing Distributed Applications

As the system architecture has grown increasingly more complex, so have the development requirements for distributed applications. The distribution of processing across a number of different tiers means that a great deal of effort must go into making the different application partitions integrate together – in fact the goal is to make each application module not know or even care whether the other modules it interacts with are local or remote. What's more, any reasonable sized application is going to require a range of additional services beyond its simple application logic. For example, it will need to be able to create and control transactions (often across multiple application modules); it will need a security layer to protect it from nefarious and accidental use; and so on.

To utilize such services, it would be necessary to add a significant amount of "plumbing" code to your applications. More often than not, you'd be required to set up and configure different middleware solutions, and make API calls to the vendor-specific APIs to access the specific services. Apart from services such as relational database access, most of these services are either proprietary or non-standard. The result is that your applications will be more complex, time consuming, and expensive to develop, manage, and maintain.

Apart from having to manage all these different APIs, there is another critical demand on server-side applications: on the server-side, resources are scarce. For example, you cannot afford to create the same number of objects that you can typically afford to create in client-side applications. Other server-side resources that require special attention include threads, database connections, security, transactions, etc. Custom-building an infrastructure that deals with these resources has always been a challenge. This task is almost impossible within the environment and economy of the Internet. Would you care to build a connection pool, or an object cache, or an "elegant" object layer for database access, when your development lifecycle is only three months?

Since these server-side requirements are common across a wide variety of applications, it is more appropriate to consider a platform that has built-in solutions. This lets you separate these infrastructure-level concerns from the more direct concern of translating your application requirements to software that works. This is where J2EE comes into the picture.

J2EE Architecture

In order to facilitate n-tier application development, Sun MicroSystems designed a new enterprise architecture that is based on the Java platform. This new architecture is called **J2EE** (the **Java 2 Platform, Enterprise Edition**). J2EE takes the basic Java concept of providing a high-level API that is agnostic of the implementation, providing it is compliant with the specification.

Thus, for the enterprise environment, the J2EE specification defines a new type of distributed application architecture that goes a long way to solve many of the problems of n-tier application development.

The J2EE Container Architecture

J2EE specifies roles and interfaces for applications, and the runtime onto which applications can be deployed. This results in a clear demarcation between the applications and the runtime infrastructure allowing the runtime to abstract most of the infrastructure services that enterprise developers have traditionally attempted to build on their own. As a result, J2EE application developers can just focus on the application logic and related services, while leveraging the runtime for all infrastructure-related services.

What's more, J2EE does not specify how a J2EE runtime should/could be built, but instead provides an abstraction of the runtime infrastructure, through what it calls the **container**.

> It is important to note that the container is not an actual physical construct but rather a theoretical representation of the architecture discussed below.

The architecture of a container can be divided into four parts:

❑ **Component contract:**
The basic purpose of the container in the J2EE architecture is to provide a runtime for application components. That is, instances of the application components are created and invoked within the Java Virtual Machine (JVM) of the container. This makes the container responsible for managing the lifecycle of application components. However, for the application components to be manageable within the container runtime, the application components are required to abide by certain **contracts** specified by the container.

❑ **Container service APIs:**
The J2EE platform defines a set of Java standard extensions that each J2EE platform must support. J2EE containers provide a service-level abstraction of the APIs. As a result, you can access the service APIs such as JDBC, JTA, JNDI, JMS, etc. within the container, as though the underlying container is implementing them. A container in the J2EE architecture provides a federated view of various enterprise APIs specified in the J2EE platform.

❑ **Declarative services:**
One of the important features of the J2EE architecture is its ability to dynamically interpose services for application components. This is based on declarations specified outside your application components. The purpose of this approach is to minimize the application programming required in order to make use of such services.

❑ **Other container services:**
Other runtime services, related to component lifecycle, resource pooling, garbage collection, etc.

Furthermore, the J2EE specification defines four types of container:

❑ An **applet container** to run applets

❑ An **application-client container** for running standard Java application clients

❑ A **web container** for hosting Java servlets and JSP pages

❑ An **EJB container** for hosting Enterprise JavaBean components

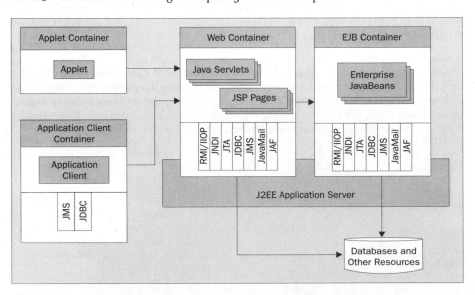

In the above figure, the vertical blocks at the bottom of each container represent the J2EE APIs. Apart from access to these infrastructure-level APIs, each container also implements the respective container-specific API (Java Servlet API for the web container, and the EJB API for the EJB container).

The stacks of rectangles (applets, application clients, servlets, JSP pages, and EJBs) in this figure are the programs that you develop and host in these containers. In the J2EE parlance, these programs are called **application components**.

The J2EE Application Architecture

With any application, the most important element is modeling the necessary business logic through the use of components – application-level reusable units. We described a container as hosting the runtime for application components, so although the container may be able to supply many of the services and much of the communication infrastructure, it is ultimately the responsibility of the developer to create the application components. However, these components will be dependent upon their container for many services, such as lifecycle management, threading, security, etc. This allows you to concentrate on providing the requisite business functionality without getting into the details and low-level semantics of containers.

The J2EE platform provides three technologies for developing components:

❑ **Servlets**
Servlets are server-side programs that allow application logic to be embedded in the request-response process of the HTTP. Servlets provide a means to extend the functionality of the web server to enable dynamic content in HTML, XML, or other web languages.

❑ **JavaServer Pages (JSP)**
JavaServer Pages (JSP) provides a way to embed components in a page, and to have them do the work to generate the page that is eventually sent to the client. A JavaServer Page can contain HTML, Java code, and JavaBean components. JavaServer Pages are in fact an extension of the servlet programming model – when a user requests a JSP page, the web server compiles it into a servlet. The web server then invokes this servlet and returns the resulting content to the web browser. Once the servlet has been compiled from the JSP page, the web server can simply return the servlet without having to recompile each time. Thus, JavaServer Pages provide a powerful and dynamic page-assembly mechanism that benefits from the many advantages of the Java platform.

❑ **Enterprise JavaBeans (EJB)**
The topic of this book – the EJB architecture is a distributed component model for developing secure, scalable, transactional, and multi-user components. To put it simply, they are reusable software units containing business logic. Just as JSP allows the separation of application and presentation logic, EJBs allow separation of application logic from system-level services thus allowing the developer to concentrate on the business domain issues and not system programming.

J2EE APIs

This book will of course focus mainly on EJBs. However, before we dive into the EJB architecture, we will first briefly review a few of the other features and APIs of J2EE which are the most relevant to EJB development:

❑ **RMI/IIOP**

RMI/IIOP is a protocol for communication between two tiers. **Remote Method Invocation (RMI)** is one of the primary mechanisms in distributed object applications. It allows you to use interfaces to define remote objects. You can then call methods on these remote objects as if they were local. The exact wire-level transportation mechanism is implementation specific. For example, Sun uses the Java Remote Method Protocol (JRMP) on top of TCP/IP, but other implementations such as BEA's WebLogic Server have their own protocol.

RMI-IIOP is an extension of RMI but over IIOP (Internet Inter-ORB Protocol), which allows you to define a remote interface to any remote object that can be implemented in any language that supports OMG mapping and ORB. The standard protocol used for communication between different tiers of J2EE architecture is IIOP. The server vendors are required to implement this protocol in their servers.

❑ **JNDI**

The role of the **Java Naming and Directory Interface (JNDI)** API in the J2EE platform is two-fold. Firstly, it provides the means to perform standard operations to a directory service resource such as LDAP, Novell Directory Services, or Netscape Directory Services.

Secondly, a J2EE application utilizes JNDI to look up interfaces used to create, amongst other things, EJBs, and JDBC connections.**JTA**

JTA stands for the **Java Transaction API**. JTA provides infrastructure for transaction management. The programmer uses this API for opening a transaction, committing a transaction, and rolling back a transaction in the case of an error. If the client transaction spans multiple beans deployed on the same server or widely dispersed servers, the server vendor is responsible for ensuring the proper implementation of the transaction control. The transaction, spanning multiple servers, requires the propagation of transaction context between servers over IIOP.

❑ **JDBC**

JDBC is not actually an acronym, although it is popularly taken to stand for Java DataBase Connectivity (actually this isn't true; but nobody will say what it *does* stand for!). The JDBC API defines several classes and interfaces for database access. It allows you to create connections to a database, create statements, run INSERT/DELETE/UPDATE queries, run stored procedures, and so on. The new JDBC API (version 3.0) even supports database connection pooling.

❑ **JavaMail and JAF**

JavaMail defines a set of abstract classes and interfaces for supporting a mail system through your Java application. The JavaMail service providers implement these interfaces and classes. With this API, you can compose a message, transport a message, retrieve the message from the store, and so on. JAF stands for JavaBeans Activation Framework and is used for mail attachments.

❑ **JMS**

In the enterprise environment, the various distributed components may not always be in constant contact with each other. Therefore, there needs to be some mechanism for sending data asynchronously. The **Java Message Service (JMS)** provides just such functionality to send and receive messages through the use of message-oriented middleware (MOM).

You'll see all these APIs, as well as a few others, at various points throughout the book.

Enterprise JavaBeans

We've talked about EJBs in rather general terms until this point. It is now necessary to address the issue of what an EJB component consists of.

> **An EJB is a collection of Java classes, following defined rules and providing specific callback methods, and an XML file, combined into one single unit.**

From the bean programmer's point of view, that's all there is to it. The EJB will run in an EJB container in an application server. The container takes responsibility for the system-level issues. This division of labor between the bean programmer and the container is the central idea of Enterprise JavaBeans technology.

EJBs are also not limited to any particular company, server implementation, middleware, or communication protocol. Enterprise JavaBeans are just a *specification* that any company can implement in any number of different ways. Your EJB, if it doesn't take advantage of any proprietary extensions, can be moved between different server implementations according to your requirements. The portability of EJB components is one of their major advantages.

EJBs can boost developer productivity for the small, workgroup application. They can help structure the model behind your company's interactive web site. They can even be made to scale to the largest e-commerce application.

EJBs versus JavaBeans

One common potential point of confusion with Enterprise JavaBeans is the name, which unfortunately is very similar to another component architecture, that of *JavaBeans*:

❑ JavaBeans define a model for creating general-purpose components that are typically used on the client side. These components may or may not contain a user interface.

In contrast:

❑ Enterprise JavaBeans define a server-side component model for creating highly specialized business logic components. EJB components do not have a graphical user interface.

Besides this, the development and deployment processes are totally different for these two types of beans.

Why Use EJBs in Your Design?

A designer of a server-side Java application needs to understand how servlets, JSP pages, and EJBs work together, and which are appropriate in different circumstances. Why, specifically, is the EJB API necessary? Countless web sites have demonstrated that it is possible to provide dynamic content using servlets or JSPs alone. It might seem that this new API adds unnecessary complexity to the development process.

It is important to understand that every API has circumstances where its use is appropriate, and circumstances where it should not be used. The EJB specification is intended to provide enterprise-level services – software services that are fundamental to an organization's purpose, regardless of the scale of those services. This specification thus has a high degree of complexity in its administration and programming model. A dynamic application with modest business-logic requirements will probably be best served by avoiding this complexity and using a strictly JSP/servlet implementation (which would use JavaBeans components for business logic and data access). To take it a step further, a simple web site with no dynamic requirements at all should probably skip server-side Java altogether, and be written in HTML.

The Enterprise JavaBeans API was designed to keep the application programmer from having to provide systems-level services, so that they are free to concentrate on business logic. A web site that simply needs to provide dynamic content to its users probably doesn't require those systems-level services in the first place. However, many applications do require those services, and the Enterprise JavaBeans technology fulfills this need.

Sun's documentation for the J2EE platform includes a publication discussing how the various Java enterprise technologies fit together *(Designing Enterprise Applications with the Java 2 Platform, Enterprise Edition*, also known as the *J2EE Blueprints*). This document lists four basic architectures for web applications:

- ❑ Basic HTML
- ❑ HTML with JSP pages and servlets
- ❑ Servlets and JSP pages that access modular JavaBeans components
- ❑ Servlets, JSP pages, JavaBeans components, and Enterprise JavaBeans

Each of these successive architectures is increasingly complex, and also increasingly robust and modular. The use of EJBs extends this modularity further. As the requirements of the application increase in complexity, access to the enterprise's business logic and data is moved to EJB components. However, the decision to use EJBs should not be based on application complexity alone. A requirement for any of the services provided by an EJB container can also indicate whether the technology is appropriate (such as transactions, scalability, persistence, security, future growth possibilities, and access from other types of clients).

If it is still unclear whether you should use EJB technology in your project, it may be of help to look at EJBs as being the *business objects* of your application. That means that they are the object representations of the rules of your enterprise: what it owns, what it owes, how it operates, who works there, who can get credit, what's for sale, how much to charge, etc. If you need to access these rules, you should do it through the business-object representation. If the application you are building needs to capture the complexity of a process – if it needs to read, validate, transform, and write data in consistent units; if it needs to be kept secure; if it needs to be reused in different contexts – then it makes sense to take advantage of the services that an EJB container can provide.

Everything about the EJB specification is designed for this task of representing business objects without making the business-logic programmer provide system-level services. EJB technology is not suited for use as a reporting system, for analytical processing, or to serve files to the web. But if you need to access business logic of any complexity, you will find that writing your business logic as EJB components will open up new possibilities in developer productivity, application deployment, performance, reliability, reusability, and more.

The EJB Architecture

EJB components are deployed in an **EJB container**. The container can be understood as the execution environment and is managed by, and embedded in, an **EJB server**, which typically runs on the middle tier and is responsible for managing one or more EJB containers.

The primary reason that you would write an Enterprise JavaBeans component is to take advantage of the services that the container provides. Understanding what these services comprise will help you understand when you should make the decision to use EJB components in your design, and what role they should play.

EJB Container Services

We mentioned earlier that the container offers various services to the application developer. So what are they?

- ❏ Component Pooling and Lifecycle Management
- ❏ Client Session Management
- ❏ Database Connection Pooling
- ❏ Transaction Management
- ❏ Authentication and Access Control
- ❏ Persistence

The important point to remember here is that most of these services are made available to the application without any coding effort from the application developer's point of view. The need for such services is declared by the application in its deployment descriptor and the server then provides the services for the application. Let's now look at these various services.

Component Pooling and Lifecycle Management

As we will see, an EJB client does not hold a direct reference to the EJB, therefore **component pooling** becomes possible. In this case, when the EJB server starts up, or whenever the EJB is deployed on the server, the server creates several instances of the bean and keeps them in a pool. When a client requests a bean, one of the pre-created bean instances is assigned to the client. If the client relinquishes control, the server returns the bean to the pool of available beans. During the lifetime of the client, the client may invoke any number of methods on the bean. It needs to obtain the reference to the bean only once and it uses this reference throughout its life span.

For each client that requests a bean, an instance from the pool is assigned. This process continues until all the bean instances from the pool are assigned to various clients.

If yet another client comes in, the server first checks if any of the previously assigned bean instances is not being actively used by the client. By 'not being actively used', we mean that the client is not currently in the middle of a method execution or transaction; in general, a client may hold the bean reference for a long time, though it may not be actively using the bean during all this time. After every execution of a business method the client may do other work before executing another business method on the bean. During this in-between time, the bean is free and may be assigned to another client. Note, however, that the client still holds a reference to the bean.

When the original client comes back and requests an execution of another business method, the server once again searches for a bean instance that is not actively used and assigns it to the client. As far as the client is concerned, it has gained access to the same bean instance it used before. Actually, a totally new instance may be assigned to the same client for each method invocation.

At certain times, it is possible that all the instances are in active use by the various clients. Such a situation arises during peak hours when you have large number of visitors to your site. When this happens, the server automatically creates another instance of the bean and assigns it to the new client. When the load increases and there are not enough instances available in the pool, the server keeps on creating additional instances and assigning them to the new clients. But what happens to all these additional instances when all these clients go away? When the load reduces, the server automatically removes the additional beans that were created thereby freeing the server resources. Thus, the server along with the container is responsible for the **lifecycle management** of the bean.

As you can see, the big advantage of this component pooling technique is that a small number of bean instances can serve a large number of clients. The ability to scale-up and serve large numbers of clients is a highly desirable feature of any application. Furthermore, the process is managed totally by the container and server, requiring no coding effort on the part of the bean developer.

Client Session Management

After the above discussion, one question still remains. What if the client is maintaining information (*state*) in the bean's instance variables? Here, if the bean instances are pooled and shared between multiple clients, the container takes responsibility for saving and retrieving the bean's state during changing assignments. When the bean is assigned to a new client, the server saves its existing state, and when the same client returns to invoke another method on the bean, the state is retrieved and re-copied into the bean before the bean is assigned back to the client. Thus, the client always sees the same state across method invocations.

During the entire lifecycle of the bean, the bean may be returned to the pool (this is called **passivation**) if the client does not actively use it. During passivation, the container assumes the responsibility of saving the client state, if any, maintained in the bean. When the client requests the bean again, the client's state is restored in the bean before it is assigned to the client (this is called **activation**). The container manages the entire process of passivation/activation. When the beans are not in use, they may be destroyed and garbage collected or simply returned to the pool of available instances. The container manages all these operations during the entire client session of our application.

Database Connection Pooling

In the same way that the components are pooled and shared, it should be possible to share the other resources on the server. Indeed, this is what the EJB server does for database connections too (although similar functionality can be implemented via other software). The system administrator decides the number of connections maintained in the pool.

Database connection pools are advantageous because database connections are usually expensive, in terms of the resources consumed by a connection and the time it takes to make it. Also, there may be a limited number of connections to a given database because of software license restrictions, or due to the limitations of the database engine itself. Therefore, if the connections are pooled and shared, it will make the middle tier more scalable and we can have large number of clients accessing the database in the same short period of time using a limited number of connections. Also, since creating database connections is computationally expensive, using a pool improves application performance.

Once again, the server takes this responsibility; it makes a number of database connections when it starts up and maintains them in a pool. These connections are then shared among various clients just as the EJB components are shared. Now, for a database connection, the client state is not important. However, a client may open a transaction on a connection; if the server has to assign this connection to another client, the process is more involved and complex. As per the J2EE specification laid out by Sun, a server vendor is not required to support connection pooling in such situations, meaning that a connection with the open transaction need not be shared.

The server maintains a connection pool for other resources too. Connections to the mail server and URL (socket) connections are pooled and shared. Again, this makes the middle tier more scalable.

Transaction Management

This is one of the most important services provided by the server to the application developer. The container supports **declarative transactions**. The meaning of a declarative transaction is that you can tell the container that specific operations (method invocations) should be transacted. The container now assumes the responsibility of starting the transaction, committing the transaction, and even rolling back any partially done operations within the transacted code in case of an error. All these are done without a single line of code written by the programmer. As you might imagine, transactions are expensive so we must be careful when deciding how many of them we will have.

Authentication and Access Control

Authentication and **Access Control** are two more great features supported by EJB containers. Just as we can declare transaction support in our deployment descriptor, similarly we can declare the security requirements for the application in our deployment descriptor. Let's look at these security requirements individually.

Authentication

You should give access to your application only to authenticated users. The users are provided with a login screen and only when their user ID and password are validated are they allowed to use the application. For our J2EE application, we need to create users and declare them in our deployment descriptor. The rest is taken care of by the EJB server. The deployment tool may even generate a login screen for the user, and authenticate the credentials of the user before granting access. Once again no coding is required on the part of the application developer.

Access Control

Once a user is granted access to the application, we'll probably want to grant access to the various business methods of the application based on the kind of user that they are. This is where we utilize the concept of **roles**, assigning users to a group that has a set of access rights to different parts of the system depending on who they are. This means that we can grant different privileges to different types of users.

For example, a bank manager will have different privileges from a bank customer for any banking application. So you define the roles for your application. If a user is currently using the application under a certain role, you assign certain privileges to the user and if another user is currently logged on under a different role, you assign a different set of permissions. Therefore, for each method, we define the access control by specifying the role under which that method may be executed. This is once again described in the deployment descriptor. The EJB server now ensures that the specified methods can be run only under the assigned privileges – no need to write any program code.

Note that the server vendors are responsible for transmitting the security context over IIOP to a remote server so you can have a single logon to your application. The logon information you have entered at the start of the application will be transmitted to a remote server and will be validated by the remote server.

The support for declarative security means that we can change the security control of our application at any time by modifying the deployment descriptor and re-deploying the application.

Persistence

We can even, should we choose, elect to have the container manage the persistence mechanism for our EJBs. At the time of deployment, we declare the desired persistence support for our bean in the deployment descriptor. We will need to specify the member variables of our bean that should be mapped to a database column. The deployment tool may even support the creation of a database table if it does not exist; we just define a one-to-one mapping between the instance variable and the database column. The rest is taken care of by the container. The container generates all the SQL statements required for database update. The container ensures the concurrency control on our database and thus also ensures the database integrity. Once again all this is done with no coding on the part of the programmer; this is a great asset to the application developer.

How the Container Provides Services

Without getting too involved with the finer details, it may help you to have some idea of the mechanisms by which the EJB container provides its various services to the EJB components. There are three basic ideas:

❑ First, there are clearly defined responsibilities between the various parts of an application using EJB components – the client, the EJB container, and the EJB component. The definition of these responsibilities is formally known as a **contract**.

❑ Second, the **services** that the container provides are defined in such a way that they are *orthogonal* to the component. In other words, security, persistence, transactions, and other services are separate from the Java files that implement the business logic of the component.

❑ Third, the container **interposes** on each and every call to an EJB component so that it can provides its services. In other words, the container puts itself between the client and the component on every single business method call.

The rest of this section explains each of these concepts in more detail.

Contracts

A contract in this context is simply a statement of responsibilities between different layers of the software. If each layer of the software follows the rules of its respective contract, it can work effectively with the layer above and the layer below, *without knowing anything else about that layer*.

This means, in general, that you can mix and match layers without rewriting your code, as long as you stick to the contract, and nothing but the contract. As shown in the figure below, there are three well-defined layers in the EJB specification: client, bean, and container. As a result of the contracts between these layers, your bean can run in different containers, unmodified, and your client can access different beans, unmodified:

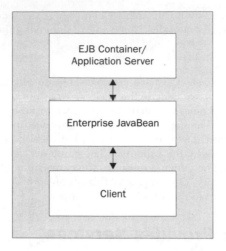

Of course, the contracts are written with more than portability in mind. The rules are carefully crafted to make it possible for server vendors to build their servers on many different technologies, with many different capabilities. The bean programmer can follow these relatively simple rules and patterns to take advantage of the services and capabilities of any of these application servers.

What kinds of rules are there for the bean programmer? We'll cover them later in the book, but the main ones are:

❑ The developer of an EJB component (also known as the 'bean provider') must implement the business methods (any method that provides access to the logic of the application) in the implementation class.

❑ The bean provider must implement the specific (and appropriate) methods if the bean is an entity with bean-managed persistence.

❑ The bean provider must define the enterprise bean's home and component interfaces.

❑ The bean provider must not use programming practices that would interfere with the container's run-time management of the enterprise bean instances.

Services

The EJB container exists to provide the bean programmer with services. For the most part, the bean programmer just needs to follow the rules to automatically take advantage of these services. They can simply tell the container the details of what should be provided. This process of "telling the container" is known as **declarative semantics**, and is one of EJB's best features. Declarative information is specified in an XML file known as the **deployment descriptor**. For many features, even this declarative information is not necessary, and the container will provide the feature without any work on the bean programmer's part at all.

In addition to the services that we have already mentioned, some containers will provide optional services. An important option for large projects is clustering for fail-over and scalability. Management tools are not part of the EJB specification, but are provided as an optional component by server vendors, and can be important to the success or failure of any project. The optional services that are available are limited only by a vendor's imagination. As the Java APIs expand to envelop the world, some of these additional services may become standardized. One example is the Java Management Extensions (JMX) API that may provide a lowest common denominator for management implementations.

The important point to understand about all these services is that they are implemented by the container developer, not by the business-logic programmer. This is possible, even though the container developer knows nothing about the business logic, because the business logic components – the Enterprise JavaBeans – follow the contract defined in the specification.

Interposition

An application developer follows the rules of the bean-development contract, and the container is then able to provide system-level services. But how exactly is this possible? There is a lot to it. Writing a quality EJB container is a difficult task. But there is one central concept that makes it easier for the bean developer to understand what is happening: **interposition**.

In the same way that, an RMI stub *interposes* between the client interface and the remote object to provide marshaling and network transport, the EJB container interposes between the client business interface and the EJB's business logic to provide services such as transactions, security, error handling, and persistence management. Let's look at this process in more detail.

First, here are the various actors involved in the process:

- ❑ The client to the EJB (this maybe a remote client or even another EJB – either way the process is the same)
- ❑ The EJB container
- ❑ A **home object**
- ❑ Either a remote or local object, which we will collectively call the **component object**
- ❑ An instance of the bean itself – this is the object that provides the business logic implementations

Each bean effectively exists within its own container, in the sense that the services provided to each bean are customized by the bean developer and application assembler (through the deployment descriptor), and by the deployer, through implementation-specific mechanisms. Remember though that a container is a theoretical construct.

An important point, with relation to EJBs, is that the client never has direct access to the bean instance – we'll see why this is important in a moment. Instead, the container generates two objects that it exposes to the client, as shown in the following diagram. These two objects are the home and component interfaces:

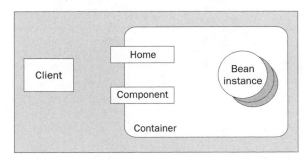

So let's follow a typical method call to an Enterprise JavaBean from a client:

> **It should be noted that a lot of the real details about how the steps below actually happen are container-specific, in other words each vendor can have its own way of doing it, therefore we can only discuss it in these general terms.**

Firstly, the client needs access to the home object, but how does a client know where to find this? When an EJB is deployed, the EJB container makes sure that the home object is available to the client through a JNDI lookup.

The home object is essentially a factory for bean instances. Therefore, the function of the home object is to return a reference to a bean instance when the client requests one. How or where the reference comes from is actually irrelevant to the client; the home object could either create a new bean instance or return a reference to an existing instance. Whether or not a bean instance is created, pooled, or whatever is dependent on the container's implementation.

Note that a client never has a direct reference to a bean instance. This is because the home object doesn't actually return a reference to the bean instance to the client, instead it returns a reference to a component object. This component object is basically a delegate or a proxy to the actual bean instance. So the client thinks it's getting a reference to the bean instance when in fact all it has is a proxy.

Once the client has a reference to the component interface, it can then call the bean's business methods as if it were accessing the bean instance directly. Each of these calls to the component interface will be delegated down to a bean instance to actually invoke.

It is in between the component object delegate and the bean instance that the container is able to interpose services required by the bean. This is shown more clearly in the diagram below:

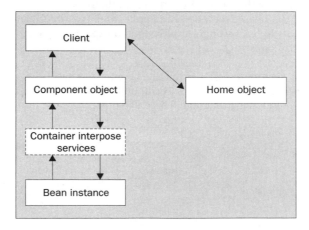

Logically the interposition will happen as follows (although some of the following steps may be optimized away):

❑ The container will examine the security credentials of the caller of that method.

❑ It will start or join with any required transactions.

❑ It will make any necessary calls to persistence functions.

❑ It will trigger various callbacks to allow the EJB component to acquire resources.

❑ Only after all of this is done will the actual business method be called.

❑ Once it is called, the container will do some more work with transactions, persistence, callbacks, and so on.

❑ Finally, the results of the business method, be it returned data or an exception, will be sent back to the remote client.

This explains the reason behind one of the less intuitive parts of Enterprise JavaBeans technology. The application developer will write an interface that declares their business logic functions, and they will write a class that implements those functions. But the class isn't required to implement the interface. In fact, the programmer is strongly discouraged from implementing that interface in their business logic class. How is it possible, then, for the client call to a function in the interface to eventually reach the corresponding business logic implementation? Basically, interface implementation has been replaced with a naming convention. The container will use Java introspection – either when you deploy your EJB or at run-time – to match methods in the interface with methods in the implementation.

EJB Types

We noted earlier that EJBs are server-side business logic components that exist on the middle tier. Actually, there are several different types of EJB:

❑ Session beans

❑ Entity beans

❑ Message-driven beans

Let us now examine each type of bean and describe its purpose.

Session Beans

Session beans, as the name suggests, have the same lifetime as the client session they are assigned to and are classified by the length of this client interaction. Thus, session beans can be divided into the following types:

❑ **Stateless** session beans – these do not declare any instance (class-level) variables. Therefore each method may operate only on its local parameters and there is no way to maintain state across method calls.

❑ **Stateful** session beans – these hold client state across method invocations. This type of bean will have instance variables declared in its class definition. The client sets the values of these variables during a method call and uses these values in other method calls.

From the above discussion, the obvious difference between stateless and stateful beans from the point of view of a bean developer is the declaration of the instance variables. More specifically, any session bean with class-level variable declarations should be treated as a stateful bean. We'll look specifically at developing session beans in Chapter 3.

It should now be clear that stateless session beans provide excellent scalability because the container does not have to remember the bean's state across method calls. However, saving the state of an EJB is a very resource-intensive process, so there is more work involved for the server in sharing stateful session beans than for stateless beans. Therefore the use of stateful beans in your application may not make your application as easily scalable as using stateless beans.

Entity Beans

Entity beans map to an underlying datastore table to create an object view of the datastore. For example, if you have a table called `Customer` in your database, you can create an entity bean to map each row of the table to a bean and each column in the table is mapped to an appropriate instance variable of the bean. Thus, an entity bean is always a stateful bean. Entity beans are classified depending on who takes the responsibility of synchronizing the bean's state (values of instance variables) with the underlying datastore. Therefore, we get entity beans of one of the following types:

- ❑ **Container-managed persistence (CMP)** – in this case the container assumes the full responsibility of synchronizing the state of the bean with the underlying datastore that it represents. The client may modify the bean's state several times during its lifespan; we may even find that multiple clients modify the bean's state at different times. It is the responsibility of the container to ensure data consistency and integrity while using a CMP bean. The container provides the code required for synchronizing the state, which basically consists of SQL statements for INSERT, MODIFY, DELETE, and so on. The container automatically generates all of these statements at the time of bean deployment. It is important to note, however, that CMP requires an underlying database that is relational in nature.

- ❑ **Bean-managed persistence (BMP)** – in this case the bean programmer has to implement the entire code for synchronization between the instance variables and the underlying datastore. The programmer must code all the necessary SQL statements and the JDBC calls in the bean's implementation class. The container assumes the responsibility of calling this code at appropriate times by way of callback methods, and keeps track of when the bean's state is dirty and needs synchronization. Accordingly, it calls the callback methods in the bean's implementation class where the programmer is responsible for providing the necessary synchronization code.

Why would a programmer take on the additional programming inherent to a BMP entity bean when the CMP container readily provides this service? Sometimes we need some flexibility in our design, or we may need to support persistence in non-relational storage. For example, version 1.1 of the EJB specification allows only one-to-one mapping between the instance variables and the columns of the table. This means that, when using this version, if you want to represent an aggregate object in an entity bean that stores its state in multiple tables, you can't use CMP. This is where BMP comes into the picture. The EJB 2.0 specification defines a sophisticated Query Language (QL) for persistence management.

There are some significant difference between the EJB 1.1 and 2.0 specifications, therefore we will discuss the 1.1 entity bean specification in Chapter 4, and the 2.0 specification in Chapter 5.

Message-Driven Beans

Messaging plays an important role in the present day architecture of distributed computing. Messages, by their very nature, are asynchronous, while method invocations are usually synchronous. If you wish to send a message to your business logic implemented in EJBs, how do you do it?

As the message delivery is asynchronous, you cannot assume the availability of the bean at the time of sending messages. It means that the bean must be activated or created whenever the message is received by the application. This is where message-driven beans are useful. These beans are driven by asynchronous message receipt.

Message-driven beans are new to EJB 2.0 specification, and we will discuss them in detail in Chapter 6.

Application Servers

Recently, we have seen a flood of **application servers** (app servers) into the marketplace. An app server is designed to manage the many facets of a business system; it can consist of many components, such as an EJB server, an HTTP server, a secured HTTPS server, and so on. Different app server vendors provide a variety of features in their servers. For example, an app server includes an HTTP server so that you don't need buy a separate web server for the deployment of your application. Similarly, a secured server (HTTPS) is generally provided as a part of the app server to enable your application to use secured web pages.

This competition between app servers leads to a lack of portability of applications between different vendor implementations. Your J2EE applications may not be portable across different vendors, thus defeating the motive behind Sun's "write once, run anywhere" products.

To ensure the portability of your J2EE applications across the app servers of different vendors, Sun has designed a compatibility suite for the vendors. The suite consists of more than 6000 tests that the server has to successfully pass through to get the compliance certificate from Sun. Some of the app servers that have achieved this certification are BEA WebLogic, IBM WebSphere, iPlanet, and SilverStream. The reader is encouraged to visit the official Sun site (http://java.sun.com/) for the latest updates.

Sun, in its J2EE specifications, gives some details about a contract between the container and the EJB server for the vendors to follow in their implementations of app servers. At the time of writing, this contract is not well defined and Sun is in the process of finalizing it. Once a suitable contract is defined and adopted, we will see the introduction of vendor-neutral EJB containers in the market. It means that you will be able to buy a container from any party and run it under another vendor's app server. At present, however, there are no independent container vendors and you are forced to use the container provided as a part of the app server.

Summary

This chapter has provided an introduction to the main concepts associated with Enterprise JavaBeans and presented an overview of the necessary architecture. After briefly setting the historical context with a discussion about the evolution of distributed computing over the last three decades, we saw why a new distributed architecture was needed.

We then briefly reviewed the J2EE platform and some relevant APIs, before looking more closely at EJBs and their architecture. This architecture provides a means to easily separate the development of application-specific business logic, from the lower-level system services that an enterprise application requires. The provision of these services by the container is one of the great advantages of the EJB architecture since it removes the onus for providing these services from the bean developer.

With so much material introduced, let us now delve into the details. In the next chapter, we will develop our first EJB, deploy it on the server, and test it.

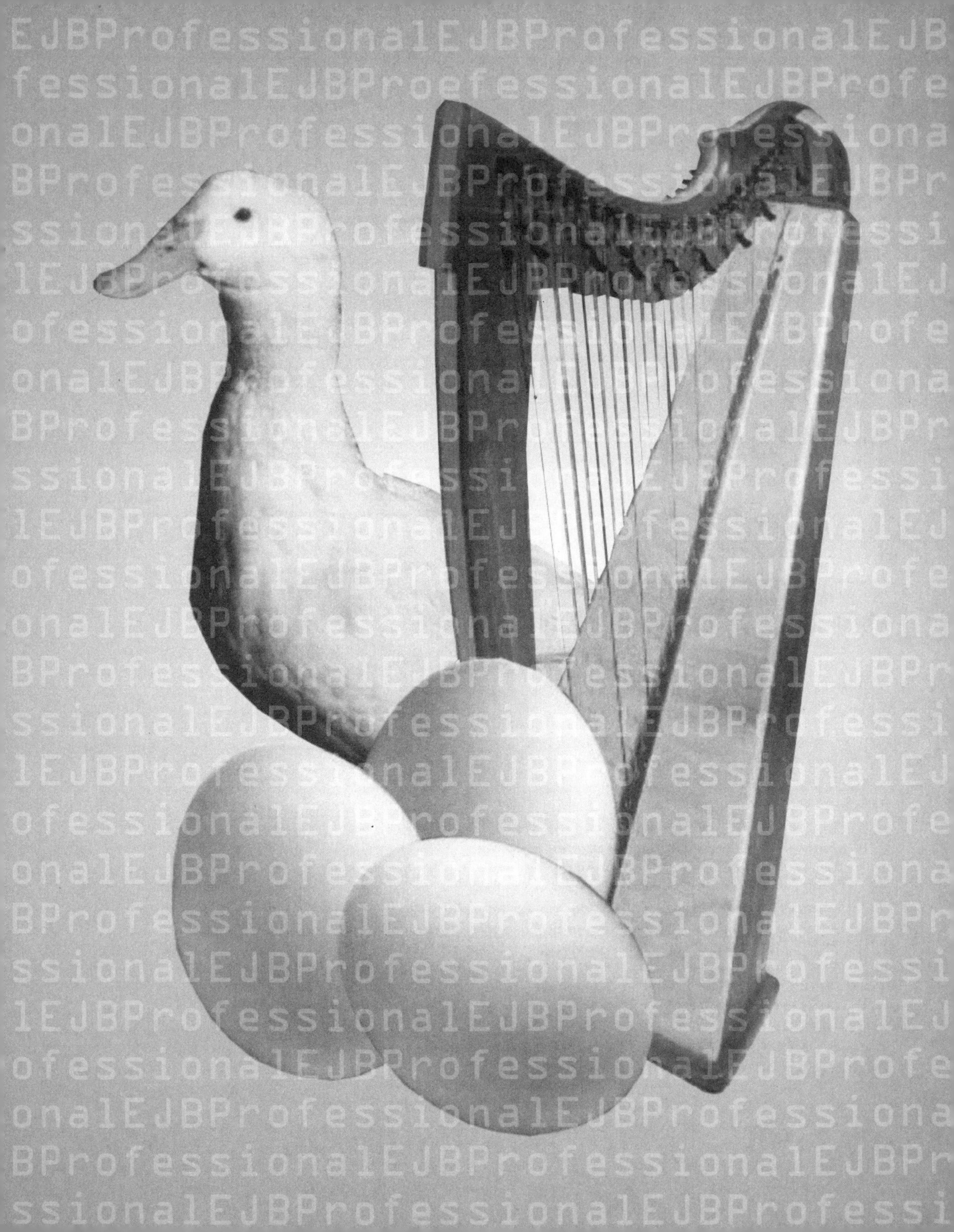

EJB Development

In the first chapter, you learned the EJB component model and the EJB architecture. Now, it's time to do some actual EJB development. In this chapter, we will be developing our first EJB. You will assemble the application containing this bean, deploy the application, write a client program, and test the application.

We will be covering the following:

- ❑ Understanding the roles involved in EJB development
- ❑ Developing a simple Enterprise JavaBean
- ❑ Understanding the deployment descriptor
- ❑ Understanding application deployment
- ❑ Writing a client program to test the application
- ❑ Understanding the various EJB interfaces and classes

Before we develop our first bean, let's first consider the different roles that need to be played in the development process.

EJB Roles

The EJB specification defines six distinct roles that are involved in the development and deployment of EJB applications:

- ❑ Enterprise Bean Provider
- ❑ Application Assembler
- ❑ Deployer
- ❑ System Administrator
- ❑ EJB Server Provider
- ❑ EJB Container Provider

Although the responsibilities of these roles are discretely divided, it is not necessary (and unlikely) that each role will map to a different individual person. For the most part you will find there are only really two relevant roles – an EJB developer (incorporating the bean provider, application assembler, and deployer) and the EJB server (incorporating the server provider and container provider).

The EJB specification also defines the contracts for each role thereby ensuring the smooth communication between the potentially different parties; compatibility is a key issue in this specification. We will discuss the various contracts as we go through the development of various kinds of beans.

The Enterprise Bean Provider

An **Enterprise Bean Provider** is nothing but you – a programmer, who does the coding of the EJBs. The bean provider is a domain expert who understands the business logic that is to be implemented in EJBs. As seen in Chapter 1, an EJB consists of three objects: the home object, component object, and an implementation object. The bean provider writes an interface to the home and component objects, as well as an implementation class that implements the various business methods defined in the remote interface. In addition, the bean provider writes an XML file called the deployment descriptor that defines the classes and interfaces that form the bean, as well as specifying the external resources required by the bean. The bean can use the system services provided by the container in its implemented methods. Finally, an EJB JAR file is created by the bean provider to contain all of the files described above.

We can now summarize the functions of a bean provider:

- ❑ Write a home interface for the bean
- ❑ Write a component interface for the bean that declares various business methods required by the application
- ❑ Write a implementation class that implements the various business methods declared in the remote interface
- ❑ Write a deployment descriptor describing the resources required by the bean and various other parameters
- ❑ Package the interfaces and implementation class along with the deployment descriptor into an EJB JAR file

The Application Assembler

The Application Assembler is a domain expert who has the knowledge of the business for which the application is being developed. The assembler gathers the beans developed by several bean providers and may even collect beans from other vendors to assemble them into an application to provide a complete solution to the business. The application assembler reads the deployment descriptors provided by the bean providers and adds the assembly instructions, such as transactional and security settings, to the deployment descriptor. The modified descriptor is later used in the deployment process.

The application assembler should understand the various interfaces declared by the bean developers; however, the assembler need not go into the coding details of the implemented methods. During application assembly, the assembler may collect other types of components, such as JavaServer Pages, HTML, and graphics files, in the application.

The Deployer

The Deployer takes an assembled application from an Application Assembler and deploys it on a specific environment. The deployer should have the operational knowledge of the specific EJB server and should be familiar with the deployment procedures for the specific server. The deployer must map the resources required by the application to the resources available at the current site. For example, an application may require a datasource that should be mapped to the existing database engine at the installation site.

The application may specify the security requirements in the deployment descriptor. The deployer should map the users and the groups defined in the system to the roles defined by the application. The deployer should set up the authentication for the application and the access control lists for the various business methods.

The EJB server vendor typically supplies a deployment tool to ease the deployment process.

The System Administrator

The System Administrator is responsible for the overall well-being of the installation. The functions of the administrator may be summarized as follows:

- ❑ Ensure the availability of the application at all times
- ❑ Configure and administer the entire installation
- ❑ Support the networking infrastructure at the installation
- ❑ Create groups and users for the system to be used by the deployer while deploying the application
- ❑ Monitor the application performance by using tools provided by server vendor
- ❑ Fine-tune the use of various resources required by the application

The EJB Server Provider

The EJB Server vendor is a system-level expert who has expertise in providing low-level system services for distributed object application and distributed transaction management. In general, the EJB server vendor is an operating system vendor or a middleware vendor. It is assumed that currently the same party plays the roles of both EJB server provider and the EJB container vendor.

The EJB Container Provider

The container provides the runtime environment for the deployed EJBs. The container provider should therefore also be a system-level expert who implements a secured, transaction-enabled, and scalable container that can be integrated with an EJB server. As mentioned in Chapter 1, the contract between the container and the server is not well defined in the current version of EJB specification. Thus, it is left up to the server and container vendors to integrate the two pieces together. The container provider is responsible for providing:

- ❑ Run-time environment for the deployed EJBs
- ❑ Deployment tool for deploying EJBs on the container

In addition to these responsibilities, the container provider may provide tools for monitoring the performance and managing the container and the deployed beans.

Developing Your First Enterprise JavaBean

We now have a reasonable amount of background into the EJB architecture and the various roles involved in working with EJBs. Therefore, it is time to start trying out the various roles that we described above and develop our first Enterprise JavaBean component. Over the course of the rest of the chapter, we will try our hand at the bean provider, application assembler, and deployer, as well as looking at what the server and container provider has supplied us with in the form of the J2EE Reference Implementation.

As we described for the bean provider, at its simplest an EJB consists of four elements:

- ❑ A home interface
- ❑ A component interface
- ❑ A bean implementation class
- ❑ A deployment descriptor

For our first bean, we will be developing a relatively simple EJB that calculates our monthly net salary based on annual salary, pension contributions, and income tax.

> *The bean that we will be developing is an example of a stateless session bean. However, we will be concentrating on the elements of EJB development that are common to all beans, no matter what type they are. Therefore, all discussions relating to the bean being a session bean will be deferred to the next chapter.*

However, before we can begin to look at implementing our first EJB, we must brief take a diversion into the realm of EJB clients.

EJB Client Views

The client view of an Enterprise JavaBean is provided by home and component interfaces. Under the 1.1 and early 2.0 drafts of the EJB specification, these interfaces always assumed the possibility that the component was remote. This had advantages, such as providing location transparency for your components. It also had disadvantages, chiefly in performance.

However, with Proposed Final Draft 2 of the EJB 2.0 specification, the concept of local interfaces was added. A local interface assumes that the client of an EJB is located in the same JVM as the component (in other words, it is another component co-located on the application server). We now, therefore, have two separately identifiable client views to an EJB.

Remote Clients

Remote clients are essentially the good-old EJB 1.1 client type. A remote client to an EJB uses the bean's remote interface and remote home interface. These remote interfaces are Java RMI interfaces, thus arguments passed from client to bean are passed by value, and each method must declare a typed exception of `java.rmi.RemoteException`. Remote clients are agnostic of the bean's location, and in fact under some load-balancing schemes, subsequent invocations can be processed by component instances located on different servers.

Local Clients

Local clients are collocated within the same JVM as the server bean, and consequently must be other server components. A local client to an EJB uses the bean's local interface and local home interface. As the client is assumed to be within the same JVM, arguments and results will now be passed by reference, which means that state is now potentially shareable between client and bean. Local interface methods never throw `java.rmi.RemoteException`.

Choosing the Type of Interface to Use

For session or entity EJBs, you may declare a remote home and component interface, a local home and component interface, or both. If you follow standard design patterns, you will write session bean façades that your clients use for all access to your business logic tier. These session beans will need to publish remote interfaces to make themselves accessible from the client tier. The remaining entity and stateless session beans can be thought of as an "implementation detail", and should probably publish only local interfaces. This will both hide the details of your object model (which makes it easier to maintain your application), and potentially improve performance.

> It is possible to provide both a local and remote client view to an EJB, but in most cases, the bean provider will need to make a design decision as to which is the most appropriate view.

Local Interfaces and CMP Persistence

Local interfaces play an important role in the new EJB 2.0 model of container-managed persistence. By avoiding the run-time penalty associated with remote semantics, they make it possible to model business objects using fine-grained entity beans. This is explained fully in Chapter 5.

Developing the Home Interface

The **home interface** is responsible for controlling the lifecycle operations upon a bean: creating, removing, and locating the bean. When using an EJB, the home interface is the first point of contact that a client has with a bean. The bean provider merely needs to write an interface to a bean's home – it is the container's responsibility to provide the implementation of the home object. The home interface is not associated with a particular instance of the bean, just with the type of bean.

A client to an EJB will acquire a reference to a bean's home interface through JNDI. As you will see when we write the deployment descriptor, each bean is registered in a JNDI server that can be used at run-time by clients to locate the bean's home interface. Once a client has a reference to the home interface it can then perform a number of operations on the bean through this interface (depending on whether it is a local or remote home). These operations are as follows:

- ❑ Create a new instance or find an existing instance of the bean (local and remote)
- ❑ Access the `EJBMetaData` interface (remote only)
- ❑ Get a serializable reference to a bean instance (remote only)
- ❑ Remove the bean instance (local and remote)
- ❑ Execute home business methods (remote entity beans only)

For our simple example, we will merely be using the home interface to create a new instance of our bean.

The home interface is extended from either the `EJBHome` interface for remote clients or the `EJBLocalHome` interface for local clients.

The EJBHome and EJBLocalHome Interfaces

The `EJBHome` interface definition is as follows:

```
package javax.ejb;

import java.rmi.Remote;
import java.rmi.RemoteException;

public interface EJBHome extends Remote {

    public abstract EJBMetaData getEJBMetaData()
        throws RemoteException;

    public abstract HomeHandle getHomeHandle()
        throws RemoteException;

    public abstract void remove(Object obj)
        throws RemoteException, RemoveException;

    public abstract void remove(Handle handle)
        throws RemoteException, RemoveException;
}
```

The `EJBLocalHome` interface is as follows:

```
package javax.ejb;

public interface EJBLocalHome {

    public abstract void remove(Object obj)
        throws RemoveException, EJBException;
}
```

In the `EJBHome` interface, the `getEJBMetaData()` method returns a reference to the `EJBMetaData` interface, which can be used for obtaining information about the bean.

> *Note that `EJBMetaData` is not a remote interface. However, the class that implements this interface must be serializable because an instance of this class is obtained by invoking a remote call on the home interface.*

The `getHomeHandle()` method returns a **handle** to the home object. A handle is basically a persistent reference to the object and can be used for re-construction of the object. A handle can be saved to local storage and used later to obtain the reference to the same home object in possibly another client session.

> *Note that the `HomeHandle` interface extends `java.io.Serializable` and thus it is possible to serialize the handle to a local storage.*

The handle may also be passed to another client running on a different virtual machine. The advantage in doing so is that the new client does not have to make a trip to the JNDI server to locate the home object. It can obtain the home object represented by this handle by invoking the `getEJBHome()` method on the handle. Thus, the client gets a readily available reference to the existing home object and can use it for creating instances of the bean.

You can remove the bean's instance by calling the `remove()` method on its home object and by passing the handle to this `remove()` method.

The effect of calling remove can have different consequences depending on the bean type. For example, calling `remove()` on a session bean merely returns the bean to the pool, but for entity beans, calling `remove()` is the equivalent of deleting records from the datastore.

Now that we have covered the basics of the home interface, let's write one for our bean.

The SalaryHome Interface

For our bean, we will be using a remote home interface, because we want our bean to be accessible by a simple standalone Java client that will be operating in a separate JVM from our bean. Our interface declaration will therefore be as follows:

```
package simpleBean;

public interface SalaryHome extends javax.ejb.EJBHome {


}
```

> *It is common EJB practice to name the home interface <bean-name>Home, the remote interface <bean-name> and the implementation class <bean-name>EJB.*

For our bean, we also need to define one method that will allow our client to access an instance of the bean – the create() method:

```
package simpleBean;

public interface SalaryHome extends javax.ejb.EJBHome {

    Salary create() throws java.rmi.RemoteException, javax.ejb.CreateException;
}
```

The create() method takes any argument necessary for initializing the state of a bean's instance (note that in this case our bean is stateless, therefore our create() method has no parameters), and returns a reference to the created remote object, or rather, the remote interface to the bean instance. The reference is returned to the client by way of an RMI stub that acts as a proxy to the server object. In fact, the client invokes methods on this proxy object completely unaware that it is only a proxy.

> *The container may not actually create new an instance of the bean but simply take a pooled instance and hand that reference back to the client. Conceptually though, it is appropriate to think of the client getting a new instance.*

Finally, create() methods can throw two exceptions: java.rmi.RemoteException (the standard RMI exception for remote calls) and javax.ejb.CreateException (should the container have problems creating a bean instance).

> *The create() methods are the primary methods that you will need to add to your bean's home interface. For entity beans you may also define finder and home business methods, which we'll look at in Chapters 4 and 5.*

Now we have our home interface, let's move on to the component interface.

Developing the Component Interface

We know that when a client calls `create()` on a home interface reference, it will get a reference to a component object – in our case, because we used a remote home interface, we get a reference to a remote object – but what can the client then do with this component reference? The bean provider uses the component interface to define what business methods the bean is to expose to the client. These methods are implemented in the bean's implementation class. Like the home interface, the container vendor creates an implementation class for this interface during the deployment process. When the program calls the `create()` method on the home object, the container creates an object of this class and returns a reference to the super interface. Using this reference, you can invoke methods on the remote object.

A remote interface is extended from the `EJBObject` interface:

The EJBObject Interface

```
package javax.ejb;

import java.rmi.Remote;
import java.rmi.RemoteException;

public interface EJBObject extends Remote {

    public abstract EJBHome getEJBHome()
        throws RemoteException;

    public abstract Handle getHandle()
        throws RemoteException;

    public abstract Object getPrimaryKey()
        throws RemoteException;

    public abstract boolean isIdentical(EJBObject ejbobject)
        throws RemoteException;

    public abstract void remove()
        throws RemoteException, RemoveException;
}
```

The `getEJBHome()` method returns a reference to the home object.

The `getHandle()` method returns a handle representing the current object. Note that the `HomeHandle` interface is implemented by all home object handles, whereas the `Handle` interface is implemented by all `EJBObject` handles. Like the home object handle, this handle may be saved to a local storage for a later use or may be passed to another client running under a different JVM. Passing the handle to another client provides a ready reference to the bean. The other client saves the trouble of locating the home interface and calling the `create()` method. It can simply call the `getEJBObject()` method on the handle to obtain the `EJBObject` reference represented by this handle. It is important to note here that the passing of the handle to another client does not pass on the security privileges of the first client to the second client.

The `getPrimaryKey()` method is used by entity beans and returns a reference of the `java.lang.Object` type that can be typecast to the `PrimaryKey` class representing the primary key used by the entity bean. If this method is called on the instance of a session bean, a `RemoteException` is thrown to the client.

The isIdentical() method is used for comparing the two EJBObject references. You cannot use Java's equals() method for comparing the object references in case of EJBs because the references could be different even if the bean is the same, as in the case of stateless session beans.

Finally, the remove() method removes the current instance of the bean. The removal does not mean that the bean is garbage-collected, it simply indicates to the container that the client is no longer interested in using this bean and the bean may be destroyed or returned to the pool of available instances. After removing a bean, your program should mark the object reference to the bean as null. If you attempt to use an object reference to a bean that has been previously removed, you will get a run-time exception.

However, for the most part you will be using the remote interface to call the business methods on your bean, so now let's go ahead and look at the remote interface for our bean.

The Salary Interface

Each business method we declare in our remote interface should throw a java.rmi.RemoteException. Thus, if any of the methods executed on the bean object throws an exception (either application or system exception), the container takes the responsibility of throwing a remote exception to the client.

For our example we will define a single business method calculateSalary().

```
package simpleBean;

public interface Salary extends javax.ejb.EJBObject {

    double calculateSalary(int annualSalary, int pensionContrib, double bonus)
        throws java.rmi.RemoteException;
}
```

The Local Interface

In our example, we are only coding for remote clients, therefore we defined our business methods through the remote interface. If, however, we were developing for local clients and had implemented our local interface through the EJBLocalHome interface then we would have needed to extend EJBLocalObject instead of EJBObject for our component interface.

As you will see the only appreciable difference between the EJBObject and EJBLocalObject interfaces is that the local interface is not an RMI remote interface (extends java.rmi.Remote):

```
package javax.ejb;

public interface EJBLocalObject {

    public abstract EJBLocalHome getEJBLocalHome()
        throws EJBException;

    public abstract Object getPrimaryKey()
        throws EJBException;

    public abstract boolean isIdentical(EJBLocalObject ejblocalobject)
        throws EJBException;

    public abstract void remove()
        throws RemoveException, EJBException;
}
```

In terms of declaring our business methods, besides not having them throw a `RemoteException`, there would be no difference, although of course when we came to implementing the methods in our implementation class we would need to be aware that arguments were being passed by reference instead of by value. We'll be seeing local interfaces again later in the book.

Developing the Bean Implementation Class

The final piece of Java coding required for our bean is to write the implementation class. This is the class that contains all the actual implementation details of our business logic. In addition to providing the implementation for these methods, there are a number of EJB-specific callbacks that we may also need to work with, depending on our type of bean.

The type of bean that we are writing determines what interface our implementation class will implement and consequently the callbacks that are required. The possible interfaces are:

❑ Session beans – `javax.ejb.SessionBean`

❑ Entity beans – `javax.ejb.EntityBean`

❑ Message-drive beans – `javax.ejb.MessageDrivenBean`

Each of these interfaces extends the basic marker interface `javax.ejb.EnterpriseBean`, which marks the class as serializable.

The SalaryEJB Interface

In our case, as we are developing a stateless session bean, we will implement the `SessionBean` interface as follows:

```
package simpleBean;

import javax.ejb.*;

public class SalaryEJB implements SessionBean {

}
```

We will be looking at the particulars of the `SessionBean` interface in the next chapter; for now all you need to know is that session beans require the following lifecycle methods (although you can probably guess the methods, such as `ejbCreate()`, that will be called when the home interface `create()` method is called):

❑   `ejbCreate()`

❑   `ejbRemove()`

❑   `ejbActivate()`

❑   `ejbPassivate()`

We also have to define another method that allows us to access the bean's context. We'll be looking at the context later in this chapter:

❑ setSessionContext(javax.ejb.SessionContext)

For our stateless session bean we do not need to provide any implementation for these methods (we will be leaving everything up to the container) so we can simply add their method signatures to our class:

```
package simpleBean;

import javax.ejb.*;

public class SalaryEJB implements SessionBean {

    public void ejbCreate() {}
    public void ejbRemove() {}
    public void ejbActivate() {}
    public void ejbPassivate() {}
    public void setSessionContext(SessionContext ctx) {}

}
```

Now the only thing left to do is provide the implementation for our calculateSalary() method:

```
package simpleBean;

import javax.ejb.*;

public class SalaryEJB implements SessionBean {

    public void ejbCreate() {}
    public void ejbRemove() {}
    public void ejbActivate() {}
    public void ejbPassivate() {}
    public void setSessionContext(SessionContext ctx) {}

    private static double taxRate = 28;

    public double calculateSalary(int annualSalary, int pensionContrib,
        double bonus) {

        double monthly = 0;
        monthly = annualSalary/12;

        //Add bonus
        monthly = monthly + bonus;

        //Remove pension contribution
        monthly = monthly - (monthly * (pensionContrib/100));

        //Remove tax
        monthly = monthly - (monthly * (taxRate/100));

        return monthly;

    }
}
```

Nothing too complex there. You should now be able to compile your three Java classes – in order to do so you will need the `javax.ejb` package in your classpath. You should find one in the library files for your EJB container implementation. For example, for the J2EE Reference Implementation it is in `%J2EE_HOME%\lib\j2ee.jar`.

> *Finally, note that we did not write the code for implementation of our two interfaces, home and remote. The container will generate the implementation for these two interfaces at deployment.*

However, in case you get the idea that you can do anything you like in the bean implementation class, there are some limitations to working with the EJB component model.

Limitations to the EJB Model

One of the principal advantages of the EJB architecture is that it relieves the bean developer from having to implement the system-level tasks, thus allowing them to concentrate more on the application-specific logic. However, this flexibility does come at a price, in that in order to hand-off the responsibility for transactions, security, etc. to the container, means sacrificing certain capabilities:

❑ Your bean must not use read/write static fields

❑ Your bean can't use threads or the threading API

❑ Your bean can't use AWT for input or output

❑ Your bean can't act as a network server, by listening, accepting, and multicasting on a socket

❑ Your bean can't use the `java.io` package

❑ Your bean can't load a native driver

❑ Your bean can't use `this` as an argument or return value

❑ Your bean can't modify the classloader; stop the JVM; change the input, output, and error streams

❑ Your bean can't access or modify security settings and objects

❑ You bean must not attempt to define a class in a package

❑ Your bean must not use the subclass and object substitution features of the serialization protocol

Most of these are limitations simply because to use them would be to compromise the container's ability to manage these things efficiently.

EJB Context

As we saw when we were writing the bean implementation class, we had to define a method called `setSessionContext()` that accepted a `SessionContext` object as a parameter. As you will discover over the next four chapters, each type of bean has a similar method. For example, entity beans require a `setEntityContext()` method, and message-driven beans have a `setMessageDrivenContext()` method.

Each of these methods accepts a subclass of an `EJBContext` object, the purpose of which is to provide the bean instance with some information about its container – the **bean's context**.

The `EJBContext` interface is as follows:

```
package javax.ejb;

import java.security.Identity;
import java.security.Principal;
import java.util.Properties;
import javax.transaction.UserTransaction;

public interface EJBContext {

    public abstract Identity getCallerIdentity();

    public abstract Principal getCallerPrincipal();

    public abstract EJBHome getEJBHome();

    public abstract EJBLocalHome getEJBLocalHome();

    public abstract Properties getEnvironment();

    public abstract boolean getRollbackOnly()
        throws IllegalStateException;

    public abstract UserTransaction getUserTransaction()
        throws IllegalStateException;

    public abstract boolean isCallerInRole(String s);

    public abstract boolean isCallerInRole(Identity identity);

    public abstract void setRollbackOnly()
        throws IllegalStateException;
}
```

Note that `getCallerIdentity()`, `getEnvironment()`, *and* `isCallerInRole()` *are deprecated.*

In addition, the `SessionContext` and `EntityContext` interfaces (but not `MessageDrivenContext`) also define:

```
    public abstract EJBLocalObject getEJBLocalObject()
        throws IllegalStateException;

    public abstract EJBObject getEJBObject()
        throws IllegalStateException;
```

The purpose of these methods is:

- The getEJBObject() and getEJBLocalObject() methods return the bean's component interface.

- The getEJBHome() and getEJBLocalHome() methods return the bean's home interface.

- The getCallerPrincipal() method returns the java.security.Principal that identifies the invoker of the bean instance's EJB object.

- The isCallerInRole() method tests if the caller of the session bean instance has a particular role.

- The setRollbackOnly() method allows the instance to mark the current transaction such that the outcome of the transaction must be a rollback. Only instances of a session bean with container-managed transaction demarcation can use this method. (This is the normal case.)

- The getRollbackOnly() method allows the instance to test if the current transaction has been marked for rollback. Only instances of a session bean with container-managed transaction demarcation can use this method. (This is the normal case.)

- The getUserTransaction() method returns the javax.transaction.UserTransaction interface. The instance can use this interface to demarcate transactions and to obtain transaction status. Only instances of a session bean with bean-managed transaction demarcation can use this method. In general, you should let the container manage your transactions.

EJB Exceptions

We've already seen a number of different exceptions used in our code so far; so let's take a quick detour to look at how to handle exceptions in our EJB applications.

The EJB specification outlines two main types of exceptions that an EJB can throw:

- **Application exceptions**
  These are application-specific exceptions relating to the executing business logic that the client should be handling. For example, invalid input augments, etc. Application exceptions must be a subclass of java.lang.Exception and never a subclass of java.lang.RuntimeException or java.rmi.RemoteException.

- **System exceptions**
  On the other hand, system exceptions are those caused by system-level faults such as JVM errors, JNDI errors, etc. System exceptions will be either a java.lang.RuntimeException or javax.ejb.EJBException wrapping the original exception.

Throwing Exceptions

Therefore, from within your EJB (or more specifically your bean implementation class) you will generally be throwing one of two exceptions:

For application exceptions, you would write your own exception class that subclasses (directly or indirectly) the basic java.lang.Exception class. So for our Salary bean, we could theoretically have defined an IllegalPensionContribution exception such as:

```
package simpleBean;

public class IllegalPensionContribution extends Exception {
  public IllegalPensionContribution();
}
```

For system exceptions, for example if we had to catch a `NamingException` on a JNDI lookup, we would have to throw an `EJBException` that wrapped the `NamingException`:

```
try {
   ...
} catch (javax.naming.Exception ne) {
  throw new EJBException(ne);
}
```

Declaring Exceptions

When it comes to defining what exceptions can be thrown in the method signatures on the home and component interfaces, things are slightly different:

❑   All application exceptions are declared in the `throws` clause as normal.

❑   `EJBException` is a subclass of `RuntimeException`, therefore you do not need to include it in the `throws` clause.

❑   The remote home and remote interfaces are RMI interfaces (they extend `java.rmi.Remote`) therefore, all methods on these interfaces must throw `java.rmi.RemoteException` to handle potential networking errors that could occur.

❑   Conversely, as the local home and local interfaces are local Java interfaces they must not throw `RemoteException`.

In addition, to these rules, there are a number of EJB lifecycle exceptions that must be declared. For example, we have already seen the `javax.ejb.CreateException` on `create()` methods. We will see the rest of these exceptions at the relevant time.

Writing the Deployment Descriptor

There's one more file that we need to write before we can deploy our EJB and that's the deployment descriptor. The deployment descriptor (which should be named **ejb-jar.xml**) is an XML file that contains the deployment instructions and lists the resources required by the components to be deployed. It also defines the security roles for the application, the authentication information, and the access control list for the various business methods.

> *Initially, under the EJB 1.0 specification, the deployment descriptor was written as a standard Java object, however from 1.1 it must be an XML document. Don't worry if you are unfamiliar with XML, the file is very easy to pick up.*

The deployment descriptor provides one of the main advantages of the EJB architecture by allowing the bean developer to declaratively determine which services the container will interpose on the bean at run-time.

Depending on what EJB server you are using, you may not even have to write this file at all. Many EJB server vendors provide their own deployment tools that provide a GUI interface for constructing this file. In addition, some servers require additional deployment descriptors beyond this one mandated by the EJB specification. For this book however, we will be providing you with the deployment descriptors that the example code requires so that you can get an appreciation of what attributes the deployment descriptor is defining.

The Document Type Definition (DTD) for ejb-jar can be found at the following URLs (depending on which EJB specification version you are using):

- ❑   http://java.sun.com/dtd/ejb-jar_2_0.dtd
- ❑   http://java.sun.com/j2ee/dtds/ejb-jar_1_1.dtd

This is what the top level of the XML root element look like:

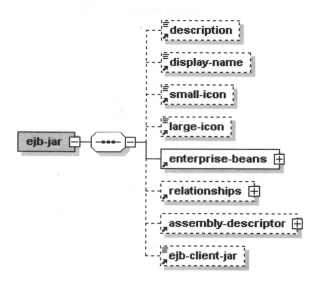

The dotted outlines represent optional elements, so you can see that <enterprise-beans> is the only required element.

Over the next eight or so chapters we will be going through all the different components of these DTDs, but for this chapter we will limit ourselves to just some of the top-level elements that we can define for our simple example bean:

DTD element	Optional	Purpose
`<ejb-jar>`		The root element of the deployment descriptor. All other elements are child elements of this.
`<description>`	Yes	Provides a textual description of the parent element. Many elements within the deployment descriptor can have an optional description.
`<display-name>`	Yes	A name that EJB deployment tools can use to display the name of the parent element. This name does not have to be unique.
`<small-icon>`	Yes	The relative path to a small (16x16) JPEG or GIF image, which can be used by deployment tools.
`<large-icon>`	Yes	The relative path to a large (32x32) JPEG or GIF image, which can be used by deployment tools.
`<enterprise-beans>`		The parent element that contains the declarations for all beans within this EJB application.
`<assembly-descriptor>`	Yes	The parent element that contains application assembly instructions for the EJB application. This includes transaction attributes, method permissions, security roles, and excluded methods.
`<ejb-client-jar>`	Yes	A JAR file that contains the classes necessary for a client to access the bean.

Our deployment descriptor will therefore initially look like this:

```
<?xml version="1.0"?>

<!DOCTYPE ejb-jar PUBLIC '-//Sun Microsystems, Inc.//DTD Enterprise JavaBeans
1.1//EN' 'http://java.sun.com/dtd/ejb-jar_2_0.dtd'>

<ejb-jar>

   <description>
       Single stateless session bean to calculate monthly salary
   </description>
   <display-name>Simple Bean</display-name>

   <enterprise-beans></enterprise-beans>

</ejb-jar>
```

Now we need to add our bean to the `<enterprise-beans>` element. The 2.0 DTD has three potential child-nodes:

DTD element	Purpose
`<session>`	The parent element for session beans
`<entity>`	The parent element for entity beans
`<message-driven>`	The parent element for message-driven beans

The EJB 1.1 DTD obviously only specifies the `<session>` and `<entity>` elements.

We will be looking at the child elements for these over the next four chapters, so we will defer most of that discussion to the relevant chapter. However, there are some basic elements that are common across all bean types that we will discuss here:

DTD element	Optional	Purpose
`<description>`	Yes	Same as before.
`<display-name>`	Yes	Same as before.
`<small-icon>`	Yes	Same as before.
`<large-icon>`	Yes	Same as before.
`<ejb-name>`		This is a unique identifying name within the ejb-jar file but is not necessarily the name that will be used to lookup the home interface. From entity beans with container-managed persistence based on the EJB 2.0 specification, the name must be a valid XML name (NMTOKEN) and not be a reserved word in the EJB Query Language.
`<home>`	Yes	The fully-qualified Java name of the remote home interface.
`<local-home>`	Yes	The fully-qualified Java name of the local home interface.
`<remote>`	Yes	The fully-qualified Java name of the remote interface.
`<local>`	Yes	The fully-qualified Java name of the local interface.
`<ejb-class>`		The fully-qualified Java name of the bean implementation class.

We can now then add the description for our Salary bean:

```
<?xml version="1.0"?>

<!DOCTYPE ejb-jar PUBLIC '-//Sun Microsystems, Inc.//DTD Enterprise JavaBeans
1.1//EN' 'http://java.sun.com/dtd/ejb-jar_2_0.dtd'>

<ejb-jar>

   <description>
        Single stateless session bean to calculate monthly salary
   </description>
   <display-name>Simple Bean</display-name>

   <enterprise-beans>
      <session>
         <description>
            Simple Salary Bean to calculate monthly net earnings
         </description>
         <display-name>Salary Bean</display-name>
         <ejb-name>Salary</ejb-name>
         <home>simpleBean.SalaryHome</home>
         <remote>simpleBean.Salary</remote>
         <ejb-class>simpleBean.SalaryEJB</ejb-class>
         <session-type>Stateless</session-type>
         <transaction-type>Container</transaction-type>
      </session>
   </enterprise-beans>

</ejb-jar>
```

Now we have all the files we need for our EJB application, the only step remaining is to package them up as an EJB JAR file.

Preparing the EJB JAR File

The final step in the EJB creation process and the product of the bean provider is to take the Java files and deployment descriptor and use the JAR utility to package them as a suitable archive.

For our example, we need to make sure that the archive has the following structure:

```
simpleBean/
          Salary.class
          SalaryHome.class
          SalaryEJB.class
META-INF/
          ejb-jar.xml
```

> Note that the EJB specification requires that the deployment descriptor must always be packaged under a directory called **META-INF**.

Deployment

The bean we have created must now be deployed into an EJB container before a client can use it. For our purposes we will be using the **J2EE 1.3 Reference Implementation (RI)**, however, you can either refer to Appendices B to G, or your container deployment instructions, which will give details on deploying the JAR file in your specific container of choice.

The Reference Implementation provides us with a GUI-based deployment tool that helps with the deployment and configuration of J2EE applications. In fact, we could have used this deployment tool to build our EJB JAR file and write our deployment descriptor for us. You can find instructions on how to use the deployment tool to do this in Appendix B. For now we will simply take our prepared JAR file and deploy it into our Reference Implementation. The overall deployment process remains proprietary, and this is why deployer becomes an important role in EJB.

Start the J2EE server running and then the deployment tool.

> *Within the* `%J2EE_HOME%\bin` *directory there are two batch executables* `j2ee.bat` *and* `deploytool.bat` *that will do this. Alternatively, the command lines* `j2ee -verbose` *and* `deploytool` *will start the server and run the Application Deployment Tool, respectively.*

Before we can deploy an EJB application using the RI we need to first create a J2EE application that will contain our EJBs. Some servers allow you to deploy an EJB JAR file straight into the EJB container; others, such as the RI, first require an Enterprise Archive (EAR) file to be created.

Using the deployment tool, create a new application by selecting the New Application... menu option under File menu. This opens a New Application dialog. Type the fully qualified path for the application file name and its display name. The deployment tool will create an EAR file with this name:

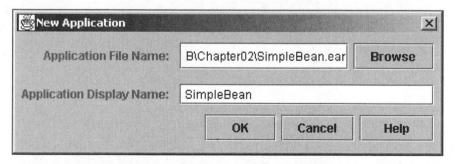

Select OK. This creates a new application with the given name and adds it to the first screen of the deployment tool. Next, we need to add our JAR file to this application. To do this select Add to Application | EJB JAR... from the File menu. This will prompt you to browse your file system for the JAR file. Select the EJB JAR file we created earlier, and hit the Add EJB JAR button. You should now see our Salary bean appear in the tree-view on the left of the tool's window:

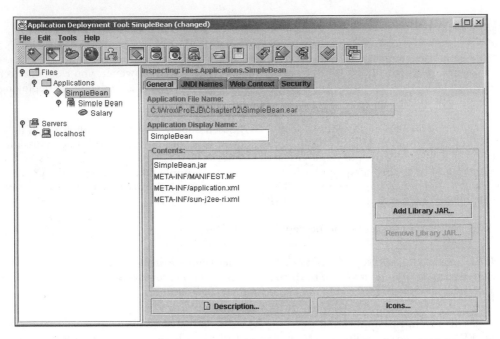

If you select the Salary bean in the tree-pane, you will see the right-hand pane adapt to display the basic properties of our bean. You will see that it has marked our bean as Session and Stateless:

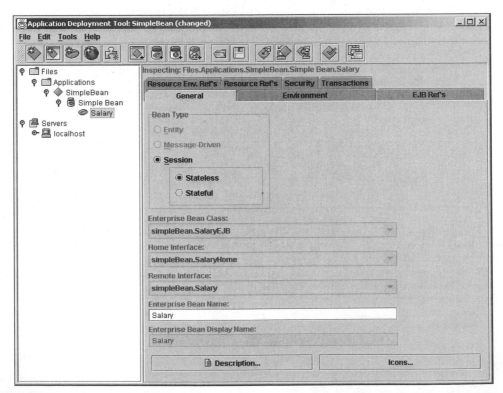

If you press the Description button you will see the description we added for our bean in the deployment descriptor:

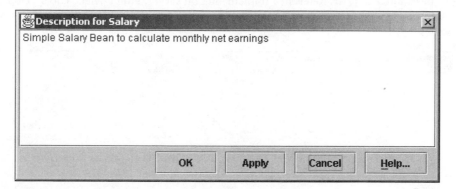

To view the deployment descriptor, select Descriptor Viewer from the Tools menu. As you will see, the simple act of adding the JAR file to the Deployment Tool has added a number of other attributes to our deployment descriptor:

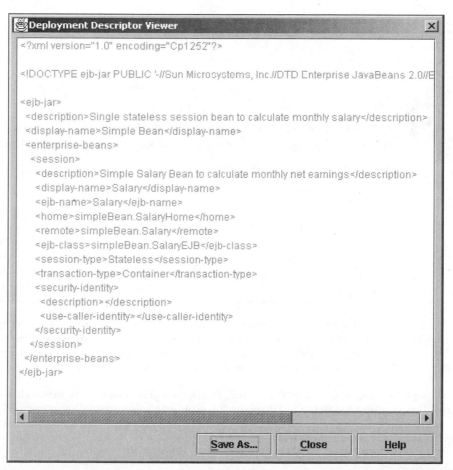

We are now ready to deploy our bean.

To deploy our bean into the J2EE Reference Implementation server, either select Tools | Deploy... or press the Deploy button on the toolbar. You will be presented with a window asking you to select which application to deploy:

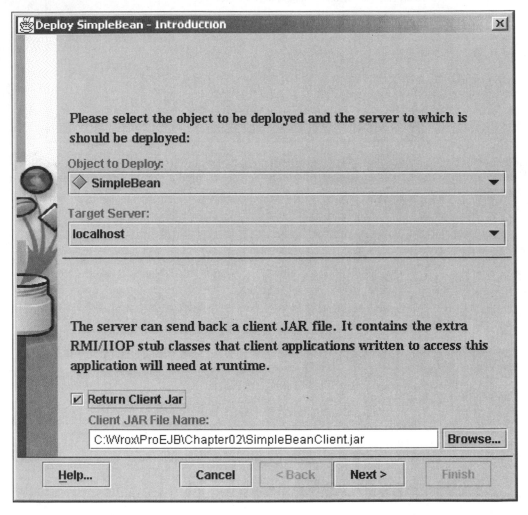

Make sure that SimpleBean is the selected application and also check the Return Client Jar box at the bottom of the window (you can also modify the location of where the client JAR file will be saved). The client JAR file contains all the required files (interfaces and stubs) for executing the methods of a remote EJB. We will need this later when we come to execute a client against our bean.

Press Next to move to the next screen of the wizard. This screen allows us to determine what name our bean is going to be registered as in the JNDI server. To avoid confusion, we will also use a JNDI name of Salary; however, we could specify almost any name we want so you can see how we can separate the deployment process from the development:

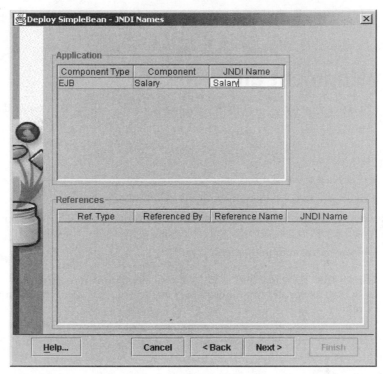

During the deployment process, the deployment tool generates several classes required by the container for the EJB to work properly. These are the additional files, such as RMI stubs and proxies, which allow the container to communicate and interpose services on your bean's behalf.

The deployment progress is displayed on your screen. The progress chart shows the various stages of the deployment. In case of errors, the tool will display an error message in a pop-up dialog:

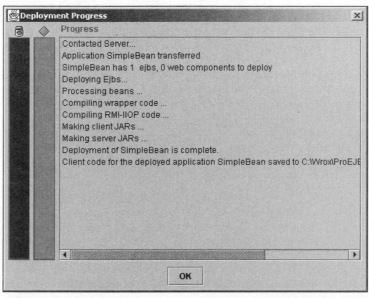

Once the application is successfully deployed, it is ready for use. Next, we will develop a client application for testing our bean.

Client Development and Lookup

In this section, we will write a Java console application to access the Salary bean created and deployed in the previous section.

In order for a client to work with an EJB, it must perform the following:

- ❑ Obtain a reference to a JNDI server
- ❑ Obtain a reference to the home object of the desired bean
- ❑ Obtain a reference to a remote object by either calling `create()` or a finder on the home object
- ❑ Invoke a business method on the bean

The consequence of this is that any client access to an EJB is always diverted through a carefully controlled path by the container, which allows the container to provide a variety of services and capabilities transparently to the client.

So now we know what is needed, let's see how we go about doing it. We'll start with the basics of our client class:

```
import javax.ejb.*;
import simpleBean.*;
import javax.naming.InitialContext;

class SalaryClient {

  public static void main(String[] args) {

  }
}
```

The first thing we need to do is obtain a reference to the JNDI server. To do this we must obtain a reference to an `InitialContext` object, which basically acts like the root to the JNDI tree. From this initial context we can search the tree for a specific entry – in this case the reference to our EJB's home.

For the Reference Implementation, we can connect to the JNDI server simply by creating a new `InitialContext` object with no arguments. However, for most other containers additional properties will be required such as the initial context factory object and the provider URL, which can be added to the initial context as a hash table. We also need to wrap our call in a `try/catch` block of course:

```
import javax.ejb.*;
import simpleBean.*;
import javax.naming.InitialContext;

class SalaryClient {

  public static void main(String[] args) {

    try {

      InitialContext ctx = new InitialContext();
      Object objRef = ctx.lookup("Salary");

    } catch (javax.naming.NamingException ne) {
      System.out.println("Naming Exception caught: " + ne);
    }
  }
}
```

Once we have our context, we can simply call the `lookup()` method to get a reference to our EJB home object. The EJB specification recommends that the EJB container register EJBs under the `java:comp/env/ejb` environment. However, for the J2EE RI, this context is only available from within a J2EE application, therefore we simply need to look up `"Salary"`:

```
import javax.ejb.*;
import simpleBean.*;
import javax.naming.InitialContext;

class SalaryClient {

  public static void main(String[] args) {

    try {

      InitialContext ctx = new InitialContext();
      Object objRef = ctx.lookup("Salary");

    } catch (javax.naming.NamingException ne) {
      System.out.println("Naming Exception caught: " + ne);
    }
  }
}
```

The next step is to take this object reference and typecast it to our home interface. The problem is that the stub returned by the `lookup()` method to the JNDI server is only of type `Object`. This is because the underlying RMI-IIOP protocol for the lookup does not support multiple interfaces – RMI-IIOP must accommodate a number of other languages, some of which to not support inheritance. Consequently we need to narrow this generalized `Object` type into something far more specific for our purposes. This is where the `narrow()` method of `PortableRemoteObject` comes in.

The `narrow()` method takes two arguments: the object reference that is to be narrowed, and the type to which the reference should be narrowed. Once the object reference has been narrowed, we are then able to do a simple class cast to our home interface:

```
import javax.ejb.*;
import simpleBean.*;
import javax.naming.InitialContext;

class SalaryClient {

  public static void main(String[] args) {

    try {

       InitialContext ctx = new InitialContext();
       Object objRef = ctx.lookup("Salary");

       SalaryHome home = (SalaryHome)javax.rmi.PortableRemoteObject.narrow(
                          objRef, SalaryHome.class);

    } catch (javax.naming.NamingException ne) {
       System.out.println("Naming Exception caught: " + ne);
    }
  }
}
```

We need to use the `PortableRemoteObject`*'s* `narrow()` *method because we are using the remote home interface. If our client is local to the EJB, we would merely need the class cast to* `SalaryHome` *as follows:*

```
SalaryHome home = (SalaryHome)objRef
```

The program then calls the `create()` method on the home object to create a bean instance. The `create()` method returns a reference to the remote object in the form of a stub:

```
import javax.ejb.*;
import simpleBean.*;
import javax.naming.InitialContext;

class SalaryClient {

  public static void main(String[] args) {

    try {

       InitialContext ctx = new InitialContext();
       Object objRef = ctx.lookup("Salary");

       SalaryHome home = (SalaryHome)javax.rmi.PortableRemoteObject.narrow(
                          objRef, SalaryHome.class);

       Salary bean = home.create();

    } catch (javax.naming.NamingException ne) {
       System.out.println("Naming Exception caught: " + ne);
    } catch (javax.ejb.CreateException ce) {
       System.out.println("Create Exception caught: " + ce);
    } catch (java.rmi.RemoteException re) {
       System.out.println("Remote Exception caught: " + re);
    }
  }
}
```

Note that the EJB server creates two objects at this time, a remote object that implements the remote interface and the object of the implementation class (our `SalaryEJB` class). The reference to the remote object is returned to the client. The EJB server may create a new object of the implementation class by calling its constructor or by assigning an existing instance from the pool to the client.

Using this remote reference, the client can invoke the business methods on the bean:

```
import javax.ejb.*;
import simpleBean.*;
import javax.naming.InitialContext;

class SalaryClient {

  public static void main(String[] args) {

    try {

        InitialContext ctx = new InitialContext();
        Object objRef = ctx.lookup("Salary");

        SalaryHome home = (SalaryHome)javax.rmi.PortableRemoteObject.narrow(
                        objRef, SalaryHome.class);

        Salary bean = home.create();

        System.out.println("Monthly net salary: " +
                bean.calculateSalary(28000, 2, 500));

    } catch (javax.naming.NamingException ne) {
      System.out.println("Naming Exception caught: " + ne);
    } catch (javax.ejb.CreateException ce) {
      System.out.println("Create Exception caught: " + ce);
    } catch (java.rmi.RemoteException re) {
      System.out.println("Remote Exception caught: " + re);
    }
  }
}
```

Note that in the above program, we do not explicitly release the reference to the bean. This is not required in this particular case as the program terminates immediately after printing the result of the method invocation. The EJB server will then return the bean instance to the pool of available beans. Your program may voluntarily relinquish control on the bean by calling the bean's `remove()` method and marking the reference variable as `null`. When you do this, the bean may not necessarily be garbage-collected; the EJB server may simply return it to the pool for later assignment to another client.

Once you have compiled the client class, you can execute; it but make sure that you place the client JAR file that the deployment tool created for us in the client's classpath:

```
C:\WINNT\System32\cmd.exe                                                    _□×

C:\Wrox\ProEJB\Chapter02\code>java -classpath %J2EE_HOME%\lib\j2ee.jar;SimpleBeanClient.jar;. SalaryClient
Monthly net salary: 2053.925

C:\Wrox\ProEJB\Chapter02\code>
```

Running the Client Application from a Remote Machine

EJBs can provide a location-independent view to the client, through the remote interface. Thus, to access an EJB from a remote machine, you do not need any code changes. However, the client still needs to obtain the initial context of the JNDI server. Thus, if you are accessing the J2EE app server from a remote machine, you will need to specify the two environment variables to bootstrap into the naming service. The command line to run our salary client from a remote machine might then look like:

```
java -Dorg.omg.CORBA.ORBInitialHost=[ip address or name of server]
     -classpath %J2EE_HOME%\lib\j2ee.jar;..\SimpleBeanClient.jar SalaryClient
```

To run the application from the remote machine, you will also need to copy the `SimpleBeanClient.jar` file onto the client machine.

EJBMetaData

As we saw earlier in the chapter, the `EJBHome` interface has a method that returns us an interface to `EJBMetaData`. The `EJBMetaData` interface declares several methods for bean introspection.

```
package javax.ejb;

public interface EJBMetaData {

    public abstract EJBHome getEJBHome();

    public abstract Class getHomeInterfaceClass();

    public abstract Class getPrimaryKeyClass();

    public abstract Class getRemoteInterfaceClass();

    public abstract boolean isSession();

    public abstract boolean isStatelessSession();
}
```

For example, the `getHomeInterfaceClass()` method returns a reference to the `Class` object representing the bean's home interface. The `getRemoteInterfaceClass()` method returns the reference to the `Class` object representing the bean's remote interface. The `isSession()` method returns `true` if the current bean represents a session bean the and `isStatelessSession()` method returns `true` for a stateless bean. In addition, there is a method called `getPrimaryKeyClass()`. This method is useful in the case of entity beans and returns the primary key class for the current bean; if called for a session bean it will throw an exception.

The `EJBMetaData` interface is mainly used by tool developers for introspection, however, let's quickly develop a client that will get the metadata for our Salary bean:

```java
import javax.ejb.*;
import simpleBean.*;
import javax.naming.InitialContext;
import java.lang.reflect.*;

class SalaryInspector {

  public static void main(String[] args) {
    try {
        InitialContext ctx = new InitialContext();
        Object objRef = ctx.lookup("Salary");
        SalaryHome home = (SalaryHome)javax.rmi.PortableRemoteObject.narrow(
                          objRef, SalaryHome.class);

        EJBMetaData data = home.getEJBMetaData();

        Class homeClass = data.getHomeInterfaceClass();
        System.out.println("The home interface is: " + homeClass.getName());
        getClassInfo(homeClass);

        Class remoteClass = data.getRemoteInterfaceClass();
        System.out.println("The remote interface is: " + remoteClass.getName());
        getClassInfo(remoteClass);

        String beanType = "";
        if(data.isSession()) {
           if (data.isStatelessSession()) {
             beanType = "Stateless Session Bean";
           } else {
             beanType = "Stateful Session Bean";
           }
        } else {
          beanType = "Entity Bean";
        }

        System.out.println("The bean is a: " + beanType);

    } catch (javax.naming.NamingException ne) {
      System.out.println("Naming Exception caught: " + ne);
    } catch (java.rmi.RemoteException re) {
      System.out.println("Remote Exception caught: " + re);
    }
  }

  private static void getClassInfo(Class cls) {

    String name = cls.getName();
    Constructor[] constructors = cls.getConstructors();
    Field[] fields = cls.getFields();
    Method[] methods = cls.getMethods();

    System.out.println(name + " has " + constructors.length + " constructors");
    for (int i =0; i < constructors.length ; i++) {
        System.out.println("" + constructors[i]);
    }
```

```
        System.out.println(name + " has " + fields.length + " fields");
        for (int i = 0; i < fields.length; i++)  {
            System.out.println("" + fields[i]);
        }

        System.out.println(name + " has " + methods.length + " methods");
        for (int i = 0; i < methods.length; i++) {
            System.out.println("" + methods[i]);
        }
    }

}
```

When you run this you'll get a result something like this:

```
C:\WINNT\System32\cmd.exe                                                                          _ □ ×

C:\Wrox\ProEJB\Chapter02\code>java -classpath %J2EE_HOME%\lib\j2ee.jar;..\SimpleBeanClient.jar;. SalaryInspector
The home interface is: simpleBean.SalaryHome
simpleBean.SalaryHome has 0 constructors
simpleBean.SalaryHome has 0 fields
simpleBean.SalaryHome has 5 methods
public abstract void javax.ejb.EJBHome.remove(java.lang.Object) throws java.rmi.RemoteException,javax.ejb.RemoveExceptio
n
public abstract void javax.ejb.EJBHome.remove(javax.ejb.Handle) throws java.rmi.RemoteException,javax.ejb.RemoveExceptio
n
public abstract javax.ejb.EJBMetaData javax.ejb.EJBHome.getEJBMetaData() throws java.rmi.RemoteException
public abstract javax.ejb.HomeHandle javax.ejb.EJBHome.getHomeHandle() throws java.rmi.RemoteException
public abstract simpleBean.Salary simpleBean.SalaryHome.create() throws java.rmi.RemoteException,javax.ejb.CreateExcepti
on
The remote interface is: simpleBean.Salary
simpleBean.Salary has 0 constructors
simpleBean.Salary has 0 fields
simpleBean.Salary has 6 methods
public abstract void javax.ejb.EJBObject.remove() throws java.rmi.RemoteException,javax.ejb.RemoveException
public abstract javax.ejb.EJBHome javax.ejb.EJBObject.getEJBHome() throws java.rmi.RemoteException
public abstract java.lang.Object javax.ejb.EJBObject.getPrimaryKey() throws java.rmi.RemoteException
public abstract javax.ejb.Handle javax.ejb.EJBObject.getHandle() throws java.rmi.RemoteException
public abstract boolean javax.ejb.EJBObject.isIdentical(javax.ejb.EJBObject) throws java.rmi.RemoteException
public abstract double simpleBean.Salary.calculateSalary(int,int,double) throws java.rmi.RemoteException
The bean is a: Stateless Session Bean

C:\Wrox\ProEJB\Chapter02\code>_
```

Summary

We started this chapter with a detailed review of the roles involved in the development and deployment of EJB applications. From this discussion, we can further generalize the various roles into those of the developer (bean provider, application assembler, and deployer) and those of the server (server and container provider). With this background knowledge in hand, it was possible to develop our first EJB.

At the initial stage of the development process we assessed the particular requirements of our application, in terms of the client view. Whether the client is going to be remote or local is an important issue as there are differences in the implementation of the two types, and the bean provider will need to decide the most appropriate view early in the design stages. For our example we used a remote home interface.

Next, we introduced all of the new code necessary for producing the home interface, the component interface, the implementation class, and the XML deployment descriptor.

Thus, we have learned that the four elements of an EJB in their sequential order of creation are:

- ❑   A **home interface** – responsible for controlling the lifecycle operations upon a bean: creating, removing, and locating the bean

- ❑   A **component interface** (local or remote) – used by the bean provider to define what business methods the bean is to expose to the client

- ❑   A **bean implementation class** – contains all the actual implementation details of our business logic

- ❑   A **deployment descriptor** – XML file containing deployment instructions, resource requirements of the deployed components, and security roles of the application

After packaging our programs into an EJB JAR file, we deployed our EJB via a J2EE application created using the highly user-friendly J2EE 1.3 Reference Implementation deployment tool. Finally, we accessed our first EJB by running a Java console application program.

In the next few chapters we will start to look in more detail at the specific types of EJB available to us, starting with session beans.

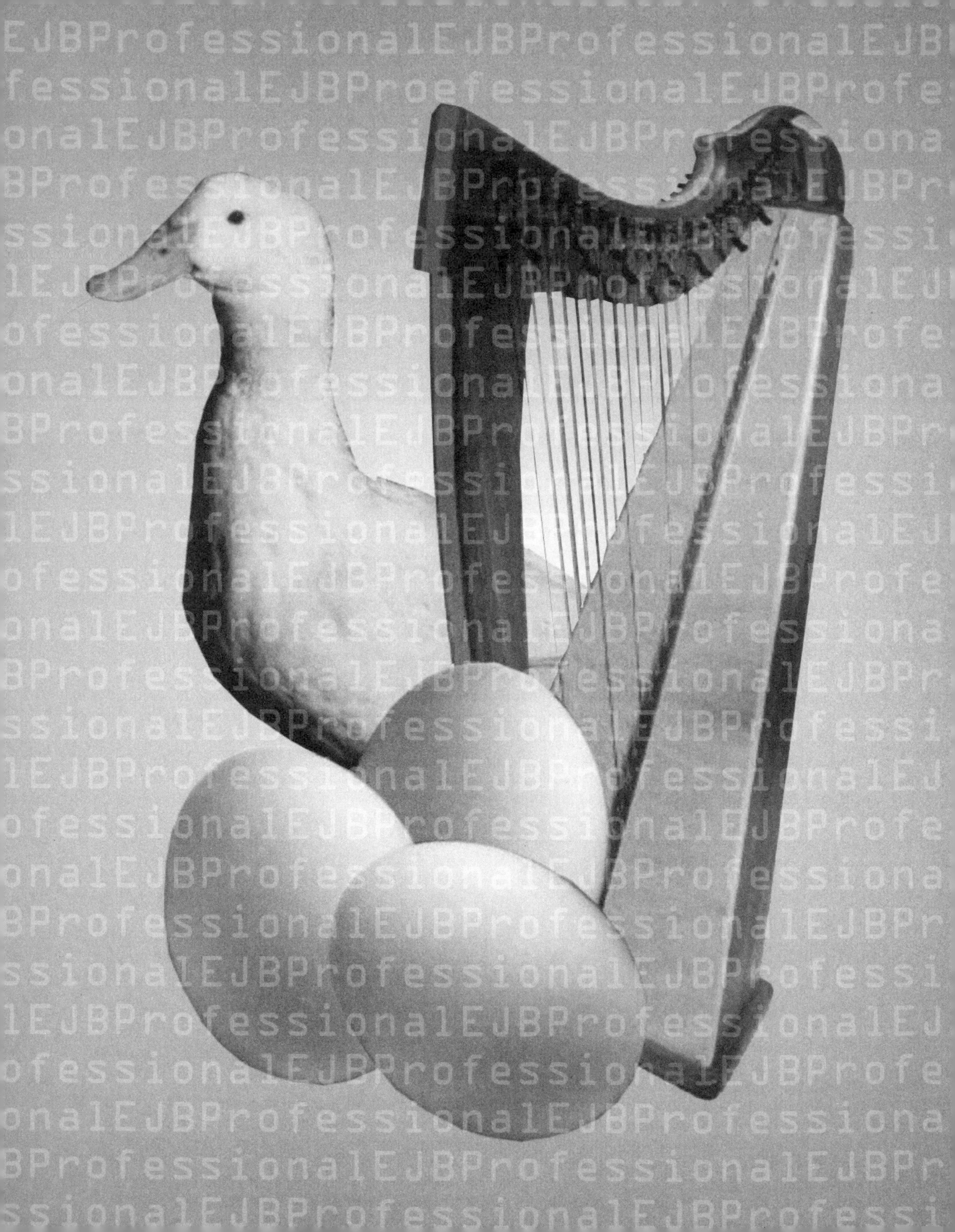

3

Developing Session Beans

In the previous chapter, we studied the development of our first Enterprise JavaBean. Although we didn't stress it, the Salary bean was in fact an example of a **session bean**. Session beans can be viewed as an extension to a client application, in that they are only ever used by one client at a time. Although they are capable of updating shared data in an underlying database, session beans do not represent that data. Any given session bean can be relatively short-lived, even though it models the session for a client.

Session beans are differentiated into either stateful or stateless depending on the intended support for the state of a client throughout its application session.

In this chapter, we will learn more about session beans, how they are developed, how they are deployed, and how to use them in a client application. We will discuss the following topics:

- ❑ Creating session beans
- ❑ Deploying session beans
- ❑ Lifecycles of session beans
- ❑ Lifecycle of a session bean from the client's point of view
- ❑ Lifecycle of a stateless session bean from the bean's point of view
- ❑ Lifecycle of a stateful session bean from the bean's point of view
- ❑ Sequence diagrams for session beans

What are Session Beans?

As discussed briefly in Chapter 1, there are two types of session beans: **stateful** and **stateless**. These two types have much in common:

❑ Both implement the `javax.ejb.SessionBean` interface, and therefore have the same container callbacks

❑ Both represent a private resource for the client that created them

❑ Both are intended to model a process or a task

❑ Both can update shared data, but do not represent that shared data in the way that an entity bean does

In fact, the only way that an EJB container can distinguish a stateless session bean from a stateful session bean is to look in the XML descriptor file to see which type the programmer intended the bean to be.

The primary difference between the two types of beans – as is obvious from their names – is how they treat **object state** (in other words, their variables). This simple but important difference has complex ramifications for the design of your system. We'll talk about this later in the chapter.

> **A stateful session bean can keep data between client accesses, whereas a stateless session bean must not.**

Stateless Session Beans

Stateless session beans are fairly straightforward, being just beans that supply business logic for one client at a time without keeping track of the state of the client across method invocations. By state we mean keeping track of values through the use of instance variables. This doesn't mean that a stateless session bean cannot hold state but rather it can't hold state across more than a single client method call – therefore for any resources that the bean uses, such as database connections, it is the bean provider's responsibility to clean up these resources before the method exits.

A simple example of a stateless session bean is one used to calculate a number; the number can be arbitrarily complicated, but won't be stored anywhere other than the client. We'll look at developing such a bean shortly.

Stateful Session Beans

As the name suggests, a stateful session bean maintains the client's state across method invocations. The client state is maintained in the instance variables of the session bean. Thus, to create a stateful session bean, you must declare instance variables in the bean's implementation class. The client invokes a business method on the bean which, along with other things, may set the values of these variables. In another method call, the client and/or other business methods can use the values stored in these variables and may further modify the values. These method calls could set the values by retrieving data from an underlying data store (database, XML files, or simple text file), or they could take them from an entity bean that is representing that data. There will be more on entity beans in Chapter 4.

A typical example of a stateful session bean is a shopping cart. Once the client logs on to a site that sells goods online, a shopping cart is assigned to the client. The client adds the purchases to the shopping cart, removes a few items at some time during the shopping process, and finally checks out all the contents of the cart before leaving the store. During the entire client session, the client is the exclusive user of the assigned shopping cart and no other user will be able to share this shopping cart with the current user. The shopping cart may be implemented in a stateful session bean. The contents of the cart represent the client's state, and such state is maintained throughout the client session.

To make the EJB architecture scalable, the container may **passivate** beans that are not used by the client for a certain period of time. Such beans may be assigned to another client when needed. In such a case, the container has to save the current state of the bean to a temporary storage before the bean is assigned to another client. When the first client requests another method invocation, some other instance (the one which is available in the pool currently) will be assigned to the client. Before the bean instance is assigned, the container restores the earlier state from the temporary storage. This process is called **activation**. The container assumes full responsibility for passivation and activation.

The container may save the bean's state in a temporary cache or in a database. Thus, there may be a considerable overhead involved in serializing/deserializing such state. This makes the use of stateful session beans less efficient compared to stateless session beans in terms of scalability of the application. Hence, we would only use stateful session beans when we specifically need to maintain the state across method invocations, like in our example of shopping cart described above. If a bean implements a simple business logic that computes a result and returns it to the user, it may not require maintaining state across method invocations. Similarly, if the bean does a simple database lookup like returning the tax percentage depending on the geographical location, it may not be required to maintain the state across method invocations. In such cases, we would use stateless session beans to produce a more efficient application.

The SessionBean Interface

Each session bean implementation class that we write, whether stateless or stateful, must implement the `javax.ejb.SessionBean` interface. This interface declares a number of callback methods that we must include in our implementation class for it to function as a session bean. Fortunately, we are not required to write them all ourselves as the container will provide implementations for us, although we can add actions that we require to be performed at certain times.

Here is the `SessionBean` interface:

```
package javax.ejb;

import java.rmi.RemoteException;

public interface SessionBean extends EnterpriseBean {

   public void setSessionContext(SessionContext ctx)
      throws EJBException, RemoteException

   public void ejbRemove() throws EJBException, RemoteException

   public void ejbActivate() throws EJBException, RemoteException

   public void ejbPassivate() throws EJBException, RemoteException
}
```

The reason the container expects these methods to be included in our session bean is because it uses them to notify the bean instance of relevant lifecycle events. In each case, the throwing of a `RemoteException` is defined for compatibility with the EJB 1.0 specification. Beans written to the EJB 1.1 or 2.0 specification should just throw an `EJBException`.

The `setSessionContext()` method is used by the container to set the session context, which the instance should store in an object variable, and is called after instance creation. The `ejbRemove()` method is invoked by the container before it ends the life of the session bean, either due to the client invoking a remove method, or the container deciding to timeout the bean. The container calls the `ejbActivate()` method when it activates an instance from its passive state, when the instance should acquire any resource that was earlier released in the `ejbPassivate()` method. The container calls the `ejbPassivate()` method before it puts the bean into the passive state, and the instance should release any resources it can re-acquire later through the `ejbActivate()` method.

Developing a Stateless Session Bean

In this section, we will go through the full development and deployment process for a simple EJB. We will be coding a stateless session bean to start with, because they are probably the simplest to develop and deploy.

You'll notice that this example is quite similar to that which we developed for the previous chapter, however, this time we'll be examining the session bean specifics.

In order to create our bean, we will have to follow these steps:

1. Write home and component interfaces for a stateless session bean

2. Write a bean implementation class for a stateless session bean

3. Compile the code

4. Assemble the bean into an application, using either a vendor-provided tool or writing the deployment descriptor by hand

5. Deploy the application on the EJB server

6. Test it using a Java application

EJB development involves writing two interfaces and one implementation class. The two Java interfaces consist of a home interface and a component interface; the home interface is used for creating a bean instance and the component interface contains the method signatures for your business methods. The bean implementation class contains the implementation of those business methods.

We will develop a bean that will help us to calculate additions to and withdrawals from an account. As noted above, this bean will consist of three parts:

- An home interface: `StatelessFundManagerHome`

- A component, or in this case remote, interface: `StatelessFundManager`

- And a bean implementation class: `StatelessFundManagerEJB`

We are developing our bean with a remote interface because it will only be accessed by a remote client.

As well as presenting a relatively simple example to follow, later in the chapter we'll be turning this stateless session bean into a stateful session bean. This will allow us to look at the differences in lifecycle between the two types of session bean, as well as keeping us focused on the implementation of the bean as opposed to the implementation of the business methods.

First, though, we will write the stateless bean, starting with the home interface.

The Home Interface of StatelessFundManager

We looked at the particulars of writing the home interface in the last chapter, so we can go straight on to look at our implementation:

```
import java.rmi.RemoteException;
import javax.ejb.CreateException;
import javax.ejb.EJBHome;

public interface StatelessFundManagerHome extends EJBHome {

    StatelessFundManager create() throws RemoteException, CreateException;

}
```

The `create()` method defined here does not take any arguments. A `create()` method with arguments would be required for initializing the bean's state during creation process, but since this is a stateless session bean, we use the no-argument `create()` method. The `create()` method returns a reference to the remote object. In case of run-time errors, the method throws a remote or a create exception to the client.

The Remote Interface of StatelessFundManager

In the remote interface for our fund-managing bean, we declare two methods, one called `addFunds()`, and the other called `withdrawFunds()`. These methods will be implemented in the bean class. Here is the remote interface in full:

```
import javax.ejb.EJBObject;
import java.rmi.RemoteException;

public interface StatelessFundManager extends EJBObject {

  public double addFunds(double balance,
                         double amount) throws RemoteException;

  public double withdrawFunds(double balance, double amount)
          throws InsufficientBalanceException, RemoteException;
}
```

The Implementation Class of StatelessFundManager

The implementation class implements the SessionBean interface. As we saw earlier, this interface has a number of callback methods we need to implement:

```
import javax.ejb.*;

public class StatelessFundManagerEJB implements SessionBean {

  public void ejbRemove() {}
  public void ejbActivate() {}
  public void ejbPassivate() {}
  public void setSessionContext(SessionContext sc) {}
  public void ejbCreate() throws CreateException {}
```

These are callback methods, called by the container at appropriate times during the bean's life span. In the current implementation, we will provide null method bodies for these. We'll explain the significance of all these methods in detail in the next section.

The implementation class defines the remote methods declared in our remote interface. Our remote interface has two methods we need to implement, addFunds() and withdrawFunds(). We'll look at addFunds() first: this method simply takes the account balance and the amount to be added, and adds them, returning the new balance:

```
public double addFunds(double balance, double amount) {

  balance += amount;
  return balance;
}
```

As we are developing a stateless session bean, we don't need to worry about keeping track of the account balance; we'll leave that to the client application.

The withdrawFunds() method is slightly more complicated, in that it needs to check that there is enough money in the account to be withdrawn. If we try to take more money out of the account than we have in, withdrawFunds() throws a user-defined exception, InsufficientBalanceException; otherwise, we subtract the withdrawal amount from the balance and return the new balance:

```
public double withdrawFunds(double balance, double amount)
                         throws InsufficientBalanceException {

  if (balance < amount) {
    throw (new InsufficientBalanceException());
  }
  balance -= amount;
  return balance;
  }
}
```

Note that the remote method implementation does not throw a RemoteException though the remote interface is required to declare this exception. The container handles the exceptions. Thus, if the business method in the bean implementation class generates an exception, the container will throw a RemoteException to the client.

This completes our coding of the session bean, but before we move on to the deployment descriptor we need to code the InsufficientBalanceException.

The InsufficientBalanceException Class

The bean class uses a user-defined exception class that is shown below:

```
public class InsufficientBalanceException extends Exception {
  public InsufficientBalanceException() { }
}
```

The Deployment Descriptor of StatelessFundManager

As we saw in the last chapter, each EJB needs a deployment descriptor, and our fund-managing bean is no different. Here is the deployment descriptor we need to include in an XML file called ejb-jar.xml. This file will be put in a directory called META-INF (the capitalization is important), immediately below the directory we saved our fund-managing bean classes in:

```
<?xml version="1.0" encoding="Cp1252"?>

<!DOCTYPE ejb-jar PUBLIC
          '-//Sun Microsystems, Inc.//DTD Enterprise JavaBeans 1.1//EN'
          'http://java.sun.com/dtd/ejb-jar_2_0.dtd'>

<ejb-jar>
   <description>Only one EJB in this file, StatelessFundBean</description>
   <display-name>StatelessFundJAR</display-name>
   <enterprise-beans>
     <session>
       <description>
         A stateless session bean to calculate balance changes
       </description>
       <display-name>StatelessFundBean</display-name>
       <ejb-name>StatelessFundBean</ejb-name>
       <home>StatelessFundManagerHome</home>
       <remote>StatelessFundManager</remote>
       <ejb-class>StatelessFundManagerEJB</ejb-class>
       <session-type>Stateless</session-type>
       <transaction-type>Container</transaction-type>
     </session>
   </enterprise-beans>
</ejb-jar>
```

As we can see, the deployment descriptor for our fund-managing bean contains some very simple information that the application server will need in order to deploy the bean correctly. The <home> and <remote> tags define the home and remote interfaces, StatelessFundManagerHome and StatelessFundManager, while the <ejb-class> tag defines the bean implementation class, StatelessFundManagerEJB. The <session-type> declares this bean to be Stateless. The <transaction-type> indicates that the container will manage the transactions, thus saving us the trouble of writing the code ourselves.

Since the deployment process varies greatly from vendor to vendor, it is important that you study the ejb-jar DTD and learn to create the deployment descriptor by hand.

The DTD for Session Beans

Here is a depiction of the <session> element from the EJB 2.0 DTD:

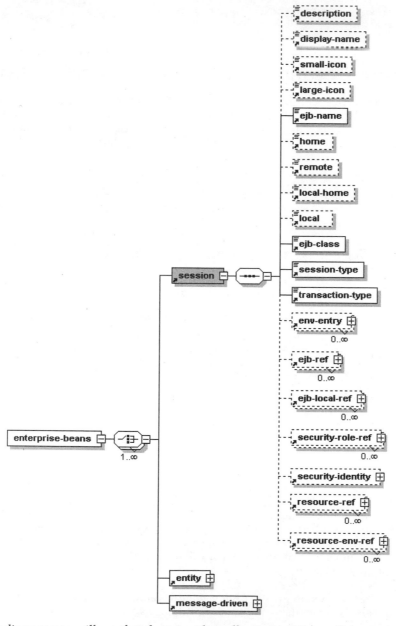

From this diagram you will see that there is only really one significant element specific to session beans:
<session-type>. We covered the other basic required elements such as <ejb-name> and <home> in
the previous chapter so let's just look at <session-type>.

The <session-type> element must contain one of two values, the purpose of which is to inform the container of the denomination of session bean:

❑   Stateful

❑   Stateless

Now we can compile and package our class files and deployment descriptor into a JAR file, called StatelessFundJAR.jar.

Deployment

The session bean we created in the previous section must be deployed on an application server before a client can use this bean. We will use Sun's J2EE 1.3 Reference Implementation provided along with the J2EE SDK for deploying and using our beans. The full deployment process for the Reference Implementation application server is discussed in detail in Appendix B. Here, we will discuss only the required steps for deploying our FundManager bean.

After starting the server running, use the deployment tool to create a new application by selecting File | New | Application... which opens a New Application dialog. Type the fully qualified path for the application file name (say, C:\ProEJB\Chapter03\StatelessFundManager\StatelessFundManager.ear), or browse to the directory you will be storing the code in, and its display name (we'll accept the default display name, which is the application file name without the .ear extension):

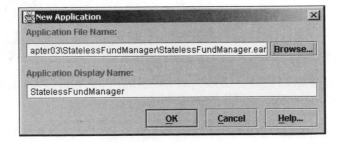

Select OK. This creates a new application with the given name and adds it to the first screen of the deployment tool, where it should be highlighted:

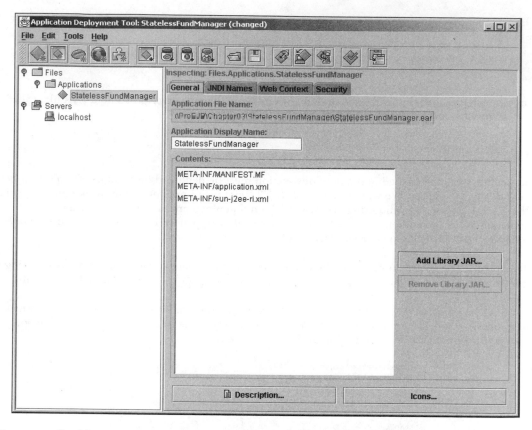

Next, we will add our `StatelessFundJAR.jar` file. Select File | Add to Application | EJB JAR... and on the following screen identify the JAR file we wish to add:

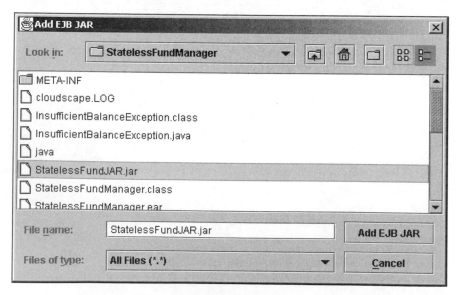

Our application contains only one EJB and no web components. Before we deploy the application, we will need to set the JNDI names for the resource references. Select the JNDI Names tab on the front screen of the deployment tool, and enter MyStatelessFundManager as the name of the reference for the shown reference item:

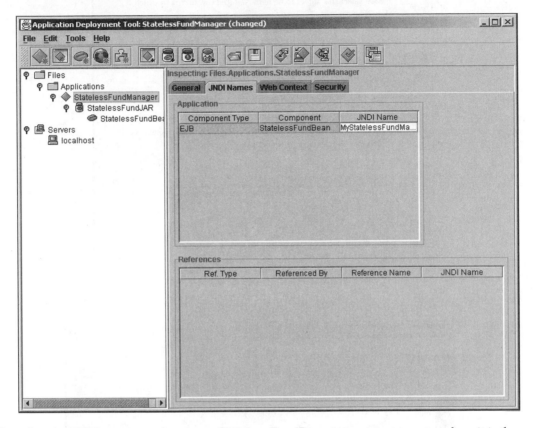

Note that the JNDI name we give to our StatelessFundBean is important to remember; it is the name we will use in the client application to look up the EJB we want.

Now we are ready to deploy the application. Select Tools | Deploy… and click on the Return Client Jar checkbox to select it. This opens a field for entering the name for the client JAR file. Either accept the default name shown or enter the name of your choice in this field. The deployment tool creates a client JAR file that needs to be copied on the client machine. The JAR file contains all the required files (interfaces and stubs) for executing the methods of a remote EJB:

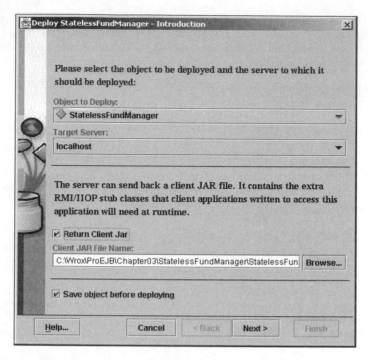

Press Next to move to the next screen of the wizard. Accept the defaults on the remaining screen:

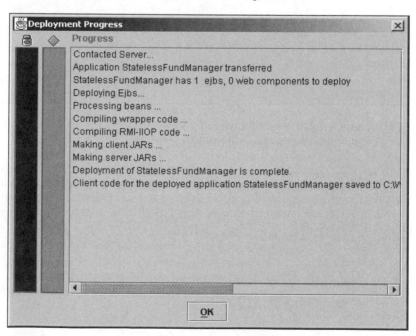

Once the application is successfully deployed, it is ready for use by a suitable client program.

The Client

We will now develop a client program that uses the `StatelessFundManager` bean developed and deployed in the previous section. Instead of developing a console-based application, we will develop a GUI based client application so that we can run multiple client copies concurrently.

For those seeking to refresh their memories on programming GUIs with Java, take a look at
Beginning Java 2, *by Ivor Horton, ISBN 1-861003-66-8, or* Professional Java Programming, *by Brett Spell, ISBN 1-861003-28-X, both from Wrox Press.*

The `StatelessFundManagerTestClient` class declares several instance variables required for building the GUI and the internal operations of the class. The `main()` method instantiates the class and calls the `init()` method.

The program uses Swing classes. The `StatelessFundManagerTestClient` class extends from `JFrame` class and implements `ActionListener`:

```java
import javax.naming.Context;
import javax.naming.InitialContext;
import javax.rmi.PortableRemoteObject;
import javax.swing.*;
import java.awt.*;
import java.awt.event.*;
import java.text.*;

public class StatelessFundManagerTestClient extends JFrame
                                    implements ActionListener {

  double balance = 0;
  JTextField amount = new JTextField(10);
  JButton addFunds = new JButton("Add Funds");
  JButton withdrawFunds = new JButton("Withdraw Funds");
  String msg = "Current account balance: ";
  String strBal = "0";
  JLabel status;
  StatelessFundManager manager;
  NumberFormat currencyFormatter;

  public StatelessFundManagerTestClient() {
    super("Fund Manager");
  }

  public static void main(String[] args) {
    new StatelessFundManagerTestClient().init();
  }
```

The init() method does the following:

1. Calls the buildGUI() method to build the GUI

2. Sets up a window listener for window closing

3. Sets up action listeners for the two buttons

4. Creates a StatelessFundManager session bean object, using the createFundManager() method

5. Formats the current account balance and displays it in the status area

6. Displays the user interface to the client and waits for client operations

```
public void init(){

    buildGUI();
```

To set up the window listener, an anonymous class based on WindowAdapter is created. On the occurrence of a 'window closing' message, the program terminates, leaving the server still available for other clients:

```
addWindowListener(new WindowAdapter() {
    public void windowClosing(WindowEvent evt) {
    System.exit(0);
    }
});
```

Next, the action listeners for the two buttons are added. The StatelessFundManagerClient object acts as a listener to these events:

```
addFunds.addActionListener(this);
withdrawFunds.addActionListener(this);

// Create fund manager
createFundManager();
// Set the starting balance to 0
try {
```

After returning from the createFundManager() method, we format an initial balance of 0 (zero) using the NumberFormat class in the current Locale, and display it in the status label field:

```
currencyFormatter = NumberFormat.getCurrencyInstance();
String currencyOut = currencyFormatter.format(0);
status.setText(msg + currencyOut);
} catch (Exception re) {
re.printStackTrace();
}
```

The program then displays the application frame window to the client by calling the show() method. The user can now enter the amount in the displayed text field and add/withdraw the displayed amount from the current account balance:

```
        pack();
        show();
    }
```

The buildGUI() Method

The `buildGUI()` method uses a `GridBagLayout` to build the GUI:

```
public void buildGUI() {

    GridBagLayout gl = new GridBagLayout();
    GridBagConstraints gc = new GridBagConstraints();
    Container container = getContentPane();
    container.setLayout(gl);

    gc.fill = GridBagConstraints.BOTH;
    JLabel label = new JLabel("Enter Amount");
    gl.setConstraints(label, gc);
    container.add(label);

    gc.gridwidth = GridBagConstraints.REMAINDER;
    gl.setConstraints(amount, gc);
    container.add(amount);

    gl.setConstraints(addFunds, gc);
    container.add(addFunds);
    gl.setConstraints(withdrawFunds, gc);
    container.add(withdrawFunds);

    status = new JLabel(msg);
    gl.setConstraints(status, gc);
    container.add(status);
}
```

Adding and Withdrawing Funds using Event Handlers

The event handler for action events does the fund addition and fund withdrawal operations:

```
public void actionPerformed(ActionEvent e){

    String str = amount.getText();

    if (str.equals("")){
        return;
    }

    try {
        if (e.getSource() == addFunds) {
```

To add funds, we call the `addFunds()` method on the manager object. After adding the funds, the new balance is displayed to the user by calling the `getBalance()` method and formatting the output to the locale currency format:

```
        balance = (double) manager.addFunds(balance,
                                Double.parseDouble(amount.getText()));

        currencyFormatter = NumberFormat.getCurrencyInstance();
        strBal = currencyFormatter.format(balance);
        status.setText(msg + strBal);
    }

    if (e.getSource() == withdrawFunds) {
```

Similarly, calling the `withdrawFunds()` method on the `manager` object does the withdrawing of funds. The new account balance is displayed to the client in the status display:

```
        balance = (double) manager.withdrawFunds(balance,
                                Double.parseDouble(amount.getText()));

        // Set new balance
        currencyFormatter = NumberFormat.getCurrencyInstance();
        strBal = currencyFormatter.format(balance);

        status.setText(msg + strBal);
        }
    } catch (Exception ex) {
      ex.printStackTrace();
    }
  }
```

Looking up and Creating the Bean Instance

Finally, we saw in the previous chapter how to access our EJB from our client program so this code should be familiar:

```
public void createFundManager() {
  try {
    Context initial = new InitialContext();
    Object objref = initial.lookup("MyStatelessFundManager");

    StatelessFundManagerHome home =
      (StatelessFundManagerHome) PortableRemoteObject.narrow(objref,
          StatelessFundManagerHome.class);
    manager = home.create();
  } catch (Exception ex) {
    System.err.println("Caught an unexpected exception!");
    ex.printStackTrace();
  }
 }
}
```

Running the Client

Compile the client and run it making sure that the client JAR file is on the classpath:

```
java -classpath %J2EE_HOME%\lib\j2ee.jar;StatelessFundManagerClient.jar;.
    StatelessFundManagerTestClient
```

Here is the first screen you should see (note that the account balance at the bottom is formatted to pounds because it was run with an English (United Kingdom) locale):

Enter the amount in the Enter Amount text field and click on the Add Funds or Withdraw Funds buttons to add/withdraw funds from the current balance. The new balance is shown immediately after every update:

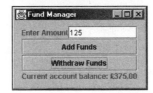

How do we get these results? When we put a number into the textbox and press the Add Funds button, our client program detects which button has been pressed. It takes the value from the box, together with the Current account balance, and passes them to the stateless session bean in a call to addFunds(). The bean adds the two numbers together and returns the new balance, which the client presents in the Current account balance section of the display. Simple, really – all the graphics are handled by the client, and the balance calculations are handled on the application server by the bean, and all the user sees is their balance going up or down by whatever amount they specify.

Lifecycle of Stateless Session Beans

In order to improve our overall understanding of EJBs, we shall now look into the lifecycle of stateless session beans. The lifecycle of a bean can be seen from the client's point of view as well as the point of view of the bean itself. For a client, it is important to know if and for how long the bean is available, and whether it can safely maintain its state in the instance variables of the bean. If a bean instance is passivated/activated by the server during the client's lifecycle, then what are the implications for the client? Such questions will be answered when we look at the client's view of the bean's lifecycle.

For a bean developer, the study of a bean's lifecycle from the bean's point of view is important. By studying the lifecycle, the bean developer will know their responsibilities while coding the bean. The programmer can then appropriately take care of the state management, transaction management, etc., in the code.

In this section, we will study the following:

- ❑ Client view of a session bean's lifecycle
- ❑ Lifecycle of a stateless session bean

Client View of a Session Bean's Lifecycle

In general, the lifecycle of a session bean is controlled by the client's session. The bean represents a non-persistent object that is accessible to the client during its entire session. As seen in the previous chapter, each bean has an identity specified by its handle that may be saved and retrieved at a later time by the client. The identity of the bean would not survive a container crash.

The following diagram shows the different stages of the lifecycle of a session bean as seen from the client's perspective:

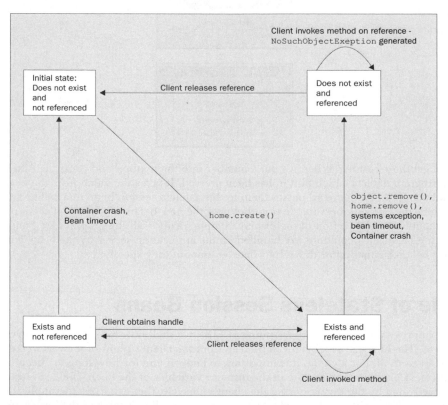

The initial state of the bean is represented by the top left-hand corner box – Does not exist and not referenced. It indicates that the bean has not been created so far and the client does not have any reference to the bean, as it does not exist.

When the client creates a bean by calling the create() method on the home object, a transition takes place to the diagonally opposite state – Exists and referenced. At this stage, the bean has been created and thus it exists. The client receives the reference to the component object of the bean and we say that the bean is **referenced**. In this state, the client may invoke any number of methods on the bean. After each method call, the bean returns to the same state.

The client may remove the bean at any time by calling its `remove()` method or by calling the `remove()` method on the home object. This causes a transition to the state **Does not exist and referenced**. Such a transition can also take place in the case of bean timeout, container crash, or a system exception in one of the bean's methods. Note that in this state, the bean has been removed from the container and thus does not exist. However, the client may still have a variable that holds a reference to the bean.

> **After removing the bean, the client should usually mark this reference to `null`. In this state, the client may use the reference variable to invoke a method on the bean. In such a case, the client will receive a `NoSuchObjectException`, or `NoSuchObjectLocalException`. When the client releases the reference by marking it `null`, the first state (Does not exist and not referenced) will be reached.**

From the **Exists and referenced** state, a transition to the **Exists and not referenced** state takes place whenever the client marks the reference as `null`. At this time, the bean still exists. However, the client will not be able to access it, as it does not hold a valid reference to the bean. If the client has previously obtained a handle to the bean, it can use this handle to obtain another reference to the bean and the transition to **Exists and referenced** state will take place.

A transition from the **Exists and not referenced** state to the initial **Does not exist and not referenced** state takes place whenever the bean times out or the container crashes.

Having seen the lifecycle from the client's view, we will now study the state diagram for the stateless session bean.

State Diagram for a Stateless Session Bean

The state diagram of a stateless session bean is very simple. The stateless bean has only two states; either it exists or it does not exist. When it exists, it is always in a method-ready pool where the client can invoke a method on the bean. After the completion of the method, the bean returns to the pooled state. As the bean does not hold any state for the client, the bean is always returned to the pool of available beans and assigned to any other client during the next method invocation. The state diagram is shown below:

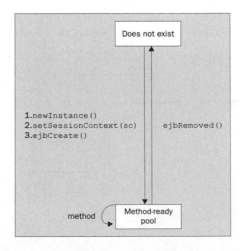

The transition from Does not exist to Method-ready pool takes place whenever the client calls the `create()` method. During the bean creation, the container will call the following methods:

- ❑ `newInstance()`
- ❑ `setSessionContext(sessionContext sc)`
- ❑ `ejbCreate()`

The `newInstance()` method is called to instantiate the bean. The container calls the `setSessionContext()` method on the bean object and passes the `SessionContext` to it. The bean uses this `SessionContext` object to introspect the context under which it is running. The server stores important information in this context for the bean's use. The bean may store this context in an instance variable for later use. The container then calls the `ejbCreate()` method on the bean that allows the bean to do any initialization or allocation of resources required during the entire lifecycle of the bean.

The transition from Method-ready state to Does not exist state takes place when the client calls the `remove()` method on the bean. During the removal process, the container calls the `ejbRemove()` method on the bean object. This gives the bean an opportunity to do any necessary cleanup such as de-allocating the resources allocated during the creation process.

Sequence Diagrams for Stateless Session Beans

Sequence diagrams help in understanding the interaction of the various classes involved in a certain operation. In this chapter we will use sequence diagrams to enhance our understanding of the various operations involved with both stateless and stateful session beans.

Here we will discuss the sequence diagrams for the following operations for stateless session beans:

- ❑ Client-invoked creation of a session bean
- ❑ Invoking business methods on a bean instance
- ❑ Removing a session bean
- ❑ Adding a bean instance to the pool
- ❑ Removing an instance from the pool

Client-Invoked Creation of a Session Bean

The client calls the `create()` method on the home object to create an instance of the bean. As you can see the bean instance is available but the client has nothing to do with it:

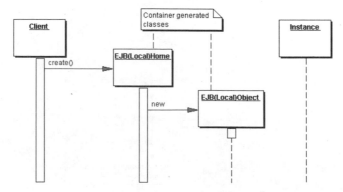

Invoking Business Methods on a Bean Instance

A client holds a reference to the component object and invokes a business method on the component object. The container delegates the method call to the bean instance. The bean method may require access to a database. In such a case, the method may do any database updates. Such database updates may be registered with the external transaction service, if the current method participates in a transaction:

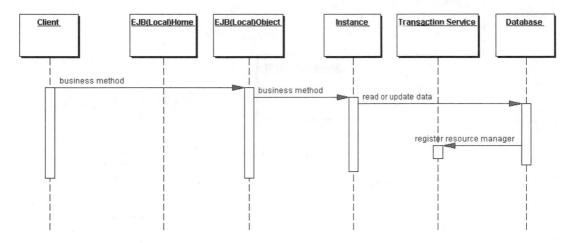

Removing a Session Bean

The sequence diagram for the remove operation is very simple. The client invokes the `remove()` method on the component object. The container then removes the component object and the bean instance:

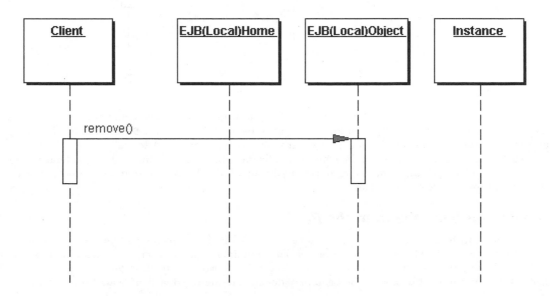

Adding an Instance to the Pool

As seen from the state diagram in the previous section, a stateless bean has only two states – Does not exist and Method ready. The container creates a bean and adds it to the pool of available beans. The sequences of events that take place during this operation are illustrated in the following diagram:

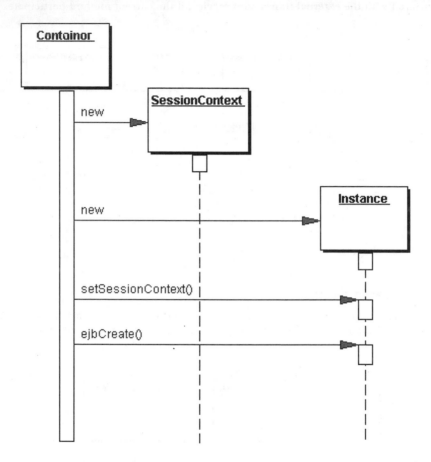

The container creates a SessionContext object and a bean instance. The container then calls the setSessionContext() method on the bean object, passing the SessionContext object as the argument to the method. The bean may store this context for later use. After calling the setSessionContext() method, the container calls the ejbCreate() method on the bean object. The bean may allocate any required resources in this method. Allocated resources will be available throughout the lifecycle of the bean.

Removing an Instance from the Pool

As seen earlier, the container may add instances to the pool whenever the load on the server increases, and thus there is a demand for more instances. The container removes such instances whenever the load reduces. During this operation, the container calls the ejbRemove() method on the bean instance. This is illustrated in the next diagram. The bean may de-allocate the previously allocated resources in this method:

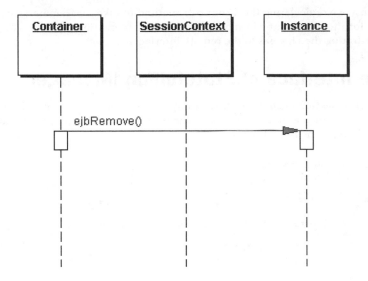

Developing a Stateful Session Bean

In this section, we will develop a stateful session bean, based upon our earlier stateless bean. As the bean is going to store the client's state across method calls, we're going to need to alter the implementation class, and also the client. Additionally, because of the new methods we'll be adding, we'll need to alter the interfaces for the bean. We won't be making any changes to the InsufficientBalanceException class.

We will call our stateful session bean StatefulFundManager. The client creates an instance of the FundManager bean for its use. The FundManager provides a variable called amount that maintains the client's account balance. The business methods of the bean allow the client to add funds to and withdraw funds from this account. The bean may be passivated/activated any number of times during the entire lifespan of the client. However, the client is assured of the correct account balance at all times.

First, let's look at the changes in the remote interface for our StatefulFundManager bean.

The Home Interface of StatefulFundManager

As we have seen in the case of a stateless session bean, the home interface of a stateful session bean is extended from the EJBHome interface. The interface for our stateful session bean declares one create() method that takes a double representing a starting balance as an argument. Thus, we only need to alter the method declaration:

```
import java.rmi.RemoteException;
import javax.ejb.CreateException;
import javax.ejb.EJBHome;

public interface StatefulFundManagerHome extends EJBHome {

   StatefulFundManager create(double amount) throws RemoteException,
                                                     CreateException;

}
```

Notice that because we're declaring the `create()` method to take a parameter, we're going to have to write some code for the `ejbCreate()` method in the implementation class. We'll take a closer look at that after demonstrating the changes to the remote interface.

The Remote Interface of StatefulFundManager

Also like the stateless session bean of our first example, the remote interface is derived from the `EJBObject` interface. For the stateful version of our bean, we need to alter the method declarations because we'll be doing something different with them:

```
import javax.ejb.EJBObject;
import java.rmi.RemoteException;

public interface StatefulFundManager extends EJBObject {

  public void addFunds(double amount) throws RemoteException;

  public void withdrawFunds(double amount)
            throws InsufficientBalanceException, RemoteException;

  public double getBalance() throws RemoteException;
}
```

The Implementation Class of StatefulFundManager

This is where we implement the changes in order to make our stateless session bean into a stateful session bean. The first thing is that we declare a variable of type `double` called `amount`. This `amount` field will be used to hold the customer's account balance. The state of this variable will be modified by the two business methods, `addFunds()` and `withdrawFunds()`. The `getBalance()` method will return the value of this variable when called. The declaration of this instance variable makes this bean a stateful session bean.

As is the case with stateless session beans, we need to implement the methods declared in the `SessionBean` interface. All these methods are implemented with a null body:

```
import javax.ejb.*;

public class StatefulFundManagerEJB implements SessionBean {

  double amount;

  public void ejbRemove() {}
  public void ejbActivate() {}
  public void ejbPassivate() {}
  public void setSessionContext(SessionContext sc) {}
```

The container calls the `ejbCreate()` method during the bean creation process. We've declared this method to take a double parameter in the home interface, so we need to provide some code to deal with that. What we'll do is use the argument to initialize the `amount` variable, enabling us to create our account with funds already there. If the input parameter is negative, a `CreateException` is thrown.

The `ejbCreate()` method is called only once during the bean creation process. Once the value for the `amount` variable is set, it may be changed using the business methods several times during the bean's lifetime:

```
public void ejbCreate(double amount) throws CreateException {

  if (amount < 0) {
    throw new CreateException("Invalid amount");
  }else {
   this.amount = amount;
  }
}
```

Remember that in the remote interface to the stateful version of this bean, we altered the signatures of the addFunds() and withdrawFunds() methods; this means we're going to change their implementation as well. The addFunds() method now accepts only one double parameter, which it will add to the current account balance. If the input parameter is less than or equal to zero, it is not added to the balance:

```
public void addFunds(double amount) {

  if (amount <= 0){
    return;
  }
  this.amount += amount;
}
```

The withdrawFunds() method now has to subtract the input value from the current account balance. In case of an insufficient balance, it throws an InsufficientBalanceException to the caller and does not modify the account balance:

```
public void withdrawFunds(double amount) throws
            InsufficientBalanceException {

  if (this.amount < amount) {
    throw (new InsufficientBalanceException());
  }
  this.amount -= amount;
}
```

We also declared an accessor method in the remote interface, getBalance(), which we need to implement. This is very simple, since it merely returns the current account balance:

```
public double getBalance(){
  return amount;
}
}
```

The Deployment Descriptor of StatefulFundManager

Create the following deployment descriptor and save it in the `<code_base>\META-INF\` directory:

```xml
<?xml version="1.0" encoding="Cp1252"?>

<!DOCTYPE ejb-jar PUBLIC '-//Sun Microsystems, Inc.//DTD Enterprise JavaBeans
2.0//EN' 'http://java.sun.com/dtd/ejb-jar_2_0.dtd'>

<ejb-jar>
  <display-name>StatefulFundManagerJAR</display-name>
  <enterprise-beans>
    <session>
      <display-name>StatefulFundManagerBean</display-name>
      <ejb-name>StatefulFundManagerBean</ejb-name>
      <home>StatefulFundManagerHome</home>
      <remote>StatefulFundManager</remote>
      <ejb-class>StatefulFundManagerEJB</ejb-class>
      <session-type>Stateful</session-type>
      <transaction-type>Container</transaction-type>
    </session>
  </enterprise-beans>
</ejb-jar>
```

Note the use of `<session-type>` element. The deployment descriptor states that the current bean is a stateful session bean by setting the `<session-type>` element. The container will now assume the responsibility of maintaining the client's state during its entire session. Otherwise, there is little difference between the deployment descriptor for a stateless and a stateful session bean, apart from the obvious interface and class name difference.

Compile and archive the code into a file called `StatefulFundManagerJAR.jar`.

Deployment

The deployment process is similar to the one described for the stateless session bean earlier. Again, we will be using the J2EE 1.3 Reference Implementation, so make sure the server is running.

Start the deployment tool and click on either File | New | Application... or select the Applications node and click on the new application icon. We'll call this application `StatefulFundManager` and store it in the application file called `StatefulFundManager.ear`:

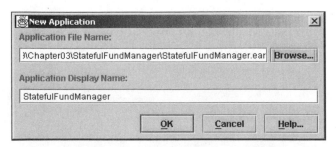

Next, select the **Add to Application | EJB JAR...** menu option. Specify the JAR file that we created above, `StatefulFundManagerJAR.jar`.

Once the JAR has been loaded, select the **JNDI Names** tab for the `StatefulFundManager` application. Give our EJB the JNDI name MyStatefulFundManager:

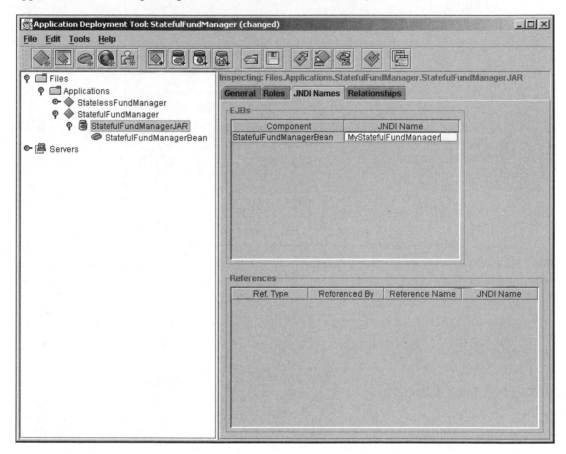

Now you are ready to deploy the application. Select **Tools | Deploy...** to begin deployment. Click on the **Return Client Jar** checkbox to select it:

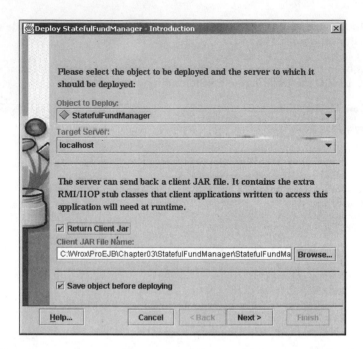

The client JAR file contains important classes that are required for running the client application. Press Next to move to the next screen of the wizard. Accept the defaults on the remaining screen, and click Finish to deploy our stateful bean.

The deployment tool tells you the success/failure of the deployment process. Once the application is successfully deployed, it is ready for client use. We will now modify our client program to access the new stateful bean.

Changing the Client

Since we've changed the implementation of the bean, we need to make some changes to our client in order for it to continue working. Let's now take a look at those changes. We'll start at the top of the class, where the only change is to the name of the class, and since we're doing the same thing as in the last client, we don't need to import any other classes:

```
public class StatefulFundManagerTestClient extends JFrame
                                    implements ActionListener {
```

As the bean will be taking care of maintaining the state, we don't need the balance variable or the strBal variable either, and StatelessFundManager manager can obviously be changed to StatefulFundManager manager. The class constructor differs only in name:

```
public StatefulFundManagerTestClient() {
   super("Fund Manager");
}
```

The next change we need to make is in the `main()` method, where we have to make sure that we are instantiating an instance of this client class, not the version we developed for the stateless bean:

```
public static void main(String[] args) {
   new StatefulFundManagerTestClient().init();
}
```

The `init()` method has only one change to make, in the initialization of the `currencyOut` variable. This change is made because when we create our bean we will be doing so with an argument representing the starting balance; therefore, instead of assuming an initial balance of zero, we should check to see what the value actually is:

```
public void init() {

// Other code as in StatelessFundManagerTestClient
   try {
      currencyFormatter = NumberFormat.getCurrencyInstance();
      String currencyOut = currencyFormatter.format(manager.getBalance());
      status.setText(msg + currencyOut);
   }
// catch block as in StatelessFundManagerTestClient
}
```

There are no changes in the `buildGUI()` method, since that doesn't deal with the session bean, so the next method we need to change is `actionPerformed()`. The conditional logic in this method remains the same, but we'll have to change what happens when the buttons are selected:

```
public void actionPerformed(ActionEvent e) {

// other code as in StatelessFundManagerTestClient
    if (e.getSource() == addFunds) {

        // Call addFunds method on manager EJB
        manager.addFunds(Double.parseDouble(amount.getText()));

        // Set new balance
        String currencyOut = currencyFormatter.format(manager.getBalance());
        status.setText(msg + currencyOut);
    }
```

As you can see, the code is a little simpler than earlier, because we don't have to worry about recording changes to the state thanks to the now stateful nature of the session bean. We can now make use of the `getBalance()` method in order to be able to display the present balance to the client, although we still format it for the locale:

```
    if (e.getSource() == withdrawFunds) {
```

```
        // Call withdrawFunds on manager EJB
        manager.withdrawFunds(Double.parseDouble(amount.getText()));

        // Set new balance
        String currencyOut = currencyFormatter.format(manager.getBalance());
        status.setText(msg + currencyOut);
    }

// catch block as in StatelessFundManagerTestClient
}
```

The last change we need to make is in the `createFundManager()` method, where we change the name of the object we're looking for, along with the object we typecast it to:

```
public void createFundManager() {

// Try as in StatelessFundManagerTestClient
    Object objref = initial.lookup("MyStatefulFundManager");

    StatefulFundManagerHome home =
        (StatefulFundManagerHome) PortableRemoteObject.narrow(objref,
            StatefulFundManagerHome.class);

    manager = home.create(2000);

// catch block as in StatelessFundManagerTestClient
}
}
```

Running the Client

Compile the above client code, and then run the client program by using the following command line:

```
java -classpath .;%J2EE_HOME%\lib\j2ee.jar;StatefulFundManagerClient.jar
    StatefulFundManagerTestClient
```

Remember that the `StatefulFundManagerClient.jar` file was created during the deployment process and contains the stub classes required for running the client.

Enter the amount in the **Enter Amount** text field and click on the **Add Funds** or **Withdraw Funds** buttons to add/withdraw funds from the current balance. The new balance is shown immediately after every update. You should see the same results as with the stateless session bean earlier.

Testing Client State Management

To test the container client state management, we can run multiple copies of the client. On each fund manager screen, enter some value and add/withdraw funds. Keep on doing this for multiple clients. When you switch between applications, the manager object (session bean) created by each application remains idle most of the time:

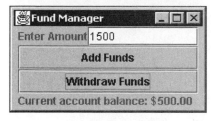

Note that the above instances of the Fund Manager were run in an English (United States) locale, hence the dollar signs in front of the account balance.

The bean object is used only when either of the two buttons of the application is clicked. As the object remains unused during the rest of the period it becomes a likely candidate for pooling, and the container, in the background, could be passivating and activating these objects several times without the user realizing that such a thing is happening. The same component instances may be shared between several of the applications that were started above. However, from the user's perspective, they always see the current account balance for each fund manager application. Note that unlike the stateless version earlier, each fund manager application (each StateFulFundManager object) maintains its own balance that is independent of others.

Lifecycle of Stateful Session Beans

As with stateless session beans, we're going to take a look at some of the key events in the lifecycle of a stateful session bean. Again, we'll look at a state diagram and several sequence diagrams. As mentioned earlier in the chapter, the client's view of a session bean is essentially the same, regardless of the ability of the bean to represent state.

State Diagram for a Stateful Session Bean

The state diagram for a stateful session bean is more complicated than that for a stateless session bean, as can be seen from the following diagram:

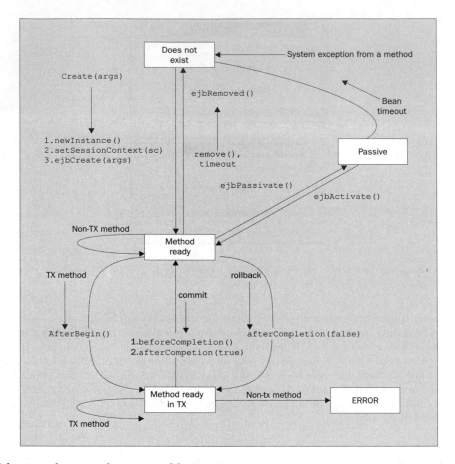

A stateful session bean can be in any of four states:

- ❑ Does not exist
- ❑ Method ready
- ❑ Method ready in transaction
- ❑ Passive

The initial state of a stateful session bean is **Does not exist**, the first state shown at the top of the diagram. When the client creates a bean, the following methods will be called in the given sequence:

- ❑ `newInstance()`
- ❑ `setSessionContext(SessionContext)`
- ❑ `ejbCreate(args)`

The methods and their calling sequence are the same as the ones discussed for stateless session beans. Once the bean is created it is ready for client method invocations and we say that the bean is in the **Method ready** state. In this state, the client may invoke several methods that do not participate in a transaction. After each method call, the bean returns to the same state. For a transacted method, a different state exists (**Method ready in TX**) that is discussed in the next section.

When the client calls a `remove()` method on the bean instance, we achieve the state **Does not exist**. During this transition, the container calls the `ejbRemove()` method on the bean instance before it is actually removed. This gives an opportunity to the bean programmer to release any previously allocated resources before the bean is destroyed.

If the client does not use the bean for a long time or the server decides to free some resources, the container passivates the bean and the bean enters the **Passive** state. The container vendor decides the algorithm for selecting beans for passivation. Generally, the bean that is least recently used will be passivated first. During the passivation process, the container is responsible for calling the `ejbPassivate()` method on the bean class. This gives an opportunity to the bean programmer to release any previously allocated resources before the bean is passivated.

The container may activate a passivated bean whenever the client requests an instance of the bean. During the activation process, the container is responsible for calling the `ejbActivate()` method on the bean instance. This once again gives an opportunity to the bean developer to allocate any resources required by the bean before it returns to the **Method ready** state.

The container may destroy a passivated bean if it times out. This brings us full circle to the **Does not exist** state. Generally, the container calls the `ejbRemove()` method on the bean instance whenever it removes the bean from the container. However, during this transition the container does not call the `ejbRemove()` method. This means that if you are de-allocating any resources in the `ejbRemove()` method, such resources will not be de-allocated. A container crash or a system exception thrown from the instance's method to the container also results in a missing call to the `ejbRemove()` method.

The Transacted Method

Let us now discuss the state in which a bean's transacted method is executed. Transactions are discussed in more depth in Chapter 9. However, we will briefly touch on transacted methods here.

The bean itself may manage a transaction. This is called **Bean-Managed Transactions (BMT)**. Alternatively, the container may manage the transaction; this is called **Container-Managed Transactions (CMT)**. In the case of a CMT, the transaction demarcation is on a per-method basis, which means that the container opens a transaction at the method beginning and commits it at the method end. The bean itself may be interested in knowing when the container starts a transaction. For this, the EJB API defines an interface called `SessionSynchronization` that the bean must implement. This interface has three methods:

- ❑ `afterBegin()`
- ❑ `beforeCompletion()`
- ❑ `afterCompletion(Boolean)`

The container calls the `afterBegin()` method after it opens a transaction. Just before committing the transaction, the container calls the `beforeCompletion()` method and after completing the transaction, it calls the `afterCompletion()` method that takes one argument. The `true` value for the method argument indicates that the transaction was completed successfully and the `false` value indicates that the transaction was rolled back.

In the state diagram shown at the beginning of this section, notice that when the bean moves from the method ready state to method ready in TX state, the above methods are called at appropriate times by the container.

A transacted method may invoke another transacted method. This will return the bean to the same state at the end of the new method. If a non-transacted method is invoked from within the body of a transacted method, an exception may be thrown to the client. This depends on the transaction attributes, which are discussed in depth in Chapter 9.

This completes our discussion on lifecycle diagrams for stateful beans. Let us now look at the sequence diagrams under various circumstances during the bean's lifecycle.

Sequence Diagrams for Stateful Session Beans

We will look at the sequence diagrams for the following operations:

❑   Creating a session object

❑   Passivating/Activating a bean

❑   Removing a bean

The sequence diagrams for stateless and stateful beans are very similar. The main difference is that for stateless beans there is no passivation and activation.

Creating a Session Object

The sequence diagram for the create operation is shown in the following diagram:

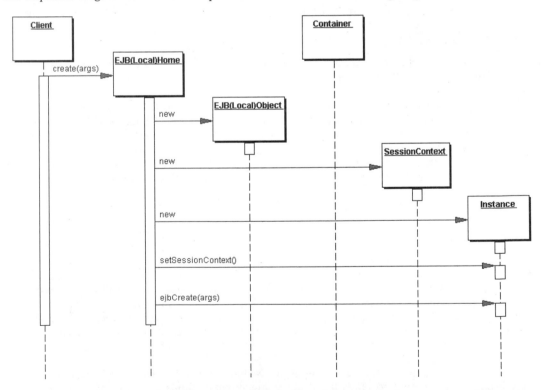

The client calls the create() method on the home object to create the bean instance. The create() method may take zero or more parameters. The container then creates three objects: a component object, a SessionContext object and a bean instance, in the given order.

The container then calls the setSessionContext() method on the newly created bean instance and passes the SessionContext object as an argument to it. Finally, the container calls the ejbCreate() method on the bean instance with the same set of arguments passed to the create() method. This completes the bean creation process.

Passivating/Activating an Object

If the client does not use the bean for a long time, that bean instance may be passivated by the container and returned to the pool of available beans. During the passivation process, the container is responsible for storing the state of the object. The container restores this state during the activation process. The sequence diagram for both the passivation and activation operations is given here:

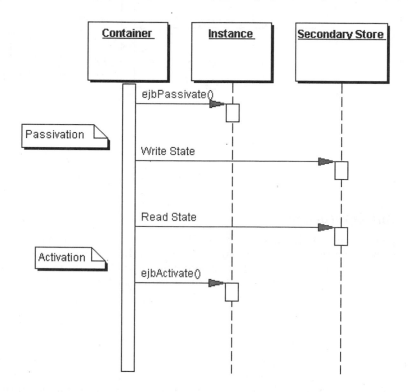

When the container passivates a bean instance, it calls the ejbPassivate() method on the instance. The bean instance can use this method to de-allocate any previously allocated resources or modify the bean's state before the container saves it. After the ejbPassivate() method is completed, the container writes the bean's state to the secondary storage.

During the activation process, the container first retrieves the bean's state from the secondary storage and sets the bean's variables to this retrieved state. After initializing the bean state, the container calls the ejbActivate() method on the bean instance. The bean may allocate the required resources in this method. It may optionally modify the state of variables to the desired values.

Removing a Bean

The client calls the `remove()` method on the component object. The container then calls the `ejbRemove()` method on the bean instance before the bean is actually removed. This gives an opportunity to the bean to do any cleaning up before it is destroyed by the container:

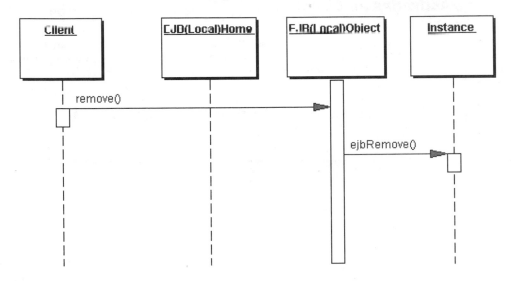

Other Important Operations

Besides the sequence diagrams discussed in the previous section, there are many more important situations in which sequence diagrams can help us understand the interaction between the various classes involved in a particular operation. One such important operation is transaction processing. The sequence diagrams for transacted methods will be discussed in Chapter 9 on transactions.

Use of Handles

As we saw in Chapter 2 when discussing the `EJBHome` and `EJBObject` interfaces, the home and remote interfaces have handles that are serializable, and thus it is possible to transfer the handles between programs using files, sockets, or RMI. So for example, they can be saved in a servlet session or messaged through JMS. However, references to remote objects in EJB are single-threaded so you cannot have simultaneous access from multiple clients or multiple threads.

The handles may be passed to other applications running under a different JVM. Such applications will not then need to do a JNDI lookup to create a bean or to obtain a reference to the home interface. Such handles can be very useful when using stateful session beans. For example, a client may add few items in its shopping cart and may decide to return at a later time for additional shopping. If the client disconnects between the two operations, the next login will be considered as another client session. The client may obtain the state of its earlier session by using the previously saved handle. Unfortunately, if the server goes down then the handle is no use for session beans, even when the server returns.

To illustrate the use of handles, we will write a small Java application that does the following:

1. Creates a `FundManager` object

2. Modifies funds

3. Obtains the object handle and saves it to a file

4. Loses a reference to the object by marking it as `null`

5. Loads the handle from a previously saved file

6. Gets the object reference from the retrieved handle

7. Confirms that the earlier object state is still available

8. Uses the object

9. Discards the object by removing it

The HandleTest Application

The complete source for our handle testing program (called `HandleTest`) is given below:

```
import javax.naming.Context;
import javax.naming.InitialContext;
import javax.rmi.PortableRemoteObject;
import java.io.*;
import javax.ejb.Handle;

public class HandleTest {

  public static void main(String[] args) {
    try {
```

In the `main()` method of our `HandleTest` program, we first obtain a reference to the JNDI server. The program then searches for `MyFundManager` object. After obtaining the object reference, it is typecast to the home object as in the case of earlier programs:

```
    // Obtain initial context of JNDI server
    Context initial = new InitialContext();
    // Search for a StatefulFundManager Home object reference
    Object objref = initial.lookup("MyStatefulFundManager");
    // Type cast to home object
    StatefulFundManagerHome home =
        (StatefulFundManagerHome)PortableRemoteObject.narrow
                    (objref, StatefulFundManagerHome.class);

    // Create a new customer account
    StatefulFundManager manager = home.create(1000);
```

The program then creates a `FundManager` object and invokes a few methods on it to modify funds:

```
// Add funds to customer's account
System.out.println("Adding 100");
manager.addFunds(100);
// Withdraw funds
System.out.println("Withdrawing 200");
manager.withdrawFunds(200);
// Add more funds
System.out.println("Adding 500");
manager.addFunds(500);

// Get current account balance
System.out.println("Current Account Balance: " +
                      manager.getBalance());
```

Next comes the important part of our discussion. The program calls its `saveHandle()` method to save the handle of the `manager` object to a file called `test`, before marking the object reference as `null`:

```
// Save the bean handle to a file
System.out.println("Storing Handle...");
saveHandle(manager);

// Mark the bean reference as null
System.out.println("Marking the reference as null...");
manager = null;
```

When the client relinquishes the control of the object this way, the object itself is not removed from the server. Since the bean object represents a session bean, the container will retain the object while the client session is active. When the client terminates, the bean will be removed and may either be garbage-collected or returned to the pool of available beans. After losing a reference to the bean, the client can obtain the reference again by using the previously stored handle. This is exactly what is done in our main program:

```
// Obtain the reference to the existing bean
System.out.println("Loading the handle...");
manager = loadHandle();
```

The main program now withdraws some funds from the `FundManager` object and prints the new balance which verifies that the earlier balance is still available. This proves the point that the server does not remove the bean as long as the client session is active. You may define a timeout for the bean at the time of deployment, although the means of doing this will vary from server to server. In such a case, the server removes the bean after the timeout:

```
// Withdraw more funds
System.out.println("Withdrawing 100");
manager.withdrawFunds(100);

// Get new balance
System.out.println("Current Account Balance: " +
                      manager.getBalance());
```

The `remove()` method removes the bean from the server. The client may not set the variable holding the bean reference to `null` and if the client tries to use this bean by using this reference variable, an `ObjectNotFoundException` will be thrown:

```
            // Discard the bean
            manager.remove();

        } catch (InsufficientBalanceException ie){
            System.out.println("Insufficient account balance");
        } catch (Exception ex) {
            System.out.println("Caught an unexpected exception!");
            ex.printStackTrace();
        }
    }
```

The Handle Handling Methods

Let us now look at the `saveHandle()` method. This method opens a file called `test` for saving the handle. An `ObjectOutputStream` is then opened on the created file output stream. The handle to the bean is obtained by calling the `getHandle()` method on the `manager` object. The object is serialized to the disk by calling the `writeObject()` method on the output stream. After writing the object, the file is closed:

```
    private static void saveHandle(StatefulFundManager manager){
        try {
            // Open a file with the name "test" for saving handle
            FileOutputStream fos = new FileOutputStream("test");

            // Create object output stream
            ObjectOutputStream out = new ObjectOutputStream(fos);

            // Get the handle and serialize to file
            out.writeObject(manager.getHandle());

            // Close the file
            out.close();

        } catch (FileNotFoundException fe) {
            System.out.println("File not found");
        } catch (IOException ie) {
            System.out.println("Error writing file");
        }
    }
```

Now let us look at the `loadHandle()` method to understand how the object reference is recovered from the handle stored in a disk file. The program opens the `test` file and creates an object input stream on it. The handle is retrieved from the file by calling the `readObject()` method on the file object:

```
    private static StatefulFundManager loadHandle (){
        try {

            // Create file input stream on "test" file
            FileInputStream fis = new FileInputStream("test");
```

```
        // Create object input stream
        ObjectInputStream in = new ObjectInputStream(fis);

        // Read handle data
        Handle handle = (Handle) in.readObject();
```

From the retrieved handle, the reference to the bean is obtained by calling the getEJBObject() method on the Handle object:

```
        // Get object reference from handle
        Object objRef = handle.getEJBObject();
        StatefulFundManager manager = (StatefulFundManager)
            handle.getEJBObject();
```

The program then closes the file and returns the object reference to the caller:

```
        // Close file
        in.close();

        // Return object reference
        return manager;

    } catch (FileNotFoundException fe) {
        System.out.println("File not found");
    } catch (IOException ie) {
        System.out.println("Error reading file");
    } catch (Exception ee) {
        ee.printStackTrace();
    }
    return null;
    }
}
```

Running the Handle Testing Application

After we've compiled HandleTest (making sure that the j2ee.jar file is still in the classpath), we can run it using the following command:

```
java -classpath .;%J2EE_HOME%\lib\j2ee.jar;StatefulFundManagerClient.jar
    HandleTest
```

The screenshot below shows the HandleTest class in action:

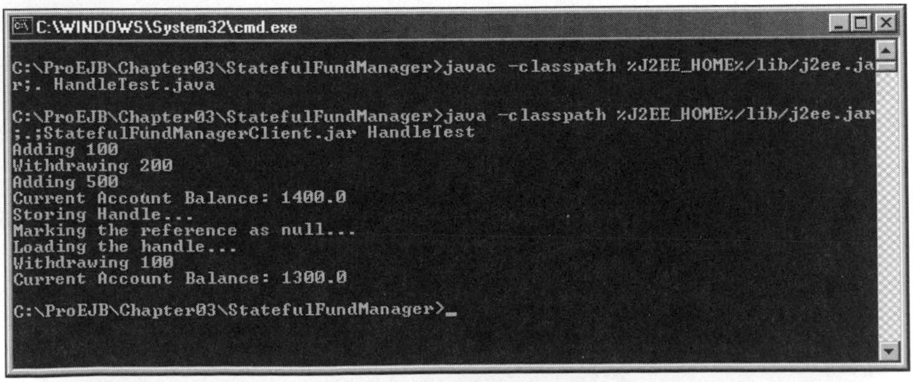

Summary

In this chapter we studied the development of both stateless and stateful session beans. The main difference between stateless and stateful session beans is that a stateful bean allows the client to maintain a conversation with the bean by preserving the bean's state across multiple method invocations. The state of the bean is embodied in the declared attributes (member variables of the class). The client uses these variables (through set and get methods) to maintain its state during its lifetime. The container may share the same bean instances between multiple clients. We also studied how component pooling is achieved with the help of passivation and activation processes.

The development and deployment of both stateless and stateful session beans was discussed at length in this chapter. The deployment of a stateful session bean does not differ much from that of a stateless session bean. We looked at the following aspects of developing session beans:

- Developing a session bean – writing two interfaces, an implementation class, and the deployment descriptor. We looked at the `SessionBean` interface that our session bean class must implement, a simple example of both stateless and stateful session beans, and what we need to add to the deployment descriptor.

- Deploying a session bean – creating the JAR file that contains the interfaces, class, and deployment descriptor. We then deployed our session bean on the J2EE Reference Implementation application server.

- Developing a client for a session bean – which demonstrated how we create, locate, and utilize a session bean.

- Lifecycle diagrams – lifecycle of a session bean from client's view, and diagrams of stateless and stateful beans from a bean's view. Here we saw some of the differences and similarities between the two types of bean in a diagrammatic form. We also looked at sequence diagrams for several operations for each type of bean.

- Using handles – to locate the same bean after we've released our original reference to it.

This completes our study of session beans. In the next chapter, we will go on to look at entity beans.

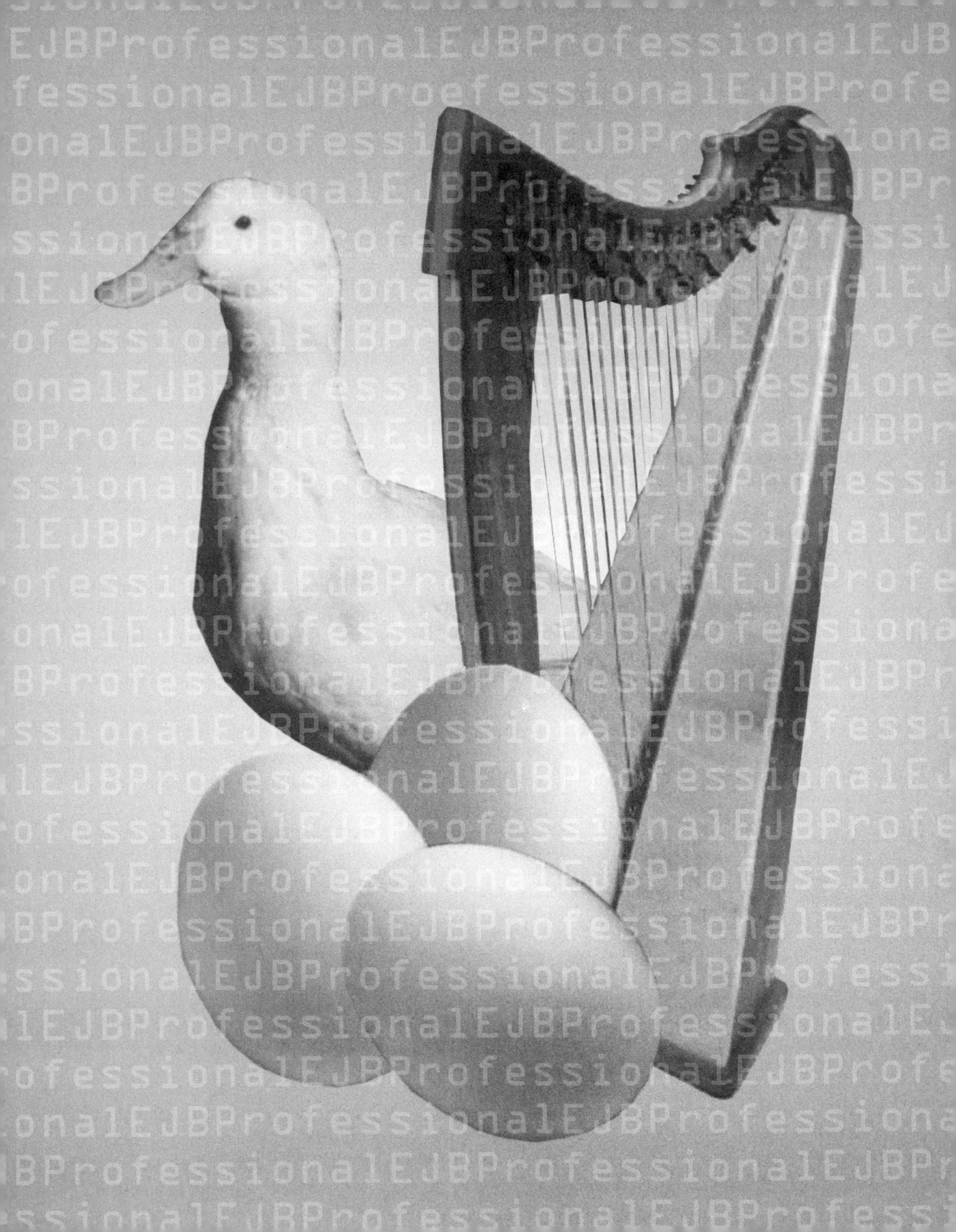

Developing EJB 1.1 Entity Beans

4

Entity beans represent data in a datastore as a Java object. Often, but not always, this translates to an entity bean representing a record within a database. The advantage of this approach is that, to manipulate the data within the datastore, we can call methods that access the datastore, instead of having to send commands to the datastore directly (which is error-prone). This technique is known as **object/relational mapping**.

This mapping implies that entity bean creation is equivalent to inserting a record into a database. Of course, since the bean and the database record correspond, any changes made to the contents of the bean must also be synchronized with the record too: this process is called **persistence**. Indeed, we noted in Chapter 1 that there were two types of entity bean, which are distinguished by how they handled persistence.

In the first type, the persistence of a bean's state to the underlying database may be automatically managed by the container itself, which leads to a **Container-Managed Persistence** (**CMP**) entity bean. The other type deals with situations where we may prefer, or need to, have better control of the persistence mechanism. Here we can ask the container to be more "hands-off", and allow us to include code in our bean to manage the manipulation of the database – this is called **Bean-Managed Persistence** (**BMP**). In this chapter we will study the development and deployment of both types of entity bean.

The EJB 2.0 specification introduces many additions to the entity bean architecture. EJB 2.0-compliant containers must still be able to support 1.1 beans. Due to the significance of the changes from 1.1 to 2.0, the entity bean contracts for each version are considered to be separate. Therefore, your entity beans must either support the 1.1 or the 2.0 specification but not a combination. Therefore, this chapter will adhere to the EJB 1.1 specification, while in the next chapter we will cover the changes introduced in 2.0.

In this chapter we will discuss:

❑   The need for entity beans, and for two types (CMP and BMP) of entity bean

❑   The development of CMP and BMP entity beans

❑   The deployment of CMP and BMP entity beans

❑   The lifecycle of entity beans

A Closer Look at Entity Beans

As we said a moment ago, an entity bean is an object-oriented representation of data. This notion of **representation** is important to understand. After all, a session bean can access any data that an entity bean can. But although a session bean can access data, it can't provide an object-oriented *representation* of that data. How then does an entity bean differ?

The basic explanation is simple, even if the details are complicated. The state that entity beans represent is a **shared, transactional** state. In contrast, if a session bean has state, it must be **private** and **conversational**. So the fundamental problem in representing an object with a session bean is in how that state is made available to clients of that bean. An entity bean is (logically, anyway) a single point of access for that data: any client that accesses the data will go through that entity bean. A session bean, on the other hand, is only accessible to a single client. If there are multiple clients, there will be multiple session beans.

This actually implies another important difference between entity beans and session beans: that the lifespan of a session bean is dependent upon the lifespan of the client session(s), while the lifespans of entity beans are determined by the existence of corresponding data.

Container- or Bean-Managed Persistence?

In the first chapter, we learned that one of the great advantages of the EJB architecture is that the EJB container can provide its beans with various useful services automatically. One of these services, should we choose to use it, is **persistence management**. In this case, at the time of deployment, the container generates all of the required SQL code for persistence management.

Obviously, the benefit of using the EJB container's built-in persistence support is that we don't ever have to write database access code for our beans. This simplifies the development of beans that take advantage of this container-managed persistence (CMP), allowing us to focus on the pure business logic of the bean.

Another advantage of using CMP is that we enhance the database independence of the bean, because the container takes care of connecting to the database. This makes these entity beans more flexible and reusable across different applications. However, you should note that we still have to map bean attributes to database fields at deployment time.

Given these advantages of container-managed persistence, why should we want to use bean-managed persistence (BMP) instead? After all, this means that we must provide all of the necessary SQL statements (database update, insert, delete, and read operations) within the bean's code.

However, bean-managed persistence is an important choice in some circumstances. The basic problem is that, although every EJB-1.1 compliant container must provide support for container-managed persistence, the specification does not indicate *how* this support must be provided. In fact, a container need not necessarily provide any CMP support for mapping your entity bean's state to columns in a database. It could use Java serialization to write the whole bean to one column and still be compliant. This would rarely be adequate for a project, and might necessitate the use of bean-managed persistence if your EJB container used serialization.

The trick is determining whether your EJB container has the level of support that you require using container-managed persistence. If it does, take advantage of this support to free your business logic programmers from writing persistence logic. The boost in productivity is potentially very large and, depending on the EJB container, the boost in application performance may be large too.

One benefit of BMP comes when it is difficult to map a bean's attributes to database fields at deployment time. This may occur if the bean state is defined by data in different databases. It can also occur if we are using a target datastore that is a legacy system, because we will probably need to access the store using a vendor-specific protocol rather than SQL commands, and the EJB container probably will not support this protocol.

The key point is that using BMP gives us more flexibility in how we manage bean state, while use of CMP speeds up bean development and increases bean flexibility.

Primary Keys

So far we've said that an entity bean is an OO representation of data and, consequently, its lifespan is dependent on the life of its corresponding data. Therefore, it should not be a surprise to learn that an entity bean has a unique identity that clients can use to locate the bean, and thus the data it represents. The identity of an entity bean is known as its **primary key**.

This primary key must be represented by a primary key class that the bean developer defines or specifies. In other words, this class contains the information necessary to find that entity in the persistent store. It is used internally by the EJB container, and also by the client to find a particular instance of the entity. The primary key class must follow certain rules.

For bean-managed persistence, the rules are exceedingly simple. The format of the class is pretty much left up to the bean developer, since it is the bean developer and not the EJB container who is going to be using it:

❑   The primary key can be any legal value type in RMI/IIOP (which implies that it must be serializable)

❑   It must also provide suitable implementations of the `hashCode()` and `equals()` methods

❑   It must have a unique value within the set of all beans of a particular type

Those are the only formal rules. Obviously, in practice, the primary key class will have state fields that correspond to the values of the entity bean's primary key. For instance, a Customer entity bean may have a primary key that has a `customerID` field of type `int`. Alternatively, the Customer entity in this example may use the type `java.lang.Integer`, which meets all the requirements.

There are a few extra rules for a bean with container-managed persistence. The basic problem is that the container is responsible for managing the entity's creation, finding, loading, saving, and deletion. To do all these things, the container needs to be able to create a primary key, so the key class must have a no-arguments public constructor.

The container also needs to be able to map the bean's state to the state of the primary key class, and vice versa. So there are a few rules that are designed to make this possible. The specification provides two different methods for providing key classes for beans using CMP. One is a general case, good for primary keys with any number of fields; the other is a special case, for convenience in dealing with a primary key with one field:

□   The general case accomplishes the mapping using a naming convention: the public fields in the primary key class correspond to the equivalent public fields in the bean class.

❑   The special case accomplishes the mapping by indicating the relevant entity bean field in the deployment descriptor, and is provided for convenience in using types such as Long, Integer, and String as the primary key, where a mapping based on a naming convention is clearly not possible.

The EJB developer may wish to use a synthetic key, such as an auto-incrementing key, as the primary key of their entity bean. There are two possible strategies. The first is to generate the key using a session bean. This session bean might retrieve a block of keys from the database, and distribute keys sequentially from this block to requesting entity beans. The second strategy is to depend on the database to automatically create the synthetic keys when the entity bean's state is inserted. If the entity bean uses container-managed persistence, the EJB container's object/relational mapping tools must support this functionality for the target database.

The EntityBean Interface

Each entity bean implementation class that we write, whether for CMP or BMP beans, must implement the EntityBean interface. As for session beans, this interface defines a number of callbacks that we must include in our implementation class. Whether or not we need to provide any implementation for these methods in our implementation class depends on which type of persistence-management we have chosen.

For CMP beans we are not likely to provide much if any implementation for these callbacks as the container will be responsible for generating all the persistence calls. However, for BMP beans, it is in these callbacks that we must write our own persistence code.

Here then is the EntityBean interface; as you can see it extends the marker interface EnterpriseBean:

```
package javax.ejb;

import java.rmi.RemoteException;

public interface EntityBean extends EnterpriseBean {

    public abstract void ejbActivate()
        throws EJBException, RemoteException;

    public abstract void ejbLoad()
        throws EJBException, RemoteException;

    public abstract void ejbPassivate()
        throws EJBException, RemoteException;

    public abstract void ejbRemove()
        throws RemoveException, EJBException, RemoteException;
```

```
        public abstract void ejbStore()
            throws EJBException, RemoteException;

        public abstract void setEntityContext(EntityContext entitycontext)
            throws EJBException, RemoteException;

        public abstract void unsetEntityContext()
            throws EJBException, RemoteException;
    }
```

In addition to the above methods, an entity bean must also define `ejbCreate()` methods to match the `create()` methods on the home interface, as well as an additional `ejbPostCreate()` method, again to match each `create()` method on the home interface. We'll see why we need an additional method for bean creation in a moment. Let's now look at how these methods make up the persistence mechanism for entity beans.

When working with data, there are four basic operations that you could want to perform on it:

- Creating
- Reading
- Updating
- Deleting

For each of these four actions, there are appropriate callback methods defined for entity beans:

Data Activity	EJB Equivalent method
Creating	`ejbCreate()` and `ejbPostCreate()`
Reading	`ejbLoad()`
Updating	`ejbStore()`
Deleting	`ejbRemove()`

One point of confusion for many programmers is why an `ejbCreate()` and an `ejbPostCreate()` are both necessary. As a general rule, the bean provider – for either BMP or CMP – will do all their work in `ejbCreate()`, leaving `ejbPostCreate()` empty. The fundamental reason that the `ejbPostCreate` method exists is because the programmer is never allowed to pass "this" as a parameter to a remote method; they must always use the remote interface instead. However, the remote interface for the bean is not available until `ejbCreate()` returns. If they needed the remote interface *during* the creation of the EJB component, there would be no way to proceed. Rather than leave this hole in the spec, an "after create" method was developed in which the remote interface would be available. This method is `ejbPostCreate()`. The same situation exists with the primary key in container-managed persistence, because the container creates the key. If the primary key is needed for some reason, that work also needs to be done in `ejbPostCreate()`. Why would you need to pass the EJB's remote reference or primary key to another EJB during its creation? Perhaps one of the main reasons is to set up relationships, for example when you create the employee you want the boss to have a reference.

In addition to these callback methods, there are a number of other methods that are declared in the `EntityBean` interface. For session (stateful) beans, the `ejbActivate()` and `ejbPassivate()` methods are used to indicate that a bean is a saved to or restored from secondary storage. However, as entity beans by definition exist in persistent storage, if the container isn't using the bean then it doesn't need to worry about preserving its state before releasing resources.

For entity beans, `ejbActivate()` provides a notification that the entity bean instance has been associated with an identity (a primary key) and it is now ready for `ejbLoad()` to be called prior to business method invocation. A matching `ejbPassivate()` method will be called to notify the entity bean that it is being disassociated froma a particular identity prior to reuse (with another identity or for finder methods), or perhaps prior to being dereferenced and made eligible for garbage-collection.

Finally we have the `setEntityContext()` and `unsetEntityContext()` methods. Similar to the `setSessionContext()` method that we discussed in the previous chapter, the `setEntityContext()` method provides a means for our bean instance to access the bean's context. This is especially relevant for entity beans because the `EntityContext` interface declares a `getPrimaryKey()` method that we need to associate a bean instance with a particular identity at certain times – we'll see when and how to use this later in the chapter. The `unsetEntityContext()` basically provides us with a way to de-allocate resources with a particular identity.

So we now have some idea of why entity beans are useful, how they differ from session beans, and how we can search for unique entity bean instances. Let's now move on to develop and deploy an example of each type of entity bean.

Developing a CMP Entity Bean

We'll start be developing a container-managed persistence entity bean because, as you will see, it is much easier to develop than a bean managing its own persistence.

In this section, we will develop a CMP entity bean that represents the sales tax rate for states in the US. We will define a Tax table that contains two columns representing the state code and the tax rate respectively. In this example, we will simply allocate the state code column to act as our primary key for the bean, so we won't have to develop a primary key class ourselves.

We will not create the database table ourselves; we will rather ask the deployment tool provided in the Reference Implementation to create the required database table at the time of deployment of our entity bean. However, you should note that not all deployment tools will provide this facility; for example, if you are using WebLogic you will need to create the database tables yourself.

Like session beans, entity beans require a component and a home interface, and an implementation class that provides the bean's business methods. We'll start with writing the interfaces first.

The Home Interface

The home interface extends `EJBHome` and defines a `create()` method as standard:

```
package cmp;

import java.util.Collection;
import java.rmi.RemoteException;
import javax.ejb.*;

public interface TaxHome extends EJBHome {

  public Tax create(String stateCode, float taxRate)
      throws RemoteException, CreateException;
```

The `create()` method receives two arguments: the state code as a String and tax rate as a float. These two arguments represent the bean's state that is mapped to the two columns of our Tax table.

It is possible, and sometimes appropriate, to have an entity bean with no `create()` methods. An entity bean is just an object-oriented view on transactional, shared data. In an environment with non-EJB applications, this data – and therefore, these entity beans – may exist without `create()` ever being called. If this data should be created *only* by these non-EJB applications, then the entity beans can be written without any `create()` methods. For instance, our database records might be created exclusively by someone with a Star Office spreadsheet linked to our database, with our EJB application being used to keep the information about owners and franchise players up-to-date. No `create()` methods would be required in this case.

Finder Methods

In addition, to the `create()` method, entity beans allow us to define any number of **finder methods** on the home interface. With entity beans, creating a bean instance through the use of a `create()` method is actually the same as inserting a record in the database. However, when you are working with data you more often want access to data rather than to create new records. Therefore, the finder methods provide a means to locate specific data (either as a specific record or a group of records). In this example, we will define two finder methods.

The `findByPrimaryKey()` method receives an argument specifying the primary key (in our case this will be the state code, which will be a `String`) that is to be searched for, and it also throws a `javax.ejb.FinderException`:

```
public Tax findByPrimaryKey(String primaryKey) throws FinderException,
    RemoteException;
```

> The **findByPrimaryKey()** finder is required to be defined by all entity beans, whereas any other finders are optional.

The `findInRange()` method accepts two parameters that specify the lower and upper limits for the tax rate. The method searches the database for the all records where the tax rate lies within the specified range. The container will then create the beans for all the matching records and return the remote references to the client:

```
    public Collection findInRange(float lowerLimit, float upperLimit)
        throws FinderException, RemoteException;
}
```

As this finder method may find more than one bean, a `Collection` is returned to the client; this `Collection` contains instances of primary key classes for all the returned beans matching the finder's search, which the container then translates into remote references for the client. Potentially, this method may return a huge collection if the table contains many records. Indeed, if the selection matches all these records you may run out of memory when you execute this method.

You can alternatively return an `Enumeration` rather than a `Collection` of primary keys should you so desire.

For CMP beans, the required SQL statements for the implementation of these methods are generated at the time of deployment, and the container executes the SQL statements during the execution of the method. Therefore, when we come to deploy our bean, we will need to provide the container with a bit more information on how to execute a SQL WHERE clause for our defined finders. Under the 1.1 specification the nature of specifying the WHERE clause is vendor-specific, however, the EJB 2.0 specification introduces a standardized way of writing them called the **EJB Query Language**, which you'll see in the next chapter.

The Component Interface

As with the previous chapter, we need to develop a remote interface to be accessed by a non-EJB client outside the container.

Our `Tax` interface defines two business methods, for setting and getting the tax rate. The `setTaxRate()` method accepts the tax rate as a floating-point number, while the `getTaxRate()` method returns the tax rate as a float:

```
package cmp;

import javax.ejb.EJBObject;
import java.rmi.RemoteException;

public interface Tax extends EJBObject {

  public void setTaxRate(float taxRate) throws RemoteException;
  public float getTaxRate() throws RemoteException;

}
```

The Bean Implementation Class

Our CMP bean class implements the `EntityBean` interface, indicating that this is an entity type of bean:

```
package cmp;

import java.util.*;
import javax.ejb.*;

public class TaxEJB implements EntityBean {
```

We then need to declare variables to represent the fields that we want our container to manage the persistence for. These variables will contain the state information for the specific database record that the bean represents. For a CMP bean class these variables must be declared as public.

For our Tax bean class we will declare two public variables: `stateCode` and `taxRate`. These variables map to the two columns of our Tax table:

```
public String stateCode;
public float taxRate;
```

The bean class next defines get and set methods that operate on the `taxRate` variable. Though these variables are declared public, the client cannot access them directly as the client never obtains a reference to the bean instance:

```
public void setTaxRate(float taxRate) {
   this.taxRate = taxRate;
}

public float getTaxRate() {
   return this.taxRate;
}
```

Now we will go through the persistence callback methods that we need to define.

Create

When a client calls `create()` for an entity bean, state data is inserted into the corresponding data store (such as a relational database). This is transactional data that is accessible from multiple clients. In contrast, when a client calls `create()` for a stateful session bean, the EJB container creates a private, non-transactional store of data in the application server's temporary storage. This difference is important to understand.

> When you call **create()** on a session bean's home interface, you are creating an instance of that session bean, whereas when you call **create()** on an entity bean's home interface, you are actually inserting a record in the database.

There can be multiple forms of the `create()` method defined in the bean's home interface, and these `create()` methods may take different parameters, which correspond to the bean's state at the time of creation. The parameters must have enough information to at least initialize the primary key of the entity. The corresponding `ejbCreate()` methods that we define in the bean implementation class must have a return type that corresponds to the primary key class type, whereas the method itself must return a `null`. This is so that the container can create a BMP bean by sub-classing the CMP bean.

On our home interface we declared a single `create()` method that took the state code and tax rate as parameters. Therefore, in our bean implementation class we need to define an `ejbCreate()` and `ejbPostCreate()` method that takes the same parameter signature:

```
public String ejbCreate(String stateCode, float taxRate)
         throws CreateException {

   if (stateCode == null) {
      throw new CreateException("The State Code is required.");
   }
```

```
        this.stateCode = stateCode;
        this.taxRate = taxRate;

        return null;

    }

    public void ojbPostCreate(String stateCode, float taxRate) {}
```

The ejbCreate() method receives two arguments, the stateCode and the taxRate, that it copies into the instance variables of the class. Note that besides this simple task, we haven't had to write any data manipulation code at all.

The stateCode variable represents the primary key of our table (which is why the ejbCreate() method returns a String) and therefore should not be null, and ideally not an empty string, so the method checks the value of stateCode, and throws a CreateException if it is not suitable. Should we try to create a new record with the same primary key we will receive a javax.ejb.DuplicateKeyException.

After creating the instance, the container calls the ejbPostCreate()method that takes the same number of arguments as the ejbCreate() method. This method can provide additional initializations and allocate resources required by the bean during its lifespan. Bean handles (discussed in the previous chapter) will be valid in this ejbPostCreate() method; if you obtain a handle in the ejbCreate() method, it will be invalid.

Read

The ejbLoad() callback method corresponds roughly to the 'read' functionality of entity beans. A simple way to look at it is that the entity will load the data from the database in correspondence to the container's ejbLoad() call. With container-managed persistence, the EJB container will take care of transferring the entity's state from the database to the entity's instance variables. In this case, the bean programmer will often leave the ejbLoad() method blank, but may choose to do some post-processing of the loaded data. With bean-managed persistence, the bean programmer will write their data-access code (probably JDBC and SQL code) in ejbLoad() to transfer the entity's state to instance variables.

This description is a good way to understand the process, but it is not the whole story. Technically, ejbLoad() doesn't tell the bean that it must actually load data: it just tells the bean that it must re-synchronize its state with the underlying data store. This is a subtle but potentially important difference.

> The bean's persistence implementation may choose to defer loading the state until that state is actually used.

Let's consider an example. An Order entity bean may have an order number, a customer name, and a list of line items. When ejbLoad() is called for an entity bean that represents a particular order, the state of that order – the number, name, and line items – must be synchronized with the database. In this example, the persistence logic may choose to update the name and number immediately from the database. But retrieving the list of related line items is a potentially expensive operation, so a 'dirty' flag is set instead. If the only method that is called on this order bean is getCustomerName(), the line items will never need to be loaded. Any method that must access the list, such as totalLineItems() for example, will need to check the dirty flag and load the list from the database if it is set.

It's possible, even likely, that your container's automatic persistence loads the entire bean when ejbLoad() *is called. (This is known as 'eager loading of state'.) This can affect both your application design and your choice of bean-managed persistence or container-managed persistence.*

The role of ejbLoad() in container-managed persistence is to process the data after it has been loaded from the database. Often, the data will not need processing at all, and your ejbLoad() method will be empty. Sometimes, however, changes will be necessary. A practical example is that you may store your String data in char database fields of a certain size, and the database may append blanks to your strings to pad them to the correct length. Although this may be more efficient than using a varchar data type, those trailing blanks can be annoying. You could use ejbLoad() to trim those trailing blanks. Alternatively you may want to provide encryption and decryption of the data.

Here is the ejbLoad() callback for our Tax bean:

```
public void ejbLoad() {

  if (stateCode != null)
    stateCode.trim();

}
```

Update

The ejbStore() callback method corresponds roughly to the 'update' functionality of entity beans. Of course, the actual modification of the entity bean's cached state will be done through calls to business methods, such as setStateCode() or calculateTax(). The container will call the ejbStore() method to notify the bean that it must synchronize its state with the database. For a bean with container-managed persistence, this method will be called directly before the container writes the altered bean state to the database, and the programmer of a CMP bean may use this opportunity to pre-process the bean's data to ensure that it is in an appropriate state for persistent storage. Typically, however, this method will be left empty.

With ejbLoad()*, the bean had the option to defer the actual loading of state until it was used. There is no such option with* ejbStore()*. Any modifications to the object's state must be written to the data store immediately. The equivalent optimization is probably something called 'tuned updates'. In other words, only the modified state need be written to the data store; if something hasn't changed, you can leave it alone.*

Here then is the ejbStore() method for our Tax bean:

```
public void ejbStore() {}
```

Delete

When a client calls remove() on an entity bean, data is deleted from the corresponding data store. In contrast, when a client calls remove() for a stateful session bean, the EJB container discards the session bean instance in the application server's temporary storage. It is important to understand this difference. You should always call remove() when you are done using a stateful session bean; otherwise, the EJB container will waste resources managing this instance.

> You should not call `remove()` on an entity bean unless you want to delete that record. The EJB container will manage the entity bean's instance in the container.

For an entity bean with container-managed persistence, the `ejbRemove()` method can usually be left empty, and the container will handle the deletion of the instance from the underlying data store. The programmer of an entity bean with container-managed persistence may use this method to implement any actions that must be done (such as updating related data or notifying other systems) before the entity object's representation is removed from the database. Here is the method for our Tax bean:

```
public void ejbRemove() {}
```

Context and Activation/Passivation

For this CMP bean we will be leaving resolving the identity of the bean up to the container and, as we are not using any additional resources in the bean, we can provide null implementation for these methods:

```
public void unsetEntityContext() {}
public void setEntityContext(EntityContext context) {}
public void ejbActivate() {}
public void ejbPassivate() {}
}
```

And that completes the coding for the Tax bean's implementation class. As you will have noticed, using CMP makes this a very simple process.

The Deployment Descriptor

We have now defined the home and remote interfaces for the bean, as well as the implementation class, so we now need a deployment descriptor before we can create a JAR file. Here it is:

```
<?xml version="1.0"?>

<!DOCTYPE ejb-jar PUBLIC
          '-//Sun Microsystems, Inc.//DTD Enterprise JavaBeans 1.1//EN'
          'http://java.sun.com/dtd/ejb-jar_1_1.dtd'>

<ejb-jar>
  <description>no description</description>
  <display-name>taxCMP</display-name>
  <enterprise-beans>
```

The first thing to note about this deployment descriptor is the `<entity>` element, which (unsurprisingly) indicates that the bean defined in this tag is an entity bean:

```
<entity>
  <description>no description</description>
```

As usual we declare the name of the bean, the home and remote interfaces, and the bean implementation class:

```
<display-name>TaxBean</display-name>
<ejb-name>TaxBean</ejb-name>
<home>cmp.TaxHome</home>
<remote>cmp.Tax</remote>
<ejb-class>cmp.TaxEJB</ejb-class>
```

Next we declare our bean to have container-managed persistence and the class that our primary key belongs to, and we also declare that the bean cannot be called upon while it is in a business method (using the `<reentrant>` tags):

```
<persistence-type>Container</persistence-type>
<prim-key-class>java.lang.String</prim-key-class>
<reentrant>False</reentrant>
```

Here we declare the fields to be persisted, and the field that will be used as the primary key:

```
<cmp-field>
  <description>no description</description>
  <field-name>taxRate</field-name>
</cmp-field>
<cmp-field>
  <description>no description</description>
  <field-name>stateCode</field-name>
</cmp-field>
<primkey-field>stateCode</primkey-field>
    </entity>
</enterprise-beans>
```

Now we need the `<assembly-descriptor>` section, which contains `<container-transaction>` tags that describe the transactional attributes of the bean. Here we are saying that transactional attributes are not supported in any of the methods in the bean (* indicates all methods):

```
<assembly-descriptor>
  <container-transaction>
    <method>
      <ejb-name>TaxBean</ejb-name>
      <method-name>*</method-name>
    </method>
    <trans-attribute>NotSupported</trans-attribute>
  </container-transaction>
</assembly-descriptor>
</ejb-jar>
```

We are now able to make our EJB JAR file, `taxCMP.jar`.

The DTD for 1.1 Entity Beans

Here is a depiction of the <entity> element from the EJB 1.1 DTD:

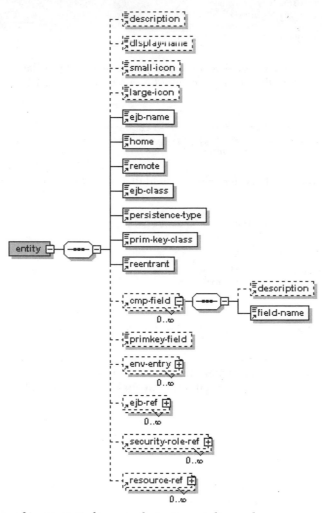

There are a number of important elements that we must discuss here.

<persistence-type>

The required <persistence-type> element can be one of two values, the purpose of which is to tell the container who is responsible for managing the bean's persistence:

❑ Container

❑ Bean

<prim-key-class> and <primkey-field>

These two elements allow you to specify for the container what the bean's primary key will be. The `<prim-key-class>` element is required for all entity beans and should be a fully qualified Java class that is serializable. For CMP beans, the primary key is one of the fields specified in the `<cmp-field>` elements and must be of the same type as the `<prim-key-class>`.

> *Under certain conditions, the bean provider may not know the type of class that will be used as the primary key, or they may want the deployer to select the primary key fields at deployment time. Under these conditions, the bean provider can choose to simply leave the primary key class as* `java.lang.Object` *in the* `findByPrimaryKey()` *method, the* `ejbCreate()` *method, and the deployment descriptor.*

<reentrant>

Unlike session beans, which are never **reentrant**, an entity bean can be specified as reentrant or non-reentrant. A reentrant bean is one that allows a 'loopback' – for example, an Order entity bean calls a LineItem entity bean, which then calls the Order bean. The initial call to the LineItem 'looped back' to the Order.

If the Order bean in this example were specified as reentrant, the call would be allowed. If the Order bean were specified as not being reentrant, the EJB container would disallow the call and throw a `java.rmi.RemoteException`.

Many programmers are used to a style of programming where child items (such as a line item) have a reference to their containing parent (such as an order). This is admittedly useful in a variety of situations, and is allowed. However, making entity beans reentrant is discouraged (not forbidden) by the specification. This is because it makes it impossible for the container to prevent a certain class of error.

If a bean is coded as reentrant, the EJB container cannot prevent a multi-threaded client operating within a single transaction from making multiple calls to the entity bean. Although entity beans are designed to be single-threaded, this could lead to a situation where two (or more) threads of control were operating on a single instance of an entity bean simultaneously. This is the type of system error that Enterprise JavaBeans technology was designed to free the business logic programmer from worrying about, which is partly why the specification suggests that bean programmers avoid reentrant beans.

The `<reentrant>` element is therefore either `True` or `False`.

<cmp-field> and <field-name>

The `<cmp-field>` element notifies the container what fields it needs to manage the persistence for, as specified in the child `<field-name>` element. Obviously these elements are only applicable to CMP beans.

Let's now turn our attention to deploying this bean.

Deployment

We start the deployment of our Tax bean by creating a new application. After starting the J2EE server, open the J2EE RI deploy tool, and create a new application by selecting the File | New Application... menu option. Specify the following names in the New Application dialog window:

❑   Application File Name: tax ear

❑   Application Display Name: taxApp

This creates a new application in the specified folder. Now select the Add to Application | EJB JAR... menu option and specify the JAR file that we created above, `taxCMP.jar`. Once the JAR has added to our application, double-click on this JAR file name. It shows that it contains a TaxBean EJB. Click on this to open the settings screen for the TaxBean. We will need to set up the database for persistence management here; click on the Entity tab to show the persistence management settings as in the following screenshot:

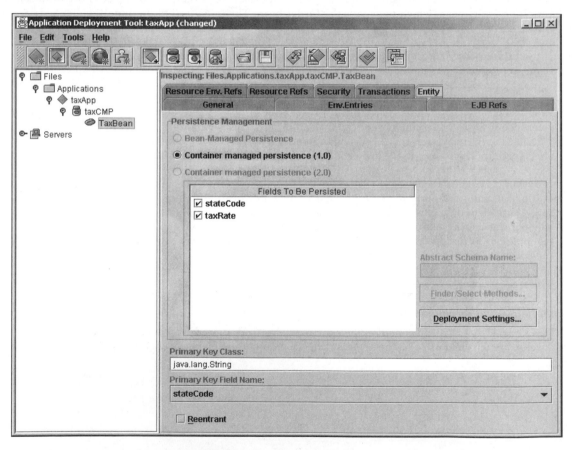

Note that the deployment descriptor marks the bean as using Container managed persistence (1.0) even though this is the J2EE 1.3 deployment tool. As we said earlier, the EJB 2.0 specification mandates that there is a separate container contract for 1.1 and 2.0 entity beans.

Now click on the Deployment Settings button:

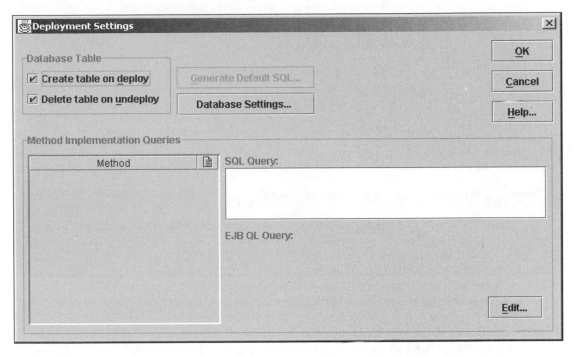

Now click on the Database Settings button. We need to select the database and to generate the required SQL statements. In the Database JNDI Name field type the following:

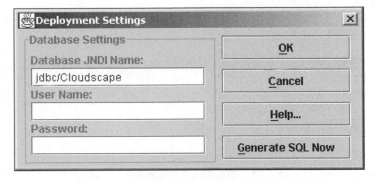

jdbc/Cloudscape is a datasource that is bound in a JNDI tree in the server and is configured to point to the underlying datastore for the bean. We'll look at specifying datasources in more detail in Chapter 8.

This is the default database installed as a part of J2EE. The JNDI name is specified in the properties file of the server. (Refer to Appendix B for details on how to set up a different database.) Before we proceed further, make sure that the database server is up and running. If not, start the database server by using the following command line:

```
%J2EE_HOME%\bin\cloudscape -start
```

Now click on OK to close the window, and then select the Generate Default SQL button to start the SQL generation process. It takes several seconds to generate the SQL statements.

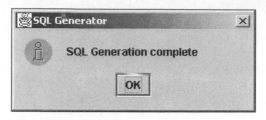

Once they are generated, the tool prompts you to provide the WHERE clause for all the SQL statements that need a parameter. In our case, there is only one method where we need to provide WHERE clause:

The deployment tool is able to generate the SQL for the findByPrimaryKey() *finder by itself because it is a simple* WHERE [Primary Key Field] = ? *query.*

Select the findInRange method and type in the following WHERE clause after the text in the statement display on the right hand side:

```
WHERE "taxRate" BETWEEN ?1 AND ?2
```

This is shown below:

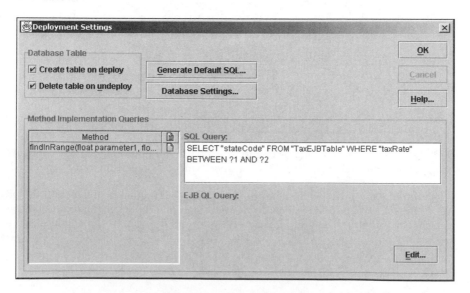

Note that in Cloudscape, database table names and column names are case-sensitive.

You can examine the generated SQL code for the rest of the methods. Note that the Reference Implementation automatically creates the database table on deployment. In case of other servers, you may need to create these tables yourself.

Close the **Deployment Settings** dialog by clicking on the **OK** button. Before we deploy our bean we need to set the JNDI name for the application. Select **taxCMP** in the left-hand tree, switch to the JNDI Names tab and enter a JNDI name for the bean:

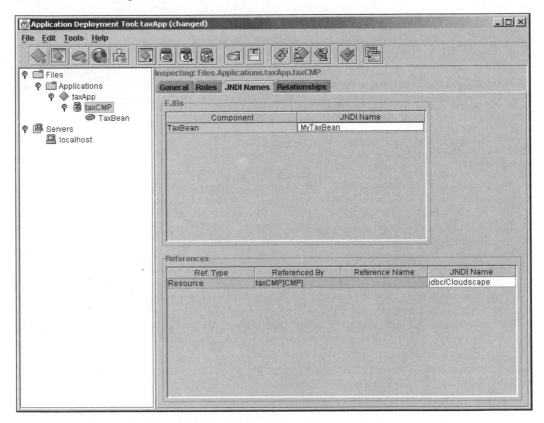

You'll also see that the deployment tool has add a resource reference for us, which represents the datasource that the bean will use to connect to the database. When we come to the BMP version of the bean, we will need to add this reference in manually.

Now we are ready to deploy the application. Click on the **Deploy...** menu option under **Tools** menu. Run through the deployment screens remembering to return a client JAR file.

Developing the Client

The client program we will develop in this section is very similar to the client programs we have developed in last two chapters. We will write a Java console application for testing our CMP entity bean. Let's take a look:

```
import cmp.*;
import java.util.*;
import javax.naming.Context;
import javax.naming.InitialContext;
import javax.rmi.PortableRemoteObject;

public class TaxClient {
  public static void main(String[] args) {
    try {
```

In the main() method, we first locate our bean by initializing the JNDI context and performing a lookup for the JNDI name MyTaxBean. This was the name used while registering our bean with the JNDI server:

```
Context initial = new InitialContext();
Object objRef = initial.lookup("MyTaxBean");
```

Once the object is located, the next step is to typecast the reference to the entity home class. We use the narrow() method of the PortableRemoteObject class to do this typecast:

```
TaxHome home = (TaxHome) PortableRemoteObject.narrow(objRef,
        TaxHome.class);

Tax tax = null;
```

We will now create a few bean instances by calling the create() method on the home object. Note that a call to the create() method creates a record in the underlying database table, creates a bean instance, and returns a remote reference to the caller. The container manages all this and we do not have to write any SQL code for inserting records in the database table.

```
tax = home.create("IL", 5.00f);
tax = home.create("CA", 6.25f);
tax = home.create("FL", 8.50f);
tax = home.create("CO", 6.75f);
```

Once the bean instances are created, we use them the same way as we've been using the session beans. For entity beans, persistent state is maintained in the database table, so we can use one of the finder methods defined in our home interface to locate an existing record and create an entity bean. The findByPrimaryKey() method is one such finder method. It searches the database for a given primary key value, and if a record with this key value is found, it creates a bean instance and initializes its state with the values from the underlying database record:

```
tax = home.findByPrimaryKey("CA");
```

A remote reference to the located bean is returned to the caller. Using this reference, the client invokes the business methods setTaxRate() and getTaxRate() on the bean in order to get the current tax rate, and to set the new value for the tax rate:

```
            System.out.println("CA tax rate: " + tax.getTaxRate());

            System.out.println("Changing tax rate for CA state");
            tax.setTaxRate(8.25f);

            System.out.println("New CA tax rate: " + tax.getTaxRate());
```

We now call another finder method to locate all the states where the tax rate is between 5 and 7. We can use the `findInRange()` method for this; this method returns a `Collection` containing the remote references to the created beans:

```
            Collection taxArray = home.findInRange(5.0f, 7.0f);
```

The program creates an `Iterator` to iterate through this collection. Remember each item in the collection is a remote reference to a bean that matched the query. Therefore, we need to perform a typecast on the reference before we use it as a Tax bean.

For each item in the collection, we print the primary key value (the state code), and the tax rate. Each located record is then permanently removed from the database by calling the `remove()` method:

```
        Iterator it = taxArray.iterator();
        while (it.hasNext()) {
          Object objRef2 = it.next();
          tax = (Tax)PortableRemoteObject.narrow(objRef2, Tax.class);

          System.out.println("Tax Rate in " + tax.getPrimaryKey() + ": "
                            + tax.getTaxRate());
          tax.remove();
        }
      } catch (Exception ex) {
        System.err.println("Caught an exception.");
        ex.printStackTrace();
      }
    }
  }
```

From this example we can see that our client program for accessing entity beans is very similar to those client programs we have already created for accessing session beans. However, in the case of entity beans, we need to use an appropriate finder method to locate and load an existing record.

Running the Client

Compile the client program and then try running it by invoking the following command:

```
    java -classpath %J2EE_HOME%\lib\j2ee.jar;taxClient.jar;. TaxClient
```

The program output is shown below:

```
C:\WINNT\System32\cmd.exe
C:\Wrox\ProEJB\Chapter04\tax>java -classpath %J2EE_HOME%\lib\j2ee.jar;taxClient.jar;. TaxClient
CA tax rate: 6.25
Changing tax rate for CA state
New CA tax rate: 8.25
Tax Rate in IL: 5.0
Tax Rate in CO: 6.75

C:\Wrox\ProEJB\Chapter04\tax>
```

When you run the program, a few records are added to the database. You can see that the program then finds the tax rate for CA state and prints it on the console. Next, a business method is invoked to change this tax rate. The new tax rate is then read and printed on the console. The program finishes by finding all the states where the tax rate lies between 5.0 and 7.0 and prints all such records on the console.

Lifecycle of Entity Beans

Having seen the development of a CMP entity bean, we will next look at the lifecycle of entity beans using sequence diagrams. First though, we must describe the client view of an entity bean. In this section we will study the following:

❑   The client view of entity bean's lifecycle

❑   The lifecycle of an entity bean instance

Client View of an Entity Bean's Lifecycle

Unlike session beans, entity beans live beyond the lifecycle of the client. Therefore, although the client creates an entity bean, invokes its business methods and releases its reference when it terminates, the entity bean itself continues to remain available in the container and may be used by other clients. Another difference between session and entity beans is that, unlike session beans, many clients can have access to an entity bean and its state is saved to persistent storage:

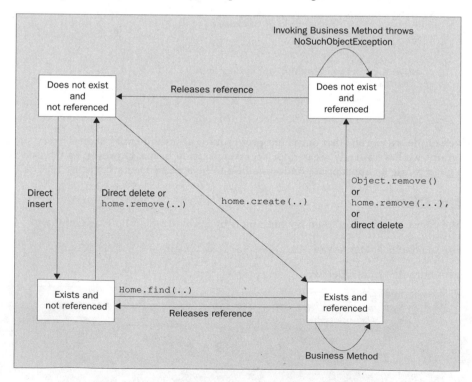

If we look at the state transition diagram shown opposite, we can see that initially the bean is in the state does not exist and not referenced (top-left in the diagram). When the client calls the `create()` method on the home object, a transition to the exists and referenced state takes place, as shown in the bottom-right corner of the diagram. The client now holds a reference to the remote object of the bean and can invoke any of the bean's remote methods. After each method call, we return to this state.

When the client invokes the `remove()` method on the object reference itself or its home object, the bean is removed. However, the client may continue to hold a reference to the bean. The block on the top-right corner of the diagram illustrates this state (does not exist and referenced). If the client tries invoking a method on the bean using a reference to it, a `NoSuchObjectException` will be thrown to the client.

A client may voluntarily relinquish the reference to the bean by marking the reference `null`. In this case, the transition to the exists and not referenced state takes place, shown in the bottom-left corner. When the client invokes a `find()` method on the home object, the transition back to the exists and referenced state takes place.

Finally, a transition from the does not exist and not referenced to the exists and not referenced state can also take place, in the case of direct inserts into the database (remember that the entity bean represents a record in the database). From this exists and not referenced state a transition can take place to the does not exist and not referenced state if the client calls the `remove()` method on the home object. In this case, the record is removed from the database. Such a transition can also take place in the case of a direct delete of the database row.

These are the various states of the entity bean from the client's perspective. We will now study the state diagram of the entity bean's instance.

The Entity Bean Instance Lifecycle

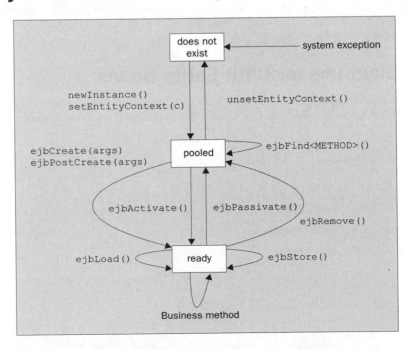

When the client invokes a create() method on the home object, the bean is created and put in the pool of available beans – a transition from **does not exist** to **pooled** state takes place. During this transition, the container calls the newInstance() method to create a bean instance and calls a setEntityContext() method in the bean implementation class to pass the context to the bean.

The container may garbage-collect a pooled bean if it decides to free the resources used by the bean, and in this case a transition back to the **does not exist** state takes place. During this transition, the container calls the unsetEntityContext() method in the bean implementation class. As seen earlier, this method can be used for deallocating the previously allocated resources.

When the client invokes one of the finder methods, the container locates the bean in the database, copies the primary key into the instance variable and returns the bean to the **pooled** state. Note that at this time, the container may not load the entire record into the bean. The container uses the ejbLoad() method to load and synchronize the bean's state with the underlying database whenever required.

When the client calls the create() method, the container calls ejbCreate() followed by ejbPostCreate() on the bean class, and the bean moves from the **pooled** to the **ready** state. In the **ready** state, the bean's state is fully initialized. At this time, the bean is ready for method invocation. After each method call, the bean returns to the same state for another method invocation. In the **ready** state the container may call the ejbLoad() and ejbStore() methods several times to ensure proper synchronization of the bean's state with the underlying database record.

If the client calls the remove() method on the bean, the container will call the ejbRemove() method on the bean class and a transition from **ready** to **pooled** state takes place.

While the bean is in the **ready** state, the container may return it to the **pooled** state, depending on the resource requirements at that time. This process, as we have seen earlier, is called passivation. During passivation, the container calls the ejbPassivate() method on the bean object. The container may activate a previously pooled bean, and in this case a transition from the **pooled** to the **ready** state takes place. This is known as activation and during this process, the container calls the ejbActivate() method on the bean object.

Sequence Diagrams for CMP Entity Beans

As we saw in Chapter 3, the sequence diagrams help us to understand the interaction of various classes involved in a certain operation. We will now discuss the diagrams for several operations on CMP entity beans.

We will discuss the following:

- ❑ Creating CMP entity objects
- ❑ Activating/Passivating CMP entity objects
- ❑ Removing a CMP entity object
- ❑ Finding a CMP entity object

Creating a CMP Entity Object

The client calls the create() method on the home object to create an instance of the bean:

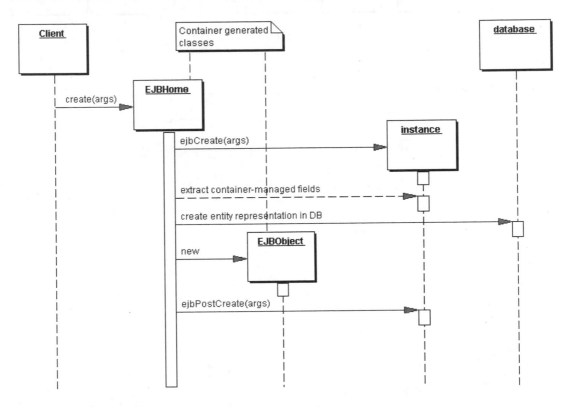

The create() method takes arguments that are the values of the variables to be persisted. The container calls the ejbCreate() method on the bean instance, passing the same number of arguments as taken by the create() method. Note that the container will not always create a new bean instance; it might use an instance available in its pool.

Since the container is responsible for persistence management, it determines the fields that need to be saved from the deployment descriptor (this is indicated on the diagram by the dotted arrow). The container then saves these fields to the database. All of these database changes will be registered with the resource manager. The container then creates a remote EJB object and calls the ejbPostCreate() method on the bean instance. Remember that this is a callback method used by the bean to do any additional initialization during the create operation. At this stage, the object is ready for method invocation. When the client invokes a business method on the remote object, the call is delegated to the bean instance.

Activating/Passivating a CMP Entity Bean

The container may activate/passivate a bean any number of times during its lifecycle. With reference to the following object interaction diagram, we will now study the interaction between the various objects during the activation/passivation process:

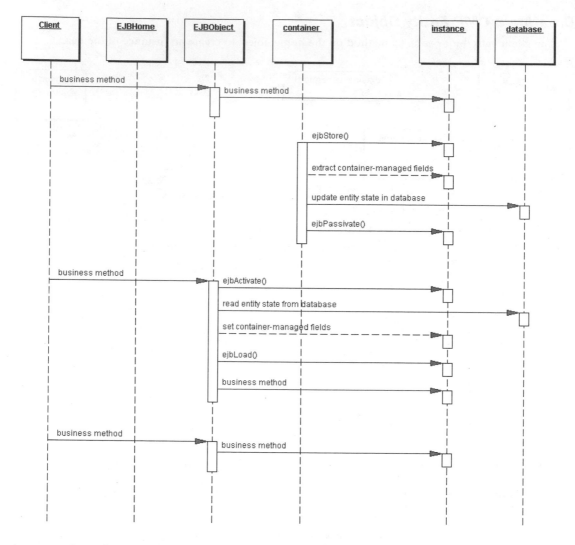

As seen earlier, whenever the client invokes a business method on the remote object, this call will be delegated to the bean instance. If the client has not invoked a business method on the bean for a while, the container may decide to passivate the bean.

During the passivation process, the container first calls the ejbStore() method on the bean instance. This gives a chance for the bean to change its state before it is actually saved to persistent storage. The container then determines the fields that need to be stored. The container updates the bean's state in the underlying database by invoking appropriate SQL statements. Once the state is saved, the container calls the ejbPassivate() method on the bean instance. The bean may use this method to free any previously allocated resources.

When the client invokes a business method on the remote object and the bean instance is not actively associated with the client, the container will call the `ejbActivate()` method on the bean instance. The client may allocate the required resources in this method. The container then reads the bean's state from the underlying database table and sets the values for those instance variables that the container is responsible for persisting. The container then calls the `ejbLoad()` method on the bean instance giving it an opportunity to modify its state, if desired. Finally, the business method that the client has invoked in the first place will now be invoked on the bean instance.

Once a bean instance gets actively associated with the client, the next business method invocation does not require the activation process and the method call is immediately delegated to the bean instance.

Removing a CMP Entity Object

Here a client invokes a `remove()` method on the remote object reference; the container then calls the `ejbRemove()` method on the bean instance, which allows the bean instance an opportunity to do any cleanup before it is removed. The container then removes the representation of the bean from the underlying database table – meaning that the database record is deleted from the underlying tables:

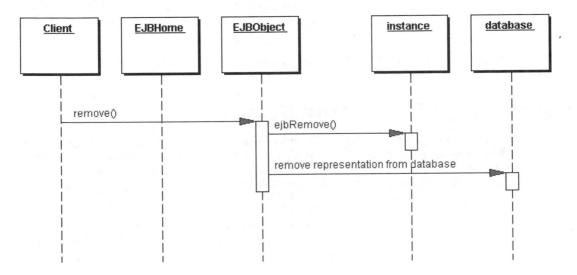

Finding a CMP Entity Bean

A client may invoke one of the finder methods defined in the home interface to locate a bean. This finder method may require one or more arguments (corresponding to specific values of persisted data). In the case of CMP, since the container is responsible for persistence management, it now searches the underlying database for the desired record(s). Once a database record is located, a new remote object is created and its reference is returned to the client:

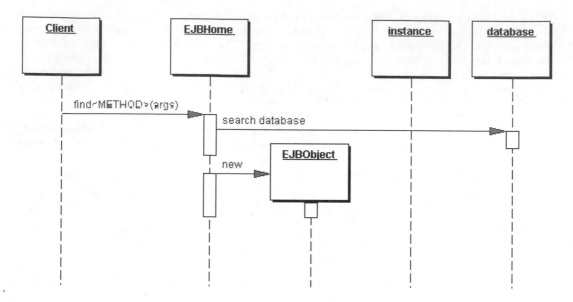

Now we will move on to look at developing the other type of entity bean.

Developing a BMP Entity Bean

In the previous section, we developed a CMP entity bean, for which the container is responsible for the persistence management. In this section, we'll see how to develop a BMP entity bean. In this case, you, the bean developer, are responsible for the persistence management. Thus, we will be required to generate appropriate SQL statements for database management and use the appropriate primary key while accessing the entity beans.

Rather than develop a new example, we'll take our existing Tax bean and modify it so that it manages its own persistence. This way we can easily compare the differences between developing a CMP bean and a BMP bean.

In this chapter we will only be going through some basics of bean-managed persistence. Later in the book in Chapter 16, we'll be looking at more complex models of managing your own persistence.

The Home Interface

The home interface is essentially unchanged from the CMP version:

```
package bmp;

import java.util.Collection;
import java.rmi.RemoteException;
import javax.ejb.*;

public interface TaxHome extends EJBHome {
```

```
    public Tax create(String stateCode, float taxRate)
        throws RemoteException, CreateException;

    public Tax findByPrimaryKey(String primaryKey) throws FinderException,
        RemoteException;

    public Collection findInRange(float lowerLimit, float upperLimit)
        throws FinderException, RemoteException;
}
```

However, when we come to the bean implementation class, this time we will need to provide an implementation for the finders. The naming convention for the finder implementations is that for each findXXX() method in the remote interface there must be an ejbFindXXX() method in the bean class.

The Remote Interface

The remote interface is similarly unchanged:

```
package bmp;

import javax.ejb.EJBObject;
import java.rmi.RemoteException;

public interface Tax extends EJBObject {

  public void setTaxRate(float taxRate) throws RemoteException;
  public float getTaxRate() throws RemoteException;

}
```

The Bean Implementation Class

Now we come to the implementation class. Unlike the CMP version, this time we are going to have to do a lot of coding to manage the persistence ourselves. We'll be doing this by using JDBC to connect to the database and execute statements that we'll write in SQL.

Therefore, first up we'll need to import some additional packages for the data handing:

```
package bmp;

import java.sql.*;
import javax.sql.*;
import javax.naming.*;
import java.util.*;
import javax.ejb.*;

public class TaxEJB implements EntityBean {
```

Then our class declares several instance variables that are used to hold the bean's state. Unlike the CMP version, these variables are declared private, as they are accessed by the bean's methods and the container should not have to access these variables directly:

```
private String stateCode;
private float taxRate;
```

Besides these, we declare four more instance variables. The `EntityContext` type variable holds the context received during object creation, `DataSource` type variable holds the reference to the JNDI lookup for the datasource, `dbName` holds the environment variable name for our database connection, and `connection` holds a connection to the database. Note that `dbName` will be mapped to the actual database name at the time of deployment:

```
private EntityContext ctx;
private DataSource ds;
private String dbName = "java:comp/env/jdbc/Cloudscape";
private Connection con;
```

As before we still have a getter and setter for the `taxRate` variable:

```
public void setTaxRate(float taxRate) {
  this.taxRate = taxRate;
}

public float getTaxRate() {
  return this.taxRate;
}
```

We can now look at how to define the entity callbacks for a BMP bean.

Create

In the CMP version all we needed to do was check that the state code was valid and then simply set the instance variables to the passed in arguments. This time we need to do all that as well as inserting a record into the table:

```
public String ejbCreate(String stateCode, float taxRate)
        throws CreateException {

  if (stateCode == null) {
    throw new CreateException("The State Code is required.");
  }

  try {
    String sqlStmt = "INSERT INTO TaxTable VALUES ( ? , ? )";
    con = ds.getConnection();
    PreparedStatement stmt = con.prepareStatement(sqlStmt);
    stmt.setString(1, stateCode);
    stmt.setFloat(2, taxRate);
    stmt.executeUpdate();
    stmt.close();
  } catch (SQLException sqle) {
    throw new EJBException(sqle);
  } finally {
     try {
        if (con != null) {
          con.close();
        }
     } catch (SQLException sqle) {}
  }
```

```
      this.stateCode = stateCode;
      this.taxRate = taxRate;

   return stateCode;

}
```

One other significant difference from the CMP bean is that instead of returning `null`, we need to return the primary key for the bean.

The `ejbPostCreate()` method is the same as before:

```
public void ejbPostCreate(String stateCode, float taxRate) {}
```

Read

The role of `ejbLoad()` in bean-managed persistence is to notify the bean that it must invalidate the current cached state and prepare for business method invocations. In practical terms, this usually means replacing the state by loading it from the database.

To find the entity bean's data in the database, you will need the primary key. By the time that `ejbLoad()` is called, the primary key has been associated with the entity and is available from its context:

```
public void setEntityContext(EntityContext context) {
   this.ctx = context;
}
```

```
public void unsetEntityContext() {
   ctx = null;
}
```

When the container activates a bean, it calls the `ejbActivate()` method in the bean class. In this method, we obtain the primary key from the previously-stored context object and assign it to the `stateCode` instance variable. The container then associates the bean instance with a particular database record specified by the primary key field. The container is responsible for initializing the state of the rest of the variables from the database record at the appropriate time. Note that the container may not load the entire record in the bean instance immediately, it may defer the database record loading to a later time:

```
public void ejbActivate() {
   stateCode = (String)ctx.getPrimaryKey();
}
```

During its lifetime, the container may passivate and activate the bean several times. Before the bean can be passivated, the container must call the `ejbPassivate()` method defined in the bean class. This method is used to free any previously allocated resources. In the current implementation, to do this we must set the primary key (the `stateCode` variable) to `null`. By setting this variable to `null`, we disassociate the current instance from the database record. The container returns such an instance to the pool of available beans and may assign it to some other database record in future:

```
public void ejbPassivate() {
   stateCode = null;
}
```

Now that we are sure that our bean instance is related to the correct primary key we can go on to code the `ejbLoad()` method. In this method we need simply to load our instance variables with the data from the database:

```
public void ejbLoad() {

   try {
      String sqlStmt = "SELECT stateCode, taxRate FROM TaxTable " +
                       "WHERE stateCode = ? ";
      con = ds.getConnection();
      PreparedStatement stmt = con.prepareStatement(sqlStmt);

      stmt.setString(1, stateCode);
      ResultSet rs = stmt.executeQuery();

      if (rs.next()) {
         this.taxRate = rs.getFloat("taxRate");
         stmt.close();
      } else {
         stmt.close();
         throw new NoSuchEntityException("State Code: " + stateCode);
      }
   } catch (SQLException sqle) {
      throw new EJBException(sqle);
   } finally {
      try {
         if (con != null) {
            con.close();
         }
      } catch (SQLException sqle) {}
   }
}
```

Update

In the `ejbStore()` method we need to update the values in the underlying database with the current instance variables of the bean:

```
public void ejbStore() {

   try {
      String sqlStmt = "UPDATE TaxTable SET "
                       + "taxRate = ? " + "WHERE stateCode = ?";
      con = ds.getConnection();
      PreparedStatement stmt = con.prepareStatement(sqlStmt);

      stmt.setFloat(1, taxRate);
      stmt.setString(2, stateCode);

      if (stmt.executeUpdate() != 1) {
         throw new EJBException("Object state could not be saved");
      }
      stmt.close();
```

```
      } catch (SQLException sqle) {
        throw new EJBException(sqle);
      } finally {
        try {
          if (con != null) {
            con.close();
          }
        } catch (SQLException sqle) {}
      }

    }
```

Delete

In the ejbRemove() method we need to delete the underlying data record for the bean:

```
public void ejbRemove() {

    try {
        String sqlStmt = "DELETE FROM TaxTable WHERE stateCode = ? ";
        con = ds.getConnection();
        PreparedStatement stmt = con.prepareStatement(sqlStmt);

        stmt.setString(1, stateCode);
        stmt.executeUpdate();
        stmt.close();

    } catch (SQLException sqle) {
        throw new EJBException(sqle);
    } finally {
        try {
            if (con != null) {
                con.close();
            }
        } catch (SQLException sqle) {}
    }

}
```

The Finder Methods

As we said when discussing the home interface, this time round we will need to write the full SQL query for the finder methods.

ejbFindByPrimaryKey()

First we will look at the ejbFindByPrimaryKey() method:

```
public String ejbFindByPrimaryKey(String primaryKey)
    throws FinderException {

    try {
        String sqlStmt = "SELECT stateCode "
                    + "FROM TaxTable WHERE stateCode = ? ";
        con = ds.getConnection();
        PreparedStatement stmt = con.prepareStatement(sqlStmt);
        stmt.setString(1, primaryKey);

        ResultSet rs = stmt.executeQuery();
```

```
            if (!rs.next()) {
                throw new ObjectNotFoundException();
            }
            rs.close();
            stmt.close();
            return primaryKey;

        } catch (SQLException sqle) {
            throw new EJBException(sqle);
        } finally {
            try {
                if (con != null) {
                    con.close();
                }
            } catch (SQLException sqle) {}
        }

    }
```

ejbFindInRange()

Now the other finder method that returns a collection of beans with a tax rate within two boundaries:

```
    public Collection ejbFindInRange(float lowerLimit, float upperLimit)
        throws FinderException {

      try {
          String sqlStmt = "SELECT stateCode from TaxTable "
                        + "WHERE taxRate BETWEEN ? AND ?";
          con = ds.getConnection();
          PreparedStatement stmt = con.prepareStatement(sqlStmt);

          stmt.setFloat(1, lowerLimit);
          stmt.setFloat(2, upperLimit);
          ResultSet rs = stmt.executeQuery();

          ArrayList list = new ArrayList();
          while (rs.next()) {
            String id = rs.getString(1);
            list.add(id);
          }

          stmt.close();
          return list;

      } catch (SQLException sqle) {
          throw new EJBException(sqle);
      } finally {
          try {
              if (con != null) {
                con.close();
              }
          } catch (SQLException sqle) {}
      }
    }
```

As mentioned earlier, the Collection that we need to return is basically just a list of primary key class instances for all the beans that match the search criteria. The container then translates these into remote references to be passed back to the client.

Initializing the Datasource

Almost all of the above methods get a connection to the database using a datasource object, but we have yet to see where this datasource comes from. The datasource is a resource registered in the server much like the EJB is itself and available through a JNDI lookup. We could perform this lookup each time we need the connection, but the lookup can be quite a costly operation, therefore, it doesn't necessarily makes sense from a performance perspective to keep creating connections. Something else to remember is that the `ejbLoad()` and `ejbStore()` methods could be called very frequently by the container even though no data access is needed.

Therefore, we will be getting our datasource in the `setEntityContext()` method as it is only called once for a bean instance. The following code can now be added to the `setEntityContext()` method seen previously:

```
public void setEntityContext(EntityContext context) {

    this.ctx = context;

    try {
        InitialContext initial = new InitialContext();
        ds = (DataSource)initial.lookup(dbName);
    } catch (NamingException ne) {
        throw new EJBException(ne);
    }
}
}
```

That's the last method of our bean. Now let's take a look at the deployment descriptor for this bean.

The Deployment Descriptor

Here is the deployment descriptor for our Tax BMP bean. It is similar in most ways to the deployment descriptor for our CMP bean earlier in the chapter. The differences have been highlighted below:

```
<?xml version="1.0" encoding="Cp1252"?>

<!DOCTYPE ejb-jar PUBLIC
        '-//Sun Microsystems, Inc.//DTD Enterprise JavaBeans 1.1//EN'
        'http://java.sun.com/dtd/ejb-jar_1_1.dtd'>

<ejb-jar>
  <description>no description</description>
  <display-name>taxBMP</display-name>
  <enterprise-beans>

    <entity>
        <description>no description</description>
        <display-name>TaxBean</display-name>
        <ejb-name>TaxBean</ejb-name>
        <home>bmp.TaxHome</home>
        <remote>bmp.Tax</remote>
        <ejb-class>bmp.TaxEJB</ejb-class>
        <persistence-type>Bean</persistence-type>
        <prim-key-class>java.lang.String</prim-key-class>
        <reentrant>False</reentrant>
```

```
      <resource-ref>
        <res-ref-name>jdbc/Cloudscape</res-ref-name>
        <res-type>javax.sql.DataSource</res-type>
        <res-auth>Container</res-auth>
      </resource-ref>
    </entity>
  </enterprise-beans>

  <assembly-descriptor>
    <container-transaction>
      <method>
        <ejb-name>TaxBean</ejb-name>
        <method-name>*</method-name>
      </method>
      <trans-attribute>NotSupported</trans-attribute>
    </container-transaction>
  </assembly-descriptor>

</ejb-jar>
```

Note that now we must declare the properties of our resource reference, the database. The contents of the `<res-ref-name>` tag describe the JNDI name of our resource, `<res-type>` indicates the Java class type of the resource, and the contents of the `<res-auth>` tag designates whether authentication is performed by the bean or the container.

> *We also no longer need the `<primkey-field>` element because our bean knows this already in its own persistence logic.*

Now we can compile and archive our bean into a JAR file called `taxBMP.jar`.

Before we deploy our bean, let's first create our database table.

Creating a Database Table

We will use Cloudscape as our database engine again. The Cloudscape database gets installed as a part of the J2EE installation; you can refer to the online documentation to learn how to use this database engine. However, we can't use the table that our CMP bean created for us because when we undeploy that application it will delete the table – anyway we don't want any legacy data from our earlier example to mess up our BMP bean.

The SQL for generating the table is given below:

```
DROP TABLE TaxTable;

CREATE TABLE TaxTable (stateCode VARCHAR(3),
                       taxRate REAL);
```

Store the above SQL statements in file called `createTable.sql`. Now we can use a utility that comes with Cloudscape to create this table. Enter the following into a batch file called `createTaxTable`:

```
set
classpath=%J2EE_HOME%\lib\system\tools.jar;%J2EE_HOME%\lib\cloudscape\RmiJdbc.jar;
%J2EE_HOME%\lib\system\cloudscape.jar;%J2EE_HOME%
```

```
%JAVA_HOME%\bin\java -Dij.connection.Cloudscape=jdbc:cloudscape:rmi:CloudscapeDB
-Dcloudscape.system.home=%J2EE_HOME%\cloudscape -ms16m -mx32m
COM.cloudscape.tools.ij createTable.sql
```

Note that it is important to specify the locations of `tools.jar`, `RmiJdbc.jar`, and `cloudscape.jar` in the classpath. When we run this batch file, `TaxTable` will be created in the Cloudscape database (you'll need to make sure that the Cloudscape database is still running first, though).

Our next task is to deploy the bean on the J2EE app server.

Deploying the Bean

We'll now take our previously created `taxApp` application, remove the CMP bean and replace it with our new BMP bean.

From the deployment tool, make sure you are connected to a running server then expand the Servers node until you can see our deployed taxApp application. Select the parent server, probably localhost, and in the right-hand pane undeploy the application.

Then under the Files node, select the taxCMP application and remove it by selecting Delete from the Edit menu. Then just as before add a new EJB JAR file to the application, but this time select our `taxBMP.jar` file:

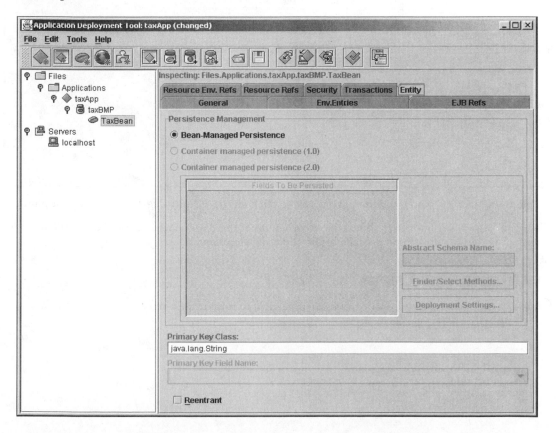

Note that this time we don't need to perform any additional deployment steps for the persistence as it's all programmed into the bean.

Next, we will need to specify the JNDI names before deploying the bean. Select the application file name, and specify the following JNDI names in the **JNDI Names** dialog:

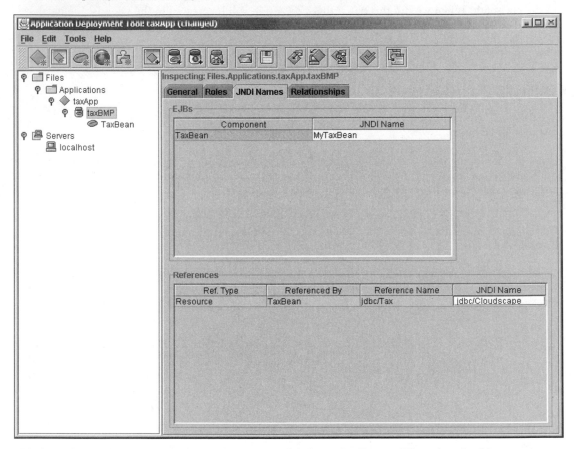

Click on the Deploy menu option, making sure to click on the Return Client Jar checkbox option.

The deploy tool will inform us about success or failure of the deployment process. Once the bean is successfully deployed, we can proceed to the client development.

Developing the Client

The only change we need to make to the client is for it to import the correct home and remote interfaces:

```
import bmp.*;
import java.util.*;
import javax.naming.Context;
import javax.naming.InitialContext;
import javax.rmi.PortableRemoteObject;
```

Otherwise, the client can remain unchanged.

Now if you run the client again, you should get the same results as before, except that this time we implemented all the persistence code ourselves.

Sequence Diagrams for BMP Entity Beans

We'll now look at how the sequence diagrams for BMP operations differ from those we saw earlier on CMP operations.

As before, we will discuss the following operations:

- ❑ Creating BMP entity objects
- ❑ Activating/Passivating BMP entity objects
- ❑ Removing a BMP entity object
- ❑ Finding a BMP entity object

Creating a BMP Entity Object

The process of creating a BMP entity bean is very similar to that for creating a CMP entity bean. However, remember that in the case of BMP, the bean itself manages the persistence. Thus, the sequence diagram for our BMP bean differs from that for the CMP bean wherever the object interactions for persistence are required:

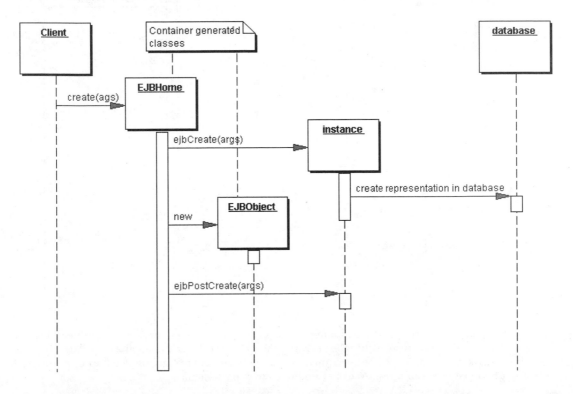

The client calls the create() method with arguments on the home object. The arguments, as in the previous case, designate the persistence state of the bean. The container calls the ejbCreate() method on the bean instance. Again, the container may use a bmp instance available in its pool, but the bean instance is now responsible for creating a representation in the database.

Once the ejbCreate() method completes by creating a representation in the database, the container creates a new remote object. A reference to this remote object will be returned to the client at the end of the creation process. The container now calls the ejbPostCreate() method on the bean instance. At this stage, the bean is ready for method invocation.

Activating/Passivating a BMP Entity Bean

The sequence diagram for activation/passivation of a BMP entity bean is very much similar to the one described above for the CMP bean. The only difference in this case is that the database read and write will be invoked by the bean instance, since the persistence is managed by the bean itself:

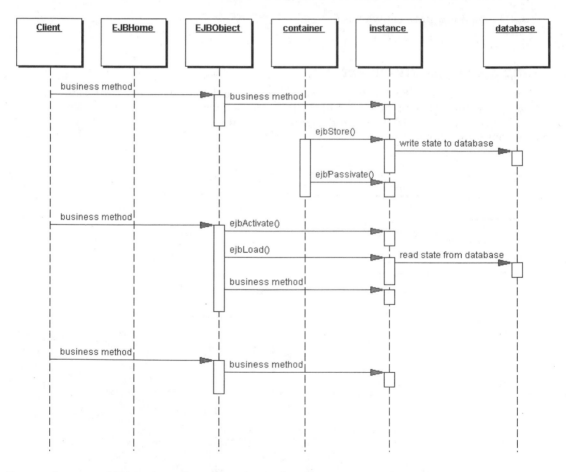

During the passivation process, the container invokes the ejbStore() method on the bean instance. The bean instance is now responsible for updating the database. After the database update, the container invokes the ejbPassivate() method on the bean instance giving itself an opportunity to free any previously allocated resources before the bean is passivated.

During the activation process, the `ejbActivate()` method on the bean instance is called followed by the `ejbLoad()` method. The bean instance now reads the data from the underlying database. Once the bean is activated and its state is properly synchronized to the underlying database record, the business method proceeds.

Any subsequent calls to the business methods will be directly delegated to the bean instance.

Removing a BMP Entity Bean

In the case of a BMP entity bean, the bean itself is responsible for removing its representation in the database. Thus, when the client calls the `remove()` method on the remote object, the `ejbRemove()` method is called on the bean instance. The bean instance now executes the required SQL statement to remove its representation from the database.

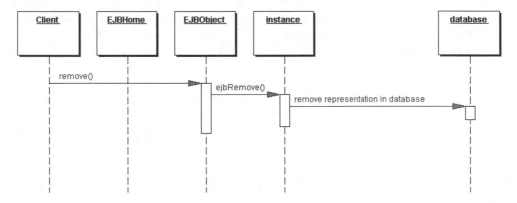

Finding a BMP Entity Bean

For the case of a BMP entity bean, the bean itself is also responsible for searching the database for the desired record(s). Thus, when the client invokes one of the finder methods on the home object, the container calls the corresponding `ejbFind()` method on the bean instance. The bean instance now searches the database for the desired record. Once a record is located, a new instance of the remote object is created and its reference is returned to the client:

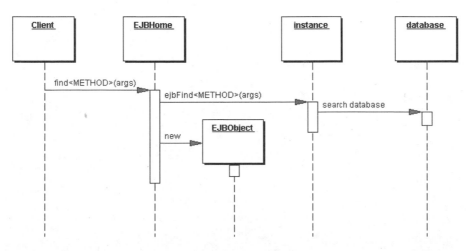

Summary

In this chapter we looked at entity beans that adhere to the EJB 1.1 specification. We learned that entity beans are commonly used to represent records within databases using object mapping and that synchronization (persistence) between corresponding bean and database record is an important issue. In fact, we demonstrated that the two types of entity bean, Container-Managed Persistence (CMP) and Bean-Managed Persistence (BMP), are distinguished by how they deal with persistence. Furthermore, an entity bean uses a primary key, specified by the developer, as a unique identity that clients must subsequently use to locate the bean (and hence the data represented).

In order to determine the level of persistence support that your EJB container might require, it is useful to keep in mind the following points:

❑ CMP – speeds up development and increases bean flexibility, although persistence management is more rigid

❑ BMP – gives more flexibility in how we manage bean state, although it requires extra coding

After the introduction, the development and deployment of both CMP and BMP was discussed at length in this chapter following the familiar formula of Chapter 3. We noted the similarities/differences between entity and session beans, and were ready for some practical examples of developing entity beans. Although there is a lot more coding required, it was noted that the deployment of a BMP entity bean is very similar to that of a CMP. There was, however, some additional work involved in creating a database table.

Following the natural progression, in the next chapter we will look at entity beans as defined in the EJB 2.0 specification.

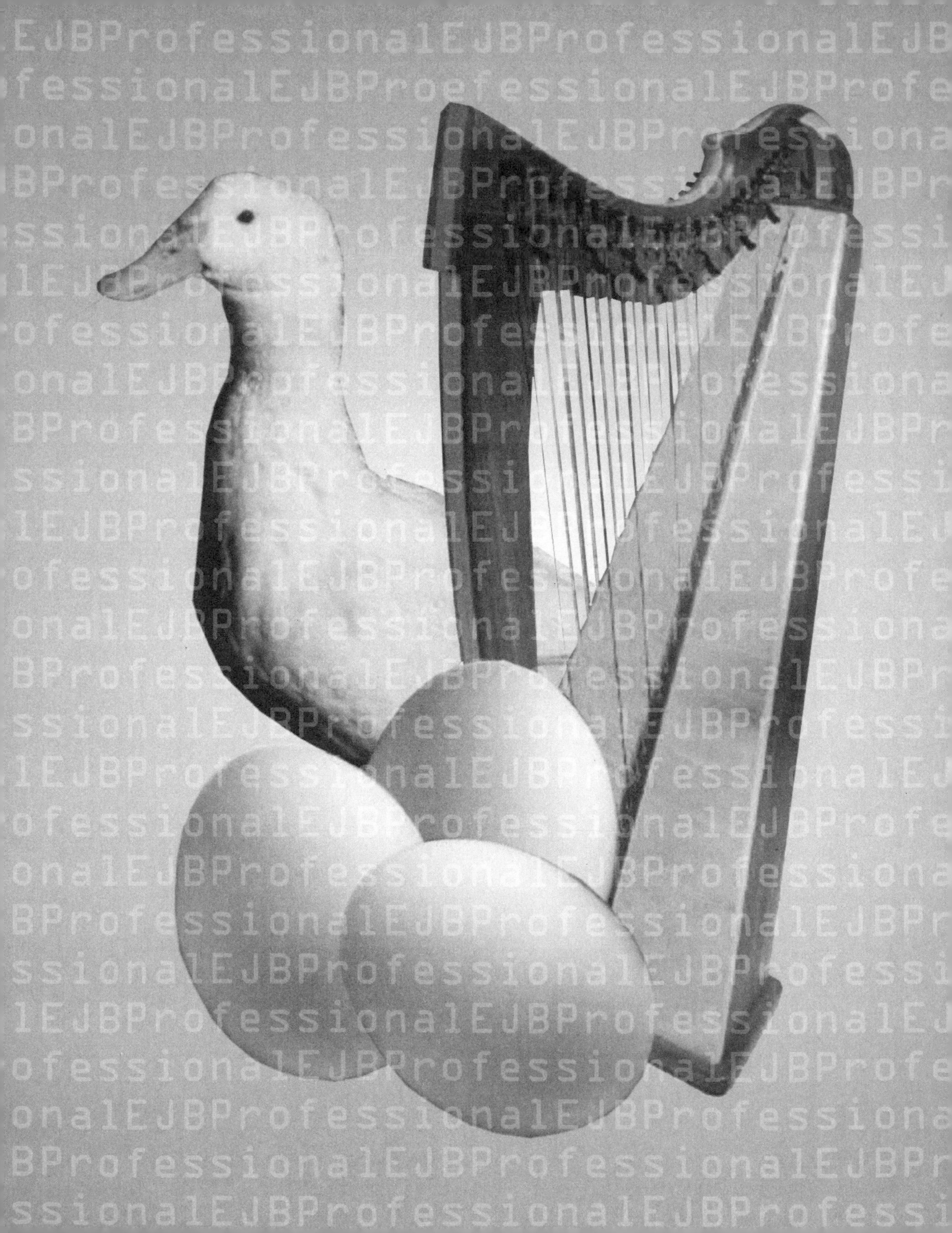

The EJB 2.0 Entity Model

The 2.0 version of the specification for Enterprise JavaBeans introduces important improvements to the bean-managed and container-managed models for entity persistence. Programmers writing entities with bean-managed persistence (BMP) may benefit from the addition of local interfaces and home-interface methods to the specification. Programmers writing entities with container-managed persistence (CMP) can choose to take advantage of an entirely new CMP model.

This new EJB 2.0 persistence model is not just a fine-tuning of features that were available in the EJB 1.1 specification. Instead, EJB 2.0 persistence is a revolutionary addition of a standards-based object-relational mapping framework to Enterprise JavaBeans technology. This chapter will concentrate on the new CMP persistence model, although it will also give an example of the new features available to entities using BMP persistence.

Some of the important points we will be covering in this chapter include:

- ❑ The differences between EJB 1.1 CMP and EJB 2.0 CMP
- ❑ Abstract methods and their role in EJB 2.0 CMP
- ❑ Local interfaces, relationships, and the client view
- ❑ The representation of relationships between entities
- ❑ The EJB 2.0 query language
- ❑ Home interface methods

As the changes the entity beans are so significant, this chapter will primarily provide an overview of the EJB 2.0 persistence model, and then look at BMP entities under the new specification. In the next chapter we will drill down in the 2.0 CMP model in greater depth.

Container-Managed Persistence Comparison

This section will briefly review the goals of container-managed persistence, and compare it to bean-managed persistence. Once we have finished this high-level review, we will look at problems with the EJB 1.1 CMP model, and how the EJB 2.0 CMP model tries to solve them.

Review of CMP Goals

One of the guiding philosophies of Enterprise JavaBeans technology is to split up the work between the EJB component developer and the EJB container. The EJB component developer focuses on business logic. The EJB container focuses on providing the systems-level services that every significant application requires – such as security, transactional integrity, remote communications, and scalability. There are at least three advantages to this division of responsibility:

❏   The component developer doesn't need to worry about these system-level services, and so they can spend more time on the business logic – which is, after all, the point of writing the application in the first place.

❏   The responsibility for developing systems-level services is in the hands of specialists, and so they will likely run faster, operate more safely, scale better, and provide more features than would otherwise be possible.

❏   The systems-level services are based on generally accepted standards, and so the EJB software components are portable between implementations of these services.

The idea behind container-managed persistence is that persistence should be considered one of the systems-level services whose implementations are provided by a vendor. In theory, all three of the preceding advantages are applicable to container-managed persistence. Consider:

The component developer can spend more time on business logic

Most organizations would rather have their programmers working on activities that contribute directly to the bottom line, rather than on writing SQL statements and JDBC code. If you work for an online bookstore, you should be writing software to manage inventory, track shipments, and enhance the customer's experience. You probably shouldn't be developing an object-relational mapping framework. It is certainly no trivial task to write, debug, and test the code that moves data from business objects and their relationships to a relational database management system. If you use container-managed persistence, you can concentrate on the business objects, and not their persistence.

The persistence services are developed by specialists

This means that they are likely to run faster, operate more safely, scale better, and provide more features. The EJB 2.0 model of persistence provides sophisticated relationship-management capabilities, a full-featured and portable query language, and a flexible object model. The EJB 2.0 specification is written to allow optimizations such as lazy loading, dirty detection, and the efficient compilation of EJB queries into native DBMS queries. Implementing all these features is not a trivial task, and neither is testing, debugging, and managing them.

Your EJB components are portable between EJB containers and data stores

If you need features that are not present in one EJB container – such as the ability to map to a particular database schema, the ability to use stored procedures, or the ability to provide a distributed read-write object-oriented cache as a front-end to your relational database – you can simply switch to another EJB container without rewriting your components. Particular EJB containers (or plug-ins) may provide support for database-specific features and optimizations. You can take advantage of this when you deploy your EJB components, without introducing database dependencies into the components themselves.

The Bean-Managed Persistence Alternative

The alternative to container-managed persistence is, of course, bean-managed persistence. The general category of bean-managed persistence encompasses several strategies for development:

❑　You might simply embed the JDBC persistence code for your database in your entities. I don't generally recommend this approach, as it compromises portability between different database schemas (and potentially between different databases). It can be appropriate for small projects where you don't intend to distribute your EJB components or change your database, and where container-managed persistence is not an option, for example because your application server does not support the features you need.

❑　You might develop a set of data-access classes to which you delegate persistence logic from your entity beans. This preserves the portability of your entity beans, but does force you to be responsible for designing, testing, debugging, and managing your data-access code.

❑　You might use a proprietary object-relational mapping framework. This approach has many of the same advantages as container-managed persistence. The disadvantages come because the framework is proprietary. This is a trade-off that is sometimes appropriate; proprietary tools are used successfully all the time. For example, one good reason to use a proprietary object-relational mapping framework might be that your organization already has a significant investment in it (in training and/or in code that has already been written). I think that you should carefully consider the advantages of EJB 2.0 CMP over a proprietary framework, such as component portability and multi-vendor support.

❑　Finally, you might use an existing enterprise application, rather than a database, as your persistent store. For example, your entity beans might save and retrieve their data from an Enterprise Resource Management (ERP) application running on your company's mainframe. With this strategy you will almost certainly need to use bean-managed persistence, unless you find a highly specialized EJB container that supports your enterprise application. In fact, with the introduction of the Connector Architecture with J2EE 1.3, even this reason is losing some impact.

It is quite likely that your new component development should use entity beans with EJB 2.0 container-managed persistence. If you have an unusual situation, you may be compelled to use bean-managed persistence for some or all of your application's persistence logic. Even this should be a temporary situation. With time, EJB containers will improve their support for the EJB 2.0 persistence model, and they will grow in sophistication and capability. As this happens, there will be fewer reasons to write your own persistence logic or to use a proprietary framework.

Problems with the EJB 1.1 CMP Model

There were two obvious problems with the EJB 1.1 model of container-managed persistence:

❑ The difficulty of modeling coarse-grained entity objects

❑ The lack of a portable way to specify finder queries

The first of these, especially, was enough to require the use of bean-managed persistence in many common circumstances.

The EJB 1.1 specification suggested that entity beans be modeled as coarse-grained objects. In other words, an entity bean should represent a business object that has an independent identity and lifecycle, and is referenced by multiple clients. In practice, this would mean that an entity bean would often map to multiple tables and records in a relational database. In the entity's implementation, the complex data would be modeled as dependent value objects.

A **dependent object** is a helper class that is used to model an entity's state. Its most obvious use is to model aspects of the entity's state that have a multiplicity greater than one. Java programmers use dependent objects all the time without thinking twice about it. Anytime we have a `Collection` class state variable (a `java.util.List` or a `java.util.Map`) its contents are dependent objects. For example, an `Order` business object might contain `LineItem` dependent objects. An `Employee` business object might have `Children` dependent objects. A `Customer` business object might have `ContactNumber` dependent objects.

In the EJB 1.1 model, a dependent object class can be represented in your entity in one of two ways:

❑ Another entity bean

❑ A simple Java class, known as a dependent value object

Representing a Dependent Object with Another Entity Bean

It is possible to model your complex objects using other entity beans. Consider the example of an `OrderEJB` entity bean with line items. Those line items could be modeled by `LineItemEJB` entity beans. The `LineItemEJB` instances could be retrieved programmatically by defining an appropriate finder method in the `LineItemEJB` home interface (`findByOrder(long orderNumber)`).

Unfortunately, there are several disadvantages to this approach:

❑ Poor performance. (This is probably the most important disadvantage.) Invocations of EJB components are heavyweight, because the EJB container has the responsibility to manage their security and transactional integrity, copy their non-remote parameters, and perform logging and exception handling.

❑ The details of the object model are unnecessarily exposed to the client. In other words, the client has access to implementation details that should be hidden behind a façade. As a result, the application is less easily changed. For example, if the client has access to those `LineItem` beans, and a future version of the application changes the `LineItem` bean to an `OrderAspect` bean with line item dependent objects, the client will need to change.

❑ The relationship between the EJB components needs to be managed in the component's code (the finder method that retrieves the line items needs to be written, and reissued whenever the contents may have changed within that transaction).

Representing a Dependent Object with a Dependent Value Class

It was also possible to define an entity that used simple Java classes (dependent value classes) to model its complex state. Consider again that example of an `OrderEJB` entity bean with line items. Those line items could be represented by a simple Java class stored in a `java.util.LinkedList` in the `OrderEJB` implementation. They are stored to, and retrieved from, the database along with the rest of the state data.

However, there were also several problems with this approach:

❏ The EJB container did not have visibility into the structure of the `OrderEJB` implementation. In other words, the contents of the linked list (line item classes) wasn't declared anywhere in the deployment descriptor. This made it more difficult for the EJB container to save the state of the bean to a normalized relational database schema.

❏ There was no foolproof way for the container to implement the load-on-demand optimization. Load-on-demand means that data is loaded from the persistent store when it is needed, and not before. For example, the line items for an order wouldn't be retrieved from the database until they were used in the code. If the line items weren't used in the transaction, that database access would be avoided. As data access operations are typically slow and expensive, this is an important optimization.

❏ There was no foolproof and efficient way for the container to implement dirty checking. Dirty checking means that data is only saved to the persistent store when it has been modified. For example, if some line items had been changed, some deleted, and some added, only the necessary SQL `UPDATES`, `DELETES`, and `INSERTS` should be issued. As data access operations are typically slow and expensive, this is also an important optimization.

❏ There was no portable way to ensure that the state of the `Collection` classes would be appropriate for the EJB container's persistence strategy. For instance, there was nothing in the EJB 1.1 specification that prevented a bean developer from saving objects of different classes in a collection or map. Vendor-imposed restrictions affected the portability of EJB components.

❏ There were potential data-aliasing problems with dependent objects used by two or more objects in the same transaction. Data aliasing basically means that there are two representations of the same data. The problem occurs when you update one, and expect the other to be updated, but it isn't. For example, consider two `Person` entities representing a husband and wife. Each has a reference to the same dependent object that stores their address. You expect that if you update the husband's address, the wife's address should also be updated. Since there was no way for the container to update the entity's data cache (such as its address object) within a transaction, logic errors could result.

Various work arounds to these problems were developed by some container vendors. One common strategy for basic dirty checking at the entity level was to add support for an `isModified()` method. Of course, this strategy, despite being common, was not (strictly-speaking) portable. However, it was not uncommon for these problems to go completely unresolved, and more than one widely-used EJB container saved entire collections of objects in serialized form, in a single database table column.

An earlier draft of the EJB 2.0 specification introduced a new type of container managed object, called a dependent object. Dependent objects were intended to be used for implementing coarse-grained entities. That concept has been removed from the specification (although many of the same problems are addressed by the addition of local interfaces). Whenever you see the words 'dependent object' in this chapter, I am referring to the general concept of a dependent object, and *not* this discarded EJB 2.0-specific concept.

Finder Queries

A finder query is a declarative expression of the appropriate behavior for a finder method in an entity bean with container-managed persistence. The EJB container is responsible for implementing these finder methods, but it needs to be told what these finder methods should do.

The EJB 1.1 specification did not provide a format for these finder queries, which meant that each application server or EJB container had its own format. This damaged an EJB component's portability. Consider an entity bean that was intended for commercial resale and reuse by multiple application programmers across multiple platforms. Each deployer of that bean would need to re-implement the business logic that was inherent in the finder query, or the bean developer would need to provide a complete set of finder queries for each potential deployment platform.

EJB 2.0 Solutions

The Enterprise JavaBeans 2.0 specification provided comprehensive solutions to the problems of EJB 1.1 container-managed persistence by introducing a new model of container-managed persistence and adding the concept of local interfaces. Here is how some of its features match up to the problems of EJB 1.1 container-managed persistence. This chapter will provide explanations for all of these features:

EJB 1.1 Problem	EJB 2.0 Solution
No appropriate way to represent dependent objects of entity beans.	Introduction of local interfaces, which mitigates some of the performance issues of entity beans and also allows you to hide your object model from a remote client.
No foolproof way to implement load-on-demand. No foolproof way to implement dirty checking.	EJB 2.0 CMP entities use abstract accessor methods to set and retrieve data. The EJB container provides an implementation of these accessor methods, where load-on-demand and dirty checking logic can be located. Furthermore, relationships are also represented by abstract accessor methods and collection classes maintained by the EJB container. This allows relationships to be intelligently managed.

EJB 1.1 Problem	EJB 2.0 Solution
No portable way to ensure that the contents of a collection are suitable for the container's persistence strategy.	Collection classes maintained by the EJB container are subject to usage rules that simplify the object-relational mapping. For instance, only a single type of entity may be contained in a persistence-manager collection class.
Potential data-aliasing problems with dependent objects and collections used by two or more entities in the same transaction.	Dependent objects are represented by entity components, whose state is managed by the EJB container. Relationships are represented by abstract accessors and special collection classes, which are also managed by the EJB container. This allows for synchronization within a transaction and solves data aliasing problems.
No portable query language for finders.	A portable query language based on a subset of SQL-92 is provided in the EJB 2.0 specification.

EJB 2.0 Container-Managed Persistence

The EJB 2.0 model of container-managed persistence did not modify the EJB 1.1 model of container-managed persistence. The specification writers did not want to break existing code. Instead, the two models for CMP exist side-by-side. The old EJB 1.1 model of CMP has not been deprecated; a compliant EJB 2.0 container must provide support for both EJB 1.1 CMP and EJB 2.0 CMP. This decision to introduce an entirely new model allowed for extensive changes to the way EJB 2.0 CMP works. The following section provides for a tour of some of these changes, before we go on to consider them in more detail. We'll look quickly at:

- ❑ The role of abstract methods in EJB 2.0 CMP
- ❑ Local and remote client views
- ❑ How relationships are represented
- ❑ The EJB 2.0 query language
- ❑ The new structure of the EJB 2.0 deployment descriptor

Abstract Methods in EJB 2.0 CMP

One of the most visible changes from the EJB 1.1 model of container-managed persistence is the introduction of abstract accessor methods.

> **An abstract accessor in the context of EJB 2.0 is an abstract get or set method used to access part of the object's persistent state. An abstract accessor is part of the bean's implementation class. Since all access to the bean's persistent state is through these abstract accessors, it allows the container to manage this state intelligently. These abstract accessors have nothing to do with the client view. They may or may not be exposed in the bean's component interface.**

For instance, an entity EJB representing a customer might have state to represent the customer's id, first name, last name, and birth date. The corresponding abstract accessors for this business object might be declared as follows (this code is not intended to be run, but just an example of accessor methods):

```
public abstract class CustomerBean implements EntityBean {

    public abstract long getId();
    public abstract void setId(long id);

    public abstract String getFirstName();
    public abstract void setFirstName(String firstName);

    public abstract String getLastName();
    public abstract void setLastName(String lastName);

    public abstract Date getBirthDate();
    public abstract void setBirthDate(Date birthDate);
}
```

The naming convention for abstract accessors corresponds to the standard naming convention for JavaBean accessors. The first letter of the state variable name is capitalized, and either get or set is prepended. Getter methods take no parameters and have a return type corresponding to the type of the state variable. Setter methods take one parameter with a type corresponding to the type of the state variable, and return void. Abstract getter and setter methods do not throw exceptions.

These abstract accessors must correspond to <cmp-field> elements in the deployment descriptor. This is no different from the EJB 1.1 container-managed persistence model. The types of these container-managed fields are determined from the parameters and return values of the abstract accessors. Legal types are limited to:

- ❏ Java primitive values (int, long, float, etc.)
- ❏ Java serializable objects (java.util.Date, java.lang.String, etc.)
- ❏ User-defined types that implement java.io.Serializable
- ❏ EJB component home and remote interfaces

You cannot have a non-serializable Java class or a local interface class as a legal type for a cmp field.

> The terms "cmp field" and "cmr field" are often used to refer to the corresponding part of an entity's persistent state and persistent relationships, represented by abstract accessor methods and declared in the deployment descriptor using the <cmp-field> or <cmr-field> elements. A cmp field represents persistent state. A cmr field represents an endpoint of a persistent relationship.

The bean developer uses these methods to access the persistent state of the bean. The implementation of these methods is left to the EJB container. In other words, the EJB component developer never writes a version of any of these accessor methods that has a body. The following is not legal for any abstract accessor method:

```
public String getFirstName() {
  return firstName;
}

public void setFirstName(String firstName) {
  this.firstName = firstName;
}
```

Of course, there is no prohibition against writing getter and setter methods that do not correspond to aspects of the EJB component's persistent state. For our customer entity, the following is perfectly legal:

```
public String getName() {
  return getFirstName() + " " + getLastName();
}
```

The EJB component developer never declares any variables representing the persistent state of the object. This, too, is left to the EJB container. All access to those state variables in the EJB component must be through the abstract accessor methods. At deployment time, the EJB container will provide some representation of the object's state and implementations of its abstract accessor methods. At runtime, calls to an abstract accessor will become calls to the appropriate method implemented by the EJB container, returning the appropriate state information.

> Note: it is still legal to have state variables, as long as that state isn't part of the object's persistent state. For instance, the EJB component might cache references to a resource that it needed.

Abstract accessor methods are used for both entity beans and their dependent objects. The resultant Java bean-implementation classes can look a little unusual to experienced programmers, because they often declare few if any object-scoped variables.

> **They must also be declared as abstract classes, because any class with an abstract method must itself be abstract. A container-supplied class will provide a concrete derivation of the component developer's abstract class.**

Abstract Methods and Relationships

Relationships are also managed through abstract accessor methods. In the case of a relationship where the multiplicity of the associated object is many, the abstract accessor's parameter or return value type is a collection class representing the relationship. This collection class implements the java.util.Set or java.util.Collection interface. (A future version of the specification may add java.util.Map and java.util.List as return types.) In the case of a relationship where the multiplicity of the collection class is one, the abstract accessor's parameter or return value type is a single instance of the related object.

For example, consider the case where an order is related to one shipment address and multiple line items. The relationship accessors might look like this:

```
public abstract Collection getLineItems();
public abstract void setLineItems(Collection lineItems);

public abstract AddressLocalEJB getShipAddress();
public abstract void setShipAddress(AddressLocalEJB shipAddress);
```

The collection classes used with relationship accessor methods are implemented and instantiated by the EJB container. You can use those collection classes to modify the relationship directly. In the example above, you could use the `java.util.Collection` object returned from `getLineItems()` to find, add, or remove line items from the order-line item relationship. You would not need to subsequently call the `setLineItems()` method. In fact, setter methods for many-valued relationships have special semantics that will be explained in the following chapter.

Just as the container-managed state fields for an EJB 2.0 CMP entity are declared as `<cmp-field>` elements in the deployment descriptor, relationship state fields are declared in the deployment descriptor as `<cmr-field>` elements. These `<cmr-field>` declarations are made in a special section of the deployment descriptor that contains all the relationship information. A `<cmr-field>` element has a name and a description, just like a `<cmp-field>`. For the case where the target object relationship has a multiplicity of many, the type of collection object (either `java.util.Collection` or `java.util.Set`) must also be specified.

Abstract ejbSelect() Methods

Along with these abstract accessor methods for the object's persistent state and its relationships, there is one other type of abstract method that the programmer may declare: zero or more instances of the `ejbSelect()` method. These `ejbSelect()` methods are similar to finder methods in that they use the EJB query language to retrieve information. However, there are two important differences:

❑ First, they are never exposed to a client. They are used only in the EJB's implementation.

❑ Second, they can return entities and the values of cmp fields, whereas finder methods just return entities.

Here is an example `ejbSelect()` method whose behavior would be specified by a query in the deployment descriptor:

```
public abstract Collection ejbSelectAllLineItems();
```

Local and Remote Client Views of the Object Model

A client (meaning either an application client, a web component, or another EJB) accesses an EJB through its home and component interfaces. There are two varieties of component interfaces: remote and local. Remote interfaces have been part of the EJB specification from the beginning. Local interfaces are an addition made by the EJB 2.0 specification. This section will first briefly review the concept of local interfaces. Then it will discuss the utility of local interfaces for developing your object model. Finally it will talk about local interfaces, remote interfaces, and their implications for the client view of your object model.

Local Interfaces Reviewed

A local interface is a component interface, much like the remote interface, for a session or entity bean. An EJB component can have both a local and remote interface. They are both described in the deployment descriptor and made available through a home interface for the component. A local interface differs from a remote interface in several important respects.

The local interface must always be located in the same Java Virtual Machine

One of the advantages of a remote interface is that it provides location transparency. In other words, the client can use that remote interface without knowing or caring if the EJB it represents is deployed in the same JVM, the same container, the same application server, or even in the same company. A local interface **must** be used on the machine to which the EJB component is deployed. This limits your flexibility during deployment, although in practice performance considerations dictate that tightly coupled EJB components should be located in the same container anyway.

Parameters and return values to a local interface are passed by reference, not by value

A remote interface must always enforce pass-by-value semantics, even if the call is in reality a local call. Pass-by-value semantics require that copies be made of all objects, unless they are immutable or they are remote references. This is to ensure that a bean's behavior is not different depending on how it is deployed, and is a requirement of location transparency. In practice, there are situations where this copying can be expensive, for example if a large XML document were passed as a parameter or returned as a result. (Potentially remote calls use pass-by-value semantics because a copy of a non-remote object must of course be made when it is streamed from one JVM to another, say across a network.)

Methods on a local interface do not throw java.rmi.RemoteException

Methods that are called remotely are subject to various interruptions, such as transport difficulties and remote object availability, which are not relevant to methods that are called locally. These interruptions are represented by a checked exception of class `java.rmi.RemoteException`, which must be declared in the `throws` clause of a remote method. A method on a local interface *must not* throw `java.rmi.RemoteException`.

Due to this rule, certain exceptions that derive from `java.rmi.RemoteException` (`TransactionRequiredException`, `TransactionRolledBackException`, and `NoSuchObjectException`) need to have local equivalents that derive from `javax.ejb.EJBException` instead (`TransactionRequiredLocalException`, `TransactionRolledBackLocalException`, and `NoSuchObjectLocalException`).

The Utility of Local Interfaces for Your Object Model

Local interfaces make it practical for entity components to represent fine-grained aspects of your object model, in terms of performance. Consider the following passage from the EJB 1.1 specification that describes why an entity should be coarse-grained:

> "*Every method call to an entity object via the remote and home interface is potentially a remote call. Even if the calling and called entity bean are collocated in the same JVM, the call must go through the container, which must create copies of all the parameters that are passed through the interface by value (i.e. all parameters that do not extend the java.rmi.Remote interface). The container is also required to check security and apply the declarative transaction attribute on the inter-component calls. The overhead of an inter-component call will likely be prohibitive for object interactions that are too fine-grained.*"

Here are the problems, and the corresponding solutions of local interfaces:

❑ **Every method call is potentially a remote call**
This is not true of local interfaces.

❑ **The container must create copies of all the parameters that do not extend `java.rmi.Remote`**
This is not true of local interfaces, which pass parameters by reference.

❑ **The container is required to check security and apply declarative transaction attributes**
This is still true of local interfaces. However, the ability to have methods without security checks was introduced to the EJB 2.0 specification, which allows the application assembler to mitigate this problem. (Use the <unchecked> element rather than a role name in the <method-permission> element to indicate that a method should not be checked for authorization.)

Local Interfaces, Remote Interfaces, and the Client View

A local client is one that is located in the same Java Virtual Machine as its component and uses a local interface. A remote client uses the remote interface of the component. The two different types of clients have different privileges for accessing details of the object model.

A local interface may use other local interfaces as parameters and return values, and may also use the collection classes that represent multi-valued relationships as parameters and return values. A remote interface *must not ever* use a local interface or relationship collection as a parameter or a return value. The reason for this rule is easily understood: a remote client may not be using the same Java Virtual Machine, but these classes are dependent on a particular virtual machine for their correct execution.

The client view of an EJB component is defined by the methods in the EJB's home and remote interface. This view is independent of the EJB's implementation – and specifically, independent of the EJB's object model. From the point of view of a client, local interfaces and relationships are just an irrelevant implementation detail. All the client of an EJB cares about are the remote methods that it can invoke.

For instance, let's consider the example of an entity bean representing an order. This entity bean might have the following remote interface:

```
import java.rmi.RemoteException;
import javax.ejb.EJBObject;

public interface Order extends EJBObject {

    public Long getOrderId() throws RemoteException;
    public String getCustomerName() throws RemoteException;
    public String getStreetAddress() throws RemoteException;
    public String getCity() throws RemoteException;
    public String getState() throws RemoteException;
    public String getZip() throws RemoteException;
}
```

The implementation class for this EJB (perhaps named `OrderEJB`) might have state variables representing the customer's street address, city, state, and zip code. On the other hand, it might have a one-to-one relationship with a local address EJB. It might have a regular Java object that gets serialized into a database column. It might even have a one-to-many relationship with local address EJBs, and use an algorithm to select an appropriate shipping address for an order based on the order's manufacturing facility. From the client's point of view, it doesn't matter. The same street, city, state, and zip code strings are returned through the public interface.

In fact, it is illegal to return a local component interface or a relationship collection class from a remote interface method in an entity. You could not simply write the above interface as follows (assuming `Address` is a local component interface):

```
import java.rmi.RemoteException;
import javax.ejb.EJBObject;

public interface Order extends EJBObject {

  public Long getOrderId() throws RemoteException;
  public Address getAddress() throws RemoteException;
}
```

The local address remote interface cannot be the return value in a remote method invocation.

Transferring State to and from the Client

Even though it is illegal to return a local interface or a relationship collection to the client, it is still often necessary to transfer a view of the entity's state to the client, or to apply an update of the entity's state from the client. A common pattern is to use a Java class to represent the state or updates to be transferred. This class might be generic (a custom `java.sql.ResultSet` implementation) or specific to the state that needs to be transported (an `AddressView` or `LineItemView` class).

For instance, the interface for the order bean might be defined as follows:

```
import java.rmi.RemoteException;
import javax.ejb.EJBObject;
import javax.ejb.CreateException;

public interface Order extends EJBObject {

  public Long getOrderId() throws RemoteException;
  public LineItemView[] getLineItemViews() throws RemoteException;
  public void addLineItem(LineItemView liv)
        throws RemoteException, CreateException;
  public void updateLineItem(LineItemView liv) throws RemoteException;
  public void removeLineItem(long lineItemID) throws RemoteException;

}
```

A class that provided a client view of the local interface line item object could transport state back and forth from the client:

```
public class LineItemView implements java.io.Serializable {

  private long id;
  private String product;
  private int quantity;

  public LineItemView() {}

  public LineItemView(long id, String product, int quantity) {
    this.id = id;
    this.product = product;
    this.quantity = quantity;
  }

  public long getId() {
    return id;
```

```
      }

      public void setId(long id) {
        this.id = id;
      }

      public String getProduct() {
        return product;
      }

      public void setProduct(String product) {
        this.product = product;
      }

      public int getQuantity() {
        return quantity;
      }

      public void setQuantity(int quantity) {
        this.quantity = quantity;
      }

    }
```

The implementation class for the `OrderEJB` component would use information in a `LineItemView` object to update its state, or initialize `LineItemView` objects and return them to the client to present a view of its data. Here is a very basic example of this technique:

```
import java.util.Iterator;
import java.util.Collection;
import javax.ejb.EntityBean;
import javax.ejb.EntityContext;
import javax.ejb.CreateException;

public abstract class OrderEJB implements EntityBean {
```

Some abstract accessor methods and entity bean methods have been elided from this example...

```
      public abstract Collection getLineItems();
      public abstract void setLineItems(Collection lineItems);
```

The `getLineItemViews()` method creates an array of `LineItemView` objects to return to the client:

```
      public LineItemView[] getLineItemViews() {

        LinkedList returnValues = new LinkedList();
        Iterator iterLineItems = getLineItems().iterator();

        while (iterLineItems.hasNext()) {
          LineItem lineItem = (LineItem) iterLineItems.next();
          LineItemView view = new LineItemView(lineItem.getId(),
                                        lineItem.getProduct(),
                                        lineItem.getQuantity());
          returnValues.add( view );
        }

        return (LineItemView[]) returnValues.toArray(new LineItemView[]{});
      }
```

The addLineItem() method uses the information in its LineItemView parameter to create a new LineItem component represented by a local interface. The implCreateLineItem() method is just a simple method that acquires a home interface and calls a create() method:

```
private LineItem implCreateLineItem(int id, String product,
                                    int quantity) {

  try {
    InitialContext initial = new InitialContext();
    LineItemLocalHome home = (LineItemLocalHome)
                      initial.lookup("java:comp/env/ejb/LineItemLocal");
    return home.create(id, product, quantity);
  } catch (Exception e) {
    throw new javax.ejb.EJBException(e);
  }
}
```

```
public void addLineItem(LineItemView liv) throws CreateException {
  try {
    LineItem l = implCreateLineItem(liv.getId(), liv.getProduct(),
                                    liv.getQuantity() );
    getLineItems().add(l);
  } catch (CreateException e) {
    e.printStackTrace();
    throw e;
  }
}
```

The updateLineItem() method uses the information in its LineItemView parameter to update an existing LineItem component (note: we would probably use an ejbSelect() method for performance reasons, rather than iterating through the collection):

```
public void updateLineItem(LineItemView liv) {
  Collection col = getLineItems();
  Iterator iter = col.iterator();
  while (iter.hasNext()) {
    LineItem li = (LineItem) iter.next();
    if (li.getId() == liv.getId()) {
      li.setProduct(liv.getProduct());
      li.setQuantity(liv.getQuantity());
      return;
    }
  }
}
```

```
public void removeLineItem(long lineItemID) {
  Collection col = getLineItems();
  Iterator iter = col.iterator();
  while (iter.hasNext()) {
    LineItem li = (LineItem) iter.next();
    if (li.getId() == lineItemID) {
      iter.remove();
      return;
    }
  }
}
```

Of course, other approaches are possible. For instance, it is possible to use an XML document to represent client views and server updates of arbitrary nesting and complexity. Whatever approach is appropriate for your project, it is important to remember that local interfaces and relationship collections are "implementation details" that are never directly exposed to a client.

How Relationships are Represented

One of the most exciting aspects of the EJB 2.0 persistence specification is the comprehensive support for relationships. Relationships are between two or more entity beans that use EJB 2.0 container managed persistence. They can be **unidirectional:**

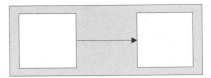

or **bi-directional:**

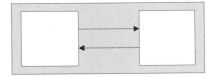

(can be navigated in one or both directions), and can have a multiplicity of **one-to-one:**

one-to-many:

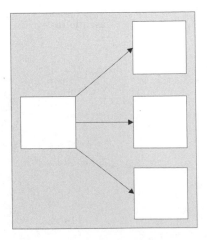

or **many-to-many:**

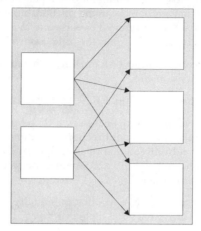

The target of a relationship must be represented by a local interface, although the source of a unidirectional relationship does not absolutely need a local interface.

Relationships are used by the EJB component developer in the following three ways:

❑ **Accessing objects and collections of objects that are associated, based on the business logic of the application**
For instance, there might be a `Collection` class that represents the line items associated with a particular order. The related objects and collections of objects are retrieved by using abstract accessor methods, as described earlier. For instance, the `Order` object would have a `getLineItems()` method and a `setLineItems()` method that had a `java.util.Set` or `java.util.Collection` as a return value or parameter.

❑ **Navigating between associated objects using the new EJB query language syntax**
A query can declaratively traverse the relationships of objects defined in an EJB JAR file. For instance, a query might retrieve only those orders that have a line item for the product "Spam", without knowing anything about the structure of the underlying database.

❑ **Managing the lifespan of entity objects**
An entity object in a relationship can be cascade-deleted when its containing object is deleted.

Relationship Descriptions

Relationships are described in the deployment descriptor. A relationship represents one meaningful association between any pair of entity beans, based on the business logic of the application. Here are some examples of relationships:

❑ Between customers and orders

❑ Between orders and line items

❑ Between teachers and students

❑ Between classes and classrooms

❑ Between automobile manufacturers and automobile makes

❑ Between automobile makes and product safety recalls

Each relationship consists of two roles. A role is essentially a traversal of the relationship in a particular direction. In other words, a role begins at one endpoint of the pair of relationship participants (known as the role source) and looks to the other participant in the relationship (known as the role target, which the container infers by using the reverse role's source). For each role in a relationship, there are potentially five pieces of information that can be specified (plus the usual assortment of names and descriptions):

❑ The **multiplicity**, which can be either One or Many. This multiplicity refers to the quantity of the source object in the relationship.

❑ The **role source**. This is the name of the EJB 2.0 CMP entity.

❑ The **<cmr-field> name**. This is only necessary if there are corresponding get and set accessors in the source object. For a unidirectional relationship, only one role will have a <cmr-field> name. For a bi-directional relationship, both roles will have a <cmr-field> name. (For any role that has a <cmr-field> name, the source entity of the reverse role must be represented by a local interface.)

❑ The **type of collection** for a <cmr-field> that potentially represents more than one target element. The legal values are java.util.Set or java.util.Collection.

❑ Whether or not the target object should, when deleted, apply a **cascade-delete** to the source objects participating in this relationship. The target object (that is, the reverse role) must have a multiplicity of one.

In the example of the Order-LineItem relationship, there would be two roles. They might be aptly named OrderHasLineItems, and LineItemInOrder. Let's take a look at the information that we would provide in the deployment descriptor for these roles:

	OrderHasLineItems	**LineItemInOrder**
multiplicity	One. There is at most one order associated with any line item.	Many. There are potentially many line items associated with a particular order.
role source	The entity OrderEJB.	The entity LineItemEJB.
<cmr-field>	lineItems	In this example, this is a unidirectional relationship between orders and line items, so no <cmr-field> is specified.
type of collection	java.util.Collection	As we did not specify a <cmr-field>, we do not need to specify a type of collection. Even if we had specified a <cmr-field>, we would not need to specify a type of collection because the reverse relationship has a multiplicity of one.
cascade-delete	It would not be legal to specify cascade-delete here, because the reverse relationship (LineItemInOrder) has a multiplicity of many.	The cascade-delete element could be specified here if we wanted to remove all of an order's line items when that order was removed.

Here is a possible deployment descriptor entry for this relationship:

```
<ejb-relation>
  <ejb-relation-name>OrderLineItem</ejb-relation-name>

  <ejb-relationship-role>
    <ejb-relationship-role-name>
        OrderHasLineItems
    </ejb-relationship-role-name>
    <multiplicity>One</multiplicity>
    <relationship-role-source>
        <ejb-name>Order</ejb-name>
    </relationship-role-source>
    <cmr-field>
      <cmr-field-name>lineItems</cmr-field-name>
      <cmr-field-type>java.util.Collection</cmr-field-type>
    </cmr-field>
  </ejb-relationship-role>

  <ejb-relationship-role>
    <ejb-relationship-role-name>
        LineItemInOrder
    </ejb-relationship-role-name>
    <multiplicity>Many</multiplicity>
    <relationship-role-source>
        <ejb-name>LineItemEJB</ejb-name>
    </relationship-role-source>
  </ejb-relationship-role>

</ejb-relation>
```

Relationship Collection Classes

Relationships with one-to-many or many-to-many cardinality are represented by an object that implements either the `java.util.Set` or `java.util.Collection` interface. The `Collection` class is used to access and modify the state of that relationship. We saw some examples of this in an earlier code example illustrating an `OrderHasLineItems` relationship. Let's take another look at a fragment of this code, to examine its use of a relationship collection:

```
public void addLineItem(LineItemView liv) throws CreateException {
    try {
        LineItem l = implCreateLineItem(liv.getId(), liv.getProduct(),
                                        liv.getQuantity());
        getLineItems().add(l);
    } catch (CreateException e) {
        e.printStackTrace();
        throw e;
    }
}
```

The `getLineItems()` method is the abstract accessor for the relationship between the order and its line items. The collection class it returns represents that relationship, and additions to or removals from the collection class immediately change the relationship. In this case, after we create a new `LineItem` component instance, we add that instance to the relationship by adding it to the collection. If we neglected to add the line item to the collection before we returned from this method, we would have created a "disconnected" line item entity that was not accessible through the relationship collection. (It would still, however, be accessible through the query language via finder or `ejbSelect()` methods.)

The Collection classes that represent a relationship are created exclusively by the EJB container. You cannot create new instances of these Collection classes, nor can you change the identity of the Collection class used to represent a particular relationship. The set accessor methods for a relationship collection do not actually set the collection. Instead, they act in a somewhat counterintuitive manner to set the contents of the collection based on another relationship collection with the same type of relationship.

This is a potentially confusing topic that will be covered in depth in the next chapter. For the most part, when you are working with a relationship that has a multiplicity of many, you will retrieve the corresponding collection with the get abstract accessor and work directly with that collection, ignoring the set abstract accessor completely.

Bidirectional Relationships

Relationships that are bi-directional have abstract accessors for both participants in the relationship. For example, an order entity might have getLineItems() and setLineItems() methods, and a line item entity object might have a getOrder() method and a setOrder() method. Changes that are made in one participant in the relationship are instantly reflected in the other participant. For instance, if you changed the order for a line item within that line item, it would be automatically removed from the relationship collection for its original order and automatically added to the relationship collection for its new order within the transaction.

Consider this somewhat facetious code example:

```
public void doTest() {
  Collection lineItems = getLineItems();
  Iterator iter = lineItems.iterator();
  if (!iter.hasNext()) {
    return;
  }
  LineItem lineItem = (LineItem) iter.next();
```

The following is, of course, true:

```
// This is of course true
if (!lineItems.contains(lineItem)) {
  throw new IllegalStateException();
}
lineItem.changeOrder();
```

This will be false, because our collection was updated by the container:

```
// This is false; the relationship collection
// was automatically updated
if (lineItems.contains(lineItem)) {
  throw new IllegalStateException();
  }
 }
```

There are many modeling situations that require bi-directional relationships (teacher-student, customer-order, employee-project, and endless others given the right business requirements). Anyone who has worked with bi-directional relationships before understands the potential for data-aliasing problems. What happens if the line item changes its order, but the order doesn't get notified and still thinks that it owns the line item? Disaster, usually. But you can confidently use bi-directional relationships in your EJB 2.0 entity beans without worrying about these problems.

The EJB 2.0 Query Language

The new **EJB 2.0 query language (EJB QL)** allows the developer to navigate entity objects and their relationships for EJB finder methods – and also to select entities and field values for use in the entity's implementation. So not only does the EJB 2.0 specification provide for a solution to the problem of portably defining the behavior of CMP finder methods, it also provides us with an exciting new querying capability.

Finder methods are familiar from their role in the EJB 1.1 specification. They are defined in the home interface of the entity bean and available for use by the client. Every entity bean must have a `findByPrimaryKey()` method that takes an instance of its primary key as a parameter and returns a single instance of that entity type (or throws a `javax.ejb.FinderException` to indicate that the object was not found). Since the behavior of this mandatory method is already well defined, the EJB component developer does not need to associate it with a query using the new query language.

Additional finder methods may be defined in the local home or remote home interfaces. Each one of these finder methods must be associated with an EJB QL query in the deployment descriptor. Additionally, the component developer may also define `ejbSelect()` methods in the entity's implementation class. These `ejbSelect()` methods are not exposed to the client, and are used only as part of the implementation. However, they provide the component developer with access to the powerful facilities of the query language to access entities and their container-managed fields.

Similarity to SQL-92

The EJB QL was based on a subset of SQL-92 and enhanced by path expressions that allow the component developer to navigate over the relationships defined between entity objects. Rather than working with relational database tables, EJB QL works with the definitions of entities (known as their schemas) and their relationships in the deployment descriptor. The schema of an entity bean is referenced in EJB QL by its abstract-schema-name, defined in the deployment descriptor using the element `<abstract-schema-name>`.

Apart from path expressions and schemas, EJB QL syntax maps fairly directly to SQL-92 syntax. This makes it easy to learn for the component developer, and also makes it possible to compile the EJB QL down to native SQL-92 code at deployment time (at which time the relational database schema is known). Like SQL, EJB QL has a `FROM` clause, a `SELECT` clause, and a `WHERE` clause.

FROM Clause

The `FROM` clause is similar to the SQL from clause in that it specifies the participants in a Cartesian join (this is explained in the next chapter). Rather than tables, the EJB QL `FROM` clause uses one of two things: the schema of an entity bean in the deployment descriptor or a path expression. A path expression specifies a navigation route from a previously referenced schema to a new schema, through a relationship that has also been declared in the deployment descriptor.

Here is an example of a simple `FROM` clause. This includes an entity schema (an order bean, with a schema name of `OrderBean`), and a path expression from that entity to a related entity schema (through the `OrderHasLineItems` relationship). This query, which would be placed in the deployment descriptor, returns all orders with any line items. The details will be explained in the section on EJB QL in Chapter 6:

```
SELECT OBJECT(o) FROM OrderBean AS o, IN(o.lineItems) AS li
```

SELECT Clause

Just as in SQL, the SELECT clause in EJB QL determines what elements to return from the Cartesian join specified in the FROM clause and qualified in the WHERE clause.

Here is a simple example of a query for an ejbSelect() method that returns a collection of entity interfaces for line item entity components that are associated with any order:

```
SELECT OBJECT(li) FROM OrderBean o, IN(o.lineItems) li
```

WHERE Clause

Just as in SQL, the WHERE clause is responsible for qualifying the results of the Cartesian join specified in the FROM clause. You can use many of the operators and Boolean expressions with which you are familiar from SQL, such as =, >=, >, <=, <, <>, BETWEEN, NOT BETWEEN, LIKE, NOT LIKE, IN, NOT IN, +, -, *, /, IS NULL, IS NOT NULL, AND, OR, (, and).

There are also extensions specifically defined for use in the context of EJBs: you can determine whether a multi-valued path expression has any elements by using the IS EMPTY expression, and you can determine whether a single valued path expression is a member of a multi-valued path expression by using the MEMBER OF expression.

You can reference the parameters to the finder or ejbSelect() method in the WHERE clause, by using a simple syntax of a question mark plus the one-based index of the parameter, as in ?1 for the first parameter.

Here is a simple example of a query for a finder method on a remote home interface that returns a collection of orders, where the orders have line items for the product passed in as a parameter. (If this were a local home interface, it could not throw a java.rmi.RemoteException.) The finder method is defined as follows:

```
public java.util.Collection findOrdersForProduct(String product)
       throws javax.ejb.FinderException, java.rmi.RemoteException;
```

Here is the query statement in the deployment descriptor:

```
SELECT OBJECT(o) FROM OrderBean o, IN(o.lineItems) li WHERE li.product = ?1
```

The Structure of the Deployment Descriptor

The deployment descriptor in EJB 2.0 has a major new section to support the new model of entity persistence. It provides for the description of the relationships between entity objects. Here is a table providing short descriptions of the major "top-level" elements of the EJB 2.0 deployment descriptor, and what has changed that is relevant to EJB 2.0 persistence:

Element	Description
<enterprise-beans>	This is the section where EJB components (session beans, message-driven beans, and entity beans) are described. The description for container-managed entity beans will include their container-managed fields. If the entity uses the EJB 2.0 model of container-managed persistence, it will also provide a name for the entity's schema and the EJB QL queries for its finder and ejbSelect() methods.

Element	Description
`<relationships>`	The relationships section of the deployment descriptor describes the relationships between entity beans using EJB 2.0, that are described in this deployment descriptor. Each relationship has two relationship roles, specifying the multiplicity, role source, cmr field if necessary, type of role collection if necessary, and cascade-delete if necessary.
`<assembly-descriptor>`	The application assembly information describes how the EJB component or components are composed into a larger application unit. The EJB 2.0 specification introduces the concept of unchecked methods, which helps to make fine-grained entities practical for your object model.
`<ejb-client-jar>`	The `ejb-client-jar` specifies an archive that contains the Java class files necessary for a client program to use the EJB components in this JAR. This section does not introduce anything relevant to EJB 2.0 persistence.

Of course, the `entity` element of the deployment descriptor changed to support the changes in EJB 2.0. The following diagram, produced using XMLSpy, shows the sub-elements of the deployment descriptor's entity element:

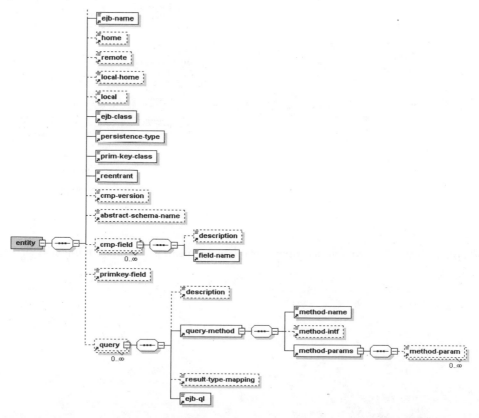

The <local> and <local-home> elements have been added to support local interfaces, and the <home> and <remote> elements have been made optional to handle the (likely) case that only local interfaces are specified. The <abstract-schema-name> element has been added to support abstract schemas in queries, and the <query> element has been added to specify EJB-QL syntax for ejbSelect() and finder methods.

Likewise, here is the visualization for the <relationships> element:

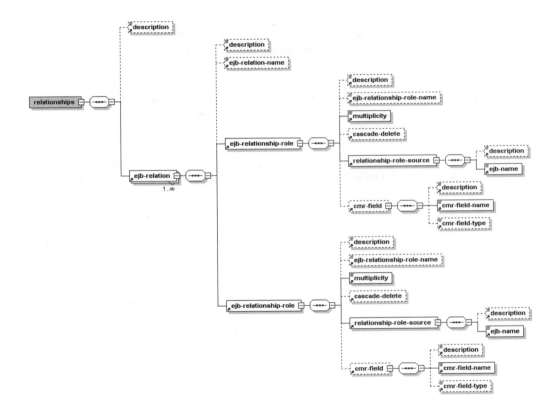

We'll be looking at the deployment descriptor for relationships in great detail in the next chapter.

Section Summary

This section provided an overview of the new model for container-managed persistence. It introduced a lot of new material that will be further described in the next chapter. After reading this section, you should understand the following:

❑ **The types and role of abstract methods in EJB 2.0 persistence**
Abstract methods play a key role in the EJB 2.0 persistence model. Abstract accessors are used to access and modify persistent state and relationship information for entity objects. Abstract ejbSelect() methods give the component developer access to the new EJB query language. Abstract methods are key to such optimizations as dirty checking and lazy loading.

❑ **The separation of the client view from the object model**
You cannot pass a local interface or a relationship collection class across a remote interface. The client never sees the structure of an entity. Instead, the entity provides a view through its remote interface, possibly by using view objects.

❑ **The representation of relationships**
Relationships are accessed through get and set accessors, and through collection classes if they have a multiplicity of many. They are also used in the EJB query language, and to manage the lifespan of entity objects (through cascade-delete). The set accessors of relationships that are represented by a collection class are only used in special circumstances. Relationships are defined in the deployment descriptor as having two roles each. A role consists of a multiplicity, a role source, a <cmr-field> if necessary, a collection type if necessary, and a cascade-delete element if necessary.

❑ **The structure of the EJB query language (EJB QL)**
The new query language is based on SQL-92, and is enhanced by path expressions that allow the component developer to navigate over the relationships defined between entity objects. Rather than working with relational database tables, EJB QL works with the definition of entities in the deployment descriptor (known as their schema). There are three parts to an EJB QL query: the SELECT clause, the FROM clause, and the WHERE clause. These queries are used to define the behavior of finder methods (which are exposed to the client), and ejbSelect() methods (which are strictly used in the implementation) for entity beans with EJB 2.0 container-managed persistence.

❑ **The structure of the deployment descriptor**
The deployment descriptor has a major new element to support the EJB 2.0 persistence model: the relationships section. In addition, there are several additions to the entity element of the enterprise-beans section to support EJB 2.0 persistence, such as an element for an abstract-schema-name and elements to specify queries. Finally, there is a new security permission type for a method, called Unchecked, which helps to make the use of fine-grained entities practical to build your object model.

The remaining part of this chapter will talk about how some of the changes in EJB 2.0 can affect your beans with bean-managed persistence.

EJB 2.0 Changes to Bean-Managed Persistence

The changes and improvements to bean-managed persistence are not nearly as extensive as those for container-managed persistence. There are basically two:

❑ A developer of an EJB entity using bean-managed persistence can take advantage of fine-grained entities using local interfaces, rather than dependent value objects, in implementing the object model. This will solve state data-aliasing problems, but not relationship data-aliasing problems.

❑ A developer can use the new **home interface business methods** to implement business methods for operations that are not specific to a particular entity; for example, methods that apply to groups of entities or that do not need any entity instances to exist.

Rules for Using Home Interface Business Methods

Home business methods are the EJB equivalent of class (static) methods in general Java development. In other words, they are an appropriate place for functionality that applies to that class of object, rather than a particular object.

For each home business method declared in the home interface, there must be a corresponding method in the implementation class with `"ejbHome"` prepended to the method name. Because there is no entity identity associated with the instance when it is executing a home business method, the bean developer must not access functionality associated with a particular entity. This includes the accessor methods and the entity context.

A BMP Example Using Home Business Methods

Let's look at an example of how an entity bean with bean-managed persistence can take advantage of the new home interface methods. We'll use a simple entity that represents measurements in the database and uses bean-managed persistence. Once it has been recorded in the database, this bean is read-only and our only requirements are for reporting. We'll access the data we need in two ways: first, using a finder method and iterating through instances on the client; and second, by using a home business method.

This example comprises five files:

File Name	File Description
Measurement.java	The entity remote component interface.
MeasurementHome.java	The entity remote home interface.
MeasurementEJB.java	The entity implementation class.
ejb-jar.xml	The deployment descriptor.
Client.java	A simple file to test the application.

Remote Component Interface

A remote interface would often replace these fine-grained accessors with a view object. We have defined our component to be read-only once created; note that there are no setter accessors in this interface.

```
package measurements;

import java.util.Date;
import java.rmi.RemoteException;
import javax.ejb.EJBObject;

public interface Measurement extends EJBObject {
```

```
      public long getId() throws RemoteException;
      public Date getEventTimestamp() throws RemoteException;
      public String getEventName() throws RemoteException;
      public double getEventMagnitude() throws RemoteException;
  }
```

Remote Home Interface

Along with the typical finder and create methods, this interface defines a business method. This is new for EJB 2.0:

```
  package measurements;

  import java.util.Date;
  import java.util.Collection;
  import java.rmi.RemoteException;
  import javax.ejb.EJBHome;
  import javax.ejb.FinderException;
  import javax.ejb.CreateException;

  public interface MeasurementHome extends EJBHome {
    public Measurement create(long measurementId, Date timestamp,
                              String eventName,
                              double magnitude) throws CreateException,
                              RemoteException;

    public Measurement findByPrimaryKey(Long measurementId)
            throws FinderException, RemoteException;
```

The `totalMagnitudeForRange()` business method is declared here. Note that it doesn't make sense for this method to be in the component interface, because it may apply to more than one measurement:

```
    public double totalMagnitudeForRange(Date from,
                                         Date to) throws RemoteException;

    public Collection findInDate(Date from, Date to)
            throws RemoteException, FinderException;
  }
```

Implementation Class

The measurement entity "bean" class has implementations for both the methods in the component interface and the methods in the home interface:

```
  package measurements;

  import java.util.Date;
  import java.util.Collection;
  import java.util.LinkedList;
  import java.sql.Connection;
  import java.sql.ResultSet;
  import java.sql.PreparedStatement;
  import javax.sql.DataSource;
  import javax.ejb.FinderException;
  import javax.ejb.ObjectNotFoundException;
  import javax.naming.InitialContext;
  import javax.ejb.EntityBean;
  import javax.ejb.CreateException;
  import javax.ejb.EntityContext;
```

```
import javax.ejb.EJBException;

public class MeasurementEJB implements EntityBean {
  private EntityContext ctx;
  private long id;
  private Date eventTimestamp;
  private String eventName;
  private double eventMagnitude;

  public long getId() {
    return id;
  }

  public Date getEventTimestamp() {
    return eventTimestamp;
  }

  public String getEventName() {
    return eventName;
  }

  public double getEventMagnitude() {
    return eventMagnitude;
  }
```

This is the implementation for the home business method. The `totalMagnitudeForRange()` method in the home interface becomes `ejbHomeTotalMagnitudeForRange()` in the implementation class. Notice that we don't use anything in this method that depends on the identity of the instance:

```
public double ejbHomeTotalMagnitudeForRange(Date from, Date to) {
  Connection con = null;
  try {
    InitialContext initial = new InitialContext();
    DataSource ds =
      (DataSource) initial.lookup("java:comp/env/jdbc/DefaultDS");
    con = ds.getConnection();
    PreparedStatement ps =
      con.prepareStatement("SELECT sum(eventMagnitude) " +
                           "FROM measurements WHERE " +
                           "eventTimestamp >= ? AND eventTimestamp <= ?");
    ps.setTimestamp(1, new java.sql.Timestamp(from.getTime()));
    ps.setTimestamp(2, new java.sql.Timestamp(to.getTime()));
    ResultSet rs = ps.executeQuery();
    if (rs.next()) {
      return rs.getDouble(1);
    } else {
      throw new EJBException("Unknown error");
    }
  } catch (java.sql.SQLException sqle) {
    sqle.printStackTrace();
    throw new EJBException(sqle);
  } catch (javax.naming.NamingException ne) {
    ne.printStackTrace();
    throw new EJBException(ne);
  } finally {
    if (con != null) {
      try {
        con.close();
      } catch (Exception ex) {}
    }
  }
}
```

With bean-managed persistence, the bean is responsible for providing the implementation of the finder methods, including the mandatory findByPrimaryKey():

```
public Long ejbFindByPrimaryKey(Long measurementId)
        throws FinderException {
  Connection con = null;
  try {
    InitialContext initial = new InitialContext();
    DataSource ds =
      (DataSource) initial.lookup("java:comp/env/jdbc/DefaultDS");
    con = ds.getConnection();
    PreparedStatement ps =
      con.prepareStatement("SELECT id FROM measurements WHERE id = ?");
    ps.setLong(1, measurementId.longValue());
    ResultSet rs = ps.executeQuery();
    if (!rs.next()) {
      throw new ObjectNotFoundException();
    }
    return measurementId;
  } catch (java.sql.SQLException sqle) {
    sqle.printStackTrace();
    throw new EJBException(sqle);
  } catch (javax.naming.NamingException ne) {
    ne.printStackTrace();
    throw new EJBException(ne);
  } finally {
    if (con != null) {
      try {
        con.close();
      } catch (Exception ex) {}
    }
  }
}
```

The findInDate() method retrieves instances between two timestamps. Like any home method implementation, it cannot use any data specific to a particular instance:

```
public Collection ejbFindInDate(Date from,
                                Date to) throws FinderException {
  Connection con = null;
  try {
    InitialContext initial = new InitialContext();
    DataSource ds =
      (DataSource) initial.lookup("java:comp/env/jdbc/DefaultDS");
    con = ds.getConnection();
    PreparedStatement ps =
      con.prepareStatement("SELECT id FROM measurements " +
                           "WHERE eventTimestamp >= ? " +
                           "AND eventTimestamp <= ?");
    ps.setTimestamp(1, new java.sql.Timestamp(from.getTime()));
    ps.setTimestamp(2, new java.sql.Timestamp(to.getTime()));
    ResultSet rs = ps.executeQuery();
    LinkedList results = new LinkedList();
    while (rs.next()) {
      results.add(new Long(rs.getLong(1)));
    }
    return results;
  } catch (java.sql.SQLException sqle) {
    sqle.printStackTrace();
```

```
        throw new EJBException(sqle);
    } catch (javax.naming.NamingException ne) {
      ne.printStackTrace();
      throw new EJBException(ne);
    } finally {
      if (con != null) {
        try {
          con.close();
        } catch (Exception ex) {}
      }
    }
  }
```

The `ejbCreate()` method is the only method in this class that modifies the database:

```
  public Long ejbCreate(long measurementId, Date timestamp,
                        String eventName,
                        double magnitude) throws CreateException {
    if ((timestamp == null) || (eventName == null)) {
      throw new CreateException("Null values not allowed.");
    }
    this.id = measurementId;
    this.eventTimestamp = timestamp;
    this.eventName = eventName;
    this.eventMagnitude = magnitude;
    Connection con = null;
    try {
      InitialContext initial = new InitialContext();
      DataSource ds =
        (DataSource) initial.lookup("java:comp/env/jdbc/DefaultDS");
      con = ds.getConnection();
      PreparedStatement ps =
        con.prepareStatement("INSERT INTO measurements (id, " +
                             "eventTimestamp, eventName, eventMagnitude) " +
                             "VALUES (?,?,?,?)");
      ps.setLong(1, id);
      ps.setTimestamp(2, new java.sql.Timestamp(eventTimestamp.getTime()));
      ps.setString(3, eventName);
      ps.setDouble(4, eventMagnitude);
      ps.executeUpdate();
      return new Long(measurementId);
    } catch (Exception e) {
      e.printStackTrace();
      throw new CreateException();
    } finally {
      if (con != null) {
        try {
          con.close();
        } catch (Exception ex) {}
      }
    }
  }

  public void ejbPostCreate(long measurementId, Date timestamp,
                            String eventName,
                            double magnitude) throws CreateException {}
```

This is a fairly standard `ejbLoad()` method. However, we do not implement `ejbStore()` because there are no circumstances in which we modify the bean instance:

```java
  public void ejbLoad() {
    Connection con = null;
    Long tmpId = (Long) ctx.getPrimaryKey();
    id = tmpId.longValue();
    try {
      InitialContext initial = new InitialContext();
      DataSource ds =
        (DataSource) initial.lookup("java:comp/env/jdbc/DefaultDS");
      con = ds.getConnection();
      PreparedStatement ps =
        con.prepareStatement("SELECT eventTimestamp, eventName, " +
                             "eventMagnitude " +
                             "FROM measurements where id = ?");
      ps.setLong(1, id);
      ResultSet rs = ps.executeQuery();
      if (!rs.next()) {
        throw new EJBException("Object not found");
      }
      eventTimestamp = new Date(rs.getTimestamp(1).getTime());
      if (rs.wasNull()) {
        throw new EJBException("Null in database not allowed.");
      }
      eventName = rs.getString(2);
      if (rs.wasNull()) {
        throw new EJBException("Null in database not allowed.");
      }
      eventMagnitude = rs.getDouble(3);
      if (rs.wasNull()) {
        throw new EJBException("Null in database not allowed.");
      }

    } catch (java.sql.SQLException sqle) {
      sqle.printStackTrace();
      throw new EJBException(sqle);
    } catch (javax.naming.NamingException ne) {
      ne.printStackTrace();
      throw new EJBException(ne);
    } finally {
      if (con != null) {
        try {
          con.close();
        } catch (Exception ex) {}
      }
    }
  }

  public void ejbStore() {}
  public void ejbRemove() {}
  public void ejbActivate() {}
  public void ejbPassivate() {}
  public void setEntityContext(EntityContext ctx) {
    this.ctx = ctx;
  }
  public void unsetEntityContext() {
    this.ctx = null;
  }
}
```

Deployment Descriptor

This deployment descriptor does not differ at all from an EJB 1.1 deployment descriptor.

```xml
<?xml version="1.0"?>

<ejb-jar>

  <enterprise-beans>
    <entity>
      <ejb-name>Measurement</ejb-name>
      <home>measurements.MeasurementHome</home>
      <remote>measurements.Measurement</remote>
      <ejb-class>measurements.MeasurementEJB</ejb-class>
      <persistence-type>Bean</persistence-type>
      <prim-key-class>java.lang.Long</prim-key-class>
      <reentrant>False</reentrant>
      <resource-ref>
        <res-ref-name>jdbc/DefaultDS</res-ref-name>
        <res-type>javax.sql.DataSource</res-type>
        <res-auth>Container</res-auth>
      </resource-ref>
    </entity>
  </enterprise-beans>

  <assembly-descriptor>
    <container-transaction>
      <method>
        <ejb-name>Measurement</ejb-name>
        <method-name>*</method-name>
      </method>
      <trans-attribute>Required</trans-attribute>
    </container-transaction>
  </assembly-descriptor>

</ejb-jar>
```

Client

This client creates some sample measurements, and then retrieves some summary data using two methods. First, it uses a finder method and iterates through the bean instances. Second, it uses the home business method that delegates the summary functionality to the database:

```java
package measurements;

import java.util.Date;
import java.util.Random;
import java.util.Collection;
import java.util.Iterator;
import java.rmi.RemoteException;
import javax.naming.InitialContext;
import javax.rmi.PortableRemoteObject;
import javax.ejb.CreateException;

public class Client {
  private static long currentId = 1;
  private static Random random = new Random();
```

```
    private static long getNextId() {
      return currentId++;
    }

    private static void createSampleMeasurements(MeasurementHome mh,
            Date timestamp, String eventName,
            int quantity) throws CreateException, RemoteException {
      for (int iter = 0; iter < quantity; iter++) {
        mh.create(getNextId(), timestamp, eventName, random.nextDouble());
      }
    }

    public static void main(String[] args) {
      try {
        InitialContext initial = new InitialContext();

        MeasurementHome measurementHome =
          (MeasurementHome) PortableRemoteObject
            .narrow(initial.lookup("Measurement"), MeasurementHome.class);

        Date currentTimestamp = new Date(); ·
        createSampleMeasurements(measurementHome, currentTimestamp,
                              "TestEvent", 25);
```

With the first method, we use a finder to iterate through the measurements we care about:

```
        Collection measurements = measurementHome.findInDate(currentTimestamp,
                              currentTimestamp);

        double total = 0.0;
        Iterator iter = measurements.iterator();
        while (iter.hasNext()) {
          Measurement measurement =
            (Measurement) PortableRemoteObject.narrow(iter.next(),
                                              Measurement.class);
          total += measurement.getEventMagnitude();
        }
        System.out.println("Results from method one: " + total);
```

With the second method, we use our home interface method:

```
        System.out.println("Results from method two: "
                + measurementHome.totalMagnitudeForRange(currentTimestamp,
                                              currentTimestamp));
      } catch (Exception e) {
        e.printStackTrace();
      }
    }
  }
```

The Database Table

Here's the schema for the table that our bean uses:

```
CREATE TABLE MEASUREMENTS ( id NUMBER NOT NULL,
                            eventTimeStamp DATE,
                            eventName VARCHAR(50),
                            eventMagnitude NUMBER
                          );
```

Deployment

Deploying this BMP bean is no different from deploying any other BMP bean. As home business methods are really an implementation detail they have no real effect on the deployment process beyond the fact that you need to look in a slightly different place for setting transactional and security attributes for your business methods:

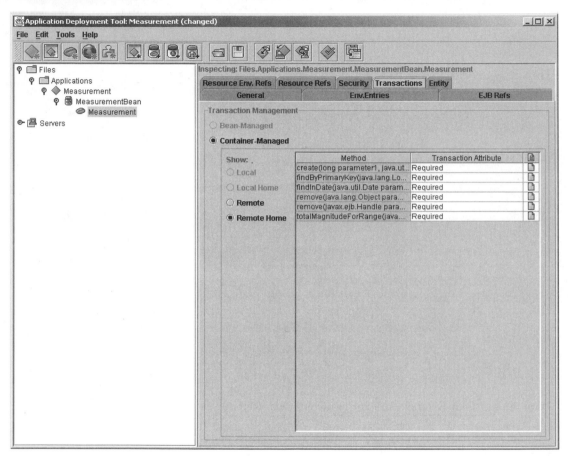

Syntactic Sugar

For the most part, anything you can do with a home business method, you could also do with a stateless session bean façade. The one exception is that a home business method for an entity bean that uses EJB 2.0 container-managed persistence can access `ejbSelect()` methods, which a stateless session bean could not. The primary advantage of home interface methods is that you don't need to write two components (an entity and its stateless session pair) for functionality that is really very tightly coupled to the entity.

Summary

This chapter talked about the changes in the entity persistence model introduced for EJB 2.0. With the exception of local interfaces and home business methods, most of the changes are specific to the new EJB 2.0 model of container-managed persistence. This chapter covered:

- **The advantages of EJB 2.0 container-managed persistence over bean-managed persistence**
  EJB 2.0 CMP is standards-based. It allows your developers to spend more time on business logic. Your object-relational mapping layer will have been developed by specialists. Your components will be portable between persistence managers and between databases.

- **The advantages of EJB 2.0 container-managed persistence over EJB 1.1 container-managed persistence**
  The EJB 2.0 model allows the portable, efficient modeling of dependent objects using entities and local interfaces. It provides a portable query language for finder methods. It solves the problem of data-aliasing for data and relationships.

- **The types and role of abstract methods in EJB 2.0 persistence**
  Abstract methods play a key role in the EJB 2.0 persistence model. Abstract accessors are used to access and modify persistent state and relationship information for entity objects. Abstract ejbSelect() methods give the component developer access to the new EJB query language. These abstract methods are key to such optimizations as dirty checking and lazy loading.

- **The separation of the client view from the object model**
  You cannot pass a local interface or a relationship collection class across a remote interface. The client never sees the structure of an entity. Instead, the entity provides a view through its remote interface, possibly by using view objects.

- **The representation of relationships**
  Relationships are accessed through get and set accessors, and through collection classes if they have a multiplicity of many. They are also used in the EJB query language, and to manage the lifespan of entities through cascade-delete. The set accessors of relationships that are represented by a collection class are only used in special circumstances. Relationships are defined in the deployment descriptor has having two roles each. A role consists of a multiplicity, a role source, a cmr-field if necessary, a collection type if necessary, and a cascade-delete element if necessary.

- **The structure of the EJB query language (EJB QL)**
  The new query language is based on SQL-92, and is enhanced by path expressions that allow the component developer to navigate over the relationships defined between entities. Rather than working with relational database tables, EJB QL works with the definition of an entity in the deployment descriptor (known as its schema). There are three parts to an EJB QL query: the SELECT clause, the FROM clause, and the WHERE clause. These queries are used to define the behavior of finder methods (which are exposed to the client), and ejbSelect() methods (which are strictly used in the implementation).

- **The structure of the deployment descriptor**
  The deployment descriptor has a new relationships element to support the EJB 2.0 persistence model. In addition, there are several additions to the entity element of the enterprise-beans section to support EJB 2.0 persistence, such as an element for an abstract schema name and elements to specify queries.

The next chapter will go into greater depth on the new model of container managed persistence. It will consist of three sections. The first of these sections will cover entity component development. The second section will talk about relationships, and the relational integrity model of EJB 2.0. The third section will describe the new query language in more depth.

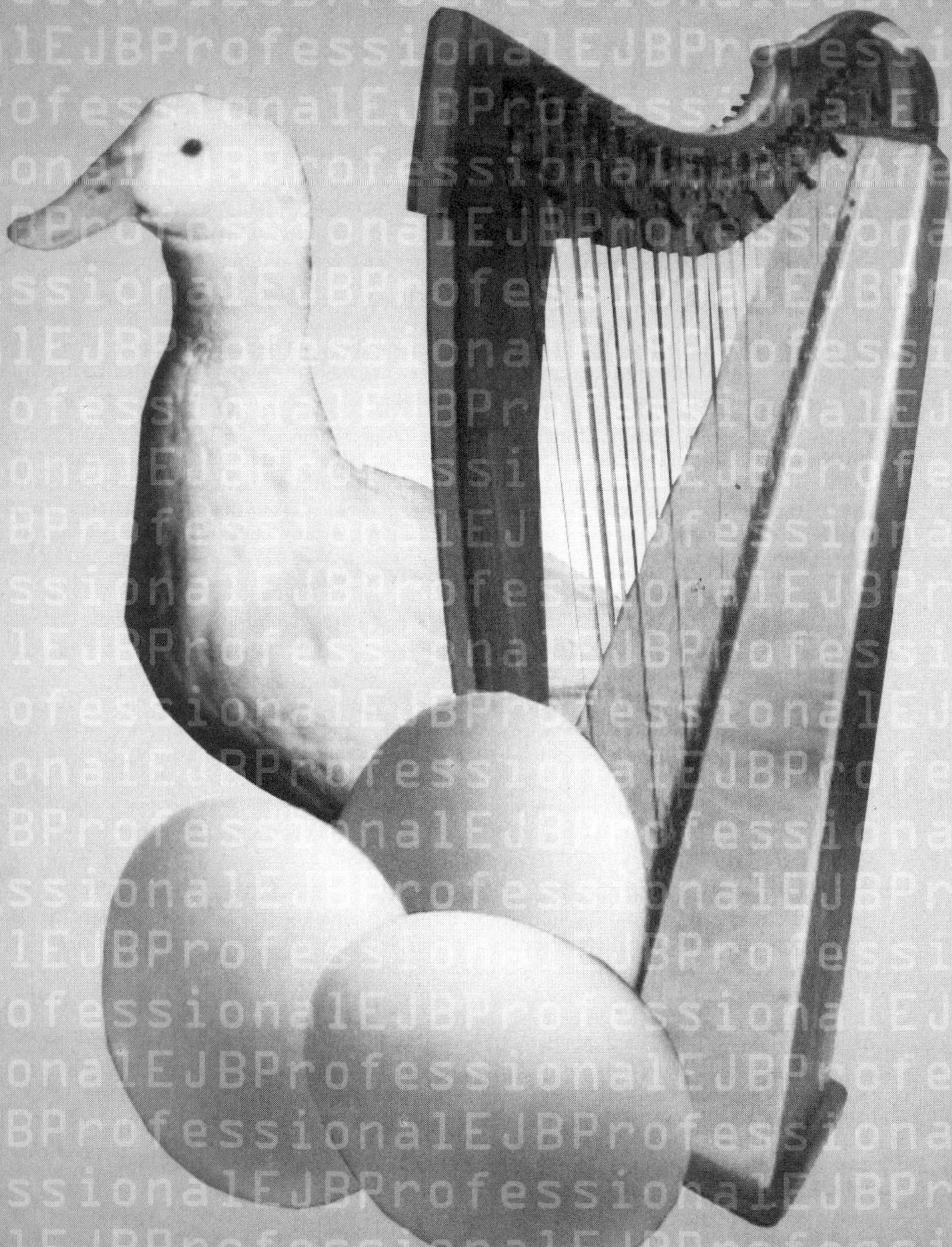

Developing EJB 2.0 CMP Entity Beans

The last chapter talked about important improvements that the 2.0 version of the EJB specification introduced to the entity bean persistence model. This chapter will examine the programming contract for EJB 2.0 CMP more closely. Having looked at developing BMP entities under the 2.0 specification, this chapter will present the details that you need to know to use EJB 2.0 container-managed persistence effectively and correctly.

Some of the important points we will be covering in this chapter include:

- ❑ A review of callbacks and their role in entity bean development
- ❑ A comparison between entities and dependent value objects
- ❑ Modeling your entity beans in terms of component granularity
- ❑ Data aliasing
- ❑ Referential integrity
- ❑ Relationship collection semantics
- ❑ Fail-fast iteration
- ❑ The details of the query language

> *This chapter (like the last) is based on a draft version of the EJB 2.0 specification (Proposed Final Draft version 2, published on April 24, 2001). The material described in this chapter is subject to change.*

Entity Components Using EJB 2.0 CMP

This section starts off by reviewing the entity bean callbacks in terms of their usage for EJB 2.0 CMP entities. Next, we will create three buildable, runnable, deployable examples of entity beans that use EJB 2.0 persistence.

These examples have the general benefit of demonstrating the use of local interfaces, abstract accessors, the structure of the deployment descriptor, and so on. In addition, the first two examples illustrate the difference between designing your object model with local interfaces versus designing it with dependent value objects. We'll implement the same entity bean twice, alternating techniques.

The final example demonstrates the "entity bean" solution to the data aliasing problem that you would experience if you used a dependent value object solution.

Review of Entity Bean Callbacks

Enterprise JavaBean components receive notifications about various lifecycle events in the form of callback methods. For an entity bean, these methods indicate that the instance is being moved into or out of the pooled state, is being associated with or disassociated from an identity, is being removed from the database, or is being saved to or restored from the database. These callback methods are declared in the `javax.ejb.EntityBean` interface, which all entity beans must implement.

For the most part, an entity bean that uses container-managed persistence does not need to do anything in these callback methods. The EJB container is responsible for the activities that would normally be triggered by these callbacks, such as saving the persistent state of the component to the database. However, there are certain circumstances in which these notifications can be useful. The following table provides a list of these callback methods, and a brief summary of how they might be used.

Callback Method	Potential Use
ejbActivate()	Associate a resource with the instance that depends on a particular identity, for example, a handle to a particular business object on a company mainframe. In general, resources should be managed by the application server.
ejbPassivate()	Free the resource acquired in ejbActivate().
setEntityContext()	(1) Cache the entity context for use in business methods. This is the most likely scenario for the use of any callback method for a bean with container-managed persistence.
	(2) Associate a resource with the instance that might be used with any identity (or by a home method that could be called without an identity), for example, a socket handle to a web-based information feed. In general, resources should be managed by the application server.
unsetEntityContext()	(1) Nullify the context cached in setEntityContext(), as per the specification.
	(2) Free a resource acquired in setEntityContext().

Callback Method	Potential Use
ejbLoad()	Cache persistent information in a component's non-persistent state. For example, an entity with a `firstName` and `lastName` field might have a cached `wholeName` field to avoid calculating the name repeatedly in business methods. In general, this usage should be avoided (because of the code complexity of maintaining a cache, and the potential run time costs of calculating unneeded information) unless the cost of dynamically producing this information is prohibitive and it will be used more than once. Note that a lazy-calculation strategy is possible, and the `ejbLoad()` method would be used to mark the non-persistent cache as dirty.
ejbStore()	Move information from the component's non-persistent state to its persistent state. For example, an entity with a modified non-persistent `wholeName` field might parse that field and move the information to its persistent `firstName` and `lastName` fields. In general, this usage should be avoided unless the cost of dynamically normalizing the object's state is prohibitive and it will be updated more than once.
ejbRemove()	(1) Additional validation before allowing a remove operation. (2) Removing related objects that are not eligible for cascade-deletion (for example, enterprise data not represented by an entity component, or an entity bean that requires additional logic to decide whether or not the delete should be cascaded). (3) Free a resource acquired in `ejbActivate()` (because `ejbPassivate()` will not be called).

Local Interfaces vs. Dependent Value Objects

We have seen that an EJB 2.0 CMP entity is an abstract class whose state is accessed by abstract getters and setters. The EJB 2.0 CMP entity is described in the deployment descriptor and can participate in relationships with other entities through its local interface. That local interface, however, cannot be part of the state of another entity. In other words, it can be the value of a <cmr-field> defined in the <relationships> section of the deployment descriptor but not the value of a <cmp field>, defined in the <entity> section of the deployment descriptor. We will shortly see an example of this: an address entity bean's local interface is used in a relationship with an order entity bean, but it could not be used as the value of a cmp field.

By contrast, a dependent value class is a concrete class whose state is defined as variables in that class. It is not described in the deployment descriptor, and cannot participate in relationships with entities. However, it can be part of the state of an entity. In other words, it can be the value of a cmp field, but not a cmr field. We will also see an example of this: an address value object is saved in a cmp field in the implementation of an Order entity bean, but could not be used in a relationship.

> Don't be confused by the term dependent value class. This is not a new concept; this is just how the Enterprise JavaBeans specification refers to any concrete, serializable Java class. Basically, dependent value classes are the familiar Java classes that you use in programming all the time.

As the EJB container knows the structure of an entity object from the deployment descriptor, it will be able to save it to the database in normalized form. This means that each state variable will get its own database column. On the other hand, the EJB container does not know the structure of a dependent value class. It may save a dependent value class to a single database column in its serialized form. Even if your EJB container has a proprietary way to decompose dependent value classes, every dependent value class must still implement `java.io.Serializable`.

Since the EJB container knows the structure of an entity object, you will be able to reference its fields in an EJB QL query. The EJB container does not know the structure of a dependent value class, so you will not be able to reference it in an EJB QL query.

The lifecycle of an entity is managed by the EJB container. This allows the container to materialize the same entity for different components participating in a transaction. As a result, data aliasing problems are prevented. The lifecycle of a dependent value class instance is managed by the component. If the same object identity is referenced by multiple EJB entities, the dependent value instances may become uncoordinated.

Local interfaces cannot travel across potentially remote boundaries. In other words, they cannot be used as a return value or a parameter in any method in an entity bean's remote home or component interface. On the other hand, dependent value classes can be used as a parameter or returned to the client.

You should usually use local entity interfaces rather than dependent value classes to model your business objects; this is due to four reasons:

- ❏ They can be portably mapped to normalized relational database tables
- ❏ They can participate in relationships
- ❏ They can be used in EJB QL queries
- ❏ Their lifecycle is managed by the EJB container to alleviate data aliasing problems

Here is a table that summarizes the differences between local entity interfaces and dependent value classes:

Local Entity Interface / Entity	Local Entity Interface / Entity	Dependent Value Class
Implements `java.io.Serializable`	Local interfaces are not serializable, nor do they have handles that can be serialized.	Must implement
Class modifier	abstract	Must not be abstract
Can be part of object's persistent state (that is, the value of a `cmp-field`)	No	Yes

Local Entity Interface / Entity	Local Entity Interface / Entity	Dependent Value Class
Can have a relationship with other entity components (that is, be the value of a cmr field)	Yes	No
Can be returned or passed as a parameter across a remote interface	No	Yes
Can be returned or passed as a parameter across a local interface.	Yes	Yes
Described in the deployment descriptor	Yes	No
Persistent state is...	...implemented by the container	...implemented by the component developer
Lifecycle is...	...managed by the container, which can prevent data-aliasing problems	...managed by the component
State can be used in EJB QL queries	Yes	No

A Dependent Value Class Example

Any concrete, rather than abstract, class that implements java.io.Serializable can be a dependent value class. In other words, any helper classes that were used to implement an EJB 1.1 CMP entity bean were probably dependent value classes. In fact, an EJB 2.0 CMP entity bean that uses dependent value classes is very similar to an EJB 1.1 CMP entity bean, except for the use of abstract accessors rather than explicit state variables. The switch from dependent value classes to entities with local interfaces is one of the most important aspects of the EJB 2.0 persistence model. The following simple example, implementing an Order entity with a dependent shipping address, illustrates this change. We'll look at two versions. The first will use a dependent value class to represent the shipping address. The second will use an entity with a local interface (and a relationship) to represent that address.

The dependent value class example comprises the following six files:

File Name	File Description
Order.java	The remote interface of the order entity bean
OrderHome.java	The remote home interface of the order entity bean
OrderBean.java	The implementation class of the order entity bean
AddressValueObject.java	The concrete, serializable class that represents the shipping address
ejb-jar.xml	The deployment descriptor
ClientDemoValueObject.java	A very simple client to test the functionality of our entity bean

The Remote Interface

Notice that the Address dependent value class can be returned directly to the client through the remote interface. In this respect, it is different from a local entity interface. That doesn't necessarily mean that you wouldn't provide a separate view mechanism, rather than directly exposing your object model to the client. However, you do have the option to reuse the `AddressValueObject` as a view as well as a dependent value of the order:

```
package examples.value_objects;

import java.rmi.RemoteException;
import javax.ejb.EJBObject;

public interface Order extends EJBObject {

  public String getCustomerName() throws RemoteException;
  public AddressValueObject getShipAddress() throws RemoteException;
}
```

The Home Interface

Again, notice that we have the option of reusing the `AddressValueObject` as a view to update or create the order entity. Here, it is being passed as a parameter to the `create()` method:

```
package examples.value_objects;

import java.rmi.RemoteException;
import javax.ejb.CreateException;
import javax.ejb.EJBHome;
import javax.ejb.FinderException;

public interface OrderHome extends EJBHome {

  public Order create(long orderID, String customerName,
                      AddressValueObject shipAddress)
            throws RemoteException, CreateException;

  public Order findByPrimaryKey( Long orderID )
            throws RemoteException, FinderException;
}
```

The Implementation Class

The state of the entity bean is represented by abstract accessor methods. The `AddressValueObject` is included in the state of the bean, and has its own pair of get and set accessors:

```
package examples.value_objects;

import javax.ejb.CreateException;
import javax.ejb.EntityBean;
import javax.ejb.EntityContext;
```

```
public abstract class OrderBean implements EntityBean {

  // CMP fields
  public abstract long getOrderID();
  public abstract void setOrderID(long orderID);

  public abstract String getCustomerName();
  public abstract void setCustomerName(String customerName);

  public abstract AddressValueObject getShipAddress();
  public abstract void setShipAddress(AddressValueObject shipAddress);
```

The `ejbCreate()` method simply takes the `shipAddress` parameter and uses it to set the value of the `shipAddress` state field:

```
  // Callback methods
  public Long ejbCreate(long orderID, String customerName,
                        AddressValueObject shipAddress)
            throws CreateException {
    setOrderID(orderID);
    setCustomerName(customerName);
    setShipAddress(shipAddress);
    return null;
  }

  public void ejbPostCreate(long orderID, String customerName,
                            AddressValueObject shipAddress)
            throws CreateException {}
```

It is common to be able to leave some or all of these notification methods empty with container-managed persistence:

```
  public void ejbActivate() {}
  public void ejbLoad() {}
  public void ejbPassivate() {}
  public void ejbRemove() {}
  public void ejbStore() {}
  public void setEntityContext(EntityContext ctx) {}
  public void unsetEntityContext() {}
}
```

The Address Value Object

This class represents an address, and is used to represent the shipping address for the order entity. It is also used as a view class for the client. Note that there is nothing special about this class; it is a typical Java class that implements `java.io.Serializable`:

```
package examples.value_objects;

public class AddressValueObject implements java.io.Serializable {

  private int addressID;
  private String street;
  private String city;
```

```java
  private String state;
  private String zip;

  public AddressValueObject() {}

  public AddressValueObject(int addressID, String street, String city,
                            String state, String zip) {
    this.addressID = addressID;
    this.street = street;
    this.city = city;
    this.state = state;
    this.zip = zip;
  }

  public int getAddressID() {
    return addressID;
  }

  public void setAddressID(int addressID) {
    this.addressID = addressID;
  }

  public String getStreet() {
    return street;
  }

  public void setStreet(String street) {
    this.street = street;
  }

  public String getCity() {
    return city;
  }

  public void setCity(String city) {
    this.city = city;
  }

  public String getState() {
    return state;
  }

  public void setState(String state) {
    this.state = state;
  }

  public String getZip() {
    return zip;
  }

  public void setZip(String zip) {
    this.zip = zip;
  }
}
```

The Deployment Descriptor–ejb-jar.xml

The interesting thing about this deployment descriptor is what it doesn't define. Notice that there are no relationships defined in this deployment descriptor. Notice also that, although the structure of the Order entity is defined in this deployment descriptor, there is no corresponding description of the structure of the Address object (because it is a dependent value object):

```xml
<?xml version="1.0"?>
<!DOCTYPE ejb-jar PUBLIC "-//Sun Microsystems, Inc.//DTD Enterprise JavaBeans
2.0//EN" "http://java.sun.com/dtd/ejb-jar_2_0.dtd">

<ejb-jar>

  <enterprise-beans>
    <entity>
      <ejb-name>ValueObjectOrderEJB</ejb-name>
      <home>examples.value_objects.OrderHome</home>
      <remote>examples.value_objects.Order</remote>
      <ejb-class>examples.value_objects.OrderBean</ejb-class>
      <persistence-type>Container</persistence-type>
      <prim-key-class>java.lang.Long</prim-key-class>
      <reentrant>True</reentrant>
      <cmp-version>2.x</cmp-version>
      <abstract-schema-name>ValueObjectOrderBean</abstract-schema-name>
      <cmp-field><field-name>orderID</field-name></cmp-field>
      <cmp-field><field-name>customerName</field-name></cmp-field>
      <cmp-field><field-name>shipAddress</field-name></cmp-field>
      <primkey field>orderID</primkey-field>
    </entity>
  </enterprise-beans>

<assembly-descriptor>
  <container-transaction>
    <method>
        <ejb-name>ValueObjectOrderEJB</ejb-name>
        <method-name>*</method-name>
    </method>
    <trans-attribute>Required</trans-attribute>
  </container-transaction>
 </assembly-descriptor>
</ejb-jar>
```

A Simple Sample Client

This client creates an order with a shipping address. It then retrieves that shipping address, and prints it out to make sure everything worked as expected:

```java
package examples.value_objects;

import javax.naming.InitialContext;
import javax.rmi.PortableRemoteObject;

public class ClientDemoValueObject {
  public static void main(String[] args) {
    try {
```

```
            InitialContext initial = new InitialContext();

        OrderHome orderHome = (OrderHome)PortableRemoteObject.narrow(
                                    initial.lookup(
                                        "ValueObjectOrderEJB"), OrderHome.class);
        Order order = orderHome.create(1, "Puddentane",
                          new AddressValueObject(25, "1132 Decimal Ave",
                                                "Evanston", "IL", "60202"));
        System.out.println(order.getCustomerName());
        AddressValueObject shipAddress = order.getShipAddress();
        System.out.println(shipAddress.getStreet());
        System.out.println(shipAddress.getCity());
        System.out.println(shipAddress.getState());
        System.out.println(shipAddress.getZip());
    } catch (Exception e) {
        e.printStackTrace();
    }
  }
}
```

Problems of using a Dependent Value Class

Using a dependent value class (rather than a local view of an entity component) for the Address object means that the EJB container does not know how the address state is represented. There are two practical consequences of this. First, EJB QL queries cannot be qualified on the basis of the street, city, state, or zip code information in the address. It's easy to see why this might be a problem. You might quite likely want to retrieve order information based on its shipping address.

Second, unless your EJB container has a proprietary mapping scheme, the shipping address information is likely to be saved in a single database column as a serialized Java object. This information would not be accessible outside of the EJB container (for example, by a reporting tool). It would also not be accessible if there were to be an incompatible change in the definition of the address value class.

Deployment

We will now go through the deployment details for the dependent value example. (See Appendix B for a basic explanation of deploying on the J2EE Reference Implementation.)

We need to ensure that the Cloudscape database is running before starting this example. Start your Cloudscape database, the J2EE server, and the deployment tool.

We will start by creating the application; we will give it the name value_objects, after the package name. Then import your JAR file into the application.

On the Entity tab for the bean, we need to configure the database settings (just as we did for a 1.1 entity):

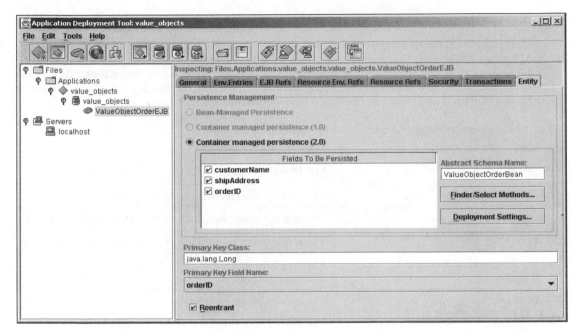

We can now see that the **Deployment Settings...** button is available: press this and in the further dialog enter the database settings for the bean. We have entered the **Database JNDI Name** from the default available to us with the J2EE RI, which is **jdbc/Cloudscape**. Press *Tab* to allow you to press OK. The **Generate Default SQL...** button is now available; we now need to create the default SQL, if we try to miss this step we are reminded with an error message.

Generate the default SQL and then press **OK**. We will then return to the main window.

Now select in the left pane of either the `value_objects` application or container nodes. Select the **JNDI Names** tab and enter the **JNDI Name** as ValueObjectOrderEJB. You can also enter the JNDI Name at deployment time.

Now to deploy the application. We need to make sure that the deployment returns a client JAR file: select the **Return Client Jar** button, then choose where you want the file to be sent.

Click **Next**; in this screen you can add the **JNDI Name** for the Component if you didn't do it earlier. Click **Next** and then the **Finish** to deploy the bean.

Once the deployment process has finished, open a console in the folder containing the returned client JAR and run the command:

```
java -classpath %J2EE_HOME%\lib\j2ee.jar;value_objectsClient.jar;.
    examples.value_objects.ClientDemoValueObject
```

You should then get the result in the console:

```
Puddentane
1132 Decimal Ave
Evanston
IL
60202
```

A Local Interface Example

A local interface represents an entity that is managed by the EJB container. You should model your EJB 2.0 CMP entity beans with fine-grained entity components, rather than dependent value classes. We'll take the Order entity that we built in the previous example, and rewrite it so that it uses a fine-grained entity object rather than a dependent value class. However, we'll reuse that dependent value class as a view that can be used as a parameter to or a return value from a remote method.

The local interface example comprises the following nine files:

File Name	File Description
Order.java	The remote interface of the Order entity bean
OrderHome.java	The remote home interface of the Order entity bean
OrderBean.java	The implementation class of the Order entity bean
AddressValueObject.java	The serializable view class to provide the client with address information
AddressLocal.java	The local interface of the Address entity bean
AddressLocalHome.java	The local home interface of the Address entity bean
AddressBean.java	The implementation class of the Address entity bean
ejb-jar.xml	The deployment descriptor, which contains information about the schemas of the entity beans and their relationship
ClientDemoDependentObject.java	A very simple client to test the functionality of our entity beans

The Order Remote Interface

The remote interface is quite similar to the earlier version. We changed the name of the method that was originally called getShipAddress() to getShipAddressView(). If we hadn't, there would have been a conflict in the implementation class, because the getShipAddress() method is also the name of the abstract accessor for the relationship to the shipping address local interface. We can't expose any relationship accessor methods that return local interfaces or collection classes in the remote interface of the entity:

```
package examples.local_objects;

import java.rmi.RemoteException;
import javax.ejb.EJBObject;

public interface Order extends EJBObject {

    public String getCustomerName() throws RemoteException;
    public AddressValueObject getShipAddressView() throws RemoteException;
}
```

The Order Remote Home Interface

This interface is identical to the earlier version, except for the package name. However, there is a subtle difference in the implementation, in that before, we knew that a copy of the `AddressValueObject` parameter to the `create()` method was going to be part of the order's state. Now, it is simply a view object that will be transformed into another entity that helps implement the object model. Of course, from the client's point of view there is no way of telling the difference. This hiding of the implementation details is one of the main points of having an interface to a component:

```
package examples.local_objects;

import java.rmi.RemoteException;
import javax.ejb.CreateException;
import javax.ejb.EJBHome;
import javax.ejb.FinderException;

public interface OrderHome extends EJBHome {

    public Order create(long orderID, String customerName,
                        AddressValueObject shipAddress)
            throws RemoteException, CreateException;

    public Order findByPrimaryKey(Long orderID)
            throws RemoteException, FinderException;
}
```

The Order Implementation Class

The implementation class replaces the `cmp`-field abstract accessors for the `shipAddress` state with `cmr-field` abstract accessors for a relationship with an address entity:

```
package examples.local_objects;

import javax.ejb.CreateException;
import javax.ejb.EntityBean;
import javax.ejb.EntityContext;
import javax.naming.InitialContext;

public abstract class OrderBean implements EntityBean {

    // cmp fields
    public abstract long getOrderID();
    public abstract void setOrderID(long orderID);

    public abstract String getCustomerName();
    public abstract void setCustomerName(String customerName);

    // cmr-fields
    public abstract AddressLocal getShipAddress();
    public abstract void setShipAddress(AddressLocal shipAddress);
```

To provide a view of the address entity in the object model, we first retrieve it using the abstract relationship accessor method. We then initialize the view class and return it to the client:

```
public AddressValueObject getShipAddressView() {
  AddressLocal shipAddress = getShipAddress();
  return new AddressValueObject(shipAddress.getAddressID(),
                      shipAddress.getStreet(), shipAddress.getCity(),
                      shipAddress.getState(), shipAddress.getZip());
}
```

The `ejbCreate()` method initializes the state of the Order object. Remember that this state no longer includes the shipping address information. Instead, that information is contained in a related entity object (represented by its local interface). We don't do anything with the `shipAddress` in `ejbCreate()` because relationships must be set up in `ejbPostCreate()`:

```
// Callback methods
public Long ejbCreate(long orderID, String customerName,
                    AddressValueObject shipAddress)
          throws CreateException {

  setOrderID(orderID);
  setCustomerName(customerName);
  return null;
}
```

The following method is an implementation helper for `ejbPostCreate()`:

```
private AddressLocal createShipAddress(int addressId, String street,
                                    String city, String state, String zip) {
  try {
    InitialContext initial = new InitialContext();

    AddressLocalHome home = (AddressLocalHome)
                              initial.lookup(
                                "java:comp/env/ejb/AddressEJB");

    return home.create(addressId, street, city, state, zip);
  } catch (Exception e) {
    throw new javax.ejb.EJBException(e);
  }
}
```

One of the subtler points of the EJB 1.1 spec was that the `ejbPostCreate()` method should be used whenever the identity of the created object was required. Those situations were uncommon in EJB 1.1 persistence. Here, we require the identity of the Order object to be established before we can form a relationship with another object (in this case, the Address object). We initialize any relationships in `ejbPostCreate()` rather than `ejbCreate()`:

```
public void ejbPostCreate(long orderID, String customerName,
                        AddressValueObject shipAddressView)
          throws CreateException {

  AddressLocal shipAddress = createShipAddress(
    shipAddressView.getAddressID(), shipAddressView.getStreet(),
    shipAddressView.getCity(), shipAddressView.getState(),
    shipAddressView.getZip());
  setShipAddress(shipAddress);
}
```

Once again, the notification callbacks do not need implementations:

```
    public void ejbActivate() {}
    public void ejbLoad() {}
    public void ejbPassivate() {}
    public void ejbRemove() {}
    public void ejbStore() {}
    public void setEntityContext(EntityContext ctx) {}
    public void unsetEntityContext() {}
}
```

The View

This view is simply the earlier dependent value class (AddressValueObject), unchanged except for the package name. Although it no longer helps us to model the Order object's persistent state, it is still quite useful for transferring information to and from the client (and provides all the benefits of the view pattern, for example, saving network round trips).

The Address Local Component Interface

The local component interface extends javax.ejb.EJBLocalObject, rather than javax.ejb.EJBObject. Its methods do not throw a RemoteException. Apart from minor details such as these, the difference between a local interface and a remote interface is in design intent. Here, we expose low-level getters and setters for the entity properties, rather than a view object or higher-level business methods.

You could also expose getter and setter methods for other local interfaces and relationship collection classes in a local interface. Notice, however, that we do not expose a setter method for any key properties. A primary key value does not change once it has been established in ejbCreate():

```
    package examples.local_objects;

    import javax.ejb.EJBLocalObject;

    public interface AddressLocal extends EJBLocalObject {

      public int getAddressID();

      public String getStreet();
      public void setStreet(String street);

      public String getCity();
      public void setCity(String city);

      public String getState();
      public void setState(String state);

      public String getZip();
      public void setZip(String zip);
    }
```

The Address Local Home Interface

Remote component interfaces have remote home interfaces. Local component interfaces have local home interfaces. Again, notice that we do not throw RemoteException from any methods:

```
package examples.local_objects;

import javax.ejb.CreateException;
import javax.ejb.EJBLocalHome;
import javax.ejb.FinderException;

public interface AddressLocalHome extends EJBLocalHome {

  public AddressLocal  findByPrimaryKey(Integer addressID)
                        throws FinderException;

  public AddressLocal  create(int addressID,  String street, String city,
                              String state, String zip)
                        throws CreateException;
}
```

The Address Implementation Class

This class looks quite different from the dependent value class that it replaces. Although it models the same state, it does it through abstract accessor methods rather than state variables. It is an abstract class whose implementation will be provided by the EJB container when the component is deployed:

```
package examples.local_objects;

import javax.ejb.CreateException;
import javax.ejb.EntityBean;
import javax.ejb.EntityContext;

public abstract class AddressBean implements EntityBean {

  public abstract int getAddressID();
  public abstract void setAddressID(int addressID);

  public abstract String getStreet();
  public abstract void setStreet(String street);

  public abstract String getCity();
  public abstract void setCity(String city);

  public abstract String getState();
  public abstract void setState(String state);

  public abstract String getZip();
  public abstract void setZip(String zip);

  public Integer ejbCreate(int addressID, String street, String city,
                           String state, String zip)
                throws CreateException {
    setAddressID(addressID);
    setStreet(street);
    setCity(city);
    setState(state);
    setZip(zip);
    return null;
  }
```

```
    public void ejbPostCreate(int addressID, String street, String city,
                              String state, String zip)
         throws CreateException {}

  public void ejbActivate() {}
  public void ejbLoad() {}
  public void ejbPassivate() {}
  public void ejbRemove() {}
  public void ejbStore() {}
  public void setEntityContext(EntityContext ctx) {}
  public void unsetEntityContext() {}
}
```

The Deployment Descriptor–ejb-jar.xml

The deployment descriptor describes the structure of the Order and Address entity beans. It also describes the relationship between the two:

```xml
<?xml version="1.0" encoding="UTF-8"?>

<!DOCTYPE ejb-jar PUBLIC '-//Sun Microsystems, Inc.//DTD Enterprise JavaBeans
2.0//EN' 'http://java.sun.com/dtd/ejb-jar_2_0.dtd'>

<ejb-jar>
  <display-name>local_objects</display-name>
  <enterprise-beans>
    <entity>
      <display-name>OrderEJB2</display-name>
      <ejb-name>OrderEJB2</ejb-name>
      <home>examples.local_objects.OrderHome</home>
      <remote>examples.local_objects.Order</remote>
      <ejb-class>examples.local_objects.OrderBean</ejb-class>
      <persistence-type>Container</persistence-type>
      <prim-key-class>java.lang.Long</prim-key-class>
      <reentrant>True</reentrant>
      <cmp-version>2.x</cmp-version>
      <abstract-schema-name>OrderBean</abstract-schema-name>
      <cmp-field><field-name>customerName</field-name></cmp-field>
      <cmp-field><field-name>orderID</field-name></cmp-field>
      <primkey-field>orderID</primkey-field>
```

Since EJB 1.0 we have needed to declare a reference to any component we acquire from within another component. The EJB 2.0 spec introduces the <ejb-local-ref> element to supplement the <ejb-ref> element:

```xml
      <ejb-local-ref>
        <ejb-ref-name>ejb/AddressEJB</ejb-ref-name>
        <ejb-ref-type>Entity</ejb-ref-type>
        <local-home>examples.local_objects.AddressLocalHome</local-home>
        <local>examples.local_objects.AddressLocal</local>
        <ejb-link>AddressEJB</ejb-link>
      </ejb-local-ref>
    </entity>
    <entity>
      <display-name>AddressEJB</display-name>
      <ejb-name>AddressEJB</ejb-name>
```

Note the usage of the new elements `<local-home>` and `<local>`:

```
        <local-home>examples.local_objects.AddressLocalHome</local-home>
        <local>examples.local_objects.AddressLocal</local>
        <ejb-class>examples.local_objects.AddressBean</ejb-class>
        <persistence-type>Container</persistence-type>
        <prim-key-class>java.lang.Integer</prim-key-class>
        <reentrant>True</reentrant>
        <cmp-version>2.x</cmp-version>
        <abstract-schema-name>AddressBean</abstract-schema-name>
        <cmp-field><field-name>addressID</field-name></cmp-field>
        <cmp-field><field-name>zip</field-name></cmp-field>
        <cmp-field><field-name>state</field-name></cmp-field>
        <cmp-field><field-name>city</field-name></cmp-field>
        <cmp-field><field-name>street</field-name></cmp-field>
        <primkey-field>addressID</primkey-field>
    </entity>
</enterprise-beans>
```

Of course, the top-level `<relationships>` element is new to EJB 2.0:

```
<relationships>
  <ejb-relation>
    <ejb-relation-name></ejb-relation-name>
    <ejb-relationship-role>
      <ejb-relationship-role-name>OrderEJB2</ejb-relationship-role-name>
      <multiplicity>one</multiplicity>
      <relationship-role-source>
        <ejb-name>OrderEJB2</ejb-name>
      </relationship-role-source>
      <cmr-field>
        <cmr-field-name>shipAddress</cmr-field-name>
      </cmr-field>
    </ejb-relationship-role>
    <ejb-relationship-role>
      <ejb-relationship-role-name>AddressEJB</ejb-relationship-role-name>
      <multiplicity>one</multiplicity>
      <relationship-role-source>
        <ejb-name>AddressEJB</ejb-name>
      </relationship-role-source>
    </ejb-relationship-role>
  </ejb-relation>
</relationships>

<assembly-descriptor>
  <container-transaction>
    <method>
      <ejb-name>AddressEJB</ejb-name>
      <method-name>*</method-name>
    </method>
    <method>
      <ejb-name>OrderEJB2</ejb-name>
      <method-name>*</method-name>
    </method>
```

```
        <trans-attribute>Required</trans-attribute>
      </container-transaction>
   </assembly-descriptor>
</ejb-jar>
```

The Client

This client creates an order with a shipping address. It then retrieves that shipping address, and prints it out to make sure everything worked as expected:

```java
package examples.local_objects;

import javax.naming.InitialContext;
import javax.rmi.PortableRemoteObject;

public class ClientDemoDependentObject {
  public static void main(String[] args) {
    try {
      InitialContext initial = new InitialContext();

      OrderHome orderHome = (OrderHome)
                              PortableRemoteObject.narrow(
                                initial.lookup("OrderEJB2"), OrderHome.class );

      Order order = orderHome.create(1, "Puddentane",
                                new AddressValueObject(25, "1132 Decimal Ave",
                                                "Evanston", "IL", "60202"));
      System.out.println(order.getCustomerName());
      AddressValueObject shipAddress = order.getShipAddressView();
      System.out.println(shipAddress.getStreet());
      System.out.println(shipAddress.getCity());
      System.out.println(shipAddress.getState());
      System.out.println(shipAddress.getZip());

    } catch (Exception e) {
      e.printStackTrace();
    }
  }
}
```

A Normalized Representation

The EJB 2.0 specification does not provide for a particular mapping from an object model to a relational database schema. However, it is quite likely (if not certain) that every EJB container will take advantage of the information in the deployment descriptor to map your entities and relationships to normalized database tables. The ability of the EJB container to map to a complicated or pre-existing schema will vary from implementation to implementation (and is one of the "value added" services on which vendors compete).

You can also portably use the entities that compose your object model (in this case street, city, state, and zip code in the address object) in EJB QL queries. This is true regardless of how your EJB container maps the object model to the relational database schema (or to another type of data store). In other words: it's not your problem how this is accomplished, but your vendor's.

Home and Component Interfaces as Value Types

Remote interfaces to other EJB components can be used as part of an entity's persistent state. In other words, they can be used as the value of cmp fields. Local entity interfaces can be used as the target of cmr fields. There is no overlap between the two.

Unless you have a highly unusual situation, you should manage other entity objects in relationships using local interfaces, rather than as part of your entity's persistent state using remote interfaces. It is possible to come up with scenarios where it is convenient to make home and remote interfaces part of your object's persistent state, for example, the remote entity type is unknown until run time. However, this will damage the portability either of your EJB components (because you depend on a proprietary mechanism to map a remote interface to a normalized table), or your database (because you are storing a vendor's proprietary handle format in a database column) .

An Important Reminder about Primary Keys

Once a key field has been set in the ejbCreate() method for that entity, it must never be modified. It is not legal to expose a setter method for that key field in either the local component interface or the remote component interface.

Deployment

We need to ensure that the Cloudscape database is running before starting this example. Start your Cloudscape database, the J2EE Server, and the Application Deployment Tool.

We will start by creating the application; we will give it the name local_objects, after the package name. Then import your EJB JAR file into the application. Most of the deployment information is similar to the previous example, so we will just briefly review the new areas. Don't forget to set up the database setting and JNDI names for the beans. We are using the same JNDI name as the bean name for this example.

If we switch to the Relationships tab for the JAR file, we can see here the relationship that allows the OrderEJB2 entity to have a 1:1 multiplicity with the AddressEJB entity:

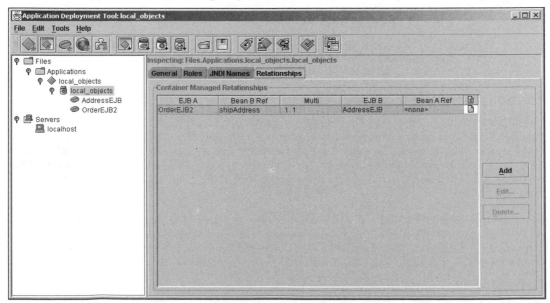

We can also see in the following screen the EJB reference that is set up to allow the OrderEJB2 entity access to the local interfaces of the AddressEJB:

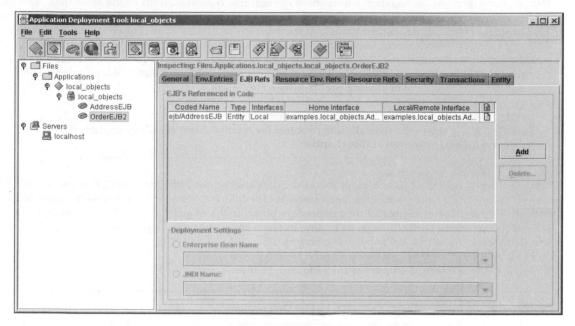

Once the deployment process has finished run the client:

```
java -classpath %J2EE_HOME%\lib\j2ee.jar;local_objectsClient.jar;.
    examples.local_objects.ClientDemoDependentObject
```

You should then again get the result in the console:

```
Puddentane
1132 Decimal Ave
Evanston
IL
60202
```

Granularity and Modeling

This section discusses whether or not an entity should have a remote component interface, a local component interface, or both. It is possible (though probably not wise) to completely translate your business model to remote objects. It is also possible to have only local interfaces, and to never expose an entity remotely. In general, we favor the second approach. In my opinion, all entity components should be hidden behind session bean façades that provide coarse-grained services to the client.

However, providing only local interfaces does limit your ability to distribute entity components on a network. In general, you should co-locate tightly coupled components in a container (such as a session bean service façade and the entity beans that help to implement this service). But you could make an argument that some entities should make their remote interfaces accessible to a client. Try to expose as little as possible in remote interfaces. (The interfaces that are exposed should probably correspond to your system-level use cases.)

A (Non) Data Aliasing Example

Data aliasing refers to the situation where there are multiple representations of the same data. This can lead to problems when you update one representation, and incorrectly expect others also to be updated. This problem exists, for dependent value objects, even in the EJB 2.0 model of container persistence. It does not exist for entity objects, which are synchronized by the EJB container. Within a transaction, if you change an entity object with a particular identity, that change must be reflected in all instances that represent that object identity. As local interfaces make it practical to use entity objects rather than dependent value objects, data aliasing problems need not occur.

> EJB 2.0 also solves the data aliasing problem for relationships, as will be explained in the relationships section of this chapter.

To demonstrate how the EJB container solves the data aliasing problem for entity beans, we'll look at a simple example. Two different entity bean instances (of different types) will each have a relationship with a third entity bean (representing a dependent object in the object model). The first entity bean will ask the second entity bean (through its remote interface) to update the "dependent object" entity bean. It will then check to see that its "copy" has changed.

The data aliasing example comprises the following 11 files:

File Name	File Description
Entity1.java	The remote component interface of the first entity
Entity1Home.java	The remote home interface of the first entity
Entity1Bean.java	The implementation class of the first entity
Entity2.java	The remote component interface of the second entity
Entity2Home.java	The remote home interface of the second entity
Entity2Bean.java	The implementation class of the second entity
CommonDependentLocal.java	The local component interface of the entity representing part of the object model
CommonDependentLocalHome.java	The local home interface of the entity representing part of the object model
CommonDependentBean.java	The implementation class of the entity representing part of the object model
ejb-jar.xml	The deployment descriptor
Client.java	A simple client to run our test

Here is a summary of what happens in this sample application:

1. The client creates an instance of Entity1.

2. During its initialization, in the `ejbPostCreate()` method, Entity1 creates an instance of the CommonDependentLocal entity and sets it as the value of its `commonDependent` cmr field.

3. The client creates an instance of Entity2.

4. During its initialization, in the `ejbPostCreate()` method, Entity2 uses an `ejbSelect()` method (`ejbSelectCommonDependent()`) to find the instance of CommonLocalDependent created by Entity1. It sets it as the value of its commonDependent cmr field. At this point, both the Entity1 instance and the Entity2 instance have a relationship to the same entity.

5. The client calls the `runTest()` method on its instance of Entity1.

6. The Entity1 instance checks a value of the CommonDependent entity.

7. The Entity1 instance uses an `ejbSelect()` method (`ejbSelectCorrespondingEntity2()`) to get the Entity2 instance, and tells that `Entity2` instance, through its remote interface, to change the value of its dependent object.

8. Entity1 checks to make sure that its CommonDependent entity instance reflects this change.

If the Entity1 instance and the Entity2 instance each had its own unsynchronized copy of the data (as would be the case with a dependent value class), you would not expect that the Entity1 instance's copy would reflect the changes made by the Entity2 instance. In this case, using an entity component rather than a dependent value class, the changes are reflected.

This sequence diagram may help you to understand how this application works:

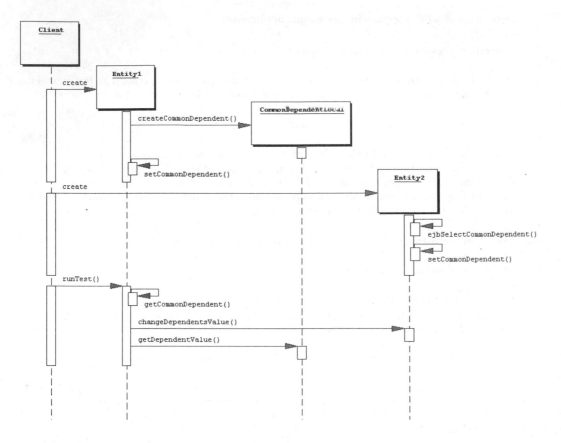

The Entity1 Remote Interface

The only exposed method of Entity1 runs the data-aliasing test. It returns true if changes in one Entity2's reference of the entity representing a dependent object in its object model are immediately reflected in the other reference. The method should return true:

```
package examples.data_alias;

import java.rmi.RemoteException;
import javax.ejb.EJBObject;

public interface Entity1 extends EJBObject {

  public boolean runTest() throws RemoteException;

}
```

The Entity1 Home Interface

This is a minimal home interface. The id for the `Entity1` and `Entity2` instances in a test should be the same:

```
package examples.data_alias;

import java.rmi.RemoteException;
import javax.ejb.CreateException;
import javax.ejb.EJBHome;
import javax.ejb.FinderException;

public interface Entity1Home extends EJBHome {

  public Entity1 create(int id) throws RemoteException, CreateException;

  public Entity1 findByPrimaryKey(Integer id)
              throws RemoteException, FinderException;
}
```

The Entity1 Implementation Class

This class is responsible for running the test to demonstrate that there is no data aliasing problem:

```
package examples.data_alias;

import javax.ejb.CreateException;
import javax.ejb.EJBException;
import javax.ejb.EJBLocalHome;
import javax.ejb.EntityBean;
import javax.ejb.EntityContext;
import javax.ejb.FinderException;
import javax.naming.InitialContext;

public abstract class Entity1Bean implements EntityBean {
```

The only state that this entity bean has is its id.

```
// cmp values
public abstract int getId();
public abstract void setId(int id);
```

This entity bean has one relationship: a one-to-one relationship with the `CommonDependentLocal` entity:

```
// cmr values
public abstract CommonDependentLocal getCommonDependent();
public abstract void setCommonDependent(CommonDependentLocal commonDependent);
```

The `ejbSelect()` method is used to get the corresponding instance of `Entity2`. (For the purposes of this test, we assume that the `Entity1` and `Entity2` instances were given the same id):

```
public abstract Entity2 ejbSelectCorrespondingEntity2(int id)
                throws FinderException;
```

The `runTest()` business method is the point of this example. It checks to make sure that the changes made by the `Entity2` instance are immediately reflected in its reference:

```
    public boolean runTest() {
      try {
        CommonDependentLocal cd = getCommonDependent();

        // Make sure we know the initial value
        if (!cd.getDependentValue().equals("initial value")) {
          return false;
        }

        // Get the equivalent entity bean
        Entity2 entity2 = ejbSelectCorrespondingEntity2(getId());

        // Tell that entity to change ITS dependent object
        entity2.changeDependentsValue("new value");

        // Check if OUR copy of the dependent object has changed
        return (cd.getDependentValue().equals("new value"));
      } catch (Exception e) {
        throw new EJBException(e);
      }
    }

    public Integer ejbCreate(int id) throws CreateException {
      setId(id);
      return null;
    }

    public CommonDependentLocal createCommonDependent(int id,
                                              String dependentValue) {

      try {
        InitialContext initial = new InitialContext();
        CommonDependentLocalHome home = (CommonDependentLocalHome)
          initial.lookup("java:comp/env/ejb/CommonDependentLocal");
        return home.create(id, dependentValue);
      } catch (Exception e) {
        throw new EJBException(e);
      }
    }
}
```

We instantiate the entity that represents a dependent object and add it to the relationship in the ejbPostCreate() method. For convenience, we use an id for the entity as part of the object model that is the same as the id for the entity:

```
    public void ejbPostCreate(int id) throws CreateException {
      CommonDependentLocal cd = createCommonDependent(id, "initial value");
      setCommonDependent(cd);
    }

    public void ejbActivate() {}
    public void ejbLoad() {}
    public void ejbPassivate() {}
    public void ejbRemove() {}
    public void ejbStore() {}
    public void setEntityContext(EntityContext ctx) {}
    public void unsetEntityContext() {}
}
```

The Entity2 Remote Interface

The changeDependentsValue() business method is used by the Entity1 instance to trigger the remote change of the entity that represents a dependent object in the object model:

```
package examples.data_alias;

import java.rmi.RemoteException;
import javax.ejb.EJBObject;

public interface Entity2 extends EJBObject {

    public void changeDependentsValue(String newValue) throws RemoteException;
}
```

The Entity2 Home Interface

This is a minimal home interface. The id for the Entity1 and Entity2 instances in a test should be the same:

```
package examples.data_alias;

import java.rmi.RemoteException;
import javax.ejb.CreateException;
import javax.ejb.EJBHome;
import javax.ejb.FinderException;

public interface Entity2Home extends EJBHome {

    public Entity2 create(int id) throws RemoteException, CreateException;

    public Entity2 findByPrimaryKey(Integer id)
                  throws RemoteException, FinderException;
}
```

The Entity2 Implementation Class

The Entity2 entity is a collaborator in the test. Its role is to change the dependent entity value on command:

```
package examples.data_alias;

import javax.ejb.CreateException;
import javax.ejb.EJBException;
import javax.ejb.EntityBean;
import javax.ejb.EntityContext;
import javax.ejb.FinderException;
import javax.naming.InitialContext;

public abstract class Entity2Bean implements EntityBean {

    // cmp values
    public abstract int getId();
    public abstract void setId(int id);
```

It doesn't matter what the cmr field is called. We could call it "ourTestObject," in which case the accessors would be getOurTestObject() and setOurTestObject():

```
// cmr values
public abstract CommonDependentLocal getCommonDependent2();
public abstract void setCommonDependent2(CommonDependentLocal commonDependent);
```

Instead of creating the dependent entity object (as Entity1 does), we assume that it already exists and call the ejbSelectCommonDependent() method to retrieve it:

```
public abstract CommonDependentLocal ejbSelectCommonDependent(int id)
                                throws FinderException;

public void changeDependentsValue(String newValue) {
  getCommonDependent2().setDependentValue(newValue);
}

public Integer ejbCreate(int id) throws CreateException {
  setId(id);
  return null;
}
```

We set up any relationship values in ejbPostCreate(), not ejbCreate(), as mandated by the EJB 2.0 specification:

```
public void ejbPostCreate(int id) throws CreateException {
  try {
    CommonDependentLocal cd = ejbSelectCommonDependent(id);
    setCommonDependent2(cd);
  } catch (FinderException fe) {
    throw new EJBException(fe);
  }
}

public void ejbActivate() {}
public void ejbLoad() {}
public void ejbPassivate() {}
public void ejbRemove() {}
public void ejbStore() {}
public void setEntityContext(EntityContext ctx) {}
public void unsetEntityContext() {}
}
```

The CommonDependent Local Home Interface

This interface provides normal factory methods for the local interface:

```
package examples.data_alias;

import javax.ejb.CreateException;
import javax.ejb.EJBLocalHome;
import javax.ejb.EntityBean;
import javax.ejb.EntityContext;
```

```
import javax.ejb.FinderException;

public interface CommonDependentLocalHome extends EJBLocalHome {

  public CommonDependentLocal findByPrimaryKey(Integer dependentID)
                            throws FinderException;

  public CommonDependentLocal create(int dependentID, String dependentValue)
                            throws CreateException;
}
```

The CommonDependent Local Interface

This entity's sole reason for existence is to have a value (here a string field called `dependentValue`) for us to change:

```
package examples.data_alias;

import javax.ejb.EJBLocalObject;

public interface CommonDependentLocal extends EJBLocalObject {

  public int getDependentId();

  public String getDependentValue();
  public void setDependentValue(String dependentValue);
}
```

The CommonDependent Implementation Class

Again, this is a minimal implementation whose sole purpose is to hold a value:

```
package examples.data_alias;

import javax.ejb.CreateException;
import javax.ejb.EJBException;
import javax.ejb.EntityBean;
import javax.ejb.EntityContext;
import javax.ejb.FinderException;

public abstract class CommonDependentBean implements EntityBean {

  public abstract int getDependentId();
  public abstract void setDependentId(int id);

  public abstract String getDependentValue();
  public abstract void setDependentValue(String dependentValue);

  public Integer ejbCreate(int id, String dependentValue)
                throws CreateException {
```

```
      setDependentId(id);
      setDependentValue(dependentValue);
      return null;
   }

   public void ejbPostCreate(int id, String dependentValue)
       throws CreateException {}

   public void ejbActivate() {}
   public void ejbLoad() {}
   public void ejbPassivate() {}
   public void ejbRemove() {}
   public void ejbStore() {}
   public void setEntityContext(EntityContext ctx) {}
   public void unsetEntityContext() {}
}
```

Deployment Descriptor–ejb-jar.xml

This deployment descriptor describes the three entities to the container. It also defines two relationships: one between the `Entity1` class and the `CommonDependentLocal`, and one between the `Entity2` class and the `CommonDependentLocal`. Notice also that the EJB QL queries for the two `ejbSelect()` methods are defined in the deployment descriptor. The EJB QL will be fully explained in the corresponding section of this chapter:

```xml
<?xml version="1.0" encoding="UTF-8"?>

<!DOCTYPE ejb-jar PUBLIC '-//Sun Microsystems, Inc.//DTD Enterprise JavaBeans
2.0//EN' 'http://java.sun.com/dtd/ejb-jar_2_0.dtd'>

<ejb-jar>
  <display-name>data_alias</display-name>
  <enterprise-beans>
    <entity>
      <display-name>Entity1EJB</display-name>
      <ejb-name>Entity1EJB</ejb-name>
      <home>examples.data_alias.Entity1Home</home>
      <remote>examples.data_alias.Entity1</remote>
      <ejb-class>examples.data_alias.Entity1Bean</ejb-class>
      <persistence-type>Container</persistence-type>
      <prim-key-class>java.lang.Integer</prim-key-class>
      <reentrant>True</reentrant>
      <cmp-version>2.x</cmp-version>
      <abstract-schema-name>Entity1Bean</abstract-schema-name>
      <cmp-field><field-name>id</field-name></cmp-field>
      <primkey-field>id</primkey-field>
      <ejb-local-ref>
        <ejb-ref-name>ejb/CommonDependentLocal</ejb-ref-name>
        <ejb-ref-type>Entity</ejb-ref-type>
        <local-home>examples.data_alias.CommonDependentLocalHome</local-home>
        <local>examples.data_alias.CommonDependentLocal</local>
        <ejb-link>CommonDependentEJB</ejb-link>
      </ejb-local-ref>
      <query>
        <query-method>
```

```
        <method-name>ejbSelectCorrespondingEntity2</method-name>
        <method-params>
          <method-param>int</method-param>
        </method-params>
      </query-method>
      <result-type-mapping>Remote</result-type-mapping>
```

The ejbSelect() method is identified by its name and parameters. The query is quite simple, saying: "select all instances of the Entity2 Bean where the id is equal to the first parameter of the SELECT method." The OBJECT operator links the result from an abstract schema to an interface for the bean.

```
      <ejb-ql>
        SELECT OBJECT(e2b) FROM Entity2Bean e2b WHERE e2b.id = ?1
      </ejb-ql>
    </query>
  </entity>
  <entity>
    <display-name>Entity2EJB</display-name>
    <ejb-name>Entity2EJB</ejb-name>
    <home>examples.data_alias.Entity2Home</home>
    <remote>examples.data_alias.Entity2</remote>
    <ejb-class>examples.data_alias.Entity2Bean</ejb-class>
    <persistence-type>Container</persistence-type>
    <prim-key-class>java.lang.Integer</prim-key-class>
    <reentrant>True</reentrant>
    <cmp-version>2.x</cmp-version>
    <abstract-schema-name>Entity2Bean</abstract-schema-name>
    <cmp-field><field-name>id</field-name></cmp-field>
    <primkey-field>id</primkey-field>
    <query>
      <query-method>
        <method-name>ejbSelectCommonDependent</method-name>
        <method-params>
          <method-param>int</method-param>
        </method-params>
      </query-method>
      <result-type-mapping>Local</result-type-mapping>
      <ejb-ql>
        SELECT OBJECT(cd) FROM CommonDependentBean cd WHERE cd.dependentId = ?1
      </ejb-ql>
    </query>
  </entity>
  <entity>
    <display-name>CommonDependentEJB</display-name>
    <ejb-name>CommonDependentEJB</ejb-name>
    <local-home>examples.data_alias.CommonDependentLocalHome</local-home>
    <local>examples.data_alias.CommonDependentLocal</local>
    <ejb-class>examples.data_alias.CommonDependentBean</ejb-class>
    <persistence-type>Container</persistence-type>
    <prim-key-class>java.lang.Integer</prim-key-class>
    <reentrant>True</reentrant>
    <cmp-version>2.x</cmp-version>
    <abstract-schema-name>CommonDependentBean</abstract-schema-name>
    <cmp-field><field-name>dependentValue</field-name></cmp-field>
    <cmp-field><field-name>dependentId</field-name></cmp-field>
```

```
                <primkey-field>dependentId</primkey-field>
        </entity>
    </enterprise-beans>
```

This section describes the relationship between the `Entity1` entity bean and the `CommonDependent` entity bean:

```
<relationships>
  <ejb-relation>
    <ejb-relation-name></ejb-relation-name>
    <ejb-relationship-role>
      <ejb-relationship-role-name>
          Entity1EJB
      </ejb-relationship-role-name>
      <multiplicity>one</multiplicity>
      <relationship-role-source>
        <ejb-name>Entity1EJB</ejb-name>
      </relationship-role-source>
      <cmr-field>
        <cmr-field-name>commonDependent</cmr-field-name>
      </cmr-field>
    </ejb-relationship-role>
    <ejb-relationship-role>
      <ejb-relationship-role-name>
          CommonDependentEJB
      </ejb-relationship-role-name>
      <multiplicity>one</multiplicity>
      <relationship-role-source>
        <ejb-name>CommonDependentEJB</ejb-name>
      </relationship-role-source>
    </ejb-relationship-role>
  </ejb-relation>
```

This section describes the relationship between the `Entity2` entity bean and the `CommonDependent` entity bean:

```
<ejb-relation>
  <ejb-relation-name></ejb-relation-name>
  <ejb-relationship-role>
    <ejb-relationship-role-name>Entity2EJB</ejb-relationship-role-name>
    <multiplicity>one</multiplicity>
    <relationship-role-source>
      <ejb-name>Entity2EJB</ejb-name>
    </relationship-role-source>
    <cmr-field>
      <cmr-field-name>commonDependent2</cmr-field-name>
    </cmr-field>
  </ejb-relationship-role>
  <ejb-relationship-role>
    <ejb-relationship-role-name>
        CommonDependentEJB
    </ejb-relationship-role-name>
    <multiplicity>one</multiplicity>
```

```
              <relationship-role-source>
                <ejb-name>CommonDependentEJB</ejb-name>
              </relationship-role-source>
            </ejb-relationship-role>
          </ejb-relation>
        </relationships>

        <assembly-descriptor>
          <container-transaction>
            <method>
              <ejb-name>Entity1EJB</ejb-name>
              <method-intf>Home</method-intf>
              <method-name>findByPrimaryKey</method-name>
              <method-params>
                <method-param>java.lang.Integer</method-param>
              </method-params>
            </method>
            <trans-attribute>Required</trans-attribute>
          </container-transaction>
          <container-transaction>
            <method>
              <ejb-name>Entity2EJB</ejb-name>
              <method-name>*</method-name>
            </method>
            <trans-attribute>Required</trans-attribute>
          </container-transaction>
          <container-transaction>
            <method>
              <ejb-name>CommonDependentEJB</ejb-name>
              <method-name>*</method-name>
            </method>
            <trans-attribute>Required</trans-attribute>
          </container-transaction>
        </assembly-descriptor>
      </ejb-jar>
```

Simple Client

The client creates the entities, runs the test, and prints out the results. It should print Dependent object preserved identity: true.

```
package examples.data_alias;

import javax.naming.InitialContext;
import javax.rmi.PortableRemoteObject;

public class Client {
  public static void main(String[] args) {
    try {
      InitialContext initial = new InitialContext();

      Entity1Home entity1Home = (Entity1Home)
        PortableRemoteObject.narrow(
          initial.lookup("Entity1EJB"), Entity1Home.class);
```

```
        Entity2Home entity2Home = (Entity2Home)
          PortableRemoteObject.narrow(
            initial.lookup("Entity2EJB"), Entity2Home.class);

        Entity1 entity1 = entity1Home.create(1);
        Entity2 entity2 = entity2Home.create(1);

        System.out.println("Dependent object preserved identity: " +
                            entity1.runTest());

    } catch (Exception e) {
      e.printStackTrace();
    }
  }
}
```

Data aliasing issues can be avoided by using entity objects, rather than dependent value objects, in your object model.

Deployment

We will start by creating the application, called `data_alias`, after the package name, and import the beans' JAR file. As before, enter the database information, this is still **jdbc/Cloudscape**, so generate the SQL for the application and then save the file.

Most of the deployment information is of a similar type to the previous example, so we will just show the altered areas.

We can see here the two relationships set up to allow both the `Entity1EJB` and `Entity2EJB` beans to have a container-managed relationship with the `CommonDependentEJB` entity, both are set with a 1:1 multiplicity.

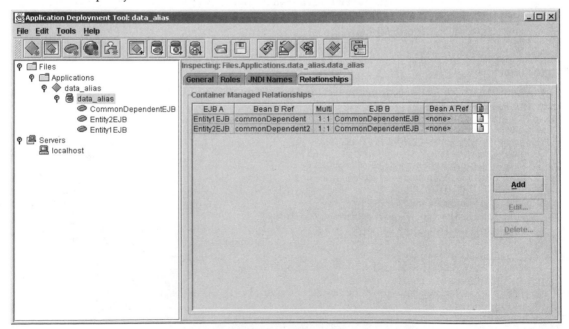

We see an EJB reference for the `Entity1EJB` allowing it to access the local interfaces of the `CommonDependentEJB` entity:

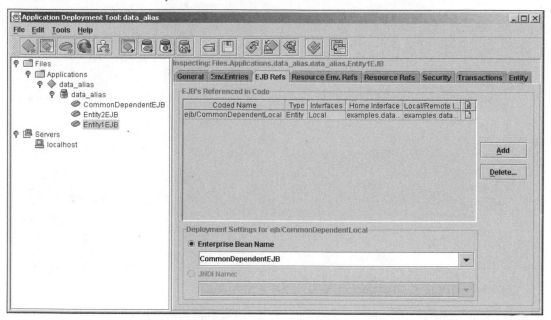

Here we see the EJB QL queries for both the `Entity1EJB` and `Entity2EJB` beans. They can be found by selectin the **Entity** tab for each bean, and then pressing the **Finder/Select Methods...** button:

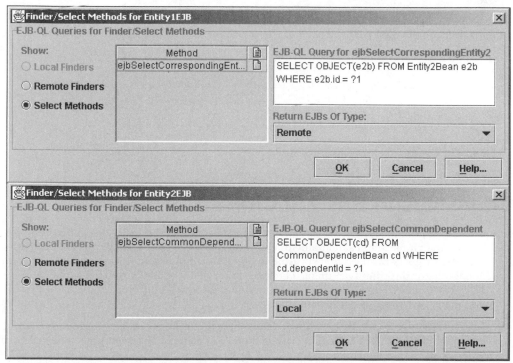

If we look at the Deployment Settings... for either bean and choose to view the Select Methods we will then see the SQL query created from the EJB QL query:

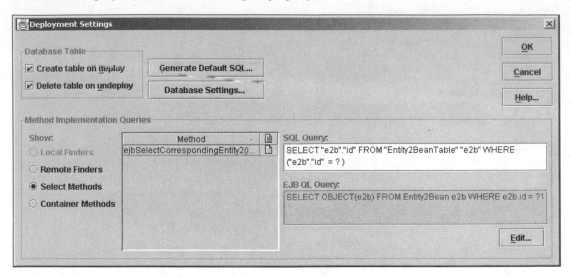

The JNDI information for the application is:

- ❏ Component: Entity1EJB   JNDI Name: Entity1EJB
- ❏ Component: Entity2EJB   JNDI Name: Entity2EJB
- ❏ Component: CommonDependentEJB   JNDI Name: CommonDependentLocal

Once the application is deployed, we need to run the client to see if the application worked.

Run the command line:

```
java -classpath %J2EE_HOME%\lib\j2ee.jar;data_aliasClient.jar;.
    examples.data_alias.Client
```

We should then get the result printed to the console:

Dependent object preserved identity: true

Relationships in EJB 2.0 CMP

In the overview of relationships in the last chapter, we learned that the EJB 2.0 specification provides for much more than a mechanical mapping of entities to database tables. Rather, it provides for the ability to model complex business objects using fine-grained entities with local interfaces, and uni- and bi-directional relationships between them. The three basic relationship cardinalities (one-to-one, one-to-many, and many-to-many) are all supported. In addition, these relationships can be navigated using the new query language of the EJB 2.0 specification.

In the previous sections, you have seen how relationships are implemented as abstract accessor methods that return either an entity or a collection class of entities. You have also seen how these relationships are described in the deployment descriptor.

This section provides additional details that you will need to model relationships correctly and effectively. The following topics are addressed:

- ❑ Relationship naming conventions
- ❑ Relationships and the JNDI namespace
- ❑ Referential integrity
- ❑ Relationship aliasing
- ❑ Fail-fast iteration

Relationship Naming Conventions

As we saw earlier, a relationship between two entities is represented in the deployment descriptor as an `<ejb-relation>` element. An `<ejb-relation>` element always consists of two `<ejb-relationship-role>` elements (because a relationship is always between two EJB component participants).

An `<ejb-relation>` element can have an `<ejb-relation-name>` element to name that relation. The name is optional, but if present it must be unique in that JAR. It has no explicit purpose in the EJB specification, typically being used for documentation. We strongly recommend that you provide names for all your relationships.

An `<ejb-relationship-role>` element can have an `<ejb-relationship-role-name>` element to name that relationship role. The name is optional, and different relationships can use the same role name for their roles. The role name has no explicit purpose in the EJB specification, again typically being used for documentation. We strongly recommend that you provide names for all your roles, and we further recommend that they be unique within a JAR.

> There is no official recommendation for relationship and role naming conventions. What follows is our recommended naming convention. You should obviously feel free to substitute your own naming convention if it makes more sense in your environment. Even if you use this naming convention, you should alter the names if a more appropriate name would provide clearer documentation for a particular case.

The relationship name is created by combining the names of the two business objects that participate in the relationship (optionally separated by a hyphen). If the relationship is navigable in one direction only, the source for the navigable relationship should be listed first. If there is an obvious parent-child relationship, the parent should be listed first. Otherwise, order doesn't matter. For instance, if there is a bi-directional relationship between a husband entity and a wife entity, the relationship could be named `Husband-Wife` or `WifeHusband`. If there was a uni-directional relationship between an order entity and a product entity, the relationship should be named `OrderProduct` (or `Order-Product`).

The role name follows the pattern of role source, followed by a verb or preposition describing the relationship, followed by the role target (in its plural form if the role target's multiplicity is `Many`). Examples of the naming convention with a one-to-many relationship are the roles for the `OrderLineItem` relationship. They would be named `OrderHasLineItems` and `LineItemInOrder`.

An example of the naming convention with a many-to-many relationship might be the roles for the Teacher-Student relationship. They would be `TeacherForStudents` and `StudentHasTeachers`. Notice that the first object in the role name is never plural. A relationship role is described from the standpoint of a single instance, so it would not make sense to have `TeachersForStudents` or `StudentsHaveTeachers`.

Relationships and the JNDI Namespace

If an EJB component uses other EJBs acquired from the JNDI namespace, it must declare its use of these EJB components using an `<ejb-ref>` or `<ejb-local-ref>` element. These references are then bound to actual EJB components at deployment time. The optional `<ejb-link>` element can be used to pre-bind a reference to a particular EJB within an application. Of course, this is not specific to EJB 2.0 persistence, and is explained in Chapter 8.

Entities that are acquired from relationship accessors or from `ejbSelect()` methods do not require the EJB component developer to directly use the JNDI namespace. As a result, no `<ejb-ref>` or `<ejb-local-ref>` declaration need be made in the deployment descriptor. If, however, the bean developer retrieves a home interface through a JNDI context (usually `javax.naming.InitialContext`), the reference must be declared in the deployment descriptor in the usual way.

It is typically unnecessary to retrieve the home interface of an EJB 2.0 CMP entity just to call a finder method, if that entity is defined in the same JAR. Instead, a corresponding `ejbSelect()` method could be used to accomplish the same purpose. However, it would be necessary to use the home interface of such an entity to create new instances or to call home-interface business methods; this concept is covered later in the chapter.

Referential Integrity

Referential integrity in EJB 2.0 relationships is similar to referential integrity in SQL databases. It means that the rules that you have declared regarding your objects are enforced by the system. In the case of EJB relationships, referential integrity is enforced by ensuring that the cardinality of relationships can't be violated by the component developer. Referential integrity also prevents dependent elements being orphaned (for example, in our earlier invoice example, removing the master should automatically clean up the detail lines).

There are three cardinalities that a relationship might have: one-to-one; one-to-many; and many-to-many. In a one-to-one relationship, the referential integrity rule is that both participants in the relationship must be referenced exclusively by their respective target. For example, if there is a one-to-one spouse relationship between an employee and a person record, no other person record may reference the employee as a spouse. Similarly, no two employees may have a spouse relationship with the same person.

In a one-to-many relationship, the referential integrity rule is that an object on the many side of the relationship may be referenced exclusively by a single target. For example, if there is a one-to-many relationship between an order and its line-items, a line-item may be referenced exclusively by a single order. It is illegal for two orders to reference the same line item. On the other hand, the object on the one side of the relationship may be referenced by multiple targets. For example, the order may be referenced by many line-items.

There are no similar referential integrity rules regarding a many-to-many relationship.

Collection Semantics and Referential Integrity

Typically the collection returned from the get accessor for a one-to-many or many-to-many relationship has the normal collection semantics. In other words, all the methods work the way you would expect them to. However, the add() and addAll() methods for a one-to-many relationship (not a many-to-many relationship) have slightly different behavior to ensure referential integrity. If you add an entity to a relationship, and it already has a relationship with a different instance, it should be removed from that original relationship. If this didn't occur, the entity would have turned its one-to-many relationship into a many-to-many relationship.

Referential integrity also applies to the ejbRemove() method. When an entity is deleted, it is also automatically removed from all the relationships in which it participates.

For instance, judges may have a one-to-many relationship with their cases. In other words, one judge has many cases, but each case must belong to at most one judge. If there were no referential integrity support from the EJB container, it would be possible to add an already-assigned case to a different judge's caseload. At this point, there would be two judges for the same case, and the business rules of the application would have been violated. However, there is referential integrity support from the EJB container. If a case is added to a judge's caseload, it will be removed from any existing relationship with a judge. Let us look at some code for this judge-case example.

The judge-case example comprises the following eight files:

File Name	File Description
Judge.java	The remote component interface for the Judge EJB
JudgeHome.java	The remote home interface for the Judge EJB
JudgeBean.java	The implementation class for the Judge EJB
CaseLocal.java	The local component interface for the Case EJB
CaseLocalHome.java	The local home interface for the Case EJB
CaseLocalBean.java	The implementation class for the Case EJB
ejb-jar.xml	The deployment descriptor
Client.java	A very simple client to test our beans

The Judge Remote Interface

The assignNewCase() method asks the judge entity to create a new case entity object and assign it to the current judge. The transferCase() method finds a case assigned to an existing judge, and transfers it to this judge through the add() method of the relationship collection. It also (for the purposes of this demonstration) verifies that the referential integrity of the judges and their caseloads has been maintained:

```
package examples.judge_case;

import java.rmi.RemoteException;
import javax.ejb.CreateException;
import javax.ejb.EJBObject;
```

```
import javax.ejb.FinderException;

public interface Judge extends EJBObject {

  public long[] getAssignedCaseLoad() throws RemoteException;

  public void assignNewCase(long docketNumber, String caseName)
            throws RemoteException, CreateException;

  public void transferCase(long docketNumber, int fromJudge)
            throws RemoteException, FinderException;
}
```

The Judge Home Interface

This is a typical home interface;

```
package examples.judge_case;

import java.rmi.RemoteException;
import javax.ejb.CreateException;
import javax.ejb.EJBHome;
import javax.ejb.FinderException;

public interface JudgeHome extends EJBHome {

  public Judge create(int judgeId, String judgeName)
            throws CreateException, RemoteException;

  public Judge findByPrimaryKey(Integer judgeId)
            throws FinderException, RemoteException;
}
```

The Judge Implementation Class

There are also three ejbSelect() methods defined. One finds a judge, given their ID. The second retrieves the cases for a particular judge. The third finds a case, given its ID.

```
package examples.judge_case;

import java.util.Collection;
import java.util.Iterator;
import javax.ejb.CreateException;
import javax.ejb.EJBException;
import javax.ejb.EntityBean;
import javax.ejb.EntityContext;
import javax.ejb.FinderException;
import javax.naming.InitialContext;

public abstract class JudgeBean implements EntityBean {

  public abstract int getJudgeId();
  public abstract void setJudgeId(int judgeId);

  public abstract String getJudgeName();
  public abstract void setJudgeName(String judgeName);
```

```
public abstract Collection getAssignedCases();
public abstract void setAssignedCases(Collection assignedCases);

public abstract CaseLocal ejbSelectCase(long docketNumber)
                          throws FinderException;

public abstract Collection ejbSelectCases(int judgeId)
                          throws FinderException;

public abstract Judge ejbSelectJudge(int judgeId)
                       throws FinderException;

public long[] getAssignedCaseLoad() {
  long[] results = new long[getAssignedCases().size()];
  Iterator iterCases = getAssignedCases().iterator();
  int iter = 0;
  while (iterCases.hasNext()) {
    CaseLocal c = (CaseLocal) iterCases.next();
    results[iter++] = c.getDocketNumber();
  }
  return results;
}


private CaseLocal createCase(long docketNumber, String caseName)
                  throws CreateException {
  try {
    InitialContext initial = new InitialContext();
    CaseLocalHome home = (CaseLocalHome)
                                      initial.lookup(
                                        "java:comp/env/ejb/CaseLocal");
    return home.create(docketNumber, caseName);
  } catch (Exception e) {
    throw new javax.ejb.EJBException(e);
  }
}

public void assignNewCase(long docketNumber, String caseName)
            throws CreateException {
  CaseLocal c = createCase(docketNumber, caseName);
  getAssignedCases().add(c);
}

private boolean verifyDocket(long[] caseLoad, long docketNumber) {
  for (int iter=0; iter<caseLoad.length; iter++) {
    if (caseLoad[iter] == docketNumber) {
      return true;
    }
  }
  return false;
}
```

This method would not typically test to ensure that the referential integrity has been maintained, as that is a mandated feature of all EJB 2.0 containers. However, we do it here to demonstrate how the feature works. Note that if the EJB container were not responsible for referential integrity, the original judge would still think the case was assigned to them:

```
    public void transferCase(long docketNumber, int fromJudge)
            throws FinderException {

      try {
        Judge judge = ejbSelectJudge(fromJudge);
        long[] assignedCaseLoad = judge.getAssignedCaseLoad();
        if (!verifyDocket(assignedCaseLoad, docketNumber)) {
          throw new EJBException("Judge didn't have case");
        }
        CaseLocal c = ejbSelectCase(docketNumber);
        getAssignedCases().add(c);

        assignedCaseLoad = judge.getAssignedCaseLoad();
        if (verifyDocket(assignedCaseLoad, docketNumber)) {
          throw new EJBException("Judge didn't lose case");
        }
      } catch (java.rmi.RemoteException re) {
        throw new EJBException(re);
      }
    }

    public Integer ejbCreate(int judgeId, String judgeName) throws CreateException {
      setJudgeId(judgeId);
      setJudgeName(judgeName);
      return null;
    }

    public void ejbPostCreate(int judgeId, String judgeName)
            throws CreateException {}

    public void ejbActivate() {}
    public void ejbLoad() {}
    public void ejbPassivate() {}
    public void ejbRemove() {}
    public void ejbStore() {}
    public void setEntityContext(EntityContext ctx) {}
    public void unsetEntityContext() {}
}
```

The Case Local Component Interface

In many respects, the case entity acts like a dependent value object. Its only purpose is to hold a docket number and a case name. However, it is a "dependent value object" with a difference: it is managed by the EJB container:

```
package examples.judge_case;

import javax.ejb.EJBLocalObject;

public interface CaseLocal extends EJBLocalObject {
  public long getDocketNumber();
  public String getCaseName();
  public void setCaseName(String caseName);
}
```

The Case Local Home Interface

Just a standard local home interface:

```
package examples.judge_case;

import javax.ejb.CreateException;
import javax.ejb.EJBLocalHome;
import javax.ejb.FinderException;

public interface CaseLocalHome extends EJBLocalHome {

  public CaseLocal findByPrimaryKey(Long docketNumber) throws FinderException;

  public CaseLocal create(long docketNumber, String caseName)
                    throws CreateException;
}
```

The Case Implementation Class

There is no significant business logic in the implementation class:

```
package examples.judge_case;

import javax.ejb.CreateException;
import javax.ejb.EntityBean;
import javax.ejb.EntityContext;

public abstract class CaseBean implements EntityBean {

  public abstract long getDocketNumber();
  public abstract void setDocketNumber(long docketNumber);

  public abstract String getCaseName();
  public abstract void setCaseName(String caseName);

  public Long ejbCreate(long docketNumber, String caseName)
            throws CreateException {
    setDocketNumber(docketNumber);
    setCaseName(caseName);
    return null;
  }

  public void ejbPostCreate(long docketNumber, String caseName)
            throws CreateException {}

  public void ejbActivate() {}
  public void ejbLoad() {}
  public void ejbPassivate() {}
  public void ejbRemove() {}
  public void ejbStore() {}
  public void setEntityContext(EntityContext ctx) {}
  public void unsetEntityContext() {}
}
```

The Deployment Descriptor–ejb-jar.xml

The deployment descriptor defines the relationship on which the referential integrity rules are based. It also defines the entities and EJB QL queries from this example:

```xml
<?xml version="1.0" encoding="UTF-8"?>

<!DOCTYPE ejb-jar PUBLIC ' //Sun Microsystems, Inc.//DTD Enterprise JavaBeans
2.0//EN' 'http://java.sun.com/dtd/ejb-jar_2_0.dtd'>

<ejb-jar>
  <display-name>judge_case</display-name>
  <enterprise-beans>
    <entity>
      <display-name>JudgeEJB</display-name>
      <ejb-name>JudgeEJB</ejb-name>
      <home>examples.judge_case.JudgeHome</home>
      <remote>examples.judge_case.Judge</remote>
      <ejb-class>examples.judge_case.JudgeBean</ejb-class>
      <persistence-type>Container</persistence-type>
      <prim-key-class>java.lang.Integer</prim-key-class>
      <reentrant>True</reentrant>
      <cmp-version>2.x</cmp-version>
      <abstract-schema-name>JudgeBean</abstract-schema-name>
      <cmp-field><field-name>judgeName</field-name></cmp-field>
      <cmp-field><field-name>judgeId</field-name></cmp-field>
      <primkey-field>judgeId</primkey-field>
```

We use the local home interface of the `Case` entity bean to create new cases, so we need to declare this reference in the deployment descriptor:

```xml
      <ejb-local-ref>
        <ejb-ref-name>ejb/CaseLocal</ejb-ref-name>
        <ejb-ref-type>Entity</ejb-ref-type>
        <local-home>examples.judge_case.CaseLocalHome</local-home>
        <local>examples.judge_case.CaseLocal</local>
        <ejb-link>CaseEJB</ejb-link>
      </ejb-local-ref>
```

Here are the query language descriptions of the behavior of the `ejbSelect()` methods. By default, they return local interfaces (which is what we want). If we needed to select a remote interface, we could use the optional `<result-type-mapping>` element, which can have the value of `Remote` or `Local`. The `<result-type-mapping>` element is a child of the `<query>` element:

```xml
      <query>
        <query-method>
          <method-name>ejbSelectCase</method-name>
          <method-params>
            <method-param>long</method-param>
          </method-params>
        </query-method>
        <result-type-mapping>Local</result-type-mapping>
        <ejb-ql>
          SELECT OBJECT(c) FROM CaseBean c WHERE c.docketNumber = ?1
```

```
          </ejb-ql>
        </query>
        <query>
          <query-method>
            <method-name>ejbSelectCases</method-name>
            <method-params>
              <method-param>int</method-param>
            </method-params>
          </query-method>
          <result-type-mapping>Local</result-type-mapping>
          <ejb-ql>
            SELECT OBJECT(c) FROM JudgeBean jb, IN (jb.assignedCases) c WHERE
            jb.judgeId = ?1
          </ejb-ql>
        </query>
        <query>
          <query-method>
            <method-name>ejbSelectJudge</method-name>
            <method-params>
              <method-param>int</method-param>
            </method-params>
          </query-method>
          <result-type-mapping>Remote</result-type-mapping>
          <ejb-ql>
            SELECT OBJECT(jb) FROM JudgeBean jb WHERE jb.judgeId = ?1
          </ejb-ql>
        </query>
      </entity>

      <entity>
        <display-name>CaseEJB</display-name>
        <ejb-name>CaseEJB</ejb-name>
        <local-home>examples.judge_case.CaseLocalHome</local-home>
        <local>examples.judge_case.CaseLocal</local>
        <ejb-class>examples.judge_case.CaseBean</ejb-class>
        <persistence-type>Container</persistence-type>
        <prim-key-class>java.lang.Long</prim-key-class>
        <reentrant>True</reentrant>
        <cmp-version>2.x</cmp-version>
        <abstract-schema-name>CaseBean</abstract-schema-name>
        <cmp-field>
          <field-name>caseName</field-name>
        </cmp-field>
        <cmp-field>
          <field-name>docketNumber</field-name>
        </cmp-field>
        <primkey-field>docketNumber</primkey-field>
        <security-identity>
          <use-caller-identity></use-caller-identity>
        </security-identity>
      </entity>
    </enterprise-beans>
```

If the multiplicity of the role were Many instead of One, there would be nothing to show in this example. When the case was added to the new judge's caseload, the original judge could also retain the case with no violation of the application's business logic:

```
<relationships>
  <ejb-relation>
    <ejb-relation-name></ejb-relation-name>
    <ejb-relationship-role>
      <ejb-relationship-role-name>JudgeEJB</ejb-relationship-role-name>
      <multiplicity>one</multiplicity>
      <relationship-role-source>
        <ejb-name>JudgeEJB</ejb-name>
      </relationship-role-source>
      <cmr-field>
        <cmr-field-name>assignedCases</cmr-field-name>
        <cmr-field-type>java.util.Collection</cmr-field-type>
      </cmr-field>
    </ejb-relationship-role>
    <ejb-relationship-role>
      <ejb-relationship-role-name>CaseEJB</ejb-relationship-role-name>
      <multiplicity>many</multiplicity>
      <relationship-role-source>
        <ejb-name>CaseEJB</ejb-name>
      </relationship-role-source>
    </ejb-relationship-role>
  </ejb-relation>
</relationships>

<assembly-descriptor>
  <container-transaction>
    <method>
      <ejb-name>JudgeEJB</ejb-name>
      <method-name>*</method-name>
    </method>
    <trans-attribute>Required</trans-attribute>
  </container-transaction>
  <container-transaction>
    <method>
      <ejb-name>CaseEJB</ejb-name>
      <method-name>*</method-name>
    </method>
    <trans-attribute>Required</trans-attribute>
  </container-transaction>
</assembly-descriptor>
</ejb-jar>
```

The Client

This provides a very simple test of the application:

```
package examples.judge_case;

import javax.naming.InitialContext;
import javax.rmi.PortableRemoteObject;

public class Client {
  public static void main(String[] args) {
    try {
      InitialContext initial = new InitialContext();
```

```
            JudgeHome judgeHome = (JudgeHome)
              PortableRemoteObject.narrow(
                 initial.lookup("JudgeEJB"), JudgeHome.class);

            Judge judge1 = judgeHome.create(1, "Antonin Scalia");
            judge1.assignNewCase(1000, "Florida Election Case");

            Judge judge2 = judgeHome.create(2, "John Paul Stevens");
            judge2.transferCase(1000, 1);

         } catch (Exception e) {
            e.printStackTrace();
         }
      }
   }
```

An exception means that your EJB container did not properly enforce referential integrity rules.

Relationship Setter Methods

Typically, you will manipulate a many-valued relationship using its collection class, and a single-valued relationship using its abstract set accessor. However, there are circumstances when you may want to use the set accessors for collection-valued relationships as well. The EJB container enforces referential integrity here, too, so the exact behavior of a relationship set accessor depends on the cardinality of the relationship.

If the setter takes a single value as an argument and it is part of a **one-to-one relationship**, its use can potentially change the relationship participation of four components. Consider the example of a husband entity and a wife entity, with the following instances and relationships:

- ❑ The husband instance John has a relationship with (is-married-to) the wife instance Susan
- ❑ The reciprocal is true: Susan is-married-to John
- ❑ The husband instance Fred has a relationship with (is-married-to) the wife instance Eileen
- ❑ The reciprocal is true: Eileen is-married-to Fred

If we call the setWife() method on the John instance with a parameter of Eileen, this has the following consequences:

- ❑ The husband instance John has a relationship with (is-married-to) the wife instance Eileen
- ❑ The reciprocal is true: Eileen is-married-to John
- ❑ The husband instance Fred has a null value for the is-married-to relationship, and a call to getWife() will return null
- ❑ The wife instance Susan has a null value for the is-married-to relationship, and a call to getHusband() will return null

If the setter takes a single value and is part of a **many-to-one relationship**, its use can potentially change the relationship participation of three components. Consider the example of a line item for the purchase of the book *"Professional EJB"*, which is originally part of order# 20057. If its setOrder() relationship accessor method is called with a value of order# 20303, it is automatically removed from 20057 to maintain referential integrity.

If the setter takes a collection class and is part of a **one-to-many relationship**, it is the equivalent of calling clear(), followed by addAll(), on the target collection. However, remember that add() and addAll() have special semantics on collections, that represent one-to-many relationships, to enforce referential integrity. The instance is removed from its current relationship, if any. In this case, it is removed from the source collection. In other words, calling the set method for a one-to-many collection-valued relationship is the equivalent of moving the instances from one to the other. In the case of Judge entity instances and their cases, calling judge2.setCases(judge1.getCases()) transfers the caseload of one judge to the other judge, and leaves the first judge without any cases at all

If the setter takes a collection class and is part of a **many-to-many relationship**, there are no referential integrity rules that need to be enforced. This simply makes the contents of the target collection equal to the contents of the source collection.

In no case is the actual collection instance changed. The lifecycle of the collection instance is managed by the EJB container and is not affected by calling set methods for it. Only the contents of the collection change.

Deployment

We will create the application giving it the name judge_case, after the package name and importing our JAR file. Now we have the beans we can enter the database information again, with is still jdbc/Cloudscape, generate the SQL for the application and then save the file.

Most of the deployment information is of a similar type to the previous example, so we will just show the altered areas.

Here we can see the relationship set up as a one-to-many allowing a single judge to have access to multiple cases, although this does not allow a case to be on more than one judge's caseload. It would be allowed if the multiplicity was set to *:* (many-to-many):

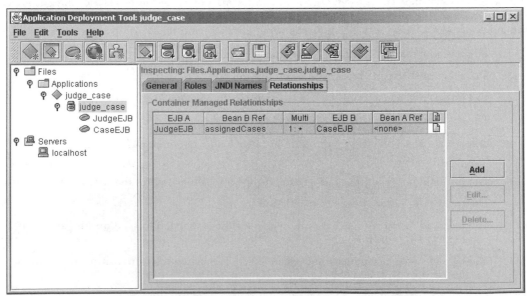

The JNDI information for the application is:

- ❑ Component: JudgeEJB   JNDI Name: JudgeEJB
- ❑ Component: CaseEJB   JNDI Name: CaseLocal

Once the application is deployed, we need to run the client to see if the application worked.

Run the command line:

```
java -classpath %J2EE_HOME%\lib\j2ee.jar;judge_caseClient.jar;.
        examples.judge_case.Client
```

If the application runs correctly we should not get any messages returned to us, if anything goes wrong with the referential integrity of the application we will get an error message sent to us.

Relationship Aliasing

Data aliasing refers to the situation where there are multiple representations of the same data. We have already seen how the EJB 2.0 model of container-managed persistence solves this problem for dependent objects. (Local interfaces make it practical to replace dependent value objects with entities in your object model.) The EJB 2.0 specification similarly requires that in cases where there are multiple representations of a relationship, all representations are kept consistent.

There will only be multiple representations of a relationship in the case of a bi-directional relationship, where (assuming both the source and the target have been instantiated) there will be exactly two representations. When a change is made to the source of a bi-directional relationship, that change will be reflected in the target.

Fail-fast Iteration

An iterator (that is, a class implementing `java.util.Iterator`) assumes that the collection class through which it is iterating does not change during the iteration, except through that iterator interface. If this assumption is violated, it could in general lead to **non-deterministic error behavior**. In other words, it could lead to bugs that only occur during demonstrations in front of major prospects, and can't be reproduced by developers or QA people.

The collection classes provided by the JDK (in the `java.util` package) instead implement **fail-fast** behavior. During iteration, the iterator detects any outside modification to the collection class and throws a `java.util.ConcurrentModificationException` exception. That way, instead of non-deterministic behavior, the developer is notified immediately that they have violated the contract with the iterator. EJB containers provide fail-fast implementations of their collections rather than allow non-deterministic behavior, although they will throw a `java.lang.IllegalStateException` instead of a `java.util.ConcurrentModificationException`.

The EJB container automatically modifies collection classes that represent relationships to ensure their referential integrity. The component developer should be aware of circumstances under which this could lead to a concurrent modification. When they are iterating through a collection representing a relationship with a one-to-many cardinality, they should be aware that adding any entity in that collection to a different instance of the collection class will result in a change to the original collection "behind their back".

> Since the `java.lang.IllegalStateException` exception is a run-time exception, it does not need to be declared in a method's signature. If thrown, it will result in a rollback of the current transaction and the ejection of the current EJB instance from the container.

An Example of Fail-fast Iteration and its Avoidance

The circumstances under which a java.lang.IllegalStateException might be thrown are easy to understand with an example. Here we have a distributor with many sales offices, each sales office having many sales representatives. We'll see a wrong way and a correct way to transfer sales reps to a different sales office.

This example comprises 11 files:

File Name	File Description
Distributor.java	The remote component interface of the Distributor entity bean
DistributorHome.java	The remote home interface of the Distributor entity bean
DistributorBean.java	The implementation class of the Distributor entity bean
SalesOfficeLocal.java	The local component interface of the SalesOffice entity bean
SalesOfficeLocalHome.java	The local home interface of the SalesOffice entity bean
SalesOfficeBean.java	The implementation class for the SalesOffice entity bean
SalesRepLocal.java	The local component interface for the SalesRep entity bean
SalesRepLocalHome.java	The local home interface for the SalesRep entity bean
SalesRepBean.java	The implementation class for the SalesRep entity bean
ejb-jar.xml	The deployment descriptor
Client.java	A simple client to test our model

This is the sequence of events that causes a ConcurrentModificationException to be thrown:

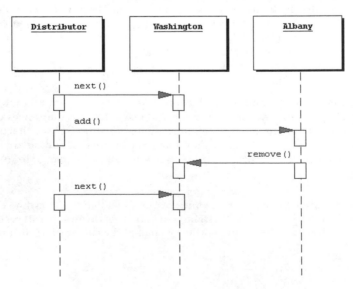

The following sequence of events successfully accomplishes the transfer:

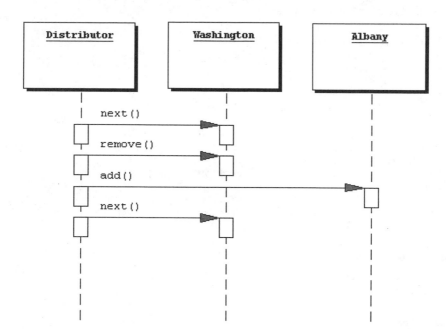

Distributor Remote Interface

This interface provides three business methods. One simply sets up an office and some sales representatives. The other two try to transfer sales representatives between two offices. The first of those (`incorrectTransferOfSalesReps()`) does so in a way that the iterator will throw an exception. The second does the transfer correctly:

```
package examples.distributor;

import java.rmi.RemoteException;
import javax.ejb.CreateException;
import javax.ejb.EJBObject;
import javax.ejb.FinderException;

public interface Distributor extends EJBObject {

  public void addOffice(String location, String[] salesReps, double[] salesVolume)
          throws CreateException, RemoteException;

  public void incorrectTransferOfSalesReps(String originalLocation,
                                    String newLocation, double minVolume)
          throws RemoteException, FinderException;

  public void correctTransferOfSalesReps(String originalLocation,
                                    String newLocation, double minVolume)
          throws RemoteException, FinderException;
}
```

Distributor Remote Home Interface

This is a standard remote home interface:

```
package examples.distributor;

import java.rmi.RemoteException;
import javax.ejb.CreateException;
import javax.ejb.EJBHome;
import javax.ejb.FinderException;

public interface DistributorHome extends EJBHome {

  public Distributor create(String distributorName)
                     throws CreateException, RemoteException;

  public Distributor findByPrimaryKey(String distributorName)
                     throws FinderException, RemoteException;
}
```

Distributor Implementation Class

The implementation class provides abstract select methods and accessor methods, as well as the implementations for the business methods:

```
package examples.distributor;

import java.util.Collection;
import java.util.Iterator;
import javax.ejb.CreateException;
import javax.ejb.EJBException;
import javax.ejb.EntityBean;
import javax.ejb.EntityContext;
import javax.ejb.FinderException;
import javax.naming.InitialContext;

public abstract class DistributorBean implements EntityBean {

  public abstract String getDistributorName();
  public abstract void setDistributorName(String distributorName);

  public abstract Collection getOffices();
  public abstract void setOffices(Collection offices);
```

This `ejbSelect()` method, `ejbSelectSalesOffice()`, will only select a sales office that belongs to this distributor. To accomplish this, we pass in the distributor's key fields (in this case, just the distributor name):

```
  public abstract SalesOfficeLocal ejbSelectSalesOffice(String distributorName,
                                                        String salesRepName)
                             throws FinderException;
```

This just sets up an office and its sales representatives:

```
    public void addOffice(String location, String[] salesReps, double[] salesVolume)
            throws CreateException {

      SalesOfficeLocal salesOffice = createOffice(location);
      for (int iter=0; iter<salesReps.length; iter++) {
        SalesRepLocal salesRep = createSalesRep(salesReps[iter], salesVolume[iter]);
        salesOffice.getSalesReps().add(salesRep);
      }
      getOffices().add(salesOffice);
    }
```

In this method, the addition of the sales representative to a different office will trigger their implicit removal from the first office. This removal alters the relationship collection "behind the iterator's back", and so the next access by the iterator will throw a `java.util.IllegalStateException`. The transaction will be rolled back and this instance will be ejected from the container:

```
    public void incorrectTransferOfSalesReps(String originalLocationName,
                                             String newLocationName,
                                             double minVolume)
            throws FinderException {

      SalesOfficeLocal originalLocation = ejbSelectSalesOffice(
                              getDistributorName(), originalLocationName);
      SalesOfficeLocal newLocation = ejbSelectSalesOffice(
                              getDistributorName(), newLocationName);

      Iterator iterRepsOriginal = originalLocation.getSalesReps().iterator();
      while (iterRepsOriginal.hasNext()) {
        SalesRepLocal rep = (SalesRepLocal) iterRepsOriginal.next();
        if (rep.getSalesVolume() >= minVolume) {
          newLocation.getSalesReps().add(rep);
        }
      }
    }
```

Here, we use the iterator (by calling `iterRepsOriginal.remove()`) to remove the sales representative from the original office before adding them to their new office. As the collection was modified with the iterator (and not implicitly), no exception will be thrown on the next access:

```
    public void correctTransferOfSalesReps(String originalLocationName,
                                           String newLocationName, double minVolume)
            throws FinderException {

      SalesOfficeLocal originalLocation = ejbSelectSalesOffice(
                              getDistributorName(), originalLocationName);
      SalesOfficeLocal newLocation = ejbSelectSalesOffice(
                              getDistributorName(), newLocationName);

      Iterator iterRepsOriginal = originalLocation.getSalesReps().iterator();
      while (iterRepsOriginal.hasNext()) {
        SalesRepLocal rep = (SalesRepLocal) iterRepsOriginal.next();
        if (rep.getSalesVolume() >= minVolume) {
          iterRepsOriginal.remove();
```

```
          newLocation.getSalesReps().add(rep);
      }
    }
  }
```

Below is a utility method to create an instance of the sales office entity. It uses the local home interface, and returns a local component interface:

```
public SalesOfficeLocal createOffice(String location) throws CreateException {

  try {
    InitialContext initial = new InitialContext();
    SalesOfficeLocalHome home = (SalesOfficeLocalHome)
                                    initial.lookup(
                                        "java:comp/env/ejb/SalesOfficeEJB");
    return home.create(location);
  } catch (Exception e) {
    throw new javax.ejb.EJBException(e);
  }
}
```

This is a utility method to create an instance of the sales rep entity. It also uses the local home interface, and returns a local component interface:

```
public SalesRepLocal createSalesRep(String repName, double salesVolume)
                  throws CreateException {

  try {
    InitialContext initial = new InitialContext();
    SalesRepLocalHome home = (SalesRepLocalHome)
                                    initial.lookup(
                                        "java:comp/env/ejb/SalesRepEJB");
    return home.create(repName, salesVolume);
  } catch (Exception e) {
    throw new javax.ejb.EJBException(e);
  }
}

public String ejbCreate(String distributorName) throws CreateException {
  setDistributorName(distributorName);
  return null;
}

public void ejbPostCreate(String distributorName) throws CreateException {}

public void ejbActivate() {}
public void ejbLoad() {}
public void ejbPassivate() {}
public void ejbRemove() {}
public void ejbStore() {}
public void setEntityContext(EntityContext ctx) {}
public void unsetEntityContext() {}
}
```

SalesOffice Local Component Interface

We can return the relationship collection class of sales reps across a local component interface. We could not do this across a remote interface:

```
package examples.distributor;

import java.util.Collection;
import javax.ejb.EJBLocalObject;

public interface SalesOfficeLocal extends EJBLocalObject {

  public String getLocation();
  public Collection getSalesReps();
  public void setSalesReps(Collection salesReps);
}
```

SalesOffice Local Home Interface

This is another standard local home interface:

```
package examples.distributor;

import javax.ejb.CreateException;
import javax.ejb.EJBLocalHome;
import javax.ejb.FinderException;

public interface SalesOfficeLocalHome extends EJBLocalHome {

  public SalesOfficeLocal findByPrimaryKey(String location)
                          throws FinderException;

  public SalesOfficeLocal create(String location) throws CreateException;
}
```

SalesOffice Implementation Class

There is little business logic in this class, which operates here much like a dependent value object:

```
package examples.distributor;

import java.util.Collection;
import javax.ejb.CreateException;
import javax.ejb.EntityBean;
import javax.ejb.EntityContext;

public abstract class SalesOfficeBean implements EntityBean {

  public abstract String getLocation();
  public abstract void setLocation(String location);

  public abstract Collection getSalesReps();
  public abstract void setSalesReps(Collection salesReps);

  public String ejbCreate(String location) throws CreateException {
    setLocation(location);
    return null;
```

```
      }

      public void ejbPostCreate(String location) throws CreateException {}

      public void ejbActivate() {}
      public void ejbLoad() {}
      public void ejbPassivate() {}
      public void ejbRemove() {}
      public void ejbStore() {}
      public void setEntityContext(EntityContext ctx) {}
      public void unsetEntityContext() {}
}
```

SalesRep Local Component Interface

We just expose the abstract getters and setters of the implementation class – except, of course, for the key field setter:

```
package examples.distributor;

import javax.ejb.EJBLocalObject;

public interface SalesRepLocal extends EJBLocalObject {
  public String getRepName();
  public double getSalesVolume();
  public void setSalesVolume(double volume);
}
```

SalesRep Local Home Interface

This is a typical local home interface:

```
package examples.distributor;

import javax.ejb.CreateException;
import javax.ejb.EJBLocalHome;
import javax.ejb.FinderException;

public interface SalesRepLocalHome extends EJBLocalHome {

  public SalesRepLocal findByPrimaryKey(String name) throws FinderException;

  public SalesRepLocal create(String name, double volume) throws CreateException;
}
```

SalesRep Implementation Class

Again, there happens to be little business logic in this class:

```
package examples.distributor;

import javax.ejb.CreateException;
import javax.ejb.EntityBean;
```

```java
import javax.ejb.EntityContext;

public abstract class SalesRepBean implements EntityBean {

  public abstract String getRepName();
  public abstract void setRepName(String repName);

  public abstract double getSalesVolume();
  public abstract void setSalesVolume(double volume);

  public String ejbCreate(String repName, double salesVolume)
              throws CreateException {
    setRepName(repName);
    setSalesVolume(salesVolume);
    return null;
  }

  public void ejbPostCreate(String repName, double salesVolume)
             throws CreateException {}

  public void ejbActivate() {}
  public void ejbLoad() {}
  public void ejbPassivate() {}
  public void ejbRemove() {}
  public void ejbStore() {}
  public void setEntityContext(EntityContext ctx) {}
  public void unsetEntityContext() {}
}
```

Deployment Descriptor – ejb-jar.xml

The deployment descriptor describes the entity schemas, the queries, the relationships, and the component's environments:

```xml
<?xml version="1.0" encoding="UTF-8"?>

<!DOCTYPE ejb-jar PUBLIC '-//Sun Microsystems, Inc.//DTD Enterprise JavaBeans
2.0//EN' 'http://java.sun.com/dtd/ejb-jar_2_0.dtd'>

<ejb-jar>
  <display-name>distributor</display-name>
  <enterprise-beans>
    <entity>
```

This section describes the Distributor entity:

```xml
<display-name>DistributorEJB</display-name>
<ejb-name>DistributorEJB</ejb-name>
<home>examples.distributor.DistributorHome</home>
<remote>examples.distributor.Distributor</remote>
<ejb-class>examples.distributor.DistributorBean</ejb-class>
<persistence-type>Container</persistence-type>
<prim-key-class>java.lang.String</prim-key-class>
<reentrant>True</reentrant>
```

```
<cmp-version>2.x</cmp-version>
<abstract-schema-name>DistributorBean</abstract-schema-name>
<cmp-field><field-name>distributorName</field-name></cmp-field>
<primkey-field>distributorName</primkey-field>
```

The Distributor entity retrieves the home interfaces of the `SalesOffice` entity and the `SalesRep` entity from its environment, so we need to declare both those references. It uses the home interfaces to create new instances:

```
<ejb-local-ref>
  <ejb-ref-name>ejb/SalesOfficeEJB</ejb-ref-name>
  <ejb-ref-type>Entity</ejb-ref-type>
  <local-home>examples.distributor.SalesOfficeLocalHome</local-home>
  <local>examples.distributor.SalesOfficeLocal</local>
  <ejb-link>SalesOfficeEJB</ejb-link>
</ejb-local-ref>
<ejb-local-ref>
  <ejb-ref-name>ejb/SalesRepEJB</ejb-ref-name>
  <ejb-ref-type>Entity</ejb-ref-type>
  <local-home>examples.distributor.SalesRepLocalHome</local-home>
  <local>examples.distributor.SalesRepLocal</local>
  <ejb-link>SalesRepEJB</ejb-link>
</ejb-local-ref>
```

This query method selects the sales offices from the relationship collection of the distributor, and not from "all sales offices" as we have previously done. With this query, we only get the offices for a particular distributor:

```
<query>
  <query-method>
    <method-name>ejbSelectSalesOffice</method-name>
    <method-params>
      <method-param>java.lang.String</method-param>
      <method-param>java.lang.String</method-param>
    </method-params>
  </query-method>
  <result-type-mapping>Local</result-type-mapping>
  <ejb-ql>SELECT OBJECT(so) FROM DistributorBean db, IN (db.offices) so
WHERE db.distributorName = ?1 and so.location = ?2</ejb-ql>
  </query>
</entity>
```

The following section describes the `SalesOffice` entity:

```
<entity>
  <display-name>SalesOfficeEJB</display-name>
  <ejb-name>SalesOfficeEJB</ejb-name>
  <local-home>examples.distributor.SalesOfficeLocalHome</local-home>
  <local>examples.distributor.SalesOfficeLocal</local>
  <ejb-class>examples.distributor.SalesOfficeBean</ejb-class>
  <persistence-type>Container</persistence-type>
  <prim-key-class>java.lang.String</prim-key-class>
```

```
        <reentrant>True</reentrant>
        <cmp-version>2.x</cmp-version>
        <abstract-schema-name>SalesOfficeBean</abstract-schema-name>
        <cmp-field>
          <field-name>location</field-name>
        </cmp-field>
        <primkey-field>location</primkey-field>
    </entity>
```

This section describes the `SalesRep` entity:

```
    <entity>
      <display-name>SalesRepEJB</display-name>
      <ejb-name>SalesRepEJB</ejb-name>
      <local-home>examples.distributor.SalesRepLocalHome</local-home>
      <local>examples.distributor.SalesRepLocal</local>
      <ejb-class>examples.distributor.SalesRepBean</ejb-class>
      <persistence-type>Container</persistence-type>
      <prim-key-class>java.lang.String</prim-key-class>
      <reentrant>True</reentrant>
      <cmp-version>2.x</cmp-version>
      <abstract-schema-name>SalesRepBean</abstract-schema-name>
      <cmp-field>
        <field-name>repName</field-name>
      </cmp-field>
      <cmp-field>
        <field-name>salesVolume</field-name>
      </cmp-field>
      <primkey-field>repName</primkey-field>
    </entity>
  </enterprise-beans>
```

The container-managed relationships between the entities are described in this section; the distributor
has sales offices:

```
  <relationships>
    <ejb-relation>
      <ejb-relation-name></ejb-relation-name>
      <ejb-relationship-role>
        <ejb-relationship-role-name>DistributorEJB</ejb-relationship-role-name>
        <multiplicity>one</multiplicity>
        <relationship-role-source>
          <ejb-name>DistributorEJB</ejb-name>
        </relationship-role-source>
        <cmr-field>
          <cmr-field-name>offices</cmr-field-name>
          <cmr-field-type>java.util.Collection</cmr-field-type>
        </cmr-field>
      </ejb-relationship-role>
      <ejb-relationship-role>
        <ejb-relationship-role-name>SalesOfficeEJB</ejb-relationship-role-name>
        <multiplicity>many</multiplicity>
        <relationship-role-source>
```

```
        <ejb-name>SalesOfficeEJB</ejb-name>
      </relationship-role-source>
    </ejb-relationship-role>
  </ejb-relation>
```

The `SalesOfficeSalesRep` relationship is one-to-many. If it were many-to-many, there would be no concurrent modification of the collection class to maintain referential integrity, and therefore no exception would have been thrown in our example:

```
    <ejb-relation>
      <ejb-relation-name></ejb-relation-name>
      <ejb-relationship-role>
        <ejb-relationship-role-name>SalesOfficeEJB</ejb-relationship-role-name>
        <multiplicity>one</multiplicity>
        <relationship-role-source>
          <ejb-name>SalesOfficeEJB</ejb-name>
        </relationship-role-source>
        <cmr-field>
          <cmr-field-name>salesReps</cmr-field-name>
          <cmr-field-type>java.util.Collection</cmr-field-type>
        </cmr-field>
      </ejb-relationship-role>
      <ejb-relationship-role>
        <ejb-relationship-role-name>SalesRepEJB</ejb-relationship-role-name>
        <multiplicity>many</multiplicity>
        <relationship-role-source>
          <ejb-name>SalesRepEJB</ejb-name>
        </relationship-role-source>
      </ejb-relationship-role>
    </ejb-relation>
  </relationships>
```

This is just the standard assembly information. Here we specify the transactional attributes for all the entities:

```
    <assembly-descriptor>
      <container-transaction>
        <method>
          <ejb-name>SalesRepEJB</ejb-name>
          <method-name>*</method-name>
        </method>
        <trans-attribute>Required</trans-attribute>
      </container-transaction>
      <container-transaction>
        <method>
          <ejb-name>SalesOfficeEJB</ejb-name>
          <method-name>*</method-name>
        </method>
        <trans-attribute>Required</trans-attribute>
      </container-transaction>
      <container-transaction>
        <method>
          <ejb-name>DistributorEJB</ejb-name>
          <method-name>*</method-name>
        </method>
```

```
            <trans-attribute>Required</trans-attribute>
          </container-transaction>
        </assembly-descriptor>
</ejb-jar>
```

Client

The client creates the distributor and two offices. It then tries to transfer some sales representatives from one office to another:

```java
package examples.distributor;

import javax.naming.InitialContext;
import javax.rmi.PortableRemoteObject;

public class Client {

  private static final String[] albanyReps = new String[] {
    "Kaylie", "Molly", "Ryan"
  };

  private static final double[] albanyVolume = new double[] {
    55000.0, 57000.0, 48000.0
  };

  private static final String[] washingtonReps = new String[] {
    "Lauren", "Brian", "Nick"
  };

  private static final double[] washingtonVolume = new double[] {
    59000.0, 60000.0, 44500.0
  };

  public static void main(String[] args) {
    try {
      InitialContext initial = new InitialContext();

      DistributorHome distributorHome = (DistributorHome)
                                          PortableRemoteObject.narrow(
                                            initial.lookup("DistributorEJB"),
                                            DistributorHome.class);

      Distributor distributor = distributorHome.create("East Coast Computers");
      distributor.addOffice("Albany", albanyReps, albanyVolume);
      distributor.addOffice("Washington", washingtonReps, washingtonVolume);

      try {
        distributor.incorrectTransferOfSalesReps("Washington", "Albany", 50000.0);
```

As the `java.util.IllegalStateException` is a run time exception, it is not passed on to the client. Instead, we will receive a `java.rmi.RemoteException`:

```
    } catch (java.rmi.RemoteException re) {
      System.out.println("First transfer failed (as expected)");
    }
    distributor.correctTransferOfSalesReps("Washington", "Albany", 50000.0);
  } catch (Exception e) {
    e.printStackTrace();
  }
}
}
```

If you are aware of the relationship integrity rules, you can easily avoid problems such as concurrent modifications to collection classes.

Deployment

We will create the application, calling it `distributor`, and importing the EJB JAR file. Now we have the beans we can enter the database information again, which is still jdbc/Cloudscape, generate the SQL for the application, and then save the file.

Most of the deployment information is of a similar type to the previous examples, so we will just show the areas that are modified to show the new information described by the section.

Here we can see the relationships set up to allow a single distributor to have access to multiple sales offices, also for each sales office to have multiple sales representatives:

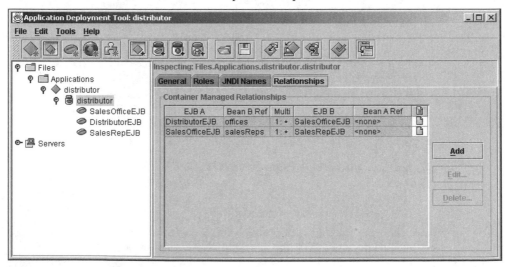

The JNDI information for the application is:

- ❑ Component: SalesOfficeEJB   JNDI Name: SalesOfficeEJB
- ❑ Component: SalesRepEJB   JNDI Name: SalesRepEJB
- ❑ Component: DistributorEJB   JNDI Name: DistributorEJB

Once the application is deployed, we need to run the client to see if the application worked.

Run the client using the command line:

```
java -classpath %J2EE_HOME%lib\j2ee.jar;distributorClient.jar;.
    examples.distributor.Client
```

We should then get the result printed to the console:

First transfer failed (as expected)

The EJB 2.0 Query Language

In the last chapter, you learned that the new EJB 2.0 query language (EJB QL) is used to define the behavior of finder methods and `ejbSelect()` methods for entity beans with container managed persistence. The EJB QL syntax and usage is based on SQL-92, with certain extensions appropriate for its purpose of navigating entities and their relationships. Like SQL, EJB QL has a FROM clause, a SELECT clause, and a WHERE clause.

> *Some of the EJB QL syntax might seem a bit counterintuitive or unnecessary. This is because the specification has been designed with the SQL-2000 standard in mind. So it should make a bit more sense in the future – not that it helps us much now.*

The FROM clause is similar to the SQL FROM clause in that it specifies the participants in a Cartesian join. Rather than database tables, the EJB QL FROM clause uses one of two things: the schema of an entity bean in the deployment descriptor; or a path expression, which uses the relationships declared in the deployment descriptor.

The SELECT clause determines the type of entity (or value object) to return from the query, and must be consistent with the corresponding finder or `ejbSelect()` method.

The WHERE clause qualifies the results of the query. You can use many of the operators and Boolean expressions with which you are familiar from SQL, such as =, >=, >, <=, <, <>, BETWEEN, NOT BETWEEN, LIKE, NOT LIKE, IN, NOT IN, +, -, *, /, IS NULL, IS NOT NULL, AND, OR,), and (. There are also extensions specifically defined for use in the context of EJBs. For instance, you can call finder methods on entity beans and use the results in an IN or NOT IN expression. You can also reference the parameters to the finder or `ejbSelect()` method in the where clause, by using a simple syntax of a question mark plus the one-based index of the parameter, for example, ?1.

This section provides additional details that you will need to use EJB QL correctly and effectively. The following topics are addressed:

- ❑   Cartesian joins
- ❑   FROM clause expressions
- ❑   SELECT clause usage
- ❑   The WHERE clause

Cartesian Joins

This is not an EJB QL innovation, but rather a concept imported directly from SQL. It is also not a difficult concept. Nevertheless, it is fundamental to understanding EJB QL (and SQL, by the way). A Cartesian join produces a Cartesian product, which is simply the set of all combinations of elements (for example, rows) from each source (for example, tables). A simple example should illustrate this. Consider two database tables, Owner and Pet. The Owner table might have the following rows:

Name	Street	Age
Johnny	Main St	8
Susie	Centre St	7
Peggy	Everett St	11

The `Pet` table might have the following rows:

OwnerName	PetType
Johnny	Dog
Johnny	Frog
Susie	Fish

A Cartesian join can be produced by the following SQL query:

```
SELECT * FROM Owner, Pet
```

The following table represents the Cartesian product:

Name	Street	Age	OwnerName	PetType
Johnny	Main St	8	Johnny	Dog
Johnny	Main St	8	Johnny	Frog
Johnny	Main St	8	Susie	Fish
Susie	Centre St	7	Johnny	Dog
Susie	Centre St	7	Johnny	Frog
Susie	Centre St	7	Susie	Fish
Peggy	Everett St	11	Johnny	Dog
Peggy	Everett St	11	Johnny	Frog
Peggy	Everett St	11	Susie	Fish

As it stands, these results are worthless. The more typical usage is to qualify this Cartesian product with a "`JOIN`" clause or a `WHERE` clause to provide a meaningful response. For instance, we might issue the following query:

```
SELECT * FROM Owner, Pet WHERE name=ownerName
```

If you look at the Cartesian product, you will see exactly three rows that meet the criteria in our `WHERE` clause, to provide the following result table:

Name	Street	Age	OwnerName	PetType
Johnny	Main St	8	Johnny	Dog
Johnny	Main St	8	Johnny	Frog
Susie	Centre St	7	Susie	Fish

Whenever you issue an SQL query or an EJB QL query, you are producing a Cartesian product using the elements of the FROM clause and then paring it down with the WHERE clause. Of course, any database or EJB container that actually did this, rather than optimizing it behind the scenes, would be completely useless in a production environment. But if you think of the queries this way, you will understand better how to write them.

Result Quantities FROM Cartesian Joins

Let's continue our hypothetical owner-pet example, and assume that both owners and pets are represented by entity beans. Consider the following simple EJB QL query to select all Pet entities for a Pet finder method:

```
SELECT OBJECT(p) FROM Pet p
```

Our Cartesian join will have only one participant, and the result set will be equivalent to the original set of Pet entities. This is just what we want. Now let's add something to the FROM clause to get our original Cartesian join:

```
. SELECT OBJECT(p) FROM Pet p, Owner o
```

Distinct Results

We're just selecting pets, but if you look at the Cartesian join table you'll see that there are three instances of each pet. It's possible that your EJB container will actually return a java.util.Collection with nine pets (six of them duplicates). However, the EJB 2.0 specification allows (but does not require) the EJB container to weed-out duplicates (like the SQL DISTINCT keyword, even if "distinct" isn't specified).

Note that the semantics of a collection class implementing java.util.Set prevent it from having duplicates, so this only applies to the case where the finder or ejbSelect() method returns an instance implementing java.util.Collection.

The keyword DISTINCT allows you to indicate that you want only distinct results in the resulting collection, so the query would look like this:

```
SELECT DISTINCT OBJECT(p) FROM Pet p, Owner o
```

An Implication of Cartesian Joins

What happens if there are no owners in our owner set? You might expect to get the same answer, because there are still three pets. But the Cartesian join to an empty set has zero result rows. So if there are no owners, the following (somewhat silly) query:

```
SELECT OBJECT(p) FROM Pet p, Owner o
```

returns no results, even though this query:

```
SELECT OBJECT(p) FROM Pet p
```

returns a collection of three pets.

FROM Clause Expressions

The FROM clause can have two types of attributes: schema entity beans, declared in the deployment descriptor; and collection member declarations, which use the relationships declared in the deployment descriptor.

Range Variables in FROM Clauses

A range variable is the EJB QL term for a schema that is used in a FROM-clause. For example, you might have an Order entity (with a schema name of OrderBean) and a line-item entity (with a schema name of LineItem). The following sample EJB QL FROM clause uses two range variables:

```
FROM OrderBean o, LineItem l
```

The concept of a range variable in EJB QL can be mapped to the concept of a table in a FROM clause in SQL. A simple Cartesian join is performed on all the range variables in the FROM clause.

In SQL you have the option to assign an alias to each table in your FROM clause. In EJB QL it is mandatory to assign an alias, known as an identification variable. You simply place the identification variable immediately after the schema. In the simple query above, the identification variables are o (for OrderBean) and l (for LineItem).

You can also declare identification variables for schemas by using the AS keyword between the schema name and the identification variable. The above query would become:

```
FROM OrderBean AS o, LineItem AS l
```

Further reference to that element of the FROM clause will use the identification variable and not the schema name. You might use the identification variable in the SELECT clause, in the WHERE clause, or later in the FROM clause.

Collection Member Declarations in FROM Clauses

A **collection member declaration** is a multi-valued path expression used with the IN operator. A **path expression** is an identification variable followed by the navigation operator (that is, a period) and a cmp field or cmr field. It is multi-valued if it ends with a cmr field represented by a java.util.Set or java.util.Collection.

Consider our order-line item example. Assume that we have declared an identification variable o for the schema OrderBean. The following would be a path expression from an order to its cmr field that has a local interface for the line item's EJB component:

```
o.lineItems
```

We can declare identification variables for objects in a many-valued relationship by using a path expression with the IN operator. For example, the following query defines the identification variable li to represent each item in the lineItems cmr field for the order entity:

```
SELECT OBJECT(o) FROM OrderBean o, IN(o.lineItems) li
```

The o is an identification variable for the OrderBean schema (for an entity bean that is probably named OrderEJB). The li is an identification variable for the line item entities in the collection class of a particular order.

How FROM Clause Path Expressions are Joined

Unlike range variables, path expressions are not blindly joined with other FROM clause elements in a Cartesian join. The whole point of path expressions is that they are navigating an existing relationship that has been declared in the deployment descriptor and is already understood by the persistence manager. The result table is formed by taking all permutations of the element referenced by the path expression's identification variable and the element referenced by the schema's identification variable.

Let's consider a simple example to make this clear. We'll consider three tables: the order table, the lineitems table, and the relationship table. These will correspond to the order entity schema, the lineitem entity schema, and the lineItems cmr field.

First, the order table:

Order Number	Customer Name
100	Dan
101	Dave
102	Jeff
103	Frank

Next, the lineitems table:

Line Item Number	Product	Quantity
1000	DeskLamp	1
1001	Chair	3
1002	Desk	5
1003	Paper	100
1004	Pencil	35
1005	Whiteboard	1
1006	Paper Clips	22

Finally, the relationship table that tells us to which order a line item belongs. (This will often be represented by foreign keys in the lineitems table instead.)

Order Number	Line Item Number
100	1000
100	1001
101	1002
101	1003
102	1004
102	1005
102	1006

The following query:

```
SELECT OBJECT(o) FROM OrderBean o, IN(o.lineItems) li
```

produces this join (which can be further qualified by your WHERE clause):

Order Number	Customer Name	Line Item Number	Product	Quantity
100	Dan	1000	DeskLamp	1
100	Dan	1001	Chair	3
101	Dave	1002	Desk	5
101	Dave	1003	Paper	100
102	Jeff	1004	Pencil	35
102	Jeff	1005	Whiteboard	1
102	Jeff	1006	Paper Clips	22

Contrast that to this query:

```
SELECT OBJECT(o) FROM OrderBean o, LineItem l
```

This query produces the Cartesian join of every element in entity one combined with every entity in element two. There are twenty-eight result rows:

Order Number	Customer Name	Line Item Number	Product	Quantity
100	Dan	1000	DeskLamp	1
100	Dan	1001	Chair	3
100	Dan	1002	Desk	5
100	Dan	1003	Paper	100
100	Dan	1004	Pencil	35

Order Number	Customer Name	Line Item Number	Product	Quantity
100	Dan	1005	Whiteboard	1
100	Dan	1006	Paper Clips	22
101	Dave	1000	DeskLamp	1
101	Dave	1001	Chair	3
101	Dave	1002	Desk	5
101	Dave	1003	Paper	100
101	Dave	1004	Pencil	35
101	Dave	1005	Whiteboard	1
101	Dave	1006	Paper Clips	22
102	Jeff	1000	DeskLamp	1
102	Jeff	1001	Chair	3
102	Jeff	1002	Desk	5
102	Jeff	1003	Paper	100
102	Jeff	1004	Pencil	35
102	Jeff	1005	Whiteboard	1
102	Jeff	1006	Paper Clips	22
103	Frank	1000	DeskLamp	1
103	Frank	1001	Chair	3
103	Frank	1002	Desk	5
103	Frank	1003	Paper	100
103	Frank	1004	Pencil	35
103	Frank	1005	Whiteboard	1
103	Frank	1006	Paper Clips	22

The best natural-language formulation of the behavior of the basic forms of the different queries might be as follows:

Query	What it does
`SELECT OBJECT(o) FROM OrderBean o`	Selects all orders
`SELECT OBJECT(o) FROM OrderBean o, LineItem l`	Selects all orders if even one single instance of the line item entity object exists
`SELECT OBJECT(o) FROM OrderBean o, l IN o.lineItems`	Selects any order that has at least one line item

Single-Valued Path Expressions vs. Multi-Valued Path Expressions

A **single-valued path expression** references a `cmp-field` or a `cmr-field` that returns a single entity.

A **multi-valued path expression** references a `cmr-field` that returns a collection class (either `java.util.Collection` or `java.util.Set`).

For example, we might have an order with a one-to-many relationship with its line items, and a one-to-one relationship with its shipping address. Assuming we have declared an identification variable o for the `OrderBean` schema, the following would be a single-valued path expression that referenced the `shipAddress` entity:

```
o.shipAddress
```

The following would be a single-valued path expression that referenced the String-valued cmp field "street":

```
o.shipAddress.street
```

The following would be a multi-valued path expression that referenced the collection of line items associated with the order:

```
o.lineItems
```

> **This distinction between single-valued and multi-valued path expressions is important, because there is little overlap in how you use single-valued path expressions and multi-valued path expressions.**

With two small exceptions, you only use multi-valued path expressions in the FROM clause. You never use them in the SELECT clause, and you almost never use them in the WHERE clause. (The two exceptions are the is [not] empty operator and the [not] member of operator in the WHERE clause.)

You only use single-valued path expressions in the SELECT clause and the WHERE clause. You never use them in the FROM clause.

You should understand that there is no reason to use a single-valued path expression in the FROM-clause, because the object is already implicitly included in the result set. For instance, there is no point to doing this:

```
    SELECT OBJECT(addr) FROM OrderBean o, IN(o.shipAddress) addr      // illegal !
```

because you can just do this:

```
    SELECT o.shipAddress FROM OrderBean o
```

Likewise, you cannot manipulate or return objects as a group. So you can't do this:

```
    SELECT OBJECT(o.lineItems) FROM OrderBean o                        // illegal !
```

but instead must do this:

```
    SELECT OBJECT(li) FROM OrderBean o, IN(o.lineItems) li
```

It is illegal to compose a path expression from a collection-valued path expression. For example, assume that a product entity object had a one-to-one relationship with lineItems. You could not do this:

```
    SELECT OBJECT(o) FROM OrderBean o WHERE o.lineItems.product.name = 'Desk'
                                                          // illegal !
```

but would instead need to do this:

```
    SELECT OBJECT(o) FROM OrderBean o, IN(o.lineItems) li WHERE li.product.name =
    'Desk'
```

By the way, although I am using the `// illegal` *notation on certain queries, there is no mechanism to actually add a comment to an EJB QL query.*

SELECT Clause Expressions

The SELECT clause partially determines the result of the query. It contains either an identification variable in the FROM clause, or a path expression rooted in one of the identification variables in the FROM clause. Optionally, it uses the keyword DISTINCT. If it uses an identification variable, it must also use the OBJECT keyword. If it uses a path expression, it must not. We've seen all this already.

Here is a select clause using an identification variable. Note that we must use the OBJECT keyword.

```
    SELECT OBJECT(o) FROM OrderBean o
```

Here is a SELECT clause using a path expression. Note that we don't use the OBJECT keyword.

```
    SELECT o.shipAddress FROM OrderBean o
```

If we use a ejbSelect() method we can return a value type. Here is an example that returns a collection of strings:

```
    SELECT o.shipAddress.city FROM OrderBean o
```

Returning Local or Remote Component Interfaces

There is no way to tell from the following query whether we are returning a collection of local or remote component interfaces:

```
SELECT OBJECT(o) FROM OrderBean o
```

The rules for determining this are very simple:

- ❏ If the query is for a finder method in a local home interface, the result must be a local component interface.

- ❏ If the query is for a finder method in a remote home interface, the result must be a remote component interface.

- ❏ If the query is for an ejbSelect() method and the optional <result-type-mapping> element is present, the result will be either a local component interface if the result type mapping is Local, or a remote component interface if the result type mapping is Remote.

- ❏ If the query is for an ejbSelect() method and the optional <result-type-mapping> element is not present, the result will be a local component interface.

The WHERE Clause

Anyone who has worked with SQL should be instantly at home with the EJB QL WHERE clause. Its typical usage consists of conditional tests on values retrieved in the FROM clause to pare down the result set. These conditional tests are grouped with parentheses and joined with AND and OR operators. The conditional tests use the = and <> operators for Boolean, numerical, and string values, as well as the >, >=, <, and <= operators for numerical values. In addition, there are IS NULL and IS NOT NULL operators that duplicate SQL's familiar three-valued logic.

A conditional test is between a cmp or single-valued cmr field and one of three things: another cmp or single-valued cmr field of the same type; a parameter to the finder or ejbSelect() method; or a literal.

> **Values are compared based on their representations in the entity, and not based on their representations in the database. For example, a cmp field of type int cannot be tested to be null, although a cmp field of type java.lang.Integer can be tested against null.**

Let's consider some examples of each of these types of conditional tests. We'll continue with our order entity component and its associated line-item entity objects. Let's also give our order two one-to-one relationships with address entities: a ship-to address and a bill-to address.

Conditional Tests against Other cmp or Single-Valued cmr Fields

Here is a possible conditional test comparing two cmp fields:

```
SELECT OBJECT(o) FROM OrderBean o WHERE o.shipAddress.city = o.billAddress.city
```

Here is a possible conditional test comparing two single-valued cmr fields:. Entities are considered equal if their primary keys are equal:

```
SELECT OBJECT(o) FROM OrderBean o WHERE o.shipAddress <> o.billAddress
```

Here is a query with a conditional test of cmp fields and a conditional test of cmr fields:

```
SELECT OBJECT(o) FROM OrderBean o WHERE o.shipAddress <> o.billAddress AND
o.shipAddress.city = o.billAddress.city
```

Conditional Tests Using Parameters

You can use the value of parameters to your finder or `ejbSelect()` method in conditional tests in your `WHERE` clause. The parameters are referred to by using a question mark, followed by the one-based index of that parameter in the method's parameter list. For example, for following `ejbSelect()` method:

```
public abstract Collection ejbSelectLineItemsForProductAndQuantity(String product,
                                                                   int quantity)
                    throws FinderException;
```

the `product` parameter would be referenced by `?1` and the `quantity` parameter would be referenced by `?2`.

Here are some queries that use these parameters (assume that the entity object `LineItem` has a cmp field called `product` with a type of `java.lang.String`, and a cmp field called `quantity` with a type of int):

```
SELECT OBJECT(li) FROM OrderBean o, IN(o.lineItems) li WHERE li.product = ?1 AND
li.quantity = ?2
```

Conditional Tests using Literals

You can use literals (also called constants) in your EJB QL queries in the `WHERE` clause. String literals are surrounded by single quotes, for example, 'Chair'. If a single quote needs to be in your literal, you can escape it by using another quote, for example, 'Dan O''Connor'. Here is an example of the use of a string literal in a query:

```
SELECT OBJECT(li) FROM OrderBean o, IN(o.lineItems) li WHERE li.product = 'Chair'
```

Exact numeric literals are represented by numeric values without a decimal point, for example, 25, -32, and +21. These literals support values in the range of the Java `long` type.

Approximate numeric literals are represented by numeric values with a decimal point, for example, 25.3, or 100.1. They can also be represented using scientific notation, for example, 8E4 or -9.3E9.

Here is an example of the use of a numeric literal in a query:

```
SELECT OBJECT(li) FROM OrderBean o, IN(o.lineItems) li WHERE li.quantity > 2
```

Boolean literals are represented by the case-insensitive values `True` and `False`.

Special Rules for Date Literals

Representing a date as a literal presents special problems because of the many different date formats in use around the world. In the EJB 2.0 specification, the problem is neatly sidestepped, at the cost of some readability. Date literals are represented as long literals that represent milliseconds since January 1, 1970, 00:00:00 GMT. That may sound a bit odd, but it's a natural fit with the behavior of the Java date classes, which represent time the same way. You can get the millisecond value by calling `getTime()` on a properly initialized instance of `java.util.Date`. This may sound like a bit of a pain, but how often will you need to include a date literal (as opposed to a date parameter, where you can just use an instance of `java.util.Date`) in a `WHERE` clause? Just write a little program to print the millisecond value out, and cut and paste it into your where clause.

Here is an example of a query that uses a date literal:

```
SELECT OBJECT(o) FROM OrderBean o WHERE o.shipDate > 979837813000
```

Arithmetic Operators

You can use the arithmetic operators +, -, *, and / for addition, subtraction, multiplication, and division in the WHERE clause. Here is an example of a possible query that uses an arithmetic operator:

```
SELECT OBJECT(o) FROM OrderBean o, IN(o.lineItems) li WHERE li.quantity * li.price
> ?1
```

BETWEEN Operator

You can use the BETWEEN and NOT BETWEEN operators in EJB QL just as you can use them in SQL. Here is an example of their use:

```
SELECT OBJECT(o) FROM OrderBean o, IN(o.lineItems) li WHERE li.quantity BETWEEN 5
AND 10
```

Note that this is equivalent to the following query:

```
SELECT OBJECT(o) FROM OrderBean o, IN(o.lineItems) li WHERE li.quantity >= 5 AND
li.quantity <= 10
```

LIKE Operator

The LIKE and NOT LIKE operators provides simple pattern matching for a cmp value of type java.lang.String. The pattern is provided by a string literal, with two types of wildcards. The underscore character (_) stands for any single character, and the percent character (%) stands for zero or more characters. If you need to use an actual underscore or percent character in your pattern, you can also declare an escape character for the like expression. The full syntax is:

```
string_valued_path_expression [NOT] LIKE 'pattern' [ESCAPE 'escape character']
```

Here is an example of its use, which gets orders with line items for Chair, HighChair, Desk Chair, Executive Chair, and so on:

```
SELECT ORDER(o) FROM OrderBean o, IN(o.lineItems) li WHERE li.productName LIKE
'%Chair'
```

Here are some examples of wild card patterns, with strings that they match and strings that they don't match:

Pattern	Matches	Does Not Match
'123_6'	12306, 12316, 12326, 123A6	123006, 22306
'123%6'	1236, 12306, 123006, 1231236, 123ABC6	12360, A1236
'CHAIR_'	CHAIRS	CHAIR
'CHAIR%'	CHAIR, CHAIRS, CHAIR1, CHAIRqqq	DESKCHAIR
'%CHAIR_'	CHAIRS, CHAIR1, DESKCHAIRS	CHAIR, DESKCHAIR

IS EMPTY Operator

The IS EMPTY and IS NOT EMPTY operators test whether a multi-valued relationship collection has no elements. For example, you could return all the orders without line items with the following query:

```
SELECT OBJECT(o) FROM OrderBean o WHERE o.lineItems IS EMPTY
```

The IS EMPTY and IS NOT EMPTY operators are the only cases where you can have a multi-valued path expression (or a multi-valued reference expression) in a WHERE clause. Otherwise, you only use them in the FROM clause of your query.

Notice that it would make no sense whatsoever to include the same path expression in the FROM clause and in an IS EMPTY expression in the WHERE clause. If the expression is in the FROM clause, it implicitly tests whether or not the collection is empty when it produces the combinations for the result set. So the following query is illegal:

```
SELECT OBJECT(o) FROM OrderBean o, IN(o.lineItems) li WHERE o.lineItems IS EMPTY
                                                                   // illegal !
```

This is contradictory because the joined result set will only include orders with line items, but the WHERE clause only allows orders without line items. Of course, you could rewrite this query to use the IS NOT EMPTY operator, in which case the test would only be redundant and not contradictory. Regardless, it would still be illegal.

MEMBER OF Operator

The MEMBER OF and NOT MEMBER OF operators test whether the result of a single-valued path expression is in a collection returned from a collection-valued path expression. For example, you could get all the orders whose customers were members of a preferred price list with the following query:

```
SELECT OBJECT(o) FROM OrderBean o, PriceListBean p WHERE o.customer MEMBER OF
p.customers AND p.type = 'Preferred'
```

By the way, the "OF" part of the keyword is optional.

IN Operator

The IN operator takes a single-valued path expression pointing to a string-valued cmp field, and checks it against a list of constants. The rules for using this in operator are quite strict. You may not, for example, use a parameter to your finder or ejbSelect() method in the IN expression. You simply compare a string-valued cmp field to a list of constants that you provide in a comma-separated list inside parentheses. Note that this is different from the IN that is used for path expressions. Here is a simple example:

```
SELECT OBJECT(o) FROM OrderBean o, IN(o.lineItems) li WHERE li.productName IN
('Chair', 'Desk', 'Lamp')
```

This is equivalent to the following query:

```
SELECT OBJECT(o) FROM OrderBean o, IN(o.lineItems) li WHERE li.productName =
'Chair' OR li.productName = 'Desk' OR li.productName = 'Lamp'
```

Note that the IN operator and the MEMBER OF operator are similar in that both test something for inclusion in a set, but their uses are quite different. The IN operator tests against constant strings, and the MEMBER OF operator tests against related entities.

Functions

There are six functions that you can use to manipulate single instances of string or numeric values in your WHERE clause. They are:

- ❑ CONCAT(string1, string2), which takes two strings and joins them together to make one string.

- ❑ SUBSTRING(string, start, length), which finds a substring of length length within a string starting at arithmetic expression start.

- ❑ LENGTH(string), which returns the length of a string.

- ❑ LOCATE(string1, string2[, start]) which finds the first occurrence of string2 in string1, starting at index start (or at the beginning if start is not specified and returns the index). If no occurrence is found, 0 is returned.

- ❑ ABS(number), which returns the absolute value of a number, as either int, float, or double.

- ❑ SQRT(number), which returns the square root of a number.

Here is a simple example that uses one of these functions:

```
SELECT OBJECT(o) FROM OrderBean o WHERE concat( o.custFirstName, o.custLastName )
= 'JohnSmith'
```

Note that in this version of the specification, there are no functions that operate on groups of string or numeric values. For example, there are no functions that sum all the values of a CMP field, or take the average of all the values of a CMP field. These will likely be added in a future version of the specification.

Finally, the following identifiers are reserved in EJB QL: SELECT, FROM, WHERE, DISTINCT, OBJECT, NULL, TRUE, FALSE, NOT, AND, OR, BETWEEN, LIKE, IN, AS, UNKNOWN, EMPTY, MEMBER, OF and IS. Also, you can not use an abstract-schema-name or an ejb-name as an identifier. You also should probably not use any other SQL reserved words as identifiers, because they may become reserved words in a future version of the EJB specification.

Summary

In this chapter we explained how to develop entity beans using the new model of container-managed persistence introduced in EJB 2.0. Some of the points we covered were:

- ❑ The role that callbacks play in developing entity beans with container-managed persistence.

- ❑ The use of local interfaces to allow entity beans to model fine grained aspects of your object model. Local interfaces represent components located in the same JVM, and they use pass-by-reference semantics. This allows the bean-developer to use entity components rather than dependent value objects to model complex business objects.

- ❑ The importance of the EJB 2.0 model of container-managed persistence in preventing data-aliasing problems for both entities and relationships.

- ❑ The actions that the container performs to maintain referential integrity.

- ❑ The correct use of iterators to modify data – it's important to avoid concurrent modification of collections by the container while it maintains referential integrity.

- ❑ The use of the EJB query language. Each part of the query – the SELECT clause, the FROM clause, and the WHERE clause – was examined in depth.

In the next chapter, we will look at the final type of Enterprise JavaBean that we can develop, which have been introduced in the 2.0 specification – message-driven beans.

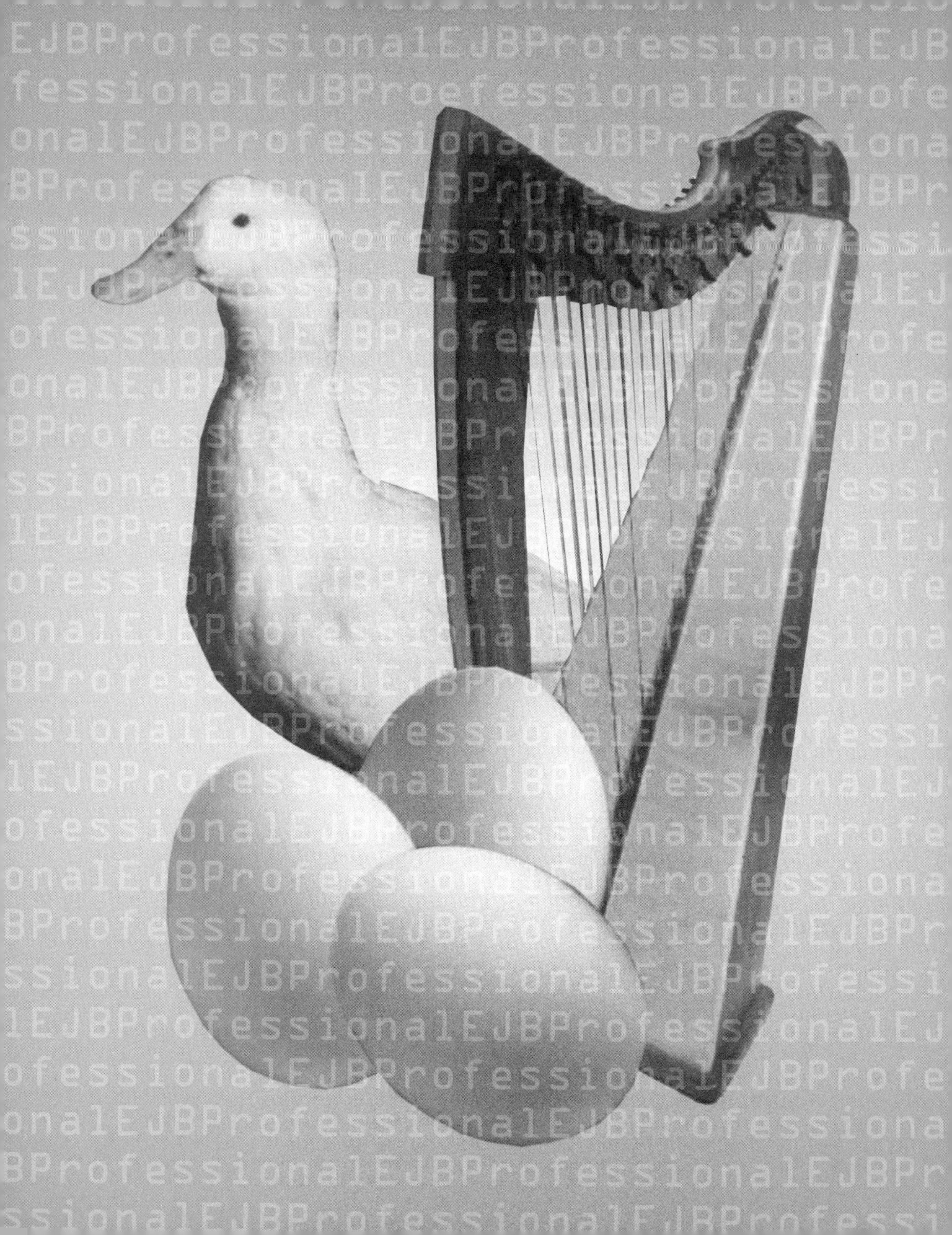

7

Asynchronous EJBs

In this chapter, we'll consider a very important addition to the EJB specification. As we have seen from the previous chapters, the business methods defined in an EJB always require a synchronous invocation by the client. However, there are many instances where an asynchronous invocation of a certain business operation is desired. For instance, if a client tries to place an order while our server is down, what happens? Does the client have to keep on trying until our server comes up again?

In this chapter, we will look at how to achieve this kind of asynchronous communication between the client and the server using newly introduced **message-driven** beans. The message-driven bean consumes the asynchronous messages generated by the client. Thus, to understand message-driven beans, a good understanding of messaging concepts and the relevant API is required.

Before we discuss the message-driven bean, we'll briefly explain the JMS API (Java Message Service) and define several terms used in messaging. In this chapter, we will cover the following topics:

- ❑ The need for asynchronous communication
- ❑ Messaging concepts and definitions
- ❑ JMS API
- ❑ Message-driven beans
- ❑ Other modes of asynchronous communication – JavaMail
- ❑ Developing an application that uses message-driven beans

So, let's start off by discussing the need for asynchronous communication.

Why is Asynchronous Communication Useful?

In everyday a life, we make several telephone calls to our business associates, friends, relatives, etc. This is **synchronous** communication. The party to which the call is made must be available, and once connected the two parties communicate with each other over the network.

This may not be always practicable and so many times, we find that the party to whom the call is made is currently unavailable. We may then send a voice mail or an e-mail to the second party. This is an **asynchronous** communication. The second party may or may not receive the message immediately and may decide not to respond immediately after reading the message. The calling party also continues their work and does not have to keep on waiting until the called party responds.

There are several situations in computing where an asynchronous communication between the client and the server is desired. In general terms, these are all situations where one part of a distributed application can't afford to wait until another part of the application sends the required information. In this section, we will look at some more specific situations.

B2C Communication

Say your company sells its products online via an electronic catalog, but your server is down because of maintenance, backup, or hardware failure. At certain times, you may even be simply disconnected from the network. If a client tries placing an order during these times, what happens to the order? As the client will not be able to invoke a business method on your server application, the server cannot receive the order. In such cases, would you expect the client to keep on trying or come back again at a later time to place the order?

In such cases, asynchronous communication comes to our rescue. The client places an order by sending a message to a messaging server and the messaging server guarantees the delivery of the message to your server whenever the latter comes back up. The client does not have to wait for the server to be ready.

B2B Communication

In a typical B2B scenario, two cooperating businesses wish to share their data. However, the two businesses are probably using different hardware and, software platforms, and altogether different application formats. In such situations, data may be shared using messaging.

A typical case could be two hospitals sharing data on one patient, or two distributors sharing their inventory. The data itself may be represented using XML. However, each business cannot assume that the other business's application server may be up and running 24 x 7. Also, the businesses may not like to give direct access to its business logic layer or to the database tier to other applications. In such cases, asynchronous communication helps in effective, reliable, guaranteed communication between the two business houses.

Saving Server Resources

Another important reason for considering asynchronous communication is to save server resources. You may not want to keep your business logic application up and running, ready to receive orders, all of the time in situations where there may not be an order for days. The orders may be received irregularly over a period of time, as with selling tickets to seasonal events. By keeping such applications running 24 x 7, you would be wasting lot of valuable resources on your server. Rather, such business logic should be invoked only when an order is received from the client.

By using messaging, the client can place an order by embedding it in a message. On receipt of the message, the messaging server will automatically invoke a service on the business tier of your application and deliver it to the business logic for processing. This can result in considerable saving of server resources because such resources will be activated on a need-only basis. The messaging approach will be ideal in the case of infrequent order receipts.

Obviously there are many more situations where asynchronous communication between client and server is desirable. Let us now study messaging more closely before we delve into asynchronous communication in Enterprise JavaBeans.

JMS Messaging

A messaging system allows a reliable asynchronous communication between two separate uncoupled applications. The communication is referred to by Sun as peer-to-peer, even though it takes place between a client machine and a server machine. An application that needs to send a message to a second application does so by first sending the message to a **messaging server**. The messaging server then delivers the message to the second application.

Similarly, if the second application wants to deliver a message back to the first party, it does so by sending a message to the messaging server first. Therefore, the messaging server plays an important role of message distribution, guaranteeing message delivery to the sender. The following diagram depicts the transfer of such messages over a generic network, with no reference to where the messaging server resides (it isn't particularly important at this stage):

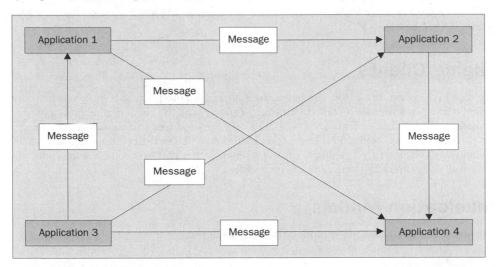

Sun has produced a standard Java-based API for such messaging servers, called **JMS – Java Message Service**. The server vendors implement this API so that different clients can communicate with each other using this Java-based standard. The following diagram shows a typical client communicating with different applications using the JMS interface:

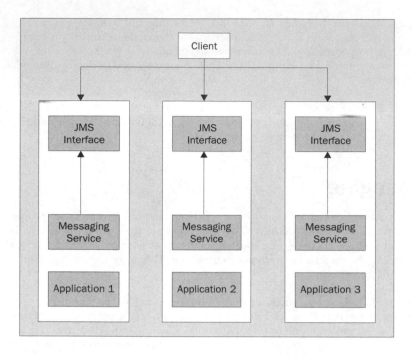

This chapter is only meant as an introduction to the key concepts behind, and objects in the JMS API. For a fuller coverage of the topic, take a look at Professional JMS Programming *from Wrox Press, ISBN 1 861004 93 1.*

Messaging Clients

As we have seen in the previous section, the messaging is always peer-to-peer. Each peer is called a **messaging client**. A client that sends a message is called a **message producer**, and the client that receives a message is called a **message consumer**. Note that a client can act as both a message producer and a message consumer. This means a client can produce messages and send them to other parties involved in the communication. Similarly, a client can act as a message consumer by listening to messages sent by other parties involved in the communication; we can have two-way communication between messaging clients.

Communication Models

There are two distinct communication models used in messaging:

❑ Point-to-Point

❑ Publish/Subscribe

Each model is used depending on the needs of the application. A client application may use either model depending on its needs; theoretically it could use Point-to-Point messaging when communicating with one server application, and Publish/Subscribe when communicating with another (although this would be unlikely to happen).

The Point-to-Point Model

A Point-to-Point communication model is used if there is one, and only one, message consumer for each message. For example, an order processing system may use this model for receiving orders from customers. It means the messaging server will deliver each message to not more than one client. A typical configuration for a Point-to-Point model is shown in the following diagram:

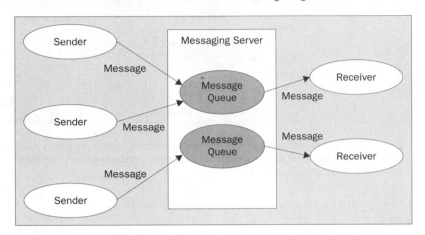

In this model, a messaging server defines one or more **message queues** for the use of its clients. Each queue will have a unique name in its server's namespace. These queues are used in a series of steps:

1. A messaging client sends a message to a desired queue

2. A message consumer registers with a specific queue

3. The server delivers the message to a registered client whenever one is available

If more than one client registers to the same queue, the message is delivered to **only one** of the clients. JMS does not define who the beneficiary is; it simply guarantees that the message is delivered to one of the registered clients. Thus, it is important that the two messaging clients must agree on a unique private queue to ensure that their messages are not lost to a third party; this is also a security issue, not just a naming issue. The messaging queue may be set by the server administrator or the messaging client itself.

Though there is only one consumer for each message, a queue may recieve messages from more than one sender. Thus, more than one sender can connect and send messages to the same queue.

The Publish/Subscribe Model

A Publish/Subscribe model is used for general broadcast type applications where a message is to be delivered to more than one client. For example, an atomic clock may periodically transmit the current time to all its subscribers. The configuration for Publish/Subscribe model is shown in the following diagram:

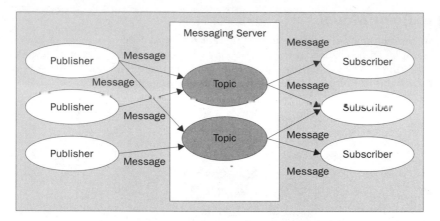

In this model, the messaging server defines a series of topics, each of which represents a defined subject for messages. Again, each topic will have a unique name in its server's namespace. Topics are used in a series of steps similar to those for message queues:

1. A message producer creates a message and publishes to a desired topic

2. A message consumer subscribes to a topic in which it is interested

3. The messaging server delivers the messages to all the parties subscribed to a particular topic

There can be more than one subscriber to each topic and the message is delivered to all those who have subscribed to a topic. A messaging client can subscribe to multiple topics. Similarly, a sender can publish to multiple topics. The topics may be defined by the server administrator or a messaging client.

Durable and Persistent Messaging

As discussed earlier, a messaging server is responsible for guaranteed delivery of messages. In the case of a virtual fully connected network, the router within the messaging server takes this responsibility. A messaging client subscribes to the messaging server indicating its interest in the messages delivered by the server. The client may request a **durable** subscription. In such a case, the messaging server holds the message for the client (a **durable subscriber**) if the client is not currently active and delivers the message to the client whenever it becomes active. We'll see more about this in the *Durable Subscribers* section later in the chapter.

At certain times, a messaging server itself may go down after it has received a message for delivery but before the message could be delivered to the client. A message may be marked as a **persistent** message; here the messaging server assumes the responsibility of storing the message to a persistent storage, and delivers the message to the client whenever the server comes up.

Now let's look into the model for the message delivery.

Message Delivery Models

The messages received by a messaging server may be delivered synchronously or asynchronously to the client. Accordingly, we have two different models for message delivery:

- ❏ Synchronous model
- ❏ Asynchronous model

Both the communication models mentioned earlier can use both of these message delivery models.

The Synchronous Delivery Model

In the synchronous delivery model, a client registers with an interesting message queue or subscribes to a topic and waits for incoming messages. If there is no message currently available, the client is blocked until the message arrives on the messaging server. The time for which the consumer is blocked ends when one of the following three criteria is fulfilled:

- ❏ Message is received
- ❏ Timeout set by consumer expires
- ❏ Consumer closes

The Asynchronous Delivery Model

In some situations, a client may not wish (or be able) to wait for the message to arrive. It may just subscribe to the messaging server, and expect the server to initiate the arrival of a message. The JMS API provides for this type of asynchronous message delivery.

The messaging client registers with a messaging server and provides a callback method for the server to call on message arrival. Whenever the message arrives, the server calls this method on the client by passing the message as an argument to the method. The client implements a `MessageListener` interface to achieve this. This is discussed further in the *Asynchronous Message Delivery* section.

Administered Objects

Having seen the message delivery model, we will now look at who provides the queues, topics, and connection factories (more on these last items shortly). We need to cover these things before we can start using them with our new message-driven beans, so we can then concentrate on the EJB specifics.

A JMS message service provider defines two types **administered objects**. These are called administered objects because they are created and managed by the messaging server administrator. The two types of administered objects are as follows:

- ❏ **Connection Factories**
  Either `javax.jms.QueueConnectionFactory` or `javax.jms.TopicConnectionFactory`
- ❏ **Destinations**
  Either `javax.jms.Queue` or `javax.jms.Topic`

The first two, Queue and QueueConnectionFactory, are used in the Point-to-Point delivery model, while the other two, Topic and TopicConnectionFactory are used in the Publish/Subscribe model. The server administrator creates these objects at server startup and registers them with the JNDI server. The messaging client looks up the JNDI server for the known names and obtains a reference to these registered objects.

> *Note that a message client can also create these objects on its own and need not use pre-defined objects. Generally, this is done for private topics and queues, which are shared between the known parties.*

Creating Messaging Clients

In order to create a messaging client, we need to take the following steps:

1. Obtain a reference to a connection factory (QueueConnectionFactory or TopicConnectionFactory as appropriate) either by looking up the JNDI server for registered name, or by instantiating the provider-specific class

2. Open a communication **session**, which is a single-threaded context for sending and receiving messages

3. Obtain a reference to the object

4. Send/receive messages on the destination

Creating Messages

To create a message, the JMS API provides a Message interface. We'll need to know about this when we come to creating message using clients for our message-driven beans.

There are several pre-defined classes that implement this interface. The objects of these classes serve as message objects for delivering messages between two messaging clients. A message object consists of three components:

❑ Header

❑ Properties

❑ Body

A **header** consists of several JMS-defined properties. These header properties are used for describing the type of message, message priority, time of creation, expiration time, destination, and so on. Some of these fields are set by the messaging client, and some are set by the server. Here is the list of properties defined in the header:

❑ JMSDestination

❑ JMSTimeStamp

❑ JMSReplyTo

❑ JMSRedelivered

- ❏ JMSCorrelationID
- ❏ JMSPriority
- ❏ JMSExpiration
- ❏ JMSMessageID
- ❏ JMSDeliveryMode
- ❏ JMSType

The **properties** component of a message consists of user-defined name/value pairs. These properties are generally used for storing additional information about a message. A message consumer can select a message based on these property values. We will discuss message selection criteria in the *Selecting Messages* section. Sun has defined certain restrictions for use when creating our own names for properties. The names beginning with JMSX are reserved by Sun for its own internal use. Similarly, the names beginning with JMS_ are reserved for the use of a messaging service provider. In addition to this, there are few pre-defined names listed in the previous paragraph.

Finally, the message **body** encapsulates the data to be transmitted. As mentioned earlier, JMS defines several classes for encapsulating different types of data. Accordingly, several message types are defined in the API.

Message Types

JMS defines the following classes for use as different message types:

- ❏ A TextMessage class is used if your message consists of strings. This may be used for simple messages such as order confirmation.

- ❏ The MapMessage class allows the client to define name/value pairs. The client defines several names and assigns a value to each name. This could be used for sending such things as account details.

- ❏ The BytesMessage is used if the message consists of series of bytes. In this case, both sender and receiver must have a prior agreement on the data format. This may be used in transmitting process control data in byte format.

- ❏ The StreamMessage class is used for sending a sequence of primitive data types. In this case, both sender and receiver must agree on the construction of data. This may be used for transmitting file contents having a well-defined format.

- ❏ The ObjectMessage class is used for sending any serialized Java object. Whenever the data to be transmitted cannot be represented by simple data types or strings, we can use this type of message.

Asynchronous Message Delivery

We shall now look briefly at how to implement asynchronous message delivery. The JMS API defines a MessageListener interface. The message consumer implements this interface for receiving messages asynchronously.

The MessageListener interface declares a method called onMessage() that takes a Message parameter. This is a callback method used by the server to initiate the receiving of the message. The message itself is sent as a parameter to this method. The consumer must typecast the message to the proper type before reading its contents. The following code snippet illustrates the implementation of an asynchronous message consumer:

```
public class messagelistener implements MessageListener {
  public void onMessage(Message message) {
    …
    System.out.println((TextMessage) message).getText());
  }
}
```

Next, we need to set the message listener for our receiver. We use the setMessageListener() method to set the listener to an instance of the above class.

```
subscriber.setMessageListener(new messagelistener());
```

Now, the messages will be delivered to the subscriber object asynchronously.

Durable Subscribers

As we saw earlier, a durable subscriber is one that does not lose an incoming message even when it is not active (through crash or voluntary shutdown). A message will be delivered to such a subscriber whenever it comes back up.

To create a durable subscriber, we use the createDurableSubscriber() method on the session object, as demonstrated in the following code snippet:

```
TopicSubscriber subscriber = session.createDurableSubscriber(myTopic,
                                                "MySubscriber");
```

Note that a message may not be delivered to a durable subscriber if it times out before the subscriber becomes active.

Persistent and Transacted Messages

A persistent message is one that is saved to a data store by the messaging server on its receipt. Therefore, even if the server goes down before the message is delivered to its consumer, the server assumes the responsibility of a delivery at a later time whenever it becomes active. A message producer must mark the message as persistent while sending the message. The message is marked as persistent by using an overloaded send() method that takes persistent mode flag as an argument:

```
Sender.send(msg, DeliveryMode.PERSISTENT, msgPriority, TimeToLive);
```

To have messages participate in a transaction, we will need to create a transacted messaging session. We create a transacted session by specifying the first parameter in the createTopicSession() or createQueueSession() method as true:

```
TopicSession ts = topicConnection.createTopicSession(true,
                                                Session.AUTO_ACKNOWLEDGE);
…
QueueSession qs = QueueConnection.createQueueSession(true,
                                                Session.AUTO_ACKNOWLEDGE);
```

Once a transacted session is created, we can commit the transaction anytime by calling the commit() method on the session object. We can also rollback a transaction by calling the rollback() method on the session object.

Selecting Messages

The method selection process may be delegated to the messaging server. The server will deliver only those messages to the consumer for which the selection criteria are matched; these criteria can be based on header and user-defined properties of a message. The selector itself is defined using a string, and uses a subset of SQL conditional expression syntax. You define the selection criteria in the deployment descriptor.

For example, the following selection criterion will deliver only those messages for which priority is greater than 4:

```
JMSPriority > 4
```

The following selection criterion will deliver messages where the value of a user-defined property called price lies in the range of 100.0 and 200.0:

```
price between 100.0 and 200.0
```

The selection criterion may consist of a complex SQL query. Once a SQL query is defined, we will need to specify the query in the create operation of a receiver or a subscriber, as illustrated below:

```
String selector = "JMSPriority > 4";
session.createReceiver(MyQueue, selector);
session.createSubscriber(MyQueue, selector, false);
```

The messaging server now ensures that only the messages matching the selection criterion are delivered to the consumer.

Having skimmed the surface of JMS, we will now proceed to study message-driven beans and JMS API implementations in the J2EE.

Message-Driven Beans

From the above discussions, it is obvious that if a message is to be sent to an EJB, that EJB instance must continue to be active and remain connected to the messaging server at all times. As the bean instances may be pooled and assigned to other clients during their lifetime, it is not possible to have a particular instance of session bean attached to a messaging server on a continuous basis.

The EJB 1.1 specification did not provide any integration points for JMS. Due to this, 1.1 EJBs cannot act as direct JMS consumers. The reason for this is that Enterprise JavaBeans are designed to be remotely accessible objects and run within the context of an EJB container.

One of the cardinal rules of EJBs is that the client of an EJB never directly accesses the bean class itself. Since this class's lifecycle, and access, is managed by the EJB container, as a client of the bean you are only allowed to access the bean *indirectly* through its remote interface.

At first glance, many developers might think the obvious solution to our issue a simple one. It would seem that we should implement the JMS MessageListener interface (and its onMessage() method) directly in our EJB bean class, along with any of our other business logic methods, and we should be all set.

But this solution will not work. Why? Because it violates the EJB specification's contract for accessing an EJB's bean class. When JMS makes an asynchronous call to our EJB, it must act as an EJB client the same as any other EJB client – meaning it must access the EJB through its remote interface (which implies a series of JNDI lookup operations, as well). So if the bean class were directly implementing the `MessageListener` interface, how would JMS locate the home or remote interfaces, to call the bean's `onMessage()` method? What's more, since the EJB's bean class may not even be instantiated, how would it be registered with JMS, and by what mechanism?

Even assuming that the EJB's bean class was perhaps registered as a `MessageListener` through some other external Java class accessing the EJB as a proper client, and that it may still exist as an instantiated instance in the object pool after the access, there is still no way for JMS to know that it is calling into an EJB when it calls the `onMessage()` method of the bean class asynchronously – and there is no way for JMS to know that it should use a JNDI lookup, and a remote interface to access the EJB.

So what would happen if we were to implement the `MessageListener` interface directly in the EJB's bean class? It is uncertain, since firstly, JMS will not access the EJB bean class through a remote interface but will call directly into the instantiated bean class, thus violating the contract for accessing the bean class only through the remote interface.

Secondly, if the particular bean instance is being reused from the pool, is in the middle of a transaction or some other internal operation, etc., it could be catastrophic. Since the container serializes access to a bean class and its methods, and provides thread safety (an EJB is single-threaded, and as per the EJB spec, must never create its own threads), when JMS calls into the bean instance's `onMessage()` method it has just violated the boundary of the EJB container and the protections it provides. The result could be unforeseen and most likely disastrous if, for example, your EJB is participating in a transaction and JMS suddenly calls directly into the same bean instance (violating the ACID properties of the transaction, that the container helps to guarantee).

This scenario obviously is not allowed, and therefore we cannot use it. Our next question then becomes, is there any way to allow your EJB to act as a JMS consumer? In EJB 2.0 this answer is yes, but for EJB 1.1 the answer is no.

There is, however, a workaround solution in EJB 1.1, which is to create a **delegator** class.

> *A delegator class acts as a surrogate for operations to be performed on a delegate class. A delegator class will act as a surrogate for receiving JMS messages through the implementation of the* `MessageListener` *interface, and delegate those messages to our EJB.*

Most application servers provide the ability register and load any number of specified Java class instances upon startup of the server. This allows you to create your own Java classes that can perform any number of operations as the application server is started, and as importantly, which run within the same VM instance as the server.

> *If want to see an example of a delegator class being used for message-consumption for EJBs, look at the EJBs and JMS chapter in* Professional JMS Programming *from Wrox Press, ISBN 1 861004 93 1.*

This startup object can act as a message consumer and continues to live at all times. However, this technique may not be available on all application servers. For this reason, Sun has introduced **message-driven beans** in the new EJB 2.0 specification.

> A message-driven bean is essentially a message consumer that implements some business logic. The bean registers interest in a `Queue` or `Topic` of its choice, implements the `MessageListener` interface, and awaits arrival of asynchronous messages.

As messages are delivered asynchronously to a bean by the messaging service provider/application server, not by invocation from a client, the message-driven bean does not require a home and a component interface. The message bean does not contain any business methods that can be invoked by the client. Thus, there is no need for home and component interfaces for a message-driven bean.

This of course implies that the bean does not have any client-visible identity by way of a reference to a home or a component interface. The bean does not have a conversational state with the client and all the instances of the bean will be equivalent while servicing a client. Typically, a server will create a pool of bean instances and keep them in a method-ready pool. On arrival of a message, one of the instances will be assigned to the client. After the method execution, the bean will be returned to the pool of available beans. Thus, the container essentially controls the lifecycle of such a bean. The component pooling of message-driven beans results in more scalable applications.

Client Interaction with a Message-Driven Bean

When a client application interacts with a message-driven bean, the following steps take place:

❑   The client obtains a reference to a `Queue` or `Topic` by looking up the JNDI namespace.

❑   The client sends a message to the messaging server.

❑   The messaging server now dispatches the message to a message-driven bean by invoking the `onMessage()` method on the bean.

❑   When the message arrives, the EJB server ensures that a message-driven bean is available for delivery of the message. This means that if the bean does not exist, the server will create an instance of the bean and will make it available for the message delivery.

The client view of a message-driven bean is illustrated in the following diagram:

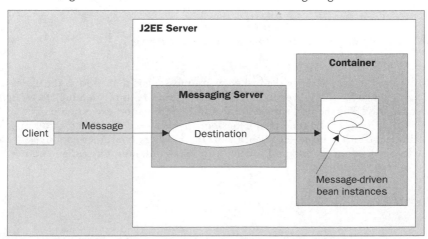

The bean provider must associate a message-driven bean with a queue or a topic by specifying the appropriate tags in the deployment descriptor. We'll see how to do this when we come to developing a message-driven remote.

Required Interfaces

A message-driven bean must implement the `javax.ejb.MessageDrivenBean` and `javax.jms.MessageListener` interfaces.

The `MessageDrivenBean` interface is as follows:

```
package javax.ejb;

public interface MessageDrivenBean extends EnterpriseBean {

    public abstract void ejbRemove() throws EJBException;

    public abstract void setMessageDrivenContext(
        MessageDrivenContext messagedrivencontext) throws EJBException;
}
```

The `MessageDrivenBean` interface declares two methods, `setMessageDrivenContext()` and `ejbRemove()`. The `setMessageDrivenContext()` method receives the context as an argument and is called by the container during the object creation time. The container calls the `ejbRemove()` method at the time of destroying the bean instance.

The `MessageDrivenContext` provided to the bean at the time of creation contains several useful methods for transaction management. These are covered in detail in Chapter 9. There are several other methods which are inherited from the `EJBContext` interface and may be irrelevant for a message-driven bean. For example, the methods such as `getEJBHome()` and `getCallerPrincipal()` should not be used in a message-driven bean.

The `MessageListener` interface defines just a single method:

```
package javax.jms;

public interface MessageListener {

    public abstract void onMessage(Message message);
}
```

This single `onMessage()` method is invoked whenever a message is delivered to the client implementing this interface. The message itself is passed in as a parameter and the implementing class can then process this message in some way. The method should not throw an application exception or a `java.rmi.RemoteException`. In general, the message-driven bean should not throw any exceptions, although it may do so if desired. From the client's view the message consumer continues to exist even if the bean does throw an application exception. In such a case, the container may assign another bean instance to the client.

The Message-Driven Bean State Diagram

The state diagram of a message-driven bean is simple, and is identical to a stateless session bean. The bean can exist in only one of the two states – Does not exist and Method-ready pool. The state diagram is shown below:

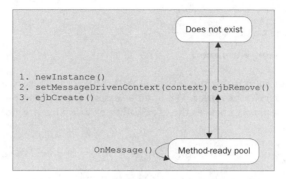

At startup, the server creates a few instances of the bean class and adds them to the Method-ready pool. During the object creation process, the server calls the newInstance() method to create a bean instance, followed by the setMessageDrivenContext() method. The setMessageDrivenContext() method receives the context as an argument. Lastly, the server calls the callback method ejbCreate() defined in the bean class. The bean may use this callback to allocate any resources it may require during its lifetime.

When the message arrives, the container will assign any one instance from the Method-ready pool to the client. After the execution of the business logic implemented in the bean instance, the bean is returned to the pool.

The container may create additional instances of the bean and add them to the pool depending on the client demand. When such instances are no longer required, the server destroys these instances to free the resources. During the destroy operation, the server calls the callback method ejbRemove() on the bean instance giving it a chance to free any previously allocated resources. Then the transition from Method-ready state to Does not exist state takes place.

JavaMail

The most popular mode of asynchronous communication is probably e-mail. E-mails are delivered asynchronously to their recipients. However, the messaging service described above is more reliable than the e-mail service as the message delivery is guaranteed and an automatic acknowledgement of the message can be provided very easily.

The ability to compose and send e-mail messages programmatically is an essential requirement for an application developer. Sun has defined an API for e-mail in the **JavaMail** specifications. Similar to the JMS API, JavaMail defines several abstract classes and interfaces, which the service provider implements. The application developer uses the API to develop applications that are portable across different vendor's application servers. In this section, we will describe this API briefly so that you will be able to compose and dispatch a mail through your program code.

Composing and Sending Mail Messages

The following steps are involved in composing and sending an e-mail message through our program code:

- ❑ Start a JavaMail session
- ❑ Create a `mail` object
- ❑ Set properties of the `mail` object
- ❑ Send the message using a transport

The J2EE specification requires support for the JavaMail API. Thus, a J2EE server provides an implementation of a JavaMail service provider. We open a session for sending e-mail by looking up the JNDI server. The application deployer ensures the availability of a service provider to our application:

```
javax.mail.Session session =
            (javax.mail.Session) initial.lookup("java:comp/env/MailSession");
```

Once a `session` object is obtained, we need to construct a mail message. The JavaMail API defines the abstract `Message` class for this purpose. The API provides a concrete implementation called `MimeMessage`, representing a **MIME (Multipurpose Internet Mail Extensions)** type of message:

```
javax.mail.Message msg = new MimeMessage(session);
```

The `MimeMessage` class contains several methods for getting/setting properties of the message. The various properties such as **From, Subject, Date**, and so on, can be set by using the appropriate set methods. The message text itself is set by calling the `setText()` method.

Once a message is composed, it can be dispatched by calling the `send()` method of the `Transport` class.

```
Transport.send(msg);
```

The mail server will now deliver the message to the recipient. We'll be seeing this in action in the example shortly.

> *For a more detailed discussion on JavaMail, the reader is referred to Chapter 17 of* Professional Java Server Programming, J2EE Edition *from Wrox Press, ISBN 1 861004 65 6.*

A Message-Driven-Bean-based Sample Application

In this section, we will develop an application that uses a message-driven bean. We will create a message queue called `OrderQueue` on our J2EE messaging server, and a message-driven bean that registers its interest in this queue. We will then develop a client that sends purchase orders to this `OrderQueue`. The messages containing the purchase orders will be delivered asynchronously to the message-driven bean. On receipt of the message, the bean will print the order details on the console and will send a thank-you note to the customer, using JavaMail API.

We will begin with the development of the message-driven bean class.

The Message-Driven Bean Class

The class `MessageBean` implements both the `MessageDrivenBean` and `MessageListener` interfaces:

```
import java.io.Serializable;
import java.rmi.RemoteException;
import javax.ejb.*;
import javax.naming.*;
import javax.jms.*;
import java.util.*;
import java.text.*;
import javax.mail.*;
import javax.activation.*;
import javax.mail.internet.*;

public class MessageBean implements MessageDrivenBean, MessageListener {

   private transient MessageDrivenContext context = null;
```

We define a no-argument constructor for the class, together with null-body implementations of the container callback methods:

```
public MessageBean() {}

public void ejbCreate() {}
public void ejbRemove() {}
```

In the implementation of the `setMessageDrivenContext()` method, we copy the received `context` object in the instance variable:

```
public void setMessageDrivenContext(MessageDrivenContext context) {
   this.context = context;
}
```

Next, comes the implementation of the important method `onMessage()`. This method contains the business logic and is invoked by the container on message receipt. The method takes the `Message` parameter containing the received message:

```
public void onMessage(javax.jms.Message msg) {
```

Note that the `Message` class is defined in both of the `javax.jms` and `javax.mail` packages. Thus, while declaring the parameter, a full qualifier for the `Message` class is required.

In the `onMessage()` method, we check if the received message is of type `MapMessage`. If the message is of type `MapMessage`, the program prints the details given in the message, by printing the various key fields defined in the message:

```
try {
  if (msg instanceof MapMessage) {
    MapMessage map = (MapMessage) msg;
    System.out.println("Order received: ");
    System.out.println("Order ID: " + map.getString("OrderID") +
                    " Item ID: " + map.getInt("ItemID") +
                    " Quantity: " + map.getInt("Quantity") +
                    " Unit Price: " + map.getDouble("UnitPrice"));
```

The program then calls the `private` method `sendNote()` to send an e-mail note to the message producer:

```
        sendNote(map.getString("emailID"));
```

If the message isn't a `MapMessage`, the program prints an appropriate message on the system console:

```
        } else {
            System.out.println("wrong message type");
        }
    } catch (Throwable te) {
        te.printStackTrace();
    }
}
```

Let's now look at the `sendNote()` method. The `sendNote()` method receives one `String` type parameter containing the e-mail ID of the recipient. The method first obtains a reference to the JNDI context and looks up the environment variable `MailSession`. The mail sessions are managed by the container and are registered with the JNDI server at the time of deployment:

```
    private void sendNote(String recipient) {
      try {
        Context initial = new InitialContext();
        javax.mail.Session session = (javax.mail.Session)
                              initial.lookup("java:comp/env/MailSession");
```

Next, the program creates a mail message by instantiating `MimeMessage` class. The various fields of the message are then set using the appropriate `set` methods:

```
        javax.mail.Message msg = new MimeMessage(session);

        msg.setFrom();
        msg.setRecipients(javax.mail.Message.RecipientType.TO,
                        InternetAddress.parse(recipient, false));

        msg.setSubject("Order Confirmation");
        DateFormat dateFormatter = DateFormat.getDateTimeInstance(
                            DateFormat.LONG, DateFormat.SHORT);

        Date timeStamp = new Date();
        String messageText = "Thank you for your order." + '\n' +
                        "We received your order on " +
                        dateFormatter.format(timeStamp) + ".";

        msg.setText(messageText);
        msg.setSentDate(timeStamp);
```

Once a message is composed, we dispatch it by calling the static `send()` method of the `Transport` class, passing our message as an argument to it:

```
        Transport.send(msg);
    } catch(Exception e) {
        throw new EJBException(e.getMessage());
    }
  }
}
```

This will deliver the mail message asynchronously to the client using a mail server.

The Messaging Client

We will now develop a client program that delivers orders asynchronously to our server by using the message-driven bean described in the previous section. The client program is a console-based application that requires one command-line argument specifying the name of the message queue to which the orders will be dispatched:

```java
import javax.jms.*;
import javax.naming.*;

public class MessageClient {

  public static void main(String[] args) {

    Context jndiContext = null;
    QueueConnectionFactory queueConnectionFactory = null;
    QueueConnection queueConnection = null;
    QueueSession queueSession = null;
    Queue queue = null;
    QueueSender queueSender = null;
    MapMessage message = null;
    final int NUM_MSGS;

    if ((args.length < 1)) {
      System.out.println("Usage: java MessageClient " + "<queue-name>");
      System.exit(1);
    }
```

The program first obtains a reference to the JNDI context by calling the `InitialContext()` method. Next, it looks the up connection factory and the queue objects in the JNDI name space:

```java
try {
  jndiContext = new InitialContext();
  queueConnectionFactory = (QueueConnectionFactory)
                 jndiContext.lookup("java:comp/env/QueueConnectionFactory");

  queue = (Queue) jndiContext.lookup(args[0]);
} catch (NamingException e) {
  System.out.println("JNDI lookup failed: " + e.toString());
  System.exit(1);
}
```

Once the factory reference is obtained, the program creates a queue connection and a session for communication. Note that we create a non-transacted session with automatic acknowledgement mode set:

```java
try {

  queueConnection = queueConnectionFactory.createQueueConnection();
  queueSession = queueConnection.createQueueSession(false,
                                      Session.AUTO_ACKNOWLEDGE);
```

Next, the program creates a sender for this queue by calling the `createSender()` method on the created session object:

```java
queueSender = queueSession.createSender(queue);
```

281

This sender is used for sending the messages to the queue. Before a message is sent, it needs to be composed. A message is created and composed by calling an appropriate method on the session object. In our case, we will compose a map message by calling `createMapMessage()`. We will add the contents to the message by defining several name/value pairs in the message body:

```
message = queueSession.createMapMessage();
message.setString("OrderID", "1");
message.setInt("ItemID", 5);
message.setInt("Quantity", 50);
message.setDouble("UnitPrice", 5.00);
// Note you'll need to change the email address for this to work
message.setString("emailID", "your.email@your.com");
```

Finally, the message is dispatched to the queue by calling the `send()` method on the sender object. The method receives the composed message as a parameter.

```
queueSender.send(message);
```

The message is now delivered to the messaging server. The server will ensure that the message is delivered to our business logic by invoking the message-driven bean defined above:

```
    } catch (JMSException e) {
    System.out.println("Exception occurred: " + e.toString());
    } finally {
    if (queueConnection != null) {
      try {
        queueConnection.close();
      } catch (JMSException e) {}
    }
  }
 }
}
```

The Deployment Descriptor

Here is the deployment descriptor we need for our message-driven bean:

```
<?xml version="1.0"?>

<!DOCTYPE ejb-jar PUBLIC
       '-//Sun Microsystems, Inc.//DTD Enterprise JavaBeans 2.0//EN'
       'http://java.sun.com/dtd/ejb-jar_2_0.dtd'>

<ejb-jar>
  <description>A simple message-driven bean</description>
  <display-name>MessageBeanJAR</display-name>
  <enterprise-beans>
    <message-driven>
      <description>The message-driven bean</description>
      <display-name>MsgBean</display-name>
      <ejb-name>MsgBean</ejb-name>
      <ejb-class>MessageBean</ejb-class>
      <transaction-type>Bean</transaction-type>
      <acknowledge-mode>Auto-acknowledge</acknowledge-mode>
      <message-driven-destination>
        <destination-type>javax.jms.Queue</destination-type>
</message-driven-destination>
      <resource-ref>
        <res-ref-name>QueueConnectionFactory</res-ref-name>
        <res-type>javax.jms.QueueConnectionFactory</res-type>
```

```
            <res-auth>Container</res-auth>
            <res-sharing-scope>Shareable</res-sharing-scope>
        </resource-ref>
        <resource-ref>
            <res-ref-name>MailSession</res-ref-name>
            <res-type>javax.mail.Session</res-type>
            <res-auth>Container</res-auth>
            <res-sharing-scope>Shareable</res-sharing-scope>
        </resource-ref>
        <resource-env-ref>
            <resource-env-ref-name>OrderQueue</resource-env-ref-name>
            <resource-env-ref-type>javax.jms.Queue</resource-env-ref-type>
        </resource-env-ref>
    </message-driven>
  </enterprise-beans>
</ejb-jar>
```

We'll cover the message-driven bean specific elements in a moment, but the only other things of interest in this deployment descriptor are the resource references. Since we're planning on using e-mail notification, we need to add a `MailSession` as a `<resource-ref>`. When we come to deploy this bean on our server, we'll need to specify the IP address of our mail server, together with an e-mail address to send from. We'll be looking are `<resource-ref>` elements in Chapter 8.

The relevant section of the DTD for message-driven beans is as follows:

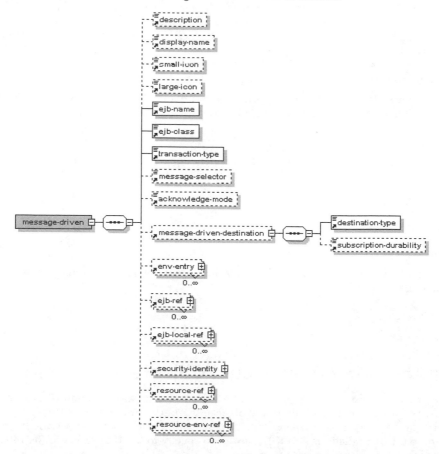

Notice that there aren't many new elements to describe our message-driven bean:

<message-driven>

The first and most obvious is the `<message-driven>` element, which is simply the parent element for our bean just like the `<entity>` and `<session>` elements.

<message-selector>

The `<message-selector>` element allows us to filter the incoming messages by writing selection criteria as we saw earlier in the section on *Selecting Messages*.

<acknowledge-mode>

We designate the way we want acknowledgements handled in the `<acknowledge-mode>` element. The value if this element can be either of:

- ❑ `Auto-acknowledge`
  The JMS session automatically acknowledges message delivery when the processing thread returns from the `onMessage()` method.

- ❑ `Dups-ok-acknowledge`
  The JMS session lazily acknowledges messages. In this case the provider may deliver a message more than once, thus this option should only be used with beans that are tolerant of duplicate messages. On the other hand, the benefit is that it reduces the session overhead by minimizing the work the session needs to do to prevent duplicate messages from being received.

<message-driven-destination>

The `<message-driven-destination>` element describes if the bean is designed for a queue or a topic. It contains two child elements `<destination-type>` and `<subscription durability>`.

<destination-type>

The destination-type element can be one of two values depending on whether the bean subscribes to a topic or queue:

- ❑ `javax.jms.Queue`
- ❑ `javax.jms.Topic`

<subscription durability>

The `<subscription-durability>` element is used to indicate if the topic subscription is durable or non-durable by having one of two values:

- ❑ `Durable`
- ❑ `NonDurable`

Setting up the JMS Administered Objects

As the application is going to use a messaging server, we will need to create the administered objects used by the application. We will create two administered objects, `QueueConnectionFactory` of type connection factory and `OrderQueue` of type queue. To create administered objects, we use the `j2eeadmin` utility supplied in the J2EE installation. This will allow us to specify to the JMS server in the reference implementation server what objects we want to create.

To create a connection factory called QueueConnectionFactory, type the following on the command line:

```
%J2EE_HOME%\bin\j2eeadmin -addJmsFactory QueueConnectionFactory Queue
```

Note that the final variable (Queue) is not case sensitive. To ensure that the object has been created, type the following on the command line:

```
%J2EE_HOME%\bin\j2eeadmin -listJmsFactory
```

This lists all the JMS factories defined in the system, as in the following screenshot:

```
Command Prompt                                                        _ □ ×
Microsoft Windows 2000 [Version 5.00.2195]
(C) Copyright 1985-2000 Microsoft Corp.

C:\>j2eeadmin -addJmsFactory QueueConnectionFactory Queue
C:\>j2eeadmin -listJmsFactory
JmsFactory
----------
< JMS Cnx Factory : QueueConnectionFactory , Queue , No properties >
< JMS Cnx Factory : jms/TopicConnectionFactory , Topic , No properties >
< JMS Cnx Factory : jms/QueueConnectionFactory , Queue , No properties >
< JMS Cnx Factory : TopicConnectionFactory , Topic , No properties >
C:\>_
```

Then, to add a message queue called OrderQueue, enter the following on the command line:

```
%J2EE_HOME%\bin\j2eeadmin -addJmsDestination OrderQueue Queue
```

As before, we should check that the object has been added, so type the following on the command line:

```
%J2EE_HOME%\bin\j2eeadmin -listJmsDestination
```

This lists all the destination objects defined in the system, as seen in the following screenshot:

```
Command Prompt                                                        _ □ ×
C:\>j2eeadmin -addJmsDestination OrderQueue Queue
C:\>j2eeadmin -listJmsDestination
JmsDestination
--------------
< JMS Destination : jms/Queue , javax.jms.Queue >
< JMS Destination : jms/Topic , javax.jms.Topic >
< JMS Destination : OrderQueue , javax.jms.Queue >
C:\>_
```

Once we have added the two objects, we are ready to create and deploy the application.

Creating the Application

The first thing to do is package our bean implementation class with the `ejb-jar.xml` descriptor, just as with session and entity beans. We'll call this JAR file `MessageBeanJAR.jar`. Next, we need to create a new application to include our bean. Again, we'll use the deployment tool supplied with the J2EE 1.3 Reference Implementation.

Start by creating a new application, which we'll start in a new file called `MessageApp.ear`.

Now select File | Add to application | EJB Jar, and select the `MessageBeanJAR.jar` file.

Next we need to specify the mail server we'll be using. Select the MsgBean object in the `MessageBeanJAR.jar` file, and select the Resource Ref's tab. For each of the entries in the Resource Factories Reference in Code pane, fill in the JNDI Name (we'll use the Coded Name). For the QueueConnectionFactory, the User Name and Password we'll be using are both j2ee:

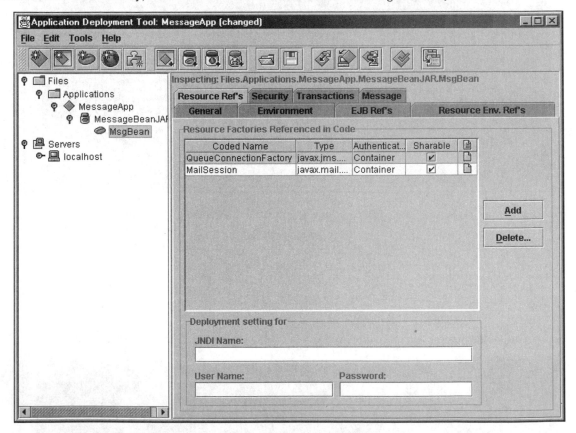

When we select the MailSession, we need to supply three additional values:

- ❑ From – this is the address our confirmation e-mail will be sent from
- ❑ Host – this is the IP address of the mail server we're using
- ❑ User name – this is the name used to connect to the mail server

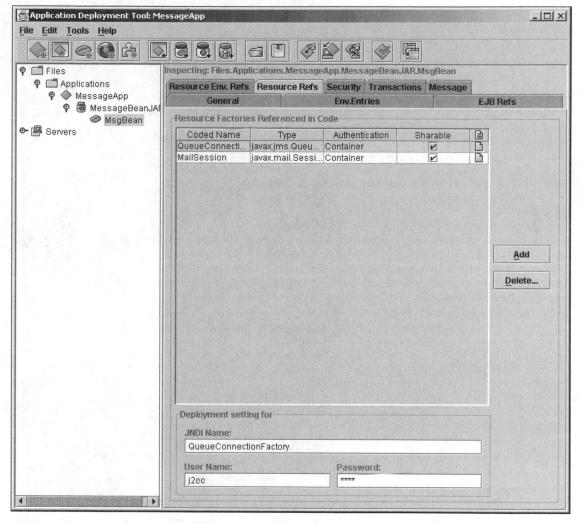

There are a couple more JNDI names that we have set, so switch to the JNDI Names tab for the JAR file and give the bean and the queue a name:

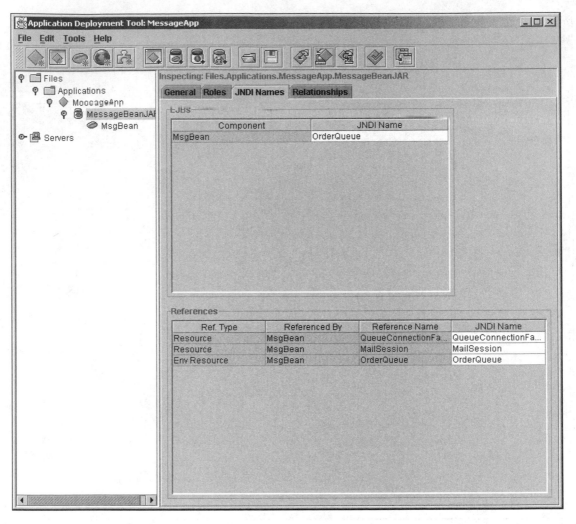

You'll see that we've actually given the bean the JNDI name of the queue. This is so that the client can find the bean by referring to a queue rather than a bean.

Creating the Application Client

Next, we will create an application client, so select File | New | Application Client. You will see the New Application Client – Jar File Contents dialog. Make sure that MessageApp is selected in the Create Archive Within Application box, and then click on Add. Browse to and select MessageClient.class, click Add and then OK in order to add the client:

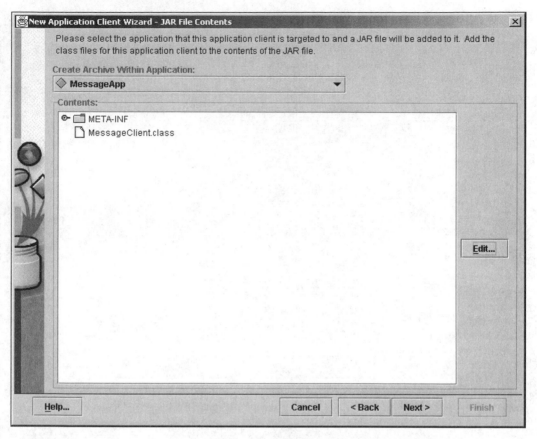

On the next three screens, we accept the defaults, until we get to the Resource References screen. Here, we add a resource reference. Select Type as javax.jms.QueueConnectionFactory. In the Coded Name field type QueueConnectionFactory. Set the Authentication as Container. In the text fields at the bottom of the screen enter the following:

- ❑ JNDI Name: QueueConnectionFactory
- ❑ User Name: j2ee
- ❑ Password: j2ee

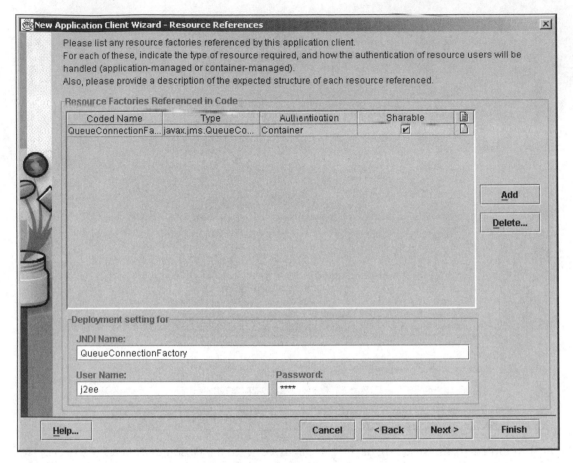

On the JMS Destination References screen, click the Add button to add a new reference. Select Type as javax.jms.Queue and in the Coded Name field type OrderQueue. In the JNDI Name field, also type OrderQueue:

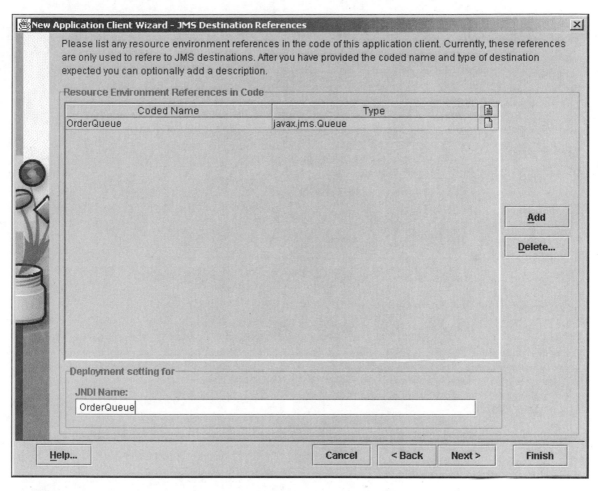

On the remaining screen we accept the defaults. Click on the Finish button to complete the creation of client application. We will see the client application added under our application name in the deployment tool:

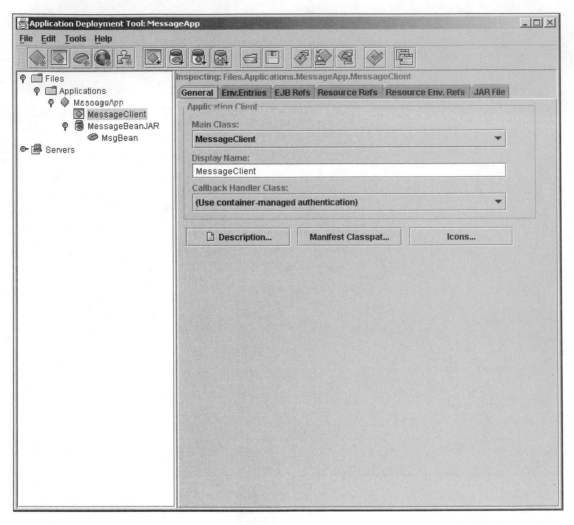

Now, we are ready to deploy the application. Select the Tools | Deploy menu option to deploy the application.

The status of deployment is displayed with the help of two vertical bars and you will be informed of the success of the deployment.

Running the Client Application

You can test the deployed message bean by running the client application. To run the client application, type the following on the command line:

```
%J2EE_HOME%\bin\runclient -client MessageApp.ear -name MessageClient OrderQueue
```

You will probably get a login box appear. Simply enter j2ee for both the username and password:

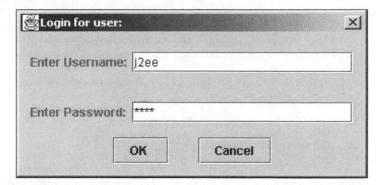

When the client program runs, a message is sent to the messaging server. This will invoke our message bean that prints the received order on the console and sends an e-mail notification to the return address specified in the message. Look up the J2EE console to confirm that our message bean prints the order:

```
C:\WINDOWS\System32\cmd.exe

C:\ProEJB\Chapter06>runclient -client MessageApp.ear -name MessageClient OrderQu
eue

Initiating login ...
Binding name:`java:comp/env/OrderQueue`
Binding name:`java:comp/env/QueueConnectionFactory`
Java(TM) Message Service 1.0.2 Reference Implementation (build b10)
Unbinding name:`java:comp/env/OrderQueue`
Unbinding name:`java:comp/env/QueueConnectionFactory`
C:\ProEJB\Chapter06>
```

```
C:\WINDOWS\system32\cmd.exe - j2ee -verbose

Order received:
Order ID: 1 Item ID: 5 Quanity: 50 Unit Price: 5.0
```

You should also receive a mail confirming the order in your inbox (assuming you have configured the bean to point to your mail server).

Summary

In this chapter we have studied an important addition made to the J2EE specification – a message-driven bean. A message driven bean is a message consumer that receives the messages asynchronously. Sun's J2EE Reference Implementation contains a messaging server based on the JMS specification. We looked at the following topics:

- ❑ We looked at a brief overview of the JMS API, and how we can use it to send and receive messages between application objects.

- ❑ We studied the use of the JavaMail API for composing and sending e-mail through program code.

- ❑ A client desiring to send an asynchronous message to a message-driven EJB does so by sending a message to a queue, or a topic, defined in the messaging server. The message-driven bean registers itself with a queue or a topic of its choice; the messaging server then delivers the message asynchronously to the message-driven bean.

- ❑ Finally, we rounded off the chapter by creating a sample application that was used to illustrate the use of a message-driven bean.

In the next chapter, we will learn more about accessing other resources, be they other beans, databases or even URLs, from our EJBs.

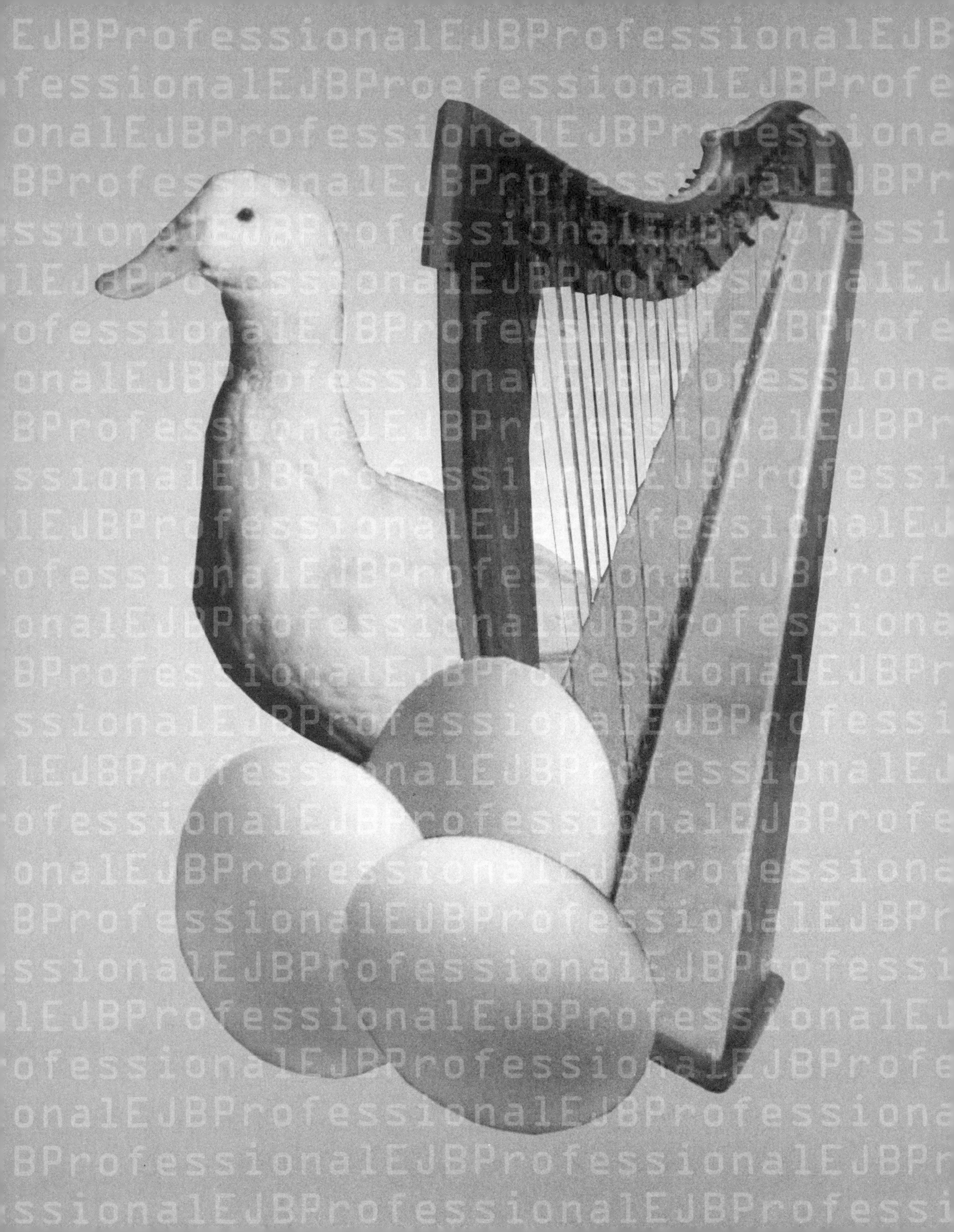

8

Resource Management and the EJB Environment

The key to the success of Enterprise JavaBeans is the container architecture that allows container vendors to provide enterprise-level services such as automatic persistence handling, transaction management, security, and a host of other key services. To allow for the maximum in flexibility and portability, the EJB specification has attempted to provide vendor-neutral standards for EJB container design. A compliant container provides an environment for enterprise beans that allows the beans to customize their business logic during deployment or assembly without the need to change the enterprise bean's source code.

Indeed, both the 1.1 and 2.0 specifications make the following statement about the EJB environment:

> *"The Application Assembler and Deployer should be able to customize an enterprise bean's business logic without accessing the enterprise bean's source code."*

This goal is achieved by allowing dynamic customization of an enterprise bean's references to other enterprise beans as well as resources external to the container. The container uses JNDI interfaces to insulate the bean's source code from the physical location of any required resources.

In this chapter we will begin with a brief look at JNDI, followed by a closer look at various means of configuring an enterprise bean's environment. While examining this customizable environment, we will cover the following topics:

- ❑ EJB environment entries
- ❑ References to other enterprise beans
- ❑ Resource manager connection factories
- ❑ Resource environment references

All of the deployment instructions and screenshots in this chapter relate to the J2EE Reference Implementation version 1.3. There are likely to be slight variations in the methodology used to deploy these applications between application servers. If you encounter any problems, be certain to consult your application server's documentation.

Let's start by looking at the EJB environment.

The Enterprise Bean Environment

As stated earlier, the J2EE container provides a variety of services to ease the work of enterprise bean developers. These services reside within a framework that exposes interfaces to be used within enterprise beans that abstract bean development from the underlying protocols, connections, and other resources. This framework is usually known as the **enterprise bean's environment**. The container implements this environment and makes its services and resources available through JNDI interfaces. The EJB specification outlines four aspects that demonstrate how this environment is made possible:

❑ The enterprise bean's business methods access the environment using the JNDI interfaces. The EJB specification mandates the use of JNDI interfaces to provide a common naming convention for referring to these resources. These names are used within the beans themselves and the deployment descriptor. The bean provider declares in the deployment descriptor all the environment properties that the enterprise bean expects to be provided with at run time. We'll cover several examples of this throughout the chapter.

❑ The container provides an implementation of the JNDI API naming context that stores the enterprise bean environment. Yet another advantage of EJB is that the bean developer need not worry about how this implementation is provided. The container also provides the tools that allow the deployer to create and manage the environment of each enterprise bean. These tools are container-specific.

❑ The deployer creates the environment properties that are declared in the enterprise bean's deployment descriptor either by hand or by using the tools provided by the container. The deployer can also set and modify the environment property values. This provides a tremendous degree of flexibility in deployment without having to touch any source code. If you choose to make these changes by hand, be sure to study your container's documentation thoroughly.

❑ The container makes the environment-naming context available to the enterprise bean instances at run time. The enterprise bean's instances use the JNDI interfaces to obtain the values of the environment properties. Notice that this is dynamically bound at run time. This is what permits the flexibility mentioned before.

Each enterprise bean defines its own set of environment properties that are shared by all instances of an enterprise bean class within the same home (an enterprise bean can be deployed within a container multiple times, resulting in multiple home interfaces). Although the deployment descriptor can be modified and the enterprise bean's environment dynamically changed, bean instances themselves are not allowed to modify the environment at run time.

Now let's take a more detailed look at how the enterprise bean's environment can be accessed by the bean's business methods.

Accessing the EJB Environment

As stated earlier, the container implements the bean's environment and makes its services available by exposing JNDI interfaces. Through these interfaces, an enterprise bean instance is able to locate the environment-naming context and subsequently, the particular service or resource desired. An instance creates a `javax.naming.InitialContext` object by using one of two constructors. The default `InitialContext` constructor has no arguments and the alternative constructor takes a single `hashtable` as a parameter. Enterprise beans use the default constructor to instantiate an `InitialContext` object that is then used to look up the environment-naming context. The `InitialContext` object is initialized by the container with the proper JNDI information necessary to create an initial context.

Clients of enterprise beans that are not, themselves, enterprise beans use the alternative constructor to establish an initial naming context. They must pass the necessary property values into the object via a `hashtable`. Enterprise beans have these properties automatically initialized by the container. Standalone clients do not have this luxury.

Once you have a reference to an initial context, you can perform the actual JNDI lookup using a registered JNDI name. The specific JNDI name used will depend upon how the resources have been mapped, but it will adhere to the following format:

```
"java:comp/env/subContext/resourceName"
```

where *subContext* represents the JNDI path and *resourceName* represents the actual JNDI name of the resource.

Consider the following code sample:

```
Context context = new InitialContext();
Object result = context.lookup("java:comp/env/ejb/EmplRecord");
```

In the above code sample, an `InitialContext` object is first instantiated (and referenced by a variable of the interface type, `Context`), and then used to perform a JNDI lookup of the `EmplRecord` resource located in the `ejb` subcontext.

> *The return type of the `lookup()` method is type `Object`. To store the result in any other type of object, we would have to cast the result to the appropriate type.*

EJB Environment Entries

Just as you can declare initialization parameters for Java servlets within the deployment descriptor, you can declare initialization parameters in the deployment descriptor for your enterprise beans. These parameters are called **environment entries** in the EJB world. The environment entries you specify for an enterprise bean are shared by all instances of the bean class within the same home (an enterprise bean can be deployed within a container multiple times, resulting in multiple home interfaces). Also, an enterprise bean cannot modify its deployment descriptor at run time. The bean deployer should do this.

An environment entry consists of a name, data type, value, and optional description. Since this entry is made in the deployment descriptor, each of these items has a corresponding XML element tag:

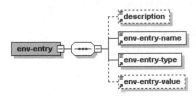

<env-entry>

The top-level element that contains the other elements.

<env-entry-name>

The name used within the bean to retrieve the environment entry value.

<env-entry-type>

The Java type expected by the bean code. Only eight data types are considered valid: the seven primitive wrapper classes (Boolean, Float, Integer, and so on) and the String class.

<env-entry-value>

The actual value that will be contained in the object returned by the JNDI lookup method.

The following is an excerpt from a deployment descriptor that specifies environment entries for a session bean:

```
<enterprise-beans>
   <session>
   ...
   <ejb-name>MyConverter</ejb-name>
   <ejb-class>ConverterEJB</ejb-class>
   ...
   <env-entry>
      <description>
         The conversion ratio from US Dollars to Japanese Yen
      </description>
      <env-entry-name>dollarsToYen</env-entry-name>
      <env-entry-type>java.lang.Double</env-entry-type>
      <env-entry-value>121.0000</env-entry-value>
   </env-entry>

   <env-entry>
      <description>
         The conversion ratio from Japanese Yen to the European Euro
      </description>
      <env-entry-name>yenToEuro</env-entry-name>
      <env-entry-type>java.lang.Double</env-entry-type>
      <env-entry-value>0.0077</env-entry-value>
   </env-entry>

   </session>
</enterprise-beans>
```

When a bean is performing an environment entry lookup, the container will use JNDI to search the registry for the requested name. If an environment property has been bound to the specified name (this is declared in the deployment descriptor), then the `lookup()` method will return the specified value. The return type is `Object`, so the result will need to be cast to the appropriate type (`Double`, `Integer`, `String`, and so on). If the requested name has not been bound to an object, then the method throws a `javax.naming.NameNotFoundException`.

The Flexible Converter Example

The J2EE Reference Implementation documentation ships with a sample application with an enterprise bean named `ConverterEJB`. This bean performs simple currency conversion on the client's behalf. In the sample code that ships with the documentation, the currency conversion ratio is hard coded into the enterprise bean's source code. In our adaptation, we will declare the conversion ratios as environment entries and retrieve the values via JNDI lookup calls.

> *Of course, if you were actually writing an enterprise application which included a currency conversion function, it would be preferable to store these conversions in a database, XML file, or somewhere on a third-party remote server, since currency conversion ratios are dynamic. This example is merely used to demonstrate how environment entries work, not as an example of best practices.*

The Remote Interface

The remote interface for our `FlexibleConverter` enterprise bean is unchanged from the original `Converter` remote interface:

```
/*
 * Copyright 2000 Sun Microsystems, Inc. All Rights Reserved.
 *
 * This software is the proprietary information of Sun Microsystems, Inc.
 * Use is subject to license terms.
 */

import javax.ejb.EJBObject;
import java.rmi.RemoteException;

public interface Converter extends EJBObject {
    public double dollarToYen(double dollars) throws RemoteException;
    public double yenToEuro(double yen) throws RemoteException;
}
```

The Home Interface

The home interface is also unchanged from the original `ConverterHome` home interface:

```
/*
 * Copyright 2000 Sun Microsystems, Inc. All Rights Reserved.
 *
 * This software is the proprietary information of Sun Microsystems, Inc.
 * Use is subject to license terms.
 */

import java.io.Serializable;
import java.rmi.RemoteException;
import javax.ejb.CreateException;
```

```
import javax.ejb.EJBHome;

public interface ConverterHome extends EJBHome {
    Converter create() throws RemoteException, CreateException;
}
```

The Enterprise Bean Class

Unlike the previous two interfaces, the enterprise bean class is significantly different from the original `ConverterEJB` class. The `FlexibleConverterEJB` is a stateless session bean that implements two business methods, `dollarToYen()` and `yenToEuro()`, as declared in the `Converter` remote interface.

Here's the declarative portion of the class definition:

```
import javax.ejb.SessionBean;
import javax.ejb.SessionContext;
import javax.naming.*;

public class FlexibleConverterEJB implements SessionBean {

}
```

Next, we must implement the two business methods declared in the remote interface. First, we'll take a look at the `dollarToYen()` method,which obtains the conversion ratio from Dollars to Yen:

```
public double dollarToYen(double dollars) {
    Context initCtx, myEnv;
    Double dollarsToYen = null;

    try {
```

We begin by obtaining a reference to an instance of the bean's initial naming context, `initCtx`. This provides a baseline from which specific naming contexts within a given namespace can be obtained. The next step obtains one such naming context. The bean's environment naming context is retrieved when we perform the actual JNDI lookup of the `"java:comp/env"` name. This returns to us an object referencing the enterprise bean's environment-naming context from which environment entries can be retrieved via JNDI lookup calls:

```
        initCtx = new InitialContext();
        myEnv = (Context)initCtx.lookup("java:comp/env");
```

By specifying the JNDI name `"dollarToYen"` as a parameter to our environment lookup, a copy of the `Double` object bound to that name is returned by the `lookup()` method call. This object is returned as type `Object` and must be cast to the appropriate type, which is `Double` in this case:

```
        dollarsToYen = (Double)myEnv.lookup("dollarsToYen");
    } catch(NamingException ne) {
        ne.printStackTrace();
    }

    return dollarsToYen.doubleValue() * dollars;
}
```

Since both of the JNDI lookup calls that we have made have had the potential to throw a `javax.naming.NamingException`, as usual we have placed the heart of this method within a `try/catch` block and prepared our code to display the run time stack trace in the event that such an exceptional circumstance occurs.

The second business method, `yenToEuro()`, used to obtain the conversion ratio from the Yen to the European Euro, is very similar to the previous method; only method and variable names have changed. Here's the method (the highlighted lines indicate differences between this method and the `dollarToYen()` method):

```java
    public double yenToEuro(double yen) {
      Context initCtx, myEnv;
      Double yenToEuro = null;

      try {
        initCtx = new InitialContext();
        myEnv = (Context)initCtx.lookup("java:comp/env");
        yenToEuro = (Double)myEnv.lookup("yenToEuro");
      } catch (NamingException ne) {
        ne.printStackTrace();
      }

      return yenToEuro.doubleValue() * yen;
    }
```

So, as you can see, the differences amount to a change in variable name or JNDI lookup name.

The final touches needed by our class are a handful of empty method implementations. We need one for the default constructor and one each for the lifecycle methods for our enterprise bean:

```java
    public FlexibleConverterEJB() {}
    public void ejbCreate() {}
    public void ejbRemove() {}
    public void ejbActivate() {}
    public void ejbPassivate() {}
    public void setSessionContext(SessionContext sc) {}
```

All three of our classes (`Converter`, `ConverterHome`, `FlexibleConverterEJB`) should compile perfectly. Once your code compiles, you are ready to deploy the application and then write a client for the enterprise bean.

The Deployment Descriptor

Here is the XML deployment descriptor that our bean will use:

```xml
<?xml version="1.0"?>

<!DOCTYPE ejb-jar PUBLIC '-//Sun Microsystems, Inc.//DTD Enterprise JavaBeans
2.0//EN' 'http://java.sun.com/dtd/ejb-jar_2_0.dtd'>

<ejb-jar>
  <description>no description</description>
```

```
    <display-name>FlexConverterJAR</display-name>

    <enterprise-beans>

      <session>
        <description>no description</description>
        <display-name>FlexConverterBean</display-name>
        <ejb-name>FlexConverterBean</ejb-name>
        <home>ConverterHome</home>
        <remote>Converter</remote>
        <ejb-class>FlexibleConverterEJB</ejb-class>
        <session-type>Stateless</session-type>
        <transaction-type>Bean</transaction-type>
        <env-entry>
          <description>A description of EntryName</description>
          <env-entry-name>dollarsToYen</env-entry-name>
          <env-entry-type>java.lang.Double</env-entry-type>
          <env-entry-value>121.0000</env-entry-value>
        </env-entry>
        <env-entry>
          <description>A description of EntryName</description>
          <env-entry-name>yenToEuro</env-entry-name>
          <env-entry-type>java.lang.Double</env-entry-type>
          <env-entry-value>0.0077</env-entry-value>
        </env-entry>
      </session>

    </enterprise-beans>

  </ejb-jar>
```

Deploying the Application

The specific steps necessary to deploy this application will vary between application servers. The important step will be setting the environment properties before actually deploying the application. While it is possible to code these by hand directly into your deployment descriptor, using your application server's deployment utility will help you to avoid making typing errors.

However your application server provides for the declaration of environment entries, you need to declare two entries for the FlexibleConverterBean to run properly. The following table identifies the name, type, and recommended values that you use in deploying the bean on your own server:

Entry Name	Data Type	Value
dollarsToYen	Double	121.0000
yenToEuro	Double	0.0077

Again, how you set these properties will vary depending upon the application server you are using. In the J2EE Reference Implementation, there are two opportunities to specify an enterprise bean's environment properties: the Bean Creation Wizard and the enterprise bean's Environment tab on the main console. Of these two, I have found that setting the properties through the wizard produced more reliable results when using version 1.2 of the J2EE RI deploy tool. With 1.3, I have found both equally easy to use.

During the creation of the bean, you are given the opportunity to specify environment properties. The screenshot below of this window shows the two environment entries that should be specified for the `FlexibleConverterBean`:

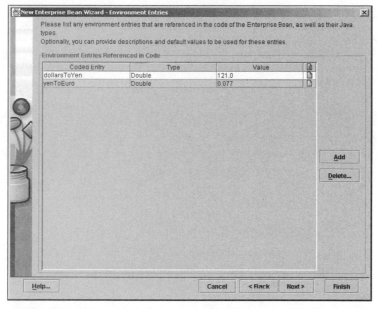

These values can be modified in the application display console of the deployment tool. If you select the enterprise bean you wish to modify, then you can access and modify the environment entries for that bean by selecting the **Envo Entries** tab in the right-hand frame:

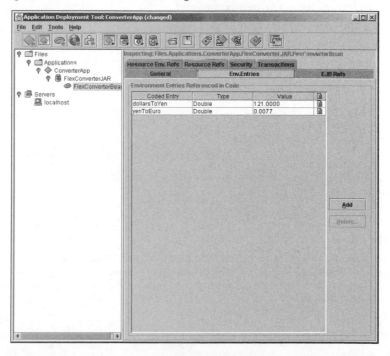

Once you have set up the bean's environment properties and successfully deployed the bean into your application server's EJB container, you are ready to write the EJB client and test the FlexibleConverterEJB.

Testing the Application

In order to test the application, we need a client to invoke the enterprise bean's business methods as defined in the remote interface. As we have kept the remote and home interfaces unchanged, then we can also use the ConverterClient client class used with the Converter sample application that ships with the J2EE documentation. Here is the source code for that class file:

```
import javax.naming.Context;
import javax.naming.InitialContext;
import javax.rmi.PortableRemoteObject;

import Converter;
import ConverterHome;

public class ConverterClient {

  public static void main(String[] args) {
    try {
      Context initial = new InitialContext();
      Object objref = initial.lookup("MyFlexConverter");
```

Be sure that the JNDI name you specify in this JNDI lookup is the same name that you specified during deployment of the FlexibleConverterEJB enterprise bean. In this case we have used MyFlexConverter.

```
      ConverterHome home = (ConverterHome)
          PortableRemoteObject.narrow(objref, ConverterHome.class);

      Converter currencyConverter = home.create();

      double amount = currencyConverter.dollarToYen(100.00);
      System.out.println(String.valueOf(amount));
      amount = currencyConverter.yenToEuro(100.00);
      System.out.println(String.valueOf(amount));

      currencyConverter.remove();

    } catch (Exception ex) {
      System.err.println("Caught an unexpected exception!");
      ex.printStackTrace();
    }
  }
}
```

Next you need to compile this class and execute the ConverterClient application. Be sure that the client JAR created by your application server's deployment wizard is directly added to your system classpath. If you used the same conversion ratio values indicated in the table above, you should see output similar to that shown:

```
Command Prompt                                                    _ □ ×

C:\ProEJB\Chapter08\FlexibleConverter>java -classpath %J2EE_HOME%\lib\j2ee.jar;F
lexibleConverterAppClient.jar;. ConverterClient
12100.0
0.77

C:\ProEJB\Chapter08\FlexibleConverter>_
```

Congratulations! You have successfully declared environment entries for an enterprise bean and used those values to modify your bean's run time execution. This is an important technique that decouples enterprise beans from the specific resources they will be accessing. The bean deployer configures the necessary values when the application is deployed, and the beans access these parameters at run time. It is important to realize that once a bean is deployed, the environment entries cannot be modified. If the bean deployer modifies them, the bean will have to be re-deployed for the changes to take effect. If the enterprise bean attempts to modify the values, then a J2EE-compliant container will throw a `javax.naming.OperationNot-SupportedException` exception.

References to Other Enterprise Beans

There are often times when enterprise beans need to communicate with one another. Many architectures use session beans to delegate work to other beans or to serve as a mediator between the client and an entity bean. Some even use entity beans that serve as an aggregate entity, communicating with other entity beans. Whatever the reason, enterprise beans need to be able to obtain a reference to other enterprise beans. Due to the nature of the container's restrictions on enterprise bean communications, it is necessary to define the nature of the bean-to-bean relationship and allow that reference to be managed by the container.

In order for a client to access an enterprise bean (regardless of whether that client is a browser, servlet, command-line application, or another EJB) it must do so via an interface. With EJB 1.1, there was only one way of doing this, via the enterprise bean's remote interface. This requires an RMI trip across the network, and creates an unnecessary degree of overhead for intra-container bean-to-bean calls. As a result, the 2.0 version of the specification has introduced a new means of referencing one EJB from another, via the bean's local interface. We'll start by taking an in-depth look at how to use the traditional remote interface and then discuss the possibilities available with the new local interface.

Referencing an EJB from another EJB via the Remote Interface

To access the remote interface of one enterprise bean from another enterprise bean, the container provides a special mechanism. Without this mechanism, if enterprise bean A needed to access enterprise bean B, then enterprise bean A would need a reference to enterprise bean B's home interface, just like a standard EJB client.

This mechanism allows a bean provider to refer to the homes of other enterprise beans using "logical" names called **EJB references**. These references are special entries declared in the application's deployment descriptor that are then used by the container to construct the environment for an enterprise bean. In the deployment descriptor, the deployer binds the EJB references used in enterprise bean A's code to the home of enterprise bean B that bean A needs to access.

So, for a bean provider to access one enterprise bean from another, a reference to the home interface of the second enterprise bean must be obtained. Once the first bean has a reference to the second bean's home interface, then the first enterprise bean obtains a remote object and invokes calls on the second bean in exactly the same way as other EJB clients that you have worked with. This is one of the assets of the distributed, network-aware nature of Enterprise JavaBeans.

A bean provider can develop a single bean, or a handful of beans that perform a useful function. A customer can then purchase this component and plug it into their current architecture wherever it is appropriate, and use the object again and again. The EJB component doesn't care if the client accessing it is in the same container, on the same server, or half way around the world! As long as the client has the appropriate security access and makes the proper JNDI lookup calls, the component will function exactly as expected.

The process of accessing one enterprise bean from another occurs in three stages:

1. Create an entry in the enterprise bean's environment that associates a JNDI lookup name with the enterprise bean your bean needs to reference. EJB references are declared in the deployment descriptor and the EJB specification recommends (but does not require) that all references to other enterprise beans be organized in the `ejb` subcontext of the bean's environment (in other words in the `java:comp/env/ejb` JNDI context).

2. Look up the home interface of the second enterprise bean in the enterprise bean's environment using the JNDI name specified in the previous step.

3. Invoke one of the `create()` methods declared in the home interface of the other enterprise bean to create a remote object through which the enterprise bean's methods may be accessed. This is of course no different from how other clients access enterprise beans.

In the next few pages, we will take a closer look at each of these steps, and see them put into practice in a sample application involving a stateful session bean that queries a stateless session bean for information.

The Deployment Descriptor

Just as environment entries use a special element within the deployment descriptor, the `<env-entry>` element, there is also an element used to identify references to other enterprise beans. This element is the `<ejb-ref>` element. The bean provider uses this element to declare all the enterprise beans referenced by a particular enterprise bean.

The `<ejb-ref>` element can have six possible child elements, four of which are mandatory:

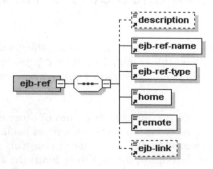

Below is a typical example of an enterprise bean reference that incorporates all seven elements:

```
...
<enterprise-beans>
   <session>
   ...
      <ejb-name>EmployeeService</ejb-name>
      <ejb-class>com.wombat.empl.EmployeeServiceBean</ejb-class>
      ...
      <ejb-ref>
        <description>
            This is a reference to the entity bean that
            encapsulates access to employee records.
        </description>
        <ejb-ref-name>ejb/EmplRecord</ejb-ref-name>
        <ejb-ref-type>Entity</ejb-ref-type>
        <home>com.wombat.empl.EmployeeRecordHome</home>
        <remote>com.wombat.empl.EmployeeRecord</remote>
      </ejb-ref>

      <ejb-ref>
        <ejb-ref-name>ejb/Payroll</ejb-ref-name>
        <ejb-ref-type>Entity</ejb-ref-type>
        <home>com.aardvark.payroll.PayrollHome</home>
        <remote>com.aardvark.payroll.Payroll</remote>
        <ejb-link>EmployeePayroll</ejb-link>
      </ejb-ref>
   ...
   </session>
   ...
</enterprise-beans>
...
```

Now let's briefly take a look at each of the elements in turn.

`<ejb-ref>`

Each `<ejb-ref>` element describes the interface requirements that the referencing enterprise bean has for the referenced enterprise bean. An enterprise bean can have zero or more `<ejb-ref>` elements. For every enterprise bean that the bean needs access to, an appropriate `<ejb-ref>` element should exist in the deployment descriptor.

`<ejb-ref-name>`

The `<ejb-ref-name>` element specifies the EJB reference name; its value is the environment entry name used in the enterprise bean code to retrieve a reference to the other bean's home interface. This retrieval is, naturally, performed using a JNDI lookup.

`<ejb-ref-type>`

The `<ejb-ref-type>` element specifies the expected type of the enterprise bean; its value must be either `Entity` or `Session`. It is the deployer's responsibility to ensure that this type declaration is accurate.

<home>

The <home> element specifies the expected Java types of the reference enterprise bean's home interface. You must use the fully qualified class name.

<remote>

The <remote> element specifies the expected Java types of the reference enterprise bean's remote interface. As with <home>, you must use the fully qualified class name.

<ejb-link>

This optional element allows a clean decoupling of your enterprise bean code from the JNDI namespace used in your deployment environment. The application assembler can use the <ejb-link> element in the deployment descriptor to link an EJB reference to a target enterprise bean. This means that the enterprise bean code needs to be aware of the name of the EJB reference (declared using the <ejb-ref-name> element above). At the time of application assembly, the application assembler will assign a JNDI name to the target bean and will use this name as the value for the <ejb-link> element for any EJB references to the target bean. The target enterprise bean can be in any ejb-jar file in the same J2EE application as the referencing application component.

Alternatively, the <ejb-link> element can help to resolve naming conflicts within a given J2EE application. Rather than renaming enterprise beans that have identical names, yet reside in different ejb-jar files, you can identify which specific ejb-jar and enterprise bean you are referencing. The <ejb-link> element allows for this by appending the enterprise bean name to the end of the path name of the containing ejb-jar file. The file name and the bean name are separated by a #. Let's look at an example:

```
<entity>
  ...
  <ejb-name>OrderEJB</ejb-name>
  <ejb-class>com.wombat.orders.OrderBean</ejb-class>
  ...
  <ejb-ref>
    <ejb-ref-name>ejb/Product</ejb-ref-name>
    <ejb-ref-type>Entity</ejb-ref-type>
    <home>com.acme.orders.ProductHome</home>
    <remote>com.acme.orders.Product</remote>
    <ejb-link>../products/product.jar#Product</ejb-link>
  </ejb-ref>
  ...
</entity>
```

A Note about EJB Reference Scope

An EJB reference is scoped to the enterprise bean whose declaration contains the <ejb-ref> element. This means that the EJB reference is not accessible to other enterprise beans at run time, and that other enterprise beans may define <ejb-ref> elements with the same <ejb-ref-name> without causing a name conflict.

EJB Reference Example

Now let's take a look at a working example of one enterprise bean referencing another enterprise bean. This application calculates compound interest based upon the following parameters:

- ❑ Initial account balance
- ❑ Annual yield
- ❑ Estimated rate of inflation
- ❑ Number of years that the account is maintained

We are also relying on a regular contribution schedule and a compounding cycle.

Our application will use two session beans to perform these calculations on behalf of the client:

- ❑ A stateful bean named `CompoundInterestAgent`
- ❑ A stateless bean named `CompoundInterestService`

The stateful session bean will collect all the relevant information from the client, delegate the calculation to the stateless bean, and finally return the result to the requesting client.

We'll begin by writing the code for the stateful session bean, `CompoundInterestAgent`.

CompoundInterestAgent

This bean collects all of the data necessary to calculate the return on the client's investment. After collecting all of this data, the bean will delegate the actual calculation to a stateless bean, `CompoundInterestService`. In reality, such a simple computation could easily be performed in the stateful bean, but this application is designed to demonstrate EJB references to other enterprise beans, not EJB design strategies.

The Remote Interface

```
package compIntAgent;

import java.rmi.RemoteException;
import javax.ejb.EJBObject;

public interface CompoundInterestAgent extends EJBObject {

  public double calculateReturn() throws RemoteException;

  public void setAnnualYield(double yield) throws RemoteException;

  public void setContribution(double contrib) throws RemoteException;

  public void setFrequency(int frequency) throws RemoteException;

  public void setInflation(double inflation) throws RemoteException;

  public void setStartingBalance(double balance) throws RemoteException;

  public void setTime(int years) throws RemoteException;

}
```

Chapter 8

The Home Interface

```
package compIntAgent;

import java.rmi.RemoteException;
import javax.ejb.CreateException;
import javax.ejb.EJBHome;

public interface CompoundInterestAgentHome extends EJBHome {
  CompoundInterestAgent create() throws RemoteException, CreateException;
}
```

The Bean Class

We'll begin with the declarative portion of the class:

```
package compIntAgent;

import javax.ejb.*;
import javax.naming.*;
import compIntService.*;

public class CompoundInterestAgentEJB implements SessionBean {

  public static final int MONTHLY        = 1;
  public static final int QUARTERLY      = 2;
  public static final int SEMI_ANNUALLY  = 3;

  double balance, yield, contrib, inflation;
  int years, frequency;

  public void ejbCreate() {}
  public void ejbActivate() {}
  public void ejbPassivate() {}
  public void ejbRemove() {}
  public void setSessionContext(SessionContext ctx) {}

}
```

Now we must implement the business methods. We'll begin with the various setter methods used to store the relevant financial data that will be used to calculate the return on investment:

```
public void setAnnualYield(double yield) {
  this.yield = yield;
}

public void setContribution(double contrib) {
  this.contrib = contrib;
}

public void setFrequency(int frequency) {
  if (frequency == MONTHLY)
    this.frequency = 12;
  else if (frequency == QUARTERLY)
    this.frequency = 4;
```

```
        else if (frequency == SEMI_ANNUALLY)
          this.frequency = 2;
    }

    public void setInflation(double inflation) {
        this.inflation = inflation;
    }

    public void setStartingBalance(double balance) {
        this.balance = balance;
    }

    public void setTime(int years) {
        this.years = years;
    }
```

The only one of these methods that is of any real interest to us is the `setFrequency()` method. When we come to write the client code, we will find that the client is asked if the compounding will occur monthly, quarterly, or semi-annually. The client will respond by typing 1, 2, or 3. This must then be converted into the number of compounding periods in each year.

Note that the `static final` variables MONTHLY, QUARTERLY, and SEMI_ANNUALLY, corresponding to '1', '2', and '3' respectively, were created earlier in the class. Thus, it is clear that if the frequency value passed into the `setFrequency()` method is 1, then the client's interest will be compounded on a monthly basis.

The final method left is the `calculateReturn()` method. This accesses the underlying EJB environment and requests a reference to the `ejb/CompoundInterestService` resource:

```
    public double calculateReturn() {

        if (yield != 0.0 && years != 0) {
            try {
                InitialContext initCtx;
                CompoundInterestServiceHome home;
                CompoundInterestService service;

                initCtx = new InitialContext();

                home = (CompoundInterestServiceHome) javax.rmi
                    .PortableRemoteObject.narrow(initCtx.lookup(
                        "java:comp/env/ejb/CompoundInterestService"),
                        CompoundInterestServiceHome.class);

                service = home.create();

                return service.calculate(balance, contrib, frequency, inflation,
                                        years, yield);
            } catch(Exception ex) {
                ex.printStackTrace();
            }
        }

        // If not enough information exists, the return value is 0.0
        return 0.0;
    }
```

After obtaining an initial context, the bean performs a JNDI lookup to retrieve a reference to the home interface of the other enterprise bean. After this, a remote object can be obtained, and the `calculate()` method declared in the `CompoundInterestService` remote interface can be called.

CompoundInterestService

This very simple bean performs one function. It exposes a `calculate()` method that is capable of computing compound interest on a regular investment schedule. Let's build this bean now.

The Remote Interface

```
package compIntService;

import java.rmi.RemoteException;
import javax.ejb.EJBObject;

public interface CompoundInterestService extends EJBObject {

    public double calculate(double balance, double contrib, int frequency,
                            double inflation, int years, double yield)
          throws RemoteException;

}
```

The Home Interface

```
package compIntService;

import java.rmi.RemoteException;
import javax.ejb.CreateException;
import javax.ejb.EJBHome;

public interface CompoundInterestServiceHome extends EJBHome {
    CompoundInterestService create() throws RemoteException, CreateException;
}
```

The Bean Class

First, here's the declarative part of the bean:

```
package compIntService;

import javax.ejb.*;

public class CompoundInterestServiceEJB implements SessionBean {

    public void ejbCreate() {}
    public void ejbActivate() {}
    public void ejbPassivate() {}
    public void ejbRemove() {}
    public void setSessionContext(SessionContext context) {}

}
```

Now for the single business method, `calculate()`:

```
   public double calculate(double balance, double contrib, int frequency,
                        double inflation, int years, double yield)
  {
    for (int i = 0; i < years; i++) {

      for (int x = 0; x < frequency; x++) {
        balance += contrib;
        balance = balance * (1.0 + (yield/frequency));
      }

      //Adjust for inflation
      balance = balance - (balance*inflation);
    }

    return balance;
  }
```

After computing the new balance based on regular contributions, compound interest, and estimated inflation, the new balance is returned to the CompoundInterestAgentEJB, which in turn returns the value to the calling client.

The Deployment Descriptor

Here's the deployment descriptor for this example:

```
<?xml version="1.0"?>

<!DOCTYPE ejb-jar PUBLIC '-//Sun Microsystems, Inc.//DTD Enterprise JavaBeans
2.0//EN' 'http://java.sun.com/dtd/ejb-jar_2_0.dtd'>

<ejb-jar>
  <display-name>CompIntJAR</display-name>

  <enterprise-beans>

    <session>
      <display-name>CompIntService</display-name>
      <ejb-name>CompIntService</ejb-name>
      <home>compIntService.CompoundInterestServiceHome</home>
      <remote>compIntService.CompoundInterestService</remote>
      <ejb-class>compIntService.CompoundInterestServiceEJB</ejb-class>
      <session-type>Stateless</session-type>
      <transaction-type>Bean</transaction-type>
    </session>

    <session>
      <display-name>CompIntAgent</display-name>
      <ejb-name>CompIntAgent</ejb-name>
      <home>compIntAgent.CompoundInterestAgentHome</home>
      <remote>compIntAgent.CompoundInterestAgent</remote>
      <ejb-class>compIntAgent.CompoundInterestAgentEJB</ejb-class>
      <session-type>Stateful</session-type>
      <transaction-type>Bean</transaction-type>
      <ejb-ref>
```

```
                <ejb-ref-name>ejb/CompoundInterestService</ejb-ref-name>
                <ejb-ref-type>Session</ejb-ref-type>
                <home>compIntService.CompoundInterestServiceHome</home>
                <remote>compIntService.CompoundInterestService</remote>
            </ejb-ref>
        </session>

    </enterprise-beans>
</ejb-jar>
```

Deploying the Application

Assuming that the above files have been packaged and compiled successfully, it is time to deploy the application. Remember, the specific steps necessary to deploy this application will vary between application servers. The important step will be setting the EJB reference properties before actually deploying the application. As we have seen, while it is possible to code these by hand directly into your deployment descriptor, using your application server's deployment utility will help you to avoid making typing errors.

However your application server provides for the declaration of EJB references, you need to declare one entry for the CompoundInterestAgent to run properly. The following table identifies the name, type, and recommended values that you should use in deploying the bean on your own server:

Coded Name	ejb/CompoundInterestService
Type	Session
Home	compIntService.CompoundInterestServiceHome
Remote	compIntService.CompoundInterestService

Again, how you set these properties will vary depending upon the application server you are using. In the J2EE Reference Implementation, the Bean Creation Wizard provides an opportunity to create EJB references, and the EJB References tab will allow you modify an already existing reference.

During the creation of the bean, you are given the opportunity to specify EJB references. The screenshot shows this window, with the EJB reference that should be specified for the CompoundInterestAgent:

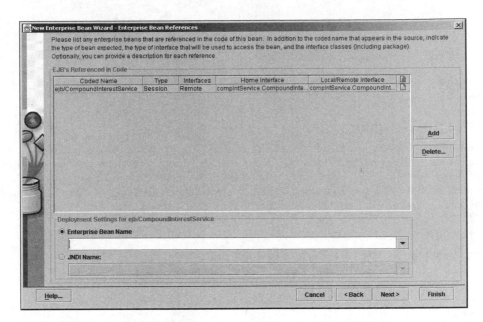

Next is the matter of the JNDI names. You have two options: you can either use the target enterprise bean name identified in the deployment descriptor with the `<ejb-name>` element as the `<ejb-ref-name>`, or you can use a different name for the EJB reference, and use the target EJB's JNDI name identified with the `<ejb-name>` element as the value of the `<ejb-link>` element. The screenshot below shows an example of the latter technique in the J2EE Reference Implementation Deployment Tool:

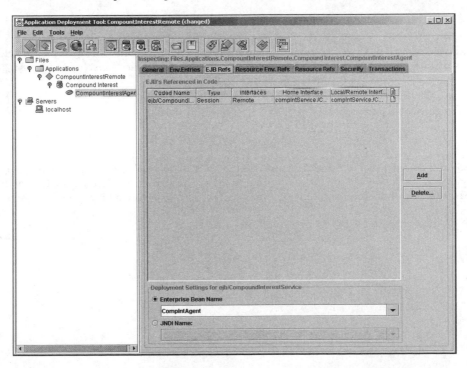

Note that the reference name used by the CompoundInterestAgent to refer to the CompoundInterestService is different from the component name declared by the CompoundInterestService.

Assuming that the application deployed successfully, you are ready to build a client class to test the application.

Testing the Application

Our client will be the CompoundInterestTester class. This class utilizes a command-line interface that collects the relevant information from the end user and stores it in the state of a stateful session bean. When all of the necessary data has been collected, the client class will query the stateful bean and request a calculation. The stateful bean will then delegate the calculation to the stateless bean and return the final result to the client. Let's take a look at the client class.

The CompoundInterestTester class

We'll begin with the declarative portion of the code:

```
import compIntAgent.*;

import java.io.*;
import java.rmi.RemoteException;
import javax.naming.*;

public class CompoundInterestTester {
  // This object will collect information from standard input
  private static BufferedReader in;

}
```

This class contains two methods, the main() method and a helper method called getInputString(). We'll take a quick look at the getInputString() method first, and then move on to the main() method:

```
private static String getInputString(String prompt) throws IOException {
  System.out.print(prompt);
  return in.readLine();
}
```

This method is a helper method used repeatedly in the main() method. The method takes a single String as an argument, displays that String as a prompt to the user, and then waits for input. The method then returns the first line of the response from the user (any text entered before hitting the *Return* key).

Now for the real workhorse, the main() method:

```
public static void main(String[] args) {
  Context initCtx;
  Object objRef;
  CompoundInterestAgentHome home;
  CompoundInterestAgent agent;

  boolean valid;
  String answer;
```

```
        double tmpDbl = 0.0;
        int tmpInt = 0;

        // This bufferedreader is set to read Standard Input (keyboard)
        in = new BufferedReader(new InputStreamReader(System.in));
```

At this point, we have declared all of the object reference types and primitive variables that we will be using in this method. We have also created a `BufferedReader` object that is collecting all input sent to Standard Input (the keyboard):

```
    try {
      initCtx = new InitialContext();
      objRef = initCtx.lookup("CompoundInterestAgent");
      home = (CompoundInterestAgentHome) javax.rmi.PortableRemoteObject.
                      narrow(objRef, CompoundInterestAgentHome.class);
      agent = home.create();
```

Here we have obtained a reference to a `CompoundInterestAgent` remote object. We will be using this agent to store the financial information as we collect it from the user:

```
        System.out.println("\nWelcome to the Compound Interest Calculator:");

        do {
          answer = getInputString("Enter a starting balance: $ ");
          try {
            tmpDbl = Double.parseDouble(answer);
            agent.setStartingBalance(tmpDbl);
            valid = true;
          } catch (NumberFormatException nfe) {
          System.out.println("Invalid Entry!");
          valid = false;
          }
        } while (valid == false);
```

This `do/while` loop prompts the user for a starting balance. If a valid balance is given, then the agent session bean sets the appropriate instance variable. After this, the code proceeds to the next `do/while` loop. If the user enters an invalid input value, then the user is informed of the problem and prompted again for a new starting balance.

The other `do/while` loops are very similar to this first one. There is one for each piece of financial information necessary to calculate the predicted investment return. Here's the code for these other loops:

```
      do {
        System.out.println("How often will the interest compound? ");
        answer = getInputString("(1) monthly, (2) quarterly, " +
                              "(3) semi-annually ");
        try {
          tmpInt = Integer.parseInt(answer);
          if (tmpInt > 3)
            throw new NumberFormatException();
          agent.setFrequency(tmpInt);
          valid = true;
        } catch (NumberFormatException nfe) {
```

```
      System.out.println("Invalid Entry!");
      valid = false;
    } //end try/catch

} while (valid == false);

// This block MUST be preceded by the frequency block.
// The tmpInt variable from the previous block is used in the switch.
do {
  System.out.print("How much will you be contributing ");
  switch (tmpInt)
  {
    case 1:
      answer = getInputString("each month? ");
      break;
    case 2:
      answer = getInputString("each quarter? ");
      break;
    case 3:
      answer = getInputString("every six months? ");
      break;
  }

  try {
    tmpDbl = Double.parseDouble(answer);
    agent.setContribution(tmpDbl);
    valid = true;
  } catch (NumberFormatException nfe) {
    System.out.println("Invalid Entry!");
    valid = false;
  }
} while (valid == false);

do {
  answer = getInputString("What is the account's annual yield? ");
  try {
    tmpDbl = Double.parseDouble(answer);
    agent.setAnnualYield(tmpDbl);
    valid = true;
  } catch (NumberFormatException nfe) {
    System.out.println("Invalid Entry!");
    valid = false;
  }
} while (valid == false);

do {
  answer = getInputString("How many years will you maintain " +
                          "this account? ");
  try {
    tmpInt = Integer.parseInt(answer);
    agent.setTime(tmpInt);
    valid = true;
  } catch (NumberFormatException nfe) {
    System.out.println("Invalid Entry!");
    valid = false;
```

```
    }
  } while (valid == false);

  do {
    answer = getInputString("What rate of inflation are you " +
                            "anticipating? ");
    try {
      tmpDbl = Double.parseDouble(answer);
      agent.setInflation(tmpDbl);
      valid = true;
    } catch (NumberFormatException nfe) {
      System.out.println("Invalid Entry!");
      valid = false;
    }
  } while (valid == false);
```

Once all of the information has been collected, the actual calculation can be performed. The request is sent to the `CompoundInterestAgentEJB` that will delegate the calculations to the `CompoundInterestServiceEJB`:

```
    tmpDbl = agent.calculateReturn();

    System.out.println("The return on this account would be $ "
                       + tmpDbl);

  } catch (NamingException ne) {
    ne.printStackTrace();
  } catch (RemoteException re) {
    re.printStackTrace();
  } catch (IOException ioe) {
    ioe.printStackTrace();
  } catch (Exception e) {
   e.printStackTrace();
  }
}
```

Now compile the `CompoundInterestTester` class and execute the class, with the client `jar` file produced by your application server in your `classpath`. If the application started successfully, you should be prompted to enter an initial balance. Try the following input values:

Starting balance: 3000
Frequency: 2 (quarterly)
Quarterly contributions: 2000
Annual yield: 0.12
Number of years: 20
Anticipated inflation: 0.04

If you use these values, you should see an output similar to that shown overleaf:

Well done! You have successfully referenced one enterprise bean from another. Unfortunately, your application has suffered a performance penalty due to the overhead of making a remote method call across the network. You may not have noticed this with such a small application, but if we were accessing a database and handling several hundred concurrent users, then we would have to pay the price. Fortunately, a solution to this problem comes in the form of local interfaces.

Referencing an EJB from another EJB via the Local Interface

When referencing an enterprise bean that resides within the same container, the container performs an unnecessary remote call over the network using the standard <ejb-ref> definition in the deployment descriptor. This causes the container to treat the communication as though it were a standard remote call leaving the container. To improve intra-container enterprise bean communication, the EJB 2.0 specification defines a new type of interface that can be used to access an enterprise bean directly – the local interface. This is a standard Java interface that does not inherit from RMI. An enterprise bean can be defined to have only a local interface, a remote interface, or both.

Just as a reference to an enterprise bean's remote object is obtained via the home interface, the local interface has a corresponding home interface. Local clients can use that local home interface as a lightweight mechanism to access another enterprise bean within the same container. This mechanism is considered lightweight because the remote method call over the network that is used in communicating via the remote interface is avoided.

Use of the local interface constitutes the creation of container-managed relationships between enterprise beans. The properties for the local home, local interface, and logical JNDI name are declared in the deployment descriptor just as they are for the remote interface. This allows the container to manage the nature of the relationship and optimize the handling of the enterprise bean references. In fact, this mechanism even allows enterprise beans to expose and pass their state to another bean instance in a typical pass-by-reference fashion. Thus, the bean has truly become a tightly coupled local object that can be referenced and manipulated by the client bean.

Deployment Descriptor

The deployment descriptor tags for an enterprise bean's local interface mirror those for an enterprise bean's remote interface. There is a containing tag, 2 optional tags, and 4 mandatory tags:

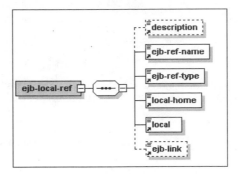

<ejb-local-ref>

The top-level element that contains the other elements.

<ejb-ref-name>

The logical name used within the bean's code to refer to this reference.

<ejb-ref-type>

The Java type expected by the enterprise bean code.

<local-home>

The fully qualified class name (full classpath) of the referenced bean's local home interface.

<local>

The fully qualified class name of the referenced bean's local interface.

<ejb-link>

This can be configured by the application assembler and allows for a greater degree of decoupling between this enterprise bean and the bean it is referencing.

The local interface provides a more efficient means of communicating between two enterprise beans that reside within the same container. This is an especially useful technique when working with entity beans. It is a well-founded EJB design technique to access entity beans through session beans, rather than allowing the client to have direct access.

EJB Local Reference Example

Now let's look at how to take our Compound Interest calculating example from before and modify it so that it's using local references instead of remote.

There are only a few slight code modifications that we need to make with the more significant changes being to the deployment descriptor.

The CompoundInterestService Home Interface

As the CompoundInterestService bean will be the local object we need to modify the home interface to be a local home:

```
package compIntService;

import javax.ejb.CreateException;
import javax.ejb.EJBLocalHome;

public interface CompoundInterestServiceHome extends EJBLocalHome {
   CompoundInterestService create() throws CreateException;
}
```

Also note that we no longer need to throw a RemoteException because this is not an RMI interface.

The CompoundInterestService Local Interface

Likewise we need to change the remote interface into a local interface by extending javax.ejb.EJBLocalObject instead of EJBObject:

```
package compIntService;

import javax.ejb.EJBLocalObject;

public interface CompoundInterestService extends EJBLocalObject {

   public double calculate(double balance, double contrib, int frequency,
                           double inflation, int years, double yield);

}
```

The CompoundInterestAgentEJB Bean Class

The only other code change that we need to make is to the CompoundInterestAgentEJB class as we no longer need to use the PortableRemoteObject's narrow() method to typecast the JNDI lookup:

```
initCtx = new InitialContext();

home = (CompoundInterestServiceHome) initCtx.lookup(
            "java:comp/env/ejb/CompIntService");

service = home.create();
```

The Deployment Descriptor

The most significant changes are in the deployment descriptor where we have to replace the <home> and <remote> elements for CompoundInterestService with those for <local-home> and <local> elements, as well as change the <ejb-ref> for CompoundInterestAgent to <ejb-local-ref>:

```xml
<?xml version="1.0"?>

<!DOCTYPE ejb-jar PUBLIC '-//Sun Microsystems, Inc.//DTD Enterprise JavaBeans
2.0//EN' 'http://java.sun.com/dtd/ejb-jar_2_0.dtd'>

<ejb-jar>
  <display-name>CompIntJAR</display-name>

  <enterprise-beans>

    <session>
      <display-name>CompIntService</display-name>
      <ejb-name>CompIntService</ejb-name>
      <local-home>compIntService.CompoundInterestServiceHome</local-home>
      <local>compIntService.CompoundInterestService</local>
      <ejb-class>compIntService.CompoundInterestServiceEJB</ejb-class>
      <session-type>Stateless</session-type>
      <transaction-type>Bean</transaction-type>
    </session>

    <session>
      <display-name>CompIntAgent</display-name>
      <ejb-name>CompIntAgent</ejb-name>
      <home>compIntAgent.CompoundInterestAgentHome</home>
      <remote>compIntAgent.CompoundInterestAgent</remote>
      <ejb-class>compIntAgent.CompoundInterestAgentEJB</ejb-class>
      <session-type>Stateful</session-type>
      <transaction-type>Bean</transaction-type>
      <ejb-local-ref>
        <ejb-ref-name>ejb/CompIntService</ejb-ref-name>
        <ejb-ref-type>Session</ejb-ref-type>
        <local-home>compIntService.CompoundInterestServiceHome</local-home>
        <local>compIntService.CompoundInterestService</local>
        <ejb-link>CompIntLocal.jar#CompIntService</ejb-link>
      </ejb-local-ref>
    </session>

  </enterprise-beans>
</ejb-jar>
```

Other than these changes we can use our bean as before.

Resource Manager Connection Factories

In addition to the services built into the container, there are external resources that the container provides access to and integration with. The EJB 1.1 and 2.0 specifications define four resources that can be accessed and managed through **resource manager connection factories**. We will discuss exactly what these are in a moment.

Both specifications also refer to the future ability to access diverse back-end systems using the Connector mechanism. The **Connector Architecture 1.0** Reference Implementation ships with the J2EE 1.3 Reference Implementation (currently in beta at the time of this writing). When the Connector API is combined with the four resources outlined in the EJB specification, we reach a total of five external resources that J2EE 1.3 compliant-containers must provide support for. These five resources are:

- ❏ JDBC 2.0 Data sources
- ❏ JavaMail sessions
- ❏ JMS queue and topic connections
- ❏ URL resources
- ❏ Legacy enterprise systems via the J2EE Connector architecture (1.3 only)

In the rest of this chapter we will concentrate on each of these five resources, exploring their purpose and capabilities, not to mention examining the coding necessary to manage these resources from enterprise beans. First though, we must present a definition of a resource manager connection factory.

What is a Resource Manager Connection Factory?

A resource manager connection factory is an object that is used to create connections to a **resource manager**.

> **A resource manager is a component of a J2EE container that manages the entire lifecycle of a particular type of resource including connection pooling, transaction support, and any necessary network protocols that make the actual connection possible.**

For example, an object that implements the `javax.sql.DataSource` interface is a resource manager connection factory for `java.sql.Connection` objects that implement connections to a database management system.

In order to use these resource factories in your enterprise bean code, you would use (logically) **resource manager connection factory references**. Let's look at a common example, a connection to a database management system:

```
// Obtain the initial JNDI context
Context context = new InitialContext();

// JNDI lookup to obtain resource manager connection factory reference
javax.sql.DataSource ds = (javax.sql.DataSource)
        context.lookup("java:comp/env/jdbc/EmployeeData");

// Invoke factory to obtain a connection.
java.sql.Connection con = ds.getConnection();
```

This does not look altogether different from the sample code we've seen earlier in the chapter. The primary differences here are that we have cast the return type from the `lookup()` method to the appropriate type (`javax.sql.DataSource`) and we have added the additional step of obtaining a `Connection` object from the factory (the connection type retrieved from the factory will vary depending on the type of resource factory). Note that the JNDI subcontext for datasources, java:comp/env/jdbc/, is discussed below, along with the subcontexts of the other external resources.

The resource manager connection factory references are defined in the deployment descriptor and are then integrated into the enterprise bean's environment at run time. By adding these entries to the deployment descriptor, the deployer binds the resource manager connection factory references to the actual resource factories that are configured in the container. These resource factories in turn allow the container to manage the specified resources to provide such services as connection pooling and automatic enlistment of the connection within a transaction context.

JNDI Subcontexts

As mentioned early in this chapter, and noted in the previous example, the EJB specification recommends organizing JNDI references into various subcontexts. Each of the five resources identified above has a corresponding subcontext that the specification recommends using. These subcontexts are as follows:

- ❑ Data sources – `java:comp/env/jdbc`
- ❑ JavaMail – `java:comp/env/mail`
- ❑ JMS – `java:comp/env/jms`
- ❑ URL – `java:comp/env/url`
- ❑ Legacy enterprise systems via Connector API – `java:comp/env/eis`

We'll work with each of these before the end of the chapter.

Now let's take a closer look at the deployment descriptor entries that must be made to bind the resource manager connection factory references to the resource factories that will be used (behind the scenes) by the container.

Setting up the Deployment Descriptor

The bean provider must define all resource manager connection factory references in the deployment descriptor. The top-level element is the `<resource-ref>` element that indicates to the container that its child elements constitute a resource factory reference for the current enterprise bean. The `<resource-ref>` element can have five possible child elements, three of which are mandatory:

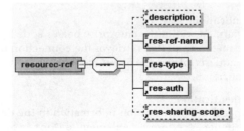

Below is a typical example of a resource manager connection factory reference for a JMS resource manager that incorporates all six elements:

```
...
<enterprise-beans>
  <session>
    <ejb-name>StockQuoteSession</ejb-name>
    <ejb-class>StockQuoteBean</ejb-class>
    ...
    <resource-ref>
      <description>
          This is a reference to a queue connection factory used
          by the StockQuoteSession enterprise bean to poll an
          external system through a JMS session.
      </description>
```

```
        <res-ref-name>jms/queueConnFactory</res-ref-name>
        <res-type>javax.jms.QueueConnectionFactory</res-type>
        <res-auth>Container</res-auth>
        <res-sharing-scope>Unshareable</res-sharing-scope>
    </resource-ref>
  ...
  </session>
</enterprise-beans>
...
```

Let's go through these elements now.

<resource-ref>

The top-level element that contains the other elements. This element is only required if you have resource references, which are themselves optional.

<res-ref-name>

The logical name used within the bean's code to refer to this resource connection factory reference.

<res-type>

The Java type expected by the bean code.

<res-auth>

When acquiring a connection to an external resource such as a database, mail server, or other resource, that resource will often require some sort of entry authorization. Typically, this manifests itself in the form of a username and password. The <res-auth> element allows you to identify one of two possible authorization schemes for your resource factory references:

❑   **Programmatic authentication**
    Authentication is performed within the enterprise bean's code by passing the appropriate sign-on information in the method call that retrieves the connection to the resource manager. Setting the deployment descriptor's <res-auth> element to Application will enable programmatic authentication.

❑   **Deployer-defined authentication**
    The bean deployer specifies authentication information in the deployment descriptor. Setting the deployment descriptor's <res-auth> element to Container will enable deployer-defined authentication.

The most commonly used method is deployer-defined authentication because it provides the greatest degree of flexibility and maintainability, without having to change the bean's source code and recompile. This follows the same pattern that we have seen before. We want to keep the actual business processes within the enterprise bean, but rely upon environment properties defined by the bean deployer to set up the specific environment that our bean(s) will operate within.

<res-sharing-scope>

This element allows the bean provider to control the sharing ability of the connections acquired from the resource manager connection factory. By default, these connections are shareable across other enterprise beans within the same application that use the same resource in the same transaction context. The bean provider can specify that connections obtained from a resource manager connection factory reference are not shareable by specifying the value of the <res-sharing-scope> deployment descriptor element to be Unshareable. The previous example demonstrates this setting.

Unless there is a compelling reason not to share connections to a particular resource (perhaps due to the way the session is being handled for the resource), it is a good idea to allow connections to be shared, as this enables the container to optimize connections and local transactions that the connections may be involved in.

Resource Managers

With a better understanding of how the bean's environment is composed and an overview of resource manager connection factory references, we are ready to look at the five types of resource managers that J2EE 1.3-compliant application servers must support. As we have seen, these resources are as follows:

❑   Database resources

❑   JavaMail sessions

❑   JMS connections

❑   URL resources

❑   Legacy resources (Connector Architecture)

In order to maintain optimum flexibility, the Java platform uses interfaces as a common communication layer between systems, allowing the implementation of that interface to be changed without modifying the code on the other side of the interface. J2EE resource managers are no different. By abstracting all communication to a common interface, both systems are insulated from the details of the other system's implementation. As long as the interface is adhered to, the components can essentially "plug and play". Changing the way a component's method is implemented, or even swapping entire components, can therefore be performed seamlessly.

Each of the five resources addressed in this section has a corresponding interface that is used to maintain optimum flexibility between the systems. When a reference to a resource manager connection factory is requested, a factory adhering to the appropriate interface is returned. This reference is then used to create a connection to the specified resource.

Database Resources

Database resources use the `javax.sql.DataSource` interface as a factory for creating database connections. This class is defined in the JDBC 2.0 Optional Package API as a substitute for the `java.sql.DriverManager` class as the primary means of creating database connections.

There is one primary difference between the `DriverManager` class and the `DataSource` interface. While both of them allow the developer to retrieve a connection to the underlying data store, the `DriverManager` class does so by loading the driver manager classes in the client code at run time, while the `DataSource` interface uses a centralized JNDI lookup to obtain the `javax.sql.DataSource` object that is then used to retrieve a connection to the database.

The benefits provided by retrieving a `DataSource` object via a JNDI lookup rather than loading the driver manager classes in the client's run time are numerous. One of the most compelling reasons is that it decouples the client code from the details of the underlying data store. So long as the JNDI lookup name remains the same, the application server can change the physical location of the database, the JDBC driver used, and even change database vendors entirely, without ever having to modify the client code! This flexibility and inherent scalability is a resounding theme within the J2EE architecture and the resource manager framework is yet another step toward those goals.

The javax.sql.DataSource Interface

Although the interface contains six methods, we are only interested in two of them: the two forms of the `getConnection()` method used to obtain database connections. Let's take a look at them:

```
public Connection getConnection() throws SQLException
```

This method returns a `java.sql.Connection` object to the `DataSource` object it is invoked on. This Connection object is used in the same manner as the Connection object returned by the `java.sql.DriverManager` class in previous JDBC versions. If the data source requires authentication (and it should) then this will have to be supplied by the bean deployer via the enterprise bean's deployment descriptor.

The second method is identical to the previous one except that a username and password are supplied as method parameters, and the authentication is established programmatically using the information supplied by the enterprise bean:

```
public Connection getConnection(String username, String password)
    throws SQLException
```

This solution is less flexible than the previous version, but more secure in that the username and password are encapsulated within the compiled code.

Data Sources and JNDI

As is the case with every EJB component, EJB resources are inherently network-aware and are accessed via JNDI, irrespective of their physical location. The steps involved in the process of making the resource available via JNDI are as follows:

1. The driver or application server vendor implements the `javax.sql.DataSource` interface.

2. The application server creates an instance of the `DataSource` implementation object and binds it with a logical name in the JNDI service. This step is container-specific and performed at deployment time by a deployer or assembler using tools provided by the container vendor.

3. The enterprise bean performs the lookup in the JNDI service, specifying the logical name of the object implementing the `DataSource` interface. The `lookup()` method returns an object conforming to the `javax.sql.DataSource` interface.

4. The object reference retrieved in the JNDI lookup is, in fact, a reference to a resource manager connection factory. This factory object is then used to retrieve a `java.sql.Connection` object that will be managed by the resource manager.

5. The Connection object is used to perform the necessary database operations on behalf of the enterprise bean.

This process is the same for the other four types of resource that we will be looking at, except that a different interface is returned by the JNDI lookup call and a different type of connection object is returned.

Now let's take a look at an example that will put all of this information into perspective.

Data Source Example

This example is merely intended as a reference, and not a complete example that can be deployed into an application server; a sample application will be demonstrated later. We'll first look at the necessary deployment descriptor entries, and then at the code that will need to be provided in our enterprise bean.

Deployment Descriptor Entries

Consider the following deployment descriptor excerpt:

```
<resource-ref>
  <res-ref-name>jdbc/EcommerceDB2</res-ref-name>
  <res-type>javax.sql.DataSource</res-type>
  <res-auth>Container</res-auth>
</resource-ref>
```

This resource reference demonstrates the minimum amount of information. Although it is generally recommended that you supply a `<description>` tag identifying the purpose and capabilities of this resource, only the three elements displayed here are mandatory children for a valid resource reference.

Of the three children elements displayed above, `<res-ref-name>` is perhaps the most interesting. It indicates the JNDI name for this resource relative to the `java:comp/env` namespace. The other two elements are very simple. The resource manager factory type implements the `javax.sql.DataSource` interface and the container handles the resource manager authorization automatically.

Application Code

Retrieving a connection from the resource manager connection factory is a very simple process. Consider the following extension to the sample code seen earlier:

```
public java.sql.Connection getConnection(String resourceName)
                          throws NamingException, SQLException {

    // Obtain the initial JNDI context
    Context context = new InitialContext();

    // JNDI lookup to obtain resource manager connection factory reference
    javax.sql.DataSource ds = (javax.sql.DataSource)
                      context.lookup("java:comp/env/jdbc/" + resourceName);

    // Invoke factory to obtain a connection and return this connection to
    // the calling method
    return ds.getConnection();
}
```

This method takes a single parameter, the JNDI resource name, and appends it to the JNDI namespace in the call to the `lookup()` method. This name is the same name specified in the `<res-ref-name>` element in the deployment descriptor, minus the `jdbc` subcontext.

Database Resource Sample Application

Now let's take a look at a real live example. This will be a very minimal stateful session bean accessed via a standard Java command-line client. The bean will access a database and print a series of messages stored in the database to the log files. If it does not, an error message will be returned to the client. First let's take a look at the enterprise bean.

The Stateful Session Bean

This bean will merely obtain a connection to the database from the container's pool of connections, retrieve every record contained in a given table, cycle through and print the contents of a single column of that table to the log files.

Why are we using a stateful as opposed to stateless bean? The reason is because the bean primarily consists of two business methods. The first obtains a resource connection object from the container and the second performs some function with that connection. Without a stateful bean, this would not be possible.

One more thing to notice is that the remote interface, home interface, and EJB class do not follow the traditional naming conventions. The reason for this is that we will be reusing the remote and home interfaces with each of the other types of resource manager connection factories. These two interfaces will remain unchanged as they are reused with each type of connection factory.

The Remote Interface

The remote interface for this bean defines two business methods. The first method initializes the resource and retrieves it from the container. The second business method tests that resource to see if it can successfully perform its task with the current configuration. The code is as follows:

```
import java.rmi.RemoteException;
import javax.ejb.EJBObject;

public interface ResourceTester extends EJBObject {

  public void initResource() throws RemoteException;
  public boolean testResource() throws RemoteException;

}
```

The first method returns nothing to the client. The second method merely informs the client as to whether or not the resource could successfully perform its task.

The Home Interface

The home interface contains only the bare minimum.

```
import java.rmi.RemoteException;
import javax.ejb.CreateException;
import javax.ejb.EJBHome;

public interface ResourceTesterHome extends EJBHome {

  ResourceTester create() throws RemoteException, CreateException;
}
```

The Enterprise Bean Class

And finally, we come to the EJB itself. We'll begin with the declarative part of the class:

```java
import java.sql.*;
import javax.ejb.*;
import javax.naming.*;
import javax.sql.*;

public class DatabaseTesterEJB implements SessionBean {

  private static final String dataSourceName =
                          "java:comp/env/jdbc/ResourceDB";

  private Connection conn;

  public void ejbCreate() {}
  public void ejbActivate() {}
  public void ejbPassivate() {}
  public void ejbRemove() {}
  public void setSessionContext(SessionContext ctx) {}

}
```

Everything here is quite standard. Notice, that we have also declared two variables. One will store the JNDI name for the database and the other will maintain a reference to the connection object retrieved in the `initResource()` method to be used whenever the `testResource()` method is called by the client.

Taking the two business methods in the order they are executed, we'll begin with the `initResource()` method:

```java
public void initResource() {
    InitialContext    initCtx;
    DataSource        ds;

    try {
       initCtx = new InitialContext();
       ds = (DataSource) initCtx.lookup(dataSourceName);
       conn = ds.getConnection();
    } catch (NamingException ne) {
       ne.printStackTrace();
    } catch (SQLException se) {
       se.printStackTrace();
    }
}
```

Aside from a bit of exception handling, there are only three lines of code that matter, and only two that are especially interesting. Those three lines of code take place within the `try` block, and the two really important lines have been indicated in boldface type. The first line in the `try` block obtains an initial naming context while the next line uses that context to request a `javax.sql.DataSource` object from the container via a JNDI lookup call and casts the return object to the appropriate type. The third line uses that `DataSource` object to obtain an actual `javax.sql.Connection` object through which the enterprise bean will be able to query the database in the next method.

The next method is the `testResource()` method where the connection to the resource is actually attempted by the enterprise bean. The method's return type is boolean, informing the client as to whether or not the test was successful.

```
public boolean testResource() {
    Statement    stmt;
    ResultSet    rs;

    try {
        stmt = conn.createStatement();
        rs = stmt.executeQuery("SELECT message FROM Resources");

        while (rs.next()) {
            System.out.println(rs.getString(1));
        }
    } catch(Exception e) {
        e.printStackTrace();
        return false;
    }
    return true;
}
```

Once a connection to the database has been obtained (as was done in the `initResource()` method), the rest of it is a piece of cake. Now, we have a reference to the database and we perform familiar JDBC functions: instantiate a `Statement` object using the `Connection` object, use the `Statement` object to perform a query on the database, take the `ResultSet` returned by the query and loop through every record, then process each record in some way.

As we loop through each record returned by the `SELECT` statement, we're only interested in the second column (the first column is referenced as 0 and the second column as 1). The database schema we'll use later is very simple. We will define a single table with two columns, one column of type `INTEGER` that will serve as the primary key, and one column of type `VARCHAR`. Our code processes this by looping through the result set, retrieving the string of characters contained in that record and sending them to Standard Out. Since this is an EJB, the data will be stored in your container's `standard.out` (or `system.out`) log file. For the Sun J2EE Reference Implementation, this is in the `%J2EE_HOME%/logs/%SERVER_NAME%/ejb/j2ee` directory.

The Client

Now that we have a nice application, we need a way to test it. For this, we will need to write a simple Java client. This client consists of a single method, `main()`:

```
import javax.naming.Context;
import javax.naming.InitialContext;
import javax.rmi.PortableRemoteObject;
import ResourceTester;
import ResourceTesterHome;

public class ResourceTesterClient {

    public static void main(String[] args) {
        Context initial;
        Object objref;
        ResourceTesterHome home;
```

```
    ResourceTester tester;

    try {
        initial = new InitialContext();
        objref = initial.lookup("DatabaseTester");

        home = (ResourceTesterHome)PortableRemoteObject.narrow
                    (objref, ResourceTesterHome.class);
        tester = home.create();
        tester.initResource();
        if (tester.testResource() == false)
          System.out.println("Test Failed!");
        else
          System.out.println("Test Succeeded!");
    } catch(Exception ex) {
        ex.printStackTrace();
        System.out.println("Test Failed!");
    }
  }
}
```

Most of the client code should look very familiar. We perform a JNDI lookup to obtain a reference to a home object that exposes the enterprise bean's home interface, then use that to eventually retrieve a remote object through which we can invoke methods on an instance of the bean. The first invocation we perform is to call the `initResource()` method. This method obtains a `javax.sql.Connection` object and since this is a stateful session bean, the Connection object is accessible by the next method call, a call to `testResouce()`.

The Deployment Descriptor

The deployment descriptor for our first resource tester example is relatively straightforward and we've seen the resource references section before. The only real changes we'll be making in the subsequent examples is to the `<resource-ref>` element:

```xml
<?xml version="1.0" encoding="Cp1252"?>

<!DOCTYPE ejb-jar PUBLIC '-//Sun Microsystems, Inc.//DTD Enterprise JavaBeans
2.0//EN' 'http://java.sun.com/dtd/ejb-jar_2_0.dtd'>

<ejb-jar>
  <display-name>ResourceTester</display-name>
  <enterprise-beans>

    <session>
      <display-name>DatabaseTester</display-name>
      <ejb-name>DatabaseTester</ejb-name>
      <home>ResourceTesterHome</home>
      <remote>ResourceTester</remote>
      <ejb-class>DatabaseTesterEJB</ejb-class>
      <session-type>Stateful</session-type>
      <transaction-type>Bean</transaction-type>
      <resource-ref>
        <res-ref-name>jdbc/ResourceDB</res-ref-name>
```

```
            <res-type>javax.sql.DataSource</res-type>
            <res-auth>Container</res-auth>
            <res-sharing-scope>Shareable</res-sharing-scope>
        </resource-ref>
    </session>


  </enterprise-beans>
</ejb-jar>
```

Now we're ready to deploy the bean, set up the database, and use the client to test the bean.

Deploying the Application

There are two steps to deploying a bean that consists of a resource manager connection factory. The first is to deploy the bean itself, and the second is to set up the external resource if necessary. We'll begin by looking at the deployment of the bean.

Deploy the Bean

Everything here will be exactly as it has been with the previous examples in this chapter. Be sure to create the bean to be a stateful session bean. Now we must also declare a resource manager connection factory to be associated with our session bean. How this is done is entirely left up to your container vendor. You'll want to consult your container's documentation if you are not using Sun's Reference Implementation (RI) to go through this chapter.

As with every other environment property covered in this chapter, the RI provides the deployer with two opportunities to associate a resource manager connection factory with an enterprise bean. The first opportunity is during the Bean Creation Wizard's creation phase and the second opportunity is via the **Resource Refs** configuration tab displayed in the right-hand portion of the deployer window. The following figure shows a screen shot of the deployment tool with the **Resource Refs** tab highlighted:

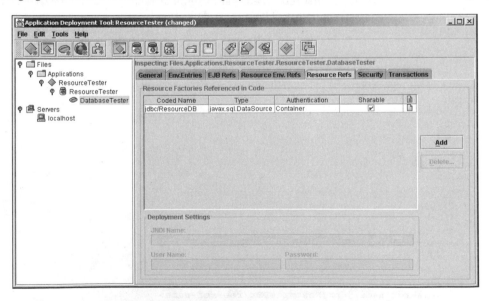

You'll want your resource reference to look the same. Here is a list of the data a tabular format:

Coded Name	Type	Authentication
jdbc/ResourceDB	javax.sql.DataSource	container

Declaring the JNDI Names

The final step necessary to deploy the bean is to set the appropriate JNDI names. Again, how you do this will vary depending upon the application server you are using and the actual mapping will be determined in part by the database you choose. You'll want to consult your documentation on how to register a data source with your application server. If you are using the RI and Cloudscape (which ships free with the RI), then the process is very simple. All you must do is use a JNDI name of jdbc/Cloudscape and the container takes care of the rest. Here's a screenshot and a table of how your JNDI variables should be defined:

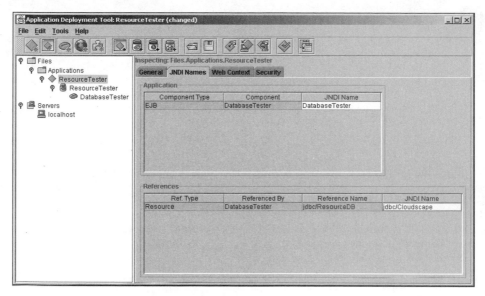

Type	Component/Reference Name	JNDI Name
EJB	DatabaseTester	DatabaseTester
Resource	jdbc/ResourceDB	jdbc/Cloudscape

Now you're ready to deploy the bean and move on to set up the database.

Set up the Database

This process will be entirely dependent upon your database vendor. The steps that you need to take are:

1. Start the database server

2. Create a database table using the schema provided (below)

3. Insert three single sentence messages (representing three individual records) into the new database table

For the Cloudscape server, a batch file or shell script is provided to start the server and an interactive command-line SQL tool is provided for creating tables and inserting records.

The SQL script for creating the Resources table is:

```
CREATE TABLE Resources (id          INTEGER NOT NULL,
                        message     VARCHAR(24),
                        PRIMARY KEY (id));
```

This creates a table called Resources, consisting of two columns. The first column is of type INTEGER and it cannot be null and must be unique as it also serves as the primary key for the table. The other column is of type VARCHAR and it will store strings of characters that represent a message that we would like to retrieve from the database via our program.

Testing the Application

Once the enterprise bean has been deployed, the JNDI environment resource references properly set up, and the database is ready, we can finally test our application. To do this, we must simply compile and run the application client displayed earlier, and be certain to include the client JAR at run time that has been created by our application server.

Your invocation of the application will probably look something like this:

```
java -cp %J2EE_HOME%\lib\j2ee.jar;ResourcesClient.jar;. ResourceTesterClient
```

If your application fails, then you can scan your system logs for more information to locate the error. If it succeeds, you can also scan your system logs to find the messages contained in your database that have how been recorded in your system log.

That's all there is to it! Now, it's just a matter of seeing how to reapply this process with the other types of resource manager connection factories.

JavaMail Sessions

In order for your enterprise beans to access a JavaMail session, they use an object of type javax.mail.Session. Objects of this class type will serve the same role for JavaMail sessions as the javax.sql.DataSource interface type served for data source connections – a resource manager connection factory.

The javax.mail.Session class behaves within an enterprise bean as it does with standard clients, as a factory for the installed Transport and Store implementations, each of which are used for different communication protocols. The only difference in this case is that the reference to the Session object is retrieved via JNDI rather than being constructed directly in the application code itself. Unlike an HttpSession object, a JavaMail Session object does not maintain state; it merely functions as a common interface between a mail-enabled client and the network, allowing them to store user properties, perform authentication, and instantiate Transport and Store objects.

Retrieving a Session object via a JNDI lookup confers the same flexibility and scalability benefits as are provided when performing a JNDI lookup for a DataSource object. This decouples the resource from the client code accessing it. So long as the JNDI lookup name remains the same, the application server can change any properties relating to the implementation of the JavaMail Store and Transport objects without touching the client code.

The javax.mail.Session Class

Although the `Session` class does contain two methods (the `getInstance()` method and `getDefaultInstance()` method), each of which return a `javax.mail.Session` instance, we will use neither of these methods to retrieve an instance of the class. Instead, we will simply perform a JNDI lookup on a JavaMail resource manager and cast the result to type `javax.mail.Session`. The benefit of doing this is that the resource manager will cooperate with the application server to ensure that resources are properly utilized and the JavaMail session efficiently handled within the scope of the other processes taking place.

Once your enterprise bean has a reference to a `Session` object then the JavaMail API can be used as it would be used in any other class file.

JavaMail Sessions and JNDI

The earlier description of the relationship between data sources and JNDI is relevant to JavaMail sessions and their relationship with JNDI. The only exception is that the `javax.mail.Session` class should be inserted in place of the `javax.sql.DataSource` interface and a `Store` or `Transport` object is produced from the resource factory rather than a `java.sql.Connection` object.

Now let's take a look at an example that will put all of this information into perspective.

JavaMail Source Example

This example is merely intended as a reference, and not a complete example that can be deployed into an application server. We'll first look at the necessary deployment descriptor entries, and then at the code that will need to be provided in our enterprise bean.

Deployment Descriptor Entries

Consider the following deployment descriptor excerpt:

```
<resource-ref>
   <description>
      This resource is used to send e-mail alerts to the system
      administrator in the event of a serious error.
   </description>
      <res-ref-name>mail/Email</res-ref-name>
      <res-type>javax.mail.Session</res-type>
      <res-auth>Container</res-auth>
</resource-ref>
```

This resource reference demonstrates a near-minimal amount of information. Of all the elements displayed above, only the `<description>` tag is optional.

The resource manager factory type implements the `javax.mail.Session` interface and the container handles the resource manager authorization automatically.

Application Code

Retrieving a `Session` object from the resource manager via JNDI is every bit as easy as retrieving a `DataSource` object. Consider the following sample code:

```
// Obtain the initial JNDI context
Context context = new InitialContext();

// JNDI lookup to obtain resource manager connection factory reference
javax.mail.Session session = (javax.mail.Session)
                context.lookup("java:comp/env/mail/MyMailSession");
```

At this point we have a reference to a `javax.mail.Session` object and there are several directions that we can go. We can either create a `Store` or `Transport` object and then use it to perform some mail-related task, or create a `Message` and use the static `send()` method defined within the `Transport` class to send the message. Now let's look at a complete sample application.

JavaMail Session Sample Application

If you haven't read through the database resource example, you'll probably want to do that. This sample application takes the code developed in that example, makes a few minor modifications, and then demonstrates how to handle a JavaMail session from within an enterprise bean.

The Stateful Session Bean

This bean obtains a JavaMail session from the container's pool of sessions, and then uses that session to send a simple e-mail message.

The Remote Interface

This is the same remote interface used previously in the database resource example, `ResourceTester`. It defines two business methods. The first method initializes the resource and retrieves it from the container. The second business method tests that resource to see if it can successfully perform its task with the current configuration.

The Home Interface

The home interface for this example is also identical to the `ResourceTesterHome` interface defined earlier.

The Enterprise Bean Class

Although this class is not identical to the `DatabaseTesterEJB` class defined as a part of the database resource example, we can use that one as a template.

Rename the file to `MailTesterEJB` (or save the `DatabaseTesterEJB` as a new file with a new name) and change the import statements to reflect the following code snippet:

```
import javax.ejb.*;
import javax.naming.*;
import javax.mail.*;
import javax.mail.internet.*;

public class MailTesterEJB implements SessionBean {

  public void ejbCreate() {}
  public void ejbActivate() {}
  public void ejbPassivate() {}
  public void ejbRemove() {}
  public void setSessionContext(SessionContext ctx) {}
}
```

Next, change the instance variables to reflect the following:

```
private static String dataSourceName =
                    "java:comp/env/mail/ResourceMail";
private static String emailAddress = "me@localhost.com";
private Session       session;
```

You may want to change the e-mail address to your own personal account, or you can leave it just as it appears here.

The `initResource()` method requires only one line to change. The connection factory object returned by the JNDI lookup call should be cast to type `Session` and the variable that stores the local reference to that connection factory object should be changed to the name `session`:

```
public void initResource() {
    InitialContext     initCtx;

    try {
        initCtx = new InitialContext();
        session = (Session) initCtx.lookup(dataSourceName);
    } catch (NamingException ne) {
        ne.printStackTrace();
    }
}
```

The `testResource()` method is very different:

```
public boolean testResource()   {
    MimeMessage         message;

    try {
        message = new MimeMessage(session);
        message.setFrom();

        message.setRecipients(Message.RecipientType.TO,
                        InternetAddress.parse(emailAddress, false));
        message.setSubject("Test Message from MailTesterEJB");
        message.setText("This is only a test message. \n" +
                    "This is only a test...");
        message.setHeader("X-Mailer", "JavaMailer");
        message.setSentDate(new java.util.Date());

        Transport.send(message);
    } catch(MessagingException me) {
        me.printStackTrace();
        return false;
    } catch(Exception e) {
        e.printStackTrace();
        return false;
    }

    return true;
}
```

The JavaMail API is very straightforward, and its method calls and static property variables are fairly intuitive. The Message object is associated with a JavaMail `Session`, that Message object is then loaded with a message, and finally that message is sent to those addresses that were specified within the message header.

The Deployment Descriptor

Here's the modified deployment descriptor. The only significant change is to point the `<resource-ref>` element to a `javax.mail.Session`:

```xml
<?xml version="1.0" encoding="Cp1252"?>

<!DOCTYPE ejb-jar PUBLIC '-//Sun Microsystems, Inc.//DTD Enterprise JavaBeans
2.0//EN' 'http://java.sun.com/dtd/ejb-jar_2_0.dtd'>

<ejb-jar>
  <display-name>ResourceTester</display-name>
  <enterprise-beans>

    <session>
        <display-name>MailTester</display-name>
        <ejb-name>MailTester</ejb-name>
        <home>ResourceTesterHome</home>
        <remote>ResourceTester</remote>
        <ejb-class>MailTesterEJB</ejb-class>
        <session-type>Stateful</session-type>
        <transaction-type>Bean</transaction-type>
        <resource-ref>
          <res-ref-name>mail/ResourceMail</res-ref-name>
          <res-type>javax.mail.Session</res-type>
          <res-auth>Container</res-auth>
          <res-sharing-scope>Shareable</res-sharing-scope>
        </resource-ref>
    </session>

  </enterprise-beans>
</ejb-jar>
```

Deploying and Testing the Application

If you have not first gone through the database resources example described earlier, you may at least want to mark those pages with a finger so that you can refer back to that material. The process of deploying and testing this application is identical to the database resources example, except that this example doesn't require access to the Cloudscape database.

Deploy the Bean

Setting up a JavaMail resource manager connection factory entails a considerable greater amount of work than does setting up a database connection factory. For one thing, there are more deployment variables that must be defined. These variables are important in order to give the container access to your system or network's SMTP server. The second factor that may need to be addressed is to make modifications to your system's SMTP server or proxy settings in order to test this application. An easy solution to this is to use your system's name (e.g. sally@mycomputer) rather than your normal e-mail address.

The following table for example identifies the properties that must be set and the values that should be assigned for this example:

Field Name	Field Value
Coded Name	mail/ResourceMail
Type	javax.mail.Session
Authentication	Container
From	(your e-mail address)
Host	(mail server host)
User Name	(your UNIX or Windows user name)

The following figure is a screenshot of the Reference Implementation GUI for this:

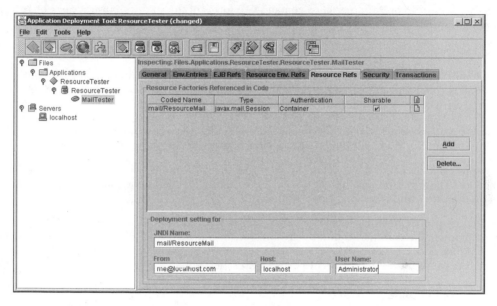

Now, assuming that the application successfully deploys, you're ready to hit the deploy button and move on to testing the application.

Testing the Application

Open the ResourceTesterClient client and change the JNDI call so that you are accessing the MailTester bean rather than the DatabaseTester bean. Otherwise, the client code goes unchanged. Recompile the file, run it, and you'll see the same type of response as before. The test will either be successful or a failure. For details, you can consult your app server's logs.

JMS Queue and Topic Connections

In order for your enterprise beans to establish a JMS connection, they must do so through an object of type javax.jms.QueueConnectionFactory (in the case of a point-to-point messaging system), or through an object of type javax.jms.TopicConnectionFactory (in the case of a publish/subscribe model). As the name suggests, objects of these classes serve as connection factories for JMS connection objects.

In terms of resource management, JMS connections are very expensive and memory-intensive. Thus, clients typically open a single connection to the message broker. In this case, the message broker is the JMS resource manager that we have accessed via JNDI and retrieved a factory object from. Although only a single connection is maintained to the message broker, multiple sessions (each with its own transaction properties and acknowledgement mode) are permitted to operate within the context of a single connection.

Retrieving a `Queue` or `TopicConnectionFactory` object via a JNDI lookup confers the same flexibility and scalability benefits as are provided when performing a JNDI lookup for a `DataSource` object or `Session` object: we obtain decoupling of the resource from the client code accessing it. So long as the JNDI lookup name remains the same, the application server can change any properties relating to the implementation of the JMS message broker.

The javax.jms.QueueConnectionFactory Class

The `QueueConnectionFactory` class contains two forms of the `createQueueConnection()` method that produces objects of type `QueueConnection`. Let's take a look at them:

```
public QueueConnection createQueueConnection() throws JMSException
```

This method creates a queue connection from the connection factory with default user identity. The connection is created in stopped mode, meaning that no messages will be delivered until the `Connection.start()` method is explicitly called:

```
public QueueConnection createQueueConnection(String username,
                    String password) throws JMSException
```

This method is identical to the previous method with the addition of two parameters that are passed into the method. These two parameters facilitate the creation of a new `QueueConnection` object using the specified username and password authorization.

Once your enterprise bean has a reference to a `QueueConnection` object then the JMS API can be used to complete the communication by creating one or more `javax.jms.Session` objects, and then using the `QueueConnection` object to create a `javax.jms.QueueSender` or `javax.jms.QueueReceiver` object to process JMS messages.

The javax.jms.TopicConnectionFactory Class

The `TopicConnectionFactory` class contains two forms of the `createTopicConnection()` method that produces objects of type `TopicConnection`. Those first form is:

```
public TopicConnection createTopicConnection() throws JMSException
```

This method creates a topic connection from the connection factory with default user identity. The connection is created in stopped mode, meaning that no messages will be delivered until the `Connection.start()` method is explicitly called.

```
public TopicConnection createTopicConnection(String username,
                    String password) throws JMSException
```

This method is identical to the previous method with the addition of two parameters that are passed into the method. These two parameters facilitate the creation of a new `TopicConnection` object using the specified username and password authorization.

Once your enterprise bean has a reference to a `TopicConnection` object then the JMS API can be used to complete the communication by creating one or more `javax.jms.Session` objects, using the `TopicConnection` object and then creating a `javax.jms.TopicPublisher` or `javax.jms.TopicSubscriber` object to process JMS messages.

JMS and JNDI

The earlier description of the relationship between data sources and JNDI is also relevant to JMS sessions and their relationship with JNDI. The only exception is that the `javax.jms.QueueConnectionFactory` or `javax.jms.TopicConnectionFactory` class should be inserted in place of the `javax.sql.DataSource` interface and a `QueueConnection` or `TopicConnection` object is produced from the resource factory rather than a `java.sql.Connection` object.

Now let's take a look at an example that demonstrates what we have learned.

JMS Source Example

Following the general format we have used so far, this example is merely intended as a reference, and not as a complete example that can be deployed into an application server. We'll look at a working sample application shortly. First though, we'll introduce the necessary deployment descriptor entries, and then look at the code that needs to be provided in our enterprise bean.

Deployment Descriptor Entries

Consider the following deployment descriptor excerpt:

```
<resource-ref>
  <description>
    This resource is used to send messages on various topics to
    any and all  subscribers for a particular resource.
  </description>
  <res-ref-name>jms/TopicSender</res-ref-name>
  <res-type>javax.jms.TopicConnectionFactory</res-type>
  <res-auth>Container</res-auth>
</resource-ref>
```

Of the elements displayed above, only the `<description>` tag is optional, so, like the database and JavaMail resources we have already seen, this resource reference demonstrates a near-minimal amount of information.

The resource manager factory type implements the `javax.jms.TopicConnectionFactory` interface and the container handles the resource manager authorization automatically.

Application Code

Here we'll focus on an example of creating a `QueueConnection` object from a `QueueConnectionFactory`. Note that the process for creating `TopicConnection` objects is nearly identical. Retrieving a `QueueConnection` object from the resource manager via JNDI is every bit as easy as retrieving a `DataSource` object. Consider the following sample code:

```
// Obtain the initial JNDI context
Context context = new InitialContext();

// JNDI lookup to obtain resource manager connection factory reference
javax.jms.QueueConnectionFactory factory =
                        (javax.jms.QueueConnectionFactory)
                    context.lookup("java:comp/env/jms/PointToPoint");

// Invoke factory object to create connection object
javax.jms.QueueConnection connection = factory.createQueueConnection();
```

At this point we have a reference to a `javax.jms.QueueConnection` object and we are free to build
`QueueSender` and `QueueReceiver` objects to be used in a point-to-point message exchange. Now let's
look at a complete application.

JMS Sample Application

Remember, if you haven't already done so, it'll be very useful to read through the database resource
example to better understand this section. This sample application makes a few minor modifications to
the code developed in that example, and then demonstrates how to handle a JMS Queue from within an
enterprise bean.

The Stateful Session Bean

This bean will merely obtain a JMS `QueueConnectionFactory` from the container's pool of resources,
and then use that factory to create connection objects and open sessions on those connection objects.

The Remote Interface

This is the same remote interface used in the Database Resource example shown above,
`ResourceTester`. As we have seen, it defines two business methods: one to initialize the resource and
retrieve it from the container, and another to test that resource to see if it can successfully perform its
task with the current configuration.

The Home Interface

The home interface for this example also is identical to the `ResourceTesterHome` interface
defined earlier.

The Enterprise Bean Class

Although this class is not identical to the `DatabaseTesterEJB` class defined as a part of the database
resource example, we can use that one as a template.

Rename the file to be `MessageTesterEJB` (or save the `DatabaseTesterEJB` as a new file with a new
name) and change the import statements to reflect the following code snippet:

```
import java.rmi.RemoteException;
import java.util.*;
import javax.ejb.*;
import javax.naming.*;
import javax.jms.*;

public class MessageTesterEJB implements SessionBean {
```

The next step is to declare any instance variables that the business methods may require. Those variables, as well as a couple of static variables, are declared in the following code segment:

```
private static final String DATASOURCENAME =
                        "java:comp/env/jms/QueueConnectionFactory";

private static final String QUEUE = "jms/Queue";

private QueueConnection conn;
private Queue queue;
```

Now, you'll want to substitute the previous implementation of the `initResource()` method with this implementation:

```
public void initResource() {
    Context initCtx;
    QueueConnectionFactory factory;

    try {
        //Establish an initial context and retrieve a reference to
        //a QueueConnectionFactory object
        initCtx = new InitialContext();
        factory = (QueueConnectionFactory)
                    initCtx.lookup(DATASOURCENAME);

        //Retrieve a Connection from the factory
        conn = factory.createQueueConnection();

        //Obtain a reference to the Queue
        queue = (Queue) initCtx.lookup(QUEUE);
    } catch (NamingException ne) {
        ne.printStackTrace();
    } catch (Exception ex) {
        ex.printStackTrace();
    }
}
```

And finally, we have the new implementation for the `testResource()` method:

```
public boolean testResource() {
    QueueSession session;
    QueueSender sender;
    TextMessage message;

    try {
        //Open the connection to the Queue
        conn.start();

        //Open a Queue session on this connection
        session = conn.createQueueSession(false, Session.AUTO_ACKNOWLEDGE);

        //Create a sender for the Queue
        sender = session.createSender(queue);

        //Create a message to be sent to the Queue
```

```
        message = session.createTextMessage();
        message.setText("The time is " + (new Date()).getTime());

        //Send the message to the Queue
        sender.send(message, DeliveryMode.PERSISTENT, 5, 0);
    } catch(Exception e) {
      e.printStackTrace();
      return false;
    }
    return true;
}
```

The Deployment Descriptor

Here are the modifications for the JMS example's deployment descriptor. Note that this time round we also have a <resource-env-ref> element:

```xml
<?xml version="1.0" encoding="Cp1252"?>

<!DOCTYPE ejb-jar PUBLIC '-//Sun Microsystems, Inc.//DTD Enterprise JavaBeans
2.0//EN' 'http://java.sun.com/dtd/ejb-jar_2_0.dtd'>

<ejb-jar>
  <display-name>ResourceTester</display-name>
  <enterprise-beans>

    <session>
      <display-name>MessageTester</display-name>
      <ejb-name>MessageTester</ejb-name>
      <home>resourceTester.ResourceTesterHome</home>
      <remote>resourceTester.ResourceTester</remote>
      <ejb-class>resourceTester.MessageTesterEJB</ejb-class>
      <session-type>Stateful</session-type>
      <transaction-type>Container</transaction-type>
      <resource-ref>
        <res-ref-name>jms/QueueConnectionFactory</res-ref-name>
        <res-type>javax.jms.QueueConnectionFactory</res-type>
        <res-auth>Container</res-auth>
        <res-sharing-scope>Shareable</res-sharing-scope>
      </resource-ref>
      <resource-env-ref>
        <resource-env-ref-name>jms/Queue</resource-env-ref-name>
        <resource-env-ref-type>javax.jms.Queue</resource-env-ref-type>
      </resource-env-ref>
    </session>
  </enterprise-beans>

</ejb-jar>
```

Deploying and Testing the Application

If you have not first gone through one of the previous examples, you may at least want to mark the deployment and testing pages for the database resource example. It will be helpful to refer back to that material as we go through the deployment of this example. The process of deploying and testing this application is identical to the JavaMail resource example and the database resources example, without the need to use the Cloudscape database in the latter.

Deploy the Bean

Setting up a JMS resource manager connection factory requires even more configuration than does a JavaMail connection factory. Although with JMS, you don't have to be concerned about the SMTP server, you do have to set up a container reference to the queue (or topic) and another reference for the connection factory from when your enterprise beans will obtain their connection objects. We'll look at these two configurations one at a time.

The Resource Envrionment

The resource environment refers to the actual queue or topic that makes the whole messaging paradigm usable. The deployment tool that ships with Sun's RI, uses a separate screen to keep track of JMS destinations:

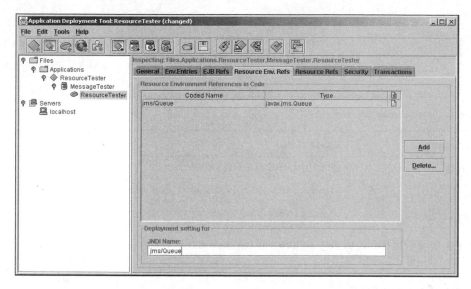

The table below identifies the properties that must be set and the values that should be assigned for the JMS queue resource we are using in our example:

Field Name	Field Value
Coded Name	jms/Queue
Type	javax.jms.Queue

The next screen in the RI Bean Creation Wizard allows the deployer to configure the resource manager connection factories. These factories are what we have been concerned with in the previous two examples, database and JavaMail, and what we will be interested in with our next resource, URLs. The following figure provides a screenshot of this stage in the Wizard:

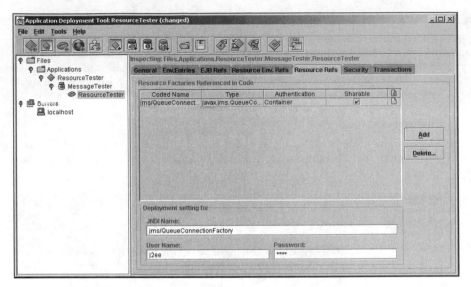

And now for the tabular version:

Field Name	Field Value
Coded Name	`jms/QueueConnectionFactory`
Type	`javax.jms.QueueConnectionFactory`
Authentication	`Container`

Now you're ready to hit the deploy button and, assuming that the application successfully deploys, move on to testing the application.

Testing the Application

Open the `ResourceTesterClient` client file and change the JNDI call so that you are accessing the `MessageTester` bean rather than the `DatabaseTester` bean or `MailTester` bean. Otherwise, the client code goes unchanged. And now for the exciting part, we must set up a JMS listener to monitor the Queue and process any messages that appear on the Queue.

The JMS Listener Class

We'll begin of course, with the declarative portion of the class:

```
import javax.jms.*;
import java.io.*;
import java.net.*;
import javax.naming.*;

public class MsgListener {
  private static final String QUEUE_CONN_FACTORY =
                         "QueueConnectionFactory";
  private static final String    QUEUE = "jms/Queue";

  public static void main(String[] args) {
```

```
Context                          initCtx;
QueueConnectionFactory           factory;
Queue                            queue;
QueueConnection                  conn;
QueueSession                     session;
QueueReceiver                    receiver;
TextMessage                      request;

    //***Body of Method here***//

  }
}
```

With all of those declarations out of the way, we can tackle the actual meat of the method, all of which is contained within a try/catch block:

```
try {
    //Obtain an initial context
    initCtx = new InitialContext();

    //Lookup Connection Factory and Queue name
    factory = (QueueConnectionFactory)
              initCtx.lookup(QUEUE_CONN_FACTORY);
    queue = (Queue) initCtx.lookup(QUEUE);

    //Create and start a Queue connection using the Factory
    conn = (QueueConnection)factory.createQueueConnection();
    conn.start();

    //Open a Queue session on this connection
    session = conn.createQueueSession(false,
                              Session.AUTO_ACKNOWLEDGE);

    //Create a listener to receive messages from the Queue
    receiver = session.createReceiver(queue);

    //Send every message received to Standard Out
    while (true) {
        request = (TextMessage) receiver.receive();
        System.out.println("Message Received: " + request.getText());
    }
} catch (NamingException ne) {
    ne.printStackTrace();
} catch (JMSException jms) {
    jms.printStackTrace();
}
```

Although it looks complicated, it is actually very similar, and in some aspects directly duplicates, the process that we coded earlier with the MessageTesterEJB. In that example we had a message object and a sender object, here we have a request object and a receiver object. Apart from that, everything else is identical!

Now you're ready to compile and start up your listener, and then fire off your EJB client. Every time you run your EJB client you should see another message printed to the console by this JMS listener.

URL Resources

A URL resource could be many things: a file located in a file system, an FTP directory, an HTTP resource, or in fact any other entity that can be referred to by a URL string. This wide array of potential resources makes the URL EJB resource mechanism a very useful aspect of a J2EE container. In order for your code to handle any of these URL resources, the `java.net.URL` class serves as the resource factory type for obtaining URL connections. Objects of this class type will serve the same role for URL connections as the `javax.sql.DataSource` interface type served for data source connections – a resource manager connection factory.

As before, by using a JNDI lookup we get flexibility and scalability benefits by decoupling the resource from the client code accessing it. So long as the JNDI lookup name remains the same, the actual location of the URL resource can change (and they often do) without affecting the client code that accesses it.

The java.net.URL Class

The URL class has well over 20 methods, but only one of them is of any real interest to us, because we need to create a new `URLConnection` object in order to access URL resources from our enterprise beans. After performing a JNDI lookup on a URL resource manager and casting the result to type `java.net.URL`, we will need to instantiate `URLConnection` objects. The URL class provides us with a single method that does just this:

> **public URLConnection openConnection() throws IOException**

This method returns a `URLConnection` object that represents a connection to the remote object referred to by the URL.

Once your enterprise bean has a reference to a `URLConnection` object then the `java.net.URL` API can be used as it would be used in any other class file.

URL Connections and JNDI

As we have seen for the other resources discussed so far, our original description of the relationship between data sources and JNDI is relevant to URL connections and their relationship with JNDI. The only exception is that the `java.net.URL` class should be inserted in place of the `javax.sql.DataSource` interface and a `java.net.URLConnection` object is produced from the resource factory rather than a `java.sql.Connection` object.

Now let's take a look at an example that will put all of this information into practice.

URL Source Example

Let's look at the deployment descriptor entries required for URL resources, and then at the code that will be needed in our enterprise bean.

Deployment Descriptor Entries

Consider the following deployment descriptor excerpt:

```
<resource-ref>
  <description>
    This URL resource is the output of a servlet.
  </description>
  <res-ref-name>url/DynamicInfo</res-ref-name>
    <res-type>java.net.URL</res-type>
    <res-auth>Container</res-auth>
</resource-ref>
```

Note that only the `<description>` tag is optional here and this resource reference therefore demonstrates a near-minimal amount of information. The resource manager factory type implements the `java.net.URL` interface and the container handles the resource manager authorization automatically.

Application Code

Retrieving a URL object from the resource manager via JNDI is every bit as easy as retrieving a `DataSource` object. Consider the following sample code:

```
// Obtain the initial JNDI context
Context context = new InitialContext();

// JNDI lookup to obtain resource manager connection factory reference
java.net.URL url = (java.net.URL)
          context.lookup("java:comp/env/url/DynamicInfo");

// Invoke factory object to create connection object
java.net.URLConnection connection = url.openConnection();
```

With this code we have a reference to a `java.net.URLConnection` object and we are free to use the `java.net.URL` API to access and process the URL's data. Now for a complete application…

URL Resource Sample Application

If you haven't read through the sample application from any of the previous examples, you'll probably find it useful to do so. This sample application takes the code developed in any of those examples, makes a few small changes, and then demonstrates how to handle a URL resource from within an enterprise bean.

The Stateful Session Bean

The following bean will simply obtain a URL object from the container's pool of resources, and then use that factory to create connection objects which will ultimately access the data stored at the URL.

The Remote Interface

This is the same remote interface used in the previous examples, `ResourceTester`.

The Home Interface

Again, the home interface for this example is identical to the `ResourceTesterHome` interface defined earlier.

The Enterprise Bean Class

As usual, although this class is not identical to the `DatabaseTesterEJB` class defined as a part of the database resource example, we will be using that one as a template. In fact, any of the other EJB class files from previous resource manager connection factory examples are fair game as templates.

Rename the file to be `UrlTesterEJB` (or save the `DatabaseTesterEJB` as a new file with a new name) and change the import statements to reflect the following code snippet:

```
import java.util.*;
import java.net.*;
import java.io.*;
import javax.ejb.*;
```

```
import javax.naming.*;

public class UrlTesterEJB implements SessionBean {

    public void ejbCreate() {}
    public void ejbActivate() {}
    public void ejbPassivate() {}
    public void ejbRemove() {}
    public void setSessionContext(SessionContext ctx) {}

}
```

The next order of business is to declare and define two variables, one a constant, and the other an instance variable:

```
    private static final String DATASOURCENAME =
                            "java:comp/env/url/ResourcesURL";

    private HttpURLConnection    conn;
```

Now we'll make a few changes to the `initResource()` method:

```
    public void initResource() {
        Context initCtx;
        URL url;

        try {
            //Obtain an initial context and retrieve a URL connection
            //factory reference
            initCtx = new InitialContext();
            url = (URL)initCtx.lookup(DATASOURCENAME);

            //Obtain an actual connection to the URL via the
            //connection factory
            conn = (HttpURLConnection) url.openConnection();
        } catch (NamingException ne) {
            ne.printStackTrace();
        } catch (Exception ex) {
            ex.printStackTrace();
        }
    }
```

And finally, we have the `testResource()` method:

```
    public boolean testResource() {
        BufferedReader reader;
        String line;

        try {
            //Use the HttpURLConnection object to feed the URL's data
            //in through a buffered data input stream
            reader = new BufferedReader(new InputStreamReader(
```

```
                               conn.getInputStream()));

         //Take each line and send it straight to Standard Out
         while ((line = reader.readLine()) != null)
            System.out.println(line);
      } catch(IOException io) {
         io.printStackTrace();
         return false;
      } catch(Exception e) {
         e.printStackTrace();
         return false;
      }

      return true;
   }
```

The Deployment Descriptor

No surprises here:

```
<?xml version="1.0" encoding="Cp1252"?>

<!DOCTYPE ejb-jar PUBLIC '-//Sun Microsystems, Inc.//DTD Enterprise JavaBeans
2.0//EN' 'http://java.sun.com/dtd/ejb-jar_2_0.dtd'>

<ejb-jar>
  <display-name>ResourceTester</display-name>
  <enterprise-beans>

    <session>
      <display-name>URLTester</display-name>
      <ejb-name>URLTester</ejb-name>
      <home>ResourceTesterHome</home>
      <remote>ResourceTester</remote>
      <ejb-class>UrlTesterEJB</ejb-class>
      <session-type>Stateful</session-type>
      <transaction-type>Bean</transaction-type>
      <resource-ref>
        <res-ref-name>url/ResourcesURL</res-ref-name>
        <res-type>java.net.URL</res-type>
        <res-auth>Container</res-auth>
        <res-sharing-scope>Shareable</res-sharing-scope>
      </resource-ref>
    </session>

  </enterprise-beans>
</ejb-jar>
```

Deploying and Testing the Application

If you have not first gone through one of the previous examples, it might be helpful to glance the deployment and testing pages for the database resource example. The process of deploying and testing this application is also identical to the JavaMail and JMS resource examples, and both of those examples derived their deployment and testing process from the original database resources example.

The table overleaf identifies the properties that must be set and the values that should be assigned for this example:

Field Name	Field Value
Coded Name	url/ResourcesURL
Type	java.net.URL
Authentication	Container
URL	http://localhost:8000/index.html

As is the case with other deployment properties, these values can be set via the wizard or afterward via the tabbed panes in the right-hand side of the deployment tool. The following figure is an example of a screenshot with the **Resource Refs** tab of the deployment tool selected:

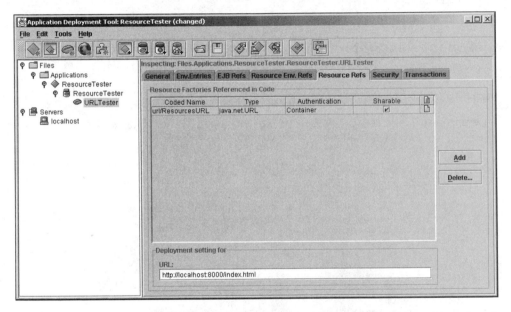

Now you're ready to hit the deploy button and move on to testing the application (assuming that the application successfully deploys).

Testing the Application

Open the `ResourceTesterClient` client and change the JNDI call so that you are accessing the `UrlTester` bean rather than one of the other beans. Otherwise, the client code goes unchanged. Recompile the file, run it, and you'll see the same type of response as before. The test will either be successful or a failure. For details, you can consult your app server's logs.

Moving On

The four types of Resource Manager Connection Factories that we have just looked at represent the most common types of outside resources that developers access directly via Enterprise Java Beans. The gaping hole in these connection factories, however, is that none of them provides seamless, standardized support for legacy systems. The solution to this is just around the corner in the shape of the Java Connector API (JCA).

Legacy Resources (Connector API)

Principally, there is a substantial need to integrate legacy systems, also referred to as **Enterprise Information Systems (EIS)**, into distributed systems utilizing a J2EE-compliant application server. The connection architecture is intended as an answer to this need.

EIS systems come in all sizes and shapes, but the specification identifies three typical examples of an EIS:

- ❑   An Enterprise Resource Planning (ERP) System
- ❑   Mainframe Transaction Processing System
- ❑   A Legacy Database System

The specification outlines a very simple architecture in which application servers and EIS vendors collaborate to produce "plug-and-play" components that all adhere to the Connector API. You'll find more information on EIS within J2EE at http://java.sun.com/j2ee/blueprints/eis_tier/. We'll now take a moment to examine the Connector architecture and API.

Architecture and API

There are two parts to this architecture:

- ❑   An EIS vendor-provided resource adapter
- ❑   An application server that allows this resource adapter to plug in to it

To be successful, both vendors must agree to support this framework and the Connector API. To make this cooperation easier, the architecture defines a set of contracts, such as connection management, transactions, and security, which a resource adapter has to support to plug in to an application server. These contracts serve as the architectural blueprints to guide both parties in the construction of their products.

The connector architecture defines three standard contracts that exist between an application server and an EIS:

- ❑   **Connection Management Contract**
  Enables an application server to pool connections to an underlying EIS, and enables application components to connect to an EIS. This leads to a scalable application environment that can support a large number of EIS clients.

- ❑   **Transaction Management Contract**
  This contract exists between the transaction manager and an EIS that supports transactional access to EIS resource managers. This contract enables an application server to use a transaction manager to manage transactions across multiple resource managers as well as supporting internal transaction management within the EIS resource manager itself.

- ❑   **Security Contract**
  Enables secure access to an EIS. This contract provides support for a secure application environment that reduces security threats to the EIS and protects valuable information resources managed by the EIS.

You might notice that these three contracts do not attempt to address any contracts that are internal to an application server implementation. The specification states that:

"The specific mechanisms and contracts within an application server are outside the scope of the connector architecture specification. This specification focuses on the system-level contracts between the application server and EIS."

The client API used by the application component for EIS access is referred to as **The Common Client Interface (CCI).** The specification defines it this way:

"The CCI defines a standard client API for application components. The CCI enables application components and Enterprise Application Integration (EAI) frameworks to drive interactions across heterogeneous EISs using a common client API."

An example of such an EIS-specific client API is the JDBC API for relational databases. As long as database vendors adhere to the JDBC API (and it suits them to do so), then developers can "plug-and-play" databases and associated JDBC drivers without having to break their code.

Now let's take a look at the two key client classes in the `javax.resource.cci` package:

javax.resource.cci.ConnectionFactory

This class implements the `ManagedConnectionFactory` interface, thus supporting a set of properties related to the configuration of the underlying EIS. These properties provide information required by the `ManagedConnectionFactory` for the creation of physical connections to the EIS.

A resource adapter can implement the `ManagedConnectionFactory` interface as a JavaBean. By doing this, deployment and management tools based on the JavaBeans framework can manage the configuration of `ManagedConnectionFactory` instances (provided that a `BeanInfo` class is also provided).

javax.resource.cci.Connection

Clearly, this class represents the actual connection to the EIS created via the `ConnectionFactory` reference found during the JNDI lookup. These two classes should not seem any different from the previous four resource types that we have examined thus far.

Next we'll look at the details of the JNDI lookup and instantiation of a `Connection` object next.

Deploying a Resource Adapter

The final product produced by the EIS vendor or resource adapter vendor is a resource adapter that should be J2EE-compliant and allow the services of the EIS to be made available to the application server.

One thing to keep in mind is that there is no restriction on who may produce J2EE resource adapters in compliance with the Connector specification. Just as there are many players in the JDBC driver market that do not sell databases, there is the potential for non-EIS companies to produce resource adapters for the EIS products of other vendors. Given that possibility, it is important that the deployer pays close attention to the resource adapter and ensures that any functionality supported by the resource adapter is also supported by the underlying EIS instance. At any rate, the functionality to be used can be declared in the resource adapter's deployment descriptor.

There is one significant difference between resource adapters and the previous four resources we've examined: a resource adapter does not require an entry in the application's deployment descriptor. The resource adapter has its own deployment descriptor and brokers its own interaction with the container.

Connector Sample Code

The process of looking up a resource manager connection factory reference via JNDI, casting the returned object to the appropriate type, and then invoking the factory reference to instantiate `Connection` objects is no different from the other types of resources that we have worked with earlier in the chapter. Consider the following example:

```
//Obtain the initial JNDI context
Context context = new InitialContext();
```

```
// Perform JNDI lookup to obtain connection factory
javax.resource.cci.ConnectionFactory connFactory =
            (javax.resource.cci.ConnectionFactory)
            context.lookup("java:comp/env/eis/MyEIS");

// Invoke the factory object to instantiate a Connection object
javax.resource.cci.Connection conn = connFactory.getConnection();
```

This concludes our exploration of the EIS Connector architecture. You should bear in mind that, at the time of writing, the Connector architecture is only in beta release and there are likely to be changes made in the API shortly after this text is published.

Resource Environment References

To access administered objects (such as JMS destinations or an open JavaMail session) from within your enterprise beans, the bean provider uses "logical" names called **resource environment references**. These references are special entries declared in the application's deployment descriptor, which are then used by the container to construct the enterprise bean's environment. In the deployment descriptor, the deployer binds the resource environment references to administered objects in the target operational environment that the bean needs to access.

Resource environment references are something of a hybrid between EJB references and resource manager connection factories. They are structured identically to EJB references, but the end result is to return a reference to an object quite similar to the connection factories we covered in the previous section.

The process of accessing an administered object from an enterprise bean has three steps:

❑   Create an entry in the enterprise bean's environment that associates a JNDI lookup name with the resource environment reference your bean needs to reference. Resource environment references are declared in the deployment descriptor and the EJB specification recommends that all resource environment references be organized in the appropriate subcontext of the bean's environment (in other words in the `java:comp/env/mail` JNDI context for a JavaMail administered object).

❑   Look up the administered object in the enterprise bean's environment using the JNDI name specified in the previous step.

❑   Convert the returned object to the appropriate type (`javax.jms.Queue`, `javax.mail.Service`, and so on).

In you've been reading this chapter from the start, you should find the concepts in this section very easy to pick up. If something doesn't seem to be explained thoroughly enough, however, the first five to ten pages of this chapter should provide the clarity you need.

The Deployment Descriptor

Just as environment entries use a special element within the deployment descriptor, the <env-entry> element, there is also an element used to identify resource environment references. This element is the <resource-env-ref> element. The bean provider uses this element to declare all administered objects referenced by a particular enterprise bean.

The <resource-env-ref> element can have three possible child elements, two of which are mandatory:

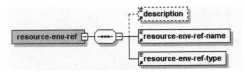

Below is a typical example of a resource environment reference that incorporates all four elements:

```
...
<enterprise-beans>
  <session>
    ...
    <ejb-name>EmployeeService</ejb-name>
    <ejb-class>com.wombat.empl.EmployeeServiceBean</ejb-class>
    ...
    <resource-env-ref>
    <description>
        This is a reference to a JMS queue used
        in the processing of Stock info
    </description>
    <resource-env-ref-name>jms/StockInfo</resource-env-ref-name>
    <resource-env-ref-type>javax.jms.Queue</resource-env-ref-type>
    </resource-env-ref>
    ...
  </session>
  ...
</enterprise-beans>
...
```

Now let's briefly take a look at each of the elements in turn.

<resource-env-ref>

Each <ejb-ref> element describes the interface requirements that the referencing enterprise bean has for the referenced administered object. An enterprise bean can have 0 to many <ejb-ref> elements. For every administered object that the bean needs access to, an appropriate <resource-env-ref> element should exist in the deployment descriptor.

<resource-env-ref-name>

The <resource-env-ref-name> element specifies the reference name for the administered object. Its value is the environment entry name used in the enterprise bean code to retrieve a reference to the object. This retrieval is, naturally, performed using a JNDI lookup.

<resource-env-ref-type>

The <resource-env-ref-type> element specifies the expected type of the enterprise bean; its value will depend upon the administered object in question. It is the deployer's responsibility to ensure that this type declaration is accurate.

Sample Application Code

So what does the administered object JNDI lookup call look like inside an enterprise bean? Not surprisingly, it looks very similar to the previous examples that we have worked with. Take a look at this sample code:

```
// Obtain the default initial JNDI context.
Context initCtx = new InitialContext();

// Look up the JMS StockQueue in the environment.
Object result = initCtx.lookup("java:comp/env/jms/MyMessages");

// Convert the result to the proper type.
javax.jms.Queue queue = (javax.jms.Queue) result;
```

Now your enterprise bean has a reference to an administered object of type `javax.jms.Queue`. The bean can now use that object as though it were local to the enterprise bean itself. It's that simple!

Summary

In this chapter, we have explored the topic of the EJB environment, the under-appreciated magician that works behind the scenes to make the lives of EJB developers easier. During this study we have covered the following:

❑   We explored the flexibility afforded by environment entries and have seen the improved functionality available by calling one enterprise bean from another.

❑   We looked at resource management and examined the way in which resource managers can extend the services provided by a J2EE container.

❑   By looking at some sample applications we saw how to access such external resources as a data store, a JavaMail session, a JMS topic or queue, and a URL resource. Additionally, we looked at the vast array of EIS resources made available via the Connector API.

❑   Finally, we took a brief look at how to utilize resource environment references to obtain a reference to an administered object such as a JMS queue.

In future chapters we will have the opportunity to put this knowledge into action, but for now, this has simply been an informative guide to the environment in which your enterprise beans exist. The material in this chapter may not be as glamorous as "EJB 2.0 Message-Driven Beans", but it is solid information that every EJB developer should have a good command of. Keep this book near your workstation and leave this chapter marked.

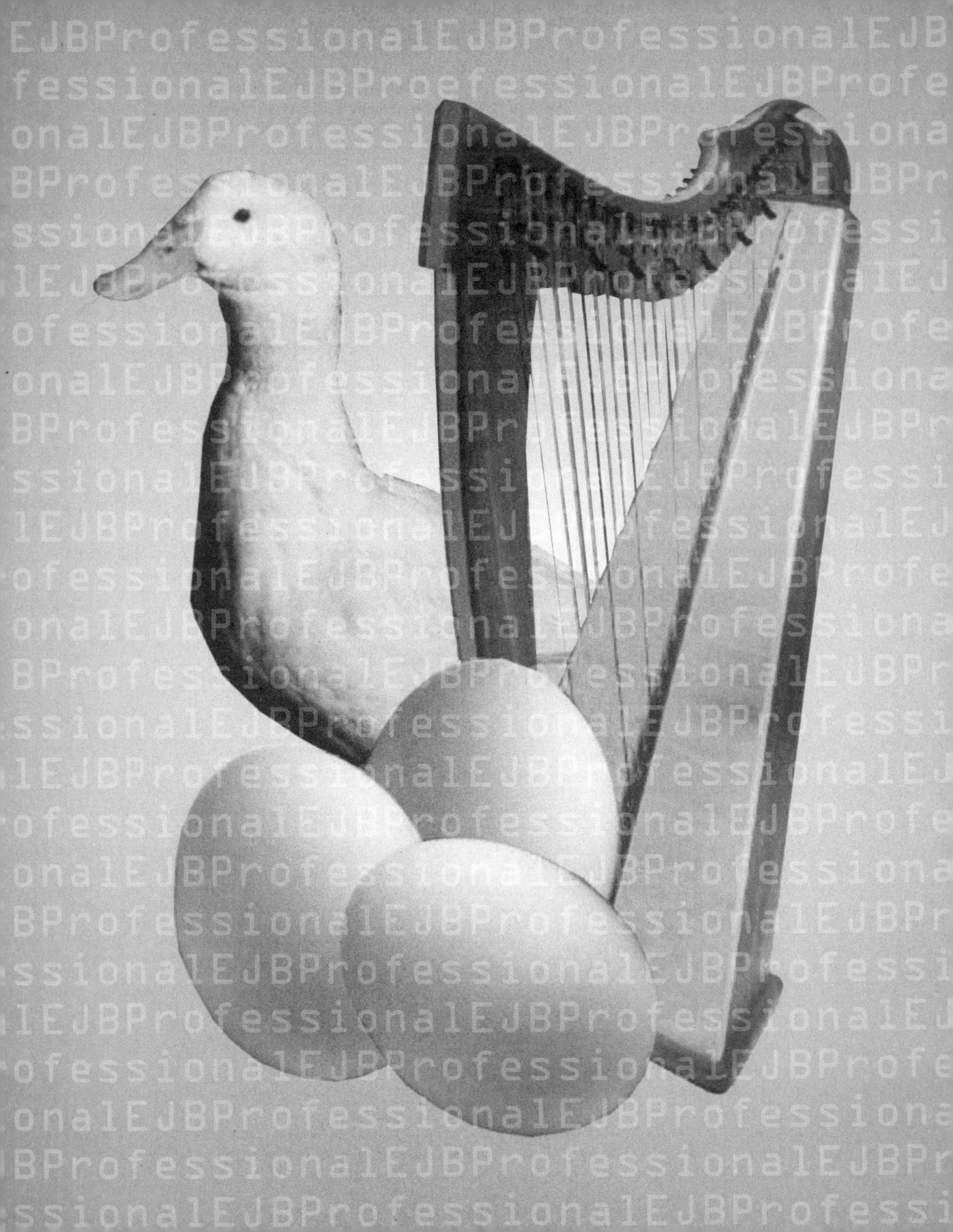

Transactions and EJB

9

Transactions play an integral role in the development of any non-trivial application. This is certainly true of EJB-based systems. The management of transactions is known as **transactional processing**.

Transactional processing can be a very complex feature to implement. However, EJB developers can consider themselves fortunate that the EJB specification requires that the container provide some measure of assistance. This doesn't necessarily mean that they do not have to be concerned with how transactions work. On the contrary, understanding transactions is vital to the development of any enterprise-class system.

This chapter aims to develop a thorough understanding of transactions, transactional systems, and how to effectively use them to improve the scalability, reliability, and dependability of EJB-based applications. It does so by examining how transactions are used within EJB systems. We begin with a discussion of just what transactions are, how they work, and what we can expect from them. Then we move on to cover the following topics:

- ❏ How transactions work in distributed systems, an area of interest in itself
- ❏ How Java supports transactions
- ❏ The API for transactions: JTA, the Java Transaction API
- ❏ EJBs and transactions

First, let's cover some basics of transactional programming.

What is a Transaction?

Simply put, a transaction is a single unit of work, composed of one or more steps. These steps have a logical relationship to each other and must be considered as a whole. Put another way, each step within a transaction depends on the success or outcome of the steps that precede it.

In the real world, a transaction represents an exchange between two entities. When you go to the grocery store and buy a loaf of bread, you are conducting a transaction. The bread must be removed from the shelf, brought to the register, paid for, put in a bag, and then removed from the store.

When you order a book online, you place your order for the book, the book is removed from inventory, your credit card is processed, the book is shipped, and you receive it.

In a banking example, we would put a hold on the account so no one else could interrupt us, check to see if there is enough money in the account, debit the appropriate amount, record the account activity, and then release the account for others to use.

We need to treat these steps as one single unit of work because each step requires the successful completion of the previous step. If one of the steps fails (for example, because of insufficient funds), we must undo any changes that were made by the previous steps. Also, we must ensure that there are no interruptions between steps.

> So, a transaction is a single unit of work that embodies the various individual steps that comprise a compose exchange.

An application or system that uses transactions is said to be a **transactional system**. The component that manages and coordinates transactions across a system is a **transaction manager** or **transaction processing (TP) monitor.** Some examples of popular TP monitors include IBM's CICS, BEA's Tuxedo, and TOP END, which was acquired by BEA from NCR in 1998.

There are many characteristics to transactions. How they work, when they're used, what behaviors they exhibit, and so on. But before we jump into the details, let's examine some of the reasons for using transactions in the first place.

Why do we Need Transactions?

Let's consider a scenario where an airline reservation application is used to book a seat on a flight. There are several steps that have to be taken to process a reservation:

- ❑ First, an appropriate flight must be found.

- ❑ Then, an available seat on the flight must be located.

- ❑ Having found the seat, the reservation is then begun. This requires getting the name of the customer as well as their credit card information, meal preference, etc.

- ❑ Once this information has been verified, the reservation can be made.

So far so good, but what happens if, while the travel agent is processing the customer information, another travel agent comes in and books the seat for another customer?

Without any proper concurrency control, it is entirely possible that the following could happen:

- ❑ Agent 1 verifies that a seat is available and begins collecting Customer 1's information.

- ❑ Meanwhile, Agent 2 also sees that the seat is available and begins collecting Customer 2's information.

- ❑ Agent 2 finishes processing Customer 2's information first and, thus, confirms the reservation.

- ❑ Agent 1 also finishes the reservation.

The result? At the very least, two travelers are inconvenienced. At the worst, the travel agents just lost two customers and, quite possibly, the airline has lost them as well.

You can easily imagine how important it is to prevent other situations such as two people trying to draw funds out of a bank account at the same time, especially when that account only has enough money to satisfy one request. Or two processes trying to update the same set of data in a database simultaneously.

Obviously this cannot be allowed to happen. Transactional processing provides us with a way to prevent scenarios such as these. Transactions provide a structured method for controlling the execution of these processes, ensuring their success or else handling their failure.

There are other reasons for using transactions. As we have already seen, one use is when we need to group various steps together into a single unit of work. This unit must either be completed successfully or not at all.

Concurrent applications, those that support multiple users at the same time, have a number of interesting issues that must be addressed. Access to data by multiple clients must be managed and coordinated. Failure to do so can, at best, yield some unexpected results and, at worst, corrupt our data.

As more and more transactions are executed, concurrency control becomes more important and crucial to the well-being of our system. Steps must be taken to ensure that work done by one client does not affect work done by another client. Likewise, changes made by one client must be shared among all clients that rely on that data. Transactions provide a mechanism by which our applications can be aware of when these changes occur.

Transactions allow us to control how several applications access the same data. It can be determined whether a client is allowed to write or even read a given set of data. Additional granularity, or control, is supported in that you can determine how a transaction's relationship to that data is controlled.

Larger systems, especially EJB systems, also have scalability needs. It is quite common, encouraged even, for various resources be located on different servers. As a system grows and provides services for more and more users, the system will have to be maintained on more and more servers in order to handle the workload. As the application "scales-up", it becomes more difficult to manage and coordinate the concurrent data requests.

> **Transactions help to alleviate the complexity of coordinating data or resource access across many clients.**

By their nature, transactions can effect changes on a system. These changes, once they have been completed, must be recorded in **transaction logs**. These transaction logs are used to support failure resolution. That is, in the event of an error or loss of data, the transaction logs can be used to rebuild or recreate the data changes from a previous backup. This is actually much more difficult in practice, but the theory is sound.

By now you have no doubt noticed that transactions exhibit certain properties – characteristics that are common across all transactions. These characteristics are commonly referred to as the **ACID properties**.

The ACID Properties

Transactions exhibit four main characteristics: **Atomicity**, **Consistency**, **Isolation**, and **Durability**. Compliance with these four properties is required in order for an entity to be considered a transaction. Why? We need to be assured that things will work as we expect them to.

Let's take a look at each of the four ACID properties.

Atomicity

Atomicity implies that a transaction will be treated as a single unit of work. You will recall that we said that a transaction could consist of several steps. By treating these steps as a single unit, we are able to put logical boundaries around a process. This will allow us to require that each step must complete successfully or the next step will not be allowed to proceed.

Each step relies on the successful completion of the step before it. Should one step fail, none of the remaining steps will be completed. This makes sense when you apply it to our real-world shopping scenario. When you want to buy that loaf of bread, and the store is out of bread, you stop the transaction and do not complete the purchase.

Likewise, in a banking application, if a check is being drawn on an account, and that account does not have sufficient funds, we halt the transaction. We do not continue processing as if the transaction were successful.

Equally as important is the requirement that, in the event of failure, any changes that were made along the way must be undone. This must be accomplished in a way that does not have any effect on the data or its clients.

A transaction will allow us to indicate the beginning and ending steps of this logical grouping. If all of the steps complete successfully, then any changes made along the way are made permanent, or **committed**. Should any one step fail, the changes are undone, or **rolled back**.

Consistency

Consistency guarantees that the transaction will leave the system or data in a consistent state. We say that data is in a consistent state when it adheres to the constraints, or rules, of the database. A **constraint** is a condition that must be true about the database when a transaction has been completed. Constraints are defined as part of the database schema and specify such things as primary keys, valid ranges for a numerical field, and whether a field may contain a null value, among others.

If the system was in a consistent state when the transaction began, it must be in a consistent state when the transaction ends. This is regardless of whether the transaction succeeds and is committed, or fails and is rolled back.

Consistency is determined against a set of business rules or integrity constraints. In order to ensure consistency, a dual effort is required by both the transaction manager and the developer of the application.

The transactional manager does its part by ensuring that a transaction is atomic, isolated, and durable (the latter terms we will discuss in a moment).

The application developer helps to ensure consistency by specifying primary keys, referential integrity constraints, and other declarative conditions.

When a transaction is to be committed, its consistency is validated by the DBMS against these rules. If it is determined that the results of the transaction will be consistent with the rules set forth by the system, the transaction will be committed. If the results do not satisfy the requirements, the transaction will be rolled back.

Consistency ensures that any changes that our transaction makes will not leave the system in an invalid state. Thus, our transactions will be more reliable. If our transaction is moving money from one account to another, it will be consistent if the total amount of money in the system remains the same (that is, the same amount of money that is removed from the first account is added to the second account).

Isolation

The isolation property of transactions provides us with one of the most powerful characteristics of transactional processing. Simply put, isolation guarantees that any data that a transaction accesses will not be affected by any changes made by other transactions until the first transaction completes.

This effectively allows our transaction to execute as if it were the only one in the system. Other database operations that are requested will only be permitted to proceed if they do not compromise the data that we are currently working with. This is vital to supporting concurrent access to data.

Due to the great opportunity for error and data corruption within a concurrent system, transactional processing must be made simple for a developer to utilize.

With the transaction manager acting as the coordinator of the executing transactions, the responsibility for ensuring isolation and managing concurrent execution is shifted away from the developer.

There are several different levels of isolation that can be applied to a transaction. Which one you use will be determined by a number of different factors. We'll examine these levels of isolation a little later on.

Durability

The durability property specifies that when a transaction is committed, any changes to data that it made must be recorded in permanent storage. This is typically implemented using a **transaction log**.

Transaction logs store data that a resource, such as a database, can use to either re-apply transactions that might have been lost as a result of some failure, or rollback transactions due to an error. Basically, a transaction log keeps track of every data operation that has occurred in the database so that the data can be returned to a known (uncorrupted) state. Once the system has been restored to a known state, the log can be used to reconstruct or replay the changes made since that state.

Durability is also very important when you consider that a committed data change is essentially a binding contract. The commitment of a transaction represents an agreement between the data source and the application. The transaction log is effectively the written record of that agreement. This is exceptionally useful when you remember that the changes themselves are not permanent – another transaction can subsequently change the data.

This analogy of legal compliance isn't just figurative, however. Some laws require that an audit trail of all data changes be maintained for as many as seven years. This is especially true within financial applications. Transaction logs provide the means by which to do this.

Transactional Processing

Let's take a look at how transactions work in code. You may already be familiar with transactional processing in databases. While not the only use for transactions, it certainly is the most common.

A transaction follows the following general flow. We shall examine this line-by-line:

```
Begin Transaction
    // Do what needs to be done
    if error, rollback
    else commit
End Transaction
```

The following state diagram helps to illustrate the general flow of a transaction:

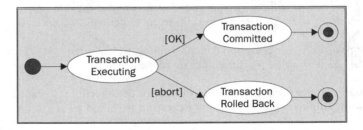

First, we indicate the beginning of the transaction. This signals that whatever instructions follow should be contained within the transaction. This procedure of identifying the beginning and ending of the transaction (also referred to as **transactional boundaries**) is known as **demarcation**:

```
Begin Transaction
```

Next we put the actual instructions that we want to have controlled by the transaction. Different design scenarios will impose different rules and restrictions on what we can do. We'll examine some of those scenarios in a little bit:

```
// Do what needs to be done
```

Once we have executed our instructions, we check to see if any errors have occurred. If they have, we rollback any changes that have been made, thus undoing the transaction:

```
if error, rollback
```

Otherwise, we commit our changes, thus making them permanent:

```
else commit
```

We then end the transaction, marking the ending boundary:

```
End Transaction
```

Now, this example is intentionally simplistic, but the point here is to understand the basic mechanism. Ideally, we would do things a little more efficiently, such as checking for an error after each instruction is executed, so as not to waste time executing steps that might be unnecessary had an error occurred somewhere along the way.

In Java, of course, we can rely on exception handling to provide a more programmer-friendly means of detecting errors that might occur while a transaction is being processed.

Transactional Processing in the Real World

Before we jump into EJB transactions, let's familiarize ourselves with how transactional processing works in a more general sense.

In the examples that follow in this chapter, we will take a look at two functionally similar but structurally different solutions. The first solution will be the traditional method of database programming via JDBC. The second will focus on an EJB-based implementation. The two examples will use the ubiquitous banking example that we are already familiar with.

The following sample program will transfer funds from one bank account to another. The transferFunds() method will start a transaction, call methods to withdraw and deposit funds, and then end the transaction by either committing or rolling back, as necessary.

We'll create a simple account table containing two fields: an account ID and a balance. Notice that we have also placed a constraint on the table such that the balance is not allowed to drop below zero. The SQL to create the database structure for this example is as follows:

```
CREATE TABLE account (
                    AccountId int,
                    Balance   double,
                    check (Balance >= 0)
);

INSERT INTO account (AccountId, Balance) values (1, 100);
INSERT INTO account (AccountId, Balance) values (2, 0);
```

The account table should now contain the following data:

```
AccountId   Balance
---------   -------
        1       100
        ?         0
```

The Bank Class

Now we'll implement the following `Bank` object. First, we'll create a general method for getting connections to a database:

```java
import java.sql.*;

public class Bank {

  public Connection getConnection(String jdbcDriverName,
                                  String jdbcURL) throws Exception {

    try {
      Class.forName(jdbcDriverName);
      return DriverManager.getConnection(jdbcURL);
    } catch (ClassNotFoundException e) {
      System.out.println(e);
    }
    return null;
  }
}
```

Next we have a simple routine for displaying all of the accounts in the database and their balances:

```java
  public void printBalances(Connection conn) {

    ResultSet rs = null;
    Statement stmt = null;

    try {
      stmt = conn.createStatement();
      rs = stmt.executeQuery("SELECT * from Account");

      while(rs.next())
        System.out.println("Account " + rs.getInt(1) +
                           " has a balance of " + rs.getDouble(2));

    } catch(Exception e) {
      e.printStackTrace();
    } finally {
```

Let's clean up our JDBC objects:

```java
      if(rs != null) {
        try {
          rs.close ();
        } catch(Exception ex) {
```

```
        System.err.println(ex);
      }
    }

    if(stmt != null){
      try {
        stmt.close ();
      } catch(Exception ex) {
        System.err.println(ex);
      }
    }
  }
}
```

The following method, `transferFunds()`, is called when funds need to be transferred:

```
public void transferFunds(int fromAccount, int toAccount, double amount,
                          Connection conn) {

  Statement stmt = null;

  try {
```

The following lines denote the beginning of the transaction, which continues until the `conn.commit()` method is reached. In JDBC, all database statements are contained within a transaction by default. Setting the connection's `autoCommit` property to `false` allows us to manually control the transaction. In the code below, we call two methods that update the database – `withdraw()` and `deposit()`. Since we want these two statements to be contained within the same transaction, we have to set the `autoCommit` property to `false` and manage the transactions ourselves:

```
conn.setAutoCommit(false);   // Beginning of transaction
withdraw(fromAccount, amount, conn);
deposit(toAccount, amount, conn);
conn.commit();
```

During the execution of our routine, if an exception is thrown, we will need to undo any database updates that we have executed. The `rollback()` method, found within our `catch` block, does just that:

```
  } catch(Exception e) {
    try {
      System.out.println("An error occurred!");
      System.out.println(e);
      conn.rollback();
    } catch(Exception ex) {
        System.out.println(ex);
    }
  }
}
```

The deposit() and withdraw() methods take three arguments each: the account number, the dollar amount to process, and a reference to the database connection. The two methods share the same database connection, thus ensuring that the transaction will be propagated, or associated, with each method. Both methods throw a SQLException so that the calling method can rollback the transaction. We could optionally handle the exception within the method and then re-throw the same method or throw a different, more business-specific exception if we wanted. However, this is sufficient for now:

```
public void deposit(int account, double amount,
                    Connection conn) throws SQLException {

  String sql = "UPDATE Account SET Balance = Balance + " + amount +
               " WHERE AccountId = " + account;
  Statement stmt = conn.createStatement();
  stmt.executeUpdate(sql);
  System.out.println("Deposited " + amount + " to account " + account);

}
```

```
public void withdraw(int account, double amount, Connection conn) throws
  SQLException {

  String sql = "UPDATE Account SET Balance = Balance - " + amount +
               " WHERE AccountId = " + account;
  Statement stmt = conn.createStatement();
  stmt.executeUpdate(sql);
  System.out.println("Withdrew " + amount + " from account " + account);

}
```

Notice that neither the deposit nor the withdraw methods are aware that they are part of a transaction. If we were to invoke either of these methods on their own, say if we were making a bank deposit, we wouldn't have to create a transaction for the database operation. This is because, by default, the database connection will automatically create a transaction for it. Only when we need to programmatically control the transaction ourselves do we need to disable the autoCommit feature.

The releaseConnection() method simply frees the database connection. You'll notice that we do not invoke conn.setAutoCommit(true). There is no need: autoCommit will be set to true automatically the next time that a new connection is retrieved from the DriverManager:

```
public void releaseConnection(Connection conn) {

  if(conn != null){
    try {
      conn.close();
    } catch(Exception e) {
    }
  }

}
```

The BankTest Class

Next we have a simple test program. After getting a database connection to work with, we invoke the `transferFunds()` method. Depending on the amount specified from the command line, money will be transferred from Account 1 to Account 2. We then print the balances for all of the accounts in the database. When all is done, regardless of success or failure, we release the database connection.

The program takes three parameters: the name of the database driver, the database's URL, and the amount to transfer. For example, if we were using a Microsoft Access database, the driver name would be "`sun.jdbc.odbc.JdbcOdbcDriver`" and the database URL might be "`jdbc:odbc:BankDB,`" depending on what we've called the ODBC datasource:

```java
import java.sql.*;

public class BankTest {

  public static void main(String args[]) {

    if(args.length < 3) {
      System.exit(1);
    }

    Connection conn = null;
    Bank bank = new Bank();

    try {
      conn = bank.getConnection(args[0], args[1]);
      bank.transferFunds(1, 2, Double.parseDouble(args[2]), conn);
      bank.printBalances(conn);
    } catch(Exception e) {
        e.printStackTrace();
    } finally {
        bank.releaseConnection(conn);
    }
  }

}
```

The first time that we run the program, all will be fine. One hundred dollars is withdrawn from Account 1 and deposited into Account 2. The balances are then displayed on the screen. The results should look like this:

```
C:\WINDOWS\System32\cmd.exe

C:\ProEJB\Chapter09>java -classpath %CLASSPATH%;. BankTest sun.jdbc.odbc.Jd
bcOdbcDriver jdbc:odbc:BankDB 100
Withdrew 100.0 from account 1
Deposited 100.0 to account 2
Account 1 has a balance of 0.0
Account 2 has a balance of 100.0

C:\ProEJB\Chapter09>
```

However, if we run the program again, the system will attempt to overdraw the first account thus producing a negative balance. Since this violates the constraints of our Account table (balance >= 0), a SQLException will be thrown. This, in turn, will result in the transaction being rolled back. The results will look like this:

```
C:\WINDOWS\System32\cmd.exe

C:\ProEJB\Chapter09>java -classpath %CLASSPATH%;. BankTest sun.jdbc.odbc.Jd
bcOdbcDriver jdbc:odbc:BankDB 100
An error occurred!
java.sql.SQLException: [Microsoft][ODBC Microsoft Access Driver] One or mor
e values are prohibited by the validation rule '[Balance]>=0' set for 'Acco
unt.Balance'. Enter a value that the expression for this field can accept.

Account 1 has a balance of 0.0
Account 2 has a balance of 100.0

C:\ProEJB\Chapter09>_
```

Note that the reference to Microsoft Access occurs because we are running this against an MS-Access database via ODBC. You would get a different error message if you used another database.

As you can see, using transactions in standard Java is quite straightforward and easy. You simply demarcate the transaction's boundaries, execute your database code, and either commit or rollback the transaction.

The database drivers handle the actual complexity of watching the operational progress of the transaction and notifying you of any errors that might occur. Of course, you could also check for other conditions that might not indicate a SQL error (failed validation perhaps) but you would most likely want to do this prior to executing your code if possible.

We'll revisit the example above and build upon it as we learn more about some of the finer control options that are available to us. But first, let's take a look at a special type of transaction called a **compensating transaction**.

Compensating Transactions

Sometimes we need to undo a transaction after it has been committed. This is usually not due to a database error, but to the fact that the user just changed their mind. **Compensating transactions** are a strategy for using transactional processing whereby committed transactions can be undone after they have been committed. They contain the necessary logic to reverse the changes made by the original transaction.

Consider the case where a bank teller makes a deposit to an account and, after the transaction has completed, realizes that the wrong account was credited. Here we have an instance where the transaction has committed but needs to be reversed nevertheless. The bank's accounting procedures won't allow us to simply delete the money from the account – we have to account for every transaction that is executed. A deletion would raise quite a few eyebrows. However, we can't simply withdraw the money back out of the account as this might upset the customer when they receive their statement at the end of the month. A compensating transaction can be used to rollback the changes that we have made.

Another use for compensating transactions comes into play when we need to wire funds between different accounts at different banks. Here we have transactions that might not get resolved quickly. In fact, wire transfers can take hours or even a few days to complete – these are referred to as **long-lived transactions**. Regardless, they still need to be protected by a transaction. However, we cannot simply tie up our resources while we wait for the transaction to complete. What to do?

We can break the transaction up into a series of smaller transactions. Each transaction must be completed in series. The transactions themselves might look like the following:

- ❑ Withdraw funds from source account
- ❑ Wire funds to federal exchange (an intermediary between the two banks)
- ❑ Wire funds from exchange to destination bank
- ❑ Deposit money into target account

Here we have four distinctly different transactions, with the second and third capable of taking a considerable amount of time. Each transaction is executed in series and can be committed. However, should one of the transactions need to roll back, we'll need a way to roll back the previously committed transactions.

By associating a compensating transaction with each of the individual transactions, we have all the information necessary to roll back each of the committed transactions, if necessary. In J2EE, we should use compensating transactions when a particular resource (such as a flat text file) does not support JTA-managed transactions.

The following state diagram illustrates the transaction life cycle using compensating transactions:

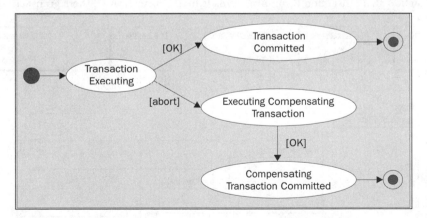

Now that we have a good understanding of how transactions work, let's take a look at some of the different ways that transactions can be used.

Transactional Models

There are many different types of and uses for transactions. How a transaction is used and how it is structured typically falls in to one of many transactional models. We'll take a look at four here, namely:

- ❑ Flat transactions
- ❑ Nested transactions
- ❑ Chained transactions
- ❑ Saga transactions

We'll start with flat transactions.

Flat Transactions

A single or atomic unit of work, composed of one or more steps, the flat transaction is the simplest of transactions. Should one of the steps fail, the entire transaction is rolled back. Flat transactions are the de facto standard for database operations, as well as Enterprise JavaBeans in general.

Nested Transactions

The nested transaction model has atomic units embedded in other transactions. This has the effect of a transaction "tree" – a root transaction that contains several branches of other transactions. The nested transaction differs from the flat transaction, in that should one of the sub-transactions roll back, it will not affect the parent transactions. In other words, the failure of a transaction is limited to just that transaction. A sub-transaction can be either a flat transaction or another set of nested transactions. The following sequence diagram illustrates using nested transactions. After Transaction A begins, it starts Transaction B. Transaction B, in turn, invokes first Transaction C, then Transaction D.

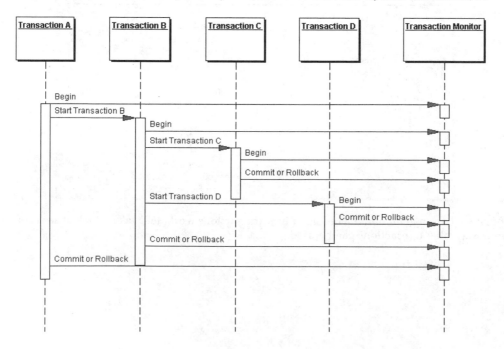

Another example of nested transactions might be an airline reservation system. Let's say that we want to book a flight from New York to San Francisco. Our first transaction (T) entails our attempt to book a direct flight. No direct flights are available, so our transaction fails. This is a flat transaction.

We then start a new transaction (U) and try to find a flight that is available between New York and Chicago. We want to hold this reservation, so we keep the transaction open. We then begin a new transaction (V), with our current one, that will attempt to book a flight from Chicago to San Francisco. There are no direct flights between the two cities, so our transaction fails and rolls back. However, since the transaction is localized at Chicago, we will not lose the New York booking. Remember, nested transactions do not roll back the transaction in which they are contained.

Another transaction (W) is started, this time attempting to book a flight between Chicago and Dallas. We are successful in finding a reservation, so we hold transaction W open.

Finally, we initiate a new transaction (X) in hopes of finding a flight from Dallas to San Francisco. If we are successful, we commit transaction X. Transaction W checks the status of transaction E and, seeing that it was successful, W commits. This continues with W's parent, transaction U, and then T. With all of the transactions committed (T, U, W, & X), we have booked our flight.

If we had decided that four flights were too many and decided to scrap the whole affair and take the train instead, X would roll back, W would see that X failed and, as part of a business rule to not accept this many layovers, would roll back, and up and up until the entire tree of transactions (T, U, W, & E) had been aborted and the entire transaction cancelled.

Chained Transactions

Chained transactions, sometimes referred to as **serial transactions**, are a set of contiguous transactions related together. Each transaction relies on the results and resources of the previous transaction. Typically, the developer identifies the boundaries of each transaction and then submits all of the transactions as a group. The transaction manager then executes each transaction in series, one after the other.

With chained transactions, when a transaction commits, its resources (say, cursors) are retained and immediately made available to the next transaction in the chain – effectively combining the `commit()` and the next `beginTransaction()` into a single atomic step. The result is that transactions outside of the chain cannot see or alter the data being affected by the transactions in the chain. This is different from committing a transaction and then starting a new one in two separate steps, as that would result in the resources used by the first transaction being released.

Another advantage of chained transactions is that resources (such as locks), used by one transaction and that are not required by subsequent transactions, can be released. This is more efficient than keeping the resources for the full length of the chain.

If one of the transactions should fail, only the currently executing transaction (the one that failed) will be rolled back – the rest of the previously committed transactions will not.

The following state diagram will give you an idea of the general progression through a chain of transactions:

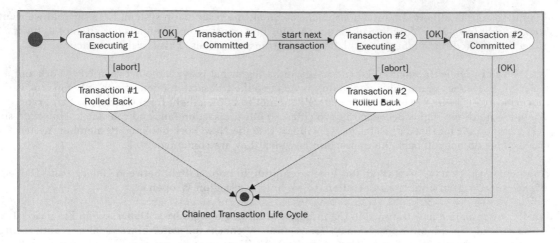

Chained Transaction Life Cycle

The downside to chained transactions is that they can potentially lock up a lot of valuable database resources, thus slowing the system down. Careful thought should be given when using these transactions.

Sagas

Sagas are long-lived transactions that model workflow processes – similar to chained transactions, in that they are composed of multiple transactions, each of which has a corresponding compensating transaction. In the event that one of the transactions fails, the compensating transaction for each transaction that successfully ran is invoked. This is done automatically by the transaction manager. Therefore, before execution of the saga, all of the associated transactions and their relationships must be identified to the transaction manager.

The state diagram below illustrates a sample saga that consists of three transactions:

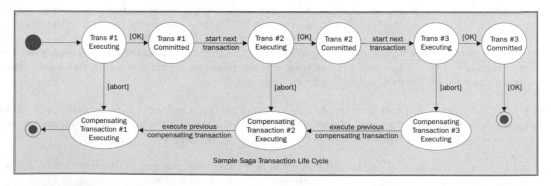

Sample Saga Transaction Life Cycle

Other Transaction Models

There are many other transaction models and strategies, but these are the most common. However, the J2EE specification only requires that flat transactions be supported. The reason this limitation was placed was to make EJB available to a wider selection of database systems, as not all of them support nested transactions. Many transactional processing systems also provide support for nested transactions. If this functionality is required, you will need to pay close attention to the features offered by a given server. You should also remember that any time you use a non-standard feature, you limit portability.

> Note that nested transactions are *not* supported by EJB. In fact, the EJB specification requires that a `javax.transaction.NotSupportedException` be thrown if a bean starts a transaction while an existing transaction is already in progress.

Transactions and EJB

As we already know, Enterprise JavaBeans provide us with a wealth of built-in functionality that we would otherwise have to develop ourselves, and transactional processing is no exception. However, like most things, we have to be willing to accept certain limitations in what we are able to do.

The J2EE's implementation of transactional processing is made available through the **Java Transaction API**, or **JTA**. JTA is an interface that provides access to an underlying transaction manager. Support for transactional processing is a standard requirement of all EJB servers, although the level of support for transactions varies. We'll examine some of those differences as we advance through this chapter. As we will shortly see, EJB offers a wide array of options when using transactions.

Demarcation

The most fundamental decision that you will need to make is whether to manage the transaction yourself or to let the EJB container manage it for you. If you are using an entity bean, the decision is an easy one – as of the EJB 1.1 specification, you are only allowed to use container-managed transactions (this is not to be confused with container-managed persistence, which is responsible for data retrieval and storage). However, for session beans, you can allow the container to manage the transactions or take on the task yourself. Either way, you will have a great deal of flexibility available to you.

The process of determining where a transaction begins and ends is called **demarcation**. If you decide to let the container manage your transactions, you are using **declarative demarcation**. They are called declarative transactions because you will declare to the container how a transaction should behave. If you opt to manage the transactions on your own, you are using **programmatic demarcation**. Programmatic demarcation is the "traditional" method of transactional programming.

Why would you choose one over the other? Declarative demarcation is simpler to use, relieving you of having to incorporate transactional processing into your code. Of course, you are not absolved of having to use transactions completely. You will still have to configure the characteristics of the transaction. However, you specify the transactional properties in the deployment descriptor.

Declarative demarcation differs from programmatic in where the boundaries are placed. With programmatic demarcation, you determine exactly where the transaction will begin and end. With declarative demarcation, the container is not able to determine the boundaries within your code. Rather than try to guess at what your intentions are by examining the instructions, it simply places the entire method into the transaction.

This should immediately suggest to you a potential source for problems. If your method invokes a long-running process (like a large loop), you will be blocking other transactions from getting access to your data. Even if the loop might seem small to you, you must remember that small delays grow to large bottlenecks very quickly in a concurrent system. Therefore, the smallest gains can have performance improvements of an order of magnitude. If your session bean's method has a slow process within it, you should consider isolating the database calls yourself and using programmatic demarcation.

Since the majority of the transactional processing that you will most likely be doing in EJB will be declarative, we'll focus on how that works first. Afterwards, we'll return to programmatic demarcation for some more advanced techniques.

Transaction Attributes

With declarative demarcation, you specify to the container which methods to subject to transactional processing. In addition, you also specify certain behavioral properties that control how and when the transaction will be created, depending on the needs of our component in relationship to the **transactional context**. Transactional context refers to the relationship between the transactional operations conducted on a given set of resources, and the clients invoking those resources. A transactional context embodies the transaction from the point of inception by the client, through to its completion. Any operation that occurs on a resource capable of participating in a transaction is said to occur within the context of that transaction, and will be subject to the rules of that context.

Enterprise JavaBeans support seven types of transactional attributes:

❑   Required

❑   RequiresNew

❑   Mandatory

❑   Supports

❑   NotSupported

❑   Never

❑   "Bean-managed"

Required

The Required transactional attribute indicates that the specified method must always be run within a transaction. If the method is called within the context of an existing transaction, that same transaction will be used, or propagated. If no transactional context exists, the container will create a new one. The new transaction will begin when the method begins and will commit when the method ends. If a rollback is required, the container will undo the transaction and throw a RollbackException. This will allow the calling method an opportunity to respond to the failure.

Required should be used whenever your method will be changing data, so as to ensure that the data operation will occur within and be protected by a transaction.

RequiresNew

The RequiresNew transaction attribute indicates that the specified method must always be executed within its own transaction. This would be used when a transaction is required, but it is not desirable for a local rollback to affect transactions outside of the method – the failure is localized. Another use is when the transaction must commit its results regardless of the outcome of the outer transactions – logging, for example.

The container will create a new transactional context for the method before it is invoked. If the method is called within the context of an existing transaction, that first transaction will be suspended and a new transaction will begin. Once the method completes, the container will commit the new transaction and then reinstate the pre-existing transaction.

Mandatory

The `Mandatory` transaction attribute indicates that your method can only be invoked within the context of a pre-existing transaction. Therefore, it is mandatory that the method's client must already have started a transaction. The transaction context will be propagated to your method. If a component tries to invoke the method and does not have a transactional context already associated with it, the container will throw a `TransactionRequiredException` or a `TransactionRequiredLocalException`.

We should use the `Mandatory` attribute when our method needs to verify that the component was invoked within the context of a client-managed transaction.

Supports

The `Supports` transaction attribute tells the container that the associated method will use a transaction if one is already available. However, if one is not previously available, that is, if a transactional context does not already exist, then the method can be invoked without a transaction.

We would use the `Supports` attribute when we do not want to incur the processing overhead of suspending and resuming a pre-existing transaction and are confident that our method will either not cause an exception or will not cause an exception that would signal a failure within the context of a transaction. Furthermore, we must be certain that our transaction will not violate any data constraints that might otherwise cause a transaction to fail.

> It is imperative to remember that, most likely, we will not know what component is invoking our bean's method and what the intention of that component is. We must always be careful to consider that our bean may be used in ways that we might not have originally intended.

Given this, it is better to support transactions and to let the client decide how failure within your bean should affect them.

NotSupported

The `NotSupported` transaction attribute tells the container that the method should not be run within a transaction. If the method is called within the context of an existing transaction, the transaction will be suspended before the method is invoked.

If the business method invokes other EJB methods, the container will not pass a transactional context with the invocation. In other words, if a bean's method is indicated as not supporting transactions, and the method is invoked from within a transaction, the transactional context will not "pass through" the method. Should an exception occur, it would not affect the suspended transaction of the caller. However, once the method has completed executing, the container will resume the original transaction. The `NotSupported` attribute should also be used when an enterprise bean needs to interact with a resource manager that does not support transactions. In this particular situation, it is recommended that the `NotSupported` attribute be used in all of the bean's methods.

Never

The `Never` transaction attribute indicates that the method should never be called within the context of another transaction. The `Never` attribute should be used when the component needs to verify that the method was not invoked within a client-managed transaction and that the container will not attempt to provide a transaction for it.

`Never` should also be used when a given method is not capable of participating in a transaction. The container will execute the method without starting a transaction for it. If a component invokes the method and a transaction context does exist, the container will throw a `RemoteException` if the client is remote or `EJBException` if the client is local. This differs from `NotSupported`, in that `NotSupported` will simply suspend a transaction if one already exists, resuming upon completion of the method. `Never` will throw an exception if a transaction exists.

"Bean-managed"

The absence of a transactional attribute in the deployment descriptor indicates that the bean will manage its own transactions. This can only be done by session beans or message-driven beans. Furthermore, a component cannot have some of its methods managed by the container, and others managed by itself.

> *Note: In EJB 1.0, there was an attribute to explicitly indicate that a transaction was bean-managed. `TX_BEAN_MANAGED` was a static value of the `ControlDescriptor` object – part of the `DeploymentDescriptor` object structure. In EJB 1.1, the `DeploymentDescriptor` was deprecated in favor of the XML-formatted deployment descriptor. The absence of a transaction entry for a given method in the deployment descriptor implies that the method's transaction is bean-managed.*

The following table summarizes the transactional attributes and the effect that they have on a component's method's transaction context, in relationship to a calling client's transactional context:

Transaction Attribute	Client's Transaction	Component Method's Transaction	Comment
`Required`	None	T2	If no transaction exists, the server creates one
	T1	T1	If a transaction exists, the server uses it
`RequiresNew`	None	T2	If no transaction exists, the server creates one
	T1	T2	If a transaction exists, the server creates a new one
`Mandatory`	None	Error	If no transaction exists, an exception is thrown
	T1	T1	If a transaction exists, the server uses it
`Not Supported`	None	None	The server does not provide transactional support

Transaction Attribute	Client's Transaction	Component Method's Transaction	Comment
	T1	None	The server does not provide transactional support
Supports	None	None	If no transaction exists, the server does not provide support
	T1	T1	If a transaction exists, the server uses it
Never	None	None	The server does not provide transactional support
	T1	Error	If a transaction exists, an exception is thrown

Transactional Attribute Usage

The differences between the various transactional attributes are sometimes slight and it can be confusing trying to determine when to use which one. Which attribute is selected will undeniably be the result of which ACID properties are required and the extent to which they are needed.

For example, `RequiresNew` provides a greater level of atomicity and isolation, albeit at the cost of performance. This is due to the overhead of creating a new transaction and managing the existing one.

Another factor that will affect which attribute is used will be the level of transactional support that is provided by the transactional processor in question. For example, if the processor does not support nested transactions, neither will the application.

As a general guideline, consider the following:

- ❑ Use the `Required` attribute when the code needs to change the value of some data.
- ❑ Use the `Supports` attribute when the code needs to read data from a data source. This will allow the caller of the component to determine whether a transaction should be used. This is appropriate because the enterprise bean really has no way of knowing what the intention of the calling method is.
- ❑ If we are communicating with resources that do not support transactional processing, then we should use the `NotSupported` attribute.
- ❑ When using message-driven beans, the transaction attributes must be specified for the bean's `onMessage()` method. Message-driven beans only support the `Required` and `NotSupported` transaction attributes. They do no support `RequiresNew` or `Supports` as they are never invoked within the context of a pre-existing transaction. Also, they do not support `Mandatory` and `Never`, as message-driven beans are only ever invoked by the container. Therefore, it would not make sense to support client-side transactions.

Declaration of Transactional Attributes

Associating an attribute with a transaction is typically done in one of two ways: either through the EJB container's deployment tool, or by directly including it in the deployment descriptor. Of course, regardless of which method you choose, the result will be the same: the deployment descriptor contains the declaration of all transaction attributes.

Here is the relevant section of the DTD for setting transactional attributes, which comes under the `<assembly-descriptor>` element:

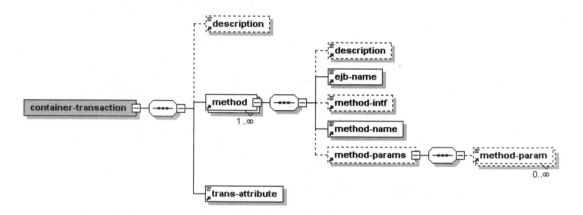

There are actually three ways to declare a transactional attribute for a given method. However, they all follow the same general format:

```
<ejb-jar>
  ...
  <assembly-descriptor>

    <container-transaction>
      <method>
        <ejb-name>someEJBean</ejb-bean>
        <method-name>someMethod</method-name>
      </method>
      <trans-attribute>transactionalAttribute</trans-attribute>
    </container-transaction>

  </assembly-descriptor>
  ...
</ejb-jar>
```

The deployment descriptor entry starts with `<container-transaction>` and contains two elements: `<method>` and `<trans-attribute>`.

The `<method>` element contains two additional sub-elements: `<ejb-name>` and `<method-name>`. The `<ejb-name>` sub-element identifies the enterprise bean that the method is part of, while `<method-name>` identifies the name of the method to apply the transactional attribute to.

The `<trans-attribute>` element indicates the transactional attribute to apply to the named method, using one of the keywords discussed above: `Required`, `RequiresNew`, `NotSupported`, `Supports`, `Mandatory`, `Never`, or `BeanManaged`.

Let's take a look at a typical deployment descriptor entry. Here we have an enterprise bean named `Customer`, with a method `getCustomerName()`. We have applied the `Supports` transactional attribute to the method:

```
<container-transaction>
  <method>
    <ejb-name>Customer</ejb-name>
    <method-name>getCustomerName</method-name>
  </method>
  <trans-attribute>Supports</trans-attribute>
</container-transaction>
```

If we have an overloaded method, we have to include the parameter declarations within the deployment descriptor as well.

The following entry applies the `Requires` transactional attribute to the `Customer` bean's `getProfile()` method. The method accepts three parameters, an `int`, a `String` and an array of `FilterType` objects. Thus, the methods signature might look like this:

```
Profile getProfile(int type, String groupId, FilterType filter[]);
```

In the deployment descriptor, notice that the <method-param> entry for the array of `FilterType` contains an empty bracket, indicating that it is an array:

```
<container-transaction>
  <method>
    <ejb-name>Customer</ejb-name>
    <method-name>getProfile</method-name>
    <method-params>
      <method-param>int</method-param>
      <method-param>java.lang.String</method-param>
      <method-param>FilterType[]</method-param>
    </method-params>
  </method>
  <trans-attribute>Requires</trans-attribute>
</container-transaction>
```

If the `getProfile()` method were to also have an overridden method that accepted no parameters, the deployment descriptor entry would have an empty <method-params> section, like so:

```
<container-transaction>
  <method>
    <ejb-name>Customer</ejb-name>
    <method-name>getProfile</method-name>
    <method-params></method-params>
  </method>
  <trans-attribute>Requires</trans-attribute>
</container-transaction>
```

> *Note that for each method with the same name that our EJB has, if we supply a transaction information entry for one, we must supply an entry in the deployment descriptor for each.*

Finally, if all of the methods in the enterprise bean are to utilize the same transactional attribute, a shortcut is provided. Simply use an asterisk, *, for the <method-name> value:

```
<container-transaction>
  <method>
    <ejb-name>Customer</ejb-name>
    <method-name>*</method-name>
  </method>
  <trans-attribute>Supports</trans-attribute>
</container-transaction>
```

Now every method within the `Customer` enterprise bean will be associated with the `Supports` attribute.

If the bean's transactions are to be managed by the bean itself, no deployment descriptor entry is required. Remember that only session beans can manage their own transactions. Also, if one method in the bean is bean-managed, they must all be bean-managed. You cannot have some methods managed by the bean and others managed by the container. This would potentially cause problems if one method called another. However, it is perfectly fine for a bean-managed method to call a container-managed method in another bean.

Unspecified Transaction Context

When a method does not have a transactional context associated with it, such as with `NotSupported` or `Never`, that transaction context is said to be **unspecified**. An unspecified transaction context can also result when a method `Supports` transactions, but is invoked without a transactional context.

When handling a method that runs with an unspecified transaction context, we must carefully plan out any data operations that might be performed. However, as it is always a bad idea to manipulate data outside the scope of a transaction, this should generally be avoided. The Enterprise JavaBeans specification does not mandate how a container should handle the execution of a method with an unspecified transaction context. It is important that we review our EJB server's documentation for specifics. However, a container might utilize the following general approaches:

❑ The container may execute the method, and access any resource managers referenced within, without a transaction context.

❑ The container may execute each call within the method to a resource manager as an individual transaction.

❑ The container may combine all calls to one or more resource managers within a single transaction.

❑ If the bean instance invokes methods on other bean instances, and those instances also have an unspecified transaction context, the container may combine all calls to all resource managers in all of the methods and execute them within a single transaction.

These methods are not absolutes, but instead are possible approaches to managing an unspecified transaction context.

We have to be careful when writing methods that may run in an unspecified transaction context. Since the EJB specification does not define how the container should handle this situation, we cannot rely on any specific behavior. Therefore, we should avoid writing our methods to rely on any set behavior. It is also important to remember that, should a failure occur during an unspecified transaction, any resource managers accessed from the method could be left in an unknown state, or corrupted.

Implementing Bean-Managed Transaction Demarcation

Sometimes it is desirable for a bean to manage its own transaction. Some reasons for managing your own transactions include:

- ❑ Maintaining transactional state across multiple methods in a stateful session bean
- ❑ Providing transactional behavior for a resource that doesn't provide transactional processing (wire services, e-mail, flat files)
- ❑ Providing support for compensating transactions

The Java Transaction API provides an interface for explicitly controlling a transaction – the UserTransaction interface:

```
public interface javax.transaction.UserTransaction {

    public void begin() throws NotSupportedException, SystemException;

    public void commit() throws RollbackException,
                                HeuristicMixedException,
                                HeuristicRollbackException,
                                SecurityException,
                                IllegalStateException,
                                SystemException;

    public void rollback() throws IllegalStateException,
                                SecurityException,
                                SystemException;

    public int getStatus() throws SystemException;

    public void setRollbackOnly() throws IllegalStateException,
                                SystemException;

    public void setTransactionTimeout (int seconds) throws SystemException;
}
```

The use of the UserTransaction interface is very straightforward, as detailed below:

1. Begin the transaction by invoking begin()

2. Execute any business logic to be contained within the transaction

3. Complete the transaction by either invoking commit() or rollback()

The setRollbackOnly() method will mark a transaction for rollback without actually rolling the transaction back. This is desirable when other methods within the transaction need to run regardless of whether the transaction will commit or rollback. When the setRollbackOnly() method is used, the transaction's status should be checked before the end of the transaction and handled accordingly. This is done by invoking the getStatus() method which will return the status of the current transaction. getStatus() returns one of the following values (embodied in the javax.transaction.Status interface):

❑   STATUS_ACTIVE
A transaction is associated with the component and is in the active state.

❑   STATUS_COMMITTED
A transaction is associated with the component and has been committed.

❑   STATUS_COMMITTING
A transaction is associated with the component and is in the process of committing.

❑   STATUS_MARKED_ROLLBACK
A transaction is associated with the component and has been marked for rollback.

❑   STATUS_NO_TRANSACTION
No transaction is associated with the component.

❑   STATUS_PREPARED
A transaction is associated with the component and has been prepared for committing in a two-phase commit (discussed later). It is waiting for a commit instruction from the transaction manager.

❑   STATUS_PREPARING
A transaction is associated with the component and is in the process of preparing for a two-phase commit, but has not yet completed the preparation.

❑   STATUS_ROLLEDBACK
A transaction is associated with the component and has been rolled back.

❑   STATUS_ROLLING_BACK
A transaction is associated with the component and is in the process of rolling back.

❑   STATUS_UNKNOWN
A transaction is associated with the component but its status cannot be determined.

The following state diagram shows the relationship of the statuses to the transaction lifecycle:

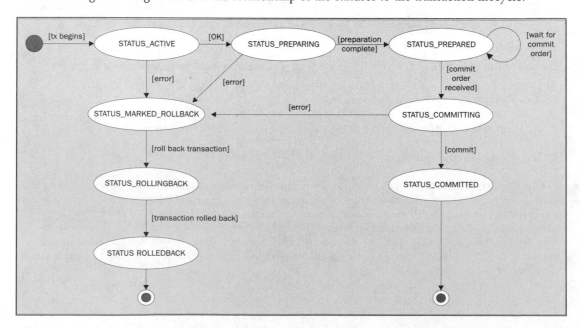

There are two ways to obtain a reference to the `UserTransaction` interface. We can get an instance via a JNDI lookup to `java:comp/UserTransaction` or via the `EJBContext.getUserTransaction()` method.

The `setTransactionTimeout()` method sets the timeout value of the transaction that is associated with the current thread. If a transaction does not complete within the specified length of time, a `SystemException` will be thrown. Generally, the timeout value for a transaction is defined through the application server's configuration. As such, it is better to set the timeout value at the server level, than at the method level.

Restrictions on the UserTransaction Interface

There are certain restrictions to using the `UserTransaction` interface:

- ❑ First, keep in mind that entity beans cannot manage their own transactions and, therefore, cannot access `UserTransaction`. Only session beans and message-driven beans can.

- ❑ A bean instance that starts a transaction must complete the transaction before starting a new one. Nested transactions are not allowed in EJB.

- ❑ Code within a transaction must not attempt to use control methods specific to a resource manager. For example, calling `commit()` on a JDBC connection is not permitted when that connection is obtained via the container's resource factory.

- ❑ A stateless session bean must close a transaction in the same invocation in which it was started. As the bean does not maintain state, it will not be able to maintain transactional state, either. This is appropriate behavior for a stateless session bean. If the method exits without finishing the transaction, the following will happen:

  - ❑ The server will log an application error
  - ❑ The transaction will be rolled back
  - ❑ The session bean instance will be discarded
  - ❑ A `RemoteException` or `EJBException` will be thrown

- ❑ A stateful session bean may start a transaction in one method without finishing the transaction before the method invocation ends. That is, the method invocation does not need to call `commit()` or `rollback()` before exiting. The container will remember the transactional context across multiple invocations. Thus, subsequent method calls will be invoked within the same transactional context.

  Furthermore, a database connection need not be kept open during the entire transaction. In fact, a method may open and close a connection several times during multiple invocations within the same transaction context. The connections will all be managed within the same transaction provided the transaction is started before all of the database operations and committed afterwards.

- ❑ A message-driven bean must close the transaction before the `onMessage()` method returns.

- ❑ A J2EE server is not required to provide access to its transaction manager to an application client. By application client we mean any client that is not contained within the J2EE server itself. Furthermore, if a JDBC transaction on the client invokes an enterprise bean, the context of that client's transaction is not required to be propagated to the EJB server.

What about JTS?

The **Java Transaction Service (JTS)** should not be confused with the Java Transaction API (JTA). JTA serves as an interface between our code and a system's transaction manager. JTS, on the other hand, provides an interface to the CORBA Object Transaction Service (OTS). JTS provides interoperability between transaction managers to support distributed transactions. An EJB server is not even required to provide a client access to its JTS implementation. In practice, JTA is used by application developers and JTS is used by the transaction manager vendors.

Distributed Transactions

So far, we have looked at transactions that are executed against a single resource (one database). This has left us with a number of questions:

❑ What happens if our transaction needs to execute against multiple resources such as two database servers?

❑ What if we need to mix resource types within a transaction? For example, a database and a message queue.

❑ What if we need to have multiple enterprise beans within the same transactional context?

❑ What issues need to be taken into consideration when working with transactions that are distributed throughout the enterprise?

❑ How are these **distributed transactions** managed in the real world?

Fortunately for us Java developers, we needn't be too concerned with the physical complexity of distributed transactions. The Java Transaction API (JTA) that we have already learned will suffice quite nicely.

Consider a session bean, `EmployeeManager`, that provides a method `createNewEmployee()`. This method performs several tasks all within a single transaction:

❑ Create a new record in the human resources employee database

❑ Create a new record in the accounting system's payroll database

❑ Send a message to the technical support group requesting the creation of a network ID and e-mail account for the new employee

We are able to include in our transaction not only the two databases, but a message server as well. If any of the tasks were to fail, we would want the entire operation to be rolled back. In order to support transactions across multiple resources, all you need to do is enclose the calls to those resources within a transaction. As long as each resource manager provides support for distributed transactions via JTA, you can be assured of the ACID benefits of transactional processing.

But what exactly are distributed transactions and, especially, how do they work?

What is a Distributed Transaction?

A distributed transaction is a transaction whose context spans more than one resource and/or whose context is propagated or shared by more than one component. Distributed transactions support scenarios such as:

❑ A component needs to communicate with multiple resources within the same atomic operation. A bank account session bean might debit funds from an account in one database and credit the funds in another database.

❑ Multiple components need to operate within the same atomic operation. Our banking system could debit the balance in one account entity bean, credit the funds to another entity bean, and create an audit log entry by calling a third session bean.

A distributed transaction requires the cooperation of several different transaction managers. A master transaction manager known as a **distributed transaction manager** coordinates the other transaction managers. It is the responsibility of the distributed transaction manager to control the propagation, demarcation, and resolution of a single transaction across several participating *local* transaction managers. A local transaction manager is a transaction manager that participates, or is "enlisted", in a distributed transaction.

The following diagram illustrates one possible configuration:

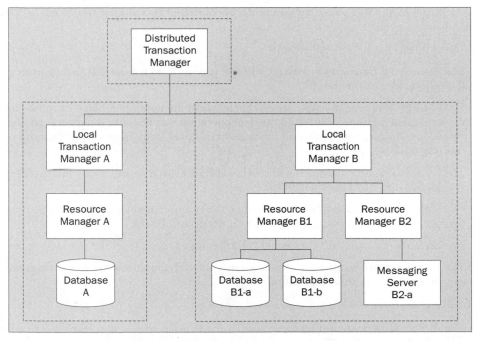

Four resources exist on two different systems. The resources are three databases (named Database A, Database B1-a, and Database B1-b) and a messaging server (Messaging Server B2-a). Database A is managed by Resource Manager A. Typically, the two together compose a database management system (DBMS). Here, they are shown separately to distinguish between the physical data and the component responsible for managing that data. Resource Manager A's transactional context is managed by Local Transaction Manager A. For almost all databases, the transaction manager is coupled with the resource manager.

This topology also applies to Database B1-a and Database B1-b. The messaging server also has an associated resource manager, B2. For the purpose of our example, the database and the messaging server are managed by the same transaction monitor (perhaps they are part of a vendor's integrated solution). However, more often than not, these resource managers will have separate transaction managers.

The Distributed Transaction Manager at the top is responsible for coordinating the efforts of the underlying local transaction managers when the resources associated with the local managers are involved within a distributed transaction.

The Two-Phase Commit Protocol

The **two-phase commit protocol** is a method of communication for the coordination of transactions across multiple servers and/or resources. The Open Group (X/Open, http://www.opengroup.org/) manages a standardized version of the two-phase commit protocol. However, not all vendors support the standardized protocol, preferring to implement their own. EJB supports the X/Open standard via the Java Transaction API. For consistency and compatibility across different platforms, you should make sure that your application server supports the X/Open specification.

When a transaction requires the services of multiple resources, the transactional processing of these resources will be managed using the two-phase commit protocol. Although we have primarily discussed databases, know that any resource manager that supports the two-phase commit protocol can participate in a distributed transaction.

As its name suggests, the two-phase commit protocol consists of two phases: the "prepare" phase and the "commit" phase.

In the prepare phase, the following happens:

❑ The distributed transaction manager tells the various local transaction managers to prepare for the requested data operations.

❑ Each local transaction manager writes the details of the data operation to a transaction log. In the event that a failure occurs and the data operation was not submitted successfully to the resource manager, the transaction manager has a 'local' copy from which it can try to recreate this transaction.

❑ The local transaction managers will create a local transaction and notify their respective resource managers of the operations.

❑ Once the data operation has been executed, the resource manager will notify its transaction manager that it is ready to commit or that it needs to rollback.

❑ The resource manager will then wait for further instructions from the transaction manager.

❑ The local transaction manager will then notify the distributed transaction manager of the success or failure of their transaction.

In the commit phase:

❑ The distributed transaction manager notifies the enlisted transaction managers to commit or rollback. This decision is based on the results from the various local transaction managers in the prepare phase.

❑ The local transaction managers notify their resource managers to commit or rollback their changes.

❑ The resource managers comply and report the outcome back to their local transaction manager.

❑ Finally, the local transaction manager reports the results to the distributed transaction manager, which likewise, returns the result to the calling application.

The following diagram summarizes this process:

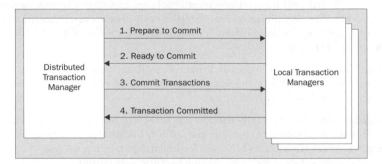

Should a local transaction manager determine that it cannot commit its transaction, the distributed transaction manager will notify the other local transaction managers to abort – as illustrated below:

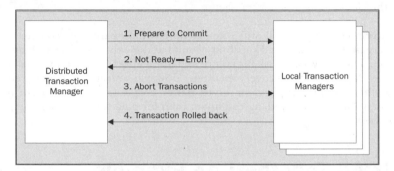

While it appears to the programmer that utilizing a distributed transaction is rather straightforward (and indeed it is), the actual implementation is extremely complex and difficult. So much so that some EJB vendors simply do not support distributed transactions. When we look at some of the problems inherent in implementing a distributed transactional system, it's easy enough to understand why:

❑ Failure recovery cannot be relied on, if it exists at all. A transaction can fail due to connection problems, server crashes, transaction timeouts, and deadlocks or other situations that might cause a transaction to get "stuck".

❑ What if our distributed transaction has three enlisted resource managers and the third resource manager fails during the commit phase? The other two resource managers have already committed their local transactions. Once data is committed, it usually cannot be rolled back. As a result, our data is now in an inconsistent, or corrupt, state. Worse still, other transactions may have executed against the now-committed data, compounding the problem and making recovery horrifically difficult if not outright impossible.

❑ If a distributed transaction does fail, how does our application determine where the failure occurred? How can we implement compensating transactions if we don't know where to apply them?

❑ While many transaction managers have logs that can be consulted to assist in recovery, this is often a manual process. In fact, you'd be surprised by how many organizations do not have a process in place to support transactional failures. The most common resolution is to restore from an earlier backup. This works provided, of course, that the organization is diligent with maintaining backups. The organization also has to be willing to accept the loss of work completed prior to the failure – most are not.

❑ The performance of distributed transactions is very slow compared to traditional, local transactions. Distributed transactions require a large amount of resources potentially spanning several servers. The two-phase commit protocol requires more communication than local transactions and this communication is conducted over a network, which can present all sorts of connectivity problems.

❑ Distributed transactions are typically longer lived than local transactions, affecting overall system response time. This is due to the increased number of enlisted transaction managers and resource managers involved.

❑ Distributed transactions typically use the strictest form of isolation due to their higher-risk nature. This increases data contention and presents additional bottlenecks. Add to these performance issues the various schemes for ensuring stability, caching, logging, and recovery support, and the performance implications become substantial.

❑ By their very nature, the design of distributed transactional systems is much more complex. Special care must be taken to ensure that one transaction does not rely on the data affected, and thus locked, by another transaction.

The use of distributed transactional processing is more complex than the code to implement it would imply. The increased scalability and capability comes at the expense of performance and the added cost of pre-planning. There is greater risk for failure and more effort required for recovery tactics. Some systems do provide support for recovery methods. However, effective recovery relies not just on the automated capabilities of the application server, but on corporate policy, as well. Without a proper contingency plan and standardized, agreed-upon, rules for data reconciliation, data recovery success will be minimal at best.

Putting It All Together: An Example

Let's take a look at a full example of a stateful session bean that manages its own transactions. What follows is a bean used for interacting with a ledger – a part of our banking system. The LedgerBean will allow us to enter account activity for checking accounts and savings accounts. It will also allow us to send messages to a bank supervisor.

All of this will be conducted within a single transaction. Also, several account activities and messages can be created all within the same transaction. If at any point an error should occur, the entire transaction will be rolled back. For the sake of simplicity, the banking activity is a simple string.

This example will illustrate a number of different things:

❑ How to manage our own transactions

❑ How to maintain a transaction across method invocations

❑ How to include different databases within the same transaction

❑ How to include other resources, such as a messaging server, in a transaction

First, we need two databases, one called CheckingDB and another called SavingsDB. For the purposes of this example, we will assume that CheckingDB is an Oracle database and SavingsDB is in Cloudscape.

Next, within each database, we create the following table:

```
CREATE TABLE Ledger(  Activity VARCHAR(100)  );
```

The `LedgerBean` class contains five remote methods that are called by the client:

- ❑ `openLedger()`
  This method starts the transaction.

- ❑ `addCheckingAccountActivity()`
  Allows us to enter activity in to the checking account ledger. Checking accounts are maintained in the `CheckingDB` database.

- ❑ `AddSavingsAccountActivity()`
  Allows us to enter activity in to the savings account ledger. Savings accounts are maintained in the `SavingsDB` database.

- ❑ `notifySupervisor()`
  Sends a copy of the activity being reported to a message queue. At some other point (and in another application) a bank supervisor will read the message from the queue. The message queue accepts messages from client programs and submits them to a workflow queue for Supervisors, named `SupervisorQueue`. For more information on messaging and the Java Messaging Service (JMS), please refer to *Professional JMS Programming*, from Wrox Press, ISBN 1-861004-93-1, or the JMS specification document available at http://java.sun.com/jms/.

- ❑ `closeLedger()`
  This method completes the transaction.

The LedgerBean Class

At various points, the bean may throw an application exception. We can assume that these exceptions simply extend `java.lang.Exception` (see below):

```
package bank.ledger;

import javax.ejb.*;
import javax.transaction.*;
import javax.sql.*;
import java.sql.*;
import javax.jms.*;
import javax.naming.*;

public class LedgerBean implements SessionBean {

  SessionContext sessionCtx = null;
```

In order for us to be able to get a reference to the `UserTransaction` interface, we must access it through the `SessionContext` object. We can get a reference to the `SessionContext` object when the container calls the `setSessionContext()` method:

```
public void setSessionContext(SessionContext ctx) {
  sessionCtx = ctx;
}
public void ejbCreate() {};
public void ejbActivate() {};
public void ejbPassivate() {};
public void ejbRemove() {};
```

The `openLedger()` method prepares the ledger for use by starting a new transaction:

```
public void openLedger() throws LedgerNotAvailableException {

   try {
     // Get a UserTransaction instance
     UserTransaction userTrx = sessionCtx.getUserTransaction();

     // Start the transaction
     userTrx.begin();
   } catch(Exception ex) {
     System.err.println(ex);
     throw new LedgerNotAvailableException();
   }
 }
```

The `addCheckingAccountActivity()` method will add an account activity record to the Ledger in the Checking account database. We look up a context for the `CheckingDB` database to give us a data source, establish a connection, insert the activity log, and close up the connection. On an exception being caught, we attempt to rollback the transaction, print the exception to the standard error log, and throw a `LedgerFailureException`; if the rollback fails, we log the error, and throw a `LedgerNotAvailableExcpetion`. We'll see these simple exceptions after we've defined the bean in full. This method can be called several times within the same transaction:

```
public void addCheckingAccountActivity(String activity)
                              throws LedgerNotAvailableException,
                                     LedgerFailureException   {

   try {
     InitialContext initialCtx = new InitialContext();

     // Get a handle to the datasource and a connection for use
     DataSource ds =
             (DataSource)initialCtx.lookup("java:comp/env/jdbc/CheckingDB");
     java.sql.Connection conn = ds.getConnection();
     Statement stmt = conn.createStatement();
     stmt.execute("INSERT INTO Ledger (activity) VALUES('" + activity +
                                                      "')");
     conn.close();
   } catch(Exception ex) {
     try {
       UserTransaction ut = sessionCtx.getUserTransaction();
       ut.rollback();
     } catch(Exception ex2) {
       System.err.println(ex2);
       throw new LedgerNotAvailableException();
     }
     System.err.println(ex);
     throw new LedgerFailureException();
   }
 }
```

The `addSavingsAccountActivity()` method adds an account activity record to the Ledger in the Savings account database; this method works just like the previous method, only it is targeted at the `SavingsDB` database. This method can also be called several times within the same transaction:

```
public void addSavingsAccountActivity(String activity)
                              throws LedgerNotAvailableException,
                                     LedgerFailureException {

  try {
    InitialContext initialCtx = new InitialContext();

    // Get a handle to the datasource and a connection for use
    DataSource ds =
    (DataSource)initialCtx.lookup("java:comp/env/jdbc/SavingsDB");
    java.sql.Connection conn = ds.getConnection();

    Statement stmt = conn.createStatement();
    stmt.execute("INSERT INTO Ledger (activity) VALUES('" + activity +
                                               "')");

    conn.close();
  } catch(Exception ex) {
    try {
      UserTransaction ut = sessionCtx.getUserTransaction();
      ut.rollback();
    } catch(Exception ex2) {
      System.err.println(ex2);
      throw new LedgerNotAvailableException();
    }
    System.err.println(ex);
    throw new LedgerFailureException();
  }
}
```

The notifySupervisor() method will send a copy of the activity to a banking supervisor. First we create a QueueConnectionFactory, which we use to create a QueueConnection. Using this connection, we then create a QueueSession, get a context for the message queue we want to send to, create a sender, create a TextMessage, set its text, and send it. On an exception being caught, we'll do much the same as with the previous methods – attempt to roll back the transaction, and print the exception to the standard error log. This is another method that can be called several times within the same transaction:

```
public void notifySupervisor(String activity)
                            throws LedgerNotAvailableException,
                                   NotificationFailureException {

  QueueConnectionFactory factory = null;
  QueueConnection connection = null;
  Queue queue = null;
  QueueSession session = null;
  QueueSender sender = null;
  TextMessage message = null;

  try {
    InitialContext initialCtx = new InitialContext();

    // Prepare the messaging objects
    factory = (QueueConnectionFactory)initialCtx.lookup
                          ("java:comp/env/jms/QueueConnectionFactory");
    connection = factory.createQueueConnection();
    session = connection.createQueueSession(true,
                                        Session.AUTO_ACKNOWLEDGE);
    queue = (Queue)initialCtx.lookup("java:comp/env/jms/SupervisorQueue");
    sender = session.createSender(queue);
```

```
      message = session.createTextMessage();
      message.setText(activity);

      sender.send(message);
    } catch(Exception ex) {
      try {
        UserTransaction ut = sessionCtx.getUserTransaction();
        ut.rollback();
      } catch(Exception ex2) {
        System.err.println(ex2);
        throw new LedgerNotAvailableException();
      }
      System.err.println(ex);
      throw new NotificationFailureException();
    }
  }
```

The closeLedger() method will close the ledger and commit the transaction:

```
  public void closeLedger() throws LedgerNotAvailableException,
                                   LedgerFailureException {

    try {
      // Get a UserTransaction instance
      UserTransaction userTrx = sessionCtx.getUserTransaction();

      // Start the transaction
      userTrx.commit();
    } catch(Exception ex) {
      try {
        UserTransaction ut = sessionCtx.getUserTransaction();
        ut.rollback();
      } catch(Exception ex2){
        System.err.println(ex2);
        throw new LedgerNotAvailableException();
      }
      System.err.println(ex);
      throw new LedgerFailureException();
    }
  }

}
```

The LedgerHome Interface

```
package bank.ledger;

import java.rmi.RemoteException;
import javax.ejb.*;

public interface LedgerHome extends EJBHome {
  Ledger create() throws RemoteException, CreateException;
}
```

The Ledger Interface

```
package bank.ledger;

import javax.ejb.EJBObject;
import java.rmi.RemoteException;

public interface Ledger extends EJBObject {

  public void openLedger()
        throws LedgerNotAvailableException, RemoteException;

  public void addCheckingAccountActivity(String activity)
        throws LedgerFailureException, LedgerNotAvailableException,
              RemoteException;

  public void addSavingsAccountActivity(String activity)
        throws LedgerFailureException, LedgerNotAvailableException,
              RemoteException;

  public void notifySupervisor(String activity)
        throws NotificationFailureException, LedgerNotAvailableException,
              RemoteException;

  public void closeLedger()
        throws LedgerFailureException, LedgerNotAvailableException,
              RemoteException;
}
```

The LedgerClient Class

Here is a simple client that will invoke our session bean. The client program will start by obtaining a reference to the Ledger session bean. Once it has a valid remote reference, it will then deposit $100 in the checking account, deposit $200 in the savings account, and withdraw $500 from the checking account. Lastly, it will send a message to a supervisor indicating that the $500 withdrawal was made:

```
import javax.naming.*;
import javax.rmi.PortableRemoteObject;
import bank.ledger.LedgerHome;
import bank.ledger.Ledger;

public class LedgerClient {

  public static void main(String args[]) {

    try {
      InitialContext ctx = new InitialContext();
      Object obj = ctx.lookup("Ledger");
      LedgerHome ledgerHome = (LedgerHome) PortableRemoteObject.narrow(obj,
                                                LedgerHome.class);
      Ledger ledger = ledgerHome.create();

      ledger.openLedger();
      ledger.addCheckingAccountActivity("$100 deposited to checking " +
                                        "account 12345");
      ledger.addSavingsAccountActivity("$200 deposited to checking " +
                                        "account 12345");
      ledger.addCheckingAccountActivity("$500 withdrawn from checking " +
                                        "account 12345");
```

```
            ledger.notifySupervisor("$500 withdrawn from checking account 12345");
            ledger.closeLedger();

        } catch(Exception e) {
            System.out.println(e.toString());
        }
    }
}
```

The Exceptions

These exceptions simply extend `java.lang.Exception`:

```
package bank.ledger;

public class LedgerFailureException extends Exception {}
```

```
package bank.ledger;

public class LedgerNotAvailableException extends Exception {}
```

```
package bank.ledger;

public class NotificationFailureException extends Exception {}
```

Running the Example

We will run this example on the J2EE 1.3 Reference Implementation. Before we actually run the code, we need to configure some data sources for our bean to use.

Click on the Tools | Server Configuration... | Data Sources | Standard:

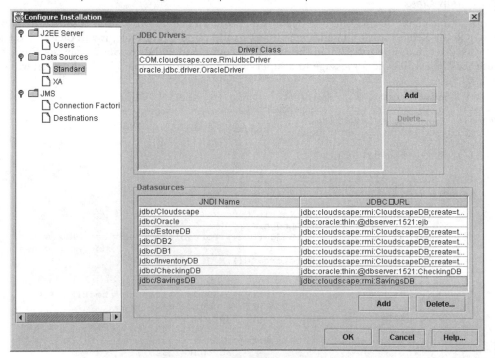

Enter the driver class for your database. In our case, we will be using Oracle, so we specify the `oracle.jdbc.driver.OracleDriver`. Next, we need to specify the JNDI names of our two database tables that are looked up in the `LedgerBean` class: `jdbc/CheckingDB` and `jdbc/SavingsDB`, and then provide them with a suitable URL for the database.

We also need to set up a destination JMS queue, which we can do on the same dialog. Select the Destinations page from the JMS folder on the left:

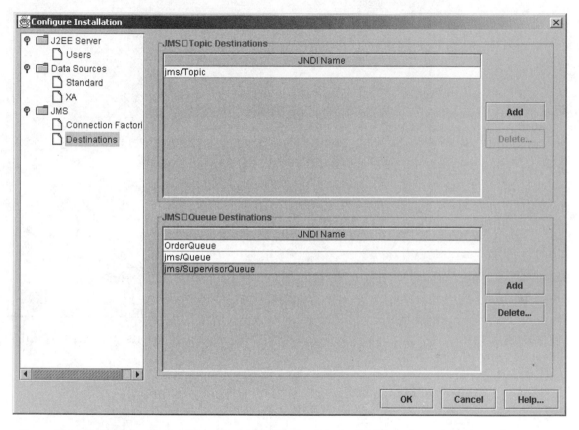

To create a JMS queue destination, all we need do is click the Add button, and then supply a name – in this case, `SupervisorQueue`. Notice that we won't worry about getting the message from the queue in this example. We'll also create a connection factory for our queue, on the tab above Destinations. Click the Add button next to the list of Queue Connection Factories to add our new entry, which we'll call `jms/QueueConnectionFactory`:

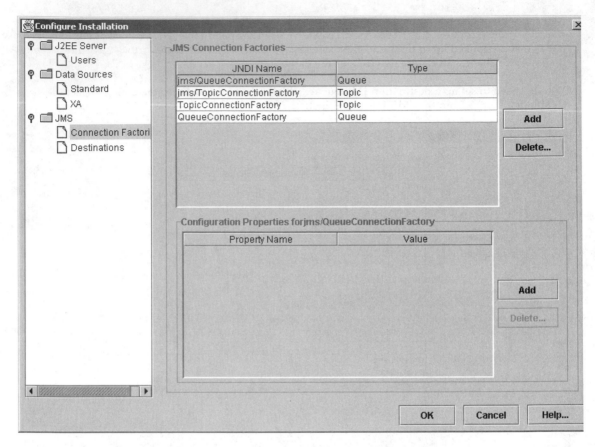

Now create a JAR file called `Ledger.jar` with the following structure (the `ejb-jar.xml` file for this example will be shown below):

```
bank/
    ledger/
            Ledger.class
            LedgerHome.class
            LedgerBean.class
            LedgerFailureException.class
            LedgerNotAvailableException.class
            NotificationFailureException.class
META-INF/
            ejb-jar.xml
```

The Deployment Descriptor

```xml
<?xml version="1.0" encoding="Cp1252"?>

<!DOCTYPE ejb-jar PUBLIC
            '-//Sun Microsystems, Inc.//DTD Enterprise JavaBeans 2.0//EN'
            'http://java.sun.com/dtd/ejb-jar_2_0.dtd'>
```

```
<ejb-jar>
  <display-name>Ledger</display-name>
  <enterprise-beans>
    <session>
      <display-name>Ledger</display-name>
      <ejb-name>Ledger</ejb-name>
      <home>bank.ledger.LedgerHome</home>
      <remote>bank.ledger.Ledger</remote>
      <ejb-class>bank.ledger.LedgerBean</ejb-class>
      <session-type>Stateful</session-type>
      <transaction-type>Bean</transaction-type>
      <resource-ref>
        <res-ref-name>jdbc/CheckingDB</res-ref-name>
        <res-type>javax.sql.DataSource</res-type>
        <res-auth>Container</res-auth>
        <res-sharing-scope>Shareable</res-sharing-scope>
      </resource-ref>
      <resource-ref>
        <res-ref-name>jdbc/SavingsDB</res-ref-name>
        <res-type>javax.sql.DataSource</res-type>
        <res-auth>Container</res-auth>
        <res-sharing-scope>Shareable</res-sharing-scope>
      </resource-ref>
      <resource-ref>
        <res-ref-name>jms/QueueConnectionFactory</res-ref-name>
        <res-type>javax.jms.QueueConnectionFactory</res-type>
        <res-auth>Container</res-auth>
        <res-sharing-scope>Shareable</res-sharing-scope>
      </resource-ref>
      <resource-env-ref>
        <resource-env-ref-name>jms/Queue</esource-env-ref-name>
        <resource-env-ref-type>javax.jms.Queue</resource-env-ref-type>
      </resource-env-ref>
    </session>
  </enterprise-beans>
</ejb-jar>
```

Deployment

Create a new application in the deployment tool called **Ledger** and import `Ledger.jar` by selecting **File | Add to Application | EJB JAR...** and specifying the correct path. Next, select the **JNDI Names** tab of the **Ledger** application. Give our EJB the JNDI name `Ledger`. Now, expand the `Ledger` bean and select the **Resource Ref's** tab. We need to provide some additional deployment information for the resource factories such as security credentials:

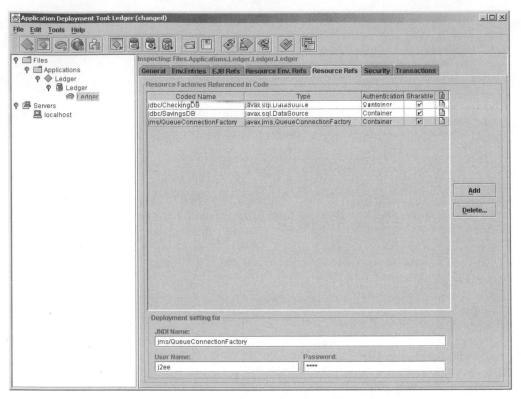

The final stage is deployment. Select **Deploy...** from the **Tools** menu, remembering to specify the directory the client will be run from as the place for the client JAR to be saved to. Here are the JNDI names we used:

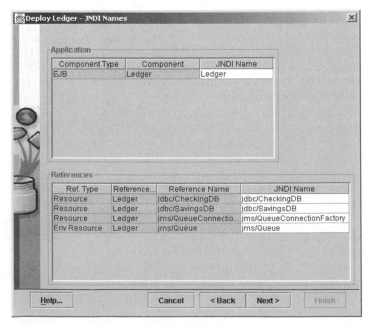

Lastly, we have to run the example:

```
java -classpath %J2EE_HOME%\lib\j2ee.jar;LedgerClient.jar LedgerClient
```

Verify that actions have been inserted into the appropriate tables by using a tool such as SQL+ to read the row entries.

Transactions and Entity Beans

When using an entity bean, special care should be taken with container-managed persistence. The ejbLoad() and ejbStore() methods are called with the same transactional context as the business method that triggered them. Since ejbLoad() is invoked as the result of another of the bean's methods being called, this is quite understandable.

The ejbStore() method is always invoked when a bean's data is to be persisted. As the data is always persisted when a commit is executed, the ejbStore() method must execute within the same transactional context. For ejbLoad() and ejbStore(), the transactional attribute is, essentially, Supports.

This raises an interesting question. What happens if the originating or calling method does *not* have a transactional context? That is, what if there is no transaction in use when ejbLoad() or ejbStore() is called? Since their transactional attribute is Supports, they will not create a new transaction.

The EJB specification does not require that ejbLoad() and ejbStore() operate within a transaction. Instead, ejbLoad() will execute in the same transaction context as the business method which causes it to be invoked. The ejbStore() method will execute in the same transaction context that ejbLoad() or ejbCreate() was executed in – whichever was called prior to ejbStore(). In fact, the specification simply states when they should be invoked. The ejbLoad() method will be called at some point between when an entity bean is associated with a context ID and a business method is called. The ejbStore() method will be called at some point between when the business method is called and the object is disassociated from the context ID.

This poses a problem in that data could be persisted without a transaction. Worse than that, since the entity bean is, for all intents and purposes, a caching mechanism between the container and the data source, if the data is not maintained within a transaction, it will be very easy for that data's state to become invalid.

This is especially problematic when you consider that it is entirely possible for the following scenario to occur:

- ❑ A client updates a bean's data
- ❑ Another process updates the data in the data store
- ❑ The bean persists the data in the database

Changes made to the data by the external process are lost. Worse, if that process is operating within a transaction, the entity bean's persistence operation could fail. However, the client will already have been told that the update completed successfully. Furthermore, the entity bean has no way of notifying the client that the persistence operation failed.

Another scenario: the database server crashes or becomes unavailable while the bean is in the middle of updating. Without a transaction, information about the update will not be stored in a transaction log. Thus, the server will not be able to recover the update at a later point. Granted, most database servers have their own internal transaction managers, but that will be of little use to a bean that has multiple update processes in the same atomic operation.

The easiest way to avoid this scenario is to require your business methods to operate within a transactional context. Again, this is all provided that you are using container-managed persistence.

Why not create our own transaction in ejbStore()? In other words, why don't we just assign the Required transaction attribute to the method and not worry about it? The answer is simple enough: We cannot Require a transaction in ejbStore() because the ejbStore() method is always invoked by the container when the bean is passivated. If a bean is passivated while it is in the middle of a transaction, the act of creating a transaction in ejbStore() would result in the data being committed. If the bean's data is in an inconsistent state, this could cause a lot of problems.

If we are using bean-managed persistence, we should not rely on ejbLoad() and ejbStore() to manage our bean's state. This can be achieved by directly interacting with the database from within a given method and not relying on the container to notify your bean when to manage its state. Effectively, the ejbLoad() and ejbStore() methods are empty. We are, of course, gaining safety at the cost of performance, but this is always going to be a tradeoff. We must always be careful to choose wisely.

Transactional Context Propagation

When a client invokes a bean's method, the client's transactional context is propagated to the bean. However, before the bean's method is invoked, the client's transaction is suspended. If the bean has container-managed transaction demarcation, the container will handle the method's transaction in accordance with the transactional attribute. If the bean has bean-managed transactional demarcation, it will be up to the bean provider to determine if, and how, to incorporate the client's transactional context.

Transactional context propagation for bean-managed transaction demarcation can be summarized as follows:

❑ If the client calling the enterprise bean instance does not have a transactional context associated with it, and the bean instance does not have a transactional context associated with it, the container will invoke the bean method with an unspecified transaction context.

❑ If the calling client is already associated with a transaction, and the bean instance is not associated with a transaction, the container will suspend the client's transaction and invoke the bean method with an unspecified transaction context.

❑ If the calling client is not associated with a transaction, and the bean instance is already associated with a transaction (one is already in progress), the container will invoke the bean method with the transaction that is already associated with the bean instance. Note that this cannot happen with a stateless session bean, as they do not maintain transactional state across method invocations.

❑ If the client is already associated with a transaction, and the bean instance is also associated with a different transaction, the container will suspend the client's transaction and invoke the bean method with the transaction that is already associated with the bean instance. Once the bean method is completed, the container will resume the client's transaction.

The general rule here is that the bean's transaction context will take priority over the client's transaction context.

Transaction Interaction

For container-managed transactions, Enterprise JavaBeans provide a set of methods that allow some interaction with the current transactional context. These are:

- ❑ setRollbackOnly()
- ❑ getRollbackOnly()

The setRollbackOnly() method marks the current transaction for rollback. It does not actually roll the transaction back, as this would be in violation of the constraints imposed by container-managed transaction demarcation. Instead, it indicates that the transaction should be rolled back. The container, at a later point, will roll back the transaction. When the transaction is actually rolled back is at the discretion of the transaction. However, it is guaranteed that the transaction will not commit.

There are some restrictions to the use of the setRollbackOnly() method:

- ❑ First, it can only be called by container-managed transaction beans.
- ❑ Second, it can only be called by methods whose transactional attributes are Required, RequiresNew, or Mandatory. If setRollbackOnly() is invoked from a method that does not have one of these transactional attributes, the java.lang.IllegalStateException will be thrown.

The getRollbackOnly() method will return the current state of the transaction, embodied by the javax.transaction.Status interface. This provides us with the opportunity to determine, at an arbitrary point, whether the transaction should be rolled back due to some error condition or if it should be allowed to continue. By having the ability to preempt the transaction, we can prevent the invocation of resource calls that would otherwise have to be rolled back at the end of the transaction.

Transaction Events

There are three basic events associated with transaction demarcation:

- ❑ The transaction has started
- ❑ The transaction is about to commit
- ❑ The transaction has ended

When using container-managed transaction demarcation with session beans, EJB provides an optional callback mechanism by which to be notified of these transaction events, namely the SessionSynchronization interface.

The SessionSynchronization interface is defined as follows:

```
public interface javax.ejb.SessionSynchronization {

    public void afterBegin() throws EJBException, RemoteException;

    public void afterCompletion(boolean committed) throws EJBException,
                                                          RemoteException;

    public void beforeCompletion() throws EJBException, RemoteException;
}
```

The afterBegin() method is invoked by the container when a new transaction has started. This method will be called prior to any of the business methods that will be invoked within the context of the transaction. This gives the session bean an opportunity to prepare data for use, such as reading it in from a database or some other source, or formatting it.

The beforeCompletion() method is called by the container just prior to when a transaction is to be committed. This provides the session bean with an opportunity to conduct any last minute data preparation, such as validation or formatting. This also gives the session bean one last chance to rollback the transaction via the setRollbackOnly() method, or by throwing an exception.

The afterCompletion() method is called by the container once the transaction has committed. A Boolean value is passed to the method indicating whether the transaction successfully committed, true, or was rolled back, false. When this method is invoked, the transaction has completed. Therefore there is no transaction context available.

Transaction Isolation

The ACID property **isolation** requires that a transaction must be able to operate without regard for and without being affected by other active transactions in the system. In a concurrent system, several transactions may be executing at once – often on the same data. It may be necessary to protect one transaction from the efforts of another. Transaction isolation is achieved via locking and the serialization of data requests.

Locking controls access to a given set of data. The two primary types of locks are read locks and write locks. Read locks are **non-exclusive** locks – they will allow multiple transactions to read data simultaneously. Write locks are **exclusive** locks – they will only allow a single transaction to update a set of data.

Serialization guarantees that concurrently executing transactions will behave as if they were executing sequentially, not concurrently. Of course, the transactions will be executing concurrently, but they will appear to be executing in series. The result of serialization is the appearance that multiple transactions are working with data one at a time, in order.

Isolation levels specify concurrency control at a high-level. The types of locks and serialization used, as well as the extent to which they are applied, determines the level of isolation that a transaction will execute under. The actual implementation is up to the resource manager and/or transaction manager. Isolation levels vary from very relaxed to very strict. As might be expected, the stricter the level of concurrency control, the greater the impact on performance. As with so many other issues in designing concurrent systems, special care must be taken when determining which isolation level to use.

J2EE provides support for four types of isolation levels, as defined in the java.sql.Connection interface (we will see how to set these later):

- ❑ TRANSACTION_READ_UNCOMMITTED

- ❑ TRANSACTION_READ_COMMITTED

- ❑ TRANSACTION_REPEATABLE_READ

- ❑ TRANSACTION_SERIALIZABLE

In transactional processing, there are three major types of concurrency issues that the isolation levels attempt to address:

❑ Dirty reads

❑ Unrepeatable reads

❑ Phantom reads

The following discusses the various problems as well as the appropriate isolation level to use to resolve these problems.

Dirty Reads

A dirty read occurs when a transaction reads data that has been written by another transaction but has not been yet been committed. This happens when there is a complete lack of synchronization on the data. We return to our banking system for an example of a dirty read:

❑ A client's bank account has $1000.

❑ Transaction 1 deposits $500 into the account, but does not yet commit the operation.

❑ Transaction 2 is posting a check for $1500, reads the account and sees the balance is $1500. It then processes the check against the account and commits.

❑ Transaction 1, which is still active, rolls back its operation. The balance is restored to the $1000 that it was at before transaction one started.

❑ The $1500 check has still been cleared and the bank just lost the money!

A dirty read can occur if we use the lowest level of transactional isolation, TRANSACTION_READ_UNCOMMITTED. The only time that this level of isolation should be used in a system is when the transaction will be the only one accessing the data. Similarly, we should also use it when the data is, and always will be, read-only.

An example of this would be a static lookup table. Even in this case, we might want to implement some sort of read/write control mechanism in the rare event that the data might need to be updated. TRANSACTION_READ_UNCOMMITTED is used by the reading transactions, but the reads are blocked when a writing transaction is active.

The use of TRANSACTION_READ_COMMITTED avoids the dirty read problem. It requires that a transaction can only read data that has been committed. It cannot read data that is in the scope of another active transaction. This is the most common level of isolation and, in fact, is the default isolation method for most databases servers. However, since we will be using Enterprise JavaBeans which are concurrent by nature, we try to avoid using TRANSACTION_READ_UNCOMMITTED whenever possible.

Unrepeatable Reads

An unrepeatable read occurs when a transaction reads data from a database, but gets a different result if it tries to read the same data again within the same transaction. This typically happens when another transaction writes over some of the data that was read in by the first transaction.

Consider an order entry system where a customer's invoice is being reviewed:

- ❑ Clerk 1 is reading an invoice.

- ❑ Clerk 2 makes changes to the invoice's line items updating the unit price.

- ❑ Clerk 1 fulfills the invoice at the original price.

- ❑ The company has charged the client the wrong amount for the order!

The second clerk should not be allowed to modify the order while the first clerk is working with it.

If this behavior needs to be prevented, the TRANSACTION_REPEATABLE_READ isolation level should be used. TRANSACTION_REPEATABLE_READ provides more reliable transactions where data must be read and subsequently re-read. This isolation level works by locking the data so that other transactions cannot make changes to it. Once the transaction is completed, the other transactions will then be permitted to continue.

Phantom Reads

A phantom read occurs when a transaction executes multiple reads against a set of data and, in between two of the read operations, another transaction slips in and inserts additional data. This differs from the unrepeatable read problem in that here data is being inserted into our data set, rather than that data merely being updated.

Returning again to our example of an order-entry system, let's say we were fulfilling an order:

- ❑ The shipping department reviews the order, packages the items, and sends them on their way.

- ❑ Meanwhile, here comes Clerk 2 again who adds an additional item to the order.

- ❑ If the shipping department were to review the order again, they would see that another item has magically appeared. The client does not get their correct order and is very upset!

It is desirable that Clerk 2 should not be allowed to add items to this invoice while another person is working on it.

Using the transaction isolation level TRANSACTION_SERIALIZABLE prevents this from occurring. This level of isolation provides the strictest form of transaction management available.

Specifying Isolation Level

In container-managed transaction demarcation, the isolation level is determined by the container. Since EJB 1.1, there is no support for specifying the isolation level in the deployment descriptor. While some containers provide the ability to specify the isolation level at the resource-manager level, you should not rely on this. It is generally best to leave this decision to the container.

In bean-managed transaction demarcation, the isolation level is specified by directly interacting with the resource manager's API. In the case where a database is being used, this would be via the java.sql.Connection.setTranactionIsolation() method.

> Be forewarned that support for transaction isolation by a resource manager is not a requirement. Therefore, caution should be used when specifying a transaction's isolation level. In fact, many resource managers will prevent you from doing this (database managers especially).

When determining the proper isolation level to use, it is important to remember that stricter levels of control will have a greater impact on performance. It is for this reason that each transaction will have to be considered on an individual basis. One isolation level will not be applicable across all transactions.

An isolation level is associated with a resource manager. As such, if a bean interacts with multiple resource managers (say, two database servers), a separate isolation level can be specified for each resource manager. However, most resource managers require that all access to that resource manager within a given transaction must be executed at the same isolation level.

It is very important that you do not attempt to switch isolation levels mid-way through a transaction, as this could cause the transaction to commit prematurely, among other erratic behavior. This is because you would be changing the rules governing locking and serialization in the middle of the transaction. This gets even more complex when you have multiple beans accessing the same resource manager within the same transaction. Certainly, a great deal of caution, coordination, and planning is required.

Alternatives to Isolation Control

Strict transaction isolation comes at a price – the greater the level of control, the greater the performance cost. When strict isolation is required, the negative performance impact could require us to seek alternative control methods. Two such methods are **optimistic locking** and **pessimistic locking**.

Optimistic locking allows many clients to access the same data concurrently. Optimistic locking is called so because we are "optimistic" that the data will not change while we are using it. When one of the clients needs to update the data, it submits the changes to a controller (say, an entity bean) for consideration. The controller compares the data in the database (or similar) to the data that was originally provided to the client. If they match, that is if no changes have occurred between the time that the client read the data and when the client requested to change the data, then the update is allowed to proceed. If, on the other hand, the data has changed since it was initially provided to the client, the client is notified that it must refresh its copy of the data and re-submit the update request. As this can result in a duplication of effort, optimistic locking is best suited for situations where most of the clients will be reading, not updating.

Pessimistic locking takes the view that there is a high probability that someone will want to change data while we are working with it, thus the data must be protected. Pessimistic locking is usually achieved through the use of transactions. However, where transactions are not available or could be very long-lived, a semaphore can be used in its place. In this case, the master data record contains a flag that indicates whether the data is currently in use by a client for either viewing or editing.

Pessimistic locking is achieved by utilizing read locks every time data is read, and write locks every time the data is to be updated. These locks are held for the duration of the transaction in which the data is being used. Clients may obtain a read lock on the data provided that no other transactions have write locks. Write locks are used to update the data and other clients are still allowed to read the data provided that they do not require a read lock. However, a write lock will not allow another transaction to read its changing data until those changes have been committed.

Behavior of Exceptions in Container-Managed Transactions

The behavior of exceptions when using container-managed transactions depends on the type of transaction being used, who initiated the transaction, and the type of exception occurring. Let's briefly review how exceptions work in EJB.

Recall that there are two categories of exceptions in EJB:

❑   Application exceptions

❑   System exceptions

Application exceptions are basically any exceptions that are declared in the throws clause of the methods of a bean's home or remote interfaces. Put another way, application exceptions are those exceptions that will be propagated to a bean's client.

The purpose of an application exception is to indicate an abnormal application-level condition. For example, an invalid account balance, an invalid account number, or attempting to access prohibited data could all result in an application exception.

Typically, an application exception is defined by the bean developer and represents a business-logic exception more than a system exception. InsufficientFundsException, AccountNotFoundException, and AccessDeniedException are all examples of application exceptions. In addition, javax.ejb.CreateException, RemoveException, and FinderException are also considered application exceptions, despite the fact that they do not represent business logic exceptions. However, it is desirable that these exceptions be propagated back to the client.

System exceptions are any non-application exceptions. When a system exception occurs, it is due to a system-level error, not a business-level error. System exceptions are not returned to the client. Instead, they are caught at the server level and dealt with there. If an exception is to be returned to the client, either an EJBException will be thrown or an application exception will be created and thrown instead.

There are no hard and fast rules regarding the behavior of system exceptions, but the following guidelines usually apply:

❑   If a RuntimeException or Error occurs, it will be propagated to the container

❑   If the exception is not a RuntimeException, it will be wrapped in an EJBException and returned to the bean

❑   Any other type of unexpected error will result in an EJBException

Exception Scenarios

When an exception occurs within the bounds of a transaction, the results vary depending on the type of error and where the transaction originated. The following sections detail the different possible exception scenarios.

Scenario One

The transaction originated on the client and the transactional attribute for the bean's method is either Required, Mandatory, or Supports.

When an application exception occurs within this context, the container will still attempt to commit the transaction. Since an application exception does not necessarily indicate an error with the data operation itself, the container cannot assume on its own that the transaction should be rolled back. Furthermore, as the container did not start the transaction itself, it cannot safely guess the use of the transaction.

If we raise an application exception and know that the transaction should be rolled back, we should invoke the setRollbackOnly() method on the EJBContext object. This should be done within our bean's method where the application exception would be raised.

It is at the discretion of the client whether or not to continue a transaction when an application exception occurs. A good example of this would be an `InsufficientFundsException` being thrown when posting a check within our banking system. The client may wish to try posting the check to another account, such as a savings account or overdraft account. When a client does receive an application exception, however, they should check the `getRollbackOnly()` or `getStatus()` methods.

When a system exception or error occurs within this context, the container will:

❑ Log the exception or error for later review by the system administrator

❑ Mark the transaction for rollback, via the `setRollbackOnly()` method

❑ Discard the instance of the bean

❑ Throw a `TransactionRolledBackException` or `TransactionRolledBackLocalException` back to the client

Scenario Two

The transaction is started by the container, with the transactional attribute `Required` or `RequiresNew`.

When an application exception is thrown, if the bean's method where the exception was thrown marked the transaction for roll back via the `setRollbackOnly()` method, the container will rollback the transaction. Otherwise the container will attempt to commit the transaction. The container will then re-throw the application exception back to the client.

When a system exception occurs, the container will:

❑ Log the exception or error for later review by the system administrator

❑ Mark the transaction for rollback, via the `setRollbackOnly()` method

❑ Discard the instance of the bean

❑ Throw a `RemoteException` or `EJBException` back to the client

This is similar to the behavior of a transaction started by the client, except that a `RemoteException` or `EJBException`, depending on client location, is thrown. Since the transactional context is limited to the bean's method, it would not make sense to return a `TransactionRolledBackException` or `TransactionRolledBackLocalException`, as above.

Scenario Three

The bean method is invoked with an unspecified transaction context, such as when the transaction attributes `NotSupported` or `Never` are used, or when the bean's method is marked as `Supports` but is invoked by an unspecified transaction context.

The container will not rollback the transaction if an application error is thrown, simply re-throwing the application exception that occurred. Remember that a transaction cannot be marked for rollback within an unspecified transaction context. The `setRollbackOnly()` method is only supported for methods with the transaction attribute `Required`, `RequiresNew`, or `Manadatory`. Attempting to set a transaction for rollback within an unspecified transaction context will result in a `java.lang.IllegalStateException`.

When a system error occurs, the container will log the exception or error, discard the instance of the bean, and throw a `RemoteException` or `EJBException`.

Scenario Four

The method is part of a session bean or message-driven bean and the transaction is bean-managed.

When an application exception is thrown, the client will receive the application exception.

When a system error occurs, the container will:

- ❏ Log the exception or error for later review by the system administrator
- ❏ Mark the transaction for rollback, via the setRollbackOnly() method
- ❏ Discard the instance of the bean
- ❏ Throw a RemoteException back to the client

When dealing with container-managed transactions, if a transaction was rolled back due to the setRollbackOnly flag being set, the container will roll the transaction back, but will not throw a RemoteException. Instead, the container will either return the normal result of the method or, if one was thrown, an application exception.

In container-managed transactions, if an exception occurs, the container will release any connections to any managed resources. A managed resource is any resource (such as a database) that the bean's instance might have obtained via the container's resource factory. However, the container cannot release any *unmanaged* resources (such as a network socket) that the bean instance might have obtained through the standard JDK APIs. Unmanaged connections will be released during regular garbage collection. If you are using unmanaged connections, you should be careful to release them in the event of an exception.

When a system exception occurs, the transaction may not necessarily be marked for rollback. For example, a communication problem prevents the remote bean from even begin called. In this case, the server won't have the opportunity to mark the transaction for rollback because it never even got the transaction in the first place.

Summary

Transactional processing is critical in any application where data is being accessed by more than one source at a time. The field of transactional processing is quite complex and we have really only scratched the surface here. Through the course of this chapter, we have seen:

❑ While the Enterprise JavaBeans framework strives to free us of a lot of the concerns involved with developing enterprise-class applications, we are still required to understand how components interact with each other and the data that they share.

❑ Different levels of isolation and concurrency control are available to our components. Each component will require individual consideration to determine the best balance of control versus balance. The stricter the control, the greater the performance cost.

❑ We can rely on the EJB container to manage our transaction for us, or we can manage them ourselves. If we choose to let the container manage our transactions, we must indicate, in the deployment descriptor, how those transactions will behave. Also, container-managed transactions are conducted at the method level. If we desire a finer level of control, we will have to manage the transactions ourselves.

❑ Finally, EJB provides developers with a considerable amount of control over the transactional processing of their components. Although entity beans can only be controlled by the container, we can still largely effect the transactions on those beans by specifying their transaction attributes.

Understanding how transactional processing works is crucial to the success of any enterprise-level system and we must ensure that we have a solid understanding of the concepts. For a more thorough exploration of transactional processing, *Transaction Processing: Concepts and Techniques* (ISBN 1-55860-190-2) by Jim Gray and Andreas Reuter is considered to be the definitive source.

In the next chapter, we will look at some of the key issues in security for EJBs.

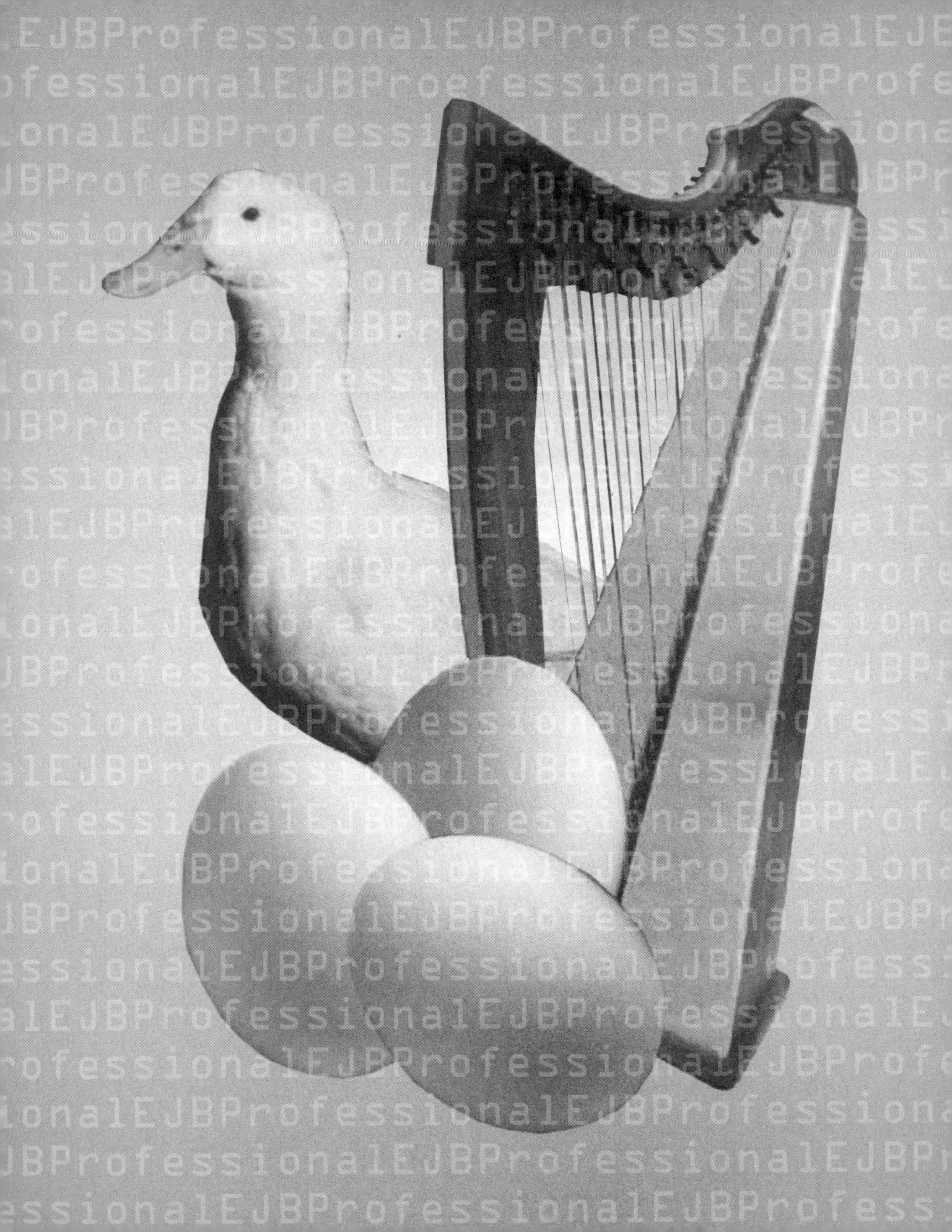

10

Security in EJB

Security is an extremely important issue in the development and deployment of enterprise-class applications. Business needs dictate that enterprise data and applications may only be accessed in a secure way by authorized users.

As anyone who has developed enterprise applications will tell you, including security measures in your application can take as long to write as the business logic itself. Given that the EJB framework (and J2EE in general) is aimed at relieving the pressure on developers to write system-level interaction code, security would be a strange part of the application to leave out of this goal. Well, it hasn't been left out, quite the opposite in fact. It is possible for the bean provider to write their bean with only the slightest reference to security (as long as it's the right type of reference), and leave it up to the application assembler and deployer to set the security levels for each method on every bean in the application.

However, before we get carried away with the notion of hardly having to work to include security in our beans, we should take a step back as it were, and look at security in a broader context. To this end, in this chapter we'll be looking at the following aspects of security:

- ❑ An overview of the EJB security model
- ❑ EJB-specific issues in security management
- ❑ Developing EJBs for security (coded security)
- ❑ Application security design (declarative security)
- ❑ Deploying secure EJB applications
- ❑ Designing and developing EJB clients

The EJB Security Model

Traditionally enterprise application developers spent a large amount of development resources on defining and implementing logic to manage the security policies at run time. Implementing this logic typically entailed the following:

- ❑ Defining users and groups
- ❑ Associating application privileges to groups, then users to groups
- ❑ Providing efficient and secure storage mechanisms for the above, usually in a database management system
- ❑ Implementing the logic to check for authorization at run time
- ❑ Implementing tools to manage users, groups, and privileges

Any time a feature was added to the application, the necessary security logic also had to be incorporated in to the system. Changing the security mechanism usually entailed a re-implementation of the security logic. This naturally placed an enormous and unreasonable burden on the application developer whose expertise, typically, lay in the business rules and logic and not necessarily in the realm of security management. Now the business rules expert was forced to be a security expert too!

Apart from the core business logic, a typical enterprise application also includes logic to manage transaction processing, persistence, security, resource management, communication, and concurrency. The EJB specification promotes a consistent philosophy that experts in each domain should be responsible for the areas of their expertise. In other words the enterprise application programmer should focus on the business logic development and let the EJB container handle the other aspects of the enterprise application.

It is one of the major goals of the Enterprise JavaBeans framework to isolate the application developer from the, sometimes low-level, details of implementing the security logic. The security policies are specified declaratively (in a deployment descriptor document) and are not hard coded in the bean. This enables the application deployer to customize or define security policies during deployment without having to modify and recompile the beans. Objects implementing the security logic enforcement are generated and instantiated using container-provided tools during deployment. The implementation of these objects is clearly influenced by the security policies, among other things, specified declaratively in the deployment descriptor.

Finally the EJB specification enables the applications to be portable across multiple EJB containers that may use a wide variety of security infrastructure implementations.

EJB Security Model Conclusions

As per the EJB 2.0 specification, EJB security management has the following three goals:

- ❑ Take away the responsibility of application security from the bean provider (application developer) to other EJB roles such as EJB container, deployer, and system administrator.
- ❑ Security policies should not be hard-coded by the bean provider at development time. The application assembler or deployer should set up the security policies. The EJB container implements the security infrastructure.
- ❑ Enable the portability of EJBs across multiple EJB Servers that use different security mechanisms.

In order to demonstrate the EJB security model we will take a relatively simple EJB application and look at the various ways in which we can secure it.

Overview of the Sample Application

We shall use a simple application from the banking domain to illustrate the security features of EJB. The application is assembled using the following Enterprise JavaBeans:

Enterprise JavaBean	EJB Type
Account Bean	Entity
AccountManager Bean	Session
Log Bean	Entity

Before we start discussing how to apply security to an EJB application, let's see what the application looks like before any security measures are in place. Each customer will have a bank account in their name, represented by the Account bean. This simple 2.0 CMP entity bean deals solely with account balances. The stateless session bean, AccountManager bean, handles all access to the Account bean. Different clients (account holding customers, and bank staff) call the AccountManager bean, which acts as a façade for the Account beans. The Log bean provides an access record of which clients have called which method.

The following diagram presents an overview of the application:

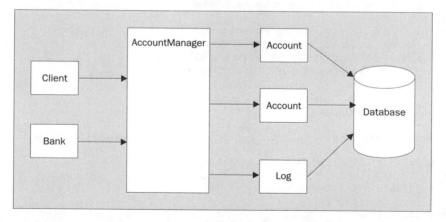

The session bean `AccountManagerEJB` serves as a façade for the application, acts to create and manage Account objects. The `AccountEJB` bean represents individual accounts. The `LogEJB` bean implements the auditing and logging logic and is used by the `AccountEJB`. Over the course of this chapter, we will look at various ways of incorporating different layers of security into the application.

The Account Bean

Using EJB 2.0 container-managed persistence makes the task of creating the Account bean a simple one. Here are the interfaces for this bean.

The Remote Component Interface

```
package banking;

import javax.ejb.EJBObject;
import java.rmi.RemoteException;

public interface Account extends EJBObject {

  public double getBalance() throws RemoteException;

  public void deposit( double amount) throws RemoteException;

  public double withdraw(double amount) throws InsufficientFundsException,
                                              RemoteException;

  public double calculateInterest() throws RemoteException;

}
```

The Home Component Interface

```
package banking;

import javax.ejb.EJBHome;

import javax.ejb.*;
import java.rmi.RemoteException;

public interface AccountHome extends EJBHome {

  public Account create(String customerName, double currentBalance)
        throws CreateException, RemoteException;
  public Account findByPrimaryKey(String key)
        throws FinderException, RemoteException;
}
```

The Bean Implementation Class

```
package banking;

import javax.ejb.EntityBean;

import javax.ejb.EntityContext;
import javax.naming.*;
import javax.rmi.*;

public abstract class AccountEJB implements EntityBean {

  private EntityContext context;
  private static final double INTEREST = 0.01;

  public AccountEJB() {}

  public void setEntityContext(EntityContext ec) {
    context = ec;
  }
```

```java
  public void unsetEntityContext() {
    this.context = null;
  }
  public void ejbActivate() {}
  public void ejbPassivate() {}
  public void ejbLoad() {}
  public void ejbStore() {}

  public String ejbCreate(String customerName, double currentBalance)
        throws javax.ejb.CreateException {
    setCustomerName(customerName);
    setCurrentBalance(currentBalance);
    return null;
  }

  public void ejbPostCreate(String customerName, double currentBalance) {}

  public void ejbRemove() {}

  public double getBalance() {
    return getCurrentBalance();
  }

  public void deposit(double amount) {
    setCurrentBalance(getCurrentBalance() + amount);
  }

  public double withdraw(double amount)
        throws InsufficientFundsException{

    if (amount < getCurrentBalance()) {
      throw new InsufficientFundsException("Account does not have "
                                      + amount);
    } else {
      setCurrentBalance(getCurrentBalance() - amount);
      return getCurrentBalance();
    }
  }

  public double calculateInterest() {
    setCurrentBalance(getCurrentBalance() +
                                (getCurrentBalance() * INTEREST));
    return getCurrentBalance();
  }

  public abstract double getCurrentBalance();
  public abstract void setCurrentBalance(double initialAmount);

  public abstract String getCustomerName();
  public abstract void setCustomerName(String customerName);
}
```

The business methods are simple implementations – we'll let the container worry about interacting with the database.

The AccountManager Bean

Since this bean sits between the clients and the Account bean instances they are interested in, there will be more to code in this bean. Let's see the interfaces first.

The Remote Component Interface

```java
package banking;

import javax.ejb.*;
import java.rmi.RemoteException;

public interface AccountManager extends EJBObject {

  public void deposit(String customerName, double amount)
     throws RemoteException;

  public double withdraw(String customerName, double amount)
     throws InsufficientFundsException, RemoteException;

  public double getBalance(String customerName)
     throws RemoteException;

  public double calculateInterest(String customerName)
     throws RemoteException;

  public account createAccount(String customerName, double initialBalance)
      throws NoAccountCreatedException, RemoteException;
}
```

The Home Component Interface

```java
package banking;

import javax.ejb.*;
import java.rmi.RemoteException;

public interface AccountManagerHome extends EJBHome {

  public AccountManager create()
  throws CreateException, RemoteException;

}
```

The Bean Implementation Class

```java
package banking;

import javax.ejb.*;
import java.util.*;
import javax.naming.*;
import javax.rmi.*;
import java.rmi.RemoteException;

public class AccountManagerEJB implements javax.ejb.SessionBean {
```

```
   private SessionContext context;
   public static final String DEPOSIT = "deposit funds";
     public static final String WITHDRAW = "withdraw funds";
     public static final String GETBALANCE = "get an account balance";
     public static final String CALCULATEINTEREST =
       "calculate interest on an account";
     public static final String CREATEACCOUNT = "create an account";
     public static final String CLIENT = "Client";
     public static final String BANK = "Bank";

     public AccountManagerEJB() {}

     public void ejbActivate() {}
     public void ejbPassivate() {}
     public void ejbRemove() {}

     public void setSessionContext(SessionContext ctx) {
       context = ctx;
     }
     public void ejbCreate() {}

     // business methods
     public void deposit(String customerName,
                         double amount) throws RemoteException {

       logActivity(DEPOSIT, customerName);

       try {
         Account account = getAccount(customerName);
         account.deposit(amount);
       } catch (NoSuchAccountException nsae) {}
       catch (RemoteException re) {
         throw new EJBException();
       }

     }

     public double withdraw(String customerName, double amount)
            throws InsufficientFundsException, RemoteException {

       double newBal;
       logActivity(WITHDRAW, customerName);

       try {
         Account account = getAccount(customerName);
         double bal = account.getBalance();

         if (amount < bal) {
           throw new InsufficientFundsException("Account does not have "
                                                + amount);
         }
         newBal = account.withdraw(amount);
       } catch (RemoteException re) {
         throw new EJBException();
       } catch (NoSuchAccountException e) {
         throw new EJBException();
       }
   }
   return newBal;
     }

   public double getBalance(String customerName) throws RemoteException {
```

```
    logActivity(GETBALANCE, customerName);

    double bal = 0;
    try {
      Account account = getAccount(customerName);
      bal = account.getBalance();
    } catch (AccountAccessDeniedException AE) {
      throw new AccountAccessDeniedException("Access Denied");
    } catch (NoSuchAccountException nsae) {}
    catch (RemoteException re) {
      throw new EJBException();
    }
    return bal;
  }

  public double calculateInterest(String customerName)
        throws RemoteException {

    logActivity(CALCULATEINTEREST, customerName);

    try {
      Account account = getAccount(customerName);
      return account.calculateInterest();
    } catch (RemoteException re) {
      throw new EJBException();
    } catch (RemoteException re) {
      throw new EJBException();
    }
  }

  public Account createAccount(String customerName, double initialBalance)
        throws NoAccountCreatedException, RemoteException {
    logActivity(CREATEACCOUNT, customerName);

    try {
      AccountHome accountHome = getAccountHome();
      accountHome.create(customerName, initialBalance);
    } catch (CreateException ce) {
      throw new NoAccountCreatedException(ce.getMessage());
    } catch (RemoteException re) {
      throw new EJBException(re);
    }
  }

  // convenience logging method
  private void logActivity(String method, String customer) {

    this.log(this.context.getCallerPrincipal().getName() + " tried to "
            + method + " for " + customer);
}

  // convenience account finder method
  private Account getAccount(String customerName)
        throws NoSuchAccountException {

    try {
```

```
            AccountHome home = getAccountHome();
            return home.findByPrimaryKey(new String(customerName));
        } catch (RemoteException re) {
            throw new EJBException(re);
        } catch (FinderException fe) {
            throw new NoSuchAccountException();
        }
    }

    private AccountHome getAccountHome() {
        try {
            InitialContext initial = new InitialContext();
            Object objref = initial.lookup("ejb/account");
            AccountHome home =
                (AccountHome) javax.rmi.PortableRemoteObject.narrow(objref,
                    AccountHome.class);
            return home;
        } catch (NamingException ne) {
            throw new EJBException(ne);
        }
    }

    private void log(String msg) {
        try {
            InitialContext ctx = new InitialContext();
            Object ref = ctx.lookup("ejb/log");
            LogHome h = (LogHome) PortableRemoteObject.narrow(ref, LogHome.class);
            h.create(msg);
        } catch (Exception e) {}
    }

}
```

Each of the business methods in this session bean needs to perform some very similar processing, so this has been gathered together in the form of two convenience methods, `logActivity()` and `getAccount()`. To make the `logActivity()` method viable, we have declared some static string variables to hold the activities that will be logged. The `getAccount()` method obtains a reference to an `AccountEJB` (through calling the `getAccountHome()` method), which it then uses to find the instance it is looking for, by utilizing the `findByPrimaryKey()` method.

Each of the business methods logs who has called it, by using the `logActivity()` method, which in turn calls the `log()` method. This method uses our last bean, the Log Bean to enter a logging message into a database.

The Log Bean

Our second entity bean, the Log bean, is another simple implementation.

The Remote Component Interface

```
package banking;

import javax.ejb.EJBObject;

import java.rmi.RemoteException;
```

```
public interface Log extends EJBObject {
  public void log(String msg) throws RemoteException;
}
```

The Home Component Interface

```
package banking;

import javax.ejb.*;
import java.rmi.RemoteException;

public interface LogHome extends EJBHome {

    public Log create(String msg)
        throws CreateException, RemoteException;

    public Log findByPrimaryKey(String key)
        throws FinderException, RemoteException;
}
```

The Bean Implementation Class

```
package banking;

import javax.ejb.*;

public abstract class LogEJB implements EntityBean {

  private EntityContext context;
  public LogEJB() {}

  public void setEntityContext(EntityContext ec) {
    context = ec;
  }

  public void unsetEntityContext() {
    this.context = null;
  }

  public void ejbActivate() {}
  public void ejbPassivate() {}
  public void ejbLoad() {}
  public void ejbStore() {}

public String ejbCreate(String logMessage) throws CreateException {
    setLogMessage(logMessage);
    return null;
  }

  public void ejbPostCreate(String logMessage) {}
  public void ejbRemove() {}

  public void log(String msg) {
      setLogMessage(msg);
  }
```

```
    public abstract String getLogMessage();
    public abstract void setLogMessage(String logMessage);
}
```

The simplest of our three EJBs, LogEJB is responsible only for inserting a logging message into a database. As with the AccountBean, this is accomplished using EJB 2.0 CMP. Notice that, like the Account bean and all EJB 2.0 CMP beans, LogEJB is declared as abstract.

The Application Exceptions

This application defines and uses the following application exception classes:

```
package banking;

public class InsufficientFundsException extends Exception {
  public InsufficientFundsException(String mesg) {
    super(mesg);
  }
}
```

```
package banking;

public class NoAccountCreatedException extends Exception {

  public NoAccountCreatedException(String reason) {
    super( reason );
  }

  public String getReason() {
    return getMessage();
  }
}
```

```
package banking;

public class NoSuchAccountException extends Exception {
  public NoSuchAccountException() {}
}
```

The Deployment Descriptor

Here is the deployment descriptor for these beans, which we can package up into one JAR file:

```
<?xml version="1.0"?>
<!DOCTYPE ejb-jar PUBLIC
  '-//Sun Microsystems, Inc.//DTD Enterprise JavaBeans 2.0//EN'
  'http://java.sun.com/dtd/ejb-jar_2_0.dtd'>

<ejb-jar>

  <enterprise-beans>

    <entity>
      <description>A bank account entity bean</description>
```

```xml
        <ejb-name>Account</ejb-name>
        <home>banking.AccountHome</home>
        <remote>banking.Account</remote>
        <ejb-class>banking.AccountEJB</ejb-class>
        <persistence-type>Container</persistence-type>
        <prim-key-class>java.lang.String</prim-key-class>
        <reentrant>False</reentrant>
        <cmp-version>2.x</cmp-version>
        <abstract-schema-name>AccountBeanSchema</abstract-schema-name>
          <cmp-field>
            <field-name>customerName</field-name>
          </cmp-field>
          <cmp-field>
            <field-name>currentBalance</field-name>
          </cmp-field>
        <primkey-field>customerName</primkey-field>
        <query>
          <query-method>
            <method-name>findByPrimaryKey</method-name>
            <method-params>
              <method-param>java.lang.String</method-param>
            </method-params>
          </query-method>
          <ejb-ql>
            SELECT OBJECT(o)
            FROM AccountBeanSchema o
            WHERE o.customerName = ?1
          </ejb-ql>
        </query>
  </entity>

  <entity>
    <description>A logging entity bean</description>
    <ejb-name>Log</ejb-name>
    <home>banking.LogHome</home>
    <remote>banking.Log</remote>
    <ejb-class>banking.LogEJB</ejb-class>
    <persistence-type>Container</persistence-type>
    <prim-key-class>java.lang.String</prim-key-class>
    <reentrant>False</reentrant>
    <cmp-version>2.x</cmp-version>
    <abstract-schema-name>LogBeanSchema</abstract-schema-name>
      <cmp-field>
        <field-name>logMessage</field-name>
      </cmp-field>
    <primkey-field>logMessage</primkey-field>
    <query>
      <query-method>
        <method-name>findByPrimaryKey</method-name>
        <method-params>
          <method-param>java.lang.String</method-param>
        </method-params>
      </query-method>
      <ejb-ql>
        SELECT OBJECT(o)
        FROM LogBeanSchema o
```

```
            WHERE o.logMessage = ?1
          </ejb-ql>
        </query>
    </entity>

    <session>
      <description>An account manager session bean</description>
      <ejb-name>AccountManager</ejb-name>
      <home>banking.AccountManagerHome</home>
      <remote>banking.AccountManager</remote>
      <ejb-class>banking.AccountManagerEJB</ejb-class>
      <session-type>Stateless</session-type>
      <transaction-type>Container</transaction-type>
      <ejb-ref>
        <ejb-ref-name>account</ejb-ref-name>
        <ejb-ref-type>Entity</ejb-ref-type>
        <home>banking.AccountHome</home>
        <remote>banking.Account</remote>
      </ejb-ref>
      <ejb-ref>
        <ejb-ref-name>log</ejb-ref-name>
        <ejb-ref-type>Entity</ejb-ref-type>
        <home>banking.LogHome</home>
        <remote>banking.Log</remote>
      </ejb-ref>
    </session>

  </enterprise-beans>

  <assembly-descriptor>
    <container-transaction>
      <method>
        <ejb-name>AccountManager</ejb-name>
        <method-name>*</method-name>
      </method>
      <trans-attribute>Required</trans-attribute>
    </container-transaction>
    <container-transaction>
      <method>
        <ejb-name>Log</ejb-name>
        <method-name>*</method-name>
          </method>
      <trans-attribute>Required</trans-attribute>
    </container-transaction>
    <container-transaction>
      <method>
        <ejb-name>Account</ejb-name>
        <method-name>*</method-name>
      </method>
      <trans-attribute>Required</trans-attribute>
    </container-transaction>
  </assembly-descriptor>

</ejb-jar>
```

Issues in Security Management with EJBs

There are three major issues that designers and developers of enterprise applications have to address while dealing with the security of their applications:

❑   Authentication and principal mapping

❑   Authorization

❑   Secure Communication

> **A principal is specified by the Java interface `java.security.Principal` and may represent, abstractly, any entity, such as an individual user, a group of users, a corporation, or a login ID.**

Let's take a closer look at these three issues.

Authentication

Authentication refers to the process of verifying that a client is who they claim to be. Authentication may either be performed on the client before it interacts with the server, or it may be performed by the server. In either case, once a client is authenticated, a **Principal object** (also called a **credential**) is associated with that client.

Authentication on the Client

A client may be authenticated before it contacts the server. This means of authentication is relevant to both EJB-based applications and non-EJB-based applications. The authentication may be performed in a number of ways as listed below:

❑   A client application container may authenticate the user by interacting with an authentication service such as Kerberos (see http://web.mit.edu/kerberos/www/ for more information)

❑   A client application container (the JVM) may inherit the authentication context which was established by the operating system when the user logged in to the system

❑   A client may utilize the user's digital certificate

The authentication mechanisms listed above may be realized by plugging in the appropriate **Java Authentication and Authorization Service (JAAS)** module. Once a client is authenticated, a `Principal` object is associated with the client. Any calls made by this authenticated client to an EJB component, via the remote reference, result in the implicit propagation of this `Principal` to the EJB server.

> *For further information on many aspects of security, have a look at* Professional Java Security, *from Wrox Press, ISBN 1-861004-25-7.*

Authentication on the Server

For those clients that do not have access to any authentication infrastructure in their environment, the client may send the authentication information to the EJB server on a secure connection. The authentication information sent to the server may be as simple as a user-name and password, or it may be as complex as a digitally signed document along with a digital certificate.

When using digital certificates, public key and private key cryptography is used. In this kind of cryptography, we have a pair of related keys called private and public. A document encrypted with one key may only be decrypted with the other key for symmetric cryptography.

For digital certificate-based authentication, a sender sends a document, say M, along with a *digested* and encrypted (in that order) copy of the document M, say M1. Digestion is basically a one-way hashing process and is performed using **Message Digest** algorithms such as MD-5 etc. The encryption is performed using the sender's private key. The receiver, upon receiving both M and M1, passes the document, M, through the Message Digest algorithm and produces a digested document, say M2. The receiver decrypts the received document, M1, using the sender's public key to obtain another document, say M3. The receiver then compares M2 and M3. If they are equal, then the receiver can authenticate the sender.

In any case, the server is now responsible for authenticating the user, perhaps accessing similar authentication services listed in the previous section. Once a client is authenticated a Principal object is, once again, associated with the client. Now it is the server's responsibility to detect call requests from clients and associate the appropriate Principal object with a thread of execution (on the server) that is selected to handle that particular request.

The association of a Principal object with a client's request can be done in a number of server-specific ways. One way to do this, after a successful login, is to store the Principal in the javax.naming.Context object that is created. Any lookup() method invoked by the caller on this Context object, can implicitly pass the Principal information to the server. The server, after instantiating (or finding) the server-side objects, returns client-side proxy objects (remote references), embedded with the Principal information, to the client. Method invocations on these remote references result in the implicit propagation of the Principal and authentication data to the server. This mechanism allows a server to always '*know*' who the caller is.

Authentication mechanisms make use of objects known as **Security Realms** to store and manage authentication information. A Security Realm is a Java object that provides access to storage areas where the definitions of users, groups, passwords and the Access Control List (ACL) are stored. Security Realms, while providing a uniform interface, may be implemented in a number of ways:

- ❑ Flat file storage
- ❑ Using the Operating System (NT, Unix, Windows 2000)
- ❑ LDAP Server-based storage
- ❑ Database storage

Conclusions

For both client-side and server-side authentication, a Principal object is associated with the client after a successful authentication. In the former case, this object is propagated to the server, while in the latter case it resides on the server. In both cases, the server associates this Principal object with the thread of execution that handles the client's request.

It is also important to note that clients do not have to be authenticated; a client may be executed in unauthenticated mode. In this case no Principal object is associated with the server's thread of execution that is selected to handle this request.

Authorization

Authorization refers to the process of checking whether a particular method call request, from a client to an EJB component, should result in the execution of that method. The EJB application assembler may define a number of **security-roles**, in the deployment descriptor, for an application composed of one or more Enterprise JavaBeans.

A security role denotes a group of users, where each member of the group has the same set of privileges, to invoke methods on the component and home interfaces, as the other members of the group. Normally these security roles are mapped to groups in the operating environment, where each member of the group has the privileges associated with the corresponding security role.

> **A security-role is a semantic grouping of method permissions that a client must have in order to successfully invoke those methods. A method permission is a permission to invoke a specified set of methods from the EJB's component interfaces.**

For example, in a banking scenario, the application assembler may define some security roles such as *Administrator, Customer, Teller, Clerk, Receptionist, Manager,* etc. The application assembler can also define declaratively, in the deployment descriptor, method permissions for each security role. These security roles provide a simplified view of the security requirements to the application deployer – the deployer now sees a limited (hopefully) number of security roles as opposed to a potentially larger number of EJB methods.

The application deployer is responsible for associating `Principals` (or groups of `Principals`), which are defined in the operational environment (these could be real users or groups as defined in the operating system), with the security roles defined by the application assembler. At run time, the server detects the `Principal` object associated with the client's method call request. This request results in the method execution if (and only if) the `Principal` object associated with the client has itself been associated by the application deployer with at least one security role that 'contains' the relevant method permission.

The application assembler may also optionally specify a specific security role to be used during execution using the `<run-as>` tag. The application deployer is responsible for associating a `Principal` for this role-name. This enables the application assembler to switch the privileges at run time. We shall discuss this further in the *Application Security Design* section.

As mentioned earlier, the container provider is responsible for providing the tools to generate the objects that enforce the security policies as defined by the application assembler and as customized by the application deployer.

The following diagram illustrates the sequence of operations that occur in a server-based authentication and EJB authorization:

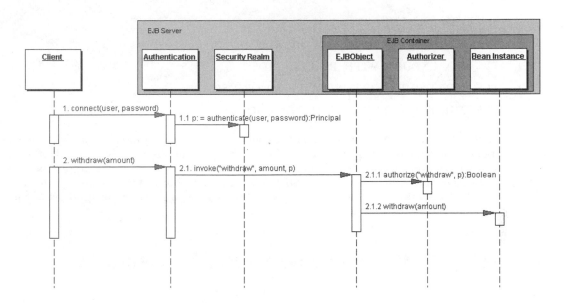

In this case, a user connects to the server specifying the user name and a credential such as a password. The server uses an authenticator and a security realm to authenticate the user. Once a user is authenticated, the server associates a `Principal` object, p, with the user.

The user, after being authenticated, invokes the `withdraw()` method on an `AccountManagerEJB`. The server handles this method call from the client. The server propagates the call to the EJB container after associating the caller's `Principal` object with the thread of execution. In the EJB container, the call is intercepted by the server-side proxy, `EJBObject`.

This proxy uses the authorizer to ensure that the caller's `Principal` object has the authorization to invoke this method, `withdraw()`. If the authorization fails, a security exception is thrown; otherwise the call is propagated to the bean instance.

Secure Communication

A third aspect of security deals with the communication mechanisms used by the EJB clients and servers. Here the EJB vendors may use secure sockets layer (SSL) and other, perhaps proprietary, means of encrypted communication.

Remote invocations to EJB objects use the IIOP protocol. The EJB 2.0 specification requires the support of SSL3.0 (Secure Sockets Layer) and TLS1.0 (Transport Layer Security) security protocols for IIOP. The following SSL and TLS cipher suites are supported:

❑   SSL_RSA_EXPORT_WITH_RC4_40_MD5

❑   SSL_RSA_EXPORT_WITH_RC4_128_MD5

❑   SSL_DHE_DSS_EXPORT_WITH_DES40_CBC_SHA

❑   SSL_DHE_DSS_EXPORT_WITH_DES_CBC_SHA

❑   TLS_RSA_EXPORT_WITH_RC4_40_MD5

❑   TLS_RSA_EXPORT_WITH_RC4_128_MD5

❑   TLS_DHE_DSS_EXPORT_WITH_DES40_CBC_SHA

❑   TLS_DHE_DSS_EXPORT_WITH_DES_CBC_SHA

Before initiating a secure connection to the EJB container, the client needs to know the hostname and port number at which the server is listening for SSL connections, and the security protocols supported or required by the server object. This information is obtained from the `EJBObject` or `EJBHome` reference's Interoperable Object Reference (IOR). It is the responsibility of the container provider to provide tools to specify the encryption strategies and also the tools to generate the appropriate client-side stubs and container classes.

Developing Enterprise JavaBeans for Security

In this section, we will look at how we can develop EJBs with security in mind. In order to incorporate security into our EJBs, we need to know about the following things (and we'll explain why as well):

❑   **Inter-bean security context propagation**
Using this approach, the EJB components, designed with restricted or limited access privileges may be accessed by switching the caller's run-time identity.

❑   **Programmatic security context**
Useful in enforcing security policies at run time through coded security measures.

❑   **Verifying security role membership**
This allows a bean implementation to verify, at run time, whether the current caller belongs to a specified security role.

❑   **Declaring security role references**
Enables the bean provider to inform the application assembler about the security roles that are being referred to from within the bean's implementation, without exposing the bean's source code.

❑   **Accessing the Principal**
This is useful if we want to use the `Principal` object associated with the caller as a key to access some information.

❑   **Resource manager access**
EJB components that access other resources, such as database management systems or message queues, need to be able to propagate the security information to these resources because these resources invariably have their own security requirements.

❑   **Issues in accessing operating-system resources**

We'll start at the top of the list

Inter-Bean Security Context Propagation

An enterprise bean may invoke the home and component interface methods of other beans. The specification does not provide any programmatic way of specifying or controlling the security context propagation.

Typically, the security context associated with the caller of a bean's method is propagated to the invoked bean for the duration of the method execution. It is useful to note that the application assembler and application deployer may override this method of security context propagation.

The management of propagating principals during inter-bean calls may be specified by the application deployer and set up by the administrator in a container-dependent way. This is generally done using deployment tools. It is the responsibility of the bean provider and the application assembler to describe in detail all the principal propagation requirements (if any), for inter-bean method invocations, in the `<description>` field of the deployment descriptor.

Since the AccountManager bean is the source of all calls to the Account bean, we will perform all of our security checking within `AccountManagerEJB`.

Programmatic Access to Security Context

For the most part, the enterprise bean developer must try to keep the bean implementation code free of any security related code. More accurately, we should say:

> **Do not hardcode any security-related logic in the bean implementation. This is important because the bean developer usually does not have sufficient information about the security requirements of the deployment environment. Also hard coding security policies may limit the reusability of a bean.**

Security policies must, where possible, be specified declaratively in the deployment descriptor, and the container must manage them at run time. However, in some (hopefully rare) cases, should the enterprise bean developer need to programmatically access the security context at run time, we may do so by invoking the appropriate methods on an `EJBContext` object. These needs arise in some applications that have special security requirements. For example, an application might make authorization decisions based on the time of day, physical location of the caller, the parameters of a call, or the internal state of an enterprise bean. Another application might restrict access based on user information stored in a database.

Note that for comparative and explanatory purposes, we will be presenting in this section some security measures that, being based in the EJBs themselves, are essentially hard coded. However, we do this in order to demonstrate how *not* to add security to an enterprise-level application. It is possible, say, for a simple bean implementation that is never going beyond your hard-drive, to use hard coded security such as this and get away with it, but not if you expect other people to use your code.

All types of Enterprise JavaBeans (entity, session, and message-driven) are provided with an object at run time called the `EJBContext` object that implements the `javax.ejb.EJBContext` interface. This context object encapsulates the security and transaction contexts and provides the methods to access them. The two methods to access the security context are:

```
    public interface EJBContext {

//Other methods

    public boolean isCallerInRole(String role_name);

    public java.security.Principal getCallerPrincipal();
}
```

isCallerInRole()

Tests if the caller has a given security role. The method returns `true` if the caller has the role specified by the `role_name` parameter. There is also a deprecated version of this method, which takes a `java.security.Identity`.

getCallerPrincipal()

Returns the `java.security.Principal` object that identifies the caller. This return value is never `null`.

These methods should normally only be invoked from those business methods of an enterprise bean for which the container has a client security context.

Verifying Security Role Membership

If the enterprise bean needs to verify at run time if the current method invoker belongs to a security role, it may do so by invoking the `isCallerInRole()` method. This method should only be used for those security checks that cannot be easily specified declaratively using method permissions in the deployment descriptor.

This is useful for encoding role-based limits on requests. The role name used may also be determined at run time, but the list of all role name references must be declared in the deployment descriptor. The example below shows a partial implementation of the `AccountManager` bean, where we verify that the `createAccount()` method is being invoked by a caller belonging to the security-role (as defined by the bean developer) `AccountCreator`:

```
public class AccountManagerEJB implements javax.ejb.SessionBean {
  javax.ejb.EJBContext myContext;

  public void setSessionContext(javax.ejb.SessionContext ctx) {
    this.myContext = ctx;
  }

  public static final String CLIENT = "Client";
  public static final String BANK = "Bank";

  public Account createAccount(String customerName,
                               double initialBalance) throws
                               NoAccountCreatedException, RemoteException,
                               MethodNotAllowedException {
  logActivity(CREATEACCOUNT, customerName);

    checkSecurity(CREATEACCOUNT, BANK);
```

```
        try {
          AccountHome accountHome = getAccountHome();
          accountHome.create(customerName, initialBalance);
        } catch (CreateException ce) {
          throw new NoAccountCreatedException(ce.getMessage());
        } catch (RemoteException re) {
          throw new EJBException(re);
        }
      }
    }
```

Since we're going to be performing a lot of security checking, we use a convenience method, checkSecurity(). The first variable passed is the same as for the logActivity() method, and details the method that is calling checkSecurity(). The second parameter represents the role in which the caller must be to be allowed to proceed. Both parameters are final static string variables, and we have added two more to the AccountManagerEJB class to represent the allowed roles. This code is simple, although the power it grants us to confirm security permissions is not to be underestimated:

```
    private void checkSecurity(String methodCalledFrom, String requiredRole)
                          throws MethodNotAllowedException {

      if (!this.context.isCallerInRole(requiredRole)) {
        throw new MethodNotAllowedException("Not a " + requiredRole +
                                            ", you're not allowed to " +
                                            methodCalledFrom);
      }
    }
```

We have also included a new exception, MethodNotAllowedException, which can be simply defined as follows:

```
package banking;

public class MethodNotAllowedException extends java.lang.Exception {
  public MethodNotAllowedException(String mesg) {
    super(mesg);
  }
}
```

The security context that is propagated can be switched by specifying a different Principal in the deployment descriptor using the XML element, <run-as>. This is discussed in greater detail later in the chapter. However, the method invocation, isCallerInRole(requiredRole), tests the Principal that represents the caller of the method and not the Principal that corresponds to the <run-as> tag.

Adding this Principal-checking code to the rest of the business methods of AccountManagerEJB is as simple as adding the call to checkSecurity() after the call to logActivity(). Here are the changed parts of the other business methods:

```
    public void deposit(String customerName,
                        double amount) throws MethodNotAllowedException {

    logActivity(DEPOSIT, customerName);
    checkSecurity(DEPOSIT, CLIENT);
// rest of method
  }
```

```
    public double withdraw(String customerName, double amount)
            throws MethodNotAllowedException, InsufficientFundsException {
    System.out.println("withdraw called");

    logActivity(WITHDRAW, customerName);
    checkSecurity(WITHDRAW, CLIENT);
// rest of method
    }


    public double getBalance(String customerName) throws MethodNotAllowedException {

        logActivity(GETBALANCE, customerName);
        checkSecurity(GETBALANCE, CLIENT);
// rest of method
    }


    public double calculateInterest(String customerName)
            throws MethodNotAllowedException {

        logActivity(CALCULATEINTEREST, customerName);
        checkSecurity(CALCULATEINTEREST, BANK);
// rest of method
    }
```

It should go without saying that the changes in the implementation methods should be reflected in the remote interface, where all these methods should also be declared to throw the new `MethodNotAllowedException`.

Declaring Security Role References

Entity and session beans that make references to security role names from within their code must have this fact declared in the deployment descriptor. This gives the application assembler (who may not have access to the bean source code) an idea of the security roles being referred to from within the guts of the enterprise bean.

It is also important to note that the security role name being referred to is an abstract security-role reference, and *not* the security role that the application assembler defines. This mechanism frees the bean developer to use any security role name that they wish to use. The bean developer is responsible for declaring, using the `<security-role-ref>` tag, all the security role names used in the bean's source code (in the call `isCallerInRole()`). The application assembler is responsible for linking this security role reference with the security role the application assembler defines.

The following example shows how the bean developer may specify the security role reference in the `ejb-jar.xml` deployment descriptor:

```
    <session>

      <security-role-ref>
        <role-name>Client</role-name>
        <role-link>Client</role-link>
      </security-role-ref>
      <security-role-ref>
```

```
            <role-name>Bank</role-name>
            <role-link>Bank</role-link>
        </security-role-ref>

    </session>
```

Note that the `<security-role-ref>` element is valid only for session and entity beans and may not be specified for message-driven beans. Message-driven beans are always invoked by the container, using the `Principal` object associated with the container and are not executed using the caller's security context.

We're taking a simple approach here – we are linking security roles to other security roles of the same name. Each `<security-role-ref>` element contains a `role-name` and a `role-link`, which, as we'll see later in more detail, serve to link the security role in the `role-name` element to a security role in the `role-link`, which is specified outside of the application. We'll come back to this in the *Mapping Security Role References to Security Roles* section.

Here is a graphical representation of the `<security-role-ref>` element:

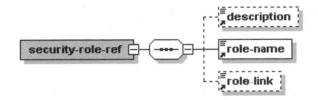

Accessing the Principal

The declarative security policies of EJB may only be specified at a class level. This can potentially be a problem if you are looking for instance-level security. In our banking example, we have an `Account` object with business methods to handle deposits and withdrawals. All members of the bank (our users) clearly need to be given privileges to execute these methods, but only on their own instances.

Unfortunately there is no way to specify this declaratively in EJB. However, the `Principal` object associated with the caller (unless it has been remapped by some intervening middleware) is available through the `EJBContext` object.

The bean developer may access the `Principal` object associated with the current thread of execution by invoking the method `getCallerPrincipal()` on its `EJBContext` object. This is another example of 'hard-coding' security logic in the bean code. The developer may access the distinguished name of the principal by invoking the `getName()` method on the `Principal` object.

We have a cmp field in the `AccountEJB` bean, called `customerName`, which represents the owner of this account. Further we also assume that this name is exactly the same as the name of the `Principal` object associated with the caller. The following partial sample code demonstrates the use of this method:

```
public abstract class AccountEJB implements EntityBean {

  private EntityContext context;

  public double withdraw(double amount)
         throws AccountAccessDeniedException, InsufficientFundsException {

    java.security.Principal p;
    p = this.context.getCallerPrincipal();

    if (!p.equals(getCustomerName())) {
      throw new AccountAccessDeniedException(p.getName() +
                                      " does not have access " +
                                      "to this account");
    }

    if (amount > getCurrentBalance()) {
      throw new InsufficientFundsException("Account does not have "
                                      + amount);
    } else {
      setCurrentBalance(getCurrentBalance() - amount);
      return getCurrentBalance();
    }
  }
}
```

The new version of this method is declared to throw another new exception, `AccountAccessDeniedException`, which can be implemented as follows:

```
package banking;

public class AccountAccessDeniedException extends java.lang.Exception {
  public AccountAccessDeniedException(String mesg) {
    super(mesg);
  }
}
```

As with the previous new exception we introduced, the addition to the `withdraw()` method in `AccountEJB` of the `AccountAccessDeniedException` will require the Account interface to be updated to reflect this. In this case, we'll also have to update the `withdraw()` method declaration in the `AccountManager` interface, and its implementation in the `AccountManagerEJB` class.

Note that in a real application, we would want to extend this security checking to *all* the methods, not just `withdraw()`. If we did this, we would probably also want to not include this code in each method, so we would write another convenience method like `logActivity()` and `checkSecurity()`, called perhaps `verifyOwner()`.

We implement this level of security checking on the `AccountEJB` as an extra check in case the `AccountManagerEJB` somehow connects to the wrong Account instance.

Resource Manager Access

Enterprise JavaBeans may need to access other enterprise-wide resources such as database management systems and message-oriented middleware. Both these kinds of resources have their own security requirements. The bean provider must use resource manager connection factories to create connections to these resources. The reference to a factory is obtained through a JNDI-based naming service.

The bean provider has two choices with regards to dealing with associating a principal with the resource manager access as shown below. The bean provider uses the `<res-auth>` tag in the deployment descriptor to indicate which of the two resource manager authentication methods are used:

❑ Allow the application deployer to set up principal mapping or resource manager sign-on information such as user name and password. In this case, the EJB code invokes a resource manager connection factory method that has no security-related parameters. Thus:

```
<res-auth>Container</res-auth>
```

❑ Sign on to the resource manager from the enterprise bean's code. In this case, the enterprise bean provides all the sign-on, authentication information as method parameters to the appropriate resource manager connection factory methods. Thus:

```
<res-auth>Application</res-auth>
```

Issues in Accessing Operating System Resources

The EJB specification does not define the operating system principal under which enterprise bean methods execute. This implies that the bean provider cannot depend on a specific principal for accessing the underlying operating system resources such as files. The EJB designers envision that data will be stored in resource managers such as database management systems and not plain files, and hence this should not affect the portability of most Enterprise JavaBeans.

Conclusions

So, we have seen that when we are developing EJBs with security, there are several things to bear in mind:

❑ Try to avoid hard-coding the security mechanisms in the bean code

❑ Let the application assembler and application deployer specify the security policies in the deployment descriptor

❑ Let the container tools generate the appropriate objects that enforce the security policies at run time

Following these simple guidelines should lead to a portable and easily maintainable EJB-based application.

The New Deployment Descriptor

Since we have a sample application to which we have been adding code, we should update the `ejb-jar.xml` file accordingly:

```xml
<?xml version="1.0" encoding="UTF-8"?>

<!DOCTYPE ejb-jar PUBLIC
    '-//Sun Microsystems, Inc.//DTD Enterprise JavaBeans 2.0//EN'
    'http://java.sun.com/dtd/ejb-jar_2_0.dtd'>

<ejb-jar>
  <display-name>HardSecuredBankBean</display-name>

  <enterprise-beans>
    <entity>
      <display-name>AccountBean</display-name>
      <ejb-name>AccountBean</ejb-name>
      <home>banking.AccountHome</home>
      <remote>banking.Account</remote>
      <ejb-class>banking.AccountEJB</ejb-class>
      <persistence-type>Container</persistence-type>
      <prim-key-class>java.lang.String</prim-key-class>
      <reentrant>False</reentrant>
      <cmp-version>2.x</cmp-version>
      <abstract-schema-name>AccountBeanSchema</abstract-schema-name>
      <cmp-field>
        <description>no description</description>
        <field-name>customerName</field-name>
      </cmp-field>
      <cmp-field>
        <description>no description</description>
        <field-name>currentBalance</field-name>
      </cmp-field>
      <primkey-field>customerName</primkey-field>
      <security-identity>
        <description></description>
        <use-caller-identity></use-caller-identity>
      </security-identity>
    </entity>

    <session>
      <display-name>HardAccountManager</display-name>
      <ejb-name>HardAccountManager</ejb-name>
      <home>banking.AccountManagerHome</home>
      <remote>banking.AccountManager</remote>
      <ejb-class>banking.HardAccountManagerEJB</ejb-class>
      <session-type>Stateless</session-type>
      <transaction-type>Container</transaction-type>
      <ejb-ref>
        <ejb-ref-name>ejb/log</ejb-ref-name>
        <ejb-ref-type>Entity</ejb-ref-type>
        <home>banking.LogHome</home>
        <remote>banking.Log</remote>
      </ejb-ref>
      <ejb-ref>
        <ejb-ref-name>ejb/account</ejb-ref-name>
        <ejb-ref-type>Entity</ejb-ref-type>
        <home>banking.AccountHome</home>
        <remote>banking.Account</remote>
      </ejb-ref>
```

```
            <security-role-ref>
              <role-name>Client</role-name>
              <role-link>Client</role-link>
            </security-role-ref>
            <security-role-ref>
              <role-name>Bank</role-name>
              <role-link>Bank</role-link>
            </security-role-ref>
            <security-identity>
              <description></description>
              <use-caller-identity></use-caller-identity>
            </security-identity>
          </session>

          <entity>
            <display-name>LogBean</display-name>
            <ejb-name>LogBean</ejb-name>
            <home>banking.LogHome</home>
            <remote>banking.Log</remote>
            <ejb-class>banking.LogEJB</ejb-class>
            <persistence-type>Container</persistence-type>
            <prim-key-class>java.lang.String</prim-key-class>
            <reentrant>False</reentrant>
            <cmp-version>2.x</cmp-version>
            <abstract-schema-name>LogBeanSchema</abstract-schema-name>
            <cmp-field>
              <description>no description</description>
              <field-name>logMessage</field-name>
            </cmp-field>
            <primkey-field>logMessage</primkey-field>
            <security-identity>
              <description></description>
              <use-caller-identity></use-caller-identity>
            </security-identity>
          </entity>
        </enterprise-beans>

        <assembly-descriptor>
          <security-role>
            <description>systems admin</description>
            <role-name>Administrator</role-name>
          </security-role>
          <security-role>
            <description>Account holding customers</description>
            <role-name>Client</role-name>
          </security-role>
          <security-role>
            <description>Employees</description>
            <role-name>Bank</role-name>
          </security-role>
        </assembly-descriptor>

      </ejb-jar>
```

As you can see, there are only a few changes to be made. In the next section, however, we'll be changing the deployment descriptor far more as we look at declarative security.

Application Security Design

In this section, we will take a look at declarative security for our simple banking application. In order to show all the elements available to us, some of the examples will be using fictional beans. Once we have implemented all the declarative security measure we are about to discuss, we will be able to remove the hard-coded security elements that we implemented in the last section.

The application assembler (as formally specified in the EJB specification) refers to the person who is responsible for building applications using the Enterprise JavaBeans. Although it is not unusual for an application assembler to implement enterprise beans (this is a scenario where the application assembler also plays the role of a bean provider), typically the application assembler collects or purchases enterprise beans from various bean providers to construct (assemble) an application.

The application assembler may define the logical security view of the application. The EJB architecture enables the application assembler to define the security view in a way that best reflects the security requirements of the application.

The **security view** basically consists of a set of security roles. A set of enterprise bean home and component interface methods are associated with each such security role. This association of a method with a security role implicitly defines a **method permission**. A caller associated with a security role is only allowed to invoke the EJB methods associated with their security role (or roles, as a caller may be associated with more than one security role). If a caller tries to invoke an enterprise bean method that does not figure in the list of methods associated with any of the security roles they are associated with, then the container throws a security exception.

It is optional for the application assembler to define the security view as described above, but in most cases the application assembler is best suited to perform this step anyway. Doing so greatly simplifies the application deployer's job as the deployer is presented with a consolidated security view of the application. All the deployer has to do, in this case, is to map the logical security roles to real users or groups in the operating environment. The mechanics of this task are container-dependent.

If the application assembler does not define the logical security roles, the deployer will need a detailed knowledge of all the home and component interface methods of all the enterprise beans that compose the application in order to securely deploy the application. Specifically, the deployer needs to understand what each of the methods does in order to determine whether a given caller may or may not invoke it. Clearly this places an unreasonable burden on the deployer who may not be very familiar with the application, its components, or their intended individual uses.

The application assembler also needs to link the security roles (if any) with the security role references (if any) made by the bean developers.

This is how the three main roles interact with regard to security:

❑ The bean provider specifies in the code which of the security roles they define in the deployment descriptor may access which methods, denying access to callers who are not in the appropriate role ("Client" or "Bank" in our case).

❑ The application assembler takes these defined roles, and maps them to the security groups they have defined, based on which groups need what level of access.

❑ Finally, the deployer maps these security groups to groups of users on the system.

In the rest of this section, we will now look at the following aspects of application security design:

- ❑ Defining application security roles

- ❑ Mapping security role references to security roles

- ❑ Specifying method-level permissions

- ❑ Specifying an exclude list

- ❑ Security identities

- ❑ Security context propagation

Let's start with the top item on the list.

Defining Application Security Roles

The application assembler may define one or more security roles using the `<security-role>` tag in the `<assembly-descriptor>` part of the deployment descriptor document. It is important to remember that these security roles are logical roles that represent the application's security view and should not be confused with the user groups, principals, or other security related concepts that may exist in the target application server's operational environment. Each security role logically represents a set of users that have identical access privileges to the application.

The security roles, as defined in the deployment descriptor, apply to all the enterprise beans specified there. Since all such enterprise beans are packaged in the same EJB JAR file, the security roles are scoped and apply to all the enterprise beans contained in the same JAR file.

Defining a security role entails the following steps:

1. Define the security role using the `<security-role>` element

2. Use the `<role-name>` element to specify the security role name

3. Use the `<description>` element to provide the documentation for the intended use of this security role. This step is optional.

Here is a graphical representation of the `<security-role>` element:

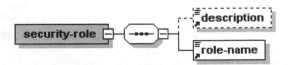

The example below demonstrates how an application assembler may define the security roles for a banking application. In this example, we shall define the following security roles:

- ❑ Administrator
- ❑ Customer
- ❑ PreferredCustomer
- ❑ Teller
- ❑ Manager

445

```
...
<assembly-descriptor>
  <security-role>
    <description>
      This role represents the system administrators of this
      application. Members belonging to this role must be given
      privileges to execute all methods of all components.
    </description>
    <role-name>Administrator</role-name>
  </security-role>

  <security-role>
    <description>
      This role represents customers of the bank. Members
      belonging to this role must be given access to query their
      accounts and also the privileged access to other member
      services offered by the bank such as currency conversion
      rates, loan information etc.
    </description>
    <role-name>Customer</role-name>
  </security-role>

  <security-role>
    <description>
      This role represents preferred customers of the bank.
      Members belonging to this role must be given all the
      privileges to the "Customer" role. The bank may also offer
      some additional personal banking services (through some
      specialized components), better interest rates etc.
    </description>
    <role-name>PreferredCustomer</role-name>
  </security-role>

  <security-role>
    <description>
      This role represents the tellers at the bank. Members
      belonging to this role must be given access to query all
      accounts and perform transfers on behalf of customers.
    </description>
    <role-name>Teller</role-name>
  </security-role>

  <security-role>
    <description>
      This role represents the managers at the bank. Members
      belonging to this role must be given all the privileges of
      a "Teller". In addition, members belonging to this role
      may also be given the privilege to create new accounts.
    </description>
    <role-name>Manager</role-name>
  </security-role>

</assembly-descriptor>
```

In the example above, the application assembler has basically defined a set of security roles that satisfy the requirements of a banking application. The <description> tag is used to provide the documentation of the security view. The application deployer is the intended audience for this documentation. It also has to be acknowledged that this is a rather informal way of presenting information.

Note that for the purposes of our example application, we shall only be using two of these roles, Customer and Manager. However, we will continue to demonstrate applying security roles with the full range shown here.

Mapping Security Role References to Security Roles

As mentioned earlier, the application assembler may use enterprise beans developed by various bean providers. The bean providers may make references to security roles' names from their code as long as they advertise this fact in their deployment descriptors. Given that bean providers are free to choose any name they want for the security role references, it is possible that two vendors of enterprise beans may use the same security role name but with different semantic interpretations.

Consider the example below:

```
<session>
  <ejb-name>AccountManager</ejb-name>
  <ejb-class>AccountManagerEJB</ejb-class>
  ...
  <security-role-ref>
    <role-name>Client</role-name>
  </security-role-ref>
  ...
</session>
```

And now a second bean we might want to use (once it's been added to the application):

```
<session>
  <ejb-name>CurrencyExchange</ejb-name>
  <ejb-class>CurrencyExchangeEJB</ejb-class>
  ...
  <security-role-ref>
    <role-name>Client</role-name>
  </security-role-ref>
  ...
</session>
```

In this example, the application assembler has collected two beans, AccountEJB and CurrencyExchangeEJB. Both these beans make references to a security role name, Client.

The application assembler might want to associate their Customer security role with the Client role as specified by AccountEJB, and their PreferredCustomer role with the Client role as specified by CurrencyExchangeEJB.

Similarly, the application assembler might also be presented with a pair of enterprise beans provided by two different vendors who make references to distinct security role names that have the same semantics. Consider the following example:

```
<session>
  <ejb-name>AccountManager</ejb-name>
  <ejb-class>AccountManagerEJB</ejb-class>
  ...
  <security-role-ref>
    <role-name>Client</role-name>
  </security-role-ref>
  ...
</session>
```

And the second bean (another one that might be added to the application later); same semantics for the security role, different name:

```
<session>
  <ejb-name>LoanArranger</ejb-name>
  <ejb-class>LoanArrangerEJB</ejb-class>
  ...
  <security-role-ref>
    <role-name>Bank</role-name>
  </security-role-ref>
  ...
</session>
```

In the example above, the application uses the two enterprise beans `AccountMAnagerEJB` and `LoanArrangerEJB` that make references to security role names `Client` and `User` respectively. The application assembler might want to associate both these roles with their own security role `Customer`.

Since bean providers in general are independently operating entities, cases such as those mentioned above are not uncommon. If the application assembler has defined security roles (like `Customer` in this case) using the `<security-role>` tag elements in the deployment descriptor, then they are responsible for linking them with the security role references made by bean providers.

In order to provide this linkage, the application assembler modifies the `<security-role-reference>` part of the deployment descriptor specified by the bean provider by inserting the tag entry `<role-link>`. For the two cases mentioned above, the application assembler should modify the deployment descriptor as shown below:

```
<session>
  <ejb-name>AccountManager</ejb-name>
  <ejb-class>AccountManagerEJB</ejb-class>
  ...
  <security-role-ref>
    <role-name>Client</role-name>
    <role-link>Customer</role-link>
  </security-role-ref>
  ...
</session>

<session>
  <ejb-name>CurrencyExchange</ejb-name>
  <ejb-class>CurrencyExchangeEJB</ejb-class>
  ...
  <security-role-ref>
```

```
            <role-name>Client</role-name>
            <role-link>PreferredCustomer</role-link>
         </security-role-ref>
         ...
      </session>

      <session>
         <ejb-name>LoanArranger</ejb-name>
         <ejb-class>LoanArrangerEJB</ejb-class>
         ...
         <security-role-ref>
            <role-name>Bank</role-name>
            <role-link>Customer</role-link>
         </security-role-ref>
         ...
      </session>
```

The example above demonstrates how the application assembler specifies that security role names defined in the previous section, Customer and PreferredCustomer, should be linked with the bean providers' security role references Client and User. It is important to note that the linkage is necessary even if the security role name and the security role reference name are identical, as they are in our sample application.

Specifying Method-Level Permissions

The application assembler, after defining the security roles, may also associate methods from the home and component interfaces of the session and entity beans with the security roles. The security roles are those that are specified by the application assembler and not the ones specified by the bean provider. Note that method-level permissions cannot be specified for message-driven beans because a message driven bean does not have either a component or home interface. Its sole 'business' method, onMessage(), is invoked by the container.

Method permissions are defined in the deployment descriptor using the <method-permission> tag. Each such permission associates one or more security roles with one or more methods of the home and component interfaces. It is useful to think of a method permission as a binary relation from the set of security roles to the set of methods of the home and component interfaces of the session and entity beans. This relation includes the tuple *(Sr, Bm)* if and only if the security role *Sr* is granted the privilege to invoke the bean method *Bm*.

Here is a graphical representation of the method-permission element:

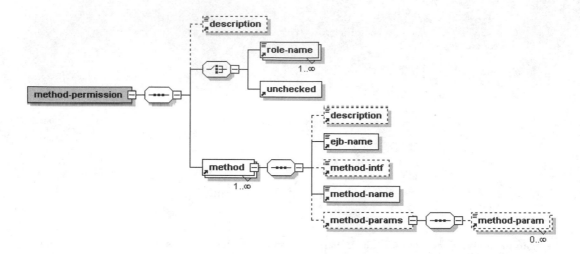

Each <method-permission> element includes one or more security roles and one or more methods. The security roles are denoted by the <security-role> element, and the methods are denoted by the <method> element. The application assembler may also include an optional <description> element.

A security role or a method may appear in more than one <method-permission> element in the deployment descriptor.

There are three ways to specify the <method> element within the <method-permission> element:

- ❑ **Style 1**:

```
<method>
  <ejb-name>AccountManager</ejb-name>
  <method-name>*</method-name>
</method>
```

This style is used to represent all the component and home interface methods (including their super-interface such as EJBObject and EJBHome) of the enterprise bean represented by the <ejb-name> AccountManager. This short hand form is useful if we want to specify the same privilege to all the methods of an enterprise bean.

- ❑ **Style 2**:

```
<method>
  <ejb-name>AccountManager</ejb-name>
  <method-name>deposit</method-name>
</method>
```

This style is used to refer to a specific method from the component or home interface of the named enterprise bean. If the method is overloaded, this description refers to all the methods (from both the component and home interface) with this name.

- ❑ **Style 3**:

```
<method>
  <ejb-name>AccountManager</ejb-name>
```

```
    <method-name>deposit</method-name>
    <method-params>
      <method-param>double</method-param>
    </method-params>
  </method>
  <method>
    <ejb-name>AccountManager</ejb-name>
    <method-name>deposit</method-name>
    <method-params>
      <method-param>double</method-param>
      <method-param>java.util.Date</method-param>
    </method-params>
  </method>
```

> This style is useful in denoting a specific method if the method name is overloaded. This method must be either in the home or the component interface of the enterprise bean. In the above example, the deposit() method is overloaded – one method takes a double as a parameter, while the other takes a double and a Date object.

For those cases where a method (with the same signature) appears both in the home and component interface of an enterprise bean, we need a way to distinguish between them. To denote a method from a specific interface, we can also use the optional <method-intf> element.

The possible values for this element are Home and Remote. Let us assume that the enterprise bean AccountManager has a method in its home interface called createAccount(), and method in its remote interface also called createAccount(). The following example shows how we may identify the version of createAccount() in the remote interface:

```
<method>
  <ejb-name>AccountManager</ejb-name>
  <method-name>createAccount</method-name>
  <method-intf>Remote</method-intf>
</method>
```

The <method-intf> element can be used with any of the three styles of denoting methods discussed above.

In the following example we will grant the security role Administrator the privilege to invoke all the methods for the beans in the application (including the yet to be added CurrencyExchange and LoanArranger). The security role Customer will be granted privileges to invoke the methods on the AccountManager bean. The security role PreferredCustomer will be granted privileges to invoke the methods on the MyAccount bean and the remote interface for the CurenncyExchange bean. The security role Manager will be granted privileges to invoke the methods on the LoanArranger bean and all the methods of MyAccountManager bean. The following table summarizes the security policy:

EJB	Administrator	Customer	PreferredCustomer	Manager
AccountManager	All methods	Some methods	Some methods	All methods
CurrencyExchange (remote)	All methods	None	All methods	All methods

Table continued on following page

EJB	Administrator	Customer	PreferredCustomer	Manager
LoanArranger	All methods	None	None	All methods
LogBean	All-methods	None	None	None

The partial deployment descriptor shown below lists all the method permissions for various roles. The permissions for the security role PreferredCustomer are defined in two distinct method permission segments:

```
<method-permission>
  <role-name>Administrator</role-name>
  <method>
    <ejb-name>AccountManager</ejb-name>
    <method-name>*</method-name>
  </method>
  <method>
    <ejb-name>CurrencyExchange</ejb-name>
    <method-name>*</method-name>
  </method>
  <method>
    <ejb-name>LoanArranger</ejb-name>
    <method-name>*</method-name>
  </method>
  <method>
    <ejb-name>LogBean</ejb-name>
    <method-name>*</method-name>
  </method>
</method-permission>


<method-permission>
  <role-name>Customer</role-name>
  <role-name>PreferredCustomer</role-name>
  <method>
    <ejb-name>Account</ejb-name>
    <method-name>deposit</method-name>
  </method>
  <method>
    <ejb-name>Account</ejb-name>
    <method-name>withdraw</method-name>
  </method>
  <method>
    <ejb-name>Account</ejb-name>
    <method-name>getBalance</method-name>
  </method>
</method-permission>

<method-permission>
  <role-name>PreferredCustomer</role-name>
  <method>
    <ejb-name>CurrencyExchange</ejb-name>
    <method-name>*</method-name>
  <method-intf>Remote</method-intf>
  </method>
```

```
    </method-permission>

  <method-permission>
    <role-name>Manager</role-name>
    <method>
      <ejb-name>AccountManager</ejb-name>
      <method-name>*</method-name>
    </method>
    <method>
      <ejb-name>CurrencyExchange</ejb-name>
      <method-name>*</method-name>
    </method>
    <method>
      <ejb-name>LoanArranger</ejb-name>
      <method-name>*</method-name>
    </method>
  </method-permission>
```

Specifying an Exclude List

For those times when you absolutely, positively have to stop a method being called, ever, use the
<exclude-list> element. This element, like most in the ejb-jar.xml file, is fairly self-
explanatory – it prevents the specified method(s) from being run.

But why, you might ask, would we want to write the method if we then don't use it? The answer is that
we might not have written the bean ourselves, and upon inspection of this third-party EJB we might
decide that one or more of the methods it implements are just not suitable for our environment. Rather
than editing the code of the bean (which may not be possible), we can declare an <exclude-list>
element in the deployment descriptor, as follows:

```
  <exclude-list>
    <description>
      An optional description of the methods we're excluding
    </description>
    <method>
      <description>
        Optional description for each method we exclude
      </description>
      <ejb-name>NameOfEJBWithMethod</ejb-name>
      <method-intf>OptionalInterfaceClarification</method-intf>
      <method-name>nameOfMethodToExclude</method-name>
      <method-params>
        <method-param>Optional parameters </method-param>
      <method-params>
    </method>
  </exclude-list>
```

Here is a graphical representation of the <exclude-list> element:

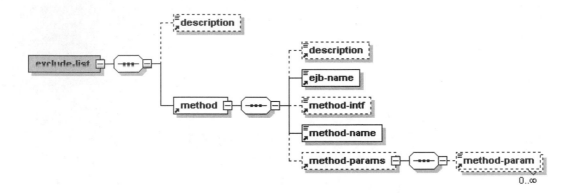

Security Identities

The application assembler may optionally specify a security identity to be associated with the thread of execution while executing the enterprise bean's home or component interface methods (and any other method calls in the chain). The security identity may be specified using the `<security-identity>` element in the deployment descriptor.

If the application assembler chooses not to pass any instructions regarding security identities to the deployer, then they need not specify this element in the deployment descriptor. The `<security-identity>` element may take one of the following two values:

❑   `<use-caller-identity>`

❑   `<run-as>`

Specifying `use-caller-identity` causes the container to use the caller's `Principal` object while executing any method on this bean. `<use-caller-identity>` cannot be specified for message-driven beans. Message-driven beans may have the `<run-as>` attribute defined.

If you want to execute a method with a specific `Principal`'s security context, you may specify it explicitly using the element `<run-as>`. This is explained in the next section.

Here is a graphical representation of the `<security-identity>` element:

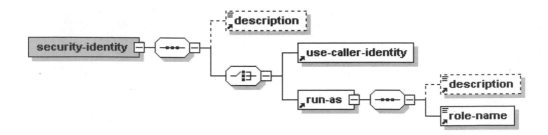

Security Context Propagation

It is useful in some cases to change the security identity associated with the thread of execution while invoking a method on the enterprise bean. Consider the following scenario in our banking application.

We may wish to provide the Manager security role, as we have done in the previous section, the privileges to execute all the methods on the AccountManager bean. Let's say that our application requires us to log all operations, performed on the Account bean, in some log database. We may implement an entity bean called LogBean to perform the logging operations and store the log information in the log database.

The entity bean LogBean may be specified as follows in the deployment descriptor.

```
<enterprise-beans>
  <entity>
    <ejb-name>LogBean</ejb-name>
    <ejb-class>LogEJB</ejb-class>
    ...
  </entity>
</enterprise-beans>
```

Since most databases support a limited number of users (and in any case we do not want to create a database user account for every customer in our bank), all the calls to the LogBean (and indirectly to the log database) must be performed as if a single user is executing them, say the Administrator. This arrangement basically enables us to get away with creating a single database user account, say Administrator, on the log database. In our simple scenario, all calls to the LogBean originate in the AccountManager entity bean. Also we do not want the Manager role (or any role other than the Administrator role) to invoke any methods on the LogBean.

To ensure that the LogBean is only available to the Administrator role, we specify the following in the deployment descriptor:

```
<assembly-descriptor>
  <method-permission>
    <role-name>Administrator</role-name>
    <method>
      <ejb-name>LogBean</ejb-name>
      <method-name>*</method-name>
    </method>
  </method-permission>
</assembly-descriptor>
```

To ensure that all operations on the AccountManager bean execute with the security identity of the Administrator role, we must update the entry for the AccountManager entity bean as shown below:

```
<entity>
  <ejb-name>AccountManager</ejb-name>
  <ejb-class>AccountManagerEJB</ejb-class>
  ...
  <security-identity>
    <run-as>
      <role-name>Administrator</role-name>
```

```
        </run-as>
      </security-identity>
    <security-role-ref>
      <description>
         This role refers to the manager of this bank
      </description>
      <role-name>Manager</role-name>
    </security-role-ref>
    ...
  </entity>
```

Note that the role name specified for the <run-as> element (Administrator) is the logical security role name defined by the application assembler in the *Defining Application Security Roles* section. This is useful since the application assembler usually does not have any information about the security environment in which the application will be deployed and executed.

The deployer assigns a security principal, defined in the deployed operational environment, to be used as the principal for the identity specified in <run-as>. The security principal, thus assigned, must be a principal that has been assigned to the security role specified by the <role-name> element.

In summary, members belonging to the AccountManager role may not access the LogBean directly, but may do so indirectly through the AccountManager bean.

The New Deployment Descriptor

Since we've made quite a few changes here (in fact, a lot since all the security for the application is now declared in the deployment descriptor), here is the new version of the ejb-jar.xml file for our BankingBean:

```xml
<?xml version="1.0" encoding="UTF-8"?>

<!DOCTYPE ejb-jar PUBLIC
    '-//Sun Microsystems, Inc.//DTD Enterprise JavaBeans 2.0//EN'
    'http://java.sun.com/dtd/ejb-jar_2_0.dtd'>

<ejb-jar>
  <display-name>DeclaredSecureBankingBean</display-name>

  <enterprise-beans>
    <entity>
      <display-name>LogBean</display-name>
      <ejb-name>LogBean</ejb-name>
      <home>banking.LogHome</home>
      <remote>banking.Log</remote>
      <ejb-class>banking.LogEJB</ejb-class>
      <persistence-type>Container</persistence-type>
      <prim-key-class>java.lang.String</prim-key-class>
      <reentrant>False</reentrant>
      <cmp-version>2.x</cmp-version>
      <abstract-schema-name>LogBeanSchema</abstract-schema-name>
      <cmp-field>
        <description>no description</description>
        <field-name>logMessage</field-name>
      </cmp-field>
      <primkey-field>logMessage</primkey-field>
```

```
      <security-identity>
        <description></description>
        <run-as>
          <description></description>
          <role-name>Administrator</role-name>
        </run-as>
      </security-identity>
    </entity>

    <session>
      <display-name>AccountManagerBean</display-name>
      <ejb-name>AccountManagerBean</ejb-name>
      <home>banking.AccountManagerHome</home>
      <remote>banking.AccountManager</remote>
      <ejb-class>banking.AccountManagerEJB</ejb-class>
      <session-type>Stateless</session-type>
      <transaction-type>Bean</transaction-type>
      <ejb-ref>
        <ejb-ref-name>ejb/log</ejb-ref-name>
        <ejb-ref-type>Entity</ejb-ref-type>
        <home>banking.LogHome</home>
        <remote>banking.Log</remote>
      </ejb-ref>
      <ejb-ref>
        <ejb-ref-name>ejb/account</ejb-ref-name>
        <ejb-ref-type>Entity</ejb-ref-type>
        <home>banking.AccountHome</home>
        <remote>banking.Account</remote>
      </ejb-ref>
      <security-role-ref>
        <role-name>Client</role-name>
        <role-link>Client</role-link>
      </security-role-ref>
      <security-role-ref>
        <role-name>Bank</role-name>
        <role-link>Bank</role-link>
      </security-role-ref>
      <security-identity>
        <description></description>
        <use-caller-identity></use-caller-identity>
      </security-identity>
    </session>

    <entity>
      <display-name>AccountBean</display-name>
      <ejb-name>AccountBean</ejb-name>
      <home>banking.AccountHome</home>
      <remote>banking.Account</remote>
      <ejb-class>banking.AccountEJB</ejb-class>
      <persistence-type>Container</persistence-type>
      <prim-key-class>java.lang.String</prim-key-class>
      <reentrant>False</reentrant>
      <cmp-version>2.x</cmp-version>
      <abstract-schema-name>AccountBeanSchema</abstract-schema-name>
      <cmp-field>
        <description>no description</description>
```

```xml
        <field-name>customerName</field-name>
      </cmp-field>
      <cmp-field>
        <description>no description</description>
        <field-name>currentBalance</field-name>
      </cmp-field>
      <primkey-field>customerName</primkey-field>
      <security-identity>
        <description></description>
        <use-caller-identity></use-caller-identity>
      </security-identity>
    </entity>
  </enterprise-beans>

  <assembly-descriptor>
    <security-role>
      <description>System administrator</description>
      <role-name>Administrator</role-name>
    </security-role>
    <security-role>
      <description>Account holding customers</description>
      <role-name>Client</role-name>
    </security-role>
    <security-role>
      <description>Employees of the bank; tellers and managers</description>
      <role-name>Bank</role-name>
    </security-role>

    <method-permission>
      <role-name>Client</role-name>
      <method>
        <ejb-name>AccountManagerBean</ejb-name>
        <method-intf>Remote</method-intf>
        <method-name>getBalance</method-name>
        <method-params>
          <method-param>java.lang.String</method-param>
        </method-params>
      </method>
      <method>
        <ejb-name>AccountManagerBean</ejb-name>
        <method-intf>Remote</method-intf>
        <method-name>deposit</method-name>
        <method-params>
          <method-param>java.lang.String</method-param>
          <method-param>double</method-param>
        </method-params>
      </method>
      <method>
        <ejb-name>AccountManagerBean</ejb-name>
        <method-intf>Remote</method-intf>
        <method-name>withdraw</method-name>
        <method-params>
          <method-param>java.lang.String</method-param>
          <method-param>double</method-param>
        </method-params>
      </method>
```

```
        </method-permission>

      <method-permission>
        <role-name>Bank</role-name>
        <method>
          <ejb-name>AccountManagerBean</ejb-name>
          <method-intf>Remote</method-intf>
          <method-name>getBalance</method-name>
          <method-params>
            <method-param>java.lang.String</method-param>
          </method-params>
        </method>
        <method>
          <ejb-name>AccountManagerBean</ejb-name>
          <method-intf>Remote</method-intf>
          <method-name>createAccount</method-name>
          <method-params>
            <method-param>java.lang.String</method-param>
            <method-param>double</method-param>
          </method-params>
        </method>
        <method>
          <ejb-name>AccountManagerBean</ejb-name>
          <method-intf>Remote</method-intf>
          <method-name>calculateInterest</method-name>
          <method-params>
            <method-param>java.lang.String</method-param>
          </method-params>
        </method>
        <method>
          <ejb-name>AccountManagerBean</ejb-name>
          <method-intf>Remote</method-intf>
          <method-name>deposit</method-name>
          <method-params>
            <method-param>java.lang.String</method-param>
            <method-param>double</method-param>
          </method-params>
        </method>
        <method>
          <ejb-name>AccountManagerBean</ejb-name>
          <method-intf>Remote</method-intf>
          <method-name>withdraw</method-name>
          <method-params>
            <method-param>java.lang.String</method-param>
            <method-param>double</method-param>
          </method-params>
        </method>
      </method-permission>

    </assembly-descriptor>

</ejb-jar>
```

Deploying Secure EJB Applications

The application deployer is responsible, among other things, for mapping the logical security roles specified by the application assembler to users or groups of users from the operational environment. The application deployer ensures that the assembled application is secure after it has been deployed on the application server.

The deployer uses the tools provided by the EJB container provider to read the security view of the enterprise application. This security view is provided by the application assembler. Once the logical security view is mapped to the security mechanisms in the operational environment, the deployer, once again using the tools provided by the EJB container provider, generates container-specific objects that encapsulate (among other services) the security logic.

These objects are responsible for the run time enforcement of the security policies that are specified declaratively in the deployment descriptor. These container-specific objects are obviously not portable, so you may not generate the objects with WebSphere tools and use them on a WebLogic application server.

There are several key elements to deploying secure EJB applications, which we will cover in this section:

- ❑ Assigning security domains and principal realms
- ❑ Assigning security roles
- ❑ Principal delegation
- ❑ Managing security during resource access
- ❑ Processing the deployment descriptor

As usual, we'll start with the first item on the list.

Assigning Security Domains and Principal Realms

In a target operational environment, there may be many principal realms. Conceptually, principal realms are similar to the concept of groups in operating systems.

Similarly, for servers that are used in Application Service Provider (ASP) environments, there might be multiple security domains. A security domain abstractly refers to a place where the definitions of principal realms, Access Control Lists (ACL), and other security related properties are stored. A security domain may contain multiple principal realms.

It is the deployer's responsibility to assign a security domain and a principal realm to the enterprise application.

Assigning Security Roles

The application deployer, in most cases, does not change the method permissions assigned to security roles by the application assembler. Neither does the deployer pay any attention to the linkages between security role references and the security role names.

The deployer is responsible for mapping the security roles defined by the application assembler to users and groups in the operational environment of the application. The EJB specification does not specify how a compliant application server must implement the security infrastructure, hence the mechanism of assigning the security roles to real users or groups is very container-dependent. The container provider must provide the tools and the documentation required to assign users and groups to logical security roles. This assignment is performed on a per-application basis.

An Example of Assigning Security Roles

To make this clearer, we'll take the example of the J2EE 1.3 beta 2 Reference Implementation server's deployment tool. For our example application, once the assembler has specified all the security roles in the deployment descriptor, we have to map them to users in the server environment. For simplicity, we'll create two new users, Bank and Client.

We need to have the server running, and the EAR file representing our application opened in the deployment tool. First, we'll create the new users. From the Tools menu, select Server Configuration, then select the Users node under J2EE Server:

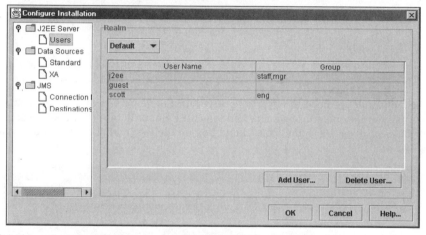

Click the Add User button, then on the following dialog specify a name and password for the new user (we'll start with the Bank), as well as selecting groups for the new user to belong to:

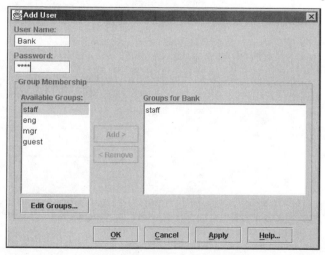

If we click Apply, we can add another user, Client. As for the Bank, we'll keep the password simple (the same as the user name). Click OK, and we can assign these new users to the security roles declared in our application. The deployment tool will show us an updated list of the users:

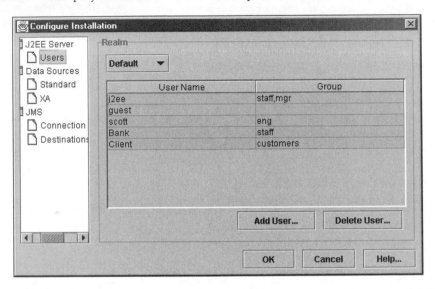

Before we can continue, we need to restart the server for the new users to become available. Finally, we return to the main deployment tool screen, and select the Security tab for the application. Here, we select one of the security roles in the Role Name box on the left, and click the Add button to select a user to assign to the role:

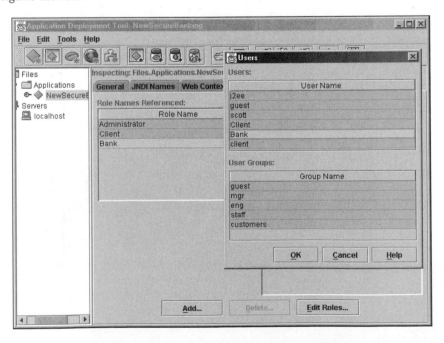

We can assign any of the users declared for the server to be part of the Bank role, one at a time. Since we only want the Bank user to be able to execute methods allowed to the Bank role, we'll leave it at that. For the Client role, however, we need to specify the Bank user as a User in Role. This is because the Bank user needs to access the methods that require the Client role. Thus we end up with the following situation for the Client role:

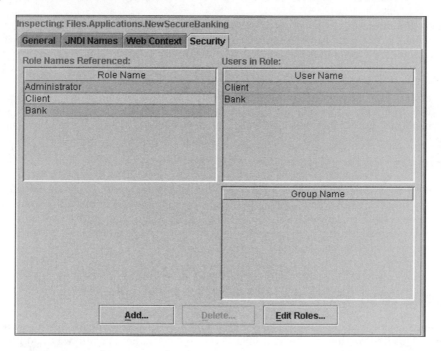

Principal Delegation

The application deployer is also responsible for configuring the `Principal` delegation for inter-bean calls. The deployer is required to follow the instructions provided by the application assembler. The instructions may have been specified in one or more of the following ways:

- ❑ Using the `<run-as>` element
- ❑ Using the `<description>` element
- ❑ In an application-specific deployment manual

If the application assembler had specified the `<use-caller-identity>` element, then the `Principal` associated with caller is propagated to the bean. If all the beans in the call chain use this `<security-identity>` element (`<use-caller-identity>`), then the call to `getCallerPrincipal()` from any of the beans in the call chain returns the same value (the `Principal` associated with the caller). However, if the application server's security infrastructure has mapped the principal to some other principal, then the method call `getCallerPrincipal()` returns the `Principal` that is a result of the mapping and not the original `Principal` object.

If the application assembler had specified, using the `<run-as>` element, a security role to be used for a bean's method invocations, then the deployer must configure a `Principal` belonging to the specified security role to be used. This `Principal` is now propagated down the call chain in the absence of any further `<run-as>` specifications.

Managing Security During Resource Access

If the enterprise bean accesses other resources such as database management systems or message queues, then the deployer might wish to propagate the `Principal` associated with the security domain and the principal realm of the enterprise bean to the resource manager being accessed.

If the value of the ‹res_auth› element is `Container`, then the deployer has to use container specific tools to map the `Principals` from the enterprise bean's security domain and principal realm to the security domain and the principal realm of the resource being accessed. This kind of mapping is not specified in the EJB specification.

If the value of the `<res-auth>` element is `Application`, then the logic to propagate the `Principal` from the enterprise bean to the resource is hard-coded in the bean's implementation; however, the values may be obtained dynamically, for instance, from the environment variables defined in the deployment descriptor.

Processing the Deployment Descriptor

The application deployer is free to treat the security view provided by the application assembler as hints, and may override the security policies defined in the deployment descriptor. While this is not the norm, it still is a possibility. In the absence of security policy definitions in the deployment descriptor (remember it is optional for the application assembler to provide this information), the application deployer has to provide this information.

Designing and Developing EJB Clients

The EJB clients usually pass authentication information to the server while establishing their connection to the server. This information is provided in a server- and container-specific way and is not specified by the EJB specification.

One common mechanism for passing the authentication information is to use the JNDI arguments `javax.naming.Context.SECURITY_PRINCIPAL` and `javax.naming.Context.SECURITY_CREDENTIALS` to provide the principal name and credentials while connecting to the JNDI-based naming service. Once a client is authenticated, the server associates the `Principal` object with that client and uses this while executing methods on behalf of the client. The following code snippet describes how you might specify these values while connecting to the name server:

```
public class SomeClient {

...

    public javax.naming.InitialContext connectToNameServer(String jndi_driver,
            String name_server_url, String user_name,
            String password) throws javax.naming.NamingException {
    java.util.Hashtable h = new Hashtable();

    h.put(javax.naming.Context.INITIAL_CONTEXT_FACTORY, jndi_driver);
    h.put(javax.naming.Context.PROVIDER_URL, name_server_url);
    h.put(javax.naming.Context.SECURITY_PRINCIPAL, user_name);
    h.put(javax.naming.Context.SECURITY_CREDENTIALS, password);
```

```
        return new javax.naming.InitialContext(h);
    }

 ...

    }
```

An alternative method to use, one that we will demonstrate here, is to include the client in the EAR file, as an application client.

Application Clients

In order to take advantage of the server authentication of a client, we need to deploy our client as part of our application's EAR file. Before we discuss how to do that, let's look at the two clients we have for this application.

Our banking application has a bank-based client, and a customer-based client. The bank-based client performs one of two tasks, either creating an account, or calculating interest on an account. The customer-based client will add funds, check the balance, and withdraw some funds. To demonstrate the application and it's security, we'll run the bank-based client to create an account, then run the customer client to play with the balance, and finally run the bank client again to calculate the interest.

Here is the bank client:

```java
package banking;

import java.util.*;
import java.rmi.RemoteException;
import javax.ejb.*;
import javax.naming.*;
import javax.rmi.PortableRemoteObject;

public class BankClient {

  public static void main(String[] args) {

    try {
      InitialContext initial = new InitialContext();
      Object objref = initial.lookup("ejb/accountManager");

      AccountManagerHome home =
        (AccountManagerHome) PortableRemoteObject.narrow(objref,
              AccountManagerHome.class);

      AccountManager accountManager = home.create();

      if (args[0] != null) {
        int i = Integer.parseInt(args[0]);

        switch (i) {
        case 1:
          System.out.println("creating account for " +
                      "Albert Finney; initial balance = 1500.0");
```

```
            accountManager.createAccount("Albert Finney", 1500.0);
          break;

        case 2:
          System.out.println("calculate interest for Albert Finney");
          accountManager.calculateInterest("Albert Finney");
          System.out.println(accountManager.getBalance("Albert Finney"));
          break;

        default:
          System.out.println("Usage: BankClient " +
                            "< 1 to create, 2 to calculate interest>");
        }

        System.out.println("Thankyou for using Java-EJB banking services");
      } else {
        System.out.println("Usage: BankClient " +
                            "< 1 to create, 2 to calculate interest>");
      }

    } catch (Exception e) {
      e.printStackTrace();
    }

    System.exit(0);
  }
}
```

And here is the customer client:

```
package banking;

import java.util.*;
import java.rmi.RemoteException;
import javax.ejb.*;
import javax.naming.*;
import javax.rmi.PortableRemoteObject;

public class CustomerClient {

  public static void main(String[] args) {

    try {
      InitialContext initial = new InitialContext();
      Object objref = initial.lookup("ejb/accountManager");

      AccountManagerHome home =
        (AccountManagerHome) PortableRemoteObject.narrow(objref,
            AccountManagerHome.class);

      AccountManager accountManager = home.create();

      System.out.println("depositing 500 in account for Albert Finney");
      accountManager.deposit("Albert Finney", 500.0);
      System.out.println("checking balance for Albert Finney: "
```

```
                                    + accountManager.getBalance("Albert Finney"));
            System.out.println("withdrawing 40");
            System.out.println("Funds withdrawn; new balance = "
                                    + accountManager.withdraw("Albert Finney", 40.00));

      } catch (Exception e) {
         e.printStackTrace();
      }

      System.exit(0);
   }

}
```

Notice that, for both these clients, we are relying on the declarative security setup in the deployment descriptor. Because of this, it is important when setting the application client up that we have also set up the necessary security mappings from users in the application environment to security roles in the application. We'll look at how to do that after we've explained how to alter these clients to use the hard-coded security we implemented in the checkSecurity() method.

As we saw earlier, when getting an initial context, we can send a Hashtable with the environment declared. For these clients, if we were working with a server that accepts the environment settings in a Hashtable (unlike the J2EE Reference Implementation), we could do this as follows; first BankClient:

```
   public class BankClient {

     public static void main(String[] args) {

       try {
          InitialContext initial = connectToNameServer("127.0.0.1:7001",
                                                "Bank", "Bank");
          Object objref = initial.lookup("ejb/accountManager");
```

And for CustomerClient:

```
   public class CustomerClient {

     public static void main(String[] args) {

       try {
          InitialContext initial = connectToNameServer("127.0.0.1:7001",
                                                "Client", "Client");
          Object objref = initial.lookup("ejb/accountManager");
```

Note, though, that this is an application-server-specific way of connecting and authenticating the client, but then just about any way will be server-specific. However, since we as bean developer don't really need to worry about how the client is authenticated on the server (as long as they **are** authenticated), for our purposes it doesn't really matter.

Using the Banking Application Clients

We'll take the example of the J2EE 1.3 beta 2 Reference Implementation server as a quick guide to running these very simple clients. First, we need to add the clients as Application Clients. This is a simple process, which involves the following steps:

Select File | New | Application Client, and then follow the wizard through a couple of simple steps. On the first screen, select the application to which we will add the client, and use the Edit button to locate the class file for the client (just like selecting the files to add to an enterprise bean using that wizard).

We can accept the defaults on all the screens apart from the Enterprise Bean References step, where we need to specify the AccountManager bean as our reference point to the whole application. This is a simple process of filling in the name from the code (ejb/accountManager), identifying the type of bean (session), its interfaces, and finally the JNDI name assigned to it (again, ejb/accountManager). Once we've deployed the application, we can use the following command to run the BankClient:

```
runclient -client DeclaredSecureBankAPP.ear -name BankClient 1
```

This will run the BankClient, which will attempt to create a new account. Before the client gets access to the server, though, it will be required to log in using a small login dialog. This is where we provide the name and password for the user we have set up on the server. For the BankClient, the user we should be using is Bank; for the CustomerClient we should use Client (not to be confused with client). Of course, if you assign other users to the security roles Bank and Client, then you can use those user names.

Issues in Transaction Processing and Security Management

A transactional client (one with its own transactional context) cannot change its principal association within that transaction. This ensures that all calls from this client within the same transaction are executed with the same security context.

If a bean receives multiple transactional requests from multiple clients within a single transaction, then all such requests must be associated with the same security context. Basically, we cannot change the security context within a transactional context; this helps to greatly simplify the integration of the container with third-party transactional resources.

Issues in Session and Security Management

Once a client has obtained a reference to a session bean while being associated with a security principal, then that client must ensure that it is always associated with that principal during all subsequent communication with that session bean. This enables the server to associate a security principal with the session bean instance at the instance creation time, and save the overhead of assigning a security principal for each invocation from the client.

Summary

In this chapter, we covered the following ground:

- ❑ Concepts in authentication and authorization

- ❑ The EJB security model and infrastructure, EJB security roles and responsibilities, and what we need to be aware of

- ❑ Security role references, security role definitions, and how to define and use them

- ❑ Method permissions, and security role associations with methods for defining security policies

- ❑ Linking security roles and role references

- ❑ Security context propagation

- ❑ Security issues in accessing external resources

- ❑ Class versus instance-level security

- ❑ Transactions and security

- ❑ Communication issues while building secure clients

Over the next few chapters, we'll be looking at approaches to designing EJB applications.

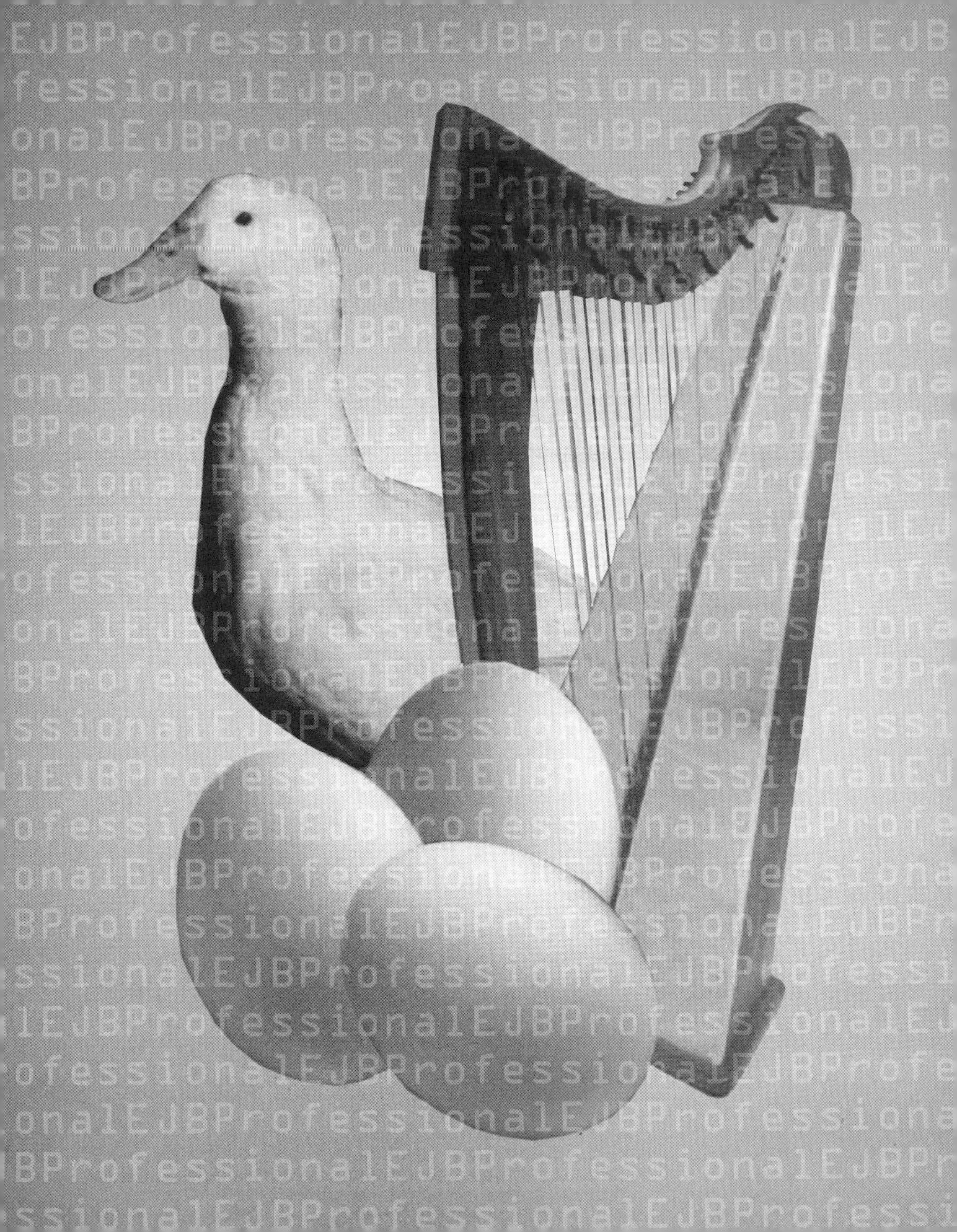

11

EJB Design Strategies

The virtues of component-based systems have been espoused time and again. Manageability, reusability, and scalability, among others, are all benefits to be gained from component-based development. But how do we know where these components should exist? How do we determine when to use such components as session beans and entity beans? What criteria should we use in deciding whether a bean should be stateless or stateful? In short, we need a strategy for designing with EJBs.

This chapter will examine several design strategies. Employing a top-down approach, we will begin by discussing the architecture in which our applications will exist. We will begin with a general look at distributed architectures, and what they have to recommend them. After this, we will move on through the chapter in the following order:

❑　We will very quickly discover that our application will not be a single entity, but rather consists of many different components spread throughout the architectural landscape.

❑　Therefore, we will need to establish guidelines that will assist us in determining how to partition our application into these components.

❑　Scalability is always an issue when building an enterprise application, so we will discuss the various challenges and design-decisions involved with ensuring that our application will be able to grow with us.

❑　Having identified the components of our applications, we will then examine different strategies for employing session and entity beans, as well as when they are not necessary.

❑　Finally, we will discuss some of the limitations and challenges presented by the EJB architecture, and also some of the general problems with regard to distributed programming.

Characteristics of Distributed Components

Components should be thought of as small, independent applications. As such, they should exhibit certain characteristics, including **autonomy** and **location transparency**. Autonomy suggests that a component should be able to perform its functions without any outside influence. That is, the component should be an independent sub-system that does not rely on a special relationship with another component that utilizes it.

This allows the component to be utilized by any other arbitrary component. Examples of this might be a centralized printing spool manager or database manager component. Neither of these components would be reliant on their callers, instead they provide distinct services autonomously, without respect to who is using them. This, in turn, promotes reuse among components. This is not to say that a component will not interact within or even be reliant on another component. However, that relationship should be known only to the component itself, and not its clients.

Enterprise JavaBeans support autonomy through the implementation of well-defined, published APIs. An enterprise bean's component interface explicitly states what the component expects and what can be expected from the component. If the internal implementation of a component should change, the clients will not be affected, provided the external characteristics (method signatures and return types) do not change. This makes it very easy to swap out or replace a component since the consent of the client is not required by virtue of the fact that no changes are required to the client. In this way, the component is said to be autonomous.

Location transparency states that where a component resides should be arbitrary to its clients. Interaction with the component should be the same regardless of whether they are on the same machine or spread apart halfway across the globe. When the concern over where a component is physically located is removed, an application system can be scaled and components relocated without disrupting the existing clients. Component development often employs the use of client- or stub-classes that encapsulate the complexity of locating or binding a client-session to a component-session at run-time.

The Enterprise JavaBeans application framework provides location transparency by decoupling a remote client from an enterprise bean via the use of home objects. An Enterprise bean home object encapsulates the complexity of locating a remote instance of a component and provides access to a remote interface to that component. The remote interface, in turn, is used in the same manner as any other object that might have been created locally. Should the physical location of an enterprise bean change, no modification to the client code will be required as the component's home object is responsible for maintaining the relationship.

Location transparency also provides a higher level of **connascence**. Connascence describes the relationship that exists between two objects. The tighter the coupling between objects, the greater the connasence. The greater the level of connascence that exists between two objects, the more likely that one object will have to be changed as a result of changes in another. One example of where this becomes an issue is when local interfaces are utilized. We'll explore the issues of implementing local interfaces later in this chapter. Suffice it to say that, for now, local interfaces require a tight coupling, or high connascence, between two objects. The net effect of connascence is that it reduces the amount of location transparency of our components – something that should be avoided if we are to ensure our components are as reuseable as possible.

The location of the home object is also transparent to the client. The location of the home object may be maintained by a Lightweight Directory Access Protocol (LDAP) server (or similar), accessed via JNDI. However, the location of the LDAP server must always be known. This is not a big deal since locating an LDAP server is accomplished with a simple URL that can be stored in a properties file, environment variable, or the like. Should the LDAP server need to be relocated, its DNS entry need only be updated to point to the new location.

When we design our components with autonomy and location transparency in mind, we will be in a much better position to partition our components among the various levels of our system's physical architecture.

The Architectural Tiers

One of the challenges in designing a component-based system is determining which components are required and where they fit in the overall system architecture. The notion of dividing a system into layers or tiers aids us in conceptualizing each component, as well as the relationship between components. By clearly dividing our application into discrete areas, it becomes easier to design and implement the system.

The architectural structure of an application describes the physical layout of that system. An application's architecture can be broken down into many layers or tiers and, as we have seen earlier in this book, this is commonly referred to as **n-tier** architecture. Such a layered approach makes for a more scalable enterprise application within which each layer can focus on a specific role. J2EE defines a set of standards to ease the development of n-tier enterprise applications. It defines a set of standardized, modular components, provides a complete set of services to those components, and automatically handles many details of the application's behavior, such as security and multithreading.

Using J2EE to develop n-tier applications may typically involve breaking the application into five layers: **client, presentation, business, integration,** and **resource**. These tiers can be thought of as being stacked on top of each other with each tier being loosely coupled to the adjacent tier. That is, a layer receives input from one tier and provides output to another tier. Similarly, a tier proxies requests between the two tiers on either side of itself. We'll examine a few examples of this shortly. The diagram below illustrates this relationship schematically:

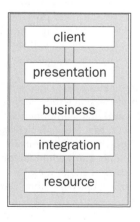

The Client Tier

The client-tier consists of the components used by the end-user of an application. The front-end interface to an application typically comprises the client tier. This may include graphical user-interfaces (GUIs), web-browsers, consoles, applets, LED panels, speakers – anything that accepts input and/or provides feedback directly to the end-user.

The Presentation Tier

The presentation-tier proxies, or delegates, requests from the client-tier to the business tier. The implementation of the presentation-tier helps to ensure that components in the client-tier do not need to be concerned with the business implementation details of the system. For example, if a client tier component in a banking application is responsible for displaying data in a spreadsheet-type table, it should not need to be concerned with the specifics of amortizing a corporate, construction-based bond whose pay-outs are calculated across a 15-year, flexible-rate payment schedule taking into consideration depreciation and additional annualized contributions. It should simply be fed data and know how to render that data in a table.

In J2EE, components in the presentation-tier are often implemented using JavaServer Pages and servlets. These components have already communicated with the business tier components (such as the aforementioned loan amortization) and prepare the raw data in a format that the client component can understand. In this case, the JSP or servlet provides HTML or XML that is subsequently rendered by the browser.

The benefit of the tiered approach is that it allows for the easy, unobtrusive changing of components on another tier. For example, the presentation-tier communicates with the business-tier to process loan amortizations. The presentation-tier receives the information in XML, renders the resulting data in HTML, and returns it to the client. If the loan calculation engine were to be replaced by a more efficient one, only the presentation-level components would need to change and only if the calculation engine required a different API or provided differently formatted result data.

Since we're using XML (a device-independent data protocol) between the presentation and client layers, we can easily swap the client component without affecting the presentation layer. Now our client can be a web browser for simplified reporting; a heavier GUI application for more elaborate presentation and interaction (say, charts and graphs); or even another system component such as a messaging publisher to WAP devices. All of these clients can use the same presentation component without requiring any special coding concessions within that presentation component. Furthermore, unknown and unspecified clients can be added at a later time, after the system has been deployed, without affecting the previously established components.

The presentation-tier can also serve as the gateway to other services such as logon and single sign-on management, session management, and more. Since the client components must access the presentation tier in order to get access to the business and data components, this is an ideal location for these security and session-related services. Note, however, that these services are actually components themselves, which may also reside on different tiers. To help visualize this, consider that the presentation-level component is essentially a client of the security component. Thus, while the presentation component exists in the presentation tier with respect to the application client, it exists in a client tier with respect to the security component. The following diagram illustrates this contextual relationship between the various clients:

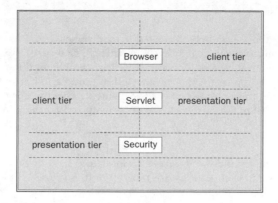

The Business Tier

The business-tier encapsulates all of the actual processing logic for a system. Components at the presentation level make requests to components in the business tier on behalf of their clients. Business-tier components also proxy requests to the integration-tier components on behalf of presentation components.

Components found within the business-tier are a logical representation of business processes. That is, they represent a business function, rather than data. When we look at any application, we can see that data operations do not happen arbitrarily; they happen for a reason. In the context of our example, these reasons might be "amortize a loan", "report the balance on an account", or "add a new customer" at the user interface. These reasons represent business functions and so, when designing our business-tier components, it is better and more intuitive to think in these terms.

Business-tier components consist of session enterprise beans (stateful or stateless) and message-driven beans. Session beans represent business processes, so this association makes sense. Message-driven beans are business process components by simple virtue of the fact that messages originate from events that are the results of business rules. The message itself is data, but the processing of that data is an execution of a business rule. Thus, message-driven beans belong in the business-tier. An important distinction at this point is that entity beans are *not* part of the business layer. However, they do play a significant role in the integration layer, as discussed in the next section.

RMI-based components, as well as CORBA components, are also included in the business-tier when they follow the same design "purpose" as session beans. That is, they expose business processes and not individual data elements. The same holds true for socket-based services.

The Integration Tier

The integration-tier is responsible for inter-operating, or connecting, an application with the outside world. In this context, the term "outside" refers to those systems that exist independently or externally to the application's system. Such external systems include databases, messaging systems, legacy systems, and other data or processing resources. Within the EJB framework, the integration-tier is supported through entity beans, as well as the J2EE Connector Architecture.

The integration-tier can also provide access to third-party systems such as rules engines, workflow managers, preference and personalization systems, Online Analytical Processing (OLAP) tools, and more. Note that the integration-tier does not contain these external systems themselves. Rather, it contains the components that provide access to these systems. Thus, the integration-tier provides a level of abstraction to external systems. Examples of integration-level components include JDBC drivers, JMS drivers, connectors, and the like. From this, we can easily see that it is the integration-tier that proxies requests between the business tier and the resource tier.

The Resource Tier

The resource-tier contains those systems referenced by components in the integration tier. Components such as databases, messaging systems, legacy systems, OLAP, Enterprise Resource Planning (ERP), news wires, stock feeds, Electronic Fund Transfer (EFT) processing, and more. Within the Enterprise JavaBeans architecture, the components that reside in the resource tier are identified in the bean's deployment descriptor using the `<resource-ref>` element. This includes not only database resources, but also JMS connections. All of these resources can be managed by the container.

Putting it Together

At this point, you should understand the different architectural tiers as well as the justification for partitioning an application into each layer. With this in mind, it is very important to understand that these partitions can be *logical* as well as physical.

It is easy enough to visualize a J2EE-based enterprise application as being divided among the several tiers. A J2EE-based n-tier application typically provides the following five layers:

❑ **Client** – Typically a browser running on the client machine handles presentation

❑ **Presentation** – JSPs, servlets, XML, or XSL

❑ **Business** – Business logic is generally implemented in session EJBs

❑ **Integration** – Data integration is generally implemented with entity EJBs and using JDBC

❑ **Resource** – the Integration-tier may use a variety of external resources, a database for example, and the best choice of accessing these resources depends upon the exact nature of the resource

These layers are illustrated in the following diagram:

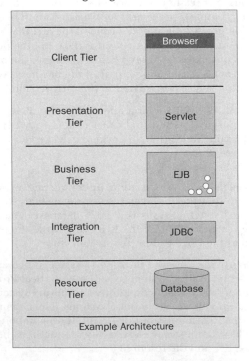

However, the same partitions can be applied to a standalone application; even something as seemingly simple as a calculator, as seen here:

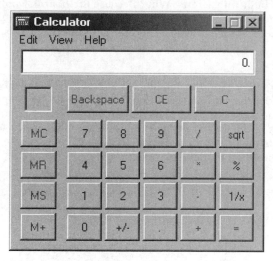

Staying with the analogy to the enterprise application, our calculator application can be divided into the following layers:

- **Client** – Buttons, display, and event listeners to button-presses of a process
- **Presentation** – Receives requests from event listeners and invokes the appropriate calculation method
- **Business** – Does the actual processing (add, subtract, divide, etc.)
- **Integration** – Receives requests from the business tier to print or store values in memory for later retrieval
- **Resource** – The printer, clipboard

This example provides us with the opportunity to understand that partitioned designs can be applied to even the most trivial of applications. Ordinarily, an application such as this calculator would be a collection of tightly coupled components. In this case, the components are just mere objects. However, if reuse and extensibility are goals of the calculator's design, then it is more appropriate to maintain a clearer division of labor. For example, the calculator could be bundled with the same objects that are used by our loan amortization's session beans to calculate loan payments. Since the loan amortization objects present a standard (that is, unchanging) interface, it should not matter who is the client of the object.

We should also understand that not all of the tiers will be required in all situations. Our application may not require a client interface, for example. Also, it is not necessarily appropriate to have one tier existing for the sole purpose of proxying requests between two other tiers. For example, it is perfectly acceptable for a presentation-tier component to directly interact with an integration-tier component if no business logic or processing is required to be applied to the resulting data. However, this is usually only applicable with smaller applications, the expandability of which could be reduced by eliminating a tier.

Do these extra levels of components increase the complexity of the design? Perhaps. Does a tiered architecture take longer to implement? Often. Does dividing an application into several discreet and independent components increase the amount of code and effort? Probably. Does the gain in performance, scalability, reusability, and maintainability resulting from partitioning more than justify the additional time and effort required to implement it? Absolutely.

To borrow from architecture of another sort, two pieces of wood will form a stronger bond together if screws are used to attach them, as opposed to nails. It might be faster to build the structure using nails, but it will be stronger if built with screws. Why? Because the boards won't pull apart with screws as easily as they will with nails. Take the time and spend the effort to build something better and it will last longer. Consider this the next time you go to design an architectural masterpiece.

An Example

Of course, it is easier to understand the benefits of a tiered approach when we look at an actual example. So, let's consider the work that would be involved with developing a loan amortization application for deployment on a web site. The design and implementation of the client tier is already completed for us thanks to the web browser. The presentation layer is a servlet that simply makes a call to a stateless session bean, which, in turn, provides the business implementation of the amortization process. Thus, our architectural model looks like this:

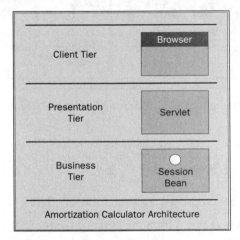

Amortization Calculator Architecture

The partitioning of the application into different layers also makes it easier to divide the required work among several developers. During development, one person can design the HTML, one person can write the servlet, and one person can concentrate on the loan calculation routines, as shown in the diagram below:

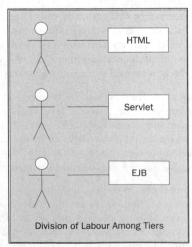

Division of Labour Among Tiers

Contrast this with a full client-side implementation of the same program where a single developer is usually responsible for writing the entire application (given that it is a small one):

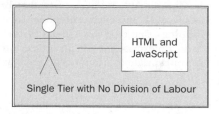

Single Tier with No Division of Labour

Here, a single developer is responsible not only for developing the HTML code, but also for writing code in JavaScript (or some similar in-browser language) to amortize the loan.

There are a number of fundamental problems with this approach. First, the amount of time required to produce the program is greatly increased, as only a single developer can work on the code. Projects that employ multiple developers to work on the same web page are often fraught with synchronization and versioning problems. Not to mention a considerable amount of finger pointing when something doesn't work correctly.

Second, changes made to one part of the HTML page can, and often do, have an effect on other code. Therefore, any time something changes in the code, the entire script must be re-submitted to a full set of regression testing. This is much more time consuming than the clean-cut, component-based approach of a tiered architecture where often only the component that has been changed needs to be re-tested. After all, if the amortization calculations produce the expected results, and we change the servlet's generation of the resulting HTML code, it should not be necessary to completely re-test the loan calculation bean all over again.

Third, our HTML page is much larger than we would like it to be, as it has all of the processing logic in it, as well as the presentation code. When you consider all of the variables that can go into amortizing a loan, the code can get considerably large and complex. This increase in page size results in longer downloads, slower (perceived) performance, and greater I/O costs on the web server. Instead, by containing the process code in a business-tier component, such as a stateless session bean, the resulting HTML code is much smaller, containing only that which is required to actually render the results.

While it is true that a greater processing load is put on the server's CPU to calculate the loan data for several clients simultaneously, the performance will still be perceived as being faster. This is because in-memory, CPU-based processing is much faster than I/O-based processing. Furthermore, should the increase in the number of requests being made to our business servers begin to degrade performance, we can easily add additional servers to our business tier. Thus, the tiered approach lends itself to better scalability.

Fourth, since the loan processing logic is completely contained within the HTML page, it cannot be utilized by any other systems or components. By deploying a business process in a centralized business tier, a greater level of reuse is supported. In addition, the development cost for that component is spread across multiple systems, thus giving us a greater return on our development investment.

Lastly, there are certain limitations inherent in using a full web-based client-side implementation. For example, access to server-side resources, such as a database, is simply not available. This greatly restricts the level of functionality that our application can provide. Should we require dynamically generated content, database support, security, or other similar services, we would need to implement components throughout some, if not all, of the remaining tiers.

479

Guidelines for EJB Design and Deployment

Should Enterprise JavaBeans be used at all? Obviously not every application is going to require the power and flexibility (and therefore complexity and high costs) that Enterprise JavaBeans provides. Careful consideration must be given to each and every component when determining an appropriate implementation. Each level of technology that exists in a given system has the effect of making that system that much more complex, and Enterprise JavaBeans are certainly no exception. Therefore, it is important to understand when it is appropriate to use Enterprise JavaBeans and when it might be better to utilize a simpler technology.

The following guidelines should help us to better prepare for this decision process.

Note that many of these are applicable not just to Enterprise JavaBeans, but to any distributed technologies.

Advantages of Enterprise JavaBeans

There are several advantages to implementing a distributed systems design in general, and using Enterprise JavaBeans in particular.

Improved Performance

It's a simple fact that application servers tend to be much more powerful than client-side, desktop machines. These servers provide support for more robust and scalable software architectures such as distributing applications across several machines, pipeline processing, collaborative computing, and so on. The capabilities of the distributed system and, particularly, Enterprise JavaBeans will provide greater performance.

Using Enterprise JavaBeans to support our large-scale, multi-user applications provides us with a number of benefits. It reduces or alleviates the need for us to implement concurrency controls, load balancing, fail-over support, and all of the other technological strategies that an application provides. The EJB server provides us with these already. This is an important advantage as we must always remember that we are in the business of providing "business solutions" – not in the "application server-building" business. A large number of distributed systems (non-EJB) projects fail because they forget this simple fact, and attempt to build their own services, rather than relying on third-party vendors to provide application server implementations.

Centralized Deployment

One of the longest standing challenges to multi-user applications has been the issue of deployment management and version control. It is a difficult and complex task to roll out an application across the enterprise. When the central resources and services are updated, every client to those resources must also be updated if any changes are made to the interfaces or resulting data.

If an application is deployed outside of the enterprise (say, the Internet, dial-up, WAP, etc.) the re-deployment process becomes almost impossible. Enterprise JavaBeans helps to alleviate this problem by allowing us to install our applications in a centralized location. Implementing a tiered architecture designed with the Model-View-Controller pattern allows us to support a larger, more disparate, user-base with less risk of anomalies. It also permits us to make changes and enhancements quicker and more often.

Centralized Business Processes

In addition to version control, there may be other reasons why it may be desirable to maintain centralized business components. It makes sense for dynamically generated business processes (often the result of business rules engines) to be located in a centralized tier and thus they are good candidates for Enterprise JavaBeans. Also, it may be necessary to protect code, algorithms, formulae and other proprietary information. Given that Java can be de-compiled rather easily, even if the code is obfuscated (it just requires more patience), Enterprise JavaBeans provides a good level of protection because the class files are not accessible by the client.

Centralized Resource Access

Access to a resource from a centralized location tends to be quicker, cheaper, and more maintainable. Enterprise JavaBeans implement connection pooling to resources and, for larger multi-user environments, a more realistic connection model. In the case of a database, an application can, and often does, maintain several simultaneous connections. Despite being allocated to each client, these connections are not used that often – at least not often enough to warrant a continuous connection. Given that databases have a finite number of connections available and licensing for many databases is based on the number of simultaneous connections, the cost of implementing that database can quickly become prohibitive. Often the database represents the most expensive component in an application system.

The notion of a centralized resource doesn't necessarily apply just to databases. News wires, stock feeds, EFT services, credit card services, and more, are all examples of resources that can benefit from connection pooling and centralization. The implementation of resource pooling by EJBs helps to reduce costs while increasing performance and improving response time. Just as importantly, the implementation details (IP addresses, user names, passwords, etc.) are hidden from the client. This provides additional security and makes scalability and re-configuration easier.

Centralized Administration and Security

Enterprise JavaBeans' centralized implementation provides for more efficient administration of a system. All security processes are hosted within the business tier and, combined with the Java security model, this provides robust and flexible management capabilities. The inclusion of roles and responsibilities control in EJB is a compelling reason for its use. Similarly, administrating an application is easier when its properties and characteristics are defined centrally and not at the client level.

Centralized Encapsulation of External Systems

The details of interacting with external systems can be rather complex. Implementing EJBs to facilitate communications with external systems is an excellent strategy. Not only are the usual administrative, security, and concurrency controls in place but, by encapsulating the implementation in an Enterprise JavaBean, the client is protected from any changes should the external system be modified or replaced.

Thinner Client Components

It is often not desirable, feasible, or even possible to have a full-blown, heavy client interface. Enterprise JavaBeans supports the implementation of an ultra-lightweight client interface by integration with technologies such as Java servlets, WAP technologies, and others. Of course, light clients have their own issues to take into consideration. We will examine the use of light clients versus heavy clients later in this chapter.

Enterprise JavaBeans are Component-based

Enterprise JavaBeans are a component-based architecture and application framework and are therefore better suited for enterprise-class systems than other technologies. This allows EJBs to support iterative development processes, easier maintenance, and faster testing. As we have seen, component-based systems are also easier to scale and optimize. Lastly, and this is critical to a distributed application system, bottlenecks and other performance problems are much easier to identify and resolve.

Vendor Independence

Not only does the Enterprise JavaBeans framework support platform independence, it also supports vendor independence. Based on an open, rather than proprietary, specification, any software vendor is free to develop products to support any of the J2EE components. We have the ability to determine the best EJB server for our needs, potentially saving a tremendous amount of money and implementation effort. We may not need an EJB server as powerful and robust as BEA's WebLogic or IBM's WebSphere when a much simpler (and less expensive) server will support our needs. This permits us to use the right tool for the right job.

Best-of-Breed Designs

By utilizing Enterprise JavaBeans as a wrapper interface to third-party products, an application system can implement functionality from components based on their individual merits. In the event that a better component should present itself, only the Enterprise JavaBean need change. This is in contrast to other solutions where a single package is used and the strengths must be accepted at the cost of its weaknesses. At the very least, changing a component (a JavaBean or an ActiveX control, for example) in these other solutions would require redeployment of the application. Using Enterprise JavaBeans as the cornerstone technology for a component framework can go a long way towards extending the life, flexibility, and usefulness of that system.

Disadvantages of Enterprise JavaBeans

As wonderful as the Enterprise JavaBeans framework is, and despite all of the many benefits of implementing an application system using the EJB platform, there are several limiting factors that must be taken into consideration. Again, as with the benefits of using Enterprise JavaBeans, these caveats could also apply to other distributed technologies as well.

Performance Costs

Out-of-process communication is expensive, requiring more time and resources than a local-based request does. Enterprise JavaBeans are based on Java's Remote Method Invocation (RMI) technology – a distributed transport protocol. Several factors, such as network latency, server loads, and communication failures to name a few, affect the performance of any network-based application. With each layer of indirection in an application system, the amount of latency increases. Server-side operations, pooling, and concurrency control can each experience performance gains from using EJBs, which, it is hoped, offsets the networking costs.

Architectural Fragility

Remembering that a chain is only as strong as its weakest link, the more servers and components that constitute the architectural structure, the greater the possibility for failure and interruptions. Again, this is not a shortcoming of EJB specifically, but of all distributed systems in general.

Greater Complexity

Developing a distributed application is by no-means easy. While Enterprise JavaBeans ease the task somewhat by providing a robust framework and rich toolset in which to work, they're not a panacea for distributed systems development problems. On the contrary, they can serve as a veritable Pandora's Box of design, programming, and implementation challenges. A more thorough understanding of a broader range of issues is required.

In addition to general OO design and analysis, other considerations such as networking and concurrency design must be taken into account. Enterprise JavaBeans don't exist in a vacuum – RMI is the communications protocol; IIOP is the networking protocol; JNDI, LDAP, JTS, JMS, JDBC, object serialization, distributed objects, distributed transactions, and more – all must be thoroughly understood in order to design and implement an enterprise-class system successfully. Moreover, if we intend to incorporate a web-based interface, we must add servlets, JSP, HTML, XML, HTTP, TCP/IP, and general Internet architecture into the mix as well.

We must make sure that we understand the significance of undertaking this task.

Greater Cost

Implementing a system across multiple tiers is more expensive than producing a standalone or traditional client-server application. This cost increase comes from several sources including hardware (servers, networks, routers), software (EJB servers, web servers, messaging servers, firewalls) and development resources (experienced distributed systems architects, OO designers, web developers, and Enterprise JavaBeans developers). In particular, these development resources are more expensive and much harder to find than more general-purpose programmers.

Technology for Technology's Sake

"Ah, she's a beaut, ain't she?" We've heard the car salesmen tell us this before. Twelve quad-head cylinders driving 490 horses from 0 to 60 in 2.4 seconds of heart-pumping, adrenaline-fueled fury. Sure, it's sexy, but if we're only going to use it to drive back and forth to the grocery store, do we really need a $250,000 Lamborghini when a Volkswagen Golf will suffice our needs just as well? Similarly, using technologies simply because they are new or exciting is wasteful and potentially dangerous. We must make sure that our application truly requires the benefits that EJBs provide. Likewise, if our application is to support a single user or small group of users, EJBs may well be overkill.

Greater Learning Curve

Using Enterprise JavaBeans is like love – easy to learn but very difficult to master. Once you have learned the general framework and the relevant J2EE APIs, you then have to go on to the much more difficult task of learning and understanding not just its application, but how to design the individual components, the overall system, distributed architecture, and much more. This is not unique to Enterprise JavaBeans but, rather, is common to all enterprise-class platforms and technologies, such as CORBA and COM+. However, EJBs are probably the easiest to learn. And, of course, the real learning comes after the books and articles and newsgroups have been read – from practical, real-world experience.

We must be careful not to discount the effort entailed in learning how to develop distributed application systems. Too many projects take on new technologies and paradigms with the attitude and naïve optimism that they can "learn it along the way". Indeed, EJBs represent a different model from what most developers are used to.

Heavy Clients vs. Thin Clients

One of the initial steps that we will need to undertake when designing our application will be deciding on whether to have a "thin" client interface or a "heavy" client interface. A **thin client** interface is a lightweight user interface, typically presented as a web browser using a combination of HTML and JavaScript. Other thin clients might include such things as wireless devices but, for the sake of simplicity, we will limit our focus to web browsers. Thin clients have a minimal amount, if any, of program logic. That which they do have is usually limited to simple data validation. Processing of data, validation against business rules, and other functionality is performed at the middle tier.

Heavy clients (often known as fat clients) are typically standalone applications, but can also include Java applets as well. Heavy clients provide a greater amount of processing that is completed at the client tier. Either interface has its advantages and disadvantages, gains and losses. Let's take a moment to examine some factors in deciding between heavy and thin clients.

HTTP and Networking Issues

On the surface, the most noticeable difference is appearance. Thin clients are limited to the standard HTML widgets – text fields, listboxes, checkboxes, and the like. Heavier clients tend to have a more robust interface and a greater deal of interactivity. Often times, such advanced widgets as spreadsheets, interactive charts and graphs, and complex graphical tree hierarchies are incorporated.

> *It's interesting to note, by the way, that while heavy clients are capable of more interactivity and complex designs, it is usually the lighter clients that demonstrate greater and more creative graphical flair. Go figure.*

Of course, this is all superficial. The real reason behind implementing a lighter client is for scalability. Due to the nature of the HTTP 1.0 protocol, each request made to a web server is a single-shot, synchronous network call. That is, for each request:

1. A network connection must be made to the web server

2. The web server begins processing the request

3. The client waits (and blocks) while the request is being fulfilled

4. The web server completes the request and returns the result to the client

5. The client closes the connection

HTTP 1.1 does not require that the connection be closed, as it permits persisted connections. However, both the client and the server must support HTTP 1.1, which is not always the case.

The process of a web server serving a file to an HTTP client is very fast indeed, once the network connection has been established. The fact is that the majority of time spent requesting a web page is spent trying to obtain that connection. The time that it takes to get a connection isn't the fault of the web server, but the amount of work required to find a network route between the client and the server. Without going into too much detail, networks (be they the Internet or a simple LAN) consist of several machines (routers, gateways, switches, etc.) that connect a given client to a server. Each request made to a server must be routed through a series of these machines. The route from a client to a server is not a straight line but, instead, is a series of any number of arbitrary paths, as illustrated in the following diagram of a networking matrix:

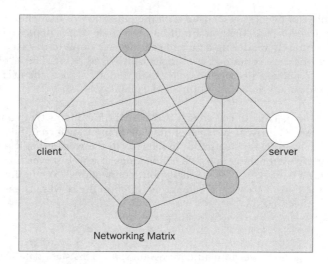

Networking Matrix

Should one element in the networking matrix become unavailable, the request can be re-routed through another element. This level of redundancy is made possible by the "web-like" design of the network routes. In fact, this is the general structure for the World Wide Web and is the source of the Web's name. All of this serves to provide a much more stable and reliable environment – but at the cost of time. Each "hop" in the route presents a delay to the networking request. These delays, known as **latency**, can be caused by traffic congestion, connection failures, and general decision-making processes, among other reasons.

However, latency is generally acceptable to most users – especially on the Web. Web servers take advantage of this latency and, as a result, are capable of handling hundreds upon thousands of requests. Users of thin clients are more accepting of delays than users of heavy clients. However, the lesson to be learned here is that thin clients support greater scalability at the cost of performance.

Heavy clients, on the other hand, connect to the application server directly and typically maintain the network connections for the duration of the application session. This reduces the time delay between requests, as the network connection does not need to be re-established every time a request is made. However, as there are a greater number of connections that are continuously in use, the application server is limited to a much smaller number of clients – typically in the tens of thousands. Thus, with heavy clients, performance is gained at the expense of scalability.

Performance

Performance is also affected by who is doing the actual processing of the client. Light clients are typically used for simple data entry and presentation. Any processing done on the client-side is usually limited to basic data validation at the field level – often date or numeric range validation. The server is required to do most of the processing. This might include calculations, business rule processing, or other similar operations, in addition to general data persistence. This increased work can greatly affect the performance of the server.

By contrast, a heavy client application is usually capable of handling a lot of the tasks that would otherwise be the responsibility of the server. The server, in turn, manages the data persistence, some final data validation in accordance with a business rules engine, and perhaps some asynchronous messaging. As the client is responsible for the more processor-intensive tasks, the server's performance is improved.

There are also a number of benefits associated with the utilization of thin clients. In addition to being able to handle a larger client-base, the amount of business logic that is deployed is minimal. The browser is relegated to merely rendering data and routing user input to the server. Software updates are easier to implement as they are contained at a single, centralized point. The application is more secure as the users' sessions are managed centrally, rather than remotely. Also, the user base is broader, with less concern required for platform compatibility and capability.

One additional performance issue to consider is that HTML documents that contain a lot of graphical elements are slow to load. This is not because of the data being transferred, but is because of the accumulated latency realized by making multiple requests to the web server. Some browsers get around this performance issue by establishing multiple connections to a web server for a single page's content (in the case of Netscape's Navigator, this is usually four connections). While this makes the page appear to load faster, it is at the cost of creating greater congestion on the server, as each client is now establishing several connections .

Session State

Light clients often rely on the server to maintain session state. This state data can be stored on the client machine, either in the form of browser cookies or embedded in the HTML document itself, or on the server. When the session state data is stored on the client machine, the browser must send the data to the server with every request. Each file referenced in an HTML document, be it other HTML documents, graphics, external script files, etc., is obtained via an independent request to the server. If you've ever watched a web page load, you will notice that first the HTML document is downloaded, the file is parsed, rendered (in the case of Microsoft's Internet Explorer), and then the individual graphical elements are downloaded. Since the cookie, which is typically limited to 4k, is sent with each request, this represents a considerable amount of overhead.

Java servlets are memory and processor intensive and provide the session state management that exists on the server-side. The client-side data is limited to an identifier that uniquely identifies the session. This reduces the amount of data that must be passed between the client and the server, but it does increase the amount of processing and resources required by the server. The result, however, is that the performance, as perceived by the client, is faster. This is because the time required to retrieve the session data on the server will be far less than that spent transmitting it from the client to the server with each request.

Callbacks

Heavy clients do have one very large advantage over light clients – they can utilize callbacks. Recall that light clients typically use HTTP, a synchronous communications protocol. When a light client makes a request, it must wait until that request completes before it can continue. While it is true that a separate thread can be used to submit a request, the server's resources will still be tied up. Some developers get around this by submitting a request to a server-side queue, then repeatedly checking to see if the job has completed. In HTML, this is achieved by causing the web page to reload periodically, displaying any new results on-screen. This creates a large amount of overhead as the same query is essentially being executed again and again. More clients with requests in the job queue means that more status queries must be handled by the server. Ultimately, this means that the server will handle fewer requests in a given period of time.

In contrast, heavy clients can submit a processing request to a queue and simply be notified by the server when the job has been completed. This is possible because heavy clients may not rely on HTTP but rather TCP or UDP, which support bi-directional, asynchronous communication. Thus, an application can take advantage of asynchronous callback methods such as messaging or other similar networking techniques.

Firewalls

The performance gains achieved through asynchronous callbacks are often rendered moot, however, by firewalls. Many applications have been prevented from being deployed simply because they could not get approval from the company's network operations group to open a port in the company's firewall. We won't go into the mechanics of how a firewall works (nor the corporate politics that can sometimes result). Suffice to say, though, that a firewall can present a considerable challenge to a heavy client. Note also that it is very common (and advised) to have firewalls *within* the corporate infrastructure – preventing unauthorized access from the inside as well as the outside. So, just because our application will not be deployed across the Internet does not free us from the constraints of a firewall.

Light clients typically avoid firewall issues because they rely on the HTTP protocol, which by default is assigned to port 80 on all web servers. Since web servers enjoy a very high level of trust among companies, there is usually very little problem with utilizing them for application deployment. Note that despite the fact that they reside in a web page, applets are considered heavy clients and are subjected to the same restrictions.

"Choose, but Choose Wisely"

What does all this have to do with designing an Enterprise JavaBean application? Simply put, the decision to use a lightweight client versus a heavyweight client determines who the EJB's client is. If a heavy client is implemented, the application rests on the client-side of the network and, thus, is the client to the EJB. If a light client is used, the application logic resides on the server-side (typically as a Java servlet) and so the server-side component is the client to the EJB. This distinction will affect the selection, utilization, and configuration of the distributed services, as each has different needs.

The decision whether to support light clients or heavy clients (or both) must be made at the beginning of an application's design phase. This is because each type has a decidedly different approach. Heavy clients require a lot of cross-network communication. The typical approach in designing heavy clients, indeed the method that is most commonly taught when learning Enterprise JavaBeans, is to establish a connection to an EJB and to utilize it as if it were a local object. This method is common in other distributed technologies as well, including RMI (which forms the basis for EJB), and technologies such as CORBA, Microsoft Transaction Server (MTS), COM+, and more. How the client interacts with the distributed or remote components, and the structure of those components, can have a dramatic effect on a system's performance and scalability.

EJB Component Design

Having identified the various components of our system and decided upon utilizing Enterprise JavaBeans to implement them, the next step is to design the individual components themselves. You may recall that a component may not necessarily reside in a single tier. In fact, it is not uncommon for a component to exist across several tiers and to consist of several sub-components.

To further complicate matters, the concept of a tier is contextual. That is, what a tier is and where it will reside will differ from component to component. Clearly, each component must be treated with independent detail. We mustn't give in to the temptation of making broad, sweeping design decisions. Each component is a separate entity and must be treated as such. In the rest of this chapter we'll assume that these components have been identified and we are now looking at the implementation of the EJB objects.

Granularity

The topic of granularity often comes up in design discussions and it is of little surprise: no single other aspect of a system's design can have a greater impact on its performance. The concept of granularity can be defined as the division of an application into its various parts. In a language such as Java, this refers to the division of a component into its constituent objects and the amount of work that each object's processing methods are responsible for. When we discuss granularity in the context of EJBs, we are concerned with how much data processing an enterprise bean will contain. This decision will lead us to the division of labor between session beans and entity beans.

So, good object-oriented design is fairly clear on how we should design our objects. Each object is a distinct representation of its real-world counterpart. However, good OO design, to some extent, comes at the cost of performance – this is especially true when dealing with remote objects. When two objects communicate with each other on the same machine, the overhead is typically negligible. However, when these two objects exist on two different machines, the amount of time, processing, and effort required to conduct that same conversation increases by an extraordinary order of magnitude. Combine that with the concurrent nature of EJB-based applications and their responsibility to potentially thousands of simultaneous clients and we have the potential for a very real performance problem.

As important as good design is, we are often faced with having to make concessions to ensure that we have suitable performance. This is not to say that all concessions are necessarily bad. As we'll see shortly, the key is to make careful decisions that will offer us an acceptable balance between good design and good performance.

There are two types of components encompassed by granularity: fine-grained and coarse-grained. Fine-grained objects are small objects that typically represent a single, simple business entity. More specifically, fine-grained objects contain the data for that entity. Examples of fine-grained components might be a customer, an employee, or a line item from an invoice. Coarse-grained components are larger objects that comprise broader business concepts. Typically, a coarse-grained object represents a set of one or more processes in which the finer-grained components will be used. Examples of coarse-grained components might be an order handler, communication manager, or messaging publisher.

Data Granularity

The EJB representation of fine-grained components is implemented through entity beans; coarse-grained objects are session beans. Entity beans by themselves should represent data elements, not the concepts within which those elements will be used. For example, an Account object is a fine-grained object, whereas the banking system in which the Account object will be utilized is more coarse-grained.

Entity beans can also be used as façade interfaces to external, third party, and legacy applications. Using entity beans to decouple the EJB system from the implementation details of interacting with an external system reduces the impact on the EJB system in the event that the external system is replaced. If it is replaced, only the entity bean-based classes must change, not the components that have a logical relationship (as opposed to physical relationship, like an entity bean) to the external component.

Session beans should represent business processes. This is in line with the design guidelines of EJBs, which suggest that session beans represent process while entity beans represent data. However, this is a guideline and not a rule. As we are about to find out, there are some significant problems with strictly adhering to this dictum.

The basic principle that entity beans should always be used to represent data is one that is closely followed by newcomers to the EJB framework. As entity beans represent data, to make this data available, an accessor method needs to be called. Let's review what happens when a client invokes one of these remote methods. Assuming that a remote reference to the entity bean has been acquired, the following occurs:

A method is invoked on the remote reference via its stub:

1. The stub locates the server, establishing a network connection if the previous connection was lost.

2. The server's object request broker service accepts the remote call and re-directs it to the appropriate server skeleton object.

3. The skeleton object redirects the request to the EJB server.

4. The EJB server locates the entity instance. If one is available in the container's cache, it uses that one. Otherwise, it instantiates a new instance, locates the data in the data store, and populates the new instance.

5. The EJB server obtains the requested data value and returns it to the skeleton object.

6. The skeleton object returns it, via the network, to the client stub.

7. The client stub returns the value to the calling object.

That's quite a bit of work for a single method call. Now consider that a typical object might have 10 properties. If you access all of them, you're repeating this process 10 times. Still think this is not a huge problem? Let's take a look at a real-world example.

Data Granularity – An Example

Consider an application that accesses a database of customers. The interface, a traditional, heavy client-side application, presents a list of all of the customers' names in a list box, from which the user will pick one customer to work with. Once the customer is selected, their full information is displayed on the screen. The typical approach to this situation is to use an entity bean's finder method to retrieve the customer objects. If there are 10,000 customers, that's one invocation of the finder method, plus 10,000 instantiations and remote calls for the name information. All this just to produce a list of customers. If there are 1000 users of our system on the screen at the same time (a very large call center, for example), that amounts to over 10,000,000 calls just to initiate the application! This is obviously not going to scale.

Here, the use of fine-grained objects, the customer entity beans, has a very negative effect on performance because they are being used improperly. Let's re-examine this interface again, this time using a coarse-grained object. Rather than interacting directly with the customer entity bean, let's create a Customer Manager session bean instead. The Customer Manager session bean provides a collection of services that are used to manager a customer's data. Our client interface calls to the session bean, which, in turn, acts as a façade to the entity bean, as in the illustration overleaf:

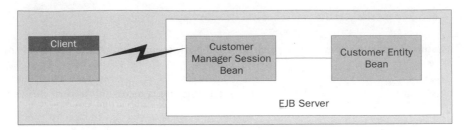

The Customer Manager session bean provides a method, `getAllCustomers()`, that returns a collection of value objects. A value object is a lightweight, read-only object that does not require the overhead that a remote object requires. Since a value object is essentially a snapshot of data, it does not need to support write functions and, since we are accepting of the fact that it *is* a snapshot, it does not need to be maintained within a transaction. Therefore, it does not need to enlist the service of an entity bean. Of course, this is not the most efficient of designs, as it could potentially return a large number of records. In a real application, we would implement search scoping, caching, and paging logic to deal with large result sets. However, for the purpose of our examination of granularity, this is sufficient.

The customer listbox in our client interface is filled by iterating through the collection of value objects and populating it with the customer's name and primary key value. When the user selects a customer to edit, then we will want to access the customer entity bean using the selected primary key. This is because our needs will require transactional support and editing of the object. This approach is acceptable because the context in which we are working has changed. Initially, we were browsing through a set of data – a read-only operation. Now, we are editing a single set of data – an interactive operation. Incidentally, the decision to use a collection of value objects is purely arbitrary. We can achieve the same improvement using XML as well.

By this point, the result on the system's performance should be fairly clear. Where before our 1000 users accessing 10,000 customers were generating 10,000,000 cross-network calls, now they are only making 1000 calls – one call per user for a client list. In addition to a reduction in the amount of network calls, the amount of data transferred is also reduced. Performance is improved because it is much faster to iterate through a collection of value objects, in order to derive the names of all the customers, than to iterate through a collection of remote references and make the cross-network requests to do the same.

We should take note here that the performance gain is achieved only when reading a large set of read-only data. The recommendation here is not to replace the entity bean finder methods with session bean methods arbitrarily, but to consider the impact of their use in certain situations. Furthermore, the use of session bean methods to retrieve collections of data comes at the price of losing the benefits of the EJB server's caching mechanism for entity beans. As different servers handle caching in different ways (if at all), it is best to do some benchmarking tests with both retrieval methods to determine which is the best approach for your application and/or component.

Process Granularity

Another aspect of using coarse-grained objects has to do with the partitioning of an application into the architectural tiers discussed earlier. The use of coarse-grained objects isn't just limited to bulk data representation. They can also be used to encapsulate larger business processes that require several steps. Let's examine a sample process where a new client is entered into a banking system. A welcome process, sometimes referred to as "on-boarding," consists of multiple sub-processes:

1. Verify that the person is, indeed, a new customer

2. Create new customer data records

3. Execute a credit check

4. Notify the Customer Relations manager at the "home branch" of the new client

5. Submit an order to a document distribution system to mail a welcome package to the new client

Over the course of the execution of these steps, the data of the client must be maintained and shared from sub-process to sub-process, as discussed in the preceding paragraph. These steps are also executed in series, with a failure or a negative response occurring in the first four steps halting the process.

Typically, the client application will utilize a stateful session bean that has a method for each of these steps. The client-side might resemble the following pseudo-code:

```
CustomerEntityBean.findBySSN(client's SSN);
        // SSN is used as the primary key
if(CustomerEntityBean == null) {
   CustomerEntityBean.create();
   :
   : // Populate entity bean
   :
   if(CustomerManagerSessionBean.passesCreditCheck(SSN) {
      if(CustomerManagerSessionBean.passesSecurityBackgroundCheck(SSN) {
         CustomerRelationsSessonBean.notifyManagerOfNewCustomer(SSN);
         DocumentationDistributionSessionBean.sendNewClientPackage(SSN);
      } else {
         throw new CustomerFailedSecurityCheckException();
      }
   } else {
      throw new CustomerFailedCreditCheck();
   }
} else {
   throw new CustomerAlreadyExistsException();
}
```

The first thing that we see here in our pseudo-code is that four Enterprise JavaBeans are referenced – one entity bean (`CustomerEntityBean`) and three session beans (`CustomerManagerSessionBean`, `CustomerRelationsSessionBean`, and `DocumentationDistributionSessionBean`). This means that our client-side interface must instantiate four instances of remote references, which results in four JNDI lookups and three create method invocations for the session beans. Furthermore, six remote method invocations are made on the Enterprise JavaBeans during this process. This results in a combined total of thirteen remote method calls.

Network-induced latency isn't the only factor affecting performance. Every call to an Enterprise JavaBean must be passed through the Enterprise JavaBeans container. On every method call, the container will enforce security, manage transactional context, retrieve the object from persistent storage, and unload other instances if necessary, as well as other services. RMI-based operations are also very expensive and time-consuming. All of this activity results in a significant amount of overhead.

In addition to this amount of network traffic, the code itself is concerned with the actual process of on-boarding a new customer. If a new step is added to the process, for example, subscribe the customer to an e-mail-based news subscription, the client code will require modification, regression testing, and re-deployment to all client installations. Instead, all of the steps required to add a new customer should be contained within a single method accessible from a single stateless session bean. Returning to our `CustomerManager` session bean from earlier, an `addNewCustomer()` method would suit this purpose quite nicely. There are several benefits to this approach.

Benefits of the New Approach

First, the complexity of the client-side code is reduced, as it now only needs to interact with a single Enterprise JavaBean. The steps comprising the on-boarding process now reside in the `CustomerManager` session bean, which will, in turn, invoke the various other beans.

Second, the code is easier to maintain as it is now only installed on the application server – not on every client machine, as was the case before. Also, the on-boarding process can now be used by multiple different systems. Should a change in the on-boarding process be required, that change need only be made in one place.

Third, and most importantly, the performance of the system is greatly improved. Initially, the client application made thirteen remote calls to complete the on-boarding process – and even more with the "e-mail news" option added. In contrast, using a coarse-grained session bean required only two calls – one to create the session connection and one to invoke the actual on-boarding method. Provided that all of the associated Enterprise JavaBeans required by the session bean are contained within the same application server instance, these objects should be treated as local objects by the container. Local calls coming from clients in the same VM, usually referred to as an **intra-VM bean method call**, are directly handed off to the container. This bypasses the network layer and serialization/deserialization phase of the call that remote method calls have to go through. Thus, such calls cause fewer overheads and achieve faster invocation times.

Of course, as our application scales, it is possible that these objects could be moved to other, separate servers and, as a result, become remote objects to our `CustomerManager` session bean. However, these servers would very likely reside on the same side of one or more firewalls, in close proximity to each other, whereas a client will typically exist on the other side of a firewall from the server, further away from the server. As a result, despite the fact that the objects would reside on a separate machine, the reduction in latency caused by the firewall would still yield improved performance. As a matter of course, care should be taken when partitioning components among different servers. Attention should be paid to the relationships that exist between components and attempts should be made to group these components together so as to reduce cross-boundary calls to other servers and/or virtual machines.

Lastly, isolating the process from the client widens the scope of who the client can actually be. In addition to the heavy user interface, other entities such as servlets, Java Server Pages, message-driven beans, and the like can interface with the same coarse-grained object. Since the purpose of a session bean is to represent "process", in this case adding a new client, the opportunity for reuse is very great. The various "clients" to the `CustomerManager` session bean should not need to be concerned with the actual implementation details of how a new customer is added. All that they care about is that a new customer *can* be added. Combining the various finer-grained steps into a single coarse-grained component results in a cleaner design that is more easily maintained and offers greater scalability and performance.

The application of coarse-grained components to a system's design is not cut-and-dried. There are a number of issues and caveats to take into consideration. To start with, it can be entirely too easy to make a component too large and complex. Just as having too many small, fine-grained components can create a situation where their use can result in a lot of cross-network and server processing overhead, so can an object that is very large. The number of simultaneous instances of a component that a container can efficiently maintain is largely influenced by the amount of memory available. Once the instance pool is depleted, the server must persist more instances of components in order to handle more client requests. This results in a greater amount of disk-based I/O, which is slower and more expensive performance-wise.

Another problem with components that are too coarse is that their scope can become too large and confusing. When a component takes on too much responsibility, its business purpose becomes less discreet and clear. This can make its interface cluttered and complex, as well as limit its reusability. If care is not taken to manage the scope of a component, it will become just as much of a problem as if it had been made too fine.

The ultimate goal is to keep the interaction between components to a minimum while, at the same time, keeping the reusability and maintainability as high as possible. Judicious use of prototyping and benchmarking will help identify bottlenecks and other areas of potential problems in your design.

Transaction Granularity

With the introduction of Enterprise JavaBeans 1.1, developers have had little control over how a container managers the transaction context for entity beans. The Enterprise JavaBeans specification only states that transactions must be managed by the container, and does not describe how this should be done. Therefore, each EJB server vendor must decide on its own how the transactions will be implemented.

As each method in an entity bean is executed in a transaction, it is possible that a new transaction will be started and destroyed on each method invocation. Furthermore, if container-managed persistence is being used, this can result in a database update occurring each time an entity bean's field is changed. Different vendors will manage this behavior in different ways and many avoid the repeated updates via the use of intelligent caching. However, there is still the issue of overhead with creating and destroying a transactional context for each method invocation. Some entity beans can have a large number of fields – say 50 to 100 or even 200 or more – and this overhead raises a considerable concern.

Another potential problem is that often the updating of an entity's attributes needs to be done atomically so as to maintain the integrity of the data. Since our transaction is only good for the duration of the accessor method, it is quite possible that another client could read a partially updated record or cause changes in-between method calls. Of course this is a very bad thing to have in our transactional system. If this is an issue in our application, we can avoid the problem by submitting the update request to a session bean instead. The session bean can start a new transaction and invoke the entity bean's method within the context of that transaction. If its transactional attribute is required, the need for the entity bean to start a new transaction each time is precluded (see Chapter 9 for more information on transactional attributes).

EJB Design Considerations

Let's take a look at some of the key decisions that we will have to make when designing our EJB components.

Entity vs. Session Beans

The decision whether to use an entity bean or a session bean is very simple; entity beans represent data, session beans represent process. More specifically, entity beans should represent single instances of transactional data. If the data must be edited or maintained in a transaction, use an entity bean. If, on the other hand, the data is essentially a "snapshot" of data, use a stateless session bean to obtain the information from an entity bean and return it as a value object. This way, the entity bean instance will only exist for the duration of the session bean's method, which is a very short time.

A large proportion of information in many applications is presented as a snapshot – a static representation of the data as it existed at the time that the request for that data was made. If the data is obtained through an entity bean, particularly for larger sets of data, unnecessary contention could occur because this data is managed by a transaction. To avoid this, the snapshot data should be obtained through a stateless session bean.

Session beans represent business processes and so this is where all business logic should be maintained – including data validation. Invariably, data validation is the result of business rules and these rules do not change from instance to instance of the data. Therefore, they should be maintained outside of the entity bean. Furthermore, we should strive to keep our entity beans as small as possible.

If our entity beans are too big, we could end up defeating or reducing the effectiveness of the EJB container's object cache. This is because the size of the cache is constrained by the amount of memory allocated to it rather than a set number of object instances. The larger the entity beans, the less that can fit into the cache, and therefore the less effective the cache will be. Even if adding the data validation code to the entity bean has an apparently small effect on its size, it is very important to remember one of the most basic rules of concurrent applications: changes, no matter how minimal, can affect the performance by orders of magnitude.

Stateful vs. Stateless Session Beans

As with everything else in EJB development, the decision to use a stateless or stateful session bean will have to be considered on an individual, component-by-component basis. While the choice to use one implementation over the other is mostly a matter of preference, there are performance implications to take into consideration with either option. Mostly, however, it comes down to this: stateful session beans require more server resources, while stateless session beans utilize more network resources.

Let's take a closer look at what using these two types of beans actually means from a design perspective.

Stateful Beans

Stateful beans maintain client data across method invocations. The data might be something as simple as a long-typed client ID, or as complex as an entire collection of objects representing an online shopper's personal information, their shopping cart, and dynamically generated pricing information for each item that they have selected. Obviously, if more state information must be maintained, more memory will be utilized by the object's instance. Since an EJB application could easily have tens of thousands of concurrent users, the memory utilization can get quite high. The nature of most business applications is transactional, and sporadic transactions at that. A typical online shopper will make a page request every 30 seconds. On average, they will interact with their shopping cart every three minutes. Knowing this allows an EJB server to maintain sessions with these tens of thousands of concurrent clients despite the fact that it would only be able to realistically handle a couple of hundred simultaneous clients.

This differentiation between concurrent and simultaneous clients is the key to an application's capability to handle large volumes of users and is achieved by persisting the state data between requests. In our online shopping example, even if the client data is requested for each page (such as the customer's name), they are only making a request every 30 seconds. The persistence-cycle, writing stateful information to storage and retrieving it on subsequent requests, requires a considerable amount of processing on the part of the server. In addition to the disk-based I/O, which is very slow and expensive compared to in-memory operations, objects must be serialized and de-serialized, and classes must be loaded and verified. All of this is in addition to the socket and RMI operational management that is required to handle the request.

Also, keep in mind that unless a special low-level file management service has been implemented on the server, most operating systems perform file I/O synchronously. That is, file operations will block the threads in which they are executing. Thus, the use of stateful beans has a potentially higher thread-count requirement. We must also be careful that we are not storing too much state data on the server. If our objects get too big, memory could be exhausted and the operating system will have to utilize a swap file (virtual memory). Should this occur, our application would suffer serious performance degradation.

This is not to say that stateful beans should not be used – it is just very important that we understand the consequences of our design decisions.

Stateless Beans

Stateless session beans have their own set of issues to take into consideration. With stateless beans, data that would otherwise be stored on the server is now stored on the client. Each time a remote method is invoked, all of the pertinent data that is required by that method must be passed as a parameter. Recall that this data might be the customer object and a collection of product items representing their shopping cart, or it might just be the customer's ID. In the case of the former, a lot of data will be crossing the network and, with the latter, any additional client information will have to be maintained in a database (or similar) and retrieved on each call. In either case, data will be passed with every request to the server. This creates an additional load on the network, which is a finite resource – unlike the server's memory area, which is dynamic (via swap files) and expandable (by adding more RAM).

Objects that are passed as parameters must be serializable and we must take care that our objects are not too large. It is much too easy to think that we are passing a simple Employee object when, in fact, we are passing in the employee, the department that Employee object references, and all of the employees that the Department object references. Before we know it, we could be passing a company's entire employee structure when we only intended to send a single entity. The lesson here is to know the extent of your object's graph and to master the use of transient object references.

Security may also be a concern when maintaining state data on the client side. Server-side data has the built-in advantage of being inaccessible to a curious end-user – not so with client-side data. If sensitive information constitutes the state data, it might be better to keep it on the server.

Bean-managed vs. Container-managed Persistence

As discussed early on in this book, one of the biggest advantages that Enterprise JavaBeans provide is the convenience of container-managed persistence (CMP). Many developers prefer CMP for the speed with which they can develop their applications. Indeed, the whole purpose of EJBs is to free the developer from the complexities of developing a distributed, multi-user application, allowing them to concentrate on the business implementations that make their applications unique. For all of its advantages, however, CMP carries with it some significant constraints that might make us consider using bean-managed persistence (BMP) instead.

First and foremost, all of the database logic of CMP beans is contained within the deployment descriptor. This eliminates the potential for reuse among non-EJB clients and hence, the logic must be duplicated among different components. A large percentage of EJB systems will have some non-EJB clients. These non-EJB clients will have to have their own database logic in order to interact with the system. BMP-based entity beans have the database access code contained directly in them. By maintaining this code in a separate package of database access objects, both the entity beans and non-EJB objects can utilize a single instance of the logic. As a result, reuse is greatly increased, the code is easier to maintain, and code duplication is avoided.

Another reason for using bean-managed persistence is that it provides us with greater control over the data implementation. Relationships are easier to manage because we develop the persistence code ourselves. Most CMP implementations will provide us with the option of creating the database schema for us, leaving us with little control or understanding of the underlying data layer. By contrast, with BMP we have complete control of the schema and how it is manipulated. There are a few good OO-to-relational-data modelers on the market to assist with a lot of the limitations that CMP has when it comes with relationships. Furthermore, the Enterprise JavaBeans 2.0 specification introduces more robust handling of relationships among entity beans.

Of course, there is still the issue of whether to even host the database processing logic in the EJB tier at all. Performance of data operations will always be faster at the database level. Most databases provide support for pre-compiled operations or stored procedures. Container-managed beans do not support the use of these stored procedures.

A lot of data validation involves comparisons to other existing data. These data constraints are part of the ANSI SQL standard and are supported by nearly all databases. When the container is given the responsibility to generate the schema, the opportunity to specify these constraints is typically not provided. Furthermore, triggers (stored procedures that are automatically invoked when an arbitrary data event occurs) are also not available.

While many database systems also provide a series of tools for analyzing and optimizing the performance of database operations, these tools will have little value if we are using CMP. If our application needs to be database neutral, as might be the case if we are developing a shrink-wrapped or lightly customized application, then portability becomes an issue. When portability is important, we should consider using dynamically generated SQL that is managed at the object level. If, on the other hand, the application will always use the same database or is likely to change only once (from Sybase to Oracle, for example), then portability is not as critical and the database logic can be maintained at the database level.

Another strategy is to provide different database-specific implementations for more popular DBMS's such as Oracle, DB2, Sybase, and Microsoft SQL Server. These layers can have database-specific routines that leverage the strengths and avoid the weaknesses of these databases. For other databases that are not supported by a specialized library, a generic set of libraries could also be provided. This gives our application the ability to take advantage of some of the more robust features of the more popular databases while still maintaining portability across other unknown systems.

If we anticipate that non-Java clients such as Perl, Visual Basic, and C++ might access the application, then the database logic is better contained in the database itself for the sake of consistency and maintainability, as well as performance.

Remote vs. Local Interfaces

With the introduction of local interfaces in the EJB 2.0 specification, developers now have another decision to make – whether to utilize local interfaces for their server-side components. Local interfaces provide certain benefits with respect to performance.

In previous versions of Enterprise JavaBeans (prior to 2.0), if an EJB component wanted to communicate with another component within the same container, it had to do so through the target bean's component (remote) interface. This meant that all communication had to be done through the RMI proxy layer – despite the fact that these objects were local to each other. Of course, this created a lot of unnecessary communications overhead, as RMI is only required for remote objects to interact with each other.

The advent of local interfaces seeks to reduce the amount of overhead by allowing components local to each other to communicate as such. This requires a little extra work on the part of the developer. Essentially, in addition to the standard `EJBHome` and `EJBObject` interfaces, local versions must now also be provided. These are the `EJBLocalHome` and `EJBLocalObject` interfaces – the details of which have been described previously.

While the use of local interfaces can offer improved performance, there are certain issues to be aware of.

Local Interfaces – Issues to be Aware Of

To begin with, local interfaces simply bypass the RMI proxy layer. They do not circumvent the container services layer that provides caching, transactions, security, and the like. The upside of this is that these benefits are still provided. The downside is that these benefits are still provided – whether we need them or not. So, the performance overhead of the container is still there.

Another difference between the behavior of remote and local interfaces to keep in mind is that while objects are passed by value in remote invocations, they are passed by reference in local method calls. Thus, a component can no longer assume that it is safe to directly modify object parameters that are passed to it.

Components that utilize a local interface will also be required to distinguish between clients that access it remotely and those that are local. The EJB 2.0 specification dictates that different exceptions apply to different interfaces. Components that support remote invocation are required to return remote exceptions, while local interfaces must support local variants of exceptions. For example, in a traditional (remote) scenario where a client accesses a component with the wrong transaction context, the component or container would throw a `javax.transaction.TransactionRequiredException`. If the client is accessing the component through a local interface, a `javax.ejb.TransactionRequiredLocalException` will be thrown. This distinction between remote and local access prevents our components from true location transparency.

Perhaps a bigger concern is that, if components are to communicate through local interfaces, they must be co-located within the same container instance. This effectively raises the level of connasence between the two components. If an application needs to be scaled up and its components are physically partitioned among several servers, they will not be able to utilize local interfaces. Instead, they will have to revert to the more traditional method of remote method invocation. This requires that the client component must be aware of its location, as well as the physical location of the remote component. Utilizing local interfaces essentially makes our component location-dependant. As a result, scalability is limited and will require that changes be made at the code level. At a minimum, the client component will have to utilize the `EJBHome` object, rather than the `EJBLocalHome` object.

Finally, there is no requirement that all methods that are exposed via the remote interface must be exposed in the local interface, and vice-versa. Thus, it is quite possible that changing from one to the other might break our component in that methods that were previously available no longer are. Even the method signatures themselves can change, and this may not even be apparent to the calling component. Recall that parameters in remote methods must be serializable. This is not the case with local interfaces. Since objects are passed by reference, rather than value, the requirement for serializability is eliminated. If a calling component is local, but needs to be re-located to another server, it may not be able to communicate with the (now) remote object in the same way that it was used to.

In conclusion, while local interfaces have a lot to offer by way of improved performance, it does come at the cost of portability and connascence. If local interfaces are to be used, these issues will have to be taken into consideration as part of the initial design, and the benefits will have to be carefully weighed against the detriments.

Summary

While Enterprise JavaBeans greatly simplifies the task of implementing a robust, scalable system, we are not alleviated of the complexities of its design. A well-planned, well-partitioned system offers several key benefits, regardless of whether our application is distributed or standalone.

We have examined some of the issues that we must take into consideration when determining which technologies to implement and, within Enterprise JavaBeans, how to design our components. In particular, we looked at the following topics:

- ❑   The granularity of our components, and how this will make a significant impact on their performance and reusability.

- ❑   Whether to implement entity beans or session beans; stateful or stateless beans; bean-managed or container-managed persistence methods; the utilization of local vs. remote interfaces.

- ❑   We cannot, *should not*, assume that we can make a blanket decision that will apply to all of our components. Design is an iterative process, and these iterations must take place with each aspect of our design.

Of course, one chapter is never sufficient to cover all of the topics germane to good distributed application design. For further discussion, the *J2EE Blueprints* from Sun Microsystems (downloadable from http://java.sun.com/) is an excellent next step.

Now that we understand what approaches to take when designing our EJB applications, in the next chapter we'll move on to examine some specific design patterns we can utilize.

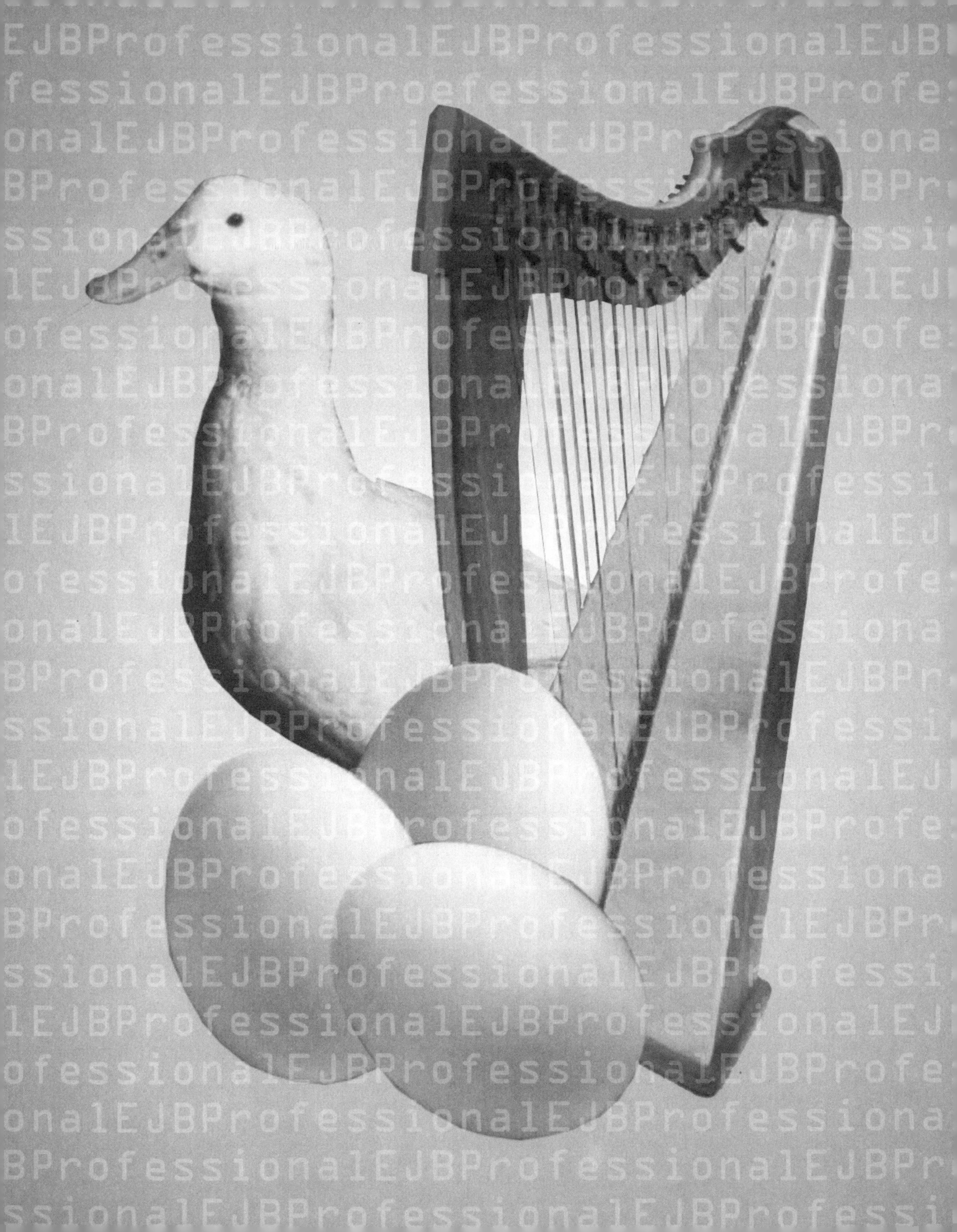

12

Common EJB Design Patterns

Design patterns provide solutions to commonly occurring problems in the design of various systems. They effectively provide programmers with a blueprint of an approachable solution to a particular problem. However, because many applications are built without applying proper design patterns, one of the main benefits of object-oriented systems – design and code reusability – is not realized. Design patterns thus enable "design reuse", although not always "code reuse". The difference between code reuse and design reuse is that the latter has a much higher return on the investment and a much higher probability of solving a business problem than the former. The latter can be used in building architectures where similar domains are involved.

In this chapter, we'll start by taking a look at what design patterns actually are, and then we'll be examining four of the more common design patterns:

- ❑ The Business Delegate pattern
- ❑ The Session Façade design pattern
- ❑ The Value Object design pattern
- ❑ The Aggregate Entity design pattern

For each of these patterns, we'll be studying the following points:

- ❑ The intent of the pattern
- ❑ The motivation behind the pattern
- ❑ The applicability of the pattern
- ❑ The participants in the pattern
- ❑ The structure of the pattern

❑   The collaborations required

❑   Any consequences of using the pattern

❑   How to implement the pattern

❑   Any related patterns

Design for Reuse

In the world of object-oriented design and development, reuse has the following three levels:

❑   **Framework reuse**
    Represents *design and code reuse*, the highest level of reuse. An EJB container can be thought as a framework because once you deploy your EJBs into the container, it takes care of all other activities such as instantiation, security, method callbacks, and so on. Thus, a container provides you with the highest level of code and design reuse. You do not have to design and code containers whenever you need to develop EJBs.

❑   **Design pattern reuse**
    Represents *design reuse*, an advanced level of reuse. This chapter covers design pattern reuse in the context of EJBs. Design patterns do not necessarily bring about code reuse, because they are conceptual design entities that need to be implemented by programmers using their choice of language and platform. A design pattern is described as a set of classes and instances that collaborate to solve a specific kind of design problem. Thus, a single class, such as the HashMap, can't constitute a design pattern. However, HashMap still contributes to reuse at the class-level.

❑   **Class reuse**
    Represents *code reuse*, the lowest level of reuse. For example, a well-designed class such as HashMap gives you code-reuse advantage because this class can be used in many programs with no (or very few) modifications.

We should note that design patterns are not always specific implementations. In fact, programmers sometimes do not realize that they are using design patterns in their code. For example, when a programmer codes a simplified interface to a complex subsystem it might not be apparent that they are actually using a pattern in their code. An understanding of various design patterns would enable the programmer to realize that they are using, for instance, the well-known façade pattern in their code. Knowledge of the various design patterns, and the ability to apply them to code design, makes a programmer's design and code highly reusable. Also, it makes life easier for another programmer who is trying to understand this design and code.

Since this is a book on Enterprise JavaBeans, we'll concentrate on the patterns related to EJB technology. The EJB framework is all about building highly specialized business logic components; therefore use of some common design patterns will obviously help to build better reusable business components. These components are traditionally distributed over the presentation, business, and integration tiers. Currently, the Java developer community has collected quite a large catalog of patterns using a tiered approach.

Cataloging and naming specific patterns helps communication between programmers. For example, mentioning to a colleague who is pattern-literate that design makes use of a Factory Method pattern, will immediately make it clear to them what you are doing and will aid their understanding of the design. Patterns are expected to be added to the present collection as an ongoing activity and there may be patterns that will be added as a part of the integration tier related to legacy integration and connectors. It is worth mentioning, however, that beginners should not use patterns for the sake of it – they're not *always* appropriate for what we're doing.

What is a Design Pattern?

In an informal sense, a **design pattern** is a convenient way of reusing designs between projects and programmers. The foremost reason for using design patterns is to keep classes separated from each other and prevent them from knowing too much about each other. Thus, a coupled system (where many dependencies exists between classes) is a bad design principle, and using design patterns helps to prevent a system from being tightly coupled.

> **Design patterns are descriptions of communicating objects and classes that are customized to solve a general design problem in a particular context.**

Further details can be found in what is perhaps one of the most important computing books of the last decade – *Design Patterns: Elements of Reusable Object-Oriented Software*, by Gamma, Helm, Johnson, and Vlissides, from Addison-Wesley, ISBN 0-201-63361-2. This book has made a powerful impact on those wanting to understand and use design patterns for building enterprise systems.

The "Gang of Four" (GoF), as Gamma et al. are commonly referred to, have catalogued design patterns into three types:

❏ **Creational Patterns**
These patterns create objects, rather than instantiating them directly. In this case, objects are created to a given context. Examples of creational patterns are Singleton, Builder, Factory Method, and so on.

❏ **Structural Patterns**
These patterns help to compose larger structures from classes and objects using inheritance to compose interfaces. Examples include Adapter, Composite, Façade, and so on.

❏ **Behavioral Patterns**
These patterns describe communication between objects and classes, characterizing the complex control flow. This characterization helps to concentrate only on the ways objects are interconnected in the system. Examples are Observer, Visitor, Mediator, etc.

Design patterns can be further distinguished into architecture, mechanisms, and idioms. They are very useful for the describing high-level concepts that will be valuable for newbie EJB system designers. Following the general principles of object-oriented design, we should additionally take note of following design tips:

❏ **Program to an interface and not to an implementation**
This means simply the top of any class hierarchy should be abstract so that derived classes will have more freedom to implement methods described in the abstract parent. More specifically, software plays roles, and interfaces are the way that we codify those roles in software.

❏ **Favor object composition over inheritance**
This means that we should include other classes inside the class we are defining, instead of using inheritance. Object composition helps to get functionality by assembling existing components and thereby avoiding creation of new components. In practice, both object composition and inheritance collaborate together to some degree.

EJB Design Patterns

The Sun Java Center is Sun's consulting organization that is focused on producing the architecture for Java technology-based solutions. It has created a catalogue of J2EE design patterns that describe typical problems encountered by enterprise application developers and provides solutions for these problems. At present, the Sun Java Center has cataloged 15 patterns in following three categories:

❑ **Presentation-tier patterns** – Contain the patterns related to servlets and JSP technology.

❑ **Business tier-patterns** – Contain the patterns related to the Enterprise Java Beans technology, the topic of this chapter.

❑ **Integration-tier patterns** – Contain the patterns related to JMS and JDBC.

Sun Java Center has identified the following seven patterns in the business tier:

Pattern Name	Intent of the Pattern
Business Delegate	Helps in decoupling the presentation and service tier in an application.
Session Façade	Helpful when complexity of objects in the business tier needs to be hidden; the main intent of this pattern is to centralize workflow.
Value Object	Useful when either the presentation, business, or integration tier needs to exchange data.
Aggregate Entity	Used in designing coarse-grained persistent business-tier objects.
Value Object Assembler	Used to compose business-tier object, which serves as a single source object to multiple data sources.
Value List Handler	Used to cache results and process them as a result of query execution.
Service Locator	Used to hide complex service lookup and network operation interfaces.

The Business Delegate, Session Façade, Value Object, and Aggregate Entity design patterns are the most common patterns used in any typical enterprise application design and, as such, this chapter will concentrate on these four patterns. Although these four patterns will solve the most commonly occurring business problems, it is useful to be aware of other options. As seen in the table above, the other design patterns catalogued by Sun under business-tier patterns are the Value Object Assembler, Value List Handler, and Service Locator.

Design Pattern Template

Design patterns are documented for users to understand them better. Common practice is to describe each object-oriented design pattern using a standard template. This practice makes choosing a design pattern much easier for users because the patterns are described in a similar manner, which makes comparing them much easier.

The table below shows a template that will be used in this chapter to describe design patterns:

Elements	Description
Name	The popular name and classification of a pattern. The name conveys the pattern's essence briefly. We can also specify other known names of the design pattern.
Intent	A pattern's rationale and aim. The intent conveys a particular design issue or problem that it addresses.
Motivation	Gives the reasons and motivations that affect the problem and the solution, including reasons why a user might choose to use the pattern.
Applicability	Situations in which the design pattern can be applied. Conveys the context.
Participants	Presents a list of the pattern's participants and their roles in the pattern.
Structure	Uses UML class diagrams to show the basic structure of the pattern participants.
Collaborations	Dynamics of the design pattern. Using UML conventions, conveys how participants collaborate to carry out their responsibilities. Participants are the classes and/or objects participating in the design pattern.
Consequences	Tradeoffs and results of using the pattern. Conveys the consequences of applying the abstract structure to a system's architecture.
Implementation	Sample code to illustrate how a user might implement the pattern.
Sample Code	Provides a sample implementation of the pattern.
Related Patterns	Design patterns that have a closely related intent. Conveys the important differences, and lists with which other patterns the pattern in question should be used.

Let's start with the details of the Business Delegate pattern.

The Business Delegate Pattern

Components in the presentation tier directly interact with services in the business tier. Thus, changes to the business tier make the presentation-tier components vulnerable to changes. The **Business Delegate design pattern** helps to solve this problem.

Intent

The Business Delegate pattern is intended to reduce coupling between the presentation and business tiers. It hides the various complex implementation details for business services like lookup and access details.

Motivation

Why would we want to use this pattern? Essentially, there are two main reasons. Firstly, presentation-tier components sometimes interact directly with business services. If such interaction is to be direct, with presentation-tier components directly calling business service methods, then whenever the business service implementation changes, the presentation-tier components will also need to be changed. Additionally, network-related performance issues arise because of too many direct invocations from the presentation to business tier and there is no client-side caching.

The second reason we might want to use a Business Delegate pattern is that, because of the multi-tiered and highly distributed architecture, clients are forced to deal with networking issues. Using this pattern helps to minimize the exposure of business-layer services to clients, avoiding network-related performance problems.

Applicability

We should look to use the Business Delegate design pattern when:

❑ Presentation-tier clients need to access business-tier components

❑ Business service implementation changes as requirements evolve

❑ A caching mechanism is needed for business service information

❑ Network traffic needs to be reduced by preventing direct invocation of business services by presentation-tier components

❑ Decoupling of the presentation- and business-tiers is desired

Participants

Let's look at the three participant objects in the Business Delegate pattern, and what they provide:

❑ **BusinessDelegate**
Shields client from the underlying implementation details of `BusinessService` and `LookupService`. Without Object ID, it uses `LookupService` to contact `BusinessService`; with Object ID, it calls `BusinessService` directly.

❑ **LookupService**
Encapsulates implementation details for `BusinessService` lookup.

❑ **BusinessService**
Implements business services in an application. An example would be a JNDI business-service layer, which provides services for the directory server. The business service is typically an EJB or a JMS component.

Structure

The following diagram represents the general structure of the Business Delegate pattern and a discussion of the process follows:

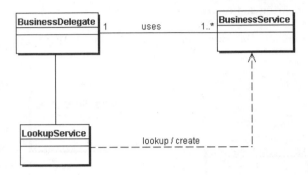

Whenever a client makes a request to `BusinessDelegate`, it can either contact `BusinessService` directly or use `LookupService` to contact `BusinessService`. This decision is based upon whether the client makes a call to the `BusinessDelegate` with or without the Object ID of the `BusinessService` object. Typically, the Object ID would be a handle to the underlying Business Service object, which is an entity or session Bean, and the `BusinessDelegate` would return this handle as a string object. If the Object ID is present as a part of the request, the `BusinessDelegate` will call the `BusinessService` directly. If an Object ID is not present, the `BusinessDelegate` will use the `LookupService` to get an Object ID.

We now present a sequence diagram showing the interactions of the Business Delegate pattern. In the first case we will consider, the client is making a request using an Object ID:

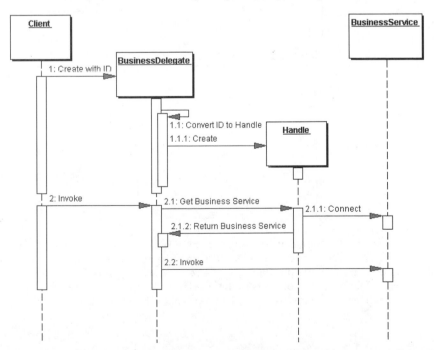

The Client requests the BusinessDelegate to create the BusinessService, the BusinessDelegate calls a get-service method on the LookupService that looks up the required BusinessService and returns the BusinessService. The Client now directly invokes the BusinessService. Next, the Client requests for the BusinessService ID, which it does through BusinessDelegate. The BusinessDelegate uses GetHandle() on the BusinessService, then converts the handle to a string and returns the ID to the Client.

Now we'll look at the Business Delegate sequence diagram with a client making a request without an Object ID:

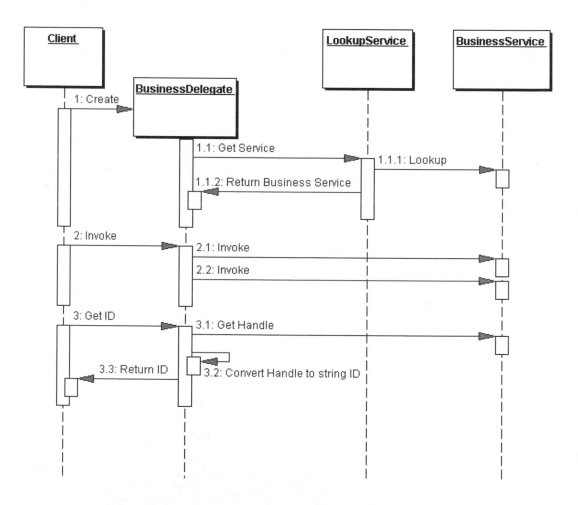

In the above diagram, the Client calls the BusinessDelegate to create the BusinessService with ID. The BusinessDelegate converts the ID to the Handle and calls the Create() method of the Handle. Next the Client invokes the BusinessDelegate which, in turn, calls the Handle to get BusinessService. The Handle connects to the BusinessService and returns the BusinessService. Then, the BusinessDelegate invokes the BusinessService.

Collaborations

We can now summarize how the various components participating in a system using the Business Delegate pattern work together. Presentation-tier components use the Business Delegate to interact with Business Service objects. If the Object ID is present in the client request, then Business Service object will be called directly. If the request contains no Object ID then the Lookup Service is used to contact the Business Service object.

Consequences

The Business Delegate pattern fulfills several roles:

❏   It decouples presentation tier and business tier objects. Centralization makes object management easier because the BusinessDelegate handles all the calls to the service layer. Thus, any changes to the service layer can easily be captured by the BusinessDelegate rather than having to worry about changing objects in the presentation tier.

❏   It is responsible for shielding clients from underlying implementation specifics, and also translates service-layer exceptions into business exceptions.

❏   It creates a simpler uniform interface.

❏   It provides caching services allowing for improved performance of common service requests from the client.

Implementation

There are many issues to be considered when implementing the Business Delegate pattern, including the following:

❏   The Business Delegate pattern presents a client-side abstraction; it may still require modification if the underlying Business Service object method changes.

❏   It must handle all the network-related exceptions and convert them into useful business exceptions that can be understood by the client.

❏   The Lookup Service that is used by the Business Delegate should be implemented as a separate component using its own design pattern (the Service Locator pattern, not covered here).

Sample Code

The following code snippet shows how a BusinessDelegate pattern acts as the delegate for the business services and how a client can invoke its methods to either create a BusinessService or invoke methods on the BusinessService or getID() of a BusinessService. Different "flavors" of the BusinessService can obviously be constructed, but here we have provided a simple example to demonstrate what is needed to construct BusinessDelegate.

```
/**
 * Class to show the Business Delegate Pattern construction.
 */
public class BusinessDelegate {
  public BusinessService Create() {
```

```
      // Look for the corresponding service using a
      // lookup service mechanism.
      BusinessService = LookupService.getService();
      return BusinessService;
    }

    public void Invoke() {
      BusinessService.invoke();
    }

    public String getID() {

      // Get the handle by calling the LookupService
      // and convert the handle to a string.
      return id;
    }

    private BusinessService BusinessService;
    private String id;

  }
```

Related Patterns

There are a number of patterns that can be effectively combined with the Business Delegate pattern:

- ❑ The Service Locator pattern (from Sun Java Center) can often be used with Business Delegate pattern for implementing the Lookup Service component of Business Delegate pattern.

- ❑ The Proxy pattern (GoF) can be used to make the Business Delegate pattern act as a proxy for objects in the business tier.

- ❑ The Adapter pattern (GoF) can be used to make the Business Delegate pattern provide coupling for disparate systems.

The Session Façade Design Pattern

When writing service-layer components on the server side we have to deal with complex enterprise beans that encapsulate the business logic and data. The exposed interfaces are complicated and therefore the complexity of the services layer increases proportionally. A **Session Façade design pattern** can help reduce such complexities.

Intent

The Session Façade design pattern is helpful when the complexity of object interactions in the business tier needs to be hidden. The main intent of the Session Façade pattern is to centralize workflow handling. This pattern manages business objects and provides uniform, coarse-grained object service access to clients. In object terminology, coarse-grained refers to an object that has its own lifecycle and manages its own relationships with other objects. Furthermore, methods from coarse-grained objects tend to be of a high level (for example, `addPerson()` rather than individual `setLastName()`, `setFirstName()`, `setSocialSecurity()`, etc. methods).

Motivation

Business objects that provide a processing service are implemented as session beans. For example, in a shopping cart application, the cart will be a session bean. Objects that represent a view of persistent storage shared across multiple sessions are implemented as entity beans. If clients interact directly with these business objects, tight coupling occurs between clients and business objects. This dependency makes the client represent and implement complex interactions for business object lookups and creations. It also makes the client manage transactions, manage relationships between the participants (business objects), and represent/implement complex interactions for business object lookups and creations.

Many method invocations between the client and the application server hosting the EJBs lead to network performance issues, as each request to an EJB goes through the network to the server. As the business objects are directly exposed to the client objects, there is no unified strategy to access the business objects; because of this, the business object can be abused.

Using a Session Façade design pattern in the architecture of the system prevents these problems.

Applicability

We would use the Session Façade design pattern if we wanted to:

❑ Prevent tight coupling between clients and business objects

❑ Prevent many remote method invocations between client and server leading to network performance problems

❑ Provide a uniform client access strategy

❑ Reduce the number of business objects in the service layer over the network

❑ Provide a centralized workflow by hiding the underlying interactions and inter-dependencies between business objects

Participants

Let's look at the key participants in the Session Façade design pattern:

❑ **SessionFacade**
Usually a session bean providing a high-level abstraction to the client, it offers coarse-grained access to the participating business objects in the system.

❑ **BusinessObject**
Can be either session beans or entity beans, or a data access object, and provides data/service to the Session Façade bean. A `DataAccessObject` abstracts the data sources available to an enterprise application, for example, an LDAP or Oracle data source, and provides transparent access to data. Sun has catalogued this under integration-tier patterns.

Structure

The following class diagram represents the structure of the Session Façade design pattern:

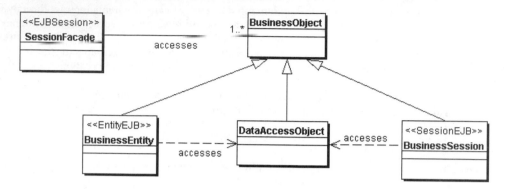

The above diagram demonstrates how a SessionFacade accesses a BusinessObject. The BusinessObject can call a session bean or an entity bean, or use a DataAccessObject to access business data. Note that all the objects in this diagram are on the server – the client only talks to the SessionFacade, which relays the requests through to the appropriate business objects.

We will now look at a sequence diagram of the Session Façade. In the diagram below, the SessionFacade acts as a façade for the underlying services. The Client invokes the SessionFacade which, in turn, invokes the get()/set() methods of the entity beans in order to get the data or invoke the other BusinessSession. This then gets data represented by the entity bean BusinessEntity2:

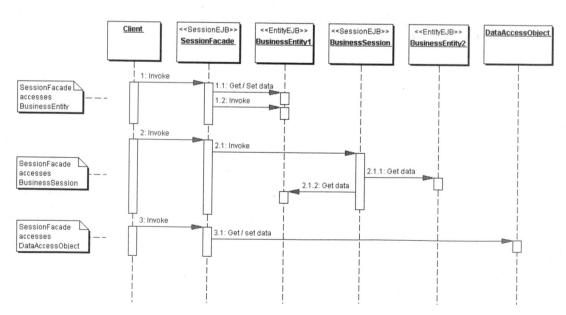

Collaboration

Now we can summarize the workings of the various components participating in a system using the Session Façade pattern. Clients use the Session Façade design pattern to interact with business objects because the Session Façade manages business objects and provides a uniform, coarse-grained service access layer to clients.

Consequences

In this section we will highlight the roles fulfilled by the Session Façade pattern:

❑ This pattern represents a boundary between clients and the business tier, and encompasses interactions between them. It adds more value to sophisticated applications rather than simple ones.

❑ In spite of the complexity of the participating business objects, it provides a simple uniform interface to the clients.

❑ It decouples the underlying business objects and systems from clients, thus reducing tight coupling. Separating workflow into a Session Façade pattern eliminates direct dependency between clients and business objects; thus workflow is centralized.

❑ It serves to reduce network overhead between client and business objects. The Session Façade manages data transfers and method invocations because of the closeness between it and the participants. The idea is that the Session Façade and the entities it accesses will likely be in the same JVM, which eliminates the need for network calls. By using local references to entity beans, in line with the EJB 2.0 specification, a call-by-value to the façade's "helper" beans can be eliminated, with replacement by call-by-reference, which increases the performance dramatically.

❑ It is a highly coarse-grained abstraction of the workflow. An application needs to be divided into logical subsystems, and each to be provided with a Session Façade.

❑ It manages security policies for the application. Because of its coarse-grained nature, Session Façade makes it easier for security management.

❑ It represents the workflow for the use cases in the system and so transaction management can be applied at this level. The Session Façade offers a central place for managing and defining transaction control in a coarse-grained fashion.

❑ It provides fewer remote interfaces to clients, which reduces the scope for application degradation because of the limited number of interactions between clients and the Session Façade when compared to the direct interaction between clients and objects in the business tier.

Implementation

There are many strategies that need to be considered when implementing a Session Façade:

❑ **Stateless Session Façade**
When implementing this pattern, a decision has to be made whether it needs to be implemented as stateless or stateful. During the analysis phase, we look how the use cases interact. If the interaction is non-conversational then a single method in the Session Façade initiates the use case, and we should implement the façade as stateless.

❑ **Stateful Session Façade**
If a use case is conversational, then a stateful Session Façade needs to be implemented. The reason for this is that there are multiple method calls and, the state needs to be saved during each client remote method invocation.

❑ **Business Object either as Session or an Entity Bean**
We should represent the `BusinessObject` as a session bean when it provides a business service/data. The `BusinessObject` as an entity bean is the most common use in Session Façade. Session Façade can wrap all the participating entity beans and provide a coarse-grained method to perform the necessary business function for the client, hiding complex entity bean interactions.

Sample Code

We now present a snippet of code that uses a Session Façade, which provides methods to the client to create a user in an LDAP system. This example code is taken from a fairly large enterprise application that has been simplified for the sake of brevity. It is therefore intended just to give a taste of the Session Façade, and to help readers to understand how the pattern is efficiently constructed.

In the entire system, LDAP services were written using JNDI architecture to interface with the directory server. Below is a Session Façade pattern that acts between the client and the LDAP service and is used to add/get users to/from the system, and to check whether users actually exist in the directory service:

```
/**
 * Code snippet for a session facade which provides the
 * interface for an underlying LDAP service.
 */
import java.util.*;
import java.io.*;
import java.rmi.*;
import java.net.*;
import javax.ejb.*;
import javax.naming.*;
import javax.naming.directory.*;

public class UserService implements SessionBean {

  private User ldapUser = null;

  /**
   * Null constructor, mandatory for serialization/activation/passivation.
   */
  public UserService() {
    try {
      if (ldapUser == null) {
        ldapUser = new User();
      }
    } catch (Exception e) {

      // do something
    }
  }

  private transient javax.ejb.SessionContext m_ctx = null;

  public User getUser(String name) throws UserException {
```

```
    User userinfo = null;

    try {
      userinfo = User.get(name);

    } catch (Exception e) {

      // do something
    }

    return userinfo;
}

public void setUser(User user, String username,
                    String password) throws UserException {

  // Code sets the user in ldap.
}

/**
 * Check if the user exists in the system
 * (userName is the associated username).
 */
public boolean isUserExists(String userName) {
  boolean userExists = false;

  if (ldapuser != null) {
    userExists = User.isUserExists(userName);
  }

  return userExists;
}

public void setSessionContext(javax.ejb.SessionContext ctx) {
  m_ctx = ctx;
}

public void ejbCreate() throws CreateException {
  try {
    if (ldapUser == null) {
      ldapUser = new User();
    }
  } catch (Exception e) {

    // do something
  }
}

/**
 * Called by the container when this instance is being destroyed due
 * to a user remove() operation, or after expiration of a timeout.
 */
public void ejbRemove() {}

/**
 * Called when the instance is activated from its "passive" state. The
 * instance should acquire any resource that it has released earlier in
 * the ejbPassivate() method.
 */
public void ejbActivate() {}

/**
 * Called before the instance enters the "passive" state. The instance
```

```
       * should release any resources that it can re-acquire later in the
       * ejbActivate() method.
       */
    public void ejbPassivate() {}

}
// end class
```

Related Patterns

The Session Façade is in fact derived from the Façade pattern (described by GoF). The Service Locator pattern can be used with Session Façade to reduce code complexity and exploit other benefits offered by this pattern. Additionally, the Business Delegate pattern uses Session Façade when the presentation tier sends requests to access the business tier. The Session Façade provides the services to the Business Delegate.

The Value Object Design Pattern

In enterprise applications built using the EJB framework, there is a necessity for exchange of data between different distributed components. Furthermore, as we have learned, the EJB framework implements enterprise application Business components as session beans and entity beans. The **Value Object design pattern** helps to ease the data exchange between the enterprise beans.

Intent

The Value Object pattern is used to encapsulate business data. When the client requests EJBs for business data, the EJB will construct the value object, populate the object with data, and pass it by value to the client. If the client needs to return the data, it will do much the same – create the value object, populate it with data, and send it to the EJB.

Motivation

A session bean is intended for a client session, and an entity bean is for multiple sessions and is representative of persistent data. Some of the service methods in a session bean may return data, so the client needs to call several accessor methods for each data element. In the case of an entity bean, it may provide accessor methods. Each call by the client to obtain data for every attribute it needs is a remote call. In both these cases, as the usage of the remote methods increase, performance will be degraded. There is also network overhead created in the process. To avoid this situation, a Value Object pattern is useful.

Applicability

We would use the Value Object design pattern when:

❑ Every remote call to get single data needs to be avoided to prevent network overheads

❑ Read transactions are most frequently used by clients for presentation, display, and other types of processing

❑ The client needs more than one attribute value of an enterprise bean

Participants

Let's now look at the key elements in the Value Object design pattern:

❑ **Client**
The client of the enterprise bean; it can therefore directly access the enterprise bean.

❑ **BusinessObject**
Can be a session bean or an entity bean; it creates and returns the value object to the client.

❑ **ValueObject**
An arbitrary, serializable Java object. It encompasses all the attribute values of an entity bean. The object can be designed to have one constructor to set all attribute values (the variables are made public). The variables can also be made protected or private. Mutator methods can be absent or present, based on the object construction requirements. The object creation is purely based on application requirements.

Structure

The following diagram represents the structure of the Value Object design pattern:

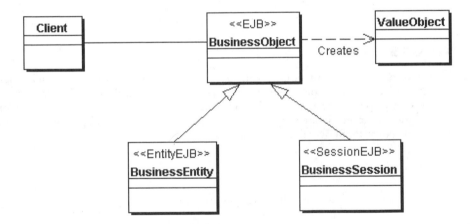

The `ValueObject` is constructed on demand by the EJB, and returned to the requesting client.

Next we turn to the interactions within the Value Object design pattern. In the sequence diagram overleaf, the `Client` requests `BusinessObject` to create a `ValueObject` and the `BusinessObject` returns the `ValueObject`. The `Client` can also call its own `ClientValueObject` to get values. As a note, there is also a "Client" version of the `ValueObject` since a call by value will give the client a local copy of the object so `get()`/`set()` methods won't occur against the "original" object:

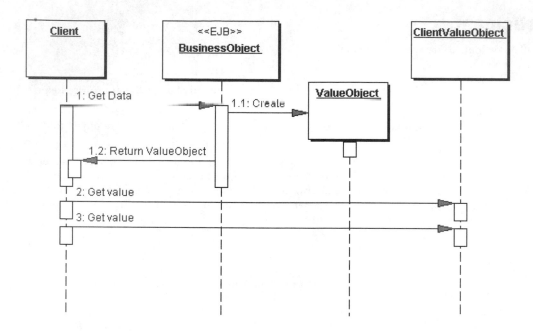

Collaborations

Following the usual format, in this section we will summarize how the various components participating in a system using the Value Object pattern work. We have seen that application clients need to exchange data with enterprise beans. To avoid making multiple calls between enterprise beans, the beans can be designed to create Value Object (or "data" place holders) and populate them with the necessary data then return them by value to the clients.

Consequences

The Value Object pattern provides the following functionality:

- Simplifies entity beans and remote interface definition. The entity beans can provide setData() and getData() methods to construct a value object and return as a single call the requested data to the client.

- Reduces duplication of code in the application.

- Reduces network calls, but transmits more data per call to the client. It is therefore important to compromise between fewer calls and more data per call.

Implementation

There are many strategies that need to be considered when implementing the Value Object design pattern; in this section we will look at two the most important ones.

Updateable Value Object Strategy

This strategy is mainly useful when the client needs to read/update data of an entity bean. In such a case, `BusinessObject` creates the `ValueObject` and provides `getData()` and `setData()` methods for the client to either get the necessary data items or update data items. Note that there will most likely be an impact on synchronization and version control of data. This strategy is illustrated in the class diagram below:

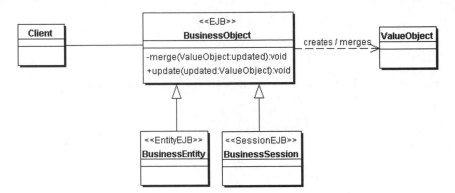

Multiple Value Object Strategy

Some application business objects can be very complex. Enterprise beans in these scenarios can produce value objects that provide data for parts of the application. As an example, in a Product-Sale Management System, objects representing the Product Price, Sale to Customer, Shipment to Customer, Delivery to Customer, Delivery-problem Report, Invoice to Customer, and Discount Agreement, can all be constructed as separate value objects and returned to the client on completing a sale.

So, with reference the following sequence diagram, when the `Client` needs `ValueObjectA` the `BusinessObject` entity bean will check for that instance of the object and return the needed data; if the client needs `ValueObjectB` that instance will be checked and returned. The `BusinessObject` thus acts as a factory, creating the needed `ValueObjects` as required:

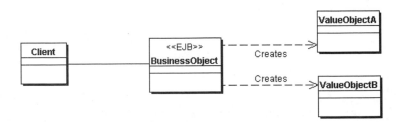

Sample Code

To demonstrate how the value object design pattern can be implemented, here is a simple example. First, we declare an `AuctionValueObject` class, which will act as our value object:

```
/**
 * A sample class shows the Value Object construction.
 */
public class AuctionValueObject implements java.io.Serializable {
```

```
    public String seller;
    public String description;
    public double startPrice;
    public String summary;
    public AuctionValueObject() {}

    // Constructor accepts all values.
    public AuctionValueObject(String seller, String description,
                             double startPrice, String summary) {
      init(seller, description, startPrice, summary);
    }

    // New constructor based on previous data.
    public AuctionValueObject(AuctionValueObject avo) {
      init(avo.seller, avo.description, avo.startPrice, avo.summary);
    }

    // Method to set the values.
    public void init(String seller, String description, double startPrice,
                    String summary) {
      this.seller = seller;
      this.description = description;
      this.startPrice = startPrice;
      this.summary = summary;
    }

    // Method creates a new AuctionValueObject.
    public AuctionValueObject getData() {
      return new AuctionValueObject(this);
    }
}
```

Then, we write our entity bean to extend our value object, thus inheriting the properties we need for the Value Object design pattern:

```
package auction;
import java.rmi.RemoteException;
import javax.ejb.*;
import java.util.*;
import java.text.NumberFormat;


public class AuctionItemBean extends AuctionValueObject
                            implements EntityBean {

  EntityContext ctx;

  // Creates the EJB.
  public void ejbCreate() throws CreateException {}

  // Standard EJB methods.
  public void ejbRemove() {}
  public void ejbActivate() {}
  public void ejbPassivate() {}
  public void ejbLoad() {}
  public void ejbStore() {}
  public void setEntityContext(EntityContext ctx) {
    this.ctx = ctx;
  }
  public void unsetEntityContext() {
```

```
    this.ctx = null;
  }

  // Client calls getData() inherited from the AuctionValueObject.
}
```

In the preceding class, we are making the entity bean `AuctionItemBean` directly inherit the value object strategy. This avoids code duplication because we are ensuring all the `AuctionItemBean` states are not duplicated in the `EntityBean` and `ValueObject` if the `ValueObject` is used as a separate class outside. The `getDataMethod()` of `AuctionValueObject`, when invoked on an object instance, will copy all the values into it and return it to the caller. In this way, we need only manage changes in the `ValueObject` alone.

Related Patterns

The Value Object design pattern has several associated patterns:

❑ Session Façade (from Sun Java Center) – Uses value objects as an exchange mechanism with participating entity beans. The façade acts as a proxy, through which the value objects from entity beans can be passed to the clients.

❑ Value Object Assembler (Sun Java Center) – Builds composite value objects from different data sources. These data sources are typically enterprise beans and are considered to be parts of the composite object.

❑ Value List Handler (Sun Java Center) – Provides a list of value objects dynamically, as and when required.

❑ Aggregate Entity (Sun Java Center) – A powerful design mechanism for EJBs when combined with the Value Object pattern because the Aggregate Entity pattern addresses complex requirements and issues involved in designing coarse-grained entity beans. We'll look at the Aggregate Entity design pattern in the next section.

The Aggregate Entity Design Pattern

As we know, entity beans are mainly used for persistent storage. While designing enterprise applications, entity beans need not represent every persistent object. They are better suited to a data structure approach. An **Aggregate Entity design pattern** is useful in designing this coarse-grained mechanism.

Intent

This pattern is used to model, represent, and manage a set of inter-related persistent objects rather than fine-grained entity beans. It represents a complete graph of objects.

Motivation

Persistent objects can be classified into two types: coarse-grained and dependent objects. The relationship between these two types of objects is a tree structure in which the coarse-grained object is the root and the dependent objects are either sub-trees or leaf-nodes. This structure reduces the number of entity beans required by the application, resulting in a highly coarse-grained entity bean that can optimize the benefits of entity beans.

Applicability

We would benefit from using the Aggregate Entity design pattern in the following cases:

- ❑ To avoid the high overhead associated with each individual entity bean.
- ❑ In applications involving entity bean attributes mapped directly to the relational database schema.
- ❑ To avoid the dependency created by the fine-grained mapping between the client and the underlying database schema. Direct mapping of the object model to a relational (that is, data) model yields fine-grained entity beans. These beans usually map to the database schema. This makes management of inter-entity bean relationships expensive.
- ❑ To decrease the "chattiness" of the applications due to inter-communication among fine-grained entity beans.
- ❑ To avoid additional chattiness occurring between the client and the fine-grained entity beans.

Participants

Let's look at the principal objects in the Aggregate Entity design pattern:

- ❑ **AggregateEntity**
  This is usually a coarse-grained object, or holds a reference to a coarse-grained object.
- ❑ **CoarseGrainedObject**
  A coarse-grained object has its own lifecycle and manages its own relationships with other objects. It can be contained within `AggregateEntity`, or the `AggregateEntity` can be coarse-grained itself.
- ❑ **DependentObject**
  Depends on the coarse-grained object, which manages the dependent object lifecycle.

Structure

The diagram below represents the general structure of the Aggregate Entity design pattern. Within this structure, the `AggregateEntity` bean contains the `CoarseGrainedObject`, which in turn contains the dependent objects:

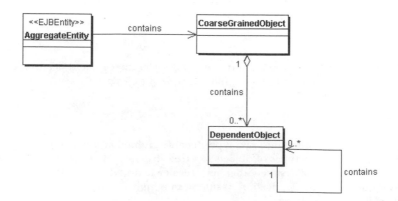

Turning our attention to the Aggregate Entity interactions, the following sequence diagram shows how the `Client` uses `AggregateEntity` to `set()`/`get()` data, which, in turn, calls the `CoarseGraineObject` to `set()`/`get()` the data, and subsequently calls various `DepedentObjects`:

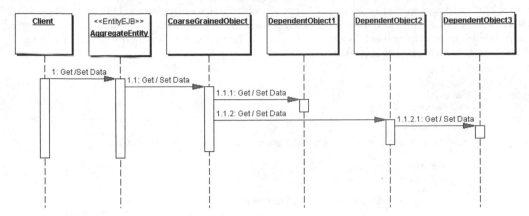

Collaborations

Summarizing how the various components of a system using the Aggregate Entity pattern works, we can state that this pattern creates coarse-grained objects that manage the lifecycle of dependent objects. The Aggregate Entity pattern takes advantage of a tree structure, and is used in designing coarse-grained persistent business-tier objects.

Consequences

The Aggregate Entity pattern provides us with the following functionality:

❑ Eliminates inter-entity bean relationships and aggregates dependent objects in to a single entity bean

❑ Improves manageability of the application by having fewer coarse-grained components

❑ Reduces the huge network overhead due to inter-entity bean communications

❑ Since the database schema is not exposed to the external world, it is hidden from the client

❑ Object granularity is created, which reduces chattiness because of the single remote method call

❑ Avoids repeated remote calls and multiple lookups

Implementation

There are a few strategies to be considered when implementing the Aggregate Entity pattern:

❑ The entity bean expresses and manages all relationships between the coarse-grained objects and dependent objects.

❑ Aggregate Entity has a tree structure. Loading all the dependencies can cause considerable strains on time and resources. This can be optimized using the lazy loading strategy, which involves loading the important dependent objects, and only loading others dynamically as and when needed.

Sample Code

The following sample code snippet shows how the Aggregate Entity design pattern can be constructed. Note that both `rpp` and `wpp` are two `PricePlan` objects that are entity beans. During `ejbLoad()` of the `DealBean`, both of the entity beans are checked and, if they are already created, they are loaded and populated into another object. When `getAllDetails()` method is called it will return the complete graph for the ID that is passed:

```
import javax.ejb.*;
import java.rmi.*;
import java.sql.*;
import java.util.*;

public class DealBean extends DetailObject implements EntityBean {

  public void ejbLoad() {

    if (wpp != null) {
      PricePlan.add(createWholePricePlanHome().findByPrimaryKey(
                                        new WholePricePlanPK(wpp)));
    }
    if (rpp != nul) {
      PricePlan.add(createRetailPricePlanHome()findByPrimaryKey(
                                        new RetailPricePlanPK(rpp)));
    }
  }

// This method returns the complete object graph of the entity bean
// Method made flexible so that you can return how many children you want.

  public DetailObject getAllDetails(int NoOfChild) {
    // In this method the detail object will be returned
    // with the complete object graph.
  }
   private RetailPricePlan rpp;
   private WholePricePlan wpp;
}
```

Related Patterns

We finish our discussion of the Aggregate Entity design pattern by mentioning the patterns that can be used with this pattern:

❑ Value Object pattern (Sun Java Center) – The Aggregate Entity pattern can use this pattern to construct value objects that are then used to serialize the coarse-grained and dependent objects tree or part of the required sub-tree.

❑ Session Façade (Sun Java Center) – If the dependent objects are entity beans, then the Session Façade pattern can be combined to manage the inter-entity bean relationships.

❑ Value Object Assembler (Sun Java Center) – If composite aggregate value objects are needed from the Aggregate Entity pattern, the Value Object Assembler pattern can be used.

Summary

In this chapter, we discussed the details and uses of design patterns in EJB component construction for the business tier. Specifically, we looked at the four frequently used design patterns in business services applications namely:

❑ Business Delegate

❑ Session Façade

❑ Value Object

❑ Aggregate Entity

Sun MicroSystems is currently documenting the patterns, categorizing into presentation-tier, business-tier, and integration tier patterns. These design patterns are available as beta Version 1.0 from http://developer.Java.sun.com/developer/technicalArticles/J2EE/patterns/.

Applying the design patterns that we've discussed in this chapter will enable projects to be built with more reusable components and ultimately provide for an efficiently tiered architecture. In fact you'll probably now be able to recognize most of these patterns as they crop up in the implementations in chapters throughout the rest of the book.

In the next chapter we'll see how to model our EJBs for our applications.

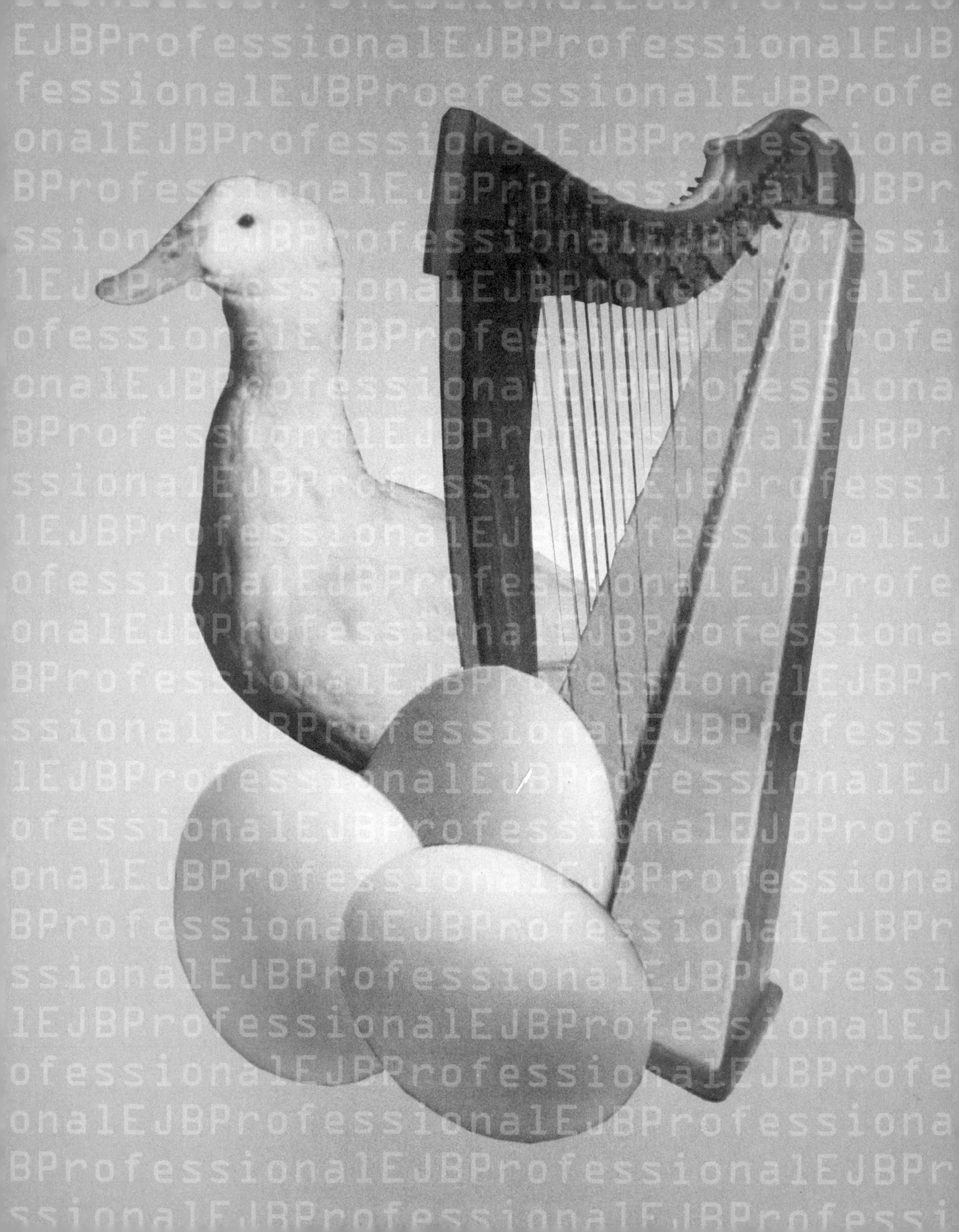

13

UML Modeling and EJBs

This chapter is about UML and EJBs. More specifically, it's about bridging the chasm between fine-grained UML models and the Enterprise JavaBean component architecture. This chapter will present and demonstrate a number of techniques, heuristics, and strategies that will help you successfully translate your UML model into a high performance, scalable EJB entity and session bean design.

In this chapter we will:

❑ Review important UML inputs into our EJB design

❑ Describe how those UML inputs influence the EJB design

❑ Review a sample application

❑ Apply strategies and heuristics to the sample application to produce an EJB design

❑ Review a possible implementation of the design

Looking Ahead

To get our bearings straight before we start, let's look at some commonly found elements in good EJB designs. We will be designing EJB entity and session beans, working to keep communications between these beans and their clients as efficient as possible.

We will define a set of components that represent objects from our problem domain. These components will be responsible for the persistence of their own state and some basic business logic. In this chapter we will demonstrate how to implement these as EJB entity bean components.

We'll also define a set of components responsible for managing our user workflow, and transaction logic. These types of components might be called *controllers* or *services* depending on the semantics of your architecture. In either case, they act as façades to the entity beans described above. These components will be implemented as EJB session beans.

When building distributed applications, we must concern ourselves with network latency and remote communication issues. Finding a balance between small discrete messages and larger chunks of work in EJB remote methods is a delicate task. The idea is to do the most we can each time we have to request or ask for some behavior to occur over the network. These larger chunks of work help minimize the performance problems associated with distributed applications. This work will result in more efficient communication among our EJB entity and session beans, and our session beans and clients be they anything from JSP or Swing clients, to external systems.

Laying the Groundwork

The **Unified Modeling Language (UML)** has become the de facto standard modeling notation succeeding a number of popular object-oriented analysis and design methods from the late eighties and nineties. The UML specification is managed by the Object Management Group (OMG). You can find additional information about UML at the OMG web site: http://www.omg.org/.

UML 1.3 provides a notation to express object oriented design using nine diagrams that are listed below:

❑   Class diagram

❑   Object diagram

❑   Use case diagram

❑   Sequence diagram

❑   Collaboration diagram

❑   Statechart diagram

❑   Activity diagram

❑   Deployment diagram

❑   Component diagram

Our focus is on a subset of these diagrams, which we will explain in the next section. Additional information about building and using UML diagrams can be found in the following resources:

❑   *UML Distilled Second Edition*, by Booch, Fowler, and Scott, from Addison-Wesley, ISBN 0-201-65783-X

❑   *Applying UML and Patterns*, by Craig Larman, from Prentice Hall, ISBN 0-137488-80-7

❑   *The Unified Modeling Language User Guide*, by Booch, Jacobson, and Rumbaugh, from Addison-Wesley, ISBN 0201571684

❑   *Instant UML*, by Pierre-Alain Muller, from Wrox Press, ISBN 1-861000-87-1

UML predates the EJB architecture. Because of this, there are currently no standardized means to represent EJBs in UML. As UML was designed to be extensible, it does provide standard extension mechanisms to define new model elements. But unless these extensions are standardized, vendor solutions will not interoperate. There is work in progress to bring EJB extensions to the UML under the Java Specification Request, JSR-026. For additional information this JSR see: http://java.sun.com/aboutJava/communityprocess/jsr/jsr_026_uml.html.

However you decide to use UML, the important thing is to ensure that UML serves you and your application development needs. In this chapter, the assumption is that your UML models have been completed independently of implementation details. Our interest is in translating these UML models into EJBs.

We have a number of steps to translating a UML object model to an EJB component model:

1. We start with a UML model

2. We iteratively and synergistically apply a number of activities to the UML model to translate it into an EJB component design

3. We implement and deploy this design

The focus of this chapter is on the second step. We assume a UML model in Step 1, and refer you to the rest of this book for details of Step 3.

Common UML Diagrams

The nine diagrams defined in UML offer varying degrees of value to modeling and our translation effort. However, time and again, other developers and I find ourselves drawn towards three common diagrams:

- ❑ Class diagrams
- ❑ Use cases and their associated diagrams
- ❑ Sequence diagrams

These three also work very well for the purpose of defining an EJB component model, and therefore we will focus on them. Let's look at the class diagram first.

UML Class Diagrams

Class diagrams describe the types of objects in the system and the static relationships among these objects. The diagram indicates navigation, dependencies, aggregation, and composition details. Class diagrams also show the attributes and operations of the class, though these can be hidden if they don't add clarity to a particular instance of a class diagram.

Some time ago I worked as a software engineer in the Application Engineering Services group at the Hewlett Packard inkjet division in Vancouver, Washington. Being in the inkjet printer division, we had easy access to Hewlett Packard inkjet printers. Not only did everyone have an inkjet on their desk, but we also had large color plotters placed through the building at twenty-five yard intervals; the kind that printed out the beautiful four-foot wide pictures of whatever suited your fancy. Being technical folks, everyone in our group had the most recent database schema of the project they were working on. These were pinned up to cube walls and laid out flat across desks everywhere. We lived and died by these data models.

A few years later, application development had shifted from client-server technologies to object-oriented technologies. Now instead of drinking morning coffee over a data model we leave the coffee cup stains on a class diagram. It replaced the data model and now provides that warm fuzzy feeling of being master of all. When I have the class diagram in hand, I understand the ways of the application.

The figure below is a portion of a class diagram from this chapter's sample application. It shows two classes from our domain, the fact they have an association, and the multiplicity of that association. In this example the line between the two classes represent an association. The 0..* states that the Category class will be associated with a zero or many instances of the Artist class, and the 1..* states that the Artist will have an association with one or more instances of a Category class:

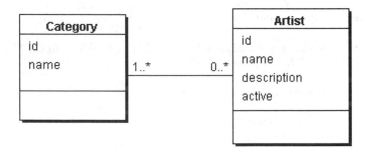

The **object diagram** is a variation of a class diagram in UML. The object diagram shows specific instances of a class, rather than the class itself. For the purposes of this chapter we will consider the object diagram to be synonymous with a class diagram.

We will spend a great deal of time discussing class diagrams, but for the moment, simply remember that the class diagram is a primary input to our EJB component model design, and will almost completely define our entity beans.

UML Use Case Diagrams

I don't think there is any other UML artifact that has caused more passion, confusion, or arguments than the **use case**. At the same time, it is continually valued as a powerful tool. Ivar Jacobson, one of the key founders of UML, originally introduced use cases in his work in the early nineties. They were soon embraced by most in the object analysis and design community. There are a number of variations on how to describe a use case. We will use a simple example.

Use cases represent a series of scenarios that are focused on user goals. The sum of the use cases represents the complete functionality of the system from the perspective of the user.

Use case diagrams are used to model the use-case view of a design, and are used to model dynamic aspects of systems. The following use case diagram shows two use cases that involve a Merchandiser:

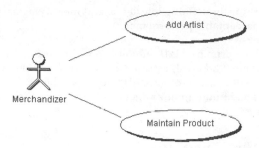

Use cases are often expressed in text form as well. For example, here's the *Add Artist* use case:

Add Artist

- ❑   A merchandiser receives a request to add a new artist to the system
- ❑   Merchandiser assigns required attributes: Artist name and description
- ❑   Merchandiser saves the new information
- ❑   System confirms save

Like class diagrams, use cases will get additional coverage later in the chapter. For now, remember that use cases will play a significant role in the design of our EJB session beans.

UML Sequence Diagrams

The last of the big three that we will look at are sequence diagrams. **Sequence diagrams** are useful for defining and observing the interactions among different objects. This diagram shows a set of objects, and the sequencing of messages sent and received by those objects. In a design with many messages being sent between many classes, it can be difficult to understand how the objects are communicating in order to fulfill the requirements set forth in use cases. A sequence diagram will display these messages as they pass from object to object, also indicating the relative timing of those messages.

The sequence diagram can be a tremendous communication and learning tool. The use of a class diagram and a sequence diagram can quickly clarify system behavior. The following is a simple sequence diagram showing messages required to display artist album titles on a user interface window:

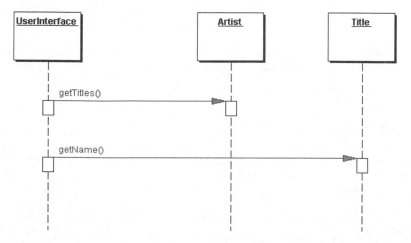

Sequence diagrams will assist us in defining interfaces, and identifying areas where large numbers of messages could result in unacceptable performance.

We've now reviewed the three primary UML models we will be using throughout this chapter. Having gained an understanding of how these will assist us in our EJB component design, you'll be well prepared to adapt that understanding to other UML models as they arise. We will return to these models throughout the text and build up our understanding of how they are used.

UML Tools

There are some fantastic UML modeling tools on the market, offering a range of features such as:

- ❑ Drag-and-drop interfaces with all nine UML models
- ❑ Reverse engineering (Generating UML diagrams from Java source)
- ❑ Code generation from UML models
- ❑ Integration with your configuration-management software

Using these tools can be a pleasure and, with enough discipline, they can produce fantastic results. But for all the good they bring, there is a flipside. They are complex to learn, and often require heavier weight methodologies that some development environments cannot, or choose not to, support. In addition, many are too expensive for a single developer or small shop to afford.

There are a variety of UML modeling tools available, ranging from open source to commercial enterprise-strength tools in integrated product suites. Here are a few sites you may want to investigate:

- ❑ http://www.rational.com/
- ❑ http://www.togetherj.com/
- ❑ http://www.nomagic.com/

Some of the best object modelers I know ignore software tools in favor of whiteboards and paper. I once worked in an office where 4 x 8" sheets of whiteboard were mounted on every wall. The developers kept the models on the whiteboards: easy to view, easy to change, easy to collaborate. Version control of the models, when considered necessary, was handled by someone copying the model from the whiteboard to a piece of paper and putting it in a notebook. It's exhilarating for several developers, each with dry erase marker in hand, to stand in front of a giant whiteboard and work through design problems together.

I've worked on projects where we've reverse-engineered code from our UML modeling tool, and I've been on projects where all UML models were kept only on whiteboards. Which was better? As an old college professor of mine used to say, "It depends on what you are trying to do…"

Review

So far we have set our sights on the goal of translating our UML model into an EJB component model. We pointed out how our class diagram will be the primary input into the design of our entity beans. Use cases will help define session beans; use cases and sequence diagrams will help define session bean and entity bean interfaces. And finally, by defining efficient messages, we'll reduce expensive network and communication overhead.

Next we'll introduce the sample application, and then we'll discuss techniques useful in achieving our EJB design goals.

Our Sample Application

Our sample application is an online record store. As a customer of the record store, you can search different music categories for an album. Albums can be added to your shopping cart, and finally you can purchase the items in your shopping cart. The record store also has employees that select products to make available online, and can manage attributes of the records such as description and images.

> **In this chapter we are assuming the UML design documents have been completed and we are now reviewing them. We're not drawing them ourselves, although we will present them for reference.**

While studying the documentation we find the domain objects described in the class diagram consist of things we might expect to find in a retail application: products, items, and categories to organize the products. These are managed by internal employees. As it has an e-commerce front end, we have order and customer objects. The commerce aspect also has a browser-based GUI used by potential customers. And as we have alliances with external partners we must include interfaces to their systems. The next sections will review the UML model of the application more closely:

- ❑ *The Application Use Cases.*
  These include the ability to add, maintain, and release product; to shop for, and purchase the products; and to make products available for strategic partners.

- ❑ *The Class Diagram.*
  This will be a static representation of our product, and the various classes in the domain supporting all we need to do with it.

- ❑ *Sequence Diagrams.*
  Used to represent important message interaction between the objects found in the class diagram.

The Use Cases

Our first use case diagram displays two different use cases: *Add Artist* and *Maintain Items.* These support the basic needs of our application, except from the customer-facing e-commerce portion.

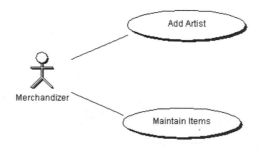

Use Case: Add Artist

- ❑ A merchandiser receives a request to add a new artist to the system
- ❑ Merchandiser assigns required attributes: artist name and description
- ❑ Merchandiser saves the new information
- ❑ System confirms save

Use Case: *Maintain Items*

- ❏ Merchandiser receives a request to update an item for an artist
- ❏ Merchandiser selects the artist of interest
- ❏ Merchandiser assigns, or modifies item's attributes
- ❏ Merchandiser saves the item

Alternative: save failed:

- ❏ The system is unable to save the information and sends an error message to the user

The next two use cases address the application functionality from the perspective of an external customer, as shown in the following use case diagram:

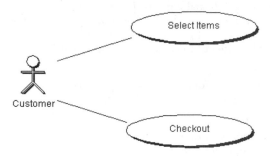

Use Case: *Select Items*

- ❏ Customer selects category to browse
- ❏ System displays available items for that category
- ❏ Customer browses through available items
- ❏ Customer selects items to add to cart

Alternative: out of inventory

- ❏ At last step, system checks inventory when customer adds to cart and alerts customer if no inventory found

Use Case: *Checkout*

- ❏ Customer goes to checkout
- ❏ System presents cart order summary and details
- ❏ Customer fills in account information
- ❏ System confirms sale

Alternative: Regular customer

- ❏ At the third step, customer enters account number
- ❏ System confirms sale

Sample Application Class Diagram

The class diagram for our sample application is shown below:

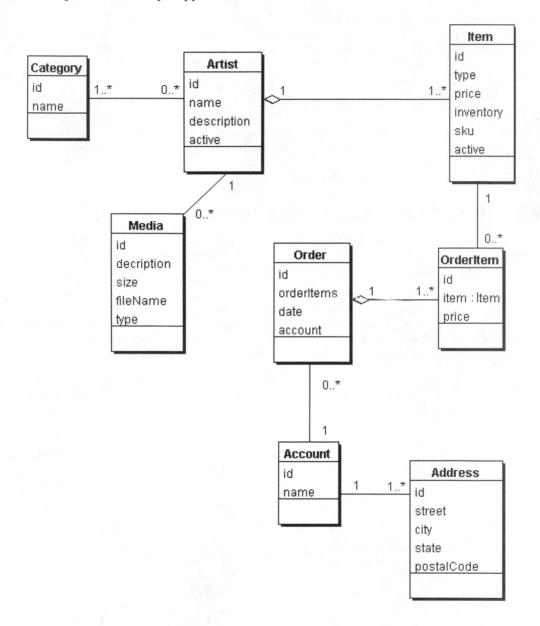

Mapping UML Models to EJBs

This section will uncover more details about our EJB design, and explain a few terms before we actually start the translation.

Our EJB model will consist of entity beans and session beans derived from our UML model. These EJBs must perform and scale well, so a great deal of attention will be given to ensure each component is properly designed.

Our system domain is defined as a set of concepts and terminology understood by the business experts in the area our system is modeling. **Domain objects** are those concepts in the domain we are modeling. Our domain objects in the UML class diagram are implemented as EJB entity beans. In EJB 1.1 and prior, we would model coarse-grained components that represent one, or often many classes from our class diagram. EJB 2.0 provides new mechanisms that allow us to implement the objects as separate entity beans, and still ensure we maintain high performance. We will be going into detail on techniques used to decide how to model our class diagram in EJB entity beans.

We must also implement use-case workflow and orchestrate communication between our clients and the entity beans. These coarse-grained services will be implemented as session beans.

Let's now explore these ideas in greater detail.

Efficient and Effective Access through Entity Beans

In business classes we learned that to be efficient does not mean to be effective, and being effective does not mean to be efficient. Being efficient means using the fewest resources to achieve the most gain. On the other hand, being effective means doing the correct thing.

For example, we might aim to drive our car from New York to Chicago. We can achieve efficiency by checking the air pressure in our tires, using good fuel and accelerating smoothly. We can also make better time if we pack food so we don't have to stop to eat. But we if we take a left leaving New York and head south to Florida, we won't be very effective in achieving our goal. We may get great fuel mileage and average 800 miles a day, but we'll never get to our destination.

We'll need both efficiency and effectiveness to achieve our goals in building EJBs. We need to be able to quickly and safely access the correct domain objects, so we are concerned about transaction security, high performance and scalability.

We have achieved this goal when we have defined the coarse-grained components that represent our fine-grained class diagram. The following diagram illustrates the idea that we begin with many small, fine-grained, objects and end with fewer coarse-grained components:

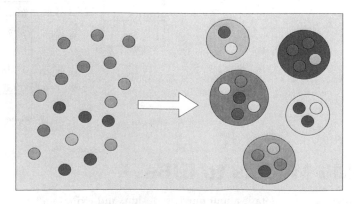

The domain objects, and access to those objects, could be implemented a number of different ways. I had the opportunity recently to build a domain abstraction layer that allowed me to switch between entity beans, an object database, and an object-relational mapping tool. The implementation does define, perhaps to a large degree, what sort of design will work. For example, using an object database like GemStone/J's Persistence Cache Architecture (PCA) as a persistence mechanism, you can retain the fine-grained objects defined in the UML class diagrams. Object-relational tools like CocoBase will also let you expose a fine-grained object model while this is mapped to a relational database behind the scenes.

However, in our case we will be working with the Enterprise JavaBeans component architecture. The techniques presented in this chapter are tailored towards that end. The components in this layer of the architecture will therefore be implemented as entity beans, and our EJB design will account for this.

Expose Coarse Grained Services in Session Beans

E-mail has become a way of life to most of us. It is quick and easy to fire off a thought to an associate. I can still remember some of my early experiences with e-mail when I was in awe about the fact I could be in conversation with someone on the phone, send them an e-mail and wait while they read it. But consider previous generations who experienced great latency in their communications: mail carried over land by horse, or letters between Americanand Europe being carried by ship. Communication was quite different when great latency was experienced.

Distributed applications have a similar concern, because each message from a remote client to the web or application server experiences network latency. Communication is therefore constricted by network speed, bandwidth, and network latency. With the additional time it takes to communicate in distributed J2EE applications, it is vital we give as much instruction as possible each time we communicate. In other words, if it is expensive to communicate, we must make the most of each communication.

Consider officers in Washington who send commands into a battlefield. Can they possibly communicate with each individual soldier? Or is it more efficient to communicate with a field commander, who in turn communicates with the individuals? In the same way, we want to decouple our domain from our clients. We don't want a drop-down list box of some client screen poking around in our domain objects. It is most likely our application will crawl to a halt as this client, and others like it, send message after message over the network. And if we somehow manage to survive that mess, we will certainly encounter problems when we try to modify a domain object only to find legions of clients inextricably coupled with fine details from our domain.

Services act as façades to our domain and persistence layers. A coarse-grained service will provide a high-level API for our client to use. Through this façade we can keep communication short and to the point, grouping as much information as is needed for a particular message, and no more. Rather than our clients asking the domain for several pieces of required information, our client asks the service for a "cohesive set" of data and that set is combined into a single message. This results in fewer, smaller, smarter messages.

Our EJB design will include services implemented as session beans. We will implement the use-case logic in these session beans, so we will have achieved one of our goals when we have built coarse-grained session bean components representing the use cases from our UML model.

Provide for Efficient Communication

While building our entity and session beans, we must always be concerned about efficient communication. We'll pay careful attention to the behavior and interfaces we are exposing to clients. With proper design we'll see reduced messaging, and with fewer messages required in our application, we will see a corresponding reduction in network latency resulting in overall better performance.

EJB Design Considerations

Now we will introduce a few concepts and considerations required in distributed EJB application design. We will discuss the concepts of cohesive classes, dependent objects, efficient communication, deployment needs, and transactional boundaries.

Remote and Local Client Views

EJB 2.0 introduces a new concept of local client views in addition to the existing remote client view. The use of remote or client views deserves certain considerations. Starting with remote client views:

❑ The remote programming model provides flexibility in component distribution.

❑ Remote calls use pass-by-value which provides isolation between the client and server roles, and can assist in preventing undesired modifications to data.

❑ Remote calls are more expensive as they require additional server resources and network latency.

Whereas for local client views:

❑ As the enterprise beans must be co-located to utilize local interfaces, the distribution of components is limited.

❑ Local calls utilize pass-by-reference, thus providing the possibility of sharing state. This results in greater performance, but also tighter coupling.

❑ As the local programming model is lighter weight in its use of server and network resources it supports finer-grained component access.

The next section on cohesive classes discusses the determining factors in deciding to build local or remote interfaces.

Cohesive Classes

First let's define cohesive classes:

> **Cohesive classes are classes that collaborate in such a manner that they would support a single, cohesive interface to other components. That is, other objects in our system could treat this collection of classes as a single entity.**

This definition gives us a number of clues about what we are after. The idea of publishing a cohesive interface or contract implies that other components should treat a collection of cohesive classes as a unified component, and indeed this is the point we're after.

A common example of cohesive classes would be an `Order` object and its associated `OrderItem` objects, as shown in the following diagram:

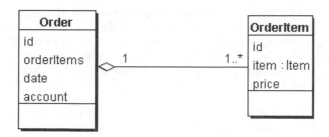

In this example, the two different classes would be considered cohesive, because a different object, for example `Customer`, could interact with the classes through a single interface treating them as if they were one.

Section 4.1.2 of the Enterprise JavaBeans Specification 2.0 states:

> *"Enterprise beans that are remotely accessible components are intended to be relatively coarse-grained business objects (e.g. purchase order, employee record). Fine-grained objects (e.g. line item on a purchase order, employee's address) should not be modeled as remotely accessible enterprise bean components, but rather as locally accessible enterprise beans or as the dependent classes of enterprise beans."*

For example, a purchase order might be implemented as an entity bean with a remote interface; the line items on the purchase order might be implemented as entity beans with a local interface, or as dependent objects, but not as entity beans with a remote interface. In this way a client wishing to access information about the `Order` and its associated `OrderItem` objects will use the `Order` object's remote interface. The `Order` object in turn will interact as needed with its `OrderItem` objects using their local interface:

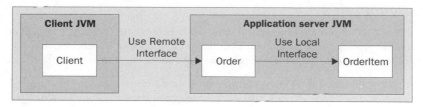

As another example, the UML class diagram below shows a common relationship between a `Person` object and an `Address` object:

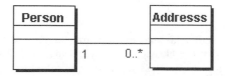

This may seem a perfectly fine example of cohesive classes that should be presented to a client through a single interface. If you were writing a magazine subscription application for a publishing house this would make sense – the address is only important because a paid subscriber lives there. The same would probably be true for a frequent flyer application for an airline. The airline might be interested in which cities you fly in and out of, but doesn't care much about your address.

How about an application for package delivery companies like UPS? This time we must pause before answering and start asking questions of the domain experts. Do they want to keep specific information such as travel time between a main street and your home address? If this is the case, they want that Address information, independent of the Person information. Consider a real estate application. The Address object would most certainly have significant meaning in that domain and would likely be implemented with a remote interface.

In a distributed application, each method call to a remote interface is potentially a remote call. One of the powerful features of EJB is that it can manage a number of things for you when performing remote method calls: EJB will manage transactions, check security, and so on.

However, one of the disadvantages of EJB is that it can manage a number of things for you when performing a remote method call. No, you didn't just read a typo; this management has both advantages and disadvantages. A disadvantage is the computational overhead required managing these additional activities.

By determining cohesive sets of classes, and providing a single remote interface for that cohesive set, we minimize the computational overhead associated with remote interfaces. We design interaction between the cohesive classes using local interfaces or dependent objects, this way we avoid the overhead associated with remote interfaces.

What about Dependent Objects?

Readers who are familiar with earlier versions of the EJB specification may have experience with **dependent objects**. The new local interfaces available in EJB 2.0 can replace much of what dependent objects were used for previously. As suggested above in section 4.1.2 of the specification, the design principles associated with the use of dependent objects and local interfaces are similar. As local interfaces will be the favored method going forward, this chapter is focused on their use.

Transaction Boundaries

We wish to share access to domain objects and data, while preserving data integrity. To achieve this goal, transactions should coincide with component boundaries. By defining transactional boundaries within, or at the borders of a component, the transaction can be kept short, minimizing required database resources.

Conversely, when a transaction does cross component boundaries, transaction management must be explicitly managed in client code. In this case a database connection is allocated when a client begins a transaction. The transaction remains open until the client is finished with its activities. During this time database resources are not available for other clients, and entire data sets may be locked from other clients.

Review use cases carefully as they will help dictate these transactional boundaries.

Deployment Issues

There may be cases where a specific class has extraordinary needs. While our first activity, to define cohesive classes, may indicate that the class potentially belongs with a set of other classes, special needs may dictate a requirement to deploy the class separately, in effect as its own component. Needs that may dictate this special treatment may include:

- ❑ Performance
- ❑ Scalability
- ❑ Failover
- ❑ Security

As an example, consider a `Transaction` object that needs to process millions of requests a day. By defining this object as a separate component, we could more easily deploy this single component to one or more higher speed processors capable of meeting the needs of this particular class. Perhaps we have complex fail-over needs for our `Order` class that far exceed the needs of other classes. Implementing and deploying the `Order` class as a separate component may allow us to meet these needs more easily.

Efficient Communication and Application Objects

We desire to keep communications between components as efficient as possible. In the EJB applications I have built, I have found the concept of application objects to be very useful in providing for efficient communications.

Application objects are similar to, and largely synonymous with, bulk accessors or value objects. If you understand the bulk accessor or value object concepts, application objects will look familiar. If not, the following section will fully explain application objects.

An application object represents a view of the model appropriate to the task at hand. Perhaps the easiest way to get a quick handle on an application object is to consider a GUI client. Consider the data attributes you'd find on a single GUI screen. An application object would provide a client with the ability to retrieve these attributes, and nothing more. The result is a single remote call doing a number of things for us.

Application objects get their name from the idea that objects passed between the services layer and the presentation layer will probably look considerably different from the data that exists in the domain layer. Thus we end up with two different views of the data: The canonical view, meaning the standard state of the objects, and the application-specific view.

While it is not necessary that the data looks different on the application side, it is possible, and sometimes desirable, that it will. The canonical view of the domain will remain consistent over time, while the application view of the data will change as required by the presentation layer.

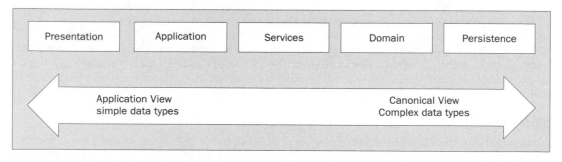

We will review why we need application views, and then provide some examples to solidify your understanding of the concept.

Distributing Objects to the Client

The following screenshot shows an example of a GUI client screen we have been asked to develop. The screen should display an artist, and all the titles for that artist:

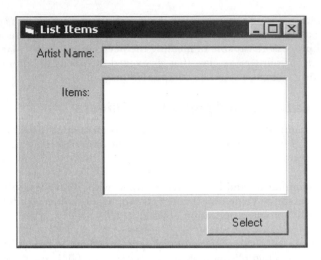

This example appears simple enough; we'll just send the objects from the domain layer to the GUI so it can populate the screen. Here are the steps required, and default resulting activities, when we send objects to the client:

1. Read the data required for the objects from the persistence layer

2. Instantiate the requested object, and all references that object holds (its object graph)

3. Serialize those objects and prepare them for network transfer

4. Send the packets to the client, using the necessary network bandwidth

5. Receive, deserialize, and reconstruct the object graph at the client

Perhaps that's more overhead than we expected. Let's look at some of the details in these steps. These details should give you a better understanding of the issues surrounding object distribution. With a strong understanding of the issues you will be able to determine the best solution to your application architecture needs, and see how application objects may benefit your own design.

Serializing the Object

When serializing an object, the default behavior is to serialize the object and its complete object graph. Here is a potential scenario where we are interested in looking up an Artist and the name attribute from the Item objects belonging to the Artist. Consider the GUI screen from the last example.

The Artist object actually contains a collection of Item objects called items. When we serialize the Artist object, we will actually serialize all of the Item objects contained in the items collection. That may surprise us, but it makes sense. And it may be fine: we are now serializing a total of six objects, but the objects are small and who knows, we may need additional item information later:

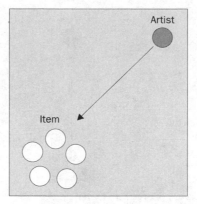

But we're not done yet. Reviewing the application class diagram (repeated below), we notice the `Artist` object contains a reference to a `Category`, and `Media` object. Maybe this is getting to be a bit more than we bargained for:

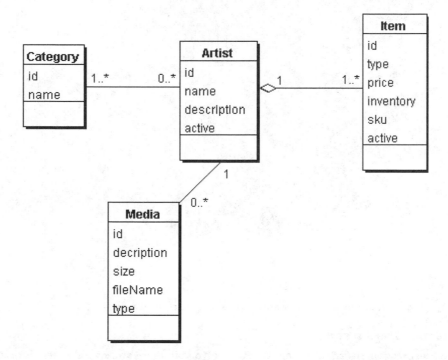

With more study, we notice that the `Category` and `Media` references are actually collections just like the items collection. So our object graph now looks like the following diagram:

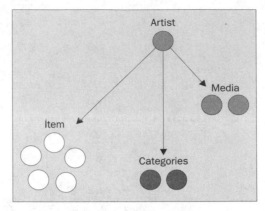

Now that we've gained some experience we can see any reference one of our classes holds could be included in the object graph we send to the client. As we continue to serialize all references, we may find our object graph becomes unbearably large as shown in the next diagram:

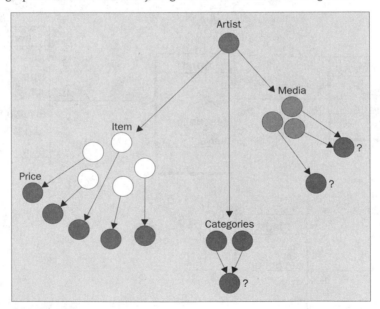

We at last concede that this makes no sense whatsoever for our simple screen.

Other Issues with Object Distribution

If the previous section on serialization did not scare you off, there are several other issues to consider when distributing objects to the client. Security is an important consideration. If we have a payroll application that contains salary information someplace in the object graph, how will we prevent that information from being transmitted back to the client? Does this information need to be pruned from the object graph before being sent to some clients but not others? How will you deal with this concern? Allowing our clients access to domain objects will result in tight coupling between the presentation and domain layers. A great deal of effort will need to be given to address these types of issues if you decide to distribute your objects throughout the different architectural layers.

Remote References

Rather than passing back the actual objects as discussed in the previous section, it is possible to give the client a remote reference to our `Artist` object, and then using this remote reference we can access other data elements as needed. This does avoid many of the issues we found in the section on serialization; for instance the EJB container can now manage security for us.

However, it also creates a new set of concerns. As we've discussed, each remote method call will incur network latency, use bandwidth, and be subject to the overhead involved with remote calls. Remote references to individual domain components will result in an application that is excessively 'chatty'. That is, the clients will end up using a tremendous amount of the available network bandwidth, resulting in sluggish response and disappointed users.

Application Objects as a Solution

Now that we have reviewed some of the issues and problems with client access of domain objects, we have some context in which to present application objects as a viable solution.

In our desire to reduce communication between components we'll define an application object that will contain just enough information within it to fulfill our needs for the task at hand. We will implement this application object as a JavaBean:

```java
package store.app;

import java.io.Serializable;

public class ArtistItems implements Serializable {

  private String artistId;
  private String artistName;
  private String itemId;
  private String itemTitle;

  public ArtistItems() {}

  public ArtistItems(String artistId, String artistName,
                     String itemId, String title, String type) {
    this.artistId = artistId;
    this.artistName = artistName;
    this.itemId = itemId;
    this.itemTitle = title;
    this.itemType = type;
  }

  public String getArtistId() {
    return artistId;
  }

  public String getArtistName() {
    return artistName;
  }

  public String getItemId() {
    return itemId;
  }

  public String getItemTitle() {
    return itemTitle;
  }
```

```
   public String toString() {
     return "Contents of ArtistItems: artistId=" + artistId
            + ", artistName=" + artistName + ", itemId=" + itemId
            + ", itemTitle=" + itemTitle;
   }

 }
```

With our completed JavaBean in hand, we can review the problems this solves for us:

❑ First, and perhaps most importantly, it reduces the conversations between the client and the domain down to a single network roundtrip. It has been my experience that this is one of the more important factors in building high performance applications.

❑ It has greatly simplified client tasks. As shown in the code the client is only required to access two different methods to retrieve all needed data from the application object.

❑ We have no security issues as only data intended for the client was sent.

❑ When we allow the session bean, rather than the client, to manage the entire database transaction, we keep transaction time to a minimum.

The JavaBean example demonstrates one way to implement application objects. Another might be to create an XML document that you pass around. Whatever method you choose will depend upon your environment. The most important concept to take away from this section on application objects is why we use them: to **make our component communication as efficient as possible**. How you achieve this goal may vary from architecture to architecture. Application objects are an implementation of this idea you may find you can use.

We've now reviewed what we expect our entity and session beans to look like, we've defined cohesive classes, local and remote interfaces, and we've brought up a few things to consider when designing EJB applications. The next section walks through our UML design with these concepts and design goals in mind.

Designing EJBs for the Sample Application

Designing our EJBs is an iterative process of reviewing UML models, implementing our findings, and allowing each new discovery to influence and perhaps change current design decisions. In this way it is similar to the UML design process itself.

It is common to find that a businesses domain model will remain more stable over time than client and workflow needs. So in practice, you'll find your entity beans remain more stable over time than your session beans. In our current case, we don't have any enterprise beans defined, so we'll start by defining the entity beans, allowing new discoveries later in the design process to influence earlier design decisions.

In this section we will begin our EJB design by allowing the UML class diagrams to drive the design of our entity beans. We'll then use our use cases to design the session beans.

Defining Entity Beans: First Pass

Let's begin with our class diagram, again repeated here for convenience:

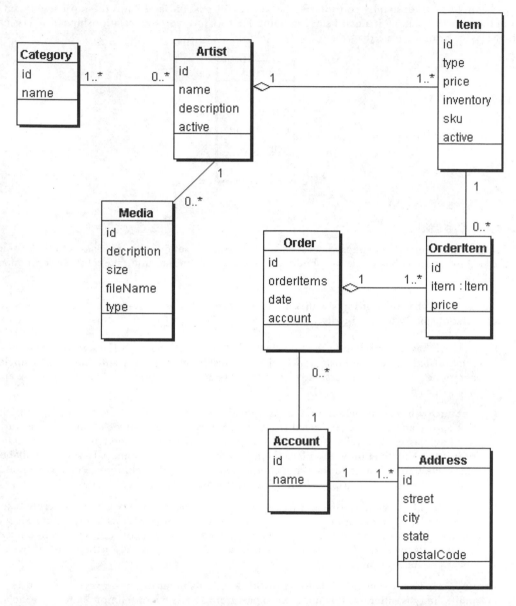

We will start our EJB design by looking for significant concepts in the class diagram. After becoming familiar with a problem domain you will be aware of important concepts from the business perspective. A useful heuristic indicates that many of these will become components, because much of the activity with the application will be centered around these concepts. Nearly all domains will have one or more conceptually significant classes. Conceptually important classes should be self-evident in the domain:

- ☐ They will be classes that may have significant message activity in sequence diagrams

- ☐ They will receive heavy use in the use cases

- ☐ These classes are probably named after their real-world counterpart in the business domain

Let's begin our EJB design by considering the `Artist` class. This is perhaps the most significant concept from the domain, making it a good starting point. First we'll review any relationships this class has with other classes from the class diagram:

Cohesive Classes

We start by defining sets of cohesive classes. We'll consider a set of cohesive classes to be a component in the sense that the cohesive classes should provide a single unified interface to other components in the architecture.

The `Artist` class has relationships with a number of other classes: `Category`, `Item`, and `Media`. Each of these relationships will now be discussed:

❑   `Artist` has an aggregation relationship with `Item`. UML aggregation and composition relationships usually indicate a lifecycle relationship and typically will end up in a single component. We also understand from the domain that a `Item` really has no meaning apart from `Artist`.

❑   `Category` has an association relationship with `Artist`. We also note the multiplicity between `Category` and `Artist`. We see that a `Category` can have an association with zero or more `Artist` classes. This tells us that `Category` has a lifecycle independent of `Artist` thus this provides no motivation yet to place them into the same component. Classes that collaborate extensively may belong to the same component. This would help reduce excessive messaging issues. Let's review the use cases that use these classes for additional clues.

❑   Reading the *Select Items* use case, we see a user can choose and navigate to different categories without consideration of product. It appears that `Category`, with its independent lifecycle indicated by the association multiplicity and this use case, is a concept significant enough to stand on its own. We'll nominate it too as a candidate component for the moment (we can always change our mind later).

❑   `Media` has an association relationship with `Artist` similar to `Category`, however its multiplicity is different. It cannot exist apart from `Artist` so we'll nominate it for inclusion in our first set of cohesive classes, which will now consist of: `Artist`, `Item`, and `Media`. We will refer to this set as our *Artist* component:

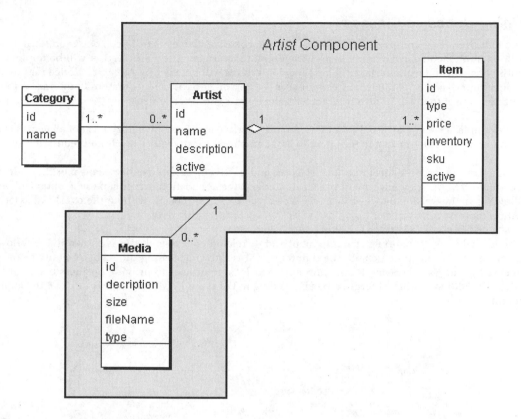

Use Cases

Let's review our use cases to determine their impact on the potential *Artist* component. As we define cohesive sets of classes into components we are drawing logical boundaries through our application. The more efficiently we can communicate over these boundaries the better our application will perform. We'll review these component boundaries in context of our use cases to see if they make sense.

- ❑ *Add Artist:*
  This use case deals exclusively with an `Artist` object alone and doesn't confirm or deny our findings to this point.

- ❑ *Maintain Items:*
  The user can read and modify much of the same information in the `Artist` and `Item` classes. In addition, they assign categories and release it to the live site. Closer scrutiny of the use case tells us that artists are assigned to categories, thus the containing relationship is from the category side. The `Category` class looks less likely to belong to with this *Artist* component.

- ❑ *Select Items:*
  This use case is from the perspective of an external customer. We note here that the category concept is most significant in this use case, as it is an enabling factor in the shopping experience. It reinforces the idea of category being a separate and significant concept from the domain.

- ❑ *Checkout:*
  The *Checkout* use case continues to confirm our findings. It has the concept of a purchased product but the category is no longer as significant in this use case.

Defining Cohesive Classes

We have defined a component consisting of three cohesive classes: Artist, Item ,and Media. Artist will be implemented as an entity bean with a remote interface. Item and Media will be implemented as entity beans with local interfaces. These local interfaces will be used by Artist. Notice that by the use of local interfaces, a remote client cannot access Item or Media. Clients may only interact with the Artist object that will in turn interact with the Media and Item objects.

For example, a client may use the Artist remote interface to ask the inventory level of all items belonging to the Artist. The Artist in turn queries its Item objects for inventory levels and returns a result.

As the Artist uses the local interface of Item and Media these three entity beans must be co-located in the same JVM. As they implement the local interface, the application server can make optimizations allowing the interaction between Artist, Item, and Media to occur without the overhead associated with remote calls.

The logical view of the *Artist* component and its related cohesive classes is shown in the following diagram. In this diagram a client in a different JVM is shown accessing the Artist entity bean. Artist may in turn access Item and Media through their local interfaces to provide business behavior for the client. In addition, other enterprise beans residing in the same JVM may access Artist through its remote interface:

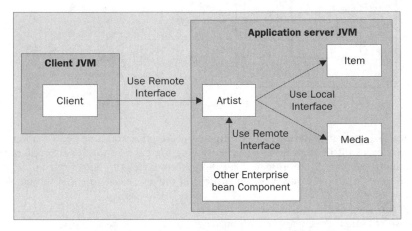

If additional performance is required, it is possible to develop a local interface for Artist designed for use by other enterprise bean components. As the local interfaces may only be used when the enterprise beans exist in the same JVM, the components would be coupled in a manner that would prevent them from being distributed in different JVMs. Your architectural needs will help determine which implementation will best suit your needs.

Defining Entity Beans: Second Pass

Moving on to our search for the next set of cohesive classes, we'll review Order. As shown in the following class diagram, Order has an aggregation relationship with OrderItem and an association relationship with Account. OrderItem appears to provide a classic example of needing a local interface or dependent objects. Its aggregation relationship indicates lifecycle dependencies. Reviewing the multiplicity of the association relation between Order and Account indicates Account has a separate lifecycle:

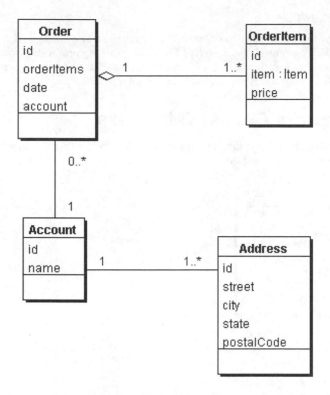

We have previously discussed the possibility of special needs constituting a need for a separate component. We are concerned about session state and fail-over needs while users are shopping. We also have higher performance requirements for this portion of our application, so we may choose to use load balancing and distribute Order across multiple servers.

With several factors suggesting Order and OrderItem belonged in a cohesive set, the fail-over need solidifies that decision. We therefore define another set of cohesive classes consisting of an Order entity bean with a remote interface, and an OrderItem entity bean with a local interface. We will refer to this set as the *Order* component:

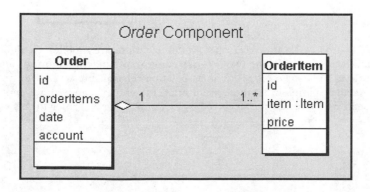

Component Interfaces

We now have two components with remote interfaces: *Artist* and *Order*. How will they communicate? Do they communicate directly? Inter-component communication will be more important when we start defining session beans that will communicate with the entity beans. We'll review this in more detail in the implementation section later in this chapter.

Defining the Entity Beans: Third Pass

We are ready to go through the class diagram again. We still have the Category class, which we earmarked as a potential component earlier, and the Account and Address classes. Let's start with the Account class:

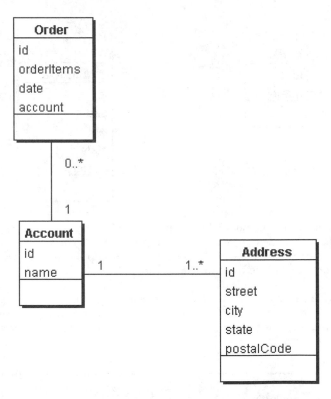

Reviewing the association with the Order class, we notice there are no lifecycle dependencies and little to moderate collaboration between the two. We are comfortable placing them in separate components. Turning to the Address class, we see it has an association relationship with Account and a lifecycle relationship. We decide to implement these as an Account entity bean with a remote interface and an Address entity bean with a local interface used by Account. We will refer to this set of cohesive classes as the *Account* component:

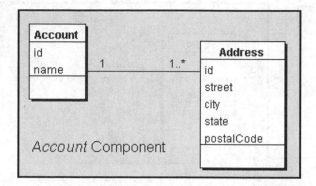

We are still left with the candidate component `Category`. As we have now reviewed all classes we see no reason to include `Category` into one of the other components, so it becomes an entity bean component consisting of a single class, called unoriginally *Category*:

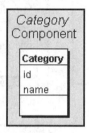

Review of Class Diagram Work

We have now developed the following components based upon our review of the class diagram:

- *Artist*
  Implemented as an `Artist` entity bean with a remote interface and an `Item` and `Media` entity beans with local interfaces.

- *Order*
  Implemented as an `Order` entity bean with a remote interface and an `OrderItem` entity bean with a local interface.

- *Account*
  Implemented as an `Account` entity bean with a remote interface and an `Address` entity bean with a local interface.

- *Category*
  Implemented as a single entity bean with a remote interface.

The components and the classes they contain are shown overleaf

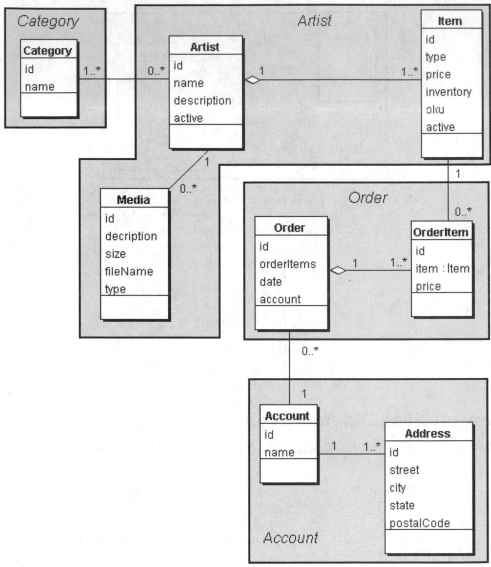

It's now time to move on to defining the services.

Defining Session Beans

We will use the use cases to define the services that will be implemented as session beans. Let's review what a service represents:

> A service is a collective group of cohesive behavior that will carry out actions on behalf of a client.

So what else will they do for our application?

- ❑ Services will help with scalability
- ❑ They help formalize what a client can do (service interfaces become the contract with the client)

The most useful UML artifact to aid us in our EJB design of service components is the use case. The use case defines a discrete unit of work to carry out, so combining all of the use cases defines the system requirements.

We'll define a set of services that will mediate between our client and our model. The service will accept a request from a client, process that request, and finally return results to the client in some form.

There are two general types of service:

- ❑ The first is an extension of the client
- ❑ The second is as system or application shared behavior

Session Bean as an Extension to the Client

In this case the service is implemented as a session bean and is tightly coupled with an intended client. You should expect minimal reuse opportunities with these services. The fact that you will get little reuse is not necessarily a negative in this context. Trying to design a session bean in an "all things to all clients" manner will result in code bloat and poor performance. Session beans designed as services based on UML artifacts will be extensions to the client, and manage workflow, business logic, and transactions – three incredibly important things.

Session Bean with Application-Wide Usefulness

Some examples of these services are logging, reporting and security. They will typically be shared among many other services or entity components, and contain application behavior that is in fact reusable.

Our discussion is focused on services that act as extensions to the client.

Use Case Review

We now review our use cases; categorizing them by the components they have significant interaction with:

Use Case	Artist	Order	Account	Category
Add Artist	Yes	No	No	No
Maintain Item	Yes	No	No	Yes
Select Items	Yes	Yes	No	Yes
Checkout	No	Yes	Yes	No

Now we select a component, `Artist`, and consider the use cases that use it. Who are the actors of those use cases? Are the use-case clients deployed in different layers or on different tiers? We are looking for commonality in the use cases.

Considering again the `Artist` component, we see three use cases access it, but in different ways. *Add Artist* and *Maintain Item* are similar in that the same actor uses them, the client for those use cases will be deployed to the same tier, and in fact it will likely be different screens of the same client. However, the *Select Items* and *Checkout* use cases may be deployed in significantly different environments.

The *Select Items* and *Checkout* use cases have these potential needs:

❑ User is an external customer

❑ May need to maintain state

❑ May have different scalability needs

❑ Collaborate with different components (`Category` and `Order`)

Because of this, we decide to build two different services, one for the *Add Artist* and the *Maintain Item* uses cases, the other for the *Select Items* use case. Here are our services:

❑ `ProductService` contains behavior to support the *Add Artist* and *Maintain Item* use cases.

❑ `ShoppingService` contains behavior to support the *Select Items* use case.

The *Checkout* use case has security needs because it may handle credit card transactions. As it is our component responsible for customer checkouts, we have fail-over needs that the other components don't require. Therefore, we build one service:

❑ `CheckoutService` will support the *Checkout* use case

Choosing Session Beans

As a result of our use-case analysis we will design three EJB components. These are services implemented as EJB session beans.

❑ `ProductService`

❑ `ShopService`

❑ `CheckoutService`

These session beans may be implemented as stateful or stateless session beans depending on our architectural design.

We will now (and later again as other components are derived) want to consider how we can simplify each bean's public interface to client components. Our goal is the reduction of messages, which as we discussed before will reduce network latency and bandwidth needs. Let's review a sequence diagram to get some ideas on how we want to construct an interface to this component.

Simplifying Communication

Review the sequence diagrams that interact with the `Artist` class. Remember that areas with a great number of messages between classes belonging to different components are the main areas of concern. The following figure shows the sequence diagram for *Maintain Item*:

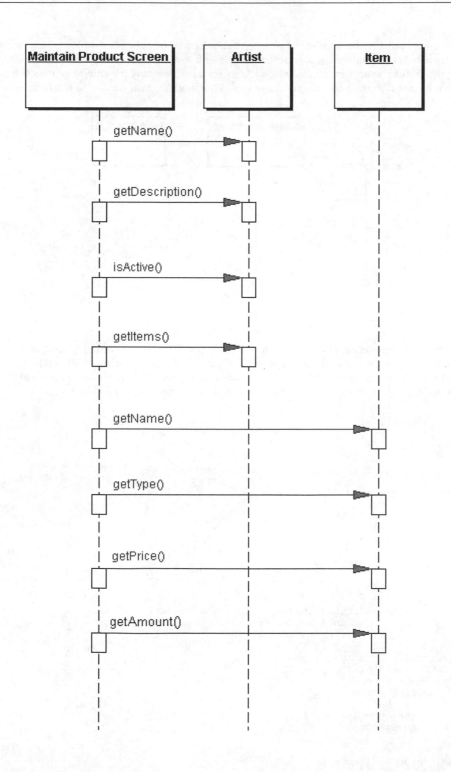

In this example you can see the number of messages required to populate a simple screen. As we are dealing with distributed components, it is possible each of these messages invokes a remote method call. If instead we can define a simpler interface in our session bean, we may be able to reduce the number of messages down to just one method call, resulting in a sequence diagram similar to the following:

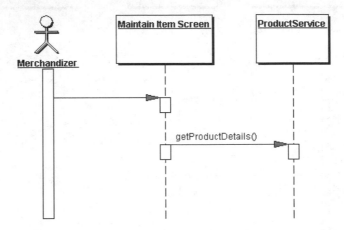

Below is an example application object implemented as a JavaBean. This could be used to return the required information for the screen in a single method call. This class consists of six attributes, with getter and setter methods for each attribute. In use, we would probably create an instance of the class, and the client would then extract the needed information using the getter methods:

```
package store.app;

import java.io.Serializable;

public class ItemDetails implements Serializable {

    private String itemId;
    private String title;
    private String activeStatus;
    private String type;
    private double price;
    private String sku;
    private int inventory;

    public ItemDetails() {}

    public ItemDetails(String itemId, String title, String type,
                       double price, String sku, int inventory,
                       String activeStatus) {

        this.itemId = itemId;
        this.title = title;
        this.type = type;
        this.price = price;
        this.sku = sku;
        this.inventory = inventory;
        this.activeStatus = activeStatus;
    }

    public String getItemId() {
```

```
      return itemId;
   }

   public void setItemId(String itemId) {
      this.itemId = itemId;
   }

   public String getTitle() {
      return title;
   }

   public void setTitle(String title) {
      this.title = title;
   }

   public String getType() {
      return type;
   }

   public void setType(String type) {
      this.type = type;
   }

   public double getPrice() {
      return price;
   }

   public void setPrice(double price) {
      this.price = price;
   }

   public String getSku() {
      return sku;
   }

   public void setSku(String sku) {
      this.sku = sku;
   }

   public int getInventory() {
      return inventory;
   }

   public void setInventory(int inventory) {
      this.inventory = inventory;
   }
   public String getActiveStatus() {
      return activeStatus;
   }

   public void setActiveStatus(String activeStatus) {
      this.activeStatus = activeStatus;
   }

   public String toString() {
      return "Item details: id=" + itemId + ", title=" + title
             + ", type=" + type + ", price=" + price + ", sku= " + sku
             + ", inventory=" + inventory + ", activeStatus="
             + activeStatus;
   }

}
```

You can see that by creating session bean services and exposing simple public interfaces designed for our client, we can greatly reduce much of the overhead associated with distributed applications.

Persisting Our Modifications

A logical question now might be, "I can see how this works for reading product information, but how do we save it?" We could persist our changes back by calling a number of methods on the remote object:

```
// Update some remote object
remoteObject.setProductName(newName);
remoteObject.setPrice(newPrice);
```

I hope you can see by now that this idea violates all we have been working towards. If we obtain a remote reference to an object and begin updating individual attributes with separate method calls, performance will suffer. Instead we define another object to be used in a simple interface again. Below we have defined a read and an update application object. First the read object as a JavaBean:

```java
package store.app;

import java.io.Serializable;

public class ReadProductData implements Serializable {

  private String productId;
  private String artistName;
  private String newArtistName;
  private String title;
  private String newTitle;
  private String description;
  private String newDescription;

  public ReadProductData(){}

  public String getProductId(){
    return productId;
  }

  public void setProductId(String productId){
      this.productId = productId;
  }

  public String getArtistName(){
    return artistName;
  }

  public void setArtistName(String name){
      this.artistName = name;
  }

  public String getTitle(){
    return title;
  }

  public void setTitle(String title){
      this.title = title;
  }

  public String getDescription(){
    return description;
  }
```

```
   public void setDescription(String desc){
       this.description = desc;
   }
}
```

The read object would be instantiated and populated, probably by some service on the server. The JavaBean would be sent to the client, which could then read required information from the JavaBean. The client might then instantiate an update object, populate its attributes using the set methods and send it to the server for processing. Here is our update object as a JavaBean:

```
package store.app;

import java.io.Serializable;

public class UpdateProductData implements Serializable{

  private String productId;
  private String artistName;
  private String newArtistName;
  private String title;
  private String newTitle;
  private String description;
  private String newDescription;

  public UpdateProductData(){}

  public String getProductId(){
      return productId;
  }

  public void setProductId(String productId){
      this.productId = productId;
  }

  public String getArtistName(){
      return artistName;
  }

  public void setArtistName(String name){
      this.artistName = name;
  }

  public String getNewArtistName(){
      return newArtistName;
  }

  public void setNewArtistName(String name){
      this.newArtistName = name;
  }

  public String getTitle(){
      return title;
  }

  public void setTitle(String title){
      this.title = title;
  }
```

```
    public String getNewTitle(){
        return newTitle;
    }

    public void setNewTitle(String title){
        this.newTitle = title;
    }

    public String getDescription(){
        return description;
    }

    public void setDescription(String desc){
        this.description = desc;
    }

    public String getNewDescription(){
        return newDescription;
    }

    public void setNewDescription(String desc){
        this.newDescription = desc;
    }
}
```

Request and Response Application Objects

The different messages between the client and services layer can be thought of as request and response objects or messages. That is, we make requests from our service, and our service sends back responses. If you take this approach, it may be easy to organize your code using a request and response suffix:

```
public class ProductDetailsRequest{
    // Code goes here
}
```

and:

```
public class ProductDetailsResponse{
    // Code goes here
}
```

When considering performance and scalability issues, the exact implementation of application objects is less important than the overall reduction in messages and bandwidth. So whether you send one request object to the service and it returns one response object, or you send the same object back and forth, you have still reduced network latency and the bandwidth resources required.

Application Objects for Session Bean Communication

The clients will communicate with our newly designed services using simplified interfaces or perhaps application objects. These will be defined while considering our use cases and service session beans.

Our use cases are:

- ❏ *Add Artist*
- ❏ *Maintain Item*
- ❏ *Select Items*
- ❏ *Checkout*

Our *defined services are:*

- ❏ `ProductService`
- ❏ `ShopService`
- ❏ `CheckoutService`

Select Items Use Case

As an example, consider a user who wants to select all products within a chosen category, and then add one of those products to their shopping cart. This would be accomplished with two application objects, one returning all products for the chosen category; the other with the product details required to add a product to the customers cart:

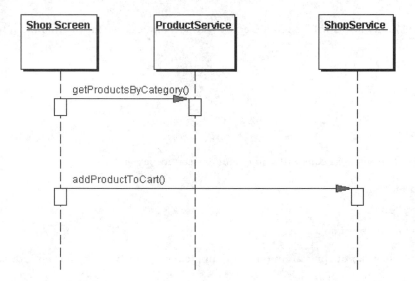

In an architecture such as we are creating, it doesn't matter what the service does with the application object. It may need to access several domain, or even service components to fulfill the goal, but the client is able to communicate each significant cohesive set of information using the fewest resources required, with the highest possible performance possible.

Application Objects

Our *Add Artist* and `Maintain Item` use cases may suggest

- ❏ `AddProduct`: Used by the *Add Artist* use case
- ❏ `ItemDetails`: Used by the *Maintain Item* use case
- ❏ `SelectProductByCategory`: Used by the *Select Items* use case
- ❏ `ArtistItems`: Used by the *Select Items* use case
- ❏ `AddProductToCart`: Used by the *Select Items* use case
- ❏ `ViewCart`: Used by the *Checkout* use case
- ❏ `ApproveCart`: Used by the *Checkout* use case

Our Final EJB Design

We now have three lists of components and objects we must implement. Let's review the list and then move on to implementation examples.

We have the following EJB entity beans with remote interfaces as the entry points into our domain components:

- ❏ Artist
- ❏ Order
- ❏ Account
- ❏ Category

The following entity beans will be implemented with local interfaces, thus hiding them from client access:

- ❏ Item
- ❏ Media
- ❏ OrderItem
- ❏ Address

The following EJB session beans will implement our service layer:

- ❏ ProductService
- ❏ ShopService
- ❏ CheckoutService

And we have a number of application objects to implement as required by our environment.

- ❏ AddProduct
- ❏ ItemDetails
- ❏ SelectProductByCategory
- ❏ ArtistItems
- ❏ AddProductToCart
- ❏ ViewCart
- ❏ ApproveCart

Overview of Potential Implementation

When complete the components in our design will look something like this:

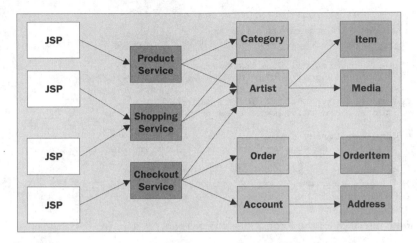

With an understanding of our design in mind, we will look at some a few points from one potential implementation in the next section.

Implementing the Sample Application

We've laid out the EJB design using the UML models as input. Now we need to implement these decisions. Just as before, during implementation we may discover issues that require us to revisit some of our previous decisions, which is perfectly normal.

There are a number of ways to implement this design. Which way you choose needs to be dictated by your architectural requirements. The code listed here is meant to show a small slice of a potential implementation of the design set forth in the preceding sections. Consider it fodder, not gospel.

The Sample Source Code

We will concentrate on demonstrating how to implement just one of the four identified components (in this case the `Artist` component) and one of the related service beans (`ProductService`). The implementation will not be exhaustive, but rather illustrative, but it should give you enough to get you started on the rest of the design should you so wish. Please refer to the rest of this book for an exhaustive reference on EJB implementation details and examples.

The ProductServiceBean Session Bean

We defined a session bean called `ProductServiceBean`. Session beans will have code for the bean itself, and the remote and home interfaces. Let's start with the remote interface:

```
package store.productService;

import store.app.*;
import java.util.Collection;

public interface ProductService extends javax.ejb.EJBObject {

  void addArtist(String artistId, String name, String description,
                 String activeStatus) throws java.rmi.RemoteException;
```

```
    void addItem(ItemDetails itemDetails,
              String artistId) throws java.rmi.RemoteException;

    void addMedia(MediaDetails mediaDetails,
              String artistId) throws java.rmi.RemoteException;

    Collection getItemsForArtist(String name)
          throws java.rmi.RemoteException;

    void updateItem(String artistId,
                ItemDetails item) throws java.rmi.RemoteException;

    ItemDetails getItemDetails(String artistId, String itemId)
          throws java.rmi.RemoteException;
}
```

Next is the home interface for the `ProductServiceBean`:

```
package store.productService;

public interface ProductServiceHome extends javax.ejb.EJBHome {

  ProductService create()
        throws java.rmi.RemoteException, javax.ejb.CreateException;
}
```

The code for the bean implementation is listed below:

```
package store.productService;

import javax.ejb.*;
import javax.naming.InitialContext;
import javax.naming.NamingException;
import store.artist.*;
import store.item.*;
import store.app.*;
import java.util.Collection;

public class ProductServiceEJB implements SessionBean {

  public Collection getItemsForArtist(String name) {

    Collection items;
    try {
      InitialContext initial = new InitialContext();
      ArtistHome home =
        (ArtistHome) initial.lookup("java:comp/env/ejb/Artist");

      Artist artist = home.findByArtistName(name);

      items = artist.getItemsForArtist();

    } catch (Exception e) {
      throw new EJBException(e);
    }
    return items;
  }

  public ItemDetails getItemDetails(String artistId, String itemId) {
```

```
    ItemDetails details;

    try {
      InitialContext initial = new InitialContext();
      ArtistHome home =
        (ArtistHome) initial.lookup("java:comp/env/ejb/Artist");

      Artist artist = home.findByPrimaryKey(artistId);

      details = artist.getItemDetails(itemId);

    } catch (Exception e) {
    throw new EJBException(e);
    }
    return details;
}

public void updateItem(String artistId, ItemDetails item) {

    try {
      InitialContext initial = new InitialContext();
      ArtistHome home =
        (ArtistHome) initial.lookup("java:comp/env/ejb/Artist");

      Artist artist = home.findByPrimaryKey(artistId);
      artist.updateItem(item);

    } catch (Exception e) {
      throw new EJBException(e);
    }
}

public void addArtist(String id, String name, String description,
                       String activeStatus) {

    try {
      InitialContext initial = new InitialContext();
      ArtistHome home =
        (ArtistHome) initial.lookup("java:comp/env/ejb/Artist");

      Artist artist = home.create(id, name, description,
                                  activeStatus);

    } catch (Exception e) {
      throw new EJBException(e);
    }
}

public void addItem(ItemDetails itemDetails, String artistId) {

    try {
      InitialContext initial = new InitialContext();

      ArtistHome home =
        (ArtistHome) initial.lookup("java:comp/env/ejb/Artist");
      Artist artist = home.findByPrimaryKey(artistId);
      artist.addItem(itemDetails);

    } catch (Exception e) {
      throw new EJBException(e);
    }
}
```

```
    public void addMedia(MediaDetails mediaDetails, String artistId) {

      try {
        InitialContext initial = new InitialContext();

        ArtistHome home =
          (ArtistHome) initial.lookup("java:comp/env/ejb/Artist");
        Artist artist = home.findByPrimaryKey(artistId);
        artist.addMedia(mediaDetails);

      } catch (Exception e) {
        throw new EJBException(e);
      }
    }

    public void ejbCreate() {}
    public void ejbRemove() {}
    public void ejbActivate() {}
    public void ejbPassivate() {}
    public void setSessionContext(SessionContext ctx) {}
}
```

Finally here is the deployment descriptor element for this session bean:

```
<?xml version="1.0" encoding="UTF-8"?>

<!DOCTYPE ejb-jar PUBLIC '-//Sun Microsystems, Inc.//DTD Enterprise JavaBeans
2.0//EN' 'http://java.sun.com/dtd/ejb-jar_2_0.dtd'>

<ejb-jar>
  <display-name>Artist Component</display-name>
  <enterprise-beans>

    <session>
      <display-name>ProductService</display-name>
      <ejb-name>ProductService</ejb-name>
      <home>store.productService.ProductServiceHome</home>
      <remote>store.productService.ProductService</remote>
      <ejb-class>store.productService.ProductServiceEJB</ejb-class>
      <session-type>Stateless</session-type>
      <transaction-type>Bean</transaction-type>
      <ejb-ref>
        <ejb-ref-name>ejb/Artist</ejb-ref-name>
        <ejb-ref-type>Entity</ejb-ref-type>
        <home>store.artist.ArtistHome</home>
        <remote>store.artist.Artist</remote>
      </ejb-ref>
    </session>
  </enterprise-beans>

  <assembly-descriptor>
    <container-transaction>
      <method>
        <ejb-name>ProductService</ejb-name>
        <method-intf>Remote</method-intf>
        <method-name>*</method-name>
      </method>
      <trans-attribute>Required</trans-attribute>
    </container-transaction>
  </assembly-descriptor>
</ejb-jar>
```

The Artist Entity Bean

The Artist entity bean and its interfaces are responsible for maintaining the Artist data elements and the tightly coupled entity beans. First we'll look at the remote interface, which exposes methods to manipulate the data:

```
package store.artist;

import java.rmi.RemoteException;
import store.app.*;
import java.util.Collection;

public interface Artist extends javax.ejb.EJBObject {

    public void setName(String name) throws RemoteException;
    public String getName() throws RemoteException;

    public void setDescription(String desc) throws RemoteException;
    public String getDescription() throws RemoteException;

    public String getArtistId() throws RemoteException;

    public void setActive(String active) throws RemoteException;
    public String getActive() throws RemoteException;

    public void addItem(ItemDetails itemDetails) throws RemoteException;
    public void addMedia(MediaDetails mediaDetails)
            throws RemoteException;

    public Collection getItemsForArtist() throws RemoteException;

    public ItemDetails getItemDetails(String itemId)
            throws RemoteException;

    public void updateItem(ItemDetails item) throws RemoteException;

}
```

Next is the home interface, used to create instances of the entity bean and finder methods to look-up instances of the entity bean:

```
package store.artist;

public interface ArtistHome extends javax.ejb.EJBHome {
    Artist findByPrimaryKey(String id)
            throws java.rmi.RemoteException, javax.ejb.FinderException;

    Artist findByArtistName(String name)
            throws java.rmi.RemoteException, javax.ejb.FinderException;

    Artist create(String id, String name, String description,
                String activeStatus) throws java.rmi.RemoteException,
                                        javax.ejb.CreateException;

}
```

And now the entity bean implementation code:

```
package store.artist;

import javax.ejb.*;
import javax.naming.InitialContext;
import store.app.*;
import store.item.*;
import store.media.*;
import java.util.Collection;
import java.util.Iterator;
import java.util.ArrayList;

public abstract class ArtistEJB implements EntityBean {

  public abstract String getArtistId();
  public abstract void setArtistId(String artistId);

  public abstract String getName();
  public abstract void setName(String name);

  public abstract String getDescription();
  public abstract void setDescription(String description);

  public abstract String getActive();
  public abstract void setActive(String active);

  public abstract Collection getItems();
  public abstract void setItems(Collection items);

  public abstract Collection getMedia();
  public abstract void setMedia(Collection media);

  public abstract ItemLocal ejbSelectItem(String itemId)
        throws FinderException;

  public abstract MediaLocal ejbSelectMedia(String mediaId)
        throws FinderException;

  public Collection getItemsForArtist() {

    ArrayList arrList = new ArrayList();
    try {
      Iterator iter = getItems().iterator();
      ArtistItems aItems = null;
      while (iter.hasNext()) {
        ItemLocal item = (ItemLocal) iter.next();
        aItems = new ArtistItems(getArtistId(), getName(),
                                 item.getItemId(), item.getTitle(),
                                 item.getType());
        arrList.add(aItems);
      }
    } catch (java.rmi.RemoteException re) {
      throw new EJBException(re);
    }

    return arrList;
  }

  public ItemDetails getItemDetails(String itemId) {

    ItemDetails details = new ItemDetails();
    try {
      ItemLocal item = ejbSelectItem(itemId);
```

```
      details.setItemId(item.getItemId());
      details.setTitle(item.getTitle());
      details.setType(item.getType());
      details.setPrice(item.getPrice());
      details.setSku(item.getSku());
      details.setInventory(item.getInventory());
      details.setActiveStatus(item.getActiveStatus());
   } catch (Exception e) {
      throw new EJBException(e);
   }

   return details;
}

public void updateItem(ItemDetails newItem) {

   try {
      ItemLocal item = ejbSelectItem(newItem.getItemId());
      item.setTitle(newItem.getTitle());
      item.setType(newItem.getType());
      item.setPrice(newItem.getPrice());
      item.setSku(newItem.getSku());
      item.setInventory(newItem.getInventory());
      item.setActiveStatus(newItem.getActiveStatus());
   } catch (Exception e) {
      throw new EJBException(e);
   }

}

public void addItem(ItemDetails itemDetails) {

   try {
      InitialContext initial = new InitialContext();
      ItemLocalHome itemLocalHome =
         (ItemLocalHome) initial.lookup("java:comp/env/ejb/Item");

      ItemLocal itemLocal =
         itemLocalHome.create(itemDetails.getItemId(),
                              itemDetails.getTitle(),
                              itemDetails.getType(),
                              itemDetails.getPrice(),
                              itemDetails.getInventory(),
                              itemDetails.getSku(),
                              itemDetails.getActiveStatus());

      getItems().add(itemLocal);

   } catch (Exception re) {
      throw new EJBException(re);
   }
}

public void addMedia(MediaDetails mediaDetails) {

   try {
      InitialContext initial = new InitialContext();
      MediaLocalHome mediaLocalHome =
         (MediaLocalHome) initial.lookup("java:comp/env/ejb/Media");

      MediaLocal mediaLocal =
         mediaLocalHome.create(mediaDetails.getMediaId(),
```

```
                                mediaDetails.getDescription(),
                                mediaDetails.getSize(),
                                mediaDetails.getType(),
                                mediaDetails.getFileName());

      getMedia().add(mediaLocal);

    } catch (Exception re) {
      throw new EJBException(re);
    }
  }

  public String ejbCreate(String id, String name, String description,
                          String activeStatus) throws CreateException {
    setArtistId(id);
    setName(name);
    setDescription(description);
    setActive(activeStatus);
    return null;
  }

  public void ejbPostCreate(String id, String name,
                            String description,
                            String activeStatus) {}

  public void ejbStore() {}
  public void ejbRemove() {}
  public void ejbActivate() {}
  public void ejbPassivate() {}
  public void setEntityContext(EntityContext ctx) {}
  public void unsetEntityContext() {}
  public void ejbLoad() {}

}
```

And finally the deployment descriptor elements:

```
<enterprise-beans>
  <entity>
    <display-name>Artist</display-name>
    <ejb-name>Artist</ejb-name>
    <home>store.artist.ArtistHome</home>
    <remote>store.artist.Artist</remote>
    <ejb-class>store.artist.ArtistEJB</ejb-class>
    <persistence-type>Container</persistence-type>
    <prim-key-class>java.lang.String</prim-key-class>
    <reentrant>False</reentrant>
    <cmp-version>2.x</cmp-version>
    <abstract-schema-name>ArtistEJB</abstract-schema-name>
    <cmp-field>
      <field-name>name</field-name>
    </cmp-field>
    <cmp-field>
      <field-name>artistId</field-name>
    </cmp-field>
    <cmp-field>
      <field-name>description</field-name>
    </cmp-field>
    <cmp-field>
      <field-name>active</field-name>
    </cmp-field>
    <primkey-field>artistId</primkey-field>
```

```xml
      <ejb-local-ref>
        <ejb-ref-name>ejb/Item</ejb-ref-name>
        <ejb-ref-type>Entity</ejb-ref-type>
        <local-home>store.item.ItemLocalHome</local-home>
        <local>store.item.ItemLocal</local>
        <ejb-link>Item</ejb-link>
      </ejb-local-ref>
      <ejb-local-ref>
        <ejb-ref-name>ejb/Media</ejb-ref-name>
        <ejb-ref-type>Entity</ejb-ref-type>
        <local-home>store.media.MediaLocalHome</local-home>
        <local>store.media.MediaLocal</local>
        <ejb-link>Media</ejb-link>
      </ejb-local-ref>
      <query>
        <description></description>
        <query-method>
          <method-name>ejbSelectMedia</method-name>
          <method-params>
            <method-param>java.lang.String</method-param>
          </method-params>
        </query-method>
        <result-type-mapping>Local</result-type-mapping>
        <ejb-ql>
          SELECT OBJECT(m) FROM MediaEJB m WHERE m.mediaId = ?1
        </ejb-ql>
      </query>
      <query>
        <description></description>
        <query-method>
          <method-name>findByArtistName</method-name>
          <method-intf>Home</method-intf>
          <method-params>
            <method-param>java.lang.String</method-param>
          </method-params>
        </query-method>
        <result-type-mapping>Local</result-type-mapping>
        <ejb-ql>
          SELECT OBJECT(a) FROM ArtistEJB a WHERE a.name = ?1
        </ejb-ql>
      </query>
      <query>
        <description></description>
        <query-method>
          <method-name>ejbSelectItem</method-name>
          <method-params>
            <method-param>java.lang.String</method-param>
          </method-params>
        </query-method>
        <result-type-mapping>Local</result-type-mapping>
        <ejb-ql>
          SELECT OBJECT(i) FROM ItemEJB i WHERE i.itemId = ?1
        </ejb-ql>
      </query>
    </entity>
</enterprise-beans>

<assembly-descriptor>
  <container-transaction>
    <method>
      <ejb-name>Artist</ejb-name>
      <method-intf>Remote</method-intf>
```

```
          <method-name>*</method-name>
       </method>
       <trans-attribute>Required</trans-attribute>
    </container-transaction>
  </assembly-descriptor>
```

The `Artist` entity bean listed above contains examples using the `Item` and `Media` entity beans, so let's display the code for them as well, starting with `Item`.

The Item Entity Bean

This is an entity bean with local and local home interfaces only. First the local interface for `Item`:

```java
package store.item;

import java.rmi.RemoteException;

public interface ItemLocal extends javax.ejb.EJBLocalObject {

  public String getItemId() throws RemoteException;

  public void setTitle(String title) throws RemoteException;
  public String getTitle() throws RemoteException;

  public void setType(String type) throws RemoteException;
  public String getType() throws RemoteException;

  public double getPrice() throws RemoteException;
  public void setPrice(double price) throws RemoteException;

  public int getInventory() throws RemoteException;
  public void setInventory(int inventory) throws RemoteException;

  public String getSku() throws RemoteException;
  public void setSku(String sku) throws RemoteException;

  public String getActiveStatus() throws RemoteException;
  public void setActiveStatus(String active) throws RemoteException;

}
```

Now the local home interface for `Item`:

```java
package store.item;

import java.util.Collection;

public interface ItemLocalHome extends javax.ejb.EJBLocalHome {
  ItemLocal findByPrimaryKey(String id)
         throws javax.ejb.FinderException;

  ItemLocal create(String itemId, String title, String type,
                   double price, int inventory, String sku,
                   String activeStatus) throws javax.ejb.CreateException;

}
```

And the code for the entity bean itself:

```
package store.item;

import javax.ejb.*;

public abstract class ItemEJB implements EntityBean {

  public abstract String getItemId();
  public abstract void setItemId(String itemId);

  public abstract String getTitle();
  public abstract void setTitle(String title);

  public abstract String getType();
  public abstract void setType(String type);

  public abstract double getPrice();
  public abstract void setPrice(double price);

  public abstract int getInventory();
  public abstract void setInventory(int inventory);

  public abstract String getSku();
  public abstract void setSku(String sku);

  public abstract String getActive();
  public abstract void setActive(String active);

  public String ejbCreate(String itemId, String title, String type,
                          double price, int inventory, String sku,
                          String activeStatus) throws CreateException {
    setItemId(itemId);
    setTitle(title);
    setType(type);
    setPrice(price);
    setInventory(inventory);
    setSku(sku);
    setActive(activeStatus);
    return null;
  }

  public void ejbPostCreate(String itemId, String title, String type,
                            double price, int inventory, String sku,
                            String activeStatus) {}

  public String getActiveStatus() {
    return getActive();
  }

  public void setActiveStatus(String status) {
    setActive(status);
  }

  public void ejbStore() {}
  public void ejbRemove() {}
  public void ejbActivate() {}
  public void ejbPassivate() {}
  public void setEntityContext(EntityContext ctx) {}
  public void unsetEntityContext() {}
  public void ejbLoad() {}

}
```

Finally the deployment descriptor:

```
<enterprise-beans>
  <entity>
    <display-name>Item</display-name>
    <ejb-name>Item</ejb-name>
    <local-home>store.item.ItemLocalHome</local-home>
    <local>store.item.ItemLocal</local>
    <ejb-class>store.item.ItemEJB</ejb-class>
    <persistence-type>Container</persistence-type>
    <prim-key-class>java.lang.String</prim-key-class>
    <reentrant>False</reentrant>
    <cmp-version>2.x</cmp-version>
    <abstract-schema-name>ItemEJB</abstract-schema-name>
    <cmp-field>
      <field-name>type</field-name>
    </cmp-field>
    <cmp-field>
      <field-name>price</field-name>
    </cmp-field>
    <cmp-field>
      <field-name>inventory</field-name>
    </cmp-field>
    <cmp-field>
      <field-name>active</field-name>
    </cmp-field>
    <cmp-field>
      <field-name>itemId</field-name>
    </cmp-field>
    <cmp-field>
      <field-name>title</field-name>
    </cmp-field>
    <cmp-field>
      <field-name>sku</field-name>
    </cmp-field>
    <primkey-field>itemId</primkey-field>
  </entity>
</enterprise-beans>

<assembly-descriptor>
  <container-transaction>
    <method>
      <ejb-name>Item</ejb-name>
      <method-intf>Local</method-intf>
      <method-name>*</method-name>
    </method>
    <trans-attribute>Required</trans-attribute>
  </container-transaction>
</assembly-descriptor>
</ejb-jar>
```

The last EJB we'll look at is `Media`.

The Media Entity Bean

The `Media` bean is very similar to `Item` in that it enjoys a 1:many relationship with `Artist`. We'll start with the local component interface:

```
package store.media;

import java.rmi.RemoteException;
```

```
public interface MediaLocal extends javax.ejb.EJBLocalObject {

  public String getMediaId() throws RemoteException;

  public String getDescription() throws RemoteException;
  public void setDescription(String description)
        throws RemoteException;

  public int getSize() throws RemoteException;
  public void setSize(int size) throws RemoteException;

  public String getFileName() throws RemoteException;
  public void setFileName(String fileName) throws RemoteException;

  public String getType() throws RemoteException;
  public void setType(String type) throws RemoteException;

}
```

Now the local home interface:

```
package store.media;

public interface MediaLocalHome extends javax.ejb.EJBLocalHome {
  MediaLocal findByPrimaryKey(String id)
        throws javax.ejb.FinderException;

  MediaLocal create(String id, String description, int size,
                    String fileName,
                    String type) throws javax.ejb.CreateException;

}
```

Of course we need the bean implementation class:

```
package store.media;

import javax.ejb.*;

public abstract class MediaEJB implements EntityBean {

  public abstract String getMediaId();
  public abstract void setMediaId(String id);

  public abstract String getDescription();
  public abstract void setDescription(String description);

  public abstract int getSize();
  public abstract void setSize(int size);

  public abstract String getFileName();
  public abstract void setFileName(String fileName);

  public abstract String getType();
  public abstract void setType(String type);

  public String ejbCreate(String id, String description, int size,
                          String fileName,
                          String type) throws CreateException {
```

```
        setMediaId(id);
        setDescription(description);
        setSize(size);
        setFileName(fileName);
        setType(type);
        return null;
    }

    public void ejbPostCreate(String id, String description, int size,
                              String fileName, String type) {}

    public void ejbStore() {}
    public void ejbRemove() {}
    public void ejbActivate() {}
    public void ejbPassivate() {}
    public void setEntityContext(EntityContext ctx) {}
    public void unsetEntityContext() {}
    public void ejbLoad() {}

}
```

And finally the deployment descriptor:

```
<enterprise-beans>
  <entity>
    <display-name>Media</display-name>
    <ejb-name>Media</ejb-name>
    <local-home>store.media.MediaLocalHome</local-home>
    <local>store.media.MediaLocal</local>
    <ejb-class>store.media.MediaEJB</ejb-class>
    <persistence-type>Container</persistence-type>
    <prim-key-class>java.lang.String</prim-key-class>
    <reentrant>False</reentrant>
    <cmp-version>2.x</cmp-version>
    <abstract-schema-name>MediaEJB</abstract-schema-name>
    <cmp-field>
      <field-name>size</field-name>
    </cmp-field>
    <cmp-field>
      <field-name>type</field-name>
    </cmp-field>
    <cmp-field>
      <field-name>description</field-name>
    </cmp-field>
    <cmp-field>
      <field-name>mediaId</field-name>
    </cmp-field>
    <cmp-field>
      <field-name>fileName</field-name>
    </cmp-field>
    <primkey-field>mediaId</primkey-field>
  </entity>
</enterprise-beans>

<assembly-descriptor>
  <container-transaction>
    <method>
      <ejb-name>Media</ejb-name>
      <method-intf>Local</method-intf>
      <method-name>*</method-name>
    </method>
```

```
        <trans-attribute>Required</trans-attribute>
      </container-transaction>
   </assembly-descriptor>
```

The Application Objects

Our component also uses three application objects, two of which we defined earlier in the chapter. The application objects we need are:

❑   `ItemDetails` – This application object is a value object for the `Item` entity and we will use this to modify and update item properties.

❑   `MediaDetails` – Likewise this application object serves the same purpose as `ItemDetails` but for the `Media` entity.

❑   `ArtistItem` – This application object contains limited information about an artist and an associated item. We will use this object when we want to browse through an artist's available items and select a particular item to download the details of.

The only one of these three that is missing is `MediaDetails` so here it is:

```java
package store.app;

import java.io.Serializable;

public class MediaDetails implements Serializable {

  private String mediaId;
  private String description;
  private int size;
  private String type;
  private String fileName;

  public MediaDetails() {}

  public MediaDetails(String mediaId, String description, int size,
                      String type, String fileName) {
    this.mediaId = mediaId;
    this.description = description;
    this.type = type;
    this.size = size;
    this.fileName = fileName;
  }

  public String getMediaId() {
    return mediaId;
  }

  public void setMediaId(String mediaId) {
    this.mediaId = mediaId;
  }

  public String getDescription() {
    return description;
  }

  public void setDescription(String description) {
    this.description = description;
```

```
      }

      public String getType() {
        return type;
      }

      public void setType(String type) {
        this.type = type;
      }

      public String getFileName() {
        return fileName;
      }

      public void setFileName(String fileName) {
        this.fileName = fileName;
      }

      public int getSize() {
        return size;
      }

      public void setSize(int size) {
        this.size = size;
      }

      public String toString() {
        return "Media details: id=" + mediaId + ", description="
               + description + ", type=" + type + ", size=" + size
               + ", fileName= " + fileName;
      }

    }
```

We are nearly finished with our implementation for the purposes of this chapter. One thing left to define for our component is the relationships.

Relationships

As we saw from our design, the `Media` and `Item` entities are closely associated with the `Artist` entity. Therefore, we want to define the `Media` and `Item` entities to have a one-to-many relationship with the `Artist` bean (each `Artist` mean can have zero or more associated `Media` and/or `Item` objects). The only difference between the `Artist-Media` and `Artist-Item` relationships is that the `Media` objects don't have a lifecycle independent of the associated artist, therefore we will want to cascade any delete operation on the `Artist` down to any associated `Media` objects.

As we saw in Chapter 6, we define relationships using the `<relationships>` element in the deployment descriptor:

```
<relationships>
  <ejb-relation>
    <ejb-relation-name></ejb-relation-name>
    <ejb-relationship-role>
      <ejb-relationship-role-name>Artist</ejb-relationship-role-name>
      <multiplicity>one</multiplicity>
      <relationship-role-source>
        <ejb-name>Artist</ejb-name>
      </relationship-role-source>
```

```
      <cmr-field>
        <cmr-field-name>items</cmr-field-name>
        <cmr-field-type>java.util.Collection</cmr-field-type>
      </cmr-field>
    </ejb-relationship-role>
    <ejb-relationship-role>
      <ejb-relationship-role-name>Item</ejb-relationship-role-name>
      <multiplicity>many</multiplicity>
      <relationship-role-source>
        <ejb-name>Item</ejb-name>
      </relationship-role-source>
    </ejb-relationship-role>
  </ejb-relation>
  <ejb-relation>
    <ejb-relation-name></ejb-relation-name>
    <ejb-relationship-role>
      <ejb-relationship-role-name>Artist</ejb-relationship-role-name>
      <multiplicity>one</multiplicity>
      <relationship-role-source>
        <ejb-name>Artist</ejb-name>
      </relationship-role-source>
      <cmr-field>
        <cmr-field-name>media</cmr-field-name>
        <cmr-field-type>java.util.Collection</cmr-field-type>
      </cmr-field>
    </ejb-relationship-role>
    <ejb-relationship-role>
      <ejb-relationship-role-name>Media</ejb-relationship-role-name>
      <multiplicity>many</multiplicity>
      <cascade-delete />
      <relationship-role-source>
        <ejb-name>Media</ejb-name>
      </relationship-role-source>
    </ejb-relationship-role>
  </ejb-relation>
</relationships>
```

Testing the Artist Component

Now that we have our *Artist* component implemented, we'll write a simple test class that we can use to check that the basic operations we have defined work successfully:

```java
package store.client;

import javax.naming.*;
import java.util.Properties;
import store.productService.*;
import java.util.Collection;
import java.util.Iterator;

import store.app.*;

public class TestArtist {
  public static void main(String args[]) {
    TestArtist aTest = new TestArtist();
    aTest.addArtists();
    aTest.maintainItem();
  }

  private void addArtists() {
```

```
      System.out.println("entering addArtists method...");
      try {
        Context initial = getRefImpContextInfo();

        Object objref = initial.lookup("ProductService");
        ProductServiceHome home =
          (ProductServiceHome) javax.rmi.PortableRemoteObject
            .narrow(objref, ProductServiceHome.class);

        ProductService ps = home.create();

        ps.addArtist("1", "Big Bad Voodoo Daddy", "Swing", "active");
        ps.addArtist("2", "The Polka Kids", "Polka swing music",
                     "active");
        ps.addArtist("3", "Dan and the Swingers", "Folk Jazz",
                     "active");

        System.out.println("Added three artists");

        // Now add some items for one artist
        ItemDetails item = new ItemDetails("1", "This Beautiful Life",
                                           "Audio CD", 14.99,
                                           "BVD-001", 10, "active");
        ps.addItem(item, "1");
        ItemDetails item2 = new ItemDetails("2",
                                           "Big Bad Voodoo Daddy",
                                           "Audio CD", 19.99,
                                           "BVD-002", 0, "ordering");
        ps.addItem(item2, "1");
        System.out.println("Added two items");

        // Now add a media object
        MediaDetails media =
          new MediaDetails("1", "MPEG of scene from movie Swingers",
                           20, "MPEG", "BBVD_Swingers.mpeg");
        ps.addMedia(media, "1");
        System.out.println("Added one media");

      } catch (Exception e) {
        System.out.println(e);
      }
      System.out.println("Finished adding artist, items and media");
    }

    private void maintainItem() {

      System.out.println("Starting to maintain item");
      try {
        Context initial = getRefImpContextInfo();

        Object objref = initial.lookup("ProductService");
        ProductServiceHome home =
          (ProductServiceHome) javax.rmi.PortableRemoteObject
            .narrow(objref, ProductServiceHome.class);
        ProductService ps = home.create();

        System.out.println("Looking up items for artist");

        // Get list of items for this artist (by name)
        Collection items = ps.getItemsForArtist("Big Bad Voodoo Daddy");

        // Iterate through collection ArtistItems object to locate the item
```

```
        // we are interested in
        Iterator iter = items.iterator();
        ArtistItems aItem;
        String itemId = "";
        String artistId = "";
        while (iter.hasNext()) {
          aItem = (ArtistItems) iter.next();
          if (aItem.getItemTitle()
                  .equalsIgnoreCase("Big Bad Voodoo Daddy")) {
            itemId = aItem.getItemId();
            artistId = aItem.getArtistId();
            System.out.println("aid=" + aItem.getArtistId());
          }
        }
        System.out.println("Getting item details for aid=" + artistId
                        + " iid=" + itemId);

        // Now we have the id for item, get the full details object
        ItemDetails details = ps.getItemDetails(artistId, itemId);

        if (details == null) {
          System.out.println("null");
        }

        System.out.println(details.toString());

        // Update details object and send back to server
        details.setInventory(20);
        details.setActiveStatus("active");
        System.out.println(details.toString());
        ps.updateItem(artistId, details);

      } catch (Exception e) {
        System.out.println(e);
      }

    }

  private Context getRefImpContextInfo() throws NamingException {
    return new InitialContext();
  }

}
```

Summary

In this chapter we discussed how to use a fine-grained UML model as the primary input into your EJB design. We discussed three goals.

❑   Definition of coarse-grained entity components as entity beans

❑   Definition of coarse-grained service components as session beans

❑   Reduction of inter-component messaging

We explained how a number of different strategies could be applied to meet these goals:

❑   Define cohesive classes

❑   Define application objects

❑   Consider deployment issues

❑   Consider transaction boundaries

❑   Simplify component interfaces

Finally we applied these techniques to design the EJBs for a sample application that included EJB session beans, entity beans, and application objects.In the next couple of chapters we will be moving on to looking at how to improve our application'sS design to improve its performance.

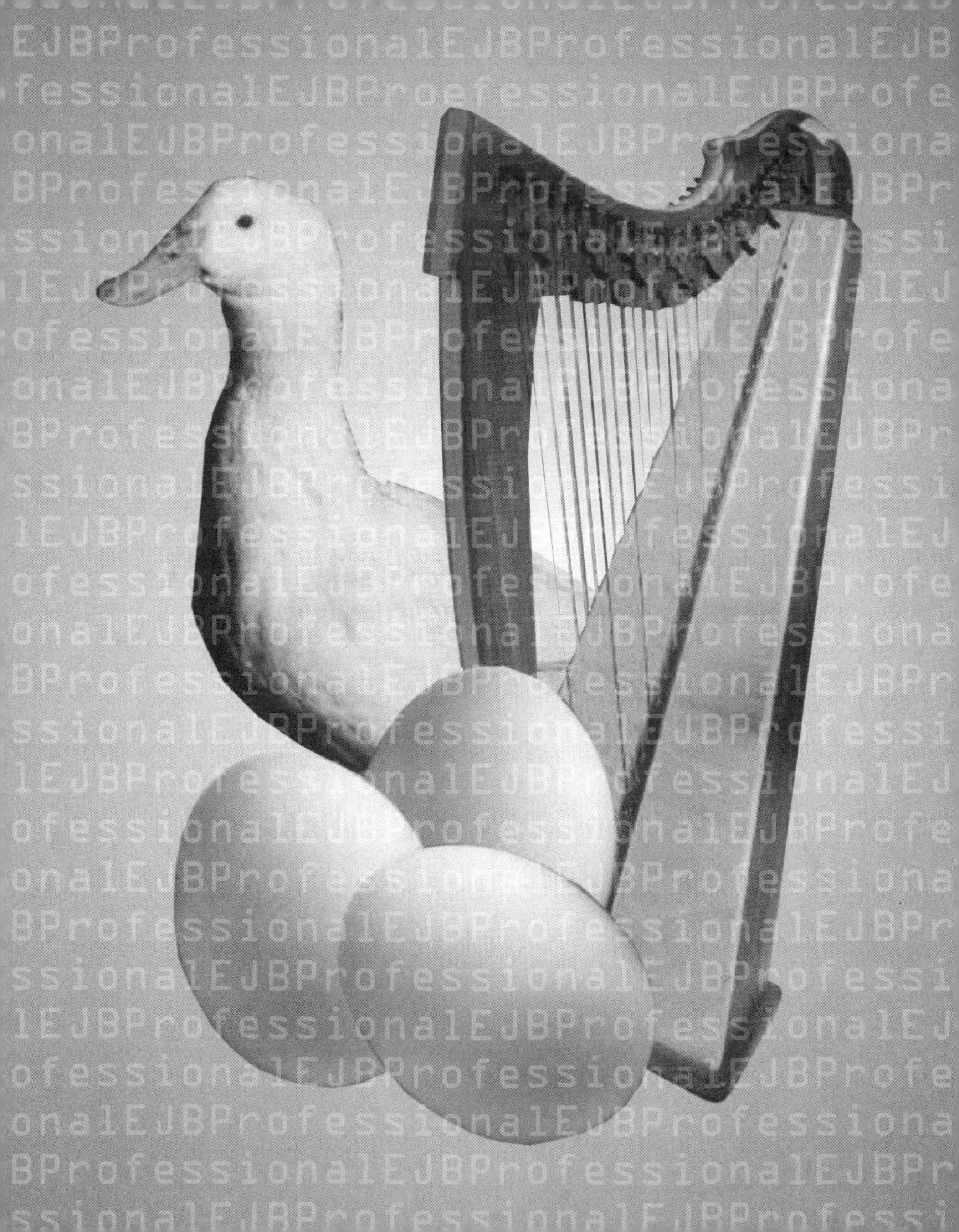

14

Testing Enterprise JavaBeans

This chapter focuses on applying common (and sometimes not so common) software testing techniques to Enterprise JavaBeans development. Here we'll try to concentrate on testing issues particular to EJB development, and offer solutions and strategies observed in common practice.

For a variety of reasons, the enterprise bean developer's work is often subject to much higher scrutiny than other kinds of work products in a J2EE project. This is partly due to the relative novelty of the EJB component model and the accompanying attention that brings, and partly due to the essential value of the application business logic that EJBs encapsulate. As businesses have placed increasing value on their IT systems and business logic over the last several years, counting it as a real market differentiator and a source of competitive advantage, that value is magnified when it is cast as portable, rapidly-developed EJB components. The EJB developer's work just naturally attracts attention because it is frequently seen as the hinge-pin of the J2EE application.

As a result, EJB development requires not only more testing, but also a different approach to testing. Thus, in the first part of this chapter, we will survey the EJB testing landscape, including:

- ❑   The motives, challenges, and requirements for testing EJBs
- ❑   The software testing tools available to the enterprise bean developer
- ❑   The EJB testing lifecycle (the "how" and "when" of testing EJBs)

In the second part of this chapter, we drill a little deeper into what it takes to test an EJB. We will begin the way most enterprise bean developers begin, by coding our own simple test driver for an EJB. In this case, we'll use one of the EJBs from Sun's Java Pet Store reference application from its J2EE Blueprints program. Along the way, we will discover:

- ❑   The requisite components of an EJB testing harness
- ❑   The measurements that are interesting for an EJB test

As we add code to our EJB test driver, it will soon become evident that there is a lot more work to creating an EJB test harness than many developers originally anticipate, leaving us with the classic "build vs. buy" dilemma. To conclude the chapter, we'll tour an EJB-specific automated testing tool, Bean-test, as a way to identify the functionality we need to develop for testing EJBs (if we choose the "build" path), and an example of leveraging currently available technology to solve the problem (if we choose the "buy" path).

An Example EJB to Test

For the EJB under test, the examples in this chapter target the `ShoppingCartEJB` *session bean that is part of the Java Pet Store reference application from Sun's Java 2 Enterprise Edition (J2EE) Blueprints program. You can download and deploy the latest Java Pet Store from* http://java.sun.com/j2ee/download.html.

More information on the J2EE Blueprints is available at http://java.sun.com/j2ee/blueprints/.

To run some of the example tests shown in this chapter, you will need to deploy the Java Pet Store application (containing the EJB under test) on a suitable J2EE-compliant application server. If you don't have access to a server, you can download and install the J2EE SDK (also available from http://java.sun.com/j2ee/download.html*) and use the Reference Implementation J2EE server. The download includes instructions for installing and configuring the reference implementation J2EE server.*

An Overview of EJB Testing

Before getting into the specific techniques of EJB testing, it helps to examine why we need to test enterprise beans differently from other software, what the particular difficulties in EJB testing are, what testing tools are available today to the enterprise bean developer, and where/when all this testing occurs in the development lifecycle of a J2EE project. With this information in hand, you will be better able to choose which types of testing to apply to your EJB project and when to apply them.

The general topic of software testing is a broad one, and obviously far beyond the scope of this chapter. For background information on software testing, including the many kinds of testing and their application, any of the following are valuable resources will serve you well:

- ❑ *The Art of Software Testing* by Glenford J. Myers (John Wiley & Sons, ISBN 0-471-04328-1)
- ❑ *The Complete Guide to Software Testing* by Bill Hetzel (John Wiley & Sons, ISBN 0-471-56567-9)
- ❑ *Testing Client/Server Systems* by Kelley C. Bourne (McGraw-Hill, ISBN: 0070066884)
- ❑ *Testing Computer Software*, 2nd ed. by Cem Kaner, Jack Falk, and Hung Quoc Nguyen (John Wiley & Sons, ISBN 0471358460)
- ❑ *Testing Object-Oriented Systems* by Robert V. Binder (Addison-Wesley, ISBN: 0-201-80938-9)

Why Unit Tests are Not Enough

It has been generally understood for some time now that the earlier you discover a bug, the cheaper it is to fix. So it should come as no surprise that this axiom holds equally true for EJB software development (perhaps more so). But in the EJB component development world there lurk unique problems that cannot be uncovered by the traditional unit test, no matter how soon you begin testing. So it not only falls on the enterprise bean developer to begin testing sooner, but also to apply functional and performance tests, which have in the past been left for others to apply much later in the application development lifecycle.

The advent of the J2EE technologies has made true n-tier development available to almost anyone. It is surprisingly easy to develop an EJB. (Not that it is so easy to develop a "good" EJB!) Development teams are able to deliver enterprise-scale, distributed applications faster than ever before. These technologies afford developers a wider range of options for architecture and design choices, for including and reusing legacy systems, and for application deployment. However, although these systems are easier to build, they are not necessarily easier to test. J2EE, and the EJB component model in particular, has enabled us to develop complicated distributed applications with far more ease, but with complex systems come complex testing problems.

Robust Components

As any component developer must do, the enterprise bean developer must deliver robust components to the application assembler. However, for EJBs, the meaning of "robust" has broadened beyond what the traditional unit test can assure. EJB components often function as the lynchpin of a J2EE application, containing the business logic that is central to an application's value. GUI's may come and go, and database servers can be replaced, but the programming logic encapsulated in business components is fundamental to the application.

As such, the EJB components must be "robust" in more ways: yes, each enterprise bean must be functionally correct as an individual component, but the EJBs must be functionally correct when they work in concert (as sub-systems of enterprise beans). Also, they must be delivered as high-performance, high-volume, distributed, transactional, scalable, portable components – all of the attributes promised by the component model must be delivered in the software that you, the enterprise bean developer, write. You may say these attributes are requirements for any software you develop, but serving as such a central piece to the J2EE application, containing the key business logic of your application, be assured the EJBs you develop will be the focus of a great deal of attention in your J2EE project.

There are also reasons to test enterprise beans beyond unit testing simply by virtue of the fact that EJBs are components. As a component developer you may not be able to predict how your component will be used in future applications. To deliver a robust component, the enterprise bean developer must understand how each business component performs and scales on its own, and how subsystems of beans function, perform, scale, etc. This is necessary if only to determine how to configure each enterprise bean in preparation for packaging and delivery to the application assembler. This information can only be obtained by designing and running tests that are beyond the bounds of traditional unit testing.

> *It is also worth being very clear and specific in the documentation you include with any EJBs you create. This way, there is less chance that they will be used for purposes they were not intended for, thus reducing the chance of your components bringing the standard of someone else's application down.*

"Measure Twice, Code Once"

There is an old saying in the carpentry trade: "Measure twice, cut once". It refers to how, by double-checking your measurements, you can eliminate wasting time, materials, and effort later. Some EJB developers choose to only run a few unit tests, and defer other kinds of testing until later in the project, when the application is fully assembled (a system test).

However, this can often be a serious mistake. Due to the "ease of use" factor provided by the J2EE technologies, the time it takes to put together a working J2EE application is amazingly shortened. Today's development cycles are compressed to the point of changing the sequence of tasks that have for years traditionally been "understood" as the necessary process for any software project. Changed too are people's expectations of how long it should/will take to develop enterprise applications.

As a result of the rapid development capability, time-to-market pressures, management expectations, and other factors, you may never get the opportunity to revisit and debug/fix a component you developed. Nor should you want or need to revisit it. Moreover, even if you could, it could be prohibitively expensive. The time spent in diagnosing and debugging is taken away from some other key development task originally planned. So you must seize this opportunity as perhaps your only chance to assure timely delivery of a component that you will not likely have to revisit later ("cut once"). That assurance can only be acquired through applying tests that yield information beyond the traditional "unit" test provides (more on this later).

Before you begin all this testing, you should note some of the challenges that await the EJB tester.

> *The term "EJB tester" refers to anyone charged with the task of testing an EJB. Often it is the enterprise bean's developer, but frequently QA engineers are assigned this task as well.*

EJB Testing Challenges

There are three general areas that represent challenges to EJB testing, detailed in the sections that follow:

❑ *Where's the GUI?*
EJBs have no GUI, just a home and remote interface. This limits the available testing tools and staffing choices. Without a user interface, an EJB developer cannot defer testing to a business analyst (who may lack the programming skills) or GUI-based capture/playback test tool.

❑ *Where has the Response Time Gone?*
Performance problems in EJBs are harder to detect when hidden in the application's middleware.

❑ *Where has the Development Time Gone?*
EJB testing must be applied much earlier than most developers anticipate.

Where's the GUI?

At its simplest, an EJB is an API – simply a chunk of business logic appearing as a collection of methods to be called and return values to be verified. This is as it should be, given our desire for coarse granularity. However, this non-graphical nature of (most) EJBs yields two testing challenges: Choosing who does the testing, and what tools they use to do it.

In order to test an enterprise bean's API, you need two things:

❑ A mechanism to drive the API programmatically (a program!)

❑ An understanding of how to drive the enterprise bean's API programmatically (what are valid arguments, return values, and exceptions for each method?)

Who does the EJB testing is largely a matter for your software development process, but for EJBs there's a twist: if you're used to passing your software downstream to a QA group, realize that an EJB requires a very different testing skill set from a client-server application with a GUI.

Some teams staff their test groups with domain experts, which is often the wisest choice. For example, business analysts are often far more capable than a developer is of devising realistic test cases for an application. Hand them an application at system test, and they'll torture it in ways its developers never dreamed of doing (or didn't have the heart to). However, hand them an EJB to test, and you are asking for an entirely different set of skills; it is unlikely that the same business analyst will have, in addition to their domain expertise, the Java programming skills to develop a test driver for the EJB, or know how that EJB's API is supposed to behave (JavaDoc that EJB!).

One of the first problems you will confront in EJB testing is one of software test tools. The majority of traditional software testing tools that are commercially available are "GUI-centric" – capture/playback tools that record a user's typing, button clicks, and mouse movements and replay them later as a test case. Most load test tools are born of this type of test tool approach. Without any visual manifestation, nothing to click on or type into, one is hard pressed to apply these tools to testing an EJB directly. At best, you must wait until servlet/JSP development is complete and integration of the presentation and middle tiers begins before you can apply these types of tools. This brings us to the second challenge of EJB testing:

Where has the Response Time Gone?

The functional and performance problems of EJBs deployed in the middle tier are inherently harder to detect. This is especially true when GUI-based load test tools are applied later in the application's development process, and performance is found to be inadequate. For example, consider performance testing the application shown in the following diagram:

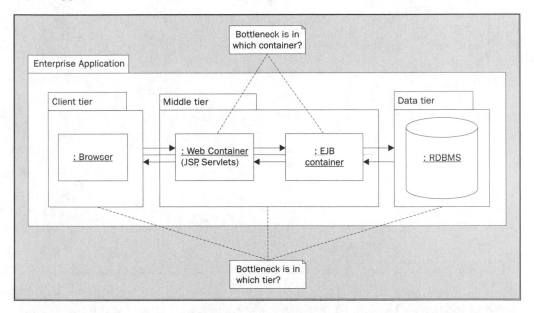

If, after applying a load test through the browser, we learned that the application's response time is too slow, we are left with little to help us identify the bottleneck. One could argue that, if you are testing the whole application, you are testing the EJBs too. This is true in a general sense, but because the EJB business logic is triggered indirectly, the test results can be ambiguous at best. For example, was slow performance due to a bug in a servlet? Or was it web container configuration, or simply network latency? Was the EJB architecture the culprit? Perhaps a stored procedure in the database is inefficient. The point is, to the browser, the application is a monolithic "black box", and testing through the browser cannot yield much diagnostic information.

"Black-box testing" and "white-box testing" are terms that can refer to test design, test implementation, or both. **Black-box** *tests are those designed without regard to the internal implementation of the object under test; the test inputs are applied only to the object's public interface (for example, a GUI, an API, or an EJB's home and remote interfaces). For an in-depth treatment of black-box testing, see* Black-Box Testing *by Boris Beizer (John Wiley & Sons, ISBN: 0-471-12094-4).* **White-box** *tests are designed with the intent to trigger specific implementation code within the object under test, and may circumvent the object's public interface to do so (including instrumenting the code being tested). Most unit tests are inherently white-box tests.*

From an EJB perspective, black-box tests require an understanding of an EJB's interfaces, and white-box tests require an understanding of the EJB's implementation.

This basic testing challenge can also be exacerbated by the complexity of the EJB architecture itself. Functional and performance problems caused by a particular enterprise bean may themselves be hidden within the collection of EJBs, as the following diagram suggests:

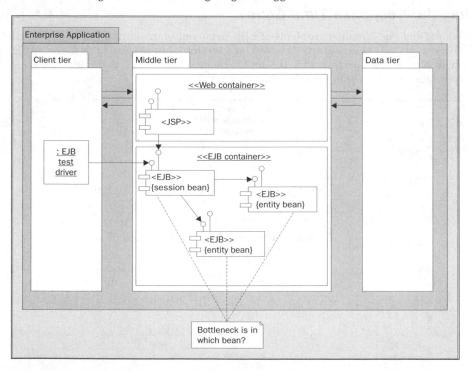

Even with such a simple three-EJB architecture, the "lead" session bean masks an entity bean causing a performance bottleneck. The EJB tier itself appears as a "black box" to the test driver.

The distributed nature of the n-tier J2EE application inherently adds complexity to the testing problem because there are more possible points of failure, within and around the EJB container, and those points of failure may be masked behind "upstream" pieces of the application. The EJB developer's challenge is to be conscious of where and how their delivered components will ultimately fit in the larger J2EE application architecture as a whole, and adopt test strategies that avoid the difficulties of finding and fixing EJB issues later (or too late) in the development cycle. This leads to the third hazard of EJB testing.

Where has the Development Time Gone?

As suggested earlier, an EJB's business logic is often the most critical piece of the entire application, and problem detection cannot wait for the system test phase. Likewise, deployment configuration of the EJB middleware, and configuration of the EJB container (server) itself, cannot be deferred, and is often more complicated than most expect. Each enterprise bean will have its own deployment descriptor, and each deployment descriptor will have several (interrelated) parameters, each of which can drastically improve or degrade the enterprise bean's performance and functionality.

The problem is a testing problem because deployment and server configuration tuning analysis often depends upon data obtained from performance tests, and performance-testing activities often commence too late in development cycles to afford the enterprise bean developer enough time. So the EJB testing challenge here is in applying performance testing to the EJB tier *during* component development. This can be accomplished, provided you have the right **testing tools**.

> *For an excellent textbook and reference on performance analysis, see* The Art of Computer Systems Performance Analys*is by Raj Jain (John Wiley & Sons, ISBN 0471503363).*

An EJB Tester's Toolbox

Despite the fact that the EJB developer faces a number of testing challenges, most can be overcome by applying the right tools at the right time. There are a growing number of Java-oriented testing tools on the market that can be applied to a variety of EJB testing activities, although an exhaustive survey of these tools is beyond the scope of this section. Instead, you may find it more instructive to survey the categories of software tools and how they fit in to the overall EJB testing. Tools useful for EJB testing can be grouped into the following categories.

❑ **Unit Test Tools**
There are a number of general tools (including your IDE) that are useful for validating code, catching Java usage errors, and other unit test activities on your EJBs.

❑ **Profilers**
Given all the attention around EJB performance, a Java profiler can yield valuable resource-utilization information.

❑ **Automated Test Tools**
There are a number of automated software test tools on the market that can make your EJB testing much more effective.

❑ **Monitoring Tools**
If you're using a tool for operational monitoring of your application server, the information it yields can be very useful for assessing the performance of your EJB middleware.

❑ **Documentation Tools**
JavaDoc and test planning just might be the biggest time saving tools of all in EJB testing.

❑ **Software Inspection**
Although a useful weapon in any testers arsenal, this is less a tool and more a process. Basically, this involves several people reading the documentation and code for a class, and making sure it matches up with the specifications.

Let's examine each of these tool categories in a little more detail.

Unit Test Tools

In most Java development projects, the "unit" in unit testing is typically a class. However, in EJB development an EJB implementation class is often not a self-sufficient entity that can be tested by itself with meaningful results. The context of the EJB container is required to create a more realistic test. For example, calling the container callback methods in the implementation class directly from a test driver (serving as surrogate for a servlet) may not uncover functional problems that would otherwise occur if the EJB were deployed in and managed by the container. More often, EJB developers prefer to treat individual enterprise beans as the "unit" to test. In this case, the familiar unit testing cycle of "code, build, test" requires an extra step for EJB development: "code, build, **deploy**, test".

> *Many EJB developers include a* main() *method within each EJB's implementation class to circumvent the container and directly test callback methods (*ejbStore()*,* ejbPassivate()*, and so forth), calling them from* main()*. This is a useful white-box testing technique, but rarely suffices as the only unit test mechanism. For example, such a test will fail to catch problems in the EJB's container-managed persistence setup, as there is no "container" to manage anything when invoking* main() *directly.*

> *To trigger the implementation of container callback methods like* ejbPassivate() *using black-box techniques (using the container services), you'll need to create the conditions that cause the method invocations (deploy the bean with the bean pool small enough to force passivation, and create a load of concurrent requests for the bean).*

Your IDE may be the best unit test tool of all for EJB unit testing. In addition to sophisticated debugging features, many integrated development environments (IDEs) now include built-in integration with leading application servers. Using these integration features, you can build, debug, deploy, and unit-test your EJB using a single development tool. Some IDEs will even generate simple client code corresponding to the EJB you have developed.

Another popular tool for unit testing Java classes is **JUnit**, a general-purpose, Java unit-testing framework written by Erich Gamma and Kent Beck. JUnit allows us to test Java code from the command line, or by using the graphical user interface. The following screenshot shows an example of JUnit's graphical user interface:

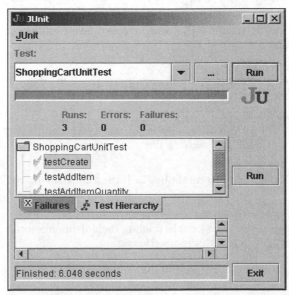

JUnit is especially popular in the **Extreme Programming (XP)** community. XP is a streamlined development methodology created by Kent Beck. Among other practices, XP advocates continual testing throughout development iterations.

> *For a nice introduction to the XP approach, read* Extreme Programming Explained: Embrace Change *by Kent Beck (Addison-Wesley, ISBN: 0201616416). You can also find more on the Web at* http://www.extremeprogramming.org *and* http://www.xprogramming.com.

Some EJB developers use JUnit to create their EJB unit test drivers. We will examine EJB test drivers and JUnit in greater detail later in this chapter (see the section Extreme EJB Testing).

Profilers

At some point in debugging and performance analysis, it becomes necessary to dig into the details of the JVM in which the EJB container is executing. A profiler can show you, in great detail, where time is being spent in methods, thread allocation, memory used by objects on the heap, and so forth. The Java 2 SDK includes its own JRE profiling capability via the -Xrunhprof switch (-Xrunhprof:help yields a list of available options):

```
java -Xrunhprof:cpu=samples,file=petstore_prof.txt -classpath %CLASSPATH% \
-Dweblogic.Domain=petstore -Dweblogic.Name=petstoreServer \
-Dbea.home=C:\bea -Dcloudscape.system.home=./samples/eval/cloudscape/data \
-Djava.security.policy==C:\bea\wlserver6.0/lib/weblogic.policy \
weblogic.Server
```

This command starts the WebLogic application server with profiling turned on, directing output to the file petstore_prof.txt. The petstore_prof.txt listing contains information similar to the following fragment:

```
CPU SAMPLES BEGIN (total = 2572) Fri Feb 23 11:16:04 2001
rank   self  accum   count trace method
   1 17.73% 17.73%    456  1389 java.net.SocketInputStream.socketRead
   2  6.57% 24.30%    169    35 java.lang.ClassLoader.defineClass0
   3  2.72% 27.02%     70    38 java.io.Win32FileSystem.getBooleanAttributes
   4  2.57% 29.59%     66   438 java.lang.Thread.yield
   5  2.41% 32.00%     62    18 java.lang.ClassLoader.findBootstrapClass
   6  2.18% 34.18%     56   252 java.lang.Class.getConstructor0
   7  2.10% 36.28%     54    37 java.util.zip.ZipFile.getEntry
   8  1.83% 38.10%     47  1406 java.lang.Class.newInstance0
   9  1.48% 39.58%     38  1401 java.io.Win32FileSystem.getBooleanAttributes
  10  1.48% 41.06%     38  1363 java.net.PlainSocketImpl.socketAccept
  11  1.48% 42.53%     38  1593 java.lang.Class.getConstructor0
```

In this case, the listing shows methods in the JRE sorted in descending order by count of calls. You can search this output for lines relating to EJB activities:

```
 398  0.04% 79.00%      1   356 java.util.Hashtable$Enumerator.<init>
 399  0.04% 79.04%      1  1681 com.sun.estore.cart.ejb.ShoppingCartEJB.getDetails
 400  0.04% 79.08%      1  1175 java.util.HashMap.put
```

In addition to the Java 2 SDK built-in profiler, there are a number of third-party Java profilers that provide greater ease-of-use and more functionality, such as Sitraka Software's JProbe (http://www.sitraka.com) or Intuitive Systems' OptimizeIt (http://www.optimizeit.com), shown overleaf:

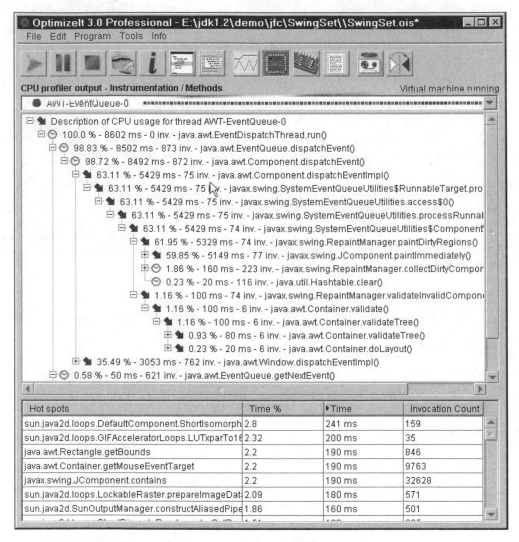

A profiler is an indispensable tool to the EJB tester/developer, especially where insight into resource allocation is required; however, a word of caution: applying a profiler too early in testing/analysis activities can be counterproductive. Profilers can provide an overwhelming collection of details about the run-time environment, leaving you with a "can't see the forest for the trees" dilemma.

In cases where there are tens or hundreds of enterprise beans involved, and hundreds of methods and objects, scouring the resource allocation details of the entire EJB deployment can take some time. This is a classic "using the right tool at the right time" issue. Many EJB developers prefer to first run higher-level tests using an automated test tool, and then use their profiler to examine the details of a problem area that the high-level test uncovered. You might think of this issue as being like using a microscope and telescope, starting broadly and narrowing your field of vision.

Automated Test Tools

Automated test tools have been available for some time now, and this is the category that most first think of when considering the software tools they need for EJB testing. In general, there are two traditional flavors of automated software test tools applicable to EJB development projects:

❑ GUI-based capture/playback tools that record and play back test cases

❑ Load-test tools that simulate multiple, concurrent users accessing the application

Capture/Playback Test Tools

GUI-based capture/playback automated test tools have been available since the days of client-server development, and most operate following the same general procedure. When you start the test tool's recorder and then invoke the application under test, the recorder logs all keyboard and mouse activity into a script that can be played back later as a test scenario.

Being born of the client-server era, most GUI-based automated test tools were oriented around the native windowing environment of the application under test (X/Motif, Windows, and so forth). But in recent years, web-based tools such as Empirix's e-Tester (http://www.empirix.com), shown below, and others have started to replace these, recording the user's actions within the browser instead of the native GUI application:

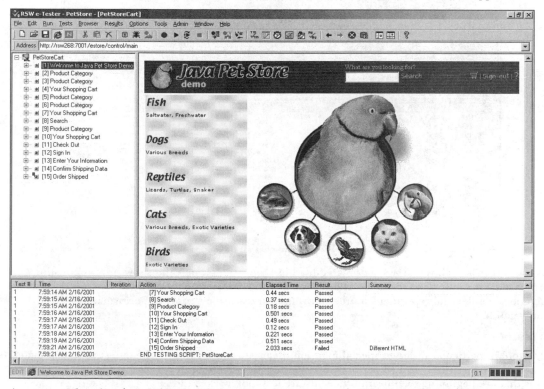

As suggested earlier (see *Where has the Development Time Gone?*), GUI-based capture/playback tools are essential to EJB testing in the context of the overall application. However, they may not suffice as the sole EJB test tool solution because of the requirement for testing to begin earlier (for independent testing of the non-graphical business logic middle tier), and the focus on performance and scalability testing that typically accompanies J2EE applications.

Automated Load Test Tools

Often, GUI-based capture/playback tools will also offer integrated load-testing solutions too (in the case of e-Tester, the corresponding load-test product is e-Load, shown below). These kinds of automated test tools are the core to scalability and performance testing that is so often the focus around most enterprise and web applications. Most integrated load-testing tools make use of the single-user test cases recorded by their capture/playback counterpart, simulating multi-user activity by multi-threading the single user test case in playback. During test execution, the load generator ramps up the number of concurrent sessions in regular increments to some specified maximum load, allowing you to track how application response time degrades as the load of user activity increases:

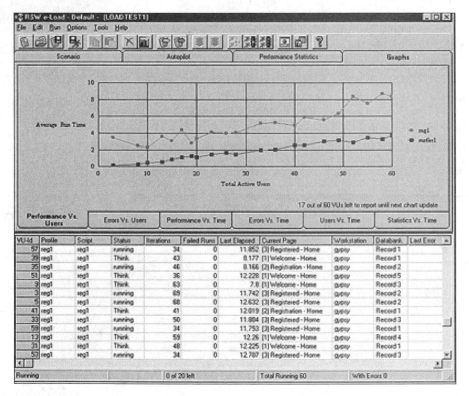

As the screenshot above shows, automated load-test tools can graphically show how application response time slows when the application is subject to an increasing load. In fact, these tools usually include several useful reporting features, allowing you to view a variety of performance-related information.

Bean-test

One tool in particular deserves special mention: Bean-test, from Empirix. Bean-test is an automated test system devoted entirely to EJB performance and functional testing. It represents the first of a handful of tools that are beginning to appear in the software test-tool market addressing EJB testing. We will examine Bean-test in greater detail later in this chapter.

Monitoring Tools

Monitoring tools are another useful type of software in EJB testing activities, where they can provide insight into the server-side operational environment. As an enterprise bean is stimulated from the client-side test driver, monitors can collect and report statistics and performance information.

There are a wide variety of tools that fall into this general category, from enterprise-wide management frameworks, to highly application- or technology-specific monitoring tools. Often, the operating system itself will have built-in monitoring tools you can use to collect and view server-side performance data as a test executes. An example of this would be performance monitoring available in Windows 2000 Professional (from the Control Panel, under the Administrative Tools menu, choose Performance):

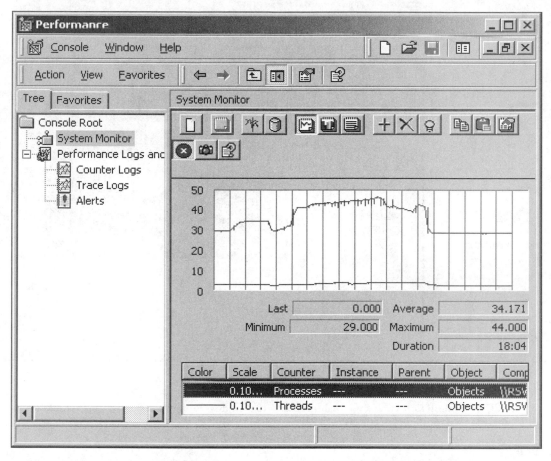

Also, the application server itself often provides monitoring and logging features via its administrative interface. For example, the WebLogic Server Console available in BEA WebLogic 6.x provides a rich assortment of monitoring and logging features:

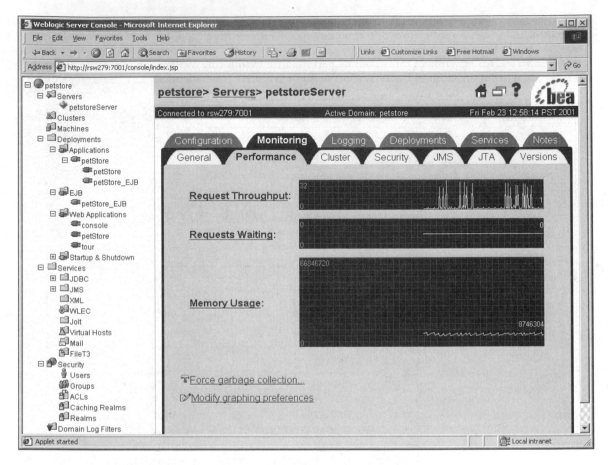

Test Documentation Tools

In general, documentation is rarely considered as a tool in development tasks, but in fact can be the most valuable tool of all.

JavaDoc

JavaDoc is an incredibly powerful tool included in the Java 2 SDK, and yet is too frequently overlooked as an EJB development tool. If colleagues are to test the EJB, we need a mechanism by which to communicate how the enterprise bean is supposed to work. As every EJB is essentially an API (in the eyes of the application assembler and of the tester), what a particular enterprise bean does or how it should be tested is not always obvious to others. And yet it's likely we will be passing our completed component to someone else in the development team, usually for the purpose of testing it. JavaDoc makes an excellent tool for this. In general, JavaDoc comments are useful for many types of project documentation, including:

- ❏ Design specifications
- ❏ Functional specifications
- ❏ Test plans
- ❏ API documentation

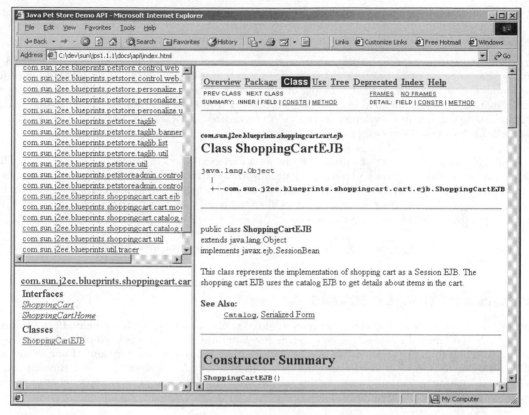

Including JavaDoc comments in your code can make a testing activity much easier later on in the development cycle. In fact, taking the time to include JavaDoc comments in EJB code is an act of self-preservation; delivering well-documented components will result in fewer untimely or unwelcome calls from team members asking how an enterprise bean is supposed to work, or claiming that the enterprise bean doesn't seem to work at all.

For the greatest EJB testing leverage, JavaDoc comments should contain the following information:

❑   A general description of the EJB and its purpose

❑   The type of enterprise bean (stateful session bean, stateless session bean, entity bean, or message-driven bean)

❑   The signatures and return types of all methods in the home interface, remote interface, primary key class (for entity beans), and any other methods available to a client of the enterprise bean

❑   Limitations, expectations, assumptions, or dependencies for every method argument and return value

❑   The default deployment descriptor configuration for the enterprise bean

❑   Limitations, expectations, assumptions, or dependencies surrounding the EJB's deployment and/or operational environment (for example, application server configuration requirements, operating system configuration requirements, external application requirements, and so forth)

❑   Performance requirements (if any have been established)

In one form or another, this information will have to be available to anyone creating an EJB test plan.

The EJB Test Plan

In any testing endeavor, the **test plan** document is an essential tool, and this is no less true for EJB testing. The very act of authoring a test plan allows you to think through the issues involved in testing a component. As mentioned at the beginning of this chapter, there are plenty of well-established testing books that describe what a good test plan should contain, and it is important to recognize that EJBs require a test plan just like any other piece of well-engineered software. At the very least, an EJB test plan will list individual test cases to be run against each enterprise bean.

Also, just like any other piece of software, there are a variety of ways to organize EJB test cases. These, too, requires careful design and planning. It's usually easiest to start by organizing groups of test cases around individual EJBs. It may sometimes make sense to create a group of test cases around a particular method in an EJB's home or remote interface. Other test cases may target a particular subset of EJBs that compose a subsystem or business process.

Regardless of the chosen design or content, the test plan will become an essential tool throughout the EJB testing lifecycle.

The EJB Testing Lifecycle

Regardless of the software development methodology at play in an EJB development effort – waterfall, spiral, Rational Unified Process (RUP), Extreme Programming (XP) – the pattern of coding, deploying, testing, and bug fixing is unavoidable. As this pattern plays out in the development of one or more EJBs, we'd like to find ways to minimize the iterations of test cycles, while at the same time ensuring delivery of high-quality components. In this section, we consider some general approaches to applying testing to an EJB development project.

Why Starting Now isn't Soon Enough

As mentioned earlier, it is imperative for EJB testing to commence sooner rather than later for the following reasons:

- A more complicated development and testing environment requires more time to set up and maintain.

- EJBs require more testing time, because of the pivotal role of these components in the overall J2EE application, and because the mission-critical business logic encapsulated in EJBs deservedly draws more attention.

- Every EJB package (JAR) in the application contains one or more files comprising its deployment descriptor. Each deployment descriptor contains parameters that must be configured, and many of these parameter values can only be determined through testing (particularly load testing). For example, what is the correct number of EJB instances to retain in the pool to accommodate the anticipated request load, but not waste valuable memory? The appropriate deployment configuration of each EJB must be ascertained well before the application is assembled, when it may or may not be readjusted.

- EJB test assets require more time to prepare. EJB test drivers are most often Java applications, which must be hand-coded or generated by a tool like Bean-test. Likewise, an EJB test framework or harness must be coded for organizing the tests into suites space and running them, logging results, generating load, and so forth.

Aside from the factors that force us to begin testing our EJB middleware sooner than we otherwise might have done, there are great benefits to be gained from taking a bottom-up approach and incorporating test development as part of the overall EJB development process.

The Bottom-up Approach

In the "bottom-up" approach to EJB testing, we begin by testing individual enterprise beans, then groups of enterprise beans, and finally the entire deployment of EJB's as a standalone application. There are a number of advantages to this testing approach:

- ❏ Finer-grained understanding of the EJB layer
- ❏ Earlier bug detection
- ❏ Development of test assets that can be reused later in the project
- ❏ More opportunities to weigh and adjust EJB architecture and design decisions

While there are clear advantages to this approach, it is sometimes difficult to apply. Nevertheless, wherever the bottom-up approach can be taken, take it.

Extreme EJB Testing

Applying the Extreme Programming (XP) approach to EJB development may be the quintessential bottom-up EJB testing strategy.

One of XP's fundamental practices is to develop a unit test driver *first*, before coding the class you intend to test. In the context of EJB development, only after coding the initial unit test does the developer begin coding the EJB itself, the unit test serving as a kind of use case or specification for the EJB. While coding and re-factoring the enterprise bean classes, the developer continually runs the unit test against the EJB (perhaps as often as every fifteen minutes or so), continuing in this manner until the test runs cleanly.

To facilitate this development approach, many XP developers use the JUnit testing framework (see the *Unit Test Tools* section earlier in this chapter) from Erich Gamma and Kent Beck. JUnit is a simple framework for writing repeatable unit tests for any Java classes, and can be used to test EJBs as well. The JUnit framework provides basic facilities for defining and grouping test cases into suites, running suites, logging, and validating test results.

> *For more on junit and to download the latest version (3.7 as this book went to press), visit the JUnit web site at http://www.junit.org/. The download includes a complete introduction to the JUnit framework, including tutorials, example code, JavaDoc documentation and more. If you are unfamiliar with JUnit, you may prefer to try the tutorial included in the download before attempting the EJB example in this section.*

The following code is an example of a JUnit test driver, adapted to test an EJB. In this example, the test driver is designed to test the ShoppingCartEJB (from Sun's Java Pet Store reference application; see the beginning of this chapter). Before writing any code for the ShoppingCartEJB itself, imagine the EJB developer taking an XP approach, and instead writing an initial unit test. It might look something like the following:

```
import junit.framework.*;
import com.sun.estore.cart.ejb.*;
import com.sun.estore.cart.model.*;
import com.sun.estore.catalog.model.*;
import javax.naming.*;
import java.util.*;
```

```java
public class ShoppingCartUnitTest extends TestCase {
  private Context jndi = null;      // JNDI initial context

  // Vendor-specific JNDI URL?modify if necessary
  // "t3" is a BEA WebLogic proprietary protocol
  private String url = "t3://localhost:7001";

  private Object homeObject;
  private ShoppingCartHome home;    // home interface
  private ShoppingCart cart;        // remote interface
  private String item, prodId;
  private int qty;

  public ShoppingCartUnitTest(String name) {
    super(name);
  }

  public static void main(String args[]) {
    junit.textui.TestRunner.run(suite());
  }

  public void setUp() throws Exception {    // before every test case
    try {
      Properties p = new Properties();

      // Vendor-specific JNDI initial context factory; modify if necessary
      p.put(Context.INITIAL_CONTEXT_FACTORY,
            "weblogic.jndi.WLInitialContextFactory");

      p.put(Context.PROVIDER_URL, url);
      jndi = new InitialContext(p);
      homeObject = jndi.lookup("estore/cart");
      home =
        (ShoppingCartHome) javax.rmi.PortableRemoteObject.narrow(homeObject,
              ShoppingCartHome.class);
      cart = home.create();
    } catch (Exception e) {
      System.out.println("Get home interface failed.");
      e.printStackTrace();
    }

    item = "EST-3";                           // item number
    prodId = "FI-SW-02";                      // item's product id
    qty = 3;                                  // item quantity
  }

  public void tearDown() throws Exception {   // after every test case
    cart.empty();
  }

  public static TestSuite suite() {
    return new TestSuite(ShoppingCartUnitTest.class);
  }

  // Test cases begin here...

  public void testCreate() throws Exception {
    cart = home.create();
    assert(!cart.equals(null));
  }
```

```
public void testAddItem() throws Exception {
  cart = home.create();
  cart.addItem(item);

  // validate
  ShoppingCartModel cartModel = cart.getDetails();
  Iterator items = cartModel.getItems();
  assert(items.hasNext());
  while (items.hasNext()) {
    CartItem i = (CartItem) items.next();
    assert(i.getProductId().equals(prodId));
  }
}

public void testAddItemQuantity() throws Exception {
  cart = home.create();
  cart.addItem(item, qty);

  // validate
  ShoppingCartModel cartModel = cart.getDetails();
  Iterator items = cartModel.getItems();
  assert(items.hasNext());
  while (items.hasNext()) {
    CartItem i = (CartItem) items.next();
    assert(i.getQuantity() == qty);
    assert(i.getProductId().equals(prodId));
  }
}
}
```

Note that this example unit test code contains vendor-specific elements required to test the EJB deployed in a specific target application server environment. In this case, the chosen target environment is BEA WebLogic Server 6.x. If you prefer to use another application server environment, you will need to modify the example unit test source accordingly.

The test driver itself participates in the JUnit framework by defining a class that extends `junit.framework.TestCase`. Within the class, individual tests are identified as methods following a standard naming convention recognized by the JUnit framework by using the "test" prefix. The `ShoppingCartUnitTest` driver defines three such unit tests: `testCreate()`, `testAddItem()`, and `testAddItemQuantity()`, each test corresponding to a planned EJB method. Like many JUnit test drivers, `ShoppingCartUnitTest` also includes `setUp()` and `tearDown()` methods to provide pre- and post-processing for each test; the framework automatically calls these methods before and after each test. Each test uses the framework's `assert()` method to validate results.

In a "pure" XP approach to EJB development, we *write this test driver first*, and only then begin to code the EJB it is supposed to test. The test driver tells us a lot about what structure and functionality we need to supply in the EJB. For example, looking at the JUnit test code's `setUp()` method, the JNDI lookup method call:

```
homeObject = jndi.lookup("estore/cart");
```

shows that we need to develop an EJB named `estore/cart` in the JNDI tree.

The home and remote field declarations:

```
private ShoppingCartHome home;    // home interface
private ShoppingCart cart;        // remote interface
```

specify a home interface named `ShoppingCartHome` and a remote interface named `ShoppingCart`. In each test, the assignment statement:

```
cart = home.create();
```

shows that we need to supply (at least) a no-argument `ejbCreate()` method.

In fact, most of the information the EJB developer needs is specified in the test code, including package names, remote interface method signatures and return values, additional classes (`ShoppingCartModel`), and more. For example, for the `ShoppingCartUnitTest` to compile, the remote interface (`ShoppingCartModel`) definition must, at a minimum, contain the following:

```
/**
 * Copyright 2001 Sun Microsystems, Inc. All rights reserved.
 */

package com.sun.estore.cart.ejb;

import java.rmi.RemoteException;
import java.util.Collection;
import javax.ejb.EJBObject;

import com.sun.estore.cart.model.ShoppingCartModel;

public interface ShoppingCart extends EJBObject {
    public ShoppingCartModel getDetails() throws RemoteException;

    public void addItem(String itemNo) throws RemoteException;

    public void addItem(String itemNo, int qty) throws RemoteException;

    public void empty() throws RemoteException;
}
```

> Note that the code above is an example remote interface meant to illustrate a preliminary stage in the development of the `ShoppingCartEJB`. The actual `ShoppingCartEJB` classes and interfaces distributed in Sun's Java Pet Store reference application contain much more than appears in this example. The Pet Store reference application is available from the following site: http://java.sun.com/j2ee/blueprints/sample_application/index.html (a version is supplied with WebLogic).

Attempting to compile and run the `ShoppingCartUnitTest` class will fail until the minimum requirements defined in the unit test are met by the EJB. All referenced classes must be available to the test class, and all method implementations must satisfy the `assert()` calls so they return `true` (see the JUnit documentation for more on the `assert()` method). This means the developer must modify, redeploy, and retest the EJB until the corresponding unit tests all pass. A likely XP-style "development episode" for an EJB would include the following sequence:

1. Write a unit test driver for the would-be EJB.

2. Code the simplest implementation of the enterprise bean (and other required classes) that you think will fulfill the requirements of the defined test cases (even starting with empty method implementations in the enterprise bean's implementation class).

3. Build and deploy the EJB on the target application server.

4. Compile and run the unit test. If the test compiles and passes, you can move forward. Otherwise,

5. Modify the EJB, and go back to Step 3. Repeat until the corresponding unit test compiles and runs without errors/failures.

After building and deploying the first iteration of the `ShoppingCartEJB`, you would want to compile and run the corresponding JUnit test cases (`ShoppingCartUnitTest`) to check your progress. The following example command compiles `ShoppingCartUnitTest` for a `ShoppingCartEJB` deployed in BEA WebLogic Server 6.x:

```
javac -classpath .;C:\junit3.6\junit.jar;petStore_EJB.jar
     ;%WL_HOME%\lib\weblogic.jar ShoppingCartUnitTest.java
```

The classpath in the example above identifies three important elements:

❏ `junit.jar` locates the JUnit framework classes (for example, `TestCase`)

❏ `petStore_EJB.jar` locates the EJB classes (for example, `ShoppingCartEJB` and `ShoppingCartModel`; for simplicity, we'll assume this has been copied to the same directory as the `ShoppingCartUnitTest.java` file)

❏ `weblogic.jar` locates the vendor-specific classes required by BEA WebLogic Server (for example, `weblogic.jndi.WLInitialContextFactory`; note that the variable `%WL_HOME%` points to the installation directory for WebLogic, which would be `C:\bea\weblogic6.0sp1` in the case of the server we're using)

If the classpath and file locations are correct, `ShoppingCartUnitTest` compiles without error and can now be executed in JUnit. The following command starts the JUnit GUI:

```
java -classpath .;C:\dev\junit3.6\junit.jar;petStore_EJB.jar
     ;C:\bea\wlserver6.0sp1\lib\weblogic.jar junit.swingui.TestRunner
```

When JUnit's GUI appears, it is pre-loaded with any JUnit tests that are on the classpath (identified as subclasses of `JUnit.framework.TestCase`):

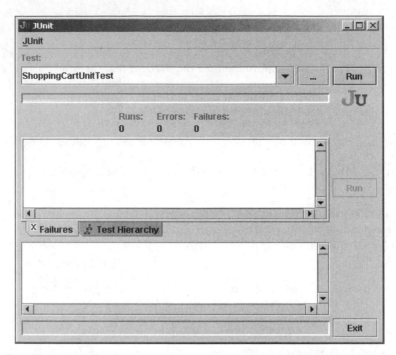

Choosing the Run button nearer the top of the window launches all the tests defined in the currently selected test case, `ShoppingCartUnitTest` (it is also possible to run individual tests within the suite).

The following JUnit result window shows errors occurred for all three of the tests (indicated by the Errors counter field value and the red progress bar) in `ShoppingCartUnitTest`:

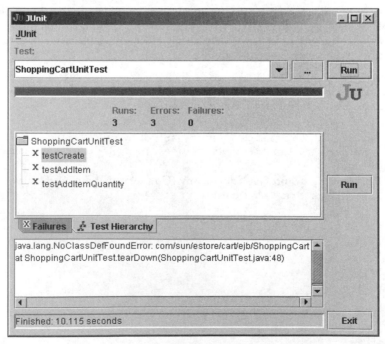

Failures usually stem from two sources:

- ❑ Run-time errors or exceptions (for example, missing/incomplete EJB classes)

- ❑ Pass/fail criteria set in the test itself (for example, `assert()` invocations that return `false`)

A few more modify/rebuild/redeploy/retest iterations in this development episode will eventually produce a successful run of all three tests, indicated in the JUnit GUI by a green progress bar and zeros in both the Errors and Failures counter fields:

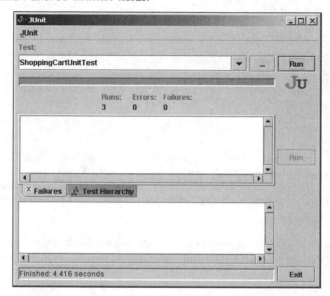

JUnit offers a nice extensible framework in which to develop unit tests for Java classes, providing easy test suite definition and execution, assert methods for test case validation, automated test setup and cleanup for each test case, and more. JUnit is increasing in popularity with EJB developers who are adapting XP techniques to their J2EE projects.

> *For more information on XP, see* Extreme Programming Explained: Embrace Change, *by Kent Beck (Addison-Wesley, ISBN: 0201616416).*

Instrumenting EJBs

Another interesting test strategy in the bottom-up approach is to instrument the EJB itself. **Instrumenting** an enterprise bean requires adding test code that logs information at key points within the enterprise bean's method implementations to collect server-side data. Consider the following code fragment from a stateful session bean's implementation class (it's one of the EJBs in Sun's J2EE Blueprints example Pet Store 1.0 application, `ShoppingCart`):

```
public void addItem(String itemNo) {
   cart.put(itemNo, new Integer(1));
}
public void addItem(String itemNo,int qty) {
   cart.put(itemNo, new Integer(qty));
}
public void deleteItem(String itemNo) {
   cart.remove(itemNo);
}
// etc.
```

609

It might be interesting to instrument this enterprise bean with added statements that track throughput by maintaining a count of shopping cart items, perhaps using a homegrown logging class, Log, that you wrote for this purpose (we will examine the requisite pieces of an EJB test harness, like a logging class, in greater detail later):

```
Log log = new Log();
public void addItem(String itemNo) {
  cart.put(itemNo, new Integer(1));
  log.incrementCounter(1);
}
public void addItem(String itemNo,int qty) {
  cart.put(itemNo, new Integer(qty));
  log.incrementCounter(qty);
}
public void deleteItem(String itemNo) {
  cart.remove(itemNo);
  log.decrementCounter(1);
}
// etc.
```

In the new, instrumented version of the ShoppingCartEJB implementation class, we simply create a new instance of our Log class and use it to track the number of items processed using the incrementCounter() and decrementCounter() methods. (The implementation details of the logger class are less important here than the technique we're trying to illustrate: adding code to the class that records performance data.)

Although this approach yields the desired data, instrumenting EJBs has some real drawbacks. For instance, it would be nice to be able to turn off the instrumentation, as one might do with a debugging flag:

```
public void addItem(String itemNo,int qty) {
  cart.put(itemNo, new Integer(qty));
  if (log.IS_ON) {      // initialized in Log constructor
    log.incrementCounter(qty);
  }
}
// etc.
```

This may seem tempting, but be aware that doing so introduces additional logic that slows down the method (remember: we added this code to turn off the overhead of logging). It may seem like a negligible price to pay, but it is not so negligible for an enterprise bean serving (hopefully!) thousands of requests. One alternative workaround would be to maintain two versions of the EJB, one with instrumentation and one without, but this too carries a price: the maintenance burden is doubled, and the cost of keeping the instrumented and non-instrumented versions of the same EJB may not be worthwhile. The conventional wisdom is: in taking a bottom-up approach to testing, it's probably best to avoid instrumenting EJBs until forced to do so.

The Top-down Approach

Of course, the opposite strategy to the bottom-up approach to EJB testing is the "top-down" approach. In the top-down approach, EJB testing begins at some chosen enterprise bean serving as an entry point to a collection of EJBs, and additional target EJBs to be tested are chosen according to chains of logic invoked by "upstream" enterprise beans. This EJB testing approach is most often applied in the following three kinds of missions:

❑ Locating the root cause of a performance bottleneck

❑ Testing a delivered EJB deployment

❑ EJB subsystem testing

In all three activities, the procedure is to apply step-wise refinement, at each step narrowing the set of enterprise beans eligible for testing. Often this goal-oriented approach results in faster completion of test activities, and more certainty around when testing is complete. The drawback is that you may get less test coverage across the set of EJBs under test, and testing starts later (the immutable law of late bug detection applies: the later bugs are detected in the development process, the more it costs to fix them).

Locating Bottlenecks

Locating bottlenecks in an assembled n-tier application most often requires a top-down approach to EJB testing. The nature of testing also changes. Performance bottlenecks are typically first discovered during the system-testing phase (or later). It is in this phase that GUI-based capture/playback load test tools (see the *Automated Test Tools* section earlier in this chapter) are applied to greatest advantage, driving the whole application end-to-end as a single entity (black-box) by running selected tests from the regression suite (we'll look at regression testing shortly).

Driving load into the application through the GUI is the "top" of the top down approach. If, during system testing, performance issues arise, problem reports found through these means are typically too ambiguous to aid in diagnosis. Complaints like, "The response time seems sluggish" or, "It takes too long for pages to display" are your only hints. Applying the stepwise refinement, the first step might be to determine if the problem lies in the presentation logic (JSP/servlet web container), the business logic (EJB container), or the data tier.

Here is a typical progression though a system with three session beans and two entity beans:

1. System tests precipitate complaints that the application's overall response time is unacceptable.

2. To isolate the presentation logic, you load-test and measure the EJB tier directly, substituting a Java test driver that simulates the method calls of the JSP/servlet it replaces. The driver calls methods on an entry point session bean, and logs response times for each call.

3. You observe that the average response time is not much less than that recorded by the overall system test, suggesting that the problem resides "downstream" of the presentation logic (EJB middleware, or data tier).

4. In a similar fashion, you develop Java test drivers for each of the three session beans called by the "lead" bean just tested, and run each individually. You observe one of the three takes surprisingly longer than the other two.

5. You develop additional test drivers for the two entity beans manipulated by the suspiciously "slow" session bean.

6. The two entity bean performance test results show response times you expected. These results warrant investigation into the semantics of the "slow" session bean, where you discover an obvious efficiency mistake (aren't they all?) and fix it. Case solved.

Note that, in this scenario, the testing goal was to pinpoint the source of an observed problem, where you knew what you were looking for (sort of), rather than the type of testing you do to expose as-yet undiscovered problems.

611

The "Low-Hanging Fruit" Approach

Another application of the top-down EJB testing approach is to pick EJBs that represent key entry points to the business logic, with the aim of surfacing big, obvious problems by testing the most frequently visited enterprise beans or bean methods first. This kind of testing is often very effective, especially when the time available to test is limited.

Starting with developing and running test drivers for these key enterprise beans, testers develop additional tests of two types, as time permits:

- ❑ Tests that drill into "suspicious" behavior observed in the first round of testing
- ❑ Tests for EJBs of secondary interest (the ones we wanted to test in the first round but didn't think we had time for)

Test development continues in this way until you run out of time, or until confidence in the application is achieved (whichever comes first).

EJB Subsystem Testing

Using a top-down approach for EJB subsystem testing usually represents more of an organizational motivation, rather than urgency. It is similar to the "low-hanging fruit" technique, except the aim here is to organize test assets (namely, test cases for EJBs) around sets of enterprise beans that represent general business functions within the overall deployment of EJBs. The subsystems of enterprise beans usually map to easily recognizable subsystems of the overall application.

After developing initial high-level test cases for each subsystem, test development proceeds to a second tier of tests within each subsystem of enterprise beans, testing each subsystem with increasing granularity. The approach stems from the traditional "functional decomposition" process of test case development.

One characteristic of this approach that differs significantly from the "low-hanging fruit" approach is in the opportunity for reuse or sharing of test cases between subsystems. Some enterprise beans may participate in more than one EJB subsystem, and where these situations occur, it usually pays to think through the organization of your test cases, refactoring where you can. In the "low-hanging fruit" approach, EJB test-case development is driven by test results; in subsystem testing, EJB test-case development is driven by application architecture.

Building a Regression Suite

As with any form of software testing, the collection of EJB test cases tends to grow over time. This is true for both the bottom-up and top-down approaches. As new functionality is added, corresponding tests are developed to verify that functionality. And as the number of developed test cases grows, it pays to regularly scan the collection for regression suite candidates.

A **regression test** is one that is likely to reveal bugs caused by changes to an enterprise bean's implementation, causing the EJB to "regress" in quality (something that worked in the past no longer works because of the change you made). A common software testing practice is to collect these kinds of tests into a **regression suite** that can be run periodically over the application's evolution.

Some teams schedule the execution of such a regression suite at key milestones in the project (for example, just before a hand-off to QA). Others choose to trigger automated regression suites from shell scripts or batch files as part of their automated build. Scheduling an automated regression suite to run at off-hours (overnight) is another common approach. In all cases, the motive is to assure that any changes did not break formerly working code. (For a more thorough treatment of regression testing techniques, refer to any of the general software testing books listed in the beginning of this chapter.)

Building an effective EJB regression suite is often the most valuable part of the overall test assets you develop, so it's worth defining a general structure and process for building and running the regression suite. As with anything else, it pays to plan. The key to the process of building a regression suite is in identifying test cases that are most likely to reveal errors.

Anatomy of an EJB Test Harness

An EJB test harness comprises all the software necessary to execute tests against an individual EJB, and collections of EJBs, to collect and compare test results for analysis. The EJB test harness can be a simple collection of utility classes, or an incredibly ornate framework, depending on the testing requirements. Deciding what kind of information to collect about the EJB will, to a large extent, dictate the degree of coding difficulty and complexity of the test harness. For example, coding a distributed, multi-threaded load engine is (for most of us) a lot harder than coding a logging class.

In this section, we examine the basic pieces most useful to an EJB test harness. To accomplish this, we will draw our examples from a commercially available EJB test tool from Empirix called Bean-test. Bean-test is an example of an already-existing, full-featured, 100% Java test harness for EJB performance and functional testing. Examining a ready-made, working example should help crystallize your understanding of what you'll need to accomplish your EJB testing goals.

The EJB Test Driver

Central to any automated software test case is the test driver. The **test driver** is the script that stimulates or drives the object under test in a particular way, through a particular sequence of operations. For EJBs, the test driver is most often a Java application (or servlet or JSP) that is a client of the EJB being tested. An EJB can (and probably should) have several different test drivers. As a client of the EJB, the test driver makes a sequence of method calls on the EJB-under-test. That sequence of method calls, combined with the unique set of argument values passed in to each of the method calls, comprises the test stimulus for the EJB.

Along the way, the test driver may collect test data for us, such as the method return values, or response time measurements, that will be useful in analyzing the results of the testing. It would also help to design the test in such a way as to maximize reuse of the driver with different test input data values for the method arguments, or to allow us to multithread the test driver to simulate load on the enterprise bean being tested.

Let's develop an EJB Java test driver to be run in the Bean-test framework. To begin, the test driver will itself be a Java application, and so must be defined as a class. Since we plan to test the `ShoppingCart` stateless session bean, it makes sense to name the class `ShoppingCartTest`.

As we suggested earlier, it would be nice to reuse this test case to simulate, say, multiple simultaneous requests on the enterprise bean coming from JSP servlet sessions in the web container. To run multiple threads of this class, we'll plan to use Bean-test's multithreaded load engine. For Bean-test to create multiple threads of this class, we will need to have the class extend the `Thread` class, override the `Thread.run` method, and include this test driver in the `com.beantest.run` package:

```
/*
 * @(#)ShoppingCartTest.java    3.1, 2/24/2001
 */
package com.beantest.run;

/**
 * Bean-test client driver for ShoppingCart bean.
 *
```

```
 * @author        tosborne@empirix.com
 * @version        1
 */
public class ShoppingCartTest extends Thread {

  /**
    * Thread entry point for EJB test
    */
  public void run() {

    // not yet implemented
  }
}
```

Note that it is just as useful to use JavaDoc to document the test case as it was to use JavaDoc to document the enterprise bean itself.

As a client of the EJB being tested, the test driver must follow the same procedure for conversing with the EJB that any servlet or other Java client of the EJB would have to follow, namely:

❑   Connect to the EJB server's JNDI naming service

❑   Lookup the EJB under test in the JNDI naming service, obtaining a reference to the enterprise bean's home interface

❑   Use the home interface methods to obtain a reference to the remote interface, containing the enterprise bean's business methods (the business logic to be tested)

❑   Use the remote interface to make the desired calls on the enterprise bean's business methods

Let's tackle these one at a time. First, we need to obtain a reference to the home interface, ShoppingCartHome. It makes sense to encapsulate the statements that get the home interface within a convenience method. This way, we can add flexibility to the test by specifying different JNDI URLs at run time (the enterprise bean may be deployed on different servers at different stages of development). We'll add a method named getHomeInterface() to accomplish this, and make use of the Bean-test framework's built-in mechanism for passing the URL to the test at run time (as we'll soon see). Let's start with adding the method implementation:

```
/*
 * @(#)ShoppingCartTest.java   3.1, 2/24/2001
 */
package com.beantest.run;
import java.util.*;
import com.sun.estore.cart.ejb.*;

/**
  * Bean-test client driver for ShoppingCart bean.
  *
  * @author        tosborne@empirix.com
  * @version        2
  */
public class ShoppingCartTest extends Thread {

  /**
    * Thread entry point for EJB test
    */
  public void run() {

// not yet implemented
```

```
    }
/**
 * Routine to get EJB home interface for BEA WebLogic Server v6.0.
 *
 * @param      urlName      machine and port that locates the
 * JNDI service (ex: "localhost:7001")
 *
 * @return      a reference to enterprise bean's home interface,
 * <code>com.sun.estore.cart.ejb.ShoppingCartHome</code>.
 *
 * @throws      Throwable
 * if an error has occurred in accessing JNDI service.
 */
ShoppingCartHome getHomeInterface(String urlName) throws Throwable {

    // [Get the initial context]
    Properties p = new Properties();
    p.put(javax.naming.Context.INITIAL_CONTEXT_FACTORY,
          "weblogic.jndi.WLInitialContextFactory");
    p.put(javax.naming.Context.PROVIDER_URL, "t3://" + urlName);
    javax.naming.Context jndi = new javax.naming.InitialContext(p);
    if (jndi == null) {
        throw (new NullPointerException("InitialContext returned null"));
    }

        // [Get the reference to the bean's home interface]
    Object homeObject = jndi.lookup("estore/cart");
    ShoppingCartHome home =
        (ShoppingCartHome) javax.rmi.PortableRemoteObject.narrow(homeObject,
            ShoppingCartHome.class);
    if (home == null) {
        throw (new NullPointerException("jndi.lookup returned null"));
    }
    return home;
}
```

Note that, in our method implementation, the `Properties` object we pass to the `InitialContext` constructor is specific to the application server on which the enterprise bean is deployed (in our example, it is BEA WebLogic 6.0). The implementation of `getHomeInterface()` might look very different using another application server. Also, notice that we included a couple of checks for things going awry in the client's dealings with the JNDI service. This error checking will save time in debugging if, for instance, the JNDI service is down, or the JNDI name bound to the enterprise bean (`estore/cart`) gets changed at some point.

Now we just need to invoke our convenience method in the driver's `run()` method:

```
/**
 * Thread entry point for EJB test.
 */
public void run() {
    try {

        // [Get a reference to the bean's home interface]
        com.sun.estore.cart.ejb.ShoppingCartHome home =
            getHomeInterface(m_sUrlName);
    } catch (Throwable t) {
```

```
        System.out.println("Error starting thread. " + t);
        return;
    }
}
```

The string argument passed to getHomeInterface is a field we have not yet defined: m_sUrlName. As we mentioned, at run time Bean-test will pass in a string representing the machine and port to use in the JNDI URL (for example, localhost:7001 to identify the WebLogic server running on the local machine). Bean-test does this by supplying (among other things) the string as an argument to the ShoppingCartTest test driver's constructor. Let's start by first defining a simple constructor that initializes a new field, m_sUrlName, with the supplied JNDI string:

```
public class ShoppingCartTest extends Thread {

    /**
     * The location (server and port) of the JNDI service
     */
    String m_sUrlName;

    /**
     * Creates a new instance of ShoppingCartTest
     *
     * @param      jndiUrl      the server and port for the JNDI URL
     */
    public ShoppingCartTest(String sUrl) {
      m_sUrlName = sUrl;
    }

    // etc.
```

Actually, Bean-test requires a constructor with a signature that handles three arguments, so this test driver is not yet ready to run in the Bean-test framework – we will need to expand this constructor implementation a bit later. In the meantime, we can add a main() method that will allow us to run this test driver as a standalone Java application.

The following listing shows the current state of our test driver implementation, including the new main() method:

```
/*
 * @(#)ShoppingCartTest.java   3.1, 2/24/2001
 */
package com.beantest.run;
import java.util.*;
import com.sun.estore.cart.ejb.*;

/**
 * Bean-test client driver for ShoppingCart bean.
 *
 * @author      tosborne@empirix.com
 * @version     3
 *
 */
public class ShoppingCartTest extends Thread {

    /**
     * The location (server and port) of the JNDI service
     */
```

```
String m_sUrlName;

/**
 * Creates a new instance of ShoppingCartTest
 *
 * @param       jndiUrl      the server and port for the JNDI URL
 */
public ShoppingCartTest(String sUrl) {
  m_sUrlName = sUrl;
}

/**
 * Starts a single ShoppingCartTest thread from the command line.
 */
public static void main(String[] args) {
  new ShoppingCartTest("localhost:7001").start();
}

/**
 * Thread entry point for EJB test.
 */
public void run() {
  try {

    // [Get a reference to the bean's home interface]
    com.sun.estore.cart.ejb.ShoppingCartHome home =
      getHomeInterface(m_sUrlName);
  } catch (Throwable t) {
    System.out.println("Error starting thread. " + t);
    return;
  }
}

/**
 * Routine to get EJB home interface for BEA WebLogic Server v6.0.
 *
 * @param       urlName      machine and port that locates the
 * JNDI service (ex: "localhost:7001")
 *
 * @return      a reference to enterprise bean's home interface,
 * <code>com.sun.estore.cart.ejb.ShoppingCartHome</code>.
 *
 * @throws      Throwable
 * if an error has occurred in accessing JNDI service.
 */
ShoppingCartHome getHomeInterface(String urlName) throws Throwable {

  // [Get the initial context]
  Properties p = new Properties();
  p.put(javax.naming.Context.INITIAL_CONTEXT_FACTORY,
        "weblogic.jndi.WLInitialContextFactory");
  p.put(javax.naming.Context.PROVIDER_URL, "t3://" + urlName);
  javax.naming.Context jndi = new javax.naming.InitialContext(p);
  if (jndi == null) {
    throw (new NullPointerException("InitialContext returned null"));

    // [Get the reference to the bean's home interface]
  }
  Object homeObject = jndi.lookup("estore/cart");
  ShoppingCartHome home =
    (ShoppingCartHome) javax.rmi.PortableRemoteObject.narrow(homeObject,
        ShoppingCartHome.class);
```

617

```
  if (home == null) {
  throw (new NullPointerException("jndi.lookup returned null"));
    }
    return home;
  }
}
```

So now we have a test driver, but what does it test? Well, it may not yet seem like this test driver is doing a lot of testing, but consider the following alternate implementation of our main() method:

```
public static void main(String[] args) {
  final int LOAD_SZ = 100;
  ShoppingCartTest[] cartClients = new ShoppingCartTest[LOAD_SZ];

  // create LOAD_SZ client threads
  for (int i = 0; i < cartClients.length; i++) {
    cartClients[i] = new ShoppingCartTest("localhost:7001");
  }

  // Launch threads
  for (int i = 0; i < cartClients.length; i++) {
    cartClients[i].start();
    System.out.println("Started client " + i);
  }
}
```

Now we have a client that can produce 100 near-simultaneous requests for the ShoppingCart bean's home interface (ShoppingCartHome). That alone is a worthwhile EJB test, before we ever call a method in the enterprise bean's home or remote interfaces, because we would want to know:

❑ Is the EJB container deploying our enterprise beans configured to deliver fast access to the ShoppingCartHome reference?

❑ Is the JNDI service configured correctly?

❑ Is the JNDI protocol we are using (here, BEA's T3 protocol in the URL t3://localhost:7001) appropriate for this load?

Already, our test driver takes us toward answering these questions, by being able to simulate load and invoke the correct sequence of methods. As a next step, we might want to add some logging code to begin getting the result data we really need for analysis. (In fact, there is much more functionality missing from this simple test driver example, functionality that Bean-test already provides.)

As we assembled this first, very simple EJB test driver, it may have occurred to you that there were many utility classes needed to aid in logging test results, making timing measurements, stepping up the number of concurrent threads, and more. If we were to begin designing these test utility classes to provide such functionality, a framework of EJB testing services would emerge. With such a framework of testing services, any EJB test drivers we create could then plug into this framework in order to:

❑ Multithread the test drivers we develop to simulate load

❑ Control test thread execution (for example, ramp up multiple threads in steps, sustain load over time, and so forth)

❑ Fetch test input data from external sources

❑ Log and compare test result data

❑ Prepare textual and graphical results reports

❑ Manage lists of testbed assets (machines, servers, client hosts)

❑ Manage suites of test cases to be executed as a group

You could probably think of more. For the remainder of this section, we will add to our test driver by making use of Bean-test's EJB test framework implementation, and examine several key Bean-test services that EJB test drivers can use.

EJB Test Logs

Before adding more to the `ShoppingCartTest` driver, it may be instructive to think about what kind of EJB test result data the driver should collect, and in what format to render it for analysis. The following three categories are a useful starting point:

❑ **Method return values**
The value (for Java primitives) or object state (for type references) returned by each non-void EJB method call. Most functional testing centers on this result data.

❑ **Response times**
The time spent waiting for each enterprise bean method call to return. This is the most essential measurement in performance testing.

❑ **Exceptions**
Any exception that wasn't caught on the EJB server-side. Seeing the errors that occurred during a test run not only accelerates problem diagnosis, but is also a requirement to performing negative tests (purposefully triggering expected errors).

Let's look at how Bean-test reports each of these.

EJB Method Return Values

Presumably the enterprise bean's methods will produce some response as a result of the test stimulus, and that response is most often a set of values returned by the method calls, one from each method. From a unit-testing and functional-testing standpoint, capturing the return values of method calls in a log is a central requirement. We may then analyze the log and see if the returned values are those that we expected.

For functionally testing an EJB, you might define a test case as the sequence of method calls, the unique set of test data passed to the methods as arguments (test input data), and the set of expected return values produced by the test driver. As an example of an EJB test framework, Bean-test provides reports that show the actual return values compared with expected values for each method call in the EJB test driver:

```
Client    Name            Expected    Actual

1         getDetails      16.5        16.5
1         updateItemQty   16.5        16.5

2         getDetails      49.5        49.5
2         updateItemQty   49.5        49.5

3         getDetails      92.5        92.5
3         updateItemQty   92.5        92.5
```

4	getDetails	74.0	74.0
4	updateItemQty	74.0	74.0
5	getDetails	18.5	18.5
5	updateItemQty	18.5	18.5
6	getDetails	0.0	18.5
6	updateItemQty	0.0	18.5

Actual vs. Expected

In most functional testing, the pass/fail criterion is determined by comparing the actual result with some predetermined expected result. When the two match, the test case passed; when they differ, the test case failed. For most EJB testing, the actual result is some value or object reference returned by the method call. The test-case pass/fail is determined by comparing a Java primitive return value (or the state of a returned object) with an expected value

In running a large number of method calls or, in the case of a scalability test, many test client threads, the result log can become quite long. In these cases, it is very useful to include a facility for filtering out the "passing" test results (actual and expected matched), and only view the failures.:

Client	Name	Expected	Actual
6	getDetails	0.0	18.5
6	updateItemQty	0.0	18.5
16	getDetails	19.95	93.5
16	updateItemQty	19.95	93.5

Response Time

For performance testing, one of the key measurements is response time. It is most useful to track the response time over an increasing load, so you can track performance degradation. In most load engines, the load increases in regular steps during test execution, toward a target load of simultaneous threads. At each step, more threads are added to the load. The size by which the number of threads increases is called the **ramp rate**.

For any given step along the way, the log should show the fastest response time achieved by any single thread, the slowest, and the average of all threads in that step. The following shows an example log:

Clients	Min	Max	Avg
10	9.283	13.048	11.943
20	10.775	18.787	16.037
30	20.069	31.796	28.093
40	24.215	36.883	33.350
50	37.644	50.282	47.282
60	39.516	54.649	52.220
70	50.092	63.751	61.374
80	52.365	71.522	68.825
90	41.249	80.305	77.248
100	76.059	85.593	83.202

It's often more convenient to render the raw log data graphically. This gives a better view of overall performance achieved during the test, and where the response time began to degrade as the load increased, as can be seen in the following graph:

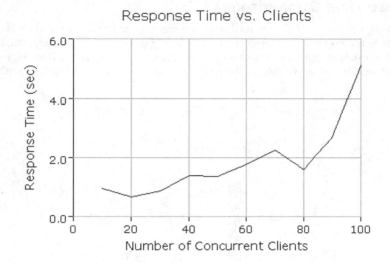

The graph above readily shows that, during the test, performance began to suffer most dramatically when the load exceeded 80 concurrent clients. This may indicate the limits of a resource constraint, such as the number of available pooled database connections.

Another important reporting capability for EJB testing is to graph a comparison showing the response time results of two different tests. This is essential for analyzing the impact on performance after changing an EJB's implementation. Comparisons are also useful in tuning deployment attributes of an enterprise bean. The following graph shows the positive effect of increasing the number of pooled database connections and re-running the same load test of 100 concurrent clients:

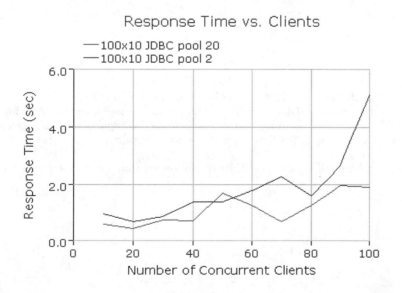

Method Response Time Comparisons

In analyzing EJB performance, an EJB's overall response time can suffer from the slow response of only one of the methods in the enterprise bean's remote interface. To detect this situation, the EJB test result log must contain the response time for every method call executed in the test driver. Here too, rendering this data graphically (as well as showing the raw log data) can be a big help with analysis:

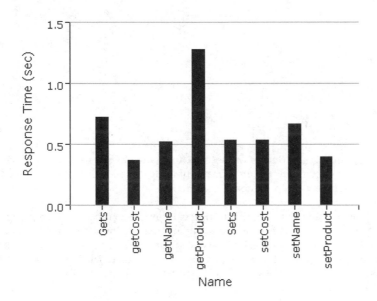

Response Time by Step vs. Clients

Viewed graphically, the log clearly shows that one method call in this EJB test (getProduct()) was nearly a full second slower on average than any other method in the remote interface. As with viewing response time data in relation to the increasing load, viewing method comparisons at any given step in the load ramp-up is an important capability that the log data must support.

To illustrate the value of this kind of log data, consider the following comparison view of two test runs of the same test driver:

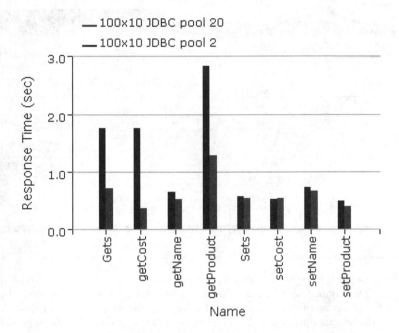

Response Time by Step vs. Clients

Being able to view response times down to the method level permits this kind of comparison. This is important for regression testing. A graphical view such as the chart shown above can help quickly identify the methods causing a performance bottleneck, or the performance impact of changes on any particular method.

Exceptions

The third major category of EJB test log data to collect is exception activity. The most obvious thing to log would be the actual exception text itself, including any trace, as shown in the following screenshot:

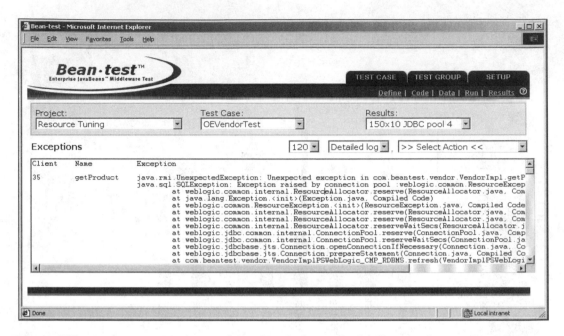

For any EJB test, the exception log needs to identify the method call or test driver activity that triggered the exception. For an EJB load test, the log also must show which client thread triggered the exception and at which step of the ramp-up the error occurred. In the above example (rendered in a browser-based report), the log shows that during the ramp of 120 concurrent threads, client thread 35 threw the exception during the getProduct() method call.

Before viewing the details of an exception, it's usually more useful to first look at the exception rate, to see when the exceptions began to occur, and how many were thrown at various points along the increasing load on the enterprise bean. Logging a simple count of exceptions can show this information, as in the following result report:

	150x10 JDBC pool 4	150x10 JDBC pool 2
Clients	Exceptions	Exceptions
50	0	0
60	0	0
70	0	0
80	0	0
90	0	0
100	0	0
110	0	11
120	3	22
130	5	31
140	14	35
150	8	34

In the log shown above, comparing the exception rates from two runs of the same test, we can see that exceptions began to occur earlier in the ramp up, and at a higher volume, in the test result labeled 150x10 JDBC pool 2 than in the result labeled 150x10 JDBC pool 4.

Perhaps an easier way to view this is graphically, as in the following example:

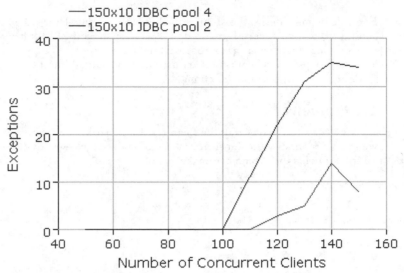

Looking at the graph, we can readily see the difference in the exception rates between the two tests results.

Using a Timer Class

Most developers begin making measurements in the driver using the following pattern:

```
// Launch threads
long t1 = System.currentTimeMillis();
for (int i = 0; i < cartClients.length; i++) {
  cartClients[i].start();
}
long t2 = System.currentTimeMillis();
System.out.println(LOAD_SZ + " Cart clients: " + (t2 - t1)
                    + " milliseconds");
```

The idiom is to surround each event of interest (a method call, a sequence of method calls, and so forth) with timer variables (`t1` and `t2`) to produce the following log output:

```
100 Cart clients: 90 milliseconds
```

The string concatenation serves to label the timed event. As testing progresses, it readily becomes apparent that a much richer logging functionality is required in order to display result data that will be useful, and most developers arrive at building a timer class. The timer class must record the duration of a timed event, as well as capturing the expected and actual return data. The Bean-test system provides just such a class, allowing you to record two types of test data with each timed event:

- ❏   Response time

- ❏   Actual and expected data

In addition, most EJB test developers desire the ability to "filter" the log data later, viewing a group of timed events and excluding all others. A useful way to do this is by associating a "folder" with each event, so that later you can select a particular group of result data in aggregate. The folder maintains a position in a hierarchy, and groups timed events that are assigned to it. In addition to its timer class, Bean-test includes a folder class to support this functionality.

Plugging into a Test Framework

To plug our `ShoppingCartTest` test driver into the Bean-test framework, and make use of its timer and logging classes, we must first modify the constructor to handle the arguments that the framework passes in, and add a couple of fields the thread can make use of:

```
public class ShoppingCartTest extends Thread {

    /**
     * The thread number of this client
     */
    int m_iClientNumber;

    /**
     * The location (server and port) of the JNDI service
     */
    String m_sUrlName;

    /**
     * The CDataSource object this thread will use
     */
    CDataSource m_ds;

    /**
     * Creates a new instance of ShoppingCartTest
     *
     * @param       iClientNumber   the thread number of this client
     * @param       sUrl            the server and port for the JNDI URL
     * @param       ds              the CDataSource object this thread will
     * use
     */
    public ShoppingCartTest(int iClientNumber, String sUrl, CDataSource ds) {
        m_iClientNumber = iClientNumber;
        m_sUrlName = sUrl;
        m_ds = ds;
    }
```

The data source object (m_ds) is just a set of test data values (a row from a table) for the thread to use for parameterized testing, fetching values from its assigned data source and passing them to methods as arguments. The data source (a CSV spreadsheet, generated values, or others) can then be specified at run time from the Bean-test GUI, and different data sources applied in different test runs to the same driver.

A data source class such as the one Bean-test provides (`com.beantest.run.CDataSource`) allows for more flexibility to the test case, allowing you to rerun the same test script multiple times, plugging in different data values for each test run. This capability is essential to functional testing, where the actual set of values supplied as arguments to a method call define the test case (boundary conditions, negative tests, and so forth).

Next, we must create a folder in which to assign result data (outside of the run method, as it will be shared between threads):

```
/**
 * The CDataSource object this thread will use
 */
CDataSource m_ds;

static CFolder m_fldTest = new CFolder("Test");

/**
 * Creates a new instance of ShoppingCartTest
 *
 * @param    iClientNumber    the thread number of this client
 * @param    sUrl             the server and port for the JNDI URL
 * @param    ds               the CDataSource object this thread will
 *                            use
 */
public ShoppingCartTest(int iClientNumber, String sUrl, CDataSource ds)
{
    m_iClientNumber = iClientNumber;
    m_sUrlName = sUrl;
    m_ds = ds;
}
```

This creates a virtual folder named "Test" into which we can assign timed log data. Lastly, we must modify our run method to create a couple of CTimer timer objects and then use their start and stop methods to log the test data:

```
/**
 * Thread entry point for EJB test.
 */
public void run() {
    CTimer timer = new CTimer(m_iClientNumber);
    CTimer timerFullTest = new CTimer(m_iClientNumber);
    timerFullTest.start(m_fldTest, "*Total");

    try {
        //[Get a reference to the bean's home interface]
        timer.start(m_fldTest, "Initialize");
        com.sun.estore.cart.ejb.ShoppingCartHome home
                = getHomeInterface(m_sUrlName);
        timer.stopAndLog();
    } catch (Throwable t) {
        timer.stopAndLog(t);
        timerFullTest.stopAndLog();
        return;
    }
    timerFullTest.stopAndLog();
}
```

In this example, one timer instance (timerFullTest) measures the overall duration of the thread, and the other timer instance (timer) can be used for timing individual events. This adds flexibility, so as we add more method calls, we can time them by reusing the timer instance while maintaining an overall time measurement with timerFullTest. Also, notice how the catch block catches Throwable. This is the mechanism by which Bean-test records exception data along with the timings.

The simple test developed thus far identifies some of the common EJB test framework elements that EJB test drivers can require. As mentioned earlier, in coding the test itself, requirements for a framework of test services begin to emerge (for example, CTimer, CFolder, and CDataSource classes).

In fact, the preceding example was intended to make an important point: with even a simple test driver, you can see that writing the test code can itself become a demanding coding effort. Many EJB developers find that, although they start out simply, before long they are enmeshed in writing more test code than the EJB code they are trying to test. This occurs as they discover the need for new kinds of measurements, reporting, and load simulation.

> **So rather than continue with the arduous task of adding more and more code and infrastructure to our example by hand-coding, we will instead abandon our simple driver and use Bean-test's code generation features to create a ready-made test client for us.**

The Value of Code Generation

Code generation is becoming an increasingly important feature in IDEs and test tools, eliminating many of the repetitive or mundane coding tasks that come with writing EJB tests (like wrapping each EJB method call in the test driver with `timer.start()` and `timer.stopAndLog()` method calls).

In addition, code generation helps overcome the problem of the sheer volume of test cases required for a typical EJB deployment. Consider a deployment of 40 EJBs, with an average of 8 home/remote interface methods in each EJB. At a minimum of one test per method, this would require 320 tests, and it is likely that would be an insufficient number of tests. The ability to automatically generate test drivers for all these methods can represent a significant productivity saving.

A Short Tour of the Bean-test Framework

Regardless of whether you choose to create your own custom test framework, or use a commercial tool, walking through the process of creating and running a simple EJB test using an existing framework like Bean-test will help you quickly identify and choose what test capabilities you will ultimately require for testing your own EJBs.

In this section we will create and run a simple EJB load test for the ShoppingCart enterprise bean, using Bean-test and BEA WebLogic Server 6.0, both available as evaluation downloads. WebLogic 6.0 also includes an example deployment of the Java Pet Store EJBs, allowing us to continue using the ShoppingCart enterprise bean as the EJB under test.

Obtaining Bean-test

You can download the latest evaluation version of Bean-test from the Empirix web site:

http://www.empirix.com

> *As you read this, there may be a newer version of Bean-test available than the version documented here (Bean-test version 4.1). However, any differences you see should be minor, and the basic steps will be the same.*

The download installer runs on Windows NT/2000 platforms (being a 100% Java application, Bean-test also runs on most Unix/Linux platforms; contact Empirix if you need the Unix version). The download software includes full documentation, a small set of demonstration EJBs, and a built-in tutorial.

You must also obtain a license before you can run Bean-test. To get a free 7-day evaluation license, send a request to ejbkey@empirix.com or call +1 781-993-8500. When you receive the license file (`license.xml`), copy it to the Bean-test installation directory (the default location is `C:\Program Files\beantest`).

For this tutorial walkthrough, you can install and run Bean-test on the same machine as the target application server (WebLogic Server 6.0), although this is not generally a good testing practice. Running a load test on the same machine as the application server hosting the EJB under test can skew the timing measurements, because the process generating the load can "steal" resources (memory, CPU cycles, disk I/O, and so forth) from the server, resources that would otherwise be available to the server in a production environment. But for our purposes, this shouldn't matter.

Obtaining WebLogic 6.0

This walkthrough uses BEA WebLogic Server 6.0 Service Pack 1 as the target deployment environment for the EJBs we plan to test, so you need to download and install WebLogic Server 6.0 to run the examples. WebLogic Server 6.0 includes a ready-made deployment of the Java Pet Store EJBs that we can use for testing the `ShoppingCart`. You can download a 30-day evaluation copy from:

http://commerce.beasys.com/downloads/weblogic_server.jsp

Follow the installation instructions that accompany the download, and verify that WebLogic 6.0 is properly installed before proceeding.

Starting Java Pet Store

Although you can always generate a Java test driver against an EJB at any time using Bean-test, the Java Pet Store EJBs must be deployed and running in the application server before you can run a load test against the `ShoppingCart` EJB. Code generation generally uses Java reflection API calls to list the EJB's home and remote interfaces, and only requires access to the Java class files and deployment descriptors in the packaged EJB (which need not be deployed and running at the time). However, actually running the test requires a running EJB, because the test driver is a Java application that makes method calls on the deployed EJB's home and remote interfaces.

Start the Java Pet Store application in the WebLogic Server now, to verify that the `ShoppingCart` EJB we want to test actually deploys correctly:

1. Stop the WebLogic Server if it is currently running.

2. Start the WebLogic Server deployment of Java Pet Store (Start | Programs | BEA WebLogic E-Business Platform | WebLogic Server 6.0 | WebLogic Server Tour | Start Pet Store).

The WebLogic Server starts, opens a new browser instance, and displays WebLogic Server Tour Overview page:

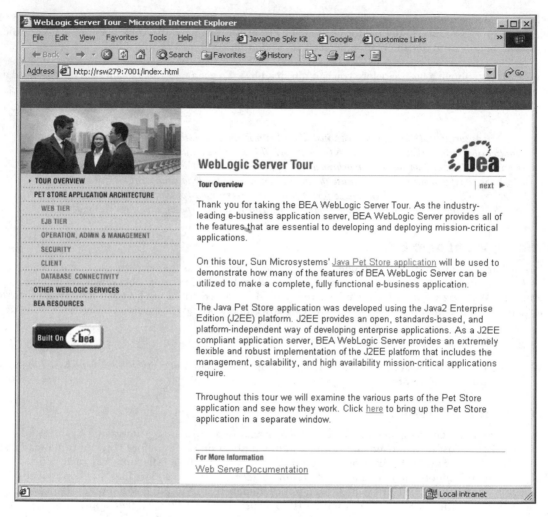

3. Click on the Java Pet Store application link that appears in the introductory text, and the main Java Pet Store application's main page opens in a new browser window:

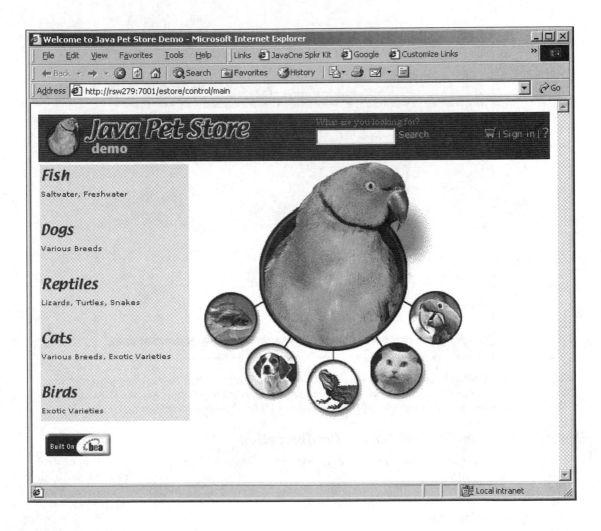

Starting Bean-test

Once we've got the Pet Store application running on WebLogic, we can start Bean-test:

1. From the Windows Start menu, locate the Bean-test submenu and select Bean-test
(UI + Server). This launches Bean-test's embedded Java web server and opens a browser
window directed to the Bean-test web server's default URL
(http://localhost:8001/Beantest.htm):

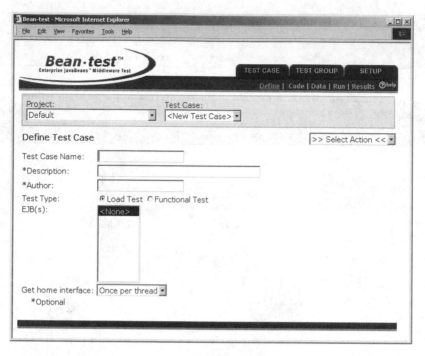

The Bean-test GUI is implemented as a servlet-based, Java intranet application, making a single installation of the tool available from any machine or architecture. In this case, we are running the Bean-test web server, browser, and application server all on the same machine.

Defining the Application Server Configuration

Using the Bean-test Server Management page lets you maintain and customize a list of application server configurations. When you later create Bean-test projects, you can choose from this list of defined server configurations. The settings for a server definition include a default initial project classpath, a Java code template obtaining a home interface reference from the server's JNDI service, and other server-specific information.

1. Click the Setup tab in the top right.

2. Click the Servers sub-tab.

3. From the list of predefined server configurations on the left, select BEA WebLogic Server v6.0.

4. Verify that Java 2 is the selected Java version.

5. Verify that the Default classpath section correctly locates the `weblogic.jar` file in the WebLogic installation directory (make sure the drive letter and directory name are both correct):

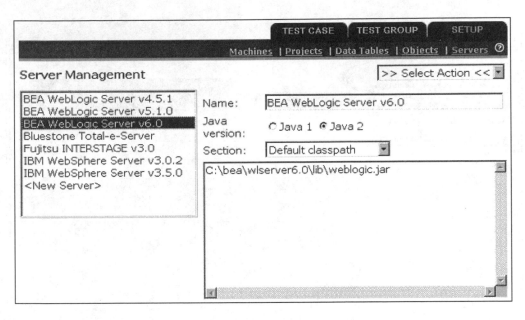

6. To save any modifications you made to the server definition, from the >> Select Action << menu, choose Save server.

Identifying Testbed Machines

Bean-test lets you test your EJBs in an environment that replicates real-world operating conditions. To better model your application's actual (or planned) physical deployment topology, you need to distribute various test software elements to match that topology.

For example, suppose you have a cluster of four web containers deployed on two machines, and they connect to a single EJB container deployed on a third machine. The more closely you model this configuration in testing, the more accurate your performance test results will be. To model such a configuration, you would likely want to distribute the test threads across four processes (JVMs) and two machines, and run the application server on a third machine.

Bean-test provides a Machine Management page for managing a list of available testbed machines to serve either of two testing functions: running test client threads, or running the application server containing the EJBs under test. You can later choose from this list of machines when you configure a test for execution, assigning the test threads to one or more predefined client machines, and directing them at one of the predefined EJB servers. Follow these steps to verify your Bean-test machine configuration:

1. Click the Setup tab:

2. Click the Machines sub-tab:

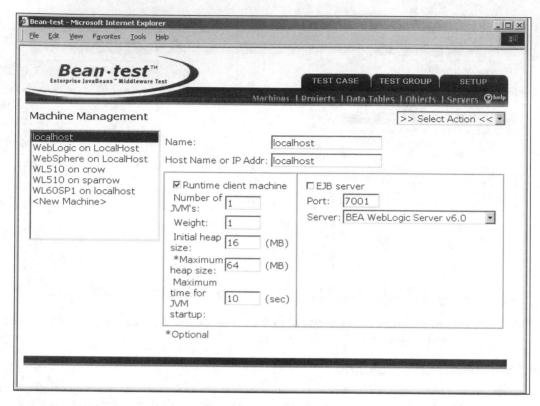

3. In the Machine Management list, select localhost.

4. Make sure Runtime client machine checkbox is enabled. This identifies the selected machine (localhost) as an available run time client for running test threads.

5. Verify the following run time client machine settings:

   ❑ Number of JVM's is set to 1

   ❑ Weight is set to 1

   ❑ Initial heap size is set to 16

   ❑ Maximum heap size is set to 64

   ❑ Maximum time for JVM startup is set to 10

   For information about these fields, click the help icon (?) that appears on upper-right corner of the page.

6. From the >> Select Action << menu, choose Save machine.

   Now verify (or set) the configuration of the machine running WebLogic Server and the EJBs to be tested (localhost).

7. In the Machine Management list, select WebLogic on LocalHost.

8. Make sure the EJB Server checkbox is enabled. This identifies the selected machine (localhost) as an available EJB server for locating the EJBs to be tested.

9. Verify (or set) the following EJB Server machine settings:

❑ The Server listbox shows BEA WebLogic Server v6.0.

❑ The Port box shows the port number on which WebLogic Server is listening (the default port is 7001).

10. From the >> Select Action << menu, choose Save machine.

Creating a Project

Projects let you organize your test cases into logical groups and associate a classpath with each project. The classpath provides important information that Bean-test requires to generate and compile the client code. This is where you specify the classes needed to connect to your server, the JAR or EAR files containing the deployed EJBs, and any other directories or archives that the deployed EJBs require.

1. On the Setup page, click the Projects sub-tab to display the Project Management page.

2. From the projects list on the left, select <New Project>.

3. In the Name field, type Wrox.

4. In the Server listbox, select BEA WebLogic Server v6.0.

5. In the Classpath box, verify that the default server classpath appears:

```
%WL_HOME%\lib\weblogic.jar
```

where `%WL_HOME%` identifies the WebLogic Server 6.0 server directory (for example, `c:\bea\wlserver6.0sp1`).

6. Add the Java Pet Store EAR (petStore.ear) to the Classpath field:

```
%WL_HOME%\config\petstore\applications\petStore.ear
```

For example, using the default WebLogic Server 6.0 Service Pack 1 installation, the file location is:

```
c:\bea\wlserver6.0sp1\config\petstore\applications\petStore.ear
```

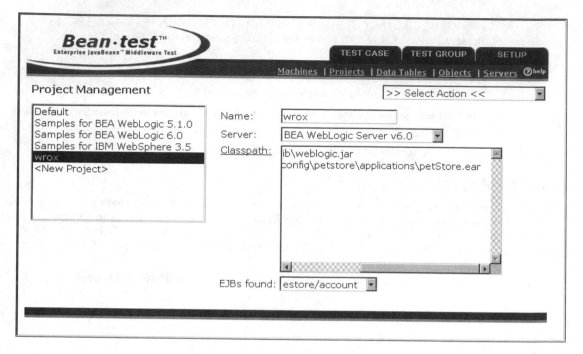

7. From the >> Select Action << menu, choose Save project, and wait a few moments for Bean-test to validate the classpath, scan it for available EJBs, and save the project.

8. Display the EJBs found list (located below the Classpath box) and verify the Java Pet Store enterprise beans (estore/account, estore/cart, etc.) appear in the list. The names correspond to the JNDI name bindings defined in each EJB's deployment descriptor.

Creating a Test Case

A test case identifies the enterprise beans to test, the test type (functional or load), the methods to call within the test driver, the test case data source to use, and other information. Using the pages on Bean-test's Test Case tab, you can now create a test case for the ShoppingCart EJB in the Java Pet Store.

1. Click the Test Case tab, to the left of the Setup tab.

2. Make sure the Define Test Case page is the current page (if not, choose the Define sub-tab to display it.)

3. In the Project field, select the Wrox project:

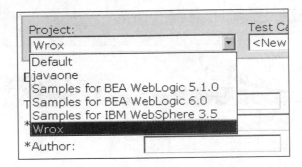

4. In the Test Case field, select <New Test Case>:

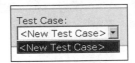

5. In the Test Case Name box, type ShoppingCartTest. This will be the class name of the automatically generated test driver.

6. In the (optional) Description box, type Simple load test for estore/cart to describe this test case.

7. In the (optional) Author box, type wrox to identify the test case author.

8. In the Test Type group, choose the Load Test radio button to run this test as a load test, and include both functional and performance data in the result logs and reports.

9. In the EJB(s) list, select estore/cart to generate test code for only the ShoppingCart EJB. (Later, you may want to experiment on your own and try generating code for multiple EJBs in a single test case by selecting more than one EJB from the list.)

10. In the Get home interface listbox, leave Once per thread selected. (See the online help for a description of this advanced option.)

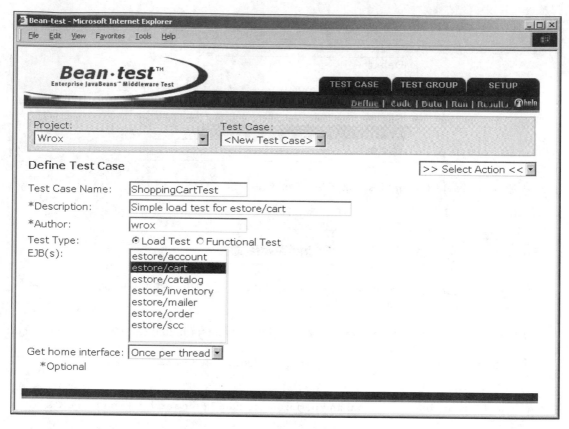

11. From the >> Select Action << menu, choose Save test case.

On saving the new test case, Bean-test adds the test case name to the project and scans the classes of the selected EJBs to generate a list of methods in the home and remote interfaces. The next task is to choose which methods to include in this test and to arrange them in sequence.

Arranging the Method Sequence

Before generating the actual Java source statements composing this test case for the `estore/cart` EJB (a.k.a. `ShoppingCart`), you have an opportunity to choose the method calls to include (or exclude) and to arrange the sequence in which they will be called in the test driver. You can always edit the generated Java code directly, but picking methods from a list is generally easier, faster, and simpler. You can use Bean-test's Test Case – Method Order page.

1. To display the Test Case – Method Order page, choose the Order sub-tab.

In creating and running an EJB test case using Bean-test, we will generally follow the left-to-right sequence of sub-tabs: Define, Order, Code, Data, Run, *and* Results.

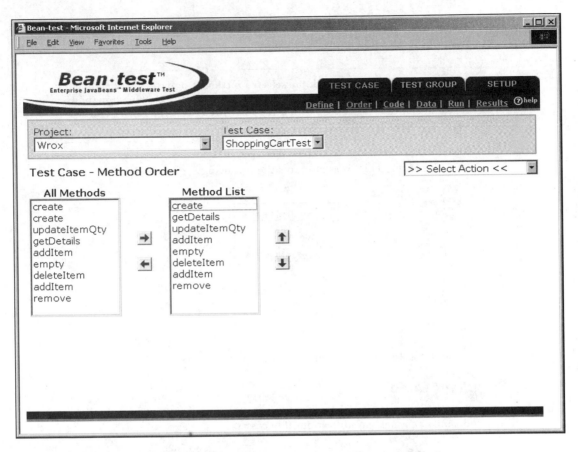

2. The Test Case – Method Order page shows two lists: the All Methods box contains a list of all available methods in the home and remote interfaces, and the Method List box shows the sequence of EJB method calls for which test code will be generated in this test case's Java test driver.

You can manipulate the **contents** of the Method List box using the left and right arrow icons: to add methods, select one or more methods in the All Methods box and click the right-arrow icon. To remove a method call from this test case, select one or more methods in the Method List box and click the left-arrow icon.

You can manipulate the **sequence** in the Method List box using the up and down arrow icons: to call a method earlier in the test sequence, select the method in the Method List box and click the up arrow. To call a method later in the test sequence, select the method in the Method List box and click the down arrow.

For this simple example, we will remove several of the method calls that appear by default in the Method List box.

3. In the Method List box, select getDetails and click the left-arrow icon.

Bean-test removes the method from the Method List box and updates the list.

4. Remove the following methods from the Method List box: updateItemQty, empty, and addItem(java.lang.String, int).

> Notice that, when you select a method, the selected method's signature and return type appears below the two lists. You can use this to correctly identify overload methods sharing the same name, as is the case with addItem(java.langString) and addItem(java.lang.String, int).

5. Verify that the Method List box contains the following sequence of calls:

6. From the >> Select Action << menu, choose Save settings.

Viewing the Client Code

Bean-test uses the specified method sequence to generate the Java code that calls the EJB methods. You can view the code and even make modifications if necessary.

1. To display the Test Case Client Code page, click the Code sub-tab.

2. Scroll through and notice how the code invokes each of the methods you specified on the Test Case – Method Order page. In reviewing the generated code, you may also notice that the general structure of the test is very similar to the EJB test driver we began coding by hand in the previous section, albeit a little more complex. For example, the generated driver uses the same performance measurement strategy as our hand-coded attempt, calling on an instance of the CTimer class to log method response times:

```
timer.start(m_fldMethods, "estore/cart.addItem");
ejbestore_cart.addItem(sArg1);
timer.stopAndLog();
```

Likewise, the generated driver also uses a CDataSource object for its test input data source:

```
String sArg1 = m_ds.getStringValue("estore/cart.deleteItem_sArg1");
```

You can specify the actual values assigned to the CDataSource object using the Test Case Data page.

Specifying Test Data

The Test Case Data page lets you specify the data values. For the `ShoppingCartTest` test case, two EJB methods will require test input data: the `addItem()` method requires a `java.lang.String` that specifies the Java Pet Store item ID to add to the cart, and the `deleteItem()` method requires a `java.lang.String` that specifies the item ID to delete from the cart. There are a variety of ways to fill the data source object with test data: you could:

- ❏ Let Bean-test generate random string values
- ❏ Create a two-column spreadsheet of values (a column of values for `addItem()`, and one for `deleteItem()` values)
- ❏ Enter data values for all threads to use
- ❏ Specify rules for Bean-test to use in generating values (string length ranges, boundaries, etc.)

For this initial test run, we will specify test data explicitly.

3. To display the Test Case Data page, click the Data sub-tab:

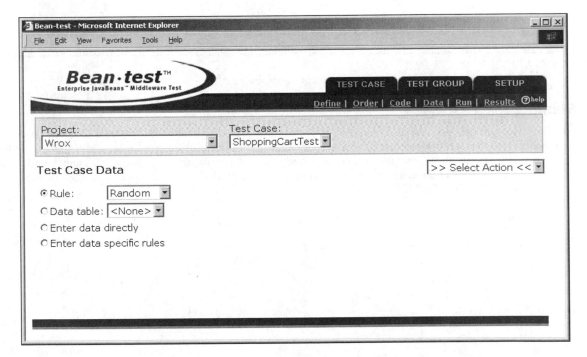

4. Choose the Enter data directly radio button.

Bean-test updates the page to show two textboxes in which you can enter values.

5. In the estore/cart.addItem_sArg1 box, type EST-5.

6. In the estore/cart.deleteItem_sArg1 box, type EST-5.

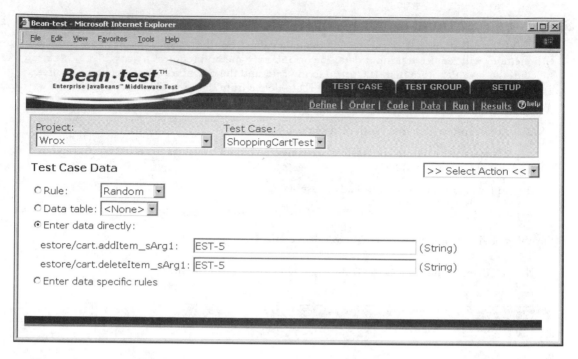

7. From the >> Select Action << menu, choose Save data.

Running the Test Case

When you run the test case as a load test, at a minimum you must specify the server and client machines, the maximum number of concurrent clients, and the ramp (for example, if you specify 1000 clients and a ramp of 100, Bean-test will run the test for 100 clients, then again for 200 clients, and so on up to 1000 clients). You must also specify a name for the result log. You can specify all the run-time attributes on the Run Test Case page.

1. To display the Run Test Case page, click the Run sub-tab.

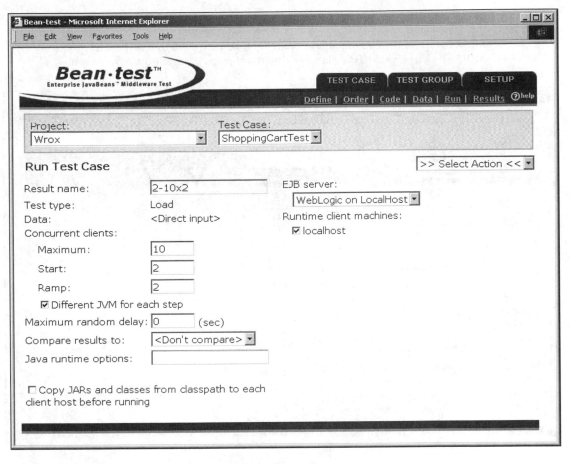

2. In the **Result name** box, type **2-10x2**. (This simple result naming convention shows that the test starts at 2 threads and grows to a maximum of 10 threads in steps of 2).

3. In the **Concurrent clients** boxes, enter the following values:

- ❏ In **Maximum** box, type **10** (the client load simulation will grow to a maximum of 10 threads)

- ❏ In **Start** box, type **2** (the first step will start at 2 threads)

- ❏ In **Ramp** box, type **2** (subsequent steps will increase by 2 – 4 threads, then 6 threads, then 8 threads, then 10)

4. In the **EJB server** listbox, make sure the correct application server is selected (**WebLogic on LocalHost**).

5. In the **Runtime client machines** list, enable the checkbox next to **localhost**.

Leave the remaining fields as shown in the screenshot above.

6. From the >> Select Action << menu, choose Run test.

Bean-test compiles the generated Java test client, launches the first two client threads, and automatically displays the Results tab's Summary page, showing the current status:

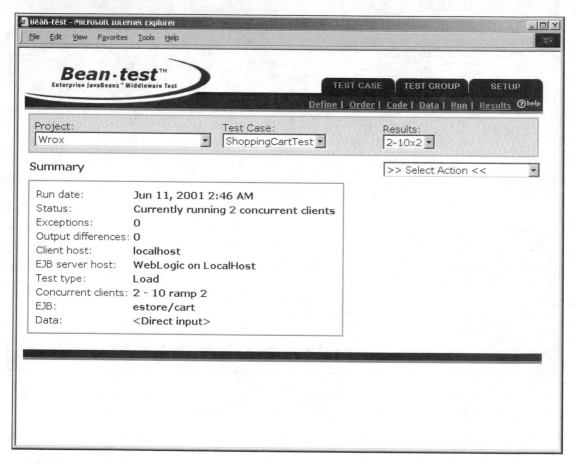

The results Summary page refreshes with each ramp increment. As you are running the client and server on the same machine, it is best to try to avoid interacting with the machine while the short test is running, to avoid skewing the test results, since any other tasks will be competing for system resources. When the test process finishes, the Status field shows Complete.

Viewing the Test Results

Bean-test can display your test results as detailed numeric result logs, and as graphs of the log data. Initially, the result summary is displayed, after which you can use these different views to analyze different aspects of the test results.

1. When the test finishes, the results Summary page shows a summary report for the ShoppingCartTest test results named 2-10x2:

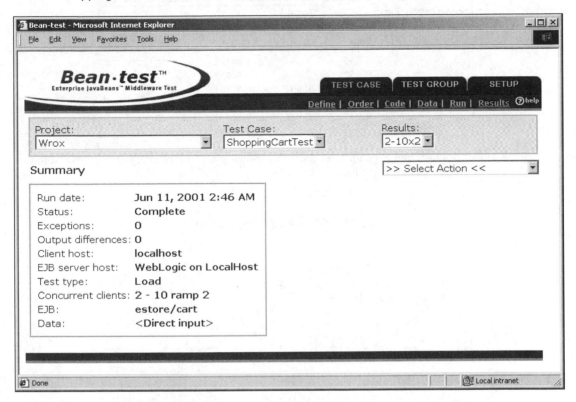

2. From the >> Select Action << menu, choose View response times. Bean-test displays the Response Time page, showing the total elapsed time values (in seconds) for each ramp step:

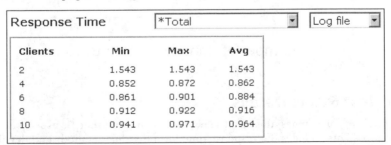

Response Time	*Total			Log file
Clients	**Min**	**Max**	**Avg**	
2	1.543	1.543	1.543	
4	0.852	0.872	0.862	
6	0.861	0.901	0.884	
8	0.912	0.922	0.916	
10	0.941	0.971	0.964	

This data represents the minimum, maximum, and average response time for the set of ShoppingCartTest threads in each ramp step. Each test driver thread includes looking up the EJB in the name service, fetching an EJB reference from the server, and making the method calls in the sequence you set up when you generated the client code. As you might expect, the response time generally increases as the number of concurrent clients increases.

3. To display this timing data graphically as a line chart, click the Log file field and select Line chart instead:

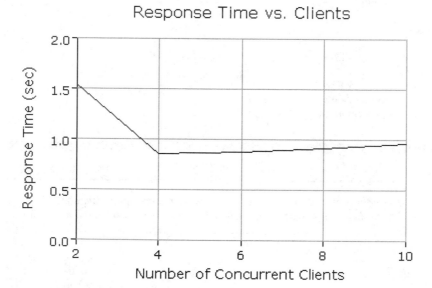

The Response Time page updates the view, showing a graph of average response time data versus the increasing client load:

Analyzing the Test Result Details

In addition to total response times, the result views let you analyze specific aspects of your enterprise bean's performance. This includes the response time for individual methods and details of any exceptions that were thrown during test execution.

1. Click the *Total field:

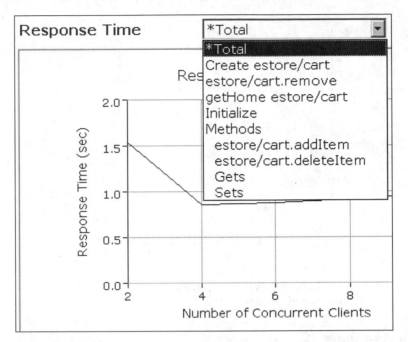

This list lets you filter the data you want to view by choosing different virtual folders that determine how to aggregate response time data. For example, the following folders represent different aggregations of data:

❑ **Initialize** – Average time to connect to the application server and obtain an initial context from the name service.

❑ **getHome estore/cart** – Average time to obtain a home interface reference using the `ShoppingCartTest`'s `getHome()` utility method (includes both the JNDI `lookup` and `javax.rmi.PortableRemoteObject.narrow()` method calls).

❑ **Create estore/cart** – Average time to obtain a remote interface reference using the EJB's `create()` method.

❑ **Methods** – Average response time for remote interface method calls.

❑ **Gets and Sets** – Average response time for all "get" and "set" methods collectively.

Note: `ShoppingCartTest` *has no calls to getter/setter methods.*

❑ **estore/cart.addItem** – Average response time for calls to remote interface method `addItem()`.

2. Select **Create estore/cart** to display only average response time data for the create method calls, and then select **HiLo chart**:

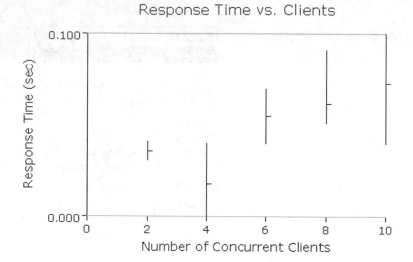

This view displays the high, low, and average response times for the `create()` method calls over an increasing load of clients.

Setting Up a Baseline

An important aspect of load testing is the ability to compare performance data obtained using different test parameters or from different versions of the enterprise bean. For example, you might want to investigate how changing the JDBC connection pool size or number of client JVMs affects response time.

Bean-test lets you designate one result log as your baseline, so that when you display other result logs from running the same test case, they appear in comparison to the baseline data.

To try this feature, you need to run the `ShoppingCartTest` again to obtain a second result log.

Increasing the Number of Client JVMs

In order to compare two sets of results, we'll need to run the same test again, but this time we'll divide the client threads across two JVMs to see the impact of multiple socket connections to the application server. With a single JVM running on the Bean-test client host, each concurrent client runs as a separate thread within that JVM. In this single-JVM case, each client request is transmitted via a single connection socket to the WebLogic Server. This provides a more accurate simulation of client requests coming from a single process, like a single web server running servlets or JSPs.

Bean-test also supports the creation of multiple JVMs on the same client host. In this case, a separate socket connection is produced by each JVM. This provides a more accurate simulation of topologies where client requests are coming from multiple sources (like a cluster of web servers, or many desktop clients). You can configure multiple JVMs for a testbed machine using the Machine Management page.

1. Click the Setup page and then click the Machines sub-tab to display the Machine Management page.

2. In the machine list, select localhost.

3. Change the Number of JVMs to 4.

4. From the >> Select Action << menu, choose Save Machine.

Running the Test Again

Before we can compare our test results, we need to generate some more to compare them against.

1. Click the Test Case tab and then click the Run sub-tab to display the Run Test Case page.

2. In the Result name field, type 2-10x2 run2.

3. Leave the remaining fields as they were before.

Notice that the Runtime client machines list now shows localhost (4 JVM's), indicating the change in the machine's configuration.

4. From the >> Select Action << menu, choose Run test, and wait for the test to finish.

Comparing Results

When the test has finished, you can compare the new (multiple-JVM) test results with the first (single-JVM) test results.

1. From the >> Select Action << menu, choose Set baseline. Bean-test adds an asterisk to the front of the result name to indicate that this is the designated baseline.

2. From the >> Select Action << menu, choose View response times. The Response Time page displays, showing response time data for the current result log (* 2-10x2 run2).

3. From the list of result logs, select the log from the previous run (2-10x2):

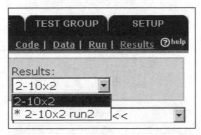

The Response Time page now shows the data from both test logs, arranged for comparison:

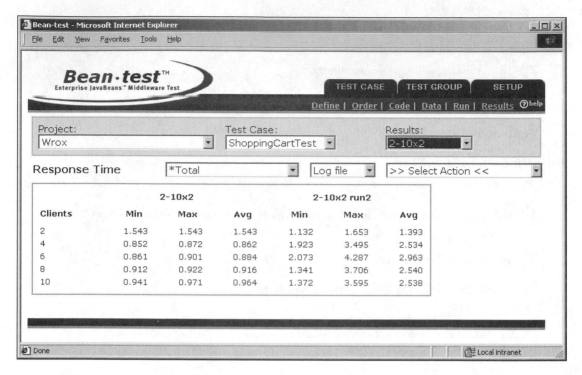

This comparison view allows you to view the actual response time values in the two sets of result data step-by-step. It is often easier to see this data rendered graphically.

4. Click Log file and select Line chart. The average response time data for both result logs are now plotted on a single graph:

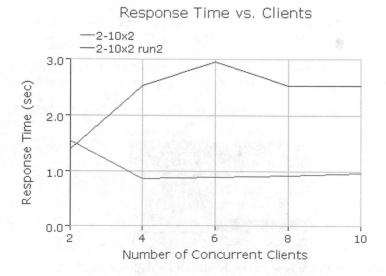

As you might have expected, the EJB performance suffered significantly when the client requests occurred over four socket connections instead of just one.

5. Change folders from *Total to Initialize and note the difference in response times for obtaining a JNDI initial context. Then view the estore/cart.addItem folder to compare the average response times only for calls to the `addItem()` method. Although the performance on each system will be different, it is likely the response times for obtaining a JNDI initial context suffered much worse from the multiple sockets than did other client requests. In general, obtaining the JNDI initial context is known to be a much more expensive request than other EJB client requests, and this expense is simply magnified when distributing the requests over multiple sockets.

6. Experiment by choosing other folders, and comparing result data between the two test runs.

Handling Object Arguments and Return Values

The two methods that we initially chose to test in the `ShoppingCart` EJB's remote interface take simple `String` arguments (item IDs) and return `void`. However, very often EJB methods require object references as method arguments and just as often return object references as their return values. One example of this situation is the `ShoppingCart` EJB's `getDetails()` method: this returns a `ShoppingCartModel` object containing details of the cart's contents.

In generating test code for these situations, two requirements arise:

❑   For object types serving as EJB *method parameters*, the test code generator must produce source statements that correctly instantiate the object and sets its state prior to passing it in as an argument.

❑   For object types serving as EJB *method returns*, the test code generator must produce source statements that correctly log and validate the object. Logging a returned object usually requires rendering the object's state as a `String` (as `toString()` would), so that it can appear in a text-based log file.

To address these requirements, Bean-test allows you to define custom code templates that map to object types occurring as EJB method parameters or return values. For any type (primitive or class), you can create templates that:

❑   Instantiate an object in preparation to passing it as an EJB method argument.

❑   Log the object's state as an expected return value, for later comparison with the actual return value. This is necessary to establish pass/fail status.

❑   Log the object's state as an actual return value.

For example, the code below is a template for logging a `ShoppingCartModel` as an actual return value:

```
// Log actual ShoppingCartModel as a String list of product IDs

timer.pause(); // pause the timer while we prepare to log
String products = "";
CartItem item;
Iterator itemList = $retName$.getItems();
while (itemList.hasNext()) {
    item = (CartItem)itemList.next();
    products += item.getProductId();
}
timer.stopAndLog(products);
```

When using the template code, the code generator will replace the $retName$ token with the actual reference variable name used to capture the return value (for example, oRet – this name being determined at the time the code is generated). This fragment pauses the timer while it builds the String to be logged, and then logs the String as the actual return value using the timer's stopAndLog() method.

This fragment is an example of using key values within an object to identify the object's state, rather than depending on toString(), or trying to determine all the available field values. In this case, we use the simple list of product IDs contained within the more complex ShoppingCartModel object to determine what items the cart holds.

To try a simple example using this template, we must do two things:

- ❑ Replace the default ShoppingCartModel template for actual return values with the customized one shown above.

- ❑ Create a new test for the ShoppingCart EJB that includes the getDetails() method call (returning a ShoppingCartModel).

Customizing an Object Template

You can customize templates for class types and primitive types using the Object Management page.

1. Choose the Setup tab, and then the Objects sub-tab to display the Object Management page.

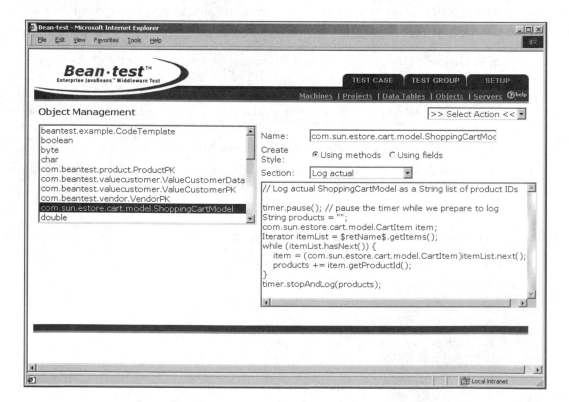

2. In the list of types on the left, select the com.sun.estore.cart.model.ShoppingCartModel entry to access its templates.

3. In the Section listbox, choose Log Actual template.

4. In the textbox containing the template code, replace the default template code with the following lines:

```
// Log actual ShoppingCartModel as a String list of product IDs

timer.pause(); // pause the timer while we prepare to log
String products = "";
com.sun.estore.cart.model.CartItem item;
Iterator itemList = $retName$.getItems();
while (itemList.hasNext()) {
    item = (com.sun.estore.cart.model.CartItem)itemList.next();
    products += item.getProductId();
}
timer.stopAndLog(products);
```

5. From the >> Select Action << menu, choose Save object.

Now, whenever Bean-test generates code for a method returning a ShoppingCartModel, the new code fragment will appear in the generated test.

Creating a Functional Test

Next, we'll need to create a test driver that calls the ShoppingCart EJB's getDetails() method. For a change of pace, we will create a functional test rather than a load test. In Bean-test, designating an EJB test as a functional test simply limits the report views to output (return) value comparisons and exceptions, and eliminates the multiple-thread load ramping (a functional test usually runs as a single thread).

1. Choose the Test Case tab, and then the Define sub-tab to display the Define Test Case page.

2. In the Test Case field, select <New Test Case>.

3. Fill in the test case fields as shown in the following screenshot, and remember to select the Functional Test radio button this time:

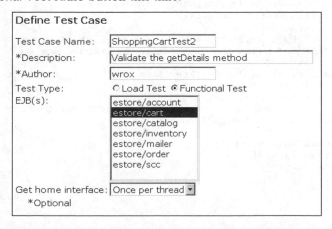

653

4. From the >> Select Action << menu, choose Save test case.

5. On the Test Case – Method Order page, arrange the method sequence as shown in the following screenshot. For this test, be sure to use the no-argument version of create (the default selection), and the single-argument version of addItem.

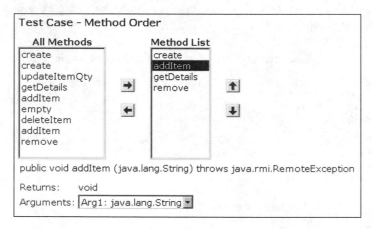

In this sequence, the client will call create() to get a remote interface reference, call addItem() to add a single item to the cart, and then call getDetails() to list the cart's contents.

6. From the >> Select Action << menu, choose Save settings.

7. Visit the Test Case Client Code page and verify that the code fragment for getDetails includes the custom template. The code generated for calling getDetails() should appear as follows:

```
//[--------- test bean method: estore/cart.getDetails --------]
try {
    String sExpectedValue
        = m_ds.getStringValue("estore/cart.getDetails_oRet");

    timer.start(m_fldMethods, "estore/cart.getDetails", sExpectedValue);
    com.sun.estore.cart.model.ShoppingCartModel oRet
        = ejbestore_cart.getDetails();

    // Log actual ShoppingCartModel as a String list of product IDs
    timer.pause(); // pause the timer while we prepare to log
    String products = "";
    com.sun.estore.cart.model.CartItem item;
    Iterator itemList = oRet.getItems();
        while (itemList.hasNext()) {
            item = (com.sun.estore.cart.model.CartItem)itemList.next();
            products += item.getProductId();
        }
    timer.stopAndLog(products);
} catch (Throwable e) {
    timer.stopAndLog(e);
}
```

Next, use the options on the Test Case Data page to specify the data used in the
CdataSource object (m_ds).

8. On the Test Case Data page, choose the Enter data directly radio button to explicitly
    specify the data values to be used in this test. Bean-test displays two fields corresponding
    to the "column labels" in the data source "row" of data that the client thread will use:

    ❏   estore/cart.addItem_sArg1 holds the String value to be supplied as an argument to
        addItem.

    ❏   estore/cart.getDetails_oRet holds the String value to be used as the expected value in
        testing the getDetails() return value. This String value will be compared with the
        String value produced by the Log actual template code you modified.

9. In the estore/cart.addItem_sArg1 box, type EST-21. This is the item ID of the product to
    add to the cart using addItem().

10. In the estore/cart.getDetails_oRet box, type FI-FM-02. This is the product ID we expect
    from the getDetails() method call. It should correspond to the EST-21 item ID, but we
    will see when we run the test.

11. From the >> Select Action << menu, choose Save data.

Running the Functional Test

To run the new functional test, display the Run Test Case page. Notice that for a Functional Test,
the Concurrent Clients fields (Maximum, Start, and Ramp) are replaced by two new fields: Total
and Concurrent.

For this test run, both of these field values should be set to 1, but Bean-test also allows you to run
multiple sets of functional test threads at the same time, where each thread uses the same Java test
driver but a different row of test data from a data table (represented by CDataSource).

Often, functional tests are differentiated only by the test input data used. For example, there might be
several test cases for addItem(), each test case supplying a different String value as an argument. In
this situation, the same test driver for all the test cases could be reused, only varying the data used for
each test thread. Running multiple functional tests concurrently can be a great time saver, especially
when there is a lot of test data to try.

1. In the Result name text box, type Run1.

2. In the Clients settings:

    ❏   Change the value in the Total box to 1

    ❏   Change the value in the Concurrent box to 1.

3. In the EJB Server list box select WebLogic on LocalHost.

4. Under Runtime client machines, enable the checkbox for localhost (4 JVM's).

*The multiple JVM setting won't matter here; we're only running a single client thread, so only a single
JVM will be spawned.*

The Run Test Case page should match the following screenshot:

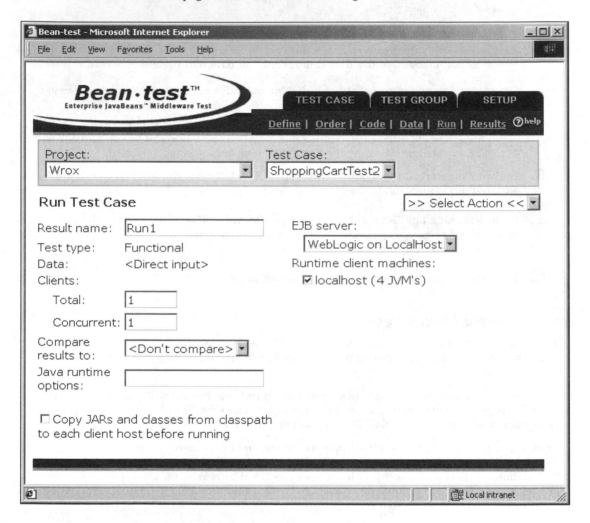

5. From the >> Select Action << menu, choose Run test and wait for the test to finish. You can examine the test results as you did before.

Viewing Functional Test Results

When the functional test ShoppingCartTest2 completes, you may notice that the Summary page shows a single output difference in the Output differences field:

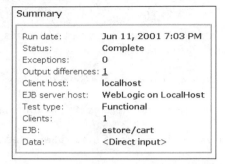

Output differences occur when the expected return value from a method call differs from the actual value returned when the test ran. The Output differences field is a tally of the number of differences that occurred in the test run.

1. To view the output difference, you can click on the field value itself (it is a hyperlink to the Output Differences page). Alternatively, you can choose View output differences from the >> Select Action << menu.

The Output Differences page filters all actual/expected comparisons to show only clients and method calls that differed in their comparisons:

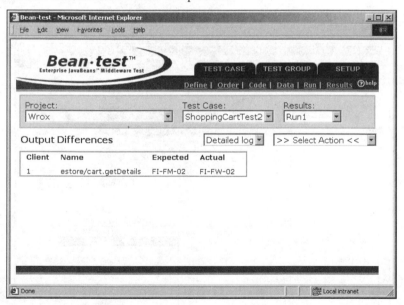

This result log shows that the actual String value (extracted from the ShoppingCartModel object that getDetails() actually returned), differs from what we set as the expected value on the Test Case Data page (the estore/cart.getDetails_oRet data source column value). However, the two Strings are *suspiciously similar*, with only a single character position separating them: M and W at the eighth character position. In fact, a little research into the Java Pet Store application uncovers a very common testing error: incorrect test data. In the Java Pet Store, the **correct product ID for item EST-21** is indeed **FI-FW-02**, and *not* FI-FM-02 as we specified on the Test Case Data page.

2. On the Test Case Data page, edit the estore/cart.getDetails_oRet field to show the correct expected String value, FI-FW-02.

3. From the >> Select Action << menu, choose Save data to save the change.

4. Rerun the functional test ShoppingCartTest2, this time naming the result log Run2.

5. When the test completes, verify that the Output differences field on the Summary page for Run2 shows 0.

Running Tests as a Group

It is useful to be able to group tests together and run them run concurrently or sequentially, allowing you to perform scenario testing, run regression test suites, and create mixed-load patterns of EJB requests to better simulate the real-world environment. Bean-test includes this functionality with features on the Test Group tab. You can also run test groups from a batch file, making it possible to perform extended, unattended testing.

1. Click the Test Group tab, and then click the Define sub-tab.

2. From the Test Group list, select <New Test Group>.

3. In the Name text box, enter CartTestGroup.

4. In the All Test Cases list, scroll to the <wrox> project. You should see your two test cases listed (ShoppingCartTest and ShoppingCartTest2).

5. Select ShoppingCartTest and then click the right-arrow icon to add that test case to the Test Group List. Repeat for ShoppingCartTest2.

6. From the >> Select Action << menu, choose Save test group.

7. Click the Data sub-tab to display the Test Group Data page.

8. Click the Project/Test Case drop-down list. Notice that your two test cases are listed. As you select each test case, the data you saved previously with each test case is displayed. You can modify the data associated with each test, but for now we'll leave it unchanged.

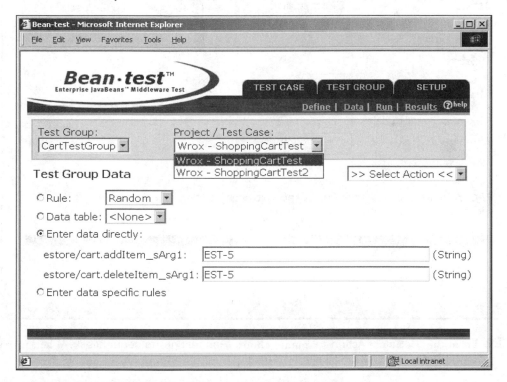

9. Next, click the Run sub-tab to display the Test Group Run page.

10. Click the Project/Test Case list. Here too, each test case retains the run settings you last set. You can modify the run settings associated with each test, but we'll leave them unchanged for this run.

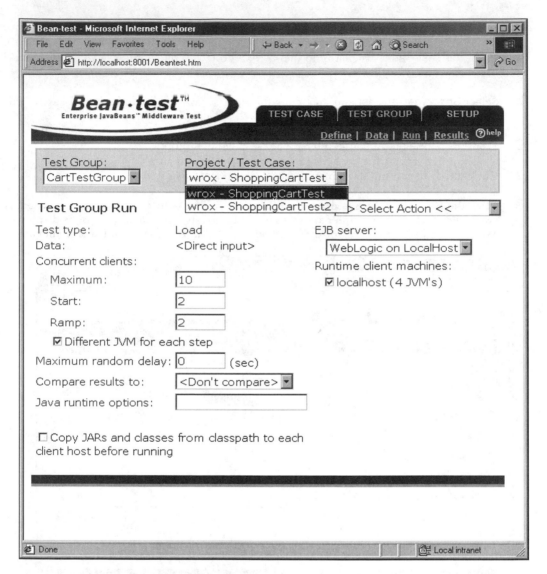

11. From the >> Select Action << menu, choose Run test group sequentially. When prompted, enter Run1 and click OK. Then wait for the test group to finish.

When the test group completes, Bean-test displays the Test Group Results Summary page:

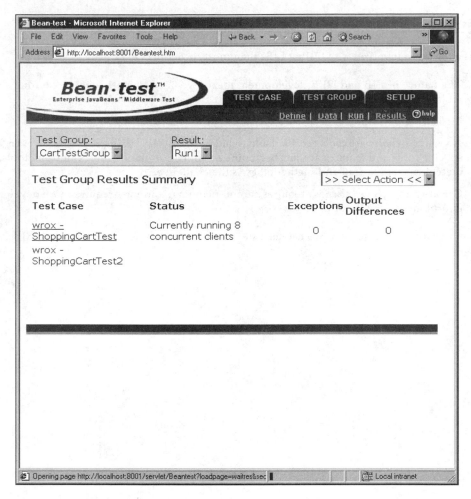

You can get detailed result information for any of the individual test cases by clicking the test case name.

Stopping Bean-test

Once we've done all the testing we're going to do for the day, stopping Bean-test is a simple task:

> Switch to the Bean-test server command prompt window, press *Ctrl-C*, and enter Y to terminate the batch job and close the command-prompt window.

This concludes our tour of the Bean-test framework. Along the way, you hopefully identified EJB test framework features that will prove useful to testing your particular EJB applications. Bean-test contains many more features than we could cover in this overview, so you may find it useful to explore the product to a greater depth on your own, perhaps running it against your own EJBs.

Summary

There is a lot more involved with testing EJBs than most developers anticipate:

- ❑ The nature of EJB and J2EE development means we need to work with new testing strategies, tools, and methodologies.
- ❑ Measuring performance and scalability are central to EJB testing.
- ❑ A variety of software tools are available to aid in the J2EE testing process. However, EJB-specific tools and features are just beginning to appear on the market. Choosing tools, and matching them to staff and methodology is the challenge.
- ❑ Creating an EJB test harness requires careful planning, and may require more development effort than originally planned.

In the next chapter, we'll see how we can take steps to improve the performance of our EJBs.

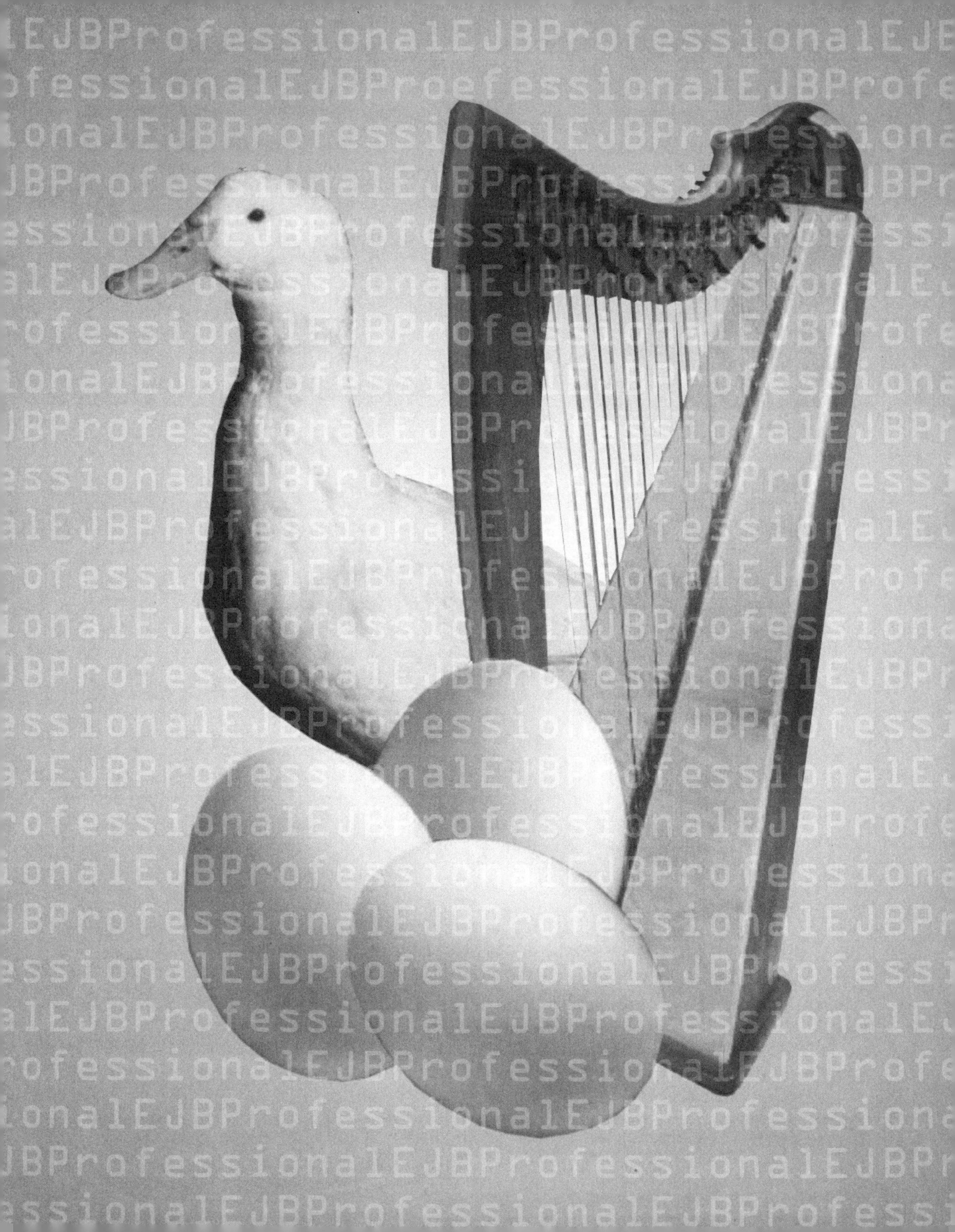

15

EJB Performance and Scalability

Performance is almost always an important topic in application development. When we think of performance, the first thought is often the **response time** from the perspective of a client. In terms of Enterprise JavaBeans, the response time is the total time from the start of a method invocation until the result is returned. The response time refers to the time needed to perform a certain amount of work and is inversely related to the throughput. **Throughput** refers to the amount of work (number of operations, for example) a component can perform in a measured period of time. The response time and throughput are certainly very important, although too often an application's performance is judged by them only. In enterprise information systems, however, the response time and throughput are not the only important measures.

Enterprise information systems are designed to serve numerous clients, and at least some of them use the application simultaneously. In web-enabled and e-commerce systems, the number of simultaneous clients can get very high. The problem is that we do not know how many clients will simultaneously use our systems, and it is very difficult to predict.

No doubt you've heard at least one of the stories about Internet startup companies (and even established companies) that were faced with a sudden rapid increase of interest. Their information systems, unprepared for such high numbers of simultaneous users, have crashed leading to a big income cutoff, not to mention a damaged image. But even if the information system would stand the high load, it is still very important that it offers acceptable response times for each client. In other words, the information system should be **scalable**.

Response time, throughput, and scalability are not the same, but they are related. A component, for example, can have a very low response time for a method invocation as long as the number of simultaneous clients is low. However, when the number reaches a certain point, the response time may degrade substantially. Scalability is the metric that refers to the amount of change in response time because of the increase or decrease in the number of simultaneous clients. The ideal is to find a balance between acceptable response time and scalability.

In this chapter we will discuss the performance and scalability of Enterprise JavaBeans (EJB) and give guidelines and advice on how to design and implement applications that will achieve good performance. We will:

❑   Look at the basic facts regarding EJBs and performance

❑   Explain some underlying concepts

❑   Discuss the remote method invocation, and fine- and coarse-grained interfaces

❑   Take a look at value objects

❑   Learn how to avoid large data transfers

❑   Understand the advantages of the façade pattern

❑   Take a look at the instance management algorithms

❑   Show how persistence and transactions affect performance

❑   Learn how to lazy-load enterprise beans

❑   Discuss the advantages of smart stubs and show how to accelerate marshaling

❑   Learn how to tune the performance when deploying EJBs

❑   Discuss the role of the containers

❑   Give practical guidelines for achieving scalability

What Can We Do About Performance?

Achieving performance in EJB technology can be difficult because EJB is a distributed architecture. Additionally, there are several specific performance considerations, such as the number of remote invocations, amount of data that is transferred, and marshaling cost of parameters/return values. To make it worse, EJB is usually used as a part of the Java 2 Platform, Enterprise Edition (J2EE), which adds several other technologies. In EJB, we get services like transaction support, security, persistence, instance management, and maybe even load balancing, and replication for "free" through the container. We have to code almost nothing of these services, because EJB provides these services in a declarative way.

To use EJB technology effectively we have to understand the underlying concepts and their limitations. We should start to think about performance as early as possible and consider performance-related questions in the design phase. Performance requirements need to be identified right along with system requirements so engineers can design to that specification. The worst mistake we can make is to ignore this question and follow the "hardware rule": if our application is too slow, we will buy a faster server (or servers). About the only thing we can guarantee is that there is no server in the market capable of compensating for really bad design.

Considering performance questions at design time requires a lot of knowledge. General knowledge regarding distributed computing, transactions, security, databases, multi-user scenarios, etc., is required, but this is not enough. It is also important to understand how the EJB architecture works under the covers. Not easy, is it? But don't be afraid. We don't want to become middleware specialists. Luckily we are using an industry-standard architecture (which EJB certainly is), and the more mature it gets the more rules we know about it. And all we have to do is follow these rules.

For achieving good performance we will follow sound design practices. Some of these are described in Chapters 11 to 13, and others are described in this chapter. If we care about design from the start, we will save time and money. Imagine that we end up with an almost finished application that does not perform well because the design has several shortcomings. Improving the design requires enormous changes to the code, which is time consuming and error prone, not to mention the related activities, like testing. Therefore it is a good idea to start testing the performance relatively early, when we develop individual EJBs.

However, it can happen that we have followed all the design patterns and our application still does not perform well enough. Then we will have to identify the bottlenecks, not an easy task. We're going to need some knowledge about the underlying concepts: about performance testing and profiling. We now have several options. First, we should find out if we can solve the problem with faster hardware. This is often the cheapest and fastest way, but the situations where faster hardware alone helps are rare. Usually hardware solves performance problems with linear time subordination, and it will certainly not solve exponential problems. We might also consider using clustering if our application server provides it.

Second, we can consider selecting another application server. Application servers and their containers can have a large influence on performance. Some containers are optimized for multi-client scalability, some for persistence, etc. At the time of writing this book almost no performance data existed with which to make an objective comparison. Things will get better when the standard performance load **ECperf Benchmark** is specified and standardized benchmark procedures are defined (both are under development in Java Community Process by the time of writing, see http://java.sun.com/j2ee/ecperf/). Therefore we should try making some performance measurements with our application on different application servers ourselves if we have the possibility. If we have followed the portability guidelines and have not used custom features, this will not be too complicated.

Other software can influence the performance, particularly database management systems (DBMS). Unfortunately we will seldom be able to select a DBMS; often we will be faced with existing data, used by other legacy applications.

The third possibility is to tune the design. Generally the application design should follow sound design practices, many of them expressed as design patterns. We should use the design patterns, not only because of performance, but also to get clean application architecture. However, it may happen that we have already followed the design patterns, but our application still does not perform well. Although this is a rare situation, our only choice then is to make performance-oriented tuning. In some cases, this will lead to solutions that are not as good looking as we would want. Sometimes we will even be forced to do ugly workarounds, but we should try not to let that happen too often. There are definitely tradeoffs between sound, clear design and performance-based solutions, and it is also useful to keep in mind that new releases of application servers (and new hardware) may improve the performance of our EJBs in future. Therefore our recommendation when compromising between clean design and performance is to primarily choose an optimum design, wherever possible.

The Underlying Concepts

Enterprise JavaBeans are written as reusable, portable components. They become distributed as soon as they are deployed in the EJB container. To access the EJB through its remote component interface, the client has to use a distributed object model – more specifically, the **object request broker** (**ORB**).

The object request broker used by EJB is the **Remote Method Invocation** (**RMI**). RMI uses the JRMP (Java Remote Method Protocol), or an application-server-specific protocol, for the actual communication. To ensure container interoperability, and interoperability with CORBA applications, the EJB 2.0 specification requires support for the **RMI-IIOP** (**RMI over Internet Inter-ORB Protocol**).

When we deploy our EJB in a container, the deployment tools generate two RMI-IIOP objects, the `EJBHome` and the `EJBObject`. To remotely access our bean, we use these two objects as typical RMI-IIOP objects. First, we locate the `EJBHome` object:

```
MyBeanHome home = (MyBeanHome) javax.rmi.PortableRemoteObject.narrow
                         (ctx.lookup ("MyBeanHome"), MyBeanHome.class);
```

Then, we use the home object to access the enterprise bean functionality:

```
// Create the MyBean EJBObject
MyBean bean = (MyBean) javax.rmi.PortableRemoteObject.narrow
                                  (home.create(), MyBean.class);

// Call the method
result = bean.myMethod();
```

Instead of creating a new bean instance, we could use finder methods to connect to an already existing entity bean instance. In each case, from the perspective of the client developer, the client code deals with the EJBs as if they are local objects, although what actually happens under the covers is remote method invocation, because we use the remote (or component) EJB interface. Thanks to the seamless integration of RMI-IIOP and Java, we do not have to be concerned with the details of remote communications. In spite of that, let us take a closer look at what happens when a client invokes a remote method.

How EJBs Work with RMI

The client gets a reference to the **stub**, as shown in the figure opposite. A stub is a local class that implements the same interface as the remote object. Therefore the client thinks that the object is local. In the earlier example, `home` has a reference to the stub of the `MyBeanHome` object. The same is true for `bean`, which points to a local `MyBean EJBObject` stub.

The stub, however, does not perform the method operations. Rather, it forwards the method invocation requests to the remote computer by converting them to a form that is suitable for transportation over the network.

The stub is thus responsible for **marshaling** remote method invocation requests so they can be transferred over the network. We can easily imagine that forming this IIOP request is not complicated for basic data types, but it can get complicated for user-defined data types. Therefore, user data types have to be serializable if we want to use them as parameters or return values of remote method invocations.

Needless to say, the IIOP request has to be transferred through several layers (as seen in the following diagram), like operating system and network layers, before it reaches the server. There the request goes through a procedure that is essentially the reverse of the one it went through on the client-side; this procedure of translating the request from an IIOP format back into a Java format is known as **unmarshaling**.

When the request travels through the network and operating system layer it is delivered to the **skeleton**. The skeleton is responsible for dispatching the request to the actual object and invoking the appropriate method. The skeleton, similar to the stub, can be a custom class, or the ORB can provide a generalized skeleton that serves all remote objects. When the server-side object processes the remote method invocation, the result is returned the same way. Note that because stubs and skeletons are tightly connected with a particular implementation, they are generated when we deploy our EJB in the container. The whole procedure is graphically presented in the following diagram:

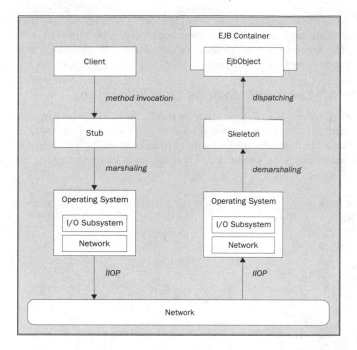

Before EJB version 2.0, Enterprise beans had **remote** interfaces only. EJB 2.0 adds the possibility to define **local** interfaces for Enterprise beans. Local interfaces do not have the described overhead, but only clients from the same JVM can access EJBs through their local interfaces. We will address the performance benefits of local interfaces shortly. EJB version 2.0 also adds a new bean type, the **message-driven** bean. Message-driven beans do not use the IIOP protocol for delivering remote method invocation requests; they do not even communicate synchronously. Rather, they communicate asynchronously through a JMS-compliant queuing system. The communication overhead is greater for message-driven beans than for synchronously communicating session and entity beans.

Remote Method Invocations are Costly

Each remote call in a distributed system imposes an overhead. This causes a considerable delay in each EJB invocation. This section will describe this with an example, and show how to reduce remote invocations. The reference bean in the following line:

```
MyBean bean = (MyBean) javax.rmi.PortableRemoteObject.narrow
                        (home.create(), MyBean.class);
```

is the logical reference to the remote EJBObject. Actually it points to the stub, which constructs an IIOP request and delivers it through several low-level layers over the network to the computer where the EJBObject is executing. Only then is the actual method on the EJBObject executed.

The problem is that all this complexity requires execution time, and time is what we care most about in this chapter. Measurements have shown that a typical local method invocation inside a single JVM takes a few hundred nanoseconds. The time required for a remote method invocation request to reach the EJBObject, however, is much longer, about half a millisecond. Taking into account the return leg, which takes approximately the same time, we soon realize that a remote method invocation can be as much as **2000 times slower** than a local method invocation.

Bear in mind that these measurements have been done on a fast, empty network. The usual network traffic slows down remote method invocation even more. Note also that these times do not include the processing time on the serverside, nor the time for transferring the method parameters and return value. Requests delivered as messages to message-driven beans usually perform even slower.

Keeping Remote Method Invocations to a Minimum

In order to achieve an acceptable performance we should keep the number of remote method invocations to a minimum. Furthermore, we should transfer only the essential data because transferring large amounts of data over the network is also very time consuming and requires heavy marshaling efforts. The best practice from the performance standpoint is to minimize the number of remote invocations as much as possible.

Let us take a closer look at the code extract already presented and try to count the number of remote method invocations:

```
MyBeanHome home = (MyBeanHome) javax.rmi.PortableRemoteObject.narrow
                    (ctx.lookup ("MyBeanHome"), MyBeanHome.class);

MyBean bean = (MyBean) javax.rmi.PortableRemoteObject.narrow
                            (home.create(), MyBean.class);

result = bean.myMethod();
```

There is no confusion over the second and third statements; they are definitely remote method invocations. What about the first statement though? It turns out that the first statement is a remote method invocation too. Actually, it requires a lookup through the JNDI, locating the remote object and returning the proxy reference. Performance measurements have shown that this statement is usually more time consuming than the last two.

Now imagine that our EJB required the setting of several attributes before we could invoke the method. This is typical for entity beans. Let us consider the following example:

```
bean.setCustomer (...);
bean.setOrderDate (...);
bean.setDeliveryDate (...);
bean.setDeliveryAddress (...);
result = bean.myMethod();
```

We can see that we have five remote method invocations. If each method invocation in a perfect environment, where only one client exists and the network is free of other traffic, takes only a millisecond, we already have five milliseconds of execution time. Then add the time taken to obtain a reference to the EJBHome object and the create or find request, to reach the EJBObject, and we soon end up with ten milliseconds. But remember this is the network latency time only. We have to add the method processing time yet.

This brings us to the conclusion that such a fine-grained approach is performance ineffective. Although the fine-grained approach is nice from the design perspective, we should consider the coarse-grained approach in order to improve performance. It is very easy to remodel the example and save three method invocations:

```
bean.setAttributes(customer,
                   orderDate,
                   deliveryDate,
                   deliveryAddress);
result = bean.myMethod();
```

Another possibility, which saves another method invocation, is:

```
result = bean.myMethod(customer,
                       orderDate,
                       deliveryDate,
                       deliveryAddress);
```

The third possibility is to set the attributes by the instance creation:

```
MyBean bean = (MyBean) javax.rmi.PortableRemoteObject.narrow (
                        home.create(customer,
                                    orderDate,
                                    deliveryDate,
                                    deliveryAddress), MyBean.class);

result = bean.myMethod();
```

There is no need to give up the fine-grained setter methods. It is enough that we add a coarse grained method for setting the whole set of attributes, or that we overload the myMethod to accept different combinations of input parameters. Typically we will combine these two approaches.

Value Objects

The proposed definition of bulk setter methods decreases the flexibility and readability of code. Instead of listing attributes one by one, we can collect them inside a class. The method invocation will then look as follows:

```
result = bean.myMethod(myOrderDetails);
```

We define OrderDetails as a class with public attributes. An object of this class has to be transferred as a parameter from the client to the remote server by each method invocation; in other words, the object has to be passed by value. We will therefore call it a value object. To be able to transfer the object's state over the wire, the state has to be serializable. The value object for our example looks like this:

```
import java.util.Date;

public class OrderDetails implements java.io.Serializable {
  public String customerName;
  public Date orderDate;
  public Date deliveryDate;
  public String deliveryAddress;
}
```

In the remote component interface of the EJB we define the setter and getter methods:

```
import java.rmi.RemoteException;
import javax.ejb.*;

public interface Order extends EJBObject {
  ...
  public void setOrderDetails(OrderDetails myOrderDetail)
                                    throws RemoteException;
  public OrderDetails getOrderDetails() throws RemoteException;
  ...
}
```

It is also useful to define the corresponding create() method with the OrderDetails class as a parameter in the home interface to initialize the newly created bean immediately, as shown in the following code extract:

```
import java.rmi.RemoteException;
import javax.ejb.*;

public interface OrderHome extends EJBHome {
  ...
  public Order create (OrderDetails myOrderDetails)
                            throws CreateException, RemoteException;
  ...
}
```

The implementation of the entity bean class depends of the persistence model used. With bean-managed persistnce, the Order class extract looks as follows:

```
import javax.ejb.*;
import javax.naming.*;

public class Order implements EntityBean {
  ...
  private OrderDetails myOrderDetails;
  ...
  public void setOrderDetails(OrderDetails myOrderDetails) {
      this.myOrderDetails = myOrderDetails;
  }

  public OrderDetails getOrderDetails() {
     return myOrderDetails;
  }
  ...
}
```

With container-managed persistence, using the EJB 1.1 persistence model, we can inherit from the OrderDetails value object:

```
import javax.ejb.*;
import javax.naming.*;
import java.util.Date;

public class Order extends OrderDetails implements EntityBean {
  ...
```

```
   // The attributes are already inherited from the Value Object
   ...
   public void setOrderDetails(OrderDetails myOrderDetails) {
      this.customerName = myOrderDetails.customerName;
      this.orderDate = myOrderDetails.orderDate;
      this.deliveryDate = myOrderDetails.deliveryDate;
      this.deliveryAddress = myOrderDetails.deliveryAddress;
   }

   public OrderDetails getOrderDetail() {
      OrderDetails myOrderDetails = new OrderDetails();
      myOrderDetails.customerName = this.customerName;
      myOrderDetails.orderDate = this.orderDate;
      myOrderDetails.deliveryDate = this.deliveryDate;
      myOrderDetails.deliveryAddress = this.deliveryAddress;
      return myOrderDetails;
   }
   ...
}
```

The implementation using the EJB 2.0 CMP model is shown in the following code extract:

```
import javax.ejb.*;
import javax.naming.*;
import java.util.Date;

abstract public class Order implements EntityBean {
   ...
   abstract public String getCustomerName ();
   abstract public void setCustomerName(String val);
   abstract public Date getOrderDate ();
   abstract public void setOrderDate (Date val);
   abstract public Date getDeliveryDate ();
   abstract public void setDeliveryDate (Date val);
   abstract public String getDeliveryAddress ();
   abstract public void setDeliveryAddress (String val);
   ...
   public void setOrderDetails(OrderDetails myOrderDetails) {
      setCustomerName (myOrderDetails.customerName);
      setOrderDate (myOrderDetails.orderDate);
      setDeliveryDate (myOrderDetails.deliveryDate);
      setDeliveryAddress (myOrderDetails.deliveryAddress);
   }

   public OrderDetails getOrderDetail() {
      OrderDetails myOrderDetails = new OrderDetails();
      myOrderDetails.customerName = getCustomerName();
      myOrderDetails.orderDate = getOrderDate();
      myOrderDetails.deliveryDate = getDeliveryDate();
      myOrderDetails.deliveryAddress = getDeliveryAddress();
      return myOrderDetails;
   }
   ...
}
```

Be aware that in EJB 2.0 you are not allowed to change the primary key in the
setOrderDetails() method.

The described approach allows clients to access all the attributes of the bean through a value object. Sometimes we are faced with entity beans that have a large number of attributes. Then it can happen that the clients do not need the whole attribute set. Entity beans with such a large number of attributes are perhaps indicative of a design flaw and we should think about modifying the design and breaking the large entity bean into several smaller beans.

If we cannot apply design changes, we can probably compensate the performance overhead of transferring the whole attribute set. Transferring unnecessary attributes has the effect of decreasing performance, mainly because of marshaling overhead. We can define specialized value objects, which should include only those attributes that are specifically relevant for certain types of clients. In complex real-world scenarios the definition and maintenance of a large number of specialized value objects can be time consuming and error prone. Therefore we should pragmatically select the number of subsets. A good approach is to base the selection on the use case scenarios.

Instead of defining several specialized value objects we can decide to use one value object with all attributes, and leave the attributes that are not useful empty (null). We have to modify the setter method, to check whether the value of an attribute is not null, before actually setting the attribute. We can apply a similar technique using the getter methods too.

Yet another possibility is to define generic value objects. Generic value objects are objects that do not store the data in statically defined attributes, but in a dynamic data structure. Most often a hashtable is used. We access and set the attributes using a key/value pair. Although generic value objects improve flexibility of code, they have a negative influence on performance. More specifically, they are very expensive for marshaling and unmarshaling because they include other objects. If performance is our first priority, we should not use generic value objects. If we nevertheless choose them, we can in fact improve the serialization performance.

Controlling Serialization

More complex value objects typically include references to other objects. When transferring such objects as parameters the whole graph of related objects is transferred. This can increase the transmission time considerably. We can use the `transient` keyword to prune the graph and control serialization. The other possibility is to provide custom serialization methods: `readObject` and `writeObject`:

```
public class OrderDetails implements java.io.Serializable {
  ...
  private void writeObject(java.io.ObjectOutputStream out)
                  throws java.io.IOException {
   ...
  }
  private void readObject(java.io.ObjectInputStream in)
                  throws java.io.IOException, ClassNotFoundException {
   ...
  }
  ...
}
```

To further improve the performance, we can install the corresponding class files on the client (in our case, `OrderDetails.class`). Otherwise, RMI-IIOP will automatically download the code to the client first time the class is used.

Why are Value Objects Advantageous?

The advantage of using value objects as described above is mainly in the increased readability and flexibility of code. A remote method invocation that has a value object as a parameter performs a little slower than a remote method invocation with a list of attributes.

Performance measurements, done by the author of this chapter, have shown that the overhead can be as high as 50%, but keep in mind that this includes only the remote method invocation latency. In other words, if we use a list of attributes, then the remote method invocation lasts approximately one millisecond plus the time needed to transfer the parameters (attributes). The latter time depends on the number of attributes and on the data length.

If we use value objects, the serialization/marshaling process is more complicated. Using RMI-IIOP, such objects are handled as RMI/IDL Value Types, and measurements have shown that the invocation lasts approximately 1.5 milliseconds plus the transmission time needed for the attributes.

Input Validation

In enterprise applications it is often necessary to validate user input. One possibility is to define the validation methods as a part of remote (or component) bean interface. At first sight this seems reasonable, because the EJB can have responsibility for doing the validation. In such a case, the EJB gets some controller responsibilities added to the model responsibilities. This is beneficial because we can make input validation independent of the client type we use.

Now imagine a servlet, applet, or Java application that tries to validate input data. It has to make a remote method invocation for each validation. We have already learned that we should minimize the number of remote invocations; therefore on the second look this decision does not seem so good.

We could implement the validation in the corresponding servlet, applet, or application and duplicate the validation code. This would save remote invocations, but would make our code (all of it) harder to maintain.

If we use value objects, as described in the above section, we have another possibility. We can add the validation logic to the value objects. True, there is no need for the value objects to be pure data objects; they can have methods, too. There are several possibilities for adding the validation logic. Maybe the most reasonable is the decision to add the input validation in the object's setter methods:

```
import java.util.Date;

public class OrderDetails implements java.io.Serializable {
  public String customer;
  public Date orderDate;
  public Date deliveryDate;
  public String deliveryAddress;

  public boolean setDeliveryDate(Date deliveryDate) {
    if (deliveryDate.compareTo(orderDate)>=0) {
      this.deliveryDate = deliveryDate;
      return true;
    } else
```

```
      return false;
    }

    public Date getDeliveryDate() {
      return this.deliveryDate;
    }

    ..
  }
```

The enterprise bean (typically the entity bean) will get the validation logic coded in the value object through either inheritance or delegation. This means that the validation logic is also available, and can be used if necessary, on the serverside.

Notice that because the OrderDetails class implements java.io.Serializable, the attributes have to be declared as public. This solution is not ideal because it violates encapsulation and information hiding. However, if we pay attention to this fact, and do not set the attributes directly, we can live with this solution.

When we use the value object by sending it to the clientside, the client (a servlet on the web server, for example) can use it to do the validation locally. This saves several remote method invocations, thus dramatically improving performance and lowering the EJB server load at the same time. Since the client can now do the validation locally, by an applet or client Java application, for example, the user interface responsiveness can be improved.

If we preinstall the corresponding .class files on the client-side, we do not even have to pay a performance penalty, compared to the previous example, where value objects have been used to store attributes data only.

For implementing the user interface, we often use JSP (Java Server Pages). In this case it is commonly necessary to do the input validation here too, and there is no obstacle to using the value objects from the JSP pages. We just have to code the value objects corresponding to the JavaBean's specification.

Input Validation using Data from the Database

When we use the value objects as described, it might be that we have to access data stored in the database in order to do the validation. Accessing the database directly from the value objects can break the tier separation rules. We can solve the problem by adding this data to the value objects, or by calling the corresponding entity bean, which can be time consuming because it can force reactivating the bean and loading the complete state from the database, even though we only need to access a single attribute (we'll discuss this soon).

Sometimes, in order to improve performance, we are forced to access the database directly. We have to be aware, however, that this is an extreme measure, which we should use with care and only in cases where performance has the highest priority. Beside making our code difficult to manage (changes in database structure, for example), this might be a potential security hole in our system, particularly if we use value objects in servlets from the web server, which is typically located in the demilitarized zone (DMZ). We shall return to this area in the *Using the Database Directly* section later in this chapter.

Avoiding Large Data Transfers

Coarse-grained bean interfaces effectively lower the number of remote method invocations. Using value objects, we can make input validation on the client-side, thus further reducing the number of remote calls. But we still transfer large amounts of data over the network.

To demonstrate the problem, let's assume that we have a simple ordering system. With reference to the following simplified class diagram, we can define the following classes: Order, OrderItem, Cutomer, and Product. These classes are modeled as entity beans and have coarse-grained interfaces:

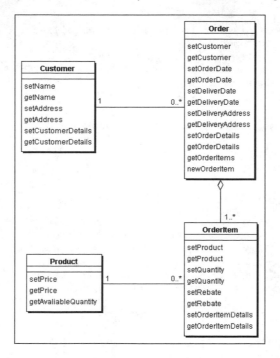

We can now look more closely at the code for each of these classes. Although we are already familiar with Order, let us look at the interface definition extract once again:

```
import java.util.*;
import java.rmi.RemoteException;
import javax.ejb.*;

public interface Order extends EJBObject {
    ...
    public void setCustomer(Customer myCustomer) throws RemoteException;
    public Customer getCustomer() throws RemoteException;
    public void setOrderDate(Date orderDate) throws RemoteException;
    public Date getOrderDate() throws RemoteException;
    public void setDeliverDate(Date deliveryDate) throws RemoteException;
    public Date getDeliveryDate() throws RemoteException;
    public void setDeliveryAddress(String deliveryAddress)
                                        throws RemoteException;
    public String getDeliveryAddress() throws RemoteException;
```

```
   ...
   public void setOrderDetails(OrderDetails myOrderDetail)
                                            throws RemoteException;
   public OrderDetails getOrderDetails() throws RemoteException;
   ...
   public Collection getOrderItems() throws RemoteException;
   public OrderItem newOrderItem() throws RemoteException;
   ...
}
```

```
import java.util.Date;

public class OrderDetails implements java.io.Serializable {
  public Customer customer_;
  public Date orderDate;
  public Date deliveryDate;
  public String deliveryAddress;
}
```

The excerpt from the `OrderItem` interface declaration looks like this:

```
import java.rmi.RemoteException;
import javax.ejb.*;

public interface OrderItem extends EJBObject {
   ...
   public void setProduct(Product prod) throws RemoteException;
   public Product getProduct() throws RemoteException;
   public void setQuantity(double quantity) throws RemoteException;
   public double getQuantity() throws RemoteException;
   public void setRebate(float rebate) throws RemoteException;
   public float getRebate() throws RemoteException;
   ...
   public void setOrderItemDetails(OrderItemDetails myOrderItemDetails)
                                            throws RemoteException;
   public OrderItemDetails getOrderItemDetails() throws RemoteException;
   ...
}
```

```
import java.util.Date;

public class OrderItemDetails implements java.io.Serializable {
  public Product prod;
  public double quantity;
  public float rebate;
}
```

The excerpt from the `Product` interface declaration looks like this:

```
import java.rmi.RemoteException;
import javax.ejb.*;

public interface Product extends EJBObject {
   ...
```

```
      public void setPrice(double myPrice) throws RemoteException;
      public double getPrice() throws RemoteException;
      ...
      public double getAvaliableQuantity() throws RemoteException;
}
```

The interface declaration of Customer is similar:

```
import java.rmi.RemoteException;
import javax.ejb.*;

public interface Customer extends EJBObject {
   ...
   public void setName(String myName) throws RemoteException;
   public String getName() throws RemoteException;
   public void setAddress(String myAddress) throws RemoteException;
   public String getAddress() throws RemoteException;
   ...
   public void setCustomerDetails(CustomerDetails myCustomerDetails)
                                              throws RemoteException;
   public CustomerDetails getCustomerDetails() throws RemoteException;
   ...
}
```

```
public class CustomerDetails implements java.io.Serializable {
  public String name;
  public String address;
  ...
}
```

What we would like to do is calculate the total of all orders. What we have to do, from the client perspective, is to iterate through all Orders. For each Order we have to access all OrderItems and, for each OrderItem, access the Product to get the price. Then we have to multiply the price by the quantity and sum the numbers.

Let us now take a look at the client code and watch out for remote method invocations, shown in **bold** below:

```
...
Collection myOrders;
Collection myOrderItems;
Iterator myOrderIter;
Iterator myOrderItemIter;
Order myOrder;
OrderItem myOrderItem;
OrderItemDetails myOrderItemDetails;
Product myProduct;
double myPrice, myQuantity;
...
myOrderIter = myOrders.iterator ();
for (int i=0; i<myOrders.size(); i++ ) {
   myOrder = (Order) PortableRemoteObject.narrow
                        (myOrderIter.next (), Order.class);
   myOrderItems = myOrder.getOrderItems();
```

```
      myOrderItemIter = myOrderItems.iterator ();
      for (int j=0; j<myOrderItems.size(); j++ ) {
         myOrderItem = (OrderItem) PortableRemoteObject.narrow
                           (myOrderItemIter.next (), OrderItem.class);
         myOrderItemDetails = myOrderItem.getOrderItemDetails();
         myProduct = myOrderItemDetails.prod;
         myPrice = myProduct.getPrice();
         myQuantity = myOrderItemDetails.quantity;

         // multiply and add
      }
   }
   ...
```

If we have only one hundred orders (myOrders.size() returns 100) with an average number of ten items per order (myOrderItems.size() returns 10), we will have to make 2,100 remote method invocations. If we have one thousand orders, the number of remote invocations raises to 21,000. If we are very optimistic and assume that each remote method invocation will last only one millisecond, the response time for one thousand orders would be around 21 seconds. We can, however, guarantee that in a production environment we will be unable to get such fast response times. More likely we will have to calculate three to five milliseconds per remote method invocation, under the proviso that we will be the only user of the system. In real-world circumstances the response time might easily get as high as 200 seconds, or more than 3 minutes for summing up one thousand orders. We definitely wouldn't want such an application.

The described problem is sometimes referred to as the **batch-processing problem**. We can recover our breath, because there is nothing wrong with the EJB architecture. The problem is that the example design, although good looking, is totally unsuitable for a scalable enterprise application. To solve the problem we will have to use the **responsibility-driven design**. Responsibility-driven design is a method for describing objects in terms of roles, responsibilities, and their collaborative behavior.

Using a Responsibility Driven Design

In the previous example, the client had the responsibility of iterating through orders. The client had to know the exact structure of the Order, OrderItem, and Product. In other words, the client had the business logic for calculating the order total incorporated within it. Does this kind of business logic belong in the client? Definitely not. It is not the client's responsibility to calculate the order total, but the responsibility of the Order bean. So let's consider adding a new method calculateOrderTotal() to the Order bean component interface:

```
import java.util.Date;
import java.rmi.RemoteException;
import javax.ejb.*;

public interface Order extends EJBObject {
   ...
   public void setCustomer(Customer myCustomer) throws RemoteException;
   public Customer getCustomer() throws RemoteException;
   public void setOrderDate(Date orderDate) throws RemoteException;
   public Date getOrderDate() throws RemoteException;
   public void setDeliverDate(Date deliveryDate) throws RemoteException;
   public Date getDeliveryDate() throws RemoteException;
```

```
    public void setDeliveryAddress(String deliveryAddress)
                                      throws RemoteException;
    public String getDeliveryAddress() throws RemoteException;
    ...
    public void setOrderDetails(OrderDetails myOrderDetail)
                                      throws RemoteException;
    public OrderDetails getOrderDetails() throws RemoteException;
    ...
    public Collection getOrderItems() throws RemoteException;
    public OrderItem newOrderItem() throws RemoteException;
    ...
    public double calculateOrderTotal() throws RemoteException;
}
```

The client does not have to iterate through order items anymore. Therefore the client code, used for calculating the total of all orders, becomes less complicated:

```
...
Collection myOrders;
Iterator myOrderIter;
Order myOrder;
double total = 0;
...
myOrderIter = myOrders.iterator ();
for (int i=0; i<myOrders.size(); i++ ) {
   myOrder = (Order) PortableRemoteObject.narrow
                     (myOrderIter.next (), Order.class);
   total += myOrder.calculateOrderTotal();
}
...
```

We have drastically reduced the number of remote method invocations from the client to the container. The client now needs only a single remote invocation to get the required information. However, the `Order` bean still has to iterate though the `OrderItems` and calculate the sum; and the `OrderItem` bean still has to access the `Product` bean. In other words, the beans still have to invoke methods remotely. To avoid the remote method invocation overhead, we can deploy the beans in the same container. In our example we would deploy the `Order`, `OrderItem`, and `Product` beans in the same container. Although it sounds reasonable, there is a trap here.

Local Access and Dependent Objects

Unfortunately, deploying enterprise beans in the same container may not be enough to reduce the remote method invocation overhead significantly. Beans are accessed through the `EJBObject` distributed object. Although two beans are located in the same container, their method invocations might still travel through the stubs and skeletons and we cannot reckon on the performance increasing. There is no guarantee that the method invocation on collocated beans will be much faster than on distributed. The EJB specification does not make any requests for container vendors to optimize this kind of method invocation.

This does not mean, however, that there will be no containers that will make local optimizations to provide great performance improvements for collocated beans. The BEA WebLogic, IBM WebSphere Advanced Server, and jBoss 2.0 ORB implementations are smart enough to optimize method invocations on beans located in the same JVM. Unfortunately we cannot count on this functionality being present in our server.

Even if the application server's ORB implements the local optimizations, the remote methods calls have to go through the container, which has to check the security and manage the declarative transaction attributes.

There are two possibilities for solving this problem. In the EJB 2.0 specification, the EJB architects have addressed this problem by introducing local interfaces to the enterprise beans. In our example, we would define a local interface for the `OrderItem` bean and use it when accessing `OrderItem` from the `Order` bean. Access through local interfaces is optimized and bypasses stubs and skeletons (actually it bypasses the whole RMI), and security checks. In contrast to remote method invocations, where the parameters are transferred by value, in local invocations they are transferred by reference. This means that, on one hand, there is no serialization overhead and, on the other hand, we can pass non-serializable arguments as parameters to methods in local interfaces. However, we have to recognize that the state of an object passed as a parameter can be changed during the method invocation.

Local interfaces allow us to create beans that preserve fine-grained interfaces for local clients. We can create beans with both local and remote (or component) interfaces. Local interfaces can be fine-grained without performance degradation. Often we will probably opt just for one type of interface. For entity beans that are accessed through a façade, we will probably define local interfaces only.

The other possibility (particularly if we do not use EJB 2.0) is to model the `OrderItem` as a simple class, instead of an entity bean, thus achieving much faster method invocations. The invocations between `Order` and `OrderItem` become local method invocations. This will make `OrderItems` accessible only through `Order` beans, which is reasonable and should not be a problem. What we actually do here is make the `OrderItem` a dependent object of the `Order` bean. Often there is a clear relationship between two objects, such that one object is contained in the other. For more information take a look at the Aggregate Detail Pattern in Chapter 12.

Distributed Façade

In the previous example, we still need as many remote invocations as we have orders. To further reduce the number of method invocations, we can move the entire business logic to the middle tier. We simply define a new bean, `OrderFacade`. The `OrderFacade` has the role of distributed façade to the system. The façade provides a unified interface to a set of interfaces in a subsystem. The `OrderFacade` bean implements the method `calculateTotal()`, as shown in the following diagram:

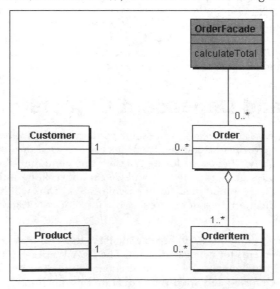

In real-world applications the façade would have more than one business method. The goal is to provide a unified interface to a set of interfaces in a subsystem, a pattern that has been defined by the "Gang of Four" in the book *Design Patterns: Elements of Reusable Object Oriented Software* (Addison-Wesley Pub Co, ISBN 0-20163-361-2).

In EJB architecture the façade is modeled as a session bean (either stateless or stateful). Session beans are appropriate for scenarios where results have to be returned to the client immediately. In EJB 2.0, façades can also be implemented using message-driven beans, thus allowing asynchronous communication. Using message-driven beans for facades is particularly useful in update operations, when the client does not need the results immediately. Another possibility in EJB 2.0 is to use entity bean home objects, which can include business methods. As home objects are bound to remote objects of a certain entity type, we would commonly use entity home objects as façades for accessing entity beans of the same type only.

The client communicates with the façade bean, which hides the entity bean interfaces from the client. The façade is a kind of a high-level gateway to the system. The distributed façade pattern further reduces the number of remote method invocations between the client tier and the middle tier, although this is far from being the only advantage. Remember that entity beans represent an object view of business entities, stored in persistent storage. Entity beans usually include methods for manipulating the bean state, as we have seen in our first examples. By their nature, entity beans are components with fine-grained interfaces.

Fine-grained interfaces are not performance effective when accessed remotely. However, using the façade pattern and proper collocation, our entity beans can have more fine-grained interfaces, without too large a performance penalty. Particularly if we use the EJB 2.0 local interfaces, we can preserve the fine-grained model for local clients. It is worth noting that a bean that implements the façade pattern is, in fact, a client for underlying beans.

Another important benefit of the façade pattern is the natural fit with the declarative transaction management offered by the EJB containers. Imagine a more complicated business logic that requires transactional integrity. A typical example is money transfer from account A to account B. Placing the logic in the client requires that a client calls a withdrawal method on the entity bean account A and a deposit method on the entity bean account B. Since we want both method invocations to happen inside a single transaction, the only choice would be to manually start a transaction inside the client code. The client code is also the place where the transaction is committed or rolled back.

It is important not to leave the transaction boundary management to the client. Rather, it would be more efficient to use the declarative transaction management. We can achieve that only if we make the bean methods transactional boundaries. The bean (session or message-driven) that is designed as a distributed façade has exactly such methods.

In other words, using session or message beans as façades for entity beans, we have forced multiple method invocations into one transaction. With this change, we have further improved the performance of the entity beans. In façade methods, entity beans are typically activated and loaded by their home interface. The finder and the state load methods are now grouped into a single transaction. This simplifies caching algorithms enormously, because the container can be sure that the data modeled by the entity bean has not changed between the find and the load method. Therefore a second database lookup can be avoided. We will say more on this in the entity beans section.

Wrapping entity beans with façade beans also ensures that we will not have transactions that are too long. In particular, transactions that span user input are very bad because, depending on the isolation level, they lock the included beans and database records for the duration of the transaction. This will be discussed in more detail shortly.

From the performance standpoint, it is ideal to have as many façade bean instances available as concurrent clients for the façade bean. Often, we cannot afford to have as many instances as concurrent clients because the number of concurrent clients is too high and our server resources do not allow us such a high number of instances. This is where the instance management algorithms come in.

Instance Management Algorithms

Let us focus on the underlying concepts once again. We have studied the remote method invocation mechanisms and understand how remote clients access the EJBObject. However, we have not yet said anything about the actual method implementations.

When we invoke a method on an EJB, we never invoke a method directly on its instance; rather, we use the EJBObject for remote invocations or EJBLocalObject for local invocations (in EJB 2.0). Neither the EJBObject nor the EJBLocalObject, however, process the method requests. They act as surrogate objects between the client and the actual EJB instance. The EJBObject (or the EJBLocalObject) only intercepts the method invocations and delegates them to the actual instances. In terms of instance management algorithms, the distinction between EJBObject and EJBLocalObject is not significant. Therefore we will refer to EJBObject only.

This is different from the distributed object architectures, like RMI and CORBA. In such cases, the clients have established a connection (through stub and skeleton) to a distributed object instance and have held the connection from the moment of binding until releasing the connection. The problem with this concept is the fact that certain clients (particularly "lazy" clients, like Java applications or applets, for instance) use the component for only a small fraction of the time compared to the time of holding the connection. This is because of user thinking time, network latency, or other similar reasons.

In multi-user enterprise information systems the number of concurrent clients can get very high and the middleware hardware has to support the increased load. If the client was directly connected with the component instance we would need as many component instances as we have concurrent clients. The instances would be used ineffectively and we would effectively be wasting expensive server resources. This is where instance pooling becomes very useful.

Instance Pooling

The EJB architecture solves this problem by decoupling the client from the component instance. Instead, the client is connected to the EJBObject. When the EJBObject receives a method invocation request, it identifies the actual bean instance, which will process the client's request.

There are several ways to identify a bean instance. One possibility would be to create a new instance just in time. The instantiation, however, requires time; therefore from the performance perspective it is favorable to already have a certain number of component instances. The EJBObject (or, more exactly, the algorithm that identifies a bean instance) can then select an instance from a pool of pre-instantiated components. It selects a free instance and allocates it to the client to process that method invocation. For the time of method processing the instance is assigned to that client. After the completion, the instance is freed and returned to the pool. This algorithm is known as the **instance-pooling algorithm** and is shown in the following diagram. It is absolutely necessary to understand the instance-pooling algorithm in order to understand the performance considerations of enterprise beans. The benefit of instance pooling is that the actual number of clients can be much higher than the number of bean instances in the pool.

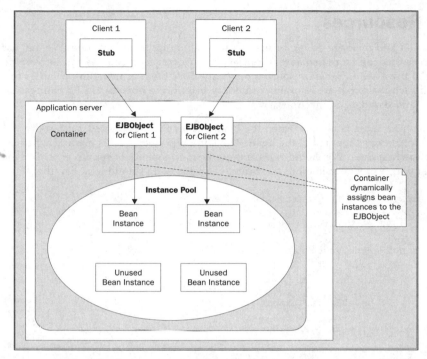

We can draw a useful analogy with a restaurant's service process. In a typical restaurant the number of waiters is much lower than the number of concurrent customers. Instead of each customer having their own waiter, the waiters are shared between customers (as bean instances are shared between clients). The waiters may not be 100% busy all the time, and may be queued up in the kitchen (instance pooling), but that's much more effective for customer service than calling a waiter at home every time a customer makes a request, and sending them back home when there are no customers to be served (just-in-time instantiation) – the cost of "instantiating" a waiter is quite high.

Usually we determine how many bean instances should be instantiated in the pool when we deploy a bean. In the majority of containers we will have to specify the minimum and the maximum number of bean instances. This complicates the instance-pooling algorithm a little. If all instances in the pool have been allocated to clients, the algorithm checks the maximum number of instances allowed. If this number is not reached yet, a new instance is created. Otherwise, the client is blocked until an instance gets freed. The instance-pooling algorithm also has to decide how many instances it will conserve in the pool between the upper and the lower limit. Usually it decides based on the available memory resources.

The instance pooling algorithm is part of the container and it is therefore the exclusive responsibility of the container to handle the instance pooling. Our bean code is not responsible for creating or destroying instances, nor is the client code. Why then, you might wonder, do we have to use the create() and remove() methods in the bean's home interface? The answer is that these methods create and destroy the EJBObjects. These methods are not related to actual bean instance creation or destruction, although to entity beans these methods cause the creation or removal of records in the database. The client is not aware of the fact that bean instances are pooled behind the EJBObject.

The described algorithm works perfectly for stateless session beans and message-driven beans. Because they do not have a client-dependent state, the instance-pooling algorithm can freely allocate them to different clients. In general, every request from a client can be served by a different stateless session or message-driven bean instance.

Reusing Resources

Stateless session and message-driven beans can store client-independent state. We can use this fact to store resources that can be reused across transactions. Acquiring resources can be very costly, therefore it is beneficial if we acquire these resources once and store them as member variables to reuse them. Examples of such resources are references to entity bean home objects, HTTP connections, socket connections, and database connections.

We should acquire these resources (when the bean instance is first created) within the `setEntityContext()` method of the bean. The container invokes this method when creating a bean instance for the first time. We should release these bean-independent resources within the `unsetEntityContext()` method of the bean. Thus, the code should look like this:

```
public class Order implements EntityBean {
  ...
  public void setEntityContext(EntityContext ctx) {
    ...
    // Acquire the resources here
    ...
  }
  ...
  public void unsetEntityContext () {
    ...
    // Release the resources here
    ...
  }
  ...
}
```

What we actually do here is resource pooling. Most application servers provide some resource pooling algorithms. Resource pooling is often delegated to other technologies. For example, the majority of application servers provide database connection pooling, which is a part of JDBC 2.0. Resource pooling, performed by the application server, can be more effective than manually storing the connections in the bean's client-independent state, and we can control the number of resource connections more accurately. To use resource pooling efficiently, we should acquire the resources as late as possible. The best way is to acquire them just in time, before we need them, and to release them immediately. Application servers, however, do not pool all the resources. They might not pool the connections to bean home objects, for example. In such cases, it is useful to do the manual resource pooling.

What About Beans with State?

Unfortunately, things get a little more complicated. Beans with state include both stateful session and entity beans. The instance-pooling algorithm cannot simply allocate an instance to a client, then return it to the pool and later allocate another instance. The client depends on the state stored in the instance, so it needs to have exactly the same instance each time. Can the instance management algorithm provide any help? Or will we need one instance for each client, as in the distributed object models?

Fortunately, it is possible to do instance pooling with stateful session and entity beans as well. The instance management algorithm, before it can allocate a bean instance to the client, has to load the corresponding state. This is called activation. And after method completion, the algorithm has first to store the state, before it can return the instance in the pool. This is called passivation. The instance-pooling algorithm has to decide which instances to passivate and which to activate. Although this depends on the algorithm implementation, most algorithms use one of the well-known strategies, like least-recently-used or most-frequently-used.

A bean instance can be passivated at any time, if the instance is not involved in a method invocation or transaction. An instance can also be activated at any time, but usually the container will wait for a client request to come in. There is however no obstacle to developing an instance-pooling algorithm that will predict a bean's instance usage and activate an instance in advance. The tricky part is only the usage prediction.

Maintaining the bean instance state has an influence on performance. This is why you might have heard so many stories about worse performance of entity beans and worse scalability of stateful session beans compared to stateless session beans. Therefore, when we use beans with state, always keep in mind what happens under the hood. This helps us make our system more efficient.

Although the procedure described applies as well to stateful session beans as it does to entity beans, there are some differences in the details. Therefore let us first take a look at the stateful session beans.

Stateful Session Beans

Stateful session beans hold conversational state with clients that spans multiple method invocations. When pooling stateful session beans, the conversational state has to be maintained. The instance management algorithm has to be able to maintain the state; therefore certain rules exist. When the bean instance gets passivated, the instance management algorithm uses serialization to convert the bean's state into a stream. It can then write the stream to permanent storage. When the algorithm decides to activate the bean instance again, it reads the stream from storage and converts it into the in-memory state representation. This is why the `javax.ejb.EnterpriseBean` interface extends `java.io.Serializable`:

```
public interface javax.ejb.EnterpriseBean extends java.io.Serializable {}
```

The container can preserve the state only if it can serialize it. Every non-transient member therefore belongs to the conversational state of the EJB. The attribute can be a primitive data type, or it can be a Java object. Serializing primitive data types is relatively simple. Serializing Java objects on the other hand can be complicated. The serialization algorithm is recursively applied on each object that is part of the bean's conversational state. Graphs of data, referred to by the bean instance, will be created.

We should remember this when we design stateful session beans. To improve the serialization procedure we should maintain only the necessary conversational state. Furthermore, we should not use particularly complicated objects and be aware of the relationships between the objects. For attributes that we do not need to serialize, we should use the `transient` keyword.

The EJB container can use custom serialization, or it can use the default serialization protocol. Sometimes, we can improve the performance by switching from using the default to using custom serialization methods. Custom serialization ought be done carefully. There is no guarantee that this will produce faster code than the default serialization, so we will need to profile serialization to ensure that we are indeed benefiting from custom serialization methods. Typically, custom serialization will give better results with complex objects if we can do the serialization smarter than the default methods. We may then have to implement the `readObject()` and the `writeObject()` methods.

The container notifies the bean before it gets passivated. For this purpose, the container calls the bean's `ejbPassivate()` method, which notifies the bean instance that the conversational state will be serialized and the bean will be swapped from the memory. In the `ejbPassivate()` method, the bean instance has the chance to free the resources that cannot be serialized. This includes database connections, sockets, etc. The following diagram illustrates this:

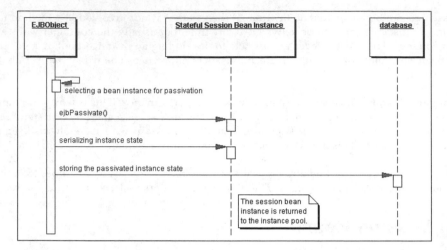

When the bean instance is activated again and the conversational state has been restored, the container notifies the instance by calling the ejbActivate() method. In this method, the bean instance can restore the resources. The sequence diagram for activating stateful session beans is shown in the diagram below:

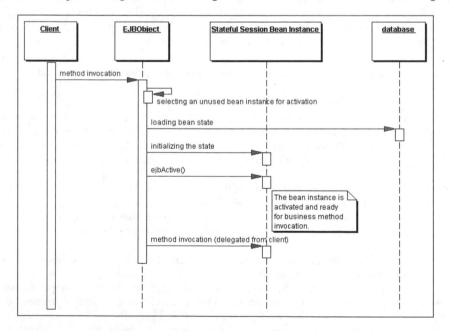

Entity Beans

Entity beans are pooled in a similar way to stateful session beans. The state of an entity bean is represented by persistent data that is stored in a database. There are two ways to persist entity bean state. We can use the bean-managed persistence (and thus write the necessary code to manage the state), or we can use the container-managed persistence and leave the work to the container algorithms.

Entity bean instance pooling works irrespective of the persistence type we've selected. It is similar to stateful session bean instance management, but a little more complicated. As with stateful session beans, the instance pooling algorithm calls the `ejbActivate()` and `ejbPassivate()` methods on entity bean instances too. The calls indicate that the entity bean instance will be activated or passivated, respectively, and that it should release or restore the resources.

When an entity bean is passivated, more is done than just releasing the resources. The instance's state has to be saved into the database. In contrast to stateful session beans, where the conversational state is saved using serialization, the entity beans state is saved using the `ejbStore()` method. The instance pooling algorithm calls the `ejbStore()` method prior to calling the `ejbPassivate()` that is before actual passivation occurs. The following diagram shows the details of passivation:

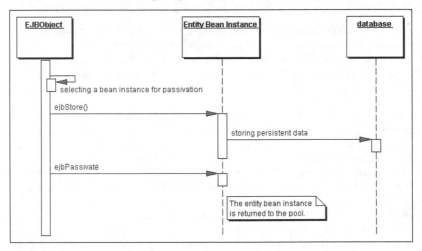

The whole procedure is reversed for activation. The instance management algorithm first calls the `ejbActivate()` method, when the bean instance has the chance to acquire the necessary resources. Then it calls the `ejbLoad()` method, in which the instance restores the state from the database. The sequence diagram is shown below:

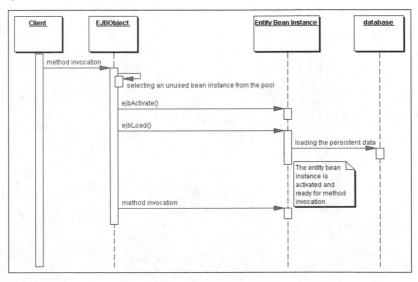

Both activation and passivation can occur at any time. The exception is that a bean cannot be passivated if it is involved in a method invocation or in a transaction. The activation will typically occur when a client requests an entity bean. (Remember that a client for the entity bean can be a servlet, applet, application, etc. If we follow the façade pattern, then a client for an entity bean will typically be a session or a message-driven bean.) The request can come from a method invocation, or it can also come from the finder method from the corresponding home object. Therefore we should make sure that we do not use the finder methods if it is not necessary. The finder method requires the entity bean instance activation. Therefore the instance management algorithm has to find a free instance in the pools. If it does not find one, it first has to store the state and passivate an existing instance. Then it can activate and load the state of the required instance, for which a database lookup is required.

Context Switching

As you might imagine, loading and storing the bean state are costly operations, as are activation and passivation. Therefore we have to minimize the number of required "context switches" to improve performance. In an ideal world we would have all our entity beans instantiated in memory. Unfortunately we do not live in an ideal world and it is not difficult to realize why it is impossible to have all entity beans in memory at the same time.

Therefore we have to carefully select the number of instances in the pool. Altering the minimum and maximum number of instances in the pool can significantly affect the performance. Unfortunately there is no formula for calculating optimal number of instances in the pool. All we can do is to experiment with our application and our application server/container. A number that works for one server might not be optimal for another. Using server logging or a profiler tool (OptimizeIt, JProbe) can help a lot. We will return to the issue of pool size in our discussion of bean deployment, later in this chapter.

Another alternative is to supervise the instance state loading and storing. It might not be necessary to store the state of an entity bean instance each time it is passivated. What if the state has not changed? For complex entity beans it pays off to keep a record of changes. We have several possibilities.

If we use bean-managed persistence, the solution is very simple. We define a Boolean attribute, that tells us if the data has changed. We check this attribute in the `ejbStore()` method:

```
public class myBMPBean implements EntityBean {
  ...
  private boolean dataHasChanged = false;
  ...
  public void ejbLoad() {
    ...
    // Load the state from the database

    dataHasChanged = false;
  }
  ...
  public void ejbStore() {
    if (dataHasChanged) {

      // Get the connection, store the data, and release the connection.

    }
  }
  ...
}
```

Another possibility is to use an application server value-added feature. For example, BEA WebLogic supports an `is-modified-method-name` method (usually `isModified()`) that tells the container if data has changed. This might be a more elegant solution, but remember, it is not portable! And we still have to write code and keep track of the changes, which is error prone.

Container-based Optimizations

A better solution is container-based optimizations. A container can, for example, inspect the data fields and decide when it is necessary to store the data. This is, however, an optional feature and we cannot rely on it. The problem with EJB 1.1 container-managed persistence is that it is very difficult for a container to supervise the changes of attributes. Therefore the majority of application servers treat persistent attributes as one unit.

IBM WebSphere Advanced Edition, in connection with IBM VisualAge for Java, offers another solution. If we use VisualAge for bean development, we can mark certain bean methods as read-only. To do this, we just have to check the **Const Method** checkbox in the control descriptor of the bean's **Properties** panel. A selected checkbox means that a method is read-only. The WebSphere container only stores the bean's state if at least one non read-only method has been invoked during a transaction. Although this is a proprietary IBM extension it is worth considering if we use the WebSphere/VisualAge combination, because it just requires us to select a checkbox and has no further influence on code portability.

The EJB 2.0 CMP model is better suited for optimizations and can easily detect modifications of CMP attributes. Still, the application server can do other things to improve the performance. In the context of persistent state management, the most obvious thing is a **data-caching algorithm**. The better the caching algorithm is, the less database lookups are required, and the faster our entity beans will perform. Unfortunately, things are not as simple as they seem. Remember that entity beans can be used to represent existing legacy data. Legacy applications do not access data through beans; they go directly into the database instead. Actually they do not even have to be legacy applications; there is nothing to stop us directly accessing a database and deleting some rows or inserting new rows.

Dealing with Legacy Systems

Now imagine a situation where we use entity beans to represent some data that is simultaneously used by a legacy system that accesses the database directly. Our application invokes the finder method on an entity home object. The container has to instantiate the entity bean. Therefore it has to select an available instance, invoke the `ejbActivate()` method, and finally invoke the `ejbLoad()` method to load the state from the database. Then our application decides to invoke a remote method on this entity instance. Let's assume that there are no other users at this time, therefore, the container does not have to passivate the bean instance in the time between the finder and remote method invocation.

Common sense tells us that because the entity bean instance is already active and has its state, the container does not have to do anything but delegate the method invocation to the instance. *Wrong!* The container indeed has to do a second database lookup, because it has to be sure that the legacy system did not change the data between the two method invocations (remember that legacy systems access the database directly). In other words, although the instance was available, a second database lookup was necessary and no cache could help here. We now have a better idea why entity beans cause a performance hit.

The container could save the second lookup, if the database would notify it of changes. Then it could also perform the data caching and this would bring enormous performance improvements. However, it is very difficult to implement a caching algorithm that is smart enough to notice direct database changes. This task becomes easier if the application server and the database management system come from the same supplier.

The situation is much simpler if we do not use any application that directly accesses the database. Then, the container can be sure that the data did not change between method invocations. Therefore, it can perform caching and reduce the number of database lookups. To make use of it, we have to tell the application server this fact. The majority of EJB application servers will let us do this, but we should be aware that if we still access the database directly, we risk data inconsistency, which can be fatal for our information system and very difficult to track down and correct. To make the database not shared in BEA WebLogic, for example, we just have to set the `db-is-shared` deployment parameter to `false`.

Be aware however, that in our example, the second database lookup can also be saved if we make both method invocations (the finder and the remote business method) inside a single transaction. This eliminates the second database lookup because the locks, acquired by the first method invocation, have not been released yet. Therefore, the container can be sure that nobody has changed the data in the meantime. This is why in the distributed *Façade Section* we have recommended that we use entity beans only through session beans.

> If we configure the façade beans so that they require a transaction, then the EJB method invocations will occur in the same transaction, thus reducing the number of database lookups.

Container-Managed Persistence

Container-managed persistence is one of the most advanced features of EJB and can simplify the application development considerably. If we use a relational database management system (RDBMS, the container has to do the object-relational mapping. Mapping simple attributes to relational schemas is not difficult, but mapping objects or even graphs of related objects can be very complicated. Several approaches exist, from mapping everything to one table, which leads to redundancy, to mapping objects to separate tables, which requires several joins when accessing the data. As a rule of thumb, from performance perspective, mapping to a single table often results in faster applications. The disadvantage is data redundancy and non-normalized data schemas.

It is recommended that we become familiar with the way the container provides persistence service. To get an idea of how much the CMP influences the performance we can compare the performance of two identical beans, once using BMP and once CMP. A well-implemented container-managed persistence should perform better than an average hand-written bean-managed persistence. The CMP can during make several optimizations, which are difficult to make when using BMP (and require additional effort by each entity bean). The EJB 1.1 persistence was not particularly good in supporting optimizations. More specifically, using EJB 1.1 CMP, it is very difficult for a container to identify attributes that have changed. Therefore the container typically treats attributes as a set – reading them all from the database by activation and writing them all during passivation. There is also no support for relationships between beans. Therefore it may happen that the activation of an enterprise bean activates all related beans too, although we do not need them.

The EJB 2.0 CMP model makes large improvements on this area. Managing persistence of attributes through getter/setter methods is more suitable for the above mentioned optimizations. Containers can more easily supervise the attributes and read and write only those that are actually needed. The support for relationships makes it easier for containers to load only beans that are actually needed (see the following section). Further improvements are possible by the concurrency control and caching.

Lazy Loading Beans

Let's spend a little more time with the entity beans. Suppose we have an entity bean that is related to other entity beans. In our earlier example (our second diagram), we had the `Order`, which was related to the `Customer`, the `OrderItem`, and the `Product`; but other similar examples can be easily found. When our application searches for a bean instance, using the finder method for example, the entity bean instance gets activated. We have already seen that the container invokes the `ejbLoad()` method. To acquire correct data, the `ejbLoad()` method instantiates (activates) the whole graph of related objects. It does that irrespective of the fact that we may only need to retrieve the delivery date (for example).

As we now understand that instantiation is costly, we can easily see that if we could find a way of not loading the whole graph of related beans, we could save time, thus getting better performance. We would then load the related beans only if we (or any other application) really needed them. In other words, we should load our related beans just-in-time; such beans are called **lazy loading beans**.

Unfortunately, a standard way for using lazy loading beans does not exist in EJB 1.1. EJB 2.0 provides support for container-managed relationships, which makes implementing automatic lazy-loading easier for application server providers. Probably most containers will provide automatic mechanisms for lazy-loading enterprise beans, although at the time of writing this book, the information on this topic was very limited. Therefore, in the meantime we can look for custom solutions from application server providers, or we can implement lazy-loading beans ourselves.

The most straightforward approach is purely manual. If we use bean-managed persistence, the proposed approach is simple and does not require large changes to the bean implementation. It is portable, too. The idea is that we do not load the related beans in the `ejbLoad()` method. We will have to provide custom load methods for related beans. These methods first check if the corresponding bean is already loaded, and if it is not, the bean gets activated via home finder methods. In the following code, we show how to lazy load a `Customer` bean within an `Order` bean, from our previous example:

```
import javax.rmi.PortableRemoteObject;
import javax.ejb.*;
import javax.naming.*;

public class Order implements EntityBean {
  ...
  public Customer customer_;
  ...

  public void ejbLoad() {
    // Do not load related beans in this method
  }

  public Customer getCustomer() {
    lazyLoadCustomer();
```

```
      return customer_;
  }

  private void lazyLoadCustomer() {
    if (customer_ == null) {
      Context initContext = new InitialContext(context.getEnvironment());
      CustomerHome home = (CustomerHome) PortableRemoteObject.narrow
                (initContext.lookup("CustomerHome"), CustomerHome.class);
      customer_ = (Customer) PortableRemoteObject.narrow
                (home.findByPrimaryKey(pk), Customer.class);
    }
    ...
  }
  ...
  public void ejbPassivate() {
    customer_ = null;
  }
  ...
}
```

Although this approach is simple, it is less than perfect because not only does it require code modifications, but it also requires that the bean developer remembers to call the lazy-load method. Another possibility, as we shall see in the *Smart Stubs* section of this chapter, is to modify the object proxy code. It might be useful to have a look at the following web site: http://www-und.ida.liu.se/~ricob684/java/ for further details.

Using the Database Directly

It is a common occurrence that we have to list all the customer names or all the orders in the user interface, regardless of whether the user interface is a web page, application, or applet. The adhoc approach is to use the finder methods of the corresponding entity bean, then to locate each instance, invoking the getter method and finally writing the string to the output.

Since we are now familiar with the way the container works, let us try to describe what happens inside the container:

❏   First, the user interface code invokes the finder method on the home object. The finder method forces a database lookup. The reference to the entity bean instance is returned to the user interface.

❏   Then, the user interface code invokes the getter method, for retrieving the name. The container has to instantiate the corresponding bean instance, for which a second database lookup is required (we already know why).

❏   Finally, the name is returned to the client (user interface). We had two remote method invocations, two database lookups, and one bean instance activation.

All this for only one name! If we assume that one remote method invocation lasts one millisecond only, and that both database lookups and the activation will be done in three milliseconds (which is very fast), then we have spent five milliseconds for one name. How many customers (or orders, or whatever else) will be in an information system? One thousand, ten thousand, or maybe even a hundred thousand? We can easily see that this approach is not optimal for performance.

Of course we have accessed entity beans directly, and this is not advisable. A better approach is to go though a façade session or message-driven bean. But the façade bean also has to locate the entity bean instances through the finder method. Since it does this in a transaction, there is only one database lookup required. However, the bean instance still has to be activated. If the façade bean is collocated with the entity beans, and if the container is capable of optimizing the remote invocations, or if local interfaces are used, then we would save the costs of remote invocations, too. This is definitely a much better approach.

However, even this approach can sometimes be too slow, mainly because each instance has to be activated (and remember there can be thousands of instances. The problem is, of course, the fact that during the instantiation *all* data is loaded into the bean. If the bean is complex, this means a lot of overhead, particularly since we're really only after the name. Implementing partial field loading would be a welcome solution. Unfortunately, implementing it "by hand" using bean-managed persistence is extremely difficult. With the EJB 1.1 container-managed persistence it is almost impossible to do it automatically, because a container cannot determine which attributes have been accessed or changed. EJB 2.0 CMP model will, however, allow application server providers to provide support for this kind of optimization.

In the mean time, the solution is to access the database via the session or message-driven façade bean, or even from a servlet, client applet, or application. Accessing the database directly, particularly from a servlet or application, is not advisable for several reasons. We bypass business logic, and our application becomes more difficult to maintain. It now directly depends on the database structure. Another reason why this is not advisable is because accessing the database, particularly from servlets on a web server, can be a possible security hole. If our server is in the DMZ, we will have to open the second firewall for direct database access. Therefore we recommend using this approach only if performance has the *highest* priority.

Transactions

The instance management algorithm is not the only algorithm that is invoked in the `EJBObject`. The container also provides declarative access to transactions and security. The `EJBObject` processes both, but for us transactions are of particular interest. Among other things, transactions assure isolation of users from each other, even if they deal with the same data in the underlying database. The isolation is achieved by concurrency control, which happens behind the scenes.

Those familiar with EJB version 1.0 might recall that when we defined a declarative transaction, by setting the corresponding attribute in the deployment descriptor, we also had to define the isolation level. We've had four options:

- ❏ `TRANSACTION_READ_UNCOMMITTED`
- ❏ `TRANSACTION_READ_COMMITTED`
- ❏ `TRANSACTION_REPEATABLE_READ`
- ❏ `TRANSACTION_SERIALIZABLE`

Newer EJB versions have, however, eliminated the transaction isolation level from the deployment descriptor. This does not mean that the isolation level does not exist anymore. Container providers can still enable the isolation-level definition, or beans can use the JDBC isolation levels directly.

Isolation is the tradeoff between safety and speed. From the previously mentioned options, `TRANSACTION_READ_UNCOMMITTED` offers the best performance, but hardly any isolation, while `TRANSACTION_SERIALIZABLE` offers the highest isolation, but the slowest performance. The isolation levels are not something that EJB invented. Those familiar with databases will already know the isolation levels mentioned, and are probably familiar with the **dirty read**, **unrepeatable read**, and **phantom read** problems. Please refer to Chapter 9 for more information about transaction isolation.

With selecting the appropriate isolation level, we can achieve great performance improvements. The maxim here is to use the lowest isolation level possible that guarantees safe operation. For example, if we do not execute the same query twice, or our application code can handle the phantom records, we can use the repeatable read isolation level.

Deadlocks

The isolation in transactions is achieved using locks. Besides the performance problem, there is also the **deadlock** problem. Deadlocks occur when two transactions place a shared lock on the same resource during a transaction. When they want to commit the transaction, they have to upgrade from a shared to an exclusive lock. This is, of course, not possible and both transactions wait for the other one to release the lock. Only then will the second be able to get the exclusive lock. Both transactions wait, and would wait forever if the lock doesn't have a timeout. The problem gets solved as soon as the first lock times out and the resource manager rolls the first transaction back, allowing the second to complete successfully.

The performance suffers considerably under deadlocks; therefore it is advisable that we try to avoid them. Resolving deadlocks is specific to the database system. However, we will try to give some general guidelines that can be applied to most databases.

It may help if we index our database tables by every attribute that is used in the finder methods (and the corresponding `SELECT` statements). We can tune the frequency with which the database performs the deadlock detection and the time an application waits for a lock. If a container provides ways to check if the bean's state has changed within a unit of work, this can help the container decide for read or read-write transactions. Read-only transactions do not have to acquire exclusive locks, which boosts performance. We have mentioned before how IBM WebSphere and BEA WebLogic solve this problem. The second benefit is that this setting prevents the unnecessary writes to the database, something that we have also looked at previously.

In some application servers we can select between **optimistic** and **pessimistic** locking. Optimistic locking acquires a shared lock at the beginning of a transaction, while the pessimistic locking acquires an exclusive lock at the beginning of a transaction. Pessimistic locking prevents deadlocks, but has other negative influences on performance. In most cases, particularly in web-based applications, optimistic locking results in better performance.

The ideal solution would be to use the highest isolation level for read-write transactions only. However, as far as we know, no application server supports this approach yet. Therefore, in order to use it, we have to implement it ourselves. The two possibilities are to use two sets of finder methods for each bean, one for read-only transactions, and one for read/write transactions; or two sets of entity beans.

Performance Guidelines for Transactions

We should use the lowest possible transaction-isolation level. Furthermore, we should also try to use as short a transaction as possible. We should not span the user interface inside a transaction. That would add the user thinking time to a transaction, which can be unpredictable and can lead to very long transactions. Because transactions place locks on the underlying data, this data is inaccessible for other users, which heavily influences performance.

To improve performance further, we can detect the transactions that have been marked for rollback. Imagine a transaction that spans several beans, and already the first bean wants to roll back. It is wise, and can save a lot of time and work, to have the other beans check for the transaction status to avoid doing work that will be rolled back at the end of transaction. We can identify if a transaction is marked for rollback using the **EJB context**. EJBContext is an object that identifies the environment and stores information related to the transaction. If we use container-managed transactions, we can use the getRollbackOnly() method to identify whether the current transaction has already been marked for rollback. The code for identifying the transaction status is simple:

```
public class Order implements EntityBean {
  ...
  public double calculateOrderTotal() {
    if (!context.getRollbackOnly()) {
      // Process the request
    } else
      return 0;
  }
  ...
}
```

For bean-managed transactions we can invoke the getStatus() method. For further explanation please take a look at Chapter 9.

If we use transactions over several distributed data sources, the transaction manager will have to use the **two-phase commit** (**2PC**) instead of the simple one-phase commit. To conclude the transaction, in the first phase of a 2PC the involved sources give their votes whether the transaction should commit or rollback. The second phase occurs if no resource voted for rollback; only then do the involved resources perform the updates. The 2PC is more complicated than the simple one-way commit, thus achieving slower performance. Therefore, if we have the choice, we would select the one-phase commit for performance.

Accelerating Marshaling

Clients invoke methods on EJBs remotely. Therefore, the method invocation requests have to be transformed and sent over the wire to the receiving object. There the requests are unmarshaled and delegated to the actual object implementations. The results are returned the same way (in reverse). User-defined classes can be particularly expensive for transferring over the wire. The marshaling and unmarshaling of serialized types uses Java serialization and this is a major overhead. It is a common occurrence that EJBs return collections of such serializable types, which makes things even worse.

In addition to serialized types, RMI-IIOP specifies **IDL data types** as well. IDL data types do not use serialization to marshal. We can therefore see that if we use the IDL data types we should be able to improve the marshaling performance and thus improve the performance of remote method invocations. This approach has a second advantage. By using IDL data types, we can easily access our EJBs from any CORBA-based system, which includes systems in C, C++, Smalltalk, COBOL, and other programming languages adopted by the CORBA language mapping specifications.

The idea is not to give up user-defined types, but to use the IDL struct data type instead of a user defined Java class. The IDL struct is a data-only structure. However, the user-defined classes that we use to return data from beans to the clients are also very data intensive. Therefore in most cases we can use IDL structs instead. Let us take a look at the serializable class first:

```
public class CustomerDetails implements java.io.Serializable {
  public String name;
  public String address;
  public int status;

  public CustomerDetails(String name, String address, int status) {
    this.name = name;
    this.address = address;
    this.status = status;
  }
}
```

Note that in this example the getter and setter methods are omitted for clarity. Typically a business method would return a collection of OrderDetails objects:

```
public java.util.Collection getAllDetails() throws RemoteException;
```

Instead, we use the following IDL struct:

```
struct CustomerDetails {
  wstring name;
  wstring address;
  long status;
};
```

We have to use the IDL-to-Java compiler to map the CORBA IDL to a corresponding Java class:

```
public final class CustomerDetails implements
                      org.omg.CORBA.portable.IDLEntity {
  public String name;
  public String address;
  public int status;

  public CustomerDetails(String name, String address, int status) {
    this.name = name;
    this.address = address;
    this.status = status;
  }

  public CustomerDetails() {
  }
}
```

The differences are minor; the most obvious is the interface IDLEntity. It is a marker interface, which implements the Serializable interface, which means that the IDLEntity is a serializable type, too. However, when marshaling an IDLEntity type, the ORB can use the standard **GIOP** (**General Inter-ORB Protocol**) procedures for construction of a GIOP/IIOP request, instead of Java Serialization, which has to serialize the whole object.

The fact that IDLEntity is a serializable type is important when using RMI with **JRMP** (**Java Remote Method Protocol**), or an application server that does not implement the RMI-IIOP completely. Both can use standard serialization and it will work properly.

The other important thing is the data type mapping. It helps if we are familiar with IDL-to-Java mapping. This is why in the `OrderDetails` IDL `struct`, `status` is declared as `long`. CORBA IDL data type `long` is mapped to Java type `int`. Mapping of important basic data types is shown in the following table:

Java	IDL	Data Size (in bits)
boolean	boolean	8
char	char and wchar	16 (8 for IDL char)
byte (signed)	octet (unsigned)	8
short	short	16
int	long	32
long	long long	64
float	float	32
double	double	64
String	string and wstring	Variable length

To do the mapping from IDL to Java, we can use any IDL-to-Java compiler. `idlj` comes as a part of Java 2 SDK version 1.3, Standard Edition. For those unfamiliar with CORBA and IDL, it is possible to write classes mapped from IDL `struct` directly. We have to declare a final class with no inheritance. The class has to implement the `IDLEntity` and all attributes have to be declared as public. We also have to provide two constructors: the default one without parameters, and the setting constructor (as shown in the example).

The business methods do not return collections anymore. Instead they return arrays:

```
public CustomerDetails[] getAllDetails() throws RemoteException;
```

With this approach, we can improve the marshaling performance considerably. Using the standard Java 2 SDK version 1.3, the improvement in method invocations returning only a single object is as much as 30%. The method invocation using Java serialization takes about 1.5 milliseconds compared to 1.1 milliseconds for using the IDL `struct`. The described approach is fully portable across different application servers and works even on servers that do not fully implement RMI-IIOP (although without the performance benefit). Furthermore, using the IDL `struct` enables seamless integration of EJBs with CORBA objects written in other programming languages.

The disadvantage of using this approach is that the IDL `struct`, because of its structural-oriented nature, may not be a perfect fit for our application. We should however be aware of this approach and use it in the performance sensitive parts of our application.

Smart Stubs

Stubs are generated as we deploy the EJBs in the container and are responsible for forwarding method invocations to the remote objects. The stubs generated by most deployment tools do exactly that and nothing more. The functionality of stubs can, however, be extended in many ways.

From the perspective of performance, the most promising ways to extend the stubs are caching remote method invocations and compressing the data before transferring it over the wire. Compressing the data can bring performance benefits only if our application transfers large amounts of data over slow communication channels. We should not think of compression as a solution for bad design. Compression also requires changes to stubs and skeletons. Remote method invocation caching requires changes to stubs only. Depending on our application, we will have to implement one caching algorithm or another.

The other possible modifications include performance monitoring, user-implemented security, etc. In this section we will not discuss the caching or compression algorithms. Rather, we will show how to modify the stubs. Their modification is transparent to the client and the server code. This approach is known in the CORBA world as **smart proxies**.

The brute force approach is to directly modify the code generated by the deployment tools. We strongly discourage this approach because it is very difficult to reapply the changes when moving to a new version or another application server. We can also lose our changes very easily if we inadvertently generate the stubs and skeletons again. Renaming the originally generated stubs and skeletons and writing our modifications using inheritance is only a marginally better approach, although some tools exist that are helpful with this approach (see http://www.white-park.freeserve.co.uk/).

In CORBA, smart proxies are implemented using a client-side factory that instantiates them. When the client requests a remote object reference, the client calls the factory, which instantiates the smart proxy. The smart proxy then implements the same interface, stores the reference in the proxy, and returns it to the client.

The drawback is that the client has to know about the server-side objects. It has to know which method invocations can be cached and which cannot. A better solution in Java is to use dynamic code downloading and implement the smart stubs on the server-side and download them to the clients.

Implementing a Smart Stub

What we need to do is to find a way to write a serializable class on the server-side that implements the same interface as the remote object for which we will use the smart stub. In our case this will be the `EJBObject` for the corresponding bean. However, the interface that will be implemented by the smart stub must not extend the `Remote` interface. If it does, we cannot transfer it by value from the serverside to the client-side, because remote interfaces cannot be transferred by value. The problem is that the `EJBObject` (and `EJBHome`) interface inherits from the `Remote` interface. Let us assume that we would like to write a smart stub for the `Product` bean that implements the `getPrice()` and `getAvaliableQuantity()` methods. The following diagram shows the relationships between interfaces and classes:

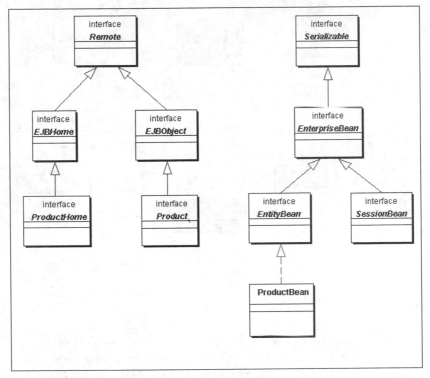

The smart stub has to implement the same `Product` interface as the bean remote component (the `EJBObject`). In the current situation the smart stub cannot implement the `Product` interface, because it inherits from the `Remote` interface. Therefore we have to re-factor the EJB design a little and first define the standalone interface `ProductIntf`:

```
import java.rmi.RemoteException;

public interface ProductIntf {
    ...
    public void setPrice(double myPrice) throws RemoteException;
    public double getPrice() throws RemoteException;
    ...
    public double getAvaliableQuantity() throws RemoteException;
}
```

Then we define the remote component interface `Product`:

```
import java.rmi.RemoteException;
import javax.ejb.*;

public interface Product extends ProductIntf, EJBObject {
    public double getPrice();
}
```

This allows us to define the `ProductSmartStub` class, which implements the `ProductIntf` interface. It also assures us that we will be able to communicate with `ProductSmartStub` locally, using local method invocations inside the client process, and that the enterprise bean (session or entity) will be able to send the smart stub to the client over the wire (because the `ProductSmartStub` can implement the `Serializable` interface too). After refactoring, the relationships between interfaces and classes look like this:

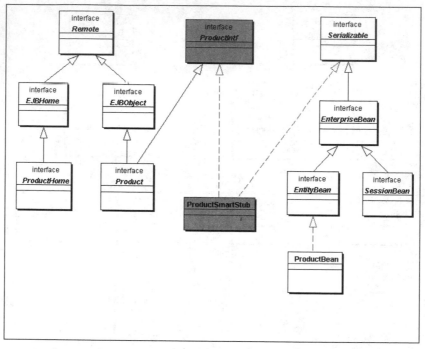

Now we have to implement the `ProductSmartStub`. Actually, we have to implement all the methods of the `ProductIntf` interface. The easiest way (in the first attempt) is to delegate the methods to the actual remote object. The example code would look like this:

```
import java.io.Serializable;
import java.rmi.RemoteException;

public class ProductSmartStub implements ProductIntf, Serializable {

  private Product ref = null;

  public ProductSmartStub(Product ref) {
    this.ref = ref;
  }

  public void setPrice(double myPrice) throws RemoteException {
    // Delegate the method to the server object
    ref.setPrice(myPrice);
  }

  public double getPrice() throws RemoteException {
    // Delegate the method to the server object
    return ref.getPrice();
  }
  ...
  public double getAvaliableQuantity() throws RemoteException {
    // Delegate the method only
    return ref.getAvaliableQuantity();
  }
  ...
  // Implement possible other methods, too.
  ...
}
```

This stub is not smart yet, because it delegates all method invocations to the remote object implementation. To make it smart, we have to implement a caching strategy. We can use everything from a very simple algorithm to complicated caching architectures with callback notification, etc. We will not discuss these alternatives here. Instead, we will show how to implement very simple caching for the getPrice() method. We will presume that the price does not change. We have to add an attribute in which we will cache the price. The simplest way is to look for the price in the constructor method. The new code looks like this:

```java
import java.io.Serializable;
import java.rmi.RemoteException;

public class ProductSmartStub implements ProductIntf, Serializable {

    private Product ref = null;
    private double price = 0;
    private boolean priceCached = false;

    public ProductSmartStub(Product ref) {
        this.ref = ref;
    }

    public void setPrice(double myPrice) throws RemoteException {
        // Delegate the method to the server object
        ref.setPrice(myPrice);
        // Update the cached value
        price = myPrice;
        priceCached = true;
    }

    public double getPrice() throws RemoteException {
        // Check if the price is cached
        if ( !priceCached ) {
            price = ref.getPrice();
            priceCached = true;
        }
        // Return the cached value
        return price;
    }
    ...
    public double getAvaliableQuantity() throws RemoteException {
        // Delegate the method only
        return ref.getAvaliableQuantity();
    }
    ...
    // Implement possible other methods, too.
    ...
}
```

In real-world scenarios we would make the smart stub even more efficient with a more complex caching strategy. We would also have to find a way to notify the stub to reread the price if another client changes it. This can lead to complications; therefore we should weigh the advantages and disadvantages and decide when the additional effort is worth the improved performance and when it is not.

To establish a connection to the bean, the client uses the following code:

```
    Product pr = (Product) PortableRemoteObject.narrow
                            (home.create(...), Product.class);
```

The reference `pr` does not point to the smart stub yet. We have to obtain a reference to the `ProductSmartStub` in the following way:

```
    ProductIntf prSmart = (ProductIntf) new ProductSmartStub(pr);
```

The reference `prSmart` now points to the smart stub and clients can use it instead of the regular `pr` reference. This solution requires that the `ProductSmartStub` is deployed on the clientside. There is, however, no obstacle to sending the smart stub to the clientside. We have to extend the `Product` interface:

```
import java.rmi.RemoteException;
import javax.ejb.*;


public interface Product extends ProductIntf, EJBObject {
    public ProductIntf getSmartStub() throws RemoteException;
}
```

We also have to implement the method in the `ProductBean` class:

```
import javax.ejb.*;
import javax.rmi.*;
import javax.naming.*;

abstract public class ProductBean implements EntityBean {
    private EntityContext ctx;
    ...
    public ProductIntf getSmartStub() {
        EJBObject eo = ctx.getEJBObject();
        Product p = (Product) PortableRemoteObject.narrow(eo, Product.class);
        return (ProductIntf) new ProductSmartStub(p);
    }
    ...
}
```

The client can now use the following code to obtain the smart stub:

```
    Product pr = (Product) PortableRemoteObject.narrow
                            (home.create(...), Product.class);
    ProductIntf prSmart = pr.getSmartStub();
```

The only imperfection of the smart stub is that it does not implement the base `EJBObject` methods, which are: `remove()`, `getEJBHome()`, `getPrimaryKey()`, `getHandle()`, and `isIdentical()`. For these methods we have to use the direct reference (`pr` in our example).

To make the smart stub support even those methods, the simplest solution would be to declare them in the `ProductIntf` interface and implement them in the `ProductSmartStub` class (actually we just have to delegate them). This solution however is not very nice, because we would have to implement these five methods in all smart stubs.

A better solution is to use inheritance. Therefore we have to redesign our example a little more. We will add the `SmartStub` interface and the `SmartStubImpl` class. The latter will implement the `Serializable` interface. The `ProductIntf` will inherit from the `SmartStub` and the `ProductSmartStub` will inherit from the `SmartStubImpl`. The whole design is shown in the following diagram:

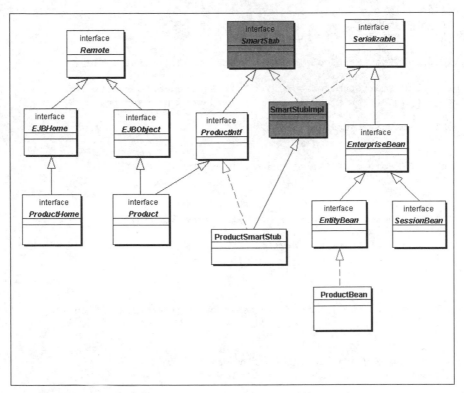

The `SmartStub` interface defines the five methods (the same as in the `EJBObject` interface):

```
import javax.ejb.*;
import java.rmi.RemoteException;

public interface SmartStub {
    public EJBHome getEJBHome() throws RemoteException;
    public Object getPrimaryKey() throws RemoteException;
    public void remove() throws RemoteException, RemoveException;
    public Handle getHandle() throws RemoteException;
    public boolean isIdentical(EJBObject obj) throws RemoteException;
}
```

The `ProductIntf` has to inherit from the `SmartStub` interface:

```
import java.rmi.RemoteException;

public interface ProductIntf extends SmartStub {
    ...
    public void setPrice(double myPrice) throws RemoteException;
    public double getPrice() throws RemoteException;
    ...
    public double getAvaliableQuantity() throws RemoteException;
}
```

We have to implement the `SmartStub` interface, which we will do in the `SmartStubImpl` class. Again, the simplest approach is to delegate the requests. However we may consider caching the primary key (`getPrimaryKey()` method):

```java
import java.io.*;
import javax.ejb.*;
import java.rmi.RemoteException;

public class SmartStubImpl implements SmartStub, Serializable {

    protected SmartStub ref = null;      // Reference to remote interface
    private Object pk = null;            // Cached primary key

    public SmartStubImpl(){
    }

    public EJBHome getEJBHome() throws RemoteException {
        return ref.getEJBHome();
    }

    public Object getPrimaryKey() throws RemoteException {
        if (pk == null)
            pk = ref.getPrimaryKey();

        return pk;
    }

    public void remove() throws RemoteException, RemoveException {
        ref.remove();
    }

    public Handle getHandle() throws RemoteException {
        return ref.getHandle();
    }

    public boolean isIdentical(EJBObject obj) throws RemoteException {
        return ref.isIdentical(obj);
    }
}
```

Some changes are required to the `ProductSmartStub`, which now inherits from the `SmartStubImpl`, too:

```java
import java.io.Serializable;
import java.rmi.RemoteException;

public class ProductSmartStub extends SmartStubImpl implements ProductIntf {

    // Reference to Product omitted
    private double price = 0;
    private boolean priceCached = false;

    public ProductSmartStub(Product ref) {
```

```
        this.ref = ref;
    }

    public void setPrice(double myPrice) throws RemoteException {
        // Delegate the method to the server object
        ((Product)ref).setPrice(myPrice);
        // Update the cached value
        price = myPrice;
        priceCached = true;
    }

    public double getPrice() throws RemoteException {
        // Check if the price is chached
        if ( !priceCached ) {
          price = ((Product)ref).getPrice();
          priceCached = true;
        }
        // Return the cached value
        return price;
    }
    ...
    public double getAvaliableQuantity() throws RemoteException {
        // Delegate the method only
        return ((Product)ref).getAvaliableQuantity();
    }
    ...
    // Implement possible other methods, too.
    ...
}
```

The client can now safely invoke the five methods, defined in the `EJBObject`, using the `prSmart` handle, for example:

```
prSmart.remove();
```

Actually, the `getPrimaryKey()` method is even cached, thus further improving performance.

The described approach for implementing smart stubs is relatively simple and can significantly improve the performance, particularly if the clients often invoke methods from the remote component interface that can be effectively cached in the smart stub.

Bean Deployment

One of the most important factors we can influence by the deployment is the pool size. Typically, we will have to specify the minimum (or initial) and maximum numbers of bean instances in the pool. Determining the right number is tricky. A small number of instances will result in heavy passivation and activation by the container, thus lowering the performance. Too large a number on the other hand will waste resources. Selecting the ideal number of instances would prevent excessive context switching and would not leave any instances unused.

We can use profilers to identify values close to the ideal number. As a rule of thumb, it is appropriate to select as many session or message-driven bean instances as we have simultaneous clients (or a few more). This limits the time that a client has to wait due to unavailability of free instances. For entity beans, we should identify how many different instances of the same entity bean we use simultaneously.

It is possible to define the timeout value for stateful session and entity beans. This value defines how long a bean instance will remain activated. After this time, the container will remove the instance. To reach the optimal value it is useful to know the delay between the client method invocations. The worst possible value is a little lower than the delay between method invocations to the same stateful session or entity bean. This requires unnecessary passivation and activation.

Another important deployment property, if offered by the container vendor, is transaction isolation. Selecting the highest isolation level will result in poor performance. Selecting a too low an isolation level can, on the other hand, result in data inconsistency. For the best performance, we should select the lowest isolation level that will guarantee error-free operation.

We should also consider shared or unshared database use. If we define the database as not shared, the container can save database lookups, thus speeding the performance. On the other hand, if we mark a database as not shared when in reality it *is* shared, this can lead to data corruption.

Sometimes we can select whether the persistent storage is updated at the end of a transaction only, or also during a transaction. The first option usually offers better performance, because it avoids unnecessary database updates. However, if we use the TRANSACTION_READ_UNCOMMITED isolation level, we might want the changes to be saved during the transaction too.

If our EJB container supports it, we can define entity beans as read-only. Read-only entity beans are never modified by an EJB client. They can, however, be modified directly through a database access, usually by a legacy application. The application server does not call the ejbStore() method on a read-only bean, thus improving the performance. In BEA WebLogic, for example, we can denote beans as read-only through concurrency-strategy deployment parameter, which we have to set to ReadOnly. If our application server does not provide this option, we could do it ourselves by using bean-managed persistence and not implementing the body of the ejbStore() method. Read-only entity beans cannot take part in transactions.

Some application servers support a setting for entity beans that are updated only occasionally. Therefore we have to define the interval in which the data is reread from the persistent storage. This saves database lookups, because the container can omit calling the ejbLoad() method too often. Again, we could implement this approach ourselves, if the application server does not provide this option.

Underlying Technology

When considering performance, we cannot forget the general performance guidelines. We should use the implementation techniques in Java known as **performance optimal**. Some of these include avoiding creating garbage, which results in less garbage collection. We can achieve that by reusing existing objects and avoiding creating unnecessary temporary objects. Further we should avoid memory leaks, that is, referenced unused objects, which cannot be garbage collected. We should avoid using finalizers for regular Java objects, and we should use performance-optimized classes where possible, like StringBuffers instead of Strings, etc. Use class preloading to avoid sending the class files over the wire. Further, use static and final keywords wherever possible.

These are only some of the options; we can find more general performance guidelines in related literature, like *Java Performance Tuning* by Jack Shirazi, from O'Reilly, ISBN 0-596-00015-4 (or see http://www.javaperformancetuning.com/); or *Enterprise Java Performance* by Steven L. Halter and Steven J. Munroe, from Prentice Hall, ISBN 0-13-017296-0.

We can influence the performance with the selection of underlying technologies as well. When we select the Java SDK, it is safe to assume that newer versions offer better performance. Java 2 SDK version 1.3 performs in almost all cases better than 1.2, which in turn performs better than version 1.1. Different implementations of the JVM offer different performance. Some performance tests have shown that the IBM JVM performs better than the others (take a look at http://www.volano.com/benchmarks.html). Just-in-time (JIT) compilers enormously speed the execution of Java programs. For EJBs, consider using the HotSpot Server JVM (see http://developer.java.sun.com/ developer/technicalArticles/Programming/JVMPerf/). However, make sure that your application server provider supports it.

JVM execution parameters influence the performance, too. If we can choose, we should select the native threads, which offer much better performance than green threads. Green threads refers to lightweight threads managed by the JVM itself, and not mapped onto multiple operating-system threads. We can tune the heap size, which can result in performance improvements. Heap size indirectly determines how often the garbage collection will be done. With Java 2, larger heap sizes often perform better because of the improved garbage collector algorithms. The heap size should, however, not be so large as to force the operating system virtual memory management into doing memory swapping. The best way is to try different heap sizes. Some application servers, like WebLogic, even support clustering on a single computer, which can prevent response blackouts due to garbage collection.

Regarding the hardware configuration, we should identify the appropriate number of physical tiers. From the performance standpoint it is desirable to combine the middle tier with the data persistence tier to form a single physical tier. We should collocate the components that have high affinities into the same container, possibly one that optimizes method invocations, and we should use local interfaces if possible. The performance can also be improved by clustering. In enterprise computing it is also very important to use the most powerful computers in the middle and the data persistence tier.

Role of Containers and Application Servers

It is clear that EJB technology, containers, application servers, and hardware equipment cannot compensate for bad design. However, containers and application servers can have a large influence on performance. The application servers provide the environment in which the EJBs execute, and JVMs and the use of JIT compilers can influence the performance. Still, in enterprise computing the processing overhead is not the most limiting to performance. More important is the communication overhead. Therefore it is particularly important that the application server provides a capable ORB on one hand and efficient communication to the persistent storage on the other hand. The application server is responsible for instance and resource management, transaction, concurrency, and security management. All these factors influence the performance.

Easing Remote Method Invocation Problems

To access EJBs via remote component interface, remote method invocation is needed, which adds several layers and is much slower than local method invocation. In spite of that, it is important that the ORB, which is responsible for remote method invocations, performs as fast as possible.

The author of this chapter has done several performance comparisons of different ORBs, including RMI, RMI-IIOP, and several CORBA implementations. In most cases there are only minor differences using very simple remote method invocations. Simple remote method invocations are those that return or accept only a few primitive data types. The differences are more significant with more complex remote invocations, for example when transferring larger amounts of data or using complex user-defined classes. Such complex classes are common in modern object-oriented applications.

When comparing RMI and IDL in Java 2 version 1.2, it has been found that RMI performs much better. In Java 2 version 1.3 the performance of IDL has been improved considerably. Now the RMI, IDL, and the newly added RMI-IIOP performances are on a par, and they are improved compared to the version 1.2. This is an additional reason to use newer Java SDKs. Large differences have been observed between commercial CORBA implementations, too. The differences were as high as six-fold. Because most commercial EJB application servers incorporate the ORBs previously offered as standalone products, these numbers are important for EJBs as well. To learn more, have a look at http://lisa.uni-mb.si/~juric/, where you can find measurement results and benchmark code.

There are several factors that can cause such differences in performance. The major sources of overhead lie in ineffective marshaling, unmarshaling, and dispatching, particularly for larger data sizes. Some ORBs have shown poor thread management algorithms. Bottlenecks can also be identified by using low-level communication routines, often accessed via Java Native Interface (JNI). For EJB developers, perhaps the most important feature is the identification and implementation of local optimizations. Local optimizations can enormously speed up the communication between collocated beans. Some application server ORBs already provide this feature; let's hope others will follow soon.

When we consider measuring the performance of remote method invocations, we should carefully plan our measurement procedure and be sure to use method invocations that are most often used in our applications. We should not forget to use complex user defined data types, try to transfer graphs of related objects by value, and measure the maximum data throughput. The latter is important if we plan to transfer larger amounts of data in method invocations over the network.

The response time alone is not, however, a representative measure for total application server performance. When the method invocation request is delivered through the ORB, it is delegated to the actual bean instance. Before the delegation, several algorithms, like instance management, transaction boundary, and security, are executed. All this requires time. On the other hand, instance management algorithms are those that guarantee a large number of clients will be able to use our applications simultaneously. In the context of enterprise computing, the performance degradation by concurrent clients – or scalability – is much more important than the response time alone.

Scalability

Application server providers can do several things to improve scalability. It seems that the most important is that instance management algorithms should be as efficient as possible. These algorithms could, for example, automatically profile the bean usage and determine the optimal number of instances in the pool. However, we soon realize that the resource management algorithms, the transaction and concurrency management, security, and others play a very important role, too.

Particularly efficient data caching algorithms can improve the performance of entity beans considerably. We should not forget the JBDC drivers, and the DBMS performance. We should identify what is responsible for transaction management (DBMS, TP monitor, etc.) and for concurrency control, and examine the needs for distributed transactions.

As there are so many factors that influence performance, it is very difficult to define testing procedures that would be as objective as possible and would include all mentioned aspects. The ECperf (http://java.sun.com/j2ee/ecperf/) promises to define the standard performance load for benechmarking application servers. However, at the time of writing this chapter it has not been finished yet. We will have to wait and see if the ECperf will objectively represent the actual performance of application servers. We should still watch out for ECperf-focused performance optimizations that will allow application servers to achieve better results on the benchmarks.

In the meantime we can develop application prototypes that imitate the final application design and test the performance ourselves. Only then will we know exactly which application server is best suited for us. Obviously, measuring performance requires time and resources; therefore we have to decide how sensitive to performance our application is.

Practical Guidelines for Achieving Scalability

We have to ensure that our application will have acceptable response times during peak usage, when there will be a large number of concurrent clients. We also have to ensure that our application will not became too slow as the persistent data in the databases grows over the years.

Therefore it is a good idea if we deploy the application in a typical environment, which includes hardware, operating system, and application server. We have to estimate the average amount of persistent data and the average number of simultaneous clients. We will not be able to measure all usage scenarios so we have to carefully select the most important ones. Furthermore, we will have to simulate the high client load using a load-testing tool. Note that the simulated number of concurrent clients usually represents a much larger number than the number of real-world clients. The load testing tools typically wait only a short time before they invoke methods again, whereas typical users have longer thinking times. To simulate a large number of records in the persistence storage, we will write scripts that populate the database.

Varying the Size of Persistent Storage

There are two variables to consider: the number of concurrent users and the size of the persistent data. To be able to infer to the possible bottlenecks, we therefore have to plan our response time measurements in two ways. First, we have to fix the number of clients and second, vary the size of the persistent storage. We usually select a small number of concurrent clients. Selecting only a single client would often not load the system enough to identify the persistent storage problems. Selecting too many concurrent clients would, on the other hand, make it very difficult to track down whether the response time becoming poor is a consequence of large database or large number of clients. With a small number of simultaneous clients we can measure the response times for:

❑   Average amount of data

❑   Large amount of data

❑   Extreme amount of data (for example, five times more than we can imagine to have in five years)

The response times should not degrade too much when moving from average to large and extreme amounts of data. If using a capable RDBMS, the response times should not differ too much from linear growth. If they do, particularly if they increase exponentially, then we probably have not indexed columns in our database accordingly. If we use bean-managed persistence, we can quickly find out if the columns are indexed. With the help of EXPLAIN, we can see when we must add indexes to tables to get a faster SELECT which, in turn, uses indexes to find the records. If we use container-managed persistence, then we have to figure out the necessary columns for indexing through examination of finder methods. We also have to get familiar with the persistence schema used by the application server.

If indexing the database columns does not help, we have two possibilities. Either our hardware configuration on which the RDBMS is executing is too slow, or the RDBMS itself cannot handle this amount of data. In the latter case, we have to think of changing the RDBMS vendor. To identify the hardware bottleneck we will typically observe the following three parameters:

❑ CPU usage

❑ Memory usage

❑ I/O usage

If the average CPU usage reaches more than 90 percent, then it is obvious that we need a faster CPU, or we need more CPUs, if applicable. Again, we can think of clustering. If the memory is fully used, then the operating system might be performing virtual memory management, which heavily influences the performance. In this case, expanding the memory is the best way to improve performance. If the I/O (like network connections, disk I/O, etc.) is overused, we have to improve on that. However, it is sometimes difficult to measure the average I/O usage. Therefore, as a rule of thumb, low CPU usage often implies I/O bottlenecks.

Varying the Number of Concurrent Clients

When we have fixed the persistent storage bottlenecks (if any), we can continue with the concurrent user tests. Now we would set the size of the database to the average number of records and vary the number of concurrent clients. As with varying the persistent storage, increasing the number of clients and measuring the response times usually takes place in three steps:

❑ Average number of concurrent clients

❑ Expected maximum number of concurrent clients

❑ Extreme number of concurrent clients

If we find that the response times increase exponentially, this most often indicates bottlenecks in the architecture and in the application. Before tracking these, however, we can check the hardware configuration of the application server, using the same procedure as when we checked the RDBMS hardware. Then we have to check the application server configuration. If we still do not succeed, we have to look for the bottlenecks in our application architecture. We can go through the design and code and try to identify the cases where we have used the techniques described in this chapter as performance ineffective. The fastest way, however, is to use a profiler, for example OptimizeIt from JProbe. With a profiler we can easily get the list of most time consuming classes, where we can start searching for bottlenecks. We also get information on memory usage, garbage collection, number of threads, etc. To make our measurements more accurate, we can also include more than three levels of workload. For those, who want to learn more, there are several books available on performance tuning:

❑ *Professional Java Programming* by Brett Spell, from Wrox Press, ISBN 1-861003-82-X.

❑ *Java Platform Performance: Strategies and Tactics* by Steve Wilson, Jeff Kesselman, from Addison-Wesley, ISBN 0-201-70969-4.

❑ *High-Performance Java Platform Computing: Multithreaded and Networked Programming* by George K. Thiruvathukal, Thomas W. Christopher, from Prentice Hall, ISBN 0-13-016164-0.

❑ *Java Performance and Scalability, Volume 1: Server-Side Programming Techniques* by Dov Bulka, from Addison-Wesley, ISBN 0-201-70429-3.

Summary

In this chapter we have discussed several strategies and techniques that influence the performance Enterprise JavaBeans. We have seen that we should start to care for performance as early as possible; it is important not to defer the performance questions until the final implementation. Specifically, we looked at the following issues:

- ❑ The discussion of underlying concepts has shown that remote method invocations are much more time consuming than local invocations inside a single JVM. Therefore we should be aware of remote invocations and control their number. We have learned how to minimize them with coarse-grained interfaces and value objects, which we can use for input validation too, in order to further improve the performance.

- ❑ We have also seen that the coarse-grained approach alone does not solve all the problems. Therefore we have introduced responsibility driven design and distributed façades. We have learned that we should use entity beans through façade beans, and how local interfaces and dependent objects can improve performance.

- ❑ We have become familiar with instance management algorithms. Understanding how they work helps us understand the possible performance bottlenecks. We have seen why the size of instance pools is important, how can we control serialization by the stateful session beans, and we have discussed how to reuse resources.

- ❑ We have learned how to improve the performance of entity beans, how to prevent unnecessary database lookups and updates, how to implement lazy-loading beans, and when to access the database directly.

- ❑ Transactions offer several performance traps. We have identified them, learned to use appropriate transaction isolation levels to avoid deadlocks, and learned to identify transactions marked for rollback.

- ❑ Improving the remote method invocation can be important, therefore we have discussed techniques for accelerating marshaling and implementing smart stubs. As a side effect, we have seen how to make EJB easily accessible from CORBA applications.

- ❑ We have discussed bean deployment parameters and the underlying technologies that influence performance.

- ❑ We have also identified the role of containers and application servers and pointed to some important issues when measuring the performance.

- ❑ Last, but not least, we have collected some practical guidelines for achieving scalability.

The performance of EJB applications is important and the EJB technology requires that we follow some rules in their development. With these rules, we can build large, mission-critical, EJB-based information systems that offer acceptable performance.

In the next chapter we will revisit the subject of EJB persistence and look at how we to use BMP to model more complex persistence mappings.

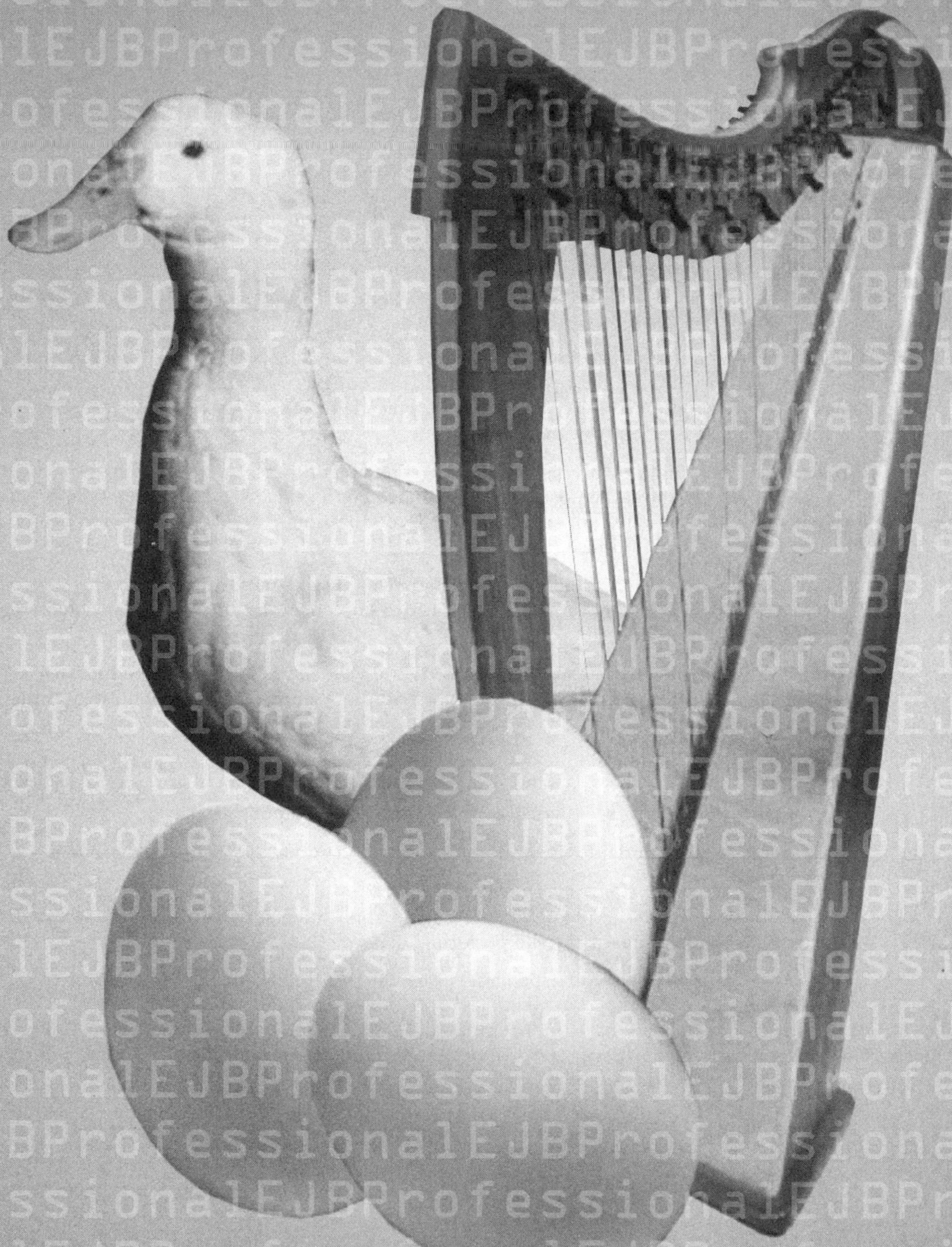

16

Advanced Bean-Managed Persistence

The EJB specification allows for the automatic persistence of entity beans using the container-managed persistence (CMP) contract. With the improvements to CMP laid out in the EJB 2.0 specification, CMP entity beans should be useful for most applications. The specification also outlines a bean-managed persistence contract, which allows an entity bean writer to implement the persistence for a bean.

The CMP contract has many advantages over the BMP solution. The time and effort saved by automatic persistence generation is the most obvious, but the potential for increased overall performance and scalability of the beans using 2.0 CMP is another important one. Unlike the EJB 1.1 specification, the new 2.0 CMP model allows the persistence implementation to use many optimizations previously achievable only using BMP. Also because the CMP implementation is not necessarily bound by the programming restrictions of BMP, it can take advantages of features like data caching, which a BMP cannot access.

There are some situations, however, where BMP is necessary. Your persistence manager provider may not support the data source in your application, or your data may be too complex to map using the automatic method. Using BMP can also be necessary to achieve better control over the performance of particular data operations that are common in your application. Since CMP can usually be used in the simple situations, it is the complex mappings that are important in BMP.

In this chapter we will be looking at the following topics:

- ❏ Mapping entity beans to a single table in a relational database
- ❏ Mapping entity beans to multiple tables
- ❏ Issues surrounding the use of lookup tables
- ❏ How to cope with object relationships
- ❏ Using value objects

While we call these mappings complex, the table structures will be similar to those commonly found in existing relational database systems. The examples will require understanding the BMP entity bean contract, which is present in Chapters 4 and 5 of this book. They will also require basic knowledge of relational database systems. For more information on relational databases, refer to a book on the subject, such as *Designing Relational Database Systems* by Rebecca Riordan, from Microsoft Press, ISBN 0-7356-0634-X.

Mapping an Entity to a Single Table

The simplest type of persistence maps an entity bean onto a single table. For every column declared in the table, there is a corresponding field declared in the bean. The lifecycle methods of the bean perform their corresponding database function in order to persist the bean's fields. This type of mapping is relatively simple, but we will use it to highlight some basic practices that are good for all BMP implementations and as a base case for more complex scenarios.

A Simple Example: A Product Bean

For our example we will use a Product bean. This example bean is very simple and includes a name, description, and price for the product, as well as the product's unique ID. It also contains an image for the product, which is represented in both the object and the table as an array of bytes:

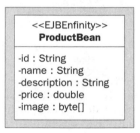

The table structure is a single table that includes all of the fields of the bean. The id field is declared as a primary key for the table. In the database table diagrams used in this chapter, the primary key field for the table will be underlined. The diagrams will contain the datatype names used by Oracle's relational database. Data types differ slightly between databases, but any database should support equivalent types. The Product table for our example is structured as follows:

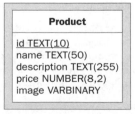

A Simple Base Class for Entity Beans

All of our entity bean examples in the chapter will share a common base class. This class provides several things:

❑   It implements the `setEntityContext()` and `unsetEntityContext()` methods from the
    `EntityBean` interface.

❑   It tracks the entity context and exposes it through a protected variable, `entityContext`.

❑   It also contains the utility methods `getConnection()` and `cleanUp()`, which we will use
    from our bean.

Here is the code for the `AbstractEntityBase`:

```
package base;

import javax.ejb.*;
import java.sql.*;
import javax.sql.DataSource;
import javax.naming.InitialContext;
import javax.naming.NamingException;

public abstract class AbstractEntityBase implements EntityBean {

  protected EntityContext entityContext;

  public void setEntityContext(EntityContext inContext) {
    this.entityContext = inContext;
  }

  public void unsetEntityContext() {
    this.entityContext = null;
  }
```

The base class also provides two utility methods to simplify the interactions with the database. First the
`getConnection()` method hides retrieving the datasource object from the bean's environment:

```
protected Connection getConnection() throws SQLException {
  try {
    InitialContext ic = new InitialContext();
    DataSource ds = (DataSource) ic.lookup("java:comp/env/jdbc/Database");
    return ds.getConnection();
  } catch (NamingException ex) {
    throw new EJBException(ex);
  }
}
```

When using the JDBC API to interact with the database, it is very important to close all of the JDBC
objects we have used. Many JDBC drivers will automatically free database resources when the objects
are garbage collected, but garbage collection is unpredictable and waiting until garbage collection to
free these resources may have a negative impact on your application performance and the overall
performance of the database. Failure to do so may cause memory leaks in both the driver and in the
database itself. We have taken an approach that uses a single `finally` block in the lifecycle method. It
uses nested `finally` blocks in the `cleanUp()` method to ensure that all objects that have been created
are properly closed, regardless of error occurrences:

```
protected void cleanUp(Connection conn, PreparedStatement ps,
                       ResultSet rs) {
  try {
    try {
      if (rs != null) {
```

```
          rs.close();
        }
      } finally {
        try {
          if (ps != null) {
            ps.close();
          }
        } finally {
          if (conn != null) {
            conn.close();
          }
        }
      }
    } catch (SQLException ex) {
      throw new EJBException(ex);
    }
  }
}
```

The ProductBean Remote Interface

Of course, no enterprise bean is complete without its home and remote interfaces. For our bean these are fairly self explainatory. The field accessors are exposed through the remote interface, as follows:

```java
package singleTable;

import java.rmi.RemoteException;
import javax.ejb.EJBObject;

public interface Product extends EJBObject {

  public String getId() throws RemoteException;

  public String getName() throws RemoteException;
  public void setName(String inName) throws RemoteException;

  public String getDescription() throws RemoteException;
  public void setDescription(String inDesc) throws RemoteException;

  public double getPrice() throws RemoteException;
  public void setPrice(double inPrice) throws RemoteException;

  public byte[] getImage() throws RemoteException;
  public void setImage(byte[] inImage) throws RemoteException;

}
```

The ProductBean Home Interface

The home interface declares the findByPrimaryKey() and create() methods. Here is our home interface for the Product bean:

```java
package singleTable;

import java.rmi.RemoteException;
import javax.ejb.*;

public interface ProductHome extends EJBHome {
```

```
      public Product findByPrimaryKey(String id) throws FinderException,
                                                         RemoteException;

      public Product create(String inId) throws CreateException,
                                                 RemoteException;

      public Product create(String inId, String inName, String inDesc,
                            double inPrice,
                            byte[] inImage) throws CreateException,
                                                   RemoteException;

}
```

The ProductBean Implementation Class

```java
package singleTable;

import javax.ejb.*;
import java.sql.*;
import javax.naming.InitialContext;
import javax.naming.NamingException;

import base.AbstractEntityBase;

public class ProductBean extends AbstractEntityBase {

  private String id;
  private String name;
  private String description;
  private double price;
  private byte[] image;

  public String getId() {
    return id;
  }

  public String getName() {
    return name;
  }
  public void setName(String inName) {
    this.name = inName;
  }

  public String getDescription() {
    return description;
  }
  public void setDescription(String inDesc) {
    this.description = inDesc;
  }

  public double getPrice() {
    return price;
  }
  public void setPrice(double inPrice) {
    this.price = inPrice;
  }

  public byte[] getImage() {
    return image;
```

```
    }
    public void setImage(byte[] inImage) {
      this.image = inImage;
    }
```

Several of the required lifecycle methods do not map to persistence operations. In the `ejbActivate()` method, the bean acquires a reference to the primary key field from the `entityContext` instance. The `ejbPassivate()` method is used to set reference fields to `null` to aid in garbage collection:

```
public void ejbActivate() {
  id = (String) entityContext.getPrimaryKey();
}

public void ejbPassivate() {
  id = null;
  name = null;
  description = null;
  image = null;
}
```

The `ejbFindByPrimaryKey()` method does not actually select any data from the table. It merely checks that a record matching the primary key exists. The following is an implementation of `findByPrimaryKey()` for the Product bean. Notice the unused constant 1 in the SELECT clause in place of any actual database column:

```
public String ejbFindByPrimaryKey(String id) throws FinderException {
  Connection conn = null;
  PreparedStatement ps = null;
  ResultSet rs = null;
  try {
    conn = getConnection();
    ps = conn.prepareStatement("SELECT 1 FROM product WHERE id = ?");
    ps.setString(1, id);
    rs = ps.executeQuery();
    if (rs.next()) {
      return id;
    } else {
      throw new ObjectNotFoundException();
    }
  } catch (SQLException ex) {
    throw new EJBException(ex);
  } finally {
    cleanUp(conn, ps, rs);
  }
}
```

The `ejbLoad()` method selects a single row from the database and sets the fields of the bean with data from the row. We must use the `next()` method on the `ResultSet` to ensure that the query returns at least one record:

```
public void ejbLoad() {
  Connection conn = null;
  PreparedStatement ps = null;
  ResultSet rs = null;
  try {
```

```
        conn = getConnection();
        ps = conn.prepareStatement("SELECT name, description, price, image "
                                    + "FROM product WHERE id = ?");
      ps.setString(1, id);
      rs = ps.executeQuery();
      if (!rs.next()) {
        throw new NoSuchEntityException();
      }
      name = rs.getString(1);
      description = rs.getString(2);
      price = rs.getDouble(3);
      image = rs.getBytes(4);
    } catch (SQLException ex) {
      throw new EJBException(ex);
    } finally {
      cleanUp(conn, ps, rs);
    }
  }
```

The `ejbStore()` method updates the database record based on the fields of the bean. Later in the chapter, we will make a significant improvement to this method by tracking field modifications. When executing this and all other statements that alter the database, we will check the row count to be sure that only the proper row was updated. While this is strictly unnecessary, as a properly written SQL statement will be unable to update more than one row, it is good to take a safety-first approach when altering the database:

```
public void ejbStore() {

    Connection conn = null;
    PreparedStatement ps = null;
    try {
      conn = getConnection();
      ps = conn.prepareStatement("UPDATE product " +
                                  "SET name=?, description=?, " +
                                  "price=?, image=? " +
                                  "WHERE id = ?");
      ps.setString(1, name);
      ps.setString(2, description);
      ps.setDouble(3, price);
      ps.setBytes(4, image);
      ps.setString(5, id);
      if (ps.executeUpdate() != 1) {
        throw new EJBException("Wrong update count");
      }
    } catch (SQLException ex) {
      throw new EJBException(ex);
    } finally {
      cleanUp(conn, ps, null);
    }
  }
}
```

The `ejbCreate()` method is a slightly more interesting case. The EJB specification allows the bean to provide more than one `create()` method for the bean. However, since there is a single table, a single INSERT statement will generally suffice for all cases.

Our implementation includes a separate method, `insertRecord()`, which contains the INSERT statement. Each call to any of the `ejbCreate()` methods will initialize all of the fields of the bean , including the primary key, based on its input parameters. They then call `insertRecord()` to actually perform the insert. Unlike CMP beans, a BMP bean is not guaranteed that all of its fields will be initialized to their Java defaults. An `ejbCreate()` method must initialize every field, or risk inserting invalid data into the database:

```
public String ejbCreate(String inId) throws CreateException {
  this.id = inId;
  this.name = null;
  this.description = null;
  this.price = 0;
  this.image = null;
  insertRecord();
  return id;
}
public void ejbPostCreate(String inId) throws CreateException {}

public String ejbCreate(String inId, String inName, String inDesc,
                        double inPrice,
                        byte[] inImage) throws CreateException {
  this.id = inId;
  this.name = inName;
  this.description = inDesc;
  this.price = inPrice;
  this.image = inImage;
  insertRecord();
  return id;
}

public void ejbPostCreate(String inId, String inName, String inDesc,
                          double inPrice,
                          byte[] inImage) throws CreateException {}

public void insertRecord() {
  Connection conn = null;
  PreparedStatement ps = null;
  try {
    conn = getConnection();
    ps = conn.prepareStatement("INSERT INTO product VALUES(?,?,?,?,?)");
    ps.setString(1, id);
    ps.setString(2, name);
    ps.setString(3, description);
    ps.setDouble(4, price);
    ps.setBytes(5, image);
    if (ps.executeUpdate() != 1) {
      throw new EJBException("Incorrect insert count");
    }
  } catch (SQLException ex) {
    throw new EJBException(ex);
  } finally {
    cleanUp(conn, ps, null);
  }
}
```

The `ejbRemove()` method executes a DELETE statement to remove the record from the database:

```
public void ejbRemove() throws RemoveException {
  Connection conn = null;
  PreparedStatement ps = null;
  try {
    conn = getConnection();
    ps = conn.prepareStatement("DELETE FROM product WHERE id = ?");
    ps.setString(1, id);
    if (ps.executeUpdate() != 1) {
      throw new EJBException("Wrong delete count");
    }
  } catch (SQLException ex) {
    throw new EJBException(ex);
  } finally {
    cleanUp(conn, ps, null);
  }
}
```

The Deployment Descriptor

Since this bean is a simple BMP entity bean, the deployment descriptor entry is also simple. To reduce repetition, we'll only show the deployment descriptor once in this chapter. As with all the code in the book, the deployment descriptors are available in the code download:

```
<ejb-jar>
  <enterprise-beans>
    <entity>
      <ejb-name>singleTable.Product</ejb-name>
      <home>singleTable.ProductHome</home>
      <remote>singleTable.Product</remote>
      <ejb-class>singleTable.ProductBean</ejb-class>

      <persistence-type>Bean</persistence-type>
      <prim-key-class>java.lang.String</prim-key-class>

      <reentrant>False</reentrant>

      <resource-ref>
        <res-ref-name>jdbc/Database</res-ref-name>
        <res-type>javax.sql.DataSource</res-type>
        <res-auth>Container</res-auth>
      </resource-ref>
    </entity>
  </enterprise-beans>

  <assembly-descriptor>
    <container-transaction>
      <method>
        <ejb-name>singleTable.Product</ejb-name>
        <method-intf>Remote</method-intf>
        <method-name>*</method-name>
```

```
        </method>
        <method>
          <ejb-name>singleTable.Product</ejb-name>
          <method-intf>Home</method-intf>
          <method-name>*</method-name>
        </method>
        <trans-attribute>Required</trans-attribute>
      </container-transaction>
    </assembly-descriptor>
  </ejb-jar>
```

Basic Improvements

Our product bean is now fully functional, but it is still missing two basic features that can be a part of any BMP implementation.

The isModified flag

In the EJB lifecycle, the container will always call `ejbStore()` to synchronize any changed state. However, in many situations the persistent data of the bean is not changed as a result of the current transaction. In this case the bean will execute an unnecessary update statement, which has no effect on the data. It will, however, still incur all of the overhead associated with an update statement.

In order to avoid performing unnecessary database updates, all BMP beans should track whether or not they have modified their state. This is one of the simplest optimizations to implement, and one of the most effective. Some containers will provide this functionality for BMP beans through custom features. Usually the container will allow individual remote methods to be declared as read-only methods in a custom deployment descriptor. The container will not call `ejbStore()` on a bean if all the methods called on that bean in a transaction are read-only methods.

Unfortunately, however, this functionality is not portable between containers. A portable version of this feature can be implemented by keeping a single `isModified` field in your bean. Methods that change the persistent fields of the bean will set the `isModified` field to `true`, as in this example:

```
// rest of variables
  private boolean isModified;
// rest of bean
  public void setName(String inName) {
    isModified = true;
    this.name = inName;
  }
```

The same addition can be made to each of the set methods in the bean.

When the `ejbLoad()` method originally loads the data for the fields, it should set the `isModified` flag to `false`, indicating that the bean's fields are unchanged from the data in the database:

```
public void ejbLoad() {
  // set variables for connecting to database
  try {
    // make connection
    }
    // get data
```

```
            // set the modified flag to false after loading the data
            isModified = false;
        // rest of method
```

When `ejbStore()` is called, the update is only executed if the `isModified` flag is set to `true`. This way, if no set methods are called in the bean, the update method may be skipped:

```
public void ejbStore() {

    // only update the database if the bean has been modified
    if (isModified) {
        // rest of method
}
```

Using an `isModified` flag is an important part of creating most scalable and optimized BMP entity beans.

Simple Lazy Loading

Lazy loading is the process of delaying the loading of fields for the bean until they are actually needed. Usually the container calls `ejbLoad()` and the bean loads all of its persistent fields. Not all of the fields, however, are necessarily used during the current transaction. When one or more of the persistent fields take a particularly long time to load or take up a large amount of memory, then the application may perform better if loading the field is delayed until it is actually used. That way the time and memory are saved if the field is not used.

Good examples of fields where this technique is useful are images or large blocks of text. In a similar way to the `isModified` flag, we will add both an `imageLoaded` and `imageModified` flag to our bean. During the `ejbLoad()` method all the properties of the bean except for the image are loaded as before, and the `imageLoaded` flag is set to `false`:

```
    // rest of variables
    private boolean imageLoaded;
    private boolean imageModified;
    // rest of bean
    public void ejbLoad() {
        Connection conn = null;
        PreparedStatement ps = null;
        ResultSet rs = null;
        try {
            conn = getConnection();

            // select all fields except image
            ps = conn.prepareStatement("SELECT name, description, price "
                                    + "FROM product WHERE id = ?");
            ps.setString(1, id);
            rs = ps.executeQuery();
            if (!rs.next()) {
                throw new NoSuchEntityException();
            }
            name = rs.getString(1);
            description = rs.getString(2);
            price = rs.getDouble(3);
```

```
        // instead of loading the image, set the imageLoaded flag
        imageLoaded = false;

        // rest of method the same as before
```

A special loadImage() method is added to the bean. The loadImage() method will execute the SQL statement to load the image only if the imageLoaded flag is false. It will then set the flag to true to prevent performing the operation multiple times:

```java
public void loadImage() {
  if (!imageLoaded) {
    Connection conn = null;
    PreparedStatement ps = null;
    ResultSet rs = null;
    try {
      conn = getConnection();

      // select the image field
      ps = conn.prepareStatement("SELECT image FROM product " +
                                 "WHERE id = ?");
      ps.setString(1, id);
      rs = ps.executeQuery();
      if (!rs.next()) {
        throw new EJBException("Zero rows in load");
      }
      image = rs.getBytes(1);

      // set flags after loading the image
      imageLoaded = true;
      imageModified = false;
    } catch (SQLException ex) {
      throw new EJBException(ex);
    } finally {
      cleanUp(conn, ps, rs);
    }
  }
}
```

Before accessing the image field of the bean, the loadImage() method must be called to ensure that the image is loaded. Also, when the image field of the bean is set, the imageLoaded flag should be set to true. Otherwise on the next call to the getImage() method, the bean will overwrite the new value with the one from the database. We will also set the imageModified flag in the setImage() method, which will be used during the ejbStore() method. Here is the code for these methods:

```java
public byte[] getImage() {
  loadImage();
  return image;
}

public void setImage(byte[] image) {
  imageModified = true;
  imageLoaded = true;
```

```
    this.image = image;
}
```

During the `ejbStore()` method, the `imageModified` flag must be taken into account. The image field in the database should only be updated if the image field in the bean has been modified. Otherwise, we should omit the image from the update. To achieve this, we will alter the `ejbStore()` method as follows:

```
public void ejbStore() {
  if (isModified) {
    // get connection to database
    ps = conn.prepareStatement("UPDATE product " +
                               "SET name=?, description=?, price=?" +
                               (imageModified ? ", image=?" : "") +
                               " WHERE id = ?");
    ps.setString(1, name);
    ps.setString(2, description);
    ps.setDouble(3, price);
    if (imageModified) {
      ps.setBytes(4, image);
      ps.setString(5, id);
    } else {
      ps.setString(4, id);
    }
// rest of method as before
```

Notice how in the above code, the index for the `id` field changes based on the `imageLoaded` field. When lazy-loading a single field the above approach works. However, if we were using lazy loading for more than one field, then the number of possible combinations becomes too large to use the hard-coded constants for the indexes. In this case a counter variable can be used to track the current index while setting the parameters for the prepared statement.

While lazy loading can improve the performance of a bean when not accessing the lazy-loaded field, it does add some overhead when the bean does access the field. Our example will see a performance improvement when fields of the product other than the image are being used. However, when the image field is accessed, two SQL statements must be executed to load the bean, one within the `ejbLoad()` method and one in the `loadImage()` method. This adds an extra round-trip to the database. Lazy-oading also complicates the code for `ejbStore()`, which can cause code clarity and maintenance problems. Therefore when deciding whether to employ a lazy-loading strategy the tradeoff between the two cases must be considered in the particular context and usage scenarios of the application.

Mapping an Entity to Multiple Tables

If your database and object schemas are exact matches, the simple mapping technique above will work. Often, however, the object schema and the database schema differ. In databases, the primary design concerns are storage size and access speed. In order to achieve these goals, the structure of the database tables often does not match the structure of the logical entities they represent.

An example of this may be creating a separate table to include product details. In order to speed the process of a search, the main Product table has just enough information to search the products. The detailed information is stored in a separate table, which is only accessed if the end user decides to view details for a product. If large data structures like images or descriptions are optional, they may be stored in a separate table to avoid allocating storage space when the data is not present.

Objects, on the other hand, have a totally different set of design criteria. As much as possible, objects are modeled to resemble the logical entities they represent. The objects will attempt to encapsulate the actual structure of the tables, so that the user of the objects need not be exposed to the details of the database implementation. Even if a product and its details are stored in two separate tables, there will often only be a single Product object.

Objects also try to capture patterns in the data and increase reusability. For example, an address may be used both in the table for an order and the table for a customer. In the database, these fields have no explicit relationship, but in the objects they should be represented by a single Address class. Even when objects differ from database tables in their exterior design, internally they still need to take advantage of the database structure to increase performance and achieve scalability. To handle these more complicated cases, additional logic is required for the object's persistence.

Splitting the Product Bean Across Two Tables

We will use the product and product details scenario described above as our example. All of the information required for searching through products is stored in the main product table. This example is similar to our previous example, but the additional detail fields have been added to the Product bean. The image field has also been removed temporarily:

In the database this information is split into a product table and a product_details table. The product table includes the name of the product, a short description, and the type of product. Like most tables it also includes a primary key. The product_details table includes information like the size and weight of the product, and a longer description:

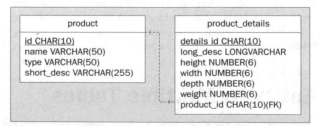

The product_details table also includes a product_id column that indicates which product the details are for. In a relational database a column that points to a primary key in another table is called a foreign key. By declaring it as a foreign key in the database, the database will make sure that every value in the foreign key column in the details table points to an existing primary key in the main table, thus maintaining referential integrity. This way, product_details records will be unable to point to non-existent records in the products table.

As a first step, let's decide what SQL statements are going to be used to implement the persistence. Here's a first attempt:

❏ Find:

```
SELECT 1 FROM Product
      WHERE id = ?
```

❏ Load:

```
SELECT name, type, short_desc, long_desc, height, width, depth, weight
      FROM Product, Product_Details
      WHERE product.id = Product_Details.product_id
      AND product.id = ?
```

❏ Store:

```
UPDATE Product SET name=?, type=?, short_desc=?
      WHERE id = ?

UPDATE Product_Details
      SET long_desc=?, height=?, width=?, depth=?, weight = ?
      WHERE product_id = ?
```

❏ Create:

```
INSERT INTO Product (id, name, type, short_desc) VALUES (?,?,?,?)

INSERT INTO Product_Details (details_id, long_desc, height, width,
                             depth, weight)
      VALUES (?,?,?,?,?,?)
```

❏ Remove:

```
DELETE FROM Product
      WHERE id = ?

DELETE FROM Product_Details
      WHERE product_id = ?
```

Notice that two UPDATE, INSERT, and DELETE statements are needed; one for each table. Most people's instinct is to use a single SELECT statement to join the tables and load the data for the bean, as above. However, by using a join both tables are accessed each time the bean is loaded. This defeats the original intent of the separate tables, which is to limit access to just the main table when the details are unused.

A better approach is to employ a lazy-loading strategy by using two separate SELECT statements instead. This allows the details table to be accessed only when the details are used. Just like the earlier lazy-loading example, there is some additional overhead to having two SQL statements, so there is a trade off between faster access time when not using the details, and slower time when using both the main table and the details table. Here is the SQL for the lazy-loading approach:

❏ Load:

```
SELECT name, type, short_desc
      FROM Product
      WHERE id = ?

SELECT long_desc, height, width, depth, weight
      FROM Product_Details
      WHERE product_id = ?
```

Let's fill in the code that surrounds these SQL statements.

The Changed EJB Code

This change is reflected in the remote and home interfaces as follows. Also notice that the `ejbCreate()` method that remains exposes both a product ID and a details ID field. We will improve on this later in the example.

The Changed ProductBean Remote Interface

We have changed the persistent fields of the bean, so the remote interface changes to include these changes:

```java
package detailRecord;

import java.rmi.RemoteException;
import javax.ejb.EJBObject;

public interface Product extends EJBObject {

  public String getId() throws RemoteException;

  public String getName() throws RemoteException;
  public void setName(String inName) throws RemoteException;

  public String getType() throws RemoteException;
  public void setType(String inType) throws RemoteException;

  public String getShortDescription() throws RemoteException;
  public void setShortDescription(String inType) throws RemoteException;

  public int getHeight() throws RemoteException;
  public void setHeight(int inHeight) throws RemoteException;

  public int getWidth() throws RemoteException;
  public void setWidth(int inWidth) throws RemoteException;

  public int getDepth() throws RemoteException;
  public void setDepth(int inDepth) throws RemoteException;

  public int getWeight() throws RemoteException;
  public void setWeight(int inWeight) throws RemoteException;

}
```

The Changed ProductBean Home Interface

```java
package detailRecord;

import java.rmi.RemoteException;
import javax.ejb.*;

public interface ProductHome extends EJBHome {

  public Product findByPrimaryKey(String id)
          throws FinderException, RemoteException;

  public Product create(String inProductId, String inDetailsId)
          throws CreateException, RemoteException;

}
```

The Changed ProductBean Implementation Class

Since we have changed the number and type of the persistent fields of the bean, the accessors must change accordingly. The accessors for the fields stored in the detail table follow the lazy-loading pattern discussed in the previous example and call `loadDetails()` before accessing their state. A `detailsLoaded` and `detailsModified` flag have also been added as part of the lazy-loading pattern. As before, we'll only show the changes:

```
package detailRecord;
// imports as before
public class ProductBean extends AbstractEntityBase {

  private String id;
  private String name;
  private String type;
  private String shortDescription;
  private String longDescription;
  private int height;
  private int width;
  private int depth;
  private int weight;

  private boolean mainModified;
  private boolean detailsLoaded;
  private boolean detailsModified;

// getId() and getName() unchanged
  public void setName(String inName) {
    mainModified = true;
    this.name = inName;
  }

  public String getType() {
    return type;
  }
  public void setType(String inType) {
    mainModified = true;
    this.type = inType;
  }

  public String getShortDescription() {
    return shortDescription;
  }
  public void setShortDescription(String inDesc) {
    mainModified = true;
    this.shortDescription = inDesc;
  }

  public String getLongDescription() {
    loadDetails();
    return longDescription;
  }
  public void setLongDescription(String inDesc) {
    loadDetails();
```

```
      detailsModified = true;
      this.longDescription = inDesc;
   }

   public int getHeight() {
     loadDetails();
     return height;
   }
   public void setHeight(int inHeight) {
     loadDetails();
     detailsModified = true;
     this.height = inHeight;
   }

   public int getWidth() {
     loadDetails();
     return width;
   }
   public void setWidth(int inWidth) {
     loadDetails();
     detailsModified = true;
     this.width = inWidth;
   }

   public int getDepth() {
     loadDetails();
     return depth;
   }
   public void setDepth(int inDepth) {
     loadDetails();
     detailsModified = true;
     this.depth = inDepth;
   }

   public int getWeight() {
     loadDetails();
     return weight;
   }
   public void setWeight(int inWeight) {
     loadDetails();
     detailsModified = true;
     this.weight = inWeight;
   }
```

The ejbLoad() method will load only from the main product table. The fields from the main product table are loaded as before. Rather than loading the detail fields, however, it sets the detailsLoaded flag to false, as follows:

```
   public void ejbLoad() {
     // make connection to database
     ps = conn.prepareStatement("SELECT name, type, short_desc " +
                                "FROM product WHERE id = ?");
     ps.setString(1, id);
     rs = ps.executeQuery();
```

```
      if (!rs.next()) {
        throw new NoSuchEntityException();
      }
      name = rs.getString(1);
      type = rs.getString(2);
      shortDescription = rs.getString(3);
      mainModified = false;
      detailsLoaded = false;
   // end of method the same
```

All of the fields from the product_details table are loaded in a special loadDetails() method. Any get and set methods for the details fields must call the loadDetails() method before accessing the persistent fields of the bean. The loadDetails() method will only execute a database query if the detailsLoaded flag is currently set to false:

```
public void loadDetails() {
  if (!detailsLoaded) {
    Connection conn = null;
    PreparedStatement ps = null;
    ResultSet rs = null;
    try {
      conn = getConnection();
      ps = conn.prepareStatement(
                   "SELECT long_desc, height, width, depth, weight" +
                   "FROM product_details WHERE product_id = ?");
      ps.setString(1, id);
      rs = ps.executeQuery();
      if (!rs.next()) {
        throw new EJBException("Zero rows in loadDetails");
      }
      longDescription = rs.getString(1);
      height = rs.getInt(2);
      width = rs.getInt(3);
      depth = rs.getInt(4);
      weight = rs.getInt(5);
      detailsLoaded = true;
      detailsModified = false;
    } catch (SQLException ex) {
      throw new EJBException(ex);
    } finally {
      cleanUp(conn, ps, rs);
    }
  }
}
```

When the ejbStore() method is called, each table is updated only if the corresponding fields have been altered. In the following code it is possible than one, both, or none of the tables are altered during the transaction:

```
public void ejbStore() {
  if (mainModified || detailsModified) {
    Connection conn = null;
    PreparedStatement ps = null;
```

```
        try {
          conn = getConnection();
          if (mainModified) {
            ps = conn.prepareStatement(
                        "UPDATE product SET name=?, type=?, short_desc=? " +
                        "WHERE id = ?");
            ps.setString(1, name);
            ps.setString(2, type);
            ps.setString(3, shortDescription);
            ps.setString(4, id);
            if (ps.executeUpdate() != 1) {
               throw new EJBException("Wrong update count");
            }
            ps.close();
            ps = null;
          }
          if (detailsModified) {
            ps = conn.prepareStatement("UPDATE product_details " +
                                  "SET long_desc=?, height=?, " +
                                  "width=?, depth=?,weight=? " +
                                  "WHERE product_id = ?");
            ps.setString(1, longDescription);
            ps.setInt(2, height);
            ps.setInt(3, width);
            ps.setInt(4, depth);
            ps.setInt(5, weight);
            ps.setString(6, id);
            if (ps.executeUpdate() != 1) {
               throw new EJBException("Wrong update count");
            }
          }
        }
      } // catch-finally block same as earlier
```

The ejbCreate() method will insert the corresponding data into both tables. Notice the details_id field for the second table that has been added to this code. This will be a subject for discussion later in this section:

```
    public String ejbCreate(String inProductId,
                            String inDetailsId) throws CreateException {
      this.id = inProductId;
      this.name = null;
      this.type = null;
      this.shortDescription = null;
      this.longDescription = null;
      this.height = 0;
      this.width = 0;
      this.depth = 0;
      this.weight = 0;
      insertRecord(inDetailsId);
      return id;
    }
```

The ejbRemove() method can simply remove the record from both of the tables, like so:

```
public void ejbRemove() throws RemoveException{
  // get ready for connection
  try {
    // same as before until after checking ps.executeUpdate()
      if (ps.executeUpdate() != 1) {
        throw new EJBException("Wrong delete count");
      }
      ps = null;
      ps = conn.prepareStatement("DELETE FROM product_details " +
                                 "WHERE product_id = ?");
      ps.setString(1, id);
      if (ps.executeUpdate() != 1) {
        throw new EJBException("Wrong delete count");
      }
      // catch-finally block as before
```

The `ejbFindByPrimaryKey()` method remains unchanged from the previous example. It still checks the main product table for the record. It does not use the details table at all.

Neither the `ejbActivate()` nor the `ejbPassivate()` method interacts with any table. Therefore they continue to follow that same pattern as before, and indeed `ejbActivate()` doesn't change at all. Here is the code for the changed `ejbPassivate()` method:

```
public void ejbPassivate() {
  id = null;
  name = null;
  type = null;
  shortDescription = null;
  longDescription = null;
  // setting the int values to 0 is strictly unnecessary,
  // but helps with debugging
  height = 0;
  width = 0;
  depth = 0;
  weight = 0;
}
```

For the sake of brevity this example contains only a single `ejbCreate()` method.

Using Database Constraints

We now have a new functioning bean, one which deals with the database in a more efficient manner. By examining the code for `ejbLoad()`, however, we can find several potential problems. The code currently assumes that each SELECT statement will return exactly one row, even though in the database there is nothing to guarantee this. Also, the `ejbFindByPrimaryKey()` method is based on only the main product table. A product_details record whose foreign key field is null will be inaccessible through this bean.

In order for this bean to work properly there must be a single record in the product table and a single corresponding record in the product_details table. Currently it is possible that only a product_details record exists, only a product record exists, or multiple product_details records exist. To help combat this problem we can use **database constraints**.

Constraints are a way to ensure data that is invalid for the application is not inserted into the database. Usually, a constraint is a limitation on the data that can go into a particular column. Two of the most common types of constraints are a **unique** constraint and a **not-null** constraint.

A unique constraint ensures that the data in a particular column is unique within the table. By declaring our foreign key column to be unique, we can guarantee that no more than one product_details record will ever exist for a given product. For multiple product_details records to exist, the product_id column would have to be repeated, which will be impossible because of the unique constraint. In our example we want to limit the product and product_details tables to a one-to-one relationship so a unique constraint is appropriate.

A not-null constraint ensures that no entires in a database column will be null. Declaring this constraint on our foreign key will guarantee that no product_details records will exist without a corresponding product record. Since the product_id column is a foreign key, a not-null value must always point to an existing product record.

In our case we want our foreign key column to be both unique and non-null, which can be done in Oracle with the following statement:

```
ALTER TABLE product_details
            ADD (UNIQUE product_id)
            MODIFY (product_id NOT NULL)
```

It is important to point out that the constraints that we use in this example are not applicable to all foreign key columns. We have analysed what are valid database states for our particular application and have declared constraints accordingly. Throughout the rest of the chapter we will consider in the examples what, if any, database constraints are appropriate for the given case.

Using a PK-FK Column

With our product and details scenario there is an even better solution to our data validity problem than simply declaring the constraints. Currently, the product_details database table has its own primary key. This details_id column does not contain meaningful application data. It is present solely to facilitate storing the data in two separate tables.

For the most part the object insulates a user from this aspect of having separate tables by declaring only a single key field in the product bean. The only place the details_id key is visible to the user of the bean is in the signature of the ejbCreate() method. It is then used in the insertRecord() method, but this method is part of the internal implementation, and is not exposed through the remote interface.

Unfortunately exposing this field is unavoidable with our current database schema, as the INSERT statement must include the primary key column for the table. In order to further insulate the user we can make the product and product_details tables share a key. We do this by removing the primary key column from our product_details table, and declaring the product_id column to be both a foreign key and the primary key for the table:

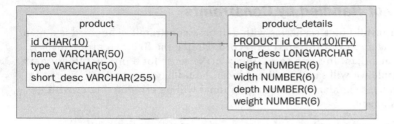

Now we can remove the `details_id` key column from both INSERT statements and from the `ejbCreate()` method, as follows:

```java
public String ejbCreate(String inProductId) throws CreateException {
    this.id = inProductId;
    this.name = null;
    this.type = null;
    this.shortDescription = null;
    this.longDescription = null;
    this.height = 0;
    this.width = 0;
    this.depth = 0;
    this.weight = 0;
    insertRecord();
    return id;
}
```

And now the `insertRecord()` method:

```java
public void insertRecord() {
    // start of method as before
    if (ps.executeUpdate() != 1) {
        throw new EJBException("Wrong insert count");
    }
    ps.close();
    ps = null;
    ps = conn.prepareStatement(
                "INSERT INTO product_details(product_id,long_desc," +
                "height,width,depth,weight) " +
                "VALUES (?,?,?,?,?,?)");
    ps.setString(1, id);
    ps.setString(2, longDescription);
    ps.setInt(3, height);
    ps.setInt(4, width);
    ps.setInt(5, depth);
    ps.setInt(6, weight);
    if (ps.executeUpdate() != 1) {
        throw new EJBException("Wrong insert count");
    }
    // rest of method as before
```

Since primary keys are both non-null and unique by definition, this kills three birds with one stone. By declaring `product_id` as the primary key for the `product_details` table we can take care of both the constraints and eliminating the extra key. Of course, in some real-life situation the database may already exist and changing the primary key may be infeasible or unacceptable for the project. In these cases, the user will have to be exposed to the extra key in the `ejbCreate()` method.

Illegal Database States not Handled by Constraints

We've taken care of two of our invalid data scenarios with database constraints. The third is a main `product` record existing without a `product_details` record. Unlike the first two problems it is unclear that this is actually invalid data. In some cases it may make sense for a product to not have details. However, for our example we will say that all products should have a `product_details` record. The case of a record in the secondary table being optional will be presented later with the scenario of the product and an image.

We have decided that a `product` record without a `product_details` record is invalid data. Unfortunately, we cannot easily guarantee this with a database constraint. We will therefore have to enforce this rule in our application logic.

Currently in our EJB it is impossible to insert or delete a main `product` record without also inserting or deleting a corresponding `product_details` record. Also, if a `product` record without a `product_details` record is detected in our `ejbLoad()` method, then an error will occur. Our `Product` bean already enforces the rule without any changes. When accessing this table directly, however, either from a session bean or outside the EJB application, we must be careful to always follow this rule, otherwise, run-time application errors may result when using the entity bean.

Alternatively, we could restrict access to the table to just the entity bean in our application, although this might take some watching to stop people adding products to the database without using the bean. We could do this by having the EJB application as the only 'front-end' to the database.

Optional Records

As mentioned in the previous section, sometimes when a bean is loaded from multiple tables, a record may not exist in every table. With the `product` and `product_details` tables, we decided that a non-existent `product_details` record was an application error. In some cases, however, not having one of the records may be a valid application state. A good example of this is an image.

In many situations an image is optional. Since images tend to be expensive to store and transmit, it also makes sense to use a lazy-loading strategy and separate an image into its own table. To make our example interesting we will include both a small image (icon) and a large image. Both images are optional, and the image will be `null` in the object if it does not exist. The following diagram represents the next version of our Product bean:

```
                    EJBEntity
              Product
-id:String
-name:String
-type:String
-shortDescription:String
-longDescription:String
-height:int
-width:int
-depth:int
-weight:int
-iconImage:byte[]
-largeImage:byte[]
```

In a database, images are generally stored in a separate table; in our example, both the images for a product are stored in a table called `product_image`. If both of the images are available, or a single one only, then there will be a record in the image table. If both images are `null`, then there should be no record in the image table for that product:

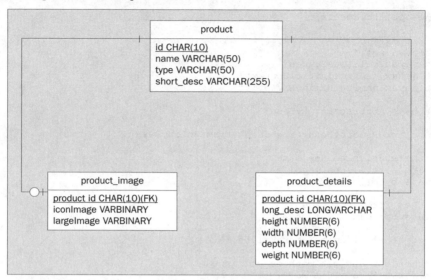

Every lifecycle method in our bean must take into account not only the possibility of the image not being loaded, but also whether a record for the image currently exists at all. Let's therefore take a look at the changes we'll need to make to accommodate the optional image.

Changes to the ProductBean for Optional Images

The home interface is unaffected and is the same as the previous example. The remote interface is also largely unchanged.

The Remote Interface

The accessor methods for the image fields have simply been added to it. The presence of the extra table is transparent through the remote interface, as seen here.

```
package optionalRecord;

import java.rmi.RemoteException;
import javax.ejb.EJBObject;

public interface Product extends EJBObject {

  // other methods as previously
  public byte[] getIconImage() throws RemoteException;

  public void setIconImage(byte[] inImage) throws RemoteException;

  public byte[] getLargeImage() throws RemoteException;

  public void setLargeImage(byte[] inImage) throws RemoteException;

}
```

The Bean Implementation Class

To facilitate these changes, three flags, `imageLoaded`, `imageChanged`, and `imageRecordExists`, are added to the bean along with its other fields

```
package optionalRecord;

import javax.ejb.*;
import java.sql.*;
import javax.sql.DataSource;
import javax.naming.InitialContext;
import javax.naming.NamingException;

import base.AbstractEntityBase;

public class ProductBean extends AbstractEntityBase {

    // other variables the same
    private byte[] iconImage;
    private byte[] largeImage;

    // other flags the same
    private boolean imageLoaded;
    private boolean imageModified;
    private boolean imageRecordExists;

    // other set and get methods unchanged
    public byte[] getIconImage() {
        loadImage();
        return iconImage;
    }
    public void setIconImage(byte[] inImage) {
        loadImage();
        imageModified = true;
        this.iconImage = inImage;
    }

    public byte[] getLargeImage() {
        loadImage();
        return largeImage;
    }
    public void setLargeImage(byte[] inImage) {
        loadImage();
        imageModified = true;
        this.largeImage = inImage;
    }
```

The `ejbLoad()` method follows the same basic lazy-loading pattern as before, and remains unchanged. The `loadDetails()` method also remains unchanged.

Unlike the `loadDetails()` method, `loadImage()` does not throw an error if there is no record in the `product_image` table. It instead sets the image fields to `null` and sets the `imageRecordExists` flag to `false`. This flag will be used in other lifecycle methods:

```
public void loadImage() {
    if (!imageLoaded) {
    // prepare to get connection
        try {
            conn = getConnection();
```

```
            ps = conn.prepareStatement("SELECT icon_image, large_icon " +
                                "FROM product_image " +
                                "WHERE product_id = ?");
        ps.setString(1, id);
        rs = ps.executeQuery();
        if (rs.next()) {
          iconImage = rs.getBytes(1);
          largeImage = rs.getBytes(2);
          imageRecordExists = true;
        } else {
          iconImage = null;
          largeImage = null;
          imageRecordExists = false;
        }
        imageLoaded = true;
      // finish the method as usual
```

The `ejbCreate()` method is the easiest of all the lifecycle methods that change data:

```
    public String ejbCreate(String inProductId) throws CreateException {
      // other initialization unchanged
      this.iconImage = null;
      this.largeImage = null;
      insertRecord();
      return id;
    }
```

Since we are just creating the `product` bean, none of the `product` records should exist, including the `product_image` record. We simply insert into the `product`, `product_details`, and `product_image` table as normal, unless both images are `null`, in which case we skip the `product_image` table. The code for this logic follows:

```
    public void insertRecord() {
        // first two database inserts as before
        if (ps.executeUpdate() != 1) {
          throw new EJBException("Wrong insert count");
        }
        ps.close();
        ps = null;

        // if both images are null, skip insert
        if (iconImage == null && largeImage == null) {
          imageRecordExists = false;
        } else {
          ps = conn.prepareStatement(
            "INSERT INTO product_image(product_id,icon_image,large_image) " +
            "VALUE (?,?,?)");
          ps.setString(1, id);
          ps.setBytes(2, iconImage);
          ps.setBytes(3, largeImage);
          if (ps.executeUpdate() != 1) {
            throw new EJBException("Wrong insert count");
          }
          imageRecordExists = true;
        }
```

```
      imageLoaded = true;
   // catch-finally block as usual
```

The ejbStore() method is the most complicated in this scenario. Instead of just containing UPDATE statements for the image, it may need to execute an INSERT or DELETE statement on the table for the image. Here is the new ejbStore() method:

```
public void ejbStore() {

   // if any part of the bean is modified, then we will need to
   // update at least one of the tables.
   if (mainModified || detailsModified || imageModified) {
     Connection conn = null;
     PreparedStatement ps = null;
     try {
       conn = getConnection();
       if (mainModified) {

         // if the main table is modified, update it as before
         ps = conn.prepareStatement("UPDATE product " +
                               "SET name=?, type=?, short_desc=? " +
                               "WHERE id = ?");
         ps.setString(1, name);
         ps.setString(2, type);
         ps.setString(3, shortDescription);
         ps.setString(4, id);
         if (ps.executeUpdate() != 1) {
           throw new EJBException("Wrong update count");
         }
         ps.close();
         ps = null;
         mainModified = false;
       }
       if (detailsModified) {

         // if the details table is modified update it.
         ps = conn.prepareStatement("UPDATE product_details " +
                               "SET long_desc=?, height=?, " +
                               "width=?,depth=?,weight=? " +
                               "WHERE product_id = ?");
         ps.setString(1, longDescription);
         ps.setInt(2, height);
         ps.setInt(3, width);
         ps.setInt(4, depth);
         ps.setInt(5, weight);
         ps.setString(6, id);
         if (ps.executeUpdate() != 1) {
           throw new EJBException("Wrong update count");
         }
         ps.close();
         ps = null;
         detailsModified = false;
       }
       if (imageModified) {
```

```
      // when the image is modified there are four possible actions,
      // do nothing, delete a record, update a record,
      // or insert a record
      if (iconImage == null && largeImage == null) {
        if (imageRecordExists) {

          // if both images are null and a record exists, the record
          // should be dcleted.
          ps = conn.prepareStatement("DELETE FROM product_image " +
                                     "WHERE product_id = ?");
          ps.setString(1, id);
          if (ps.executeUpdate() != 1) {
            throw new EJBException("Wrong delete count");
          }
          imageRecordExists = false;
        }

        // if both images are null and a record does not exist, then the
        // database is in the proper state and no action is required
      } else {
        if (imageRecordExists) {

          // if there is a non-null image and a record is currently
          // present, update it with the current image data
          ps = conn.prepareStatement("UPDATE product_image " +
                                     "SET icon_image=?, large_image=? "
                                   + "WHERE product_id = ?");
          ps.setBytes(1, iconImage);
          ps.setBytes(2, largeImage);
          ps.setString(3, id);
          if (ps.executeUpdate() != 1) {
            throw new EJBException("Wrong update count");
          }
        } else {

          // if there is a non-null image an no record currently exists,
          // insert a new record with the image data
          ps = conn.prepareStatement(
              "INSERT INTO product_image(id, icon_image,large_image) " +
              "VALUES (?,?,?)");
          ps.setString(1, id);
          ps.setBytes(2, iconImage);
          ps.setBytes(3, largeImage);
          if (ps.executeUpdate() != 1) {
            throw new EJBException("Wrong update count");
          }
          imageRecordExists = true;
        }
      }
      imageModified = false;
    }
// catch-finally block as usual
```

First the method checks the image fields to see what the current state of the product_image table should be. If both are null, then as described above there should not be a record in the image table. If the record currently does not exist, then we can do nothing. Otherwise we should delete the current record from the table to satisfy our specified application semantics. If either of the images has a non-null value, then there should be a record in the table. If there is currently a record in the table, we can simply update the existing record. Otherwise, we must insert a new record into the table.

The ejbRemove() method is simple. We can still execute a DELETE statement for all three of the tables, including the product_image table. If the record does not currently exist, the DELETE statement will have no effect, but also causes
no harm:

```
public void ejbRemove() {
    // start the same
    if (ps.executeUpdate() != 1) {
        throw new EJBException("Wrong delete count");
    }
    ps.close();
    ps = null;
    ps = conn.prepareStatement("DELETE FROM product_image " +
                               "WHERE product_id = ?");
    ps.setString(1, id);

    // may delete either 0 or 1 row
    if (ps.executeUpdate() > 1) {
        throw new EJBException("Wrong delete count");
    }
    ps.close();
    ps = null;
    ps = conn.prepareStatement("DELETE FROM product WHERE id = ?");
    ps.setString(1, id);
    // rest of method the same
```

The ejbFindByPrimaryKey(), ejbActivate(), and ejbPassivate() methods, as usual, are straightforward. The presence of an extra image table has no effect on them. They remain the same as the previous examples.

Now our Product bean with two optional images is complete. As we can see, mapping a bean to multiple tables complicates the bean's lifecycle considerably. Alternative options should be considered carefully before deciding to take
this approach.

While there are reasons for a single logical entity to be split across multiple tables, often multiple tables are an indication of multiple entities. For example, in many cases a product and an image would be considered separate entities. One major indication is the key structure in the table.

In both our examples above, the secondary tables used a single column as a combination primary key and foreign key. This meant that neither an image nor details could exist without a corresponding product. If one of the tables had its own independent primary key, we would have a strong indication that it was meant to be an independent entity. The final test, however, is always a subjective one that depends both on the usage of the data in the current application and on the original intent of the database designer.

Isolation Problems

Now that we have explored some more complicated mappings between entity beans and database tables, we can consider one of the more subtle problems with complex mappings, **isolation**. In database terms, isolation means that one action is unaffected by changes that result from another action. Usually isolation is used in reference to multiple transactions.

Transaction isolation is the extent to which changes in one transaction affect the execution of another transaction. Ideally, the transactions would not affect each other at all, but for performance reasons most databases will allow the transaction isolation level to be set on a per transaction basis. We will not deal with isolation between transactions, as this is taken care of by the database for us. Instead we have a problem of bean isolation.

Our bean loads data from a database record into its fields. The bean later updates the database record based on this in-memory data. These updates assume that the data in the database has not been changed since the original read. If it has changed, then these changes may be undone by the update. Between transactions, we can take care of this by setting the proper transaction isolation level in the database. However, we still have a problem if another part of the application updates the database record.

Therefore, we have the basic rule that a database record that is loaded and updated based on an in-memory representation of the data cannot be updated outside the bean in the same transaction. In terms of entity beans, this usually means preventing multiple bean instances from having the same database record loaded into memory simultaneously.

In terms of our beans, we must be sure that there is a one-to-one relationship between the records in the two tables. Without this, any of the SELECT statements that are not based on the primary key of the bean being matched to the primary key of the table may cause problems. Since no two beans share a primary key and no two records share a primary key, we are sure that no two beans will reference the same database record. Without this, a one-to-one relationship between the bean's primary key and the database record can be established by using a unique constraint, as described earlier in the chapter.

Lookup Tables

Although updating the same database row from more than one bean instance will cause isolation problems, there are times when bean instances can share read-only access to a single row in memory. The most common example of this case is a **lookup table**.

A lookup table maps data that is roughly equivalent to an enumerated complex type in the object world. A common example is a status field. Often status is represented as one of a predefined set of IDs: ID 1 is pending, ID 2 is shipped, ID 3 is received, etc. Of course the IDs are meaningless to most users of the system. To alleviate this problem, a lookup table is created that has the status ID as its primary key. The other fields of the table map to additional data about that status, usually human-readable information like a name for the status and a description of what the status means.

An Order Bean with a Status Lookup

An entity that contains a status, such as an order, will have a foreign key to the status table. This scenario is similar to the to the product_details example above, but notice that the foreign key is present in the primary table, instead of in the detail table as before. We have named the table order_data because order is a reserved word in most databases. Here is the database schema we will be using:

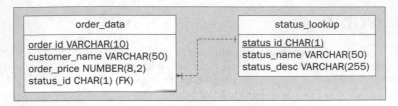

The foreign key direction only allows an order to have a single status, but multiple orders can have the same status. This is correct, and unlike the `product_details` example, we would not want to declare the foreign key column to be unique. Let's start with a SQL statement to load the data:

❑ Load:

```
SELECT ORDER_ID, CUSTOMER_NAME, ORDER_PRICE,
       ORDER_DATA.STATUS_ID, STATUS_NAME, STATUS_DESC
       FROM ORDER_DATA, STATUS_LOOKUP
       WHERE ORDER_ID = ?
       AND ORDER_DATA.STATUS_ID = STATUS_LOOKUP.STATUS_ID
```

This statement joins the two tables and returns a single row in the result set. This statement will work as long as the foreign key column is not `null`. However, this statement will not return a row if the status code foreign key column for the order is `null`. This is because this join syntax represents an **inner join**, the default type of join for relational databases. An inner join only returns a row if a corresponding record exists in *all* of the tables being joined.

A more appropriate join would be an **outer join**. In an outer join, a record is returned even if one of the joined tables doesn't contain a corresponding record. In this case an outer join would return a record even the `status_id` field in `order_data` is null. The biggest problem with using an outer join is that the syntax for specifying one can differ greatly between databases. Here is an example of outer join syntax for Oracle:

```
SELECT order_data.order_id, status_lookup.status_id
       FROM order_data, status_lookup
       WHERE order_data.status_id (+)= status_lookup.status_id
```

The following code produces the same results for SQL Server:

```
SELECT order_data.order_id, status_lookup.status_id
       FROM order_data
       LEFT JOIN status_lookup
       ON order_data.status_id = status_lookup.status_id
```

To avoid requiring an outer join, the `status_id` foreign key column in the `order_data` table can be declared to have a NOT NULL constraint, as described earlier in the chapter.

Although the Order bean loads data from the `status_lookup` table, this data is not really part of the order. When updating the status of an order we would not want to change the `status_lookup` table. This would change the information for all orders with that status code.

To solve this problem in our example, we should change the foreign key column in the database instead. Therefore a bean will only include an UPDATE statement for the `order_data` table, as follows:

❑ Store:

```
UPDATE order_data
    SET customer_name=?, order_price=?, status_id=?
    WHERE order_id = ?
```

The same goes for both the create and remove statements. These statements will have no interaction with the status_lookup table at all:

❑ Create:

```
INSERT INTO order_data(order_id,customer_name,order_price,status_id)
    VALUES (?,?,?,?)
```

❑ Remove:

```
DELETE FROM order_data
    WHERE order_id = ?
```

None of the statements that write to the database affects the status_lookup table. Therefore, this mapping does not cause the isolation problem described in the previous section even though the record is shared. It is only updating a shared record that causes isolation problems.

Since the store, create, and remove statements do not include the columns status_name or status_description, the bean should not include set methods for these fields. These fields are slightly more complicated than standard read-only fields, however.

If a user calls setStatusId() with a new status code, the status_name and status_description entries must change to reflect this. The only way for the bean to know the name and description for a new status code is to go back to the database and reload these fields, as follows:

❑ Reload status:

```
SELECT status_name, status_desc
    FROM status_lookup
    WHERE status_id = ?
```

Since this involves an extra database operation we do not want to reload the data unless it is actually going to be used, so a lazy-loading strategy should be employed here. We will base the reload on whether a statusChanged flag is set in the setStatusId() method. Now we can fill in the surrounding code.

The Order Bean for the Status Lookup Table

There are no set accessors for fields from the lookup table, a detail which is reflected in the remote interface and the implementation class.

The Remote Interfaces

Also the getStatusId() method is exposed through the remote interface, as seen here:

```
package basicLookupTable;

import java.rmi.RemoteException;
import javax.ejb.EJBObject;

public interface Order extends EJBObject {
```

```
    public String getOrderId() throws RemoteException;

    public String getCustomerName() throws RemoteException;
    public void setCustomerName(String inName) throws RemoteException;

    public double getOrderPrice() throws RemoteException;
    public void setOrderPrice(double inPrice) throws RemoteException;

    public String getStatusId() throws RemoteException;
    public void setStatusId(String statusId) throws RemoteException;

    public String getStatusName() throws RemoteException;
    public String getStatusDescription() throws RemoteException;

}
```

The Home Interface

```
package basicLookupTable;

import java.rmi.RemoteException;
import javax.ejb.*;

public interface OrderHome extends EJBHome {

    public Order findByPrimaryKey(String id)
            throws FinderException, RemoteException;

    public Order create(String inId) throws CreateException, RemoteException;

}
```

The Bean Implementation Class

The non-lookup fields follow the same pattern as our previous example. The fields involving status, however, follow a new pattern. The getStatusId() method is as normal, but the setStatusId() method also sets the statusChanged flag to true. In both the getStatusName() and getStatusDescription() methods, if the statusChanged flag is set, then the values are reloaded from the database. The code for all of the fields follows:

```
package basicLookupTable;

import javax.ejb.*;
import java.sql.*;
import base.AbstractEntityBase;

public class OrderBean extends AbstractEntityBase {

    private String orderId;
    private String customerName;
    private double orderPrice;
    private String statusId;
    private String statusName;
    private String statusDescription;

    private boolean isModified;
    private boolean statusChanged;
```

```
   public String getOrderId() {
     return orderId;
   }

   public String getCustomerName() {
     return customerName;
   }
   public void setCustomerName(String inName) {
     isModified = true;
     this.customerName = inName;
   }

   public double getOrderPrice() {
     return orderPrice;
   }
   public void setOrderPrice(double inPrice) {
     isModified = true;
     this.orderPrice = inPrice;
   }

   public String getStatusId() {
     return statusId;
   }
   public void setStatusId(String inStatusId) {
     isModified = true;
     statusChanged = true;
     this.statusId = inStatusId;
   }

   public String getStatusName() {
     if (statusChanged) {
       reloadStatus();
     }
     return statusName;
   }

   public String getStatusDescription() {
     if (statusChanged) {
       reloadStatus();
     }
     return statusDescription;
   }
```

Note that there are no methods to set either the `statusName` or the `statusDescription` field.

Unlike in the lazy-loading case, all the fields of the bean are originally loaded in `ejbLoad()`. Although the gets and sets look similar to the lazy-loading pattern, the differences in the lifecycle methods make them behave quite differently. Our code for `ejbLoad()` uses an outer join to load data from both tables simultaneously. If desired, the lookup table could be used in combination with a lazy-loading strategy:

```
public void ejbLoad() {
   Connection conn = null;
   PreparedStatement ps = null;
   ResultSet rs = null;
   try {
     conn = getConnection();

     // select all fields except image
     ps = conn.prepareStatement(
             "SELECT customer_name, order_price, order_data.status_id, " +
```

```
                    "status_name, status_desc " +
              "FROM order_data, status_lookup " +
              "WHERE order_data.status_id (+)= status_lookup.status_id" +
              "AND order_data.order_id = ?");
      ps.setString(1, orderId);
      rs = ps.executeQuery();
      if (!rs.next()) {
        throw new NoSuchEntityException();
      }
      customerName = rs.getString(1);
      orderPrice = rs.getDouble(2);
      statusId = rs.getString(3);
      statusName = rs.getString(4);
      statusDescription = rs.getString(5);
      if (rs.next()) {
        throw new EJBException("Multiple rows in load");
      }
      // set the modified flag to false after loading the data
      isModified = false;
      statusChanged = false;
    } catch (SQLException ex) {
      throw new EJBException(ex);
    } finally {
      cleanUp(conn, ps, rs);
    }
  }
```

As mentioned above, when the status ID changes the other lookup fields must be reloaded. The code for the reloadStatus() method simply selects from the lookup table, as seen here:

```
    public void reloadStatus() {
      Connection conn = null;
      PreparedStatement ps = null;
      ResultSet rs = null;
      try {
        conn = getConnection();
        ps = conn.prepareStatement("SELECT status_name, status_desc " +
                                   "FROM status_lookup " +
                                   "WHERE status_id = ?");
        ps.setString(1, statusId);
        rs = ps.executeQuery();
        if (!rs.next()) {
          throw new EJBException("Invalid status id: " + statusId);
        }
        statusName = rs.getString(1);
        statusDescription = rs.getString(2);
        if (rs.next()) {
          throw new EJBException("Multiple rows in reloadStatus");
        }
      } catch (SQLException ex) {
        throw new EJBException(ex);
      } finally {
        cleanUp(conn, ps, rs);
      }
    }
```

It is important to realize that the status_ID field cannot be set to just any ID. If the status_ID does not correspond to an id that is currently in the status_lookup table, then a database error will occur when attempting to update the foreign key column. Since the end user will probably need to know what status ids are valid, a getStatusIds() method can be added to the order bean. It will select all of the IDs from the status_lookup table, as follows:

```
    public Collection getValidStatusIds() {
      Collection ret = new LinkedList();
      Connection conn = null;
      PreparedStatement ps = null;
      ResultSet rs = null;
      try {
        conn = getConnection();
        ps = conn.prepareStatement("SELECT status_id FROM status_lookup");
        rs = ps.executeQuery();
        while (rs.next()) {
          ret.add(rs.getString(1));
        }
      // standard catch-finally block
```

This method is similar to an `ejbSelect()` method when using container-managed persistence. An `ejbSelect()` method is similar to a `ejbFind()` method in that it executes an database query. It may, however, select arbitrary data from the database and it does not use any fields of the bean, not even the bean's primary key, to locate the data.

In our scenario, a user of the Order bean can call this method to determine what the valid status IDs are. Unlike an `ejbSelect()` method from a CMP implementation, which can only be called from a business method and cannot be exposed through the home or remote interface, we can (and do) expose our method directly through the remote interface.

The `ejbStore()`, `ejbCreate()`, and `ejbRemove()` lifecycle methods that alter the database completely ignore the lookup table. They follow the same pattern as the most basic example and treat `status_id` as they would any other persistent field:

```
    public void ejbStore() {
      if (isModified) {
        Connection conn = null;
        PreparedStatement ps = null;
        try {
          conn = getConnection();
          ps = conn.prepareStatement("UPDATE orderData " +
                          "SET customer_name=?, order_price=?, " +
                          "status_id=? " +
                          "WHERE order_id = ?");
          ps.setString(1, customerName);
          ps.setDouble(2, orderPrice);
          ps.setString(3, statusId);
          ps.setString(4, orderId);
          if (ps.executeUpdate() != 1) {
            throw new EJBException("Incorrect update count");
          }
        } catch (SQLException ex) {
          throw new EJBException(ex);
        } finally {
          cleanUp(conn, ps, null);
        }
      }
    }
```

```
    public String ejbCreate(String inId) throws CreateException {
      this.orderId = inId;
      this.customerName = null;
```

```
      this.orderPrice = 0;
      this.statusId = null;
      insertRecord();
      return inId;
  }


  public void ejbRemove() throws RemoveException {
    Connection conn = null;
    PreparedStatement ps = null;
    try {
      conn = getConnection();
      ps = conn.prepareStatement("DELETE FROM order_data " +
                                 "WHERE order_id = ?");
      ps.setString(1, orderId);
      if (ps.executeUpdate() != 1) {
        throw new EJBException("Wrong delete count");
      }
    } catch (SQLException ex) {
      throw new EJBException(ex);
    } finally {
      cleanUp(conn, ps, null);
    }
  }
```

Not surprisingly, this pattern also has no effect on the ejbFindByPrimaryKey(), ejbActivate(), and ejbPassivate() methods. They follow the standard pattern, like so.

```
  public String ejbFindByPrimaryKey(String id) throws FinderException {
    Connection conn = null;
    PreparedStatement ps = null;
    ResultSet rs = null;
    try {
      conn = getConnection();
      ps = conn.prepareStatement("SELECT 1 " +
                                 "FROM order_data " +
                                 "WHERE order_id = ?");
      ps.setString(1, orderId);
      rs = ps.executeQuery();
      if (rs.next()) {
        return id;
      } else {
        throw new ObjectNotFoundException();
      }
    } catch (SQLException ex) {
      throw new EJBException(ex);
    } finally {
      cleanUp(conn, ps, rs);
    }
  }


  public void ejbActivate() {
    orderId = (String) entityContext.getPrimaryKey();
  }


  public void ejbPassivate() {
    orderId = null;
    customerName = null;
```

```
    orderPrice = 0;
    statusId = null;
    statusName = null;
    statusDescription = null;
}
```

Using a Reverse Lookup

One potential complaint about our object schema for order_data and status_lookup is that we expose the status_id to the user of the bean. Some would complain that this exposes an artifact of the persistence to the user and does not fully satisfy our goal of persistence encapsulation. This really depends on the actual data exposed. If the status IDs are somewhat meaningful, this may not be true. For example, the status IDs may be strings where P means pending, S means shipped, R means received, etc. In this case exposing these IDs will probably make sense to the user of the entity bean.

If the codes are arbitrary integers, however, then the user may be confused. In this case it would be preferable for the user to have only status names exposed in the bean. It is important to emphasize that in this case the user refers to another developer using the beans and not an application user. Because of this, it may be acceptable to expose this ID. If not, one solution is to base the update on one of the other fields in the status_lookup table. For example instead of exposing a setStatusId() method, we may expose a setStatus() method that takes in a status name.

When updating and creating the bean, we still want to update the foreign-key column. Therefore, we must lookup the ID for the status based on the foreign key. This is called a **reverse lookup**. Since the ID will be required in update, the reload of the ID and description based on the name should be performed immediately in the setStatusName() method. There is no advantage to using lazy loading in this scenario.

Changes to the Accessor Methods

The setStatusId() method is replaced with a setStatusName() method. This method now calls reloadStatus() immediately, so the other accessors do not need to:

```
public String getStatusName() {
  return statusName;
}

public void setStatusName(String inStatusName) {
  isModified = true;
  this.statusName = inStatusName;
  reloadStatus();
}

public String getStatusDescription() {
  return statusDescription;
}
```

Changes to the reloadStatus() Method

Now the reloadStatus() method does a lookup in the status table based on the statusName field to determine the ID and description, rather than based on the statusId field to determine the name and description. This method will only work if the values in the statusName field are unique. The changes to this method are simply to replace id with name (and Id with Name).

It is important to realize that performing lookups that are not based on the primary key field of a table can have a serious performance and scalability impact. If the set of potential statuses is small, then the impact is likely to be minimal. However, in many situations an index would need to be built on the name column to achieve acceptable performance when using a reverse lookup. As general rule, a reverse lookup should only be performed on column that is unique and has an index built for it.

Addition of the getValidStatusNames() Method

Another potential problem caused exposing this `String` datatype is misspellings of the status keys, which are probably regular English words. Setting the status name to any value that is not an exact match for a value in the status table will cause an application error. To avoid this problem, we must still use a method to get the valid status values. We will need to change this method to return valid status strings, as follows:

```
public Collection getValidStatusNames() {
  Collection ret = new LinkedList();
  Connection conn = null;
  PreparedStatement ps = null;
  ResultSet rs = null;
  try {
    conn = getConnection();
    ps = conn.prepareStatement("SELECT status_name FROM status_lookup");
    rs = ps.executeQuery();
    while (rs.next()) {
      ret.add(rs.getString(1));
    }
  } catch (SQLException ex) {
    throw new EJBException(ex);
  } finally {
    cleanUp(conn, ps, rs);
  }
  return ret;
}
```

This technique for mapping a lookup table does not allow the bean to update the lookup table. It therefore assumes that the status table does not need to change as part of the application. For most lookup tables this will hold true. Generally, lookup table updates are few and far between and the tables are populated via direct database statements as part of the implementation of the application. If the table needs to be updated in the application, then mapping that table as a separate entity bean with a relationship to the Order bean may be more appropriate. This way the lifecycle for a status is well defined. We will talk about object relationships in the next section.

Object Relationships

Entities rarely exist in a vacuum. Nearly all logical entities will have a relationship with another entity. In fact in most applications, all of the logical entities are related to each other, either directly or indirectly. An application can almost be defined as operating on a set of related entities. Relational databases were designed with this is mind; one of the major advantages they have over file-based storage systems is that they can directly represent relationships. When designing entity beans, these same relationships should be directly modeled in the entity bean class as well.

Relationships are already defined as part of the container-managed persistence contract. CMP-based entity beans can define relationships in their deployment descriptor and it is the responsibility of the persistence manager to maintain the proper semantics for them. When using bean-managed persistence, relationships, like most other aspects of persistence, are up to the bean provider.

It is useful, as much as possible, to maintain the same semantics as defined in the container-managed persistence case. However, implementing the full relationship system described in the container-managed persistence specification would be particularly difficult for us and would probably be overkill for the majority of situations. In our examples we will analyze the semantics required by the scenario and alter our implementation as appropriate to simplify the task.

Relationships have many intrinsic properties. The two that we are most concerned with are **navigability** and **multiplicity**. These properties are generally expressed in terms of the ends of the relationship.

Navigability indicates whether the relationship can be accessed from a given relationship end. A relationship that can be accessed from both ends is said to be **bi-directional**, while if one end or the other cannot access the relationship it is said to be **uni-directional**.

For our purposes, a relationship end can have one of two values for multiplicity: **one** or **many**. A **one** multiplicity indicates that the relationship end can contain at most one value. If the relationship end can contain more than one value, then it is said to have a **many** multiplicity.

Relationship Navigability

Navigability is represented differently in the object model and the database structure. In the object model, navigability corresponds to having an accessor method and field for the relationship in one or both of the objects participating in the relationship. An end is navigable if it contains a field for a relationship, and it is non-navigable if it does not. In a database, relationships between tables are modeled as foreign keys.

It is always possible to navigate these database relationships in either direction through a SQL statement. However, the index structure in your database most closely corresponds to navigability. In most databases there is always an index on the primary key column. Therefore, navigating from the foreign key to the primary key will always use an index.

If you want to navigate from the primary key to the foreign key, then an index should be built on the foreign key column. The SQL statement used to navigate the relationship will work with or without the index, but may have a large performance impact if an index is not built on the foreign key column.

Any time a column is used in the WHERE clause of a SQL statement it should be considered for an index. Depending on your application and the number of records in a table, the impact of building the index can vary. Other factors, such as the number of distinct values present in the column are also important to consider. In order for an application to scale to a large number of rows, proper use of indexes is essential. For more information on this topic refer to a book on relational database design, such as the one mentioned in the introduction to this chapter.

Using a Finder for Relationship Navigation

In entity beans, relationships are modeled as get and set methods. These methods return a reference to the interface of another bean or a collection of interfaces depending on the multiplicity of the relationship. In container-managed persistence, relationships are built in terms of the local component interface for the entity bean. With BMP, they can be modeled either with the remote or local component interface at the choice of the bean provider. See Chapters 5 and 6 for more information on local and remote interfaces.

In our example, we will model our relationship in terms of the remote interface. The only way for the bean provider to get a reference to a remote interface is through calling a finder. Therefore, we will model our relationship navigation in terms of finder methods.

A common mistake is to use the `findByPrimaryKey()` method to do this in all cases. If we were to use this method, we would execute one SQL statement to get the list of related beans and one SQL statement per related bean during `findByPrimaryKey()`. This means we will execute 1+*n* SQL statements, where *n* is the number of related beans.

If a custom finder is used to load the relationship, then both getting the list of related beans and their remote interfaces is combined into a single step. This way only a single SQL statement is used, which is an obvious advantage. Using `findByPrimaryKey()` is only appropriate in a one-to-one relationship where the primary key is already known. Any time a new database query must be executed to find related beans, it should be wrapped in a custom finder.

Table Relationship Types

As mentioned above, the relationships between tables in a database are represented as foreign keys. However, the relationships in your table structure and the relationships in your object model do not always directly correspond. In the previous sections we have explored mapping multiple related tables to a single entity bean. A relationship between two logical entities has two basic representations in the database: one-to-many (1-M) and many-to-many (M-M). For the first, we use a direct foreign key; for the latter, we use a reference table.

Direct Foreign Key (1-M) Relationship

A direct foreign key relationship is the most basic and common representation. This is the same type of table relationship we saw in the single entity mappings. One table has a foreign key, which points to the primary key for another table. This structure's canonical mapping is a one-to-many relationship. The table that contains the foreign key can point to only a single primary key. However, one primary key can have multiple foreign keys pointing to it. A common example of this pattern is an order and its line items, as demonstrated in the following database diagram:

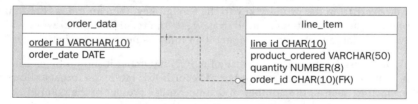

Since a line item can belong to only a single order, the `line_item` table contains the foreign key. It also contains a `line_item` primary key field that contains an arbitrary unique value that identifies the line item in the table. To find the line items for a particular order, we select primary keys from the `line_item` table based on the foreign key, as follows:

```
SELECT line_id
       FROM line_item
       WHERE order_id = ?
```

Since the WHERE clause is based on the foreign key we will want to build an index on the foreign key if the relationship is navigable from order to line item. The following statement will add an index in Oracle. We have named the index `order_index`, but the name is arbitrary:

```
CREATE INDEX order_index
       ON line_item.order_id
```

Note that this is shown to enable you to run the samples in this chapter, not because you should be expected to know how to create an index on a database table. That's the job of the database developer.

To navigate from line item to order (say, if we wanted to check how often a given item has been ordered in the past), we will select the foreign key from the `line_item` table:

```
SELECT order_id
       FROM line_item
       WHERE line_id = ?
```

This statement is very similar to the standard load query for the bean. It selects from the line item table based on the primary key. Here is the main load query for a line item:

```
SELECT product_ordered, quantity
       FROM line_item
       WHERE line_id = ?
```

To reduce the number of SQL statements executed, we can combine this statement to load the relationship and the main load for the bean into a single statement:

```
SELECT order_id, product_ordered, quantity
       FROM line_item
       WHERE line_id = ?
```

Now we can navigate the relationship, but the relationships are more than just wrappers around custom finders. Relationships between entities can be altered. Altering a direct foreign key relationship in the database means updating the foreign key column. To set the order for a line item, update the foreign key column for that line item:

```
UPDATE line_item
       SET order_id = ?
       WHERE line_id - ?
```

This statement could be used to set the order for a line item to `null`. Also, since relationships are symmetrical in the object model, setting the order for a line item is equivalent to adding that line item to the order. Setting the order to `null` for a line item is equivalent to removing the line item from its current order. All of these operations correspond to the above SQL statement. On top of that, this UPDATE statement is very similar to the main update for the line item bean:

```
UPDATE line_item
       SET product_ordered = ?, quantity = ?
       WHERE line_id = ?
```

Like the load queries, these queries can be combined into a single SQL statement:

```
UPDATE line_item
       SET order_id = ?, product_ordered = ?, quantity = ?
       WHERE line_id = ?
```

Since relationships are by definition shared between two beans, we must deal with the isolation problems of two beans updating the same table. Details on this problem were presented in the *Isolation Problems* section earlier in this chapter. The isolation problem stems from reading data into memory at one time and then performing updates based on the originally read data at a later time. To solve this problem, we will only update the relationship in one of the two beans.

As mentioned above, all of the operations on one side of the relationship are logically equivalent to operations on the other side and we will use this to our advantage. In the direct foreign key case we have already noted that the load and update for the line item can be combined with one of the finds and the update for the relationship. This makes the line item the natural choice as the owner of this relationship.

Bi-Directional Relationships

Given our above findings, we can now fill in the persistence code for both of the beans. The following code represents a bi-directional relationship between order and line item.

The LineItem Bean Remote Interface

```
package directOneToMany;

import java.rmi.RemoteException;
import javax.ejb.EJBObject;

public interface LineItem extends EJBObject {

  public String getLineId() throws RemoteException;

  public String getProductOrdered() throws RemoteException;
  public void setProductOrdered(String inProduct) throws RemoteException;

  public double getQuantity() throws RemoteException;
  public void setQuantity(double inQuantity) throws RemoteException;

  public Order getOrder() throws RemoteException;
  public void setOrder(Order inOrder) throws RemoteException;

}
```

The Line ItemBean Home Interface

```
package directOneToMany;

import java.rmi.RemoteException;
import javax.ejb.*;
import java.util.Collection;

public interface LineItemHome extends EJBHome {

  public LineItem findByPrimaryKey(String inLineId) throws FinderException,
                                                           RemoteException;

  public Collection findRelatedLineItems(String orderId)
                                      throws FinderException,
                                             RemoteException;

  public LineItem create(String inLineId) throws CreateException,
                                                 RemoteException;

}
```

The LineItem Bean Implementation Class

We use both a `relatedOrderId` field and a `relatedOrderField`. The `relatedOrderId` field is loaded as part of the standard load, but the `relatedOrder` field is only set when `getOrder()` is called:

```
package directOneToMany;

import javax.ejb.*;
import java.sql.*;
import java.rmi.RemoteException;
import javax.rmi.PortableRemoteObject;
import javax.naming.InitialContext;
import javax.naming.Context;
import javax.naming.NamingException;
import java.util.Collection;
import java.util.LinkedList;

import base.AbstractEntityBase;

public class LineItemBean extends AbstractEntityBase {

  private String lineId;
  private String productOrdered;
  private double quantity;
  private String relatedOrderId;
  private Order relatedOrder;

  private boolean isModified;

  private EntityContext entityContext;

  public String getLineId() {
    return lineId;
  }

  public String getProductOrdered() {
    return productOrdered;
  }
  public void setProductOrdered(String inProd) {
    isModified = true;
    this.productOrdered = inProd;
  }

  public double getQuantity() {
    return quantity;
  }
  public void setQuantity(double inQuantity) {
    isModified = true;
    this.quantity = inQuantity;
  }
```

The `getOrder()` method differs greatly from other accessors. Accessors for a relationship are mapped into calls on finder methods. Since this method is expensive and the line item is the owner of the relationship, we will cache the result of this method call:

```
public Order getOrder() throws RemoteException {

  // we delay instantiating an Order object as long as possible
  if (relatedOrder == null) {
```

```
      if (relatedOrderId == null) {

        // line item is not related to an order
        return null;
      } else {
        try {
          Context ic = new InitialContext();
          OrderHome oHome =
            (OrderHome) PortableRemoteObject
                          .narrow(ic.lookup("java:comp/env/ejb/OrderHome"),
                                  OrderHome.class);
          relatedOrder = oHome.findByPrimaryKey(relatedOrderId);
        } catch (NamingException ex) {
          throw new EJBException(ex);
        } catch (FinderException ex) {
          throw new EJBException(ex);
        }
        return relatedOrder;
      }
    } else {
      return relatedOrder;
    }
  }
```

The setOrder() method acts like a regular accessor, with the addition that it updates both the remote interface and the ID version of the relationship
fields together:

```
public void setOrder(Order inOrder) throws RemoteException {
  this.relatedOrderId = inOrder.getOrderId();
  this.relatedOrder = inOrder;
}
```

All of the standard lifecycle methods for the LineItem bean handle the relatedOrderId field in the same way as the other fields of the bean. The relationship has little impact on these methods, so we'll just show the ejbFindByPrimaryKey() method:

```
public String ejbFindByPrimaryKey(String id) throws FinderException {
  Connection conn = null;
  PreparedStatement ps = null;
  ResultSet rs = null;
  try {
    conn = getConnection();
    ps = conn.prepareStatement("SELECT 1 FROM line_item " +
                               "WHERE line_id = ?");
    ps.setString(1, id);
    rs = ps.executeQuery();
    if (rs.next()) {
      return id;
    } else {
      throw new ObjectNotFoundException();
    }
  } catch (SQLException ex) {
    throw new EJBException(ex);
  } finally {
    cleanUp(conn, ps, rs);
  }
}
```

All the other lifecycle methods can be found in the code download for the book, along with the rest of the code.

A custom finder method is also added. We will use this finder method later in the Order bean to navigate the relationship from order to line items:

```
public Collection ejbFindRelatedLineItems(String orderId)
        throws FinderException {
  Collection ret = new LinkedList();
  Connection conn = null;
  PreparedStatement ps = null;
  ResultSet rs = null;
  try {
    conn = getConnection();
    ps = conn.prepareStatement("SELECT line_id FROM line_item " +
                               "WHERE order_id = ?");
    ps.setString(1, orderId);
    rs = ps.executeQuery();
    while (rs.next()) {
      ret.add(rs.getString(1));
    }
  } catch (SQLException ex) {
    throw new EJBException(ex);
  } finally {
    cleanUp(conn, ps, rs);
  }
  return ret;
}

}
```

The Order Bean Remote Interface

The accessors for the relationship, like the other field accessors, are exposed through the remote interface. They are also defined in terms of the remote interface, making it easy to navigate from one remote object to another. For brevity, this interface isn't shown, although it can be found in the code download.

The Order Bean Home Interface

Unlike most previous examples, the relationship does have an effect on the home interface. Because custom finders are used to implement the relationship, these finder methods are visible in the home interface. A user of the bean may call these methods, but the preferred way to navigate the bean is through the relationship accessors in the remote interface:

```
package directOneToMany;

import java.rmi.RemoteException;
import javax.ejb.*;

public interface OrderHome extends EJBHome {

  public Order findByPrimaryKey(String id)
        throws FinderException, RemoteException;

  public Order create(String inId) throws CreateException, RemoteException;

}
```

The Order Bean Implementation Class

The Order bean does not declare any fields corresponding to the relationship. All of the remaining fields follow the same pattern as before:

```
package directOneToMany;

import javax.ejb.*;
import java.sql.*;
import javax.rmi.PortableRemoteObject;
import java.rmi.RemoteException;
import javax.naming.InitialContext;
import javax.naming.Context;
import javax.naming.NamingException;
import java.util.Collection;

import base.AbstractEntityBase;

public class OrderBean extends AbstractEntityBase {

  private String orderId;
  private Date orderDate;

  private boolean isModified;

  private EntityContext entityContext;

  public String getOrderId() {
    return orderId;
  }

  public Date getOrderDate() {
    return orderDate;
  }

  public void setOrderDate(Date inDate) {
    isModified = true;
    this.orderDate = inDate;
  }
```

The Order bean maps all of its methods that access the relationship into the equivalent calls of the item bean. The getOrder() method is mapped to the findRelatedLineItems() customer finder. The addLineItem() and removeLineItem() methods are mapped into calls to setOrder() on LineItem This eliminates both the repetition of SQL between the beans, and the isolation problems with both beans accessing the relationship data:

```
public Collection getLineItems() throws RemoteException {
  try {
    Context ic = new InitialContext();
    LineItemHome liHome =
      (LineItemHome) PortableRemoteObject
        .narrow(ic.lookup("java:comp/env/ejb/LineItemHome"),
            LineItemHome.class);
    return liHome.findRelatedLineItems(orderId);
  } catch (NamingException ex) {
    throw new EJBException(ex);
  } catch (FinderException ex) {
    throw new EJBException(ex);
  }
```

```
    }

    public void addLineItem(LineItem item) throws RemoteException {
        item.setOrder((Order) entityContext.getEJBObject());
    }

    public void removeLineItem(LineItem item) throws RemoteException {
        Order oldOrder = item.getOrder();

        // should only set order to null if this order actually
        // contains the line item
        if (oldOrder != null && oldOrder.getOrderId().equals(orderId)) {
            item.setOrder(null);
        }
    }
}
```

Notice that in the Order bean, the finder method that corresponds to the relationship load for line items is called each time that `getLineItems()` is called. We must go back to the database each time, because it is possible that a line item has been moved to a different order since the last time `getLineItems()` was called. It is important that users of the `order` bean understand that each call to `getLineItems()` corresponds to a new database query and eliminate unnecessary calls to this method from their code.

As has been the case with many of our examples, the pattern for the majority of the lifecycle methods is not affected by this relationship type. From here to the end of the chapter, any lifecycle method which simply follows standard pattern will be mentioned by name and omitted from the text. This is for the sake of brevity; the full source for the examples is available from the web site for the book.

The following lifecycle methods follow the standard pattern and have been omitted:

❑   `ejbLoad()`

❑   `ejbStore()`

❑   `ejbCreate()`

❑   `ejbRemove()`

❑   `ejbFindByPrimaryKey()`

❑   `ejbActivate()`

❑   `ejbPassivate()`

Unidirectional Relationships

So far we have discussed only bi-directional relationships. To alter our example from bi-directional to unidirectional from line item to order is a simple task. We can remove all of the methods corresponding to the line items relationship from the `Order` bean. We can also remove the `findRelatedLineItems()` finder method from the `LineItem` bean. Doing this is probably a good idea if an index is not built on your foreign key. However, in our example it logically makes more sense for the relationship to be unidirectional from order to line item.

This solution of removing the methods will not work for order to line item in our example, because the `Order` bean methods depend on the `LineItem` bean methods to function. In this case making the relationship unidirectional would be complicated to implement. If the `Order` bean is responsible for updating the relationship, then when a line item is moved from one order to another, two `Order` beans would try to update the same line item record. This introduces the possiblity of isolation problem, as described earlier in the chapter.

Leaving the relationship bidirectional causes little performance impact because the navigation from line item to order is based on the primary key, and therefore will always have an index defined on it. If desired we could remove the `getOrder()` method from the `LineItem` bean to indicate that it is not intended to be navigable, but leaving the `setOrder()` method in place greatly simplifies the implementation of the relationship and causes no significant harm.

Reference Table (M-M) Relationship

Another common database table structure used to represent relationships between entities is a reference table. In this case neither of the tables for the entities contains a foreign key. The foreign keys are kept in separate table called a **reference table**. The table contains a foreign key for both tables. These tables are also called **junction tables** by some databases (notably SQL Server).

This structure offers several advantages over the direct foreign key case. In the direct foreign key case, one of the ends is limited to pointing to a single object. To represent a many-to-many relationship, a reference table must be used. Another major advantage is that a reference table can be added after the original table structure is already complete and in use.

Generally speaking, altering database tables after they have production data in them is considered bad practice. It is an expensive operation from a time perspective and has the potential of corrupting the existing data. It may also mean taking a production system offline during the operation. Since neither of the main tables differs as a result of adding the reference table, a new reference table can be added between two existing tables without affecting the original table structure or data.

Of course, reference tables have disadvantages as well. Since neither of the foreign keys resides in the entity tables, neither of the navigation queries can be combined with the main load for the bean. Also, the implementation of the relationship in code is more complex and requires a larger number of SQL statements to be constructed.

The canonical mapping for the reference table structure is a many-to-many relationship. Our example of a many-to-many relationship will consist of a meeting entity and a person entity. A meeting will consist of more than one person, and one person may be invited to more than one meeting, hence it is a many-to-many relationship:

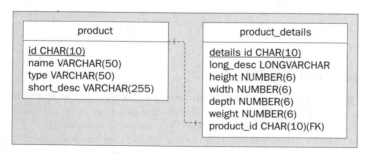

Here is the database table structure we will use in this case. The reference table (`person_meeting_ref`) achieves the many-to-many functionality:

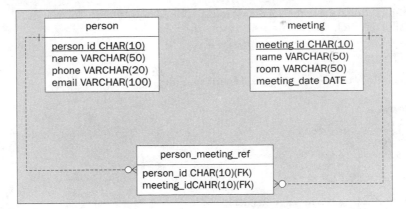

Again we will start with navigating the relationship. Navigating in either direction will be a SELECT on the reference table, as it contains both of the foreign keys. To find the people involved in a meeting we must select the people foreign key based on the meeting foreign key:

```
SELECT person_id
        FROM person_meeting_ref
        WHERE meeting_id = ?
```

To find all meetings that a particular person is invited to, we will switch the foreign key involved in the SELECT clause with the one in the WHERE clause:

```
SELECT meeting_id
        FROM person_meeting_ref
        WHERE person_id = ?
```

Adding a person to a meeting or adding a meeting to a person's agenda are logically equivalent operations. Both correspond to inserting a record into the reference table as follows:

```
INSERT INTO person_meeting_ref (person_id,meeting_id)
        VALUES (?,?)
```

The same symmetry applies to removing a person from a meeting and vice-versa. These correspond to deleting a record from the reference table, as follows:

```
DELETE FROM person_meeting_ref
        WHERE person_id = ?
        AND meeting_id = ?
```

Unlike in the direct foreign key case, neither bean really owns the relationship. This is because the relationship is not stored in either bean's table. We still have the same isolation problems however, as both beans may need to update the relationship table. In the previous example we avoided this problem by delegating all relationship updates to a single bean. This bean was free to store data for the relationship in memory and not worry about consistency, since it was the only bean updating the relationship table.

For the reference table case we will take a different approach. Neither bean will cache data about the relationship in memory. Since no updates are based on previous reads, proper consistency can be maintained even if both beans update the same table.

As with the bi-directional case, the relationship is visible in both remote interfaces. The customer finders are visible in the home interfaces.

The Person Bean

The Person bean does not declare any fields corresponding to the relationship.

The Remote Interface

```
package refTableManyToMany;

import java.rmi.RemoteException;
import javax.ejb.EJBObject;
import java.util.Collection;

public interface Person extends EJBObject {

  public String getPersonId() throws RemoteException;

  public String getName() throws RemoteException;
  public void setName(String inName) throws RemoteException;

  public String getPhone() throws RemoteException;
  public void setPhone(String inPhone) throws RemoteException;

  public String getEmail() throws RemoteException;
  public void setEmail(String inEmail) throws RemoteException;

  public Collection getMeetings() throws RemoteException;
  public void addMeeting(Meeting inMeeting) throws RemoteException;
  public void removeMeeting(Meeting inMeeting) throws RemoteException;

}
```

The Home Interface

```
package refTableManyToMany;

import java.rmi.RemoteException;
import javax.ejb.*;
import java.util.Collection;

public interface PersonHome extends EJBHome {

  public Person findByPrimaryKey(String inPersonId) throws FinderException,
                                                           RemoteException;

  public Collection findMeetingAttendees(String meetingId)
                                        throws FinderException,
                                               RemoteException;

  public Person create(String inPersonId) throws CreateException,
                                                 RemoteException;

}
```

The Bean Implementation Class

The accessor methods for non-relaltionship fields follow the same basic pattern as before:

```
package refTableManyToMany;

import javax.ejb.*;
import java.sql.*;
import javax.rmi.PortableRemoteObject;
import java.rmi.RemoteException;
import javax.naming.InitialContext;
import javax.naming.Context;
import javax.naming.NamingException;
import java.util.Collection;
import java.util.ArrayList;

import base.AbstractEntityBase;

public class PersonBean extends AbstractEntityBase {

  private String personId;
  private String name;
  private String phone;
  private String email;

  private boolean isModified;

  public String getPersonId() {
    return personId;
  }

  public String getName() {
    return name;
  }
  public void setName(String inName) {
    isModified = true;
    this.name = inName;
  }

  public String getPhone() {
    return phone;
  }
  public void setPhone(String inPhone) {
    isModified = true;
    this.phone = inPhone;
  }

  public String getEmail() {
    return email;
  }
  public void setEmail(String inEmail) {
    isModified = true;
    this.email = inEmail;
  }
```

The `getMeetings()` method on the Person bean is implemented as a call to a custom finder on the Meeting bean:

```
public Collection getMeetings() throws RemoteException {
  try {
    Context ic = new InitialContext();
```

```
        MeetingHome mHome =
          (MeetingHome) PortableRemoteObject
            .narrow(ic.lookup("java:comp/env/ejb/MeetingHome"),
                  MeetingHome.class);
        return mHome.findMeetingsForPerson(personId);
      } catch (NamingException ex) {
        throw new EJBException(ex);
      } catch (FinderException ex) {
        throw new EJBException(ex);
      }
    }
```

The addMeeting() method will immediately insert a record into the reference table. If we attempted to delay the insert of the record until the call to ejbStore(), then we would need a mechanism to track what changes had occurred to the relationship. We greatly simplify the implementation by performing the operations immediately:

```
    public void addMeeting(Meeting meeting) throws RemoteException {
      Connection conn = null;
      PreparedStatement ps = null;
      try {
        ps = conn.prepareStatement("INSERT INTO person_meeting_ref" +
                                   "(person_id,meeting_id) VALUES(?,?)");
        ps.setString(1, personId);
        ps.setString(2, meeting.getMeetingId());
        if (ps.executeUpdate() != 1) {
          throw new EJBException("Wrong insert count");
        }
      } catch (SQLException ex) {
        new EJBException(ex);
      } finally {
        cleanUp(conn, ps, null);
      }
    }
```

Just as with the addMeeting() method, the removeMeeting() method removes a record from the reference table immediately:

```
    public void removeMeeting(Meeting meeting) throws RemoteException {
      Connection conn = null;
      PreparedStatement ps = null;
      try {
        conn = getConnection();
        ps = conn.prepareStatement("DELETE FROM person_meeting_ref" +
                                   "WHERE person_id = ? " +
                                   "AND meeting_id = ?");
        ps.setString(1, personId);
        ps.setString(2, meeting.getMeetingId());

        // may delete 0 or 1 row
        if (ps.executeUpdate() > 1) {
          throw new EJBException("Wrong delete count");
        }
      } catch (SQLException ex) {
```

```
        throw new EJBException(ex);
    } finally {
        cleanUp(conn, ps, null);
    }

}
```

As in the previous example, a custom finder is added to the bean, which will be used in the `getAttendees()` method on the Meeting bean:

```
public Collection ejbFindMeetingAttendees(String meetingId) {
    Collection ret = new ArrayList();
    Connection conn = null;
    PreparedStatement ps = null;
    ResultSet rs = null;
    try {
        conn = getConnection();
        ps = conn.prepareStatement("SELECT person_id " +
                                   "FROM person_meeting_ref " +
                                   "WHERE meeting_id = ?");
        ps.setString(1, meetingId);
        rs = ps.executeQuery();
        while (rs.next()) {
            ret.add(rs.getString(1));
        }
        return ret;
    } catch (SQLException ex) {
        throw new EJBException(ex);
    } finally {
        cleanUp(conn, ps, rs);
    }
}
```

The following methods have been omitted for brevity, but are available as part of the code download for the book:

❑   ejbLoad()

❑   ejbStore()

❑   ejbCreate()

❑   ejbRemove()

❑   ejbFindByPrimaryKey()

❑   ejbActivate()

❑   ejbPassivate()

The Meeting Bean

Just like the Person bean, no fields corresponding to the relationship are declared in the Meeting bean.

The Remote Interface

```
package refTableManyToMany;

import java.rmi.RemoteException;
import javax.ejb.EJBObject;
import java.sql.Date;
import java.util.Collection;

public interface Meeting extends EJBObject {

  public String getMeetingId() throws RemoteException;

  public String getName() throws RemoteException;
  public void setName(String inName) throws RemoteException;

  public String getRoom() throws RemoteException;
  public void setRoom(String inRoom) throws RemoteException;

  public Date getDate() throws RemoteException;
  public void setDate(Date inDate) throws RemoteException;

  public Collection getAttendees() throws RemoteException;
  public void addAttendee(Person attendee) throws RemoteException;
  public void removeAttendee(Person attendee) throws RemoteException;

}
```

The Home Interface

```
package refTableManyToMany;

import java.rmi.RemoteException;
import javax.ejb.*;
import java.util.Collection;

public interface MeetingHome extends EJBHome {

  public Meeting findByPrimaryKey(String inId) throws FinderException,
                                                      RemoteException;

  public Collection findMeetingsForPerson(String personId)
                                          throws FinderException,
                                                 RemoteException;

  public Meeting create(String inId) throws CreateException,
                                            RemoteException;

}
```

The Bean Implementation Class

Non-relationship fields are represented as normal:

```
package refTableManyToMany;

import javax.ejb.*;
import java.sql.*;
import javax.rmi.PortableRemoteObject;
```

```
import java.rmi.RemoteException;
import javax.naming.InitialContext;
import javax.naming.Context;
import javax.naming.NamingException;
import java.util.Collection;
import java.util.ArrayList;

import base.AbstractEntityBase;

public class MeetingBean extends AbstractEntityBase {

  private String meetingId;
  private String name;
  private String room;
  private Date date;

  private boolean isModified;

  public String getMeetingId() {
    return meetingId;
  }

  public String getName() {
    return name;
  }
  public void setName(String inName) {
    isModified = true;
    this.name = inName;
  }

  public String getRoom() {
    return room;
  }
  public void setRoom(String inRoom) {
    isModified = true;
    this.room = inRoom;
  }

  public Date getDate() {
    return date;
  }
  public void setDate(Date inDate) {
    isModified = true;
    this.date = inDate;
  }
```

Since we have chosen to make the person the owner of the relationship, the relationship calls in the Meeting bean are delegated to the Person bean:

```
public Collection getAttendees() throws RemoteException {
  try {
    Context ic = new InitialContext();
    PersonHome pHome =
      (PersonHome) PortableRemoteObject
        .narrow(ic.lookup("java:comp/env/ejb/PersonHome"),
                PersonHome.class);
    return pHome.findMeetingAttendees(meetingId);
  } catch (NamingException ex) {
    throw new EJBException(ex);
```

```
    } catch (FinderException ex) {
      throw new EJBException(ex);
    }
  }

  public void addAttendee(Person person) throws RemoteException {
    person.addMeeting((Meeting) entityContext.getEJBObject());
  }

  public void removeAttendee(Person person) throws RemoteException {
    person.removeMeeting((Meeting) entityContext.getEJBObject());
  }
```

The Meeting bean also contains the custom finder used earlier to implement the getMeetings()
method on the Person bean:

```
  public Collection ejbFindMeetingsForPerson(String personId) {
    Collection ret = new ArrayList();
    Connection conn = null;
    PreparedStatement ps = null;
    ResultSet rs = null;
    try {
      conn = getConnection();
      ps = conn.prepareStatement("SELECT meeting_id " +
                                 "FROM person_meeting_ref " +
                                 "WHERE person_id = ?");
      ps.setString(1, personId);
      rs = ps.executeQuery();
      while (rs.next()) {
        ret.add(rs.getString(1));
      }
      return ret;
    } catch (SQLException ex) {
      throw new EJBException(ex);
    } finally {
      cleanUp(conn, ps, rs);
    }
  }
```

In this case every call to a relationship (get, add, or remove) causes an immediate database operation.
Again users of the entity bean must take this into account when writing client code for the bean.

The following methods have been omitted for brevity, but are available as part of the code download
for this book:

❑   ejbLoad()

❑   ejbStore()

❑   ejbCreate()

❑   ejbRemove()

❑   ejbFindByPrimaryKey()

❑   ejbActivate()

❑   ejbPassivate()

Using the Unique Constraint

The above examples show the simplest mapping for the direct foreign key and reference table database structures. By applying a unique constraint to a foreign key column, however, any end of a relationship that has a many multiplicity can be limited to one multiplicity.

We employed a similar technique previously in the chapter with product and details to ensure that when loading data from multiple tables for a bean the records has a one-to-one correspondence. By using a unique constraint, a direct foreign key structure can represent a one-to-one relationship, and a reference table structure can represent either a one-to-one or a one-to-many relationship. When a unique constraint is used, code must be added to ensure that the constraint is not violated when updating the relationship.

The Unique Contraint and Direct Foreign Keys

For a one-to-one example will use the manager of a department. The relationship will be between an Employee object and a Department object:

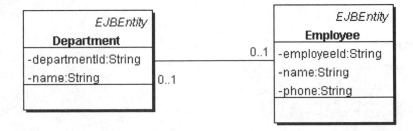

Note that in this instance, the Employee represents a manager, and the Department is one that they manage. We will use the following table structure, which uses a direct foreign key, to represent the relationship:

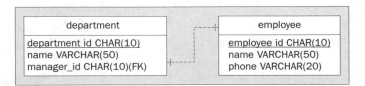

We will declare the `manager_id` field to be unique, which can be done in Oracle with the following statement:

```
ALTER TABLE department
    ADD (UNIQUE manager_id)
```

We'll look at the code for this example next. The home interfaces show the customer finders for the relationship, and otherwise follow the standard pattern. The remote interfaces show the relationship as a object-oriented programmer would expect it. There is no sign of the work going on to maintain the unique constraint within the remote interface. To complete the example, code for all of the home and remote interfaces is provided.

The Department Bean

Just as before with the LineItem bean, the Department bean will load and update the foreign key field with the other fields of the bean.

The Remote Interface

```
package directOneToOne;

import java.rmi.RemoteException;
import javax.ejb.EJBObject;

public interface Department extends EJBObject {

  public String getDepartmentId() throws RemoteException;

  public String getName() throws RemoteException;
  public void setName(String inProduct) throws RemoteException;

  public Employee getManager() throws RemoteException;
  public void setManager(Employee inManager) throws RemoteException;

}
```

The Home Interface

```
package directOneToOne;

import java.rmi.RemoteException;
import javax.ejb.*;
import java.util.Collection;

public interface DepartmentHome extends EJBHome {

  public Department findByPrimaryKey(String inDepId) throws FinderException,
                                                     RemoteException;

  public Department findManagedDepartment(String employeeId)
                                    throws FinderException,
                                           RemoteException;

  public Department create(String inDepId) throws CreateException,
                                           RemoteException;

}
```

The Bean Implementation Class

This bean will declare a variable to hold the cached remote object reference, in this case relatedManager. All other accessors follow the standard pattern:

```
package directOneToOne;

import javax.ejb.*;
import java.sql.*;
import java.rmi.RemoteException;
import javax.rmi.PortableRemoteObject;
import javax.naming.InitialContext;
import javax.naming.Context;
import javax.naming.NamingException;
```

```
import java.util.Collection;
import java.util.LinkedList;

import base.AbstractEntityBase;

public class DepartmentBean extends AbstractEntityBase {

  private String departmentId;
  private String name;
  private String relatedManagerId;
  private Employee relatedManager;

  private boolean isModified;

  public String getDepartmentId() {
    return departmentId;
  }

  public String getName() {
    return name;
  }

  public void setName(String inName) {
    isModified = true;
    this.name = inName;
  }
```

The getManager() and setManager() methods also follow the same pattern as the line item bean. They update the relatedManagerId and relatedManager fields simulataneously, to maintain both the foreign key value and a cached reference to the remote interface for the related object:

```
public Employee getManager() throws RemoteException {

  // we delay instantiating a Person object as long as possible
  if (relatedManager == null) {
    if (relatedManagerId == null) {

      // department does not have a manager
      return null;
    } else {
      try {
        Context ic = new InitialContext();
        EmployeeHome eHome =
          (EmployeeHome) PortableRemoteObject
            .narrow(ic.lookup("java:comp/env/ejb/EmployeeHome"),
                    EmployeeHome.class);
        relatedManager = eHome.findByPrimaryKey(relatedManagerId);
      } catch (NamingException ex) {
        throw new EJBException(ex);
      } catch (FinderException ex) {
        throw new EJBException(ex);
      }
      return relatedManager;
    }
  } else {
    return relatedManager;
  }
}
```

```
public void setManager(Employee inManager) throws RemoteException {
  this.relatedManagerId = inManager.getEmployeeId();
  this.relatedManager = inManager;
}
```

Notice that when the setManagedDepartment() method is called on the Employee bean, it must set its previous relationship to null before setting the new relationship. Without the extra step, it is possible that one employee would be set to manage two departments. This would violate our unique constraint and cause a database error.

This example also declares a custom finder like the LineItem example. Here is our first noticeable difference, however; the finder returns a single object rather than a Collection. This is because of the unique constraint declared on the foreign key column. Other than that the method is very similar, as seen below:

```
public String ejbFindManagedDepartment(String managerEmployeeId)
                                       throws FinderException {
  Connection conn = null;
  PreparedStatement ps = null;
  ResultSet rs = null;
  try {
    conn = getConnection();
    ps = conn.prepareStatement("SELECT department_id " +
                               "FROM department " +
                               "WHERE manager_id = ?");
    ps.setString(1, managerEmployeeId);
    rs = ps.executeQuery();
    if (rs.next()) {
      return rs.getString(1);
    } else {
      throw new ObjectNotFoundException();
    }
  } catch (SQLException ex) {
    throw new EJBException(ex);
  } finally {
    cleanUp(conn, ps, rs);
  }
}
```

Again the lifecycle methods are uninteresting and have been omitted for space. The full source is included in the code download for this book. The following methods have been omitted:

❑ ejbLoad()
❑ ejbStore()
❑ ejbCreate()
❑ ejbRemove()
❑ ejbFindByPrimaryKey()
❑ ejbActivate()
❑ ejbPassivate()

The Employee Bean

The Employee bean declares no special fields for the relationship. It uses methods on the Department bean to control the relationship.

The Remote Interface

```
package directOneToOne;

import java.rmi.RemoteException;
import javax.ejb.EJBObject;
import java.sql.Date;
import java.util.Collection;

public interface Employee extends EJBObject {

  public String getEmployeeId() throws RemoteException;

  public String getName() throws RemoteException;
  public void setName(String inName) throws RemoteException;

  public String getPhone() throws RemoteException;
  public void setPhone(String inPhone) throws RemoteException;

  public Department getManagedDepartment() throws RemoteException;
  public void setManagedDepartment(Department inDepartment)
                                   throws RemoteException;

}
```

The Home Interface

```
package directOneToOne;

import java.rmi.RemoteException;
import javax.ejb.*;

public interface EmployeeHome extends EJBHome {

  public Employee findByPrimaryKey(String id) throws FinderException,
                                                     RemoteException;

  public Employee create(String inId) throws CreateException,
                                             RemoteException;

}
```

The EmployeeBean Implementation Class

The declarations for the standard fields follow:

```
package directOneToOne;

import javax.ejb.*;
import java.sql.*;
import javax.rmi.PortableRemoteObject;
import java.rmi.RemoteException;
import javax.sql.DataSource;
import javax.naming.InitialContext;
import javax.naming.Context;
import javax.naming.NamingException;
import java.util.Collection;
```

```
import base.AbstractEntityBase;

public class EmployeeBean extends AbstractEntityBase {

  private String employeeId;
  private String name;
  private String phone;

  private boolean isModified;

  public String getEmployeeId() {
    return employeeId;
  }

  public String getName() {
    return name;
  }
  public void setName(String inName) {
    isModified = true;
    this.name = inName;
  }

  public String getPhone() {
    return phone;
  }
  public void setPhone(String inPhone) {
    isModified = true;
    this.phone = inPhone;
  }
```

The big difference caused by using a unique constraint in this relationship is in the relationship methods for the Employee bean. Rather than declaring add and remove methods here, the Employee bean defines getManagedDepartment() and setManagedDepartment() methods. The getManagedDepartment() method is similar to the previous cases. It calls a custom finder in the Department bean to navigate the relationship. The difference is the finder now returns a single value rather than a Collection:

```
public Department getManagedDepartment() throws RemoteException {
  try {
    Context ic = new InitialContext();
    DepartmentHome dHome =
      (DepartmentHome) PortableRemoteObject
        .narrow(ic.lookup("java:comp/env/ejb/DepartmentHome"),
                DepartmentHome.class);
    return dHome.findManagedDepartment(employeeId);
  } catch (NamingException ex) {
    throw new EJBException(ex);
  } catch (ObjectNotFoundException ex) {

    // if there is no department found for this employee, then its
    // managed department is null
    return null;
  } catch (FinderException ex) {
    throw new EJBException(ex);
  }
}
```

The setManagedDepartment() method differs quite a bit. An employee managing two departments simultaneous would violate our unique constraint. Therefore, we must be sure to unset the previously managed department for the employee, before setting the new managed department. The code for this logic is as follows:

```
public void setManagedDepartment(Department newDepartment)
                               throws RemoteException {

    // Calling setManager will update the foreign key column in the
    // department table.  To avoid violating the unique constraint on
    // this column, the previously managed department must first
    // be set to null
    Department currentDepartment = getManagedDepartment();
    if (currentDepartment != null) {
      currentDepartment.setManager(null);
    }
    newDepartment.setManager((Employee) entityContext.getEJBObject());
}
```

Once again, the lifecycle methods are irrelevant to our discussion. The following methods are omitted, but are with the code download for the book:

- ❑ ejbLoad()
- ❑ ejbStore()
- ❑ ejbCreate()
- ❑ ejbRemove()
- ❑ ejbFindByPrimaryKey()
- ❑ ejbActivate()
- ❑ ejbPassivate()

Our example indicates one of the common caveats with one-to-one relationships. Usually requiring both ends to be exactly one is overly restrictive. Most applications would be able to handle a single employee managing more than one department, and an application that does not may fall short in a real-life situation when this exact state occurs.

The most common types of one-to-one relationships are between two entities that are inseparably linked. A user and a user profile are a good example. In these cases there is a fuzzy line between a single entity and multiple related entities. Some guidelines for making this decision between a single entity and two related entities were presented earlier in this chapter.

The Unique Contraint and Reference Tables

Using a unique constraint on a reference table will require a similar change to our persistence code. When set is called on a one multiplicity end, a check is performed to see if the end currently has a relationship. If so, we cannot insert a new record into the reference table, as it would violate the unique constraint. We will simply update the existing record instead. As an example we will use Category and Item entities:

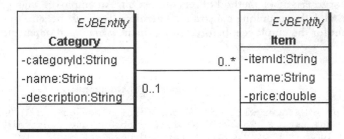

These objects are represented in the database as follows:

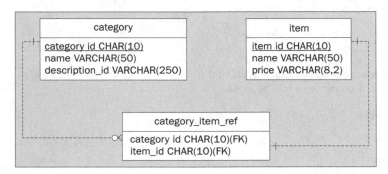

To limit an item to being in only one category, we place a unique constraint on the item foreign key:

```
ALTER TABLE category_item_ref
    ADD (UNIQUE item_id)
```

In this case, we will choose the Item bean as the relationship owner. We will actually map this one-to-many relationship in a similar way to the one-to-many relationship with the direct foreign key. However, since the relationship is stored in a separate table, it will be like mapping a join with an optional record in the secondary table. We covered this case with the product and image example earlier in the chapter.

The home and remote interfaces follow the same pattern as the `Order` and `LineItem` one-to-many relationship. This is significant, because to an outside user of the bean it is transparent whether the relationship is modeled as a direct foreign key or a reference table. The object-oriented developer has been completely isolated from this detail.

The Item Bean

Here is an extract of the code for this bean, together with the full interfaces.

The Remote Interface

```
package refTableOneToMany;

import java.rmi.RemoteException;
import javax.ejb.EJBObject;

public interface Item extends EJBObject {
```

```
    public String getItemId() throws RemoteException;

    public String getName() throws RemoteException;
    public void setName(String inName) throws RemoteException;

    public double getPrice() throws RemoteException;
    public void setPrice(double inPrice) throws RemoteException;

    public Category getCategory() throws RemoteException;
    public void setCategory(Category inCategory) throws RemoteException;

}
```

The Home Interface

```
package refTableOneToMany;

import java.rmi.RemoteException;
import javax.ejb.*;
import java.util.Collection;

public interface ItemHome extends EJBHome {

  public Item findByPrimaryKey(String inId) throws FinderException,
                                                    RemoteException;

  public Collection findItemsInCategory(String categoryId)
                                    throws FinderException,
                                           RemoteException;

  public Item create(String inId) throws CreateException, RemoteException;

}
```

The Bean Implementation Class

Both `relatedCategoryId` and `relatedCategory` fields are added to represent the relationship. Three flags are also added to help manage the relationship, `categoryReferenceLoaded`, `categoryReferenceChanged`, and `categoryReferenceRecordExists`. These fields follow the same pattern as the optional detail table:

```
package refTableOneToMany;

import javax.ejb.*;
import java.sql.*;
import java.rmi.RemoteException;
import javax.rmi.PortableRemoteObject;
import javax.naming.InitialContext;
import javax.naming.Context;
import javax.naming.NamingException;
import java.util.Collection;
import java.util.LinkedList;

import base.AbstractEntityBase;

public class ItemBean extends AbstractEntityBase {

  private String itemId;
  private String name;
```

```
      private double price;

      private String relatedCategoryId;
      private Category relatedCategory;

      private boolean categoryReferenceRecordExists;
      private boolean categoryReferenceLoaded;
      private boolean categoryReferenceChanged;

      private boolean isModified;

      public String getItemId() {
        return itemId;
      }

      public String getName() {
        return name;
      }
      public void setName(String inName) {
        isModified = true;
        this.name = inName;
      }

      public double getPrice() {
        return price;
      }
      public void setPrice(double inPrice) {
        isModified = true;
        this.price = inPrice;
      }
```

The getCategory() and setCategory() methods are a cross between optional record and order-line item reference patterns. The getCategory() method lazy-loads the the relatedCategoryId field through the loadCategoryRef() method. Once it loads the ID field it uses it to call the finder on the Category object and caches the result:

```
      public Category getCategory() throws RemoteException {
        loadCategoryRef();
        if (relatedCategory == null && relatedCategoryId != null) {
          try {
            Context ic = new InitialContext();
            CategoryHome cHome =
              (CategoryHome) PortableRemoteObject
                .narrow(ic.lookup("java:comp/env/ejb/CategoryHome"),
                        CategoryHome.class);
            relatedCategory = cHome.findByPrimaryKey(relatedCategoryId);
          } catch (NamingException ex) {
            throw new EJBException(ex);
          } catch (FinderException ex) {
            throw new EJBException(ex);
          }
        }
        return relatedCategory;
      }
```

The setCategory() method also needs to call loadCategoryRef(). Just like in the optional record case this method sets the categoryReferenceRecordExists flag, which is needed during ejbStore():

```
public void setCategory(Category inCategory) throws RemoteException {

  // need to call this to set categoryRecordExists flag
  loadCategoryRef();
  categoryReferenceChanged = true;
  relatedCategoryId = inCategory.getCategoryId();
  relatedCategory = inCategory;
}
```

The lazy loading for the reference is achieved in the loadCategoryRef() method. It treats the reference table like an optional detail table and select either 0 or 1 row from the table. If it selects 0 rows, it sets the categoryReferenceRecordExists flag accordingly:

```
public void loadCategoryRef() {
  if (!categoryReferenceLoaded) {
    Connection conn = null;
    PreparedStatement ps = null;
    ResultSet rs = null;
    try {
      conn = getConnection();
      ps = conn.prepareStatement("SELECT category_id " +
                                 "FROM category_item_ref " +
                                 "WHERE item_id = ?");
      ps.setString(1, itemId);
      rs = ps.executeQuery();
      if (rs.next()) {
        relatedCategoryId = rs.getString(1);
        categoryReferenceRecordExists = true;
      } else {
        relatedCategoryId = null;
        categoryReferenceRecordExists = false;
      }
      if (rs.next()) {
        throw new EJBException("Multiple rows in loadCat");

        // this variable is set in getCategory
      }
      relatedCategory = null;
      categoryReferenceLoaded = true;
      categoryReferenceChanged = false;
    } catch (SQLException ex) {
      throw new EJBException(ex);
    } finally {
      cleanUp(conn, ps, rs);
    }
  }
}
```

Because of the lazy -oading strategy, the ejbLoad() method does not load the category fields, but instead simply sets the categoryReferenceLoaded flag:

```
public void ejbLoad() {
  Connection conn = null;
  PreparedStatement ps = null;
```

```
        ResultSet rs = null;
        try {
          conn = getConnection();
          ps = conn.prepareStatement("SELECT name, price FROM item " +
                                "WHERE item_id = ?");
          ps.setString(1, itemId);
          rs = ps.executeQuery();
          if (!rs.next()) {
            throw new NoSuchEntityException();
          }
          name = rs.getString(1);
          price = rs.getDouble(2);
          categoryReferenceLoaded = false;
          isModified = false;
        } catch (SQLException ex) {
          throw new EJBException(ex);
        } finally {
          cleanUp(conn, ps, rs);
        }
    }
```

When the category reference has been changed, the ejbStore() method may need to insert, update, or delete a record in the reference table. The logic is the same as the optional record logic described earlier in the chapter:

```
    public void ejbStore() {
      Connection conn = null;
      PreparedStatement ps = null;
      try {
        conn = getConnection();
        ps = conn.prepareStatement("UPDATE item SET name=?, price=?" +
                              "WHERE item_id = ?");
        ps.setString(1, name);
        ps.setDouble(2, price);
        ps.setString(3, itemId);
        if (ps.executeUpdate() != 1) {
          throw new EJBException("Wrong update count");
        }
        ps.close();
        ps = null;
        if (categoryReferenceChanged) {
          if (relatedCategoryId == null) {
            if (categoryReferenceRecordExists) {
              ps = conn.prepareStatement("DELETE FROM item_category_ref " +
                                    "WHERE item_id = ?");
              ps.setString(1, itemId);
              if (ps.executeUpdate() != 1) {
                throw new EJBException("Wrong delete count");
              }
            }
          } else {
            if (categoryReferenceRecordExists) {
              ps = conn.prepareStatement("UPDATE item_category_ref " +
                                    "SET category_id=? " +
                                    "WHERE item_id = ?");
```

```
                    ps.setString(1, relatedCategoryId);
                    ps.setString(2, itemId);
                    if (ps.executeUpdate() != 1) {
                      throw new EJBException("Wrong update count");
                    }
                  } else {
                    ps = conn.prepareStatement("INSERT INTO item_category_ref" +
                                               "(category_id,item_id) VALUES (?,?)");
                    ps.setString(1, relatedCategoryId);
                    ps.setString(2, itemId);
                    if (ps.executeUpdate() != 1) {
                      throw new EJBException("Wrong insert count");
                    }
                  }
                }
              }
            }
          } catch (SQLException ex) {
            throw new EJBException(ex);
          } finally {
            cleanUp(conn, ps, null);
          }
        }
```

A custom finder is added to the item bean for use by the Category bean. This code follows the same pattern as the standard reference table case:

```
    public Collection ejbFindItemsInCategory(String categoryId)
            throws FinderException {
      Collection ret = new LinkedList();
      Connection conn = null;
      PreparedStatement ps = null;
      ResultSet rs = null;
      try {
        conn = getConnection();
        ps = conn.prepareStatement("SELECT item_id " +
                                   "FROM item_category_ref " +
                                   "WHERE category_id = ?");
        ps.setString(1, categoryId);
        rs = ps.executeQuery();
        while (rs.next()) {
          ret.add(rs.getString(1));
        }
      } catch (SQLException ex) {
        throw new EJBException(ex);
      } finally {
        cleanUp(conn, ps, rs);
      }
      return ret;
    }
```

The other lifecycle methods are irrelevant to this case and have been omitted for space. The full source is available as part of the code download for this book. The following methods have been omitted:

- ❏ ejbCreate()
- ❏ ejbRemove()
- ❏ ejbFindByPrimaryKey()
- ❏ ejbActivate()
- ❏ ejbPassivate()

The Category Bean

The Category bean follows the same pattern as the standard reference table case. To keep away from too much repetition, we will show none of this bean. The full source for the bean is available on the web site for the book.

A reference table structure can also be mapped into a one-to-one relationship. Although a direct foreign key relationship is usually more appropriate for both one-to-one and one-to-many relationships, a reference table may be used in some special cases. As an example, if two tables that already exist need to have a relationship added to them, a reference table may be used since it requires no changes to the structure of the existing tables. In the code for the one-to-one relationship, the Category bean would map its set and get calls into calls for Item. This case is similar to the one-to-one direct foreign key relationships mentioned earlier in the section.

Value Objects

Thus far we have discussed mapping entity beans and relationships between two entity beans to the database. Entity beans are appropriate for most database mappings, as the BMP contract for the entity bean allows the container to manage the object's lifecycle.

However, in some situations the contract for BMP entity beans is too limiting. For one, all entity beans are required to have a primary key. However, the biggest problem with the entity bean is the regimented lifecycle itself. The find, load, update, and relationship update phases are all done separately. In many cases we would like to combine some of these operations, for example to find and load an object simultaneously.

In both of these situations we can use regular serializable objects to represent what is logically an entity. These objects will be managed within the lifecycle of the containing entity bean. Because these objects depend on the containing entity bean for their lifecycle and persistence, many object frameworks would name these objects dependents. However, pre-release drafts of the EJB 2.0 specification used the term dependent object to mean a very specific type of object, which had its own lifecycle. Even though this concept was removed from the specification, there is still some confusion about what does and does not qualify as a dependent.

To attempt to alleviate some of this confusion, we will refer to our objects as **value objects**. For our purposes, the value object will simply mean a serializable object that we are mapping to persistent data.

Because a value object has no identity outside the context of a particular entity bean, the entity bean's end of the relationship with a value object will always have a multiplicity of one. Only the containing bean may have a reference to it. Also, for simplicity the value object tends not to have navigability back to the entity bean. Since the value object is always used in the context of a particular entity bean, this reference is generally unnecessary. This leaves us two types of relationships to consider, one-to-one and one-to-many unidirectional.

Value Objects in a Single Table

The one-to-one value object relationship is easiest to think of as packaging multiple fields of the bean into a single object. Take a customer and address relationship. In many cases the address data will not have its own table. Data for both objects will be stored in a single `customer` table as follows:

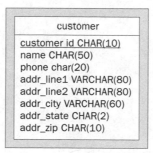

However, because logically a customer and address can be thought of a separate, we will model this pattern using two objects. In the object model, data will be split between Customer, which is a full-fledged entity bean, and Address, which is a value object:

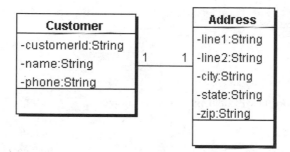

The Address Value Object

Because the Address object is not an entity bean, it will not contain persistence logic or SQL statements. It will simply follow the standard Java pattern for get and set methods:

```java
import java.io.Serializable;

public class Address implements Serializable {
    private String line1;
    private String line2;
    private String city;
    private String state;
    private String zip;

    public String getLine1() {
        return line1;
    }
    public void setLine1(String inLine1) {
        this.line1 = inLine1;
```

```
  }

  public String getLine2() {
    return line2;
  }
  public void setLine2(String inLine2) {
    this.line2 = inLine2;
  }

  public String getCity() {
    return city;
  }
  public void setCity(String inCity) {
    this.city = inCity;
  }

  public String getState() {
    return state;
  }
  public void setState(String inState) {
    this.state = inState;
  }

  public String getZip() {
    return zip;
  }
  public void setZip(String inZip) {
    this.zip = inZip;
  }
}
```

The Customer Bean

Now let's look at the EJB that will be using the value object.

The Remote Interface

The Address value object is exposed directly through the remote interface:

```
package valueObjectSingleTable;

import java.rmi.RemoteException;
import javax.ejb.EJBObject;

public interface Customer extends EJBObject {

  public String getCustomerId() throws RemoteException;

  public String getName() throws RemoteException;
  public void setName(String inName) throws RemoteException;

  public String getPhone() throws RemoteException;
  public void setPhone(String inPhone) throws RemoteException;

  public Address getAddress() throws RemoteException;
  public void setAddress(Address inAddr) throws RemoteException;

}
```

The Home Interface

We do not do so here, but the `Customer` create and finder methods could also use the `Address` value object, if desired:

```java
package valueObjectSingleTable;

import java.rmi.RemoteException;
import javax.ejb.*;

public interface CustomerHome extends EJBHome {

  public Customer findByPrimaryKey(String id) throws FinderException,
                                                     RemoteException;

  public Customer create(String inId) throws CreateException,
                                             RemoteException;

}
```

The Bean Implementation Class

The Customer object will define its own fields as per the standard pattern. The fields that correspond to the address will all be stored in a single Address object, which is also stored in a field:

```java
package valueObjectSingleTable;

import javax.ejb.*;
import java.sql.*;
import javax.naming.InitialContext;
import javax.naming.NamingException;

import base.AbstractEntityBase;

public class CustomerBean extends AbstractEntityBase {

  private String customerId;
  private String name;
  private String phone;
  private Address address;

  private boolean isModified;

  public String getCustomerId() {
    return customerId;
  }

  public String getName() {
    return name;
  }
  public void setName(String inName) {
    isModified = true;
    this.name = inName;
  }

  public String getPhone() {
    return phone;
  }
  public void setPhone(String inPhone) {
    isModified = true;
    this.phone = inPhone;
```

```
  }

  public Address getAddress() {
    return address;
  }
  public void setAddress(Address inAddr) {
    isModified = true;
    this.address = inAddr;
  }
```

It will be the responsibility of the Customer bean to manage the persistent data in the Address object. It will manage the fields of the Address object the same way it manages its own fields. To illustrate this, here are the implementations of the `ejbLoad()` and `ejbStore()` methods:

```
public void ejbLoad() {
  Connection conn = null;
  PreparedStatement ps = null;
  ResultSet rs = null;
  try {
    conn = getConnection();
    ps = conn.prepareStatement("SELECT name, phone, addr_line1, " +
                               "addr_line2, addr_city, addr_state, " +
                               "addr_zip " +
                               "FROM customer WHERE customer_id = ?");
    ps.setString(1, customerId);
    rs = ps.executeQuery();
    if (!rs.next()) {
      throw new NoSuchEntityException();
    }
    name = rs.getString(1);
    phone = rs.getString(2);
    address = new Address();
    address.setLine1(rs.getString(3));
    address.setLine2(rs.getString(4));
    address.setCity(rs.getString(5));
    address.setState(rs.getString(6));
    address.setZip(rs.getString(7));
    isModified = false;
  } catch (SQLException ex) {
    throw new EJBException(ex);
  } finally {
    cleanUp(conn, ps, rs);
  }
}

public void ejbStore() {
  if (isModified) {
    Connection conn = null;
    PreparedStatement ps = null;
    try {
      conn = getConnection();
      ps = conn.prepareStatement("UPDATE customer SET name=?, phone=?, " +
                                 "addr_line1=?, addr_line2=?, " +
                                 "addr_city=?, addr_state=?, " +
                                 "addr_zip=? " +
                                 "WHERE cutomer_id = ?");
```

```
        ps.setString(1, name);
        ps.setString(2, phone);
        ps.setString(3, address.getLine1());
        ps.setString(4, address.getLine2());
        ps.setString(5, address.getCity());
        ps.setString(6, address.getState());
        ps.setString(7, address.getZip());
        ps.setString(8, customerId);
        if (ps.executeUpdate() != 1) {
          throw new EJBException("Wrong update count");
        }
      } catch (SQLException ex) {
        throw new EJBException(ex);
      } finally {
        cleanUp(conn, ps, null);
      }
    }
  }
```

The `ejbCreate()` method for the `Customer` bean also follows this same pattern. It inserts all the values in the set Address object:

```
public String ejbCreate(String inId) throws CreateException {
  this.customerId = inId;
  this.name = null;

  // all field of address are null by default
  this.address = new Address();
  insertRecord();
  return customerId;
}

public void insertRecord() {
  Connection conn = null;
  PreparedStatement ps = null;
  try {
    conn = getConnection();
    ps = conn.prepareStatement("INSERT INTO customer " +
                               "VALUES(?,?,?,?,?,?,?,?)");
    ps.setString(1, customerId);
    ps.setString(2, name);
    ps.setString(3, phone);
    ps.setString(4, address.getLine1());
    ps.setString(5, address.getLine2());
    ps.setString(6, address.getCity());
    ps.setString(7, address.getState());
    ps.setString(8, address.getZip());
    if (ps.executeUpdate() != 1) {
      throw new EJBException("Incorrect insert count");
    }
  } catch (SQLException ex) {
    throw new EJBException(ex);
  } finally {
    cleanUp(conn, ps, null);
  }
}
```

The pattern for the other lifecycle methods remains unchanged. Therefore the following methods are omitted from the text, but are available in the full code download:

- ❑ ejbRemove()
- ❑ ejhFindByPrimaryKey()
- ❑ ejbActivate()
- ❑ ejbPassivate()

A Caveat with Value Objects

One important thing to notice about this implementation is which methods set the isModified flag to true. None of the set methods that are declared in the Address object will set this flag. If a user writes the following block of code, then the database will not be updated:

```
Address addr = customerX.getAddress();
addr.setCity("Pittsburgh");
```

This is because the isModified flag on the Customer bean was not set to true, and no update statement will be executed. To set the isModified flag, call setAddress() after changing the values in the Address object, like this:

```
Address addr = customerX.getAddress();
addr.setCity("Pittsburgh");
customerX.setAddress(addr);
```

Now the isModified flag will be set to true and the database will be updated.

Splitting One-to-One Value Objects Over Multiple Tables

It is also possible to map this same object model to a database that has separate tables for customer and address:

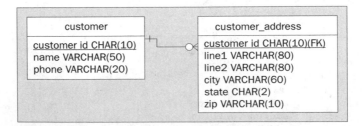

This has the added benefit that the address can be null. If there is no corresponding record in the customer_address table, then the address should be set to null. Since two separate tables are involved we would employ a lazy-loading pattern to load the address. Also when updating the address table, it is possible that we will need to insert a new record into the address table or remove the existing record.

We have already seen this pattern in both the product-image and item-category examples earlier in the chapter. By keeping an addressRecordExists flag we will be able to know whether to execute an INSERT, UPDATE, or DELETE in ejbStore(). This difference is this scenario packages several of the fields into a new value object.

A One-to-Many Value Object Relationship

When using a one-to-many value object relationship, two tables will be used to establish the multiplicity of "many" on the side of the value object. The lifecycle of the value object will be tied to the lifecycle of the relationship, rather than directly to the lifecycle of the bean.

When a value object is added to the relationship, a new record will be inserted into the database. When a value object is removed from the relationship, a record will be deleted. Because of this no value objects will exist that are not participating in a relationship. To illustrate this scenario we will re-implement the order and line item pattern using value objects for the line items. The database tables stay pretty much the same:

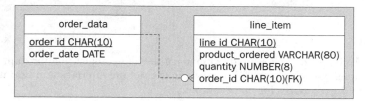

The difference now is that because all line items must participate in a relationship, the foreign key column should be declared to have a NOT NULL constraint. We can do this in Oracle with the following statement:

```
ALTER TABLE line_item MODIFY (order_id NOT NULL)
```

The object model will also be very similar to the previous example, with line item now being a value object. The implementation, however, will be quite different.

The Line Item Value Object

Previously, we managed the relationship in the line item bean. Now the LineItem is a value object and will contain no persistence logic. It will follow the simple get and set pattern, like our Address value object did in the last scenario:

```
package valueObjectOneToMany;

import java.io.Serializable;

public class LineItem implements Serializable {
  private String lineId;
  private String productOrdered;
  private int quantity;

  public String getLineId() {
    return lineId;
  }
  public void setLineId(String inLineId) {
    this.lineId = inLineId;
  }

  public String getProductOrdered() {
```

```
      return productOrdered;
  }
  public void setProductOrdered(String inProd) {
    this.productOrdered = inProd;
  }

  public int getQuantity() {
    return quantity;
  }
  public void setQuantity(int inQuant) {
    this.quantity = inQuant;
  }

}
```

The Order Bean

The Order bean declares no explicit fields to manage the value object relationship. As with our other value object example, the value object is exposed in the remote interface and optionally in the home interface. Here are the interfaces for our example.

The Remote Interface

```
package valueObjectOneToMany;

import java.rmi.RemoteException;
import javax.ejb.EJBObject;
import java.sql.Date;
import java.util.Collection;

public interface Order extends EJBObject {

  public String getOrderId() throws RemoteException;

  public Date getOrderDate() throws RemoteException;
  public void setOrderDate(Date inDate) throws RemoteException;

  public Collection getLineItems() throws RemoteException;
  public void addLineItem(LineItem item) throws RemoteException;
  public void removeLineItem(LineItem item) throws RemoteException;
  public void updateLineItem(LineItem item) throws RemoteException;

}
```

The Home Interface

```
package valueObjectOneToMany;

import java.rmi.RemoteException;
import javax.ejb.*;

public interface OrderHome extends EJBHome {

  public Order findByPrimaryKey(String id)
```

```
              throws FinderException, RemoteException;

    public Order create(String inId) throws CreateException, RemoteException;

}
```

The Bean Implementation Class

The Order bean declares its non-relationship fields using the standard pattern:

```
package valueObjectOneToMany;

import javax.ejb.*;
import java.sql.*;
import javax.naming.InitialContext;
import javax.naming.NamingException;
import java.util.Collection;
import java.util.ArrayList;

import base.AbstractEntityBase;

public class OrderBean extends AbstractEntityBase {

  private String orderId;
  private Date orderDate;

  private boolean isModified;

  public String getOrderId() {
    return orderId;
  }

  public Date getOrderDate() {
    return orderDate;
  }
  public void setOrderDate(Date inDate) {
    isModified = true;
    this.orderDate = inDate;
  }
}
```

For this scenario, we will need to manage the relationship of the Order bean to the `LineItem` value object through relationship accessor methods. Also, the database actions involved in this scenario are quite different from those in the previous order and line item example. Instead of updating the foreign key column, we will be inserting records into and deleting records from the line item table. The logic is actually relatively straightforward.

The `getLineItems()` method simply selects records from the line item table:

```
public Collection getLineItems() {
  Collection ret = new ArrayList();
  Connection conn = null;
  PreparedStatement ps = null;
  ResultSet rs = null;
  try {

    conn = getConnection();
```

```
          ps = conn.prepareStatement("SELECT line_id, product_ordered, " +
                                      "quantity " +
                                      "FROM line_item WHERE order_id = ?");
        ps.setString(1, orderId);
        rs = ps.executeQuery();
        while (rs.next()) {
          LineItem item = new LineItem();
          item.setLineId(rs.getString(1));
          item.setProductOrdered(rs.getString(2));
          item.setQuantity(rs.getInt(3));
          ret.add(item);
        }
        return ret;
      } catch (SQLException ex) {
        throw new EJBException(ex);
      } finally {
        cleanUp(conn, ps, rs);
      }
    }
```

The addLineItem() method inserts data for the line item into the line_item table. The method does not check if there is a line item with the given ID is already in the table. Therefore, adding a duplicate line item will result in a database error for a duplicate item ID:

```
    public void addLineItem(LineItem item) {
      Connection conn = null;
      PreparedStatement ps = null;
      try {
        conn = getConnection();
        ps = conn.prepareStatement("INSERT INTO " +
                    "line_item (line_id,product_ordered,quantity,order_id) " +
                                   "VALUES (?,?,?,?)");
        ps.setString(1, item.getLineId());
        ps.setString(2, item.getProductOrdered());
        ps.setInt(3, item.getQuantity());
        ps.setString(4, orderId);
        if (ps.executeUpdate() != 1) {
          throw new EJBException("Wrong insert count");
        }
      } catch (SQLException ex) {
        throw new EJBException(ex);
      } finally {
        cleanUp(conn, ps, null);
      }
    }
```

The removeLineItem() method deletes a record from the line item table. If the item does not actually exist in the table, no record will be deleted and no error will be thrown:

```
    public void removeLineItem(LineItem item) {
      Connection conn = null;
      PreparedStatement ps = null;
      try {
        conn = getConnection();
        ps = conn.prepareStatement("DELETE FROM line_item " +
                                   "WHERE line_id = ?");
        ps.setString(1, item.getLineId());
```

```
            if (ps.executeUpdate() > 1) {
              throw new EJBException("Wrong delete count");
            }
        } catch (SQLException ex) {
          throw new EJBException(ex);
        } finally {
          cleanUp(conn, ps, null);
        }
    }
```

Just as with the address, simply setting values into a line item will not update the database. A method must be called on the Order bean to initiate a change in the database. If the values within a line item change after being added to the order, then the updateLineItem() method should also be called. Here is that method:

```
public void updateLineItem(LineItem item) {
  Connection conn = null;
  PreparedStatement ps = null;
  try {
    conn = getConnection();
    ps = conn.prepareStatement("UPDATE line_item " +
                               "SET product_ordered=?, quantity=? " +
                               "WHERE line_id = ?");
    ps.setString(1, item.getProductOrdered());
    ps.setInt(2, item.getQuantity());
    ps.setString(3, item.getLineId());
    if (ps.executeUpdate() != 1) {
      throw new EJBException("Wrong update count");
    }
// standard catch-finally block
```

Because the relationship is managed entirely within the accessor methods for the relationship, the other lifecycle methods remain unchanged. For brevity the following methods have been omitted:

- ❑ ejbLoad()
- ❑ ejbStore()
- ❑ ejbCreate()
- ❑ ejbRemove()
- ❑ ejbFindByPrimaryKey()
- ❑ ejbActivate()
- ❑ ejbPassivate()

The main reason to take the value object approach in a one-to-many relationship is performance. When two separate entity beans were used, getting the list of line items and accessing their data involved many SQL statements: one to load the primary keys of the related beans and one per bean to load the actual data for the bean. With the value object pattern getting the list of line items has been reduced to a single SQL statement.

At first glance, this might seem like a great place to use nested classes since the line item is dependent on the order. However, the problem with using a nested class here is that the LineItem class is exposed to the client, while the OrderBean class is part of the internal implementation. If LineItem were a nested class the client would need to have access to the OrderBean class, which it really shouldn't. Also it presents even more of a problem if the client is in a different VM, because in a more realistic scenario an OrderBean may use libraries that are not available on the server, which may lead to "class not found" errors if an attempt is made to load OrderBean or its nested classes.

Summary

The mapping and persistence code for many common database structures has been presented in this chapter. We have covered the following:

- ❑ Mapping an entity to a single table
- ❑ Using an `isModified` flag
- ❑ Lazy loading
- ❑ Mapping an entity to multiple tables:
- ❑ With a required secondary table
- ❑ With an optional secondary table
- ❑ Using the not-null and unique constraints on foreign key columns
- ❑ Using a primary key-foreign key combination column
- ❑ Dealing with bean isolation issues
- ❑ Mapping lookup tables
- ❑ Mapping entity relationships modeled:
- ❑ As a direct foreign key relationship
- ❑ As a reference or junction table
- ❑ Use of value objects:
- ❑ To decompose a single table into multiple objects
- ❑ To model dependent relationships

At one level, these examples are not realistic. It is rarely that the cases will be so isolated. In fact objects will usually employ one or more of the above patterns simultaneously.

Objects also often participate in multiple relationships, which may be implemented with different strategies. However, these isolated examples establish a series of techniques, which can be applied in tandem to implement persistence for many database structures. For better or worse, there is a great deal of variation in way that data has been stored, even within the scope of relational databases.

The basic skills used in this chapter, like recognizing key structures and employing lazy-loading in a variety of situations, are the building blocks for extending these techniques and even developing new techniques to implement persistence for an application's unique data structure.

In the next chapter, we will delve into the world of container internals.

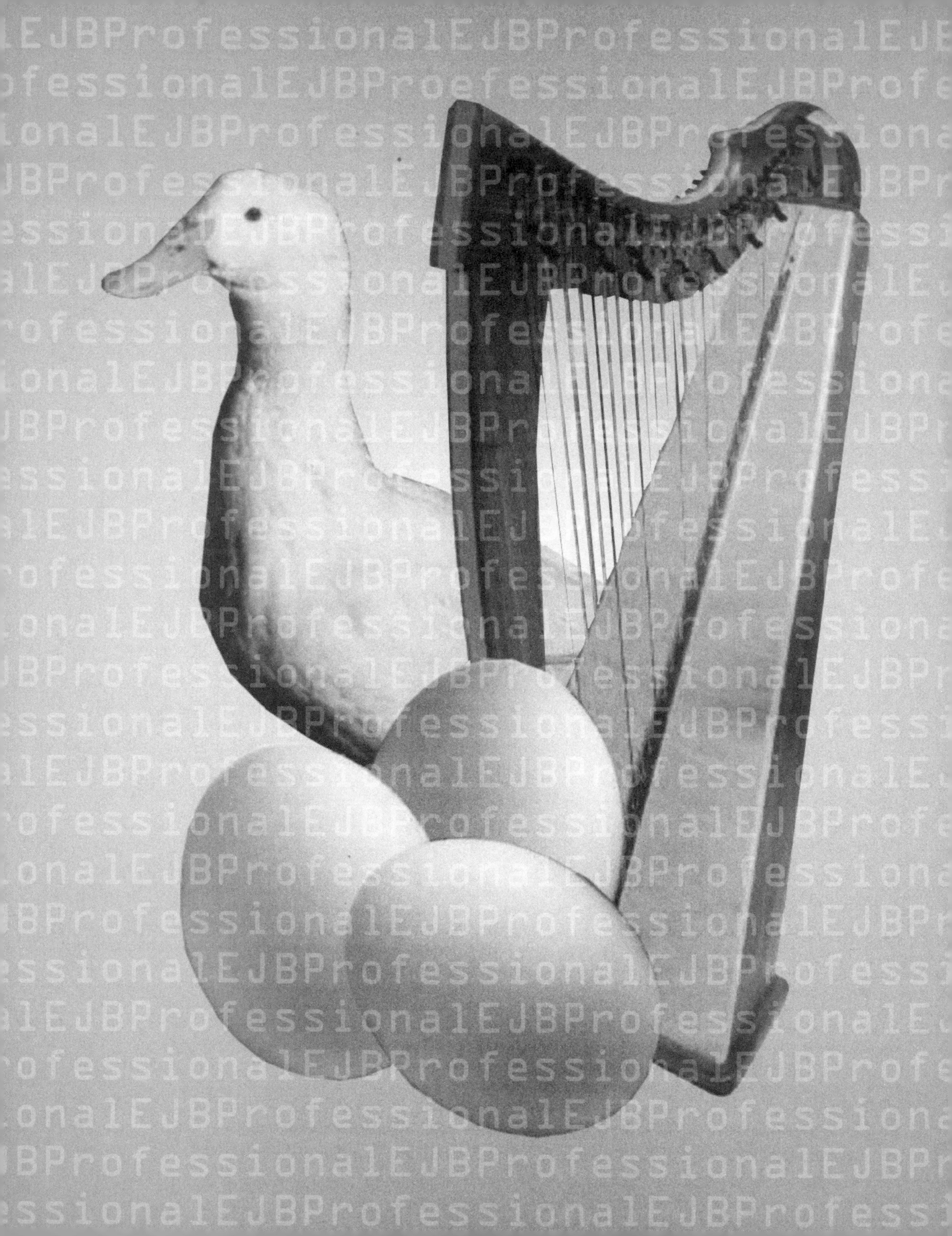
EJBProfessional

17

The EJB Container

In this chapter, we're going to look at how a typical EJB container operates. The EJB container is commonly regarded as a "black box", a service whose implementation is neither obvious nor interesting to the developer. To some degree, this is unavoidable since all containers are implemented differently, and we're not privy to the design of every one. However, there are a number of areas that are specifically addressed by the EJB specification, and a number of areas that lend themselves to common implementations. We'll look into these common areas in detail, since a working knowledge of the container gives us a better understanding of how to integrate our beans with the container. Armed with this insight, we can make better design decisions when modeling our beans, and better implementation decisions when coding them. Thus, we can improve the efficiency of the entire development process.

We will therefore be taking the following path through the workings of a container:

❑   Firstly, in order to clarify which aspects of the container we'll be looking at, we must briefly review the lifecycle of an EJB. A bean is developed, assembled, deployed, and finally used and managed. The container is not involved during development and assembly, but becomes involved during deployment, use, and management.

❑   Then, we'll look at the container's role and implementation for these three phases of the bean's lifecycle.

❑   We'll start with the deployment process, where the assembled beans are customized to the specific server environment, including generating container-specific classes and deployment descriptors.

❑   Then we'll look at the techniques and services that a container uses to process calls to running beans.

❑   Finally, we'll look at the management situation for EJB containers, the clustering options for scalability and fault tolerance, and take a brief look at what's coming in the next specification release.

Although some of the material might be familiar from earlier chapters of this book, this chapter will be focusing specifically on the role of the EJB container.

First though, we'll briefly review the function of an EJB container.

Introduction to the EJB Container

The J2EE architecture draws a distinction between **servers** and **containers**, but the difference is not always obvious. In brief, a server is a collection of services, whereas a container applies those services to specific components of our application. For example, an EJB server includes a transaction service and a security service, and the EJB container is the specific logic that applies transactions and security to EJB components.

J2EE applications are multi-tiered and web-enabled, and each application consists of one or more components, which are deployed in containers. J2EE supports the following four types of containers:

- ❑ EJB container – hosts enterprise beans
- ❑ Web container – hosts JavaServer Pages (JSP) and servlet components, as well as static documents (including HTML pages)
- ❑ Application client container – hosts standalone applications
- ❑ Applet client container – hosts applets, which may be downloaded from a web site

The J2EE specification has not yet clearly delineated the roles of the container and the server, so currently an application server is tied to the particular container implementations with which it ships. It is hoped that future revisions to the J2EE architecture may support a specific container API, which would allow middleware vendors to focus on aggregating best-of-breed containers, while container vendors may focus on developing specific containers in their area of expertise. This might also allow the end user to select the best container to meet their needs, and replace a specific component of their server.

In any case, as the container and server are currently so closely tied, the terms are often used interchangeably. You might notice this later in this chapter, since some of the topics we discuss, such as clustering, are more appropriately the province of the server as opposed to the container; we would typically cluster one application server on each server machine, not one container on each server machine. On the other hand, we do not discuss the implementations of the services provided by the server, such as transactions and security, except insofar as they affect the implementation of the EJB container itself.

Next, continuing our examination of the EJB container, we'll discuss the deployment process.

Deployment

The first time we interact with the container is when we customize our beans to the specific environment of the container, and deploy them into the container. This includes two main tasks for the container.

First, we need to customize the configuration of the assembled beans to the container's current environment. That is, any external references (such as remote EJBs, databases, and security roles) must be resolved to specific resources in the container's operational environment. The container needs to track this information somehow so that we don't have to repeat the process every time the container is restarted.

Second, the container must generate implementations for the classes that it needs to provide. For example, since a client interacts with a bean's component interface and the bean implementation doesn't have to implement that interface, the container has to provide a class that does.

In the following sections, we'll look at how the container handles both of these tasks, and the Java APIs that make it all work.

Configuration

When we deploy a bean, we need to start by fleshing out the deployment information. For example, the standard deployment descriptor lists EJB references, resource references, and security role references. However, these references just declare what resources or roles the bean needs; it doesn't link them up to specific database pools or actual roles in the container's security system.

In general, many EJB containers have some sort of graphical tool we use to handle this configuration. However, at this time, there is no standard format for the container to indicate what resources are available to resolve the outstanding references. The container's tools generally either leave it to you, the developer, to type in the correct values, or use a proprietary interface into the container to gather the available options for each setting that you need to make.

The EJB specification also does not address the storage of that additional information, so each container handles the information it gathers in a different way. The most common approach is to store the information in one or more XML files in the EJB JAR. These files are sometimes referred to as server-specific deployment descriptors (for example WebLogic's `weblogic-ejb-jar.xml`) as they work in the same way as the standard EJB deployment descriptor. Other products, such as certain versions of WebSphere, store that information in files in a different format, or in a central repository such as a database.

This means that there is no way to take beans deployed on one vendor's container, and deploy them into another vendor's container without repeating the same configuration process. Further, we can't even set up an automated build and deploy script that will compile, package, configure, and deploy our beans in a standard way that will work across all container products. In fact, it's suggested that we don't even try to access the vendor-specific information at all. The reason being that once we customize our beans to a specific server, there's no telling whether that information would be valid on a different server – and if we deployed an EJB JAR full of inconsistent information, there's no way to predict how or where it may fail. Possibilities of where it may fail include during deployment, at run time with a JNDI exception, at run time with an `SQLException`, at run time with an internal container exception, etc.

Ultimately, it's up to us to check our product's documentation carefully to determine whether it's wise, or even possible, to manipulate the vendor-specific deployment information. Generally, it's safest to stick to the tools the vendor provides.

The future will bring some improvements in the area of standardizing the deployment process. These improvements are the responsibility of JSR-88 (see http://www.jcp.org/jsr/detail/88.jsp), which aims to provide a standard interface for deployment tools, meaning that a single tool will be able to assemble and deploy EJB JARs into server products from different vendors. The scope of this JSR includes a common format for the container to provide all the information that the deployer needs to complete the configuration, and that should be enough to allow tools to provide automated deployment features. Even beyond standard deployment tools, this functionality could easily be integrated into development environments, making the deployment process that much more accessible. The API defined by JSR-88 will be included in J2EE 1.4, and it should greatly reduce the vendordependence of the deployment process.

Developer Classes vs. Container Classes

The container's other task during deployment is to generate any additional classes required to run the EJBs. To understand why this is necessary, let's review the client and container views of a deployed EJB, as depicted in the diagram below:

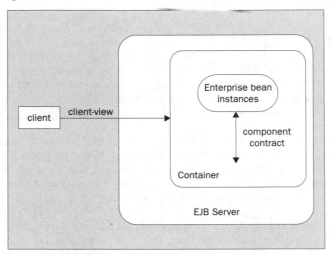

The client only interacts with the container, and the container ultimately forwards those calls to specific bean instances. Further, the client only interacts with beans through their home and component interfaces, so the bean instances are never exposed to the client. However, the EJB developer does not supply all the classes required to implement this policy. The developer provides only the home and component interfaces, and the bean implementation class. Since the bean instances don't implement the home and component interfaces, the developer isn't providing anything with which the client can interact. Instead, the container needs to create some classes that implement those interfaces. So, the client will interact with the classes generated by the container, and then the container will, in turn, interact with the instances of the bean implementation class.

We'll see later that this architecture is essential to the container. It can use the generated classes to intercept calls to the beans and provide security and transactions for each call. The container can also use pools and caches of bean instances to improve performance, rather than always creating a new instance to handle every call. The following diagram gives an idea of the classes involved in a call to the container:

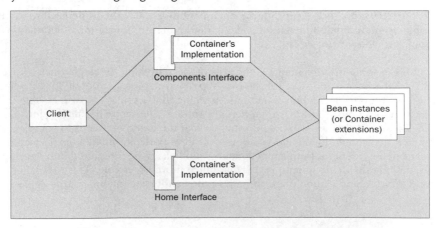

Here we can clearly see that the client only interacts with the home and component interfaces, and the container provides the implementation of those interfaces. The container's implementations, in turn, forward the calls to individual bean instances for handling. In some cases, the container may also extend the bean implementation classes to provide extra functionality – we'll see an example of this when we discuss the EJB 2.0 container-managed persistence architecture.

Generating Container Classes

There are two possible approaches for the container to use when it generates these container classes. It can write and compile the classes during deployment time, or it can generate them on the fly at run time. There are advantages and disadvantages to each approach, and there are containers today that use each approach. We'll look at both approaches, and then look at the APIs that make them work in more detail.

Generating Classes during Deployment

The first approach is to process as much of this as possible ahead of time, and generate code that handles the specifics. For example, the container can generate Java classes that implement the home and component interfaces. In the container's implementation of each interface method, the container can code a call that acquires an instance of the bean implementation, and directly calls the appropriate method on that instance. The security and transaction settings can also be coded directly into each method, for optimal performance.

In order for this to work, the container has to generate source code for each of these classes, compile the generated Java code, and add the resulting classes to the EJB JAR. Then it must add these class names to its custom configuration information (whether stored in a server-specific deployment descriptor or elsewhere). Finally, the container must also make some of these classes available to the client. For example, the client needs RMI stubs for the classes that it will be interacting with directly, such as the container's implementation of the bean's component interface.

This approach has both advantages and disadvantages. It minimizes the use of reflection at run time, which can improve speed (as we'll see when we discuss reflection in more detail). It can also be easier to debug, since the source code for all the classes used is physically written to disk (see the *Java Compiler* section) and you can usually instruct the code generator to leave the files instead of deleting them once compiled. On the other hand, this means that a JAR configured for a specific server has many additional files in it. It also means that the container needs to make the generated client stubs available to the clients, whether by download at run time or by including the classes in the client's classpath. Finally, it introduces an extra step into the assembly and deployment process, which may or may not be easy to run in an automated fashion.

This is the approach most commonly used by commercial EJB containers. For example, with WebLogic, we run the `ejbc` tool to generate the container-specific classes.

Generating Classes at Run Time

The second approach is to avoid writing and compiling additional code using a technology introduced in JDK 1.3 known as **dynamic proxies**. This methodology lets you construct a class on the fly that implements any interface. The container uses it to construct implementations of the home and component interfaces from scratch at run time. This entails a much more extensive use of reflection, since all method calls on a dynamic proxy are handled entirely via reflection.

This approach also has both advantages and disadvantages. The primary advantage is that no additional classes are generated, and the client does not need any additional bean-specific classes or stubs to be available. When there is a significant change to a bean that affects the home or component interface, the clients need only the updated interface. It is also much faster to assemble and deploy beans when the container uses this approach because the container does not need to generate and compile Java code. On the other hand, the greater use of reflection imposes a run time performance penalty compared to direct method invocation.

This is the approach most commonly used by open source EJB containers. Under JBoss, for example, you need only copy an EJB JAR to a directory to deploy it; JBoss has no equivalent to the `ejbc` tool. We shall return to the subject of dynamic proxies within our more detailed discussion of the various tools for generating container classes, which comes next.

Tools for Generating Classes

As obvious as it may sound, the only general-purpose solution to the problem of generating Java classes is to use a Java compiler. Fortunately, the JDK includes a compiler that can be invoked by Java programs. On the other hand, it is not very convenient to use the compiler in that manner, so dynamic proxies provide a way to work around the compiler, and generate classes directly without using any source code. As we shall see, the penalty for this power is that dynamic proxies are extremely specialized, and lean heavily on reflection. Without these limitations, implementing and using dynamic proxies would be just as difficult as implementing classes using the compiler.

In this section, we'll look at how to generate classes with the compiler, and with dynamic proxies, and examine the benefits and pitfalls of both methods. We'll also see how these techniques could be used outside implementing an EJB container. The specific example we'll discuss in each section is how the container might handle calls to a trivial session bean. Although the example code is not complete, it gives some insight into how the container might use each technique.

Here is the code for the session bean:

```
public interface MyBean extends EJBObject {
  public String sayHello() throws RemoteException;
}

public class MyBeanImpl extends SessionBean {
  public String sayHello() {
    return "Hello";
  }
  ...
}
```

The Java Compiler

In order to create a Java class in the traditional way, you have to write your code into a `.java` file on disk, set the classpath to allow the use of the compiler, and then run the compiler on the file. At that point, the compiler produces a `.class` file on disk.

When a container wants to generate a class with the compiler, you'd think there was a better way. The disk is slow, and the container is writing the source code on the fly anyway, so why not store the Java code in memory, and operate entirely without the disk? All the class files that need to be compiled are loaded in the current environment already. Why bother with a classpath full of files and directories on disk? The container just wants to directly load the output class, so why write it to disk. Since the compiler presumably reads through the source code from top to bottom, why can't the container just feed in code as it generates it?

Unfortunately, none of that is possible with the current JDK compiler. It operates only with files and classes on disk, and only outputs to disk. If you specify an output location, it outputs into a subdirectory structure based on package names. It makes more than one pass through the source code; so spooling code as it's generated is only of limited use. There has been a fair bit of talk about the ways to improve the Java compiler, but even if those suggestions are ultimately accepted, we can't expect to see the results soon.

At present, the container needs a working directory to write code into. It needs to launch the compiler, and note that some versions of the compiler actually call `System.exit()` when they're finished compiling, which means the compiler must be run in a separate Java virtual machine. Finally, the container must read in the class files from disk in order to use them. The code that the container would generate for the example session bean might look something like this:

```
public class ContainerBeanImpl extends UnicastRemoteObject
                               implements MyBean {
  public String sayHello() throws RemoteException {
    try {
      checkCallerInRole("HELLO_CALLER_ROLE");
      MyBeanImpl impl = new MyBeanImpl();
      impl.setSessionContext(...);
      impl.ejbCreate();
      createTransaction();
      String result = impl.sayHello();
      commitTransaction();
      impl.ejbRemove();
      return result;
    } catch(RuntimeException c) {
      throw new RemoteException(e);
    }
  }
  ...
}
```

You can see the container can code some logic right into the method calls. Here it includes code to handle security and transactions, and also to create, initialize, and dispose of a bean instance in addition to performing the method call in question. The container has access to the deployment descriptors when it generates the code for this method, so it can include handling for the specific security and transaction settings of the method. The example above may not represent the best design, but it would certainly be speedy at run time.

Even beyond EJB containers, the fact that invoking the compiler at isn't as convenient as it could be doesn't mean it's not useful. We might use a similar technique to implement an interactive Java shell, where we could just type in some code and have it executed for us on the fly. The system could wait for us to enter a full method or block, and then run it. It would write a shell of a class to disk that contains the code, then compile it, load it, and run it. We could even use this as an interactive test bed for manipulating EJBs as we develop them.

Dynamic Proxies

As mentioned previously, the alternative to using the compiler to generate code is to use dynamic proxies, a concept first introduced in the *Swing Connection*, in an article about dynamic event listeners (see http://web2.javasoft.com/products/jfc/tsc/articles/generic-listener/). They were later introduced into JDK 1.3 as a general-purpose technology – so perhaps the article was simply the first glimpse of the work in progress. Since their introduction in JDK 1.3, several open-source packages have been developed to implement the same functionality for JDK 1.2.

The concept is very simple – a dynamic proxy is an object generated at run time which implements a list of interfaces that we specify, and then forwards all calls to a handler we provide (to clarify this terminology, note that we refer to the proxy as being the object and the proxy class being the class). The proxy itself doesn't do any work other than routing the call – our handler looks at what method was called, decides what to do, and returns the appropriate result. Using reflection, each method call on the proxy is dissected to its component parts, and then passed along to our handler for processing.

A simple non-reflection implementation would invoke the compiler at run time as above, but that's less useful since it is slow, it requires disk access, the compiler must be on your path or classpath, and the resulting classes would have to be distributed to other JVMs if you wanted to serialize them across the network. Instead, dynamic proxies are created by assembling bytecode directly, and then loading the resulting class. This is clearly not a general-purpose technique, or it would be a regular compiler. But it works well enough for the small scope of implementing interfaces, and it's quite fast as well.

Dynamic proxies make significant use of reflection and, in order to fully understand them, we first need to take a closer look at reflection.

Reflection API

Reflection is a way to inspect an unknown object or class, and manipulate its fields and methods at run time. A key part of reflection is the ability to operate on classes, fields, or methods when you are given their name but nothing else. For example, given the name of a class, you can create an instance of the class, check whether the instance has a method called "start" and call it, if it exists.

The main use of reflection is to separate areas of the code that are logically independent. For example, the developers of an application server vendor have a lot of detailed knowledge about how EJB containers should work, and application developers have a lot of detailed knowledge about how their application should work. Without reflection, someone has to write the linking code that joins the two together, and then if either party changes their interface, the code breaks. With reflection, the two domains can focus on their areas of expertise and interoperate without any specific code tying them together.

An example relevant to an EJB container concerns indexing all of the methods in the component interface of a bean. The container might want to store the corresponding bean implementation methods in a map indexed by name and parameters, so that when a call comes in for a method the container can quickly invoke the correct method of a bean instance. This is demonstrated with the following code, where additional comments are included for clarity:

```
/**
 * This class is used as the hash key for a reflection Method object.
 */
public class MethodKey {
  public String name;
  public Class[] params;

  public MethodKey(String name, Class[] params) {
    this.name = name;
    this.params = params;
  }

  /**
   * Return a function of the method name and parameter types.
   */
  public int hashCode() {
    return name.hashCode() + params.length;
  }
```

```
    /**
     * Checks whether the method names and parameter types are equal.
     */
    public boolean equals(Object o) {
      MethodKey other = (MethodKey)o;
      if(!other.name.equals(name) || other.params.length != params.length) {
        return false;
      }
      for(int i-0; i<params.length; i++) {
        if(!params[i].equals(other.params[i])) {
          return false;
        }
      }
      return true;
    }
}
...

/**
 * The container gets calls from the bean's remote interface, and must
 * translate those to calls on the bean's implementation class. This method
 * makes a map where the key is the key for the remote interface method, and
 * the value is the bean implementation method. Thus, when the container
 * receives a call to a remote interface method, it can use the map to look
 * up the corresponding bean implementation method.
 */
public static Map indexMethods(String remoteClassName,
                               String implClassName) {
  Map map = new HashMap();
  try {
    Class remoteInterface = Class.forName(remoteClassName);
    Class implClass = Class.forName(implClasName);
  // get all the remote interface methods
    Method methods = remoteInterface.getMethods();
    for(int i=0; i<methods.length; i++) {
      MethodKey key = new MethodKey(methods[i].getName(),
                                    methods[i].getParamaterTypes());

    // for each method, map it to a bean implementation method
      Method implMethod = implClass.getMethod(key.name, key.params);
      map.put(key, implMethod);
    }
  } catch(Exception e) {
    return null;
  }
  return map;
}
...
```

Since the container gets the component interface and bean implementation names from the deployment descriptor, the `indexMethods()` method here just takes the class names as strings. It loads the classes, loops through all the methods in the component interface, and for each one finds the analogous method in the implementation class. All the methods are stored in the map indexed by an object that holds both the method name and parameter types.

Performance of Reflection

The most common objection to using reflection to locate and call methods is that it is dramatically slower than direct (that is, compiled) method invocation. On the other hand, it does offer unparalleled flexibility. With these points in mind, the main questions we need to answer are: what does reflection really get you, and how slow is slow?

We've already covered the first question in the case of an EJB container. By leaning more on reflection and dynamic proxies, we can provide a faster and simpler deployment process, and make client distribution easier. So we just need to evaluate the impact on performance. The important thing to keep in mind is what we're comparing it to. Method invocations are so fast that the number is almost meaningless, but if reflection means that method invocations are taking the bulk of the time for a call to an EJB, then reflection is simply not acceptable.

An informal test performed on a 750 MHz Pentium III provides some concrete numbers to discuss. This test ran a plain `for` loop, to establish the baseline overhead of the loop. The same `for` loop was then run invoking a simple method directly, and subsequently invoking the same method via reflection. The table below shows our results:

Reflection versus Direct Method Invocation (Total time for 10 million iterations)		
	HotSpot JIT	No JIT
`for` loop	64 ms	387 ms
Direct invocations	230 ms	2046 ms
Reflection invocations	45379 ms	56106 ms

From this data, it is clear that reflection is slower than direct method calls, by up to several orders of magnitude. Furthermore, a **Just In Time (JIT) compiler**, included in modern JDKs, was seen to speed up a direct method call to a much greater degree than a call via reflection. In concrete terms, taking into account the overhead of the loop itself, reflection was over 30 times slower than a direct method call without a JIT, or more than 270 times slower with a JIT (this is the more relevant number). In both cases, dividing the time taken for the reflection calls by the total number of calls, we find that a call via reflection cost about five microseconds (assuming about 10 million iterations), so the difference between the JIT and no JIT results was mainly due to the JIT speeding up the direct method call.

Five microseconds is a lot in today's terms, where the same CPU is supposed to be completing instructions nearly every nanosecond. But what else is going on as part of the same overall call? The same call is likely to involve a lot of work on the container's part, such as creating and managing transactions, checking security roles, and so on. Ultimately, there is probably a database call, which typically involves network access and possibly even disk access. Each of those is measured in milliseconds. In fact, another test showed that a client retrieving a field from an entity bean on an EJB container on the same machine took about five milliseconds, so the cost of reflection was around 0.1% of the total cost of the call.

So ultimately, compared to everything else that's going on, the extra time taken by reflection is generally negligible. We can also reduce the other CPU times with techniques like double buffering. Note, however, that debugging becomes very difficult with reflection. Before we decide to write any additional code to avoid reflection, we should have tried out a good Java profiling tool like OptimizeIt (http://www.vmgear.com/) or JProbe (http://parker.sitraka.com/software/jprobe/) and seen where our time is really spent, and whether reflection is really causing any performance problems. Certainly our time may be better spent on things like creating better application architecture, tuning database access, or changing the granularity of our beans (that is, how many remote calls we make for a particular operation). We may be able to realize substantial performance gains simply by changing the Commit option on our beans alone, if that's appropriate.

Finally, note that the JDK team is well aware of the performance issues with reflection. Reflection has been significantly reworked for the JDK 1.4 release, so the performance penalty will hopefully decrease even further in the future.

Using Dynamic Proxies

Now that we've established that reflection is a viable alternative to writing and compiling code at deployment time, we can look at using dynamic proxies. This technology makes it possible to generate classes at run time, instead of at deployment time.

First, we'll discuss what the handler looks like. As shown in the following code snippet, it implements `java.lang.reflect.InvocationHandler`:

```
public interface InvocationHandler {
  public Object invoke(Object proxy, Method method, Object[] args)
               throws Throwable;
}
```

As there's only one method in the handler, we can tell that the same handler method is called regardless of which interface method was called. The handler method gets the following three parameters:

- ❑ `proxy` – the proxy instance on which the interface method was called.

- ❑ `method` – the `java.lang.reflect.Method` instance corresponding to the method that was invoked on the proxy.

- ❑ `args` – an array of objects containing the values of the arguments that were passed into the method invocation on the proxy. This argument is null if there are no parameters in the proxy method invocation.

It needs to return an appropriate value if the method that was called doesn't return void, and it should just return `null` if the method that was called does return void.

The other class we use is the `java.lang.reflect.Proxy` class, which has one method of interest to us here:

```
public static Object newProxyInstance(ClassLoader loader,
                                  Class[] interfaces,
                                  InvocationHandler h)
                 throws IllegalArgumentException
```

The `newProxyInstance` method creates a new proxy that implements all the interfaces we list and uses the invocation handler we provide. It returns the proxy instance as an Object, but we can cast this to any of the interfaces we passed in. Note that we must pass in a `ClassLoader`, as the generated proxy's class will be created in that `ClassLoader`. Of course, the interfaces we pass in must be visible to that `ClassLoader` as well.

Here's an example of creating a dynamic proxy to handle calls to our sample bean. It does the same things as the sample provided for generating classes at deployment time, but there's more code and it involves more reflection since the exact classes and methods aren't compiled. Note the comments which indicate the sequence of events associated with a dynamic proxy:

```
/**
 * This is the class that will be used to handle all calls to the dynamic
 * proxy for the bean's home or component interface. The code for this
 * class is not specific to any single bean, so its constructor takes an
 * identifier for the bean as a parameter and uses that to customize itself
 * to the bean in question. However, this class as written is specific to
 * a session bean (though we could also make it generic in that regard).
```

```
*/

public class ContainerHandler implements InvocationHandler {

  // Maps the interface methods to the implementation methods
  private Map methods;
  private Class beanImplClass;

  public ContainerHandler(Object beanIdentifier)
        throws ClassNotFoundException {

    // The code for indexMethods is discussed in the reflection section
    methods = indexMethods(getComponentInterface(beanIdentifier),
                        getBeanImplementation (beanIdentifier));

    // In practice, we wouldn't use Class.forName like this since the
    // bean class does not live in the System ClassLoader
    beanImplClass = Class.forName(getBeanImplementation(beanIdentifier));
  }

  /**
   * This method is called every time a client calls a method on the bean's
   * home or component interface. It has to forward the call to an instance
   * of the bean implementation class. Note that it assumes there is no
   * caching or pooling of bean instances going on.
   */
  public Object invoke(Object proxy, Method method, Object[] args)
              throws Throwable {
    try {

      // 1: If the security system denies the call, throw an exception.
      checkSecurity(method);

      // 2: Identify a bean instance to handle the call.
      Object beanInstance = beanImplClass.newInstance();

      // 3: Call setSessionContext on the instance.
      Method setCtx = (Method)methods.get(
                      new MethodKey("setSessionContext", new Class[]{
                                        SessionContext.class
                                    }));
      setCtx.invoke(beanInstance, new Object[]{...});

      // 4: Call ejbCreate on the instance.
      Method create = (Method)methods.get(new MethodKey("ejbCreate",
                                            new Class[0]));
      create.invoke(beanInstance, new Object[0]);

      // 5: See whether we need to start and/or suspend a transaction, or
      //    or perhaps throw an exception.
      checkTransactionStart(method);

      // 6: Identify and call the business method.
      Method businessMethod = (Method)methods.get(
                              new MethodKey(method.name, method.params));
      Object result = businessMethod.invoke(beanInstance, args);

      // 7: See whether we need to commit, rollback, and/or
      //    resume a transaction.
      checkTransactionEnd(method);
```

```
         // 8: Call ejbRemove on the instance.
         Method remove = (Method)methods.get(
                               new MethodKey("ejbRemove", new Class[0]));
         remove.invoke(beanInstance, new Object[0]);

         // 9: Return the result.
         return result;
      } catch(...) {...}
   }
}

/**
 * These methods are located in the container's internals.
 */
public class SomeContainerClass {

   /**
    * Given some token to identify a bean, the container produces a class
    * that implements the component interface of the bean by generating a
    * dynamic proxy for that interface.
    */
   public EJBObject getComponentInterfaceImplementation(
                                          Object beanIdentifier) {
      InvocationHandler handler = new ContainerHandler(beanIdentifier);
      try {
         Class componentInterface = Class.forName(getComponentInterface(
                                                   beanIdentifier));
         EJBObject impl = (EJBObject)Proxy.newProxyInstance(
                                 componentInterface.getClassLoader(),
                                 new Class[]{componentInterface},
                                 handler);
         return impl;
      } catch(ClassNotFoundException e) {}
   }

   /**
    * Given some token to identify a bean, the container looks up the name of
    * the component interface class for that bean. This is originally loaded
    * from the deployment descriptor, and stored in the container's internal
    * metadata structures for the bean.
    */
   public String getComponentInterface(Object beanIdentifier) {...}

   /**
    * Given some token to identify a bean, the container looks up the name of
    * the bean implementation class for that bean. This is originally loaded
    * from the deployment descriptor, and stored in the container's internal
    * metadata structures for the bean.
    */
   public String getBeanImplementation(Object beanIdentifier) {...}
}
```

The getComponentInterfaceImplementation() method that actually generates the proxy is fairly straightforward. It creates an InvocationHandler, passing in some sort of identifier for the current bean. Then it looks up the component interface for the bean, which is what the proxy needs to implement. Finally, it calls newProxyInstance() with the interface, its class loader, and the handler. It has to cast the result to an EJBObject, since that's a common super-interface for all EJB component interfaces.

The invocation handler implemented by ContainerHandler is much more complex. Its constructor indexes all the methods using the sample we discussed in the reflection section. It also records the bean implementation class, so when it comes time to dispatch the method it can create an appropriate instance to do so.

The meat of the work is done in the invoke() method. In this example, we assume that any call coming in is a business method call, though in reality that may not be the case. In order to handle the call, we first check security, passing in the method identifier because we'd need to look up the security settings for that particular method. Then we create a new bean instance, and prepare it by looking up and invoking the setSessionContext and ejbCreate() methods. We check whether a transaction needs to be started, again passing in the method identifier since we'd need to look up the transaction attribute for the method.

Note that we can't just call invoke() on the method that was passed to the handler, because that represents a method on the original component interface. Instead, we have to look up the appropriate method from our method index, which gives us the same method on the bean implementation class. This is the one we invoke, on the bean instance we created, using the arguments that were used on the original call to the proxy. Finally, we clean up the transaction and the bean instance, and return the result.

RMI and Dynamic Proxies

One of the subtleties of dynamic proxies is that they are serializable, as long as their invocation handler is also either serializable or remote. It's a little odd to think that a class generated from scratch could be transmitted to another JVM, but the reality is that the proxy is simply regenerated on the other end. A surprising side effect of this is that the class of the proxy constructed on the other end may in fact have a different name, but it implements the same interfaces and uses the same InvocationHandler, so it works as you would expect. The generated proxy classes are cached so that each deserialized instance only has to really generate a new class if the particular combination of interfaces that it implements is new to the receiving JVM.

Dynamic Proxies in the EJB Container

As we've seen, an EJB container can take advantage of dynamic proxies to avoid generating additional classes to deploy EJBs. The container identifies the home and component interfaces for a bean from the deployment descriptor, and creates a dynamic proxy for each using a custom invocation handler, just as we did in the example. The container's invocation handler is a remote object, so the proxy can be serialized.

When our client looks up the bean's home in JNDI, or looks up a specific bean, the container returns the dynamic proxy for the appropriate interface. Next, when the client calls methods on the bean or the home interface, those calls get forwarded to the invocation handler and, since it is a remote object, the call is processed on the container side of the network. At that point, the invocation handler can identify an appropriate instance of the bean implementation class, then make the call on the implementation using the method name and parameters it was passed, returning the results to the client.

We can double-check that the client doesn't need to be configured with access to any container-generated classes in this scenario. The classes that the client needs are the bean's home and component interfaces, the proxy class, the invocation handler RMI stub, and the interfaces that the proxy implements. So the question is, are any of these container-generated classes specific to a deployed bean? They would be the classes that we'd have to package with the client. The home and component interfaces are not container-generated. The invocation handler is the same for all beans, or at least all beans of the same type. The interfaces implemented by the proxy are just the home and component interfaces. That leaves the proxy itself as the only container-generated class that's specific to the bean. However, the proxy class is regenerated on the client side at run time, so the client doesn't need to have it ahead of time. In the end, there is no need for the container to generate, compile, or distribute extra classes during the deployment process.

Where to Use Dynamic Proxies

Outside of an EJB container, there are a number of potential applications for dynamic proxies. One example would be creating a JDBC driver wrapper that logs all SQL statements. Since all the JDBC classes are interfaces, we can create dynamic proxies to implement them. We'd create proxies for each major JDBC class (`Connection`, `Statement`, and so on), and our invocation handlers would keep a reference to the "real" `Connection`, `Statement`, etc. Whenever a call was made on the proxy, the invocation handler would just dispatch it to the real object. However, any time a call involved SQL (such as `Statement.executeQuery()`), we would log the SQL to a file before dispatching the call to the real object.

This would allow us to log all SQL calls by simply changing the JDBC URL in the database configuration. We might insert a trace: after the jdbc: part of the URL, and leave the rest unchanged so that our proxies can create the correct database objects they need just by stripping out that additional trace:. If we implemented this without proxies, we'd have to override hundreds of methods. With proxies, on the other hand, we need only write the reflection code to redirect the method call once, in a common superclass, and then provide additional handling of the methods that we want to log. The dynamic proxy code would also be much less error-prone, since it either all works or all breaks – we'd avoid the endless cut and paste routine.

In conclusion, although dynamic proxies have a steep learning curve, they offer a significant benefit in return.

Run Time

Once our beans have been deployed, we're interested in how the container behaves at run time. We've seen some of this already, in the examples of how the container implements the bean's home and component interfaces. Here we'll take a closer look at each step the container takes when it handles a request, as well as some of the other run-time issues such as reloading classes and throwing exceptions.

Handling a Request

Every time a client makes a call to a bean, the container receives the call and dispatches it to a bean instance to handle. The container does more than just redirect the call, however. It takes this opportunity to apply the security and transaction settings configured for the bean, and to optimize the access to bean instances to improve performance.

In this section, we'll follow the request process from a client and look at each of the services the container provides:

- ❑ **Naming** – the client looks up the bean in JNDI
- ❑ **Security** – the container checks whether the client is authorized to call the method
- ❑ **Bean Instances** – the container selects a bean instance to handle the request
- ❑ **Transactions** – the container manages transactions for the call
- ❑ **Resources** – the bean uses any resources it requires
- ❑ **Persistence** – the container manages persistence for CMP entity beans

Before we dive in, though, let's look at the thread-local variables API, which is used in virtually all of the areas of the EJB container mentioned above.

Thread-Local Variables API

The EJB container needs to track information for the current user or request at a number of different stages. Ideally, we could just put that information in a static location, and then any component that needed it could access it. Unfortunately, with numerous requests being processed at the same time, any such static location would be overwritten too often to be of any use. So we could create a static map rather than a static location, where the key identified the current request. This way each request could store a different value. However, what would happen if the map grows without bound?- and it's not clear what a natural key would be to identify a request.

A common solution to these problems is to identify the current user or request by the thread that is executing. Though a container may be handling multiple requests at the same time, a single thread is dedicated to a single request for the lifetime of the request. The Java standard library includes the class java.lang.ThreadLocal, which was introduced in JDK 1.2. This class holds a thread-local variable: a variable that can have a different value for every thread in the JVM. Each thread can set a value in what appears to be the same place, but in reality a different value is stored for each thread, and when the calling thread gets the value again it is the value for that specific thread; it has not been overwritten by other threads.

This example piece of code demonstrates the use of a ThreadLocal:

```
public class ThreadLocalTest {
  static ThreadLocal tLocal = new ThreadLocal();
  public static class Runner extends Thread {
    private int value;
    public Runner(int value) {
      this.value = value;
    }

    public void run() {
      tLocal.set(new Integer(value));
      System.out.println("Set Value: "+value);
      try {
        sleep(500*value);
      } catch (InterruptedException e) {
      }
      System.out.println("Got Value: "+tLocal.get());
    }
  }

  public static void main(String args[]) {
    new Runner(1).start();
    new Runner(2).start();
  }
}
```

If tLocal was a normal variable, the two threads would overwrite each other with their set calls, and after waiting a while they'd both get the same value. However, with a ThreadLocal, a different value is stored for each thread, and the output is:

Set Value: 1
Set Value: 2
Got Value: 1
Got Value: 2

The container can use a ThreadLocal to store the current user or caller, the current bean, the current transaction, and a number of other parameters of the request. That way, every part of the container that's involved in processing the request has access to the information it needs. For example, resources acquired by the bean can be authenticated using the current caller's credentials, and can be added to the correct transaction. This is a very useful API for many of the services we'll discuss here.

Now we can proceed with detailing how the container behaves at run time, starting with a discussion of the naming service.

Naming

In order for a client to interact with a bean, it must first look up a reference to the bean. The client uses a naming service to locate a reference to a bean based on the name of the bean it is looking for. The Java Naming and Directory Interface (JNDI) is the standard naming service for locating external resources in J2EE. This covers clients looking up beans, and also beans looking up the resources they need to handle client requests, including database connection, environment variables, and more.

JNDI works a bit differently in J2EE from how it does in most other areas. In most JNDI implementations, everything in the JNDI directory is visible to all callers. There may be security restrictions that prevent a client from accessing certain parts of the directory without specific credentials, but it's not possible, for example, for two different callers to ask for an entry at the same location and receive two different results.

The JNDI entries in J2EE work in exactly the opposite way. In all cases where the specification dictates that JNDI should be used in J2EE, the entries are specific to a single component. For example, an environment variable declared in one EJB is not visible to any other EJBs, and an EJB reference declared in one web application is not visible to any other web applications. Furthermore, it is possible for several components to map different things to the same JNDI location, and each component sees only the items it has placed in JNDI. Though this example is obviously contrived, one EJB could map an environment variable to `java:comp/env/MyLocation` and another EJB could map a database reference to the same location. Each bean's implementation would see only what it expected at run time; the two entries would not cause any conflicts. If another bean or a client looked up that same JNDI location, it wouldn't see anything at all.

Implementing Component-Local JNDI

It's actually not obvious how to implement a JNDI context that returns different results for the same location depending on who's asking. After all, how can a piece of code tell who called it? The solution lies with thread-local variables.

Since each thread in an EJB container can only be operating on one bean at a time, the container can put an identifier for the current bean in a `ThreadLocal`, and then the JNDI context can use that to determine which results to display. If the same context gets calls from different threads at the same time, the `ThreadLocal` will show that the current bean is different for each thread, and each bean will see the appropriate entries in JNDI.

Application (and Applet) Containers

One corollary of this is that if an EJB container went no further than the specification requires it would not be possible for a simple client program to access an EJB. The reason is that there's nothing in J2EE that is globally visible – there's no way for a simple client to get a reference to a bean. The JNDI tree would appear to be empty to the client, since all the references are local to specific application components, and a standalone client is not an application component.

This is the purpose of the application container (or equivalently, the applet container) defined in the J2EE specification. If a client runs within one of those containers, it includes a deployment descriptor that identifies the EJBs that the client needs to access, and gives JNDI locations where the client will look each one up. The application container uses a proprietary mechanism to map the real bean on the server to the location specified by the client's deployment descriptor. Again, the result of this is a JNDI entry specific to the client, which is not visible to other clients, whether they're running in the same container or not.

Avoiding Application Containers

Most EJB containers allow us to avoid using application containers by making a global JNDI entry for each bean. This is part of the container-specific phase of the deployment process – again the specification does not provide for global JNDI entries. However, if our container does let us create a global JNDI entry, then any client can just create a new JNDI context and look up the beans. The application may still need to provide authentication information to use the beans (see the *Security* section below), but it doesn't have to run within a container itself. The important thing to remember is that this is outside the specification, so a container may not support it, or may mandate that any beans must fall within a certain JNDI sub-context, and so on.

Security

Once the client has looked up a bean or home interface, any methods it calls are handled by the container. When a container receives a call for a bean, one of the first things it must do is establish whether the caller is allowed to call the bean. If not, there's no point in selecting a specific bean instance to process the call, managing the transactions for the call, and so on. Of course, in order for the container to figure out whether the caller is authorized, it has to know who the caller is; the caller must be authenticated with the container.

At this point, we must make a distinction between web clients and application clients. While standard mechanisms are in place for web clients to authenticate to web containers, there is no comparable standard for an application client to authenticate to an EJB container.

Web Clients

A web container must support three authentication mechanisms for web clients:

❑ HTTP Basic Authentication

❑ HTTPS Client Authentication

❑ Form-based Authentication

Most modern web browsers support all of those methods of authentication. There are additional optional authentication mechanisms, but between the three required options, it should be easy for a web client to authenticate in a standard manner.

The problem comes when a web component such as a JSP page invokes an EJB. The EJB container has no idea what web authentication may have occurred, and it needs to know the identity of the caller (known as the principal) so it can determine whether to allow access to the EJB in question. On the other hand, we don't want the EJB to authenticate the user all over again (that is, check their credentials, such as their password) on every call, as that would slow down the whole process.

The solution is to set up trust relationships between containers. If you configure an EJB container to trust a particular web container, then the EJB container assumes that the web container has performed any necessary authentication. Thus the web container can simply pass the caller's principal to the EJB container, and the EJB container will assume that the principal has been properly authenticated. It is also possible to configure separate EJB containers to trust each other so that calls from an EJB in one container to an EJB in another container are handled properly.

Unfortunately, while the EJB specification requires that EJB containers must support trust relationships and provide tools to manage trust relationships, the actual implementation of those tools is left to the container vendor. In other words, it's left to the system administrator to figure out how to configure these trust relationships for the particular EJB container we're using.

Application Clients

Since there is no standard for application clients to authenticate to EJB containers, this is also left to the container vendor to implement. In this case, the user's credentials (often a password) are sent to the container on every bean invocation. However, before we even get that far, the application client itself needs to acquire the proper credentials for the current user.

If the application client is running in an application container, the application container may use one of a number of mechanisms to acquire the credentials for the current user. It may inherit the user's information from the operating system, prompt the user at startup time, read a certificate from a store in the user's home directory, or use any other mechanism. The client container may use the Java Authentication and Authorization Service (JAAS), or another implementation of its choice. The important thing is that once the client container establishes the principal and credentials for the client, it stores them to be used for subsequent calls to EJB containers (rather than retrieving that information from scratch for each EJB call). Once again, this information can be stored in a thread-local variable, so it is maintained for the duration of the current thread of execution.

If the application client is not running in an application container, it's outside the specification already so there certainly is no standard method of authentication. Generally, the client must be coded to make some container-specific authentication call. How this works and how often it must be done is up to the container vendor.

In either an application container or a standalone application, the application client ultimately submits a principal and credentials to the EJB container. Then the container must authenticate these using its own security service. At that point, the situation is the same as when the EJB container is called by a different trusted container with a valid principal for the current caller.

Container-Managed Authorization

Once the container has a valid principal for the current caller, it has to determine whether that caller is authorized to call the method in question. EJB uses a role-based authorization scheme, so the container needs to find out what roles the caller is in. Then it must determine whether any of those roles have been granted access to the method.

The first problem here is how the container gets a list of roles for a user. That as well is left to the container vendor. The container is required to provide tools that associate users with roles, but no implementation is specified. The container may allow us to map the roles defined in the underlying operating system or an external LDAP directory to the roles defined in the deployment descriptor, or we may just drag and drop users into roles in some sort of graphical tool, and so on.

The next question is which roles are allowed to access the method that's being called. The permissions on each method are set up in the deployment descriptor, using the <method-permission> element. For each method permission, we list a number of beans or methods, and then a list of roles that are allowed to invoke the specified beans or methods. The container processes all the method permissions when it deploys the EJB JAR, and makes a list of all the roles that are allowed to access each method (combining multiple method permission declarations for the same method if required). Any method that is not listed in any method permission element is assumed available to all callers.

When a call comes in for a method, the container gets a list of roles that the caller is in, using the principal for the caller, and checks these one by one against the list of roles allowed to invoke the method. As soon as any one role matches, the call is allowed to proceed. The call is only stopped if none of the user's roles match.

Once again, the container can store the current principal in a thread-local variable so that any other bean calls or resource accesses performed in the current method will propagate the correct principal. The deployer can also configure a bean so it always uses a particular principal and always passes that to other beans that are invoked.

Bean-Managed Authorization

The system of authorizing users to call particular methods is easy on the bean developer, but not particularly flexible. For example, a user can either call a particular method on all instances of a particular entity bean, or none. There's no way for the container to decide whether to allow a call based on specific data. If we wanted to restrict access to employee records to employees or administrators in the same department, the container's authorization system doesn't go far enough.

The container provides two methods (discussed in Chapter 10) that allow beans to manage their own security. Both are in the EJBContext class, and they allow you to get the current caller Principal and check whether the current caller is in a particular role:

❑   java.security.Principal getCallerPrincipal()

❑   boolean isCallerInRole(String role)

The methods above allow the bean to use code like this to manage security:

```
if(getCallerPrincipal().getName().equals(username) ||
                          isCallerInRole("Administrator")) {
  updateUser(username);
} else {
  throw new AccessDeniedException();
}
```

These methods are fairly straightforward for the container, based on the container-managed authorization implementation. The container has the current principal because it was set when the current method was invoked, and it has to be maintained in case the current bean calls any other beans (or attempts to use protected resources, and so on). The container knows how to get a list of roles that the current principal has, because it needs that to check permissions for the current method call.

Bean Instances

Once the container has established that the caller is authorized for the method that's being called, it has to select an instance of the bean implementation class to handle the call. In the simplest case, the container could create a brand new object of the appropriate type, initialize it, let it handle the call, and then save the work, if necessary, and dispose of the instance. That's what we did in the examples in the deployment section above. However, this approach means a lot of extraneous object creation, and it doesn't perform well. Instead, many servers use pools and caches of EJB instances to serve requests. This way, an individual instance can be reused many times, resulting in better performance and better memory usage.

Since the pooling and/or caching mechanism differs for different types of EJBs, we'll look at each of the four types of EJBs individually. For each type of bean, we'll look at the states that an instance of the bean can be in – states such as: does not exist, ready in a pool, in a transaction, and so on.

Stateless Session Beans

Stateless session beans are ideal for pooling. Since they store no state, there's no need for an object to be assigned to a particular caller. A different instance can handle every method invocation, and go right back into the pool. This way, you only need as many objects in the pool as there are simultaneous requests, instead of as many as there are active clients or entities in the database. A small number of pooled objects can handle a relatively large number of client requests.

Looking more closely at the lifecycle of a stateless session bean, the states of a bean instance are depicted in the following diagram:

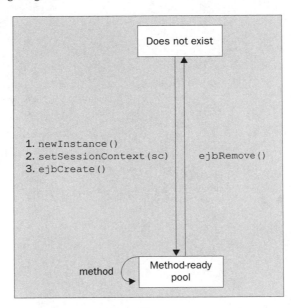

Preparation is minimal: all the container needs to do is set the session context and call `ejbCreate()` on the instance, and then it is ready to serve clients. When the container receives a method call, it selects an instance from the pool, lets it handle the call, and then immediately returns it to the pool. When the container wants to shrink the pool, the container simply calls `ejbRemove()` on the instances that will be removed.

Since the container is so efficient at managing stateless session beans, we should always consider whether it would be possible to use a stateless bean instead of a stateful bean. Perhaps the state can be stored in the client (for example, in a servlet's session) or an entity bean, leaving the session bean stateless.

Stateful Session Beans

Stateful session beans are more complicated because they are tied to an individual client. Every time that client calls a method on the bean, the instance that handles the call must remember all the state from any previous calls (or if the state was saved, it must be reloaded in order to handle the call). Since only one client can interact with a stateful session bean at a time, the container can't pool instances to handle any incoming call. The active stateful session beans are in a cache instead, so only the most recently used beans are in memory.

If we look closely at the states of a stateful session bean in the cache, they are complicated by the special transaction restrictions imposed on entity beans, but basically an instance is devoted to handling a particular client until it is passivated or times out, as shown schematically in the following diagram:

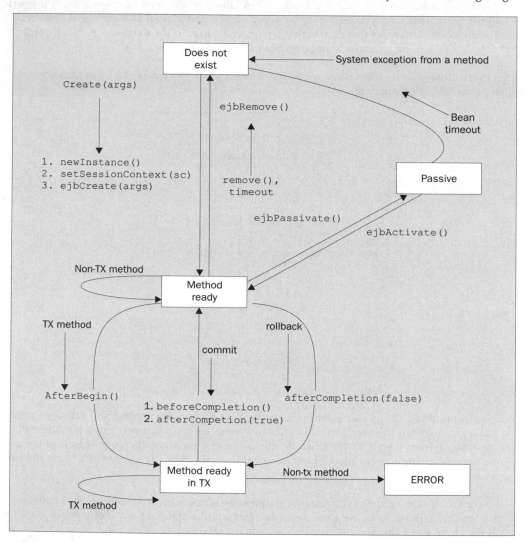

Start with no sessions when a client calls `create()` to initialize a new session, the container prepares an instance by calling `setSessionContext()` followed by the appropriate `ejbCreate()` method. At this point the instance represents a ready and active session.

If the client calls non-transactional methods on the stateful bean (such as read-only business methods), the instance handles the calls and is once again ready for subsequent calls from the same client. If the client calls a transactional method (such as a business method that writes to a database), or begins a user transaction before calling the bean, special rules apply. The client is not allowed to call methods that require a different transactional context (including no transactional context), and is not allowed to call `remove()`, until the transaction is committed or rolled back.

There are also several special transaction notification methods that the container calls on the instance as part of this process. Those methods are afterBegin(), beforeCompletion(), and afterCompletion() (all referring to the beginning or completion of the transaction). They may be used, for example, to roll back the state of the bean to the state that existed at the beginning of a transaction when the transaction is rolled back. In any case, once the transaction is completed, the instance is again ready for any type of call from the same client.

If the bean has not been used recently enough to keep it in the cache, the container passivates it and frees up the instance. If the client subsequently calls another method on the same session bean, the container creates or acquires a free instance and activates it, restoring all state to the instance and returning it to the cache of ready instances, whereupon the method call is handled as above. The client never knows that the instance was passivated and activated again.

If the bean goes unused for such a long time that the timeout period elapses, the instance is removed. If the instance was in the cache, it is removed. If the instance was passivated, then the passivated state is removed from storage. Further calls to the bean will result in exceptions.

Finally, if the client calls remove() on the bean, the container calls ejbRemove() and removes the instance from the cache.

Entity Beans

Entity beans have similarities to both stateful and stateless session beans. The methods of an entity's home interface, such as finders, are effectively stateless. On the other hand, the methods of the entity's component interface are stateful. So the container can benefit by maintaining both a pool and a cache of entity instances. The pooled instances handle the stateless methods of the home interface, and the cached instances represent to the most recently used entities and handle the stateful methods of the component interface. The states of an entity bean instance are represented in the diagram below:

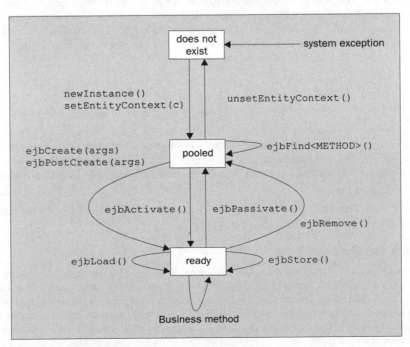

Initialization is straightforward again here. When the container needs to add an instance to the pool, it simply calls setEntityContext() on the new instance.

Pooled instances are available to handle methods of the home interface. The container gets an instance from the pool, calls the method on it, and returns it to the pool.

When the client creates a new entity, the container gets an instance from the pool, calls ejbCreate() and ejbPostCreate() on it, and adds it to the cache.

When the client calls a method on a particular entity that is not in the cache, the container gets an instance from the pool, calls ejbActivate() on it, and adds it to the cache. The container will call ejbLoad() on it before using it to service the method call.

When the client calls a business method on an entity that's in the cache, the container simply uses the cached instance to handle the call, and the instance stays in the cache. The container calls ejbLoad() and ejbStore() as often as it needs to in order to keep the entity's state synchronized with persistent storage. There is no specific guarantee when or how often these methods will be called. How the container optimizes when it should call these methods can be what distinguishes a fast container from a slow container. Some important points to keep in mind are:

❑   When a finder is called, the container must call ejbStore() on every entity in the same transaction as the finder, so the state of the changed entities is accessible to the finder.

❑   With BMP beans, we should consider adding a "changed" flag that we update when we modify the bean, so that we needn't actually make any database calls in our ejbStore() unless the bean has been changed.

❑   Some containers support a method such as isModified() to give the container hints about when stores are unnecessary, but as this is not part of the spec, it will only help in those containers.

❑   Since the container controls what order our beans will be stored in, we can run into trouble with referential integrity in the database. For example, we might change a foreign key reference and then delete the previously referenced record and, depending on when the container executes the ejbStore(), we may be deleting the record while it's still in use. If our database supports deferring referential integrity checks to the end of the transaction, we should definitely consider enabling that.

❑   The commit option for a bean is a primary factor in determining how often the container must load and store beans. Commit option A is the fastest, but it assumes that the container has exclusive access to the database. Even triggers and cascading deletes can rule out the use of commit option A.

When a particular entity has not been used recently enough to keep it in the cache, the container calls ejbPassivate() on the instance, removes it from the cache, and returns it to the pool. At that point, it is like any other pooled instance and can only be used to handle home interface methods until it is created or activated again.

When the client calls remove() on an entity, the container removes the instance from the cache, calls ejbRemove() on it, and returns it to the pool.

Finders and Entity Caches

Sometimes a client calls a finder on an entity that returns a very large number of results. The specification does not provide specific guidelines for the container in this regard. The simplest implementation would just instantiate all the beans that were found, but that would clear everything else out of the cache and then start passivating instances representing active results in order to make room for more results. Worse, if the container processes the results in ascending order, the first results the client sees will already be passivated in order to make room for the last results!

Fortunately, the specification does leave room for the container to manage this situation. Our bean returns an enumeration or collection of primary key objects, and the container's implementation of the home interface converts that into an enumeration or collection of bean objects. However, the container doesn't have to do that up front. The container can put off resolving the keys to beans until the client actually requests them. For example, if the method returns an Enumeration, the container might wrap it with an implementation like this to return from the finder:

```
public class ContainerEnumeration implements Enumeration {
  private Enumeration pks;

  public ContainerEnumeration(Enumeration keys) {
    pks = keys;
  }

  public boolean hasMoreElements() {
    return pks.hasMoreElements();
  }

  public Object nextElement() {
    Object key = pks.nextElement();
    return resolveBean(key);
  }

  //Look up the bean using findByPrimaryKey() in some manner.
  private Object resolveBean(Object primaryKey) {...}
}
```

We can see here that the primary key is not converted to a bean until the client actually asks for it. This may be somewhat less efficient in the case where the client asks for all the results, but works well if the client finds a large data set and only uses the first few rows (as would be typical if the user performs a search that returns an unmanageable result set, and then goes on to refine the criteria).

There really is no good way for the container to manage its resources if the client requests a huge result set and goes on to use all of those results immediately. In that case, we may need to reconsider whether a finder returning beans is the appropriate model for the situation. Perhaps a stateless session bean could execute a query and return an array of data structures, for example, without the overhead of a bean for each row.

Message-Driven Beans

Message-driven beans are the only way that the EJB specification supports asynchronous processing. A message-driven bean is not invoked by a client, but rather associated with a single JMS destination. This means that a message-driven bean has no home or component interface – it only receives requests from the container itself, upon the arrival of a JMS message. From the JMS point of view, a message-driven bean is just another message consumer.

Individual instances of a message-driven bean are indistinguishable, and the container may use as many as it feels appropriate to handle the incoming messages. There is no guarantee as to which messages will be delivered to which instances, or in which order messages will be delivered. So ultimately, a message-driven bean behaves very similarly to a stateless session bean. The container can maintain a pool of available instances, and any instance can handle any message. The states of a message-driven bean instance are shown in the diagram overleaf:

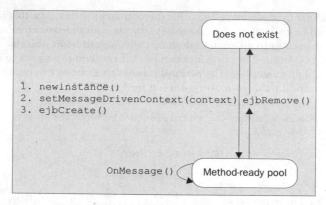

In order to prepare a new message-driven bean instance, the container calls `setMessageDrivenContext()` and `ejbCreate()` on the instance. From that point on, the instance is pooled and available to handle messages.

When a message arrives, the container selects an instance from the pool and calls its `onMessage()` method. If the container is managing transactions for the bean, it will acknowledge the message if the transaction commits successfully. Otherwise, the container will always acknowledge the message. In no case should the bean acknowledge the message. Once the message has been handled, the container returns the instance to the pool.

When the container needs to shrink the pool, it calls `ejbRemove()` on any instances that are being removed from the pool. We cannot rely on `ejbRemove()` getting called, though, since under certain circumstances the container may bypass it (for example, if the instance throws a system exception).

Note that the JMS configuration is an important factor in the reliability of a message-based application. If a message-driven bean is attached to a durable topic subscription or queue, the container guarantees that every message will be handled, even if the container goes down for some time. Queues and durable topic subscriptions are important for reliable applications. On the other hand, the container cannot guarantee that a message will be handled for non-durable topic subscription (if the message is sent during a period when the container is not available).

Transactions

Once the container has authorized the caller and selected a bean instance to handle the call, it needs to manage transactions for the call. Transactions are a key aspect of the J2EE platform. With transaction support, beans that work together can save (commit) or cancel (roll back) their work together. This keeps our data in a consistent state, so we don't save someone's address without their name, or charge their credit card without recording any items to ship to them.

The container implements the Java Transaction API (JTA) to provide transaction support. JTA defines the API for a `TransactionManager`, a `Transaction`, and all the resources that participate in a transaction.

The use of JTA is generally driven by the container transaction settings we specify in an EJB's deployment descriptor. You may recall that in a container transaction entry, we select one transaction attribute, and then list as many beans or methods as we want that attribute to apply to. There can be any number of these container transaction entries, for different transaction attributes or just different groups of beans and methods. It's also possible for a bean, or in some cases a client, to control transactions directly using a `UserTransaction` (as discussed in Chapter 9), but that is less common than letting the container manage the transactions for us based on the deployment descriptors.

Container Preparation Action

When a request comes in to a container, one of the actions it must perform is checking the transaction setting for the method that's being called. If there's a container transaction setting for the method in question, the container uses that; otherwise it falls back to its default setting. The default, unfortunately, varies from container to container, but is usually either REQUIRED or SUPPORTS. Knowing the transaction setting for the method it's about to call, the container checks the current transaction state and decides whether to do nothing, create a new transaction, suspend the current transaction, or throw an exception, as shown in the following table:

Existing Transaction	Transaction Attribute	Container Preparation Action
Yes	Not Supported	Suspend current transaction
No	Not Supported	Nothing
Yes	Required	Nothing
No	Required	Create new transaction
Yes	Supports	Nothing
No	Supports	Nothing
Yes	RequiresNew	Suspend current transaction and create new transaction
No	RequiresNew	Create new transaction
Yes	Mandatory	Nothing
No	Mandatory	Throw exception
Yes	Never	Throw exception
No	Never	Nothing

Note that a suspended transaction will not be resumed until the call is completed. So, for example, if a method marked Required (new transaction generated), calls a method marked Not Supported (transaction suspended), which calls a method marked Required, then a second transaction will be created for the call to the second method marked Required. On the other hand, if one method marked Required calls another method marked Required directly, only one transaction is used.

Container Cleanup Action

After the method call is complete, the container must step in again to clean up. It must commit, rollback, or leave alone the current transaction, and then possibly restore a previous suspended transaction. This table shows the cleanup action necessary according to the transaction state that existed when the method was first called:

Original Transaction	Transaction Attribute	Container Cleanup Action
Yes	Not Supported	Resume original transaction
No	Not Supported	Nothing
Yes	Required	Nothing

Table continued on following page

Original Transaction	Transaction Attribute	Container Cleanup Action
No	Required	Commit or roll back new transaction
Yes	Supports	Nothing
No	Supports	Nothing
Yes	RequiresNew	Commit or roll back new transaction and resume original transaction
No	RequiresNew	Commit or roll back new transaction
Yes	Mandatory	Nothing
No	Mandatory	N/A
Yes	Never	N/A
No	Never	Nothing

For all of this to work, the container needs to remember what the current transaction is at the beginning and end of each method call. In order to manage resources such as database connections properly, the container needs to know which is the current transaction during each method call, so any resources used in the call can be registered with the current transaction (if there is one). So in effect, the container needs to know the current transaction state at all times. This can be tracked quite easily with a ThreadLocal variable, discussed above, where each thread of execution has a transaction associated with it.

The container needs to be careful to propagate this transaction state across calls from one bean to another. In some cases, this may be easy (for example, if the same thread just executes the call to the other bean). In other cases, this involves a "distributed transaction", where the container must call a bean on another container, and pass the transaction information along with the call to the other container. The one thing JTA doesn't address is how to implement these distributed transactions. There is a further specification for the Java Transaction Service (JTS), which maps JTA transactions to the CORBA Object Transaction Service (OTS), which is one possible way to distribute transactions. But while JTA support is required for a container, the container is not required to use JTS, so it may choose to distribute transactions in some other manner. This problem often comes up in a clustered environment. We will discuss approaches to clustering towards the end of this chapter.

Managing Resources

Once the call has cleared security, an instance has been selected to handle it, and the container has done any necessary transaction initialization, the call is forwarded to the bean instance for processing. Often the bean needs to access a database or other resource to process the request.

In the early days of J2EE, managing resources was pretty much left to individual vendors. Everyone knew that EJBs would be using databases, but beyond that, it really wasn't clear what might be supported. Each J2EE release has cleared up this picture a little more, adding specific APIs for handling databases, e-mail sessions, and now Enterprise Information Systems (EISs) of any type, including messaging, ERP, non-relational databases, and more.

The latest effort, as of J2EE 1.3, is the J2EE Connector Architecture, which provides a generic framework for accessing connection-based resources of any type, with security, transactions, and connection pooling managed by the container. Fortunately, this integrates well with the JDBC 2.0 Optional Package (formerly known as the JDBC 2.0 Standard Extension), which was the API presented for accessing databases in J2EE 1.2.

In this section we'll look at both of these technologies as they relate to databases, and investigate how other resources might be used as well.

Accessing Resources

From a bean's perspective, all resources should be acquired via JNDI. This ensures that the container can manage all resource access to provide appropriate security; include those resources in the current transaction as appropriate; pool resource connections; and generally provide the highest possible quality of service. Of course, implementing all of these features requires some degree of support from the resource vendor – the container can't very well include a resource in a transaction if it doesn't have any way to commit or roll back the work done to that resource. Even in the case where the vendor hasn't provided support for some of these services, the container is better off knowing so, so that it can use this knowledge to manage its other resources. In other words, even if our connection doesn't support transactions, we're better off declaring that it doesn't support transactions and acquiring the connection through JNDI instead of managing it on our own.

The JDBC 2.0 Optional Package

If we look at database connections in particular, the JDBC specifications included in JDK 1.x through Java 2 Standard Edition version 1.3 (JDBC 1.0-2.0) include fairly simplistic transaction support. A connection can be either committed, or rolled back. This is fine when we're using one connection at a time, but it doesn't work so well when we try to scale that up. If we have several connections in one transaction, we'd like to be able to check all of them to see whether they *can* be committed before we actually commit them all. That way, if one in the middle has a problem, we can roll everything back instead of committing the ones ahead of it and rolling back the ones after it.

You might ask if this is really necessary, since the vast majority of beans use, at most, a single resource at a time. It becomes important, for example, when a session bean method makes several calls to a single entity bean, or makes calls to several session or entity beans, all in the context of the same transaction. In that case, each individual method may be acquiring and using separate database connections, or even calling further methods with further connections under the covers.

Unfortunately, each connection in the JDBC 1.0 and 2.0 APIs is associated with its own transaction at all times. There's no way to join two connections under the umbrella of a single transaction. Likewise, there's no way to check whether a connection can be committed before we actually commit it. Thus was born the JDBC 2.0 Optional Package.

The JDBC 2.0 Optional Package works with the JTA specification to provide a mechanism for managing multiple connections in the scope of a single transaction. The container can add multiple connections to the transaction, and when the transaction ends, it can check them all (using a method called `prepare`) before it tries to commit any. Thus, it either commits them all, or rolls them all back together. In fact, JTA provides that support for any transactional resource, so the JDBC 2.0 Optional Package, strictly speaking, just provides a mapping of JDBC objects to JTA objects.

Of course, this new API required support from database vendors before it became a reality, and that support was slow in coming. Though some major vendors provided early implementations, their performance was generally rather poor. Only now are those implementations reaching a good quality. Unfortunately, none of the specifications addressed what to do with partially compliant or non-compliant JDBC drivers, so it was left to the container vendor to support the situation in the best way they could. Often that ended up being transparent when things worked well, but in the case of problems, we weren't always assured that everything would be cleaned up properly. Sometimes simple tricks like trying to select a row from a table to see whether that table exists had unpredictable results (like rolling back the whole transaction).

J2EE Connector Architecture

First introduced with J2EE 1.3, the J2EE Connector Architecture provides a brand new interface for managing resources. Unlike the JDBC 2.0 Optional Package before it, it is designed to handle resources other than databases, with different levels of transaction support. In particular, it gives guidelines for supporting database connections that don't support the JDBC 2.0 Optional Package in an environment where multiple beans may be requesting connections in the context of the same transaction.

The J2EE Connector Architecture goes even further, including specific facilities and direction for security, connection pooling, and configuring and deploying resources into the container, as well as supporting transactions. It manages to accommodate the specific implementation of the JDBC 2.0 Optional Package for databases, as well other resource implementations for other EIS resources.

With this specification, the container finally has concrete guidelines and a useful API for supporting resources of all types. From the opposing point of view, vendors of resources other than relational databases now have a specific API to implement in order for J2EE applications to use their resources in a container-neutral manner. The container provides one or more implementations of the `ConnectionManager` interface (potentially one for each level of transaction support, for example), and the resource vendor provides a **Resource Adapter** (the vendors's implementation of the resource side of the J2EE Connector contract – essentially a driver – typically packaged into a `.RAR` file). Additionally, the container may provide a Resource Adapter implementation that wraps a JDBC resource, since all JDBC drivers implement common APIs (either JDBC 1-2 or JDBC 2.0 Optional Package).

The key milestone reached with the J2EE Connector Architecture is that all resources can be managed in the same way, and the container can offer an equally high quality of service to all types of resources. After the previous sections on security, bean instances, and transactions, this should look familiar: the container can provide security, connection instance pooling, and transaction support to resources used by the beans. We'll take this opportunity to look at how the container provides each of those services.

Security

When a bean needs to access a resource, it generally needs to authenticate to the resource adapter in order to open a connection. The EJB and J2EE Connector Architecture specifications provide two options for authentication. The bean can handle the authentication itself (bean-managed authentication), or the container can manage authentication on the caller's behalf (container-managed authentication).

A bean using bean-managed authentication must pass authentication information (usually a user name and password) to the resource adapter every time it tries to acquire a connection. This lets the bean customize resource access much more extensively, but it also means the bean developer or deployer needs to know the correct resource accounts to use, and the bean is tied to that specific environment. An example of bean-managed authentication would be a bean getting a `DataSource` from JNDI and then passeingusername and password to get a connection:

```
Context ctx = new InitialContext();
DataSource ds = (DataSource)ctx.lookup("java:comp/env/jdbc/MyDB");
Connection con = ds.getConnection(username, password);
```

A bean using container-managed authentication leaves the resource authentication configuration to the system administrator. The container can be configured to use the current caller's principal and credentials to access any resources, or it can be configured to always connect as the same user regardless of the caller. The specification also allows for principal mapping, where the administrator can create arbitrary mappings between callers and the accounts used to connect to resources. That is an optional feature for the container though, so it isn't always available.

An example of container-managed authentication would be configuring the container to always use a specific username and password to connect to a database. Then the bean implementation can omit the username and password parameters when it tries to get the connection:

```
Context ctx = new InitialContext();
DataSource ds = (DataSource)ctx.lookup("java:comp/env/jdbc/MyDB");
Connection con = ds.getConnection();
```

Beyond simply deciding what user account to use to connect to the database or EIS, there's also the matter of what format the resource adapter expects its security information to be in. The most common form is a simple username and password pair, and that's all that the container is required to support. However, there is a mechanism in place for supporting other authentication systems, such as Kerberos or a public key infrastructure system. Containers may support additional configuration options for those systems as well.

Connection Pooling

Similar to managing instances for a bean, the J2EE Connector Architecture provides an API for pooling connections to a resource adapter. With most databases, opening and closing connections is a relatively expensive operation. For starters, there's usually a network connection involved. And beyond that, the database itself has to process the authentication information, and may need to allocate specific internal resources to support the new connection. With almost all databases, a quick benchmark will show that pooling connections results in a significant performance gain.

Most containers have provided this facility all along. First, there were "wrapper" drivers so that when you opened a connection from the `DriverManager` it would be pooled. Then there were JDBC 2.0 Optional Package drivers that pooled connections, or wrapped and pooled JDBC 1-2 connections. However, until the J2EE Connector Architecture, the implementation of connection pooling was outside of the J2EE specification. Some hooks were provided in the JDBC 2.0 Optional Package, but no implementation guidelines were given, and there was no attempt to address pooling in the context of an EJB container. Now though, connection pooling is addressed in the specification and implemented in the container's implementation of the J2EE Connector Architecture. This has the additional advantage that any type of connection (database or otherwise) with any level of transaction support can be pooled.

Note that the J2EE Connector Architecture requires that containers manage pooling rather than resource adapters managing pooling. This lets the container and applications deal with different types of resources consistently, as well as making it easier to manage configuring and deploying pooled resources.

Using Pooled Connections

A pooled connection works just like any other connection. There are no additional operations required to use it, or in particular, to close it. When you call `close()` on the pooled connection, the container intercepts the call and the connection is returned to the pool instead of being truly closed. Then the next time a bean asks for a connection, the container can reuse the same connection rather than creating a new one. In order to use these pooled connections effectively, our beans should not get a connection until they need to use it, and should close it as soon as they're done using it. In particular, we shouldn't keep a connection in an instance variable to store across numerous calls to the database.

The container may create dozens or hundreds of instances of a bean: in the case of entity beans, to represent entities with different primary keys, and in the case of session beans, to support multiple users. If each bean implementation stores a connection in an instance variable, the connection pool could be exhausted quickly. Ninety nine percent of those instances may not be in use at any given moment, but the connections still wouldn't be available for other beans to use until the instances with connections were passivated. This sort of behavior completely defeats the point of connection pooling, which is to reuse a small number of database connections across a large number of bean instances, and bypass the overhead of creating new connections for each call.

Instead, our beans should get connections only when they're needed, and close them as soon as possible so the connections can be returned to the pool. The less time a connection spends in the hands of a particular bean instance, the more it can be shared across multiple bean instances. That's the way to get the best use out of our connection pools.

Connection Pool Tuning

Most containers allow you to adjust the connection pool parameters in order to fine-tune the pool's performance. This also may help with databases whose connections expire after a certain period of inactivity. You can usually adjust things like the minimum and maximum number of connections in the pool, the maximum length of time a connection should be in the pool before being replaced, whether the container shrinks the pool after periods of high utilization (and if so, how), and so on. How we adjust these parameters depends on the specific patterns of use for our application. We'd like the minimum size to be large enough that there's no hit during peak sign-on periods. We'd like the maximum to be small enough that we don't cripple other applications that may be using the same database server, even under peak loads, but high enough that our beans aren't waiting for connections to free up. If the usage pattern changes rapidly during the day, the container can aggressively shrink the pool after peak times, whereas if the usage is relatively constant the container should be more conservative. All the parameters are specific to a single application.

Transactions

Any resource connections that a bean acquires will be included in the current transaction, if there is one and if the resource adapter supports transactions. Resource adapters can specify one of three levels of transaction support:

- ❑ **No transactions**

- ❑ **Local transactions** – the resource adapter doesn't support for access to more than one resource in the context of the same transaction (the equivalent of JDBC 1-2 database connections).

- ❑ **XA transactions** – the resource adapter does provide support access to more than one resource, that is, two-phase commit (the equivalent of JDBC 2 Optional Package database connections).

The specification doesn't provide any guidelines for mixing connections to resources with different levels of transaction support within one transaction. It's simply recommended that we don't do that. However, there is one special approach that a container can use for the case where a transaction includes one or more XA transaction connections and a single local transaction connection. What the container would do in this case when it goes to commit the work, is first to prepare all the XA connections. If any of them need to roll back, all the connections are rolled back. If they can all commit, the container attempts to commit the local transaction connection. If that succeeds, all the XA connections are committed, while if it fails, all the XA connections are rolled back. This single case preserves transactional integrity with mixed local and XA connections. Again, support for this special case is not required by the specification, but containers may support it.

Container-Managed Persistence

For entity beans, the container can handle persistence for us. This includes creating and removing beans, saving and loading beans, and finding sets of beans by specific criteria. It frees us from the need to write SQL in order to persist our entities to a database. On the other hand, it's not as flexible as writing SQL directly. In this section, we'll look at the approaches the container can take to container-managed persistence, the obstacles it faces, and the advances made with EJB 2.0.

The container has two main options for supporting container-managed persistence. In either case, the container must provide some sort of persistence framework that knows how to perform the basic SQL operations on a bean. The difference is how this framework is invoked. First, the container can turn all CMP beans into BMP beans by adding some extra logic to them, and then handle them as it would any other BMP bean. Second, the container may just include the necessary logic itself and handle CMP beans in a different manner from BMP beans.

Neither approach is clearly superior; they both have advantages and disadvantages, and there are some containers that use each approach. As we'll see shortly, they both face the same obstacles.

Converting CMP Entities to BMP

If the container chooses the first approach, it needs to subclass the beans during deployment to provide this support. This is a better fit if the container is already generating code at deployment time (refer back to the section on *Generating Container Classes*, earlier in this chapter), as opposed to using dynamic proxies at run time. The container would implement the usual BMP calls to perform its CMP logic. For example, let's look at how the container might implement loading and saving a CMP bean in a subclass of the bean:

```
public void ejbLoad() throws EJBException {
    framework.loadBean(this, DB_JNDI_NAME);
    super.ejbLoad();
}

public void ejbStore() throws EJBException {
    super.ejbStore();
    framework.storeBean(this, DB_JNDI_NAME);
}
```

When the container invokes `ejbLoad()` on the CMP bean as it would on a BMP bean, the container first calls its persistence framework to load all the container-managed fields from the database. Then the container calls the original bean implementation's `ejbLoad()` command to perform any post-load processing. The `ejbStore()` implementation is similar, except it reverses the order so the bean can adjust the values before they are saved.

Since the code is generated at deployment time, the container can include specific configuration settings such as the database connection to use for the bean. This makes this approach quite efficient, and since the container doesn't need different request processing logic for CMP beans and BMP beans it makes for a cleaner container implementation as well. On the other hand, it does involve generating classes during deployment.

This approach is a better fit for the container-managed persistence model in EJB 2.0. Here, the entity class is abstract, and doesn't actually define variables to store the container-managed fields. A natural approach is for the container to extend the entity class with an implementation class that provides the appropriate variables, method implementations, and persistence logic.

Handling CMP Entities Separately

The alternative is to create special request processing logic for CMP beans. In this case, when a request comes in for a CMP bean, the container must make some calls to the persistence framework in addition to any other calls. In pseudocode, this might look like:

```
checkSecurity();
EnterpriseBean instance = getBeanInstance();
startTransaction();
framework.loadBean(instance);
instance.ejbLoad();
Object value = instance.businessMethod();
instance.ejbStore();
framework.storeBean(instance);
endTransaction();
return value;
```

Compared to the request processing for a BMP entity, this just adds some additional calls to the persistence framework. Looking at the code above, there's not a significant change. But in a real implementation, the logic is likely to be more complex, making decisions on when to load a bean instance based on the commit option and so on. All of this logic is already in place for BMP entities, so why code it again? If the container takes this approach, it needs to be more careful with its design, if it is to avoid extraneous duplication of complex logic. On the other hand, the differences have a purely run-time effect, so the deployment process is not changed.

Obstacles to Container-Managed Persistence

The main problem for any CMP implementation is the differences between different database products. It seems trivial at first, since all vendors use SQL. Unfortunately, no vendors completely implement the latest SQL standards (not even SQL-92). This raises various problems, including:

❑   Handling tables where the primary key is an automatically generated number.

❑   Handling data types such as Boolean, byte, and short that are not supported in all databases.

❑   Handling unusually long fields in the database (often anything over 255 bytes, known as Large Objects (LOBs), which can be both binary (BLOBs) and character-based (CLOBs). These are supported differently in different products.

❑   Storing Java objects in the database: what column types to use, whether to use byte arrays or streams, etc.

❑   Managing specific vendor or driver requirements, such as limitations on the number of columns of a certain type in a table, or the way large strings are searched.

❑   Handling database products that do not support features such as transactions, referential integrity, or outer joins, etc.

In the end, the container vendor usually compiles some sort of configuration information for each database product that's supported for CMP, but then you're limited to using one of those products. Often the workaround for a problem with one product is safe enough to use on other products, so sometimes they're just included directly in the persistence frameworks. In any case, it is best to be sure that a container claims full CMP support for your database.

Performance of CMP

In its initial implementations, CMP was often significantly slower than BMP. This was mainly because of the fact that a container couldn't easily establish when a bean had changed, or which fields had changed, so it had to take a very heavy-handed approach by loading and storing all of the fields with an alarming frequency.

With the changes in EJB 2.0, and the advancement of CMP implementations, this is much less of a concern and often the performance of CMP can exceed the performance of BMP. For example, in EJB 2.0, the container is responsible for storing all the data values for a CMP entity – the bean is simply not allowed to declare variables to hold the CMP fields, or implement methods to access those fields. This means that all access to the fields must go through the container, and it is quite easy for the container to determine when specific fields have changed. In this way, the container can skip writing a bean to the database if none of the fields have changed, and optimize its SQL to refer only to primary key fields and any fields that have changed.

Of course, a cleverly crafted BMP bean could implement the same functionality. But there are further optimizations available to the container that are simply not available to BMP beans. For example, the findByPrimaryKey() method always returns a bean object (assuming that the primary key was valid). In BMP, this is always executed as two separate queries: one in the ejbFindByPrimaryKey() method to determine whether the key is valid, and one in ejbLoad() to initialize an appropriate bean instance. In CMP, the container could combine these into a single query, and load all the fields at the same time as it checks whether the key is valid.

Another argument against CMP is that through EJB 1.1 it didn't support relationships between beans with any cardinality other than one-to-one. For example, an order with a number of line items in another table could not be modeled as a single EJB with CMP. We could have modeled each line item as a bean and the order as a whole as another bean, with no particular relationship between them, but that introduces a lot of overhead in making remote calls to manipulate line items.

EJB 2.0 introduced local entities and container-managed relationships to address this issue. Local entities are simply entities that are not accessed remotely, so their method parameters can be passed by reference and there is no RMI overhead to call them. Container-managed relationships allow a bean to set up a relationship with a group of local entities, which is perfect for modeling a parent-child relationship like the order and line items mentioned above. Since the relationship associates a parent entity with a group of local entities, there is not such a significant performance penalty for interacting with the child entities. These additions expand the scope of CMP to handle a whole new class of entities.

Overall, CMP saves us a tremendous amount of coding and often implements enough optimizations to run faster than equivalent BMP entities. One of the major limitations to modeling entities with CMP has been removed in EJB 2.0. At this point, it's definitely attractive to use CMP wherever possible, reserving BMP for those cases that are simply too complex to model in CMP.

Generating Unique IDs

Many databases have a facility for creating unique IDs for the values in a particular column, often the primary key. However, every database does this in a different way, and there is no standard for it. Not all products include clear SQL to insert the next ID, or retrieve the next ID to be used, and JDBC itself doesn't have any method to accommodate this anyway. In the end, CMP implementations simply do not provide this functionality.

That doesn't mean we can't do it, however. The easiest way to insert a unique ID is to implement the `ejbCreate()` method of a CMP bean to retrieve the next ID and write it to the appropriate field. Since the `ejbCreate()` method is called before the bean is actually created, this ID will be written to the database in the initial `INSERT` statement. That only leaves the question of how to retrieve the next ID in our `ejbCreate()`.

This topic has been discussed extensively in forums such as TheServerSide (http://www.theserverside.com/), and there are a number of possible solutions. The simplest would be for the entity to just execute a SQL statement to retrieve the value in its `ejbCreate()`, though this could get complex if the database doesn't automatically increment the value every time you retrieve it. As well, you would have to implement that in every such CMP bean. A better solution might be to include a static object or session bean that generates IDs.

One common strategy is to use a stateless session bean that grabs a block of IDs for each table. This improves performance not only by avoiding hitting the database every time we need a new ID, but also by allowing the container to pool bean instances. It even avoids serializing access to the method that allocates IDs. However, it does mean that IDs will not be allocated sequentially, and some IDs may be skipped altogether. Usually this is not a significant issue.

However you choose to implement it, this is one of the clear holes in CMP, and hopefully it will be addressed in a future revision of the CMP specification.

CMP in EJB 2.0

We've already touched on most of the CMP improvements in EJB 2.0 in earlier chapters, but let's take another look, this time in the context of the container. First, the container is responsible for access to, and storage of, all CMP fields. This makes the container aware of all changes to container-managed fields, and that lets the container better optimize its database access. This can significantly reduce the number of stores to the database, and reduces our reliance on container-specific mechanisms such as the `isModified()` method of letting the container know what's changed.

Second, the container supports local entity views. This is an important step forward, as the performance overhead for remote calls and copying all method parameters (to support pass -by-value) was significant. It often didn't make sense for a method call between two closely related beans to be treated as remote and, as such, a number of containers support specific flags to override the behavior. For example, some containers can pass by value for calls between beans in the *same* container. This could improve performance significantly, at the risk of directly violating the specification. Equivalent optimization is now supported by the specification, and will be present in all compliant containers.

Third, the container supports relationships between entities. Although the container could handle one-to-one mappings between beans before, it was unable to handle the more common many-to-one relationship. This addition extends CMP support to a new class of entities.

Finally, EJB 2.0 provides standard syntax for finders and selectors (the manner in which a bean identifies other beans that it is related to for container-managed relationships). In the past, one of the most painful aspects of switching containers was rewriting the finder syntax for the new container. The standard EJB QL syntax is an important addition to EJB 2.0, as it brings us still closer to true container independence. The main outstanding difference between vendors is the mapping of tables and columns to container-managed beans and fields, but that is a relatively small problem compared to the finder syntax.

Reloading Classes

The final run-time issue we will consider, one that comes up frequently during development, is reloading classes. We might fix a bug in an EJB implementation, and it would be most convenient to have the container reload that class immediately, leaving the rest of the deployed classes intact. Unfortunately, this is another area in which the EJB specification provides no guidance. In most cases, however, it is not actually possible to implement this in as simple a way as it is described. The problem is due to `ClassLoaders`.

Every class in Java must be loaded by a `ClassLoader`, and since every object is an instance of a class, each object belongs to the `ClassLoader` that loaded its class. Unfortunately, once a class is loaded into a `ClassLoader`, we can't ever remove it. Strictly speaking, that's not quite true; in fact, the Java language specification says something along the lines of, "if you can force all instances of a class to be unloaded, the `ClassLoader` can remove that class, but we don't provide a way for you to force all instances to be unloaded". So in essence, in order to reload a class, you have to discard its whole `ClassLoader`, and then reload the class in a new `ClassLoader`.

However, it's not so practical to create every single class in its own `ClassLoader`, so ultimately the container will group related classes into the same `ClassLoader`. Often this amounts to one `ClassLoader` per EJB JAR, or per J2EE application, but different containers do it differently. Thus, the smallest group of classes that can be reloaded together is generally an EJB JAR.

That's not the only restriction on reloading, however. Any classes that form part of the bean's interface need to be loaded into the `ClassLoaders` for all the clients of the bean. Those classes include the bean's home and component interface, the primary key for entities, any application-specific exceptions or data structures, and so on. If any of those classes change, then simply discarding the bean's `ClassLoader` is not enough. The container would have to also discard all the client `ClassLoaders`, and since the container doesn't have any way of tracking or enforcing that, we generally can't reload beans if we change their interface. At that point, we would need to undeploy and then redeploy the bean, or restart the container.

Unfortunately, since this process is not standardized, we have to do any reloading in a server-specific way. In some cases, the server's tools allow this, and some IDEs support certain servers for this purpose, but usually it comes down to figuring out how our specific container operates. The deployment changes in J2EE 1.4 may standardize this process, making it easier to reload classes in EJB containers.

Finally, it is interesting to note that the Java Platform Debugger Architecture (JPDA) interface has been updated in JDK 1.4 to allow limited reloading of classes at run time during debugging. This raises the possibility that class reloading could be easier to implement using similar methods. However, in JDK 1.4, class reloading is strictly a feature of the debugger, and it only works in debug mode, so it is not available to classes running normally in the JVM. It's worth keeping an eye on this for future developments.

Management

The J2EE specification does not yet provide a standard mechanism for managing EJBs or EJB containers. The management strategy and tools are left to the container vendor. Some vendors have chosen to use the **Java Management Extensions (JMX)**, but while this is indeed a standard, it is not a standard for J2EE servers. What this means is that a generic JMX client can interact with the server, but it is not customized in any way to a J2EE server (or EJB container). That is, we'd like to be able to interact with a management tool that provides easy access to deployed beans and web apps, lets us manage clusters and resource pools, and so on. With a plain JMX client, all these management features are just operations on MBeans, and there's no way to customize the UI the way we'd like. Even if we were to create a specialized client, there's no standard set of JMX managed beans for a running EJB container, and no standard for the information or operations available. Instead of working with a generic management client, we typically rely on the vendor's particular management tools. Those are often specialized in the way we like, but don't offer universal integration into larger management systems.

Our hope for interoperability in the area lies with the future. The upcoming J2EE 1.4 specification will add a management interface to the standard. That interface is currently being designed under the auspices of JSR-77 (http://www.jcp.org/jsr/detail/77.jsp). This spec request aims to provide a standard interface for management tools, covering at least two distinct sets of tools:

❑ A dedicated J2EE management tool that will be able to manage J2EE servers from different vendors. Though the level of support will likely be left to the vendor, you should expect some level of reporting and control over individual EJBs and EJB JARs.

❑ Systems and network management software, such as IBM's Tivoli, CA's Unicenter, and HP's OpenView, that will be able to manage J2EE Servers just the same as any other servers or resources on the network.

The current focus of JSR-77 is on creating a UML model to represent a J2EE server. As such, the final spec would not focus on a specific Java API for management, but rather a model for a specific set of objects and services that the server should provide. This model could be mapped to any particular implementation, such as Java, JMX, Simple Network Management Protocol (SNMP), or Web Based Enterprise Management (WBEM). Thus, the interoperability for J2EE management tools is provided by a standard object model that translates to a standard set of Java classes. The interoperability for network management software is provided by mapping the J2EE management model to a protocol that the particular software understands. Vendors will still be free to extend the basic model to provide more information or functionality, but the standard model will be inclusive enough to allow for feature-rich standard tools.

Clustering

Though clustering support is not mandated by the EJB specification, most servers do implement it. Clustering is advantageous in two main areas: performance, and fault tolerance. If we can't get enough performance out of one server (at least, one economical server), perhaps adding more servers is the solution. Moreover, if a J2EE application needs maximum availability, duplicating all the data and beans on another server means that if one server fails then another can take over.

The intricacies of clustering are, for the most part, not covered by the EJB specification, and could easily be the subject of a book themselves. We'll just take a brief look at some of the approaches to, and implications of, clustering.

Approaches to Clustering

Stateless session beans and message-driven beans are easy to cluster. They can be spread across as many servers as we have, and any request or message can be delivered to any instance on any server.

Stateful session beans and entity beans are trickier to cluster, because they contain state. The container can't allow two clients to interact with two copies of the same instance on two different servers simultaneously. Additionally, the data on the different servers has to be kept in sync so that if a series of clients calls "instances" on a series of different servers, there should be no data integrity problems. Both of these requirements mean that the container has to spend a fair bit of effort synchronizing access to different copies of the same bean instance.

For that reason, it's often beneficial to minimize the number of servers that have copies of the same instance of the same bean. That is, an entity bean may be deployed on ten servers, but the entity with the primary key 108470, say, does not necessarily need to be active on all ten servers at the same time. If it is active, then the overhead of synchronizing is greater, but the fault tolerance is also greater.

So, one common approach is to replicate an instance of a bean to all the machines in a cluster, which is easier to manage and more fault tolerant. Another common approach is to replicate an instance of a bean to exactly two servers, with the provision that if one fails, the instance is replicated to a new live server, always keeping a primary and backup active at any time. This requires a little more work to manage, but needs much less overhead for each method call. On the other hand, it is not as fault-tolerant as the fully replicated cluster.

Often the decision regarding which type of replication is best for a particular application depends on the characteristics of the hardware for the servers. For a small number of very powerful servers, the additional fault tolerance of full cluster replication outweighs the additional overhead. For a large number of less powerful servers, the overhead could be burdensome and a single backup to ensure fault tolerance may be enough. Ultimately, the selection of hardware may depend on the nature and value of the application and the data it manages. These criteria will have more of a bearing on the design of the overall system, and how it will be budgeted. If your data is highly critical you would most likely go for "big iron". On the other hand, for economic reasons you may have to opt for clusters of separate boxes. The following discussion may apply to both approaches.

Distributed JNDI

The JNDI tree needs to be more "intelligent" for a cluster. We wouldn't want a JNDI context to always point to the same server in a cluster, or else we're losing all the benefits of the cluster. The JNDI context needs to be able to identify the servers in a cluster, and distribute calls accordingly. If a server goes down, the JNDI context should drop it and only call other servers until it recovers.

As for JNDI within a container, it needs to be more intelligent as well. If a bean calls another bean, odds are the performance will be better if that call is handled locally inside the same container rather than being distributed to a container in a different server, within the cluster. However, it may be the case that a particular bean or container is overloaded or broken in one server, and calls that should ordinarily stay local must be rerouted to a remote server to avoid that.

Here is a sample of how a distributed JNDI context might differ from a normal JNDI context:

```
// Normal
public Object lookup(String name) {
    return data.get(name);
}

// Distributed
public Object lookup(String name) {
    // First check if we're already on a server in the cluster.
    if(currentServer != null) {
        return currentServer.data.get(name);
    }

    // Select a server to call, using round robin or a load
    // measurement or whatever.
    final ServerData server = pickAServer();
    Object o = server.data.get(name);

    // If there's a communication error, remove this server
```

```
        // from the rotation.
        if(o instanceof EjbReference) {
            ((EjbReference)o).setErrorHandler(new ErrorHandler() {
                public void handleError() {
                    removeServer(server);
                }
            });
        }
        return o;
    }
```

In this example, we assume there's some sort of data structure holding the appropriate object stubs for each server. The normal JNDI behavior is pretty simple – it just looks up the object from the only such data structure there is. In the clustered case, it gets more complicated. First, if this JNDI context is actually running on a server, we want to resolve the call to another object on the same server. Of course, a real implementation would be somewhat more complicated including cases in which no objects were present on any server, or the home server was unusually loaded, and the call would need to be redirected. However, the general idea is the same.

Next, if the lookup was not resolved to this server, then the JNDI context needs to select an appropriate server to direct to. The simplest implementation would just be "round robin", but more advanced algorithms might take into account the capabilities of each server, the server's current load or response time, and perhaps even the network topology between the current node and each available server. Finally, the context must somehow install a hook so that it is notified of any communication errors. It may be the case that the returned object stub simply calls into the JNDI context again and identifies the problem node, but in this example the context just registers itself as a listener for connection errors.

In practice, real distributed JNDI implementations are still more complex because they often work hand in hand with smart object stubs to transparently redirect failed calls to any node in the cluster. In this case, the stub cannot be tied to a single node, but must itself be aware of the distributed JNDI tree so it can look up a new server to connect to in case of failure. If a server does go down, backup containers may need to be notified to promote new instances to active status and perhaps to replicate data. This would ensure continued fault tolerance.

Clustered Services

The basic services a container provides, such as security, transactions, and resource management, are no different in a clustered environment. However, there are new challenges in each of these areas that the cluster must address.

With regard to security, the cluster clearly needs to ensure that all servers are using the same data for authentication and authorization. However, we don't want that data to all come from the same place (that is, from a single file or a service on a single machine) because it would just represent another single point of failure. So, the clustered machines should rely on distributed security information.

Security also needs to be tighter for communication between beans. Whereas in a single container environment, calls between beans don't need to traverse the network, in this case they do. We may want those calls to be encrypted, or we may need to re-authenticate a caller principal instead of trusting what another "container" claims is an authenticated principal.

As for transactions, a cluster must similarly use distributed transactions. Bean-to-bean calls that relied on the thread carrying the transaction context must now pass the transaction context to a different container. User transactions that span several bean calls must also propagate to different servers. As in the non-clustered environment, the container may pass the transaction context across calls using JTS on OTS, or it may use another mechanism. The specification does not dictate a distributed transaction implementation, but the requirement for IIOP support for calls to the beans is a definite hint that OTS may be appropriate.

Finally, clusters introduce new challenges to resource management as well. It's extremely important that the resource configuration on the different servers in the cluster is the same, or, in any case, close enough that a deployer can map something to all the resources that a bean requires, and that a bean instance won't get different results depending on which server in the cluster its container is running on. The resources also need to make use of the distributed transaction and security facilities.

Summary

In this chapter, we've taken a detailed look at common implementations of EJB container features. We started by reviewing the characteristics of containers in the context of the J2EE architecture, and highlighted the difference between servers and containers. A server can be regarded as a collection of services, while a container applies those services to specific components of our application.

Next, we looked at how the container handles deployment, how it provides services to the beans and the developers at run time, and how it implements management and clustering. We also examined some of the Java APIs that the container uses to fulfill its end of the EJB component contract. With this background, we should be able to design and develop our applications to take full advantage of the container's strengths, and work around its limitations.

Over the next few chapter we will be looking at how to take our EJBs and integrate them with a number of alternative component models, starting with the bigger J2EE picture.

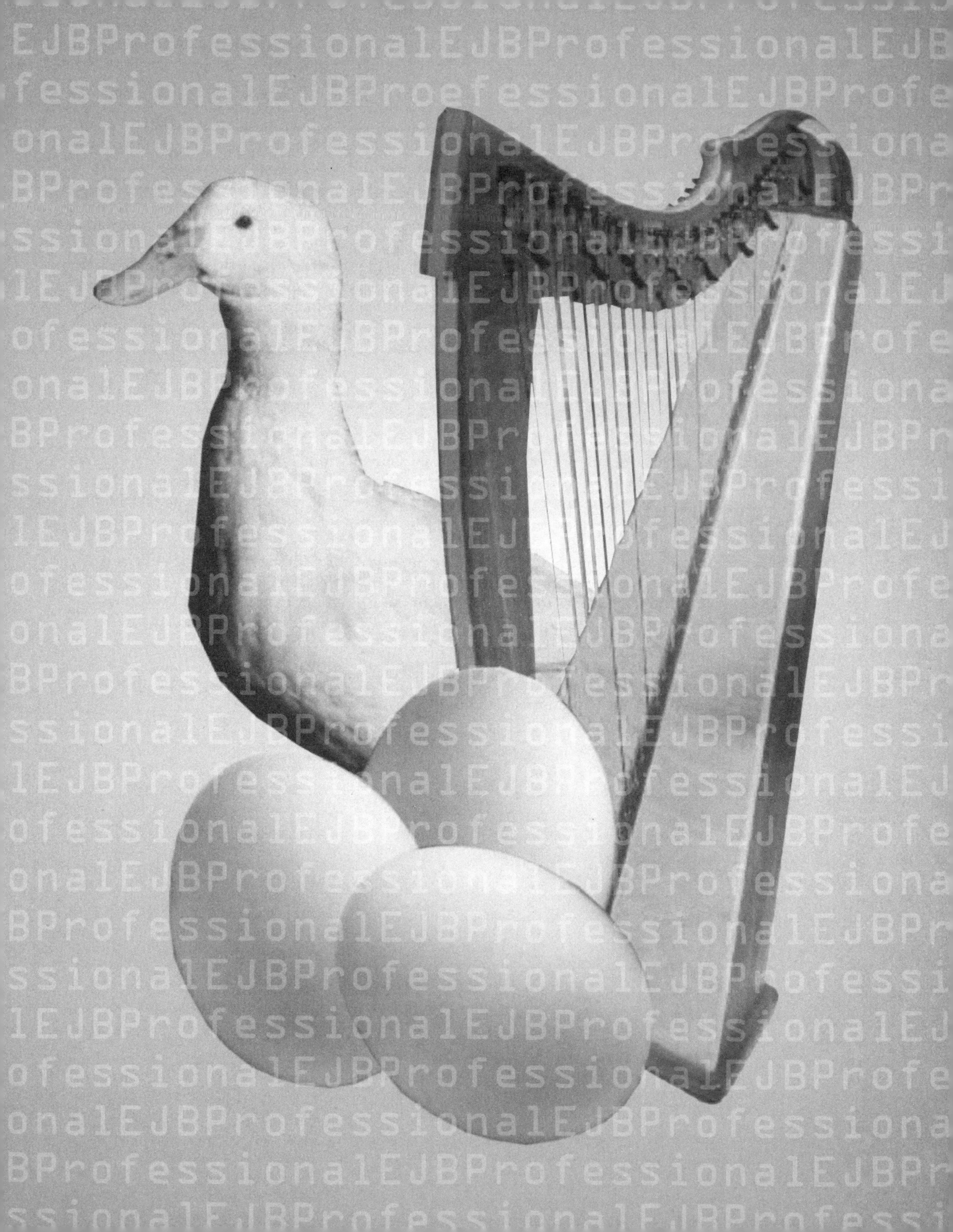

18

J2EE Applications

Since its introduction in 1999, the Java 2 Platform, Enterprise Edition (J2EE) has achieved remarkable popularity. J2EE is a set of coordinated specifications that enable solutions for developing multi-tier enterprise applications, simplifying enterprise applications by basing them on standardized, modular components. The J2EE architecture comprises a number of components, which separate the essential parts of an enterprise application. The separate components are intended to ease the development cycle, and to foster reuse between applications. Broadly, the architecture includes the components for the presentation layer, and the components for the business logic layer. It is in the latter that EJBs fit into the J2EE architecture.

In addition to the components, the J2EE architecture specifies the services and communications technologies that must be supported. Finally, the specification also outlines a number of roles in the application and deployment lifecycle, in order to aid in the identification of the tasks performed by various parties during the development and deployment of the J2EE application.

This chapter will introduce an example to illustrate the different components, show how they integrate together, and how to use them to separate business logic from data-access logic. The chapter will give the reader a basic understanding of the technologies, their roles, and the issues associated with them; thus the services and communications APIs will not be looked at thoroughly, as they are addressed elsewhere in this book.

J2EE Architecture

The J2EE architecture can be broken up into the following components:

- ❑ **Application Components** – these components execute within a container.
- ❑ **Containers** – these provide the run-time environment for the application components. The container also provides access to additional resources via the J2EE APIs.

❑ **J2EE APIs** – Containers must support the APIs listed below. These APIs are essential in providing a comprehensive platform for development as they integrate containers together. The J2EE platform 1.3 specification outlines the Java APIs that must be supported – this does not mean that the J2EE server must implement each API itself, but simply that it must provide access to the APIs so that implementations by other vendors can be plugged in.

❑ **Enterprise JavaBeans 2.0** – An enterprise bean is used to implement modules of business logic. We already know about these.

❑ **JDBC 2.0 API** – The JDBC API lets you invoke SQL commands from Java methods.

❑ **Java Servlet 2.3** – Java servlet technology lets you define HTTP-specific servlet classes. Although servlets can respond to any type of request, they are commonly used to extend the applications hosted by web servers.

❑ **JavaServer Pages (JSP) 1.2** – JSP pages technology lets you put snippets of servlet code directly into a text-based document.

❑ **Java Message Service (JMS) 1.0** – The JMS API is a messaging standard that allows J2EE application components to create, send, receive, and read messages in an asynchronous manner.

❑ **Java Transaction API (JTA) 1.0** – The JTA API provides a standard demarcation interface for demarcating transactions.

❑ **JavaMail 1.2** – JavaMail API can be used by application components to send Internet mails.

❑ **JavaBeans Activation Framework 1.0** –This provides standard services to determine the type of an arbitrary piece of data, encapsulate access to it, discover the operations available on it, and create the appropriate JavaBean component to perform those operations.

❑ **Java API for XML (JAXP) 1.1** – This is used to handle and read XML data.

❑ **J2EE Connector API 1.0** – The Connector API is used to create resource adapters that support access to enterprise information systems. These APIs are generally used by J2EE tools vendors and system integrators.

❑ **Java Authentication and Authorization Service (JAAS) 1.0** JAAS provides a way for a J2EE application to authenticate and authorize a specific user or group of users to run it.

The application components can be broken up further, as follows:

❑ **Client Components** – These are components that can be used to access services within a J2EE application server. Among them are browser-based applications, applets, and standalone applications.

❑ **Web Components** – These are components that execute within a web container, and are used to service clients that request information over the web. The requests are usually serviced in the form of HTML or XML. The two primary component types are Java servlets and JavaServer Pages, which we will discuss in this chapter.

❑ **Business Components** – The primary component within this tier is the EJB component; since this is the topic of the book we only need to discuss how it fits into the J2EE specifications. Other technologies that are encompassed within business components are the JMS, JDBC, JNDI, JTA, and RMI-IIOP APIs.

The following diagram shows how these components fit together to form the whole:

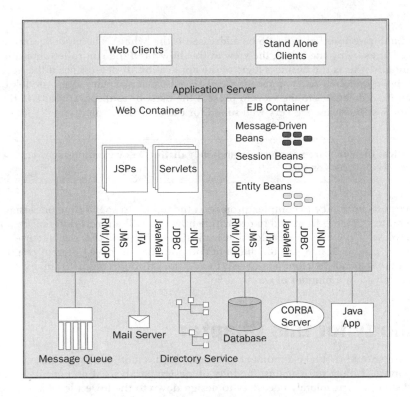

Another Look at the J2EE Architecture: The Model-View-Controller Pattern

Let's look at the J2EE architecture again. Instead of breaking it up based on the system responsibilities, let's be more abstract and break it up based on just application responsibility.

In this chapter, our example will be implemented with the **Model-View-Controller (MVC)** pattern. The MVC pattern attempts to separate the roles of an application into three distinct areas and then address them with different solutions. The terminology is very straightforward, but we'll briefly explain it.

❏ **Model**
This is concerned with the actual data model for the application. The model is not concerned with how it presents itself, or when it is accessed, it is simply concerned with the integrity of its data and from where it is obtained. Entity and session beans are directly designed for this.

❏ **View**
As the term implies, this is only concerned with the presentation. When developing EJBs so far, it should have become apparent that they are not very well suited for presentation. If we were to start including code for HTML formatting for example, our EJB would become very confusing very quickly. This is where the web components come in. JSP and servlets were designed with the intent that they would address presentation issues.

❑ **Controller**
The final question that needs to be addressed is the 'when'. The model component can be looked at as being the 'what', the view as the 'how', and the controller determines the 'when'. Essentially, this is the business logic of the application. It determines if the necessary criteria have been met, before an application can access particular data in the model; based on the situation, it delegates to the view to present the data, or to display an alternative course of action. Session beans are very well suited for the controller role.

> In practice, the roles are not always completely distinct. For example, servlets usually play a controller role as well.

Perhaps the largest hindrance to complex projects is the failure to spend time on design – it is absolutely critical to spend the time up front and to determine how you will address different requirements. In the case of this book we have already decided that we will be using the J2EE architecture, which will obviously impact on our design – as the different components will have different response times, scalability thresholds, and development needs. In addition, through the APIs, many of our requirements can usually be solved in a number of ways.

Methodology for this Chapter

At this point, we should first take a moment to briefly discuss methodology. Although I firmly believe design is important, I must warn against the folly of 'design paralysis'. I do not think that when designing a system, it is absolutely necessary to design down to the lowest level and flesh out all of the design patterns, and so on – this is best left to development time. I am also an advocate of **Extreme Programming (XP)** and find that these issues cannot be fully addressed prior to implementation; however, there is great value in setting some common design standards based upon the architecture being used (in this case J2EE). For example, depending upon the team skills, and the needs of the project, it may be wise to decide that all HTML will be placed in JSP pages only – thus eliminating the need to refactor for a common design later in the project.

I would highly recommend looking at the following books: *Refactoring: Improving the Design of Existing Code* by Martin Fowler (Addison-Wesley, 1999) ISBN: 0-201-48567-2, and *Extreme Programming Explained: Embrace Change* by Kent Beck (Addison-Wesley, 1999) ISBN: 0-201-61641-6. Information can also be found at http://www.extremeprogramming.org.

A UML diagram such as the one in the next section provides an excellent starting point to ensure that everyone has the basics of the business model. It provides a means for business needs and requirements to be expressed, updated, or modified. As a tool for communication between business analysts and developers, this is very useful.

Where projects start to run aground is when these diagrams become the project themselves. Nothing can replace open communication between parties – the diagrams should only be used to capture the basics of the system, and in some cases when signoff from a higher authority is needed. The finer details should be captured as the design and implementation progresses. Having an open dialog continuing between the business and development teams is essential keeping everyone on the same page ensuring that the finer details come to light.

For the examples in this chapter, we assume that you are using the BEA WebLogic 6.1 server and the accompanying Cloudscape DB on Windows; however, the examples can be run in any other server that supports Java Servlets 2.3 and JSP 1.2. You can download an evaluation copy of the WebLogic server from http://www.bea.com.

The Model – The Online Cinema Booking System

To help us understand the MVC pattern, and how the J2EE technologies and APIs fit into it, let's consider an example of an online cinema booking system. In this system, registered users can retrieve the names of the movies that will be playing (for simplicity's sake, we will assume that all movies start at the same time) and then proceed to book a maximum of four seats.

The system will have a predefined number of seats available for each cinema room, where a fixed amount will be pre-reserved; however, when the number of available seats falls below ten, the manager must be notified, at which point the manager can then decide to release reserved seats thus increasing the number available. In this chapter we will develop the service using the J2EE architecture, looking at the differences in design and implementation choices available.

The following is a UML diagram to express this example:

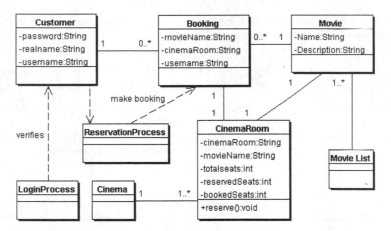

The diagram is by no means complete, but it does provide us a starting point for developing the system. It does not illustrate the implementation classes, but rather higher-level concepts and processes, which may or may not directly map onto our implementation.

Implementing the Example

So, we know what we need to implement, but how are we going to implement these objects? Which of the tools at our disposal will we be using? The J2EE architecture provides a great deal of flexibility, allowing us to implement the model layer a number of different ways. Let's look more closely at each of the objects from the UML diagram.

Movie

Since we're going to store information about the movies in a database, entity beans are the most obvious choice for developing the Movie object.

Customer

Due to the nature of the Customer object in this application, we're going to use entity beans for our implementation. The Customer object will be a fine-grained object, which will provide additional information about the customer, such as their real name. We will assume that a table containing pre-registered customers already exists, thus we will not need to implement a facility to do this, although it would be a simple task.

Booking

When we come to implement the Booking object and its functions, we might not find it so easy to keep to just one API. This is because, although we could, we are better advised to use those APIs that are designed for a specific purpose for each aspect of the Reservation process. Therefore, we will be using JSP and servlets to handle the user interaction, entity beans to represent the database objects we will need to keep track of, and a session bean to liaise between the servlets and the entity beans.

Our application is going to take reservation input using a browser-based model. This means that we have one basic choice to make: JSP pages or servlets?

At the most basic level, we could use a JSP or servlet to access the database directly and retrieve the information. This approach has a number of drawbacks:

- ❑ Firstly, it would tie our web component directly to the database – meaning that it would need to know the schema for the database and if the database were ever altered, the web components would have to be modified.

- ❑ Secondly, we know that we are going to need to perform some business processes, thus using the direct access approach, we would be mixing the control and model layers.

- ❑ And finally, the web component still needs to deal with presenting the information.

All of this can get very messy very quickly. Let's implement the reservation submssion part using a servlet and JSP and delegate the processing of the reservation to a session bean.

CinemaRoom

The CinemaRoom object is another good candidate for entity beans, because it maps on to a real world object. We will create a table in the database that lists each of the available cinema rooms and the movie showing in them.

Database Schema

The example database, MovieDB, will use the following database schema:

```
CREATE TABLE BOOKING (
      CINEMAROOM VARCHAR(255) ,
      QUANTITY INT ,
      USERNAME VARCHAR(255) ,
      MOVIENAME VARCHAR(255)
);
CREATE TABLE CINEMAROOM (
      ROOM VARCHAR(255) ,
      TOTALSEATS INT ,
      RESERVEDSEATS INT ,
```

```
        BOOKEDSEATS INT ,
        MOVIENAME VARCHAR(255)
);
CREATE TABLE CUSTOMER (
        PASSWORD VARCHAR(255) ,
        REALNAME VARCHAR(255) ,
        USERNAME VARCHAR(255)
);
CREATE TABLE MOVIES
        NAME VARCHAR(255) ,
        DESCRIPTION VARCHAR(255)
);
```

And we will assume that it is populated with information like the following:

Movies Table

Name	Description
Gladiator	Period Epic – Russell Crowe
Shrek	The greatest story never told
Swordfish	Hackers gone crazy – John Travolta, Halle Barry
The Wedding Planner	J-Lo at her best, need we say more?

CinemaRoom

Room	MovieName	TotalSeats	ReservedSeats	BookedSeats
A	Gladiator	100	25	0
B	Shrek	100	25	0
C	The Wedding Planner	100	25	0
D	Swordfish	100	25	0

Ensure that the entries in the MovieName column correspond to the Name column in the Movies table.

Customer Table

Username	RealName	Password
John	John Doe	myPass
Critic	The Critic	myPass

Since we will not be including the functionality to create new customers, you will need to manually add more to the database if you want to. Usually, you would not keep sensitive information such as the password unencrypted in the database, but for our purposes it will be all right.

Before we can use the database, we must specify the JDBC pool in `config.xml` file. In WebLogic 6.1, this file can be found in the `%WEBLOGIC_HOME%\config\mydomain` directory. You can either use the WebLogic console or add the following entry to between the <Domain> tags:

```
<JDBCDataSource
    JNDIName="MoviesPool"
    Name="MoviesPool"
    PoolName="MoviesPool"
    Targets="myserver"
/>
<JDBCConnectionPool
    CapacityIncrement="1"
    DriverName="COM.cloudscape.core.JDBCDriver"
    InitialCapacity="1"
    MaxCapacity="1"
    Name="MoviesPool"
    Properties="user=none;password=none;server=none"
    Targets="myserver"
    URL="jdbc:cloudscape:MovieDB"
/>
```

You will have to modify the above to reflect the name of the database that you created.

The first tag we're using is the <JDBCDataSource> tag. Data sources are a feature of the JDBC Optional Package API. They provide a transparent mechanism for creating, managing, and accessing a database. Using this method, as opposed to directly creating a database connection in the client, the client is able to abstract the details and work with a simple logical name for the data source.

The <JDBCDataSource> tag specifies the name by which our data source will be bound to the JNDI service, and the database connection pool that it will be part of.

The second tag is the <JDBCConnectionPool> tag. The attributes of this tag specify where the database is located (which database), and the parameters with which it should be started.

The View

To start, we will look at the options that we have for the user to interact with the application. The J2EE architecture gives us two technologies: Java servlets and JSP. Both have their strengths and weaknesses, and in many cases the choice of which to use will come down to personal preference.

Java Servlets

This section will briefly discuss the **Java Servlet API** (v2.3) and we will look at servlets in a bit more detail later in the chapter. Java servlets are similar to CGI (Common Gateway Interface) scripts – they are a server-side technology used to process and respond to requests from web clients. However, servlets have some very important differences that make them much better than CGI scripts, namely:

❑ Servlets run within a web container and have access to the other J2EE components.

❑ Servlets provide a structured framework for dealing with client requests and responses.

❏   Servlets are more scalable – the run-time execution of the servlet is handled by the web container, which along with taking advantage of the multi-threading capabilities of Java, also implements pooling algorithms to share servlet instances. On the other hand, if a servlet is only called once, then the benefit may not be noticed since servlets are slower to start up on the initial request than typical CGI scripts.

There are two primary packages in the Java Servlet API – `javax.servlet`, and `javax.servlet.http`. The `javax.servlet` package also contains two sub-packages – `javax.servlet.jsp` and `javax.servlet.jsp.tagext` that will be discussed in the section on *JavaServer Pages*.

In this section we will quickly introduce the primary classes needed to develop a servlet and the servlet lifecycle, and then we will illustrate with an example. Since this is only intended to be an introduction to Java servlets, we will only discuss servlets requested via HTTP. If you want to learn more about servlets (and JavaServer Pages), take a look at *Professional JSP, Second Edition*, from Wrox Press, ISBN 1-861004-95-8. For now, let's start with the lifecycle of a servlet.

The Servlet Lifecycle

Servlets are usually invoked by a client HTTP request via a web server (actually it is by a web container that resides in the web server). The web container is responsible for the run-time control of the servlet. The servlet will go through the following stages during its lifecycle:

❏   **Instantiated** – the web container creates an instance of the servlet.

❏   **Initialized** – the web container calls the `init()` method on the servlet.

❏   **Serviced** – the web container delegates client requests to the servlet's `service()` method. The servlet processes the requests and returns an appropriate response. A servlet instance may be used to service requests from multiple clients.

❏   **Destroyed** – the web container will call the servlet's `destroy()` method when the it is no longer needed; the servlet can now be cleaned up by the garbage collector.

The Servlet API Interfaces

In order to enable the web container to control the lifecycle of servlets, all servlets must implement the interface `javax.servlet.Servlet`.

For HTTP requests, the Java Servlet API provides another class, `javax.servlet.http.HttpServlet`, an extension of the class `javax.servlet.GenericServlet`, which provides default implementations for each of the methods in `javax.servlet.Servlet`. The `HttpServlet` class processes the requests in a `service()` method and delegates them to an appropriate method corresponding to the HTTP specification. The `HttpServlet` provides default implementations for `doGet()` and `doPost()` to support HTTP 1.0, and `doOptions()`, `doTrace()`, `doPut()`, and `doDelete()` for HTTP 1.1 support.

In most cases when developing a servlet, we will simply extend the `HttpServlet` class and override the necessary methods. The container implements a number of additional interfaces to support the servlet, and provides access to run-time and deployment information. As we said earlier, the servlet API is based on a simple request-response architecture – meaning that the container provides input data to the servlet via a Request object, and the servlet responds using a Response object. In the case of HTTP sessions, these objects are implementations of `HttpServletRequest` and `HttpServletResponse` respectively.

All access to the necessary run-time information, or additional objects, for controlling sessions and for tracking is obtained from the Request or Response objects, with the exception of one object – the ServletConfig object. The ServletConfig object is implemented by the web container, and provides access to initialization information specified during deployment (it also allows access to the ServletContext object which we will discuss later). During initialization, the HttpServlet retains a reference to the ServletConfig object.

Tracking Sessions

So far we have only looked at a basic servlet. We must still add functionality to control the sessions and user logins. Both the Java Servlet API and JavaServer Pages API provide additional mechanisms to allow for controlling the flow of applications.

The JSP API is designed for dynamic presentation, and although we can put control code on a JSP page, this would be like putting display code in a servlet – not what it's designed for. Instead, it would make more sense to use a servlet for our control (a practice which is common in web applications).

The Servlet API also provides three facilities that can be manipulated to achieve the desired level of monitoring.

The HttpSession Interface

The javax.servlet.http.HttpSession interface is an implementation of a client session. When a client accesses a servlet, the server starts a session with the user, which is active for the duration of the client's current communication with the application. If the client's browser is restarted, their session will be restarted. The session is useful for supplying information through multiple servlet or page requests for tracking purposes or to reduce the amount of user input.

The session object can be accessed from within a servlet by calling the HttpServletRequest.getSession() method. If the session does not exist yet, the server will create a new one and return that to the servlet. In order to track the session over multiple client requests, the server stores a reference to the session in a **cookie** on the client, thus if a client has turned their cookie support off, the server will return a new session object for each request. In this case, the session object will return true to the method call isNew(). The servlet should be able handle such cases (usually by using URL rewriting as an alternative).

The Cookie Class

Cookies are a simple way for server-side processes to store and retrieve information on the client invoking the process. When a server responds to a client, it is able to attach a piece of information (usually state information) within a Cookie object, which is stored locally on the client's machine. The next time the server is invoked, the client also sends the associated cookies for that URI, where the servlet can then perform some processing based upon them.

The cookie differs from the Session object in that cookies can be long lived – meaning that the cookie will still be valid after the current session is complete. By using the Cookie.setMaxAge() method, the server can specify the duration for which the cookie will be valid. On a security note – because the cookie resides in an ASCII file on the client side you should never use it to store sensitive information such as passwords, credit card numbers, and so on.

Servlet Context

The `javax.servlet.ServletContext` interface defines yet another way to track a user. In addition to tracking information, the servlet can also use the `ServletContext` interface to access application-specific information such as supported MIME types, logging facilities, servlet environment, and so on. The `ServletContext` is specific to a particular path, and can be used as a shared resource between all servlets in that path.

The following table summarizes the different mechanisms for tracking:

Type	Scope
Session	Valid only for the current session of a given client
Cookies	Valid for all requests from the same client
ServletContext	Valid across an entire application

Before we start writing our first servlet, there are a couple of extra things that the specifications mandate. These are the location of our servlet files, and how we describe them to the servlet engine.

Locating a Servlet File

The Java Servlet API specifications say that we have to place our compiled servlets in a directory named `WEB-INF`. Web applications that utilize Java technologies such as servlets and JSP pages have a specific directory structure, to which we must adhere. The following table explains this directory structure:

Path	Description
/	The root directory of the application, where we can put our (X)HTML and JSP files
/WEB-INF	A special directory that contains our web deployment descriptor file, `web.xml`, and two sub-directories
/WEB-INF/classes	The directory into which we place our servlets; any package structure we impose on our servlets will start from this directory
/WEB-INF/lib	A directory for placing resources in JAR files that our web application needs; files in here will be included in the web application's classpath

As with EJBs, servlets require a deployment descriptor, which we provide in the form of the `web.xml` file. This file can also contain deployment information for other parts of a web application, but we'll come to that later. Let's look at a simple example:

```
<?xml version="1.0" ?>
<!DOCTYPE web-app
    PUBLIC "-//Sun Microsystems, Inc.//DTD Web Application 1.2//EN"
    "http://java.sun.com/j2ee/dtds/web-app_2_3.dtd">
<web-app>
</web-app>
```

This is the almost empty web.xml file from the
%WEBLOGIC_HOME%\config\mydomain\applications\DefaultWebApp_myserver\WEB-INF
directory, and it is to this file that we shall be making additions when we create our servlets. As with
most J2EE deployment descriptor files, most of the entries we'll make in here are designed to be fairly
human-readable, but we'll explain them as we add them.

The directory above the WEB-INF directory (DefaultWebApp_myserver\) will be the root directory
for our web application, and the classes directory below WEB-INF is where we will put our first
servlet. Let's now look an example using the API to control the presentation layer. We will see the
limitations, and then show how JSP pages fit in to make development easier and more manageable.

The LoginServlet

We will need to present a login page to the user. Let's create a servlet to provide the initial page, from
which we will see the problems.

We'll start with just the login form, and come back to the authentication method shortly. Create the
following Java file:

```java
package movie.servlets;

import javax.servlet.*;
import javax.servlet.http.*;
import java.io.*;
import java.util.*;

public class LoginServlet extends HttpServlet {

  // Should override 'doGet' if only want to process get requests
  public void doGet(HttpServletRequest req, HttpServletResponse res) {

    res.setContentType("text/html");

    try {
      PrintWriter writer = res.getWriter();    // obtain output stream
      writer.println("<html><head><title>");
      writer.println("LoginServlet");
      writer.println("</title></head>");

      writer.println("<body>");
      writer.println("<form method=\"post\" action=\"LoginServlet\">");
      writer.println("<br>");
      writer.println("Username: ");
      writer.println("<input type=\"text\" name=\"username\"><br>");
      writer.println("Password: ");
      writer.println("<input type=\"password\" name=\"password\"><br>");
      writer.println("<input type=\"Submit\"></form>");
      writer.println("</body></html>");
      writer.close();                          // Do not forget to close!!
    } catch (IOException io) {
      io.printStackTrace();                    // Usually we would use better
                                               // error handling
    }
  }
}
```

The LoginServlet is really quite simple – it only implements one method, doGet(), which it uses to display a login form for the client. At the moment, it doesn't do much else – we'll add more functionality soon, but for now the main thing to notice is how ugly the presentation code makes it look.

Compile the servlet. Make sure that you have all of the necessary classes added to your classpath (we can use j2ee.jar, or WebLogic provides an implementation of the Servlet API in weblogic.jar).

Create a directory named classes within the %WEBLOGIC_HOME%\config\mydomain\applications\DefaultWebApp_myserver\WEB-INF\ directory and place the compiled class into it observing the package structure; remember that the classes directory should contain sub-directories corresponding to the package structure of our servlets.

The web.xml File

In order to deploy the servlet into the server, we first need to create the following web.xml file and place it into the %WEBLOGIC_HOME%\config\mydomain\applications\DefaultWebApp_myserver\WEB-INF\ directory. If a web.xml file already exists, simply add the information between the <web-app> and </web-app> tags to the existing file:

```
<?xml version="1.0" ?>

<!DOCTYPE web-app
    PUBLIC "-//Sun Microsystems, Inc. //DTD Web Application 1.2//EN"
    "http://java.sun.com/dtd/web-app_2_3.dtd">

<web-app>
  <servlet>
   <servlet-name>Login</servlet-name>
   <servlet-class>movie.servlets.LoginServlet</servlet-class>
  </servlet>
  <servlet-mapping>
    <servlet-name>Login</servlet-name>
    <url-pattern>CinemaLogin</url-pattern>
  </servlet-mapping>
</web-app>
```

Start WebLogic and use your browser to go to http://localhost:7001/CinemaLogin.

Let's look at what is happening. Our class LoginServlet extends the HttpServlet class, which provides default implementations of all the methods in the Servlet interface. The only functionality that we wanted to change was for GET requests from a browser, therefore we only provided an implementation for doGet() method – POST requests will not return a valid response.

The doGet() method is straightforward. It retrieves the writer from the Response object and then delivers the HTML to be displayed. This is where the drawback is – the presentation logic is already cluttering up the code and we have not even started to do anything interesting yet.

The page that the servlet presents is devoid of any extra HTML tags to make it more appealing to the user. In addition, the presentation may need to change depending upon the type of client or depending on business rules, thus we would have a servlet full of presentation logic surrounded by conditional flow statements. This would be very ugly indeed.

It would be more manageable if we directed processing to another layer for presentation and simply used the servlet for control. Project needs and teams are never cast from the same mold, therefore the availability of two different facilities for implementing the presentation layer is very helpful in providing the flexibility we need for success.

Typically, a team will have a separation of roles for the presentation layer and for the business layer. In some cases those who are responsible for the presentation will have some basic understanding of Java and servlets. However, they will rarely want to immerse themselves in the Java design and implementation world, therefore it is usually desirable to limit the amount of Java experience necessary to a minimum and to allow them to focus on what they do best – making sure the presentation meets the users' needs. Since most application development teams will have an HTML designer to write presentation code, they're not going to be too happy at having to write it in a servlet!

JavaServer Pages (JSP)

This section will explain the JavaServer Pages 1.2 specification. JavaServer Pages is the second technology contained within the J2EE group referred to as 'web components'. JSP pages attempt to merge the design world with the programming world. In contrast to servlets, which embed presentation information into the Java code, JSP pages allow Java code to be embedded within the presentation logic.

When a client requests a JSP page, the web server executes the JSP code within a web container. The JSP page is then compiled into an implementation of the `javax.servlet.Servlet` interface. Once the JSP page is compiled, the corresponding servlet is used for all subsequent requests, unless the JSP page is changed, in which case it is recompiled.

JSP Lifecycle

The JSP lifecycle is similar to the servlet lifecycle. The primary difference is that if the web container realizes that you have changed the original JSP file, it will force the lifecycle to start at the beginning:

- ❑ **Pre-translation** – this is the actual file that we develop.

- ❑ **Translated** – The JSP container compiles the page down to a servlet. Each time the JSP page changes, it is recompiled resulting in a new servlet.

- ❑ **Initialized** – before it handles a service call, the translated JSP page (now a JSP servlet) must be initialized (which the container does by calling `jspInit()`).

- ❑ **Servicing** – The request is serviced via the `jspService()` method. This method is created during the compilation of the file. This method will be used for all subsequent requests. If the JSP servlet is already instantiated in the JSP container, the `jspInit()` method is not called.

- ❑ **Out of service** – Before destroying the JSP, the JSP container will call the `jspDestroy()` method. This method is not called after each client request; it is left to the container to decide when to call the destroy method.

To get a better understanding of how a JSP works we will create a simple one to start with.

Login.jsp

```
<html>
  <head>
    <title>Login</title>
  </head>
  <body>
```

```
<form method="post" action="CinemaLogin">
<br>Username:   <input type="text" name="username"><br>
<br>Password:   <input type="password" name="password"><br>
<br><br>

<input type="submit" name="Submit" value="Submit">
<input type="reset" value="Reset">
<br>
</form>

</body>
</html>
```

The Login.jsp displays a simple form requesting a username and password. To view Login.jsp, simply copy it into the %WEBLOGIC_HOME%\config\mydomain\applications\DefaultWebApp_myserver\ directory and then use your browser to go to http://localhost:7001/Login.jsp – notice the response time on subsequent requests. The first time you request the file, it should take noticeably longer, since the container has to compile the JSP into a servlet; however subsequent requests will not have this overhead, and the response will be much quicker.

Usually, you do not want to direct a user straight to a JSP; you would first want to perform some sort of business operations to control the flow of events. To do this, we can direct requests to a servlet, where if need be, some processing can be done, and then the request can be redirected to an appropriate JSP.

LoginServlet (with JSP)

The new LoginServlet using JSP (but with control still omitted) would look like:

```
package movie.servlets;

import java.io.*;
import java.util.*;
import javax.servlet.*;
import javax.servlet.http.*;

public class LoginServlet extends HttpServlet {

  public void doGet(HttpServletRequest req, HttpServletResponse res)
            throws IOException, ServletException {

    res.setContentType("text/html");

    RequestDispatcher rd =
                 getServletContext().getRequestDispatcher("/Login.jsp");
    rd.forward(req,res);
  }
}
```

We will need to redeploy the servlet into our server. Now reload the location http://localhost:7001/CinemaLogin in our browser. It doesn't look much different does it? It shouldn't, but it was a lot easier to implement. In addition, instead of having to recompile the servlets to include additional HTML tags, we can now modify the JSP with ease.

At this point you're probably thinking that we could have simply directed the linked to an HTML file, but that would then restrict us in using any of the wonderful features of JSP such as taglibs, and cookies, which we will see a little bit later in the chapter.

Other Parts of the JSP API

The JSP architecture also provides a large number of additional facilities that give it considerable flexibility. Many articles advocate the use of JSP pages as the solution for all problems, and you may be asking why not. Let's look at the JSP API closer and then look at an example that bypasses the servlet tier.

JSP pages also provide a number of mechanisms to provide additional functionality:

- ❑ Directives
- ❑ Actions
- ❑ Scriptlets
- ❑ Implicit objects

Directives

Generally, directives allow the JSP developer to indicate to the container that required classes or information must be obtained from another source. In the last example we used the **page** directive with the attribute **import** to notify the container that the JSP will need the class `java.util.Iterator`.

There are three directives supported with JSP 1.2. We will not get into the different attributes available for each one because it is beyond the scope of this chapter.

Directive Name	Description
Page	This directive allows the author to manipulate the compiled JSP. For example, we can define the package imports, content types, default error pages and more. This is probably the most used directive.
Include	This allows the inclusion of another page directly into this one. The directive indicates that the specified resource should be included at compile time.
Taglib	Used to specify additional tag functionality through the addition of a tag library file.

Actions

Actions are tags that can be embedded within the JSP to allow the author to control its run-time execution. Actions are very powerful, however; they introduce considerable complexity to the JSP defeating the goal of keeping the JSP simple enough for web developers to use.

The JSP API specifies the following predefined actions:

Action Name	Description
`<jsp:useBean>`	The `useBean` tag is used to provide access to a bean instance, by specifying an existing ID and/or class name.
`<jsp:setProperty>`	This is used in conjunction with the `useBean` tag. The `setProperty` tag is used to set an attribute within the bean – this requires that the bean confirms to the JavaBean specification and provides a corresponding setter method.
`<jsp:getProperty>`	This is also used with the `useBean` tag. It requires the bean to have a corresponding get method.
`<jsp:param>`	The `param` tag is used in conjunction with the include, forward, and plugin actions. Usually, those actions invoke a resource, which needs particular parameters to be set. This tag is used to set them. The difference between this and attributes within the action tags, is that the attributes are for the action itself, while `<jsp:param>` is for setting values on the invoked resource.
`<jsp:include>`	The `include` action tag allows for another resource to be included within this JSP. The included resource is evaluated at run-time (in contrast to the `include` directive).
`<jsp:forward>`	Sometimes, during processing it becomes necessary to forward the processing to another JSP. This tag provides the functionality to do this.
`<jsp:plugin>`	The `plugin` tag allows the JSP to use functionality not contained within the JSP specification, such as applets, shockwave files, and other third party plug-ins.

The JSP API also supports additional tag actions via the `taglib` directive.

Scriptlets

Scriptlets are portions of Java code that are embedded within the HTML of a JSP page. When the JSP is compiled for the first time, the scriptlet is encoded into the resulting servlet and is executed for every incoming request. Scriptlets look similar to JavaScript with the primary difference being that the code is executed on the server rather than on the client.

Implicit Objects

The JSP architecture provides nine implicit objects that can be used to access information associated with the run-time environment. Similar to the Servlet API, which wraps requests and response information in `HttpServletRequest` and `HttpServletResponse` objects, also providing implementations for `ServletContext` and session information, the JSP architecture provides the following implicit objects. They are referred to as implicit because the JSP author can use them without specifying where to obtain them from – the JSP container understands the nature of the objects and provides access to the required implementations.

JSPs will generally use implicit objects within scriptlets to provide run-time information.

Object Name	Description
request	This object wraps the `request` information from the client and supplies it to the JSP via the `jspService()` method. Similar to the `HttpServletRequest` object, it provides access to HTTP header information, request parameters, cookies, and so on.
response	This object is an implementation of the `javax.servlet.ServletResponse` interface for servicing the client's request.
pageContext	This provides access to the current instance of the compiled JSP.
session	This object provides the same functionality as the `Session` interface in the Servlet API.
application	Similar to the `ServletContext` object in the Java Servlet API. It allows access to information that can be shared across an entire application.
out	The `out` object is an instance of the `javax.servlet.jsp.JspWriter`, which is an implementation of the `java.io.PrintWriter` class. It provides a buffered output stream to the client.
config	The `config` object is an implementation of the `javax.servlet.ServletConfig` interface. It provides the JSP with access to the configuration information specified during deployment.
page	The `page` object is similar to the `this` reference in a Java class. It provides access to the compiled JSP servlet class.

JSP Database Access Example

Now let's look at accessing a database from within a JSP file. For the following example, we have used the Cloudscape database (you can download an evaluation copy from their web site at http://www.cloudscape.com); however, you can use any other JDBC 2.0-compliant database.

Create the following JSP file with the name `RetrieveMovies.jsp`:

```
<%@ page import=
    "java.util.*,
    javax.naming.*,
    javax.sql.*,
    java.sql.*" %>

<%  // This is a scriptlet

   Connection conn = null;
   ResultSet results = null;
   try {
     Context ctx = new InitialContext();        // Get JNDI context

       // Get DataSource
     DataSource dataSource = (DataSource)ctx.lookup("MoviesPool");

       // Get JDBC connection
     conn = dataSource.getConnection();
```

```
      // Create SQL statement
      Statement stmt = conn.createStatement();
      String select = "SELECT * from Movies";

      results = stmt.executeQuery(select);

   } catch (Exception e) {
      out.println(e);
   }
%>

<html>
   <head><title>Movies</title></head>

   <body>

   <% try {
      while (results.next()) {          // Process results
   %>

   <b><i>Name:</b></i> <%=results.getString("Name")%> <br>
   <b><i>Description:</b></i> <%=results.getString("Description")%> <br><br>

   <%
      }
      conn.close();
   } catch (Exception e) {
      out.println(e);
   }
   %>
   </body>
</html>
```

To start off, we use the page directive with the import attribute for the necessary packages. Next we create a scriptlet, which first obtains a reference to the JNDI context, requests the DataSource for the name MoviesPool and then opens a connection.

Once we have the JDBC connection, we can execute a SQL statement and retrieve a corresponding result set. The remainder of the JSP simply processes the results.

The example assumes that you have populated the database with the valid information from the tables given at the beginning of the chapter. Ensure that the films in the NAME column in the MOVIES table correspond to those in the MOVIENAME column in the CINEMAROOM table.

To ensure that WebLogic will be able to find the database we need to add to the WebLogic startWebLogic.cmd file the following line:

```
-Dcloudscape.system.home=<your database path>
```

So that the section after setting the classpath reads, for example:

```
"%JAVA_HOME%\bin\java" -hotspot -ms64m -mx64m -classpath %CLASSPATH% -
Dweblogic.Domain=mydomain -Dweblogic.Name=myserver "-Dbea.home=C:\BEA " -
```

```
Dcloudscape.system.home=.\samples\eval\cloudscape\data "-
Djava.security.policy==C:\BEA\wlserver6.1_beta/lib/weblogic.policy" -
Dweblogic.management.password=%WLS_PW% weblogic.Server
goto finish
```

Place the JSP file into the same path as the Login.jsp. Start the server and call the JSP,
http://localhost:7001/RetrieveMovies.jsp.

We will get returned to us all of the movies and descriptions contained in the Movies table of the database.

Although JSP pages provide these powerful mechanisms, it is not always appropriate to use them. The
JSP is now cluttered with database access code, control code, and presentation code and we haven't
even done anything difficult yet such as session validation. Depending upon the complexity of the
project, JSP pages are usually not the place for control or model code.

Before continuing with our presentation tier, this would be a good time to create our model tier and
implement our EJBs.

The Movie Object

Although many people might think of the user-interaction part of our application as the obvious place to
start, we're not going to continue doing that. Instead, we're going to create the objects that represent the
actual movies and their descriptions. This will make it easier for us to introduce the remaining
presentation classes, followed by the control tier.

As we've already seen, these are going to be entity EJBs. Although we could just access the database
directly from our servlet objects, in order to make our application scalable we should mediate all
database access through entity beans (that is what they're for).

However, entity beans are not always the most desirable choice. They may provide a very robust solution for
modeling business objects, but they also introduce a considerable amount of complexity in development.

If our sole desire was simply to display the contents of the database and we were not concerned about
how current the data was (additions and changes to the data did not need to be reflected immediately)
then it could be argued that entity beans and perhaps EJBs in general may be overkill. On the other
hand, most financial services require the secure and transactional environment that EJBs provide for
even the most basic applications.

The Movie Bean Home Interface

```
package movie.ejb;

import java.rmi.*;
import java.util.*;
import javax.ejb.*;

public interface MovieHome extends EJBHome {

  public Movie create() throws CreateException, RemoteException;

  public Movie findByPrimaryKey(String pk)
```

```
                        throws FinderException, RemoteException;

    public Collection findAllMovies() throws FinderException, RemoteException;
}
```

As usual, we only need to declare those methods we plan on implementing. For this bean, we're going to implement our own `create()` method, and two finder methods: `findByPrimaryKey()` and `findAllMovies()`. These will be fairly standard finder methods.

The Movie Bean Remote Interface

```
package movie.ejb;

import java.rmi.*;
import javax.ejb.*;

public interface Movie extends EJBObject {

  public String getMovieName() throws RemoteException;

  public String getMovieInfo() throws RemoteException;
}
```

In the remote interface, we have declared two accessor methods, which we will implement to return the name of a movie (`getMovieName()`), and a description of that movie (`getMovieInfo()`).

The Movie Bean Implementation Class

```
package movie.ejb;

import javax.ejb.*;

abstract public class MovieBean implements EntityBean {

  private EntityContext _ctx;

  //contract methods
  public String ejbCreate() throws CreateException {
    throw new CreateException("MovieBean: Create Not Implemented");
  }
```

We are not going to provide the functionality to add movies through our service, thus we will just throw an exception – however, it would be a simple implementation to provide if you wanted to expand the service:

```
  public void ejbPostCreate() {}
  public void ejbActivate() {}
  public void ejbPassivate() {}
  public void ejbRemove() {}
  public void ejbLoad() { /*CMP*/}
  public void ejbStore() { /*CMP*/}
  public void setEntityContext(EntityContext ctx) {
```

```
    _ctx = ctx;
  }
  public void unsetEntityContext() {
    _ctx = null;
  }
```

The rest of the contract methods are simple implementations.

The two finder methods we declared do not need to be implemented here since we are using CMP. Both finder methods will be defined in the deployment descriptor:

```
    abstract public String getMovieName();
    abstract public void setMovieName(String val);
    abstract public String getMovieInfo();
    abstract public void setMovieInfo(String val);
}
```

These are the accessor methods for the member variables that the container will need to handle. The methods will be implemented by the container upon deployment:

ejb-jar.xml

Here we start the deployment descriptor file:

```xml
<?xml version="1.0"?>
<!DOCTYPE ejb-jar
      PUBLIC "-//Sun Microsystems, Inc.//DTD Enterprise JavaBeans 2.0//EN"
      "http://java.sun.com/dtd/ejb-jar_2_0.dtd">

<ejb-jar>

  <enterprise-beans>
    <entity>
      <ejb-name>movie</ejb-name>
      <home>movie.ejb.MovieHome</home>
      <remote>movie.ejb.Movie</remote>
      <ejb-class>movie.ejb.MovieBean</ejb-class>
      <persistence-type>Container</persistence-type>
      <prim-key-class>java.lang.String</prim-key-class>
      <reentrant>False</reentrant>
      <cmp-version>2.x</cmp-version>
      <abstract-schema-name>MovieBean</abstract-schema-name>
      <cmp-field><field-name>movieName</field-name></cmp-field>
      <cmp-field><field-name>movieInfo</field-name></cmp-field>
      <primkey-field>movieName</primkey-field>
      <query>
        <query-method>
          <method-name>findAllMovies</method-name>
          <method-params></method-params>
        </query-method>
        <ejb-ql>
          <![CDATA[WHERE movieName like '%']]>
        </ejb-ql>
      </query>
    </entity>
  </enterprise-beans>
```

and we add the following between the `<assembly-descriptor>` tags

```
<assembly-descriptor>
  <container-transaction>
    <method>
      <ejb-name>movie</ejb-name>
      <method-intf>Remote</method-intf>
      <method-name>*</method-name>
    </method>
    <trans-attribute>Required</trans-attribute>
  </container-transaction>
</assembly-descriptor>

</ejb-jar>
```

The above entry needs to be made into the `ejb-jar.xml` file for the deployment of the `MovieBean`. For each of the beans we will only give the entries for the `ejb-jar.xml`, with the WebLogic-specific deployment descriptors given at the end of the chapter.

Accessing the Movie Entity Bean

The `MovieBean` entity is a fine-grained object, representing a single table within the database. Later in the chapter, we will say how to access it directly from a servlet. We will also show how other beans can use this bean. Later we will show how custom tags can be used to retrieve information from EJBs.

The Customer Object

Our second object is also going to be represented by an entity bean. The `Customer` bean is also a fine-grained object, with each `Customer` bean instance representing one customer of our application.

The Customer Bean Home Interface

```
package movie.ejb;

import javax.ejb.*;
import java.rmi.*;

public interface CustomerHome extends EJBHome {

  public Customer create() throws CreateException, RemoteException;

  public Customer findByPrimaryKey(String pk)
                  throws FinderException, RemoteException;
}
```

The Customer Bean Remote Interface

```
package movie.ejb;

import javax.ejb.*;
import java.rmi.*;

public interface Customer extends EJBObject {
```

```
  public String getUsername() throws RemoteException;

  public String getPassword() throws RemoteException;

  public String getRealname() throws RemoteException;
}
```

In the remote interface for our `Customer` bean we declare three accessor methods, which we will use to get information about the user from the bean. In reality, we would probably want to have other information, such as preferences or contact information.

The Customer Bean Implementation Class

```
package movie.ejb;

import javax.ejb.*;

abstract public class CustomerBean implements EntityBean {

  private EntityContext _ctx;

  //Contract methods
  public String ejbCreate() throws CreateException {
    throw new CreateException("User: Create not implemented in this app");
  }
```

Again, similar to the `MovieBean`, we will throw an exception in the `ejbCreate()` method, because we will not be providing the functionality in our system:

```
  public void ejbPostCreate() {}
  public void ejbActivate() {}
  public void ejbPassivate() {}
  public void ejbRemove() {}
  public void ejbLoad() {}
  public void ejbStore() {}
  public void setEntityContext(EntityContext ctx) {
    _ctx = ctx;
  }
  public void unsetEntityContext() {
    _ctx = null;
  }
```

As with our `MovieBean`, these contract methods are simple implementations since we are using Container-Managed Persistence (CMP).

The `ejbFindByPrimaryKey()` method will be defined in the deployment descriptor:

```
  abstract public String getUsername();
  abstract public void setUsername(String val);
  abstract public String getPassword();
  abstract public void setPassword(String val);
  abstract public String getRealname();
  abstract public void setRealname(String val);
}
```

The accessor methods are used to indicate to the container which member variables need to be handled. Note that although we will not be providing access to all of these methods through the remote interface, they still need to be declared here for the container to implement. This is for the container that may use the methods for internal use.

ejb-jar.xml

Add the code below to our deployment descriptor file:

```
<entity>
  <ejb-name>customer</ejb-name>
  <home>movie.ejb.CustomerHome</home>
  <remote>movie.ejb.Customer</remote>
  <ejb-class>movie.ejb.CustomerBean</ejb-class>
  <persistence-type>Container</persistence-type>
  <prim-key-class>java.lang.String</prim-key-class>
  <reentrant>False</reentrant>
  <cmp-version>2.x</cmp-version>
  <abstract-schema-name>CustomerBean</abstract-schema-name>
  <cmp-field><field-name>username</field-name></cmp-field>
  <cmp-field><field-name>realname</field-name></cmp-field>
  <cmp-field><field-name>password</field-name></cmp-field>
  <primkey-field>username</primkey-field>
</entity>
```

and the following between the `<assembly-descriptor>` tags:

```
<container-transaction>
  <method>
    <ejb-name>customer</ejb-name>
    <method-intf>Remote</method-intf>
    <method-name>*</method-name>
  </method>
  <trans-attribute>Required</trans-attribute>
</container-transaction>
```

CinemaRoom

The `CinemaRoom` object represents an individual room within a cinema. Information such as the available seats, the name of the movie showing, and the number of seats that have been pre-reserved can be accessed from this object.

CinemaRoomHome.java

```
package movie.ejb;

import java.rmi.*;
import java.util.*;
import javax.ejb.*;

public interface CinemaRoomHome extends EJBHome {

  public CinemaRoom create() throws CreateException, RemoteException;
```

```
    public CinemaRoom findByPrimaryKey(String room)
                    throws FinderException, RemoteException;

    public CinemaRoom findByMovieName(String movieName)
                    throws FinderException, RemoteException;
}
```

CinemaRoom.java

```
package movie.ejb;

import java.rmi.*;
import javax.ejb.*;

public interface CinemaRoom extends EJBObject {

  public String getMovieName() throws RemoteException;
  public void setMovieName(String movieName) throws RemoteException;
  public int getRemainingSeats() throws RemoteException;
  public int getTotalSeats() throws RemoteException;
  public int getReservedSeats() throws RemoteException;
  public void setReservedSeats(int quantity) throws RemoteException;
  public void bookSeats(int quantity) throws RemoteException;
  public void unbookSeats(int quantity) throws RemoteException;
}
```

The remote interface of our `CinemaRoom` defines eight methods to access information about the room. As we will see, not all of them map onto accessor methods, but instead use the accessor methods to derive additional information.

CinemaRoomBean.java

```
package movie.ejb;

import java.rmi.*;
import java.util.*;
import javax.ejb.*;
import javax.naming.*;

abstract public class CinemaRoomBean implements EntityBean {

  private EntityContext _ctx;

  public String ejbCreate() throws CreateException {
    throw new CreateException("CinemaRoom: Create not implemented");
  }
```

By now, the exception being thrown in the `ejbCreate()` method should be familiar; our service will not support the creation of new cinema rooms:

```
    public void ejbPostCreate() {}
    public void ejbActivate() {}
    public void ejbLoad() {}
```

```
    public void ejbPassivate() {}
    public void ejbRemove() {}
    public void ejbStore() {}
    public void setEntityContext(EntityContext ctx) {
      _ctx = ctx;
    }
    public void unsetEntityContext() {
      _ctx = null;
    }
```

The contract methods for CMP:

```
    abstract public String getMovieName();
    abstract public void setMovieName(String movieName);
    abstract public int getTotalSeats();
    abstract public void setTotalSeats(int val);
    abstract public int getReservedSeats();
    abstract public void setReservedSeats(int quantity);
    abstract public int getBookedSeats();
    abstract public void setBookedSeats(int quantity);
    abstract public String getRoom();
    abstract public void setRoom(String val);
```

Again, for CMP we only need to specify the accessor methods for the member variables that we want the container to be able to manipulate:

```
    public int getRemainingSeats() {
      return getTotalSeats() - getReservedSeats() - getBookedSeats();
    }

    public void bookSeats(int quantity) throws RemoteException{
      if (getRemainingSeats() > quantity) {
        setBookedSeats(getBookedSeats() + quantity);
      } else {
        throw new RemoteException("Not enough seats remaining");
      }
    }

    public void unbookSeats(int quantity) {
      setBookedSeats(getBookedSeats() - quantity);
    }
  }
```

The methods are the implementations of the other methods that we specified in the remote interface. Although they do not directly map directly onto columns in the database, they do logically fit into the CinemaRoom object.

ejb-jar.xml

Add the code below to our deployment descriptor file:

```
    <entity>
      <ejb-name>cinemaRoom</ejb-name>
      <home>movie.ejb.CinemaRoomHome</home>
      <remote>movie.ejb.CinemaRoom</remote>
```

```
    <ejb-class>movie.ejb.CinemaRoomBean</ejb-class>
    <persistence-type>Container</persistence-type>
    <prim-key-class>java.lang.String</prim-key-class>
    <reentrant>False</reentrant>
    <cmp-version>2.x</cmp-version>
    <abstract-schema-name>CinemaRoomBean</abstract-schema-name>
    <cmp-field><field-name>movieName</field-name></cmp-field>
    <cmp-field><field-name>totalSeats</field-name>cmp-field>
    <cmp-field><field-name>reservedSeats</field-name></cmp-field>
    <cmp-field><field-name>bookedSeats</field-name></cmp-field>
    <cmp-field><field-name>room</field-name></cmp-field>
    <primkey-field>room</primkey-field>
    <query>
      <query-method>
        <method-name>findByMovieName</method-name>
        <method-params>
          <method-param>java.lang.String</method-param>
        </method-params>
      </query-method>
      <ejb-ql>
        <![CDATA[WHERE movieName like ?1]]>
      </ejb-ql>
    </query>
  </entity>
```

and the following between the `<assembly-descriptor>` tags:

```
<container-transaction>
  <method>
    <ejb-name>cinemaRoom</ejb-name>
    <method-intf>Remote</method-intf>
    <method-name>*</method-name>
  </method>
  <trans-attribute>Required</trans-attribute>
</container-transaction>
```

Booking

The final class that we need to implement to round out our model tier is the `Booking` object. The `Booking` object represents a reservation made by a customer for a movie in a particular cinema room. It may seem redundant to maintain references to both the cinema room and the movie name, but in practice it is possible for the same movie to be showing in more than one room, and in the case of conflicts, it would be desirable for the manager to have both pieces of data.

BookingHome.java

```java
package movie.ejb;

import java.rmi.*;
import java.util.*;
import javax.ejb.*;

public interface BookingHome extends EJBHome {

  public Booking create(String movieName, String userName,
```

```
                              int quantity, String cinemaRoom)
                throws CreateException, RemoteException;

   public Booking findByPrimaryKey(String username)
                throws FinderException, RemoteException;
}
```

Booking.java

```
package movie.ejb;

import java.rmi.*;
import javax.ejb.*;

public interface Booking extends EJBObject {

  public String getMovieName() throws RemoteException;

  public String getUsername() throws RemoteException;

  public int getQuantity() throws RemoteException;

  public String getCinemaRoom() throws RemoteException;
}
```

The remote interface is straight forward, providing four methods to retrieve the value of each of the member variables the container will be maintaining.

BookingBean.java

```
package movie.ejb;

import java.util.*;
import javax.ejb.*;

abstract public class BookingBean implements EntityBean {

  private EntityContext _ctx;

  public String ejbCreate(String movieName, String username,
                          int quantity, String cinemaRoom )
                throws CreateException {

    this.setMovieName(movieName);
    this.setUsername(username);
    this.setQuantity(quantity);
    this.setCinemaRoom(cinemaRoom);
    return null;
  }
```

This is the first entity bean for which we will provide the implementation of the ejbCreate() method. We simply use the accessor methods, which we define overleaf, to assign the values of each of the member variables:

```
public void ejbActivate() {}
public void ejbLoad() {}
public void ejbPassivate() {}
public void ejbRemove() {}
public void ejbStore() {}
public void setEntityContext(EntityContext ctx) {
  _ctx = ctx;
}
public void unsetEntityContext() {
  _ctx = null;
}
public void ejbPostCreate(String movieName, String username,
                          int quantity, String cinemaRoom) {}
```

Again, the contract methods are simple because we are using CMP. Note, that the signature of the `ejbPostCreate()` method must correspond to the signature of the `ejbCreate()` method:

```
abstract public String getMovieName();
abstract public void setMovieName(String val);
abstract public String getUsername();
abstract public void setUsername(String val);
abstract public String getCinemaRoom();
abstract public void setCinemaRoom(String val);
abstract public int getQuantity();
abstract public void setQuantity(int val);
}
```

These are the accessor methods to be implemented by the container. In our remote interface we have only exposed the get methods, but if the system wanted to support modifying a booking, the remote interface would need to expose the set methods as well.

ejb-jar.xml

Add the code below to our deployment descriptor file:

```
<entity>
  <ejb-name>booking</ejb-name>
  <home>movie.ejb.BookingHome</home>
  <remote>movie.ejb.Booking</remote>
  <ejb-class>movie.ejb.BookingBean</ejb-class>
  <persistence-type>Container</persistence-type>
  <prim-key-class>java.lang.String</prim-key-class>
  <reentrant>False</reentrant>
  <cmp-version>2.x</cmp-version>
  <abstract-schema-name>BookingBean</abstract-schema-name>
  <cmp-field><field-name>movieName</field-name></cmp-field>
  <cmp-field><field-name>username</field-name></cmp-field>
  <cmp-field><field-name>quantity</field-name></cmp-field>
  <cmp-field><field-name>cinemaRoom</field-name></cmp-field>
  <primkey-field>username</primkey-field>
</entity>
```

and the following between the `<assembly-descriptor>` tags:

```
<container-transaction>
  <method>
    <ejb-name>booking</ejb-name>
    <method-intf>Remote</method-intf>
    <method-name>*</method-name>
  </method>
  <trans-attribute>Required</trans-attribute>
</container-transaction>
```

So, now we have a representation of our objects in the database, what else do we need to do? We need some way for the customer to interact with the application, which brings us back to the to servlets and JSP pages.

LoginServlet doPost()

As we saw in Login.jsp, the form will post to CinemaLogin, resulting in the doPost() method in LoginServlet being called. We will hardcode a username and password for now. On a successful login, the servlet will add an attribute to the session object so that other servlets can verify that the login has been successful.

Our servlets will use doGet() methods to supply the requesting client either just with information, or with a form that posts back to the same servlet. The doPost() will be used to process the form-based requests. Let's now implement the doPost() method for our LoginServlet:

```
public void doPost(HttpServletRequest req, HttpServletResponse res)
          throws IOException, ServletException {
    res.setContentType("text/html");

    try {

      // Extract parameters from req object
      String username = (String)req.getParameter("username");
      String password = (String)req.getParameter("password");

      String goTo="/Error.jsp";

      // Check password
      // if successful go to home page
      // this is TOO much for the servlet.
      if ((username.compareTo("defaultUser")== 0) &&
         (password.compareTo("defaultPW")== 0)) {

        req.getSession().setAttribute("isLoggedIn", "true");

        BasicUserInfo user = new BasicUserInfo("The Default User",
                                               "defaultUser");

        req.getSession().setAttribute("realname",user);

        Cookie chocChip = new Cookie("username", username);
        chocChip.setMaxAge(24*60*60*30);
        res.addCookie(chocChip);
        goTo = "/Home";
      } catch (Exception e) {
        e.printStackTrace();
```

```
            goTo = "/Error.jsp";
        }
        RequestDispatcher rd = getServletContext().getRequestDispatcher(goTo);
        rd.forward(req,res);
    }
}
```

The servlet is straightforward, but it doesn't do anything complex yet, such as retrieve user preferences or other personalization. In addition, for validating the user we may want to send the request elsewhere before returning control to the servlet. The cookie can be used to help identify the user when they first arrive at the site.

HomeServlet

When the user successfully logs in, they are then directed to another servlet, CinemaHome. The HomeServlet uses the attribute in the session object to verify the session state:

```
package movie.servlets;

import java.io.*;
import java.util.*;
import javax.ejb.*;
import javax.naming.*;
import javax.servlet.*;
import javax.servlet.http.*;

import movie.ejb.*;

public class HomeServlet extends HttpServlet {

  private static final String CONTENT_TYPE = "text/html";

  // Process the HTTP Get request
  public void doGet(HttpServletRequest req, HttpServletResponse res)
            throws ServletException, IOException {

    String goTo = "/CinemaHome.jsp";
    String val = (String)req.getSession().getAttribute("isLoggedIn");
    if ((val == null) || (val.compareTo("true") != 0)) {
      goTo = "CinemaLogin";
    } else {
      res.setContentType(CONTENT_TYPE);
      Collection c = getMovies();
      req.setAttribute("movies",c.iterator());
    }
    RequestDispatcher rd = getServletContext().getRequestDispatcher(goTo);
    rd.forward(req,res);
  }

  // Process the HTTP Post request
  public void doPost(HttpServletRequest req, HttpServletResponse res)
            throws ServletException, IOException {

    doGet(req, res);
```

```
    }

    public Collection getMovies() {
      Collection c = null;
      try {
        Context ctx = new InitialContext();
        MovieHome home = (MovieHome)ctx.lookup("MovieHome");
        c = home.findAllMovies();
      } catch (Exception e) {
        e.printStackTrace();                // Better exception handling required
      }
      return c;
    }
  }
```

In order to deploy the servlet, we first need to create the entry in the web.xml file. The file should already exist from our previous example. Add the following between entry between the <web-app> and </web-app> tags:

```
  <servlet>
    <servlet-name>Home</servlet-name>
    <servlet-class>movie.servlets.HomeServlet</servlet-class>
  </servlet>
  <servlet-mapping>
    <servlet-name>Home</servlet-name>
    <url-pattern>Home</url-pattern>
  </servlet-mapping>
```

The servlet directs the user back to CinemaLogin if they have not logged in already – this prevents users from going to pages within the site directly. In practice, the system should use the Java Authentication and Authorization Service (JAAS) for enforcing the security of the system, but we will not go into the details of that API due to its complexity.

If the user has already logged in, the home servlet retrieves a list of movies, stores them in the request object, and then directs the processing to CinemaHome.jsp to handle the presentation:

```
<%@page import = "java.util.Iterator, movie.ejb.*" %>
<%
  Iterator i = (Iterator)request.getAttribute("movies");
%>
<html>
  <head><title>CinemaHome</title></head>
  <body>
  <table>
    <tr>
      <td>Movie name</td>
      <td>Description</td>
    </tr>
    <%
      while (i.hasNext()) {
        try {
          Movie current = (Movie)i.next();
          String name = current.getMovieName();
          String desc = current.getMovieInfo();
```

```
  %>
  <tr>
    <td><%=name%></td>
    <td><%=desc%></td>
    <td><a href="/BookMovie?movieName=<%=name%>">Book Seats</a></td>
  </tr>
  <%
      } catch (Exception ex) {
        ex.printStackTrace();
      }
    }
  %>

  </table>
  </body>
</html>
```

The `CinemaHome.jsp` expects an iterator of `movies` from the `request` object and then lists them in a table. The JSP also presents them with links to book seats for the individual movies.

Can We Improve?

Looking at the implementation above, we can see that the code can get very messy very quickly. The functionality in the above is limited, but as the functionality increases (for example, we may decide to provide a reviews table to store reviews submitted by the user) we will see that the flexibility of this approach is also limited.

Control

At this point, let's look at how we are implementing our control. Servlets are handling both the presentation layer and data access in the EJB entity tier. As the functionality of the system increases, it will become desirable to separate the two different types of control from each other. The request-response structure of servlets makes them ideal to control presentation logic; however, the entity tier access control can be delegated to a session tier.

Helper Bean for the LoginServlet

Let's jump back to our `Login` Servlet. Earlier we only implemented the `doPost()` method by hard-coding the username and password. Realistically, we would like to defer processing to a session tier to control the flow.

First, we need to determine the flow – What happens on a successful login, and what happens on an unsuccessful login? In our case, we will direct the customer to a home page on a successful login, and back to the login page on an unsuccessful login. Usually, we would implement some sort of security such as blocking a user after three failed login attempts, or providing a password request page, and so on. We could implement this in the servlet, but that can become very complicated. This is where using the session bean layer for control is useful. The session bean can authenticate the user as well provide information from the corresponding `Customer` bean for presentation purposes.

The method for validating the user could return a reference to the `Customer` entity bean, but usually we would only want to provide a subset of the customer information. This allows different applications to access different information based upon the level of accessibility granted. Design patterns are discussed in more detail in Chapter 12.

Below is a class we will use to return user information for this application:

```java
package movie.beans;

import java.io.Serializable;

public class BasicUserInfo implements Serializable {

  private String realname;
  private String username;

  public BasicUserInfo(String realname, String username) {

    this.realname = realname;
    this.username = username;
  }

  public String getRealname() {
    return realname;
  }

  public String getUsername() {
    return username;
  }
}
```

We will now implement a session bean to use for user validation. We will start with a straightforward home interface.

UserValidationHome.java

```java
package movie.ejb;

import java.rmi.*;
import java.util.*;
import javax.ejb.*;

public interface UserValidationHome extends EJBHome {

  public UserValidation create() throws CreateException, RemoteException;
}
```

UserValidation.java

```java
package movie.ejb;

import java.rmi.*;
import javax.ejb.*;

import movie.beans.*;

public interface UserValidation extends EJBObject {

  public BasicUserInfo getUser(String username, String password)
                    throws RemoteException;
}
```

The remote interface only provides one method to retrieve the customer's information. Although JAAS could be used to authenticate the customer, it would still need a similar method to access the `Customer` object to retrieve the additional information.

UserValidationBean.java

```
package movie.ejb;

import java.rmi.*;
import javax.ejb.*;
import javax.naming.*;

import movie.beans.*;

public class UserValidationBean implements SessionBean {

  private SessionContext _ctx;

  public void ejbCreate() {}
  public void ejbActivate() {}
  public void ejbPassivate() {}
  public void ejbRemove() {}
  public void setSessionContext(SessionContext ctx) {
    _ctx = ctx;
  }
```

We are not doing anything special in our contract methods and therefore the code is quite straightforward:

```
// Method defined in Remote interface
public BasicUserInfo getUser(String username, String password)
                    throws RemoteException {

  Customer cust = findCustomer(username);

  if ((cust == null) || (password.compareTo(cust.getPassword()) != 0)) {

    throw new RemoteException("Does not exist, or bad PW");
  }
  BasicUserInfo returnInfo =
                new BasicUserInfo(cust.getRealname(),cust.getUsername());
  return returnInfo;
}
```

The method below allows access to the Entity tier:

```
private Customer findCustomer(String username) throws RemoteException {

  InitialContext ctx = null;
  Customer returnCustomer = null;
  try {
    ctx = new InitialContext();
    CustomerHome home = (CustomerHome)ctx.lookup("CustomerHome");
    returnCustomer = home.findByPrimaryKey(username);
  } catch (FinderException fe) {
    fe.printStackTrace();
```

```
            returnCustomer = null;
        } catch (Exception e) {
            throw new RemoteException(e.getMessage());
        }
        return returnCustomer;
    }
}
```

As projects get larger and different applications are permitted to access different parts of the model, bean classes such as the `BasicUserInfo` class provides a way to limit the visibility of sensitive information. Usually on larger projects, the team responsible for the development of the enterprise object model is not the same as the team responsible for the development of the applications, thus it is the responsibility of the model to prevent access when necessary.

ejb-jar.xml

Add the code below to our deployment descriptor file:

```xml
<session>
  <ejb-name>userValidation</ejb-name>
  <home>movie.ejb.UserValidationHome</home>
  <remote>movie.ejb.UserValidation</remote>
  <ejb-class>movie.ejb.UserValidationBean</ejb-class>
  <session-type>Stateless</session-type>
  <transaction-type>Container</transaction-type>
</session>
```

and the following between the `<assembly-descriptor>` tags:

```xml
<container-transaction>
  <method>
    <ejb-name>userValidation</ejb-name>
    <method-intf>Remote</method-intf>
    <method-name>*</method-name>
  </method>
  <trans-attribute>Required</trans-attribute>
</container-transaction>
```

So far we have looked at how JSP and servlets can be used to present screens to the user; however, our servlets have already started to get complex. The servlets are performing control logic already, although they are not too complex yet. Consider the situation where the user was required to submit a credit card number and the system was required to verify that the number was valid. This would require interfacing, not only with the model, but with external services for credit verification and a messaging service to satisfy our earlier request of notifying the manager on seat shortages. This is where session beans are advantageous for implementing control.

Reservation

Now let's focus on the reservation process. From the initial outline of the example, the reservation process creates a booking for a customer, and if the number of remaining seats for a movie reduces to below ten, it should send a message to a manager facility. We will look at the second part later in the chapter, but keep it in mind for our design.

Our home servlet references the `BookSeats` servlet for creating a booking, so we will need to implement a servlet for that. Since we know that the complexity of the process will increase, we will delegate the processing to a session tier when making the booking. Let's create the session bean first.

ReservationHome Interface

```
package movie. ejb;

import java.rmi.*;
import javax.ejb.*;

public interface ReservationHome extends EJBHome {

  public Reservation create() throws CreateException, RemoteException;
}
```

Reservation Remote Interface

```
package movie.ejb;

import java.rmi.*;
import javax.ejb.*;

public interface Reservation extends EJBObject {

  public void bookSeats(String movieName, String userName, int quantity)
          throws RemoteException;
}
```

The remote interface will only provide a single method, which will encapsulate the functionality for making the booking.

ReservationBean Implementation

```
package movie.ejb;

import java.rmi.*;
import javax.ejb.*;
import javax.naming.*;

public class ReservationBean implements SessionBean {

  private SessionContext _ctx;

  public void ejbCreate() {}
  public void ejbActivate() {}
  public void ejbPassivate() {}
  public void ejbRemove() {}
  public void setSessionContext(SessionContext ctx) {
    _ctx = ctx;
  }

  public void bookSeats(String movieName, String userName, int quantity)
          throws RemoteException {

    try {
```

```
        Context ctx = new InitialContext();
        CinemaRoomHome cinemaHome =
                          (CinemaRoomHome)ctx.lookup("CinemaRoomHome");
        CinemaRoom rm = cinemaHome.findByMovieName(movieName);

        int remainingSeats = rm.getRemainingSeats();

        if (remainingSeats > quantity) {
          rm.bookSeats(quantity);
          BookingHome home = (BookingHome)ctx.lookup("BookingHome");
          Booking booking = home.create(movieName, userName,
                                  quantity, (String)rm.getPrimaryKey());

          remainingSeats = remainingSeats - quantity;
        } else {
          throw new RemoteException("There are only " + remainingSeats
                              + "available for " + movieName);
        }
    } catch (Exception e) {
      throw new EJBException(e);           // We should handle errors better
    }
  }
}
```

The implementation of the method provides the functionality for the booking process. It determines the cinema room in which the movie is playing, verifies that that there are enough seats available, and then creates a new booking.

ejb-jar.xml

Add the code below to our deployment descriptor file:

```
<session>
  <ejb-name>reservation</ejb-name>
  <home>movie.ejb.ReservationHome</home>
  <remote>movie.ejb.Reservation</remote>
  <ejb-class>movie.ejb.ReservationBean</ejb-class>
  <session-type>Stateless</session-type>
  <transaction-type>Container</transaction-type>
</session>
```

and the following between the <assembly-descriptor> tags:

```
<container-transaction>
  <method>
  <ejb-name>reservation</ejb-name>
    <method-intf>Remote</method-intf>
    <method-name>*</method-name>
  </method>
  <trans-attribute>Required</trans-attribute>
</container-transaction>
```

Now that we have a session bean implementing the business flow for creating a booking, we can implement the corresponding servlets and JSP pages to provide the presentation view and control.

BookMovie Servlet

```java
package movie.servlets;

import java.io.*;
import java.rmi.*;
import java.util.*;
import javax.ejb.*;
import javax.naming.*;
import javax.servlet.*;
import javax.servlet.http.*;

import movie.beans.*;
import movie.ejb.*;

public class BookMovieServlet extends HttpServlet {

  public void doGet(HttpServletRequest req, HttpServletResponse res)
              throws ServletException, IOException {

    String goTo = "/BookSeats.jsp";

    // Verify user has logged in.
    String val = (String)req.getSession().getAttribute("isLoggedIn");

    if ((val == null) || (val.compareTo("true") != 0)) {
      goTo = "CinemaLogin";
    } else {
      res.setContentType("text/html");
    }
    RequestDispatcher rd = getServletContext().getRequestDispatcher(goTo);
    rd.forward(req,res);
  }

  public void doPost(HttpServletRequest req, HttpServletResponse res)
              throws ServletException, IOException {

    String goTo = "Error.jsp";

    // Verify user has logged in.
    String val = (String)req.getSession().getAttribute("isLoggedIn");

    if ((val == null) || (val.compareTo("true") != 0)) {
      goTo = "CinemaLogin";
    } else {
      res.setContentType("text/html");
      String quantity = (String)req.getParameter("quantity");
      String movieName = (String)req.getParameter("movieName");

      BasicUserInfo user =
                  (BasicUserInfo)req.getSession().getAttribute("realname");

      String username = user.getUsername();

      try {
        bookSeats(movieName, username, quantity);
```

```
            goTo = "/Booked.jsp";
        } catch (CreateException ce) {
            throw new ServletException(ce);
        } catch (NamingException ne){
            throw new ServletException(ne);
        } catch (RemoteException re) {
            throw new ServletException (re);
        }
        RequestDispatcher rd = getServletContext().getRequestDispatcher(goTo);
        rd.forward(req,res);
    }
}

public void bookSeats(String movieName, String username, String quantity)
            throws CreateException, NamingException, RemoteException {

    Context ctx = new InitialContext();
    ReservationHome home = (ReservationHome)ctx.lookup("ReservationHome");
    home.create().bookSeats(movieName,username,Integer.parseInt(quantity));
  }
}
```

Again we have used the doGet() method to send the user to a form requesting additional information and the doPost() to process the form. Our doGet() method sends the user to the BookSeats.jsp, which will ask the user for to verify the movie and specify the number of seats to book.

To deploy the servlet, you will need to add the following entry to the web.xml file:

```
<servlet>
  <servlet-name>BookSeats</servlet-name>
  <servlet-class>movie.servlets.BookMovieServlet</servlet-class>
</servlet>
<servlet-mapping>
  <servlet-name>BookSeats</servlet-name>
  <url-pattern>BookMovie</url-pattern>
</servlet-mapping>
```

BookSeats.jsp

```
<html>
  <head><title>BookSeats</title></head>
  <body>
  <form method="post" action="BookMovie">
  <input type="text" name="movieName">
  <select name="quantity">
  <option>1</option>
  <option>2</option>
  <option>3</option>
  <option>4</option>
  </select>
  <input type="submit" name="Submit" value="Submit">
  <input type="reset" value="Reset">
  </form>
  </body>
</html>
```

Again, this simple JSP submits the criteria via a form. This is by no means comprehensive – in a real-world application, you would want to take some further information to verify the user, such as a credit card number.

The JSP uses a form to post back to `BookSeats`, which is processed by the `doPost()` method of the `BookMovieServlet` that we just saw. The JSP only allows the user to reserve a maximum of four seats, but for testing purposes, you may want to add an option with a higher value. In addition, since we have stored a `BasicUserInfo` object in the session object, additional information about the customer could be displayed.

On completion of the `doPost()` method in the `BookMovieServlet`, the customer is forwarded to the `Booked.jsp`, which is a simple HTML page that displays a confirmation.

Booked.jsp

```
<html>
  <head><title>Booked</title></head>
  <body>
  Your seats have been booked.
  You must bring proof of id and payment on pickup
  </body>
</html>
```

You will also need to provide an implementation of `Error.jsp`, which is used as the default error page to display for all erroneous behavior.

Complex Architectures

In practice, J2EE applications are more complex than what we have provided so far. The session tier provides us with a place to implement further control code. In this section, we will not get into too much detail about design issues since that was covered in an earlier chapter.

Let's look at the scenario where the number of available pre-reserved seats falls to below ten. A message needs to be sent to a manager who can then choose to increase the number of seats – this could be a second application with a common model. However, it would not make sense to implement this as being synchronous. For example, imagine a real theater – the manager is not just waiting around for something to do, therefore a system that required an immediate response would cause problems, because it would prevent the system from servicing other customers.

This is when we can use JMS. The functionality we want is for the system to simply send a message about the low number of seats, then to continue serving more users. JMS provides us with the asynchronous messaging service that we need. Using JMS, we can create a topic for seat shortages. The manager would be listening to that topic and when a shortage of seats message arrived, could react to it. The implementation of the manager does not necessarily have to be human; the manager could be another server, which reacts to asynchronous calls, alternatively, there could be a process that simply displays the message on the manager's private terminal. Let's implement this to illustrate how the JMS can be used. This section is not intended to be a comprehensive look at JMS.

> *For more information on JMS see* Professional Java Server Programming J2EE Edition, *published by Wrox Press, Professional JMS Programming, ISBN 1-861004-65-6.*

First, let's create a session bean, `MessageController`, which has a method to send a message to a Queue that is defined for this service.

MessageControllerHome Interface

```
package movie.ejb;

import java.rmi.*;
import javax.ejb.*;

public interface MessageControllerHome extends EJBHome {

  public MessageController create() throws CreateException, RemoteException;

}
```

MessageController Remote Interface

```
package movie.ejb;

import java.rmi.*;
import javax.ejb.*;

public interface MessageController extends EJBObject {

  public void sendMessage(String msg) throws RemoteException;

}
```

The method in the remote interface only takes one argument, but it could be expanded to take a second argument specifying the queue to which this message should be posted. For simplicity, in our example we will always post to the same queue.

MessageController Implementation

```
package movie.ejb;

import java.rmi.*;
import javax.ejb.*;
import javax.jms.*;
import javax.naming.*;

public class MessageControllerBean implements SessionBean {

  private SessionContext _ctx;
  private QueueSession qsession;
  private QueueSender qsender;
  private Queue queue;

  public void ejbActivate() {}
  public void ejbPassivate() {}
  public void ejbRemove() {}
  public void setSessionContext(SessionContext ctx) {
    _ctx = ctx;
  }

  public void ejbCreate() throws RemoteException {
    try {

      String JMS_FACTORY="wrox.examples.jms.QueueConnectionFactory";
      String QUEUE="wrox.examples.jms.Queue";
```

```
        Context namingCtx = new InitialContext();
        QueueConnectionFactory qconFactory =
                        (QueueConnectionFactory)namingCtx.lookup(JMS_FACTORY);

        QueueConnection qcon = qconFactory.createQueueConnection();
        qsession = qcon.createQueueSession(false, Session.AUTO_ACKNOWLEDGE);
        queue = (Queue) namingCtx.lookup(QUEUE);
    } catch (Exception e) {
        e.printStackTrace();
        throw new RemoteException(e.getMessage());
    }
}
```

The `ejbCreate()` method, looks up the `QueueConnectionFactory`, the `Queue`, and sets up the `QueueSession`. These are needed for all messages, so it makes sense to set them up in the `create()` method and use the remote method only to send the message:

```
    public void sendMessage(String message) throws RemoteException {
        try {
            TextMessage msg = qsession.createTextMessage();
            msg.setText(message);
            qsender = qsession.createSender(queue);
            qsender.send(msg);
        } catch (Exception e) {
            e.printStackTrace();
            throw new RemoteException(e.getMessage());
        }
    }
}
```

This is the implementation of the method defined in the remote interface. It simply creates a `QueueSender` and then sends a message to it.

ejb-jar.xml

Add the code below to our deployment descriptor file:

```
    <session>
        <ejb-name>messageController</ejb-name>
        <home>movie.ejb.MessageControllerHome</home>
        <remote>movie.ejb.MessageController</remote>
        <ejb-class>movie.ejb.MessageControllerBean</ejb-class>
        <session-type>Stateless</session-type>
        <transaction-type>Container</transaction-type>
    </session>
```

and the following between the `<assembly-descriptor>` tags:

```
    <container-transaction>
        <method>
            <ejb-name>messageController</ejb-name>
            <method-intf>Remote</method-intf>
            <method-name>*</method-name>
        </method>
        <trans-attribute>Required</trans-attribute>
    </container-transaction>
```

The `MessageController` assumes that you have set up the appropriate Factory and Destinations in your server. You will need the following values to set it up:

JMS Connection Factory

Name: QConFactory
JNDIName: wrox.examples.jms.QueueConnectionFactory

JMSServer

Name: JMSServer
Target: myserver

Destination

Name: wroxQueue
JNDIName: wrox.examples.jms.Queue

Now let's modify our `Reservation` session bean implementation to use the `MessageController` bean. Add the following code to the end of the `bookSeats` method in the `ReservationBean` right before the `catch` clause:

```
            if (remainingSeats < 10) {
                MessageControllerHome mgHome = (MessageControllerHome)
                                        ctx.lookup("MessageControllerHome");

                mgHome.create().sendMessage("The number of seats available for "
                                + "cinemaRoom " + (String)rm.getPrimaryKey()
                                + " has reached "
                                + remainingSeats);

            }
```

This simply tells the `MessageController` to send a message that the number of seats left available for a particular cinema room has dropped to below ten. For testing purposes, you might want to increase the threshold level to send a message even when it reduces to below eighty.

Finally, we will need a class that will receive messages from the Queue and display them on a terminal.

Receiver class

```
package movie;

import java.io.*;
import java.util.*;
import javax.jms.*;
import javax.naming.*;

public class Receiver implements MessageListener {

  public void onMessage(Message message) {
    try {
      String messageString;
      if (message instanceof TextMessage) {
        messageString = ((TextMessage)message).getText();
      } else {
```

```
            messageString = message.toString();
        }

        System.out.println("Message Received: "+ messageString );
    } catch (JMSException e) {
        e.printStackTrace();
    }
}

public static void main(String[] args) throws Exception {

    String QUEUE ="wrox.examples.jms.Queue";

    Hashtable env = new Hashtable();
    env.put(Context.PROVIDER_URL, "t3://localhost:7001");
    env.put(Context.INITIAL_CONTEXT_FACTORY,
            "weblogic.jndi.WLInitialContextFactory");

    InitialContext ctx = new InitialContext(env);

    Receiver receiver = new Receiver();
    QueueConnectionFactory qconFactory = (QueueConnectionFactory)
                    ctx.lookup("wrox.examples.jms.QueueConnectionFactory");

    QueueConnection qcon = qconFactory.createQueueConnection();
    QueueSession qsession =
                    qcon.createQueueSession(false, Session.AUTO_ACKNOWLEDGE);

    Queue queue = (Queue)ctx.lookup(QUEUE);
    QueueReceiver qreceiver = qsession.createReceiver(queue);

    qreceiver.setMessageListener(receiver);
    qcon.start();

    System.out.println("Ready To Receive Messages (To quit, press CTRL-C)");

    // Loop until a CTRL-C is pressed
    synchronized(receiver) {
      while (true) {
        try {
          receiver.wait();
        } catch (Exception e) {}
      }
    }
  }
}
```

The Receiver class simply sets up a QueueReceiver on the appropriate queue and has it waiting in a loop. When it receives a message it writes it to the screen.

To start the class, the server will need to be running, and then you should type the following command from your application directory:

```
java movie.Receiver
```

Let's look at this a little bit more. Implementing the service this way decouples the system, allowing it to expand more easily. For example, let's say that a year from the date of the original service, the owners decide that they want to implement a feature that lists the movies with limited seating on a digital billboard. Using the JMS, we would simply have to develop the piece to allow the software controlling the digital billboard to receive messages from the queue already established in the JMS. A service such as this could be implemented using a message-driven bean, which can accept messages and perform some sort of processing based on them.

Advanced JSP Pages

Although the JSP architecture provides a very comprehensive API to develop web front ends, the pages can become very messy when trying to perform more complex operations. It is very easy for the pages to become cluttered with scriptlets trying to handle different scenarios. JSP 1.1 added a very powerful feature to the API – the `taglib` directive.

Taglibs

The `taglib` (tag libraries, also known as custom tags) allows a developer to specify new tags to be used within the JSP pages. The tags can be used in a number of ways; however, the most common and practical are:

❑   To perform repetitive logic

❑   For presentation purposes such as internationalization or formatting

❑   To encapsulate complex operations, such as data access

Taglibs are a very powerful addition to the JSP API. However, JSP pages can become extremely complex; the size of scriptlets can sometimes get overwhelming. Along with the lack of tools even an advanced developer will find them difficult to program. In this section we will create our own tag library, allowing us to use the movies iterator in our `CinemaHome.jsp`, and helping us to understand how a tag works. There are a large number of pre-written taglibs available on the market and we recommend that you become familiar with them. Quite often you will find that someone else has already created a tag with the functionality that you need and has released it for public use. Sun will be releasing a Standard Tag Library late in 2001; currently it is in review in the Java Community Process.

Other sources for libraries can be found at http://www.jsptags.com.

Taglibs are useful for processing repetitive information, and to dynamically modify the presentation of information based upon different client types, although they have a number of other uses. Consider the HTML tag pair <b></b>. This tag pair has been defined by the W3C to display enclosed text as bold. When the browser encounters the start tag <b>, it calls some implementation-specific code to determine what to do, and when it encounters the end tag </b> it knows that it should conclude that specific activity. Taglibs work in pretty much the same way – when the JSP container encounters a start tag, it delegates to a **tag handler** to determine what to do until it reaches the corresponding end tag.

As with the other HTML tags that we are familiar with, such as <img>, we can specify that our custom tags use attributes as well, such as the `align` attribute for the <img> tag.

The `taglib` package is specified by `javax.servlet.jsp.tagext`. Within this package, there are two primary interfaces: the `Tag` interface and the `BodyTag` interface.

The `Tag` interface defines the methods that must be implemented so that the container knows what to do when it encounters the start tag and end tag (it also defines other methods, but we will not go into them here).

The `BodyTag` interface is actually an extension of the `Tag` interface. It defines additional methods for handling the content supplied between the start tag and end tag. Typically, we will not implement these interfaces directly; the package also supplies shell implementations of the `Tag` and `BodyTag` interfaces named `TagSupport` and `BodyTagSupport`, respectively. When developing a new tag we generally subclass these, and override the necessary methods.

Consider our `CinemaHome.jsp` for retrieving the movies from the database and then displaying them within the browser. The portion of the JSP page that dealt with the result set was very messy. Ideally, what we would want to do is simply provide the iteration of movies to a tag, which will know how to display them.

To start we will need to define the tag. What we want for our example is a tag to which we can pass an `Iterator` containing the movies. Lets look at what the JSP would look like:

```jsp
<%@ page import = "java.util.Iterator, movie.ejb.*" %>

<%@ taglib uri="/Movies" prefix="movieTags" %>

<%
  Iterator i = (Iterator)request.getAttribute("movies");
%>
<html>
  <head><title>CinemaHome</title></head>
  <body>
  <table>
    <tr>
      <td><b>Movie name</b></td>
      <td><b>Dexcription</b></td>
    </tr>
  <movieTags:forEach movieIterator="<%=i%>">
    <tr>
      <td><%=currentMovieName%></td>
      <td><%=currentDescription%></td>
      <td><a href="BookMovie?movieName=<%=currentMovieName%>">
                                        Book Seats</a>
      </td>
    </tr>
  </movieTags:forEach>

  </table>
  </body>
</html>
```

This JSP is similar to our previous `CinemaHome.jsp` but we have replaced the `while` loop.

The second line of the JSP also is new. The structure is that of a directive (starts with `<%@`), the type is `taglib`, and the two attributes are `uri` and `prefix`. The `uri` identifies to the JSP the Uniform Resource Identifier (URI) location of a `taglib` definition – as we go through this section we will reveal the process by which this is determined. The `prefix` attribute specifies that for any tag beginning with this prefix, we should use the aforementioned `taglib` definition – this is useful when using multiple tag libraries.

The lines replacing the `while` loop are unfamiliar:

```
<movieTags:forEach movieIterator="<%=i%>">
  <tr>
    <td><%=currentMovieName%></td>
    <td><%=currentDescription%></td>
    <td><a href="BookMovie?movieName=<%=currentMovieName%>">Book Seats</a>
    </td>
  </tr>
</movieTags:forEach>
```

Normally, to the JSP, these would be unknown tags, and would be ignored. However, in our case the container will search through the known tag libraries to determine what to do. If the tag definition is still not found, then it will be ignored.

The start tag:

```
<movieTags:forEach movieIterator="<%=i%>">
```

uses the prefix `movie`, therefore from the `taglib` directive at the start, it will search for the tag's definition within the `uri` `/Movies`. In addition, the start tag specifies an attribute:

```
movieIterator="<%=i%>"
```

When an attribute is specified, it requires that the `taglib` definition specifies that the attribute is allowed for the tag, and the tag implementation must provide get and set methods for the attribute conforming to the JavaBean specification.

Let's now look at the **tag library definition (TLD)**. The tag library definition is an XML file that we will name `Movies.tld` that describes the class that implements the functionality for a custom tag. It also specifies the attributes that are valid for the class.

The following is the tag library definition, (`Movies.tld`), for the tag that we used in our JSP file:

```
<?xml version="1.0" encoding="ISO-8859-1"?>

<!DOCTYPE taglib
        PUBLIC "-//Sun Microsystems, Inc.//DTD JSP Tag Library 1.1//EN"
        "http://java.sun.com/j2ee/dtds/web-jsptaglibrary_1_1.dtd">

<taglib>
  <tlibversion>1.0</tlibversion>
  <jspversion>1.1</jspversion>
  <shortname>movies</shortname>

  <info>Simple example library</info>

  <tag>
    <name>forEach</name>
    <tagclass>movie.customTags.ForEachTag</tagclass>
    <teiclass>movie.customTags.ForEachTagExtraInfo</teiclass>
    <bodycontent>JSP</bodycontent>
    <info>Simple example</info>
```

```
      <attribute>
        <name>movieIterator</name>
        <required>true</required>
        <rtexprvalue>true</rtexprvalue>
      </attribute>
    </tag>
  </taglib>
```

The first two lines define the XML and DTD versions that are to be used.

Following is the `<taglib>` tag. A tag library can contain a version for itself, a version for the JSP specifications that it supports, a name by which it can be referred to (similar to an alias), and some additional information. In addition, the `<taglib>` tag can contain one or more `<tag>` tags. It is in this tag that we specify names of new custom tags, the classes that implement them, the allowed attributes, and the type of content that can be between the start and end tags.

Our `taglib` defines a tag named `forEach` and its implementing class as `movie. customTags.ForEachTag`. Associated with the tag is another class `movie. customTags.ForEachTagExtraInfo` that will supply the JSP with the attributes that it can access in a similar fashion to other declared variables. We define the `bodycontent` (the content between the start and end tags) to be JSP. This means that the container should process the content. The value could also be `none`, meaning that no content is allowed, or `tagdependant` where the content is passed straight to the tag for processing. The default value is JSP.

Within our tag we also defined an attribute. The attribute has a name `movieIterator`, and `true` as the value for the `<required>` and `<rtexprvalue>` tags. The `<required>` tag indicates whether the custom tag must provide this attribute or not. The `<rtexprvalue>` tag indicates whether the value of this attribute can be the result of a JSP expression or not.

Tag library definition files should be placed in a `tld` sub-directory of the `WEB-INF` directory for the corresponding application. If there is no directory named `tld` within the `WEB-INF` directory, create one, and place the `Movies.tld` file in it.

We must also specify the URI location of the `taglib` within the `web.xml` file. The specification is placed between the `<web-app>` tags and looks like the following.

```
    <taglib>
      <taglib-uri>
        /Movies
      </taglib-uri>
      <taglib-location>
        /WEB-INF/tld/Movies.tld
      </taglib-location>
    </taglib>
```

This simply states the URI for the tag library and the `tld` location. This is the same URI that is referenced in the JSP directive at the top of the `CinemaHome.jsp` above.

Finally, we must provide the actual implementation of the tag, also known as the tag handler.

The two methods that the `Tag` interface defines which we must implement are the `doStartTag()` and `doEndTag()` methods. These methods are called when the start and end tags are encountered respectively. The `BodyTag` interface has the `doBodyContent()` method, which we must also implement.

When the start tag is encountered, the container first examines the attributes. For each of the attributes, the container calls the corresponding set method on the tag handler (only if the attribute is specified in the TLD). If the attribute is specified in the TLD, but the tag handler does not implement the corresponding set method, an exception will be thrown. After setting the attributes, the container then calls the doStartTag() method.

Let's look at our implementation. As we said earlier, usually we would extend the BodyTagSupport class since it provides default implementations for all the methods, some of which we are not interested in here. Name the file ForEachTag.java:

ForEachTag

```java
package movie.customTags;

import java.io.*;
import java.util.*;
import javax.servlet.jsp.*;
import javax.servlet.jsp.tagext.*;

import movie.ejb.*;

public class ForEachTag extends BodyTagSupport {

  private Iterator movieIterator;
  private StringBuffer output = new StringBuffer();

  public int doStartTag() throws JspTagException {
    try {
        Movie currentMovieObj = (Movie)movieIterator.next();
        String currentMovieName = currentMovieObj.getMovieName();
        String currentDescription = currentMovieObj.getMovieInfo();
        pageContext.setAttribute("currentMovieName",currentMovieName);
        pageContext.setAttribute("currentDescription",currentDescription);
        currentMovieObj = null;
    } catch (Exception e) {
      throw new JspTagException(e.getMessage());
    }
    return EVAL_BODY_BUFFERED;
  }

  public Iterator getMovieIterator() {
    return movieIterator;
  }

  public void setMovieIterator(Iterator i) {
    movieIterator = i;
  }

  public int doAfterBody() throws JspTagException {
    BodyContent bodyContent = getBodyContent();
    try {
      if (bodyContent != null) {
        output.append(bodyContent.getString());
        bodyContent.clear();
```

```
        }

      if (movieIterator.hasNext()) {
        Movie currentMovieObj = (Movie)movieIterator.next();

        String currentMovieName = currentMovieObj.getMovieName();
        String currentDescription = currentMovieObj.getMovieInfo();
        pageContext.setAttribute("currentMovieName",currentMovieName);
        pageContext.setAttribute("currentDescription",currentDescription);
        currentMovieObj = null;
        return EVAL_BODY_AGAIN;
      }
    } catch (Exception e) {
      throw new JspTagException(e.getMessage());
    }
    return SKIP_BODY;
  }

  public int doEndTag() throws JspTagException {
    try {
      bodyContent.getEnclosingWriter().write(output.toString());
    } catch (Exception e) {
      throw new JspTagException(e.getMessage());
    }
    return EVAL_PAGE;
  }
}
```

When our JSP page, using the custom tags, is compiled, the JSP container will recognize from the taglib directive that custom tags are being used. When the start tag <movies:forEach movieIterator="<%=i%>"> is encountered, the container realizes from the prefix movies that it should look in the /Movies URI location for the definition of the forEach tag.

On startup, the server would read the web.xml file that is in the WEB-INF directory, and register that the taglib for the URI /Movies is tld/Movies.tld. The TLD file indicates that the class movie.customTag.ForEachTag is to be instantiated. The servlet then calls the setMovieIterator() method corresponding to the movieIterator attribute and then calls the doStartTag() method.

The doStartTag() method extracts the first Movie object from the iterator and stores it as an attribute in the pageContext object. The doStartTag() method returns EVAL_BODY_BUFFERED which indicates to the container that it should process the contents between the start and end tag. If you did not want to process the body content, you could return SKIP_BODY.

Our TLD indicates that the body should be evaluated; therefore the JSP container will evaluate the body, insert it into a BodyContent object, and proceed to call the BodyTag methods. The BodyTagSupport class provides default implementations for three methods – setBodyContent(), doInitBody(), and doAfterBody() – that we override to provide the desired implementation.

Usually, we will only need to implement the doAfterBody() method. The method will be continually called as long as it returns EVAL_BODY_AGAIN. Prior to calling this method, the container processes the contents between start and end tags. It will stop when the return value is SKIP_BODY. In our example, we use this method to get the next item from the iterator and update the attributes in the pageContext. Note that before each iteration, the bodycontent is placed in a StringBuffer. To do this we had to explicitly convert the bodyContent variable to a String and place it in the buffer.

Our body content contains references to variables that we do not appear to have defined anywhere in our JSP. The variables, currentMovieName and currentDescription are defined in the ForEachTagExtraInfo class.

ForEachTagExtraInfo

```
package movie.customTags;

import javax.servlet.jsp.tagext.*;

public class ForEachTagExtraInfo extends TagExtraInfo {

  public VariableInfo[] getVariableInfo(TagData data) {

    return new VariableInfo[] {

      new VariableInfo("currentMovieName","java.lang.String",true,
                       VariableInfo.NESTED),
      new VariableInfo("currentDescription","java.lang.String",true,
                       VariableInfo.NESTED)
    };
  }
}
```

The class defines two variables that can be used by the JSP container and they are given scope of NESTED meaning that they will only be valid within the specified tag.

The container then encounters the end tag </movies:forEach>, which indicates that it should call doEndTag() on the ForEachTag tag handler. In our example we use this method simply to print the contents of the StringBuffer.

Packaging

The J2EE architecture specifies several layers for packaging and deploying individual components as well as an entire application.

WebLogic Deployment

We will need the two following additional files for deploying in WebLogic. If you use a different server, you will need to ensure that you include all of the necessary files.

weblogic-ejb-jar.xml

```
<?xml version="1.0"?>

<!DOCTYPE weblogic-ejb-jar PUBLIC
     "-//BEA Systems, Inc.//DTD WebLogic 6.0.0 EJB//EN"
     "http://www.bea.com/servers/wls600/dtd/weblogic-ejb-jar.dtd" >

<weblogic-ejb-jar>
  <weblogic-enterprise-bean>
    <ejb-name>userValidation</ejb-name>
    <stateless-session-descriptor>
      <pool>
```

```
        <max-beans-in-free-pool>100</max-beans-in-free-pool>
      </pool>
    </stateless-session-descriptor>
    <jndi-name>UserValidationHome</jndi-name>
  </weblogic-enterprise-bean>

  <weblogic-enterprise-bean>
    <ejb-name>reservation</ejb-name>
    <stateless-session-descriptor>
      <pool>
        <max-beans-in-free-pool>100</max-beans-in-free-pool>
      </pool>
    </stateless-session-descriptor>
    <jndi-name>ReservationHome</jndi-name>
  </weblogic-enterprise-bean>

  <weblogic-enterprise-bean>
    <ejb-name>messageController</ejb-name>
    <stateless-session-descriptor>
      <pool>
        <max-beans-in-free-pool>100</max-beans-in-free-pool>
      </pool>
    </stateless-session-descriptor>
    <jndi-name>MessageControllerHome</jndi-name>
  </weblogic-enterprise-bean>

  <weblogic-enterprise-bean>
    <ejb-name>customer</ejb-name>
    <entity-descriptor>
      <entity-cache>
        <max-beans-in-cache>1000</max-beans-in-cache>
      </entity-cache>
      <persistence>
        <persistence-type>
          <type-identifier>WebLogic_CMP_RDBMS</type-identifier>
          <type-version>6.0</type-version>
          <type-storage>META-INF/weblogic-cmp-rdbms-jar.xml</type-storage>
        </persistence-type>
        <persistence-use>
          <type-identifier>WebLogic_CMP_RDBMS</type-identifier>
          <type-version>6.0</type-version>
        </persistence-use>
      </persistence>
    </entity-descriptor>
    <jndi-name>CustomerHome</jndi-name>
  </weblogic-enterprise-bean>

  <weblogic-enterprise-bean>
    <ejb-name>movie</ejb-name>
    <entity-descriptor>
      <entity-cache>
        <max-beans-in-cache>1000</max-beans-in-cache>
      </entity-cache>
      <persistence>
        <persistence-type>
          <type-identifier>WebLogic_CMP_RDBMS</type-identifier>
```

```
      <type-version>6.0</type-version>
      <type-storage>META-INF/weblogic-cmp-rdbms-jar.xml</type-storage>
    </persistence-type>
    <persistence-use>
      <type-identifier>WebLogic_CMP_RDBMS</type-identifier>
      <type-version>6.0</type-version>
    </persistence-use>
  </persistence>
</entity-descriptor>
<jndi-name>MovieHome</jndi-name>
</weblogic-enterprise-bean>

<weblogic-enterprise-bean>
  <ejb-name>cinemaRoom</ejb-name>
  <entity-descriptor>
    <entity-cache>
      <max-beans-in-cache>1000</max-beans-in-cache>
    </entity-cache>
    <persistence>
      <persistence-type>
        <type-identifier>WebLogic_CMP_RDBMS</type-identifier>
        <type-version>6.0</type-version>
        <type-storage>META-INF/weblogic-cmp-rdbms-jar.xml</type-storage>
      </persistence-type>
      <persistence-use>
        <type-identifier>WebLogic_CMP_RDBMS</type-identifier>
        <type-version>6.0</type-version>
      </persistence-use>
    </persistence>
  </entity-descriptor>
  <jndi-name>CinemaRoomHome</jndi-name>
</weblogic-enterprise-bean>

<weblogic-enterprise-bean>
  <ejb-name>booking</ejb-name>
  <entity-descriptor>
    <entity-cache>
      <max-beans-in-cache>1000</max-beans-in-cache>
    </entity-cache>
    <persistence>
      <persistence-type>
        <type-identifier>WebLogic_CMP_RDBMS</type-identifier>
        <type-version>6.0</type-version>
        <type-storage>META-INF/weblogic-cmp-rdbms-jar.xml</type-storage>
      </persistence-type>
      <persistence-use>
        <type-identifier>WebLogic_CMP_RDBMS</type-identifier>
        <type-version>6.0</type-version>
      </persistence-use>
    </persistence>
  </entity-descriptor>
  <jndi-name>BookingHome</jndi-name>
</weblogic-enterprise-bean>

</weblogic-ejb-jar>
```

weblogic-cmp-rdbms-jar.xml

```xml
<!DOCTYPE weblogic-rdbms-jar PUBLIC
    '-//BEA Systems, Inc.//DTD WebLogic 6.0.0 EJB RDBMS Persistence//EN'
    'http://www.bea.com/servers/wls600/dtd/weblogic-rdbms20-persistence-600.dtd'>

<weblogic-rdbms-jar>

  <weblogic-rdbms-bean>
    <ejb-name>movie</ejb-name>
    <data-source-name>MoviesPool</data-source-name>
    <table-name>Movies</table-name>
    <field-map>
      <cmp-field>movieName</cmp-field>
      <dbms-column>Name</dbms-column>
    </field-map>
    <field-map>
      <cmp-field>movieInfo</cmp-field>
      <dbms-column>Description</dbms-column>
    </field-map>
  </weblogic-rdbms-bean>

  <weblogic-rdbms-bean>
    <ejb-name>customer</ejb-name>
    <data-source-name>MoviesPool</data-source-name>
    <table-name>Customer</table-name>
    <field-map>
      <cmp-field>username</cmp-field>
      <dbms-column>Username</dbms-column>
    </field-map>
    <field-map>
      <cmp-field>realname</cmp-field>
      <dbms-column>Realname</dbms-column>
    </field-map>
    <field-map>
      <cmp-field>password</cmp-field>
      <dbms-column>password</dbms-column>
    </field-map>
  </weblogic-rdbms-bean>

  <weblogic-rdbms-bean>
    <ejb-name>cinemaRoom</ejb-name>
    <data-source-name>MoviesPool</data-source-name>
    <table-name>CinemaRoom</table-name>
    <field-map>
      <cmp-field>movieName</cmp-field>
      <dbms-column>MovieName</dbms-column>
    </field-map>
    <field-map>
      <cmp-field>totalSeats</cmp-field>
      <dbms-column>TotalSeats</dbms-column>
    </field-map>
    <field-map>
      <cmp-field>reservedSeats</cmp-field>
      <dbms-column>ReservedSeats</dbms-column>
    </field-map>
    <field-map>
```

```
            <cmp-field>bookedSeats</cmp-field>
            <dbms-column>bookedSeats</dbms-column>
        </field-map>
        <field-map>
            <cmp-field>room</cmp-field>
            <dbms-column>room</dbms-column>
        </field-map>
    </weblogic-rdbms-bean>

    <weblogic-rdbms-bean>
        <ejb-name>booking</ejb-name>
        <data-source-name>MoviesPool</data-source-name>
        <table-name>Booking</table-name>
        <field-map>
            <cmp-field>movieName</cmp-field>
            <dbms-column>moviename</dbms-column>
        </field-map>
        <field-map>
            <cmp-field>username</cmp-field>
            <dbms-column>Username</dbms-column>
        </field-map>
        <field-map>
            <cmp-field>quantity</cmp-field>
            <dbms-column>quantity</dbms-column>
        </field-map>
        <field-map>
            <cmp-field>cinemaRoom</cmp-field>
            <dbms-column>cinemaRoom</dbms-column>
        </field-map>
    </weblogic-rdbms-bean>

</weblogic-rdbms-jar>
```

The two files need to be placed into the META-INF directory associated with the EJBs and other classes.

The deployment descriptors assume that you have set up a Connection Pool and Data Source using the following values:

JDBC Connection Pool

Name : MoviesPool
URL : jdbc:cloudscape:MoviesDB
Driver Classname: COM.cloudscape.core.JDBCDriver
Properties: user=none
        password=none
        server=none

JDBC Datasource

Name : MoviesPool
JNDI Name: MoviesPool
Pool Name : MoviesPool

Java Archive Files (JARs)

JAR files are used to quick-deploy EJBs. To repeat, we package all of the required classes, the ejb-jar.xml, weblogic-ejb-jar.xml, and weblogic-cmp-rdbms-jar.xml files (the last two are specific to WebLogic) into a single archive using the Java jar tool.

The structure below shows the file placement for the JAR:

```
movie\
        Receiver.class
        beans\
                BasicUserInfo.class
        ejb\
            Booking.class
            BookingBean.class
            BookingHome.class
            Cinema.class
            CinemaBean.class
            CinemaHome.class
            Customer.class
            CustomerBean.class
            CustomerHome.class
            MessageController.class
            MessageControllerBean.class
            MessageControllerHome.class
            Movie.class
            MovieBean.class
            MovieHome.class
            Reservation.class
            ReservationBean.class
            ReservationHome.class
            UserValidation.class
            UserValidationBean.class
            UserValidationHome.class
    META-INF\
            ejb-jar.xml
            weblogiv-ejb-jar.xml
            weblogic-cmp-rdbms-jar.xml
```

To create the unDeployedBeans.jar file we use the command:

```
jar -cvf unDeployedBeans.jar movie META-INF
```

In WebLogic we can use the following command to create the Movie.jar for deployment into the server:

```
// For this line ensure that the . is removed from the classpath
java weblogic.ejbc unDeployedBeans.jar Movie.jar
```

Web Archive Files (WARs)

In order to deploy web components (servlets or JSP pages) we need to package them into WAR files. WAR files are basically just JAR files with a different extension and a specific internal structure. Let's take our example. To deploy the web components as a WAR file, we need to create the WAR with the directory structure as given opposite:

```
\
Booked.jsp
BookSeats.jsp
CinemaHome.jsp
Error.jsp
Login.jsp
WEB-INF\
        web.xml
        classes\movie\
                        beans\
                                BasicUserInfo.class
                        customTags\
                                ForEachTag.class
                                ForEachTagExtraInfo.class
                        ejb\
                            Booking.class
                            BookingHome.class
                            CinemaRoom.class
                            CinemaRoomHome.class
                            Customer.class
                            CustomerHome.class
                            MessageController.class
                            MessageControllerHome.class
                            Movie.class
                            MovieHome.class
                            Reservation.class
                            ReservationHome.class
                            UserValidation.class
                            UserValidationHome.class
                        servlets\
                                BookMovieServlet.class
                                HomeServlet.class
                                LoginServlet.class
        tld\
                Movies.tld
```

We can then create the WAR by executing the following call:

```
jar -cf webFiles.war WEB-INF *.jsp
```

In this case, `webFiles.war` will be the name of the new package, with the contents of the `WEB-INF` directory. We can place the WAR file in the `application` directory and the server will automatically detect and deploy the servlet.

To call the servlet enter http://localhost:7001/*<war file name>*/*<servlet uri-mapping name>*.

In this case, *<war file name>* is the name of the WAR file without the extension and *<servlet uri-mapping name>* is the name that we specified in the `<servlet-mapping>` tag in the `web.xml` file.

So for our example we would type http://localhost:7001/webFiles/CinemaLogin in the browser.

Enterprise Archive Files (EARs)

The highest level of deployment in the J2EE architecture is the EAR file. The EAR file packages all of the JAR and WAR files, and along with a directory containing an `application.xml` file describing the contents, providing a mechanism to deliver an self-contained application.

Let's create an EAR file for our entire chapter. Create the following directory structure:

```
\
Movie.jar
webFiles.war
META-INF\
        application.xml
```

Where the `application.xml` file is as follows:

```xml
<?xml version="1.0"?>
<!DOCTYPE application
        PUBLIC "-//Sun Microsystems, Inc.//DTD J2EE Application 1.2//EN"
        "http://java.sun.com/j2ee/dtds/application_1_2.dtd">

<application>
  <display-name>Movie App</display-name>

  <module>
    <ejb>Movie.jar</ejb>
  </module>

  <module>
    <web>
      <web-uri>webFiles.war</web-uri>
      <context-root>movie</context-root>
    </web>
  </module>

</application>
```

We can use the following command to create the archive:

```
jar -cf movieApp.ear webFiles.war Movie.jar META-INF
```

We can then deploy the `movieApp.ear` file into the `applications` directory of our server.

The above `application.xml` file is very simple. The first two lines are the XML and DTD versions for the document, which are specified in the J2EE architecture.

The next tag, `<application>`, is the root tag for the document, which contains an optional `<display-name>` tag, and one or more `<module>` tags.

The `<module>` tags identify the JAR and WAR files that are used. The WAR files are described within a `<web>` tag, which identifies the location of the WAR, and assigns a context for the file. Thus, after packaging our chapter and deploying the EAR into the server, we could access our `CinemaLoginServlet` class by typing http://localhost:7001/movie/CinemaLogin into the location path of the browser. Note that when deploying the WAR file by itself, the context is automatically the same as the WAR file name, but when using an EAR, we can assign our own.

Summary

This chapter has provided us with an introduction to the J2EE architecture. It was meant to give us a basic understanding of the different technologies and how they integrate together using the MVC architecture. The J2EE architecture attempts to address the entire application development cycle by defining the environment, the structure, and the components required.

Among the primary topics that we covered were:

❑   Java servlet architecture

❑   JavaServer Pages

❑   J2EE API access

❑   EJB integration with JSP and servlets

In addition to the above, we briefly touched on some more advanced subjects, such as:

❑   Session tracking

❑   Tag libraries and extensions

❑   JMS messaging

Many things can be done using all the different technologies of the J2EE architecture; we have only given a small example of the power of the platform.

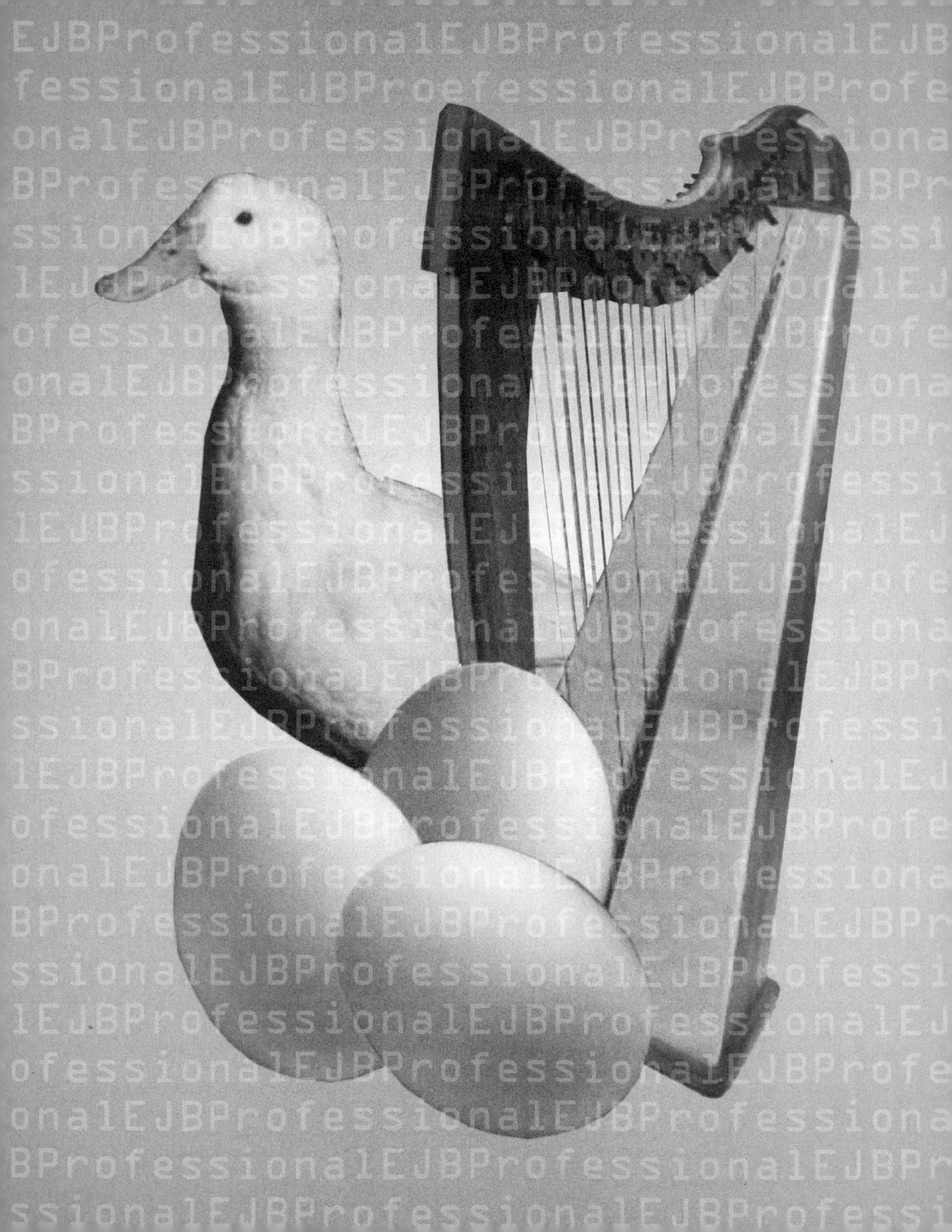

19

COM-Based EJB Clients

In the last chapter we looked at how we can use our EJBs to work with their sibling J2EE components, and in the next chapter we'll look at their not too distant cousin CORBA. However, in this chapter we are going to take a look at integrating EJBs with Microsoft's **Component Object Model (COM)**, which probably couldn't even be considered a long lost relative, as its operating model is not obviously compatible with the JVM.

There's no denying Microsoft's monopoly of the desktop. If you purchase a PC then you will almost certainly get a copy of some version of Windows with it. With a situation such as this, it is quite possible that at some point you may have to figure out how to get your EJBs to communicate with some piece of Microsoft software such as Visual Basic (VB) application or MS Office. Therefore, in this chapter we'll look at a number of ways that we can bridge the communication gap between Java and COM.

We will be looking at:

- ❏ An overview of COM
- ❏ How to get Java and COM to work together
- ❏ Using J-Integra to create a Visual Basic client to an EJB
- ❏ Using the Sun J2EE COM Bridge to create an Excel client to an EJB

Let's start by looking at COM in a bit more detail.

An Overview of COM

If you peel back the layers of most pieces of Microsoft software, you'll find that they are all dependent on COM. COM, previously known as OLE and then ActiveX, and now technically COM+, is Microsoft's own component model, not dissimilar to the way that JavaBeans and EJBs are Java's component models.

COM is all about a binary level of interoperability between clients and COM objects – in other words, how they talk to each other. In many ways COM is analogous to EJB and CORBA, in that they are all able to encapsulate implementation details behind a well-defined interface that conforms to an exacting specification.

However, while Java and COM both share the concept of specifications to provide a known communication interface, they differ in how the specification is implemented. As we have already said, COM provides a binary-level of interoperability through a binary specification and a run time.

Binary Specification

As we've mentioned several times, COM is a binary specification. This binary specification covers the description of how an interface is represented in memory and accessed at run time.

Virtual Method Tables

When you define an interface, the order of the methods, the parameters of each method, and the various other attributes you define form the interface signature. When you compile a COM component, that signature (**binary layout**) is burnt (so to speak) into the created file. The information is used to build a virtual method table (**vtable**), which is how the methods of an interface are invoked at run time by a client. In very simple terms, you can think of a vtable as an array with n elements that contains functions, where n is the number of methods in an interface:

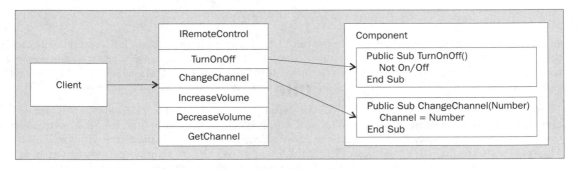

The array doesn't contain the code, but it does contain a pointer that describes where the code is actually located. So by using the vtable, we know that the entry at index 0 points us to the `TurnOnOff` method, the entry at index 1 points us to the `ChangeChannel` method and so forth.

When client code using an interface is compiled, these array elements (0, 1, ...) are what are placed into the compiled component. This is known as **early binding**. The client knows how to invoke a method in an interface by accessing a function at a given offset. The client doesn't have to query for any additional information at run time to be able to make the call once it has an interface pointer. The interface pointer is effectively a pointer to the array of functions that we can call.

Run time / The COM

The COM run time is an implementation of the COM specification and is provided with all versions of Windows. The run time itself resides in many DLLs, although the core API is in `ole32.dll`. We use the COM run time, and all of the functions provided in DLLs like `ole32.dll`, in our COM developments all the time without even knowing about it – the calls are made *transparently* on our behalf.

Bridging the COM-Java Gap

One way for a Java developer to work with a COM-component is to bind their code to native libraries (through the **Java Native Interface**) that will make native calls to a COM component. This task can be difficult as it binds the Java code to a machine-specific binary that is not portable between different platforms and results in the need for multiple installation tasks for each supported platform.

Although this task is complex, pure Java programmers are fortunate to have available a few third party solutions that help eliminate this problem and also help ease programming complexity. Linar has developed one such product called **J-Integra** (http://www.intrinsyc.com/products/deviceintegration/jintegra.html). J-Integra supports bi-directional communication between Java and COM components without requiring a native library. This means J-Integra works not only on the Microsoft platform, but also on any platform with a Java VM. This forms a good solution for Java developers who need to use distributed COM components from non-Microsoft operating systems.

Another solution currently being developed by Sun is the **J2EE Client Access Services (CAS) COM Bridge** (http://developer.java.sun.com/developer/earlyAccess/j2eecas/download-com-bridge.html). This solution allows developers using Microsoft Visual Basic, and other Windows-based tools, to use standard Java objects as if they were Microsoft COM components. It is another great solution that allows developers to reuse components.

These are more than just this couple of bridges available, such as Bridge2Java from IBM's Alphaworks (http://alphaworks.ibm.com/tech/bridge2java) and the JACOB Project (http://users.rcn.com/danadler/jacob/). However, we will limit our discussion in this chapter to just J-Integra and the J2EE CAS COM Bridge, as they have obvious support for EJBs.

The Example Amazon Application

To demonstrate combining COM with EJB we will write a relatively simple bean and then use two different approaches to achieve two different results using the bean.

Our example will be based around a Visual Basic (VB) utility that browses the Amazon.com web site and records the sales rank for selected book titles. The titles for which it searches are listed by ISBN in a flat file. In order to facilitate database access we will write a simple entity bean that the VB program will use to save the data. Then we will write an Excel client that reads the data from the beans so that we can plot the sales of the titles.

For the saving of data from the VB application, we will be using the J-Integra bridge, while for the Excel client we will use the CAS COM Bridge that Sun is developing:

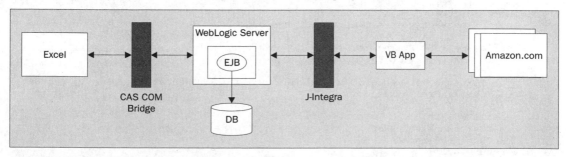

We'll start by looking at the EJB that acts as the data proxy.

The AmazonRank EJB

For simplicity we'll develop our bean as an entity bean with EJB 2.0 CMP. What's more our EJB doesn't have any significant business methods so the code is all very straightforward.

The Home Interface

```
package ranking;

public interface AmazonRankHome extends javax.ejb.EJBHome {

  public AmazonRank create(String id, String isbn, int salesRank, String rankDate)
      throws javax.ejb.CreateException, java.rmi.RemoteException;

  public AmazonRank findByPrimaryKey(String key)
      throws javax.ejb.FinderException, java.rmi.RemoteException;

}
```

The Remote Interface

```
package ranking;

public interface AmazonRank extends javax.ejb.EJBObject {

  public String getISBN() throws java.rmi.RemoteException;
  public int getSalesRank() throws java.rmi.RemoteException;
  public String getRankDate() throws java.rmi.RemoteException;

}
```

The Bean Implementation Class

```
package ranking;

import javax.ejb.*;

public abstract class AmazonRankEJB implements EntityBean {

  public abstract String getISBN();
  public abstract void setISBN(String isbn);

  public abstract String getRankDate();
  public abstract void setRankDate(String rankDate);

  public abstract int getSalesRank();
  public abstract void setSalesRank(int rank);

  public abstract String getId();
  public abstract void setId(String id);

  public String ejbCreate(String id, String isbn, int salesRank, String rankDate)
      throws CreateException {

    setISBN(isbn);
    setSalesRank(salesRank);
    setRankDate(rankDate);
    return null;
  }
```

```
    public void ejbPostCreate(String id, String isbn, int salesRank,
                              String rankDate) {}

    public void ejbStore() {}
    public void ejbLoad() {}
    public void ejbRemove() {}

    public void setEntityContext(EntityContext ctx) {}
    public void unsetEntityContext() {}

    public void ejbActivate() {}
    public void ejbPassivate() {}

}
```

The Deployment Descriptors

We'll be running the bean on WebLogic 6.0, so we need the additional deployment descriptors `weblogic-ejb-jar.xml` and `weblogic-cmp-rdms-jar.xml` besides the standard `ejb-jar.xml`.

ejb-jar.xml

We are using the `id` field as the primary key for our bean, and we'll leave it up to the VB application to provide it:

```
<?xml version="1.0"?>

<!DOCTYPE ejb-jar PUBLIC
                  '-//Sun Microsystems, Inc.//DTD Enterprise JavaBeans 2.0//EN'
                  'http://java.sun.com/dtd/ejb-jar_2_0.dtd'>

<ejb-jar>
  <enterprise-beans>
    <entity>
      <ejb-name>AmazonRank</ejb-name>
      <home>ranking.AmazonRankHome</home>
      <remote>ranking.AmazonRank</remote>
      <ejb-class>ranking.AmazonRankEJB</ejb-class>
      <persistence-type>Container</persistence-type>
      <prim-key-class>java.lang.String</prim-key-class>
      <reentrant>False</reentrant>
      <cmp-version>2.x</cmp-version>
      <abstract-schema-name>AmazonRankEJB</abstract-schema-name>
      <cmp-field>
        <field-name>id</field-name>
      </cmp-field>
      <cmp-field>
        <field-name>iSBN</field-name>
      </cmp-field>
      <cmp-field>
        <field-name>salesRank</field-name>
      </cmp-field>
      <cmp-field>
        <field-name>rankDate</field-name>
      </cmp-field>
      <primkey-field>id</primkey-field>
    </entity>
  </enterprise-beans>
```

```
  <assembly-descriptor>
    <container-transaction>
      <method>
        <ejb-name>AmazonRank</ejb-name>
        <method-intf>Home</method-intf>
        <method-name>*</method-name>
      </method>
      <trans-attribute>NotSupported</trans-attribute>
    </container-transaction>
    <container-transaction>
      <method>
        <ejb-name>AmazonRank</ejb-name>
        <method-intf>Remote</method-intf>
        <method-name>*</method-name>
      </method>
      <trans-attribute>NotSupported</trans-attribute>
    </container-transaction>
  </assembly-descriptor>
</ejb-jar>
```

weblogic-ejb-jar.xml

```
<?xml version="1.0"?>

<!DOCTYPE weblogic-ejb-jar PUBLIC
        "-//BEA Systems, Inc.//DTD WebLogic 6.0.0 EJB//EN"
        "http://www.bea.com/servers/wls600/dtd/weblogic-ejb-jar.dtd" >

<weblogic-ejb-jar>
  <weblogic-enterprise-bean>
    <ejb-name>AmazonRank</ejb-name>
    <entity-descriptor>
      <persistence>
        <persistence-type>
            <type-identifier>WebLogic_CMP_RDBMS</type-identifier>
            <type-version>6.0</type-version>
            <type-storage>META-INF/weblogic-cmp-rdbms-jar.xml</type-storage>
        </persistence-type>
        <persistence-use>
            <type-identifier>WebLogic_CMP_RDBMS</type-identifier>
            <type-version>6.0</type-version>
        </persistence-use>
      </persistence>
    </entity-descriptor>

    <jndi-name>AmazonRank</jndi-name>
  </weblogic-enterprise-bean>

</weblogic-ejb-jar>
```

weblogic-cmp-rdbms-jar.xml

```
<?xml version="1.0"?>

<!DOCTYPE weblogic-rdbms-jar PUBLIC
    '-//BEA Systems, Inc.//DTD WebLogic 6.0.0 EJB RDBMS Persistence//EN'
    'http://www.bea.com/servers/wls600/dtd/weblogic-rdbms20-persistence-600.dtd'>

<weblogic-rdbms-jar>

  <weblogic-rdbms-bean>
```

```
      <ejb-name>AmazonRank</ejb-name>
      <data-source-name>Amazon</data-source-name>
      <table-name>AmazonRankingTable</table-name>
      <field-map>
        <cmp-field>id</cmp-field>
        <dbms-column>id</dbms-column>
      </field-map>
      <field-map>
        <cmp-field>iSBN</cmp-field>
        <dbms-column>isbn</dbms-column>
      </field-map>
      <field-map>
        <cmp-field>salesRank</cmp-field>
        <dbms-column>salesrank</dbms-column>
      </field-map>
      <field-map>
        <cmp-field>rankDate</cmp-field>
        <dbms-column>rankdate</dbms-column>
      </field-map>
    </weblogic-rdbms-bean>

</weblogic-rdbms-jar>
```

Now you can compile the Java files, archive them into a JAR and run the WebLogic generator utility on it before deploying in WebLogic:

```
java -classpath %WL_HOME%\lib\weblogic.jar weblogic.ejbc Amazon.jar Amazon_WL.jar
```

For more information on the deployment process for WebLogic refer to Appendix C.

This example also requires that you set up a datasource called Amazon for your database of choice. This is shown in the `<data-source-name>` tag in the `weblogic-cmp-rdms-jar.xml` file.

A Visual Basic EJB Client

We will be writing the Amazon-browsing portion of the application using Visual Basic, to browse to each book page and screen-scrape the sales rank off the output. From within VB we will instantiate a local instance of the Microsoft Internet Explorer browser that we can point at Amazon.com URLs. We will then be able to process the resulting browser display text and by some cunning string manipulation retrieve the sales rank for a particular book.

From the VB application, once we have accumulated all the data, we'll be using J-Integra 1.4 (available from http://www.intrinsyc.com/products/deviceintegration/jintegra.html) to bridge the gap between VB and our EJB running in WebLogic.

J-Integra

J-Integra is a Java-based run time that translates Java calls to COM calls, and vice versa, by using DCOM (Distributed COM) calls, through the use of basic Java networking classes:

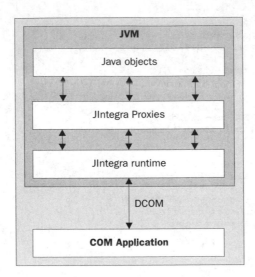

Therefore, it is possible to have your Java code running on a Unix machine and communicate with a COM-based client running on Windows. All J-Integra needs from the client perspective is some run time libraries (but no JVM) and to be pointed to the server where the Java code is running.

In order for J-Integra to interface with both our bean in WebLogic and our VB application, we will create a bridging class called COMtoWebLogic, that intercepts the (D)COM calls to the J-Integra run time and passes them on to our bean in WebLogic:

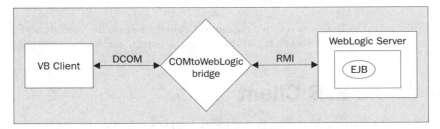

The COMtoWebLogic class is quite simple, in that all it really has to do is perform the client lookup for our bean in WebLogic. All the interception and translation takes places behind the scenes in the J-Integra run time.

This class, as well as others for accessing other application servers, is available on the J-Integra documentation site: http://www.linar.com/jintegra/doc/

```java
import javax.naming.*;
import java.util.Hashtable;
import com.linar.J-Integra.*;

public class COMtoWebLogic {
  public static void main(String[] args) throws Exception {
    Jvm.register("ejb", new EjbInstanciator());
    Thread.sleep(10000000);
  }
}
```

The class simply consists of a `main()` method that registers an instance of user-defined class called `EjbInstanciator` into the JVM run time under the name `ejb`. This will be what our VB client uses to get a reference to the EJB home object, as you will see later.

The `EjbInstanciator` class really isn't all that different from the clients we've seen so far in this book, in that all it does is perform a JNDI lookup on the EJB container. It can be included in the same `.java` file as `COMtoWebLogic`:

```
class EjbInstanciator implements Instanciator {
  Context ctx;

  EjbInstanciator() throws NamingException {
    Hashtable env = new Hashtable(11);
    env.put(Context.INITIAL_CONTEXT_FACTORY,
            "weblogic.jndi.WLInitialContextFactory");
    env.put(Context.PROVIDER_URL, "t3://localhost:7001");
    ctx = new InitialContext(env);
  }

  public Object instanciate(String javaClass) throws AutomationException {
    System.out.println("instanciate called for class: " + javaClass);
    try {
      return ctx.lookup(javaClass);
    } catch (NamingException e) {
      e.printStackTrace();
      throw new AutomationException(e);
    }
  }
}
```

To compile these classes you'll need the `J-Integra.jar` file – found in the J-Integra install directory's `\lib` folder – in your classpath.

Don't run this quite yet as we need to write the VB client first.

The Amazon Browser Application

The Amazon Browsing VB application needs to perform a number of steps:

1. First, it opens a flat file that contains a list of ISBNs for the books we are interested in, and reads them into local memory

2. It then uses these ISBNs to browse the Amazon.com web site and locate the sales rank figure on the page

3. It loops through all the ISBNs until all the data has been read

4. Finally it uses our AmazonRank EJB to save all this data into the database

We'll now look at how to build our VB application.

I will take you through all the steps necessary to construct this application but I will not be explaining the VB portion of the code.

Creating the Project and Form

First create a new Standard EXE project in Visual Basic 6.0 and call it something appropriate such as AmazonBrowser, and the default form something like frmBrowser:

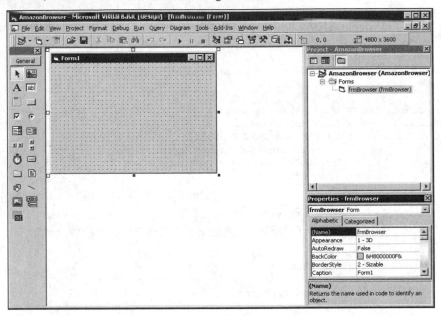

Although we don't need to display the browsing process to the user, we will provide a progress bar to give some indication as to how the program is doing.

The progress bar is not in the default control palette, so we need to add it to our VB environment. To do this, right-click the control tool bar on the left-hand edge of the IDE and select Components. This will bring up the Components dialog. Scroll down and check the Microsoft Windows Common Controls 6.0 box:

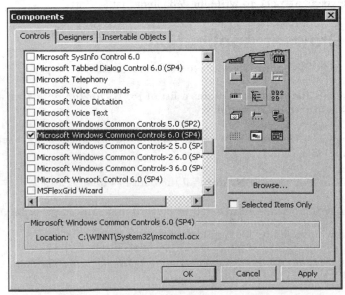

Once you OK this dialog you will be presented with some additional controls in the palette. Select the progress bar control and place one onto the form, and call it ProgressBar. Also add a label to the form called lblForm:

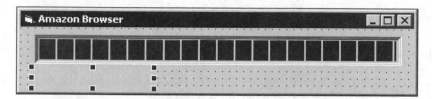

We are just about ready to start coding, but first we need to add some references to the project. In the same manner that we need to import packages into our Java classes, we can add references to other COM libraries to make use of their objects.

From the Project menu select References to bring up the References dialog. Select the libraries for the Microsoft Scripting Run time and Microsoft Internet Controls (you will also see that VB has automatically included its run time libraries):

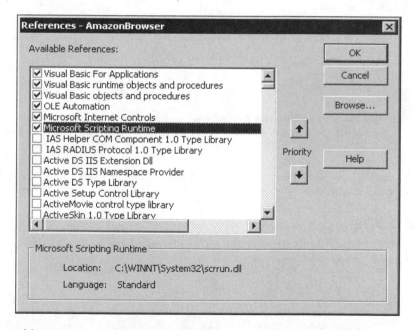

We'll start by adding some variables at form-level scope to be used by the various routines we'll add shortly. Open the code window for the form and add the following declarations:

```
Option Explicit

Private WithEvents m_ie As SHDocVw.InternetExplorer
Private mstrISBNs() As String
Private mstrData() As String
Private mstrURL As String
Private mintCounter As Integer
Private mintTotal As Integer
```

❑   The m_ie variable will hold a reference to an internal instance of Internet Explorer that
    we'll create

❑   mstrISBNs and mstrData are String arrays that we'll use to hold the local memory copies
    of the books to be searched for and their sales ranks

❑   mstrURL holds the basic URL to browse the web site for

❑   The mintCounter and mintTotal variables are used to keep track of the application's progress

Now we can start coding the various routines that we need. We'll start with the Form_Load routine that
is called when the program first starts and the form is loaded:

```
Private Sub Form_Load()

    'Instantiate new instance of Internet Explorer
    If m_ie Is Nothing Then Set m_ie = New SHDocVw.InternetExplorer

    'Load ISBNs from flat file into a local array
    LoadISBNArray

    'Navigate the browser instance to the first ISBN at Amazon
    mstrURL = "http://www.amazon.com/exec/obidos/ASIN/"
    m_ie.Navigate mstrURL & mstrISBNs(0)
    lblForm = "Browsing..."

End Sub
```

First we create a new instance of Internet Explorer for our application to use. Then we call another
routine called LoadISBNArray that reads in all the ISBNs that we are interested in browsing for. We'll
see this routine in a moment.

We then build the URL for the Amazon web site. We can access the book page for any title by browsing
to http://www.amazon.com/exec/obidos/ASIN/ with the ISBN appended onto the end.

Loading the ISBNs

We load the ISBNs that we are interested in recording the sales rank for from a basic text file that has
all the ISBNs listed on a separate line. For example:

```
1861005083
1861004931
...
```

We will use the FileSystemObject that is part of the VB Scripting run time to open and read this file
in a routine called LoadISBNArray. Add the following to the form's code window:

```
Private Sub LoadISBNArray()

    Dim objFSO As FileSystemObject
    Dim objFile As File
    Dim objStream As TextStream
    Dim i As Integer
```

```
Set objFSO = New FileSystemObject
Set objFile = objFSO.GetFile("c:\isbn.txt")
Set objStream = objFile.OpenAsTextStream(ForReading)

Do While Not objStream.AtEndOfStream
  ReDim Preserve mstrISBNs(i)
  mstrISBNs(i) = objStream.ReadLine
  i = i + 1
Loop

mintTotal = i

End Sub
```

We're currently reading the data in from a file called isbn.txt in the root of the C: drive but you can modify the path to wherever you like.

Having read the contents of the file into an array the application then iterates through the array browsing for each ISBN in turn. The next step is to capture the sales rank.

Recording the Sales Rank

You may recall that we declared our Internet Explorer variable m_ie using the WithEvents keyword. This is the equivalent of registering our form as an event listener to this object. Consequently we can have our form be called when the Internet Explorer object raises certain events. The event we are interested in is called DocumentComplete and is called when the page the Internet Explorer object is browsing for has been downloaded fully. We need to wait for the whole page to download so we can guarantee that the information we want is available.

In the DocumentComplete event handler m_ie_DocumentComplete, we perform a basic If operation dependent on where in the ISBN array the program is. Add the following to the form's code window:

```
Private Sub m_ie_DocumentComplete(ByVal pDisp As Object, URL As Variant)

    If mintCounter = UBound(mstrISBNs) Then
    '    Last one
        RecordSalesRank
        ProgressBar = 100
        SaveData
        End
    ElseIf mintCounter < UBound(mstrISBNs) Then
        RecordSalesRank
        mintCounter = mintCounter + 1
        ProgressBar = ((mintCounter / mintTotal) * 100)
        m_ie.Navigate mstrURL & mstrISBNs(mintCounter)
    End If
End Sub
```

If we are not at the end of the array then we simply want to record the sales rank into a local array and move on to the next ISBN, whereas if we've reached the end of the array we also want to save the data to the database.

To record the sales rank into a local array we have a routine called RecordSalesRank that performs some complex string manipulation to pull out the sales rank from the page:

```
Private Sub RecordSalesRank()

    Dim strBody As String
    Dim intPlace As String
    Dim strRank As String

    strBody = m_ie.Document.body.outertext

    intPlace = InStr(strBody, "Amazon.com Sales Rank")

    strRank = Trim(Mid(strBody, intPlace + 23, 8))

    If InStr(strRank, vbCr) Then
        strRank = Trim(Left(strRank, InStr(strRank, vbCr) - 1))
    End If

    ReDim Preserve mstrData(mintCounter)
    mstrData(mintCounter) = strRank

End Sub
```

Saving the Data

Finally, we come to the interesting routine that connects to our EJB to save the data to the database. If you examine the code below you'll see that is actually very simple:

```
Private Sub SaveData()

    Dim i As Integer
    Dim dtmNow As Date
    Dim home As Object
    Dim ranking As Object

    dtmNow = Now

    lblForm = "Saving data..."

    Set home = GetObject("ejb:AmazonRank")

    Do Until i > UBound(mstrISBNs)
        Set ranking = home.Create(GetGUID, mstrISBNs(i), CLng(mstrData(i)), _
                                  CStr(dtmNow))
        i = i + 1
    Loop

    Set m_ie = Nothing

End Sub
```

The GetObject() method allows us to connect our object variable home to an existing process. This process is the J-Integra run time, to which we pass in the name of the EJB that we want. If you remember the COMtoWebLogic class from earlier, this is basically doing our JNDI lookup on the WebLogic server for us. Once we have a reference to the home object we can simply call create() just as we would for any EJB client. The J-Integra run time will intercept these calls and translate them into Java calls that our bean will understand.

If you recall when we were constructing our EJB, I mentioned that we would be leaving the primary generation up to the VB client. We needed to add a specific id field to be used for the primary key because we could not guarantee that the other fields would be unique. As you can see from the code above, we make another call to a routine we're going to develop, called getGUID to generate the primary key value.

As we are going to be running our client on Windows, I thought it was appropriate to make use of COM **GUIDs** to provide us with a unique ID. GUID stands for **Globally Unique Identifier** and is a 128-bit number that can be expressed in a string format such as {7CF0B6A9-6152-11D3-8126-00105A6FA316}. GUID's are generated by a complex algorithm that uses the system clock and network card's MAC address. Supposedly the algorithm could generate 10 million GUIDs each second until the year 5770 AD, and each one would be unique in the world. If, however, you don't have a network card then they are only guaranteed to be unique on that machine.

Unfortunately, GUID generation by VB is normally automatic and it is not that easy to simply generate one for use by our program itself. However, we can get round this by making a call to a Windows API method called CoCreateGuid and then processing the results into a string we can understand.

Add a new standard module to our VB project by selecting **Add Module** from the **Project** menu, and call it something like basGUID. Then add the following code that I found in a MSDN Knowledge Base article:

```
Private Type GUID
  Data1 As Long
  Data2 As Integer
  Data3 As Integer
  Data4(7) As Byte
End Type

Private Declare Function CoCreateGuid Lib "OLE32.DLL" (pGuid As GUID) As Long

Public Function GetGUID() As String
'(c) 2000 Gus Molina

  Dim udtGUID As GUID

  If (CoCreateGuid(udtGUID) = 0) Then

    GetGUID = _
    String(8 - Len(Hex$(udtGUID.Data1)), "0") & Hex$(udtGUID.Data1) & _
    String(4 - Len(Hex$(udtGUID.Data2)), "0") & Hex$(udtGUID.Data2) & _
    String(4 - Len(Hex$(udtGUID.Data3)), "0") & Hex$(udtGUID.Data3) & _
    IIf((udtGUID.Data4(0) < &H10), "0", "") & Hex$(udtGUID.Data4(0)) & _
    IIf((udtGUID.Data4(1) < &H10), "0", "") & Hex$(udtGUID.Data4(1)) & _
    IIf((udtGUID.Data4(2) < &H10), "0", "") & Hex$(udtGUID.Data4(2)) & _
    IIf((udtGUID.Data4(3) < &H10), "0", "") & Hex$(udtGUID.Data4(3)) & _
    IIf((udtGUID.Data4(4) < &H10), "0", "") & Hex$(udtGUID.Data4(4)) & _
    IIf((udtGUID.Data4(5) < &H10), "0", "") & Hex$(udtGUID.Data4(5)) & _
    IIf((udtGUID.Data4(6) < &H10), "0", "") & Hex$(udtGUID.Data4(6)) & _
    IIf((udtGUID.Data4(7) < &H10), "0", "") & Hex$(udtGUID.Data4(7))
  End If

End Function
```

And that's it for our VB client. We are now able to run our example.

Running the VB Client

In order to make sure that our application works properly we need to make sure that all the relevant pieces are running:

- ❑ Firstly, make sure that WebLogic is running with the deployed bean (and also the database engine if it is required)

- ❑ Secondly, we need to start the COMtoWebLogic bridge running in the J-Integra run time. To do this run the class with the following command, replacing the path to the JAR files as appropriate:

```
java -classpath %WL_HOME%\lib\weblogic.jar;%J-INTEGRA_HOME%\lib\J-Integra.jar;.
    -DJ-INTEGRA_DCOM_PORT=7050 COMtoWebLogic
```

- ❑ Thirdly, on the VB client machine, we need to tell J-Integra about the location of the JVM and the name of the service running in it. This can be done with the regjvmcmd.exe utility that comes with J-Integra. If the VB client is on a different machine from the server then replace localhost as appropriate, and you will also need some DLLs from the J-Integra installation:

```
%J-INTEGRA_HOME%\bin\regjvmcmd.exe ejb localhost[7050]
```

We are finally now able to run our VB client application, either from within the VB IDE or compiled as a separate executable. Don't forge to create the isbn.txt file first though, or you can use the one we provide with the source download from http://www.wrox.com/.

Now let's look at how we can take our entity beans and build an Excel-based client to help study the data.

An Excel EJB Client

Having got all our data into our database, it would now be useful if we could somehow perform some analysis on it, or be able to plot it in a chart. One common tool that many people are familiar with is Microsoft's Excel application that comes as part of MS Office. In this section, we'll therefore look at how we can use Excel to access the data using our EJB.

Integrated into the Excel application, is an execution engine for Visual Basic for Applications (VBA). This is basically a cut down version of VB that runs within the Excel process space and allows you to automate the various features of Excel. Therefore, we could if we wanted simply use the same J-Integra bridge that we developed before to get at the EJB, but for a bit of variety we'll use a different bridging product.

The CAS COM Bridge

Sun has been developing a COM bridge called the **J2EE Client Access Services (CAS) COM Bridge**, which at the time of writing was at the Early Access 3 stage:

http://developer.java.sun.com/developer/earlyAccess/j2eecas/download-com-bridge.html

The CAS COM Bridge works by turning the COM client into a J2EE application client. It does this by creating a JVM within the process space of the client. The bridge then acts as a COM server to the COM client by exposing an OLE automation interface (the same things that allow us to automate Excel from VBA), which translates COM-based calls into their Java equivalents and the COM-client can access the J2EE application as if it were a native Java application:

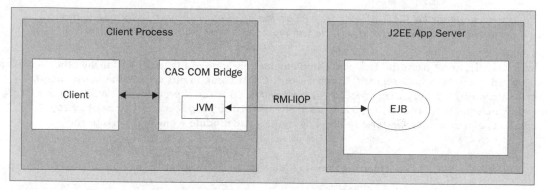

The COM bridge itself is composed of a number of layers of services:

- **COM Bridge Core Services**
  This is the core of the COM bridge that is responsible for creating and accessing the basic services of the JVM

- **Java Services**
  The second level provides a more convenient method of working with the COM bridge than the interfaces the bridge exposes. These services include class lookup, object creation, and type casting.

- **Enterprise Services**
  The top layer of services provides the means for the bridge to work with various J2EE application servers. Each app server will have a different module that contains the server-specific connection information.

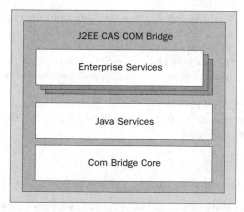

Each enterprise module is tightly integrated with an EJB container implementation. Thus although many enterprise modules exist, you will only ever use the relevant module for your application server. Fortunately, the CAS COM installation comes with a number of these modules for some of the main applications servers:

- The J2EE Reference Implementation
- iPlanet
- Silverstream
- WebLogic
- WebSphere

If you wish to use the CAS COM Bridge with another application server, then the installation comes with instructions and sourcecode to help you write the enterprise module for your server.

Unfortunately, apart from the Reference Implementation none of the modules for the other servers are registered in the Windows registry (in other words COM components are unable to use them). Fortunately, this is a very easy process. All you need to do is run the `regsvr32` utility on the DLL you need, which can be found in the `%J2EE_CAS_BRIDGE%\doc\appserver-connectivity-samples\bin` directory. So for our WebLogic enterprise module we would need to run:

```
regsvr32
    %J2EE_CAS_BRIDGE%\doc\appserver-connectivity-samples\bin\weblogic-services.dll
```

Now we are ready to create the Excel client using this DLL to communicate with our bean deployed in WebLogic.

The Excel Client

What we will be doing in this part of our example is loading the data for each book title into an Excel worksheet. We can then use this data to draw a chart, do some analysis, or whatever we wish.

Before we start writing the VBA code, however, we will take advantage of a tool that comes with the CAS COM Bridge that allows us to generate a type library for our Java components. A type library is a file that contains descriptions of COM interfaces. These descriptions provide the binary mapping of the component's public methods that are available for use by other COM components.

We can use this type library to early-bind our object variables and thus help our development effort. If you remember from the J-Integra example earlier, all our variables that represented Java objects were declared as type `Object`, thus we were using **late binding**. This meant that VB was unaware of the exact object type until run time. With **early binding** we can declare our variables as `java.util.Collection` type and thus have access to all the object's public properties and methods at design time, as you will see.

In the `\bin` directory of the CAS COM Bridge installation is a tool called `gentypelib` that takes a Java object and generates the respective COM type library for it. We will use this tool to generate the type libraries for the following objects:

- Our bean's remote interface `ranking.AmazonRank`
- Our bean's home interface `ranking.AmazonRankHome`
- The Java Collections class `java.util.Collection` so we can call our `findByISBN()` finder method
- The Java `Iterator` class `java.util.Iterator` so we can iterate over the collection

To do this run the `gentypelib` tool with the following options:

```
gentypelib -n ranking.AmazonRank -n ranking.AmazonRankHome -n java.util.Collection
           -n java.util.Iterator -lib AmazonLibs
```

You will also need our Amazon bean's JAR file (`Amazon_WL.jar`) as well as the `javax.ejb.*` packages in the classpath.

This will generate the type libraries in a file called `AmazonLibs.tlb` that can be found in the `%J2EE_CAS_BRIDGE%\output` directory.

Now we are ready to code our Excel client, so start up Excel and open the VBA editor by either pressing *Alt+F11* or going Tools | Macros | Visual Basic Editor:

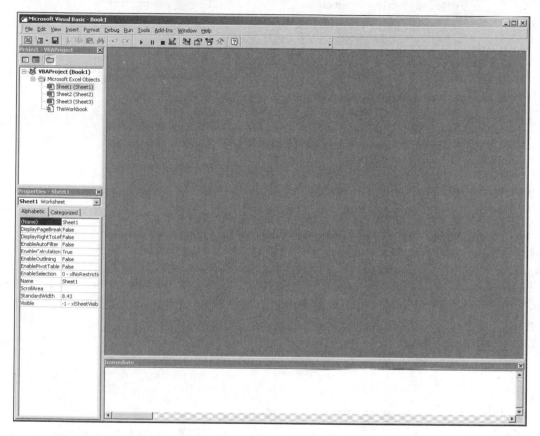

We now need to add the various references to the type libraries we generated earlier as well as CAS COM Bridge components. So open the References dialog by going to the Tools | References menu option and checking the boxes for the type libraries in the following figure (again some of these will be pre-selected by the VBA editor):

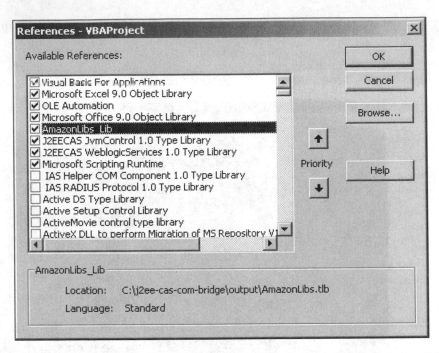

Now open the **ThisWorkbook** code window to start coding our client routines. Our client will be a very simple couple of routines that loads all the data from the beans into the workbook sorted by ISBN. To start with we'll use the same `LoadISBNArray()` routine from our VB client to get a list of the available ISBNs:

```
Option Explicit

Private mstrISBNs() As String

Private Sub LoadISBNArray()

   Dim objFSO As FileSystemObject
   Dim objFile As File
   Dim objStream As TextStream
   Dim i As Integer

   Set objFSO = New FileSystemObject
   Set objFile = objFSO.GetFile("c:\isbn.txt")
   Set objStream = objFile.OpenAsTextStream(ForReading)

   Do While Not objStream.AtEndOfStream
     ReDim Preserve mstrISBNs(i)
     mstrISBNs(i) = objStream.ReadLine
     i = i + 1
   Loop

End Sub
```

Now we will get to the main routine that is responsible for the bean access. Our routine needs to perform a number of functions:

1. Create a client JVM

2. Initialize the enterprise module

3. Look up our bean's home object

4. Look up the beans by ISBN

5. Enter the data onto the workbook

Creating a Client JVM

The CAS COM Bridge works by creating a JVM within the client process, which is responsible for actually calling the Java components. To do this, the CAS COM Bridge has a component called the **JVM Control**, which allows us to create and configure a local JVM. For the JVM to access our EJB in WebLogic we will need to make sure that the `weblogic.jar` file (so that the JVM can perform the JNDI lookup on the bean) and the `Amazon_WL.jar` file are in the JVM's classpath. Add the following code to the code window:

```
Public Sub LoadData()

    Dim JvmCtl As New JvmControl
    JvmCtl.Classpath = "%WL_HOME%\lib\weblogic.jar" & _
                        ";%WL_HOME%\config\mydomain\applications\Amazon_WL.jar"
    JvmCtl.StartJvm
```

Initializing the Enterprise Module

The next step is to initialize the enterprise module to connect to the application server where our bean is deployed. For WebLogic, this is a simple as creating a new `WeblogicServices` object:

```
    Dim service As WeblogicServices
    Set service = New WeblogicServices
```

Once the enterprise module is initialized we need to set the provider URL for the naming service and also any necessary security credentials:

```
    service.ProviderURL = "t3://localhost:7001"
    'service.SecurityCredentials = ""
    'service.SecurityPrincipal = ""
```

Look up our Bean's Home Object

Having configured our reference to the application server we are now able to look up our EJB's home object. With the CAS COM Bridge this as easy as calling the `LookupEjbHome()` method on the enterprise module passing in the JNDI name for the EJB and the home interface class name:

```
    Dim home As ranking_AmazonRankHome
    Set home = service.LookupEjbHome("AmazonRank", "ranking.AmazonRankHome")
```

Look up the Beans by ISBN

Now we have a reference to our home object we can use it in pretty much the same was as we would from a Java client, and call the `findByISBN()` finder method for each ISBN in the text file:

```
    'Load the list of ISBNs from the text file
    LoadISBNArray

    Dim row, i As Integer
    Dim books As java_util_Collection
    Dim objIter As java_util_Iterator
    Dim rank As ranking_AmazonRank

    Do While i <= UBound(mstrISBNs)

        Set books = home.findByISBN(mstrISBNs(i))
        ' more code to be added here, in next section
        i = i + 1
    Loop
End Sub
```

Enter the Data onto the Workbook

Once we have a reference to the collection of beans that represent the data for that ISBN we can iterate through the collection using our new VB typed `java_util_Iterator` object and calling the getter routines on the bean:

```
    Do While i <= UBound(mstrISBNs)

        Set books = home.findByISBN(mstrISBNs(i))
        Set objIter = books.iterator
        row = row + 1
        While objIter.hasNext
            Set rank = objIter.Next
            row = row + 1
            Application.Cells(row, 1).Select
            ActiveCell.FormulaR1C1 = mstrISBNs(i)
            Application.Cells(row, 2).Select
            ActiveCell.FormulaR1C1 = rank.getRankDate
            Application.Cells(row, 3).Select
            ActiveCell.FormulaR1C1 = rank.getSalesRank
        Wend
        i = i + 1
    Loop
End Sub
```

Now we can run the Excel client by switching back to the main Excel window and selecting Tools | Macros | Macros | LoadData, making sure to have the WebLogic server running. We should then get all the data from the beans loaded onto the active workbook, and we can write an additional macro to present the data in a graphical form, which might look something like the following screenshot.

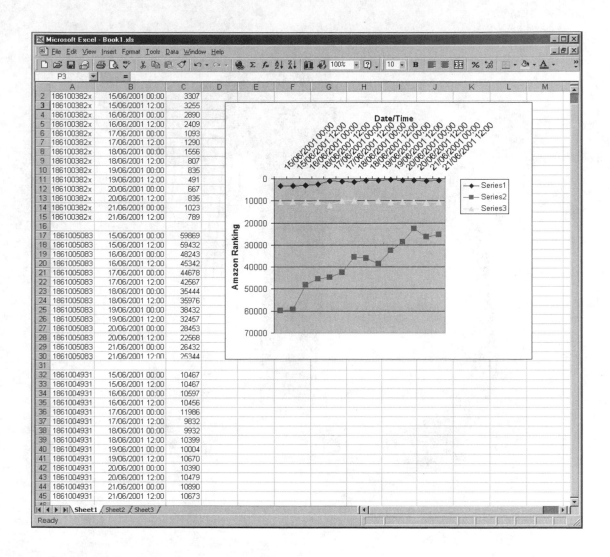

Summary

In this chapter, we've taken a look at a number of ways that we can extend our EJB clients out beyond the obvious Java and CORBA-based clients into the realm of Microsoft COM-based environments. The jump from the Java component model to the Microsoft component model can be quite complex but through the use of third-party bridging products such as J-Integra and the J2EE CAS COM Bridge, the process can be greatly simplified.

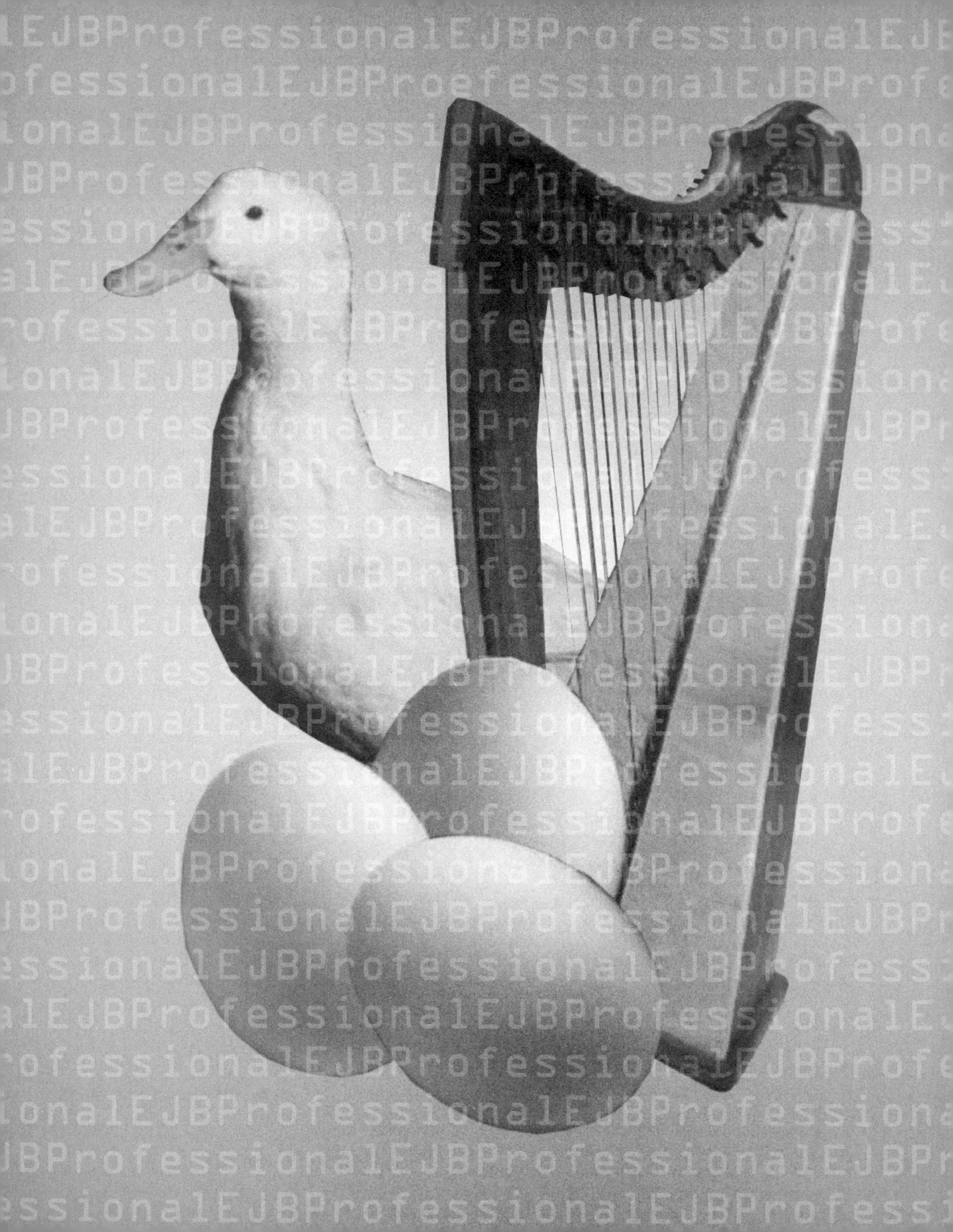
EJBProfessional

Integrating EJBs and CORBA

The Enterprise JavaBeans framework, as you are no doubt aware by now, provides the developer with a very powerful tool for deploying software – the ability to deploy the same component onto various hardware and software platforms. This can be a tremendous advantage when introducing EJBs into existing software architecture. However, when attempting to utilize these new EJBs you will most likely find that the "write-once, run-anywhere" benefit that is achieved through the EJBs' use of Java also introduces one small problem:

> EJBs are always written in Java. Unfortunately, legacy software usually isn't.

The goal of this chapter is to demonstrate how to integrate your EJBs with non-Java software through the use of CORBA. In order to do this, we'll be looking at the following:

- ❏ An overview of CORBA
- ❏ A small CORBA example
- ❏ A simple EJB to be accessed using CORBA
- ❏ A C++ client to access the EJB through CORBA

Tools Required for this Chapter

Some of the code examples in this chapter make use of C++ and the Interface Definition Language (IDL) and, for the sake of brevity, we will not attempt to teach these languages. For instance, Wrox publishes a number of introductory guides which will give you a strong background in programming with C++. See www.wrox.com for further details.

We will need several tools to support the examples presented in this chapter:

- ❑ The JavaIDL ORB that is bundled within the Sun Java SDK (http://java.sun.com) – for our simple CORBA example

- ❑ BEA WebLogic Server 6.0, Service Pack 1 (http://www.bea.com) – to deploy our EJB example.

- ❏ ORBacus C++ ORB from Object Oriented Concepts, Inc. (http://www.ooc.com) – for our C++ client

- ❑ A C++ compiler for your particular platform – for compilation of the ORBacus product as well as our sample client application

CORBA Overview

CORBA, an acronym for **Common Object Request Broker Architecture**, is a specification for a distributed application framework that is not dependent on any particular programming language. Developed by the Object Management Group (OMG), CORBA, along with other OMG specifications such as the **Internet Inter-ORB Protocol (IIOP)**, provides a language-independent, vendor-independent architecture for distributed object computing.

Since CORBA is a specification, we will need to obtain a specific implementation in order to build a system using CORBA. There are several production-grade CORBA implementations available, including Iona's Orbix and OrbixWeb (http://www.iona.com), and Inprise/Borland's Visibroker. http://(www.inprise.com). There are also many public-domain implementations to choose from. The OMG maintains a pretty extensive list of these at its web site, http://www.omg.org. It's important to realize that CORBA is simply a *specification* and, like many other specifications, it has gone through several revisions since its introduction. The documents describing these specifications are available for downloading at the OMG web site. As we will see later, compliance with these specification revisions will play a major part in the compatibility between CORBA and our EJBs.

Central to the CORBA architecture is the **Object Request Broker**, or **ORB** for short. The ORB provides connectivity between clients and remote object implementations. Conceptually, a simple distributed application can be viewed as a client and remote object both being attached to the ORB, allowing the client's requests for remote object method invocations to be passed from the client through the ORB to the remote object:

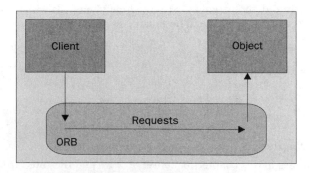

Now that we've introduced the ORB at a conceptual level, let's take a closer look at distributed applications and how they are implemented using CORBA.

Implementing Distributed Applications with CORBA

One of the main reasons for building a distributed application is to allow clients and objects to reside in different locations, allowing them to communicate whether they are located in different processes on the same computer or different hosts within a network. A primary concern when designing these types of applications is to determine just how the client and object will communicate, how they will work together.

As with EJBs, this is accomplished by defining an interface. This interface is basically a contract between an object and its clients, which defines the functionality of the object in terms of the operations and attributes that the client can access. It is important to realize that the interface does not describe how the operations will be performed; this is strictly the responsibility of the object's implementation. The client should make no assumptions as to how the functionality is carried out since the object is free to alter its implementation at any time. In simple terms, the interface defines 'what', not 'how'.

Unlike EJBs, where the interface is defined in Java, in CORBA an interface is defined in a programming-language-neutral manner, using the **Interface Definition Language** (IDL). The CORBA interface defines the attributes, operations, exceptions, structures, etc. that the client and object use to interact. An object implementing a CORBA interface is called a **CORBA object**. As described above, a client and CORBA object communicate only according to the IDL defined interface and the client makes no assumptions as to how the object's implementation provides the functionality.

Now, those of you new to CORBA may already be a bit disgruntled since we have barely started reviewing CORBA and already there is another language to learn, namely IDL. Before getting too upset, let me mention a couple of things. Firstly, IDL is not a large language in comparison to programming languages like Java or C++. In fact, it resembles Java to some degree, so it won't be terribly painful to pick up. Secondly, and this is the important part, it is the IDL that makes possible one of the biggest benefits of CORBA: the client and object implementation can be written in different programming languages.To see how this is possible, let's examine what happens once we've defined an interface and want to implement our distributed application.

Using the CORBA Interface

Once the interface is defined in IDL, it can be compiled and used to provide interfaces between our client and object implementation code and the ORB. More specifically, compiling an IDL interface with a utility called an IDL compiler will yield two important pieces of source code, namely an **IDL stub** and an **IDL skeleton**.

The **IDL stub** is source code generated in a target programming language, such as Java or C++, that allows our client source code to invoke operations, access attributes, etc., defined in the interface on a proxy object which, in turn, directs these invocations through the ORB. The **IDL skeleton**, on the other hand, is source code generated in a target programming language that allows the ORB to invoke operations, access attributes, etc., defined in the interface on an object's implementation. The key to these objects is that since the IDL stub and IDL skeleton reside in different applications, they don't need to be in the same target language.

Given a single IDL interface, compiling it using IDL compilers for different target languages will yield stubs and skeletons for different programming languages. We could, for instance, generate a Java IDL stub and a C++ IDL skeleton, which would allow us to build our client in Java and our object implementation in C++. New clients can be written later in different programming languages that access our original CORBA object. Alternatively, another CORBA object could be implemented in a different programming language and used in place of the existing one without affecting the client applications. Hence, IDL-defined interfaces combined with the IDL-to-language mappings provide the ability to develop clients and CORBA objects in different programming languages.

The following diagram represents a conceptual view of a client connecting to a CORBA object, using IDL stubs and skeletons:

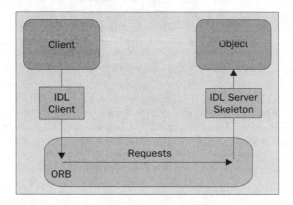

Locating and Using a CORBA Object

Now that we understand how a client interacts with a CORBA object, we need to answer two questions: how do we find a CORBA object and, once we've found it, how do we use it? To make it easier to understand, we are going to answer the second question first.

CORBA can pass object references across the network by creating a string of bytes called an **interoperable object reference (IOR)**. This object reference is the data needed by the ORB to locate and access the CORBA object within the network. We'll see why it is called an 'interoperable' object reference in a little while.

The IOR is an encoded sequence containing several pieces of information about the CORBA object that, from the programmer's perspective, are not very important because they aren't used directly by the programmer. It is, however, worth noting that an IOR can be thought of as encapsulating following elements:

❑   **Hostname** – The name of the host on which the server is running. If you run the server on a new host, the previously published IOR of an object gets invalidated.

❑   **Port number** – The port number on which the server listens for incoming requests. If you rerun a server, the previously published IOR may become invalidate.

❑   **Object key** – A unique key for a particular instance of an object.

The ORB uses the data from the IOR to direct method invocations from our client application to the CORBA object. Once the IOR is obtained, we are free to use the CORBA object (through the proxy object provided by the IDL skeleton) without regard for its actual location in the network. Thus, it is the responsibility of the ORB to direct our invocations properly.

Since we've now introduced the object reference, let's discuss how to retrieve one. The CORBA architecture provides several mechanisms for obtaining object references, the most common of which are:

❑   Using an object location service, such as the OMG Naming Service

❑   Recreating an object reference from its string form

❑   Receiving an object reference from another CORBA object

Although there are others, we'll concentrate on these three mechanisms here. To begin with, let's discuss object location services.

Object Location Services

In general, an object location service is any source that provides object references upon request. Most common, however, is the OMG-defined Naming Service. The OMG has defined a set of common object services that are most likely to be needed within distributed systems. This set of services is called the **CORBAServices**.

The most prominent and commonly used of these services is the **Naming Service**. It is itself a CORBA object, which provides the ability to associate a string name with an object reference. When a CORBA object is created, its object reference is added to the Naming Service under some well-known name. When a client needs to access the CORBA object, it queries the Naming Service for the object reference associated with the well-known name. Once the client receives the object reference, it can then begin to interact with the CORBA object. Note that the CORBA Naming Service is very similar in functionality to a JNDI naming service.

An Object Reference's String Form

The second mechanism that a client may use is to reconstruct an object reference from its string form. An object reference's string form is the entire contents of its internal data serialized into a string data type. To do this, we can make use of two methods that are accessible through the CORBA implementation's ORB object. An object reference can be converted to its string form by invoking the ORB's object_to_string() method. To reconstruct this string into the original object reference, we can use the string_to_object() method. This mechanism can be utilized in a similar fashion to the object location service described above:

❑ First, the CORBA object upon creation would create the string form of its object reference using the ORB and then copy this string to an agreed-upon location, such as a file or database record.

❑ Next, when the client needs the object reference, it can obtain the string from this agreed-upon location and convert it back to the original object reference.

Object References Returned from Other CORBA Objects

The third mechanism that a client may use to obtain an object reference is to invoke a method on a CORBA object that returns an object reference, similar to the Naming Service we saw earlier. This is possible because IDL interfaces can define attributes, parameter types, and return types that are themselves object references. However, this implies that the client already has an object reference, so this mechanism cannot be used until the client has already obtained an object reference through some other mechanism.

Other Ways of Obtaining an Object Reference

In addition to these methods, many CORBA implementations provide their own non-CORBA-compliant object location mechanisms that will provide clients with object references. Although these are certainly acceptable, they are not CORBA-compliant, and therefore cause our source code to become ORB vendor-specific. This may cause difficulties if porting among different vendor's CORBA products is necessary.

The object location mechanisms, along with the encapsulation of information within the object reference, provide one of the major benefits of using CORBA – object location transparency. These object location mechanisms act as intermediaries between the client and the CORBA object. Using the Naming Service as an example, the CORBA object publishes its object reference to a Naming Service and the client, in turn, retrieves it from the Naming Service. Since the object reference encapsulates the network location of the CORBA object, this allows the client to access the CORBA object without explicit knowledge of where it resides in the network. When a CORBA object is moved to a different location within the network, it will only need to update its object reference within the Naming Service. From that point on, clients will use the new object reference just as they did the previous one, ignorant of the fact that the CORBA object has moved.

ORB Interoperability

We have briefly introduced the data that the ORB requires to locate and access a CORBA object in the form of an interoperable object reference (IOR). We must therefore discuss the notion of **ORB Interoperability** and provide a clearer definition. What this means simply is that clients running within one ORB are not restricted to accessing only the CORBA objects running within the same ORB. ORB Interoperability ensures that a client running in one ORB may interact with any CORBA object running within any other ORB; provided of course that network connectivity exists.

The reason why this functionality is possible is because all CORBA-compliant ORBs are required to interact using the OMG-defined Internet Inter-ORB Protocol (IIOP). This requirement forces all ORBs, regardless of platform or vendor, to speak the same language when interacting with each other. Since every CORBA object in a CORBA-compliant architecture is referenced using an IOR, these object references are valid and meaningful regardless of the ORB in which they originated, and regardless of the ORB in which they are being used.

Extending our diagram of our distributed application to include ORB interoperability, we now have:

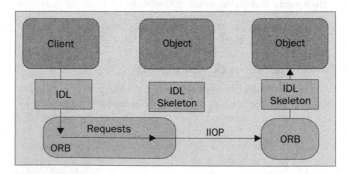

Benefits of CORBA

Distributed applications built using the CORBA architecture enjoy several benefits:

❑ **Language independence**
Clients and objects can interact regardless of the programming language used to implement each. This feature is not possible with EJBs.

❑ **Location transparency**
Similar to EJBs, clients and objects are not directly aware of their respective locations within the network, allowing relocation of one (or both) without impacting on theother.

❑ **Support for heterogeneous networks**
Due to the platform ndependence of the CORBA architecture and support from many different vendors, CORBA-compliant products and frameworks exist for most operating systems and hardware platforms (like Java and EJB), allowing CORBA applications to span many different types of computers, from small handhelds to large mainframes.

❑ **Interoperability**
Clients and objects running within ORBs from different vendors can communicate just as if they were located within the same ORB. This feature is also available with EJBs.

For more information about CORBA itself, visit the CORBA web site at http://www.corba.org. There you can find the specifications that we've spoken about as well as links to additional references and implementations.

CORBA Example

Before we begin examining how to use CORBA and EJBs together, let's take a look at a simple pure CORBA example. Since Java is the language used in developing EJBs, we'll ease the transition of learning CORBA by using Java as the programming language for both the client and server applications. For our ORB, we can make use of the JavaIDL ORB that is bundled with the Sun JDK. This is a basic "Hello World" type example designed as a starting point for those who are unfamiliar with CORBA development. It consists of a Java server application containing an object that exposes a single method in its IDL interface and a Java client that invokes this method.

Let's start with the IDL interface.

The Example IDL Interface

Our CORBA object will expose one method, namely `hello()`, that takes a string as an input parameter and returns a string as its return type. We'll save this interface in a file named `Test.idl`:

```
#if !defined TEST_IDL
#define TEST_IDL

interface Test
{
  string hello(in string name);
};

#endif
```

This interface is compiled using the IDL-to-Java compiler, `idlj` provided as part of the JDK. This will generate the Java stubs and skeletons necessary to build our client and server applications. To compile this interface, run the following command:

```
idlj -fall Test.idl
```

The `-fall` option instructs the IDL compiler to generate both client stubs and server skeletons. More specifically, this will create the `_TestImplBase` class, which is used as the base of our `Test` implementation class. It will also create the `Test` interface (derived from a `TestOperations` interface) that the client application will use to access the CORBA object and the `TestHelper` class that will provide the `narrow()` method we'll use when recreating the IOR from a text string.

For more information on how IDL is mapped to Java, please see the IDL-to-Java mapping specification provided by the OMG.

Given this IDL interface and the generated code we just created, we now need to create the implementation object that exposes this interface.

The Example Implementation Object

Our implementation object will extend the _TestImplBase class generated by the IDL compiler:

```
class TestImpl extends _TestImplBase {
  public String hello(String name) {
    System.out.println("Received a request for name '" + name + "'");
    return "Hello " + name;
  }
}
```

The implementation object will echo the input string in the return string, verifying that everything is working correctly. Once we have the CORBA object implementation completed, we'll need to create a CORBA server to contain the object.

The Example CORBA Server

The CORBA server can be thought of as the container for our CORBA object. There are several steps that we must perform in coding the server class. First, we must initialize the ORB class by calling ORB.init(). Then we instantiate the CORBA object implementation. Once this is done, we must make the IOR of the implementation object available for clients. To expose our CORBA object's IOR, we will create the string form of the IOR using the ORB and write it to a text file, making it available to any clients who are interested. Finally, we can wait for incoming requests. The code for our server is as follows:

```
import org.omg.CORBA.*;
import org.omg.CosNaming.*;
import java.io.*;

class TestServer {
  public static void main(String args[]) {
    try {

      // Retrieve objectIORfile from command line arguments
      if (args.length == 0) {
        System.err.println("Usage : TestServer <objectIORfile>");
        System.exit(-1);
      }
      String iorFile = args[0];

      // Initialize ORB
      ORB orb = ORB.init(args, null);

      // Create Test implementation object
      System.out.println("Creating Test object");
      TestImpl impl = new TestImpl();
      orb.connect(impl);

      // Write Test object reference to text file
      String ior = orb.object_to_string(impl);
      FileWriter fw = new FileWriter(iorFile);
      fw.write(ior);
      fw.close();
```

```
      // Wait for incoming requests
      System.out.println("Ready to accept requests");
      java.lang.Object syncObj = new java.lang.Object();
      synchronized (syncObj) {
        syncObj.wait();
      }
    } catch (Exception e) {
      System.err.println("Exception caught : " + e);
      e.printStackTrace(System.err);
    }
  }
}
```

The next stage is to construct our client application.

The Example Client

Our client application obtains the IOR string of the remote object from the file written by our server, recreates the object reference, and invokes the method. Note that the IOR retrieved from the string_to_object() method is of type org.omg.CORBA.Object. To convert this to a Test object, we must use the TestHelper.narrow() method:

```
import org.omg.CORBA.*;
import org.omg.CosNaming.*;
import java.io.*;

class TestClient {
  public static void main(String args[]) {
    Test testObj = null;

    try {

      // Retrieve objectIORfile from command line arguments
      if (args.length == 0) {
        System.err.println("Usage : TestClient <objectIORfile>");
        System.exit(-1);
      }
      String iorFile = args[0];

      // Initialize ORB
      ORB orb = ORB.init(args, null);

      // Read TestObject IOR from file and recreate IOR
      System.out.println("Retrieving object IOR from " + iorFile);
      BufferedReader reader = new BufferedReader(new FileReader(iorFile));
      String ior = reader.readLine();

      org.omg.CORBA.Object obj = orb.string_to_object(ior);
      testObj = TestHelper.narrow(obj);
    } catch (Exception e) {
      System.err.println(e.getMessage());
    }

    try {

      // Invoke method on remote object
      String result = testObj.hello("CORBAClient");
      System.out.println("Response from server : " + result);
```

```
            // Release object resources when finished
            testObj._release();
        } catch (Exception e) {
            System.err.println(e.getMessage());
        }
    }

}
```

Building the CORBA Client and Server

To avoid confusion and possible overwriting of files, especially with the introduction of generated source code, it is usually best to keep the client, server, and IDL-generated source code separated into their own subdirectories. With this in mind, a possible directory structure (in Windows) for the above example could be as follows:

Directory	Files
C:\CORBAsample\Client	TestClient.java
C:\CORBAsample\Server	TestImpl.java
	TestServer.java
C:\CORBAsample\IDL	Test.idl

After compiling the client, server, and generated Java files, we are ready to test our example.

Running the CORBA Example

To run this example, start the CORBA server as follows (from the \Server folder):

```
java -classpath .;..\IDL TestServer objectior.txt
```

You should see the following output from the server application:

When the server starts, it creates the Test object's IOR file, in our case in a file called objectior.txt. Here's a look at the "stringified" IOR that is created by the server (you'll probably get something slightly different):

```
IOR:000000000000000d49444c3a546573743a312e30000000000000000001000000000000000054000101
000000000d3139322e3136382e312e3931000005750000018afabcafe0000000217ddcc5500000008
000000000000000000000001000000010000001400000000000010020000000000000101000000000
```

Once the server is running, we can start the CORBA client as follows (from the Client folder):

```
java -classpath .;..\IDL TestClient ..\Server\objectior.txt
```

You should see the following output from the client application:

```
C:\WINDOWS\System32\cmd.exe                               _ □ ×
Microsoft Windows 2000 [Version 5.00.2195]
(C) Copyright 1985-2000 Microsoft Corp.

C:\ProEJB\Chapter20\CORBAsample\Client>java -classpath .;..\IDL
TestClient ..\Server\objectior.txt
Retrieving object IOR from ..\Server\objectior.txt
Response from server : Hello CORBAClient

C:\ProEJB\Chapter20\CORBAsample\Client>
```

And, to prove that the server has received a request, the following line should be output from the server application:

```
C:\WINDOWS\System32\cmd.exe - java -classpath .;..\IDL TestServer objecti...  _ □ ×
C:\ProEJB\Chapter20\CORBAsample\Server>java -classpath .;..\IDL
TestServer objectior.txt
Creating Test object
Ready to accept requests
Received a request for name 'CORBAClient'
```

In this example we have seen how simple CORBA can be. Using a Java client, we have invoked a method from the IDL interface of an object contained within a Java server application. Next we will turn our attention to using CORBA to access EJBs.

Accessing EJBs using CORBA

Before we begin writing our client application, let's pause for a moment and examine how this CORBA-to-EJB communication is possible. After all, at the surface it may appear that CORBA clients and EJBs are incompatible.

So far, we have seen the following inconsistencies between the CORBA and EJB frameworks:

❑ In our CORBA example, all communication between client and server via CORBA is specified by an interface defined in IDL. Our EJBs don't have IDL interfaces. All EJB communication is specified by interfaces defined in Java.

❑ We also know from our overview of CORBA that messages pass between client and server using the IIOP protocol. However, our EJB messages are achieved through the use of Java RMI, which may not have been using the IIOP protocol.

So how is this integration possible? Given the above, you may begin to think that accessing EJBs from CORBA clients is not impossible. In fact, initially it wasn't possible, until the introduction of a few new specifications, as well as a few changes to existing specifications that combined to open up EJBs to clients outside the Java programming language. More specifically, these specifications (and their associated URL links) are:

- ❑ The Java Language Mapping to OMG IDL Specification (http://www.omg.org/technology/documents/formal/java_language_mapping_to_omg_idl.htm)

- ❑ Object-by-Value parameter passing (http://cgi.omg.org/cgi-bin/doc?formal/99-10-07)

- ❑ The RMI over IIOP specification (http://java.sun.com/j2se/1.3/docs/guide/rmi-iiop/index.html)

These specifications pull the CORBA and EJB distributed frameworks together, allowing us to overcome the above inconsistencies as follows:

- ❑ The Java-to-IDL language mapping specification details how to convert a Java interface, such as the remote interface of an EJB or an RMI object, into an IDL interface.

- ❑ This language mapping from Java to IDL requires the adoption of Object-by-Value parameter passing to the CORBA specification in order to support passing of complex types in and out of interface methods.

- ❑ The RMI over IIOP specification (RMI-IIOP) defines how to issue Java RMI invocations using the IIOP protocol.

Although compliance with these specifications is becoming very common, as an architect or developer you need to be concerned that the above specifications have been implemented in the tools and platforms you choose to use.

The RMI over IIOP specification and the Java-to-IDL language mapping are implemented as part of the `rmic` compiler included with J2SE version 1.3. Using the `rmic` compiler you can generate either IIOP or JRMP stubs for your EJB (or RMI object). You can also use the `rmic` compiler to generate IDL interfaces from your existing Java interfaces. Also note that many application server products provide their own compiler tools. Consult the vendor's documentation if any compliance-related questions arise. In practice, this is rarely an issue.

The Objects-by-Value specification was added to version 2.3.1 of the CORBA specification, which has been implemented in the latest versions of many of the ORB products available today. However, use of an ORB product compliant with an earlier version of the specification may prevent use of the IDL interface generated from your EJB (or RMI object) remote interfaces.

If your choice of products (or lack of choice, as is often the case) does not support these specifications, we will outline a technique for working around this problem below.

An EJB Example

Now that we've seen a simple Java CORBA client to Java CORBA object example, let's get started on the Enterprise JavaBean part of our CORBA to EJB example. We'll develop an Enterprise JavaBean that accepts log messages from its clients and writes these messages to the EJB container's log file.

Here are the EJB remote and home interfaces:

The Remote Interface: LoggerBean

```
import javax.ejb.EJBObject;
import java.rmi.RemoteException;

public interface LoggerBean extends EJBObject {

  public boolean log(String level, String appName,
                     String message) throws RemoteException;
}
```

The Home Interface: LoggerBeanHome

```
import javax.ejb.EJBHome;
import javax.ejb.CreateException;
import java.rmi.RemoteException;

public interface LoggerBeanHome extends EJBHome {

  public LoggerBean create() throws CreateException, RemoteException;
}
```

The Bean Implementation Class: LoggerBeanImpl

Here is the implementation of our EJB:

```
import javax.ejb.SessionBean;
import javax.ejb.SessionContext;
import java.rmi.RemoteException;

import weblogic.logging.NonCatalogLogger;

public class LoggerBeanImpl implements SessionBean {

  public LoggerBeanImpl() {}

  public boolean log(String level, String appName,
                     String message) throws RemoteException {

   NonCatalogLogger logger = new NonCatalogLogger(appName);

    if (level.equalsIgnoreCase("info")) {
      logger.info(message);
    } else if (level.equalsIgnoreCase("warning")) {
      logger.warning(message);
    } else if (level.equalsIgnoreCase("error")) {
      logger.error(message);
    } else {
      logger.debug(message);
    }

    return true;
  }

  public void ejbCreate() {}
  public void ejbRemove() {}
  public void ejbActivate() {}
  public void ejbPassivate() {}
  public void setSessionContext(SessionContext sc) {}
}
```

To access the WebLogic Server's log file, we will use the `NonCatalogLogger` class. It provides several methods for writing log messages of varying levels, namely info, warning, error, and debug.

Building and Deploying the EJB

Once we have our code written, there are several steps that we'll need to perform to deploy into the WebLogic server. The WebLogic server installation includes several example web applications. For simplicity, we'll deploy our EJB into one of these apps, namely, the 'examples' app.

For further information regarding installing and deploying with WebLogic, refer to Appendix C.

Before building and deploying the EJB, run the `setExamplesEnv` script in the `config\examples` directory of the WebLogic Server installation. This will set up the path and other environment variables WebLogic needs to run, and also make sure that `weblogic.jar` is in our classpath – we'll need to reference this in order to compile our beans.

Now we can build our EJB. There are two deployment descriptors that are needed for deploying the EJB. The first is the normal `ejb-jar.xml` and can be configured as follows:

```xml
<?xml version="1.0"?>

<!DOCTYPE ejb-jar PUBLIC
        '-//Sun Microsystems, Inc.//DTD Enterprise JavaBeans 1.1//EN'
        'http://java.sun.com/j2ee/dtds/ejb-jar_1_1.dtd'>

<ejb-jar>
  <enterprise-beans>
    <session>
      <ejb-name>LoggerBean</ejb-name>
      <home>LoggerBeanHome</home>
      <remote>LoggerBean</remote>
      <ejb-class>LoggerBeanImpl</ejb-class>
      <session-type>Stateless</session-type>
      <transaction-type>Container</transaction-type>
    </session>
  </enterprise-beans>
  <assembly-descriptor>
    <container-transaction>
      <method>
        <ejb-name>LoggerBean</ejb-name>
        <method-intf>Remote</method-intf>
        <method-name>*</method-name>
      </method>
      <trans-attribute>Required</trans-attribute>
    </container-transaction>
  </assembly-descriptor>
</ejb-jar>
```

The next deployment descriptor, which is specific to WebLogic, is called `weblogic-ejb-jar.xml`, and can be set up as follows:

```xml
<?xml version="1.0"?>

<!DOCTYPE weblogic-ejb-jar PUBLIC
        '-//BEA Systems, Inc.//DTD WebLogic 5.1.0 EJB//EN'
        'http://www.bea.com/servers/wls510/dtd/weblogic-ejb-jar.dtd'>
```

```
<weblogic-ejb-jar>
  <weblogic-enterprise-bean>
    <ejb-name>LoggerBean</ejb-name>
    <caching-descriptor>
      <max-beans-in-free-pool>10</max-beans-in-free-pool>
    </caching-descriptor>
    <jndi-name>LoggerBeanHome</jndi-name>
  </weblogic-enterprise-bean>
</weblogic-ejb-jar>
```

Once we've created our JAR file, we can create the EJB stub code and deploy:

```
java -classpath %WL_HOME%\lib\weblogic.jar weblogic.ejbc -compiler javac
     loggerbean.jar %WL_HOME%\config\examples\applications\loggerbean.jar
```

Testing the LoggerBean EJB

Before we attempt to access this bean via CORBA, let's verify that everything is working correctly by constructing and running an EJB client application:

```java
import java.rmi.RemoteException;
import javax.rmi.PortableRemoteObject;

import javax.ejb.CreateException;
import javax.ejb.RemoveException;

import javax.naming.Context;
import javax.naming.InitialContext;
import javax.naming.NamingException;

import java.util.Properties;

public class Client {

  private LoggerBeanHome home;
  private static final String JNDI_NAME = "LoggerBeanHome";

  public Client(String url) throws NamingException {

    // Use the JNDI to retrieve the LoggerBean Home interface
    Context ctx = null;
    try {

      // Get an InitialContext
      Properties h = new Properties();
      h.put(Context.INITIAL_CONTEXT_FACTORY,
            "weblogic.jndi.WLInitialContextFactory");
      h.put(Context.PROVIDER_URL, url);
      ctx = new InitialContext(h);
    } catch (NamingException ne) {
      System.err.println("Unable to get initial context of server at "
                         + url);
      throw ne;
    }

    try {
      Object homeObj = ctx.lookup(JNDI_NAME);
      home = (LoggerBeanHome) (PortableRemoteObject.narrow(homeObj,
             LoggerBeanHome.class));
```

943

```
      } catch (NamingException ne) {
        System.err.println("Failure looking up " + JNDI_NAME);
        throw ne;
      }
  }

  public void test()
          throws CreateException, RemoteException, RemoveException {

    System.out.println("Creating a LoggerBean");
    LoggerBean logger =
      (LoggerBean) (PortableRemoteObject.narrow(home.create(),
                                                LoggerBean.class));
    boolean result;

    result = logger.log("info", "LoggerBeanClient",
                        "This is an 'info' message");
    result = logger.log("warning", "LoggerBeanClient",
                        "This is a 'warning' message");
    result = logger.log("error", "LoggerBeanClient",
                        "This is an 'error' message");
    result = logger.log("debug", "LoggerBeanClient",
                        "This is a 'debug' message");

    System.out.println("Removing the LoggerBean");
    logger.remove();
  }

  public static void main(String[] args) throws Exception {

    System.out.println("\nBeginning LoggerBean Client\n");
    String url = null;

    // Parse the argument list
    if (args.length != 1) {
      System.out.println("Usage: java Client t3://hostname:port");
      return;
    } else {
      url = args[0];
    }

    Client client = null;
    try {
      client = new Client(url);
    } catch (NamingException ne) {
      System.exit(1);
    }

    try {
      client.test();
    } catch (Exception e) {
      System.err.println("Exception caught while using the LoggerBean.");
      System.err.println(e);
    }

    System.out.println("\nEnd LoggerBean Client\n");
  }

}
```

After compiling, to run the client, enter the following at the system prompt:

```
java -classpath .;.\build;%WL_HOME%/lib/weblogic.jar Client
    t3://localhost:7001
```

The `t3://localhost:7001` *identifies the location of the WebLogic Server to allow the client access to the JNDI naming directory.*

The results output from the `Client` application should resemble the following:

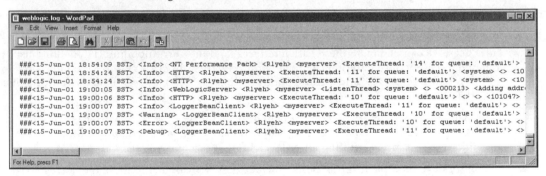

If we check the end of the `weblogic.log` file in the log directory of our server, we should see similar results to those in the following screenshot:

Now that we have successfully developed and deployed our EJB, our next step is to examine how CORBA clients and EJBs are able to interact.

C++ CORBA Client

We will be using ORBacus 4.0.5 for C++ from Object Oriented Concepts as the ORB product for our C++ client. This ORB product is compliant with the CORBA 2.3 standard, and therefore supports the Objects-by-Value specification allowing us complete access to our EJB via an IDL interface.

There are several steps that we need to perform in order to construct our client application. First we'll use the EJB's home and remote interfaces to generate the IDL interfaces of our EJB. Next we'll discuss how to modify these generated IDL interfaces to simplify compilation. Once we've created our final IDL interface file(s), we will use an IDL-to-C++ compiler to generate C++ header and source files from the IDL files. Finally, we will code our C++ client application, compile it, and link these C++ files together to build our client application executable.

Creating the IDL

In order to build a CORBA client that can access our EJB, we'll need to create an IDL interface on which our client application can invoke its methods. To generate the IDL interfaces, we'll use the `ejbc` compiler provided as part of the WebLogic server installation. Working with the JAR file we created earlier during the compilation of our EJB, we can generate the IDL using the following command from within your source code directory:

```
java -classpath %WL_HOME%\lib\weblogic.jar weblogic.ejbc -idl -idlOverwrite
    -idlDirectory .\IDL loggerbean.jar loggerbeanidl.jar
```

Since we have already deployed our EJB, the `loggerbeanidl.jar` file created above is not of much interest to us. Running the above command will create an IDL directory containing quite a few interface definitions. Remember that our EJB interfaces extend base EJB interfaces. In addition, some of the methods of these interfaces make use of classes within the Java API, for example `javax.ejb.CreateException`. Note that the Java-to-IDL compiler generates IDL interface definitions for every Java interface/class visible from your EJB's remote interfaces.

Simplifying the IDL Compilation

Compiling all of the above IDL interfaces can be very tedious, due to the numerous files that are created. Although this is sometimes necessary, if you don't expect to use certain parts of an interface or if you don't need any of the methods defined in base interfaces, it is possible to simplify the compilation process by making several pre-compilation modifications to the IDL.

To simplify our IDL definitions, we can do the following:

❑ Since we will not be directly invoking the methods defined in the `EJBObject` and `EJBHome` interfaces, we can eliminate these base interfaces (and the corresponding IDL definitions) by removing the interface inheritance in the `LoggerBean` and `LoggerBeanHome` interfaces (in `.IDL\LoggerBean.idl` and `.IDL\LoggerBeanHome.idl`), as seen below in our modified IDL definitions.

❑ Removing the `printStackTrace()` methods from the `Throwable` interface definition (in `.\IDL\java\lang\Throwable.idl`) will eliminate the need to compile most of the IDL definitions that coincide with the lower-level `java.lang` and `javax.ejb` packages.

❑ When we have multiple levels of nested include files, we can merge these into a single IDL file to reduce the include search path that must be specified when compiling. An example of this is our `LoggerBeanHome` interface file that includes the `CreateEx` file. `CreateEx.idl` in turn includes the `CreateException.idl` file, and so on. We can merge these files into one file to make our include search path simpler.

Applying the first two steps will reduce the needed IDL files to the following set of IDL files:

❑ `LoggerBean.idl`
❑ `LoggerBeanHome.idl`
❑ `CreateEx.idl`
❑ `CreateException.idl`
❑ `_Exception.idl`
❑ `Throwable.idl`

The contents of these files can be merged into a single file as shown below. It is important to ensure that all definitions are defined before being used, for example since `LoggerBeanHome` references `LoggerBean`, make sure to include the `LoggerBean` definition first. If, as in some cases, this is impossible, you must then add forward reference statements to the IDL file. To do this, simply add a line including the name of the interface, exception, etc. followed by a semicolon. For example, to create a forward reference for `LoggerBean` before the definition of `LoggerBeanHome`, add the following line to the IDL:

```
// Forward reference for LoggerBean
interface LoggerBean;

// Interface definition for LoggerBeanHome, which references LoggerBean
interface LoggerBeanHome { ... };

// Interface definition for LoggerBean
interface LoggerBean{ ... };
```

Below are the IDL definitions merged into a single file called `LoggerBean.idl`. Note that the definitions have been ordered such that forward references are not necessary:

```
#include "orb.idl"

//**********************************************************
// Throwable valuetype definition

#ifndef ___java_lang_Throwable
#define ___java_lang_Throwable

module java {
module lang {
  valuetype Throwable {
    readonly attribute ::CORBA::WStringValue localizedMessage;

    readonly attribute ::CORBA::WStringValue message;

    factory create__CORBA_WStringValue(in ::CORBA::WStringValue arg0);
    factory create__();
    ::CORBA::WStringValue toString();

#pragma ID Throwable "RMI:java.lang.Throwable:A348DE9411E6EEEA:D5C635273977B8CB"

};
};
};

#endif

//**********************************************************
// Exception valuetype definition

#ifndef ___java_lang__Exception
#define ___java_lang__Exception

module java {
module lang {
  valuetype _Exception : ::java::lang::Throwable {
    factory create__CORBA_WStringValue(in ::CORBA::WStringValue arg0);
    factory create__();
```

```
#pragma ID _Exception "RMI:java.lang.Exception:4C2F1EED1A593904:D0FD1F3E1A3B1CC4"

};
};
};

#endif

//********************************************************************
// CreateException valuetype definition

#ifndef ___javax_ejb_CreateException
#define ___javax_ejb_CreateException

module javax {
module ejb {
  valuetype CreateException : ::java::lang::_Exception {
    factory create__CORBA_WStringValue(in ::CORBA::WStringValue arg0);
    factory create__();

#pragma ID CreateException
"RMI:javax.ejb.CreateException:7C78AA9E9FB0D1B7:575FB6C03D49AD6A"

};
};
};

#endif

//********************************************************************
// CreateEx exception definition

#ifndef ___javax_ejb_CreateEx
#define ___javax_ejb_CreateEx

module javax {
module ejb {
exception CreateEx {
    CreateException value;

};
};
};

#endif

//********************************************************************
// LoggerBean interface definition

#ifndef ___LoggerBean
#define ___LoggerBean


interface LoggerBean{

    boolean log(in ::CORBA::WStringValue arg0,
                in ::CORBA::WStringValue arg1,
                in ::CORBA::WStringValue arg2);

#pragma ID LoggerBean "RMI:LoggerBean:0000000000000000"
```

```
};

#endif

//*********************************************************
// LoggerBeanHome interface definition

#ifndef  ___LoggerBeanHome
#define  ___LoggerBeanHome

interface LoggerBeanHome {
    ::LoggerBean create() raises (::javax::ejb::CreateEx);

#pragma ID LoggerBeanHome "RMI:LoggerBeanHome:0000000000000000"

};

#endif
```

Compiling the IDL

Once the above is complete, we can compile the IDL file into C++ stub files. This is done to provide C++ source code that our client application can use when attempting to access the EJB. Note that since we are only interested in the client-side CORBA stubs, we can use the `--no skeletons` option on the IDL compiler provided with the ORBacus installation.

Assuming that your ORBacus installation is located in `C:\OOC`, the following commands executed from within the generated IDL directory will compile our newly modified IDL into the necessary C++ stub classes:

```
set PATH=c:\OOC\OB-4.0.5\bin;%PATH%
set OOCIDL=c:\OOC\OB-4.0.5\idl
idl -I%OOCIDL% -I%OOCIDL%\OB --output-dir .\.. --no-skeletons *.idl
```

The `--output-dir` option will allow you to direct the newly created files to a separate directory. In our case we want to create our source files one directory up from our IDL directory created earlier, hence the use of the `-output-dir .\..` option. Given that our IDL interface file is named `LoggerBean.idl`, the compilation above will generate two files, `LoggerBean.h` and `LoggerBean.cpp`.

Creating the C++ Client

Now that we have our C++ stub files, we can write our C++ CORBA client. We will obtain our `LoggerBeanHome` object reference using the `CosNaming` interface of the WebLogic server. This is simply a CORBA Naming Service interface exposed by the WebLogic Server naming service usually accessed via JNDI. To do this, we'll make use of the `host2ior` utility of the Weblogic server:

```
java -classpath %WL_HOME%\lib\weblogic.jar utils.host2ior localhost 7001
    > wl-ior.txt
```

The `wl-ior.txt` file will contain the following:

```
IOR:000000000000002849444c3a6f6d672e6f72672f436f734e616d696e672f4e616d696e67436f6e
746578743a312e3000000000001000000000000000700001010000000a3132372e302e302e31001b59
0000003800574c53000000010000002849444c3a6f6d672e6f72672f436f734e616d696e672f4e616d6d
696e67436f6e746578743a312e30000000080000000100000010000001400000000000100200000
0000000101000000000
```

IOR for IIOP/SSL:
```
IOR:000000000000002849444c3a6f6d672e6f72672f436f734e616d696e672f4e616d696e67436f6e
746578743a312e3000000000001000000000000000ec0001010000000a3132372e302e302e31001b5a
0000003800574c53000000010000002849444c3a6f6d672e6f72672f436f734e616d696e672f4e616d6d
696e67436f6e746578743a312e300000000008000000030000000100000140000000000010020000
0000000101000000000000000190000006200000000000005a68747470733a2f2f3132372e302e30
2e313a373030312f636c61737365732f44656661756c745765624170705f6578616d706c6573536572
7665724044656661756c745765624170705f6578616d706c65735365727665722f0000000000001400
0000080000013a013a1b5a
```

We are only interested in the first IOR, so we'll create a new file, called `ior.txt`, containing only the first IOR above. Our client can convert this text (using `string_to_object()`) into a CORBA object reference and then narrow (the CORBA equivalent of casting) it into a Naming Service context object reference.

Here is the client source code, which we'll save in a file called `Client.cpp` in the same directory in which we have just created our C++ stub files:

```cpp
#include <OB/CORBA.h>
#include <OB/CosNaming.h>
#include <stdlib.h>

// Header files generated by compiling IDL

#include <LoggerBean.h>
#include <CreateException.h>

#ifdef HAVE_STD_IOSTREAM
using namespace std;
#endif

int run(CORBA::ORB_ptr orb, int argc, char* argv[])
{
    // Get NamingService Context object

  cout << "Retrieving the root naming context" << endl;

  CORBA::Object_var obj = orb->string_to_object("relfile:/ior.txt");
  if(CORBA::is_nil(obj))
  {
  cerr << argv[0] << ": cannot read IOR from ior.txt" << endl;
  return EXIT_FAILURE;
  }

  CosNaming::NamingContext_var rootnc =
                          CosNaming::NamingContext::_narrow(obj.in());
  if(CORBA::is_nil(rootnc.in()))
  {

    cerr << argv[0] <<
    ": IOR is not a NamingContext object reference" << endl;
    return EXIT_FAILURE;
  }
```

```cpp
const char *objName = "LoggerBeanHome";

CosNaming::Name name;
name.length(1);
name[0].id = CORBA::string_dup(objName);
name[0].kind = CORBA::string_dup("");

LoggerBeanHome_var home = LoggerBeanHome::_nil();

try {

  cout << "Resolving the name " << objName <<
      " in the NamingService" << endl;

  obj = rootnc->resolve(name);

  home = LoggerBeanHome::_narrow(obj.in());

  if(CORBA::is_nil(home.in()))
  {
    cerr << argv[0] << ": retrieved IOR is not a LoggerBeanHome object "
                                          << "reference" << endl;
    return EXIT_FAILURE;
  }
} catch(const CosNaming::NamingContext::NotFound&) {
  cerr << "CosNaming::NamingContext::NotFound caught" << endl;
}

try {
  cout << "Retrieving a LoggerBean from the LoggerBeanHome object" <<
  endl;

  LoggerBean_var bean = home->create();

  if(CORBA::is_nil(bean.in()))
  {

    cerr << argv[0] <<
        ": failed to retrieve a LoggerBean from the LoggerBeanHome object"
        << endl;

    return EXIT_FAILURE;
  }

  CORBA::WStringValue_var infolevel =
        new CORBA::WStringValue(CORBA::wstring_dup(L"info"));

  CORBA::WStringValue_var warnlevel =
        new CORBA::WStringValue(CORBA::wstring_dup(L"warning"));

  CORBA::WStringValue_var errorlevel =
        new CORBA::WStringValue(CORBA::wstring_dup(L"error"));

  CORBA::WStringValue_var appName =
        new CORBA::WStringValue(CORBA::wstring_dup(L"C++Client"));

  CORBA::WStringValue_var infomsg =
        new CORBA::WStringValue(
            CORBA::wstring_dup(L"This is an info message"));
```

```
        CORBA::WStringValue_var warnmsg =
            new CORBA::WStringValue(
                CORBA::wstring_dup(L"This is a warning message"));

        CORBA::WStringValue_var errormsg =
            new CORBA::WStringValue(
                CORBA::wstring_dup(L"This is an error message"));

        cout << "Invoking the log method on EJB" << endl;

        bean->log(infolevel, appName, infomsg);
        bean->log(warnlevel, appName, warnmsg);
        bean->log(errorlevel, appName, errormsg);

    } catch(javax::ejb::CreateEx &ex) {
        cerr << "javax::ejb::CreateEx caught : " << ex._to_string() << endl;
    }

    return EXIT_SUCCESS;
}

int main(int argc, char* argv[], char*[])
{
    int status = EXIT_SUCCESS;
    CORBA::ORB_var orb;

    try {
        orb = CORBA::ORB_init(argc, argv);
        orb->register_value_factory(javax::ejb::CreateException::_OB_id(),
                                    new CreateExceptionFactoryImpl);

        status = run(orb, argc, argv);
    } catch(const CORBA::Exception& ex) {
        cerr << ex << endl;
        status = EXIT_FAILURE;
    }

    if(!CORBA::is_nil(orb)) {
        try {
            orb -> destroy();
        } catch(const CORBA::Exception& ex) {
            cerr << ex << endl;
            status = EXIT_FAILURE;
        }
    }

    return status;
}
```

Before we can build our client, we have one more bit of work to do. As you can see in the merged IDL file (LoggerBean.idl), there is a CORBA valuetype named CreateException, which is declared this way:

```
module javax {
module ejb {
    valuetype CreateException : ::java::lang::_Exception {
        factory create__CORBA_WStringValue(in ::CORBA::WStringValue arg0);
        factory create__();
```

```
#pragma ID CreateException
"RMI:javax.ejb.CreateException:7C78AA9E9FB0D1B7:575FB6C03D49AD6A"

};
};
};
```

CORBA valuetypes are the means by which CORBA implements the Object-by-Value specification. The IDL valuetype is used to pass state data over the wire. This is of concern to us because CORBA valuetypes require an implementation of the valuetype and a factory mechanism to be created for each target programming language that the IDL definition is applied to. As a result, we will need to provide an implementation and factory for the CreateException valuetype.

For simplicity, we can place both the implementation and factory into one header and one source file. The header file for the implementation and factory is shown below. We'll call this file CreateException.h and again place in the same directory as our other C++ source files:

```cpp
#if !defined CREATE_EXCEPTION_H
#define CREATE_EXCEPTION_H

#include <LoggerBean.h>

class CreateExceptionImpl : public OBV_javax::ejb::CreateException,
              public virtual CORBA::DefaultValueRefCountBase
{
public:

  CORBA::ValueBase* _copy_value();

  CORBA::WStringValue* localizedMessage();
  CORBA::WStringValue* message();
  CORBA::WStringValue* toString();

};

class CreateExceptionFactoryImpl : public javax::ejb::CreateException_init
{
public:
  CreateExceptionFactoryImpl();

  virtual ~CreateExceptionFactoryImpl();

  javax::ejb::CreateException*
                    create__CORBA_WStringValue(CORBA::WStringValue* arg0);

  javax::ejb::CreateException* create__();

  CORBA::ValueBase* create_for_unmarshal();
};

#endif
```

Here is the source file for CreateException.cpp, and we will once more place it in our C++ source files directory:

```
#include <OB/CORBA.h>
#include <CreateException.h>

CORBA::ValueBase* CreateExceptionImpl::_copy_value()
{
  CreateExceptionImpl* result = new CreateExceptionImpl;
  return result;
}

CORBA::WStringValue* CreateExceptionImpl::localizedMessage()
{
  return new CORBA::WStringValue(
                    CORBA::wstring_dup(L"javax::ejb::CreateException"));
}

CORBA::WStringValue* CreateExceptionImpl::message()
{
  return new CORBA::WStringValue(
                    CORBA::wstring_dup(L"javax::ejb::CreateException"));
}

CORBA::WStringValue* CreateExceptionImpl::toString()
{
  return new CORBA::WStringValue(
                    CORBA::wstring_dup(L"javax::ejb::CreateException"));
}

CreateExceptionFactoryImpl::CreateExceptionFactoryImpl()
{
}

CreateExceptionFactoryImpl::~CreateExceptionFactoryImpl()
{
}

javax::ejb::CreateException*
        CreateExceptionFactoryImpl::create__CORBA_WStringValue(
                                        CORBA::WStringValue* arg0)
{
  return new CreateExceptionImpl;
}

javax::ejb::CreateException* CreateExceptionFactoryImpl::create__()
{
  return new CreateExceptionImpl;
}

CORBA::ValueBase* CreateExceptionFactoryImpl::create_for_unmarshal()
{
  return new CreateExceptionImpl;
}
```

Building the Client

All that is left to do now is to build the client application. To ensure that we use the correct libraries that were created as part of our ORBacus build and installation, we'll make use of the base makefile that is provided with the ORBacus installation, namely Make.rules.mak. Following is the makefile (Makefile.mak) for our client application, which is used with the nmake utility. Remember to place this in the same directory as our C++ source files. Note that Makefile.mak contains a variable named top_srcdir that must be set to point into your ORBacus application directory:

```
# Make sure to set the following variable based on
# your ORBacus installation location
top_srcdir = c:\OOC\OB-4.0.5\ob

CLIENT_NAME = client.exe

TARGETS = $(CLIENT_NAME)

!include $(top_srcdir)\..\config\Make.rules.mak

OB_LIBVER   = 405

CXXFLAGS         = $(CXXFLAGS) /GR

OB_CPPFLAGS      = /I$(top_srcdir)\include
OB_IDLFLAGS      = -I$(top_srcdir)\idl
OB_LIBS          = $(top_srcdir)\lib\ob$(LIBSUFFIX).lib
IDL              = $(top_srcdir)\bin\idl.exe
IDLDIR           = $(top_srcdir)\idl

!if "$(DLL)" == "yes"
PATH             = $(top_srcdir)\lib;$(PATH)
!endif

!if "$(WITH_JTC)" == "yes"
OB_CPPFLAGS      = $(OB_CPPFLAGS) /I$(JTC_DIR)\include
OB_LIBS          = $(OB_LIBS) $(JTC_DIR)\lib\jtc$(LIBSUFFIX).lib
OB_DLLLIBS       = $(OB_DLLLIBS) $(JTC_DIR)\lib\jtc$(LIBSUFFIX).lib

!if "$(DLL)" == "yes"
PATH             = $(JTC_DIR)\lib;$(PATH)
!endif

!endif


CLIENT_OBJS = Client.obj LoggerBean.obj CreateException.obj

ALL_CXXFLAGS    = $(CXXFLAGS)
ALL_CPPFLAGS    = /I. /I$(top_srcdir)\..\naming\include $(OB_CPPFLAGS) $(CPPFLAGS)
ALL_LIBS        = $(top_srcdir)\..\naming\lib\CosNaming$(LIBSUFFIX).lib $(OB_LIBS)
$(LIBS)


$(CLIENT_NAME): $(CLIENT_OBJS)
    -del $@
    $(LINK) $(LINKFLAGS) /out:$@ \
    $(CLIENT_OBJS) $(ALL_LIBS)
```

Running the Client

Once built, to execute the client simply type `client` at the command prompt. You should see the following output:

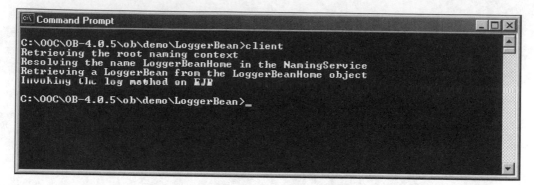

Examining the WebLogic log file, you should see the following entries:

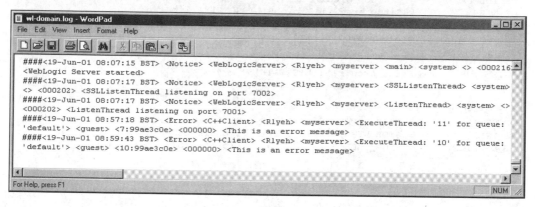

It is important to keep in mind during your development cycle that any changes to the LoggerBean or LoggerBeanHome interfaces in your EJB will require re-creating the IDL interface definitions. This will in turn require re-modifying the IDL (if you chose to do so), recreating the C++ stubs and recompiling the client. Although this is very inconvenient during the development process, this should not be an ongoing problem since once an EJB interface is published it should not change.

An Alternative Solution

When using earlier versions of an ORB product and/or an application server, non-compliance with the latest specifications listed above can create several issues. For example, if your CORBA ORB product does not support the Objects-by-Value specification, your CORBA client will not be able to use the IDL interface generated from your EJB or RMI object. Alternatively, if your application server or SDK does not support RMI over IIOP, the EJB will not be able to understand the messages sent from the CORBA client. Either of these issues will most likely prevent you from using the solution described above. If any of these issues are present, an alternative solution is to build a **bridge server**.

The bridge server, in this case, is a CORBA server developed in Java that acts as an intermediary between the CORBA client and the EJB. The CORBA server can expose a developer-defined IDL interface that is fully supported by the CORBA product. In turn, the CORBA server is implemented using Java so that it can access the EJB through its native Java interfaces and protocol.

Conceptually, you will have the following:

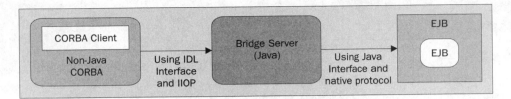

An explicit demonstration of the bridge server technique is beyond the scope of this chapter. We will, however, note that the design of a bridge server consists of three parts: a non-Java CORBA client, a Java CORBA server, and an EJB, each of which we have already built in our earlier examples. Using the bridge server is comparable to implementing the Adapter design pattern. In this case though, we are adapting EJB interfaces to CORBA IDLs.

It is also worth mentioning that from a performance standpoint, the bridge server is not an ideal solution since we have introduced an additional 'hop' for each method invocation that is performed. In a production environment, this is also one additional piece to be monitored and maintained. However, in the absence of an up-to-date ORB and/or application server, this solution will permit connectivity between non-Java clients and EJBs.

Summary

As we have learned throughout this book, Enterprise JavaBeans provide developers with the ability to create server-side components that, once written, can be deployed on almost any platform available. As a result, and as a byproduct of the growing support of Java as a server-grade programming language, EJBs are rapidly becoming the design technique of choice for providing functionality in enterprise applications. In doing so, this begs the question – how do we integrate EJBs with our existing software?

In this chapter, we have established that an effective method of doing so is to couple the platform-independence of EJBs with the language-independence of CORBA. To this end, we have accomplished the following:

❑ Introduced CORBA and used it to build a sample client and server

❑ Discussed how emerging specifications have bridged the gap between the EJB and CORBA frameworks

❑ Accessed an EJB from a CORBA client written in C++

❑ Discussed an alternative approach when support for the latest specification revisions is not present

In the next chapter we'll be taking a look at combining EJBs with wireless applications.

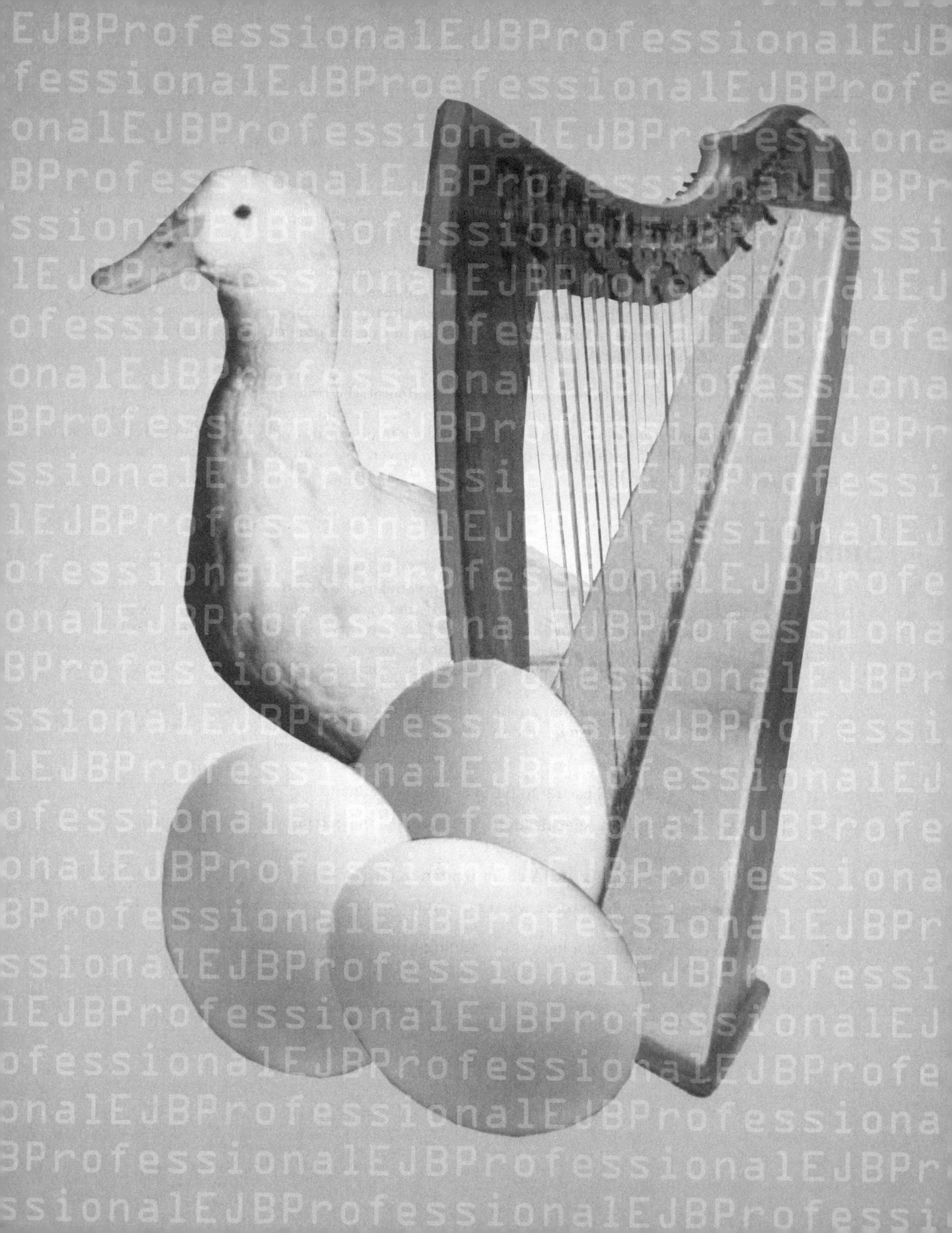
EJBProfessional

21

Wireless EJB Clients

The point of this case study is to highlight that EJBs, and the J2EE architecture in general, can be used to deploy applications to clients other than just the desktop. The world is increasingly becoming mobile with more people accessing services and applications via a wireless device such as a mobile phone, or a personal digital assistants (PDA), and even through embedded systems aboard automobiles to a limited extent.

Already in Japan, there are more people accessing the Internet via a wireless phone than on a desktop, thanks to Japanese wireless giant NTT DoCoMo's successful i-Mode service. DoCoMo (the acronym "DoCoMo" is often interpreted as "Do Communications over Mobile network") is a subsidiary of Japan's telephone operator corporate NTT. First introduced in Japan in February 1999 by NTT DoCoMo, i-Mode is one of the world's most successful services offering wireless web browsing and e-mail from mobile phones in Japan. The number of subscribers to topped 20 million on March 4, 2001 making up almost half of all Internet subscribers in all of Japan. In Finland, the government is removing public pay phones since such a high percentage of their population has a mobile phone, and although they are primarily used for voice services, it will only be a matter of time before users start demanding data services in mass numbers.

Wireless Introduction

Today the media has plenty to say about the wireless wonders that we can expect; but if these services are so desired, why haven't companies been developing them until now? There are a number of factors that are contributing to make the wireless Internet a slow reality:

❑   **Standards**
    Over the past few years, the industry has focused on developing standards that will promote the development of applications. The advent of technologies such as the extensible Markup Language (XML), Wireless Application Protocol (WAP), and Short Message Service (SMS), has reduced the barriers of entry for independent application developers to provide services on a wide scale.

❑ **Bandwidth**
Although currently data services on wireless devices are very disappointing, the introduction of next-generation wireless networks such as General Packet Radio Services (GPRS) and third generation (3G) networks will increase the bandwidth, and move from a circuit-switched network to a packet-based network, all of which should provide for a much better user experience.

Much has been said about the success of DoCoMo's i-Mode and how it is better than WAP. The reality is that i-Mode and WAP are not directly competing – i-Mode is a service that uses cHTML (a compacted form of HTML) for displaying content. WAP on the other hand is a protocol, thus particular implementations of WAP would better suited for a comparison to i-Mode. DoCoMo chose to use cHTML for their i-Mode service because of its ease of conversion from existing web pages; however, in their next service rollout of a 3G network scheduled for October 2001, they will be using WAP 2.0.

WAP

The **Wireless Application Protocol (WAP)** was first developed by the WAP Forum, a consortium including Ericsson, Motorola, Nokia, and OpenWave (formerly Phone.com). The protocol is a collection of specifications outlining protocols for the application, session, transaction, security, and transport layers of a telecommunications network.

WAP was designed to be an open, interoperable, industry-wide specification for use on the widest number of wireless networks and operating systems possible. The WAP protocol uses the **Wireless Markup Language (WML)**, **WMLScript**, and in version 2.0, **XHTML** for presenting information to the user.

WML is a lightweight markup language defined as an XML document. WML like all XML documents, only describes the structure of the data to be displayed, not the way in which the data is to be displayed; later in the chapter we will look at the structure of a valid WML document. WAP also defines a **Wireless Application Environment (WAE)** for displaying information on the client via a user-agent, which is any piece of software (such as a browser) that can retrieve and interpret network referenced content such as WML or WMLScript (similar to JavaScript for HTML).

WAP is a specification that is in ongoing development with version 2.0 now being advocated. To get the latest information visit the WAP forum site at http://www.wapforum.com.

The following table shows how it compares to the Internet Protocol:

Internet Protocol	Wireless Application Protocol
XHTML	Wireless Application Environment (**WAE**)
HTML	Wireless Markup Language (**WML**), WMLScript, XHTML
Javascript	
HTTP	Wireless Session Protocol (**WSP**)
	Wireless Transaction Protocol (**WTP**)
SSL	Wireless Transport Layer Security (**WTLS**)
TCP/IP	WDP, UDP
UDP/IP	SMS, GPRS, USSD, HSCSD, CSD...

In addition, WAP also loosely outlines the hardware architecture. Typically, a client does not communicate directly with the web server; it communicates via a **gateway** (that physically may reside on the same machine as the web server), which translates the communication.

The client makes WAP requests to the gateway, which converts the request to an HTTP request and propagates it to the web server. The web server then responds with an HTTP response to the gateway, which encodes it and delivers a WAP response to the client where it is displayed by the user-agent:

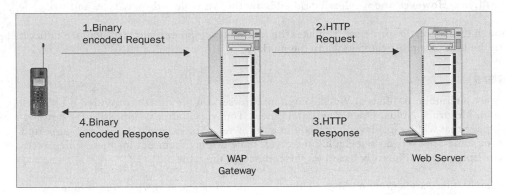

J2EE and Wireless

The J2EE architecture is ideal for the wireless world. The entire architecture of J2EE is designed to separate the presentation from the business logic – the wireless world simply introduces an additional presentation medium. Your application can still model the business in the entity layer, control the business logic in the servlet and session layers, and then finally determine the presentation in the JSP layer by determining the client type.

This simple piece of code can be used to determine the client's user-agent:

```
String clientType = request.getHeader("User-Agent");
if (clientType.indexOf("Nokia7110") {
  ....
}  // Can continue to check for different browsers
```

Thus in the above WAP architecture design, the J2EE server would take the role of the web server, and interact with the WAP gateway. The gateway would provide the wireless client's request to the servlet container, and the JSP container would return its responses to the gateway to be encoded for the client.

The role of the J2EE server is arguably much more important in the wireless world. In the wired world, more processing can be offset to the client as is happening with the peer-to-peer arena today; this is not possible today for wireless, since in comparison, wired devices have much greater processing power.

Design Considerations

Developing for wireless users is still in its infancy. The one key area that WAP has purposely omitted from the protocol is the way in which to display WML on the client. Since wireless devices will be appearing in much more varied forms than the traditional desktop monitor, it makes more sense to leave the task of presenting content to the device itself.

When a device receives a WML document (known as a **deck**, which is separated into **cards** like individual pages in a web site), its browser can determine how to display the components that it is able to support, and omit those that it doesn't. In addition, if a particular device has its own standard for displaying components (for example actions), it will be able to make the WML conform to its standard. The difference between browsers can be compared to the WWW in 1996, where users had to develop and test their pages to be viewed on Netscape Navigator and Microsoft Internet Explorer, which were using different HTML versions, and also having to support the large number of text based browsers such as Lynx. However, the wireless world adds another variable – display type and size.

Although this is great in principal, it makes the task of development and testing more difficult at present due to the lack of sophisticated tools on the market.

Browsers

There are a number of different WAP-compliant browsers on the market provided by Microsoft, Ericsson, Motorola, Nokia, OpenWave, and others. Today, it is almost impossible to develop a useful WML page that will be displayed correctly in all browsers. For example, tables are supported in WML; however some browsers do not display them yet, some display them but formatted incorrectly, while others display them differently based on the contents of the table.

Fortunately, there are a great number of emulators out there and it is wise to test your pages on as many of them as possible. You can find a list of emulators from http://www.gelon.net/ – an invaluable site for wireless developer resources. Some of the tools that we prefer are:

- ❑ Nokia Toolkit – http://www.nokia.com/
- ❑ UP.SDK – http://www.openwave.com/
- ❑ Mobile Application Development Kit – http://www.motorola.com/

Finally, you should test your pages on the actual devices prior to launching, since most emulators have slight variances from their actual counterparts.

Usage Analysis

The underlying theme that we are trying to express to you in the last few paragraphs is that the wireless world is a different animal from the wired world. In the last couple of years we have become spoiled with the increased amount of bandwidth available, and developers have no longer had to consider users who cannot download large images. Although user navigation is taken into consideration, the size of individual pages is usually not.

In any case, the design issues for WWW pages are more concerned about the time a user has to spend to find the information they are interested in. The wireless world introduces another complexity here as well. Wireless access is generally much more expensive than wired access; thus if a user downloads a WML deck that contains unnecessary information, they will not be happy since it will directly contribute to their bill.

As we will see, a single WML deck will usually contain multiple cards, which may all be related. In today's networks, connections are **circuit switched connections**, meaning that every request requires the device to re-establish a connection to the server, which takes time. Since the user is charged for the duration of the entire session, rather than the amount of data that is actually retrieved, there is a tradeoff between downloading multiple cards, as opposed to retrieving information as you need it.

The next generation of networks will be packet-based, similar to the TCP/IP protocol, thus the connection time will be reduced, and the user will be charged only for the information that they request, not the duration. Our design will vary depending upon the network that our expected users will be on, and in any case we should concentrate on content over presentation due to the small size of the displays it will be seen on.

The Taxi Service Example

The following example is a simple application relevant to a wireless environment – a location-based service. In this example, the client will request the name of a taxi company that services a given area. The example will show how the J2EE web components can handle requests from a WAP client, process the request using EJBs, and then return a response back to the client formatted in WML.

This example is definitely not comprehensive – it does not deal with any issues such as personalization, user interface constraints, or network capabilities. We will come back to this after the example and discuss what is still lacking.

This example will show the full lifecycle from requirements to implementation.

Requirements

Before we start coding anything, we need to be aware of what is expected from the application. Assume that through further analysis and user requirements gathering, we are able to define the following requirements for the application:

❑   The system will be able to give the taxi service number associated with each area. An area is defined to be a borough within a city. It could be expanded to define a set of postcodes.

❑   The first time the user asks for a taxi, they give the area that will be used as their default.

❑   This is an example, and thus the system will only supply content for a limited area in London (based on the following table). We will assume that there is only one taxi service for each area:

Taxi Company Name	Service Area	Phone Number
Battersea Taxi Company	Battersea	020 7111 1111
Camden Taxi Company	Camden	020 7222 2222
Kensington Taxi Company	Kensington	020 7333 3333
Knightsbridge Taxi Company	Knightsbridge	020 7444 4444
Richmond Taxi Company	Richmond	020 7555 5555
West End Taxi Company	West End	020 7666 6666
Westminster Taxi Company	Westminster	020 7777 7777
Wimbledon Taxi Company	Wimbledon	020 7888 8888

❑ An account should be created for the user, where their phone number is their ID.

❑ The next time the user enters the site the system should return the same taxi name and number that they retrieved on their previous visit to the site.

❑ The user should be able to change their default location after retrieving a match.

❑ We will assume that the user will be accessing the system via a WAP-compliant browser. (We will assume that the user is using a Nokia 7110 phone, which provides access to WAP-based services via an inbuilt WML microbrowser.)

Business Requirements

Let's look at the above requirements and develop the use cases:

1. User accesses site for first time to request a taxi

Basic Course of action:

❑ The user accesses the site by entering their phone number
❑ The user is asked to enter their area
❑ The system searches for a taxi company that serves that area
❑ The system returns the name and number for the taxi firm for the given area

2. The user accesses the site a subsequent time to request for a taxi

Basic Course of action;

❑ The user enters the site and submits their phone number
❑ The system detects that this is a return visit from the phone number
❑ The system automatically returns the same taxi firm name and number as the previous time

Optional extra step;

❑ The user selects to change their default location and resubmit the query

The requirements have been captured in the following use case diagram:

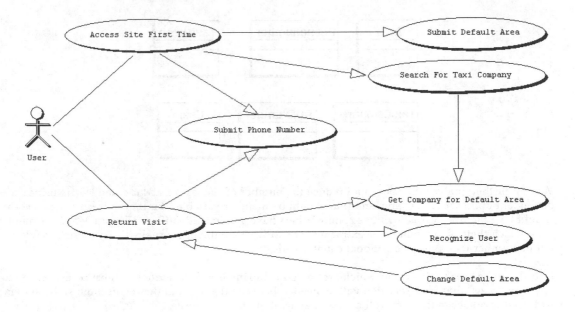

Let's now look at our technical requirements based on the business requirements.

Technical Requirements

In order to simplify the application, we're going to make a few assumptions here:

❑ The user will be accessing the site via mobile WAP-enabled phone, thus we will need to format our response in WML (WAP 2.0 defines XHTML as the markup language for clients; however, at this point, there are few devices that support it). In order to develop and view the pages on your computer you will need to install an emulator and a gateway.

We will use the Nokia WAP Toolkit 2.1 with the Nokia 7110 Simulator, available after registration from http://forum.nokia.com/wapforum/main/1,,1_1_30_2_3,00.html.

The Nokia WAP toolkit offers developers a PC environment for creating, testing, and demonstrating WAP applications. It allows you to configure the suite not to use an external gateway.

❑ We will use the BEA WebLogic 6.0 application server, downloadable for a 30-day trial from http://www.bea.com.

❑ We require a database to store the content. In this example we will use the Cloudscape database that comes with the WebLogic installation.

Let's begin by defining our object model.

Object Model

From our requirements and use cases we can extract the nouns and use them as the starting point for determining our objects:

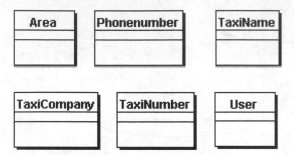

We can further analyze the above and reduce the number of classes. TaxiName and TaxiNumber are dependent upon TaxiCompany, and thus should be member variables. Further more, Phonenumber should be a member variable of User. Subscribers have a unique identifier called an MSISDN number from which their phone number is extracted. The MSISDN number is usually the subscriber's full phone number including international country code.

In order to be able to determine which area a taxi company is able to service, it must be associated to an Area object, thus an association will be needed between them. From the requirements, the system will need to associate the user with a particular area on all return visits.

With these changes, our class diagram will look as follows:

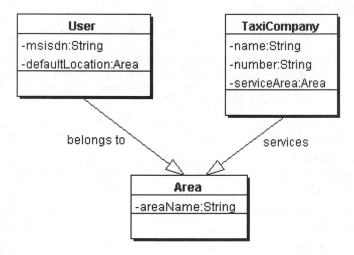

To provide the functionality for this, we will use the J2EE architecture to separate the application using MVC (Model-View-Controller). The following diagram shows the structure we will adhere to:

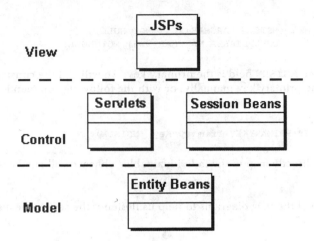

To begin let's create the database. We are fortunate here since we will be creating the database from scratch and will not have any legacy issues to deal with. Our needs are very simple. We can begin by creating the database to directly reflect our object model.

Use the following DDL (Data Definition Language – an industry standard language used to specify a database scheme) to create the tables. We will create three tables, which directly reflect the needs of our object model. Start the `Cloudview` tool using the following command:

```
java COM.cloudscape.tools.cview
```

You will need to have the Cloudscape libraries `cloudscape.jar` and `tools.jar` in your classpath.

Create a new database (We will call ours `exampleDB` and create it in the server directory `C:\bea\wlserver6.0sp2\config\mydomain\applications\database`), and then execute every command separately to create the database tables:

```
CREATE TABLE SERVICEAREAS (AREANAME VARCHAR(255) NOT NULL)
```

We will have to manually add the constraints to the table once we have created it. For the `SERVICEAREAS` table the `AREANAME` field is the primary key; we will call the constraint `AREANAMEPRIMARY`. To create the primary key, you can add it manually with the tool, or execute the following `ALTER` command:

```
ALTER TABLE SERVICEAREAS
    ADD CONSTRAINT AREANAMEPRIMARY Primary Key (AREANAME)
```

The `TAXILOCATIONS` table:

```
CREATE TABLE TAXILOCATIONS (TAXICOMPANYNAME VARCHAR(255) NOT NULL,
                            SERVICEAREA VARCHAR(255) NOT NULL,
                            NUMBER VARCHAR(100))
```

The USERS table:

```
CREATE TABLE USERS (MSISDN VARCHAR(255) NOT NULL,
                    DEFAULTAREA VARCHAR(255) NOT NULL)
```

For the USERS table the MSISDN field is the primary key; we will call the constraint PRIMARYKEY. Again, you can add the primary key manually, or with the following command:

```
ALTER TABLE USERS
    ADD CONSTRAINT PRIMARYKEY Primary Key (MSISDN)
```

Our entity beans will directly map to the individual tables, thus we will need entity beans for User, Area, and TaxiCompany.

Let's now create some of the flow diagrams to help us flesh out the session beans:

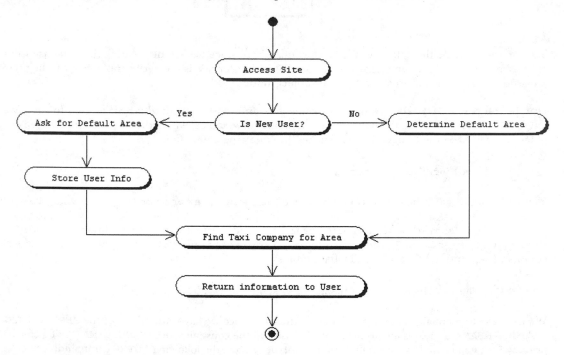

To start, the user enters the site. Whether it is the first time, or a return, we would need a servlet that extracts the necessary information from the request and then passes it on to the session bean layer to determine the control flow. We will call the servlet IndexServlet and the session bean in the session layer CentralController, and since the bean does not need to maintain any state on behalf of the user, we will make it a stateless session bean.

The CentralController bean will need to be able to determine if the user is a first-time user or a return user. If the user is new, the system should request the user to enter their location via another servlet. We will call this servlet UserDetailsServlet.

If the user is a return user, the `CentralController` session bean should determine their associated area, and then extract the taxi name and number from the `TaxiCompany` entity bean and return the information via a servlet. The servlet will be named `TaxiMatchServlet`. The user can then choose to change their location by returning to the `UserDetailsServlet`.

Let's go back to the scenario where the user is a first-time user, and they submit their default area in which they are interested. The servlet that handles the submission should extract the necessary information and again pass it along to the `CentralController` session bean. We will use the same `UserDetailsServlet` to handle the request.

The `CentralController` bean should now create a new `User` entity and save the appropriate information. It will then return the taxi name and number. We can use the same servlet that was used for return users, `TaxiMatchServlet`.

Let's look at the sequence diagrams for the two different scenarios. For the scenario where the user is a first-time user the sequence diagram would be as follows:

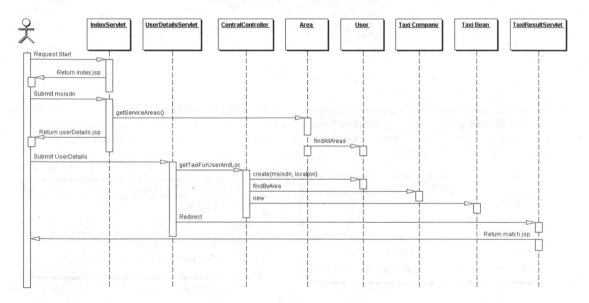

For the scenario where the user is a return user, the sequence diagram would look similar to the following diagram:

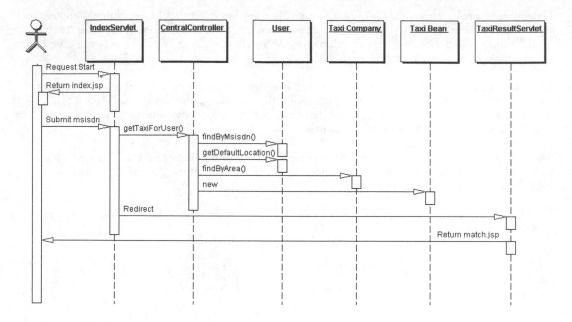

We can use the sequence diagrams to complete our class diagram with methods. We will consolidate the requests for taxi name and taxi number from the `CentralController` into a single method, and we will create another method that will implicitly create a new user. To pass the information back we will create a new class `TaxiBean`:

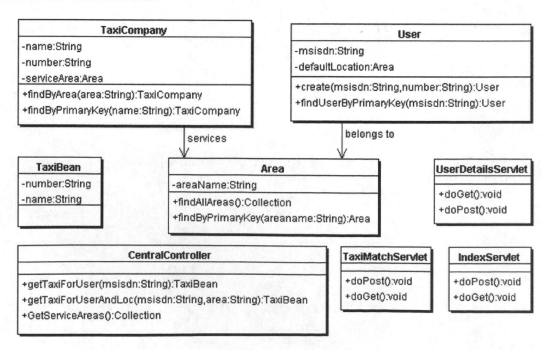

We can now start with the implementation.

Implementation

Let's start with the bntity beans; since we already have the database schema mapped to our object model, this will be very simple.

User

We'll look at the User EJB first, starting with the home interface.

The Home Interface

```
package examples.taxis;

import java.rmi.*;
import javax.ejb.*;

public interface UserHome extends EJBHome {

  public User create(String msisdn, String location)
            throws CreateException, RemoteException;

  public User findByPrimaryKey(String MSISDN)
            throws FinderException, RemoteException;
}
```

The Remote Interface

For our application, we will need to have the ability to retrieve the MSISDN and the defaultLocation, and we will need to be able to change the defaultLocation. To enable this, we will add the appropriate get and set methods:

```
package examples.taxis;

import java.rmi.*;
import javax.ejb.*;

public interface User extends EJBObject {

  public String getMsisdn() throws RemoteException;

  public String getDefaultLocation() throws RemoteException;

  public void setDefaultLocation(String location) throws RemoteException;
}
```

The Bean Implementation

```
package examples.taxis;

import javax.ejb.*;

public class UserBean implements EntityBean {

  private EntityContext ctx;
  public String msisdn;
  public String defaultLocation;
```

```
  public void setEntityContext(EntityContext ctx) {
    this.ctx = ctx;
  }

  public void unsetEntityContext() {
    this.ctx = null;
  }

  public void ejbActivate() {}
  public void ejbPassivate() {}
  public void ejbLoad() {}
  public void ejbStore() {}
  public void ejbRemove() {}

  public String ejbCreate(String msisdn, String location) {
    this.msisdn = msisdn;
    this.defaultLocation = location;
    return msisdn;
  }

  public void ejbPostCreate(String msisdn, String location) {}

  public String getMsisdn() {
    return msisdn;
  }

  public String getDefaultLocation() {
    return defaultLocation;
  }

  public void setDefaultLocation(String location) {
    defaultLocation = location;
  }
}
```

Entry in ejb-jar.xml

The entry in the ejb-jar.xml file is as follows. We can use the phone number of the user as the primary key, but both the msisdn and the defaultLocation need to be maintained by the container:

```xml
<?xml version="1.0"?>

<!DOCTYPE ejb-jar PUBLIC '-//Sun Microsystems, Inc.//DTD Enterprise JavaBeans
1.1//EN' 'http://java.sun.com/j2ee/dtds/ejb-jar_1_1.dtd'>

<ejb-jar>
  <enterprise-beans>

  <entity>
    <ejb-name>UserEntityBean</ejb-name>
    <home>examples.taxis.UserHome</home>
    <remote>examples.taxis.User</remote>
    <ejb-class>examples.taxis.UserBean</ejb-class>
    <persistence-type>Container</persistence-type>
    <prim-key-class>java.lang.String</prim-key-class>
    <reentrant>False</reentrant>
    <cmp-field>
      <field-name>msisdn</field-name>
    </cmp-field>
    <cmp-field>
```

```
        <field-name>defaultLocation</field-name>
      </cmp-field>
      <primkey-field>msisdn</primkey-field>
    </entity>

...

    </enterprise-beans>
</ejb-jar>
```

Area

Now we will take a look at the `Area` EJB.

The Home interface

We will need to add an additional finder method to be able to retrieve all of the supported areas:

```
package examples.taxis;

import java.rmi.*;
import java.util.*;
import javax.ejb.*;

public interface AreaHome extends EJBHome {

  public Area create(String area) throws CreateException, RemoteException;

  public Area findByPrimaryKey(String areaName)
              throws FinderException, RemoteException;

  public Collection findAllAreas()
                    throws FinderException, RemoteException;

}
```

The Remote interface

We only need one method in the remote interface, since there is only one variable that will be maintained:

```
package examples.taxis;

import java.rmi.*;
import javax.ejb.*;

public interface Area extends EJBObject {

  public String getAreaName() throws RemoteException;

}
```

The Bean Implementation

```
package examples.taxis;

import javax.ejb.*;

public class AreaBean implements EntityBean {
```

```
    private EntityContext ctx;
    public String area;

    public void setEntityContext(EntityContext ctx) {
      this.ctx = ctx;
    }

    public void unsetEntityContext() {
      this.ctx = null;
    }

    public void ejbActivate() {}
    public void ejbPassivate() {}
    public void ejbLoad() {}
    public void ejbStore() {}
    public void ejbRemove() {}

    public String ejbCreate(String area) throws CreateException {
      throw new CreateException();   // We do not support creating new areas
    }

    public void ejbPostCreate(String area) {}

    public String getAreaName() {
      return area;
    }
}
```

Entry in ejb-jar.xml

The ejb-jar.xml entry needs to manage the area variable, which is also the primary key:

```
<entity>
  <ejb-name>AreaEntityBean</ejb-name>
  <home>examples.taxis.AreaHome</home>
  <remote>examples.taxis.Area</remote>
  <ejb-class>examples.taxis.AreaBean</ejb-class>
  <persistence-type>Container</persistence-type>
  <prim-key-class>java.lang.String</prim-key-class>
  <reentrant>False</reentrant>
  <cmp-field>
    <field-name>area</field-name>
  </cmp-field>
  <primkey-field>area</primkey-field>
</entity>
```

TaxiCompany

Third on the list is the TaxiCompany EJB.

The Home Interface

This will also need an additional finder method. We need to be able to search for a TaxiCompany based on an area. In our example we have restricted this to one taxi company per area, thus we can make the return type a single class; however, if there were more than one we would need to provide a collection:

```
package examples.taxis;

import java.rmi.*;
import javax.ejb.*;

public interface TaxiCompanyHome extends EJBHome {

  public TaxiCompany create(String name)
                    throws CreateException, RemoteException;

  public TaxiCompany findByPrimaryKey(String name)
                    throws FinderException, RemoteException;

  public TaxiCompany findByArea(String area)
                    throws FinderException, RemoteException;

}
```

The Remote Interface

To keep our classes as simplistic as possible, we will only provide get methods that we know we will need, but if we wanted to provide a comprehensive solution, we would also provide a get method for the area:

```
package examples.taxis;

import java.rmi.*;
import javax.ejb.*;

public interface TaxiCompany extends EJBObject {

  public String getName() throws RemoteException;

  public String getNumber() throws RemoteException;

}
```

The Bean Implementation

```
package examples.taxis;

import javax.ejb.*;

public class TaxiCompanyBean implements EntityBean {

  private EntityContext ctx;
  public String name;
  public String number;

  // Needed to match fields in ejb-jar.xml
  // Needed for container to implement findByArea
  public String serviceArea;

  public void setEntityContext(EntityContext ctx) {
    this.ctx = ctx;
```

```
  }

  public void unsetEntityContext() {
    this.ctx = null;
  }

  public void ejbActivate() {}
  public void ejbPassivate() {}
  public void ejbLoad() {}
  public void ejbStore() {}
  public void ejbRemove() {}

  public String ejbCreate(String name) throws CreateException {
    throw new CreateException("Not Implemented");
  }

  public void ejbPostCreate(String name) {}

  public String getName() {
    return name;
  }

  public String getNumber() {
    return number;
  }
}
```

Entry in ejb-jar.xml

The ejb-jar.xml entry has three variables that it must identify to manage. Usually, you would develop a more robust solution to ensure that the value for area is from the ServiceArea table, but for our purposes we can assume that the submissions have been checked:

```
<entity>
  <ejb-name>TaxiCompanyEntityBean</ejb-name>
  <home>examples.taxis.TaxiCompanyHome</home>
  <remote>examples.taxis.TaxiCompany</remote>
  <ejb-class>examples.taxis.TaxiCompanyBean</ejb-class>
  <persistence-type>Container</persistence-type>
  <prim-key-class>java.lang.String</prim-key-class>
  <reentrant>False</reentrant>
  <cmp-field>
    <field-name>name</field-name>
  </cmp-field>
  <cmp-field>
    <field-name>number</field-name>
  </cmp-field>
  <cmp-field>
    <field-name>serviceArea</field-name>
  </cmp-field>
  <primkey-field>name</primkey-field>
</entity>
```

Now let's move on to the session layer. We only needed one bean in this layer to handle our requests – the CentralController bean.

CentralController

The implementation for this will be straightforward, like the other EJBs in this example.

The Home Interface

```
package examples.taxis;

import java.rmi.*;
import javax.ejb.*;

public interface CentralControllerHome extends EJBHome {

  public CentralController create() throws CreateException, RemoteException;

}
```

The Remote Interface

We will add another method here, which will allow us to obtain all of the areas listed in the database. This will be used to provide a selection to our users. We also will use a new class TaxiBean, which will encapsulate all of the necessary information for a TaxiCompany:

```
package examples.taxis;

import java.rmi.*;
import java.util.*;
import javax.ejb.*;

public interface CentralController extends EJBObject {

  public TaxiBean getTaxiForUser(String msisdn)
              throws NoUserException, RemoteException;

  public TaxiBean getTaxiForUserAndLoc(String msisdn, String location)
              throws RemoteException;

  public Collection getServiceAreas() throws RemoteException;

}
```

The Bean Implementation

```
package examples.taxis;

import java.rmi.*;
import java.util.*;
import javax.ejb.*;
import javax.naming.*;
import javax.rmi.*;

import examples.taxis.*;

public class CentralControllerBean implements SessionBean {

  public void ejbCreate() {}
```

```
public void setSessionContext(SessionContext ctx) {}
public void ejbRemove() {}
public void ejbActivate() {}
public void ejbPassivate() {}

public TaxiBean getTaxiForUser(String msisdn)
               throws NoUserException {
  try {

    // Find user
    UserHome home = (UserHome)PortableRemoteObject
                              .narrow(getHome("UserHome"), UserHome.class);
    User user = home.findByPrimaryKey(msisdn);

    // Find taxi for default location
    TaxiCompanyHome taxiHome = (TaxiCompanyHome)PortableRemoteObject
                        .narrow(getHome("TaxiCompany"), TaxiCompanyHome.class);

    TaxiCompany taxi = taxiHome.findByArea(user.getDefaultLocation());

    return new TaxiBean(taxi.getName(), taxi.getNumber());

  } catch (ObjectNotFoundException onfe) {
    throw new NoUserException();
  } catch (FinderException e) {
    throw new EJBException();
  } catch (NamingException ne) {
    throw new RemoteException(ne.getMessage());
  }
}

public TaxiBean getTaxiForUserAndLoc(String msisdn, String location)
               throws NoUserException {
  try {

    UserHome home = (UserHome)PortableRemoteObject
                              .narrow(getHome("UserHome"), UserHome.class);

    try {
      User user = home.findByPrimaryKey(msisdn);

      // User exists, just change default location
      user.setDefaultLocation(location);
    } catch (FinderException fe) {

      // User does not exist, create new one
      User user = home.create(msisdn, location);
    }

    // Find taxi company
    TaxiCompanyHome taxiHome = (TaxiCompanyHome)PortableRemoteObject
                        .narrow(getHome("TaxiCompany"), TaxiCompanyHome.class);

    TaxiCompany taxi = taxiHome.findByArea(location);

    return new TaxiBean(taxi.getName(), taxi.getNumber());
```

```
      } catch (ObjectNotFoundException onfe) {
        throw new NoUserException();
      } catch (FinderException fe) {
        throw new EJBException(fe);
      } catch (CreateException ce) {
        throw new EJBException(ce);
      } catch (NamingException ne) {
        throw new EJBException(ne);
      }
    }

    public Collection getServiceAreas() {
      Vector returnVector = new Vector();
      try {

        // Get areas from entity beans, and create return Vector
        AreaHome home = (AreaHome)PortableRemoteObject
                            .narrow(getHome("AreaHome"), AreaHome.class);
        Collection c = home.findAllAreas();

        Iterator i = c.iterator();
        while (i.hasNext()) {
          Area currentArea = (Area)i.next();
          returnVector.addElement(currentArea.getAreaName());
        }
      } catch (FinderException fe) {
        throw new EJBException(fe);
      } catch (NamingException ne) {
        throw new EJBException(ne);
      }
      return returnVector;
    }

    // Simply to make things easier
    private Object getHome(String beanName) throws NamingException {
      Context ctx = new InitialContext();
      return ctx.lookup(beanName);
    }
  }
```

Additional Exception Class

We use the following exception class:

```
package examples.taxis;

public class NoUserException extends Exception {

  public NoUserException() {}
}
```

Additional JavaBean

We also used a bean, TaxiBean, which is defined as follows:

```
package examples.taxis;

import java.io.*;

public class TaxiBean implements Serializable {
  private String name;
  private String number;

  public TaxiBean(String name, String number) {
    this.name = name;
    this.number = number;
  }

  public String getName() {
    return name;
  }

  public String getNumber() {
    return number;
  }
}
```

Entry in ejb-jar.xml

The `ejb-jar.xml` file should look as follows. Ensure that you specify that it is a stateless session bean:

```
<session>
    <ejb-name>CentralControllerSessionBean</ejb-name>
    <home>examples.taxis.CentralControllerHome</home>
    <remote>examples.taxis.CentralController</remote>
    <ejb-class>examples.taxis.CentralControllerBean</ejb-class>
    <session-type>Stateless</session-type>
    <transaction-type>Container</transaction-type>
</session>
```

The WML Documents

Before looking at the servlets, let's look at the necessary WML (Wireless Markup Language) to be sent back to the client. The client you are developing this for has decided that they would like to have WML designers specifically for the front-end look and feel. The designer does not have any knowledge of Java, and thus you will be given the mock-ups in plain WML format.

As discussed earlier, a WML document is an XML document, and thus it must follow the same rules. First, the file must specify the XML version and DTD that it is for followed by the body of the document. The body of the WML file is comprised of a single deck specified by the <wml> tag, which contains one or more cards specified by the <card> tag.

A WML browser downloads an entire deck, and displays a single card at a time. The text to be displayed must be inside a paragraph element <p> within the <card> tag.

For submitting forms, we will use the <do> tag. This tag may have an attribute type defined. In addition the <go> tag may also be defined. The <go> tag will indicate how to submit the information to the server (POST or GET) and the resource to retrieve. The <go> tag is similar to the <form> tag in HTML. The input variables are submitted via the <postfield> tag.

We will need an initial page named index.wml, which will simply ask for the user's phone number using the <input> tag, and submit the information through the <postfield> tag.

index.wml

```
<?xml version="1.0"?>
<!DOCTYPE wml PUBLIC "-//WAPFORUM//DTD WML 1.1//EN"
                     "http://www.wapforum.org/DTD/wml_1.1.xml">

<wml>
  <card>
    <p align="center">
    Enter your Mobile Phone Number
    <do type="accept" label="GetTaxi">
      <go method="post" href="Index">
        <postfield name="msisdn" value="$(number)"/>
      </go>
    </do>
    <input name="number"/>
    </p>
  </card>
</wml>
```

We will also need a page for user input named userDetails.wml – allowing the user to register for the first time.

userDetails.wml

```
<?xml version="1.0"?>
<!DOCTYPE wml PUBLIC "-//WAPFORUM//DTD WML 1.1//EN"
                     "http://www.wapforum.org/DTD/wml_1.1.xml">

<wml>
  <card id="register" title="Register">
  <p>
  Submit your info:
    <do type="confirm" label="Register User">
      <go method="post" href="UserDetails">
        <postfield name="msisdn" value="$(userNumber)" />
        <postfield name="area" value="$(userLocation)" />
      </go>
    </do>

  Your Number:
  <input name="userNumber"/>
  Areas:
  <select name="userLocation" title="Areas">
  <option value="someValue">someName</option>
  </select>
  </p>
  <do type="prev" label="Back">
    <prev/>
  </do>
  </card>
</wml>
```

Finally, we will need a page to display the result of a query; we will call this match.wml.

match.wml

```
<?xml version="1.0"?>
<!DOCTYPE wml PUBLIC "-//WAPFORUM//DTD WML 1.1//EN"
                     "http://www.wapforum.org/DTD/wml_1.1.xml">
<wml>
  <card id="match" title="Match">
  <p>
  For your area:<br/>
  Tel: <b>TaxiName</b><br/>
  Name: <b>TaxiNumber</b> <br/>
  </p>
  <do type="prev" label="Back">
    <prev/>
  </do>
  </card>
</wml>
```

Serving our WML Content

We will be serving our pages via JSP so we can embed our logic within the pages and change the extensions.

index.Jsp

For the index.wml file, we do not need to add any logic; however, since it will be parsed by the JSP container, we need to change the content type. To do this we use the `<page contentType>` directive at the top of the page and rename the index.wml file to index.jsp:

```
<%@ page contentType="text/vnd.wap.wml" %>
```

userDetails.jsp

The userDetails.wml requires a bit more code. The page will need to allow the user to select the area to be used as their default area. We will assume that our servlet will provide a Collection containing all of the areas in the request object (we will see later that it does!). We need to add to the file the `<page contentType>` directive and the `<page import>` directive for the Collection. We also assume that the request contains the number that was input on the initial page:

```
<%@ page contentType="text/vnd.wap.wml" %>
<%@ page import="java.util.Iterator" %>
```

We also need to add the code to extract the Collection from the Request object. We also check to see if the number is already contained in the Session object:

```
<%
String num = (String)session.getAttribute("msisdn");
Iterator i = (Iterator)request.getAttribute("areas"); %>
```

Lastly, we need to modify the `<select>` tag to use the values in the Collection. The final page userDetails.jsp should look as follows:

```
<?xml version="1.0"?>
<!DOCTYPE wml PUBLIC "-//WAPFORUM//DTD WML 1.1//EN"
                     "http://www.wapforum.org/DTD/wml_1.1.xml">

<%@ page contentType="text/vnd.wap.wml" %>
<%@ page import="java.util.Iterator" %>

<%
String num = (String)session.getAttribute("msisdn");
Iterator i = (Iterator)request.getAttribute("areas"); %>

<wml>
  <card id="register" title="Register">
  <p>
  Submit your info:
    <do type="confirm" label="Register User">
      <go method="post" href="UserDetails">
        <postfield name="msisdn" value="$(userNumber)" />
        <postfield name="area" value="$(userLocation)" />
      </go>
    </do>

  Your Number:
  <input name="userNumber" value="<%=num%>"/>
  Areas:
  <select name="userLocation" title="Areas">
  <% while (i.hasNext()) {
      String currentElement = (String)i.next(); %>
      <option value="<%=currentElement%>"><%=currentElement%></option>
  <% } %>
  </select>
  </p>
  <do type="prev" label="Back">
    <prev/>
  </do>
  </card>
</wml>
```

We will also need to make some modifications to the match.wml file.

match.jsp

The resulting JSP, match.jsp, will assume that the servlet layer has provided the match in the Request object, as two separate strings – one for the name of the taxi company, and another for the phone number. Again, we will need to add the <page contentType> directive, and the code to extract the two values that we need. We will also add a <do> tag for going back to the userDetails.jsp to change locations. The resulting JSP, match.jsp will look as follows:

```
<%@ page contentType="text/vnd.wap.wml" %>

<?xml version="1.0"?>
<!DOCTYPE wml PUBLIC "-//WAPFORUM//DTD WML 1.1//EN"
                     "http://www.wapforum.org/DTD/wml_1.1.xml">
```

```
<% String name = (String)request.getAttribute("CompanyName");
   String number = (String)request.getAttribute("CompanyNumber"); %>

<wml>
  <card id="match" title="Match">
  <p>
  For your area:<br/>
  Tel: <b><%=number%></b><br/>
  Name: <b><%=name%></b> <br/>
  <do type="accept" label="Change Location">
   <go method="get" href="UserDetails" />
  </do>
  </p>
  <do type="prev" label="Back">
    <prev/>
  </do>
  </card>
</wml>
```

Lastly let's look at our servlets.

IndexServlet

The IndexServlet will be the start point for the application. On a GET request, it will simply forward the request to index.jsp.

On a POST, it will extract the values it is looking for and use them to retrieve a TaxiBean from the CentralController session bean. If the user (msisdn attribute) does not exist, then a NoUserException is thrown, and the servlet forwards to the userDetails.jsp. Before doing so, the servlet retrieves a vector of all supported areas from the CentralController and attaches an Iterator to the Request object.

If the user does exist, then the CentralController bean will return a matching TaxiBean object. The servlet will then forward the bean and request to the TaxiMatchServlet:

```
package examples.taxis;

import java.io.*;
import java.util.*;
import javax.naming.*;
import javax.servlet.*;
import javax.servlet.http.*;

public class IndexServlet extends HttpServlet {

  public void doGet(HttpServletRequest req, HttpServletResponse res)
            throws ServletException, IOException {

    getServletContext().getRequestDispatcher("/index.jsp").forward(req, res);
  }

  public void doPost(HttpServletRequest req, HttpServletResponse res)
            throws ServletException, IOException {
```

```
        HttpSession session = req.getSession();
        String msisdn = (String) req.getParameter("msisdn");

        // Save for other servlets
        session.setAttribute("msisdn", msisdn);
        TaxiBean bean = null;

        try {
          Context ctx = new InitialContext();
          CentralControllerHome home = (CentralControllerHome)
                                       ctx.lookup("CentralController");
          CentralController control = home.create();
          try {
            bean = control.getTaxiForUser(msisdn);
          } catch (NoUserException ne) {

            // User does not exist, send back userDetails
            // Need to include serviceAreas
            Collection c = control.getServiceAreas();
            req.setAttribute("areas", c.iterator());
            RequestDispatcher dispatcher =
                    getServletContext().getRequestDispatcher("/userDetails.jsp");
            dispatcher.forward(req, res);
            return;
          }
        } catch (Exception e) {
          e.printStackTrace();            // Should have better error handling
        }

        // Include in session to be available to other servlets
        session.setAttribute("bean", bean);
        RequestDispatcher dispatcher =
                getServletContext().getRequestDispatcher("/TaxiResult");
        dispatcher.forward(req, res);
      }
    }
```

UserDetailsServlet

The UserDetailsServlet accepts the post from the userDetails.jsp file. It expects that the user has provided a phone number and an area. If an error occurs, we simply forward to an error page, error.jsp. In practice you would have better control. If a successful registration and match occurs, the servlet forwards the resulting TaxiBean and request to the TaxiMatchServlet:

```
package examples.taxis;

import java.io.*;
import java.util.*;
import javax.naming.*;
import javax.servlet.*;
import javax.servlet.http.*;

public class UserDetailsServlet extends HttpServlet {
```

```java
public void doGet(HttpServletRequest req, HttpServletResponse res)
              throws ServletException, IOException {

  HttpSession session = req.getSession();

  // If the msisdn is already known, use it.
  String msisdn = (String) session.getAttribute("msisdn");
  try {
    Context ctx = new InitialContext();
    CentralControllerHome home = (CentralControllerHome)ctx
                                      .lookup("CentralController");
    CentralController control = home.create();
    Collection c = control.getServiceAreas();
    req.setAttribute("areas", c.iterator());
    RequestDispatcher dispatcher = getServletContext()
                              .getRequestDispatcher("/userDetails.jsp");
    dispatcher.forward(req, res);
    return;
  } catch (Exception e) {
    RequestDispatcher dispatcher = getServletContext()
                                .getRequestDispatcher("/error.jsp");
    dispatcher.forward(req, res);
    return;
  }
}

public void doPost(HttpServletRequest req, HttpServletResponse res)
              throws ServletException, IOException {

  HttpSession session = req.getSession();
  String msisdn = (String) req.getParameter("msisdn");
  session.setAttribute("msisdn", msisdn);  // In case the user modified it
  String area = (String) req.getParameter("area");

  TaxiBean bean = null;

  try {
    Context ctx = new InitialContext();
    CentralControllerHome home = (CentralControllerHome)ctx
                                  .lookup("CentralController");
    CentralController control = home.create();
    bean = control.getTaxiForUserAndLoc(msisdn, area);
  } catch (Exception e) {
    RequestDispatcher dispatcher = getServletContext()
                                  .getRequestDispatcher("/error.jsp");
    dispatcher.forward(req, res);
    return;
  }

  // Include in session to be available to other servlets
  session.setAttribute("bean", bean);
  RequestDispatcher dispatcher = getServletContext()
                                  .getRequestDispatcher("/TaxiResult");
  dispatcher.forward(req, res);
}
}
```

TaxiMatchServlet

The `TaxiMatchServlet` simply extracts a `TaxiBean` from the request, determines the values for the name and phone number, embeds them into the request object, and then forwards it to `match.jsp`. We could have done this directly in both the `UserDetailsServlet` and `IndexServlet`, but it is cleaner to do this here. It allows the control over formatting to be kept in one place:

```
package examples.taxis;

import java.io.*;
import javax.servlet.*;
import javax.servlet.http.*;

public class TaxiMatchServlet extends HttpServlet {

  public void doPost(HttpServletRequest req, HttpServletResponse res)
            throws ServletException, IOException {

    TaxiBean bean = (TaxiBean) req.getSession().getAttribute("bean");
    req.setAttribute("CompanyName", bean.getName());
    req.setAttribute("CompanyNumber", bean.getNumber());

    RequestDispatcher dispatcher = getServletContext()
                                       .getRequestDispatcher("/match.jsp");
    dispatcher.forward(req, res);
  }
}
```

Packaging and Deploying

We will provide the entire application as a single EAR file. We will first need to package the EJBs into a JAR file, and the web components into a WAR file.

Additional Files for BEA WebLogic 6.0

For deploying in BEA WebLogic 6.0, you will need these additional files for deployment in the META-INF directory. If you are going to use another server, note the JNDI names, the container-managed fields, and the finder method declarations that I have used here – you will need them for deploying to the server that you choose, so that the rest of this example works with it.

weblogic-ejb-jar.xml

```
<?xml version="1.0"?>

<!DOCTYPE weblogic-ejb-jar PUBLIC
        '-//BEA Systems, Inc.//DTD WebLogic 5.1.0 EJB//EN'
        'http://www.bea.com/servers/wls510/dtd/weblogic-ejb-jar.dtd'>

<weblogic-ejb-jar>
  <weblogic-enterprise-bean>
    <ejb-name>CentralControllerSessionBean</ejb-name>
    <caching-descriptor>
      <max-beans-in-free-pool>100</max-beans-in-free-pool>
```

```xml
      </caching-descriptor>
      <jndi-name>CentralController</jndi-name>
</weblogic-enterprise-bean>

<weblogic-enterprise-bean>
   <ejb-name>UserEntityBean</ejb-name>
   <caching-descriptor>
     <max-beans-in-cache>1000</max-beans-in-cache>
   </caching-descriptor>
   <persistence-descriptor>
     <persistence-type>
       <type-identifier>WebLogic_CMP_RDBMS</type-identifier>
       <type-version>5.1.0</type-version>
       <type-storage>META-INF/weblogic-user-rdbms-jar.xml</type-storage>
     </persistence-type>
     <persistence-use>
       <type-identifier>WebLogic_CMP_RDBMS</type-identifier>
       <type-version>5.1.0</type-version>
     </persistence-use>
   </persistence-descriptor>
   <jndi-name>UserHome</jndi-name>
</weblogic-enterprise-bean>

<weblogic-enterprise-bean>
   <ejb-name>AreaEntityBean</ejb-name>
   <caching-descriptor>
     <max-beans-in-cache>1000</max-beans-in-cache>
   </caching-descriptor>
   <persistence-descriptor>
     <persistence-type>
       <type-identifier>WebLogic_CMP_RDBMS</type-identifier>
       <type-version>5.1.0</type-version>
       <type-storage>META-INF/weblogic-area-rdbms-jar.xml</type-storage>
     </persistence-type>
     <persistence-use>
       <type-identifier>WebLogic_CMP_RDBMS</type-identifier>
       <type-version>5.1.0</type-version>
     </persistence-use>
   </persistence-descriptor>
   <jndi-name>AreaHome</jndi-name>
</weblogic-enterprise-bean>

<weblogic-enterprise-bean>
   <ejb-name>TaxiCompanyEntityBean</ejb-name>
   <caching-descriptor>
     <max-beans-in-cache>1000</max-beans-in-cache>
   </caching-descriptor>
   <persistence-descriptor>
     <persistence-type>
       <type-identifier>WebLogic_CMP_RDBMS</type-identifier>
       <type-version>5.1.0</type-version>
       <type-storage>META-INF/weblogic-tc-rdbms-jar.xml</type-storage>
     </persistence-type>
     <persistence-use>
       <type-identifier>WebLogic_CMP_RDBMS</type-identifier>
       <type-version>5.1.0</type-version>
```

```
        </persistence-use>
      </persistence-descriptor>
      <jndi-name>TaxiCompany</jndi-name>
    </weblogic-enterprise-bean>
</weblogic-ejb-jar>
```

weblogic-area-rdbms-jar.xml

```xml
<!DOCTYPE weblogic-rdbms-bean PUBLIC
    '-//BEA Systems, Inc.//DTD WebLogic 5.1.0 EJB RDBMS Persistence//EN'
    'http://www.bea.com/servers/wls510/dtd/weblogic-rdbms-persistence.dtd'>
<weblogic-rdbms-bean>
  <pool-name>CaseStudyPool</pool-name>
  <table-name>ServiceAreas</table-name>
  <attribute-map>
    <object-link>
      <bean-field>area</bean-field>
      <dbms-column>areaname</dbms-column>
    </object-link>
  </attribute-map>
  <finder-list>
    <finder>
      <method-name>findAllAreas</method-name>
      <finder-query><![CDATA[(isNotNull area )]]></finder-query>
    </finder>
  </finder-list>

  <options>
    <use-quoted-names>false</use-quoted-names>
  </options>
</weblogic-rdbms-bean>
```

weblogic-tc-rdbms-jar.xml

```xml
<!DOCTYPE weblogic-rdbms-bean PUBLIC
    '-//BEA Systems, Inc.//DTD WebLogic 5.1.0 EJB RDBMS Persistence//EN'
    'http://www.bea.com/servers/wls510/dtd/weblogic-rdbms-persistence.dtd'>
<weblogic-rdbms-bean>
  <pool-name>CaseStudyPool</pool-name>
  <table-name>TaxiLocations</table-name>
  <attribute-map>
    <object-link>
      <bean-field>name</bean-field>
      <dbms-column>taxicompanyname</dbms-column>
    </object-link>
    <object-link>
      <bean-field>number</bean-field>
      <dbms-column>number</dbms-column>
    </object-link>
    <object-link>
      <bean-field>serviceArea</bean-field>
      <dbms-column>servicearea</dbms-column>
    </object-link>
  </attribute-map>
  <finder-list>
    <finder>
```

```
            <method-name>findByArea</method-name>
            <method-params>
              <method-param>java.lang.String</method-param>
            </method-params>
            <finder-query><![CDATA[(= serviceArea $0)]]></finder-query>
          </finder>
        </finder-list>
        <options>
          <use-quoted-names>false</use-quoted-names>
        </options>
      </weblogic-rdbms-bean>
```

weblogic-user-rdbms-jar.xml

```
<!DOCTYPE weblogic-rdbms-bean PUBLIC
    '-//BEA Systems, Inc.//DTD WebLogic 5.1.0 EJB RDBMS Persistence//EN'
    'http://www.bea.com/servers/wls510/dtd/weblogic-rdbms-persistence.dtd'>
<weblogic-rdbms-bean>
  <pool-name>CaseStudyPool</pool-name>
  <table-name>USERS</table-name>
  <attribute-map>
    <object-link>
      <bean-field>msisdn</bean-field>
      <dbms-column>MSISDN</dbms-column>
    </object-link>
    <object-link>
      <bean-field>defaultLocation</bean-field>
      <dbms-column>DEFAULTAREA</dbms-column>
    </object-link>
  </attribute-map>
</weblogic-rdbms-bean>
```

Packaging Our Application

As you remember, we need to package our EJB components into a JAR file, and our web components into a WAR file. We'll deal with the JAR file first.

Creating the JAR File

The required files for the EJB JAR are as follows:

```
examples/
        taxis/
              Area.class
              AreaBean.class
              AreaHome.class
              CentralController.class
              CentralControllerBean.class
              CentralControllerHome.class
              NoUserException.class
              TaxiBean.class
              TaxiCompany.class
              TaxiCompanyBean.class
              TaxiCompanyHome.class
              User.class
              UserBean.class
```

```
              UserHome.class
META-INF/
        ejb-jar.xml
        weblogic-area-rdbms-jar.xml
        weblogic-ejb-jar.xml
        weblogic-tc-rdbms-jar.xml
        weblogic-user-rdbms-jar.xml
```

Create the JAR file and name it unDeployedBeans.jar, then compile the JAR for deployment using the following command (ensure that you have included weblogic.jar, and weblogic_sp.jar, if necessary, in your classpath). From within the classes directory execute the following command line:

```
    java weblogic.ejbc unDeployedBeans.jar CentralController.jar
```

Creating the WAR File

A WAR file contains the files for the web tier of an applications, thus all JSPs and servlets must be included. The files we'll be including in the WAR are as follows:

```
index.jsp
match.jsp
userDetails.jsp
WEB-INF/
        web.xml
        classes/
                examples/
                        taxis/
                                Area.class
                                AreaHome.class
                                CentralController.class
                                CentralControllerHome.class
                                IndexServlet.class
                                NoUserException.class
                                TaxiBean.class
                                TaxiCompany.class
                                TaxiCompanyHome.class
                                TaxiMatchServlet.class
                                User.class
                                UserDetailsServlet.class
                                UserHome.class
```

The web.xml file is as follows. Note the JNDI names given to the servlets; they must match those that were used in the JSP files. In addition, you must add the MIME type mappings to support WML. In WebLogic this is done in this file:

```
<?xml version="1.0" ?>
<!DOCTYPE web-app PUBLIC
        "-//Sun Microsystems, Inc.//DTD Web Application 1.2//EN"
        "http://java.sun.com/j2ee/dtds/web-app_2_2.dtd">
<web-app>
  <servlet>
    <servlet-name>IndexServlet</servlet-name>
    <servlet-class>examples.taxis.IndexServlet</servlet-class>
  </servlet>
  <servlet-mapping>
    <servlet-name>IndexServlet</servlet-name>
```

```
      <url-pattern>Index</url-pattern>
    </servlet-mapping>

    <servlet>
      <servlet-name>UserDetailsServlet</servlet-name>
      <servlet-class>examples.taxis.UserDetailsServlet</servlet-class>
    </servlet>
    <servlet-mapping>
      <servlet-name>UserDetailsServlet</servlet-name>
      <url-pattern>UserDetails</url-pattern>
    </servlet-mapping>

    <servlet>
      <servlet-name>TaxiMatchServlet</servlet-name>
      <servlet-class>examples.taxis.TaxiMatchServlet</servlet-class>
    </servlet>
    <servlet-mapping>
      <servlet-name>TaxiMatchServlet</servlet-name>
      <url-pattern>TaxiResult</url-pattern>
    </servlet-mapping>

    <mime-mapping>
      <extension>wml</extension>
      <mime-type>text/vnd.wap.wml</mime-type>
    </mime-mapping>
    <mime-mapping>
      <extension>wmls</extension>
      <mime-type>text/vnd.wap.wmlscript</mime-type>
    </mime-mapping>
    <mime-mapping>
      <extension>wmlc</extension>
      <mime-type>application/vnd.wap.wmlc</mime-type>
    </mime-mapping>
    <mime-mapping>
      <extension>wmlsc</extension>
      <mime-type>application/vnd.wap.wmlscript</mime-type>
    </mime-mapping>
    <mime-mapping>
      <extension>wbmp</extension>
      <mime-type>image/vnd.wap.wbmp</mime-type>
    </mime-mapping>

  </web-app>
```

To create the WAR, execute the following command:

```
jar c0f webFiles.war index.jsp match.jsp userDetails.jsp WEB-INF
```

Creating the EAR File

Now to create the EAR; we will need to create an `application.xml` file. This file should look as follows:

```
<?xml version="1.0"?>
<!DOCTYPE application PUBLIC
          "-//Sun Microsystems, Inc.//DTD J2EE Application 1.2//EN"
```

```
                    "http://java.sun.com/j2ee/dtds/application_1_2.dtd">

<application>
  <display-name>My WirelessApp</display-name>

<module>
  <ejb>CentralController.jar</ejb>
</module>

<module>
  <web>
    <web-uri>webFiles.war</web-uri>
    <context-root>wireless</context-root>
  </web>
</module>

</application>
```

The directory structure should be as follows:

```
CentralController.jar
webFiles.war
META-INF/
        application.xml
```

To create the EAR file, execute the command:

```
jar c0f Wireless.ear CentralController.jar webFiles.war META-INF
```

Deploying our Application

To deploy the EAR simply drop the file into the application directory of your server; in our example this is `C:\bea\wlserver6.0sp2\config\mydomain\applications`. However, before the EJBs will be useable, we will need to create the data source and JDBC entries into the `config.xml` file for WebLogic. WebLogic provides a console tool that you can use to create the data source and update the `config.xml` file.

In this example, we used the values:

JDBC Connection Pool

JDBC Connection pool name: CaseStudyPool
URL : jdbc:cloudscape:exampleDB (modify the URL to reflect the name of your database)
Driver Classname: COM.cloudscape.core.JDBCDriver

In the Properties section we have:

user=none
password=none
server=none

JDBC Datasource

Name : CaseStudyPool
JNDI Name: CaseStudyPool
Pool Name : CaseStudyPool

The example assumes that you have populated the database with the valid areas and the taxi companies from the tables given at the beginning of the chapter. Ensure that the names in the AREANAME column in the SERVICEAREAS table correspond to those in the SERVICEAREA column in the TAXILOCATIONS table.

To ensure that WebLogic will be able to find the database we need to add to the WebLogic startWebLogic.cmd file the following line:

```
-Dcloudscape.system.home=<your database path>
```

So that the section after setting the classpath reads, for example:

```
"%JAVA_HOME%\bin\java" -hotspot -ms64m -mx64m -classpath %CLASSPATH% -
Dweblogic.Domain=mydomain -Dweblogic.Name=myserver "-Dbea.home=C:\BEA " -
Dcloudscape.system.home=.\samples\eval\cloudscape\data "-
Djava.security.policy==C:\BEA\wlserver6.0sp1/lib/weblogic.policy" -
Dweblogic.management.password=%WLS_PW% weblogic.Server
goto finish
```

Start the default WebLogic 6.0 server, launch your emulator and request the file http://localhost:7001/wireless/index.jsp

Note the directory wireless. This is needed because the application.xml in the EAR file specifies wireless as the context-root.

How the Application Responds

The first screen that you will receive will look something like the one below – the exact specifics may very depending on what emulator and version you are using. You can use the mouse to select items on the phone:

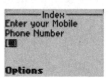

On the middle of the phone there is a dark black square, which is called a jog dial. Similar to the real Nokia 7110, the jog dial is a dial that you can press in three different directions – up, center, and down – to navigate through pages. Select the center of the jog dial to enter text into the input field. You will receive a screen similar to the following:

Enter a phone number into the field:

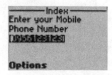

When you have finished, select the key directly below OK. This will return you to the original screen. Now, select Options to be taken to the options menu, where you will see the GetTaxi option, which was defined in the WML. Select the option to submit and go to the next screen:

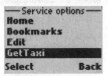

This will send a query back to the server with the parameter msisdn included in the Request object. Since this is the first time that you are accessing the system, the server will forward the request to the userDetails.jsp for you to submit the user location. The screen should look as follows:

The first field for the user number should already be filled in. To select your location, scroll to the Areas field and select it. This will take you to the next screen, which will provide you with a list of all the service areas:

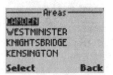

Select the appropriate one, return to the UserDetails screen, and select Options. The Options screen will have a listing for Register User defined from our WML:

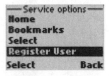

By selecting this, the user details will be sent to the server to be processed, taking you to the Match screen:

The Match screen provides the number and name for the taxi company for your area. Realistically, there would be more than one match, and the system should provide a list for the user to choose from. On subsequent visits, it could default to the same company. The Nokia 7110 provides the ability to select a number displayed in the browser. To do this, you can select the Options button, scroll to the Use number option, and select it:

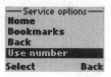

This will bring the number up on the screen ready to dial:

Second Time Around

Now that we have used the system once, when we use the site again, the system will recognize our number and take us directly from the Index page to the Match page. The taxi company that will be displayed will be for the same area that was used the previous time; however, if the user wants to modify their details, they can use the Options tab to choose the Change Location option, which will return the user to the UserDetails screen. If the device supports sessions, the number field will already be filled in:

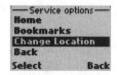

Summary

This very simple service is only meant to show how the J2EE architecture can be used to deliver services to wireless users. However, in practice this service is lacking in a number of ways. Ideally, you would not want the user to have to enter their present location – as the market evolves, this information will be provided by the network operator of the device that you are using. Unfortunately, this is not widely available information yet, due to privacy concerns, and operators are still dealing with how they will be able to make money from the data. The phone number (MSISDN) can also be extracted from the user's device but this is also not widely supported.

However, the more difficult part is going to be integrating this service with other services to provide a more comprehensive solution to an end user. For example, in the case study above, the user may want further personalization and security, they may want to take advantage of other services such as navigation and GIS (Geographic Information Systems). They may also want to request additional content such as reviews, and time of operations, and in addition the provider of the applications must be able integrate the services with the operators' network components for billing, customer care, and tracking. As the mobile world grows, these issues will become much more complex, and the costs of integration and migration will become too high for application developers to justify. There are a number of companies attempting to solve this issue by providing platforms and toolsets to ease the development cycle and reduce the time to market for wireless application development.

Some of the companies that are working on this are:

❑ **Bonita Software** (http://www.bonitasoftware.com/): Headquartered in San Francisco, CA, Bonita Software is a supplier of mobile solutions software for the wireless industry. Bonita develops Java-based solutions, and has established partnerships with many companies, including Sun Microsystems and Motorola.

❑ **eVector** (http://www.evectormobile.com/): eVector is a wireless enabler out of Bangalore (India). Its product provides a scalable enterprise platform to mobile-enable corporate, enterprise, transaction-based applications for a variety of mobile and handheld devices and other service delivery-channels.

❑ **Lokah** (http://www.lokah.com/): Lokah is a software middleware developer headquartered in London, UK. Its primary product is a middleware solution for the rapid development of wireless location-based applications. Lokah's platform integrates best-of-breed services from third parties to provide a flexible and scalable solution for entry into multiple markets.

❑ **Openwave Systems** (http://www.openwave.com/): Headquartered in Redwood City, CA, Openwave is one of the original four firms that co-founded the WAP forum (the other three being Nokia, Motorola, and Ericcson). Openwave Systems is a leading provider of Internet-based communication infrastructure software and applications. Their Mobile Browser is licensed to 25 of the 40 major phone manufacturers.

In the final chapter we will be looking at extending the service-based model out across the web and accessing our EJBs using the HTTP protocol instead of RMI as web services.

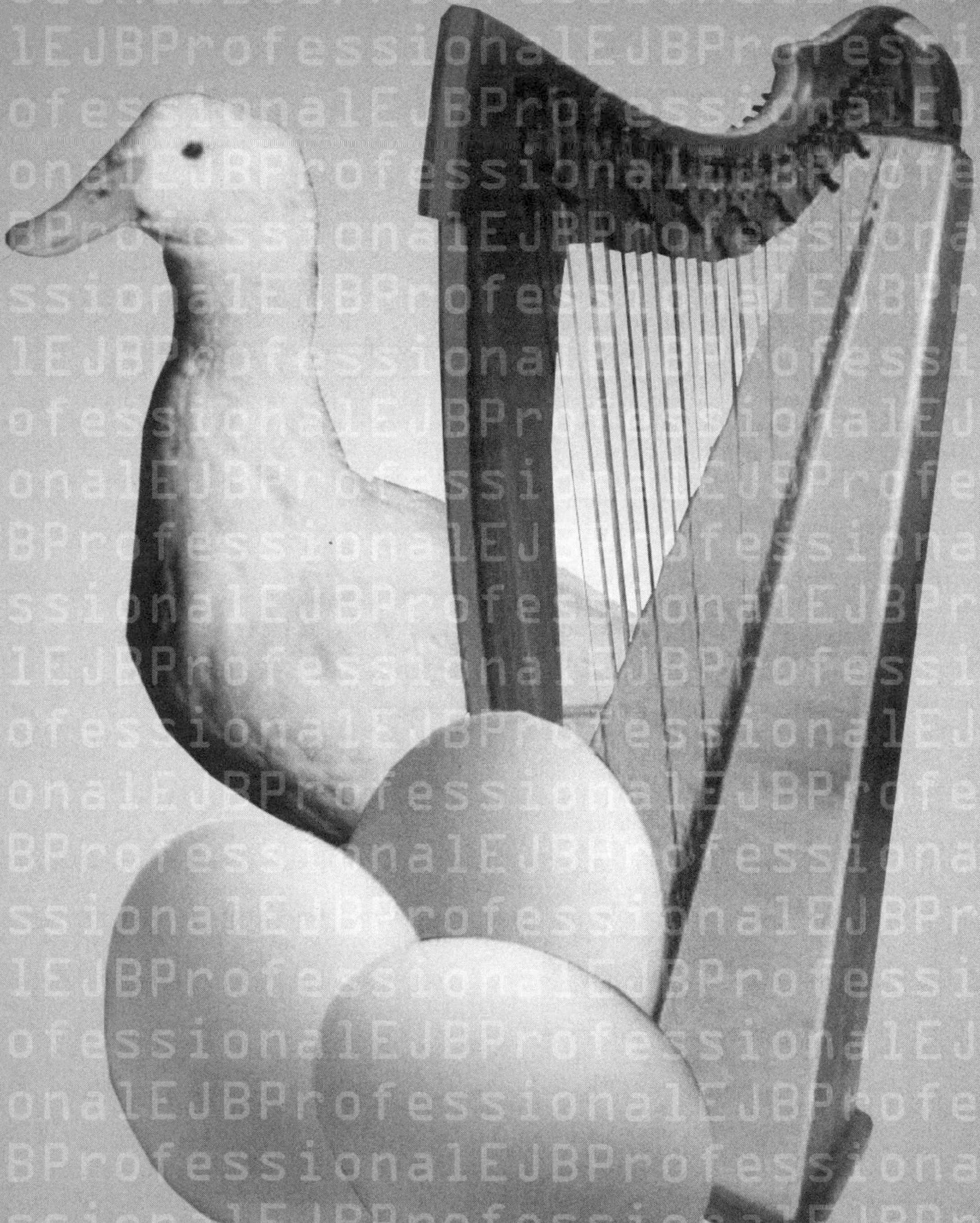

22

EJBs as Web Services

Over the course of this book, we've learned how to create and use Enterprise JavaBeans. However, we have primarily been accessing our EJBs with Java clients via a protocol called RMI over IIOP. In this chapter, we'll see how we can allow non-Java clients to access our EJB environment using multiple network protocols, most notably HTTP. The mechanism that we will introduce to make this possible is known as **web services**.

In simple terms, a web service describes any computational functionality that can be found and invoked over the Internet (or, indeed, *any* network) in a standard way. Typically, a web service represents a self-describing, self-contained application that can be mixed and matched with other web services to create innovative processes and value chains. In an Internet-based enterprise system, each web service represents an application that can execute one or more specific functions, and can interoperate with other web services to accomplish a business transaction.

In this chapter, we will look at the following:

❑   The architecture of web services

❑   The specifications that have been created to help implement and use web services technology

❑   How we can deploy and publish an EJB application as a web service using IBM's Web Services Toolkit

❑   Using CapeClear's CapeConnect product and BEA's WebLogic Application Server to accomplish the same task

Since the technology of web services is relatively new, not to mention rapidly evolving, the tools that we use to implement our examples in this chapter will most likely change over time too. For this reason emphasis is placed on fundamental details about web services here, and the deployment issues of specific application servers are reserved for the appendices of this book.

Web Services Architecture

The web services architecture spans services that encapsulate all levels of business functionality. This can go from simple request-reply sequences to fully integrated business processes. In other words, the granularity of a web service is not limited in any way.

Another goal of the architecture is to allow multiple web services to be automatically composed into new functionality; this integration must happen without manual intervention and should be possible for both new and existing applications. To make this architecture pervasively useful, open and widely-adopted standards must be used for the publication, discovery, and invocation of a service. More specifically, for a service to be useful to any client anywhere on the Internet, a number of standards must be maintained:

❑ A registry mechanism must exist that allows us to search for a service providing a well-defined function; logically, a similar mechanism is also needed to allow the publication of a service.

❑ The offered function must be fully described so that a client knows how to invoke it.

❑ A protocol must exist that allows the invocation of the service over the Internet.

❑ These descriptions and protocols must be neutral to both platform and programming language.

Given these goals, three distinct roles can be defined that interact with each other in a web services scenario: a service provider, a service requestor, and a service broker. Let us look at these roles and their interactions in more detail:

❑ **Service provider**
Creates the service and makes it accessible for clients over the Internet. The service can be created in any language on any platform as long as the Publish and Bind interactions are supported (see below). The service provider is similar to the bean provider as defined in the J2EE specification.

❑ **Service requestor**
The client that uses a web service. This client can also be written in any language and run on any platform, as long as it can Find and Bind to a web service. It is worth noting that a web service implementation can take advantage of other web services and thus take on the role of a requestor.

❑ **Service broker**
Brings the requestor and the provider together. It provides an interface between existing Publish and Find services.

So how do these roles interact with each other? As mentioned above, they use 'Publish', 'Find', and 'Bind' operations. The following diagram shows these three roles and their associated interactions:

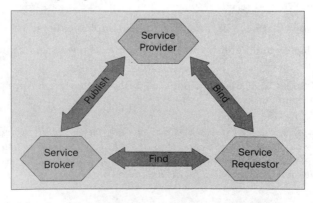

Now we need to define these interactions:

❑ **Publish**
A service provider can tell the service broker about the services it provides by using the publish interface of the service broker. The published information includes data about the service itself and the location where it can be accessed.

❑ **Find**
The service requestor, on the other hand, communicates with the service broker to find a particular web service. Services can be found by specifying a variety of search parameters.

❑ **Bind**
Represents the actual invocation of a web service. It is important to note that the term 'bind' is used differently here than from it is in some other environments. In JNDI, for example, 'binding' an object refers to its publication in the naming server. Binding in the web services context can be compared to a function call, where parameters are passed to the function and a return value is received as a result.

A service requestor may not always invoke a Find operation followed by a Bind operation. Finding a service could be something that is done only once, and the results could be cached. Only in cases where the Bind step fails, because the service may have been moved to a different location, would the requestor have to go back to the broker and refresh the cached information. Both the 'Publish' and 'Find' operations are described in a standard called **Universal Description, Discovery and Integration** (**UDDI**), which we will look at in more detail later in this chapter.

Having identified the different roles and operations, we can now look at what kind of services can exist. It's important to realize that a service-oriented architecture can be used internally within an enterprise as well as externally. That is, all three roles can exist within an intranet as opposed to the Internet. For example, a company might decide to make parts of its internal software functionality accessible via web services. In this case it could use an internal service broker to help connect requestors and providers of services.

Internally-provided systems might include services such as an enterprise messaging service, or an internal business workflow service. Moreover, legacy applications could provide part of their interface as a service to allow integration with other applications.

This principle can be expanded to include the entire Internet, where services are retrieved from anywhere on the network. For the requestor of a service this makes no difference, since the protocols used are the same in both cases: in order to find some required functionality, it would still access the same service broker. The service broker can check for internally provided services first and then contact other brokers on the Internet if they don't exist locally. This works similarly to the way the Domain Name System (DNS) works to resolve names into IP addresses.

You can find more information about the web services architecture in the IBM developerWorks Web Services section, at http://www.ibm.com/developerWorks/webservices.

The Web Services Specifications

In the previous section we defined the three operations that may be executed in a web services environment: Publish, Find, and Bind. Now we will turn our attention to the specifications that have been created to standardize these operations. As we will see, they are all XML-based, which ensures language and platform neutrality.

Rather than having one specification for each of the operations mentioned above, the Publish and Find mechanisms have been merged into a single specification and another describes the Bind step. A third specification defines the service itself or, more specifically, describes the supported interface.

These specifications cover the following:

❑   **Simple Object Access Protocol (SOAP)** – A way to invoke a web service.

❑   **Web Service Definition Language (WSDL)** – A way to describe what a web service does.

❑   **Universal Description, Discovery, and Integration (UDDI)** – A way to publish and find a web service.

Next we'll look at each of these specifications in more detail.

The Simple Object Access Protocol (SOAP)

The SOAP protocol supports the invocation of a web service implementation over the Internet. The SOAP specification is at release 1.1 at the time of this writing, released as a joint effort by IBM and Microsoft. SOAP was submitted to the W3C organization to become a standard and is currently evolving into the 'XML Protocol' standard.

> See http://www.w3.org/TR/SOAP for the latest information on SOAP, and http://www.w3.org/2000/xp/ for more information on XML Protocol-related activities at W3C.

At its core, SOAP is a transport-independent messaging protocol using one-way messages (though they can obviously be combined into request/response sequences). It is not defined what the receiver of a SOAP message does with this message.

The Structure of a SOAP Message

The structure of a SOAP message is very simple: each SOAP message contains one XML document. The following diagram shows the structure of this XML document:

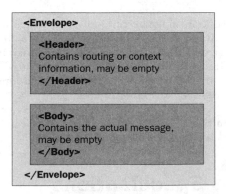

The SOAP message XML document has a root element called `<Envelope>` (the name of this element is the reason why a SOAP message is often referred to as a 'SOAP envelope'). The `<Envelope>` element contains two elements: `<Header>` and `<Body>`. The `<Header>` is a generic mechanism for adding features to a SOAP message without prior agreement between the communicating parties, while the `<Body>` is a container for information intended for the ultimate recipient of the message.

Interestingly enough, both these elements can be empty! In other words, the following is a perfectly valid SOAP message:

```
<Envelope>
  <Header/>
  <Body/>
</Envelope>
```

Of course, this does not make much sense, it is just to show that the core SOAP specification is very simple and leaves most of its elements optional.

Both <Header> and <Body> can also contain additional content. Before we look at that, however, we need to spend a moment talking about namespaces. Typically, elements in a common XML document are assigned a 'namespace'. This will prevent collisions between elements with the same name in one XML document, if they are imported from different sources. In other words, by adding a namespace prefix to each element, we can give our elements a unique name. This prefix is associated with a unique URI – the namespace.

In the case of a SOAP message, a namespace URI has been defined that uniquely identifies the contained elements. This way, if we want to add XML content that contains a <Body> element to the SOAP message, the namespace prefix ensures that this is not confused with the SOAP-defined <Body>.

The following XML document shows exactly the same (rather empty) message as before, but this time a namespace prefix called 'SOAP-ENV' has been added:

```
<SOAP-ENV:Envelope
      xmlns:SOAP-ENV="http://schemas.xmlsoap.org/soap/envelope/">
  <SOAP-ENV:Header/>
  <SOAP-ENV:Body/>
</SOAP-ENV:Envelope>
```

The <Header> element is used mainly to add more information to the context of a SOAP message, like authentication or transactional information, for instance. The <Body> element contains the actual message, although its format is not strictly defined. The only element contained by the body element that is defined in the specification is an error indicator element, called <Fault>.

An interesting attribute that can be contained by both <Header> and <Body> is the encodingStyle attribute. This attribute is needed because the data that is sent inside a SOAP message must be encoded into XML format. Although the SOAP specification does not enforce a specific style of how data is encoded into XML content, SOAP does define a default encoding style that works for most simple cases. The encodingStyle attribute allows us to define our own style for encoding, or we can simply extend the SOAP default style.

SOAP is network transport protocol independent and it therefore only defines the format of an XML message, not how it is actually sent. However, the SOAP specification describes how SOAP messages would be routed over HTTP. In other words, the specification goes from defining the core messaging model, to how messages can be routed, and then to how SOAP messages over HTTP can be used for Remote Procedure Calls (RPC). As we will see later, RPC is a mechanism to invoke method calls on a remote system over network.

If run over HTTP, the SOAP header gets an additional field called `SOAPAction`, and it is carried in an HTTP POST request. The only defined response to the request is the error case, where an HTTP 500 error code must be returned, together with the `<Fault>` element in the response envelope. So why is there only a defined return value for the error case? Remember that SOAP is essentially a one way messaging protocol. A sent message does not necessarily lead to a response message, unless something went wrong while sending it.

While SOAP supports any kind of network protocol, it is mainly used over HTTP at this time. Note that SOAP is a stateless protocol; there is no context information passed with messages (unless, of course, we add it manually). There is also no guaranteed delivery of messages, and SOAP messages are not transactional. For some environments, however, these things are needed. Thus, SOAP is expected to be implemented over other transport protocols in the future, which will provide these additional levels of functionality.

The next level of refinement addressed by the SOAP specification is the use of SOAP for RPC. In essence, this means that a client makes a call to a remote method by sending a SOAP message to it and getting the result of the call back in another SOAP message. To make this work, additional elements are needed in the SOAP message. SOAP for RPC does not depend on the network protocol. In most cases it will be used with HTTP, but it could also use other network protocols. If HTTP is used, the target of the method call is defined in a `SOAPAction` header field. The `<body>` element of the message contains the method name and all parameters encoded into XML. An example of a SOAP RPC call, carried in a HTTP POST request, is shown in the code below. A call is made to a method named `GetLastTradePrice`, which takes the requested stock symbol as a parameter:

```
POST /StockQuote HTTP/1.1
Host: www.stockquoteserver.com
Content-Type: text/xml; charset="utf-8"
Content-Length: nnnn
SOAPAction: "urn:stock-quote-services"

<SOAP-ENV:Envelope
        xmlns:SOAP-ENV="http://schemas.xmlsoap.org/soap/envelope/"
        SOAP-ENV:encodingStyle="http://schemas.xmlsoap.org/soap/encoding/">

   <SOAP-ENV:Body>
        <m:GetLastTradePrice xmlns:m="Some-URI">
            <symbol>DIS</symbol>
        </m:GetLastTradePrice>
   </SOAP-ENV:Body>
</SOAP-ENV:Envelope>
```

How the SOAP Message Calls the Remote Method

This is a good point to leave the specification alone and look at how it works in the real world. First of all, we certainly don't want to build and parse these SOAP messages manually in our applications. For this reason, an Apache project is underway to define and implement a Java API for SOAP. For more information, see http://xml.apache.org/soap.

This API allows us to write a SOAP client without having to deal with any XML at all. As we will see in a little while, most of this code can be generated. The Apache SOAP package contains a complete run time environment for running SOAP.

We have not yet talked about how a SOAP message is received and how the actual remote method gets invoked. As application and EJB developers, we don't want to have to write a servlet to pick up SOAP HTTP requests and interpret them. Again, the Apache SOAP package helps us to deal with this. It contains a servlet called `rpcrouter`. Note that `rpcrouter` is the name under which the servlet is registered in the application server. The class name of the servlet, on the other hand, is `org.apache.soap.server.http.RPCRouterServlet`. This servlet retrieves information about known SOAP services from a file (there is a separate administration tool to register an existing SOAP service).

In our case, each service is represented by a class name and a method name on that class. When a SOAP message arrives, the `rpcrouter` servlet instantiates a so-called 'Pluggable Provider' object for the requested service. The provider knows how to invoke the actual method. For example, there might be a provider that simply instantiates a Java object and then calls one of its methods. In the case of an EJB, however, the provider acts as the EJB client, using the home interface to get access to the EJB before invoking the method on it. After the execution has been complete, the `rpcrouter` servlet packages the returned result into another SOAP envelope that is eventually passed back to the caller.

The following diagram shows this process schematically:

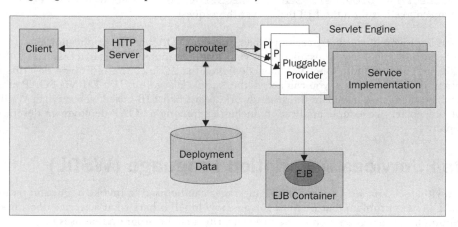

Thus, the most important thing we need to do is to create a class with a method that can be invoked remotely. Then we need to define a data structure that describes the service and register it with the SOAP server environment. For example, the service description contains the name of the Pluggable Provider that should be used. The description is an XML document, and we can think of it as the deployment descriptor for a SOAP service. Typically, this deployment descriptor will be created through a tool, so that we should not have to do this manually. Here is what this deployment descriptor looks like for the `StockQuoteService` that we used above:

```xml
<?xml version="1.0"?>

<isd:service xmlns:isd="http://xml.apache.org/xml-soap/deployment"
             id="urn:stock-quote-services">

  <isd:provider type="org.apache.soap.providers.StatelessEJBProvider"
                scope="Application"
                methods="GetLastTradePrice">
```

```
        <isd:java class="services/StockQuoteService"/>

        <isd:option key="FullHomeInterfaceName"
                    value="services.StockQuoteServiceHome" />
        <isd:option key="ContextProviderURL" value="iiop://localhost:900" />
        <isd:option key="FullContextFactoryName"
                    value="com.ibm.websphere.naming.WsnInitialContextFactory" />

    </isd:provider>

    <isd:faultListener>
       org.apache.soap.server.DOMFaultListener
    </isd:faultListener>

  </isd:service>
```

The `id` attribute in the `<service>` element is used by the client in the `SOAPAction` header field. The `<provider>` element specifies which class handles the actual request. In this example, an EJB provider (`org.apache.soap.providers.StatelessEJBProvider`) is used, which will receive the SOAP message and make a call on the EJB that serves the request.

The actual deployment is usually accomplished using the SOAP admin application that comes with the Apache SOAP package. If you installed it on your local computer, you can access it at http://localhost/soap/admin. Once you have deployed the `StockQuoteService` described by the deployment descriptor above, you can access the `StockQuoteService` EJB via SOAP messages over HTTP, which means we have laid the groundwork to our first EJB-based web service! We'll go through a complete web service sample application, including creating a SOAP deployment descriptor, later in this chapter.

The Web Services Description Language (WSDL)

In the previous section, we saw how SOAP messages can be used to invoke a function remotely over the Internet. The next problem that we must solve is how to tell others what a service does; in other words, a description that is exact enough so that we can write a client program that uses it.

You may have noticed that the Apache SOAP deployment descriptor that we have just seen does not contain a definition of the data that is passed to the function, nor does it indicate what kind of data comes back. The SOAP specification itself does not provide any mechanism for doing that either. This is exactly the reason for the **WSDL** specification. Originally developed by IBM and Microsoft, this spec has been submitted to the W3C to become a standard, and the current version can be found at http://www.w3.org/TR/wsdl.

WSDL describes the data and message contracts that a web service offers. Notice that the WSDL specification uses an approach similar to the one SOAP took: in order to avoid strict dependencies on underlying protocols, it does not force us into any particular type of messaging system. In the real world though, XML schemas are used to describe the data types and SOAP (over HTTP) is used for the messaging. This way, the standard is open to future enhancements and provides a working solution today. To keep things simple, we will assume for the remainder of this section that XML schemas and SOAP are used to describe and invoke a web service.

Each WSDL document has two parts, a reusable one and a specific one. The reason for this is that we can assume that certain services will be standardized in the future. The interfaces of these services can be described in a generic way, without specifying the exact location of the SOAP server that provides the service. This allows us to deploy the service in multiple locations, without having to duplicate the definition of the interface. As we will see shortly, this is particularly useful in the context of Universal Description, Discovery, and Integration (UDDI).

The diagram below shows all elements of a WSDL document in one view, and the following subsections go into a more detailed explanation:

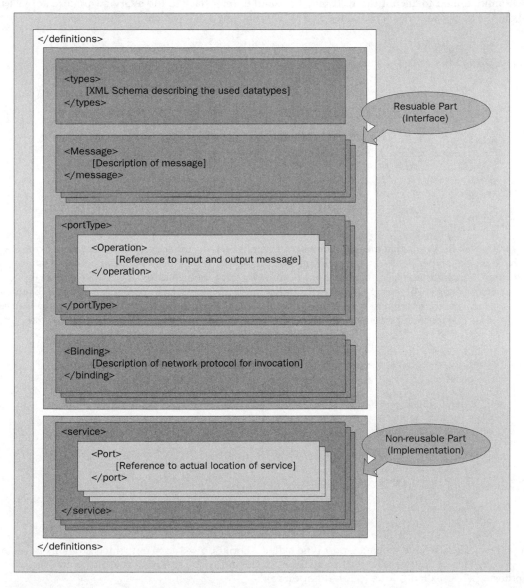

Let's look at the reusable part first.

The Reusable Part of a WSDL Definition

At the highest level, we need a definition of the data types that are used by the described web service. In the simplest case, these are basic data types defined by the XML schema standard, but can also include complex data types. All that we need to do is describe the required data types as an XML schema: There are a number of tools on the Internet that can help create and edit an XML schema, or generate it from an existing DTD, or even a JavaBean. The following sample shows how a schema is used within a WSDL document. It defines an element called `GetLastTradePrice`, which can later be used in the definition of the message that is part of the service (the definition of the element itself has been omitted here to keep it short). It may be useful to refer back to the overview picture above as we look at the various elements contained in a WSDL document. Here's our sample code:

```
<?xml version="1.0"?>
<definitions name="StockQuoteService-interface"
        targetNamespace="http://www.getquote.com/StockQuoteService-interface"
        xmlns:xsd="http://www.w3.org/1999/XMLSchema"
        xmlns:soap="http://schemas.xmlsoap.org/wsdl/soap/"
        xmlns="http://schemas.xmlsoap.org/wsdl/">

<types>
  <xsd:schema targetNamespace="http://my.org/stockquote.xsd">
      <element name="GetLastTradePrice"> ...</element>
  </xsd:schema>
</types>
...
</definitions>
```

This example also shows that the root element of every WSDL document is called `<definitions>`. Once we have the data types defined, we can define `<message>`. A WSDL document can contain many `<message>` definitions, each containing one or more `<part>` elements. Messages are can contain `<operation>` tags, where each `<operation>` has an `<input>` and an `<output>` message. Eventually, one or more operations build a `<portType>`, which basically represents a set of functions that a web service can process. The following example shows a web service that has one operation named `getQuote`:

```
<message name="SymbolRequest">
  <part name="symbol" type="xsd:string"/>
</message>

<message name="QuoteResponse">
  <part name="quote" type="xsd:string"/>
</message>

<portType name="StockQuoteService">
  <operation name="getQuote">
    <input message="SymbolRequest"/>
    <output message="QuoteResponse"/>
  </operation>
</portType>
```

As you can see, we have defined a port type called `StockQuoteService`, which contains a `getQuote` operation. This operation takes a `String` called `Symbol` (`SymbolRequest`) as input and returns another `String` called `Quote` (`QuoteResponse`).

So far, we have concentrated on describing the operation, but we still don't know how to access it. The WSDL specification defines an element called `<binding>` for this. A `<binding>` describes the message protocol with which the service can be reached. One WSDL document can contain multiple different bindings for the same port type. The following example shows a binding that states how the `StockQuoteService` service, which we described above, can be reached via SOAP (remember that the WSDL specification lets us choose the protocol we want to use):

```
<binding name="StockQuoteServiceBinding"
         type="StockQuoteService">
  <soap:binding style="rpc"
                transport="http://schemas.xmlsoap.org/soap/http"/>
  <operation name="getQuote">
    <soap:operation soapAction="http://www.getquote.com/GetQuote"/>
    <input>
      <soap:body use="encoded"
                 namespace="urn:live-stock-quotes"
                 encodingStyle="http://schemas.xmlsoap.org/soap/encoding/"/>
    </input>
    <output>
      <soap:body use="encoded"
                 namespace="urn:live-stock-quotes"
                 encodingStyle="http://schemas.xmlsoap.org/soap/encoding/"/>
    </output>
  </operation>
</binding>
```

While it is important to understand the contents of the WSDL document, we will most likely use a tooling environment to create and manage these definitions. Later in this chapter we will see how the IBM Web Services Toolkit lets us generate WSDL files. Since it is likely that there will be even newer versions of the SOAP and WSDL specifications available by the time you read this, using such tools should take account of any changes to these standards over time.

We consider the binding as being within the reusable part of the definition because we can safely assume that SOAP will be used to access the service. If that is not the case, however, we can certainly store the binding in a separate file and import it into the WSDL document.

The Non-Reusable Part of a WSDL Definition

The non-reusable part of the WSDL definition contains the actual network endpoint that is used. In other words, this is the address of the actual SOAP server handling the request. The name of the element is `<port>`; here is the corresponding code for our `StockQuoteService` example:

```
<port name="JoesPort" binding="StockQuoteServiceBinding">
  <soap:address
       location="http://demohost.mydomain.net:8080/soap/servlet/rpcrouter"/>
</port>
```

This non-reusable part of the definition is also called the **implementation** part, whereas the reusable part is called the **interface** part.

At this point, we have a definition of the service in WSDL, and we can use SOAP to invoke it. The only part that is missing is a way to find the service, or, if we are the provider of the service, a way to publish it so that others can find it. This is covered by UDDI, which we look at next.

Universal Description, Discovery and Integration (UDDI)

The success of web services depends on the capability of a provider to publish the existence of a service, and for a requestor to find a service. In that respect, the service broker plays an essential role using UDDI. So what is UDDI? It describes a registry that contains information about web services and the businesses that offer these services. The content structure of the registry and the APIs to access it are clearly specified. These specifications are backed by a group of 220 companies (including all of the big IT companies) that have committed to support them. For more information about UDDI, have a look at http://uddi.org.

The UDDI Data Structure

All information contained in a UDDI registry is formatted in XML and the API to access it is implemented using SOAP. In other words, each UDDI registry has some kind of server process that receives and responds to SOAP messages. Before we take a closer look at the UDDI API, let us look at what kind of information is stored in a UDDI registry.

The content of a UDDI registry can be described using an analogy to the different types of phone directories:

❑ White Pages – Information such as the name, address, telephone number, and other contact information of a given business.

❑ Yellow Pages – Information that identifies the type of a business and categorizes it according to the industry.

❑ Green Pages – Data about the specific services a business offers.

As part of the UDDI specification, XML Schemas were defined for all of these types of information. This makes sense since, as was mentioned above, all information in the registry is stored in XML documents. Thus, we can view a UDDI registry as one big XML document. So what is the structure of this document?

Before we can dig into this structure, we need to define a few concepts that are used in UDDI. One important concept is that of a **TModel**, which represents an arbitrary data structure. In other words, it serves as a container for abstract data, for example, technical specifications. Each TModel has a unique identifier and can be referred to by a so-called **TModelKey**. Moreover, a TModel can contain 'IdentifierBags' and 'CategoryBags'. Now we'd better define these terms.

IdentifierBags contain Identifiers, which are simply named key-value pairs. Using Identifiers, we can add additional descriptive information to a TModel. **CategoryBags** contain Category information. A Category is similar to an Identifier, but it uses a predefined taxonomy. In plain English, this means that a number of Categories have been defined that allow us to further classify the information in a TModel. For example, let's assume that we're creating a TModel that specifies a standard data protocol between a car manufacturer and a parts supplier. To indicate that our specification is focusing on the car manufacturing industry, we could add a Category to the TModel that represents this particular industry.

To wrap up what we discussed so far, we can think of a TModel as a piece of information that is categorized and has a unique key. We can now return to our discussion about the structure of a UDDI registry, and see how the TModel, Identifier, and Category concepts are relevant.

The following diagram shows the structure of a UDDI registry as an overview, further below we will look at each of the entries in more detail:

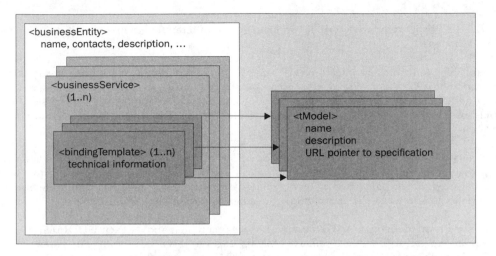

At its root, a UDDI registry contains <businessEntity> entries. These entries contain information about a business, its name, address, and so forth. We can think of this as the white pages style information we mentioned earlier. A UDDI registry can be used just for that: finding the phone number of a business of which we only know the name (and, you guessed it, there is a specific API that allows us to make queries like this one, but we'll get back to that later). On top of the contact information, a <businessEntity> element can also contain identifiers and categories. This allows performing searches for all businesses in a registry that deal with a specific industry, or which are found in a certain location (geographical categorization is another of the predefined taxonomies for which categories already exist).

Each business entry also contains zero or more <businessService> entries. Each business service entry represents a family of technical services. In other words, it shows the services that a certain business provides. Besides a description, it contains <bindingTemplates> and an optional <categoryBag> element. The <categoryBag> allows us to categorize a particular service.

The <bindingTemplates> element contains a number of <bindingTemplate> elements. These elements provide references to technical information about a service. For example, in a <bindingTemplate> we specify an access point for the service. This access point can be a URL, or a simple e-mail address or telephone number. Moreover, a <bindingTemplate> can contain references to <tModel> elements. This way, we can link an existing <tModel> to a <businessService> entry. For example, if we assume that a standardized way of doing a specific business transaction exists, this standard will be stored in the UDDI registry in a <tModel>. Every business that provides an implementation for the standard can refer to this <tModel> through the <bindingTemplate>. A requestor that searches the registry for this standard will get returned the <businessService> entry that contains a reference to the appropriate <tModel>.

An interesting aspect of this is how WSDL documents are stored in UDDI. The UDDI specification does not define this. Typically, a WSDL document will be referenced from within a <tModel>, which in turn is referenced by the <bindingTemplate> as described above. However, this only applies to the reusable, or interface part of the WSDL document. The non-reusable, or implementation part is directly referenced from within the <bindingTemplate>. The exact details of this are still being worked on and need to be clarified further.

The UDDI API

The UDDI API specification describes two main groups of interfaces, namely publishing functions and inquiry functions.

The publishing functions allow us to create (and delete) the types of entries in the registry that we have described above. We can create new <businessEntity> entries to register a business, and we can register additional <businessService> entries with information about the technical services the business offers. We can also create and store reusable <tModel> entries with specification information about web services.

The inquiry APIs provide a means to search for entries in the registry. Searches can be done based on a large variety of search criteria. For example, we can find businesses based on their location or name. We can also search for businesses or services based on categories. Finally, we can locate businesses that offer services, that refer to specific <tModel> elements.

All of the APIs are defined as XML messages. As we mentioned above, each UDDI registry has a SOAP access point, and all API calls are sent as SOAP messages to this access point. The parameters and return values of the individual functions match the XML data structures contained in the registry. This means that as soon as we are familiar with the data structure of UDDI, we are ready to use the API. The API itself is language-neutral, because it is defined in XML. A link to the latest UDDI API specification can be found at http://uddi.org.

If we are looking for a way to access a UDDI registry from within a Java application, we need Java bindings for the UDDI API. There is an open source project underway, called UDDI4J, which defines and implements a Java client API for both inquiry and publish functions. The IBM implementation of this project can be found at http://oss.software.ibm.com/developerworks/projects/uddi4j. The parameters and return values for the methods in UDDI4J are simple mappings of the XML structures into Java. Again, the advantage here is that once we are familiar with the data structure of UDDI, we can easily write a Java application accessing it via UDDI4J.

It is worth noting that nothing in the specification for either SOAP, WSDL, or UDDI forces us into one programming language.

UDDI Registries

It is the declared goal of the UDDI community to create a network of UDDI registries that resembles the Domain Name System (DNS). In other words, all UDDI registries exchange information among one another, so that accessing any registry provides the information contained in all registries. This way, it does not matter which registry we choose to publish in, we can be assured that any requestor will find our published service.

At the time of writing, three production UDDI registries exist: one from IBM (http://www.ibm.com/services/uddi), one from Microsoft (http://uddi.microsoft.com), and one from Ariba (http://uddi.ariba.com). However, Ariba's registry will be replaced by one from Hewlett-Packard soon. Eventually the number of registries will grow, and all UDDI registries will form a hierarchical tree.

Each of the three registry providers also hosts a test registry that we can use for testing purposes. To be able to publish in any of them, we must register with a userId and password combination, which are then required on the publishing APIs. For inquiries, no userId/password is needed.

We can also run a UDDI registry on our local computer or within an intranet. For example, the IBM Web Services Toolkit (WSTK) comes with a locally installable UDDI registry that stores its data in a DB2 database. Local registries are useful if we want to develop and/or demonstrate our web services without requiring a connection to the Internet.

Putting the Pieces Together

So what does this all mean? In the web services world, applications can consist of independent pieces that are separately developed and implemented, in different languages on different platforms. They can then be dynamically assembled into new solutions across a network. This is made possible by the fact that standardized descriptions of services exist, there is a standard way to invoke them, and we can find them in a common registry.

Web services can be thought of as a programming environment similar to that of EJBs and J2EE, just on a larger scale:

EJBs	Web Services
Communicate with an EJB via RMI over IIOP.	Communicate with a web service via SOAP, which can run over multiple different network protocols.
EJBs have well defined interfaces, specifically their remote interface.	A web service is described in WSDL, which can be used with different programming languages.
EJBs are registered in a JNDI name server.	Web services are stored in UDDI.

OK, these comparisons might be farfetched, but you get the general idea… why don't we just develop everything as a web service? First of all, the protocols described here have some shortcomings that make them less useful in certain cases. For example, we are talking about services, not objects. A web service does not necessarily have state, and SOAP does not carry any contextual information. This means that there are no definitions yet for transactional invocation of a service within, say, a secure context.

This is not to say that it cannot be done, but the core specifications do not cover it. Moreover, since calls to a web service go potentially across a large network, the performance of the network and the number of service calls play an important role. Not every EJB should be wrapped into a web service; a service will typically need a fairly high-level interface to be useful.

Examples of typical web services are information providers (stock quotes, weather reports, etc.), simple data services (currency exchange, mathematical computations), and also complex business functionality. For example, an Enterprise Resource Planning (ERP) application could expose some of its interfaces as web services, so that other applications can easily be integrated. This integration can happen in intranets, extranets, and the Internet. A large company could facilitate web services as a means to simplify reuse of existing software in new applications. Alternatively, an enterprise could communicate with e-marketplaces on the Internet via web services, thus using them for B2B integration. An Internet portal is another good example. In this case, the portal provider could use a UDDI registry to look for available services and offer them to be integrated into the portal.

Creating a Web Service from an EJB

After all this theory, let us see how an existing EJB application can be wrapped into a web service. Because of the stateless and connectionless nature of the SOAP protocol, stateless session beans are the best candidates to be exposed as a web service. In our example, we will develop, deploy, and install an application that stores information about music albums and the tracks that are on them. This information is stored via a number of persistent entity beans. A stateless session bean is provided that returns a list of tracks for a given CD name in an XML document. We will wrap the interface of the session bean in a web service.

The EJB Application

We'll quickly run through the code for the application. It consists of four beans:

❑   InfoService – a stateless session bean façade to the entity beans

❑   IDGenerator – a stateless session bean that provides us with an incremental index ID for the entity beans

❑   Track – an entity bean for CD track listings

❑   Album – an entity bean for album information

A client will ask the InfoService bean to get CD information based on a unique CD key. The InfoService bean will return this information back to the client as an XML structured String:

```
<album>
      <album-title></album-title>
      <artist></artist>
      <genre></genre>
      <tracks>
          <track>
              <track-title></track-title>
              <track-length></track-length>
          </track>
          <track>
              <track-title></track-title>
              <track-length></track-length>
          </track>
          ...
      </tracks>
</album>
```

> *We are going to be deploying onto WebSphere so we will make our beans compliant with only the 1.1 specification.*

The InfoService Bean

This is the bean that we will be wrapping in a web service, which acts as a façade to the entity beans.

The Home Interface

```
package infoservice;
```

```
import javax.ejb.*;

public interface InfoServiceHome extends EJBHome {

    InfoService create() throws java.rmi.RemoteException, CreateException;

}
```

The Remote Interface

There is only one significant business method to be declared here, getCDInfo():

```
package infoservice;

public interface InfoService extends javax.ejb.EJBObject {

    String getCDInfo(String identifier) throws java.rmi.RemoteException;

}
```

The Bean Implementation Class

As well as the business method declared in the remote interface, there is one other method in the implementation class; this method returns the XML structured String:

```
package infoservice;

import javax.ejb.*;
import javax.naming.*;
import java.util.Collection;
import java.util.Iterator;
import java.util.Properties;
import album.*;
import track.*;
import javax.xml.parsers.*;
import org.w3c.dom.*;
import javax.xml.transform.*;
import javax.xml.transform.stream.*;
import javax.xml.transform.dom.*;
import java.io.StringWriter;
import javax.rmi.*;

public class InfoServiceEJB implements SessionBean {

    public void ejbCreate() {}
    public void ejbRemove() {}
    public void ejbActivate() {}
    public void ejbPassivate() {}
    public void setSessionContext(SessionContext ctx) {}
```

Firstly, the getCDInfo() method takes the CD identifier and uses it to locate the appropriate album using the Album bean. Then it takes the album ID and locates the relevant tracks through the Track bean. It passes the album and tracks collection to a private method that parses the data into an XML document:

```
public String getCDInfo(String identifier) {

  Context ctx = null;
  try {
    ctx = new InitialContext();

    //Find album details
    Object objRef = ctx.lookup("java:comp/env/ejb/Album");
    AlbumHome ahome = (AlbumHome)PortableRemoteObject.narrow(objRef,
                        AlbumHome.class);
    Album a = ahome.findByCDIdentifier(identifier);

    //Find tracks for this album
    objRef = ctx.lookup("java:comp/env/ejb/Track");
    TrackHome thome = (TrackHome)PortableRemoteObject.narrow(objRef,
                        TrackHome.class);
    Collection tracks = thome.findByParentAlbumID(a.getAlbumID());

    return buildXMLDoc(a, tracks);

  } catch(NamingException ne)  {
    throw new EJBException("Naming Exception: " + ne);
  } catch (FinderException onfe) {
    throw new EJBException("Finder Exception: " + onfe);
  } catch(java.rmi.RemoteException re) {
    throw new EJBException("Remote Exception: " + re);
  }

}
```

The `buildXMLDoc()` method uses JAXP to create a DOM document, which it loads with the album and track information:

```
private String buildXMLDoc(Album a, Collection allTracks) {

  Document doc;
  Element album;
  Element track;
  Element albumtitle;
  Element artist;
  Element genre;
  Element tracktitle;
  Element tracklength;
  Element tracks;

  try {

    //Start building XML doc
    DocumentBuilderFactory dbf = DocumentBuilderFactory.newInstance();
    DocumentBuilder db = dbf.newDocumentBuilder();

    doc = db.newDocument();
```

```
      album = doc.createElement("album");

      albumtitle = doc.createElement("album-title");
      albumtitle.appendChild(doc.createTextNode(a.getAlbumTitle()));
      album.appendChild(albumtitle);

      artist = doc.createElement("artist");
      artist.appendChild(doc.createTextNode(a.getAlbumArtist()));
      album.appendChild(artist);

      genre = doc.createElement("genre");
      genre.appendChild(doc.createTextNode(a.getAlbumGenre()));
      album.appendChild(genre);

      //Iterate through tracks and add them to XML doc
      Iterator it = allTracks.iterator();
      tracks = doc.createElement("tracks");
      while(it.hasNext()) {
        Object objRef2 = it.next();
        Track t = (Track)javax.rmi.PortableRemoteObject.narrow(objRef2,
                  Track.class);

        track = doc.createElement("track");

        tracktitle = doc.createElement("track-title");
        tracktitle.appendChild(doc.createTextNode(t.getTrackTitle()));
        track.appendChild(tracktitle);

        tracklength = doc.createElement("track-length");
        tracklength.appendChild(doc.createTextNode(t.getTrackLength()));
        track.appendChild(tracklength);

        tracks.appendChild(track);
      }
      album.appendChild(tracks);
      doc.appendChild(album);

      //Transform XML doc into a String to return to client
      TransformerFactory tFactory = TransformerFactory.newInstance();
      Transformer t = tFactory.newTransformer();

      StringWriter sw = new StringWriter();

      t.transform(new DOMSource(doc), new StreamResult(sw));
      return sw.toString();

    } catch (ParserConfigurationException pce) {
      throw new EJBException(pce);
    } catch (TransformerConfigurationException tce) {
      throw new EJBException(tce);
    } catch (TransformerException te) {
      throw new EJBException(te);
    } catch (java.rmi.RemoteException re) {
      throw new EJBException(re);
    }
  }

}
```

The IDGenerator Bean

The IDGenerator bean is called by the Album and Track beans during their create() method. It maintains a database table that contains an ID number to assign to the next album or track created.

The Home Interface

```
package id;

public interface IDGeneratorHome extends javax.ejb.EJBHome {
  IDGenerator create() throws java.rmi.RemoteException,
                              javax.ejb.CreateException;
}
```

The Remote Interface

```
package id;

public interface IDGenerator extends javax.ejb.EJBObject {

  int getNextID(String objectType) throws java.rmi.RemoteException,
                                           javax.ejb.ObjectNotFoundException;

}
```

The Bean Implementation Class

```
package id;

import java.sql.*;
import javax.sql.DataSource;
import javax.naming.*;
import javax.ejb.*;

public class IDGeneratorEJB implements SessionBean {

  public void ejbCreate() {}
  public void ejbRemove() {}
  public void ejbActivate() {}
  public void ejbPassivate() {}
  public void setSessionContext(SessionContext ctx) {}

  public int getNextID(String objectType) throws ObjectNotFoundException {

    Connection conn = null;
    try {

      Context initial = new InitialContext();
      DataSource datasource = (DataSource)
                initial.lookup("java:comp/env/jdbc/musicDB");
      conn = datasource.getConnection();

      String sql = "SELECT NEXTOBJECTID FROM IDTRACKER WHERE OBJECTNAME = '"
                + objectType + "'";
      Statement statement = conn.createStatement();
      ResultSet rs = statement.executeQuery(sql);

      if (!rs.next())
        throw new ObjectNotFoundException();

      int nextID = rs.getInt("NEXTOBJECTID");
```

```
        rs.close();

        sql = "UPDATE IDTRACKER SET NEXTOBJECTID=" + (nextID + 1) +
              " WHERE OBJECTNAME = '" + objectType + "'";
        if (statement.executeUpdate(sql) != 1) {
          throw new EJBException("Failed to update ID");
        }

        conn.close();
        return nextID;

    } catch (javax.naming.NamingException ne)  {
      ne.printStackTrace();
      throw new EJBException(ne);
    } catch (SQLException sqle) {
      sqle.printStackTrace();
      throw new EJBException(sqle);
    } finally {
      try {
        if (conn != null)
          conn.close();

      } catch (SQLException sql) {}
    }

  }
}
```

Note that the `IDGenerator` bean requires us to create a database with the following SQL:

```
CREATE TABLE IDTRACKER (OBJECTNAME VARCHAR(25),
                        NEXTOBJECTID NUMBER)

INSERT INTO IDTRACKER(OBJECTNAME, NEXTOBJECTID)
          VALUES ('Album', 1)
                  ('Track', 1)
```

The Track Bean

This is the first of the two entity beans, and represents the information we have stored for a track. The information includes the track ID, the ID of the album it comes from, the track name, and the track length.

The Home Interface

```
package track;

import javax.ejb.*;
import java.util.Collection;

public interface TrackHome extends EJBHome {

  Track create(String title, String trackLength, Integer parentAlbumID)
      throws CreateException, java.rmi.RemoteException;

  Track findByPrimaryKey(Integer id) throws FinderException,
                                  java.rmi.RemoteException;

  Collection findByParentAlbumID(Integer ID) throws FinderException,
                                      java.rmi.RemoteException;

}
```

The Remote Interface

```
package track;

public interface Track extends javax.ejb.EJBObject {

  Integer getTrackID() throws java.rmi.RemoteException;
  Integer getTrackParentAlbumID() throws java.rmi.RemoteException;
  String getTrackTitle() throws java.rmi.RemoteException;
  String getTrackLength() throws java.rmi.RemoteException;

}
```

The Bean Implementation Class

```
package track;

import javax.ejb.*;
import javax.naming.*;
import java.util.Properties;
import id.*;

public class TrackEJB implements EntityBean {

  public Integer trackID;
  public Integer parentAlbumID;
  public String trackTitle;
  public String trackLength;

  public void ejbStore() {}
  public void ejbRemove() {}

  public void ejbActivate() {}
  public void ejbPassivate() {}

  public void setEntityContext(EntityContext ctx) {}
  public void unsetEntityContext() {}

  public Integer ejbCreate(String title, String trackLength,
                           Integer parentAlbumID) {

    Context ctx = null;
    try {
      ctx = new InitialContext();

      Object objRef = ctx.lookup("java:comp/env/ejb/IDGenerator");
      IDGeneratorHome home = (IDGeneratorHome)
          javax.rmi.PortableRemoteObject.narrow(objRef,
            IDGeneratorHome.class);

      IDGenerator idGen = home.create();

      this.trackID = new Integer(idGen.getNextID("Track"));
      this.parentAlbumID = parentAlbumID;
      this.trackTitle = title;
      this.trackLength = trackLength;
```

```
        return null;

    } catch(NamingException ne)  {
      throw new EJBException(ne);
    } catch (CreateException onfe) {
      throw new EJBException(onfe);
    } catch (ObjectNotFoundException onfe) {
      throw new EJBException(onfe);
    } catch(java.rmi.RemoteException re) {
      throw new EJBException(re);
    }

  }
  public void ejbPostCreate(String title, String trackLength,
                          Integer parentAlbumID) {}

  public void ejbLoad() {
    if(trackTitle != null)
      trackTitle.trim();
    if(trackLength != null)
      trackLength.trim();
  }

  public Integer getTrackID() {
    return this.trackID;
  }

  public Integer getTrackParentAlbumID() {
    return this.parentAlbumID;
  }

  public String getTrackTitle() {
    return this.trackTitle;
  }

  public String getTrackLength() {
    return this.trackLength;
  }
}
```

The Album Bean

This second entity bean represents our stored information about an album, including the title, artist, and genre, as well as relational identifiers so we can refer to the correct album from the other beans.

The Home Interface

```
package album;

import javax.ejb.*;

public interface AlbumHome extends EJBHome {
```

```
    Album create(String cdID, String title, String artist, String genre)
        throws CreateException, java.rmi.RemoteException;

    Album findByAlbumTitle(String title) throws FinderException,
        java.rmi.RemoteException;
    Album findByCDIdentifier(String identifier) throws FinderException,
        java.rmi.RemoteException;
    Album findByPrimaryKey(Integer id) throws FinderException,
        java.rmi.RemoteException;
}
```

The Remote Interface

```
package album;

public interface Album extends javax.ejb.EJBObject {

  Integer getAlbumID() throws java.rmi.RemoteException;
  String getAlbumCDID() throws java.rmi.RemoteException;
  String getAlbumTitle() throws java.rmi.RemoteException;
  String getAlbumArtist() throws java.rmi.RemoteException;
  String getAlbumGenre() throws java.rmi.RemoteException;

}
```

The Bean Implementation Class

```
package album;

import javax.ejb.*;
import javax.naming.*;
import java.util.Properties;
import id.*;

public class AlbumEJB implements EntityBean {

  public Integer albumID;
  public String cdID;
  public String albumTitle;
  public String artist;
  public String genre;

  public void ejbStore() {}
  public void ejbRemove() {}

  public void ejbActivate() {}
  public void ejbPassivate() {}

  public void setEntityContext(EntityContext ctx) {}
  public void unsetEntityContext() {}

  public Integer ejbCreate(String cdID, String title, String artist,
                           String genre) {

    Context ctx = null;
```

```
   try {
     ctx = new InitialContext();

     Object objRef = ctx.lookup("java:comp/env/ejb/IDGenerator");
     IDGeneratorHome home = (IDGeneratorHome)
         javax.rmi.PortableRemoteObject.narrow(objRef,
             IDGeneratorHome.class);

     IDGenerator idGen = home.create();

     this.albumID = new Integer(idGen.getNextID("Album"));
     this.cdID = cdID;
     this.albumTitle = title;
     this.artist = artist;
     this.genre = genre;
     return null;

   } catch(NamingException ne)  {
     throw new EJBException(ne);
   } catch (CreateException onfe) {
     throw new EJBException(onfe);
   } catch (ObjectNotFoundException onfe) {
     throw new EJBException(onfe);
   } catch(java.rmi.RemoteException re) {
     throw new EJBException(re);
   }
}

public void ejbPostCreate(String cdID, String title, String artist,
                          String genre) {}

public void ejbLoad() {
  if(albumTitle != null)
    albumTitle.trim();
  if(artist != null)
    artist.trim();
  if(genre != null)
    genre.trim();
}

public Integer getAlbumID() {
  return this.albumID;
}

public String getAlbumCDID() {
  return this.cdID;
}

public String getAlbumTitle() {
  return this.albumTitle;
}

public String getAlbumArtist() {
  return this.artist;
```

```
  }

  public String getAlbumGenre() {
    return this.artist;
  }
}
```

The Deployment Descriptor

Finally here is the deployment descriptor for this application:

```xml
<?xml version="1.0"?>

<!DOCTYPE ejb-jar PUBLIC
          '-//Sun Microsystems, Inc.//DTD Enterprise JavaBeans 1.1//EN'
          'http://java.sun.com/j2ee/dtds/ejb-jar_1_1.dtd'>

<ejb-jar>
  <enterprise-beans>

    <session>
      <ejb-name>IDGenerator</ejb-name>
      <home>id.IDGeneratorHome</home>
      <remote>id.IDGenerator</remote>
      <ejb-class>id.IDGeneratorEJB</ejb-class>
      <session-type>Stateless</session-type>
      <transaction-type>Container</transaction-type>
      <resource-ref>
        <res-ref-name>jdbc/musicDB</res-ref-name>
        <res-type>javax.sql.DataSource</res-type>
        <res-auth>Container</res-auth>
      </resource-ref>
    </session>

    <session>
      <ejb-name>InfoService</ejb-name>
      <home>infoservice.InfoServiceHome</home>
      <remote>infoservice.InfoService</remote>
      <ejb-class>infoservice.InfoServiceEJB</ejb-class>
      <session-type>Stateless</session-type>
      <transaction-type>Container</transaction-type>
      <ejb-ref>
        <ejb-ref-name>ejb/Album</ejb-ref-name>
        <ejb-ref-type>Entity</ejb-ref-type>
        <home>album.AlbumHome</home>
        <remote>album.Album</remote>
      </ejb-ref>
      <ejb-ref>
        <ejb-ref-name>ejb/Track</ejb-ref-name>
        <ejb-ref-type>Entity</ejb-ref-type>
        <home>track.TrackHome</home>
        <remote>track.Track</remote>
      </ejb-ref>
    </session>
```

```xml
<entity>
  <ejb-name>Album</ejb-name>
  <home>album.AlbumHome</home>
  <remote>album.Album</remote>
  <ejb-class>album.AlbumEJB</ejb-class>
  <persistence-type>Container</persistence-type>
  <prim-key-class>java.lang.Integer</prim-key-class>
  <reentrant>False</reentrant>
  <cmp-field>
    <field-name>albumID</field-name>
  </cmp-field>
  <cmp-field>
    <field-name>albumTitle</field-name>
  </cmp-field>
  <cmp-field>
    <field-name>artist</field-name>
  </cmp-field>
  <cmp-field>
    <field-name>genre</field-name>
  </cmp-field>
  <cmp-field>
    <field-name>cdID</field-name>
  </cmp-field>
  <primkey-field>albumID</primkey-field>
  <ejb-ref>
    <ejb-ref-name>ejb/IDGenerator</ejb-ref-name>
    <ejb-ref-type>Session</ejb-ref-type>
    <home>id.IDGeneratorHome</home>
    <remote>id.IDGenerator</remote>
  </ejb-ref>
  <resource-ref>
    <res-ref-name>jdbc/musicDB</res-ref-name>
    <res-type>javax.sql.DataSource</res-type>
    <res-auth>Container</res-auth>
  </resource-ref>
</entity>

<entity>
  <ejb-name>Track</ejb-name>
  <home>track.TrackHome</home>
  <remote>track.Track</remote>
  <ejb-class>track.TrackEJB</ejb-class>
  <persistence-type>Container</persistence-type>
  <prim-key-class>java.lang.Integer</prim-key-class>
  <reentrant>False</reentrant>
  <cmp-field>
    <field-name>trackID</field-name>
  </cmp-field>
  <cmp-field>
    <field-name>parentAlbumID</field-name>
  </cmp-field>
  <cmp-field>
    <field-name>trackTitle</field-name>
  </cmp-field>
  <cmp-field>
    <field-name>trackLength</field-name>
```

```
            </cmp-field>
            <primkey-field>trackID</primkey-field>
            <ejb-ref>
              <ejb-ref-name>ejb/IDGenerator</ejb-ref-name>
              <ejb-ref-type>Session</ejb-ref-type>
              <home>id.IDGeneratorHome</home>
              <remote>id.IDGenerator</remote>
            </ejb-ref>
            <resource-ref>
              <res-ref-name>jdbc/musicDB</res-ref-name>
              <res-type>javax.sql.DataSource</res-type>
              <res-auth>Container</res-auth>
            </resource-ref>
          </entity>

      </enterprise-beans>

      <assembly-descriptor>
        <container-transaction>
          <method>
            <ejb-name>IDGenerator</ejb-name>
            <method-name>*</method-name>
          </method>
          <trans-attribute>Required</trans-attribute>
        </container-transaction>
        <container-transaction>
          <method>
            <ejb-name>Album</ejb-name>
            <method-name>*</method-name>
          </method>
          <trans-attribute>Required</trans-attribute>
        </container-transaction>
        <container-transaction>
          <method>
            <ejb-name>Track</ejb-name>
            <method-name>*</method-name>
          </method>
          <trans-attribute>Required</trans-attribute>
        </container-transaction>
        <container-transaction>
          <method>
            <ejb-name>InfoService</ejb-name>
            <method-name>*</method-name>
          </method>
          <trans-attribute>Required</trans-attribute>
        </container-transaction>
      </assembly-descriptor>
    </ejb-jar>
```

Compile all the classes and archive all the files with the deployment descriptor into a file called musicDB.jar. Before running the application, we're going to need some information for our bean to return to us. Once the database is set up, using the SQL code shown previously, we can populate it with any information we care to.

Creating the Web Service

For this example, we will use the IBM Web Services Toolkit2.2.1 and IBM WebSphere Application Server 4.0, which has built-in support for web services. The Web Services Toolkit (WSTK) is an environment that enables the design and execution of web service applications that will find one another and collaborate in business transactions.

> *When I first developed this example everything ran like a dream. Then later on I discovered that subsequent releases of the toolkit have temporarily broken the ability to access EJBs on WebSphere Application Server 4.0. Until a corrected version of the toolkit is released, you can get hold of a copy of the 2.2.1 version with the book's source code from the Wrox site (http://www.wrox.com).*

Installing the WSTK is an easy process, and the only potentially problematic part is configuring it to use a UDDI registry. For this, we'll need to enter a user ID and password. Any ID and password will do, since there doesn't seem to be any documentation telling us otherwise.

Creating the WSDL Description

First, we will create a WSDL document that describes the offered service. The Web Services Toolkit provides a tool called the serviceWizard that can take an EJB JAR file and generate WSDL files for the EJBs contained in that JAR file.

The serviceWizard.bat file should be found in the \bin directory of the toolkit (note that the name of this batch file was changed to wsdlgen.bat in later versions of the WSTK). The serviceWizard begins with the following window:

We specify that we want to use an EJB JAR file and click on the Next button. In the topmost text box, if we type in the path to our MusicDB.jar file, the wizard will automatically inspect the JAR and fill some of the properties:

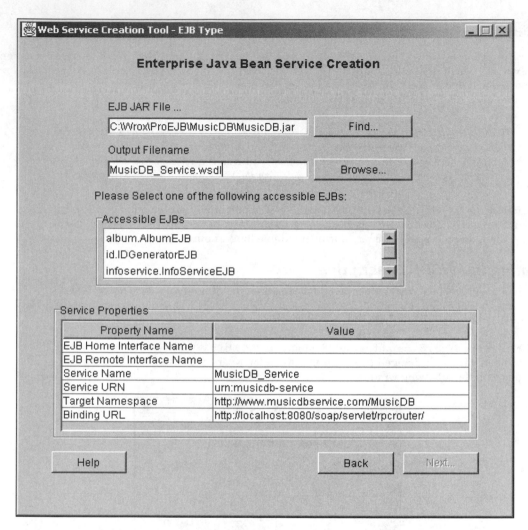

The EJB that implements the web service is called InfoServiceEJB, from the infoservice package (hence it is displayed as infoservice.InfoServiceEJB). We do still need to modify some of the Service Properties, however.

First type in the qualified path to the home and remote interfaces (infoservice.InfoServiceHome and infoservice.InfoService respectively). Then edit the Binding URL to be http://localhost:9080/MusicDB/servlet/rpcrouter, as shown here:

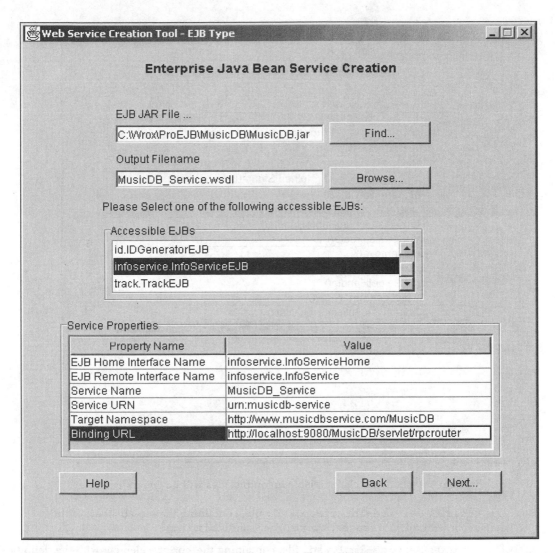

We change the port number to 9080 because the application server is configured to listen to that port. The first part of the URL – **MusicDB** in this example – has to match the context root URI that is used later with the SOAPEAREnabler tool, and then again when the enterprise application is installed. The SOAPEAREnabler tool comes with WebSphere Application Server 4.0 and is covered soon.

Next, select the getCDInfo() method to be wrapped as a web service:

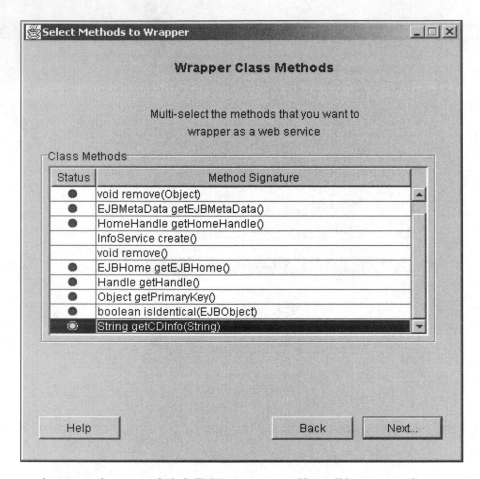

After we confirm our selection and click Finish, two output files will be generated:

❑ The `musicDB_Service-interface.wsdl` file, containing the reusable part of the definition, with the `<message>`, `<portType>`, and `<binding>` elements.

❑ The `musicDB_Service-impl.wsdl` file, containing the `<port>` element with the definition of the SOAP target address.

Creating the SOAP Deployment Descriptor

Now we need to create the deployment descriptor that will tell the Apache SOAP server (which is included in the WebSphere Application Server) how to invoke the service when a SOAP request arrives. Unfortunately, there is no tool that would automatically generate the appropriate deployment descriptor for us, so we have to manually create it. It will be stored in a file called `musicDB_DD.xml` and looks like this:

```
<?xml version="1.0"?>
<isd:service xmlns:isd="http://xml.apache.org/xml-soap/deployment"
             id="urn:musicdb-service">
```

```
   <isd:provider type="com.ibm.soap.providers.WASStatelessEJBProvider"
                  scope="Application" methods="getCDInfo">
    <isd:java class="InfoService"/>
    <isd:option key="FullHomeInterfaceName"
                value="infoservice.InfoServiceHome"/>
    <isd:option key="ContextProviderURL" value="iiop://localhost:900"/>
    <isd:option key="FullContextFactoryName"
                value="com.ibm.websphere.naming.WsnInitialContextFactory"/>
  </isd:provider>
  <isd:faultListener>
    org.apache.soap.server.DOMFaultListener
  </isd:faultListener>
</isd:service>
```

Note that the value of the class attribute in the `<isd:java>` element is the JNDI name of the EJB, not its class name. The SOAP router will use this value to find the Home reference.

Deploying the EJB JAR File

To assemble and deploy the EJB JAR file, we will use the same procedure that we would use for any EJB JAR file. The appendices of this book give detailed descriptions of EJB deployment using several different application servers. In particular, Appendix D provides details of the using the IBM WebSphere Application Server that we will use for the first part of this example. The following screenshot shows the EJB JAR file loaded into the Application Assembly Tool (`assembly.bat` in the /bin directory) of the app server:

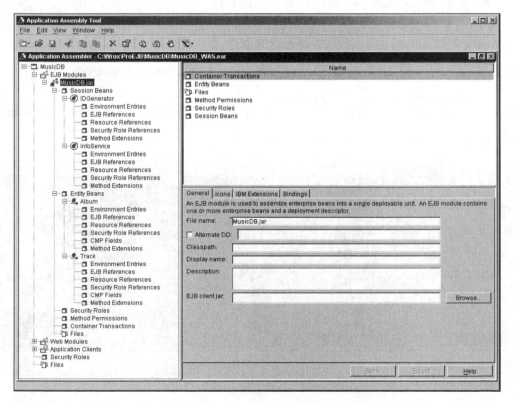

Next, we must generate the deployment code (File | Generate code for deployment) and, before installing the EAR file into the application server, we need to enable the application for use as a web service. This is where SOAP comes into the picture.

Enabling an EAR File for SOAP and Installing It

We will have to add the SOAP server run time and the correct deployment descriptor to the enterprise application before we can install and run it. WebSphere comes with a tool called `SoapEarEnabler` that does this for us. It runs as a command-line tool and prompts us to make a number of decisions. Providing that the `SoapEarEnabler.bat` file is available in your path, run the tool in the same directory in which you have your deployed EAR file (probably called `Deployed_MusicDB.ear`) and the SOAP deployment descriptor file.

Here's what you should select when prompted:

Please enter the name of your ear file: **Deployed_MusicDB.ear**

*** Backing up EAR file to: Deployed_MusicDB.ear~

How many services would you like your application to contain (1...n)?**1**

Now prompting for info for service #1:
    Please enter the file name of the deployment descriptor xml file: **musicDB_DD.xml**
    Is this service an EJB (y = yes /n = no)? **y**
    Please choose an EJB Jar file ([1] MusicDB.jar): **1**
    How many jarfiles are required for this service (0...n)? **1**
    Classpath requirement #1: Please choose a file ([1] MusicDB.jar): **1**
    Should this service be secured (y = yes/n = no)? **y**

Please enter a context root for your secured services (e.g. /soap-sec): **/MusicDB**

Do you wish to install the administration client?
Warning, you should not install this client in a production ear unless you intend to secure the URI to it.

Install the administration client (y = yes/n = no)? **n**

The `SoapEarEnabler` tool adds a web module to our EAR file with the SOAP implementation in it. The SOAP `rpcrouter` servlet is accessible under /MusicDB/servlet/rpcrouter.

We are now ready to install the application into the application server. Appendix D gives instructions on how this is accomplished, so we won't go into too much detail here. We should, however, note that it is important to define the datasource that we are using.

One additional step you'll notice when we install the EAR file into the server is that we will be prompted about the SOAP WAR file that the SOAP enabler added for us:

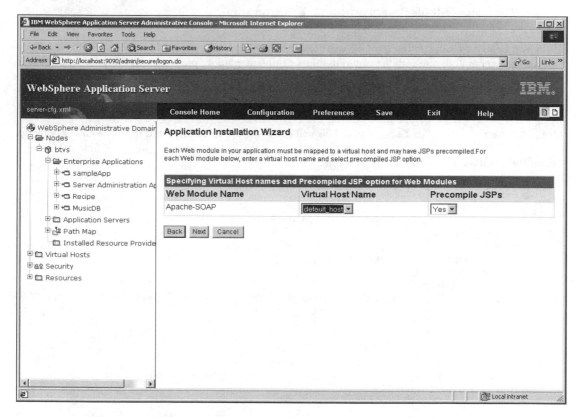

Now that we have the service deployed and installed, the only thing left to do is check if it really works!

Creating a Test Client

We will use another tool from the Web Services Toolkit to generate a Java test client for our service. More specifically, we'll be using a code generator from the WSDL toolkit that uses the WSDL definition as input as it contains all of the information that is needed.

We can invoke the code generator, assuming that the appropriate classpath is set (see below), by entering the following on the command line:

```
java com.ibm.wsdl.Main -in MusicDB_Service-impl.wsdl
```

For this to work we need to add;

- ❑ The WSDL toolkit (`%WSTK_HOME%\wsdl-toolkit\lib\wsdl.jar`)
- ❑ The SOAP JAR file (`%WSTK_HOME%\soap\lib\soap.jar`)
- ❑ The BSF JAR file (`%WSTK_HOME%\lib\bsf.jar`)
- ❑ The Xerces JAR file (`%WSTK_HOME%\lib\xerces.jar`)
- ❑ The Xalan JAR file (`%WSTK_HOME%\lib\xalan.jar`)

However, before we can run this tool, we will have to make some changes to the WSDL file. Remember that two files are generated, one with the non-reusable, or implementation, part of the WSDL definition and one with the reusable, or interface, part. The implementation file contains an element that imports the interface file, and the WSDL generator assumes a particular location for the interface file. To make this work properly, we must change the location attribute of the import element in the `musicdb_Service-impl.wsdl` file from `http://localhost:8080/wsdl/MusicDB_Service-interface.wsdl` to `MusicDB_Service-interface.wsdl`. This will cause the file to be imported from the current directory.

Secondly, we need to amend the `rpcrouter` URL:

```
<service name="MusicDB_Service">
  <documentation>
      IBM WSTK 2.0 generated service definition file
  </documentation>
  <port
      binding="MusicDB_ServiceBinding"
      name="MusicDB_ServicePort">
      <soap:address
      location="http://localhost:9080/MusicDB/servlet/rpcrouter"/>
  </port>
</service>

<import
    location="MusicDB_Service-interface.wsdl"
    namespace="http://www.musicdbservice.com/MusicDB-interface">
</import>
```

The generated file is called `MusicDB_ServiceProxy.java`. You should notice that this file has no dependency on the target EJB JAR file. In fact, it does not know that it is making a call to an EJB, or even to a Java application, since all communication is done via SOAP.

Here's what it should look like:

```
import java.net.*;
import java.util.*;
import org.apache.soap.*;
import org.apache.soap.encoding.*;
import org.apache.soap.rpc.*;
import org.apache.soap.util.xml.*;

public class MusicDB_ServiceProxy
{
  private Call call = new Call();
  private URL url = null;
  private String SOAPActionURI = "";
```

```
      private SOAPMappingRegistry smr = call.getSOAPMappingRegistry();

      public MusicDB_ServiceProxy() throws MalformedURLException
      {
         call.setTargetObjectURI("urn:musicdb-service");
         call.setEncodingStyleURI("http://schemas.xmlsoap.org/soap/encoding/");
         this.url = new URL("http://localhost:9080/MusicDB/servlet/rpcrouter");
         this.SOAPActionURI = "urn:musicdb-service";
      }

      public synchronized void setEndPoint(URL url)
      {
         this.url = url;
      }

      public synchronized URL getEndPoint()
      {
         return url;
      }

      public synchronized java.lang.String getCDInfo
         (java.lang.String meth1_inType1) throws SOAPException
      {
         if (url == null)
         {
            throw new SOAPException(Constants.FAULT_CODE_CLIENT,
            "A URL must be specified via " +
            "MusicDB_ServiceProxy.setEndPoint(URL).");
         }

         call.setMethodName("getCDInfo");
         Vector params = new Vector();
         Parameter meth1_inType1Param = new Parameter("meth1_inType1",
            java.lang.String.class, meth1_inType1, null);
         params.addElement(meth1_inType1Param);
         call.setParams(params);
         Response resp = call.invoke(url, SOAPActionURI);

         // Check the response.
         if (resp.generatedFault())
         {
            Fault fault = resp.getFault();

            throw new SOAPException(fault.getFaultCode(), fault.getFaultString());
         }
         else
         {
            Parameter retValue = resp.getReturnValue();
            return (java.lang.String)retValue.getValue();
         }
      }

   }
```

The last thing we will do is to create a command-line client that uses the generated class to make a call to the service. The client code is very simple and looks like this:

```
import org.apache.soap.SOAPException;
import java.net.MalformedURLException;

public class MusicServiceClient {

  public static void main(String args[]) {

    try {
      MusicDB_ServiceProxy proxy = new MusicDB_ServiceProxy();
      String s = proxy.getCDInfo(args[0]);
      System.out.println("Result string is : " + s);
    } catch (java.net.MalformedURLException me) {
      System.out.println(me);
    } catch (org.apache.soap.SOAPException se) {
      System.out.println(se);
    }
  }
}
```

To run this example, compile the `MusicDB_ServiceProxy` and `MusicServiceClient` classes, making sure you have all the JAR files listed earlier still in your classpath. Then simply run the `MusicServiceClient` class (from the IBM JVM that ships with the WebSphere server) passing in the CD ID as a parameter (you will also need the `j2ee.jar` file in your classpath now):

```
%WAS_HOME%\java\bin\java MusicServiceClient GlassDracula1999
```

Assuming you have some data in your tables you will get a result back like the following:

What we have not shown here is the publishing of our service into a UDDI registry. There are multiple registries existing, for example, at http://www.ibm.com/services/uddi/, which we can use to register a service, including a test registry for testing purposes.

EJB Web Services on CapeConnect

CapeClear, http://www.capeclear.com, has a product called CapeConnect that provides another easy means to expose our EJBs as web services. This tool enables us to dynamically create SOAP Web Services from EJB, J2EE, and CORBA components. One of the advantages of CapeConnect is that, although it is a J2EE engine itself, we can also take the web services engine and lay it on top of other J2EE containers, such as BEA's WebLogic. This way we don't even need to touch our existing beans to expose them as web services.

In this part of the chapter we will take our musicDB beans and expose them as a web service deployed in WebLogic 6.0.

The CapeConnect Architecture

The CapeConnect product (currently in version Two) is based around the concept of making HTTP(S) the standard protocol for accessing EJBs. The consequence of this is that our EJBs are thus exposed on the web to any client that can communicate using SOAP.

The CapeConnect architecture is primarily composed of three components:

❑ The gateway is a servlet that intercepts incoming SOAP calls

❑ The XML engine is a translation engine between the SOAP calls and the EJBs

❑ The EJB server contains the EJBs hosted for access (the EJB server may or may not be CapeConnect)

This architecture, and the interactions between the three components, can be visualized more clearly with the following diagram:

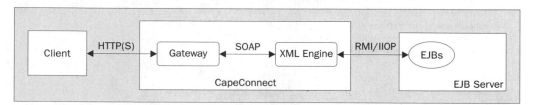

SOAPDirect

In addition to its basic architecture, CapeConnect also comes with a Java API called SOAPDirect. SOAPDirect is an easy means to write SOAP clients for the CapeConnect system by providing a way to handle the XML documents needed for transport without explicitly handling the XML. We'll be looking at how to use SOAPDirect later when we write a client for our musicDB beans through CapeConnect.

Deploying the MusicDB Beans in WebLogic

We need to modify our beans slightly and write some additional deployment descriptors to deploy them in WebLogic 6.0.

The only coding change we need to make is to make sure that WebLogic uses the correct DocumentBuilder implementation.

To do this we need to set the system property in the `buildXMLDoc()` method of `InfoServiceEJB`:

```
try {

        //For Weblogic
        System.setProperty("javax.xml.parsers.DocumentBuilderFactory",
                    "org.apache.crimson.jaxp.DocumentBuilderFactoryImpl");

        //Start building XML doc
        DocumentBuilderFactory dbf = DocumentBuilderFactory.newInstance();
        DocumentBuilder db = dbf.newDocumentBuilder();

        doc = db.newDocument();
```

Now we need three additional deployment descriptors for our WebLogic deployment. Refer to Appendix C for more information on deploying EJBs in WebLogic.

weblogic-ejb-jar.xml

```xml
<?xml version="1.0"?>

<!DOCTYPE weblogic-ejb-jar PUBLIC
        '-//BEA Systems, Inc.//DTD WebLogic 5.1.0 EJB//EN'
        'http://www.bea.com/servers/wls510/dtd/weblogic-ejb-jar.dtd'>

<weblogic-ejb-jar>
  <weblogic-enterprise-bean>
    <ejb-name>IDGenerator</ejb-name>
    <reference-descriptor>
      <resource-description>
        <res-ref-name>jdbc/musicDB</res-ref-name>
        <jndi-name>musicDB</jndi-name>
      </resource-description>
    </reference-descriptor>
    <jndi-name>IDGenerator</jndi-name>
  </weblogic-enterprise-bean>

  <weblogic-enterprise-bean>
    <ejb-name>InfoService</ejb-name>
    <reference-descriptor>
      <ejb-reference-description>
        <ejb-ref-name>ejb/Album</ejb-ref-name>
        <jndi-name>Album</jndi-name>
      </ejb-reference-description>
      <ejb-reference-description>
        <ejb-ref-name>ejb/Track</ejb-ref-name>
        <jndi-name>Track</jndi-name>
      </ejb-reference-description>
    </reference-descriptor>
    <jndi-name>InfoService</jndi-name>
  </weblogic-enterprise-bean>

  <weblogic-enterprise-bean>
    <ejb-name>Album</ejb-name>
    <persistence-descriptor>
```

```
      <persistence-type>
        <type-identifier>WebLogic_CMP_RDBMS</type-identifier>
        <type-version>5.1.0</type-version>
        <type-storage>
              META-INF/weblogic-cmp-rdbms-jar-album.xml
        </type-storage>
      </persistence-type>
      <persistence-use>
        <type-identifier>WebLogic_CMP_RDBMS</type-identifier>
        <type-version>5.1.0</type-version>
      </persistence-use>
    </persistence-descriptor>
    <reference-descriptor>
      <resource-description>
        <res-ref-name>jdbc/musicDB</res-ref-name>
        <jndi-name>musicDB</jndi-name>
      </resource-description>
      <ejb-reference-description>
        <ejb-ref-name>ejb/IDGenerator</ejb-ref-name>
        <jndi-name>IDGenerator</jndi-name>
      </ejb-reference-description>
    </reference-descriptor>
    <jndi-name>Album</jndi-name>
  </weblogic-enterprise-bean>

  <weblogic-enterprise-bean>
    <ejb-name>Track</ejb-name>
    <persistence-descriptor>
      <persistence-type>
        <type-identifier>WebLogic_CMP_RDBMS</type-identifier>
        <type-version>5.1.0</type-version>
        <type-storage>
              META-INF/weblogic-cmp-rdbms-jar-track.xml
        </type-storage>
      </persistence-type>
      <persistence-use>
        <type-identifier>WebLogic_CMP_RDBMS</type-identifier>
        <type-version>5.1.0</type-version>
      </persistence-use>
    </persistence-descriptor>
    <reference-descriptor>
      <resource-description>
        <res-ref-name>jdbc/musicDB</res-ref-name>
        <jndi-name>musicDB</jndi-name>
      </resource-description>
      <ejb-reference-description>
        <ejb-ref-name>ejb/IDGenerator</ejb-ref-name>
        <jndi-name>IDGenerator</jndi-name>
      </ejb-reference-description>
    </reference-descriptor>
    <jndi-name>Track</jndi-name>
  </weblogic-enterprise-bean>

</weblogic-ejb-jar>
```

weblogic-cmp-rdbms-jar-track.xml

```xml
<?xml version="1.0"?>
<!DOCTYPE weblogic-rdbms-bean PUBLIC
    '-//BEA Systems, Inc.//DTD WebLogic 5.1.0 EJB RDBMS Persistence//EN'
    'http://www.bea.com/servers/wls510/dtd/weblogic-rdbms-persistence.dtd'>

<weblogic-rdbms-bean>
  <pool-name>musicDB</pool-name>
  <table-name>tracks</table-name>
  <attribute-map>
    <object-link>
      <bean-field>trackID</bean-field>
      <dbms-column>trackID</dbms-column>
    </object-link>
    <object-link>
      <bean-field>trackTitle</bean-field>
      <dbms-column>trackTitle</dbms-column>
    </object-link>
    <object-link>
      <bean-field>trackLength</bean-field>
      <dbms-column>trackLength</dbms-column>
    </object-link>
    <object-link>
      <bean-field>parentAlbumID</bean-field>
      <dbms-column>parentAlbumID</dbms-column>
    </object-link>
  </attribute-map>

  <finder-list>
    <finder>
        <method-name>findByParentAlbumID</method-name>
        <method-params>
          <method-param>java.lang.Integer</method-param>
        </method-params>
        <finder-query><![CDATA[(= parentAlbumID $0)]]></finder-query>
    </finder>
  </finder-list>

</weblogic-rdbms-bean>
```

weblogic-cmp-rdbms-jar-album.xml

```xml
<?xml version="1.0"?>

<!DOCTYPE weblogic-rdbms-bean PUBLIC
    '-//BEA Systems, Inc.//DTD WebLogic 5.1.0 EJB RDBMS Persistence//EN'
    'http://www.bea.com/servers/wls510/dtd/weblogic-rdbms-persistence.dtd'>

<weblogic-rdbms-bean>
    <pool-name>musicDB</pool-name>
     <table-name>albums</table-name>
     <attribute-map>
       <object-link>
         <bean-field>albumID</bean-field>
         <dbms-column>albumID</dbms-column>
```

```
          </object-link>
          <object-link>
            <bean-field>albumTitle</bean-field>
            <dbms-column>albumTitle</dbms-column>
          </object-link>
          <object-link>
            <bean-field>artist</bean-field>
            <dbms-column>artist</dbms-column>
          </object-link>
          <object-link>
            <bean-field>cdID</bean-field>
            <dbms-column>cdID</dbms-column>
          </object-link>
          <object-link>
            <bean-field>genre</bean-field>
            <dbms-column>genre</dbms-column>
          </object-link>
        </attribute-map>
        <finder-list>
          <finder>
            <method-name>findByAlbumTitle</method-name>
            <method-params>
              <method-param>java.lang.String</method-param>
            </method-params>
            <finder-query><![CDATA[(= albumTitle $0)]]></finder-query>
          </finder>
          <finder>  `
            <method-name>findByCDIdentifier</method-name>
            <method-params>
              <method-param>java.lang.String</method-param>
            </method-params>
            <finder-query><![CDATA[(= cdID $0)]]></finder-query>
          </finder>

        </finder-list>
      </weblogic-rdbms-bean>
```

To deploy the beans, we need to take the `musicDB.jar` file with the additional deployment descriptors in the `META-INF` directory and use it to generate a new WebLogic specific JAR file that contains all the stubs and skeletons as well as WebLogic wrapper code for our beans. To do this we need to run the `ejbc` utility in `weblogic.jar`:

```
java -classpath c:\bea\wlserver6.0sp1\lib\weblogic.jar;
     c:\j2sdkee1.3\lib\j2ee.jar weblogic.ejbc musicDB.jar musicDB_WL.jar
```

Once we have our `musicDB_WL.jar` file we can copy it into the `applications` directory of our WebLogic domain (`c:\bea\wlserver6.0sp1\config\mydomain\applications`) to deploy the beans. However, before the beans can run successfully, we need to define the JDBC datasource and connection pool called `musicDB` to connect to our database. To do this in WebLogic, either use the web application administration console or edit the `config.xml` file. Again, refer Appendix C or the WebLogic documentation for instructions on how to do this.

Connecting WebLogic with CapeConnect

Now we have our beans deployed in WebLogic, we want to add the CapeConnect web services layer on top of WebLogic to expose our beans as a web service.

To do this we need to configure CapeConnect to work with WebLogic, which involves two steps:

❑ Configure CapeConnect to communicate with WebLogic

❑ Configure WebLogic to communicate with CapeConnect

Configuring CapeConnect

If you had WebLogic installed when you installed CapeConnect you should have already gone through the process to allow CapeConnect to automatically configure itself to connect with WebLogic.

If not then you will need to modify a few files:

❑ In the `console/conf/console.properties` file, add the following line to point to your WebLogic home directory, for example `c:\bea\wlserver6.0sp1`:

```
com.capeclear.capeconnect.console.env.WL_HOME=[weblogic directory]
```

❑ In the `xmlengine/conf/server.policy` file you need to add the following permission:

```
grant codeBase "file:${WL_HOME}/classes/-" {
  permission java.net.SocketPermission "[host]",
                                "connect,accept,listen,resolve";
```

where `[host]` is the name of your local XML engine host.

Configuring WebLogic 6.0

WebLogic requires a proxy bean from CapeConnect to act as an interface between the deployed EJBs in WebLogic and the CapeConnect XML engine:

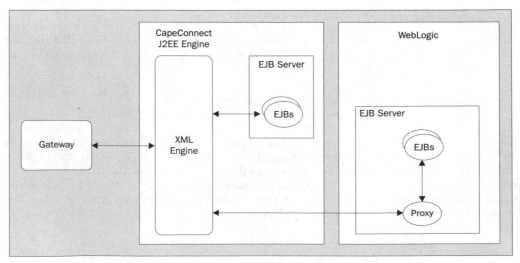

Therefore, we need to deploy this bean into WebLogic and make a few additional tweaks to enable this bean to run successfully.

Deploying the bean is easy. Merely copy the `ccproxybean-weblogic.jar` file from the `lib/cccallbean` directory of CapeConnect into your WebLogic domain's applications directory as we did before, or use the administration console to achieve the same thing.

Since this bean is a CapeConnect product, it requires some additional JAR files to execute successfully, therefore we need to modify the `startWebLogic.cmd` file for the WebLogic domain by adding the following:

```
set CCTWO_HOME=[cape connect installation directory]

set CLASSPATH=%CLASSPATH%;
              %CCTWO_HOME%/lib/capeconnect.jar;%CCTWO_HOME%/lib/common.jar
```

We are now ready to set up our web service.

Configuring the Web Service

Once the above two configuration steps are complete, setting up our EJBs as a web service is as easy as a few clicks of the mouse button.

First we need to make sure that all the various pieces of software are running:

❑   Start the WebLogic server using the Start menu, or by running the `cmd` file that we have just modified.

❑   Start the CapeConnect Console server using the Start menu, or the `start-console-server` batch file in the `\bin` directory.

❑   Start the CapeConnect Console using the Start menu, or the `start-console` batch file in the `\bin` directory.

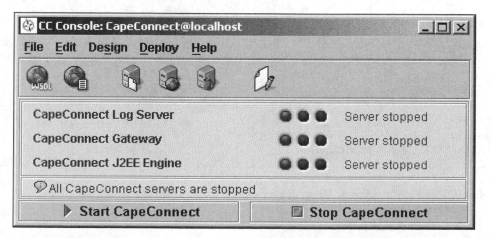

❑   Press the Start CapeConnect button on the console, as shown above.

Now, to configure our web service choose the Deployed Web Application Settings option from the Edit menu on the console. This will bring up the Deployed Web Application Settings window:

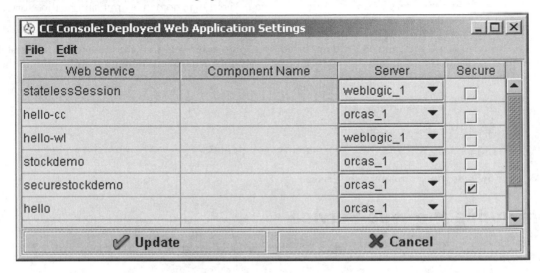

Now choose, Edit | Insert New Application Setting. In the Web Service column enter the name of the service CDInfo_Service, and in the Server column drop-down the box and select our WebLogic mapping, in our case weblogic_1:

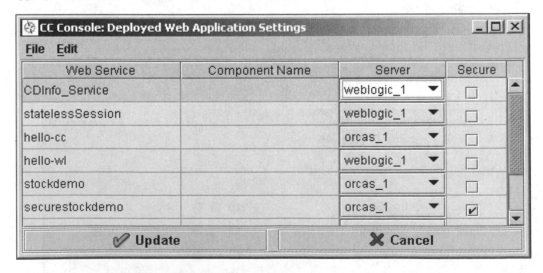

We can leave the Component Name column blank because our client will be using the default CapeConnect SOAPAction format.

Finally, just hit the Update button and our WebLogic bean is configured as a web service.

Generating WSDL with CapeConnect

Unlike in the WebSphere example, we have yet to generate any WSDL for our web service. This is because using CapeConnect we only need to generate WSDL if we are using clients that read WSDL or we are using a custom-format version of SOAPDirect. The client we will be developing uses standard SOAPDirect, so WSDL generation will be unnecessary. However, it is very easy to do in CapeConnect.

From the console go to Design | Generate WSDL. This will bring up the CapeConnect WDSL Generator:

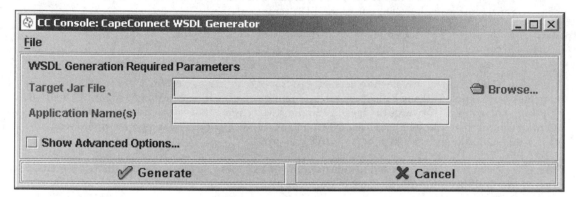

To generate WSDL, enter a path to the EJB JAR file that contains the beans to be exposed and give it a unique application name (which becomes the web service name), before hitting the Generate button:

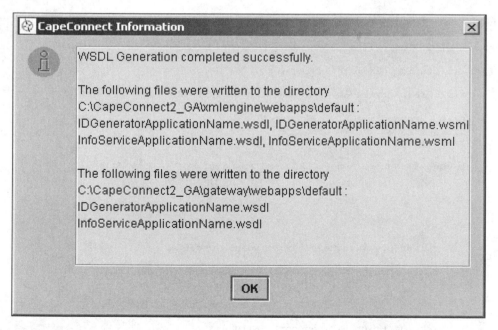

By default, the generator writes the WSDL files to `xmlengine/webapps/default` and `gateway/webapps/default` but this can be changed in the Advanced Options section of the generator, if necessary.

Testing the Web Service using SOAPDirect

We will be using the SOAPDirect API provided by CapeConnect to write a simple client for our beans that will handle all the complexities of communicating via SOAP.

SOAPDirect is primarily based around two objects that encapsulate the request/reply mechanism:

- ❑ SDRequest – This object allows us to create and send requests, where each request represents a single call to one of the EJBs remote methods.

- ❑ SDReply – This object allows us to examine the return results from the EJB, or any exceptions raised.

Under the CapeConnect architecture, a client sends a SOAP message to the gateway. This message indicates which bean is being called, the method being called, and any arguments that the method requires. The gateway forwards the message to the XML engine that translates the message into the method call on the requested bean. The XML engine also accepts any response from the bean and passes it back to the gateway as another SOAP message.

Therefore, from our client we need to construct the SOAP message that indicates the bean method we wish to call and then pass this message to the gateway.

Let's now look at how we do this using SOAPDirect. Here's our complete client class, which we'll discuss shortly:

```
import com.capeclear.soapdirect.*;

public class MusicClient_SOAPDirect {

  public static void main(String[] args) {

    String soapServiceURL = "http://localhost:8080/ccgw/GWXmlServlet";

    String appName = "CDInfo_Service";
    String beanName = "InfoService";
    String methodName = "getCDInfo";

    SDRequest request = new SDRequest(appName + ":" + beanName + "#" +
                                      methodName);

    request.add("id", args[0]);

    try {

      SDReply reply = request.invoke(soapServiceURL);

        System.out.println("CDInfo: " + reply.getString());

    } catch (SDInvalidSOAPException ise) {
      System.out.println("Invalid SOAP Exception: " + ise);
    } catch (SDTransportFailureException tfe) {
      System.out.println("Transport Failure: " + tfe);
    }
  }
}
```

First let's look at the variables we declared:

```
String soapServiceURL = "http://localhost:8080/ccgw/GWXmlServlet";
```

The `soapServiceURL` variable is the URL to the CapeConnect gateway servlet. This is the destination to which we send our SOAPMessage.

```
String appName = "CDInfo_Service";
String beanName = "InfoService";
String methodName = "getCDInfo";
```

The `appName`, `beanName`, and `methodName` variables are used to construct a URI that represents the method call that we want to make. This URI takes the format:

```
capeconnect:application_name:bean_name#method_name
```

Note how the `appName` variable maps the new web application that we defined earlier using the administration console. The `beanName` and `methodName` are self-evident.

The next step is then to create our request object. We do this by passing in the target URI to the constructor:

```
SDRequest request = new SDRequest(appName + ":" + beanName + "#" +
                                  methodName);
```

The final step is to add the identifying CD key as an argument to the method call. To do this we need to call the `add()` method on the `SDRequest` object, passing in the name of the parameter and the value:

```
request.add("id", args[0]);
```

We are now ready to pass the SOAP message to the gateway servlet. To do this, we simply need to call the `invoke()` method passing in the URL to the gateway servlet:

```
SDReply reply = request.invoke(soapServiceURL);
```

When we run this client, we should get the same result as before, except this time we are going through CapeConnect, to WebLogic, and back again. Depending on what your MusicDB data source contains, you might get an output that looks something like this:

```
C:\WINNT\System32\cmd.exe                                        _ |□| x|

C:\Wrox\ProEJB\MusicDB>java -classpath C:\CapeConnect2_GA\client\soapdirect.jar;
. MusicClient_SOAP "GlassDracula1999"
CDInfo: <?xml version="1.0" encoding="UTF-8"?>
<album><album-title>Dracula</album-title><artist>The Kronos Quartet</artist><gen
re>The Kronos Quartet</genre><tracks><track><track-title>Dracula</track-title><t
rack-length>1:00</track-length></track><track><track-title>Journey to the Inn</t
rack-title><track-length>1:00</track-length></track><track><track-title>The Inn<
/track-title><track-length>1:00</track-length></track><track><track-title>The Cr
ypt</track-title><track-length>1:00</track-length></track><track><track-title>Th
e Carriage without a driver</track-title><track-length>1:00</track-length></trac
k><track><track-title>The Castle</track-title><track-length>1:00</track-length><
/track><track><track-title>The Drawing Room</track-title><track-length>1:00</tra
ck-length></track></tracks></album>

C:\Wrox\ProEJB\MusicDB>
```

Summary

In this chapter, we have taken a brief look at web services, and how we can expose existing EJBs to the world of web services. We have seen that:

❑ Web services are similar to EJBs, in that they are both designed to be run in a distributed environment (web services more so), and both need a specific interface mechanism.

❑ Web services involve several specifications: SOAP for communication, WSDL for description, and UDDI for registering and finding web services.

❑ We can expose existing EJB applications as web services in a number of ways. Specifically, we looked at using IBM's Web Services Toolkit and CapeClear's CapeConnect product.

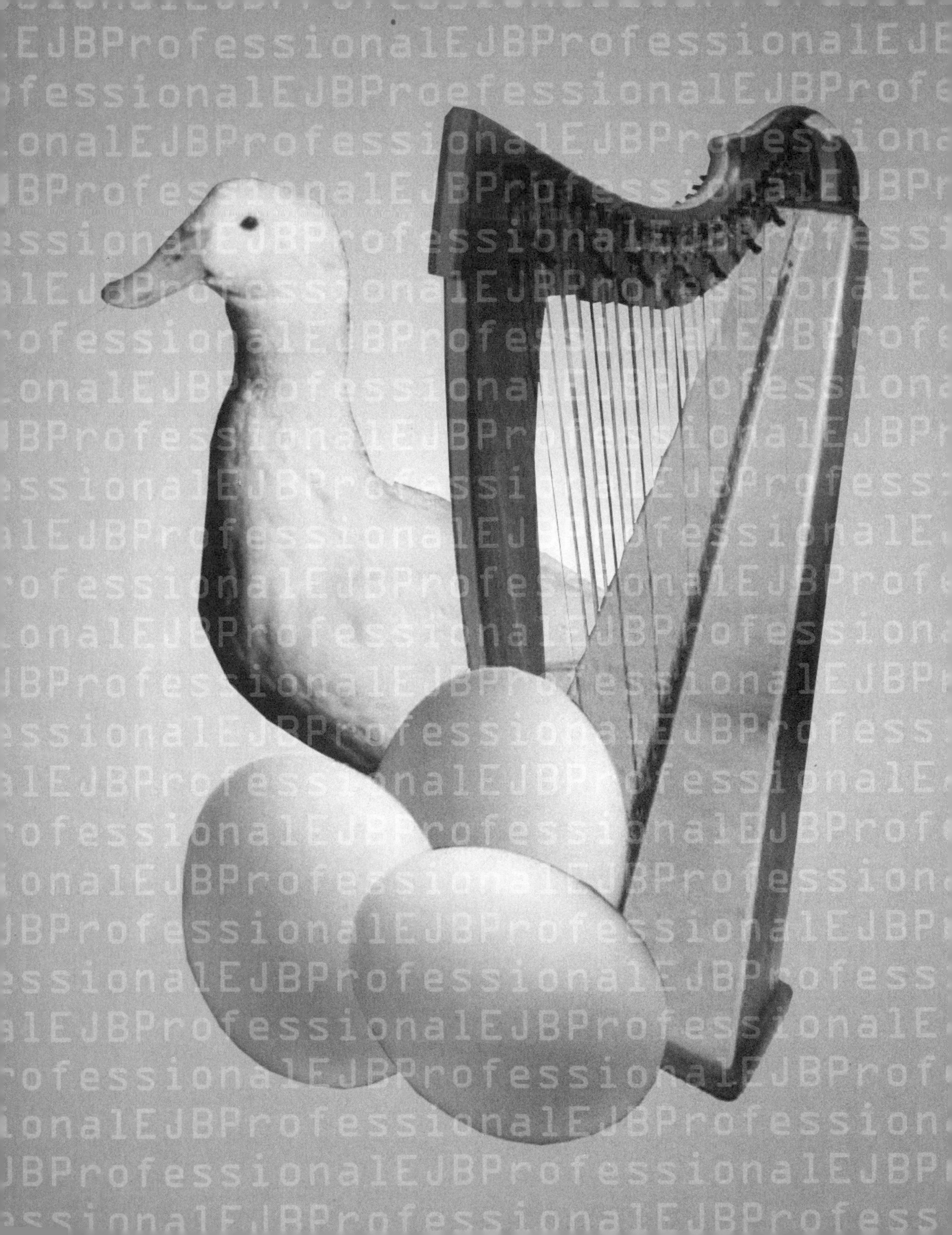
EJBProfessional

The Recipe Beans

In the following appendices, we shall be taking a look at deployment issues with a number of the leading application servers. In order to get a good comparison, we'll be using one set of beans to deploy on each server. This appendix presents code listings for all the beans involved (there are four of them), the SQL scripts used to generate tables for the entity bean persistence, and the client code that uses the beans.

At the time of writing most application servers only supported the EJB 1.1 specification, therefore, most of the appendices will be based on the following 1.1 beans. We have also provided a 2.0 version of the beans for those servers that have produced updates for the latest specification.

The Recipe Beans for EJB 1.1

The application, Recipe Beans, models the actions and interactions of a small restaurant – there are recipes for various dishes, a larder to store the ingredients in, a kitchen in which to prepare the dishes, a menu listing what dishes are on offer, and finally a chef to do the work. In the first four of these objects, the EJBs, we find BMP and CMP entity beans, and stateless and stateful session beans.

The CookBook EJB

The CookBook EJB is an entity bean that represents just that, a cookbook. The bean uses BMP to store recipes in a database table, and read them out on demand. Here is the SQL to generate the RECIPEBOOK table the bean uses:

```
CREATE TABLE RECIPEBOOK (
                RECIPENAME VARCHAR(30),
                INGREDIENTS VARCHAR(500)
);
```

The CookBook Home Interface

```
package recipeBook.cookBook;

public interface CookBookHome extends javax.ejb.EJBHome {
  CookBook findByPrimaryKey(String recipeName)
          throws java.rmi.RemoteException, javax.ejb.FinderException;

  CookBook create(String recipeName, String ingredients)
          throws java.rmi.RemoteException, javax.ejb.CreateException;
}
```

The CookBook Remote Interface

```
package recipeBook.cookBook;

public interface CookBook extends javax.ejb.EJBObject {
  public String[][] getIngredients() throws java.rmi.RemoteException;
}
```

The CookBook Implementation Class

```
package recipeBook.cookBook;

import java.sql.*;
import javax.naming.*;
import javax.ejb.*;
import javax.sql.DataSource;

public class CookBookEJB implements EntityBean {
  public String recipeName;
  public String ingredients;

  EntityContext ctx;

  public void setEntityContext(EntityContext ctx) {
    this.ctx = ctx;
  }

  public void unsetEntityContext() {
    ctx = null;
  }

  /**
   * Standard EJB callbacks not implemented
   */
  public void ejbStore() {}
  public void ejbRemove() {}
  public void ejbActivate() {}
  public void ejbPassivate() {}
  public void ejbPostCreate(String key, String relatedData) {}

  /**
   * Retrieve ingredient list from RecipeBook table using recipename
   */
  public void ejbLoad() {
```

```
   recipeName = (String) ctx.getPrimaryKey();
   Connection conn = null;

   try {
     conn = getConnection();

     String sql = "SELECT INGREDIENTS FROM RECIPEBOOK WHERE RECIPENAME = '"
                  + recipeName.toLowerCase() + "'";
     Statement statement = conn.createStatement();
     ResultSet rs = statement.executeQuery(sql);

     if (!rs.next()) {
       throw new EJBException("Object not found");
     }
     ingredients = rs.getString(1);
     rs.close();
     statement.close();

   } catch (SQLException sqle) {
     throw new EJBException(sqle);
   }
   finally {
     try {
       if (conn != null) {
         conn.close();
       }
     } catch (SQLException sqle) {}
   }
}

/**
 * Store new recipe in the RECIPEBOOK table
 */
public String ejbCreate(String recipeName, String ingredients)
        throws javax.ejb.CreateException {

  this.recipeName = recipeName;
  this.ingredients = ingredients;

  Connection conn = null;
  try {
    conn = getConnection();
    PreparedStatement stmt =
      conn.prepareStatement("INSERT INTO RECIPEBOOK" +
                          " (RECIPENAME, INGREDIENTS) VALUES (?, ?)");
    stmt.setString(1, recipeName);
    stmt.setString(2, ingredients);

    if (stmt.executeUpdate() != 1) {
      throw new javax.ejb.CreateException("Failed to create recipe");
    }
  } catch (SQLException sqle) {
    throw new javax.ejb.EJBException(sqle);
  }
  finally {
```

```
        try {
          if (conn != null) {
            conn.close();
          }
        } catch (SQLException sqle) {}
      }

    return recipeName;
  }

  /**
   * Locate bean by primary key, in this case the recipename field
   */
  public String ejbFindByPrimaryKey(String primaryKey)
          throws FinderException {

    Connection conn = null;
    try {
      conn = getConnection();
      String sql = "SELECT * FROM RECIPEBOOK WHERE RECIPENAME = '"
                    + primaryKey.toLowerCase() + "'";
      Statement statement = conn.createStatement();
      ResultSet rs = statement.executeQuery(sql);

      if (!rs.next()) {
        throw new ObjectNotFoundException();
      }
      rs.close();
      conn.close();
      recipeName = primaryKey;
      return primaryKey;

    } catch (SQLException sqle) {
      throw new EJBException(sqle);
    }
    finally {
      try {
        if (conn != null) {
          conn.close();
        }
      } catch (SQLException sql) {}
    }
  }

  /**
   * Takes the string stored in the database listing
   * required ingredients and amount required
   * in the form "ingredient1, amount1|ingredient2, amount2|"
   * and splits it into a 2D array of
   * the ingredient name and the recipe requirement, of the form:
   * [ingredient1][amount1]
   * [ingredient2][amount2]
   */
  public String[][] getIngredients() {

    int i = 0;
```

```
      //Convert ingredients list into a StringTokenizer
      StringTokenizer parser = new StringTokenizer(ingredients, "|");

      //Count number ingredients to make array
      String[][] arrIngredients = new String[2][parser.countTokens()];

      //Parse delimited ingredients string into an array of ingredient
      //and quantity needed
      while (parser.hasMoreTokens()) {
        try {
          StringTokenizer line = new StringTokenizer(parser.nextToken(), ",");
          arrIngredients[0][i] = line.nextToken();
          arrIngredients[1][i] = line.nextToken();
        } catch (StringIndexOutOfBoundsException e) {}
        i++;
      }
      return arrIngredients;
    }

    /**
     * Gets the datasource to the db
     */
    private Connection getConnection() {
      try {
        Context initial = new InitialContext();
        DataSource datasource =
          (DataSource) initial.lookup("java:comp/env/jdbc/recipeJDBC");
        return datasource.getConnection();
      } catch (javax.naming.NamingException ne) {
        ne.printStackTrace();
        throw new EJBException(ne);
      } catch (SQLException sqle) {
        sqle.printStackTrace();
        throw new EJBException(sqle);
      }
    }
  }
```

When a CookBook EJB is created, it takes the name and ingredients passed, and loads them into the RECIPEBOOK table, returning the name of the recipe as proof of completion. Upon loading, a CookBook EJB connects to the database and extracts the ingredients list from the database for the recipe stored in the context.

Since the database stored the ingredients in the form of a single string, the getIngredients() method parses the string into a two-dimensional array of strings.

The Larder EJB

The Larder EJB is another entity bean, this time using CMP to store the stock information on ingredients required for the various recipes that will be created. Here is the SQL to create the LARDER table required to store this information:

```
CREATE TABLE LARDER (
                INGREDIENTNAME VARCHAR(20),
                STOCK INT
);
```

Each instance of the Larder bean will add an ingredient to the database, along with the amount in stock, check for stock levels meeting a requirement, check for general stock levels, and identify itself.

The Larder Home Interface

```
package recipeBook.larder;

import java.util.Collection;

public interface LarderHome extends javax.ejb.EJBHome {
  Larder findByPrimaryKey(String ingredientName)
        throws java.rmi.RemoteException, javax.ejb.FinderException;

  Collection findLowStockLevels(int stockLevel)
            throws java.rmi.RemoteException, javax.ejb.FinderException;

  Larder create(String ingredientName, int stock)
        throws java.rmi.RemoteException, javax.ejb.CreateException;
}
```

The Larder Remote Interface

```
package recipeBook.larder;

public interface Larder extends javax.ejb.EJBObject {
  public int checkInventoryFor(int amountNeeded)
throws java.rmi.RemoteException;
  public String getIngredientName() throws java.rmi.RemoteException;
  public int getStockLevel() throws java.rmi.RemoteException;
}
```

The Larder Implementation Class

```
package recipeBook.larder;

import javax.ejb.*;

public class LarderEJB implements EntityBean {

  public String ingredientName;
  public int stock;

  /**
   * Standard EJB callcacks, not implemented
   */
  public void ejbStore() {}
  public void ejbRemove() {}
  public void ejbActivate() {}
  public void ejbPassivate() {}
  public void setEntityContext(EntityContext ctx) {}
  public void unsetEntityContext() {}
  public void ejbPostCreate(String ingredientName, int stock) {}

  /**
   * Retrieve ingredients data from Larder table
```

```
   * and trim any extra space characters
   */
  public void ejbLoad() {
    if (ingredientName != null) {
      ingredientName.trim();
    }
  }


  /**
   * Save new ingredient stock in Larder table
   */
  public String ejbCreate(String ingredientName,
                          int stock) throws CreateException {
    this.ingredientName = ingredientName;
    this.stock = stock;
    return null;
  }


  /**
   * Compare stock level in Larder table with
   * the value required and return the difference
   */
  public int checkInventoryFor(int amountNeeded) {
    if (amountNeeded < stock) {
      return 0;
    } else {
      return (amountNeeded - stock);
    }
  }

  public String getIngredientName() {
    return this.ingredientName;
  }

  public int getStockLevel() {
    return this.stock;
  }
}
```

Since the Larder EJB takes advantage of CMP, we don't need to specify how it saves the information it is given – that's the container's problem. When a Larder bean is created, it stores the name of the ingredient it is to represent and the amount of stock it has in its ingredientName and stock variables, which the container will save into the database for us. When we come to use the bean, the container again takes care of retrieving the stored information from the database.

The Kitchen EJB

The Kitchen EJB is a stateless session bean that will get a list of ingredients from a CookBook bean, and will check the level of stock in a Larder bean.

The Kitchen Home Interface

```
package recipeBook.kitchen;

public interface KitchenHome extends javax.ejb.EJBHome {
  Kitchen create() throws java.rmi.RemoteException,
                          javax.ejb.CreateException;
}
```

The Kitchen Remote Interface

```
package recipeBook.kitchen;

public interface Kitchen extends javax.ejb.EJBObject {
  String[][] getIngredients(String dishName)
        throws java.rmi.RemoteException;

  int checkStockLevel(String item, int requirement)
      throws java.rmi.RemoteException;
}
```

The Kitchen Implementation Class

```
package recipeBook.kitchen;

import javax.naming.*;
import javax.ejb.*;
import recipeBook.larder.*;
import recipeBook.cookBook.*;

public class KitchenEJB implements SessionBean {

  /**
   * Standard EJB callbacks, not implemented
   */
  public void ejbCreate() {}
  public void ejbRemove() {}
  public void ejbActivate() {}
  public void ejbPassivate() {}
  public void setSessionContext(SessionContext ctx) {}

  /**
   * Return the list of ingredients for a recipe as 2D array
   */
  public String[][] getIngredients(String dishName) {

    try {
      InitialContext initial = new InitialContext();
      CookBookHome home =
        (CookBookHome) javax.rmi.PortableRemoteObject
          .narrow(initial.lookup("java:comp/env/ejb/CookBook"),
                  CookBookHome.class);

      CookBook book = home.findByPrimaryKey(dishName);
```

```
        String ingredients[][] = book.getIngredients();

        return ingredients;

    } catch (NamingException ne) {
      throw new EJBException(ne);
    } catch (java.rmi.RemoteException re) {
      throw new EJBException(re);
    } catch (FinderException fe) {
      throw new EJBException(fe);
    }
  }


  /**
   * Check is there is sufficient quantities of an ingredient
   * in the larder using the Larder entity bean
   */
  public int checkStockLevel(String ingredient, int amountNeeded) {

    try {
      InitialContext initial = new InitialContext();
      LarderHome home =
        (LarderHome) javax.rmi.PortableRemoteObject
          .narrow(initial.lookup("java:comp/env/ejb/Larder"),
                  LarderHome.class);

      Larder larder = home.findByPrimaryKey(ingredient);

      return larder.checkInventoryFor(amountNeeded);

    } catch (NamingException ne) {
      throw new EJBException(ne);
    } catch (java.rmi.RemoteException re) {
      throw new EJBException(re);
    } catch (FinderException fe) {
      throw new EJBException(fe);
    }
  }
}
```

The Kitchen bean simplifies ingredient listing and stock checking for the client by directing the requests to the appropriate bean. In the case of getting the ingredients, it finds the relevant CookBook bean and queries it for its list of ingredients; the process is similar for stock checking with the Larder beans – find the bean, query it for stock levels.

The Menu EJB

The Menu EJB is a stateful session bean that stores a list of dishes, and uses the Kitchen EJB to check for the ingredients.

The Menu Home Interface

```
package recipeBook.menu;

public interface MenuHome extends javax.ejb.EJBHome {
  Menu create() throws java.rmi.RemoteException, javax.ejb.CreateException,
}
```

The Menu Remote Interface

```
package recipeBook.menu;

public interface Menu extends javax.ejb.EJBObject {
  void addDish(String dishName) throws java.rmi.RemoteException;

  String checkStock() throws java.rmi.RemoteException;
}
```

The Menu Implementation Class

```
package recipeBook.menu;

import javax.ejb.*;
import javax.naming.InitialContext;
import javax.naming.NamingException;
import recipeBook.kitchen.*;

public class MenuEJB implements SessionBean {
  private String menu[] = new String[0];
  private int menuSize = 0;

  /**
   * Standard EJB callbacks, not implemented
   */
  public void ejbCreate() {}
  public void ejbRemove() {}
  public void ejbActivate() {}
  public void ejbPassivate() {}
  public void setSessionContext(SessionContext ctx) {}

  /**
   * Load dishs into an array
   */
  public void addDish(String dishName) {

    // Create temporary array and load in current menu array values
    String tempMenu[] = new String[menuSize + 1];

    for (int i = 0; i < menuSize; i++) {
      tempMenu[i] = menu[i];
    }

    // Add new dish to menu
    tempMenu[menuSize] = dishName;
```

```
      // Assign temporary menu to menu
   menu = null;
   menu = tempMenu;
   menuSize++;
}

/**
 * Takes the previously defined menu and checks
 * if there is sufficient stock in the larder
 * for the recipes by using the Kitchen bean
 */
public String checkStock() {
   String shoppingList = "You are missing: ";

   try {
      InitialContext initial = new InitialContext();
      KitchenHome home =
        (KitchenHome) javax.rmi.PortableRemoteObject
          .narrow(initial.lookup("java:comp/env/ejb/Kitchen"),
                  KitchenHome.class);

      Kitchen kitchen = home.create();

      // Loop through menu to check ingredients and stock level
      for (int i = 0; i < 3; i++) {
         String dish = menu[i];
         String ingredients[][] = kitchen.getIngredients(dish);

         // Loop through ingredients to check stock level
         for (int j = 0; j < ingredients[1].length; j++) {
            String ingredientToCheck = ingredients[0][j];
            int levelToCheck = Integer.parseInt(ingredients[1][j].trim());
            int missing = kitchen.checkStockLevel(ingredientToCheck,
                                                  levelToCheck);

            // If difference is greater than 0 there is a deficit
            // and add to shopping list
            if (missing != 0) {
               shoppingList += ingredients[0][j] + "(" + missing + "), ";
            }
         }
      }

      return shoppingList;

   } catch (NamingException ne) {
      throw new EJBException(ne);
   } catch (java.rmi.RemoteException re) {
      throw new EJBException(re);
   } catch (CreateException ce) {
      throw new EJBException(ce);
   }
}
```

The Menu bean provides the methods with which the client can specify what dishes to cook, and query the kitchen for available ingredients.

The Chef Client

In keeping with the sensible naming structure for the beans, the client application is called Chef. The first thing the chef does is to stock the larder with goods, then proceeds to check if there are sufficient quantities for the recipes on the menu. Finally, after the menu has been prepared, the chef checks the larder for low stocks.

Here is the code for the application client – note that the final method (getContextInfo()) may need modifying depending on which application server is being used:

```
package recipeBook.client;

import javax.naming.*;
import java.util.Properties;
import recipeBook.menu.*;
import recipeBook.larder.*;
import recipeBook.cookBook.*;
import java.util.Collection;
import java.util.Iterator;

public class Chef {
  public static void main(String args[]) {
    Chef thisChef = new Chef();

    // First stock the larder
    System.out.println("Stocking...");
    thisChef.stockLarder();

    // Then create a menu and check the stock
    System.out.println("Checking...");
    thisChef.checkLarder();

    // Test finder method by checking for low stock levels
    System.out.println("Searching for low stocks...");
    thisChef.checkForLowStock();
  }

  /**
   * Runs the main example that calls
   * the two session beans and entity beans.
   * Will return the shopping list of what is needed
   */
  private void checkLarder() {

    try {

      Context initial = getContextInfo();

      Object objref = initial.lookup("Menu");

      MenuHome home =
        (MenuHome) javax.rmi.PortableRemoteObject.narrow(objref,
```

```
            MenuHome.class);

    Menu menu = home.create();

    menu.addDish("Tomato Soup");
    menu.addDish("Sausage and Mash");
    menu.addDish("Apple Pie");
    System.out.println(menu.checkStock());

  } catch (Exception e) {
    System.out.println(e);
  }
}

/**
 * Stocks the two tables with data using the two entity beans
 */
private void stockLarder() {

  try {

    Context initial = getRefImpContextInfo();

    // Stock Larder table with Larder bean
    Object objRef = initial.lookup("Larder");
    LarderHome home =
      (LarderHome) javax.rmi.PortableRemoteObject.narrow(objRef,
          LarderHome.class);
    Larder larder = null;

    larder = home.create("onions", 4);
    larder = home.create("sugar", 200);
    larder = home.create("butter", 500);
    larder = home.create("milk", 2000);
    larder = home.create("tomatoes", 40);
    larder = home.create("basil", 50);
    larder = home.create("sausages", 10);
    larder = home.create("potatoes", 25);
    larder = home.create("apples", 5);
    larder = home.create("flour", 1000);
    larder = home.create("stock", 10);

    // Stock RecipeBook table with CookBook bean
    objRef = initial.lookup("CookBook");
    CookBookHome home2 =
      (CookBookHome) javax.rmi.PortableRemoteObject.narrow(objRef,
          CookBookHome.class);

    CookBook cb = null;
    cb = home2.create("tomato soup", "tomatoes, 20|basil, 25|");
    cb = home2.create("sausage and mash",
                "sausages, 15|potatoes, 15|milk, 50|onions, 5|stock, 4|");
    cb = home2.create("apple pie",
                    "apples, 20|flour, 500|butter, 200|sugar, 25|");

  } catch (Exception e) {
```

```
            System.out.println(e);
        }

        System.out.println("Larder stocked");
    }

    /**
     * Tests the custom finder method to check for stock below a certain level
     */
    private void checkForLowStock() {

        try {

            Context initial = getContextInfo();

            Object objRef = initial.lookup("Larder");
            LarderHome home =
                (LarderHome) javax.rmi.PortableRemoteObject.narrow(objRef,
                    LarderHome.class);

            Collection supplies = home.findLowStockLevels(10);
            Iterator it = supplies.iterator();
            while (it.hasNext()) {
                objRef = it.next();
                Larder ingredient =
                    (Larder) javax.rmi.PortableRemoteObject.narrow(objRef,
                        Larder.class);
                System.out.println("There is only " + ingredient.getStockLevel()
                            + " of " + ingredient.getIngredientName());
            }
        } catch (Exception e) {
            System.out.println(e);
        }
    }

    /**
     * This method sets up the JNDI context used to locate the EJBs.
     * It will need modifying depending on what EJB container is being used.
     */
    private Context getContextInfo() throws NamingException {
        return new InitialContext();
    }
}
```

The checkLarder() method, having got a reference to the Menu bean, creates three dishes, and checks the current stock.

The stockLarder() method performs two tasks: first it stocks the larder with ingredients, and then it creates the recipes in the cookbook. In the first of these operations, we obtain a reference to the home interface for the Larder bean, which we use to create several entries in the larder. The second operation is similar, except that the beans created are CookBook beans, each to represent a recipe.

The checkForLowStock() method does just that; it contacts the larder and searches for stock with low levels, printing out the resulting list of low stock together with the levels.

The Deployment Descriptor

And here is the deployment descriptor for the beans:

```xml
<?xml version="1.0"?>

<!DOCTYPE ejb-jar PUBLIC '-//Sun Microsystems, Inc.//DTD Enterprise JavaBeans
1.1//EN' 'http://java.sun.com/j2ee/dtds/ejb-jar_1_1.dtd'>

<ejb-jar>

  <enterprise-beans>

    <session>
      <ejb-name>Menu</ejb-name>
      <home>recipeBook.menu.MenuHome</home>
      <remote>recipeBook.menu.Menu</remote>
      <ejb-class>recipeBook.menu.MenuEJB</ejb-class>
      <session-type>Stateful</session-type>
      <transaction-type>Container</transaction-type>
      <ejb-ref>
        <ejb-ref-name>ejb/Kitchen</ejb-ref-name>
        <ejb-ref-type>Session</ejb-ref-type>
        <home>recipeBook.kitchen.KitchenHome</home>
        <remote>recipeBook.kitchen.Kitchen</remote>
        <ejb-link>Kitchen</ejb-link>
      </ejb-ref>
    </session>

    <session>
      <ejb-name>Kitchen</ejb-name>
      <home>recipeBook.kitchen.KitchenHome</home>
      <remote>recipeBook.kitchen.Kitchen</remote>
      <ejb-class>recipeBook.kitchen.KitchenEJB</ejb-class>
      <session-type>Stateless</session-type>
      <transaction-type>Container</transaction-type>
      <ejb-ref>
        <ejb-ref-name>ejb/CookBook</ejb-ref-name>
        <ejb-ref-type>Entity</ejb-ref-type>
        <home>recipeBook.cookBook.CookBookHome</home>
        <remote>recipeBook.cookBook.CookBook</remote>
        <ejb-link>CookBook</ejb-link>
      </ejb-ref>
      <ejb-ref>
        <ejb-ref-name>ejb/Larder</ejb-ref-name>
        <ejb-ref-type>Entity</ejb-ref-type>
        <home>recipeBook.larder.LarderHome</home>
        <remote>recipeBook.larder.Larder</remote>
        <ejb-link>Larder</ejb-link>
      </ejb-ref>
    </session>

    <entity>
      <ejb-name>CookBook</ejb-name>
      <home>recipeBook.cookBook.CookBookHome</home>
      <remote>recipeBook.cookBook.CookBook</remote>
```

```xml
            <ejb-class>recipeBook.cookBook.CookBookEJB</ejb-class>
            <persistence-type>Bean</persistence-type>
            <prim-key-class>java.lang.String</prim-key-class>
            <reentrant>False</reentrant>
            <resource-ref>
              <res-ref-name>jdbc/recipeJDBC</res-ref-name>
              <res-type>javax.sql.DataSource</res-type>
              <res-auth>Container</res-auth>
            </resource-ref>
        </entity>

        <entity>
          <ejb-name>Larder</ejb-name>
          <home>recipeBook.larder.LarderHome</home>
          <remote>recipeBook.larder.Larder</remote>
          <ejb-class>recipeBook.larder.LarderEJB</ejb-class>
          <persistence-type>Container</persistence-type>
          <prim-key-class>java.lang.String</prim-key-class>
          <reentrant>False</reentrant>
          <cmp-field><field-name>ingredientName</field-name></cmp-field>
          <cmp-field><field-name>stock</field-name></cmp-field>
          <primkey-field>ingredientName</primkey-field>
        </entity>

    </enterprise-beans>

    <assembly-descriptor>
        <container-transaction>
          <method>
            <ejb-name>CookBook</ejb-name>
            <method-name>*</method-name>
          </method>
          <trans-attribute>Required</trans-attribute>
        </container-transaction>
        <container-transaction>
          <method>
            <ejb-name>Larder</ejb-name>
            <method-name>*</method-name>
          </method>
          <trans-attribute>Required</trans-attribute>
        </container-transaction>
    </assembly-descriptor>

</ejb-jar>
```

Converting the Recipe Beans to EJB 2.0

There as some significant changes between the EJB 1.1 and EJB 2.0 (Proposed Final Draft 2) specifications, which means that we need to make a number of changes to our beans and deployment descriptor to make them executable in a EJB 2.0 container.

At the time of writing there were only a handful of EJB 2.0 container implementations available and even less supporting the Proposed Final Draft 2. Here we will go over the changes we need to make to our Recipe Beans to make them compatible with Proposed Final Draft 2 (PFD2), however, in some of the deployment environments we may need to make further tweaks for them to execute in that container implementation.

There are basically three significant changes that we need to make to our Recipe Beans to upgrade them to EJB 2.0 PFD2:

❑ The addition of local interfaces

❑ Updating the CMP Larder bean to use the 2.0 persistence model

❑ Modifying the deployment descriptor accordingly

Adding Local Interfaces

We want to add local interface support for bean-to-bean communications. Ideally we would be hiding our entity beans behind a session bean façade, however, for the purposes of simplicity in this demonstration example we allowed our Chef client to create new entities.

Therefore, our Recipe Beans will now expose the following interfaces:

❑ Menu – Remote interface only (no change)

❑ Kitchen – Local interface only

❑ Larder – Local and remote interfaces

❑ CookBook – Local and remote interfaces

In addition to adding/modifying the interface classes we will need to change some of the bean implementation classes to access the local objects instead of the remote objects.

The Menu Bean

The interfaces for the Menu bean do not change in the upgrade so we can leave them as they are. However, the MenuEJB class uses the Kitchen bean within its code, therefore, we need to change the class cast on the home object as we no longer need to use PortableRemoteObject:

```
try {
    InitialContext initial = new InitialContext();
    KitchenHome home = (KitchenHome)
                        initial.lookup("java:comp/env/ejb/Kitchen");

    Kitchen kitchen = home.create();
```

We no longer need to catch a RemoteException in this call in the catch block.

The Kitchen Bean

We are going to change the Kitchen bean so that it can only be accessed locally. This means modifying the home and component interfaces to be local:

```
package recipeBook.kitchen;
```

```
public interface KitchenHome extends javax.ejb.EJBLocalHome {
  Kitchen create() throws javax.ejb.CreateException;
}
```

```
package recipeBook.kitchen;
```

```
public interface Kitchen extends javax.ejb.EJBLocalObject {
  String[][] getIngredients(String dishName);
  int checkStockLevel(String item, int requirement);
}
```

As with the Menu bean we also need to modify the calls to the other EJBs (Larder and CookBook) from with the KitchenEJB class:

```
public String[][] getIngredients(String dishName) {

    try {
        InitialContext initial = new InitialContext();
        CookBookLocalHome home = (CookBookLocalHome)
                        initial.lookup("java:comp/env/ejb/CookBook");

        CookBookLocal book = home.findByPrimaryKey(dishName);

...

public int checkStockLevel(String ingredient, int amountNeeded) {

    try {
        InitialContext initial = new InitialContext();
        LarderLocalHome home = (LarderLocalHome)
                        initial.lookup("java:comp/env/ejb/Larder");

        LarderLocal larder = home.findByPrimaryKey(ingredient);
```

The Larder Bean

The Larder bean requires the addition of a local home and local interface in addition to the existing remote home and remote interface:

```
package recipeBook.larder;

import java.util.Collection;

public interface LarderLocalHome extends javax.ejb.EJBLocalHome {

  LarderLocal findByPrimaryKey(String ingredientName) throws
      javax.ejb.FinderException;
```

```
    Collection findLowStockLevels(int stockLevel)
            throws java.rmi.RemoteException, javax.ejb.FinderException;

    LarderLocal create(String ingredientName, int stock)
throws javax.ejb.CreateException;
}
```

```
package recipeBook.larder;

public interface LarderLocal extends javax.ejb.EJBLocalObject {

    public int checkInventoryFor(int amountNeeded);
    public String getIngredientName();
    public int getStockLevel();
}
```

The CookBook Bean

Likewise for the CookBook bean, we need to add a local home and local interface:

```
package recipeBook.cookBook;

public interface CookBookLocalHome extends javax.ejb.EJBLocalHome {
    CookBookLocal findByPrimaryKey(String recipeName)
throws javax.ejb.FinderException;

    CookBookLocal create(String recipeName, String ingredients)
throws javax.ejb.CreateException;
}
```

```
package recipeBook.cookBook;

public interface CookBookLocal extends javax.ejb.EJBLocalObject {
    public String[][] getIngredients();
}
```

CMP 2.0 Persistence

The EJB 2.0 specification requires that all CMP fields be declared with abstract setters and getters. Therefore, we must modify LarderEJB.java the following way:

```
package recipeBook.larder;

import javax.ejb.*;

public abstract class LarderEJB implements EntityBean {

    Standard EJB callbacks, not implemented

    public void ejbStore() {}
    public void ejbRemove() {}
    public void ejbActivate() {}
```

```
    public void ejbPassivate() {}
    public void setEntityContext(EntityContext ctx) {}
    public void unsetEntityContext() {}
    public void ejbPostCreate(String ingredientName, int stock) {}

  /** Note ejbLoad() becomes blank as well since there are no stockLevel
   * or ingredientName variables
   */  public void ejbLoad() {  }

  /**
   * Save new ingredient stock in Larder table
   */
  public String ejbCreate(String ingredientName, int stock) throws CreateException{
    setIngredientName(ingredientName);
    setStock(stock);
    return null;
  }

  /**
   * Compare stock level in Larder table with
   * the value required and return the difference
   */
  public int checkInventoryFor(int amountNeeded) {
    if (amountNeeded < getStock()) {
      return 0;
    } else {
      return (amountNeeded - getStock());
    }
  }

  public abstract String getIngredientName();
  public abstract void setIngredientName(String ingredientName);

  public abstract int getStock();
  public abstract void setStock(int n);

  public int getStockLevel() {
    return getStock();
  }
}
```

Note the following:

❑ We no longer have fields called `stockLevel` and `ingredientName`

❑ Instead, we created two pairs of accessors for each: `get/setIngredientName()` and `get/setStock()`

❑ These accessors have been declared abstract (and the `LarderEJB` class too)

❑ We modify and read these CMP fields only through the accessors

❑ We have altered the `getStockLevel()` method to call the `getStock()` method, rather than re-write the Larder bean home interface and the client

That's all we need as far as Java code is concerned. Now, let's turn to the deployment descriptor.

The EJB 2.0 Deployment Descriptor

We need to add the reference to local interfaces, change some of the `<ejb-ref>` elements to be `<ejb-local-ref>` as well as define the EJB QL for the Larder bean's finder method:

```xml
<?xml version="1.0" encoding="UTF-8"?>

<!DOCTYPE ejb-jar PUBLIC '-//Sun Microsystems, Inc.//DTD Enterprise JavaBeans
2.0//EN' 'http://java.sun.com/dtd/ejb-jar_2_0.dtd'>

<ejb-jar>
  <display-name>RecipeBeans</display-name>
  <enterprise-beans>

    <entity>
      <display-name>CookBook</display-name>
      <ejb-name>CookBook</ejb-name>
      <home>recipeBook.cookBook.CookBookHome</home>
      <remote>recipeBook.cookBook.CookBook</remote>
      <local-home>recipeBook.cookBook.CookBookLocalHome</local-home>
      <local>recipeBook.cookBook.CookBookLocal</local>
      <ejb-class>recipeBook.cookBook.CookBookEJB</ejb-class>
      <persistence-type>Bean</persistence-type>
      <prim-key-class>java.lang.String</prim-key-class>
      <reentrant>False</reentrant>
      <resource-ref>
        <res-ref-name>jdbc/recipeJDBC</res-ref-name>
        <res-type>javax.sql.DataSource</res-type>
        <res-auth>Container</res-auth>
        <res-sharing-scope>Shareable</res-sharing-scope>
      </resource-ref>
    </entity>

    <session>
      <display-name>Kitchen</display-name>
      <ejb-name>Kitchen</ejb-name>
      <local-home>recipeBook.kitchen.KitchenHome</local-home>
      <local>recipeBook.kitchen.Kitchen</local>
      <ejb-class>recipeBook.kitchen.KitchenEJB</ejb-class>
      <session-type>Stateless</session-type>
      <transaction-type>Bean</transaction-type>
      <ejb-local-ref>
        <ejb-ref-name>ejb/Larder</ejb-ref-name>
        <ejb-ref-type>Entity</ejb-ref-type>
        <local-home>recipeBook.larder.LarderLocalHome</local-home>
        <local>recipeBook.larder.LarderLocal</local>
        <ejb-link>Larder</ejb-link>
      </ejb-local-ref>
      <ejb-local-ref>
        <ejb-ref-name>ejb/CookBook</ejb-ref-name>
        <ejb-ref-type>Entity</ejb-ref-type>
        <local-home>recipeBook.cookBook.CookBookLocalHome</local-home>
        <local>recipeBook.cookBook.CookBookLocal</local>
```

```
        <ejb-link>CookBook</ejb-link>
      </ejb-local-ref>
  </session>

  <entity>
    <display-name>Larder</display-name>
    <ejb-name>Larder</ejb-name>
    <home>recipeBook.larder.LarderHome</home>
    <remote>recipeBook.larder.Larder</remote>
    <local-home>recipeBook.larder.LarderLocalHome</local-home>
    <local>recipeBook.larder.LarderLocal</local>
    <ejb-class>recipeBook.larder.LarderEJB</ejb-class>
    <persistence-type>Container</persistence-type>
    <prim-key-class>java.lang.String</prim-key-class>
    <reentrant>False</reentrant>
    <cmp-version>2.x</cmp-version>
    <abstract-schema-name>LarderEJB</abstract-schema-name>
    <cmp-field>
      <description>no description</description>
      <field-name>ingredientName</field-name>
    </cmp-field>
    <cmp-field>
      <description>no description</description>
      <field-name>stock</field-name>
    </cmp-field>
    <primkey-field>ingredientName</primkey-field>
    <query>
      <description></description>
      <query-method>
        <method-name>findLowStockLevels</method-name>
        <method-intf>Home</method-intf>
        <method-params>
          <method-param>int</method-param>
        </method-params>
      </query-method>
      <result-type-mapping>Local</result-type-mapping>
      <ejb-ql>
        SELECT OBJECT(o) FROM LarderEJB o WHERE o.stock &lt;= ?1
      </ejb-ql>
    </query>
  </entity>

  <session>
    <display-name>Menu</display-name>
    <ejb-name>Menu</ejb-name>
    <home>recipeBook.menu.MenuHome</home>
    <remote>recipeBook.menu.Menu</remote>
    <ejb-class>recipeBook.menu.MenuEJB</ejb-class>
    <session-type>Stateful</session-type>
    <transaction-type>Bean</transaction-type>
    <ejb-local-ref>
      <ejb-ref-name>ejb/Kitchen</ejb-ref-name>
      <ejb-ref-type>Session</ejb-ref-type>
      <local-home>recipeBook.kitchen.KitchenHome</local-home>
      <local>recipeBook.kitchen.Kitchen</local>
```

```
                <ejb-link>Kitchen</ejb-link>
            </ejb-local-ref>
        </session>
    </enterprise-beans>

    <assembly-descriptor>
        <container-transaction>
            <method>
                <ejb-name>CookBook</ejb-name>
                <method-name>*</method-name>
            </method>
        <trans-attribute>Required</trans-attribute>
        </container-transaction>
        <container-transaction>
            <method>
                <ejb-name>Larder</ejb-name>
                <method-name>*</method-name>
            </method>
        <trans-attribute>Required</trans-attribute>
        </container-transaction>
    </assembly-descriptor>
</ejb-jar>
```

Compiling and Archiving

We can now compile the Recipe beans using a reference to the `javax.ejb` package on the classpath. For example:

```
javac -classapath %J2EE_HOME%\lib\j2ee.jar;. recipeBook\menu\*.java
javac -classapath %J2EE_HOME%\lib\j2ee.jar;. recipeBook\kitchen\*.java
javac -classapath %J2EE_HOME%\lib\j2ee.jar;. recipeBook\larder\*.java
javac -classapath %J2EE_HOME%\lib\j2ee.jar;. recipeBook\cookBook\*.java
```

Then archive the class files and the deployment descriptor into a JAR file called `Recipe.jar` with the following structure:

```
META-INF/
        ejb-jar.xml
recipeBook/
        menu/
                Menu.class
                MenuEJB.class
                MenuHome.class
        kitchen/
                Kitchen.class
                KitchenEJB.class
                KitchenHome.class
        larder/
                Larder.class
                LarderEJB.class
                LarderHome.class
        cookbook/
                CookBook.class
                CookBookEJB.class
                CookBookHome.class
```

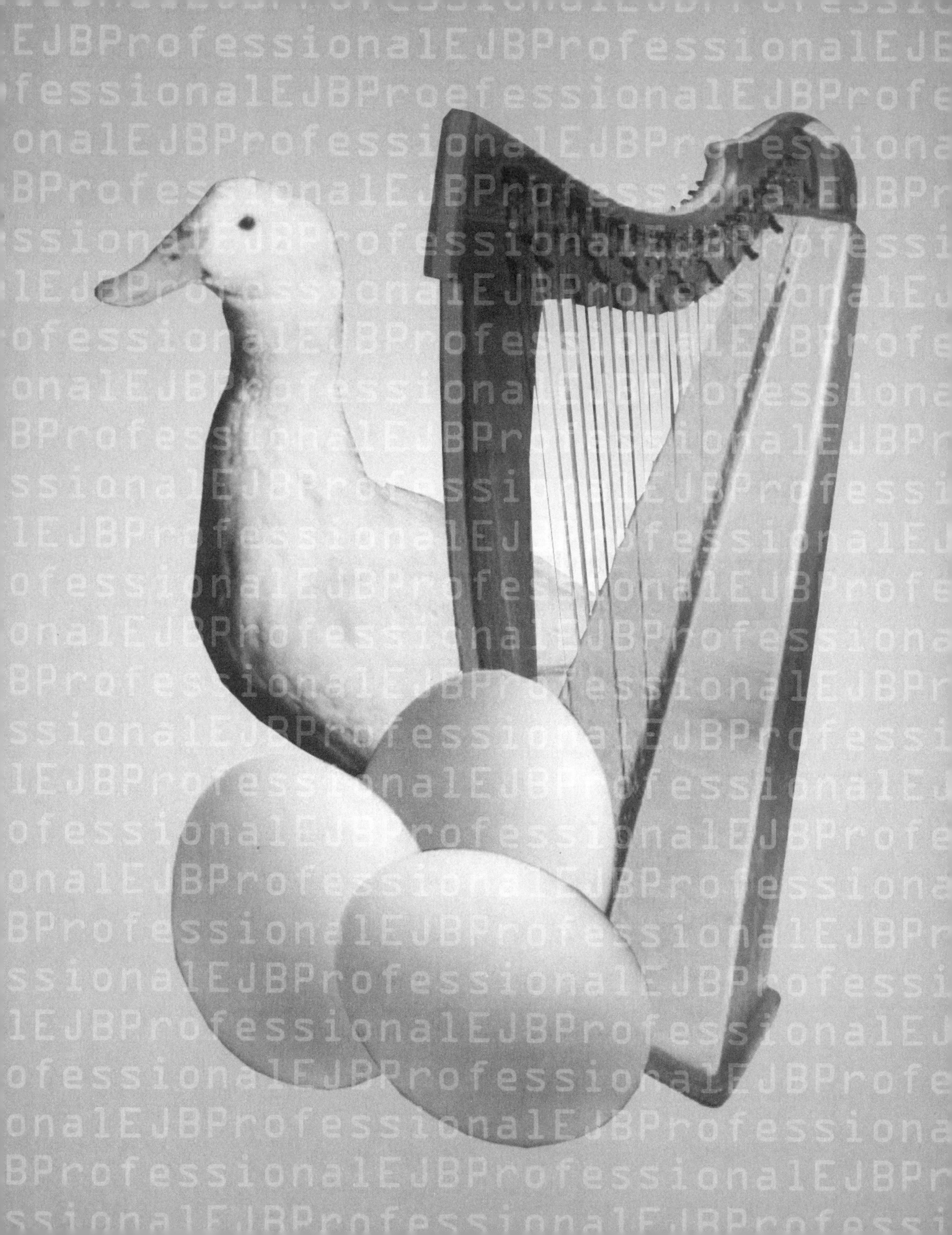

B

The J2EE Reference Implementation

Along with the J2EE SDK, Sun has provided a **Reference Implementation (RI)** of an application server and the deployment tool for the benefit of server vendors. This serves as a guideline for the vendors to implement their servers and development tools. Though this is mainly developed for server vendors, it is an excellent implementation for anybody learning J2EE technology. In this appendix, we will walk through how to deploy the Recipe beans onto the RI.

> At the time of publication the Reference Implementation was in beta 2. Therefore you may find that the deployment tool screenshots may look a little different from the final release.

The J2EE Reference Implementation is available for download from the Sun Java site. At the time of writing it was available from http://java.sun.com/j2ee/j2sdkee-beta/index.html.

Starting the J2EE Server

Starting the J2EE RI is a very simple process. Before doing so, make sure that you have two system settings for JAVA_HOME and J2EE_HOME pointing at your install locations for your JVM (preferably version 1.3 or above) and the J2EE SDK respectively.

Start the server by opening a command shell and typing the following at the command line:

    %J2EE_HOME%\bin\j2ee –verbose

This starts the server. During the startup, the progress is printed on the console. If you have previously deployed any applications, those will be re-deployed and the status will be displayed on the console:

```
C:\WINNT\System32\cmd.exe - j2ee -verbose                                    _ □ x

C:\j2sdkee1.3b2\bin>j2ee -verbose

J2EE server listen port: 1050
Naming service started:1050
Binding DataSource, name = jdbc/Oracle, url = jdbc:oracle:thin:@dbserver:1521:ejb
Binding DataSource, name = jdbc/DB1, url = jdbc:cloudscape:rmi:CloudscapeDB;create=true
Binding DataSource, name = jdbc/DB2, url = jdbc:cloudscape:rmi:CloudscapeDB;create=true
Binding DataSource, name = jdbc/Cloudscape, url = jdbc:cloudscape:rmi:CloudscapeDB;create=true
Binding DataSource, name = jdbc/EstoreDB, url = jdbc:cloudscape:rmi:CloudscapeDB;create=true
Binding DataSource, name = jdbc/InventoryDB, url = jdbc:cloudscape:rmi:CloudscapeDB;create=true
Binding DataSource, name = jdbc/XACloudscape, url = jdbc/XACloudscape__xa
Binding DataSource, name = jdbc/XACloudscape__xa, dataSource = COM.cloudscape.core.RemoteXaDataSource@4df764
Starting JMS service ... Initialization complete - waiting for client requests
Binding : < JMS Destination : jms/Topic , javax.jms.Topic >
Binding : < JMS Destination : jms/Queue , javax.jms.Queue >
Binding : < JMS Destination : OrderQueue , javax.jms.Queue >
Binding : < JMS Cnx Factory : QueueConnectionFactory , Queue , No properties >
Binding : < JMS Cnx Factory : jms/QueueConnectionFactory , Queue , No properties >
Binding : < JMS Cnx Factory : TopicConnectionFactory , Topic , No properties >
Binding : < JMS Cnx Factory : jms/TopicConnectionFactory , Topic , No properties >
Starting web service at port:8000
Starting secure web service at port:7000
Apache Tomcat/4.0-b4-dev
Starting web service at port:9191
Apache Tomcat/4.0-b4-dev
J2EE server startup complete.
```

Starting the Deployment Tool

The Reference Implementation comes with a Swing-based deployment tool that we can use to create, deploy, and administer J2EE components, including EJBs.

You start the deployment tool by using the following command line:

```
%J2EE_HOME%\bin\deploytool
```

After a while, the deployment tool opens with the following screen:

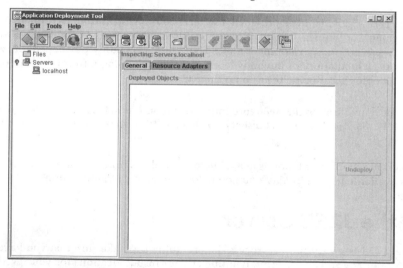

Configuring the J2EE Server

We know that our Recipe beans application contains a couple of entity beans so we need to configure the server to connect to our database of choice. In this case we will be using Oracle as our database – if you don't have Oracle then the steps are very similar for any database, you merely need to change the driver, URL, and security information as specific to your database.

In the deployment tool, select the **Server Configuration** menu option from the **Tools** menu. This will open the **Configure Installation** window that allows us to configure various resource factories and security settings for the server:

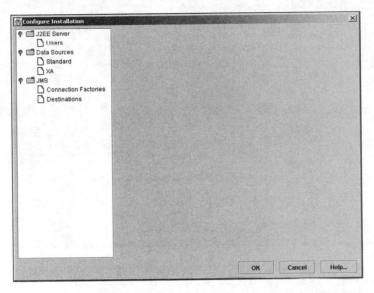

Select the **Standard Data Sources** node in the left-hand pane to bring up a list of the installed JDBC drivers and configured data sources for this server. As you can see the server has some data sources for Cloudscape pre-configured:

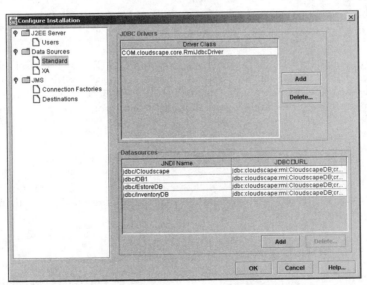

We need to add both a driver and a data source. To add a new driver, press the **Add** button to the left of the JDBC Drivers pane and enter the fully qualified name for your database driver. In my case I am using the Oracle Thin driver. Then press the **Add** button below the **Datasources** pane to add a new data source:

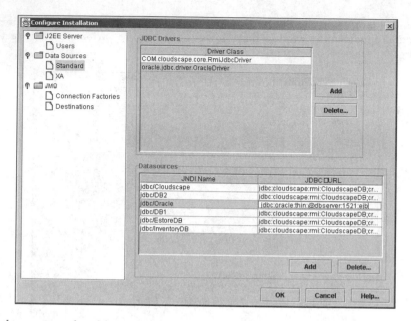

In order for the server to be able to use this new driver it needs the driver class to be in its classpath. To achieve this, open then the setenv.bat file in the %J2EE_HOME%\bin directory and add the path to the driver file in the CPATH variable.

Now restart the server to load the new driver and datasource – you should see them appear in the command window if you use the -verbose switch.

Preparing the Database

The J2EE RI is capable of creating any tables needed by any CMP beans by itself, therefore we do not need to worry about the Larder bean's persistence. However, the CookBook bean uses BMP, therefore we need to create the table manually in the database ourselves. Refer back to Appendix A for the table schema and your database vendor's documentation for how to create it in you database of choice.

Deploying the Recipe Beans

Now we have the server configured and the database primed, we are ready to start the deployment process for our beans. We'll start by deploying the 1.1 version of the beans and then look at the difference for deploying the 2.0 version.

Creating the Application

The J2EE RI does not allow you to deploy an EJB outside of an Enterprise application, in other words packaged in an EAR file. Therefore, we must first create a new application before we can start to deploy our beans.

To create a new application, select the Application... menu item under File | New menu:

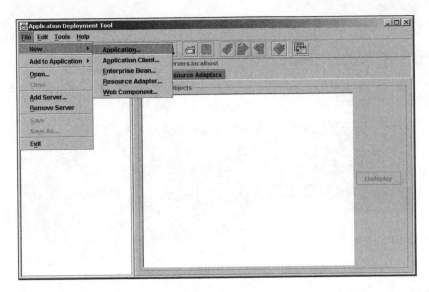

This opens a new dialog as shown below. Click on the **Browse** button to navigate to a folder where you wish to create your application. Specify the file name and display name for the application as shown in the following screen shot. Click **OK** to return to the previous screen:

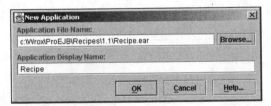

Note that the newly created application name is added under the **Applications** icon in the left-hand pane. At this stage, we are ready to add EJBs (and other components if we had them) to our application:

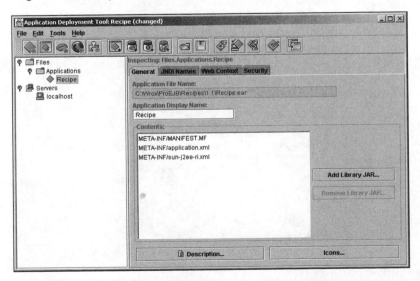

As you can see the deployment tool has added some descriptors to our EAR file for us already.

Adding the Kitchen Bean

The Kitchen bean is a stateless session bean. To deploy the bean, select the Enterprise Bean... option under the File | New menu:

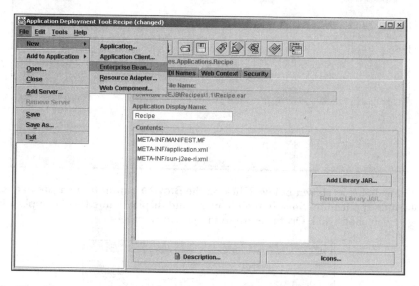

This starts the New Enterprise Bean Wizard that we can use the build the deployment information for our bean:

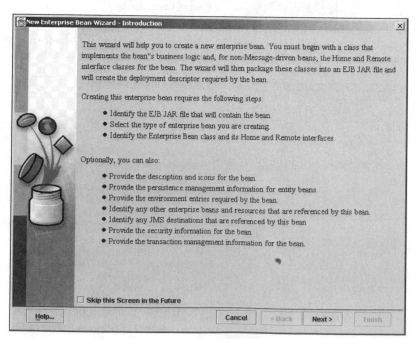

Press Next to get past the introduction screen to the first proper screen of the wizard:

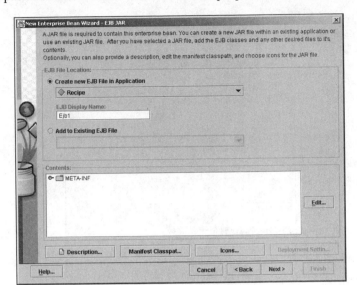

In this screen we specify the source files that make up our EJB (the home interface, remote interface, and bean implementation classes), as well as basic information for the JAR file such as the display name and description.

Press the Edit button to bring up a browser window to select the source files:

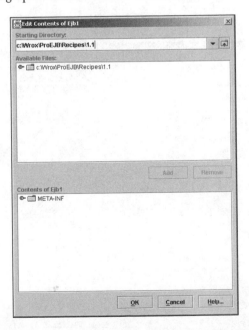

User the top pane to navigate to the desired folder where the .class files for the Kitchen bean are stored. Select and add following files to the JAR:

- Kitchen.class
- KitchenHome.class
- KitchenEJB.class

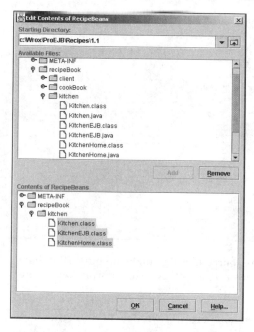

Click OK to return to the previous screen. The Contents pane now shows the three added files.

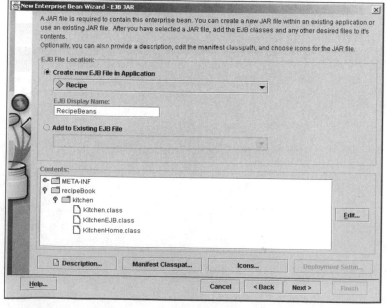

Press Next to move to the next screen:

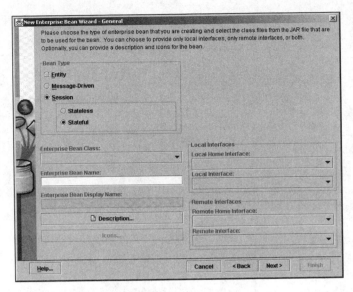

On this screen, we will select the home, remote home, and bean classes for the Kitchen bean, as well as set the bean type and additional name and description information. Select the following on this screen:

- ❏ Bean Type: Session | Stateless
- ❏ Enterprise Bean Class: recipeBook.kitchen.KitchenEJB
- ❏ Remote Home Interface: recipeBook.kitchen.KitchenHome
- ❏ Remote Interface: recipeBook.kitchen.Kitchen
- ❏ Enterprise Bean Name: Kitchen

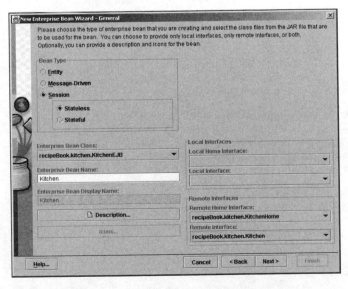

Press Next to move to first of the container services deployment screens:

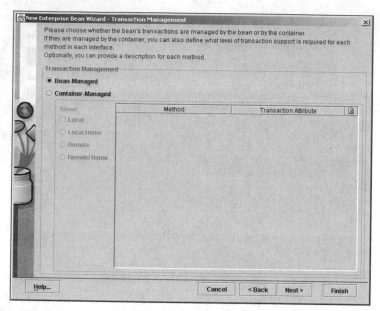

On this screen, we set up the transaction support required by our bean. The transactions may be managed by the bean itself, or we can request the container to manage transactions for us.

If we select Bean-Managed Transactions on this screen, we will not need to set anything else here. If we select Container-Managed Transactions, all the bean's methods will be displayed in the table below. For each method, we will need to select the desired transaction attribute from the drop-down list. The transaction attributes and their use are discussed in Chapter 9.

For the Kitchen bean, we do not need any transacted code, so accept the default setting of Bean-Managed Transaction and proceed to the next step:

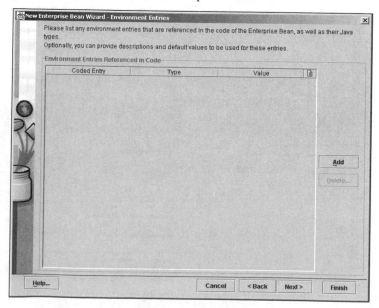

On this screen, we can define any environment variables required by our bean. When we click on the Add button, an entry will be added to the displayed table. We will need to select the data type from the drop-down list and enter its name and value in the other two fields. Likewise, we may add any number of environment variables required by our bean:

The Kitchen bean does not require any environment variables. Thus, we can skip this screen by clicking on the Next button.

On the next screen, we can specify any references to EJBs used by Kitchen bean. The Kitchen bean references two EJBs: CookBook and Larder. We will deploy these two beans later. To add the references, click on the Add button. An entry will be added to the table on the left. Select and/or type following on this screen:

- ❑ Coded Name: ejb/CookBook
- ❑ Type: Entity
- ❑ Home Interface: recipeBook.cookbook.CookBookHome
- ❑ Local/Remote Interface: recipeBook.cookbook.CookBook

This sets up a reference to the CookBook EJB. The server will now look for this bean in the local namespace rather than going through JNDI. Similarly, add one more entry for Larder EJB and specify following on the screen:

- ❑ Coded Name: ejb/Larder
- ❑ Type: Entity
- ❑ Home Interface: recipeBook.larder.LarderHome
- ❑ Local/Remote Interface: recipeBook.larder.Larder

For each referenced EJB, we can specify the JNDI name on the bottom of the screen. All the JNDI names must be specified at a later time before deployment:

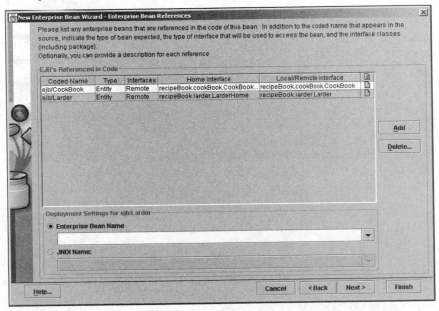

Press Next to move to the next screen:

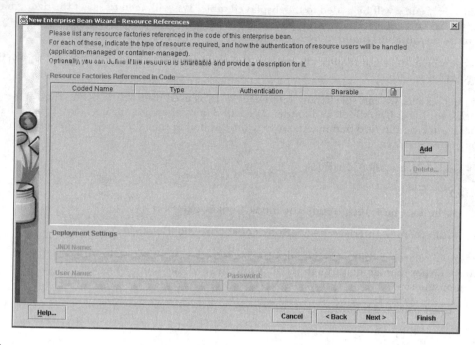

On this screen, we can enter any resource factory references required by our bean. Here we can select the type for the factory. The type can be any of the following:

❑   `javax.sql.DataSource` – for connecting to a database

❑   `javax.mail.Session` – for connecting to a mail server

❑   `java.net.URL` – for making a socket connection to specified URL

❑   `javax.jms.QueueConnectionFactory` – for obtaining a reference to JMS queue connection factory

❑   `javax.jms.TopicConnectionFactory` – for obtaining a reference to JMS topic connection factory

For each selected resource, we will need to specify the coded name, authentication, whether the resource is shareable, and its JNDI name.

The Kitchen bean does not require any of these factory resources, so we skip to the next screen again:

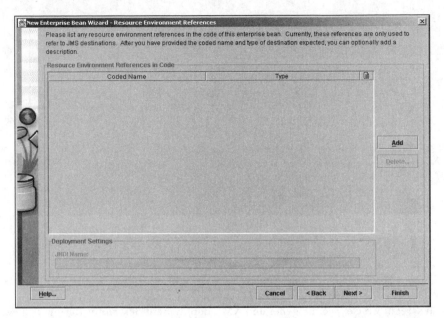

On this screen, we can set up any resource environment references required by our bean. If we were deploying a message-driven bean, we would need to set up the JMS references on this screen. For each reference, we will have to enter the type, coded name, and JNDI name. The Kitchen bean does not require any JMS references, so we can skip to the next screen by clicking on Next button:

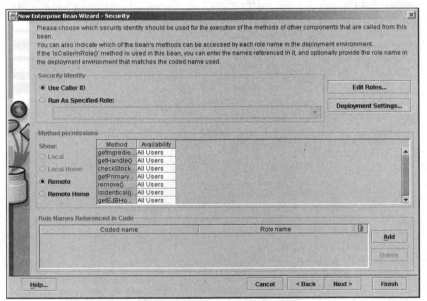

On this screen, we can define the security for our application by specifying the permissions for the various methods of the current EJB. Before setting the permissions on methods, we will need to specify the roles for your application. Once these are defined, we can select each method and apply the permissions under each available role. For the Kitchen bean and our Recipe application, we will not set any security restrictions. Thus, accept the defaults and skip to the next screen:

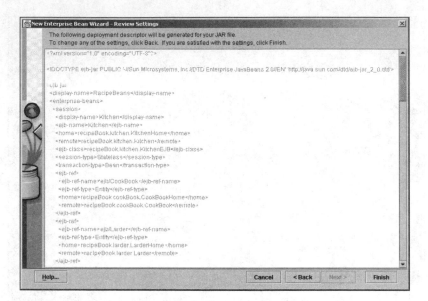

On this final screen, we can see the generated XML deployment descriptor for our review. After examining the descriptor, we can click on Finish button to complete the EJB JAR creation process.

The deployment tool now returns to the main screen. Note that the newly created JAR file is shown under the Recipe application. This completes the creation and addition of the Kitchen JAR file to our Recipe application, and if you expand the JAR file you can see our Kitchen bean which you can inspect using various tabs on the right-hand pane:

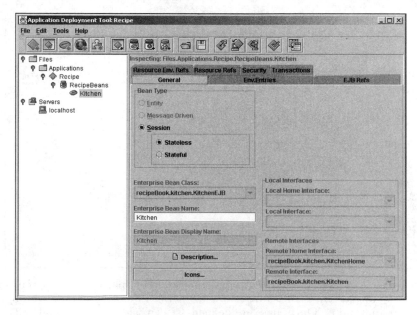

Adding the Menu Bean

The Menu bean is a stateful session bean. The procedure for adding a stateful session bean is very similar to that for adding a stateless session bean.

Open the New Enterprise Bean Wizard again by going File | New | Enterprise Bean. On the second screen, make sure to select to add the new bean to the existing RecipeBeans JAR file:

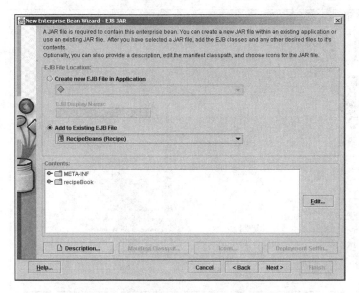

As before, select the class files to add for the bean (in this case Menu.class, MenuHome.class, and MenuEJB.class):

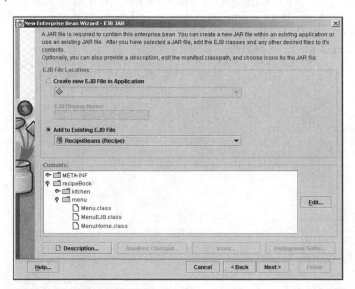

On the next screen, we will select the type for the bean and the various bean classes. Select and type the following on this screen:

- ❏ Bean Type: Session | Stateful
- ❏ Enterprise Bean Class: recipeBook.menu.MenuEJB
- ❏ Remote Home Interface: recipeBook.menu.MenuHome
- ❏ Remote Interface: recipeBook.menu.Menu
- ❏ Enterprise Bean Name: Menu

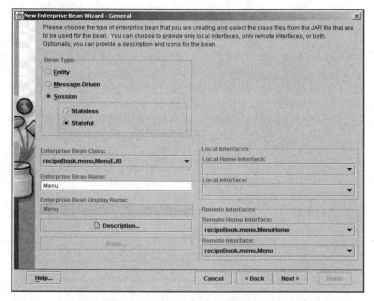

Accept the defaults on the following screens until you reach the screen for setting EJB references. We will add a reference to the Kitchen bean. This is because the Menu bean uses the Kitchen bean, and telling the deployment tool wizard about this reference will mean that when it comes to be used, the Menu bean will be able to find the Kitchen bean:

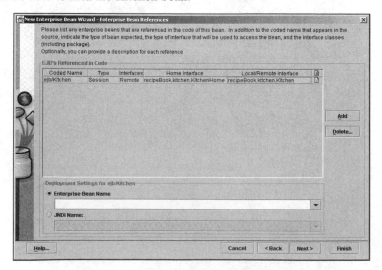

On the remaining screens, we accept the defaults until we come to the review screen. Check out the generated deployment descriptor and click on Finish button to complete the bean creation process.

Adding the Larder Bean

The Larder bean is a CMP entity bean. The process for adding entity beans is very similar to that for session beans except that there is some additional configuration required for CMP entities.

Again, start the New Enterprise Bean Wizard and select to add a bean to the RecipeBeans JAR file. This time add the class files for the Larder bean:

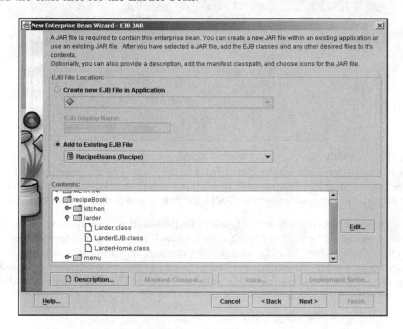

On the New Enterprise Bean Wizard-General screen, set the following parameters:

- ❏ Bean Type: Entity
- ❏ Enterprise Bean Class: recipeBook.larder.LarderEJB
- ❏ Remote Home Interface: recipeBook.larder.LarderHome
- ❏ Remote Interface: recipeBook.larder.Larder
- ❏ Enterprise Bean Name: Larder

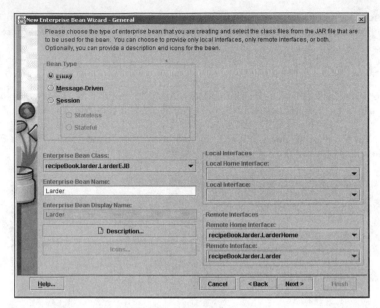

On the next screen, we will need to select the persistence management for the bean. For the Larder bean, the persistence is managed by the container. For the container-managed persistence, we have two options: **Container managed persistence (1.0)** and **Container managed persistence (2.0)**. The Larder bean uses CMP 1.0 coding, so we select the **Container managed persistence (1.0)** option.

The moment we select the CMP, the list of fields to be persisted will be shown below. Select both the fields as container-managed persistence fields. Next, we will need to select the primary key type for our bean record. Type `java.lang.String` as the data type and select the **Primary Key Field Name** as `ingredientName`. The entity bean code may be defined as **Reentrant**. However, JavaSoft recommends against the use of reentrant code, so leave this field unchecked. The following screenshot shows the wizard after these settings have been made:

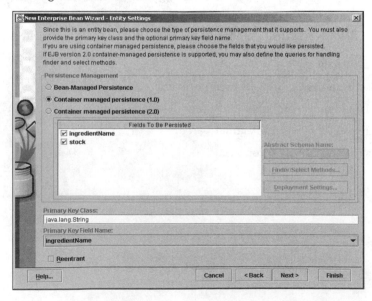

We'll accept the defaults on the next screens. Note on the Transaction Management screen that the default transactional attributes set by the container for each method is Required:

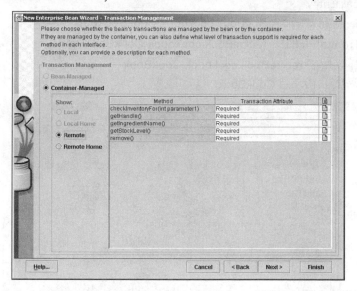

We'll accept the defaults on the remaining screens and click on Finish button after reviewing the deployment descriptor. This creates and adds the Larder bean to the application.

Adding the CookBook Bean

The CookBook bean is a BMP entity bean. Again the steps required to add this bean to our JAR file are very similar to those that went before.

Start the New Enterprise Bean Wizard again and add the three required class files: CookBook.class, CookBookHome.class, and CookBookEJB.class to our RecipeBeans JAR file:

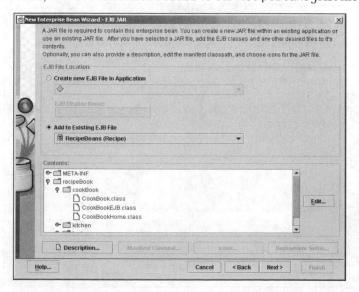

On the New Enterprise Bean Wizard-General screen, set the following parameters:

- ❑ Bean Type: Entity
- ❑ Enterprise Bean Class: recipeBook.cookbook.CookBookEJB
- ❑ Remote Home Interface: recipeBook.cookbook.CookBookHome
- ❑ Remote Interface: recipeBook.cookbook.CookBook
- ❑ Enterprise Bean Name: CookBook

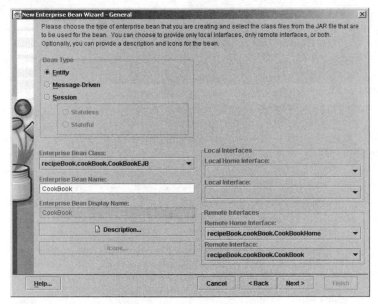

On the Entity Settings screen, select Bean Managed Persistence, and set the Primary Key Class to java.lang.String:

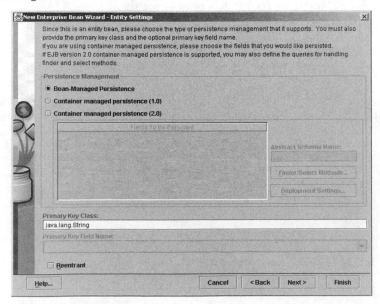

On the next screens, we accept the defaults until we come to **Resource References** screen. The CookBook bean requires a datas ource for persistence management. On this screen, click on **Add** button to add a resource factory. Set the following parameters on this screen:

- ❏ Type: javax.sql.DataSource
- ❏ Coded Name: jdbc/recipeJDBC
- ❏ Authentication: Container
- ❏ Sharable: checked
- ❏ JNDI Name: jdbc/Oracle (or whatever data source you configured earlier to connect to your database of choice)
- ❏ Username and Password: If necessary for you database connection

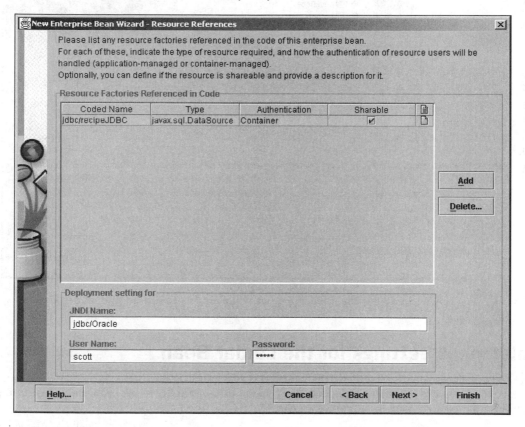

Accept the defaults for any other screen. Click on the **Finish** button on the last screen to create and add the JAR file to the application.

At this stage, we will have four beans in a JAR file added to our application:

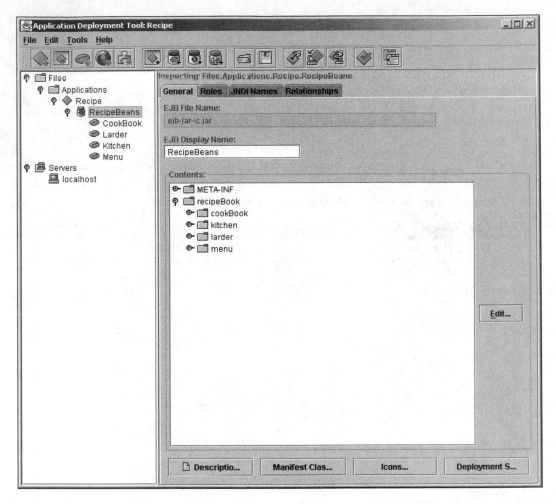

However, before we can deploy the application, we will need to provide additional deployment settings for the CMP entity bean.

Deployment Settings for the Larder Bean

Expand the RecipeBeans JAR file in the left-hand pane and select the Larder bean. This brings up a variety of tabs in the right-hand pane that allow you to further configure the bean. Select the Entity tab to bring up the entity properties that we set earlier:

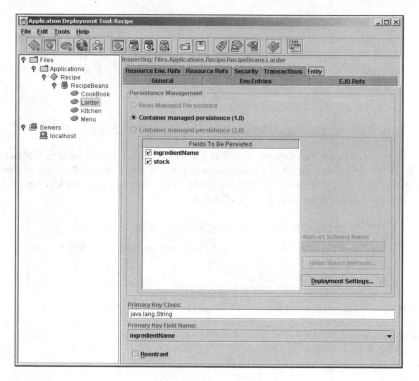

Now click on the **Deployment Settings** button to set the database required by this bean:

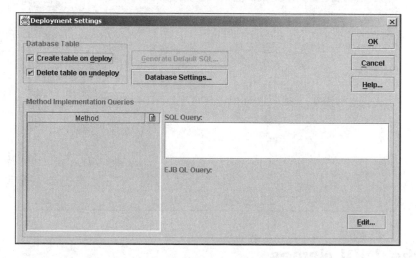

First we will need to set up the database. We do this by clicking on the **Database Settings...** button. This opens up another dialog where we will specify the JNDI name, user name, and password for the database connection. Database connections are pooled and managed by the EJB server. We will be using the data source we created earlier to connect to the database.

Type the JNDI name as **jdbc/Oracle** (or whatever you called your data source). Since we're using the Oracle, we'll need to supply additional security settings:

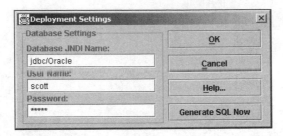

Click **OK** to return to the previous screen. On this screen, click on the **Generate Default SQL...** button to generate the SQL code for container-managed persistence. After the SQL is generated, you will be informed of the status of SQL generation. If your bean code contains any finder methods, you will be prompted to enter the SQL WHERE clause for all such methods:

To add the WHERE clause, click on the method name, in this case `findLowStockLevels()`, and you will see the generated SQL code on the right-hand side. As you can see it is only partially complete. The RI uses a fairly standard SQL-like syntax where the only thing to remember is that to access parameters to the finder method you need to use ?N where N is the parameter number reading left-to-right. So to complete our finder query we need to add the following:

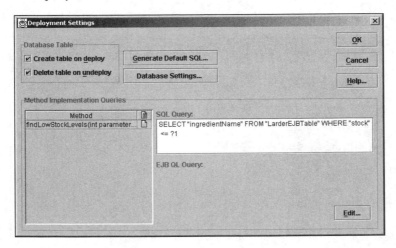

Setting the JNDI Names

We will be required to set the JNDI names for the various resources defined in our application. Select the **Recipe** application and click on **JNDI Names** tab. You will see the various resources required by our application along with the coded name for each resource. You may have set up these names earlier while adding the beans; if not, you should add them now. The following screenshot shows the settings for our application:

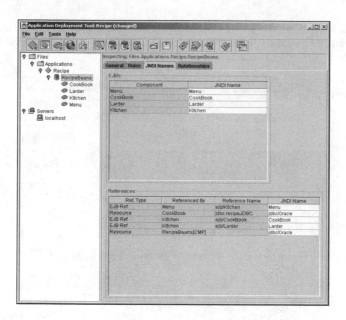

Deploying the Application into the Server

Now we are ready to deploy our Recipe application. Click on the Deploy menu option under the Tools menu.

Select Recipe under the Object to Deploy option. Select the localhost under Target Server. Click on the Return Client Jar checkbox. In the Client JAR File Name field type the desired name and path for the client JAR file:

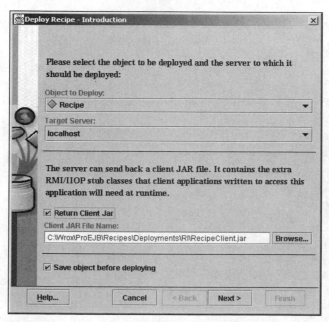

On the next screen, we will see the JNDI names for the various resources. This allows us to defer setting the JNDI names until the actual deployment process and thus this can be handled by a deployer separate from the bean provider and assembler:

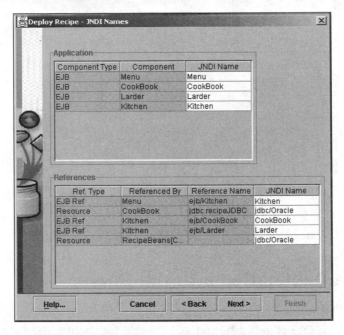

On the next Review screen click Finish. This starts the deployment process. During the deployment, the progress status is printed on the server console and the Deployment Progress dialog:

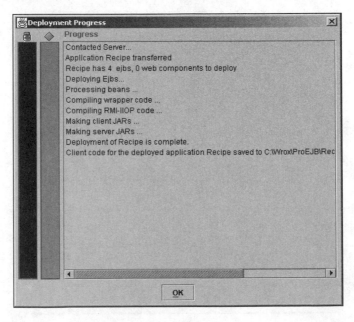

Deploying the EJB 2.0 Recipe Beans

The process for deploying the EJB 2.0 beans compared to the 1.1 version is very similar. There are a few things we need to do differently, which correspond to using local interfaces and EJB QL.

The Kitchen Bean

In our 2.0 version of the beans, the Kitchen bean only exposes local interfaces. Therefore, when we allocate the classes to interface types we need to be sure to set `KitchenHome` and `Kitchen` as local interfaces:

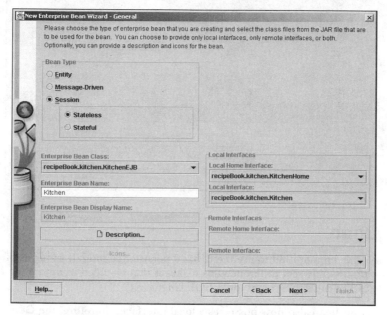

We also need to modify the EJB references screen to access the Larder and CookBook beans through a local reference:

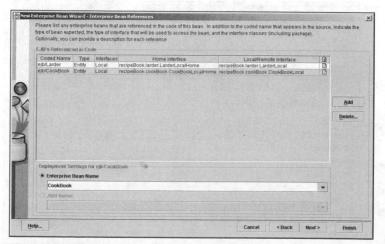

The Menu Bean

The only change for the Menu bean is in the **EJB References** screen. We need to change the reference to the Kitchen bean to be local:

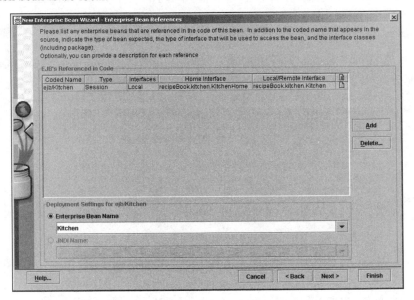

The Larder Bean

The Larder bean has been modified to use the EJB 2.0 persistence model. In terms of deployment on the deployment tool, the only real difference this makes is that we need to define the finder method using EJB QL instead of the deployment tool's SQL language.

In addition, the Larder bean also now possesses a local interface; therefore, the General screen of the wizard will look like this:

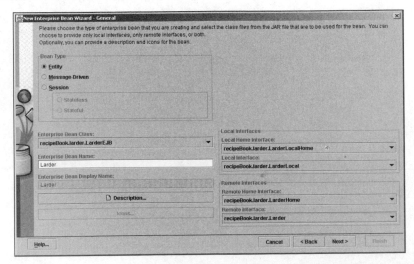

Now on the Entity Settings screen, select Container managed persistence (2.0) and as well as setting the managed fields and primary key as for the 1.1 version, also provide an Abstract Schema Name:

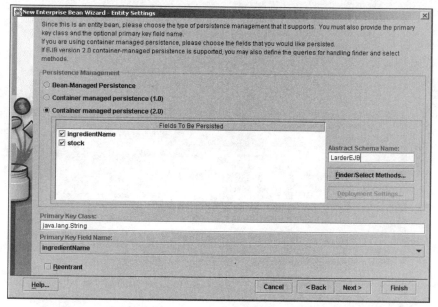

Now to define the EJB QL for the findLowStockLevels() finder, press the Finder/Select Methods button to bring up another window. Select the Remote Finders option, to see the findLowStockLevels() method listed. Now enter the following EJB QL in the window:

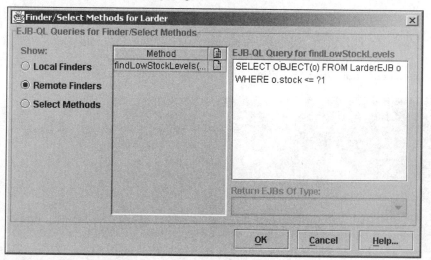

You can find out how to write EJB QL in Chapter 6.

The CookBook Bean

The only change to the deployment for the CookBook bean is to make sure that its local interfaces are specified:

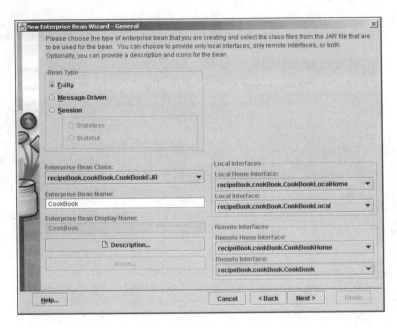

Besides these modifications to the deployment steps, the process is the same as for the 1.1 version of the beans.

Running the Client Application

Once the application is deployed, you can run the client application by typing the following command:

```
java -classpath %J2EE_HOME%\lib\j2ee.jar;.;recipeClient.jar recipeBook.client.Chef
```

This runs the client application and prints the result to the console:

```
C:\Wrox\ProEJB\Recipes\1.1>java -classpath %J2EE_HOME%\lib\j2ee.jar;..\Deployments\RI\RecipeClient.jar;. recipeBook.clie
nt.Chef
Stocking...
Larder stocked
Checking...
You are missing: sausages(5), onions(1), apples(15).
Searching for low stocks...
There is only 4 of onions
There is only 10 of sausages
There is only 5 of apples
There is only 10 of stock

C:\Wrox\ProEJB\Recipes\1.1>
```

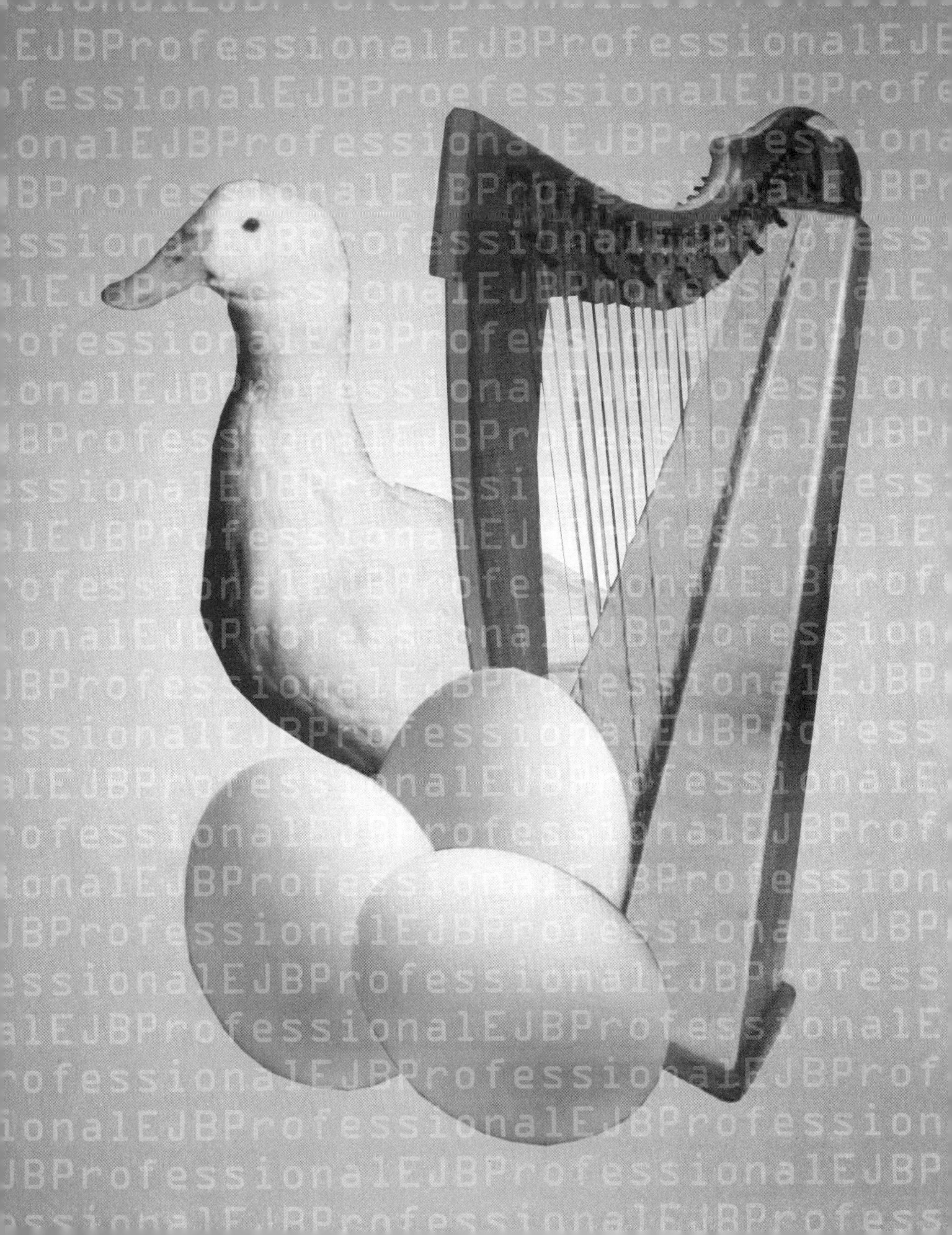

C

WebLogic Server 6.0

BEA WebLogic Server 6.0 is a fully J2EE-compliant server. Even though J2EE 1.2 only mandates the implementation of EJB 1.1, WebLogic Server 6.0 also includes a patch for an EJB 2.0 container. However, at the time of writing this patch was only up to date with the Proposed Final Draft version of the specification.

In this appendix, we will demonstrate how to deploy the 1.1 Recipe beans and a variant of the 2.0 beans into the WebLogic 6.0, server with service pack 1m

You can download WebLogic from http://commerce.beasys.com/downloads/weblogic_server.jsp#wls.

Deploying the Recipe Beans on WebLogic 6.0

This porting of our Recipe beans to WebLogic might seem a bit intimidating at first but once you understand how things work, most of it will make much more sense.

The first thing you will notice is that we are hardly changing any of the Java code that we have written so far. Most of the work will be spent in the deployment descriptors that are specific to WebLogic and configuring external resources on the server, such as the JDBC connection pool.

Let's start with the deployment descriptors.

Deployment Descriptors

As we learned earlier in the book, an EJB needs to contain at least one deployment descriptor, `ejb-jar.xml`. However, the information contained in this descriptor is not sufficient to deploy the EJB, so more descriptors are needed. Unfortunately, these other descriptors are not covered by the EJB specification, so each server provides its own set of descriptors.

WebLogic needs the following additional descriptors:

❑   `weblogic-ejb-jar.xml`.

❑   One or more container managed-persistence deployment descriptors (if the EJB is a CMP entity bean). These descriptors can have arbitrary names chosen by the bean provider.

Let's start with `weblogic-ejb-jar.xml`.

The weblogic-ejb-jar.xml File

Our Recipe application contains four beans, which means that we will have four different entries in the deployment descriptor. For two of our beans (both of the session beans), these entries are straightforward:

```xml
<?xml version="1.0"?>

<!DOCTYPE weblogic-ejb-jar PUBLIC
  '-//BEA Systems, Inc.//DTD WebLogic 6.0.0 EJB//EN'
  'http://www.bea.com/servers/wls600/dtd/weblogic-ejb-jar.dtd'>

<weblogic-ejb-jar>

  <weblogic-enterprise-bean>
    <ejb-name>Menu</ejb-name>
    <reference-descriptor>
      <ejb-reference-description>
        <ejb-ref-name>ejb/Kitchen</ejb-ref-name>
        <jndi-name>Kitchen</jndi-name>
      </ejb-reference-description>
    </reference-descriptor>
    <jndi-name>Menu</jndi-name>
  </weblogic-enterprise-bean>

  <weblogic-enterprise-bean>
    <ejb-name>Kitchen</ejb-name>
    <reference-descriptor>
      <ejb-reference-description>
        <ejb-ref-name>ejb/Larder</ejb-ref-name>
        <jndi-name>Larder</jndi-name>
      </ejb-reference-description>
      <ejb-reference-description>
        <ejb-ref-name>ejb/CookBook</ejb-ref-name>
        <jndi-name>CookBook</jndi-name>
      </ejb-reference-description>
    </reference-descriptor>
    <jndi-name>Kitchen</jndi-name>
  </weblogic-enterprise-bean>
```

Notice that each `<weblogic-enterprise-bean>` element contains an `<ejb-name>` element that corresponds to the `<ejb-name>` element in our `ejb-jar.xml` file. The other element we need to complete the definition of these simple session beans for WebLogic is `<jndi-name>`, which declares the JNDI name for the bean.

The entry for our BMP entity bean is slightly more complicated since we need to declare the data resource the bean uses. In order to do this, we need a `<reference-descriptor>` element, which is composed of a `<resource-description>` element. The `<resource-description>` element contains two further elements: a name for the resource (`<res-ref-name>`) and a JNDI name for the resource (`<jndi-name>`). Thus, the `<reference-descriptor>` element tells the container the JNDI name of the JDBC resource that should be used in order to connect to the table. The JDBC connection is an entity that represents a connection to the database. We will define this JDBC connection later.

The entry for the `CookBook` EJB is as follows:

```
<weblogic-enterprise-bean>
  <ejb-name>CookBook</ejb-name>
  <reference-descriptor>
    <resource-description>
      <res-ref-name>jdbc/recipeJDBC</res-ref-name>
      <jndi-name>jdbc/recipeJDBC</jndi-name>
    </resource-description>
  </reference-descriptor>
  <jndi-name>CookBook</jndi-name>
</weblogic-enterprise-bean>
```

The fourth bean, the CMP entity bean `Larder` is a bit more complicated, since we have to specify the persistence mechanism we'll be using (or rather that WebLogic will be using), and where the server can find further information:

```
<weblogic-enterprise-bean>
  <ejb-name>Larder</ejb-name>
  <entity-descriptor>
    <persistence>
      <persistence-type>
        <type-identifier>WebLogic_CMP_RDBMS</type-identifier>
        <type-version>5.1.0</type-version>
        <type-storage>META-INF/weblogic-cmp-rdbms-jar11.xml</type-storage>
      </persistence-type>
      <persistence-use>
        <type-identifier>WebLogic_CMP_RDBMS</type-identifier>
        <type-version>5.1.0</type-version>
      </persistence-use>
    </persistence>
  </entity-descriptor>

  <reference-descriptor>
    <resource-description>
      <res-ref-name>jdbc/recipeJDBC</res-ref-name>
      <jndi-name>jdbc/recipeJDBC</jndi-name>
    </resource-description>
  </reference-descriptor>

  <jndi-name>Larder</jndi-name>
</weblogic-enterprise-bean>

</weblogic-ejb-jar>
```

The `<entity-descriptor>` element for this bean points to a separate XML file where we will provide the persistence information on how this EJB should be stored. We'll look at this file (`weblogic-cmp-rdbms-jar11.xml`) next. The `<reference-descriptor>` element is the same as for the `CookBook` bean.

Now let's turn to the other WebLogic specific descriptor: `weblogic-cmp-rdbms-jar11.xml`.

The weblogic-cmp-rdbms-jar11.xml File

In this descriptor, we tell the container how our EJB should be mapped to the database:

```xml
<?xml version="1.0"?>

<!DOCTYPE weblogic-rdbms-bean PUBLIC
    '-//BEA Systems, Inc.//DTD WebLogic 5.1.0 EJB RDBMS Persistence//EN'
    'http://www.bea.com/servers/wls510/dtd/weblogic-rdbms-persistence.dtd'>

<weblogic-rdbms-bean>

  <pool-name>larderPool</pool-name>
  <table-name>LARDER</table-name>

  <attribute-map>
    <object-link>
      <bean-field>ingredientName</bean-field>
      <dbms-column>INGREDIENTNAME</dbms-column>
    </object-link>
    <object-link>
      <bean-field>stock</bean-field>
      <dbms-column>STOCK</dbms-column>
    </object-link>
  </attribute-map>
```

This section is straightforward: we simply map our Java fields to columns in the database. We do this in the `<attribute-map>` element, each `<object-link>` element specifying the bean's variable (`<bean-field>`) and the corresponding database column (`<dbms-column>`).

The `ConnectionPool` defined in the `<pool-name>` element is used to configure the connection that our EJBs will have with the database. We will get back to this very soon, when we start configuring the server. Next we define our finder.

When we are writing a container-managed persistence EJB, we want to be abstracted from lower-level details related to the database, and more particularly, we want to avoid writing SQL. However, the EJB container cannot guess how our finder methods should retrieve data from the database. Therefore, we need an intermediate language to define those operations.

This might look like we're only pushing the problem further: instead of learning SQL, you have to learn yet another database language. This is true, but this new language has an important advantage: it is genuinely database-neutral. Unlike SQL, which is based on standards but to which most RDBMS vendors add their own enhancements, **WebLogic Query Language** (WL-QL) is proprietary and fixed in WebLogic 6.0. You don't need to know that your EJB is stored in an Oracle or Sybase database: all you need to do is define your query and the container will take care of generating SQL for you.

Older beans using WL-QL still work, but new beans should be written using the EJB 2.0 specification, which defines a standard query language for EJBs, called **EJB-QL**. We will come back to this language when we convert our EJBs to EJB 2.0. Let's now look at the definition for our finder method:

```
<finder-list>
  <finder>
    <method-name>findLowStockLevels</method-name>
      <method-params>
        <method-param>int</method-param>
      </method-params>
    <finder-query><![CDATA[(<= stock $0)]]></finder-query>
  </finder>
</finder-list>

</weblogic-rdbms-bean>
```

In this stanza, we define the Java name of the method (`<method-name>`), its parameter (`<method-params>`, which in turn contains a `<method-param>` element for each parameter the method takes; in this case we use just one integer parameter, and its definition in WL-QL (in a `CDATA` section so that the XML parser doesn't interpret characters such as "<"). The expression is straightforward: it will return `true` for all the stocks that are less than the given parameter.

We are now done with our deployment descriptors: the three XML files we created (`ejb-jar.xml`, which can be found in Appendix A, `weblogic-ejb-jar.xml`, and `weblogic-rmp-rdbms-jar11.xml`) are sufficient to describe the deployment of our EJB to WebLogic. However, we still have some work to do before we can deploy and run our EJBs.

Java Code

This section will be very short since our EJBs have been written in a way that is compliant with the EJB 1.1 specification. However, this specification doesn't cover everything, as we already saw in the previous section, and one area that is not defined is how a client connects to the application server. Every server has its own way to make this connection.

All we need to establish a connection to a J2EE server is a `Context`. The following method will create one for us; assuming our server is running on our local machine and that it is listening to port 7001 (the default for WebLogic):

```
private Context getContextInfo() {
  Context result = null;
  String url = "t3://localhost:7001";
  try {
    // Get an InitialContext
    Properties h = new Properties();
    h.put(Context.INITIAL_CONTEXT_FACTORY,
          "weblogic.jndi.WLInitialContextFactory");
    h.put(Context.PROVIDER_URL, url);
    result = new InitialContext(h);
  } catch (NamingException ne) {
    System.out.println("We were unable to get a connection to " +
                       " the WebLogic server at " + url);
    ne.printStackTrace();
  }
  return result;
}
```

We can either change the call `getContextInfo()` to a call to `getWeblogicContextInfo()`, or we can alter the `getContextInfo()` method to call our `getWeblogicContextInfo()` method, as below:

```
private Context getContextInfo() throws NamingException {
  return getWeblogicContextInfo();
  }
}
```

This is the only modification that our code needs. Everything else can be reused without any modification.

Configuring WebLogic Server 6.0

In the previous steps, our deployment descriptors have declared two entities that we need to create within the server:

❑   The JDBC Connection (`jdbc/jdbcRecipe`)

❑   The Connection Pool (`larderPool`)

All the configuration information in WebLogic 6.0 is gathered in a file called `config.xml`, in the directory for the server domain (`%WL_HOME%/config/[domain_name]/`). There are two ways we can modify this file:

❑   By editing the XML file by hand

❑   With the web-based console

We will illustrate both ways in the following sections.

Modifying the config.xml File Directly

You should be aware that modifying your `config.xml` file directly is dangerous, especially if you are running several instances of WebLogic Server in a cluster. Any errors we make while editing this file might cause our server not to start again. That being said, sometimes we don't have access to the Console, therefore editing the XML by hand is our only option.

With this warning in mind, here are the two XML stanzas that declare the `DataSource` and the `ConnectionPool`. They can appear anywhere within a `<domain>` element:

```
<JDBCConnectionPool CapacityIncrement="1"
                    DriverName="oracle.jdbc.driver.OracleDriver"
                    InitialCapacity="1"
                    MaxCapacity="2"
                    Name="larderPool"
                    Properties="user=scott;password=tiger"
                    Targets="myserver"
                    URL="jdbc:oracle:thin:@dbserver:1521:ejb"/>

<JDBCDataSource JNDIName="jdbc/recipeJDBC"
                Name="jdbc/recipeJDBC"
                PoolName="larderPool"
                Targets="myserver"/>
```

You will need to configure the respective elements of this for your particular database.

You will also need to add the database driver into the WebLogic classpath. You can do this by editing the startup command file for the WebLogic domain.

You'll have to restart your server for these changes to take effect. Don't be alarmed by the number of options that are specified here, consider them as defaults that we can safely ignore. The important ones are:

❑　For the `JDBCConnectionPool`, the name of the driver (here we are using WebLogic's JDBC drivers for an Oracle database), the host/user/password of the database and the URL and name of the pool (it must match the one we used in our deployment descriptors: `jdbc/recipeJDBC`).

❑　For the `DataSource`, we need to define the name of the data source and its JNDI name (`jdbc/recipeJDBC`) and the `ConnectionPool` we will be using for the connection (`larderPool`, the one defined above).

Using the Web-based Console

The other way to modify our WebLogic settings is through the WebLogic default console. This is a browser-based console that offers us a full range of administration tasks for WebLogic servers. The console can be launched by pointing a web browser at http://127.0.0.1:7001/console/, or through the Start menu, under BEA WebLogic E-Business Platform | WebLogic 6.0 | Start Default Console.

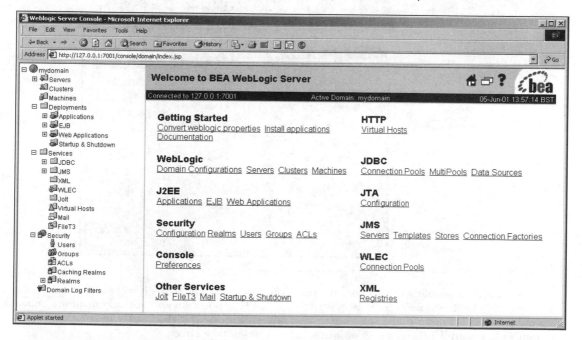

As you can see, there are a lot of options open to us, but we only need to concentrate on a couple to configure our server ready for deploying the recipe application. First, we'll set up a new connection pool. Select Connection Pools under JDBC (under the Services node on the left), and click the Create a new JDBC Connection Pool... link.

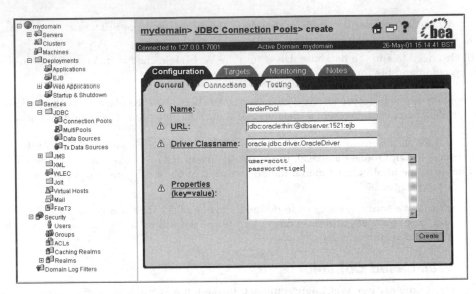

When we've filled in the appropriate entries (here for a default Oracle database using Oracle drivers, in a pool called larderPool), click Create and move to the Connections tab:

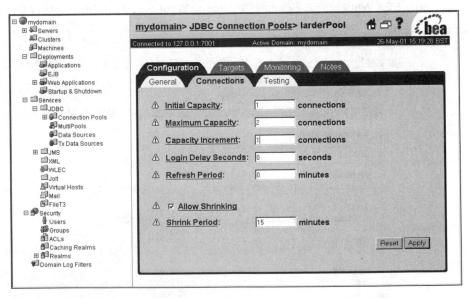

Here, we specify how many connections the pool will start with, how many it will hold, and what the increment will be. Since we're only demonstrating a simple application and are only planning on using one client, we've set these values low. Click Apply to finish this step, which will cause the console to prompt us to restart the server in order for our new values to take effect:

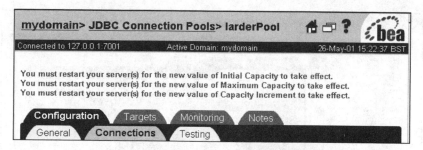

We'll not restart the server until we've set up our data source and finished setting up our connection pool, for which we require one last step. On the Targets tab, select the server we're using (in this case, myserver):

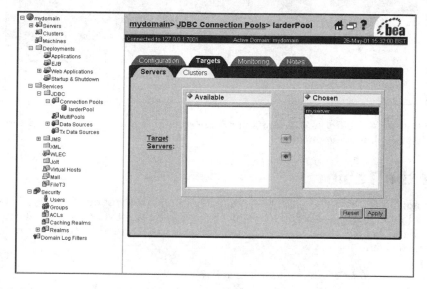

Next, we'll define a new JDBC data source. Select Data Sources under JDBC, and select Create a new JDBC Data Source..., which will bring us to the following dialog:

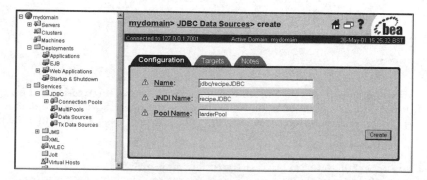

Once we have filled in the fields with the appropriate information (values that match those our application will be using for the data source Name and JNDI Name, and the Pool Name we specified earlier), we can click on Create. The next step is to select a target server on the Targets tab; again, we'll use myserver:

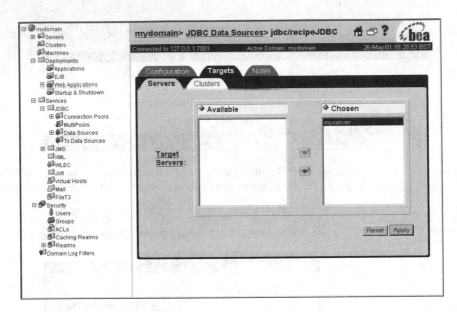

Click on Apply and we've finished defining our connection pool and data source; we can now restart our server, ready to deploy our application.

Creating the Table

In case it is not already done, we need to create the table that will host our EJBs. We have two entity beans, each of them mapped to a different table. Note that the latest version of WebLogic can create those tables for us as our EJBs are being deployed, but we will ignore this feature for now in order to illustrate the procedure.

The SQL statements to create the tables are as follows:

```
CREATE TABLE RECIPEBOOK (RECIPENAME VARCHAR(30),
                         INGREDIENTS VARCHAR(500)
);

CREATE TABLE LARDER (INGREDIENTNAME VARCHAR(20),
                     STOCK INT
);
```

The simplest way to create those two tables in our database is to use the `utils.Schema` tool that is shipped with WebLogic. All we need to do is use the same parameters we used to define our `DataSource` in the previous section. Assuming the SQL instructions are stored in a file called `db.sql`, here is the command line to create the tables:

```
java -classpath %WLS_HOME%\lib\weblogic.jar utils.Schema
     jdbc:oracle:thin:@dbserver:1521:ejb oracle.jdbc.driver.OracleDriver
     -u scott -p tiger db.sql
```

You will obviously need to modify this to use the respective URL to your database, as well as making sure the driver is in the classpath when you run this command.

Compiling the Recipe JAR for WebLogic

Now we can compile and archive the additional deployment descriptors ready for deployment in the WebLogic server. Make sure the `weblogic-ejb-jar.xml` and `weblogic-cmp-rdbms-jar11.xml` are included in the `META-INF` directory for the JAR file along with the standard `ejb-jar.xml`. Call the JAR file `std-recipe.jar`.

At this point, the previous versions of WebLogic Server required us to run the EJB compiler (`weblogic.ejbc`) on our JAR file. This is no longer needed in WebLogic Server 6.0 and above. All we need to do is deploy this JAR file (see the next section) and the server will automatically detect if it has to run `weblogic.ejbc` on the file.

You might still want to perform this operation as an exercise, and also in order to make sure that your EJB is compliant (otherwise, the errors will show up in the server log). To invoke the EJB compiler, type:

    java weblogic.ejbc -verbose std-recipe.jar recipe.jar

The `weblogic.jar` file (from the `wlserver6.0\lib\` directory) needs to be in the classpath for this command to work. If we haven't made any mistakes, this should create a new JAR file, `recipe.jar`, which we can deploy just the same as the original one. Ensure that when running this step that there is not a `'.'` at the start of your classpath.

Deploying the Recipe EJB

There are several ways you can deploy an EJB with WebLogic Server 6.0:

1. Statically (declaring your EJB in `config.xml`)

2. Programmatically (using `MBeans`)

3. Dynamically (copying your JAR file into the `%WL_HOME%\config\%WL_DOMAIN%\applications` directory)

4. Using the web-based administration console

Examining the strengths and weaknesses of these four approaches is beyond the scope of this appendix, so we'll just explain quickly what they do.

Static Deployment

A deployment is considered to be static if its definition is specified in the `config.xml` file. We can specify several sorts of applications to be deployed in WebLogic; EJBs are just one of them. There are two ways we can modify this file: either directly (using a text editor, or better, an XML editor) or through the console. If we deploy an EJB using the console, the corresponding definition will be inserted automatically in our `config.xml`.

If we wanted to deploy our Recipe EJB statically, we would need to add the following to our `config.xml`:

```
<Application Name="Recipe"
             Path="c:/ProEJB/Recipes/">

  <EJBComponent Targets="myserver"
                URI="recipe.jar" />

</Application>
```

Static deployment should be the preferred way to deploy EJBs in a production environment.

Programmatic Deployment

Once an EJB has been deployed statically, we still have a certain amount of control over it, either through a command-line tool such as the EJB Deployer, or from Java code. Using the JMX API, it is very easy to perform administration tasks from a Java client.

The following code illustrates how we can find a particular EJB deployed in the server and modify the attribute of its corresponding Mbean (in this particular case, we toggle the attribute IsDeployed, which causes the container to deploy the EJB if it is not currently deployed, or undeploy it if it is deployed):

```
import weblogic.management.Admin;
import weblogic.management.DeploymentException;
import weblogic.management.DistributedManagementException;
import weblogic.management.UndeploymentException;
import weblogic.management.MBeanHome;
import weblogic.management.WebLogicMBean;
import weblogic.management.configuration.EJBComponentMBean;
import weblogic.utils.Debug;
import weblogic.jndi.Environment;

import javax.management.InstanceNotFoundException;
import javax.management.InvalidAttributeValueException;
import javax.naming.Context;
import javax.naming.AuthenticationException;
import javax.naming.CommunicationException;
import javax.naming.NamingException;

import java.util.Iterator;
import java.util.Set;

/**
 * This client looks for an EJB deployed with a certain URI
 * in WebLogic 6 and switched its "IsDeployed" status at each call.
 * The String variables will have to be changed to appropriate values
 * for your system.
 */

 public class MBUndeploy {

    public static final String URI = "recipe.jar";
    public static MBeanHome getHome() {
    String url = "t3://localhost:7001";   // URL of the Administration server
    String username = "system";        // Only works if guest logins are enabled
    String password = "javajava"; // Change as appropriate
```

```
      MBeanHome result = null;

      try {
        Environment env = new Environment();
        env.setProviderUrl(url);
        env.setSecurityPrincipal(username);
        env.setSecurityCredentials(password);
        Context ctx = env.getInitialContext();
        result = (MBeanHome) ctx.lookup(MBeanHome.ADMIN_JNDI_NAME);
      } catch (AuthenticationException e) {
        e.printStackTrace();
      } catch (CommunicationException e) {
        e.printStackTrace();
      } catch (NamingException e) {
        e.printStackTrace();
      }

      return result;
    }

    public static void main(String argv[]) {
      try {

        // Find all MBeans of type EJBComponent
        MBeanHome home = getHome();
        Set mbeans = home.getMBeansByType("EJBComponent");

        // Try to find our EJB
        Iterator it = mbeans.iterator();
        while (it.hasNext()) {
          EJBComponentMBean cmb = (EJBComponentMBean) it.next();
          if (URI.equals(cmb.getURI())) {

            // Found it. If it is deployed, undeploy it,
            // if it is undeployed, deploy it
            boolean currentState = cmb.getApplication().isDeployed();
            System.out.println("Found " + URI + ". Deployed:" + currentState);
            cmb.getApplication().setDeployed(!currentState);
            System.out.println("Now:" + cmb.getApplication().isDeployed());
          }
        }
      } catch (DeploymentException ex) {
        ex.printStackTrace();
      } catch (UndeploymentException ex) {
        ex.printStackTrace();
      } catch (DistributedManagementException ex) {
        ex.printStackTrace();
      }
    }
  }
```

In order to compile and run this code, we need the `weblogic.jar` file in the classpath; other than that, we can run it from anywhere.

Dynamic Deployment

A deployment is considered to be dynamic if instead of declaring the EJB in our `config.xml`, we simply copy the JAR (or EAR) file into the `applications/` directory corresponding to our server. Similarly, deleting the file from the directory will cause the EJB to be undeployed, and copying a new version over the old one will undeploy the old EJB and deploy the new one. Dynamic deployment is the easiest way to develop and test EJB. The server can either be running or down when we copy the file into the directory. If it is running it will hot deploy the beans, otherwise the beans will be automatically deployed the next time the server is started.

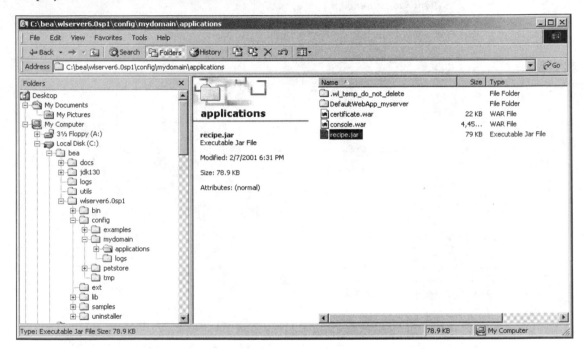

Web-based Deployment

The web-based administration console also provides a means to deploy an EJB application. All the console really does is create the descriptor for the `config.xml` file for us.

With the WebLogic server running, open the web-based console at http://localhost:7001/console and select the EJB link under the J2EE heading. This will bring up the EJB Deployments page:

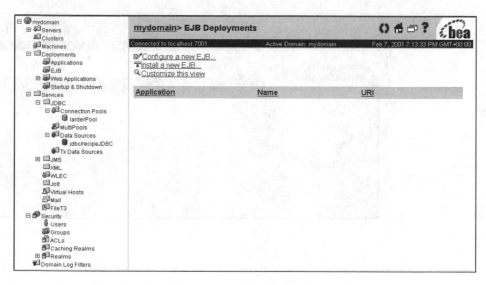

Select the Install a new EJB link to navigate to the application installation page:

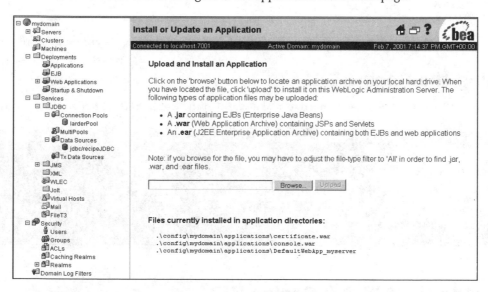

Browse to the JAR file to install then hit the Upload button. When the JAR file has been successfully deployed you can examine its properties by using the tree in the left-hand pane:

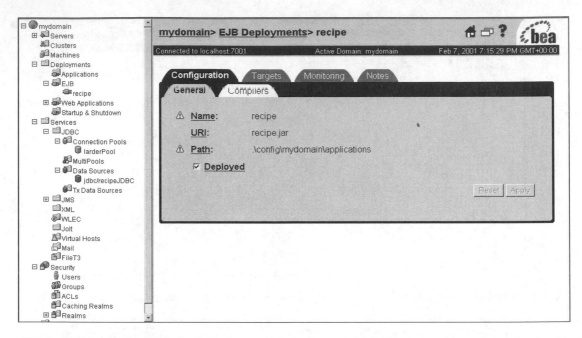

When we have deployed the beans using one of the four methods above, we are ready to run the client.

Running the Recipe EJB

To run the Chef client, we merely need to make sure that the weblogic.jar file is in the classpath:

```
C:\WINNT\System32\cmd.exe                                                    _ □ ×
C:\Wrox\ProEJB\Recipes\Deployments\WebLogic>java -classpath c:\bea\wlserver6.0sp1\lib\weblogic.jar;. recipeBook.client.C
hef
Stocking...
Larder stocked
Checking...
You are missing: sausages(5), onions(1), apples(15).
Searching for low stocks...
There is only 5 of apples
There is only 4 of onions
There is only 10 of stock
C:\Wrox\ProEJB\Recipes\Deployments\WebLogic>
```

Deploying the EJB 2.0 Recipe EJB

Before we deploy our new EJB 2.0 Recipe application, we need to make sure that our WebLogic server has the necessary EJB 2.0 enhancements. There are two ways we can do this:

❑   Try to deploy the bean – if we don't have the upgrade, then WebLogic will tell us to go to the following web page and download the EJB 2.0 upgrade:

http://commerce.bea.com/downloads/weblogic_server.jsp#wls

❑   Secondly, we can look in the /lib directory of our WebLogic installation for the `ejb20.jar`
file – if we've got that, then we don't need to download it (obviously).

The process deploy our 2.0 version of the Recipe beans is virtually identical to that for the 1.1 version.
The only difference is with the WebLogic deployment descriptors. Here are the new deployment
descriptors to be used with the 2.0 beans:

```
<!DOCTYPE weblogic-ejb-jar PUBLIC "-//BEA Systems, Inc.//DTD WebLogic 6.0.0
EJB//EN" "http://www.bea.com/servers/wls600/dtd/weblogic-ejb-jar.dtd" >

<weblogic-ejb-jar>

  <weblogic-enterprise-bean>
    <ejb-name>Menu</ejb-name>
    <reference-descriptor>
      <ejb-local-reference-description>
<ejb-ref-name>ejb/Kitchen</ejb-ref-name>
<jndi-name>KitchenLocalHome</jndi-name>
      </ejb-local-reference-description>
    </reference-descriptor>
    <jndi-name>Menu</jndi-name>

  </weblogic-enterprise-bean>

  <weblogic-enterprise-bean>
    <ejb-name>Kitchen</ejb-name>
    <reference-descriptor>
      <ejb-local-reference-description>
<ejb-ref-name>ejb/Larder</ejb-ref-name>
<jndi-name>LarderLocalHome</jndi-name>
      </ejb-local-reference-description>
      <ejb-local-reference-description>
<ejb-ref-name>ejb/CookBook</ejb-ref-name>
<jndi-name>CookBookLocalHome</jndi-name>
      </ejb-local-reference-description>
    </reference-descriptor>
    <jndi-name>Kitchen</jndi-name>
    <local-jndi-name>KitchenLocalHome</local-jndi-name>
  </weblogic-enterprise-bean>

  <weblogic-enterprise-bean>
    <ejb-name>CookBook</ejb-name>
    <reference-descriptor>
      <resource-description>
        <res-ref-name>jdbc/recipeJDBC</res-ref-name>
        <jndi-name>jdbc/recipeJDBC</jndi-name>
      </resource-description>
    </reference-descriptor>
    <jndi-name>CookBook</jndi-name>
    <local-jndi-name>CookBookLocalHome</local-jndi-name>
  </weblogic-enterprise-bean>

  <weblogic-enterprise-bean>
    <ejb-name>Larder</ejb-name>
    <entity-descriptor>
```

```
          <persistence>
    <persistence-type>
      <type-identifier>WebLogic_CMP_RDBMS</type-identifier>
      <type-version>6.0</type-version>
      <type-storage>META-INF/weblogic-cmp-rdbms-jar20.xml</type-storage>
    </persistence-type>
    <persistence-use>
      <type-identifier>WebLogic_CMP_RDBMS</type-identifier>
      <type-version>6.0</type-version>
    </persistence-use>
        </persistence>
      </entity-descriptor>

      <reference-descriptor>
        <resource-description>
          <res-ref-name>jdbc/recipeJDBC</res-ref-name>
          <jndi-name>jdbc/recipeJDBC</jndi-name>
        </resource-description>

      <ejb-local-reference-description>
  <ejb-ref-name>ejb/Kitchen</ejb-ref-name>
  <jndi-name>KitchenLocalHome</jndi-name>
        </ejb-local-reference-description>

      </reference-descriptor>


      <jndi-name>Larder</jndi-name>
      <local-jndi-name>LarderLocalHome</local-jndi-name>
    </weblogic-enterprise-bean>

</weblogic-ejb-jar>
```

```
<!DOCTYPE weblogic-rdbms-jar PUBLIC  '-//BEA Systems, Inc.//DTD WebLogic 6.0.0 EJB
RDBMS Persistence//EN' 'http://www.bea.com/servers/wls600/dtd/weblogic-rdbms20-
persistence-600.dtd'>

<weblogic-rdbms-jar>
  <weblogic-rdbms-bean>
    <ejb-name>Larder</ejb-name>
    <data-source-name>jdbc/recipeJDBC</data-source-name>
    <table-name>LARDER</table-name>

    <field-map>
      <cmp-field>ingredientName</cmp-field>
      <dbms-column>INGREDIENTNAME</dbms-column>
    </field-map>
    <field-map>
      <cmp-field>stock</cmp-field>
      <dbms-column>STOCK</dbms-column>
    </field-map>

  </weblogic-rdbms-bean>

</weblogic-rdbms-jar>
```

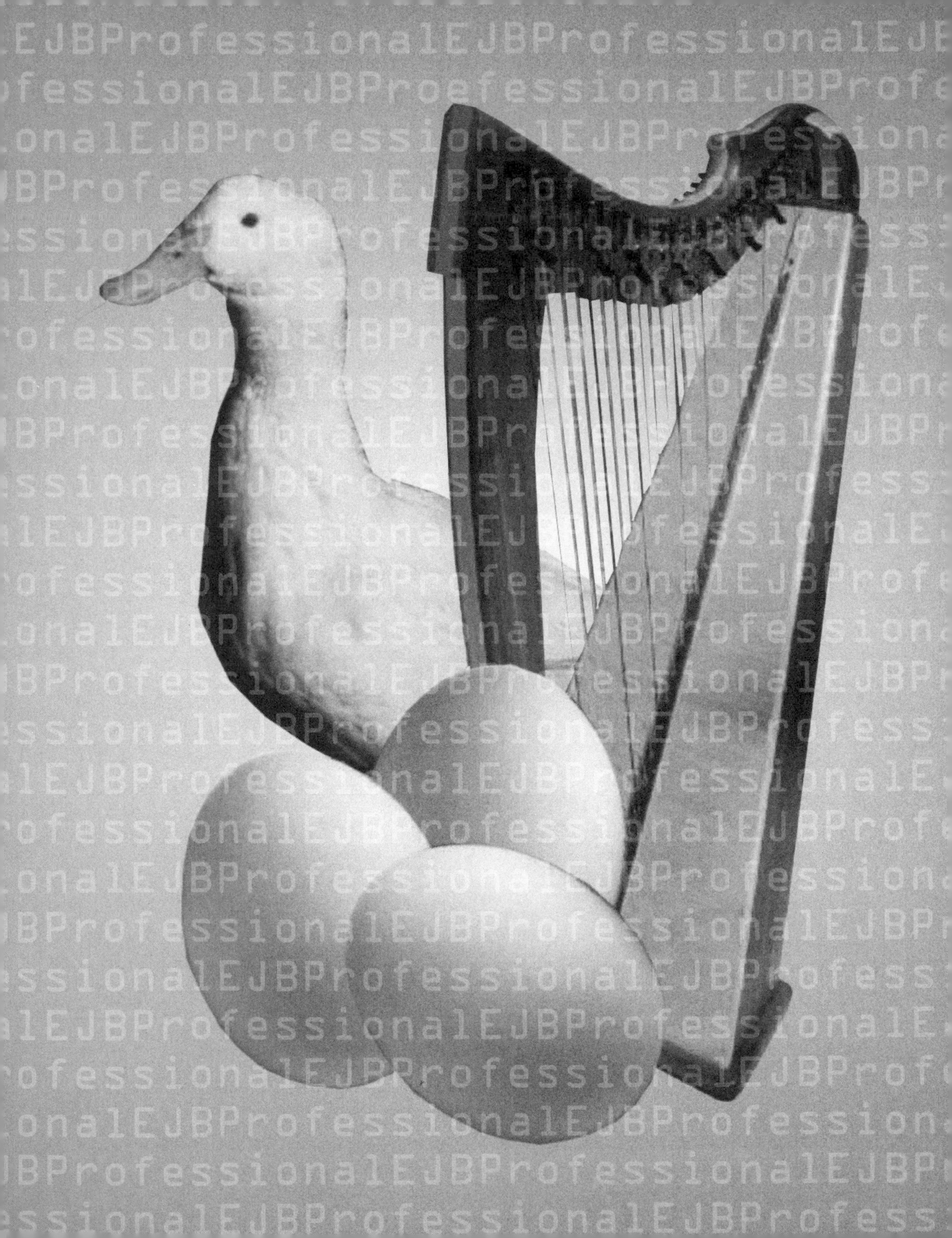
EJBProfessional

IBM WebSphere Application Server 4.0

The IBM **WebSphere Application Server** is part of IBM's WebSphere Software Platform, which contains numerous products for building and running 'e-business' software. The application server is one of the core parts of this platform, providing the means to run things like servlets, JavaServer Pages, and, obviously, Enterprise JavaBeans.

Version 4.0 of WebSphere is J2EE 1.2-compliant and supports the EJB 1.1 specification. The WebSphere Application Server (**WAS**) comes in three different editions:

- ❑ The Advanced Edition (AE)
- ❑ The Advanced Edition Single Server (AEs)
- ❑ The Advanced Edition for Development Only (AEd)

The Single Server Edition is single-server only and thus does not support the distribution of Enterprise JavaBeans across several servers for workload management. It stores all administration data in XML-based files, which can be changed manually or through the use of a browser-based user interface.

The Development Only Edition is identical to the Single Server Edition, but its license prohibits its use in a production environment, and it can be downloaded electronically only.

The Advanced Edition, comes with a complete environment for workload management and load balancing. It stores all administrative data in a relational database (DB2, Oracle 8i, or Sybase). Administration can be done via a Java client application, via command line using XML configuration files, or using 'WSCP', a scripting language and application for WebSphere administration.

It is intended that EJB development be done on the single server editions so we will focus on that edition for the remainder of the appendix.

Deploying the Recipe Beans

In this section, we will look at how the Recipe application can be installed in the WebSphere Application Server. The actual assembly and deployment process works the same way for both the Advanced Edition and the Advanced Edition Single Server. We will then look at how the deployed application can be installed into an application server instance via the web-based admin client as shipped with the Advanced Edition Single Server.

Making the Recipe beans work in the application server requires us to perform the assembly and the deployment steps as outlined in the EJB specification. There is no predefined sequence in which this must be done for WebSphere. You can first deploy the EJBs and then add the assembly information later. However, the recommended approach is to first do the assembly and then deploy the entire application, so that is what we will do in our sample here.

The code for the Recipe beans comes in an EJB JAR file. The assembly step leads to an enterprise archive file, with the extension .ear. The deployment step updates the EAR file and adds the generated classes to it. Finally, the EAR file is installed into WebSphere as an enterprise application.

Enterprise Application Assembly

This assembly is done with the **Application Assembly Tool** (**AAT**). This is a Java application that is started via a batch file called assembly.bat, located in the server's /bin directory.

The AAT offers several wizards for the creation of EAR, JAR, and WAR files. A complete application will typically be stored in an enterprise archive, so in the case of the Recipe application we'll start the Create Application Wizard:

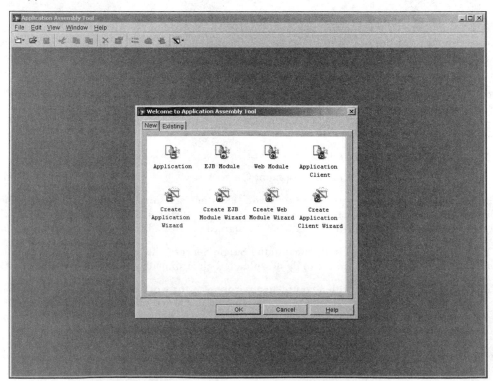

The wizard will first ask us for the name of the enterprise application that we want to create, which EAR file will be created, and a description of the application:

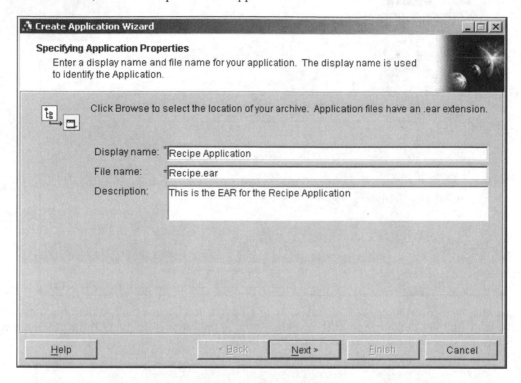

The next several steps in the wizard let us specify additional files, for example, WAR files that are part of the enterprise application. The only input file in our case is the Recipe.jar file with our EJBs in it. Skip past the **Adding Supplementary Files** and **Choosing Application Icons** screens, and on the **Adding EJB Modules** screen click on the **Add...** button. This will bring up a file dialog where we can browse to the file we want (Recipe.jar), select it, and add it to our EAR file. Before it add the JAR file however, you will be prompted if you want to enter an alternate DD:

In our case just leave it as it is and press OK:

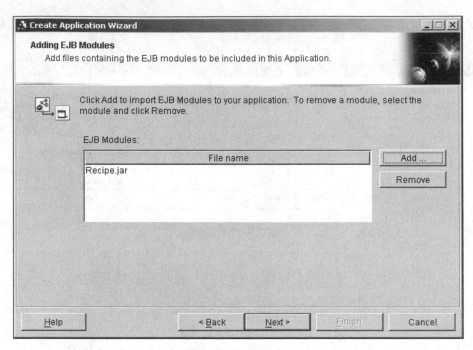

All the other screens (Adding Web Modules, Adding Application Clients, and Adding Security Roles) can be left with their defaults, and after we press Finish in the last screen, the JAR file gets imported and the following view is displayed in the AAT main window:

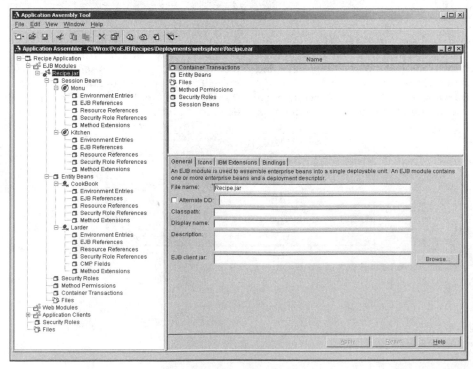

This display contains pretty much the entire information given in the deployment descriptor, and it lets us define assembly and binding information.

The properties of an EJB are displayed in a notebook with four tabs: General, Icons, IBM Extensions, and Bindings. Let us have closer look at each one:

- ❑ The General tab contains information about the bean that is read from the deployment descriptor, like the class name of the bean, its home interface name, etc.

- ❑ The Icons tab lets us specify the names of icon files for the bean.

- ❑ The IBM Extensions tab contains things that are WebSphere specific:

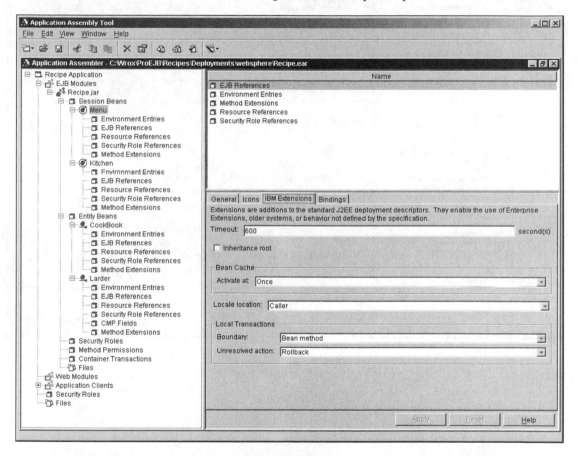

- ❑ The Binding tab lets us define what name in JNDI the EJB should be bound to once it gets installed. If we do not enter any information here, we will be asked for it later when we install the enterprise application.

For the Recipe application, we will define plain JNDI names. So for each of the four beans, switch to its Bindings tab and change the pre-configured JNDI name to its simpler variant. So, for example Kitchen for the Kitchen EJB, Menu for the Menu EJB and so forth:

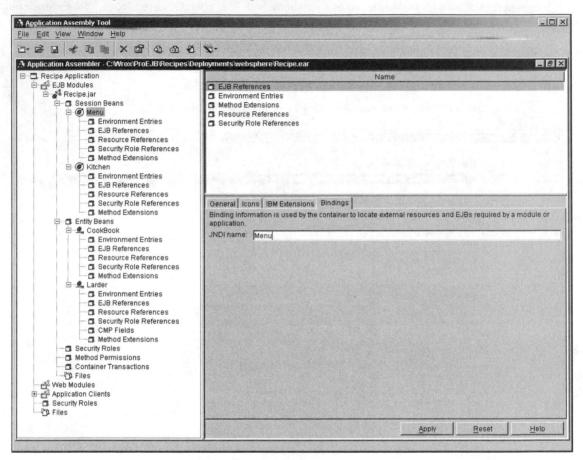

Here is an example that shows how EJB references are mapped using the **EJB References** node. The Bindings page, not shown here, allows you to define which actual JNDI name the bean refers to:

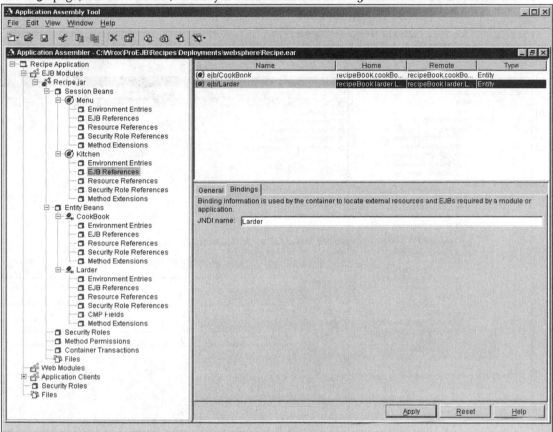

Go through the **EJB References Bindings** for the Menu and Kitchen beans and set the JNDI name to that for each bean name.

We also need to configure the datasources references for our entity beans. On the Bindings page for the Larder bean you may have noticed that as well as supplying the JNDI name for the bean we also need to provide the JNDI name and security credentials for the datasource:

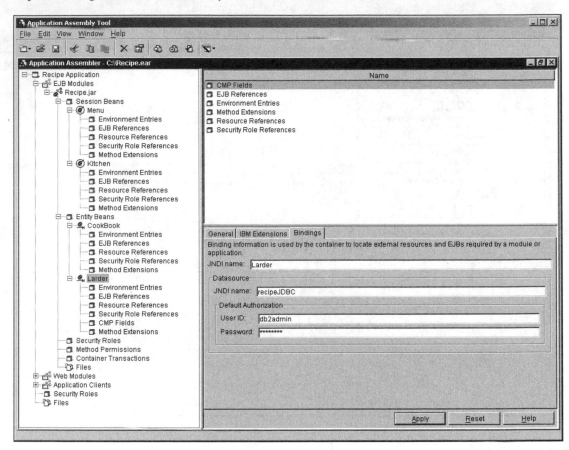

We also need to provide this information for the `jdbc/recipeJDBC` resource reference for the CookBook bean under the **Resource References | Bindings** page:

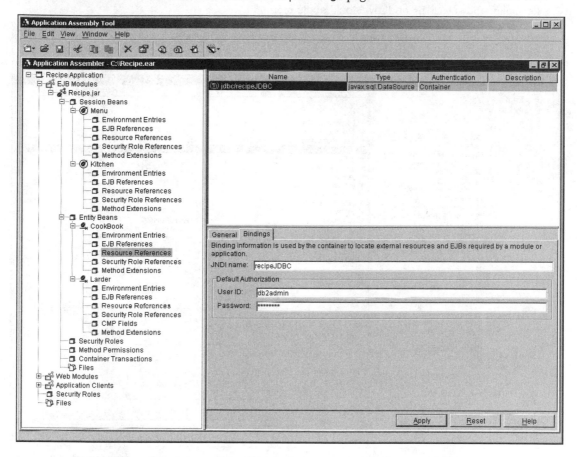

The final configuration we need to make is to define how the container should implement our `findLowStockLevels()` finder. To do this open the properties page for **Method Extensions** for the Larder bean, and select the **findLowStockLevels** method:

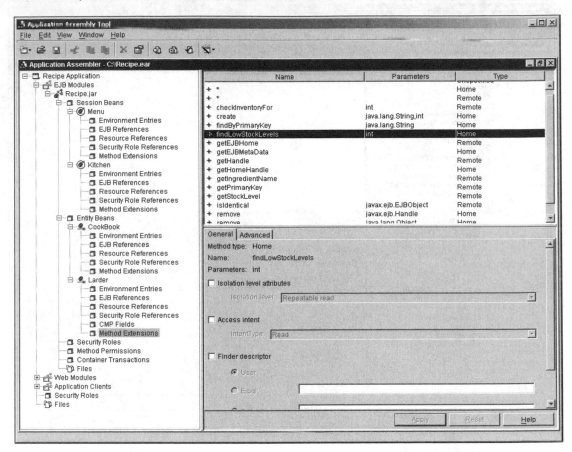

Check the Finder descriptor box and in the Where clause box enter stock <= ?:

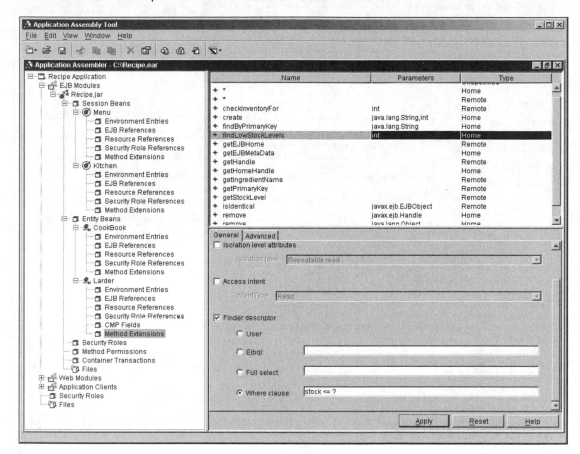

Now we can save the archive and prepare for deployment.

Deployment

After we have entered all of the required assembly information and have configured our beans and their methods and extensions, we are ready to create deployed code for our beans. The deployment tool is separate from the AAT, but you can call it from within the AAT, by using the File | Generate code for deployment menu option. This will bring up a dialog that lets you enter the name of the EAR file that should be processed, together with some additional options. Accept the defaults and press the Generate Now button to start the process:

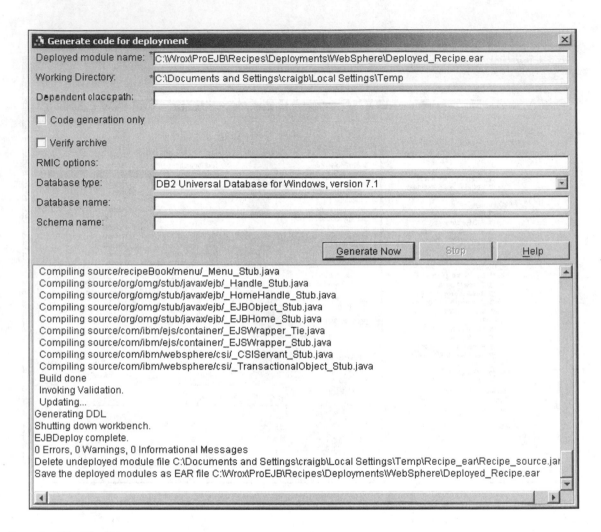

Installation

Once the deployment process is complete, the application can be installed into the application server. All the resources that build the application are contained in an EAR file. To load and configure the application, we can use several approaches, namely a browser-based client, a Java client, a command-line XML interface, or a scripting interface called 'WSCP'. Here we will look at the browser-based client that comes with the Advanced Edition Single Server (AEs).

To start the admin console, open a browser window and enter the following URL: http://localhost:9090/admin/. The following page will appear:

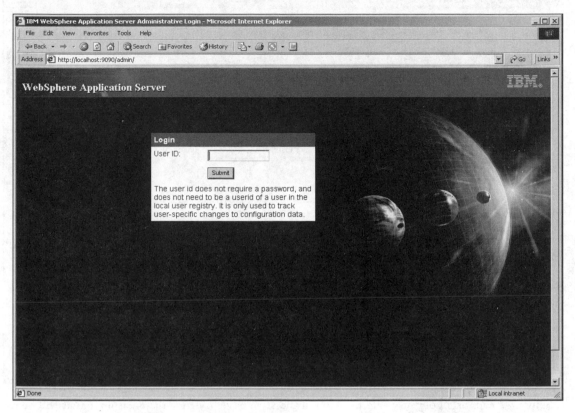

As the text says, you can enter any userId here, because it is only kept to log activities on a per user basis.

Once you've register your userId, the main page of the Administration Console looks like this:

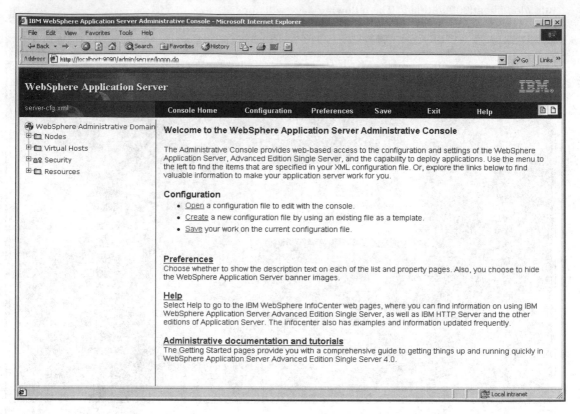

Before we can install our new enterprise application, we have to define the datasource that will be used by our application. Datasources are defined for the database driver that is used to access them. We will use the Db2JdbcDriver that was installed with the system to connect to a DB2 database.

Expand first the Resource node, then JDBC Providers, until you can see the Data Sources folder, and open the Data Sources page:

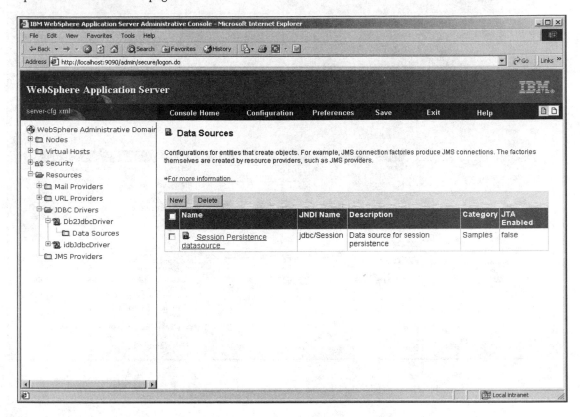

Press the New button to create a new datasource within our WebSphere server. For our example, we will call the datasource recipeJDBC with the same JNDI name. Also specify the database that you wish to use (you will have to create the tables in the database yourself using something like the DB2 command window):

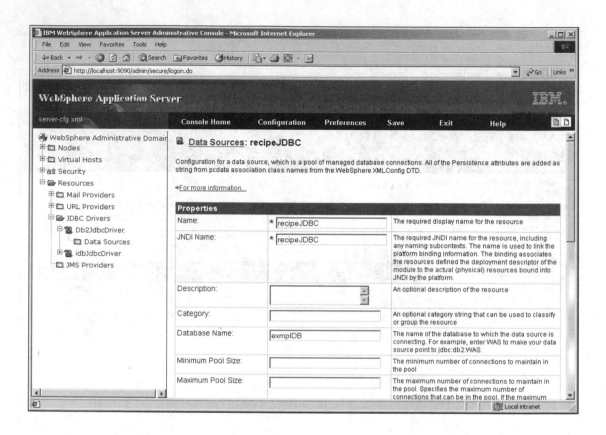

Once you have OKed the new datasource, remember to save the new configuration:

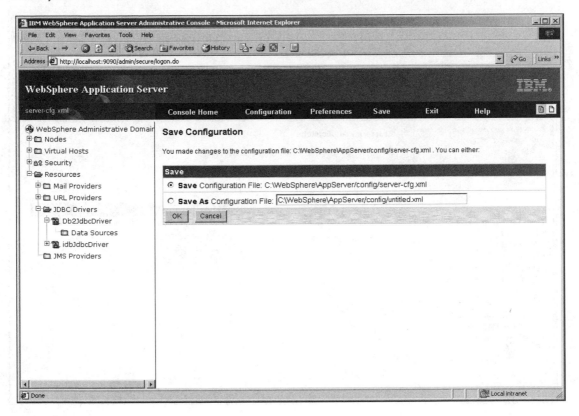

We are now ready to install our Recipe application. To do that, you navigate to the Enterprise Applications node in the tree on the left of the window.

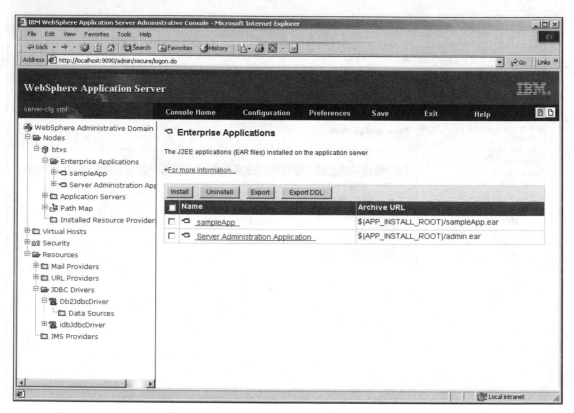

Click on the Install button to start the installation wizard. In the first screen, we can define the location of the EAR file with the application that we want to install. Make sure that you select the file with the deployed generated code in it (the one prefixed with Deployed_):

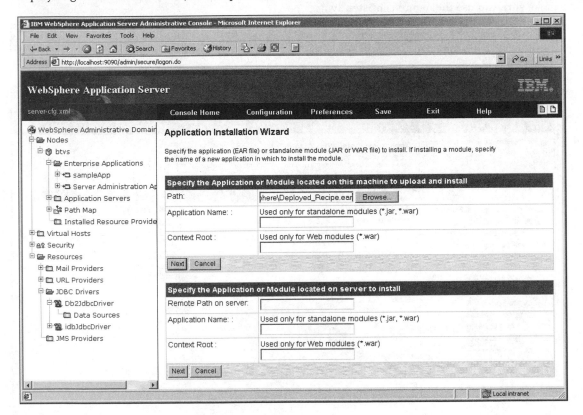

The console will then ask you to enter or verify the JNDI bindings for the contained EJBs. If you did not specify any of these bindings in the AAT, you can still enter the appropriate values here. You can enter any value here for the JNDI names, since they are referred to via java:comp lookups in the code. Just make sure you use the names consistently:

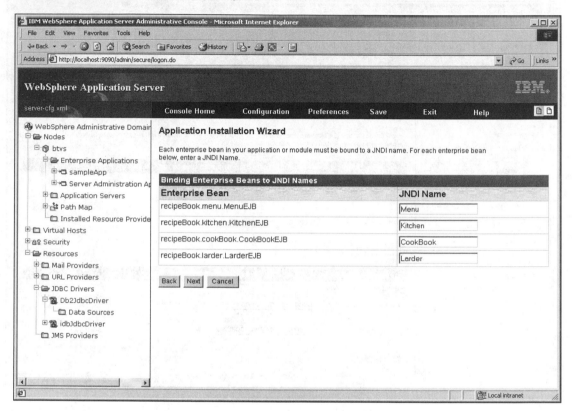

Then we need to confirm the JNDI names for the resource references. Again this should have already been set in the AAT:

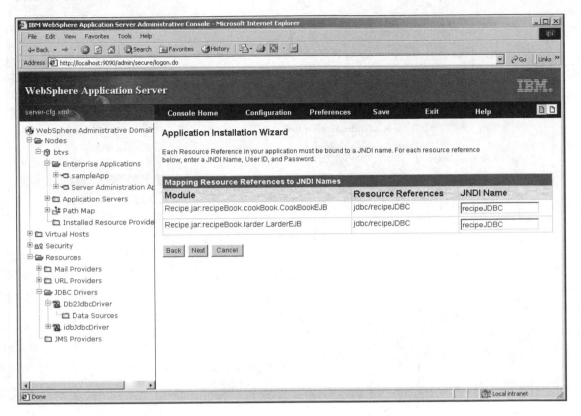

The next screen is very similar in that we now get a chance to set the JNDI names for the EJB references elements:

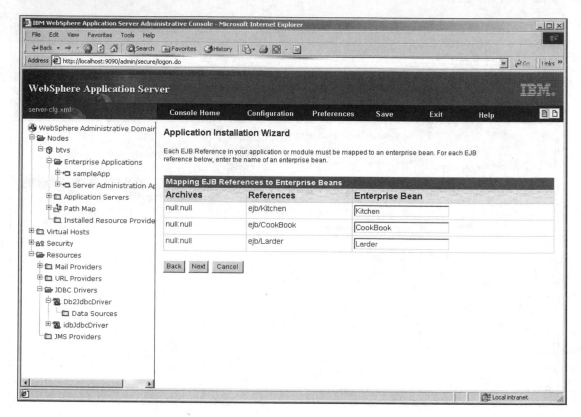

There are a number of screens that show you the various places where JNDI bindings are needed. The following picture shows the screen where you enter the datasource names for the entity beans contained in the application. Again, if you specified them in the AAT then you should not have to make any changes now:

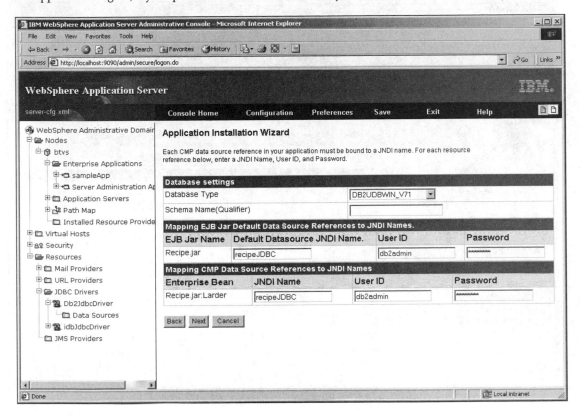

Before the application is installed, you have a chance to redeploy it. In our case, this is unnecessary as we already deployed it in the assembler, so we can uncheck that option:

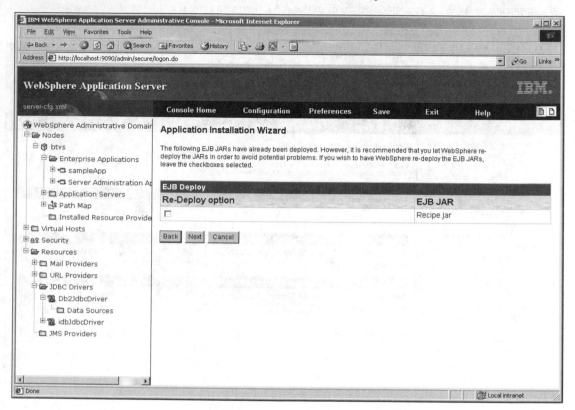

After you click on Finish on the last screen, the application is installed. Make sure you save the changes by selecting the Save menu option at the top of the screen:

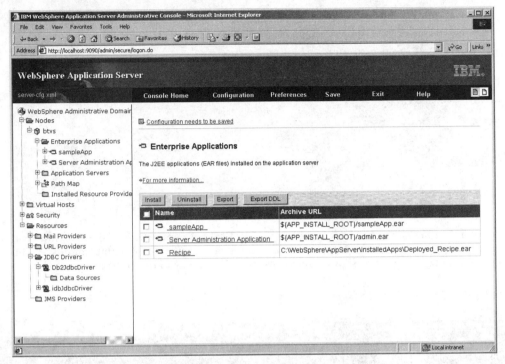

Preparing the Command-Line Client

Before we can run the client to test the successful deployment and installation of the recipe application we need to modify the client slightly so that it can correctly perform the JNDI lookup.

Modify the client code accordingly:

```
private Context getWebSphereContextInfo() {

  Context ctx = null;

  try {
    Properties prop = new Properties();
    prop.put(Context.INITIAL_CONTEXT_FACTORY,
            "com.ibm.websphere.naming.WsnInitialContextFactory");
    prop.put(Context.PROVIDER_URL, "iiop://localhost:900");

    ctx = new InitialContext(prop);

  } catch(NamingException ne)  {
    System.out.println(ne);
  }

  return ctx;
}

private Context getContextInfo() throws NamingException {
  return getWebSphereContextInfo();
}
```

Now you need to set the classpath to recompile and run the Chef class. The entries you need in your classpath to run the client are the following:

- ❑ The deployed Recipe.jar file. You can find in the /installedApps directory, at \installedApps\Deployed_Recipe.ear\Recipe.jar.

- ❑ A number of JAR files, all located in the \WebSphere\AppServer\lib directory:

   a. j2ee.jar

   b. ns.jar

   c. ejbcontainer.jar

   d. jts.jar

   e. csicpi.jar

   f. xerces.jar

   g. xalan.jar

Now we can run the client, but make sure to use the JVM that comes with WebSphere and can be located in the /java directory of /AppServer. So we can run the client with a command something like this (Assuming the JAR files listed above are already present in the classpath property):

```
%WAS_HOME%\java\bin\java recipeBook.client.Chef
```

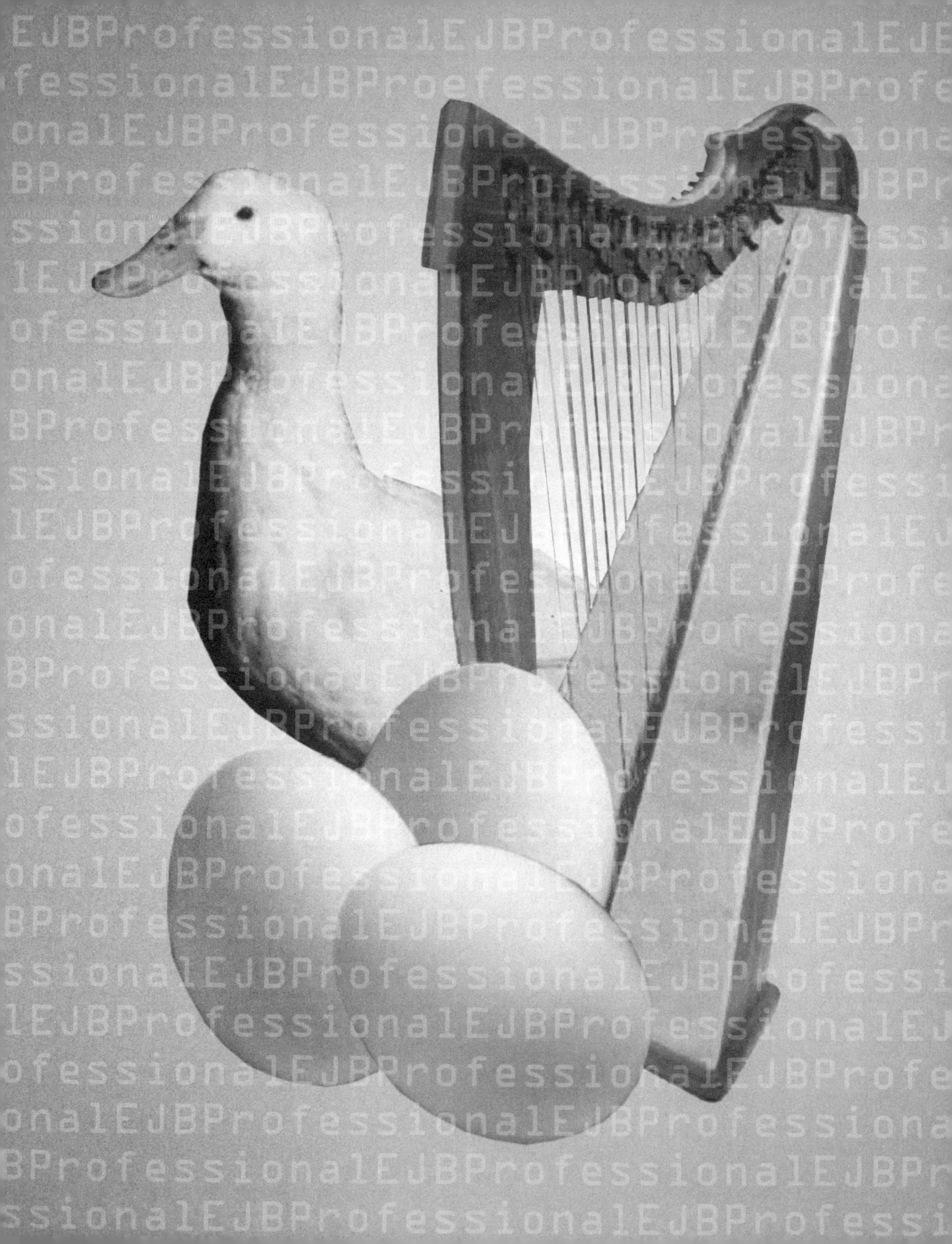
EJBProfessional

SilverStream Application Server

The SilverStream Application Server is a fully J2EE-compatible, highly scalable application server written in Java. A full suite of development and administration tools accompanies SilverStream and it includes many features and technologies to promote application performance and stability. In production environments, the SilverStream Application Server is used to host a wide variety of Java-based applications ranging from Java thin-client-based intranet applications to large scale high-hitting web sites.

At the time of writing, SilverStream was in version 3.7.2, which only supports the EJB 1.1 specification. Therefore we will only be demonstrating how to deploy the 1.1 version of the Recipe beans.

Go to http://www.silverstream.com to download the application server and the development workbench.

Beyond the base J2EE products, SilverStream provides an additional set of tools and services that run on any J2EE-compatible application server. These tools and services are encapsulated in a single product called **eXtend**. eXtend is a component-based framework and integrated development environment that enables development teams to deliver web services based on Java, J2EE , CORBA and XML technologies such as SOAP and ebXML. The framework includes:

- ❑ A Rules Engine
- ❑ A Workflow Engine
- ❑ A Content Management & Caching System,
- ❑ A Personalization System
- ❑ A B2B/XML Integration Server

Applications are built for this framework using the SilverStream eXtend Studio, which is a complete integrated development environment based upon SilverStream's core J2EE Workbench.

The SilverStream Development Workbench

SilverStream's eXtend Studio contains a complete development environment for building applications for the eXtend framework. eXtend Studio uses SilverStream's core J2EE **Development Workbench** as its foundation and provides additional modules to enable full access to the services provided by the eXtend framework. The core J2EE Development Workbench is provided for developers who are just using the SilverStream or another application server for J2EE development.

The Development Workbench is a J2EE Integrated Development Environment (IDE) that runs independently of an application server. The Workbench can be used to develop and deploy EJBs and J2EE applications to multiple remote application server instances. In a standards-based approach, SilverStream's Workbench also supports deployment to some of the other common J2EE application servers. The real strength of the J2EE Development Workbench is that it is not a generic Java IDE; it is specifically designed to build and deploy portable J2EE-based applications. The Workbench provides many useful tools and wizards to automate and simplify the many complicated and repetitive tasks that are required when developing J2EE applications.

The SilverStream Server Management Console

SilverStream provides the **Server Management Console** tool to assist server administrators in performing configuration and problem-diagnosis tasks. The Server Management Console is a standalone tool that can be used to maintain the configuration, security, and deployed Enterprise JavaBean properties for a SilverStream Application Server. A particular strength of the Server Management Console lies in its ability to administrate multiple remote application server instances. The Server Management Console provides many server-configurable options, which include:

- ❑ Database connection pools
- ❑ Event logging and tracing
- ❑ Client connection thresholds
- ❑ Client connection ports and protocols
- ❑ Security users and groups and third-party security integration
- ❑ EJB enablement/disablement
- ❑ Cluster management
- ❑ Graphical diagnostics

Configuring SilverStream for the Recipe Beans

As the Recipe beans include a couple of entity beans we need to configure our application server with the required datasource (`jdbc/recipeJDBC`) and the JDBC driver that the datasource uses.

SilverStream provides a tool called the SilverStream Designer that we can use to configure our datasources. The system administrator uses a wizard to specify the JDBC driver for the target database, and any other connection details such as username and password. A datasource is based on a particular database user. The database user may or may not already contain schema objects such as tables and views. The SilverStream application server will automatically detect the presence of such schema objects, for use in mappings with CMP Entity Beans. Additionally the SilverStream Designer tool allows an administrator to add further objects to the schema, through the use of a graphical Entity-Relationship modeling tool and Table Designer tool. If the user chooses to create or modify the schema externally, the Designer tool can be used to synchronise the application's schema mappings with the database's new schema.

First, launch the SilverStream server by running the `SilverServer.exe` executable (for Windows systems) in the `/bin` directory. Once the server is up and running, launch the Designer tool (`SilverDesigner.exe`):

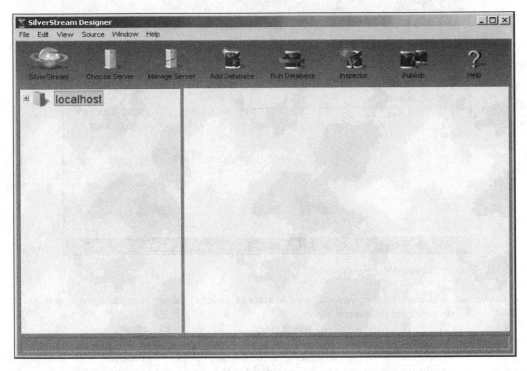

Now hit the **Add Database** link in the main toolbar to bring up the **Add Database** window. Provide a name and security credentials, and choose the database type and driver:

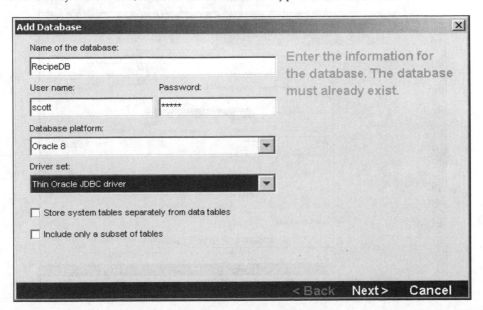

Then press the Next link to move to the second page. Here, provide the URL to the database:

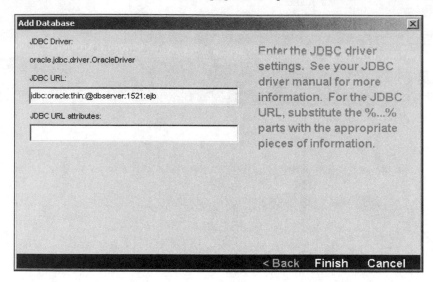

Finally hit Finish to create the datasource.

> *As with any application server, you will need to make sure that the driver is in the server's classpath before you can create the datasource.*

SilverStream datasources are actually connection pools, which implement the JDBC interface `javax.sql.DataSource`. The Server Management Console provides graphical tools to enable the minimum and maximum connections to be specified for the database connection pool:

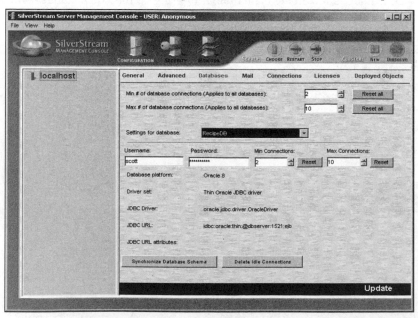

Deploying the Recipe EJBs

This example demonstrates how to deploy the Recipe bean application in the SilverStream environment.

We will demonstrate how to deploy the application both using the SilverStream Development Workbench, and from the command line using `SilverCmd`.

Deploying from the SilverStream Development Workbench

The Development Workbench provides all necessary tools to create Enterprise Java Beans and J2EE-oriented applications.

To deploy a pre-built EJB JAR, you need to:

- ❑ Create a server profile
- ❑ Create a new project
- ❑ Add the pre-built EJB JAR to the project
- ❑ Create a SilverStream deployment plan
- ❑ Deploy the EJB JAR using the SilverStream deployment tools

Creating a Server Profile

Start the SilverStream Development Workbench, by choosing it from the Start menu:

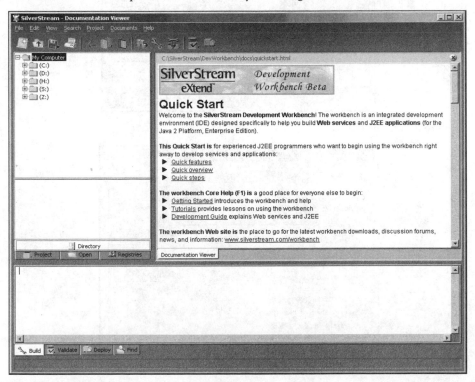

From the Edit menu choose the Profiles option and Profiles window will appear. In this dialog, press the New button to create a new profile:

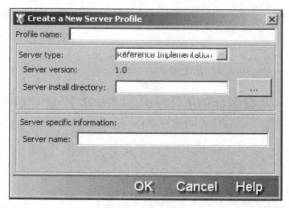

Enter the information for the profile name and installation directory, select the server type as SilverStream 3.7, server name (in this case `localhost:82`), and database (`RecipeDB`):

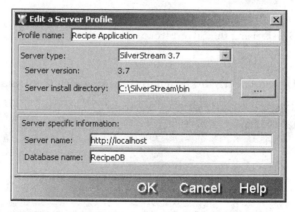

Press OK to create the profile:

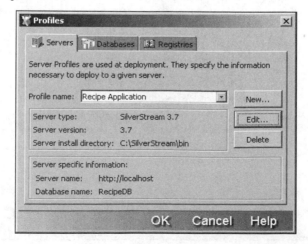

Creating a Project

Back in the main window of the Development Workbench select the New Project option from the File menu:

Check the Archive is read-only box, then select the EJB option and press Next. Provide a project name and a location. You can select any directory on the file system. Then select our source Recipe.jar file from wherever it is located on your file system:

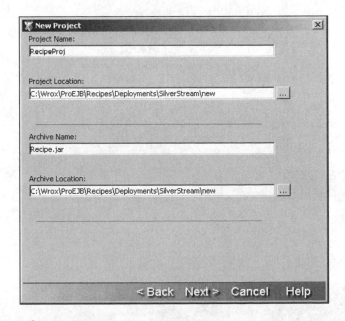

Press Next to move to the next screen:

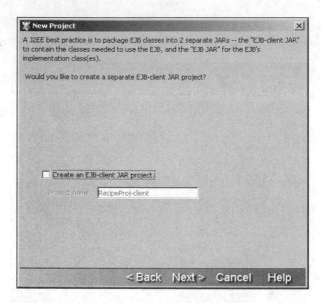

Uncheck the client JAR file option and move to the final summary screen. Finish the New Project wizard and a new EJB project workspace is opened in the workbench:

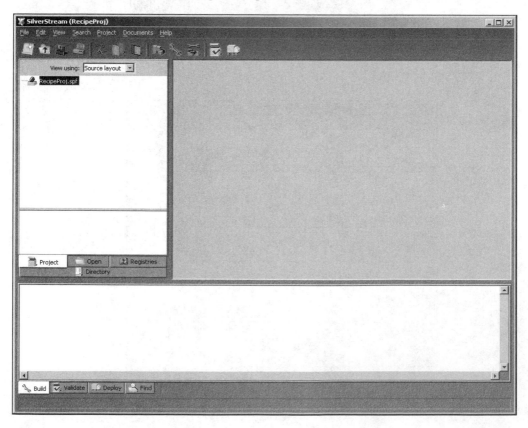

Creating a Deployment Plan for Recipe.jar

To deploy the `Recipe.jar` file to the SilverStream application server, you need to create a SilverStream deployment plan. This deployment plan is used to map the dependencies that exist in the deployment descriptor, to real entities on the target application server. These dependencies may include things like database resource references, env-entries, stateless session bean pool sizes, and CMP entity bean table/column mappings and finder method WHERE clauses.

Invoke the Deployment Plan Editor by right-clicking on the project (**RecipeProj.spf**) and selecting **Open Deployment Plan**:

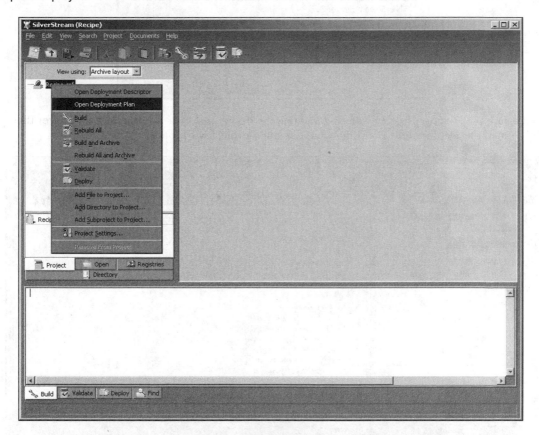

You will be prompted if you want to create a new deployment plan:

Select **Yes**:

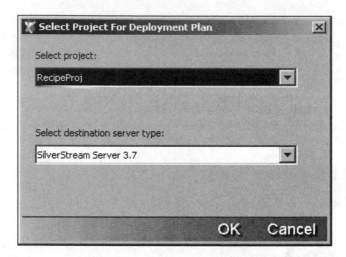

Make sure the Recipe project is selected and that the destination type is SilverStream Server then press OK to load the Deployment Plan Editor into the main project workspace:

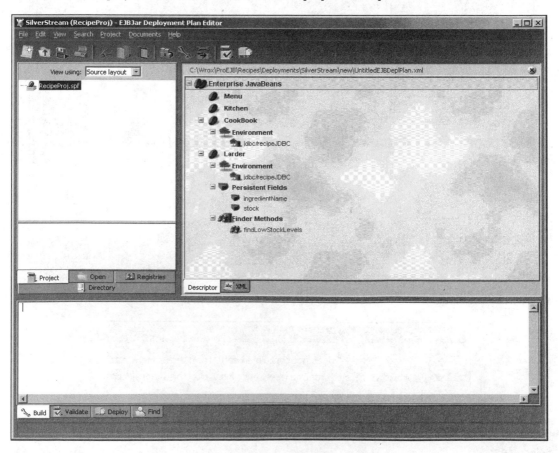

The Deployment Plan Editor is able to look at the deployment descriptor contained in the `Recipe.jar` file to determine what server dependencies need to be entered by the user. In this case, the user needs to specify the JNDI names and the mapping of the Larder container-managed persistence entity bean to the appropriate database datasource table and columns.

First however, we need to tell the deployment plan which server profile to use for deployment. To do this right-click on the top-level **Enterprise JavaBeans** element in the right-hand pane and select **Properties** from the pop-up menu:

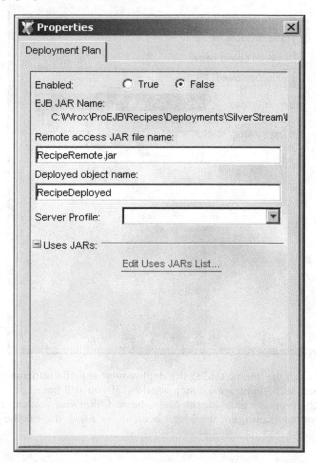

On this property page we can set the names for the generated deployment and client files as well as importantly pointing the deployment plan at a particular profile. Use the drop-down box to select the Recipe Application profile that we created earlier and enable the deployment plan using the option button at the top of the page:

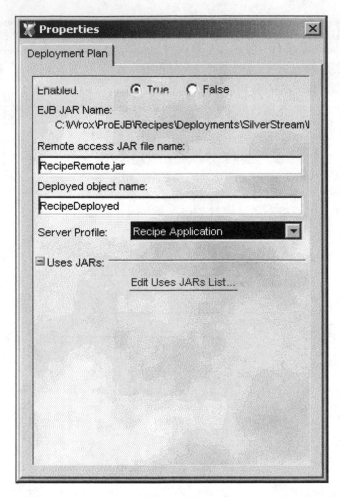

Now we can move through the beans, setting the deployment-specific information for each. Start by selecting the Menu bean in the main workbench window. If you still have the Properties window open it will adjust to show the property page for the Menu bean. Otherwise you can right-click on the bean name and choose Properties again. For the Menu bean all we need to set is the JNDI name:

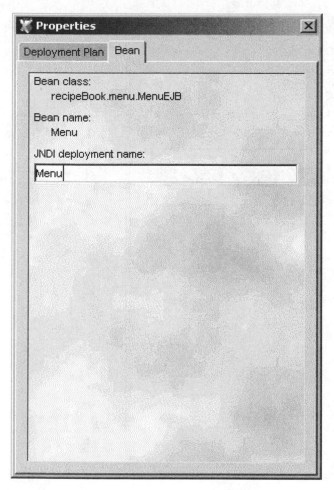

For each of the four beans we will specify the JNDI name to be the same as the bean name. When we get to the properties for the CookBook bean we also need to point the jdbc/recipeJDBC resource reference at our datasource. To do this, switch to the **Resource Reference** tab, and using the dropdown box choose our **RecipeDB** datasource that we configured earlier:

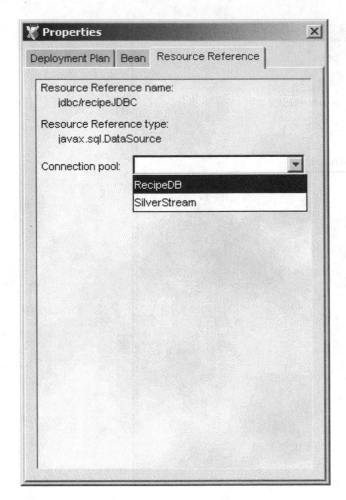

Likewise we need to perform the same step for the Larder bean. The Larder bean also requires us to map the CMP fields to columns in a database. In the Bean property page for the Larder bean there is an additional setting that allows us to specify which table in the database the bean maps to (make sure you have pre-created the LARDER table before you do this step):

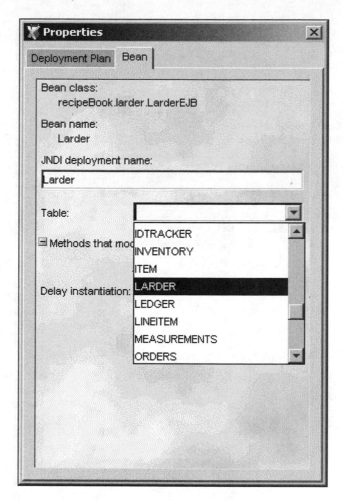

Now you can open the property page for the **Persistence Fields** and map the fields to a database column:

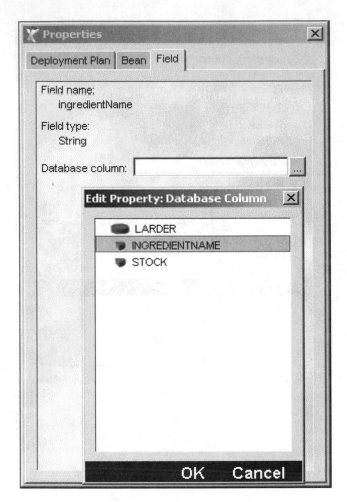

The final piece of configuration needed for the deployment plan is the implementation of our finder method `findLowStockLevels()`. On the property page you can see that SilverStream defines two different types of finder:

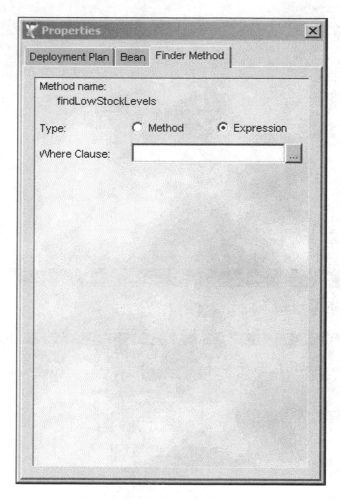

We are going to be writing an **Expression** type. We could write the finder by hand but SilverStream provides a little utility to help us with the process and verify that we've got it right:

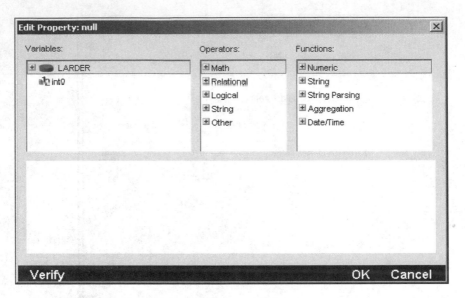

We define our finder as the following:

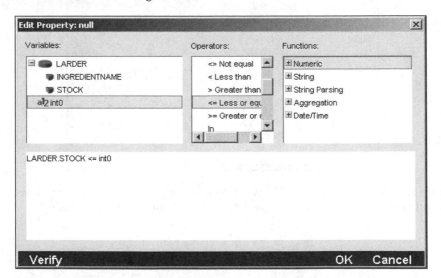

Now if you hit the Verify link you can check that our finder is valid:

So here is what our completed deployment plan looks like:

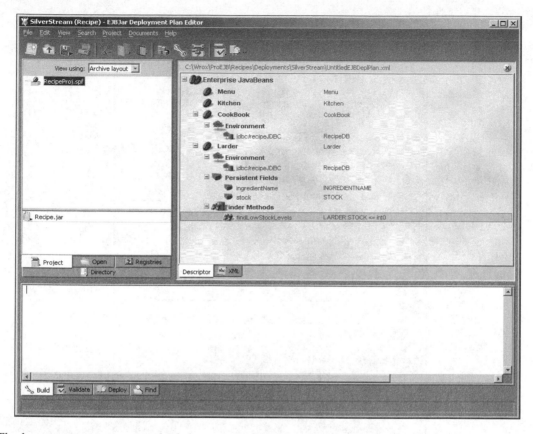

The last step is just to save it do disk using the File menu. We'll call it RecipeDeplPlan.xml.

Deploying the Recipe.jar

We have choice in how to deploy the project, either from the Workbench directly or using a command-line tool called SilverCmd. While we have the workbench open we'll look at how to deploy it directly first.

From the Workbench either choose the Deploy toolbar icon or Deploy Archive from the Project menu.

On the Deployment window, choose the application server profile that we want to deploy to, and our newly created deployment plan:

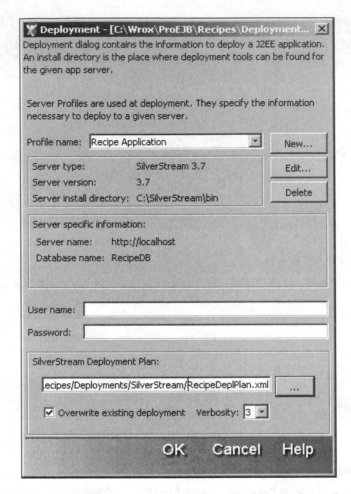

Click OK to deploy the project. The output window of the Workbench shows the progress of the deployment and shows any success or error messages that occur.

Deploying from the Command Line Using SilverCmd

This example provides an alternative method for deploying the Recipe EJB JAR to a SilverStream application server. This is achieved using SilverStream's command-line tool `SilverCmd.exe`.

To deploy from the command line, you need:

❑ An EJB JAR with deployment descriptor

❑ A SilverStream deployment plan (you can use the file generated from the previous section)

Open a command prompt at the directory where you saved the Recipe project. We can deploy our JAR file to the server using the following command:

```
SilverCmd DeployEJB localhost:80 RecipeDB Recipe.jar -f
        RecipeDeplPlan.xml -o -r RecipeRemote.jar -R .\ -v 3
```

This instructs `SilverCmd` to deploy an EJB JAR (`DeployEJB`) to the `localhost:80` application server for the database `RecipeDB`. The name of the EJB JAR file to deploy is `Recipe.jar` and the deployment plan is `RecipeDeplPlan..xml`. The deployment process will automatically generate a 'remote stub' JAR, which in this case is to be named `RecipeRemote.jar`.

You should see the following script appear when you run this command:

Deploying jar
Uploading deployed object 'Recipe' to server...
Analyzing JAR file 'Recipe' ...

Compiling and creating stubs...
RMIC status 0
Analyzing JAR file 'Recipe' ...

The JAR was successfully saved and activated.

You can confirm that the deployment has been successfully by looking up the database in the SilverStream Designer application:

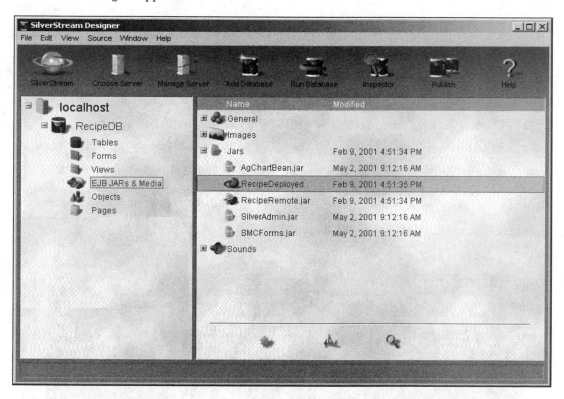

Running the Client

For this example application, the EJB client will be run as a regular standalone Java application. In real environments, it is more likely that the superior deployment capabilities of SilverStream's client container would be used to run a CAR version of the EJB client application.

Modifying the Java Client for the SilverStream EJB Container

Before compiling and running the `Chef.java` file, the source code will need modified for the appropriate JNDI lookup:

```java
private Context getSilverStreamContextInfo() {

  Context ctx = null;
  InitialContext ictx = null;

  try {
    Properties prop = new Properties();
    prop.put(Context.INITIAL_CONTEXT_FACTORY,
             "com.sssw.rt.jndi.AgInitCtxFactory");
    prop.put(Context.PROVIDER_URL, "sssw://localhost:80");

    ictx = new InitialContext(prop);
    ctx = (Context)ictx.lookup("sssw://localhost:80/RMI");

  } catch(NamingException ne)  {
    System.out.println(ne);
  }

  return ctx;
}

private Context getContextInfo() throws NamingException {
  return getSilverStreamContextInfo();
}
```

In order to run the client we need the following in the classpath:

❏ The `SilverRuntime.zip` file, located in the SilverStream `/lib` directory

❏ The `javax.ejb` package located in the `ejb.jar` file in the SilverStream `/lib` directory

❏ The client JAR file that was created at deployment time – in this case `RecipeRemote.jar`

In addition, we must run the client using the JVM that ships with SilverStream, which is located in the SilverStream `/JRE` directory. Our client command will therefore look something like this:

```
%SILVER_HOME%\JRE\bin\java -classpath
RecipeRemote.jar;%SILVER_HOME%\lib\SilverRuntime.jar;%SILVER_HOME%\lib\ejb.jar;.
recipeBook.client.Chef
```

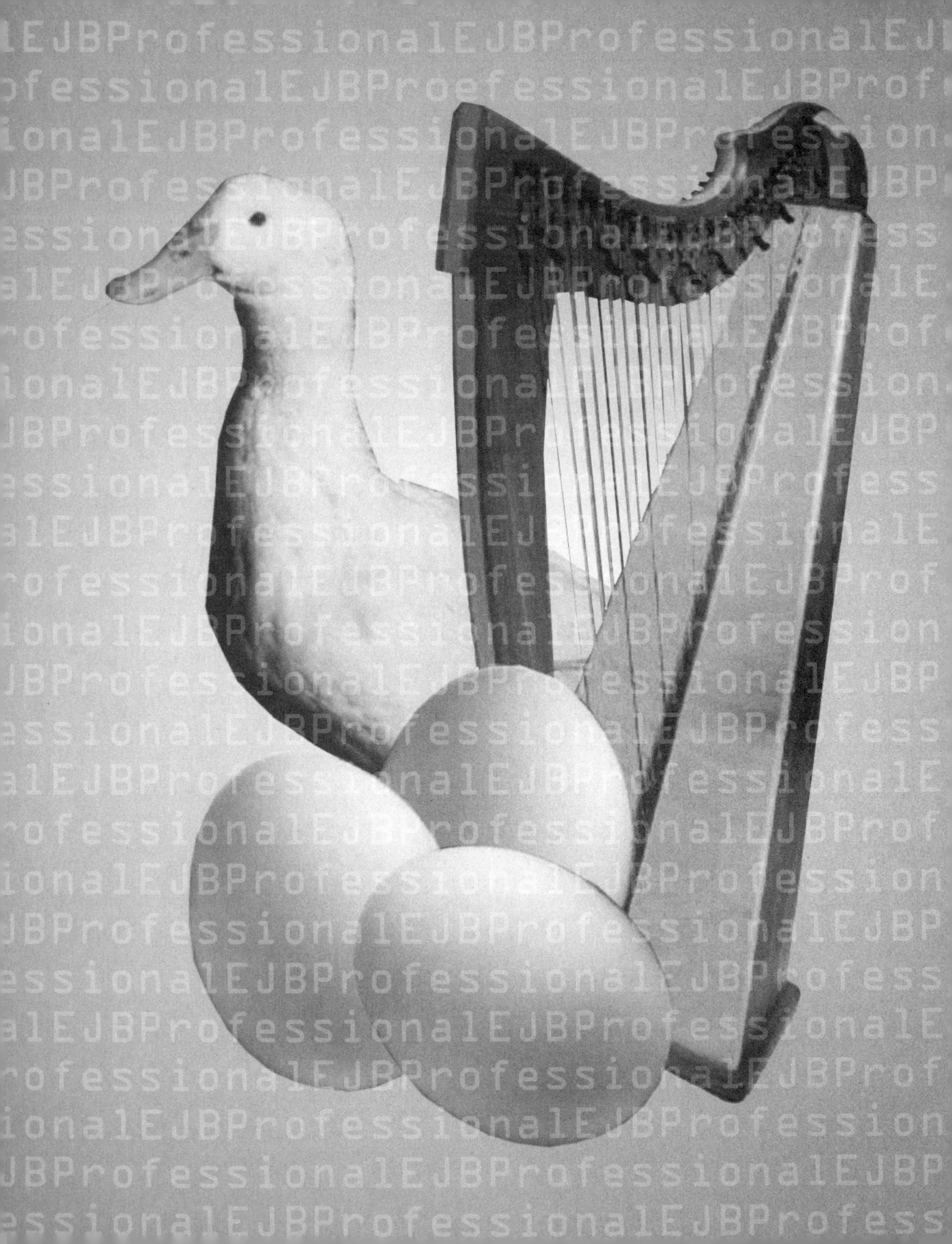

Sybase's EAServer

EAServer provides the high-performance, productive, secure, and flexible platform essential for web-enabling your back-office systems. It is based on proven Sybase application-server technology, Open Server, which is used to run thousands of successfully deployed applications around the world. EAServer can be used with components developed with a wide variety of EJB, C++, PowerBuilder, and COM development tools. It provides the comprehensive security features essential when providing access to applications from beyond the firewall. Finally, EAServer is built on open standards such as J2EE, CORBA, COM, ODBC, and JDBC to provide an open and flexible environment.

EAServer consists of two applications, the server and the management tool. The server application is called Jaguar; the management tool is called Jaguar Manager.

Deploying the Recipe Beans

This section goes into the process of deployment and configuration of the EJBs in EAServer 3.6. At the time of publication, EAServer only supported the 1.1 version of the EJB specification. However, EAServer 4.0 will be supporting the 2.0 EJB specification and the deployment process will be quite similar to that outline below for EAServer 3.6

Configuring EAServer 3.6

Make sure you are running a JDK 1.2 version of the Jaguar server, otherwise it will not be able to cope with the Collections classes we've used in the Recipe beans.

To deploy the beans, we need to use the Jaguar Manager application, so launch the manager and log onto your running Jaguar server (JDK 1.2):

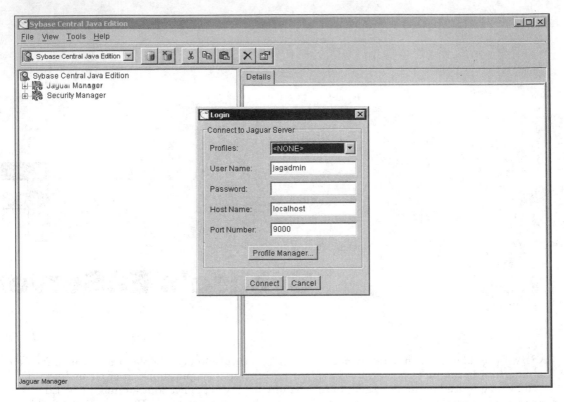

We want to set up our database connection (in this case to an Oracle database installation). In EAServer these database connections are called **connection caches**. Therefore, to create a new connection, right-click on the Connection Caches folder and select New Connection Cache:

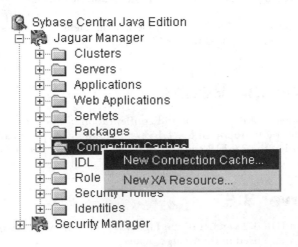

You will be prompted to give the new cache a name. Call it something appropriate like OracleCache:

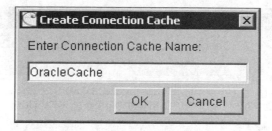

You will then be taken to the main properties dialog for the cache. Here we need to set the URL, driver class, and type as well as the security credentials. The General tab allows us to set the URL and user details. The **Server Name** box is where we need to enter the database URL for this connection cache:

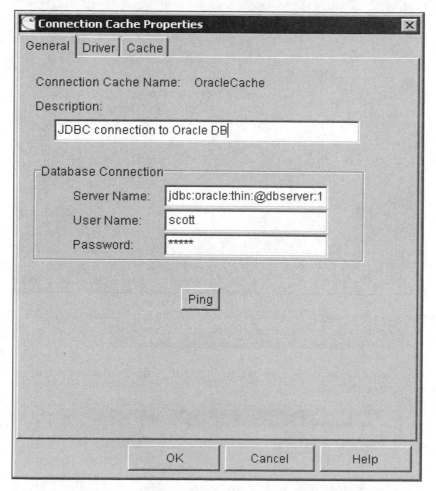

Now flip to the **Driver** tab, and enter the database driver class and select the type as JDBC:

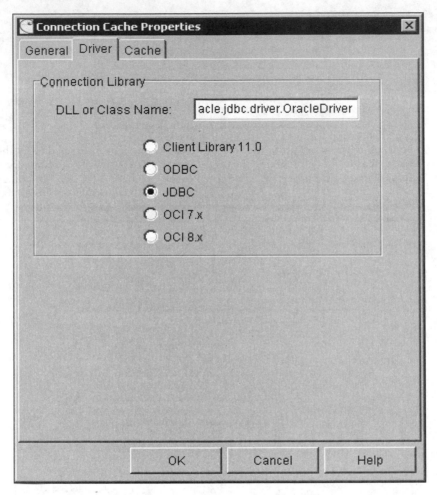

In order for the Jaguar server to load the driver class it needs to be in the server's classpath. You need to add the path to the driver class into both the classpath and bootclasspath settings. The easiest way to do this is probably to edit the batch files that load the server.

Once you have created the cache you can use the Ping button on the General tab to test if the configuration is correct:

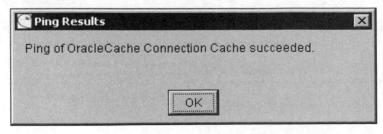

Now we are ready to deploy our Recipe beans.

Bean Deployment

Right-click on the Packages folder and select Deploy EJB | 1.1 Jar:

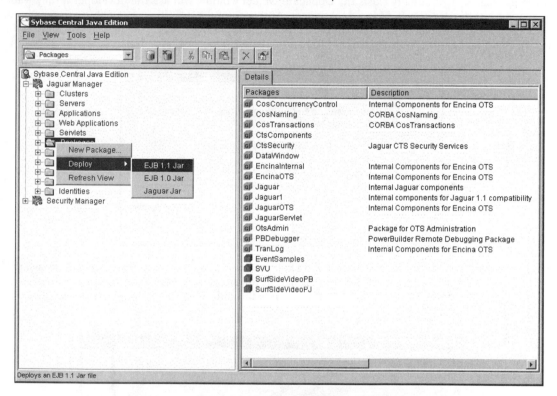

Once you have selected the deployment option, the deployment wizard will walk you through the deployment process. The wizard first asks you for the location of the Recipe JAR file. You can either type the location in or click the Browse button and locate the JAR that way:

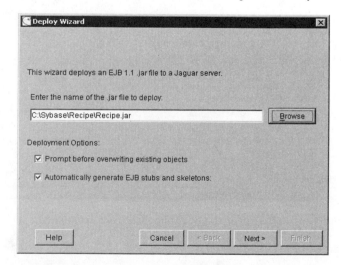

Once we have selected the JAR file, the wizard lets us define the deployment options, as can be seen above. Once you have all of our deployment options set, hit the Next button to continue the process.

If the package or EJB already exists the Duplicate Object window will ask the developer if they want to overwrite a particular object during deployment. At this point the developer can choose to rename the package with an alternative name or overwrite the existing package. If this dialog is not displayed then the EJB has not been deployed before:

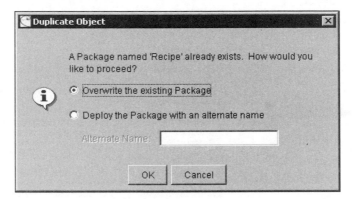

If the Automatically generate EJB stubs and skeletons deployment option was checked, the wizard will automatically create both the stubs and skeletons for the objects. Once each stub/skeleton creation is complete, the deployment process will also compile the stubs and skeletons for all of the EJBs in the JAR file:

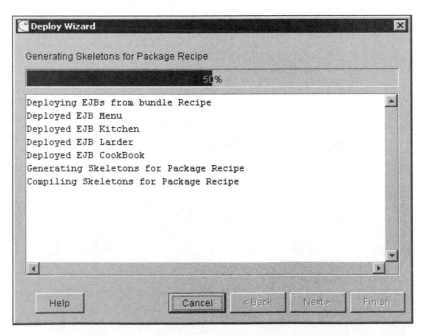

Once all of these processes are complete the deployment wizard is finished.

The deployment wizard creates the following:

❑ **The Package**
This object is used simply for grouping of objects. It is based on the JAR name that you are importing.

❑ **The Component**
These are the EJBs that are deployed. It contains all properties for the component.

❑ **The IDL**
This includes IDL definitions of all of EJBs. It includes the definition of structures that make up the data and primary key. It also defines all of the methods that make up the bean.

We can now see our new package and the deployed beans in the main Jaguar Manager window:

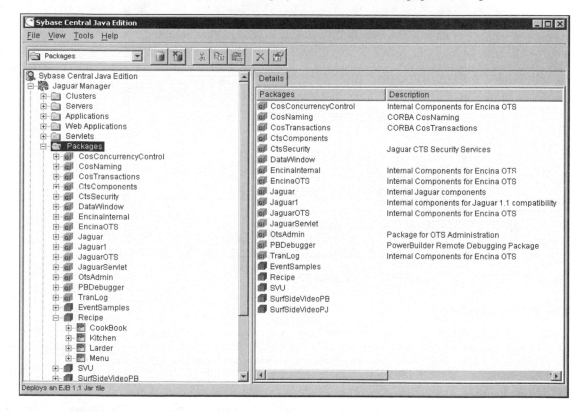

Deployment Configuration

We now need to take our deployed beans in the new package and configure elements such as the JNDI names etc.

Resource References

The CookBook and Larder beans both have resource references to JDBC datasources. Therefore, we now need to map these resource references to the connection cache we created earlier.

To map a resource to a connection cache, right-click on the component (we'll start with CookBook) and select the Component Properties option. Once the component properties window is displayed, click on the Resource Refs tab. This will allow the association of the resource with the connection cache. To do the association, highlight the resource for the data source and enter the connection cache name in the Connection Cache field:

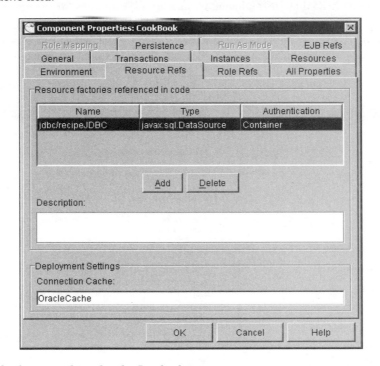

Press OK and do the same thing for the Larder bean.

CMP Bean Mapping

The deployment process creates nearly everything we need to manage the persistence of our Larder bean. The final thing that needs to be done is miscellaneous configuration of the component. This configuration includes verifying/setting the persistence information and the finder method SQL statements.

Persistence Settings

The Persistence tab defines the storage information for the Larder component. The entries for the fields are as follows:

❑ Persistence
This field defines the type of persistence EAServer is to use with the component. For CMP you must use Automatic Persistence State.

❑ Primary Key
This is the IDL that represents the primary key field.

❑ State
This is the IDL that represents the columns in the table.

❑ State Methods

This must be set to default. Default tells EAServer to use the default lifecycle methods to save and restore the state information in the component. The word default must be in all lowercase.

❑ Storage Component

This is the component that is used for storage of the state information for the component. There are two options for this field. The first is CtsComponents/JdbcStorage that uses a JDBC connection cache to provide persistent storage of component state. This component has the Requires transaction attribute. The component's state is saved in the context of any existing transaction associated with the component. The second is CtsComponents/JdbcStorageReqNew which is a copy of the CtsComponents/JDBCStorage component that has the RequiresNew transaction attribute. The component's state is saved using a separate transaction from that used to manage any database work performed by the component.

❑ Connection Cache

This is the name of the connection cache that should be used to talk to the database where the table is located. This field is case-sensitive.

❑ Table

This is the table name that the bean is mapped to. The table name must be prefixed with map: This field may be case sensitive-depending on your database.

After the deployment, most of the persistence settings should be correct. We should verify that connection cache setting and the table to which the bean is to be mapped to are OK. The connection cache should be OracleCache:

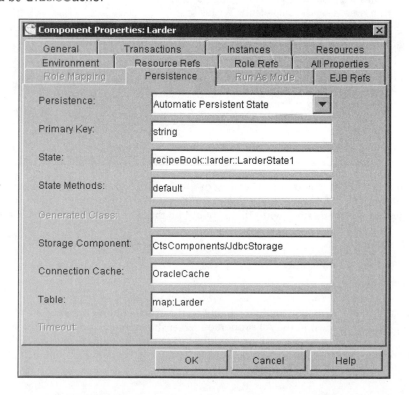

The Table property is the database table that we are mapping the object to. The format is map:TableName. For example, if you are mapping to the Larder table the entry would be map:Larder. Again, depending on the database you are using this may be case-sensitive as well. If the table does not exist in the database, EAServer will create it for you based on your field mappings.

Field Mapping

One of the final things that must be done is to ensure that the finder SQL and the fields are correctly mapped. This is done on the **All Properties** tab of the component:

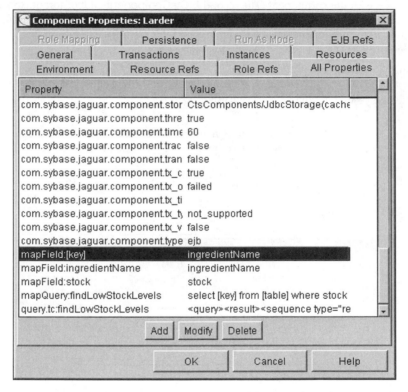

Fields are properties mapped with a prefix of mapField followed by the field name. The primary key is denoted with the suffix of [key]. Field names are denoted simply with the field name as their suffix. In the example that we are dealing with, there should be three entries. These entries are:

- ❑ mapField:[key]
- ❑ mapField:ingredientName
- ❑ mapField:stock

The value for each one of the field properties should be the actual column name of the field. In our example the correct mappings are shown in the **All Properties** screenshot above. Upon deployment they should all be the correct with the possible exception of the [key] field. If one of the fields is not correct simply highlight the property and press the **Modify** button. You can then enter the correct field name in the value field.

Finder Settings

The associated SQL must be given for the finder methods that have been defined in the example bean. The finder methods are also mapped using the **All Properties** tab. You will find entries for `mapQuery:findxxx`. There will also be a `mapQuery` for each find method in the home interface that is going to return either an enumeration or a collection.

We need to modify the `findLowStockLevels()` finder for this example. Modify the setting for the **mapQuery:findLocStockLevels** property, and set the value to be:

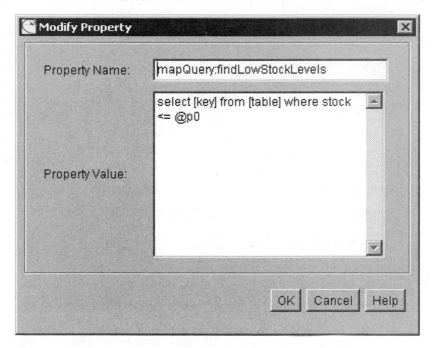

When modifying the SQL be sure *not* to change the [key] or [table]. These are mapped to the key that is defined in the IDL, and the table defined on the **Persistence** tab.

JNDI Bindings

We can also change the JNDI names that our beans have been assigned with. If you look under the **General** tab for any of the beans you can see its JNDI name in the **Bean Home Name** property. This is what a client to this bean will need to use to look up the bean:

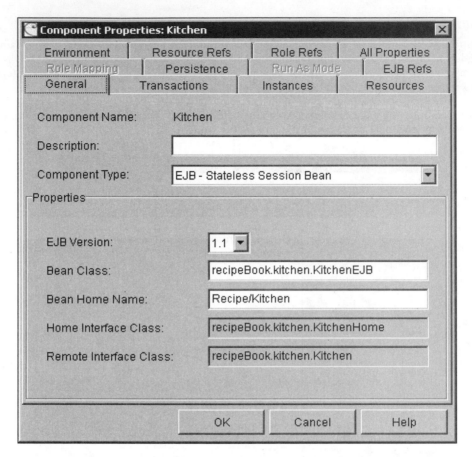

As you can see, EAServer has mapped the beans under a Recipe/ context. The client that we wrote for our beans is only looking up the beans by their basic name, so we either have to change the client code or change the deployed name. In this case, despite the fact that it involves changing code, we will update the client lookup calls as we will be changing the initial context lookup factory code anyway.

EJB References

The EJB Refs tab allows us to configure the JNDI names for the EJB references. If we had elected to change the Bean Home Name properties for our bean, then we would also have had to update the EJB references appropriately as well:

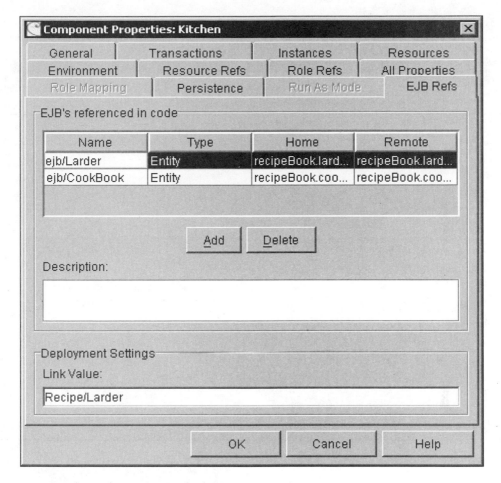

We are now nearly ready to test our deployment.

Helpful Hints

Here are a few helpful hints:

❑   To see the SQL and any additional data that is used by the container set the com.sybase.jaguar.component.debug property to true. Not only will it show the SQL, but it will also show the methods that are called by the EAServer container.

❑   If you prefer to have the container return an Enumeration instead of a Collection set com.sybase.jaguar.component.ejb.keys to java.util.Enumeration instead of java.util.Collection

Installing the Beans

The final step in our deployment process is to take our created deployments and install them into the running server.

This is as simple as expanding the Servers folder until you can see the Installed Packages. Right-click on this folder and select Install Package:

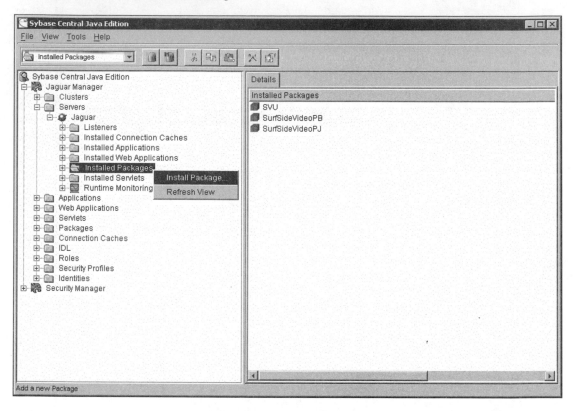

Select to install an existing package and choose our newly created Recipe package:

This will then install our Recipe beans into the Jaguar server:

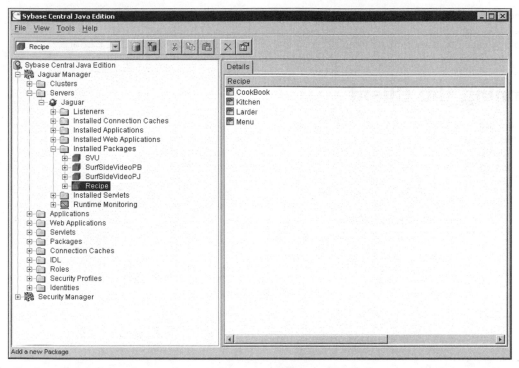

The final step is to remember to also install our connection cache. Following a similar procedure as for packages, right-click the **Installed Connection Caches** folder and select **Install Connection Cache**:

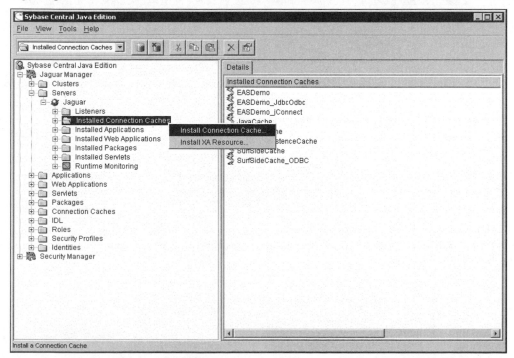

Choose to install an existing cache and select our OracleCache to install it into the server.

Now we are ready to configure our client to use the Recipe beans deployed in EAServer.

Running the Client

The code for the examples runs fine, but requires some modifications. First we must add the package name to each of the JNDI lookup values. There are four places this has to be done. To run the example, we simply need to add `Recipe/` to each lookup name. So instead of `"Menu"`, it should read `"Recipe/Menu"`:

```
...

    private void checkLarder() {

        try {
            Context initial = getContextInfo();
            Object objref = initial.lookup("Recipe/Menu");
            MenuHome home = (MenuHome) javax.rmi.PortableRemoteObject.narrow(
                                objref, MenuHome.class);

...

    private void stockLarder() {

        try {
            Context initial = getContextInfo();
            Object objRef = initial.lookup("Recipe/Larder");
            LarderHome home = (LarderHome) javax.rmi.PortableRemoteObject.narrow(
                                objRef, LarderHome.class);

...

            //Stock RecipeBook table with CookBook bean
            objRef = initial.lookup("Recipe/CookBook");
            CookBookHome home2 = (CookBookHome) javax.rmi.PortableRemoteObject.narrow(
                                objRef, CookBookHome.class);

    private void checkForLowStock() {

        try {

            Context initial = getContextInfo();
            Object objRef = initial.lookup("Recipe/Larder");
            LarderHome home = (LarderHome)javax.rmi.PortableRemoteObject.narrow(
                                objRef, LarderHome.class);
```

The second change that needs to occur is to change the code to get the initial context. The code that needs changing is to point to the EAServer initial context and to support a username and password. The code should look like:

```
    private Context getContextInfo() {
        return getSybaseContextInfo();
    }

    private Context getSybaseContextInfo() {
```

```
    Context ctx = null;

    try {
      Properties prop = new Properties();
      prop.put(Context.INITIAL_CONTEXT_FACTORY,
             "com.sybase.ejb.InitialContextFactory");
      prop.put(Context.PROVIDER_URL, "iiop://localhost:9000");
      prop.put(Context.SECURITY_PRINCIPAL, "jagadmin");
      prop.put(Context.SECURITY_CREDENTIALS, "");

      ctx = new InitialContext(prop);

    } catch(NamingException ne)  {
      System.out.println(ne);
    }

    return ctx;

  }
```

To run the client we need to have the following directories available in the classpath:

❑   %JAGUAR_HOME%\html\classes

❑   %JAGUAR_HOME%\java\classes

So we can run the client with a command something like this:

```
java -classpath %JAGUAR_HOME%\html\classes;%JAGUAR_HOME%\
     java\classes; recipeBook.client.Chef
```

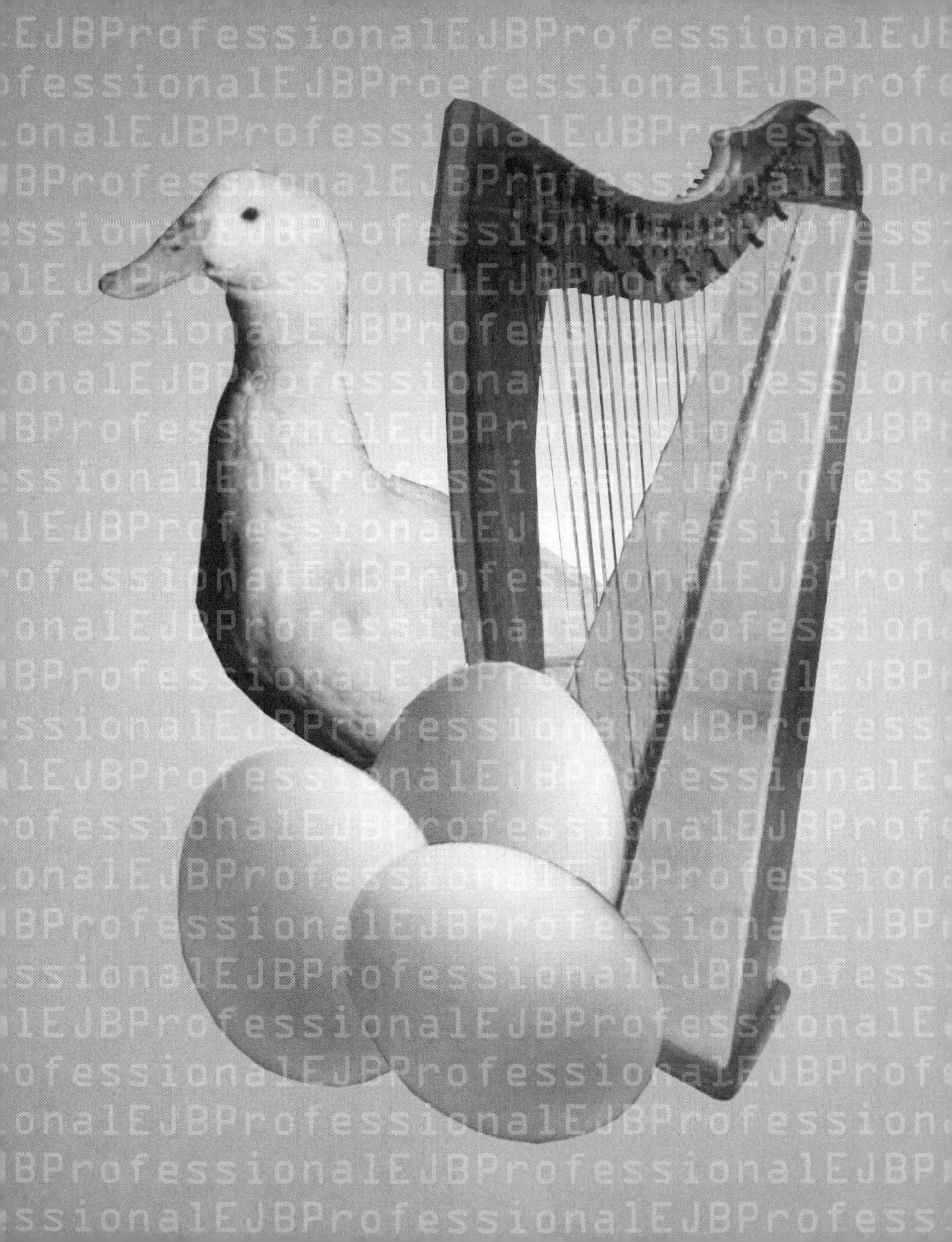

G

JBoss

In this appendix, we're going to deploy the sample beans into the JBoss EJB container. JBoss is an opensource container that can be downloaded from http://www.jboss.org/. At the time of publication, the current version of JBoss was 2.2.2. In this tutorial, we'll work with the Recipe sample beans, which are packaged into an EJB JAR with the Chef client. We'll set up JBoss with an Oracle database for the beans to use (and we assume that the database has already been set up). The steps we need to take to get the Chef cooking are:

- ❑ Install JBoss
- ❑ Testing the Installation
- ❑ Configure JBoss
- ❑ Allowing Remote Access
- ❑ Configuring a Database
- ❑ Package the EJBs
- ❑ Packaging Utility Classes
- ❑ The JBoss Deployment Descriptor
- ❑ Deploy the EJB JAR
- ❑ Start JBoss
- ❑ Configure and Run the Client

Install JBoss

JBoss is distributed as a simple archive, in formats including ZIP (best for Windows), and compressed TAR files (best for UNIX). To install JBoss, we only need to extract the files to disk. This will create a directory called `jboss-version` containing all the JBoss files.

Testing the Installation

Before we go on to configure JBoss and deploy our beans, we'll just start JBoss up to make sure it's installed properly. We can start it with the scripts in the `/bin` directory. The `run.bat` script runs in Windows, and the `run.sh` runs under UNIX. We need to either double-click on the script or go to a command prompt, change to the `/bin` directory, and run it from there. It doesn't work properly if it's run from a different directory.

If JBoss doesn't start at all, confirm that the `java` executable is on the system path, by running `java -version`. If it's not there, it can be added to the system path, or we could alter the startup scripts to use the correct path to the `java` executable.

Once JBoss starts up, it generates a lot of output, which should look something like this:

```
Shortcut to run.bat                                                    _ □ x
[BlackBoxDS] Started
[JMX RMI Adaptor] Starting
[JMX RMI Adaptor] Started
[JMX RMI Connector] Starting
[JMX RMI Connector] Started
[Mail Service] Starting
[Mail Service] DEBUG: not loading system providers in <java.home>/lib
[Mail Service] DEBUG: not loading optional custom providers file: /META-INF/javamail.providers
[Mail Service] DEBUG: successfully loaded default providers
[Mail Service]
DEBUG: Tables of loaded providers
[Mail Service] DEBUG: Providers Listed By Class Name: {com.sun.mail.smtp.SMTPTransport=javax.mail.Pr
ovider[TRANSPORT,smtp,com.sun.mail.smtp.SMTPTransport,Sun Microsystems, Inc], com.sun.mail.imap.IMAP
Store=javax.mail.Provider[STORE,imap,com.sun.mail.imap.IMAPStore,Sun Microsystems, Inc], com.sun.mai
l.pop3.POP3Store=javax.mail.Provider[STORE,pop3,com.sun.mail.pop3.POP3Store,Sun Microsystems, Inc]}
[Mail Service] DEBUG: Providers Listed By Protocol: {imap=javax.mail.Provider[STORE, imap,com.sun.mai
l.imap.IMAPStore,Sun Microsystems, Inc], pop3=javax.mail.Provider[STORE,pop3,com.sun.mail.pop3.POP3S
tore,Sun Microsystems, Inc], smtp=javax.mail.Provider[TRANSPORT,smtp,com.sun.mail.smtp.SMTPTransport
,Sun Microsystems, Inc]}
[Mail Service] DEBUG: not loading optional address map file: /META-INF/javamail.address.map
[Mail Service] Mail Service 'Mail' bound to java:/Mail
[Mail Service] Started
[Service Control] Started 22 services
[Default] JBoss 2.2.2 Started in 0m:5s
```

At that point, we can just use *Ctrl-C* to shut down JBoss, and go on to the configuration.

Configure JBoss

There are a number of settings we need to change from the default configuration shipped with JBoss. All the configuration information for JBoss itself is stored in the `/conf` directory under the main JBoss directory. You can create more than one configuration, so most of the configuration files go in a subdirectory under `/conf`, and the configuration name is the name of that subdirectory. JBoss ships with one configuration, known as `default`, so the files we'll be editing are in the directory `/conf/default/`.

Allowing Remote Access

By default, JBoss is configured to support only clients on the same machine as the JBoss server. We would rather support clients both on the local machine and on remote machines. We need to change the `jboss.properties` file in order to allow clients on different machines to access beans on the JBoss server. This file includes a number of lines at the top, all commented out by default. We need to remove the comment mark (#) from the beginning of the line `#java.rmi.server.hostname=localhost`, and then change the word `localhost` to the host name of the JBoss server. So the beginning of the updated file should look like this:

```
# System properties
# These will be loaded and set by jBoss
#java.rmi.server.useLocalHostName=true
java.rmi.server.hostname=myhostname.mydomain.com
#java.rmi.server.codebase=http://localhost:8080/
#jboss.xa.xidclass=oracle.jdbc.xa.OracleXid
```

Configuring a Database

By default, JBoss comes configured for two database products, InstantDB and Hypersonic SQL. We would rather configure it for another product, such as Oracle, and to do that we need to change the file `jboss.jcml`. There are several sections of this file that need to change. The file is an XML file, with blocks of the format:

```
<mbean code="classname" name="servicename">
   <attribute name="name">value</attribute>
   ...
</mbean>
```

We'll identify the blocks by their `classname` value, and then we'll need to change some of the attribute names and values.

Removing Hypersonic SQL

Since we don't plan to use the Hypersonic SQL database product, we can comment out the block with the class name `org.jboss.jdbc.HypersonicDatabase`. We just add the XML comment begin `<!--` before the `<mbean>` tag, and add the XML comment end `-->` after the `</mbean>` tag:

```
<!--
   <mbean code="org.jboss.jdbc.HypersonicDatabase"
          name="DefaultDomain:service=Hypersonic">
   <attribute name="Port">1476</attribute>
   <attribute name="Silent">true</attribute>
   <attribute name="Database">default</attribute>
   <attribute name="Trace">false</attribute>
   </mbean>
-->
```

Removing Default Database Pools

Likewise, we can comment out the blocks that define the two default database pools, which both have the classname `org.jboss.jdbc.XADataSourceLoader`.

Configuring JDBC Drivers

Next, we need to update the JDBC drivers that JBoss will load. This is controlled by the block with the classname `org.jboss.jdbc.JdbcProvider`. Specifically, we need to update its attribute named `Drivers`.

The default value includes the InstantDB and HypersonicSQL driver class names, and we need to replace those with the class name for the driver we want to use, which for Oracle is `oracle.jdbc.driver.OracleDriver`. The revised block looks like this:

```
<mbean code="org.jboss.jdbc.JdbcProvider"
       name="DefaultDomain:service=JdbcProvider">
    <attribute name="Drivers">oracle.jdbc.driver.OracleDriver</attribute>
</mbean>
```

In order for JBoss to load this driver you will need to make sure that you add it to the classpath when JBoss starts, by editing the `run` script in the `/bin` directory.

Adding a Database Pool

Finally, we need to add an entry for the correct database pool. We need to add the following block to the file, after the `JdbcProvider` block that we just changed:

```
<mbean code="org.jboss.jdbc.XADataSourceLoader"
       name="DefaultDomain:service=XADataSource,name=SamplePool">
  <attribute name="PoolName">SamplePool</attribute>
  <attribute name="DataSourceClass">
      org.opentools.minerva.jdbc.xa.wrapper.XADataSourceImpl
  </attribute>
  <attribute name="URL">
      jdbc:oracle:thin:@oraclehost.mydomain.com:1521:instance
  </attribute>
  <attribute name="JDBCUser">scott</attribute>
  <attribute name="Password">tiger</attribute>
  <attribute name="MinSize">2</attribute>
  <attribute name="MaxSize">10</attribute>
  <attribute name="IdleTimeoutEnabled">true</attribute>
</mbean>
```

Looking through this block, on each of the first two lines, we have to specify a name for the database pool, and the two values need to match. In this case, we used `SamplePool`. The `DataSourceClass` attribute should be specified as shown. The URL attribute needs to be the JDBC URL used to connect to the database, and we give a standard Oracle URL here. The `JDBCUser` and `Password` attributes should be set to the username and password used to connect to the database at the URL we specified. The `MinSize` and `MaxSize` attributes control the size of the database pool. The last attribute specifies that idle connections will be closed and replaced after a period of time (30 minutes, by default). This value can be either `true` or `false`, and though it's usually not necessary for Oracle, some other DB products time out their connections, so it's safest to turn it on.

If we look at the database pools that we commented out before, there are a number of additional attributes available, but since we don't need to override their default values, we just leave them out.

Package the EJBs

Now that we've configured JBoss, we need to prepare the sample beans for deployment. JBoss accepts beans packaged into the standard EJB JAR format. In our case, the sample beans are already packaged into the correct format, including the standard `ejb-jar.xml` deployment descriptor. If that wasn't the case, we could just JAR the necessary classes, and use the EJX tool that ships with JBoss to generate the standard deployment descriptor at the same time as we create the JBoss deployment descriptor (see below).

Packaging Utility Classes

If our beans were packaged into separate EJB JARs, but they all needed to access common utility classes, we could package those into a separate utility JAR. Then we'd need to write a custom Manifest file for each of the EJB JARs that included the utility JAR on the classpath. Here's an example of a custom Manifest file:

```
Class-Path: utilities.jar
```

Then, to include our custom manifest file when we create the EJB JAR, we'd use a command like:

```
jar -mf manifest-file-name ejb-jar-name files-to-include
```

Which would use our manifest instead of generating a default one. Now when we deployed the EJB JARs, we'd just have to include the utility JAR as well. Since the sample beans are all packaged into a single EJB JAR, this is not an issue for them.

The JBoss Deployment Descriptor

Once the beans are in an EJB JAR, we need both a standard `ejb-jar.xml` deployment descriptor and JBoss-specific deployment descriptors. All EJB JARs need a `jboss.xml` deployment descriptor, and any EJB JAR that includes CMP entity beans needs a `jaws.xml` deployment descriptor. Since the sample includes a CMP entity bean, we need both JBoss deployment descriptors.

Since the deployment descriptors are simply XML files, we can write them by hand or create them with tools or IDEs that generate EJBs. JBoss includes a graphical configuration tool called **EJX**, which can generate deployment descriptors in place in the EJB JAR. That's what we'll use here to create the JBoss deployment descriptors. To start EJX, we need to run the `ejx.jar` file in the `/bin` directory. You can either double-click on `ejb.jar` or go to a command prompt, change to the `/bin` directory, and run

```
java -jar ejx.jar.
```

This will bring up the main EJX screen:

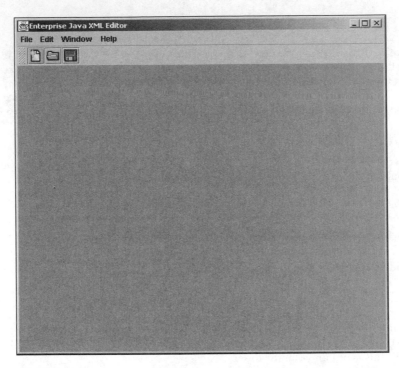

Use the File | Open menu command to bring up the Open dialog. In this dialog, you need to select the correct file type for the deployment descriptor that you want to edit. Your options are:

Files of type	Deployment Descriptor
EJB 1.1 XML	`META-INF/ejb-jar.xml`
EJB 1.1 XML with JBoss XML	`META-INF/jboss.xml`
JAWS XML	`META-INF/jaws.xml`

The jboss.xml Deployment Descriptor

If we were starting with a new EJB JAR, we could use the EJB 1.1 XML setting to create our standard deployment descriptor. Since the sample beans already have that one, though, we'll select EJB 1.1 XML with JBoss XML to create the first JBoss deployment descriptor. After we've selected the correct file type, we'll navigate to the sample bean's EJB JAR and select it:

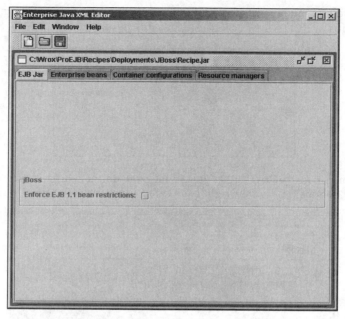

Our main goals here are to resolve the EJB references and resource references in the sample beans. JBoss manages resource references by linking each one to a resource manager, where any number of beans may share a single resource manager. So the first thing we need to do is create a resource manager for our database.

We need to select the Resource managers tab at the top of the screen, and then click the Actions menu in the top-left corner of that tab and select the Add resource manager action:

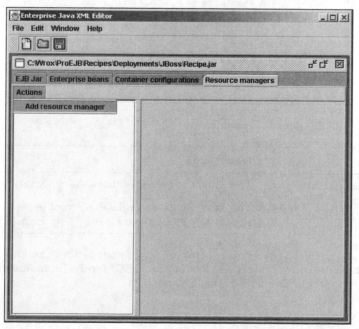

When the Add resource manager dialog appears, we select JDBC as the Resource manager class, and click Ok to create it:

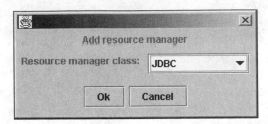

This adds a new entry called **JDBC datasource** to the pane on the left-hand side. If we click on that entry, it shows the options for it on the right-hand side:

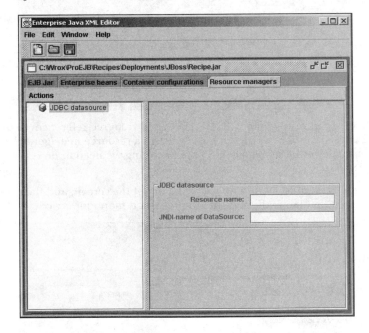

There are two values that we need to provide:

Name	Description
Resource name	The name our beans will use to identify this resource manager.
JNDI-name of DataSource	The name we gave our database pool in the *Configuring JBoss* step above, with an extra `java:/` at the beginning.

For the sample beans, we'll call our resource manager `jdbc/recipeJDBC`; and we called our database pool `SamplePool`, so the correct values are "jdbc/recipeJDBC" for the Resource name, and "java:/SamplePool" for the JNDI-name of DataSource:

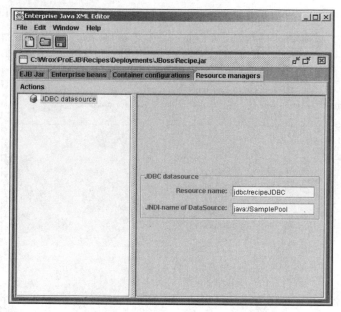

With the resource manager configured, we'll head over to the Enterprise beans tab and resolve all the references.

First we go on to the Kitchen bean, where we need to resolve two EJB references. Since the EJBs that are referenced are in the same EJB JAR, we only need to enter the JNDI names under which they are registered. A bean's JNDI name defaults to the name of the bean, and though you can change that here in EJX, we haven't done so, so we enter Larder as the JNDI name for the ejb/Larder EJB reference, and CookBook as the JNDI name for the ejb/CookBook EJB reference:

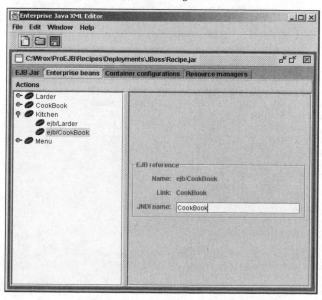

Likewise, we update the ejb/Kitchen reference of the Menu bean to use the JNDI name Kitchen:

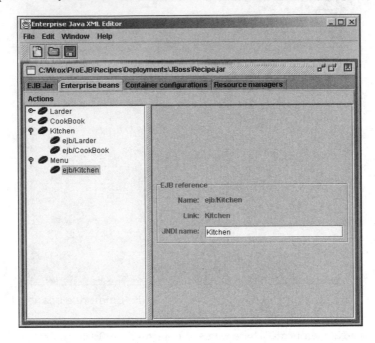

At this point we're done creating the jboss.xml deployment descriptor, so we use the File | Save menu option to write the file into the EJB JAR. If we extract that file from the JAR and look at it, we see that all the settings we made are reflected in the file:

```xml
<?xml version="1.0" encoding="Cp1252"?>

<jboss>
    <secure>false</secure>
    <container-configurations />
    <resource-managers>
      <resource-manager res-class="org.jboss.ejb.deployment.JDBCResource">
<res-name>jdbc/recipeJDBC</res-name>
<res-jndi-name>java:/SamplePool</res-jndi-name>
      </resource-manager>
    </resource-managers>
    <enterprise-beans>
      <session>
<ejb-name>Kitchen</ejb-name>
<jndi-name>Kitchen</jndi-name>
<configuration-name></configuration-name>
<ejb-ref>
  <ejb-ref-name>ejb/Larder</ejb-ref-name>
  <jndi-name>Larder</jndi-name>
</ejb-ref>
<ejb-ref>
  <ejb-ref-name>ejb/CookBook</ejb-ref-name>
  <jndi-name>CookBook</jndi-name>
</ejb-ref>
      </session>
      <session>
<ejb-name>Menu</ejb-name>
```

```
<jndi-name>Menu</jndi-name>
<configuration-name></configuration-name>
<ejb-ref>
  <ejb-ref-name>ejb/Kitchen</ejb-ref-name>
  <jndi-name>Kitchen</jndi-name>
</ejb-ref>
    </session>
    <entity>
<ejb-name>Larder</ejb-name>
<jndi-name>Larder</jndi-name>
<configuration-name></configuration-name>
<resource-ref>
  <res-ref-name>jdbc/recipeJDBC</res-ref-name>
  <resource-name>jdbc/recipeJDBC</resource-name>
</resource-ref>
    </entity>
    <entity>
<ejb-name>CookBook</ejb-name>
<jndi-name>CookBook</jndi-name>
<configuration-name></configuration-name>
<resource-ref>
  <res-ref-name>jdbc/recipeJDBC</res-ref-name>
  <resource-name>jdbc/recipeJDBC</resource-name>
</resource-ref>
    </entity>
    </enterprise-beans>
</jboss>
```

The jaws.xml Deployment Descriptor

Since we have an entity bean using container-managed persistence, we also need to create a `jaws.xml` file. To do this, we need to go back to the File | Open dialog, and select the file type JAWS XML, and then select the sample EJB JAR again. This brings up the JAWS editor for the JAR:

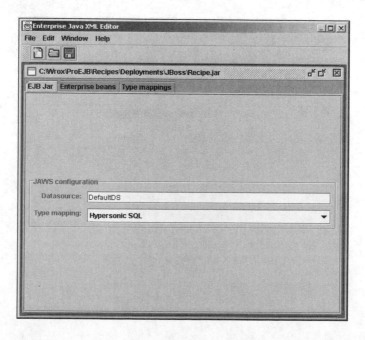

We'll start here on the EJB Jar tab, where we need to tell it which database pool to use, and what type of database that is. Again, we'll need to prefix java:/ to the name of the database pool, so in this case we set the Datasource to java:/SamplePool and the Type mapping to Oracle:

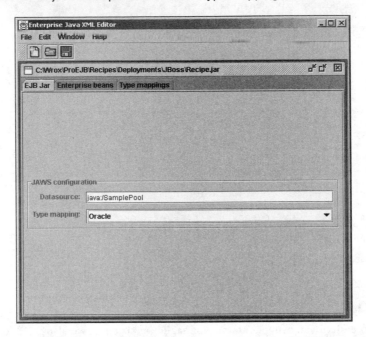

Next we need to go to the Enterprise beans tab, where we see only the CMP entities listed. In our case, this is just the Larder bean. If we select the Larder bean, we see another set of tabs on the right-hand side of the window:

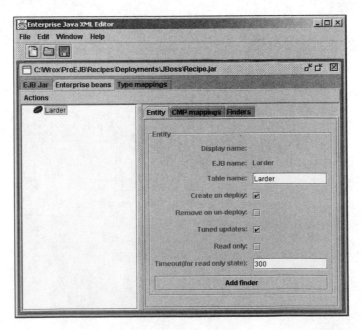

We'll start on the Entity tab there, and set the fields as follows:

Field	Value
Table Name	Larder
Create on deploy	unchecked (JBoss shouldn't try to create the table in the database.)
Remove on un-deploy	unchecked (JBoss *certainly* shouldn't drop the table when it shuts down!)
Tuned updates	unchecked (JBoss should always use the same SQL for updates, rather than customizing it to the fields that have changed. This is safest.)
Read-only	unchecked

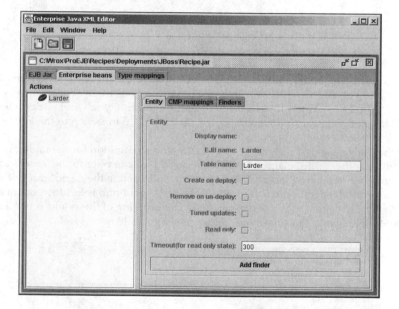

Then we need to go to the **CMP mappings** tab and link up each of the CMP fields in the bean to a column in the database. In our case, we map the `ingredientName` field to the `ingredientName` column, and the `stock` field to the `stock` column. We can also update the data types to reflect the appropriate Oracle values. In this case we set the ingredient name column to use the `VARCHAR2(20)` data type, though the default `NUMBER` data type is fine for the stock column:

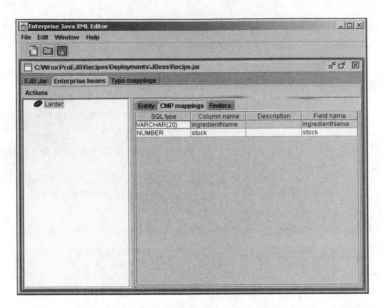

Next, we need to define the finder for the Larder bean. JBoss automatically provides implementations of `findByPrimaryKey()` and `findAll()`, if those are present, but we need to manually add `findLowStockLevels()`. To do this, we need to start on the **Entity** tab and click the **Add finder** button at the bottom. This won't appear to do anything, but then we need to switch to the **Finder** tab to define it.

Here, we enter the finder name `findLowStockLevels`, and a definition for the finder. In the definition, we are essentially entering the WHERE clause of a SQL query, and we can refer to the finder's arguments using curly braces around the zero-based index of the argument. So to define the `findLowStockLevels()` finder, we want to return all items where the value in the `stock` column is less than or equal to the method argument, and the finder definition is `stock <= {0}`. The ordering of the results is not important here, so we leave the **Order** field blank. This means our finder screen looks like:

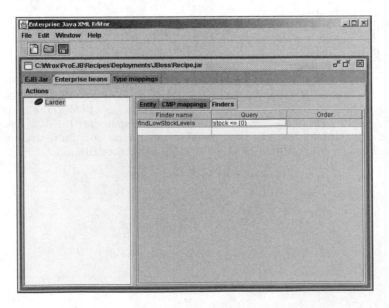

That's all we need to do for the container managed persistence configuration, so we just use File | Save to write the jaws.xml file into the EJB JAR.

Unfortunately, the version of EJX shipping with JBoss 2.2.2 has a bug that causes it to write bad jaws.xml files, so we need to extract the jaws.xml file from the EJB JAR. We see that EJX included a large group of database data type mappings, between the tags <type-mappings> and </type-mappings>, and we need to remove all of those (since JBoss by default has valid mappings for a number of database products). Also, it wrote the <type-mapping> name to use as "Oracle" (our only option in the GUI), and that needs to be changed to "Oracle7" for Oracle 7.x, or "Oracle8" for Oracle 8.x, 8i, and 9i.

Hopefully this bug will be fixed in later versions of JBoss.

After making those changes, we need to insert the updated jaws.xml file back into the EJB JAR. The final jaws.xml file looks like this. Note that the < in the finder definition is encoded so the whole document is still valid XML:

```xml
<?xml version="1.0" encoding="Cp1252"?>

<jaws>
    <datasource>java:/SamplePool</datasource>
    <type-mapping>Oracle8</type-mapping>
    <type-mappings>
            <!-- all type mappings removed -->
    </type-mappings>
    <enterprise-beans>
      <entity>
<ejb-name>Larder</ejb-name>
<table-name>Larder</table-name>
<create-table>true</create-table>
<remove-table>false</remove-table>
<tuned-updates>false</tuned-updates>
<read-only>false</read-only>
<time-out>300</time-out>
<pk-constraint>false</pk-constraint>
<cmp-field>
   <field-name>stock</field-name>
   <column-name>stock</column-name>
   <sql-type>NUMBER</sql-type>
   <jdbc-type>INTEGER</jdbc-type>
</cmp-field>
<cmp-field>
   <field-name>ingredientName</field-name>
   <column-name>ingredientName</column-name>
   <sql-type>VARCHAR(20)</sql-type>
   <jdbc-type>VARCHAR</jdbc-type>
</cmp-field>
<finder>
   <name>findLowStockLevels</name>
   <query>stock &lt;= {0}</query>
   <order></order>
</finder>
      </entity>
    </enterprise-beans>
</jaws>
```

Deploying the EJB JAR

Now that we've generated the deployment descriptors for the EJB JAR, it's time to deploy it into JBoss. That is a simple matter of copying the EJB JAR into the `/deploy` directory. If JBoss is already running, the beans will be deployed or redeployed immediately. Otherwise, they will be deployed the next time JBoss is started.

Start JBoss

If JBoss isn't running, we can start it with the scripts in the `/bin` directory. We use `run.bat` file for Windows, or `run.sh` for UNIX.

If you've deployed the sample beans, you should see sections like this in the startup sequence:

```
...
[SamplePool] Starting
[SamplePool] XA Connection pool SamplePool bound to java:/SamplePool
[SamplePool] Started
...
[Container factory] Deploying CookBook
[Container factory] Deploying Larder
[Container factory] Deploying Menu
[Container factory] Deploying Kitchen
...
```

The first section indicates that the database pool was initialized successfully, and the second section indicates that all the beans were deployed successfully.

Configure and Run the Client

Additionally, we need to configure the JNDI lookup in the Chef client with the relevant properties for JBoss. Add the following method to the Chef class:

```
private Context getJBossContextInfo() {

  Context ctx = null;

  try {
    Properties prop = new Properties();
    prop.put(Context.INITIAL_CONTEXT_FACTORY,
             "org.jnp.interfaces.NamingContextFactory");
    prop.put(Context.PROVIDER_URL, "localhost:1099");

    ctx = new InitialContext(prop);

  } catch(NamingException ne)  {
    System.out.println(ne);
  }

  return ctx;
}
```

And modify the `getContextInfo()` method to call this one:

```
private Context getContextInfo() {
    return getJBossContextInfo();
}
```

In order to get a client to communicate with JBoss, the client needs to have a number of files found in the /client subdirectory of the JBoss installation directory. Specifically we need:

❑   jboss-client.jar

❑   jnp-client.jar

❑   jbosssx-client.jar

So we can run the client with the following command:

```
set JBOSS_HOME=c:\JBoss-2.2.2

java -classpath %JBOSS_HOME%\jboss-client.jar;%JBOSS_HOME%\jnp-
client.jar;%JBOSS_HOME%\jbosssx-client.jar;Recipe.jar recipeBook.client.Chef
```

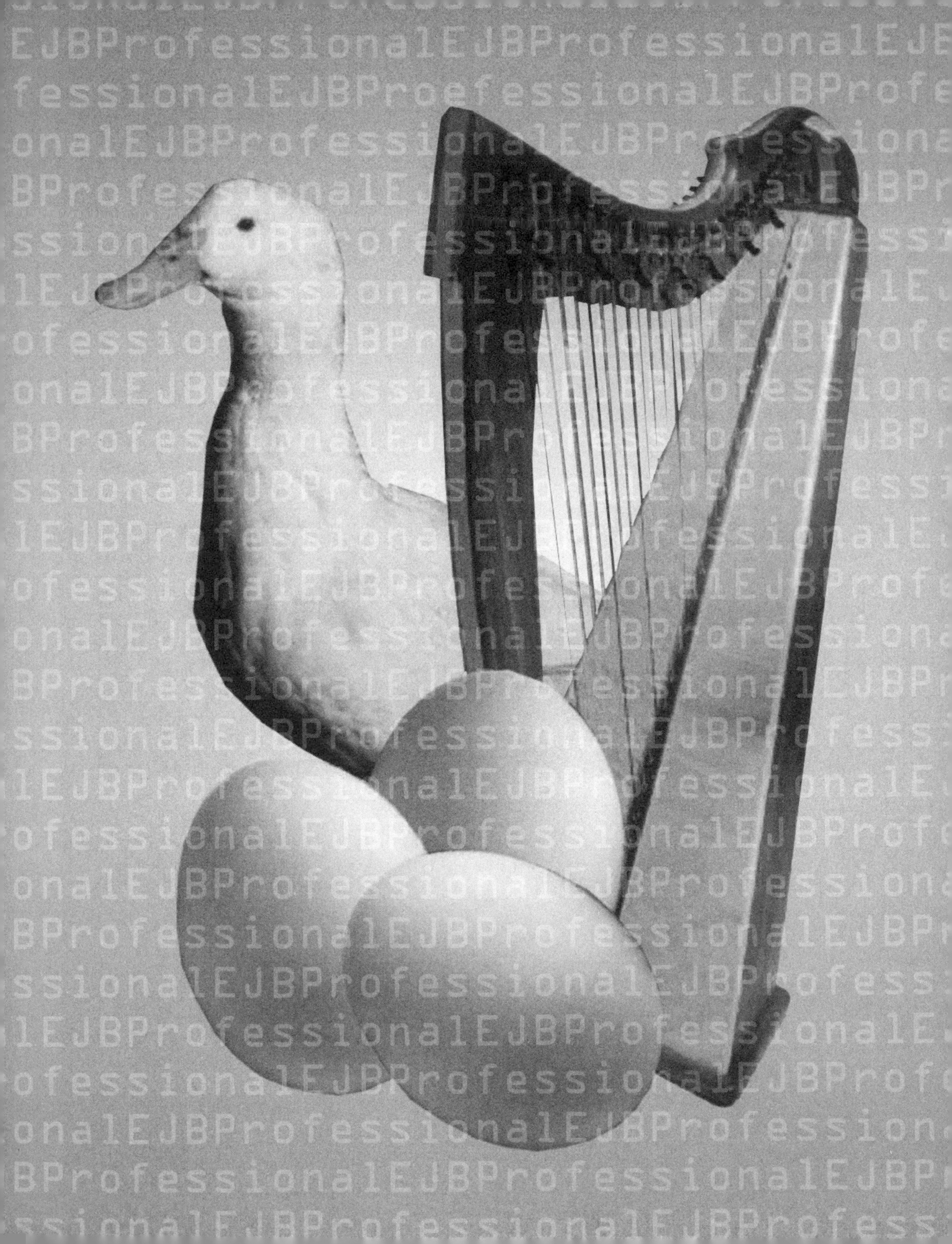
EJBProfessional

Index

A Guide to the Index

The index covers all numbered chapters and the Appendices. It is arranged alphabetically, word-by-word, with numerals preceding the letter A. Angle-bracket tag delimiters and hyphens have been ignored in alphabetizing. Acronyms, rather than their expansions, have been preferred as main entries, on the grounds that unfamiliar acronyms are easier to construct than to expand. Plural forms have also been preferred for concrete terms, although the alphabetization process will often separate these from the singular form occurring in phrases and combinations.

D

J

white-box testing, 592
wildcard characters, 258
window listener
StatelessFundManagerTestClient class, 76
wireless applications
characteristics affecting their design, 962
circuit and packet-switched connections, 962
companies, 997
suitability of J2EE, 959, 961
withdraw() method
AccountManager interface
AccountAccessDeniedException, 440
authorization sequence, 433
Bank class, 371
withdrawFunds() method
StatefulFundManager interface, 86, 87
StatelessFundManager interface, 68, 78
WithEvents keyword
Visual Basic EJB client, Amazon Browser application,
916, 917
wizards
application deployment tool, J2EE, 49
WML (Wireless Markup Language)
documents organized as decks of cards, 961, 980
index.wml initial page, 981
match.wml results page, 981
must follow XML rules, 980
tags, 980
used by WAP, 960
userDetails.wml input page, 981
WMLScript, 960
workflow handling
Session Façade design pattern, 510, 513
writeObject() method
serializing an object handle, 101

WSDL (Web Services Definition Language)
creating the description document
music CD web service application, 1027
document structure, 1007
files from IBM Web Services toolkit, 1009
generating with CapeConnect, 1045
status, 1006
web services specification, 1002
WSTK *see* **IBM Web Services toolkit.**

X

XA transaction support, 832
XHTML (Extensible HTML)
WAP 2.0 uses, 960
XML (Extensible Markup Language)
see also application.xml; config.xml; ejb-jar.xml;
web.xml; weblogic-*.xml.
between presentation and client layers, 474
deployment descriptor an XML file from EJB 1.1, 44
deployment descriptor is an XML file, 20
representing client views in, 164
SOAP messages, 1002
tag library defintions are XML files, 891
UDDI APIs in, 1012
UDDI registry in, 1010
web services specifications based on, 1001
XML schemas used in WSDL, 1006, 1008
XP (Extreme Programming), 595
extreme testing using, 603
J2EE methodology and, 846

Y

yenToEuro() method
Converter interface, 303

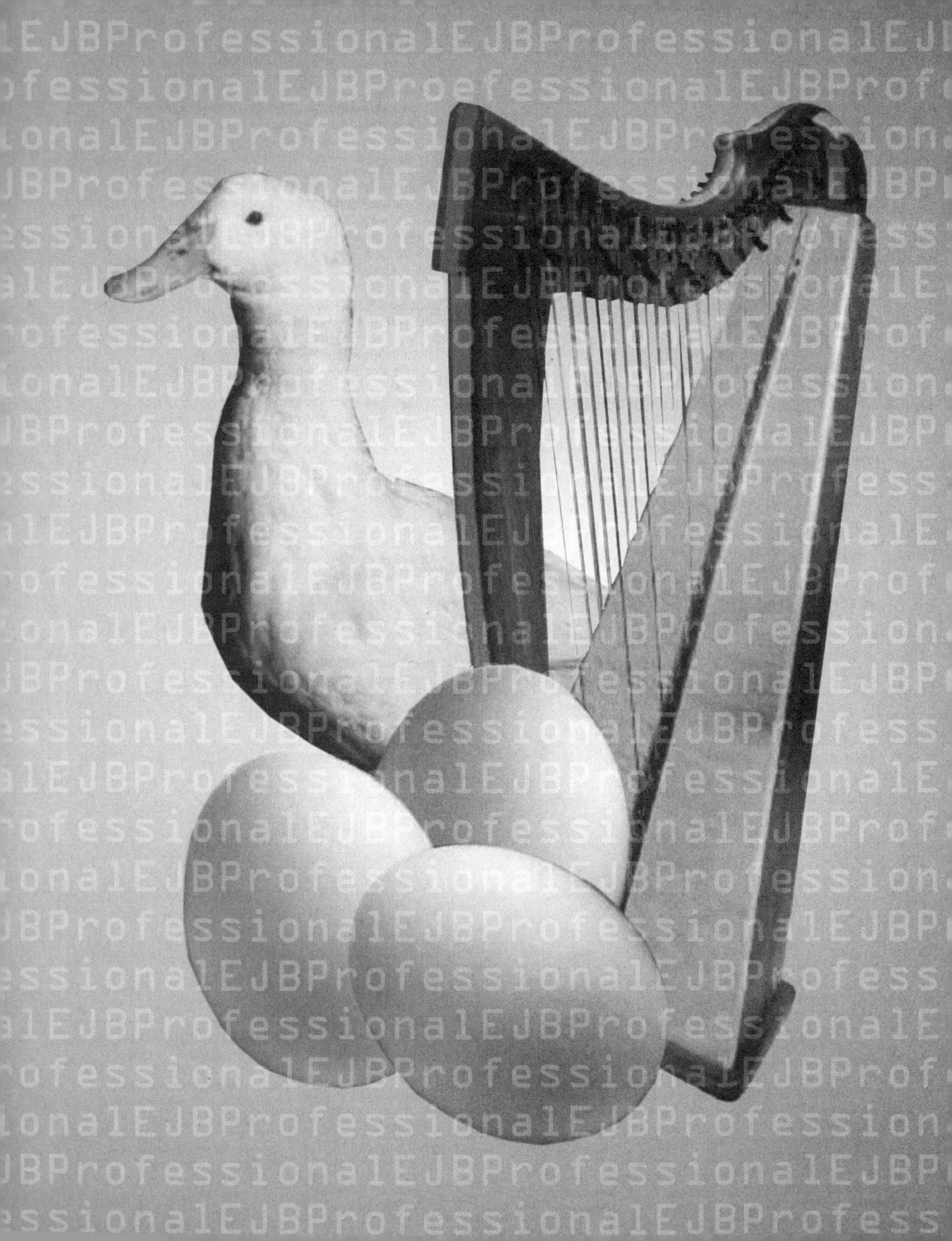

p2p.wrox.com
The programmer's resource centre

A unique free service from Wrox Press
with the aim of helping programmers to help each other

Wrox Press aims to provide timely and practical information to today's programmer. P2P is a list server offering a host of targeted mailing lists where you can share knowledge with your fellow programmers and find solutions to your problems. Whatever the level of your programming knowledge, and whatever technology you use, P2P can provide you with the information you need.

ASP — Support for beginners and professionals, including a resource page with hundreds of links, and a popular ASP+ mailing list.

DATABASES — For database programmers, offering support on SQL Server, mySQL, and Oracle.

MOBILE — Software development for the mobile market is growing rapidly. We provide lists for the several current standards, including WAP, WindowsCE, and Symbian.

JAVA — A complete set of Java lists, covering beginners, professionals,and server-side programmers (including JSP, servlets and EJBs)

.NET — Microsoft's new OS platform, covering topics such as ASP+, C#, and general .Net discussion.

VISUAL BASIC — Covers all aspects of VB programming, from programming Office macros to creating components for the .Net platform.

WEB DESIGN — As web page requirements become more complex, programmer sare taking a more important role in creating web sites. For these programmers, we offer lists covering technologies such as Flash, Coldfusion, and JavaScript.

XML — Covering all aspects of XML, including XSLT and schemas.

OPEN SOURCE — Many Open Source topics covered including PHP, Apache, Perl, Linux, Python and more.

FOREIGN LANGUAGE — Several lists dedicated to Spanish and German speaking programmers, categories include .Net, Java, XML, PHP and XML.

How To Subscribe

Simply visit the P2P site, at **http://p2p.wrox.com/**

Select the 'FAQ' option on the side menu bar for more information about the subscription process and our service.

Programmer to Programmer

wrox

Programmer to Programmer™

Wrox writes books for you. Any suggestions, or ideas about how you want information given in your ideal book will be studied by our team. Your comments are always valued at Wrox.

Free phone in USA 800-USE-WROX
Fax (312) 893 8001

UK Tel.: (0121) 687 4100   Fax: (0121) 687 4101

Professional EJB – Registration Card

Name _____

Address _____

_____

_____

City _____ State/Region _____

Country _____ Postcode/Zip _____

E-Mail _____

Occupation _____

How did you hear about this book?

☐ Book review (name) _____

☐ Advertisement (name) _____

☐ Recommendation _____

☐ Catalog _____

☐ Other _____

Where did you buy this book?

☐ Bookstore (name) _____ City _____

☐ Computer store (name) _____

☐ Mail order _____

☐ Other _____

What influenced you in the purchase of this book?

☐ Cover Design ☐ Contents ☐ Other (please specify):

How did you rate the overall content of this book?

☐ Excellent ☐ Good ☐ Average ☐ Poor

What did you find most useful about this book? _____

_____

What did you find least useful about this book? _____

_____

Please add any additional comments. _____

_____

What other subjects will you buy a computer book on soon?

_____

What is the best computer book you have used this year?

_____

Check here if you DO NOT want to receive support for this book ■

wrox

Programmer to Programmer™

Note: If you post the bounce back card below in the UK, please send it to:

Wrox Press Limited, Arden House, 1102 Warwick Road,
Acocks Green, Birmingham B27 6HB. UK.

Computer Book Publishers

BUSINESS REPLY MAIL
FIRST CLASS MAIL   PERMIT#64   CHICAGO, IL

POSTAGE WILL BE PAID BY ADDRESSEE

WROX PRESS INC.
29 S. LA SALLE ST.
SUITE 520
CHICAGO IL 60603-USA